CHILD PSYCHOLOGY

A CONTEMPORARY VIEWPOINT

CHILD PSYCHOLOGY

A CONTEMPORARY VIEWPOINT

Fourth Edition

E. Mavis Hetherington
University of Virginia

Ross D. Parke
*University of California
Riverside*

McGraw-Hill, Inc.
New York St. Louis San Francisco Auckland
Bogotá Caracas Lisbon London Madrid Mexico
Milan Montreal New Delhi Paris San Juan
Singapore Sydney Tokyo Toronto

CHILD PSYCHOLOGY
A Contemporary Viewpoint

Acknowledgments appear on pages xvi–xvii, and on this page by reference.

2 3 4 5 6 7 8 9 0 DOW DOW 9 0 9 8 7 6 5 4 3

ISBN 0-07-028444-X

This book was set in Palatino by Monotype Composition Company.
The editors were Jane Vaicunas and David Dunham;
the designer was Karen K. Quigley;
the production supervisor was Friederich W. Schulte.
The photo editors were Elyse Rieder and Kathy Bendo;
the photo researcher was Ede Rothaus.
New drawings were done by Fine Line Illustrations, Inc.
R. R. Donnelley & Sons Company was printer and binder.

Cover credit: Maurice Prendergast, FLYING HORSES, ca. 1901, watercolor on paper; Art Resource, New York.

Library of Congress Cataloging-in-Publication Data

Hetherington, E. Mavis (Eileen Mavis), (date).
Child psychology: a contemporary viewpoint/E. Mavis Hetherington, Ross D. Parke.—4th ed.
p. cm.
Includes bibliographical references and indexes.
ISBN 0-07-028444-X
1. Child psychology. I. Parke, Ross D. II. Title.
[DNLM: 1. Child Psychology. WS 105 H589c]
BF721.H418 1993
155.4—dc20
DNLM/DLC
for Library of Congress 92-21106

INTERNATIONAL EDITION

When ordering this title, use ISBN 0-07-112958-8.

ABOUT THE AUTHORS

E. Mavis Hetherington is a professor of psychology at the University of Virginia. She was trained as a developmental psychologist and as a clinical psychologist at the University of California at Berkeley where she obtained her Ph.D. She is a past President of Division 7, the Developmental Psychology Division of the American Psychological Association, and of the Society for Research in Child Development and the Society for Research in Adolescence. She has been editor of *Child Development*, associate editor of *Developmental Psychology*, and currently is associate editor of the *Journal of Abnormal Child Psychology*. She has authored and edited many books in the area of child development, two of the most recent being *The Separate Social World of Siblings* with David Reiss and Robert Plomin and *Family Transitions* with Phillip Cowan. Her research interests are in the areas of childhood psychopathology, personality and social development, and stress and coping in families. She is well known for her work on the effects of divorce, one-parent families, and remarriage on children's development.

Ross D. Parke is a professor of psychology and director of the Center for Family Studies at the University of California, Riverside. He is a past President of Division 7, the Developmental Psychology Division of the American Psychological Association. He has been editor of *Developmental Psychology* and associate editor of *Child Development*. Professor Parke is author of *Fathers* and editor of *The Family, Review of Child Development Research*, Volume 7, and most recently is co-editor of *Family-Peer Relationships: In Search of the Linkages* with Gary Ladd and *Children in Time and Place* with Glen Elder and John Modell. His research has focused on early social relationships in infancy and childhood. He is well known for his early work on the effects of punishment, aggression, and child abuse and for his work on the father's role in infancy and early childhood. His current work focuses on the links between family and peer social systems.

WITHDRAWN
GLASGOW
Departmental
Libraries
UNIVERSITY

To John and Barbara and our children:
Grant, Eric, and Jason
Gillian, Timothy, Megan, Sarah, Jennifer, and Zachary

CONTENTS

PREFACE

This book is a product of a continuing collaboration that began nearly twenty-five years ago. In the late 1960s when we started work on the first edition of *Child Psychology*, there were few topically oriented books. Instead, we and many other instructors who were interested in teaching a more process-oriented course on child psychology would assign sections from each chapter of chronological books that would provide an overview of the issues on a single topic. Needless to say, this was not a very satisfactory solution for either instructors or students. Our solution was, of course, a new book that reflected more clearly the contemporary nature of the field with a focus on research-based findings about the central processes that account for developmental shifts within different topical domains of development. Through successive editions we have tried to continually reflect the dynamic and shifting nature of the field. We hope *Child Psychology: A Contemporary Viewpoint*, fourth edition, lives up to its title—as an up-to-date and exciting overview of the best that our field has to offer to instructor and student.

It is with great excitement that we present the new edition. Our goals for this edition are consistent with those of past editions. Our primary aim is to present the most important contemporary ideas and issues in child psychology in a way that will be understood and appreciated by students at all levels. It is our hope that the academic community will find this new edition to be a comprehensive and current resource as well as an invaluable teaching tool. In order to attain these goals, we have employed a special approach to the material which is comprised of the following elements:

1. TOPICAL APPROACH—Instead of being chronologically organized, this book examines child psychology by utilizing a topical orientation. *Child Psychology*, 4/e, is organized around such topics as cognition, intelligence, language, genetics, sex typing, and moral development. Within each specific topic area, we discuss the significant developmental changes that occur during various stages of children's lives.

2. MULTIPLE THEORETICAL VIEWPOINTS—Topical organization allows for a more adequate and sophisticated presentation of the theories that guide research in each area. By utilizing a topical approach, we acknowledge that there are few universal theories of child behavior. Instead, we realize that there are smaller theories to guide research in specific topic areas. In this vein, this edition includes a diverse survey of the theories in the opening chapter. In Chapter 1, for example, we present a range of viewpoints including psychoanalytic theory, Piagetian theory, information processing, behavioral views and Vygotskian theory.

   While some books choose one special theoretical viewpoint, such as a behavioral bent, a social stance, a biological bias, or a cognitive cast, *Child Psychology*, 4/e, strives to be theoretically eclectic. This text succeeds in exposing students to a wide range of theoretical viewpoints. A number of theoretical orientations are represented, but in varying degrees depending on the topic introduced for discussion. For example, biological factors predominate in our coverage of genetics and early development. These same factors, however, also receive attention in our discussion of other topics, such as language, sex typing, and psychopathology. Similarly, while social factors predominate in our coverage of the family and peers, we are equally concerned with cognitive, behavioral, and biological issues. While cognitive factors are the primary focus of the section on intellectual and language development the social dimension always plays a prominent role. This approach to theoretical material reflects the discipline's increasing recognition of the interplay among biological, cognitive, and social factors in children's development and reflects the fact that development in all domains is multiply determined.

3. PROCESS ORIENTATION—*Child Psychology*, 4/e, features a special emphasis on the processes of development. Within each topic, we stress the processes that are responsible for changes in the child's development. As a result, the student knows not only the content of development and what changes take place across chronological age but will also understand the processes underlying development as well. This process focus is the distinguishing feature of child psychology in the last two decades and continues to be the organizing orientation for understanding development in the 1990s.

4. RESEARCH ORIENTATION—Because we present child psychology as a scientific discipline, this text illustrates and discusses the research methodology utilized by psychologists in the field. By doing this, we ensure students' understanding of the methodological approaches unique to child psychology. In order to reflect recent methodological advances, *Child Psychology*, 4/e, includes new approaches in sampling and the use of naturalistic field studies and laboratory studies for understanding development. This revision also features a greater emphasis on observational strategies and innovative usage of parental reports in order to better understand children's behavior.

5. THE APPLIED-BASIC RELATIONSHIP—Some instructors like a basic research focus while others prefer an applied approach. We think that this is an unnecessary and artificial distinction. Instead, we have attempted to show how basic information about the processes of development can assist in understanding a wide range of real-life problems and vice versa. Examples abound throughout the text. Social learning theory and basic research on imitation have helped us better understand the effects of TV on children's cognitive and social development, as illustrated in several chapters (Chapters 1 and 14, for example). In similar fashion, theories of early mother-infant attachment have clear implications for understanding the effects of day care. Child abuse, school desegregation, and computers in the classroom are other examples of applied topics that are highlighted in this edition. Chapter 17, which discusses the development and treatment of psychopathology and deviant behavior in children, provides extensive illustrations of the linkage between basic and applied research. Teachers and students will find fascinating examples throughout *Child Psychology*, 4/e, that demonstrate the dynamic interplay between basic and applied research.

6. DIVERSITY IN DEVELOPMENT—In this fourth edition, we have increased our coverage of the diverse ethnic, racial, and cultural groups that characterize our own highly heterogeneous society as well as in societies around the globe. Our increased focus on Vygotskian theory with its strong emphasis on the role of culture in development provides a framework for understanding how culture and development interact. Recent research on schooling in Japan, China, and the United States is highlighted in our exploration of achievement (Chapter 11), while cross-cultural differences in temperament are explored in chapters on biological development and infancy (Chapters 4 and 5). In our exploration of childhood psychopathology (Chapter 17), we examine how mental illness is treated and defined differently in different cultures.

Child Psychology, 4/e, has been completely rewritten to feature the most recent developments in research and theory. We have included new information in every chapter. The following chapter-by-chapter list gives specific examples of new areas of coverage:

Chapter 1: THEMES AND THEORIES. Our range of theories is extended with new sections on information processing and Vygotskian theory in the opening chapter.

Chapter 2: METHODS OF CHILD PSYCHOLOGY. Several new features are added—a new section on sampling and a discussion of the value of national representative samples for research on children. Greater coverage of the designs that combine laboratory and field approaches are included. Our discussion of ethical issues is expanded as well.

Chapter 3: THE BIOLOGICAL BASES OF BEHAVIOR. New material on the effects of nonshared environment is highlighted in our discussion of behavior genetics.

Chapter 4: PRENATAL BIRTH AND DEVELOPMENT. The impact of cocaine on the fetus and young infant as well as recent studies of the impact of AIDS on development are included.

Chapter 5: INFANCY: THE EMERGENCE OF SENSATION, PERCEPTION, AND LEARNING. New developments in the emergence of expectations in very young infants as well as recent studies of the bimodal perception continue to underscore the remarkable achievements of the young infant.

Chapter 6: BRAIN DEVELOPMENT: PHYSICAL MATURATION AND MOTOR SKILLS. Recent advances in the emergence of motor skills such as reaching, stepping, and walking that have been guided by a dynamics systems theory viewpoint are given extensive coverage in this edition. New work on the impact of timing of onset of puberty in adolescence is highlighted as well.

Chapter 7: EMOTIONAL DEVELOPMENT. The explosion of new studies of cross-cultural and cross-generational perspectives on infant-parent attachment as well as recent studies on the controversial effects of day care on infants and children are included. A new section focuses on the development of children's cognitive understanding of emotions.

Chapter 8: LANGUAGE AND COMMUNICATION. Recent work on the role of critical periods on second-language learning reflects the continuing interest in the biological basis of language. New studies on motherese and pragmatics underscore the contribution of early social interactions between parent and child to the emergence of language. The emergence of meaning is given expanded focus in this edition as well.

Chapter 9: THEORIES OF COGNITIVE DEVELOPMENT. In this new chapter we focus on alternative theoretical approaches to cognition. Piaget, of course, continues to receive in-depth coverage, but some of the recent work on object permanence that challenges Piaget's classic findings are highlighted. Information processing approaches receive extensive attention as a major approach to cognitive development in the 1990s. Two new theoretical viewpoints make their debut in this edition. Case's neo-Piagetian theory is described and Vygotskian theory—a major influence in current research—is given a major role in this fourth edition.

Chapter 10: PROCESSES OF COGNITIVE DEVELOPMENT. Recent work on analogies, problem solving, prospective memory, and children's "theory of mind" are new highlights of this edition. The interplay between social and cultural factors in cognitive development is given increased attention, especially in studies from a neo-Vygotskian perspective. Recent cross-cultural studies of mathematics among poor young street vendors are examined.

Chapter 11: INTELLECTUAL DEVELOPMENT AND ACHIEVEMENT. In this chapter, new views on multiple intelligences are explored as well as new work on achievement that emphasizes the role of children's theories of intelligence and their attributional styles.

Chapter 12: THE FAMILY. This fourth edition continues to emphasize diversity and change in contemporary families with new work on maternal employment, divorce and stepparenting, job loss, and family violence. A new section examines the impact of war on children and families.

Chapter 13: PEERS AND FRIENDS. Recent evidence of the long-term effects of early rejection by peers is highlighted as well as recent studies of loneliness in children. New studies of children's friendships, the links between families and peers, and research on group hierarchies are included.

Chapter 14: SCHOOLS, TECHNOLOGY, AND TELEVISION. New work includes studies of how teaching style interacts with children's cultural backgrounds as well as recent studies on cooperative learning. Computers in the classroom are given expanded coverage. A new section on television highlights the impact of TV advertising on children's behavior, the impact of TV on children's time use, and the educational benefits of TV.

Chapter 15: THE DEVELOPMENT OF GENDER ROLES AND GENDER DIFFERENCES. The continuing story of shrinking differences across gender in academic and social outcomes is updated. Expanded coverage is given to recent work on cognitive approaches to gender roles, as well as recent studies of gender segregation.

Chapter 16: MORALITY, ALTRUISM, AND AGGRESSION. The continuing controversy surrounding the Kohlberg-Gilligan debate about male and female differences in moral orientation is updated. New work on the early signs of moral understanding in family disputes is included as well as recent work on social conventions and the emergence of self-control strategies. Our coverage of prosocial development is updated with new studies of prosocial reasoning, empathy, and cross-cultural work on responsibility taking. Finally, new studies on proactive and reactive aggression, the impact of witnessed anger, and new school-based strategies for reducing aggression are highlights of this fourth edition.

Chapter 17: DEVELOPMENTAL PSYCHOPATHOLOGY. New studies of stress and coping as well as recent advances in classification and treatment update this chapter. Recent work on depression and autism are included in this edition, as well as recent cross-cultural perspectives on developmental abnormalities.

These new areas of coverage provide a current view of basic research and theory on the principal topics of child psychology as well as an up-to-date review of recent trends in socially relevant problem areas.

SPECIAL FEATURES

Child Psychology, 4/e, includes a number of excellent pedagogical features that will enhance student learning and aid instructors in their presentation of important material:

1. Chapter Outlines—A detailed chapter outline will be found at the opening of each chapter. These outlines allow students to become better acquainted with chapter material and assist them as they study from the text.
2. Bulleted Chapter Summaries—At the end of each chapter, we have provided bulleted summaries that reiterate the chapter's key concepts and main ideas. These summaries are excellent study aids for students and useful reference points for instructors.
3. Boxes—Throughout the text, we have utilized boxed material to illustrate timely issues in child psychology. The aim of these boxes—which contain thought-provoking discussions of a particular psychological study or special issue—is to give students some of the flavor of research in child psychology. These boxes also provide in-depth, multidimensional discussions, of a variety of compelling topics such as sex differences in spatial perception, computers in the classroom, the effects of cocaine on infants, learning in the womb, the development of sign language, and the effects of war on children. To highlight the interplay between research and application, some boxes are labeled *"Psychology in Action."* These boxes illustrate how basic research can be applied to helping children.
4. Separate Author and Subject Indexes—We have included separate indexes in this text for authors cited and topics discussed. Both the author and subject indexes will help students and instructors locate related material throughout the text.

SUPPLEMENTS

Child Psychology, 4/e, features a new and innovative ancillary package which is comprised of the following elements:

- — Study Guide by Janis Jacobs.
- — Instructor's Manual by Janis Jacobs.
- — Test Bank by Cynthia Legin-Bucell. Computerized Test Banks for use with IBM and Macintosh computers are also available.
- — McGraw-Hill Overhead Transparencies.

In addition, a book of readings, *Contemporary Readings in Child Psychology* (ISBN: 0-07-028437-7), edited by Professors Hetherington and Parke, is available as a companion volume to this text. The readings are organized topically to complement the organization of the text, and brief introductions highlight the main features of each reading. Both original research papers and recent reviews of major topics are included. Its softback format is designed to keep the total cost reasonable for the text-reader combination.

A COMMENT ON THE USE OF THE TEXT: THE SHORT VERSUS THE LONG COURSE

This volume is organized around the one-semester or quarter course. There are ways, however, in which the book can be used for shorter courses. A brief course, for example, might emphasize early development. In this case, one would concentrate on Chapters 1 through 7. Alternatively, a short, cognitively oriented course could use Chapters 1, 2, 8, 9, 10, and 11. Similarly, an instructor with a social orientation might focus on Chapters 1, 2, 12, 13, 14, 15, 16, and 17.

ACKNOWLEDGMENTS

Special acknowledgment is given to Wendy Haight at the University of Utah for her contribution to the revision of Chapter 8, Mary Jo Ratterman at Hampshire College for her contributions to Chapters 9 and 10, Kathleen Cain at Gettysburg College who contributed to the revision of Chapter 11, and to Janis Jacobs at the University of Nebraska at Lincoln who compiled the chapter outlines and summaries. A special thanks to Chris Strand in Riverside, California, for her patient and professional assistance in preparing the manuscript.

A number of individuals have reviewed various parts of the manuscript for the fourth edition. Thanks are extended to the following individuals for their constructive comments and suggestions: Brian P. Ackerman, University of Delaware at Newark; Bennett I. Bertenthal, University of Virginia; John D. Bonvillian, University of Virginia; Celia A. Brownell, University of Pittsburgh; Victor P. Caliri, University of Massachusetts at Dartmouth; Linda A. Camras, DePaul University at Chicago; Cynthia M. Connine, State University of New York at Binghamton; Patrick T. DeBoli, Nassau Community College; Ganie B. DeHart, State University of New York at Geneseo; Judith F. Dunn, Pennsylvania State University; Nancy Eisenberg, Arizona State University at Tempe; Jon B. Ellis, East Tennessee State University; Beverly Fagot, University of Oregon; Tiffany Field, University of Miami; Margery B. Franklin, Sarah Lawrence College; Mary Gauvain, Scripps College; Jean Berko Gleason, Boston University; William J. Gnagey, Illinois State University; Joan Grusec, University of Toronto; Margaret Stanley Hagan, University of North Carolina at Charlotte; Norman H. Hamm, University of Nebraska at Omaha; Vernon F. Haynes, Youngstown State University; Carol Nagy Jacklin, University of Southern California; Gary W. Ladd, University of Illinois at Urbana-Champaign; Joseph C. LaVoie, University of Nebraska at Omaha; Mark R. Lepper, Stanford University; Richard M. Lerner, Michigan State University; Lynn S. Liben, Pennsylvania State University; Robert B. McCall, University of Pittsburgh; Kevin MacDonald, California State University at Long Beach;

Sarah C. Mangelsdorf, University of Michigan; Jayanthi Mistry, Tufts University; Wayne Moellenberg, University of New Mexico at Albuquerque; Stuart I. Offenbach, Purdue University; Michele Paludi, Hunter College; Anne C. Petersen, Pennsylvania State University; Suzanne M. Phillips, University of Pittsburgh at Johnstown; Bradford Pillow, University of Pittsburgh; Robert Plomin, Pennsylvania State University; Mabel L. Rice, University of Kansas at Lawrence; Carolyn Saarni, Sonoma State University; Eduard Schludermann, University of Manitoba; Robert S. Siegler, Carnegie Mellon University; Patricia Smiley, Pomona College; Mary P. Hughes Stone, San Francisco State University; Ross A. Thompson, University of Nebraska at Lincoln; Spencer K. Thompson, University of Texas of the Permian Basin; Jonathan Tudge, University of North Carolina at Greensboro; Allan Wigfield, University of Maryland at College Park; and H. Jean Wilkinson, State University of New York at Albany.

E. Mavis Hetherington
Ross D. Parke

CHILD PSYCHOLOGY

A CONTEMPORARY VIEWPOINT

CHAPTER 1

INTRODUCTION: THEMES AND THEORIES

WHAT IS CHILD DEVELOPMENT?

Child development involves the scientific study of changes in the child's biological, social, cognitive, and emotional behavior across the span of childhood. Two central questions about development concern all child psychologists. First, how do children change as they develop? Second, what are the determinants of these developmental changes? Child psychology involves both the description *and* explanation of changes in children's development. It is interesting to be able to state that older children can learn to solve logic problems better than younger children, to detail how an infant's ability to grasp objects improves, or to describe children's increasing skill in understanding the feelings of others. These are the products of development or the observable end states that tell us what children know and can do at different points in development. But it is not enough to simply describe the outcomes of development. Contemporary child psychologists are committed to an exploration of the reasons and processes that underlie such developmental changes. It is this emphasis on the *processes* that explains developmental shifts that best characterize the current field. This book is organized around developmental processes, and throughout our exploration of contemporary child psychology we will illustrate how specific processes may account for different aspects of children's development.

WHY STUDY CHILDREN?

There are many reasons to study children. Some reasons are scientific while others are practical. From the scientist's viewpoint, we study children to increase our knowledge about the ways that development proceeds and the processes that alter this progression. Many behavioral scientists focus on children because some processes can be observed in simpler forms in children than in adults. Others study children under the assumption that a better understanding of children's behavior will lead to a better understanding of adult behavior. Developmental psychologists find children puzzling and fascinating. For these scientists, unraveling the mysteries of childhood is a goal in itself. Others are concerned with certain practical and policy implications of the study of children. Better information about child development can assist all members of society who care about the well-being of children, such as parents, teachers, legislators, and health professionals. Research findings can lead to helpful advice on a wide range of current issues, from selecting day-care programs and handling children's temper tantrums to the impact of busing and the effects of television violence. Finally, information on normal development facilitates early detection of problems and helps in the prevention of deviant development.

For a sample of facts and findings about children's development and a brief overview of the range of insights that you will gain as we begin our exploration of development, turn to Box 1-1.

THEMES OF DEVELOPMENT

Description versus Process

Developmental scientists have many goals in their search for answers to children's development. One aim of research is to provide a description of

BOX 1-1 A SAMPLER OF FACTS AND FINDINGS ABOUT CHILDREN'S DEVELOPMENT

The facts and findings about children's development are sometimes fascinating, other times puzzling or even surprising. Below is a sample of recent facts and findings about developing children that we will explore in depth in later chapters in this volume.

Fact 1: Adolescents reach puberty two years earlier than their grandparents did.

Fact 2: Newborns can tell their own mothers by smell.

Fact 3: Children can learn a new language easier than their parents.

Fact 4: Waterbeds can aid the development of babies who are born prematurely.

Fact 5: Divorce adversely affects the development of boys more than girls.

Fact 6: Even one experience with cocaine can adversely affect the developing fetus.

Fact 7: Babies can learn in the womb.

Fact 8: Even 2-year-olds experience jealousy.

Fact 9: Aggression at age 8 can predict criminality at age 30.

Fact 10: Newborn infants possess the ability to walk.

behavior and how it changes across development. For example, the description of how children's play changes or how many words children can remember or when children learn to crawl, sit, and walk are all of interest to child psychologists. This information is valuable in developing norms concerning the timing of developmental changes for children. Norms provide important guidelines against which to measure the individual child's progress in relation to other children of similar age. If developmental delays are detected, interventions to correct the problem can often be instituted.

Most students of development see the descriptive task as important, but only a starting point toward understanding development. At the same time, the child developmentalist is concerned with the identification of the processes or causes of development. Instead of being concerned about how many words a child can remember, they are interested in the strategies that children use to help them remember at different points in development. For example, do older and younger children organize a list of words differently to help them remember? If children have to remember "shirt," "carrot," "potato," "shoes," "hat," "peas," and "tie," older children group them into vegetables and clothing; young children do not use this simple trick. In another area, what strategies do children use to make friends? Do they share ideas, take turns, suggest activities? Understanding the processes that underlie developmental changes is of central interest to most developmental psychologists.

However, the answers to either the descriptive or process questions are by no means always clear-cut and child development, like most areas of scientific inquiry, is marked by a variety of controversies. These controversies can be stated as a series of recurring themes or questions that are debated over time as new information about development becomes available. Are some periods of development more influential than others? Do children play an active role in their own development or do they play only a passive role? Do the laws that govern development shift as society changes over time? Does development take place in similar ways in all children? These questions reflect some of the issues and themes that the developmental researchers ask about children and the study of children. Since we will encounter these themes in many forms throughout the book, it is useful to preview these themes at the beginning. The controversy that surrounds many of these

Modern theories of development recognize the importance of cross-cultural differences.

questions reminds us that the scientific study of development is an ongoing search for answers. Not everyone agrees about the answers to these recurring questions, but our understanding is enhanced by the attempts that researchers make to solve these puzzles of development.

Biological versus Environmental Influences

Most modern viewpoints recognize that both biological and environmental factors are influential, but there is disagreement over the relative importance of these factors for different aspects of development. Earlier biological extremists argued that biology is destiny and development is merely a matter of maturation. *Maturation* is the term used to describe the biological processes that these theorists assume govern development. They believed that the course of development is largely predestined and predetermined by genetic factors. One early advocate of this view was Arnold Gesell, who suggested: "All things considered, the inevitableness and surety of maturation are the most impressive characteristics of early development. It is the hereditary ballast which conserves and stabilizes the growth of each individual infant" (Gesell, 1928, p. 378). At the other extreme, some early theorists, such as the behaviorist John B. Watson (1928), placed their emphasis strictly on the environment. Watson assumed that biological genetic factors place no restrictions on the ways that environmental events can shape the course of development. By proper organization of the environment, a Mozart, a Babe Ruth, or an Al Capone could be produced.

Today neither of these extreme positions has any supporters. The question for modern developmental psychologists is to explore how biological and environmental factors interact to produce developmental differences in various children. The interplay between biology and environment is evident in many ways, including the interaction between hormones and exposure to aggressive experiences in the development of aggression, the relation between genetics and nutrition in physical and social development, and the interaction between infant temperament and the home environment on social and personality development.

The Passive versus the Active Child

Some developmental psychologists view the child as a passive organism who is shaped mainly by external forces in the environment. Children are assertive or shy largely as a result of parental childrearing practices. Delinquency is caused by being associated with an antisocial peer group. Children's interest in history and geometry is the product of a talented teacher. Others sharply disagree with this view of children as playing a very minor role in shaping their own development. Instead of assuming that children are only passive recipients of environmental influence, they believe that children are often active agents who shape, control, and direct the course of their own development. Children are seen as curious information seekers who intentionally try to understand and explore the world about them. Moreover, in the social world the child is not simply molded by socializing agents, such as parents, peers, or teachers; instead, influence is a two-way process, with children actively modifying the actions of their parents and other people that they encounter in their daily lives.

Continuity versus Discontinuity

One of the major questions that confronts developmental psychologists is how to characterize the nature of change across development. Some theorists view development as a continuous process, whereby each new event or change builds upon earlier experiences in an orderly way. Development is smooth and gradual, without any abrupt shifts along the path. Others view development as occurring in a series of discrete steps or stages, with the organization of behavior being qualitatively different at each new stage or plateau. In this case, the concerns and developmental skills are different at each phase of development. According to this view, we should treat adolescence, for example, as a distinctive phase of development that marks an abrupt change in biological, social, and cognitive functioning. Some argue that adolescents are able to engage in deductive reasoning and to think in abstract terms—ways that are qualitatively distinct from the concrete thinking patterns of younger children. In this case, development is a discontinuous process rather than a smooth or continuous one. In contrast, those who endorse the continuous view think of the changes in adolescence as part of an ongoing series of smaller shifts that have been going on throughout childhood. We will encounter theorists later in this chapter, such as Piaget and Freud, who see both cognitive and social development as proceeding through a series of stages. At each stage, new strategies for understanding and acquiring knowledge and for managing interpersonal relationships come into play and displace the prior ways of dealing with the world. Other theorists, such as Bandura, advocate the continuous view of development.

Early versus Later Experience

A related question concerns the relative importance of different periods of development. Are some phases more important than others for acquiring certain types of skills, abilities, or knowledge? A more extreme way of putting this question would be: Are there critical periods in which the child must experience certain kinds of social and sensory input if development is to proceed normally? In recent years, hospitals have allowed mothers and infants to have close contact in the minutes and hours immediately after birth in order to permit bonding between the mother and baby to take place. It was assumed that the emotional attachment between mothers and infants could not develop adequately if the mother was deprived of this opportunity for contact with her baby during this early critical period. Careful evaluation of the bonding notion has yielded little support for the necessity of early mother-baby contact (Goldberg, 1983). The human mother-child relationship is malleable and plastic, and opportunities at a variety of time periods can promote good parent-child relations. Similarly, if the child is deprived of many opportunities for normal social and cognitive development in infancy, the effects are not necessarily irreversible. In a classic study, Skeels (1966) found that infants who were reared in a very impoverished orphanage, but later transferred to stimulating adoptive homes, grew up without any identifiable intellectual deficits. Those who continued in the orphanage grew up to be retarded. This work illustrates that the deleterious effects of adverse early experience can be modified. However, the issue remains a controversial one (Bornstein, 1989). Some behaviors, such as the acquisition of a second language, may be more open to modification at certain periods of development. We can think of these as sensitive, rather than critical periods. Other behaviors, such as human social relationships, may be highly plastic and open to change across all points of development.

Situational Influences versus Individual Characteristics

Children grow up in a variety of diverse settings such as homes, schools, streets, and playgrounds. How much do the contexts in which we study children affect what we learn about them? Do children shift their behavior from one setting to another, or do individual predispositions and personality characteristics cause them to behave in a similar fashion across a broad range of situations? Can we describe certain children as honest, dependent, aggressive, or helpful? How will these traits be manifested as children move from one situation to another—a difficult test, a confrontation with an angry parent or teacher, a competitive game, or a friend in need? Developmental psychologists differ in terms of the importance they assign to personality or person factors in contrast to situational or setting variables. Many resolve this controversy by adopting an interactionist viewpoint which stresses the dual role of personality and situational factors (Magnusson, 1988). For example, children who have aggressive personality traits may often seek out contexts in which they can display these characteristics and so are more likely to join a gang or enroll in a karate class than join the local church choir or sign up for a stamp club!

Cultural Universals versus Cultural Relativism

Children who grow up on a farm in China, on a kibbutz in Israel, or in a village in Peru have very different kinds of experiences from children who spend their childhood in a suburb in the United States. Developmental psychologists differ in how they view the importance of culture. Some argue that culture-free laws of development can be discovered that apply to all children in all cultures. Others argue that the cultural setting in which children grow up will have a profound influence on the laws governing development. Between these extreme views is one suggesting that development proceeds in the same orderly fashion, but the rates at which children in different societies progress may vary. In some cultures, children are encouraged to walk very early and are given opportunities to exercise their new skills. In other cultures, infants are carried or swaddled, which reduces their chances to walk until they are older.

Cultural contexts do not necessarily mean exotic and distant places. It is important to remember that within single countries, such as the United States, Australia, or Russia, there is a wide range of subcultural groups representing very diverse racial and ethnic traditions. In the United States, for example, it is not uncommon to find Native American, African American, Japanese American, Hispanic American, as well as Euro-American children together in a single school or classroom. In spite of the controversy about how culture influences develop, today most child developmentalists recognize the importance of considering cultural contexts in their accounts of development. In Chapter 9, we will encounter a theorist, Lev Vygotsky, who has emphasized the important role that culture plays in development.

Status of Secular Trends

Cultures are, of course, constantly undergoing change. In our own society, a series of dramatic changes have taken place over the last thirty years. Television is available to 99 percent of households, the majority of women work outside the home, divorce and remarriage are more common, delayed childbearing is on the rise—to mention only a few recent changes. Are the laws that govern children's behavior affected by these changes, or do children develop in much the same way regardless of the time? Theories differ considerably in how seriously they take these kinds of changes into account, but all recognize that these changes may play a part in influencing a child's development.

Basic Research versus Application of Knowledge

Some people want to know about the laws that govern how children think, feel, and behave. Others want to know how knowledge of child development can help solve practical problems. Recently the lines between these two positions have blurred. Consider the problem of day care for infants and toddlers. From a practical perspective, we would want to know how early infants should enter day care, how large the "class" should be, what kind of curriculum should be used. Often, answers to these questions come from basic research in social, emotional, and cognitive development. Moreover, the effects of being in day care on children's intellectual development or peer relations can often help us understand the effects of different types of early rearing experiences on children's development. In this case, there is a constant interplay between basic and applied research—an interplay that is common in contemporary child development.

These themes, issues, and controversies will emerge repeatedly throughout the book as we discuss the many sides of development—biological, cognitive, linguistic, and socioemotional.

THEORETICAL PERSPECTIVES ON DEVELOPMENT

Theories of development play a central part in the scientific process of understanding children's development. Theories serve two main functions. First, they help organize and integrate existing information into a coherent and interesting account of how children develop. Second, they lead to testable hypotheses or predictions about behavior. No theory is able to account for all aspects of human development. Developmental theories usually try to explain and predict a limited area of behavior, such as language development, cognition, or social behavior. Different theories vary in the emphasis and interpretations they place on the previously discussed themes of development.

We will now explore some of the principal theories that have guided research in child psychology. First we will examine the behavioral approaches of Pavlov, Skinner, and Bandura and touch briefly on the theory of cognitive development of Jean Piaget. Then we will move on to the psychoanalytic theory of Sigmund Freud and its social extension in the work of Erik Erikson. Finally, ethological, ecological, and life span approaches will be briefly explored.

Behavioral Perspectives

EARLY VIEWS

The behaviorist approach to development is exemplified in the early work of John B. Watson, Ivan Pavlov, and B. F. Skinner. Behaviorists view development as a continuous, rather than a discontinuous, or stagelike, process. The same principles of learning are assumed to shape development across the life span. Children play a relatively passive role in their own development. Just as the computer can do only as much as the programmer directs it to do, so children do only what the environment directs them to do. These behavioristic theorists developed central ideas of learning and applied these principles to children's development. Watson and Pavlov used the concepts of classical conditioning to explain children's behavior. In a famous demonstration, Pavlov showed that a dog would learn to salivate at the sound of a bell as a result of the bell's always being associated or paired with food; if this pairing occurred frequently, eventually the bell alone produced the salivation. This type of learning is called *classical conditioning*. Watson used classical conditioning to explain many aspects of children's behavior, especially emotions such as fear. For example, a child may become afraid of doctors as a result of associating the pain of an injection with the sight of the doctor.

Another form of conditioning—*operant conditioning*—studied by B. F. Skinner, focuses on the impact of the consequences of behavior, rather than the simple co-occurrence of stimuli. According to Skinner, behavior is modified by the type of rewarding or punishing events that follow it. Positive reinforcement, such as a friendly smile, praise, or a special treat, can increase the likelihood that a behavior will occur again, while punishment, such as a frown, criticism, or the withdrawal of such privileges as watching television, tends to decrease the chance that the behavior will recur. Skinner has explained a wide range of behaviors using operant reinforcement principles. Although Skinner did not apply his principles to children, many later researchers have shown the value of this approach for understanding both how children's behavior develops and how to change it. Gerald Patterson (1982), for example, has shown how the attention that hitting and teasing elicits from parents and siblings in the home often functions as a positive reinforcer and can increase children's aggressive behavior. Similarly, he has shown that punishment of this behavior by "time-out"—a brief period of isolation away from other family members—can help diminish aggressive actions. Operant conditioning has been incorporated into many applied programs to help teachers and parents change children's behavior. For an illustration of how operant principles have been used in the classroom, see Box 1-2.

Social Learning Theory

Another version of the behavioral approach is *social learning theory*. According to this view, children learn not only through classical and operant conditioning but also by observing and imitating others (Bandura, 1989). In a series of classic studies, Bandura showed that children's aggressive behavior could be increased by exposing them to another person behaving aggressively. Nursery school children watched an adult punch, kick, and pummel a large inflated Bobo doll. In contrast to children who had not seen the model, the children who watched the adult assault the doll were more aggressive when given the chance to play with the inflated toy. Moreover, many of the bizarre and novel responses that the adult model had exhibited were accurately

BOX 1-2 OPERANT PRINCIPLES CAN HELP HYPERACTIVE CHILDREN

In nearly every classroom in the country there is a hyperactive child—a child who has difficulty sitting still, attending to the teacher, finishing school tasks. Drug therapy has been a popular solution to this problem. However, not only may drugs produce undesirable side effects, such as growth suppression and increased blood pressure, but in 30 to 50 percent of the cases, drug treatments are ineffective. An alternative is the use of operant learning principles to control this type of child. Daniel O'Leary and his colleagues (1976) assigned nine children to a therapy program for ten weeks and compared them with a group of eight nontreated but equally hyperactive children in the third to fifth grades. In the authors' words:

> The primary treatment consisted of a home-based reward program. This program had five components: (1) specification of each child's daily classroom goals; (2) praising the child for efforts to achieve those goals; (3) end-of-day evaluation of the child's behavior relevant to the specified goals; (4) sending the parents a daily report card on their child's daily progress; and (5) rewarding of the child by the parent for progress toward his goals. (p. 511)
>
> During the program period, the teacher advised the parents on their child's progress by means of a daily report card. At the end of each day, the teacher completed the daily report, to be taken home by the child to his parents. They, in turn, rewarded him every time he had met his goals for the day, as indicated by the teacher's report. (p. 512)

To assess the effectiveness of using parents as therapists, two measures were made before and after treatment. First, a teacher's rating scale was employed that measured the degree of inattentiveness, anxiety, conduct problems, and hyperactivity displayed by the child. Second, a specifically designed problem-behavior rating scale was established for each; this consisted of an 8-point rating of the severity of four or five problem behaviors for each child.

The results were clear: In comparison to the nontreated children, the children in the operant therapy group showed significant improvement on both of the rating scales. They were rated as less hyperactive by their teachers and exhibited fewer problem behaviors. In a related study, Susan O'Leary and William Pelham (1977) have made an even more dramatic demonstration. Hyperactive children who were being treated by medication were taken off their drug and were given behavior therapy. The children who received behavior modification therapy improved just as much as those children who were treated with medication. Together, these studies not only demonstrate the value of operant principles in real-life settings but illustrate that operant principles can be an effective alternative way of treating hyperactivity.

Sources: O'Leary, K. D., Pelham, W. E., Rosenbaum, A., & Price, G. H. (1976). Behavioral treatment of hyperkinetic children. *Clinical Pediatrics*, **15**, 510–515; O'Leary, S. G., & Pelham, W. E. (1977). Behavior therapy and withdrawal of stimulant medication with hyperactive children. *Pediatrics*, **60**, 101–115.

Observational learning such as that on *Sesame Street* has been found to be effective in teaching children cognitive skills.

BOX 1-3 *PSYCHOLOGY IN ACTION* THE EFFECTS OF "SESAME STREET"

Can children learn new intellectual skills from watching television? To answer this question, "Sesame Street" was introduced to millions of American children in the late 1960s. The aim of the show was to improve the cognitive skills of preschoolers so that they would be better prepared for elementary school education. By using TV as a medium, the Children's Television Workshop hoped to bring the educational message to a large portion of preschool children. In fact, among its target group of 3- to 5-year-olds, "Sesame Street" is very popular with children averaging three to four hours per week of viewing. Over 1.4 million households watch this program. The show introduced Cookie Monster, Bert, Ernie, and their zany companions. However, it was not merely puppets and a host of clever attention-holding tactics but a well-defined set of educational goals that made "Sesame Street" so successful. And it has worked, as demonstrated in evaluations conducted by Ball and Bogatz (1972). Children were tested on a variety of items such as identifying body parts, letters, numbers, geometric forms, sorting, and classification before and after a six-month viewing period.

Although there was an initial concern that not enough children would watch to permit an evaluation, nearly everyone watched occasionally. Therefore, children were divided into four groups based on their frequency of watching the program: group 1 watched "Sesame Street" rarely, group 2 watched two or three times a week, children in group 3 viewed four or five times a week, and group 4 viewers saw the program more than five times a week. Children who watched "Sesame Street" showed a marked improvement in a variety of cognitive skills; more important, as Figure 1-1 clearly shows, as viewing became heavier, the amount of improvement increased. The more one watched, the more one learned. Finally, the results were not restricted to middle-class children; disadvantaged children who watched showed marked improvements as well. Perhaps one of the most interesting outcomes is that reading skills improved, even though this was not specifically taught on "Sesame Street." Later studies underscored the continuing benefits of "Sesame Street" viewing for children today. One recent study (Rice, Huston, Truglio, & Wright, 1990) found that 3- to 5-year-old viewers of "Sesame Street" demonstrated larger vocabularies over a two-year viewing period and the effects were not due to other factors, such as parent education, parent attitudes, or family size. The impact on 5- to 7-year-olds was more modest, which suggests that the impact of the program is greatest for preschoolers. These results leave little doubt that children learn by observation and that TV can be an important educational tool.

Sources: Ball, S., & Bogatz, J. (1972). Summative research of Sesame Street: Implications for the study of preschool children. In A. D. Pick (Ed.), *Minnesota Symposia on Child Psychology* (Vol. 6). Minneapolis: University of Minnesota Press; Rice, M. L., Huston, A. C., Truglio, R. T., & Wright, J. C. (1990). Words from *Sesame Street*: Learning vocabulary while viewing. *Developmental Psychology*, **26**, 421–428.

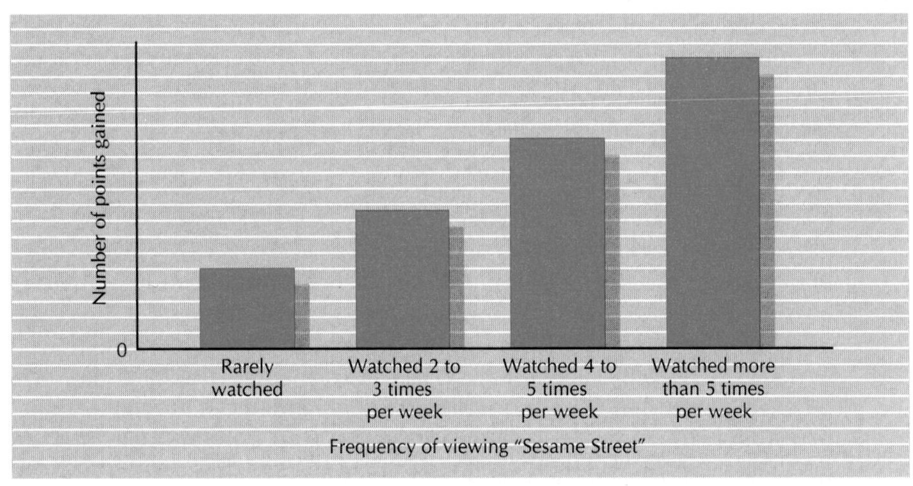

FIGURE 1-1

Improvement in total test scores for children with differing amount of viewing ("Sesame Street") experience.

reproduced by the child observers. Learning, in the absence of any apparent reinforcers delivered to either the model or the viewer, clearly had taken place. For an example of social learning theory in action, turn to Box 1-3 for a demonstration of the impact of the television program "Sesame Street" on children's intellectual development. As these studies dramatically illustrate, social learning theory both focused our attention on the beneficial as well as potentially harmful effects of television viewing on young children.

Moreover, this theory provided a set of clues or ideas about how the process of imitation works. That, in turn, led to a number of experiments that tested these ideas. According to social learning theory, imitation is not automatic; children are selective about which behaviors they imitate, and they don't imitate every behavior they observe. In order to understand some of these variations in modeling, contemporary social learning theorists have become increasingly interested in the role of cognitive factors in imitation. Children interpret and process the social behaviors they observe. Their personalities and past experience, their relationship with the model, the situations in which the children are involved will all have a part in determining whether imitation occurs. In addition, cognitive skills play an important role in observational learning. In order to imitate, children must be capable of remembering the behavior the model is displaying and those who use active strategies in trying to rehearse, organize, and recall the observed behaviors are more effective learners.

Together, classical, operant, and social learning approaches have been highly influential in helping researchers understand children's development. These processes will be encountered repeatedly throughout this book as we examine the social, emotional, and intellectual development of children.

Organismic Perspective

We have noted that dissatisfaction with traditional behavior theory led to greater concern with cognitive factors in modern social learning theory. This trend was largely the result of the impact of organismic theories of development. The best-known organismic theory of development is the cognitive structural theory of Jean Piaget. The student will have the opportunity to examine this theory in greater depth in Chapter 9. The relatively brief presentation of organismic theory in this section does not reflect its importance; it has had a profound influence on our thinking about human development.

According to Piaget's organismic theory, two complementary processes play a role in development in order to promote change and increase cognitive understanding. On the one hand, children use their current understanding of how the world works as a framework for absorbing or assimilating new events and experiences. On the other hand, children modify their existing knowledge base by incorporating new information into existing knowledge frameworks or mental structures and at the same time they accommodate or modify existing mental understanding in response to new input. Across development, children reach a better and more meaningful understanding of their world as a result of the interplay of these complementary processes.

According to this viewpoint, children actively construct the reality of their world. This means that children are not passive receivers of experience, but instead are actively interpreting and making sense out of the information and events that they encounter. Children are not passively shaped by the reinforcements and models to which they are exposed; they actively seek experience and construct their cognitive world. Objective reality is of little importance in explaining children's responses because children construct their own reality by interpreting and reorganizing their experiences. The way in which information is organized depends on the level of cognitive development of the child. Children go through different stages of cognitive development, each characterized by qualitatively different ways of solving problems and organizing knowledge. Young children, in contrast to adolescents and adults, are more bound to sensory and motor information, less flexible, and less able to think symbolically and abstractly. Moreover, young children are more egocentric, more centered on their own perspectives, and less able to take the viewpoints or understand the feelings and perceptions of others than are older children. Piaget has suggested that cognitive development could be thought of as a decentering process involving a shift from a focus on the self, on immediate sensory experience, and on single components in problems to a broader, more multifaceted, and more abstract view of the world.

Since the organization of intellect, knowledge, and cognitive strategies differs in different stages, cognitive development is discontinuous. Adolescence, for example, is viewed as a distinctive period of development with its own unique ways of thinking about problems and events. The adolescent, in contrast to the child in an earlier stage of development, can think in a logical fashion when approaching a new problem. The ability to engage in deductive reasoning, for example, distinguishes the child in this period of development. Children across development do not change in the amount of thinking; they shift in the kind or quality of their thought processes. To summarize, cognitive development results from the progression of the child's intelligence through a series of qualitatively different and increasingly complex reorganizations as a child moves on to more advanced levels of cognitive functioning.

Information Processing Perspective: An Alternative Approach to Cognition

In contrast to Piaget's theory of cognitive development, a popular approach to understanding cognitive development is the information processing approach. Instead of focusing on stages of development, this type of theory emphasizes "the information that children represent, the process that they use to transform the information, and the memory limits that constrain the amount of information they can represent and process. The quality of children's thinking at any stage depends on what information they represent in a particular situation, how they operate on the information to achieve their goal and how much information they can keep in mind at one time" (Siegler, 1991, p. 59).

Theorists in this tradition often use computer analogies and flowcharts which help them describe the precise steps that a child must take to solve a problem and generate an answer. This does not mean that children (or adults) think the same way as computers operate, but the use of these strategies helps the researcher plot the expected steps in an exact manner. Figure 1-2 provides one example of an information processing model in which the steps in thinking are spelled out in detail. As we will see in Chapters 9 and 10, this approach has been applied to a wide range of problems of cognitive development, including attention, memory, problem solving, and planning. Moreover, it is proving a highly valuable approach to the study of how children develop an understanding of reading, mathematics, and science

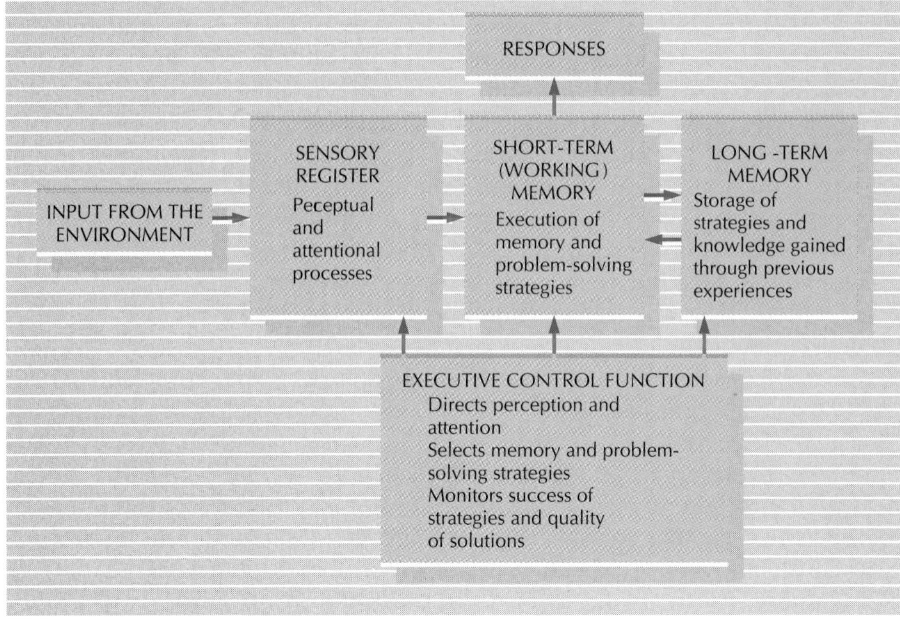

FIGURE 1-2
Modified information processing model with executive control function. *(From Atkinson & Shiffrin, 1968.)*

(Siegler, 1991). Finally, this approach has provided a powerful analytic tool for understanding social behavior, such as social problem solving and aggression (Dodge, 1985).

Psychodynamic Perspective

With his introduction of psychoanalytic theory, Sigmund Freud initiated a revolution in thinking about human motivation and personality. His emphasis on the critical role of the preschool years in the development of personality and on the role of instinctual and unconscious motivation was viewed as radical in the early decades of this century, when his theory was first becoming known.

According to Freud, development is governed by unconscious drives and instincts. Freud stressed the role of biological influences and how biologically based drives, such as sex, aggression, and hunger, were shaped by encounters with the environment, especially with other family members. For Freud, the structure of the developing personality consists of three interrelated parts: the id, the ego, and the superego. The role that each of these three aspects of personality plays changes across development as the infant, who is largely under the control of instinctual drives, gradually becomes more rational and reality-bound. The infant is guided by the id, which is the instinctual component of personality and operates on the pleasure principle. The pleasure principle is oriented toward maximizing pleasure and satisfying needs immediately. As the infant develops, the ego, or the rational controlling part of personality, emerges. The ego attempts to gratify the needs of the person through appropriate socially constructive mechanisms. The third component of personality, the superego, emerges when the child internalizes parental or societal morals, values, and roles. This acceptance, or internalization, results in the development of conscience.

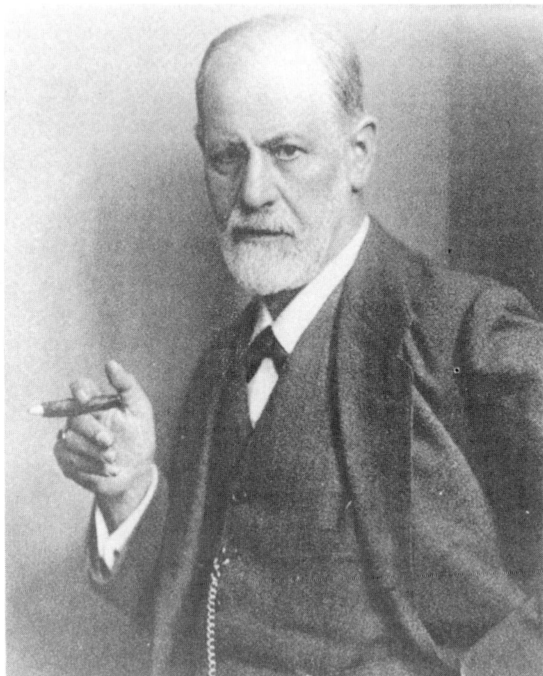

Sigmund Freud.

To Freud, development was a discontinuous process that proceeded in a series of discrete stages. In each stage, certain biological forces play a central role in organizing how the infant and child relate to the world. In the first phase, the *oral stage*, which covers the first year of life, the infant is preoccupied with activities such as eating, sucking, and biting, and with objects, such as food, associated with the mouth, which Freud calls the oral zone. Freud assumed that the infant derived great enjoyment and satisfaction from these oral-related behaviors. In the second year, priorities change and the *anal stage* begins. The infant and toddler is now involved with anal activities. At this time, too, parents are concerned with toilet training. In the third year, and until approximately the fifth year, the infant's focus shifts again from elimination and retention to the *phallic* or *Oedipal stage*: the child's sexual curiosity is aroused and attention is drawn to the genitals. Pleasure from stimulation of the genitals is discovered. At the same time, children's awareness of their sexual anatomy, and particularly of anatomical differences between the sexes, begins. In this period, boys experience the emergence of the Oedipus complex, which consists of sexual feeling for the mother and jealousy of the father and rivalry with him for the mother's attention. Girls, in the Electra complex, experience similar dynamics in relation to their parents but to a less severe degree than boys. Freud called the next stage the *latency period* because he believed that sexual drives are submerged or latent in this period. It is partly to avoid reminders of sexual feelings that occurred during the phallic phase that children avoid relationships with opposite-sex peers and become intensely involved with same-sex peers during this period from 6 years of age to puberty. This is an issue to which we will return in our exploration of peer relations in Chapter 13. This turning from the family to the peer group is associated with the acquisition of social skills, which are necessary to function effectively in the social world. Finally, in the last period, the *genital stage*, sexual desires reemerge, but this time more appropriately directed to opposite-sex peers. As at earlier stages, the onset of biological changes—in this case, puberty—plays a significant role in defining the focus of the particular stage of development.

According to Freud, the ways in which each of these stages is managed by the child will have a profound impact on the later adult personality. For example, infants who have unsatisfied needs for oral stimulation may be more likely to smoke as adults. Or toddlers who were toilet trained very early may be obsessively concerned with neatness and cleanliness. Few of these predictions have in fact been supported, but the general view that events in infancy and childhood may have a formative impact on later development remains a central issue about the nature of development.

Freud was an innovative theorist who constantly revised his theory, and his followers have moved toward a decreased emphasis on instinctual forces and an increased emphasis on the effects of social experience.

This general shift is well illustrated by the stage theory of Erik Erikson, one of Freud's most influential disciples. Table 1-1 presents a comparison of the stages of Freud and Erikson. In contrast to Freud, whose stage theory covers only the years up to adolescence, Erikson's stages encompass the full life span. Moreover, Erikson devoted much more attention to cultural, in contrast to biological, influences in development. Erikson's theory is organized around the basic personal and social tasks that need to be solved at each stage of development rather than around ways of dealing with instinctual needs.

In the first stage, the challenge of acquiring a sense of *basic trust versus mistrust* is the main task. For infants, who are highly dependent organisms, the central concern is "Is the world to be trusted"? Through their parents' handling of infants' early needs, infants' basic sense of trust in their environment is determined. In the next stage, the phase of *autonomy versus shame and doubt*, children deal with their emerging sense of autonomy but remain worried and concerned about their continuing dependency on adults and their inability to live up to adult demands and expectations. At 3 to 5 years of age, the stage of *initiative versus guilt*, children struggle with learning to take responsibility and master their environment, but often at the price of offending their loved parents. Just as in Freud's theory, rivalry with the same-sex parent occurs, but resolves itself by an increased orientation to other social partners, such as peers. *Industry versus inferiority* is the next stage, which spans the middle years of childhood (age 6 to 12). Again as in Freud's latency phase, children become increasingly oriented to peers and mastery

TABLE 1-1 **FREUD AND ERIKSON: STAGES OF DEVELOPMENT**

AGE	FREUD	ERIKSON
Infancy	Oral	Basic trust vs. mistrust
1–2	Anal	Autonomy vs. shame, doubt
3–5	Phallic	Initiative vs. guilt
6–12	Latency	Industry vs. inferiority
12–8	Genital	Identity vs. role confusion
Young adulthood		Intimacy vs. isolation
Adulthood		Generativity vs. stagnation
Maturity		Ego integrity vs. despair

of intellectual, social, and physical skills. It is also a period of constant social comparison whereby children evaluate their skills in relation to their peers. The result is sometimes a feeling of inferiority to others. In adolescence, the stage of *identity versus role confusion* ensues, and the main focus is the search for a stable definition of the self. Unlike Freud, who emphasizes the childhood stages of development, Erikson has three additional stages of development that cover the adult years. In young adulthood, the task is to form an intimate relationship with another adult. Hence, the name of this stage is *intimacy versus isolation*. This stage is followed by the stage of *generativity versus stagnation*, where the focus is on the bearing and rearing of children. In this period, the provision of clear guidelines and assistance of the next generation is a central concern. Stagnation is the outgrowth of failing to achieve this goal. *Ego integrity versus despair* is the final stage in Erikson's eight ages of man. Reflection on one's past accomplishments and failures organizes this last phase of life.

Psychodynamic theories have helped shape many of the concerns of modern child psychology, including the impact of early experience on later behavior, the role of the family in socialization, and—particularly through Erikson's work—the impact of culture on children's development. Until recently few modern researchers were actively testing these theories and their importance was largely as historical influence. Currently, there has been a revival of interest in some issues, such as adolescent identity formation, that were originally raised by psychodynamic theorists (Grotevant, 1986; Waterman, 1985). In spite of the recent interest, these theories emerged from a clinical tradition and have been more difficult to integrate into the mainstream of scientific child psychology than have the other empirically based theories of development discussed in this chapter.

Ethological Perspective

The ethological perspective is a biologically oriented position that seeks to understand the evolution of behavior, the causes of behavior, the developmental course, and the use or function of behavior (Hinde, 1987, 1989). This viewpoint has emerged from the earlier pioneering work of two famous European animal scientists, Konrad Lorenz and Niko Tinbergen, and in the last two decades there has been an increasing interest among child developmental researchers in this perspective. Humans as well as animals have a variety of behaviors that are "species-specific" or unique to their species and may aid us in understanding how children develop. One of the goals of ethology is the search for these cross-cultural universals—those behaviors which are common to all human children across a wide range of different cultures. Recent studies have found that emotional expressions such as joy, sadness, disgust, and anger are universal and are similar across a wide range of modern cultures such as Brazil, Japan, and the United States, as well as older cultures such as the Fore and Dori tribes of New Guinea (Ekman, 1972; Ekman et al., 1987).

Moreover, many universal behaviors such as smiling and crying that are seen across a range of cultures have a biological basis and play an important role in ensuring that children's needs are met by their caregivers. Crying can be viewed as an "elicitor" of parental behavior; it serves the function of communicating the fact that a child is distressed or hungry. In evolutionary terms it has clear survival value by ensuring that the young infant receives the kind of attention necessary for adequate development. In Chapter 7, we

Ethological theories suggest that similar emotional expressions are universal, as shown by this smiling girl from the Masai tribe in Kenya.

will examine, in detail, John Bowlby's theory of attachment—a significant example of an ethological approach to early social relationships. Although ethologists view many elicitors such as crying as biologically based, they assume that these types of behaviors are modified by environmentally based experiences. For example, children may learn to mask their emotions by smiling even when they are unhappy, or expressing surprise even when they knew what was expected (Saarni & Crowley, 1990). The important point is that modern ethologists view children as open to learning and input from the environment; children are not solely captives of their biological roots. Another concept that we have already encountered—the notion of critical periods—is derived from ethology. This has been a very powerful construct which has led us to focus on the importance of the timing of events in early development.

Ethologists use the observation of children in their natural surroundings as their basic methodology and their goals are to develop detailed descriptions and classifications of behavior. They seek to understand how behavior is organized into meaningful patterns. For example, high rates of hitting, poking, kicking, and yelling are often used to define the construct of aggression, whereas a slight lift of the eyebrows, a suggestive smile, and a tilt of the head suggest a pattern of flirtatious behavior. Ethology, in fact, has been very influential in increasing the popularity of observational approaches in modern developmental psychology.

One of the major interests of ethologists is in the organization of social behavior between individuals (e.g., mother and child, brother and sister). Ethologists frequently study the role of nonverbal behavior in regulating social exchanges among children. Monkeys often use threat gestures, such as a stare and bared teeth, to ward off attackers or appeasement signs, such as baring the neck, to call a halt to a struggle. As the famous evolutionary theorist, Charles Darwin, observed over a century ago, "making oneself smaller" is an appeasement gesture that can inhibit aggression. Do children use similar tactics in appeasing an aggressor? When elementary school boys were observed at play during school recess, it was found that such behaviors as kneeling, bowing, lying down—all behaviors that involved making themselves smaller—were successful appeasement tactics (Ginsburg, Pollman, & Wauson, 1977). When the playground bully was on a rampage, boys who displayed these behaviors were more likely to successfully stop an attack. Darwin was right—and modern ethologists continue to explore ways in which social behavior is regulated by gestures, postures, expression, and other nonverbal cues. As we will see in our later examination of peer groups, ethologists have also made important contributions to our understanding of how children's groups are organized. It turns out that monkeys are not the only ones to develop dominance hierarchies; children develop specific organization structures, including "pecking orders," as well! Ethology is becoming an increasingly useful and influential perspective for understanding children's development.

Ecological Perspective

Closely related to the ethological view is another perspective that emphasizes the study of development in context, namely, the ecological perspective. This viewpoint stresses the importance of understanding the relationship between the organism and various environmental systems, such as the family and the community. In turn, the relationships that exist among environmental systems are also of interest. Children are seen as active participants in creating their own environments. Moreover, children's subjective experiences of their relationships and surroundings are just as important as the objective aspects of the environment.

A major advocate of this approach is Urie Bronfenbrenner (1979, 1986, 1989), who has offered a framework for organizing sets of environmental systems. In his view, the child's world is organized "as a set of nested structures, each inside the next, like a set of Russian dolls" (Bronfenbrenner, 1979, p. 22). As Figure 1-3 illustrates, he proposes four contexts, or layers, which range from the most immediate settings, such as the family or peer group, to the more remote contexts in which the child is not directly involved, such as the local government. These systems and the relationships among them can change over the course of development. The most immediate setting is termed the *microsystem*, which refers to the actual setting in which the child lives and interacts with other people. The nature of the microsystem changes across development; while family and home may be most important in infancy, the school and the peer group may become additional focuses in middle childhood and adolescence. The next level, the *mesosystem*, comprises the interrelations among contexts of the microsystems in which the child actively participates. For example, the relationships among the microsystems of the home, school, and peer group form the child's mesosystem. For an adult, the links among the microsystems of family, work, and friends define the mesosystem. In the next level, the *exosystem*, are settings that influence a child's development but in which the child does not play a direct role. The workplace of parents is a prime example of a setting that has a profound impact on the child even though the child's own involvement and participation is minimal. When a father has to travel a great deal or suddenly goes on shift work, the nature of the child's family life may change. Other examples of the exosystem might include the local school board, the zoning commission, or a school class attended by an older sibling. If a planning commission runs

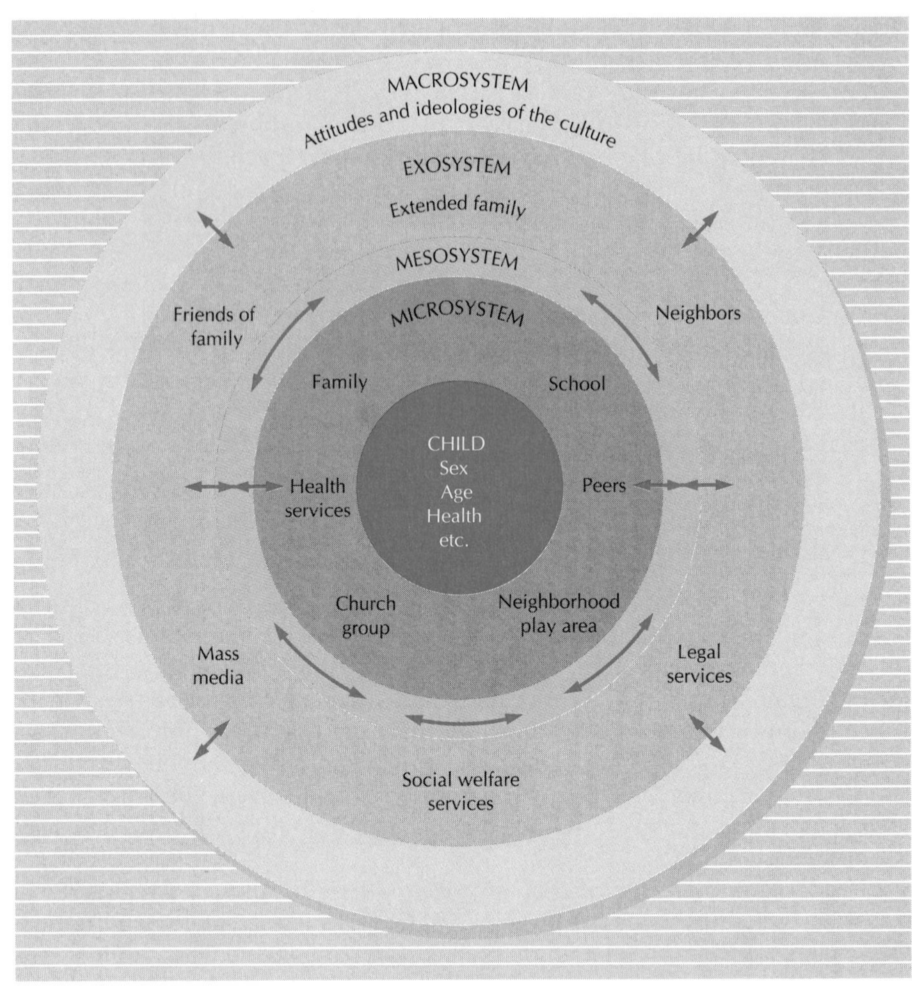

FIGURE 1-3
Bronfenbrenner's ecological model. The ecological system: microsystem refers to relations between the child and the immediate environment; mesosystem refers to the network of interrelationships of settings in the child's immediate environment; exosystem refers to social settings that affect the child but do not directly impinge upon him or her; and macrosystem refers to the attitudes, mores, beliefs, and ideologies of the culture. *(From Garbarino, 1982, by permission of the author and publisher.)*

a highway through the local playground, the child's recreational life may deteriorate. Finally, both mesosystem and exosystem are embedded within a set of ideological and institutional patterns of a particular culture or subculture, which Bronfenbrenner terms the *macrosystem*. This level recognizes that broad patterns of beliefs and ideology distinguish different cultures and countries, as well as different subcultures within a country. Children who grow up in China experience a different social ideology than children who grow up in the United States. Children who live in an inner-city ghetto are exposed to a different set of values and beliefs than children in an affluent suburb. The importance of Bronfenbrenner's ecological scheme stems from the fact that it stresses the importance of analyzing relationships between the child and a variety of environmental systems, as well as relationships among these systems. In addition, it emphasizes that the ecology of the child is never static. Development involves the interaction of a changing child with a changing matrix of ecological systems.

Life Span Perspective

A perspective that has gained increasing recognition in recent years is the life span viewpoint. In contrast to traditional development perspectives, which focus mainly on infancy through adolescence, the life span view recognizes that development is a process that continues throughout the life cycle into adulthood and old age (Baltes, 1987).

The unique focus of this perspective is on tracing the ways in which people develop and change across the life course. Childhood is not viewed as a shaping or formative period that dictates later stages of development. Instead, all periods of life from childhood to old age are viewed as important periods of development. At all points in development, the individual is open or susceptible to change. According to a life span perspective, change over development can be traced to three sets of causes. First, there are normative, age-graded events, which are experiences that most children and adults undergo at roughly the same age or time in their lives. Some of these experiences are biological or maturational. The onset of walking in infancy is one example of a normative biological event. Similarly, the onset of menarche in adolescence is another event that occurs at approximately the same age period for most girls. Individual differences, of course, are present, but there is an average or normative schedule for these biological events. Programmed by our society are other normative events which have schedules, or agenda that most individuals follow as they progress across development. For example, children enter school at approximately age 5 and begin college at 17 or 18 years of age. In turn, marriage is generally postponed until the early or mid-twenties or even later.

However, development does not always conform to a previously prescribed schedule; unexpected events often intervene to push development in new directions. Life span theorists term these *nonnormative events,* since they neither happen to everyone in the normal course of development nor follow any preset schedule. Instead, these are events that can happen to any child or family at any time and often without much warning or anticipation. Divorce, job loss, or residence change are events that may have a profound

Life-course theories emphasize cohort or historical effects on development. Events such as the Great Depression of the 1930s provided a unique set of experiences for developing children.

BOX 1-4 CHILDREN OF THE GREAT DEPRESSION

What happens to children when economic disaster strikes? To find out, Elder (1974) studied children who were part of an ongoing longitudinal project concerning social and intellectual development in California. These children were involved in the study when the economy collapsed at the time of the Great Depression. Some of the children were just entering school at the time of the Depression while others were teenagers. Not all families suffered or lost their jobs, and Elder compared families who were severely deprived with those who remained relatively well off.

In the economically deprived families, dramatic changes in family roles and relationships occurred that affected the child's development. The division of labor and power within the family shifted. As fathers' jobs disappeared and income dropped, mothers entered the labor market or took in boarders. As a result, the mother's power increased and the power, prestige, and emotional significance of the father decreased. Divorce, separation, and desertion rose, especially among couples with a poor relationship before the onset of bad economic times (Liker & Elder, 1983).

Roles changed for children too. Girls were drafted into more household work while the older boys took more outside jobs. Parent-child relationships changed in response to economic hardship, especially for fathers, who became more indifferent, more punitive, and less supportive of their children. In turn, boys, not girls, tended to shift away from the family and became more peer-oriented. However, both boys and girls were moodier, more easily slighted, and less calm. Boys often became ill-tempered and angry (Elder, 1984). The effects of the Depression were greater for the children who were young when catastrophe struck. This was due to the fact that the younger children were more dependent on their parents and were exposed to the altered situation in the home for a longer time span.

Nor were these effects short-lived. When these children became adults their values, work patterns, and marriages remained affected by these earlier experiences. Men who were forced to enter the job market as teenagers because of economic hardship preferred secure but modest jobs over riskier but higher-status positions. However, they were also less satisfied with their work and income. In addition to vocational problems, men and women who had experienced adjustment problems in response to the Depression in the 1930s had less-successful marriages. Men and women who were ill-tempered children had less-stable marriages, while women with childhood difficulties married men who were lacking in ambition and achievement (Caspi, Elder, & Bem, 1987). Finally, girls who were prone to temper outbursts as children became ill-tempered parents; thus we see a three-generational impact of the Depression. Clearly, economic hardship left its mark on the lives of many of these families. On the other hand, some families managed well in spite of economic hardship, particularly if the family ties were strong before the onset of the Depression. Studies of this kind help us appreciate the impact of unexpected historical changes on children and families.

Sources: Caspi, A. Elder, G., & Bem, D. (1987). Life-course patterns of explosive children. *Developmental Psychology*, 23, 308–313; Elder, G. (1974). *Children of the Great Depression*. Chicago: University of Chicago Press. Elder. G. (1984). Parent-child behavior in hard times and the life course: A multi-generational perspective. In P. B. Baltes & O. G. Brim, Jr. (Eds.), *Life-span development and behavior*. New York: Academic; Liker, J. K., & Elder, G. (1983). Economic hardship and marital relations in the 1930s. *American Sociological Review*, 48, 343–359.

impact on the child, but are not part of the normal, expected occurrences. We will examine one of the nonnormative events—divorce—in detail in Chapter 12. Finally, according to the life span perspective, a third set of factors influences development, namely, cohort effects. Cohort is a term used to describe a group of children who were born in the same year (for example, 1950) or the same general period (1960–1965). As cohorts develop, they share the same set of historical experiences that are unique to each group born in a particular era. Children who were born in 1950, for example, were adolescents during the 1960s—the turbulent Vietnam era in American society. In contrast, children who were born in 1940 or 1960 were either children or young adults during this period and their adolescence was not marked by the upheaval and social unrest that the adolescents of the 1950 cohort encountered. Therefore, the historical context is an important source of influence on the developing child. Development may be different for different cohorts of children. In summary, the life span viewpoint focuses on three sources of influence on development: (1) normative age-graded factors, (2) nonnormative events, and (3) cohort or historical effects. These effects on development are illustrated in Elder's (1974) study, presented in Box 1-4, of children who lived through the Great Depression of the 1930s.

DEVELOPMENTAL THEMES AND THEORETICAL PERSPECTIVES: AN OVERVIEW

Before closing this chapter, we turn to Table 1-2. In this chart we summarize the ways in which alternative theoretical perspectives emphasize the different themes outlined at the beginning of this chapter. As we will stress throughout the remaining pages of this book, the understanding of children's development can be approached from many perspectives. Some perspectives offer better and more complete accounts of some aspects of development than do others. For example, Piaget's cognitive organismic theory is especially helpful in explaining children's cognitive development, while Bandura's social learning theory offers a useful perspective for explaining social development. Freudian theory is especially useful for understanding problems of emotional dysfunction, while ethological approaches have been particularly helpful in describing the development of emotional expression and communication. Many problems and issues benefit from the application of several different theoretical perspectives. Increasingly we recognize that different aspects of development such as language and emotional and social behavior are interlinked. For example, children's learning takes place in social contexts with other people—parents and peers. The ways that children perceive the environment may be influenced by the development of their motor skills. Similarly, language and cognitive development are better understood by recognizing their mutual interdependence. In short, different aspects of development are interrelated. Therefore, it is often helpful to draw upon several theories to help understand these interrelated aspects of development. All perspectives have a place in the researcher's repertoire. In combination, they can tell us a great deal more about the course and causes of children's development than any single theory alone can tell us.

SUMMARY

WHAT IS CHILD DEVELOPMENT?

- *Child development* is the scientific study of changes in the child's biological, social, cognitive, and emotional behavior during the period of childhood. Child psychologists try to answer two major questions: How do children change as they develop, and what are the determinants of these developmental changes? Recent emphasis has been on the processes that produce and account for these changes.

WHY STUDY CHILDREN?

- We study children to increase our scientific knowledge about the ways in which development proceeds and the processes that may alter its progress. We also study children to provide practical information to assist everyone

TABLE 1-2

OVERVIEW OF MAJOR DEVELOPMENTAL THEMES AND THEORETICAL PERSPECTIVES

THEMES	BEHAVIORISTIC		ORGANISMIC (PIAGET)	INFORMATION PROCESSING	PSYCHODYNAMIC		ETHOLOGICAL	ECOLOGICAL	LIFE SPAN
Description vs. process	Process (emphasis on conditioning)	Process (emphasis on observational learning	Description and process (emphasis on adaptation)	Process (emphasis on analytic strategies)	Both process and description of types of personality and psychopathology	Both process and description	Both description of behavior in natural settings and process	Description of levels of environmental organization and processes of modification and change	Description of the impact of normative, nonnormative, and historical events on development and processes emphasizing changing individual in a changing world
Biological vs. environmental	Environmental	Environmental	Interaction between biology and environment	Focus on environment, but recognizes biological constraints	Interaction between biology and environment		Biological emphasis, but environment plays a role in eliciting and modifying behavior patterns	Biology is recognized but the main emphasis is on environmental factors	Biological constraints are recognized but the main emphasis is on environmental factors
Continuity vs. discontinuity	(1) Conditioning Continuous (nonstage view)	(2) Social learning Continuous (nonstage view)	Discontinuous stages of development	Continuous	(1) Freud: discontinuous (stages of development across childhood)	(2) Erikson: discontinuous (stages of development across life space)	Discontinuous	Continuous (nonstage view)	Continuous (nonstage view)
Early vs. later experience	Experience at all points in development is important		Impact of experience is limited by stage of development	Experience at all points in development is important	Early experience is of special importance		Early experience is of special importance	Experience at all points in development is important	Experience throughout the life span is important

Passive vs. active child	Passive child	Moderately active child	Highly active child	Active, reflective child	Passive but increasingly active across development	Passive but increasingly active across development	Moderately active child	Highly active child	Highly active child
Situational Influences vs. individual characteristics	High in situational influences	High in situational influences	High in emphasis on individual characteristics (cognitive structures)	Both individual characteristics (skills and strategies) and situational influences (how problem is presented) are important.	High on individual traits		High on situational influences	High on situational influences (e.g., environmental settings)	High on situational influences
Cultural-bound vs. cross-cultural universal principles	Cross-cultural universals	Cross-cultural universals	Cross-cultural universals	Cross-cultural universal processes but cultural-bound products	Cross-cultural universals	Cultural-bound principles	Cross-cultural universals	Culture-bound principles	Culture-bound principles
Status of secular trends	Low emphasis	Medium emphasis	Low emphasis	Low emphasis	Low emphasis		Low emphasis	Medium emphasis	High emphasis
Applied/basic	High in basic research; high in application to clinical and educational problems		High in basic research; some application to education	High in basic research; high in education applications	Low in basic research; high in clinical applications		High in basic research; low in applications	High in basic research; high in social policy applications, prevention, and social intervention programs	High in basic research; most applications to problems associated with aging or to changes associated with historical shifts (e.g., war, depression)

who cares for children, including parents, teachers, health professionals, and policy makers.

THEMES OF DEVELOPMENT

- The two goals of research on child development are to describe changes in behavior across development, and to identify the processes or causes of development. The answers to these two questions involve a variety of controversies which were presented as recurring themes or issues that continue to be debated as new research or development becomes available.
- *Biological versus environmental influences* have long been debated. Most modern viewpoints recognize the importance of both factors, but disagree over their relative contributions. The question of interest today is *how* biological and environmental factors interact to produce developmental differences.
- *The passive versus the active child*. Some developmental psychologists believe that children actively shape, control, and direct the course of their own development; others believe that children are passive recipients of environmental influence.
- The issue of *continuity versus discontinuity* concerns the way in which developmental psychologists characterize the nature of change across development. Some theorists view development as a continuous process, whereby change is smooth and gradual. Others see development as a series of qualitatively different steps or stages.
- A related issue is the relative importance of *early versus later experience*, or how critical early experience is for later development. Although the issue remains controversial, most psychologists believe that there are sensitive periods for some behaviors, while other behaviors remain open to change across all periods of development.
- The relative importance of *situational influences versus individual characteristics* in determining how stable a child's behavior will be across contexts is another highly debated issue. Many resolve it by using an interactionist viewpoint which stresses the complementary roles of personality and situational factors.
- Developmental psychologists differ in how they view the importance of culture. Some emphasize *cultural universals* while others stress *cultural relativism*. The former lead to discovering culture-free laws of development while the latter emphasizes the effects of the cultural setting on children's development. Despite the controversy, most agree that cultural contexts must be considered in any account of development.
- Theories vary on how much they consider long-term changes in society, or *secular trends*, in their account of the laws that govern children's behavior. However, many theories recognize that societal changes have some influence on development.
- Researchers differ in their goals. Some want to know about the laws that underlie children's behavior; others want answers to practical problems concerning children. Recently, distinctions between *basic research versus applications of knowledge* have become blurred because often basic research can be used to address practical questions and issues.

THEORETICAL PERSPECTIVES ON DEVELOPMENT

- Theories serve two functions. First, they help organize and integrate existing knowledge into a coherent account of how children develop.

Second, they foster research by providing testable predictions about behavior. Theories differ on many of the issues discussed in the earlier part of the chapter. Different theoretical perspectives can be viewed as complementary, rather than competing, since each can account for different aspects of development.

- According to traditional *behavioral perspectives*, development is a continuous process, which uses the same principles of learning across the lifespan. The child is relatively passive and is molded by environmental factors that modify behavior in the form of either classical or operant conditioning. These principles have often been applied to changing children's behavior, as in the example in Box 1–2 of rewarding hyperactive children for meeting daily classroom goals.
- *Social learning theory* extended the behavioral perspective to include imitation as an additional form of learning. Studies based on this perspective have focused our attention on both the positive and negative aspects of television, a common source of models for children. According to this theory, children are selective about who and what behaviors they imitate. Contemporary versions of social learning theory have included the role of cognitive factors in their accounts of learning. Albert Bandura is a leading spokesperson for this viewpoint.
- *Organismic theory* describes the child as actively seeking information and new experiences. Children adapt to their environment by accommodating to new information and by assimilating experiences to fit existing knowledge structures. Development results from increasingly complex reorganizations of mental structures as the child moves through an invariant sequence of stages to more advanced levels of cognitive functioning. Jean Piaget is the best known advocate of this approach.
- *Information processing theories* focus on children's representations of information and how they operate on the information to achieve their goals in particular situations. Theorists in this tradition often use computer analogies and flow charts to help describe the steps involved in solving a problem. This approach has been applied to a wide range of problems in studies of cognitive development and social behavior.
- Freud's *psychodynamic theory* presents a discontinuous view of development in which the child is motivated by a set of basic biological drives that are focused on different sensory zones and different activities during the early years of development. According to this theory, later adult personality is a direct result of whether or not the child's drives were deprived or satisfied at each earlier stage.
- Erikson expanded Freud's theory to include development throughout the lifespan and to include social and cultural factors. Erikson's theory is organized around the basic personal and social tasks that need to be resolved at each stage rather than around instinctual drives.
- The *ethological perspective* takes a biological-evolutionary approach to describing development. Ethologists often study the organization of social behavior between individuals by observing and describing behavior in natural settings. They often look for similar patterns of behaviors across human and nonhuman species and across cultures to understand the origins of development.
- The *ecological perspective* stresses the importance of understanding the relationship between the organism and various environmental systems, such as the family, school, community, and culture. Development involves the interplay between changing children and their changing relationships

with different ecological systems. The child's subjective experience or understanding of the environment and the child's active role in modifying the environment are important aspects of this perspective.

- The *life span perspective* emphasizes development over the full life course rather than just during childhood. According to this view, developmental change can be traced to (1) normative age-graded events (e.g., menarche), (2) nonnormative events (e.g., divorce), and (3) historical or cohort events (e.g., the Great Depression).

CHAPTER

2

THE METHODS OF CHILD PSYCHOLOGY

Theories provide insights, hunches, and ideas about development, but the next step is to determine whether the theories are correct. Do children behave and develop in the ways that theories suggest? Child psychologists have a variety of strategies and techniques that they use to evaluate the hypotheses or predictions derived from theories of development. In this chapter we will examine some of the techniques, methods, and designs that are used to understand children's development.

First, we will examine the initial step in testing our theories—selecting a sample of children. Next, we will explore ways of gathering the data or basic information that we need about children. Parental reports, self-reports, and direct observations each provide a different perspective on the child. Next, we will examine two research strategies: the correlational and experimental methods. Then, research designs used for studying development will be described. Two principal designs are used to investigate children's development: a cross-sectional design and a longitudinal design. In the cross-sectional approach, different children at different ages are selected and studied, while in the case of the longitudinal approach, the investigator studies the same children at a variety of ages as they develop. These approaches represent plans or designs for gathering information about children at different developmental levels. Finally, we examine the ethical principles that guide the conduct of research with children.

Now we turn to a detailed look at an example of each approach.

STEPS IN THE RESEARCH PROCESS: SELECTING A SAMPLE

There are a variety of steps that an investigator takes in evaluating a theory. One of the first considerations is choosing a sample. A sample is a selected portion or set of individuals from a larger group or population that the researcher hopes is representative of this larger group. Sampling is necessary since it is impossible to test all of the infants or children from a particular region or country. This is an important first step since it will determine to a large extent the types of individuals to which the conclusions of your research can legitimately apply. As we noted in the last chapter, child psychologists are increasingly aware of the importance of the impact of culture and context on development, and the choice of the sample of children to study must take these issues into account. To illustrate the problems of selecting a sample, consider the following scenarios.

Example 1. An investigator decides to study how children's vocabulary changes over age. For convenience she goes to a private (and expensive) nursery school that is located in an affluent suburban community which serves the children of professionals, such as doctors and lawyers. She selects thirty 3-year-olds and thirty 5-year-olds and carefully tests their vocabulary levels. Based on her findings she decides that she now has a set of norms or guidelines concerning what would be expected of 3-year-olds and 5-year-olds in terms of vocabulary. What's wrong with this conclusion?

In this case the sample is not representative of children in the wider population of children in the country. You may be overestimating the vocabulary skills of 3- and 5-year-olds because they were all drawn from a school that served only children of professionals, who may encourage their children to learn new words at home and may value verbal skills in their

Selecting a sample is an important step in the research process. By including children from different cultures, statements about the universality of the issue are possible.

children more than less well educated parents. Or perhaps the nursery school helps children with their vocabulary through direct teaching. What about children of other parents who are less educated or children who don't attend nursery schools? Clearly we can't generalize about the average vocabulary accomplishment of 3- and 5-year-olds unless we sample a wide range of different types of children from various social class and ethnic groups.

Consider another example.

Example 2. You are interested in the development of aggressive behavior. You select a sample of children who have been brought into a psychological clinic because of family problems. You carefully set out to evaluate various aspects of their behavior by watching them play with other children and asking them how they would resolve a dispute over a toy with a peer. To begin the search for causes, you assess how well the parents get along and how much TV their children watch. You have thirty boys and five girls in your sample and all come from a poor part of a large urban area. You conclude that boys are more aggressive than girls and you also note that high rates of fighting between the parents as well as large doses of TV viewing are related to aggression in the children. Again what's wrong with this sample?

Problems plague our study of aggression. Perhaps these children who appear in a clinic are different from children whose families do not request this kind of help. Maybe boys are more aggressive than girls, but the sample of girls may be too small to determine whether this is really the case. Similarly, you can't conclude that TV viewing and parental conflict are characteristic of all aggressive children. To be sure that your conclusions apply to children in general, you would need to test a larger number of girls as well as children who are not attending a clinic.

These examples illustrate one of the major problems that the researcher faces in selecting a sample, namely to try to recruit a group of children that is representative of the population about which you wish to make general statements concerning their development. Great care must be taken in generalizing from a sample that is restricted in some way (for example, race, sex, social class, or region of the country) to all children in the country. Increasingly investigators are becoming aware that it is helpful to select a variety of samples of children who vary in race, sex, and social class. By selecting multiple samples, we can be more certain that our conclusions about development do, in fact, apply to a broad range of children. This strategy is often used in child psychology research when investigators in different parts of the country tackle the same issues using different samples of children. When the conclusions are similar, it gives us greater confidence in the generality of our insights about development. In Box 2-1, another solution to the problem of nonrepresentative samples is discussed, namely, the use of national samples that are representative of the total population. These strategies of replication across different samples and a national sample approach are both ways of helping us be more certain about the generality of our conclusions.

METHODS OF GATHERING DATA ABOUT CHILDREN

The methods used to collect information about children include self-report measures, such as questionnaires and interviews, and direct observations. All of the methods have some limitations and some advantages. The choice of method will depend on the questions being asked by the investigators.

Self-Report Measures

PARENTAL REPORTS

A common approach to understanding development is the use of parental interviews, questionnaires, and ratings. Parents are asked to provide a verbal report of some aspect of their children's behavior or their own behavior, such as their childrearing practices.

BOX 2-1 OVERCOMING SAMPLING PROBLEMS: THE NATIONAL SURVEY APPROACH

In recent years developmental psychologists have increased their awareness of sampling limitations. One significant and innovative solution to the sampling problem is the national survey approach. In this case a nationally representative sample of families is selected. To take one example, consider the National Longitudinal Survey of Youth (NLSY), which is a study of young men and women between the ages of 14 and 24 who have been interviewed annually since 1979. The individuals were drawn from 235 sample areas comprising 485 counties and independent cities representing every state in the United States. The advantage of this strategy is clear: You are able to make general statements that apply to the general population in the United States. But it was costly: Nearly 13,000 people were interviewed. In 1986 approximately 5000 children below age 11 whose mothers were in the sample were interviewed. The sample of children may be considered representative of all children born to a nationally representative cross section of women 21 to 29 years of age in 1986.

Recently issues such as the impact of day care, maternal employment, and divorce have been examined (Chase-Lansdale, Mott, Brooks-Gunn, & Phillips, 1991). For example, maternal employment during the first year of life has significant long-term effects on both cognitive and socioeconomic development of children. However, since both middle-class and lower-class families were included, investigators were able to show that the effects varied across social class. Early employment had positive effects among poor families and negative effects among middle-class families (Desai, Chase-Lansdale, & Michael, 1989; Desai, Michael, & Chase-Lansdale, 1990). We will discuss many of these findings in greater detail in later chapters. The importance of findings that emerge from this type of sample is the degree to which we can convincingly demonstrate that the "effects" on children are generalizable across the general population of young women and their children in the United States. Without these large representative samples we would not know whether any findings are confined to particular groups such as well-educated children, individuals residing in urban or rural areas, or members of a particular ethnic group. National surveys are useful as a way of characterizing and describing the population, but are less suited to answer questions about the processes that may account for different aspects of development. Therefore, national survey approaches are sometimes used in combination with smaller samples where there is more intensive measurement of some aspect of development. In this case, a subsample of 100 or 200 families would be selected and observed, studied, and tested in more detail in order to better understand the processes that may underlie some aspect of their development.

Sources: Chase-Lansdale, P. L., Mott, F. L., Brooks-Gunn, J., & Phillips, D. A. (1991). Children of the National Longitudinal Study of Youth: A unique research opportunity. *Developmental Psychology,* **27,** 918–931; Desai, S., Chase-Lansdale, P. L., & Michael, R. T. (1989). Mother or market: Effects of maternal employment on intellectual abilities of four year old children. *Demography,* **26**, 545–561; Desai, S., Michael, R. T., & Chase-Lansdale, P. L. (1990). *The home environment: A mechanism through which maternal employment affects children.* Unpublished manuscript.

The task that the parents are asked to perform during an interview or questionnaire is a difficult one. Often, the parents are asked to recall details that have occurred in the past, to rate themselves and the child in relation to dimensions of childrearing that are meaningful to psychologists but may have little to do with the way the parents think about parenthood, and to formulate attitudes or principles that determine their behavior toward the child. In the face of such a challenge, it is not surprising to find little agreement of reports over time or between different sources of information and distortion in the direction of idealized expectations, precocity, and cultural stereotypes. Unless their child is grossly retarded, few parents report their child's development as slow. Instead the child is recalled as having walked and talked a little earlier and as having attained better grades in school than was actually the case, and may be described as active and playful, a "real boy," rather than more aptly as the scourge of the neighborhood. In a 1963 study by Robbins, the retrospective reports of childrearing practices of parents of 3-year-old children were compared with those that had previously been gathered over the course of the first three years as part of a longitudinal study. It was found that parental distortions in recall of what occurred were in the direction of greater agreement with the opinions of experts and the writings of Dr. Benjamin Spock. For example, Dr. Spock, in his 1957 book, *Baby and Child Care,* approves of the use of a pacifier and disapproves of thumb-sucking. In this study all mothers who were inaccurate in their reports of thumb-sucking, and even those who, at the time, were recorded as having reported their concern to their physicians about their children's thumb-sucking, denied that their children had ever sucked their thumbs. In contrast, most of the mothers who inaccurately recalled their use of pacifiers reported that they had used one when the actual records showed that they had not.

Parents with more than one child are also likely to have confused memories of their children's past behaviors. On being asked to describe an individual child, often what the parent produces is a composite child. Just as parents sometimes confuse their children and call them by each other's names, they confuse who did what, when, and to whom. Although parent-attitude questionnaires and reports of early child-training practices or details of the timing of developmental events are seldom able to predict independently assessed child behavior (Holden & Edwards, 1989), some improvement in such predictions is obtained by focusing on specific current practices rather than broad retrospective attitudes and behavior (Maccoby & Martin, 1983).

Recently a number of strategies have been utilized to increase the accuracy of parents' and children's reports of behavior and the range of situations in which they are sampled. These strategies involve having the family member report very recent or immediate events and also may involve training a family member as an observer. Parents may be phoned each evening and asked which of a list of specific behaviors such as hitting, crying, yelling, or noncompliance their children have exhibited in the past twenty-four hours (Patterson & Bank, 1989); or parents or children may be asked to carry a structured diary and every half hour to record in it where they are, whom they are with, what they are doing, and what they are feeling (Hetherington, 1991). Even the kind of mobile monitors carried by physicians for emergency calls have been used in research. Parents or children carry a monitor and are "beeped" at random times and asked to record their activities or feelings (Larson & Lampman-Petraitis, 1989). This permits a random sampling not only of behavior but also of the situations and the social contexts in which these behaviors occur. Finally, parents have been trained to describe and report all of certain specified events occurring in the home over a period of months (Zahn-Waxler & Radke-Yarrow, 1982). They may be asked to record what led up to an event, what the specific sequence of behaviors of the parent and child was, and what the outcome of the situation was. This is particularly useful for gathering information on infrequently occurring behavior such as temper tantrums, aggression toward the parent, or bedwetting behaviors that are unlikely to occur when parents and children are observed for short periods of time. In addition, it can be seen that these methods reduce the problem of retrospective distortion in reporting past events, behaviors, or attitudes.

CHILDREN'S REPORTS

Another strategy is to use children's reports of their own behavior or their parents' behavior. Children are more difficult to interview than adults; children are less attentive, are slower to respond, and have more difficulty understanding questions than adults. Not surprisingly, these difficulties are more evident with younger children. Just as the accuracy of adult reports was questioned, it is fair also to ask whether children's answers can be trusted. In a recent interview study of a national sample of 2279 children between 7 and 11 years of age, Zill (1985) found that interviewers rated the apparent truthfulness of parents and children equally. However, younger children were rated as less reliable and truthful reporters than older children. One way to improve the truthfulness of children's answers is to interview them alone. Children were rated as less truthful if the parent was present and listening closely during the child's interview.

Some Advantages of Self-Reports

In spite of the limited usefulness of self-report data in predicting the behavior of parents or children, it should be remembered that some kinds of information are difficult to obtain other than through self-reports. As Zill (1985) said, interviewing children directly "permits a glimpse at a child's life from his or her unique perspective. The child is the best authority on his own feelings, even if he has some trouble verbalizing those feelings. And even in matters of fact—where adults have the advantage of a more fully developed sense of where, or when and of how many—there are aspects of a child's daily life that his parents or teacher know little or nothing about" (1985, pp. 23–24). Another strength of self-reports by children or parents may be that they are based on a large number of observations of the family members over time in a variety of situations. In contrast, in most observational studies the observer sees the subject for only a short time in a single situation.

It also has been proposed that although family members may not be accurate reporters, their perceptions, expectations, beliefs, and interpretation of events and behavior may be just as important as what really occurred (Goodnow & Collins, 1991). A son may feel rejected by a father who really loves him but believes that men don't show emotion and that high standards and strict discipline are necessary to develop strong moral character in the young. The child's belief that his father does not find him worthy of love, rather than the father's real attitude, might result in the development of feelings of inadequacy and low self-esteem in the son.

Measures of such things as the image family members have of each other and of how the family functions can be used to differentiate problem families from families that are functioning well. If family members perceive the family and each other in very different ways, these discrepancies tend to be associated with conflict and distress (Grych & Fincham, 1990). This might be expected since each family member is perceiving and responding to his or her individualistic view of the family. Many family therapists focus on helping families discover the discrepancies in their perceptions of each other and the way to communicate as a means of reducing family conflict.

Clearly, self-reports have limitations, but in recent years researchers have found that many issues can be understood best through the use of this approach. As we will see, however, self-reports are often used in conjunction with other strategies such as direct observation.

Peer and Teacher Reports

Another strategy is to employ reports from teachers, supervisors, friends, and peers. For many, questions such as how well a child attends to her schoolwork, how helpful she is on the playground, or how she gets along in a study group, parents may be a poor source of information. Parents are often unaware of whether their child is the class clown, the neighborhood pot dealer, or the most feared bully on the playground! Instead teachers, peers, and supervisors can be a valuable source of information. One common use of this approach is peer ratings to assess how well a child is accepted by classmates: Children are asked to rate their peers in terms of "how much they like to play with them" for example. The ratings of all the classmates are combined to yield a picture of the child's social status in her classroom (Coie & Dodge, 1988; Terry & Coie, 1991). Or teachers often rate their pupils on a series of dimensions such as their disruptiveness, attentiveness, dependence, or sociability. Both peers and teachers can provide important reports about children's behaviors that are useful supplements to parental and child reports.

Direct Observation

Researchers are interested not only in what parents say they do or how they perceive or feel about their children's behavior, they are interested in what parents actually do. To find out how parents and children behave, researchers have resorted to the use of direct observation of parents and children in a variety of situations ranging from naturalistic home settings to highly structured tasks in the laboratory. Of course, those observational data are valid only to the extent that representative patterns of interaction have been selected and not disrupted or distorted by the presence of the observer or the demands of the situation.

There are few studies in which the same children are observed in a variety of different settings, although we know that children often behave differently in different settings. A mother's response to her child's tantrum in the glare of disapproving eyes at the checkout counter in the supermarket will be quite different from that in the privacy of her home. Studies suggest that when families are shifted from familiar to unfamiliar settings, from the home to the laboratory, or from unstructured to structured situations, there is a tendency for family members to express less negative emotion, exhibit more socially desirable responses, and assume socially prescribed behavior (Johnson & Bolsted, 1973; Lamb, Suomi, & Stephenson, 1979). Mothers are more directive and less passively attentive in the home than in the laboratory (Moustakas, Sigel, & Schalock, 1956). Similarly, with a shift from the laboratory to the home, there is a change from stereotyped gender-role behavior to an increase in the expression of emotion by fathers and more active participation in decision making by mothers (O'Rourke, 1963).

Many investigators have expressed concern that when parents are being observed, they may attempt to act in a more socially acceptable way than that in which they ordinarily behave. Most of us tend to exhibit more of our Dr. Jekyll side in public and our Mr. Hyde side in private. Recent research (Russell, Russell, & Midwinter, 1991) confirms that parents tend to behave in ways that enhance their image as a parent and to inhibit their negative behavior when they are being observed. Fathers are especially likely to be affected by the presence of an observer—even when the observations are made in the home. However, even mothers behave in a warmer, more involved style with their children when they know they are being observed than when they are unaware that they are being observed (Zegoib, Arnold, & Forehand, 1975).

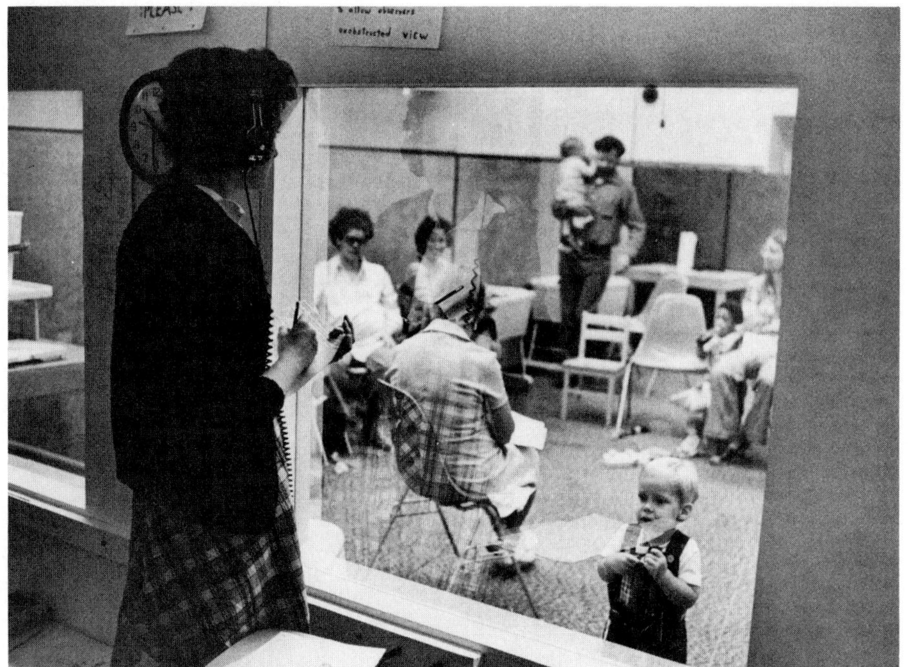

Observational methods are a commonly used technique for gathering information about children's development.

Most parents like to "show off" their children to reveal them in the best possible light. How successful are parents in doing this? Parents seem to be able to change their own behavior more readily than that of their children. Studies in which parents have been directed to make their children appear "good" or "bad" have found that parents are able to manipulate their children to appear socially undesirable, but not to appear more socially desirable (Lobitz & Johnson, 1975). In addition, nonverbal behavior is much more difficult to fake than verbal behavior, even for adults (Vincent, Harris, Cook, & Brady, 1979). There is also some evidence that in extremely disrupted families deviant family processes will remain. Reid, Taplin, and Lorber (1981) reported that mothers of abused children hit their children ten times more often than did normal mothers, in spite of knowing that they were being observed because they were abusive.

Attempts to minimize such distortions have been made by observing families in familiar situations, permitting a long period of adaptation through frequent, sustained observations, and using unobtrusive measures (Patterson, 1982; Patterson & Bank, 1989). Some experimenters have monitored homes by television or tape recorder during the entire waking hours of the family for periods as long as a month. Other studies have had observers appear at each dinner hour over a period of several weeks (Feiring & Lewis, 1987). Although it seems anyone would be a little disconcerted when an observer, wearing dark glasses to conceal the direction of his gaze and making notes on a clipboard, appeared regularly with the entree, families report that they gradually become almost unaware of the observation. This is reflected in increases in less socially accepted behaviors, such as quarreling, criticizing, punishing, and using obscene language.

There are many ways of recording observations (Bakeman & Gottman, 1986). In some cases the observer uses a specimen record, in which a description of everything the family is doing is written down. In other cases the observer may be interested in studying only a particular type of behavior, such as how the child responds to commands by parents. The observer then might use event sampling, in which he or she begins recording only when a particular event occurs. The observer would start when the parent issues a command and terminate when the child has clearly obeyed or disobeyed the parent's directive. Alternatively, the observer may use a sheet containing a list of behaviors; on this sheet the observer checks off which behaviors are occurring in a predetermined period of time. This is the time-sampling approach. For example, if the family was going to be observed for an hour, the observer might divide the hour into 120 thirty-second units. Each time any of the behaviors on the list occurred in a single thirty-second time period, the observer would put a check beside the behavior on the list. This yields the frequency of different kinds of behaviors of family members in the hour session. If you wish to examine the ordering or stream of behavior, a better strategy is to record the order of events in sequence as they actually occur (Mann et al., 1991). For example, a look at the sequence of behaviors within several five-minute time units over the hour of observation will reveal a good picture of the interactions among family members. If in the first five seconds the baby throws his cereal, next the mother slaps the baby, then the baby cries, and finally the mother picks the baby up and cuddles and pats him, a clear stream of behavior is apparent. The analysis of behavioral sequences allows us to answer such questions as the following: When the mother criticizes her son, what is the most frequent response of the son? Does he ignore her? Argue with her? Yield and accept her criticism or show remorse?

What do we do when we are interested in behavior which occurs infrequently and which we have only a slight chance of picking up in naturalistic observations? We can wait around for a long time before a child steals from her mother's purse, cheats, expresses sympathy, or helps her little sister. One method is to structure situations in such a way that these behaviors are likely to occur. For example, if we are interested in parents' responses to their children's help-seeking behavior, we might increase the chance of children asking for help by giving them tasks or problems that are very difficult to solve (Zahn-Waxler et al., 1992).

Because of the limitations in all of the methods of gathering data about children, many investigators have recently begun using multiple measures of the same behavior. For example, one might ask a child whether he is afraid of snakes, check with his friends, observe him closely on a field trip to the local woods, and watch his reaction when his zoology class adopts a snake as a classroom pet! Or you could see how he responds to pictures of snakes. It is hoped that convergence of the findings based on different assessment techniques implies greater validity of the results and that different methods may reveal different facets about children's development.

ESTABLISHING RELATIONSHIPS AND CAUSES: STEPS TOWARD UNDERSTANDING DEVELOPMENT

Theories of development not only provide clues to the kinds of data we should collect but also provide a guide concerning the relationships among different behaviors and the probable causes of various behaviors. In this section we examine two strategies that are commonly used in child psychology: correlational and experimental strategies.

The Correlational Strategy

To illustrate the *correlational* approach, consider the study of TV viewing habits and aggression among the preschool set reported by Singer and Singer (1981). Parents were asked about the TV habits of their sons and daughters. Specifically, information about how much TV children watched and the kinds of TV programs they usually watched was obtained from these parental interviews. In order to determine whether variations in TV viewing were related to aggression, observers rated how aggressive the children were with their classmates in the nursery school. Not only did the children spend a lot of time watching TV—an average of twenty-three hours a week—but TV viewing was clearly related to aggression. However, not just any kind of TV viewing was related to aggression. As the children increased the extent to which they watched action and adventure shows, they were rated more aggressive by their peers. However, there was no relationship between watching "Sesame Street" and "Mr. Rogers' Neighborhood"—shows that stress prosocial and nonaggressive themes—and the amount of aggression. Clearly, some kinds of TV programs are related to the amount of preschool aggression while other types of TV fare are not.

Now that we have seen an example of the correlational approach, a more formal definition will be helpful. A correlation is an index, or estimate, of how two factors or measures vary; it is expressed in terms of the direction and size of the relationship. Correlations can range from +1.00, which indicates that as one measure increases the other shows a fixed predictable increase, to 0, which shows only a chance relationship between the two variables, to −1.00, which shows that as one measure increases the other shows a fixed predictable decrease. Thus the plus and minus signs show the direction of the relationship and indicate a positive or negative correlation, while the size of the correlation shows the extent to which two variables are related. In our TV-aggression example, increases in aggression among the nursery schoolers are positively correlated with the extent to which the children watched action and adventure shows. To take another example, height and weight are positively correlated since increased height implies that increases in one variable are associated with increases in the second variable. To illustrate a negative correlation, consider the relationship between smoking and life expectancy. The more cigarettes an individual smokes, the shorter is his or her life expectancy. Finally, if changes in one variable are not related in any systematic way to changes in another variable, we speak of a zero correlation. Height, for example, has a zero correlation with intelligence. Knowledge of how tall a person is gives us no information about the person's level of intelligence.

A word of caution is necessary. The fact that two factors are correlated does *not* mean that one factor *caused* the other. It means only that the two factors are related in some systematic way to each other. To return to our TV example, can we conclude that watching violent TV causes increases in aggressive behavior? Absolutely not! The results of this study merely tell us that there is a relationship between the kind of TV program children watch and aggressive behavior in school. The direction of the relationship is not clear. An equally plausible explanation could be that children who watch violent programs are already aggressive and simply prefer watching aggressive shows. Their TV viewing may have had little effect on their level of aggressiveness. Correlational findings cannot establish causal relationships! This type of correlational study is only one step in the course of establishing an understanding of the TV violence–aggressive behavior puzzle. To clarify the causal links, we need to turn to another approach, namely, the *experiment*.

The Laboratory Experiment

In order to illustrate the laboratory experiment as a method for investigating the TV-aggression question, consider an investigation by Liebert and Baron (1972). One hundred thirty-six boys and girls ranging from 5 to 9 years old participated in this study. Let us follow the course of events experienced by the children. In this study, parents and children came to a laboratory where the experiment was being conducted. The next step in the study was to randomly assign children to various experimental treatment conditions. In other words, some children were designated the experimental subjects, while others were assigned to the control condition—on a purely chance basis. By this procedure, children in the two conditions should not differ in any systematic fashion; therefore, the results should be due to effects of the experimental conditions, not to initial differences in the children. Next, the experimenter escorted each individually to a room, turned on the TV and suggested that the children watch TV for a few minutes until they were ready to begin. All children watched two brief commercials selected for their humor and attention-getting value. Then the critical part of the procedure began. Half the children, the experimental group, observed $3\frac{1}{2}$ minutes of a program from the TV series "The Untouchables." The sequence contained a chase, two fistfighting scenes, two shootings, and a knifing. The children in the control group watched a highly active $3\frac{1}{2}$-minute vidoetaped sports sequence in which athletes competed in hurdle races and high jumps. Then all the children watched another sixty seconds of a tire commercial. Two aspects of the procedure merit comment. First, the *single* difference in treatment between the children in the experimental and control conditions involved the particular type of program they were exposed to. In all other ways their experience was similar. By carefully equating the treatments, one is reasonably certain that any subsequent differences in behavior are, in fact, *caused* by the type of TV program that the children watched. There is another important aspect of the procedure: the TV viewing was presented as part of the waiting period prior to the onset of the "real" part of the experiment. In this way, the subject's suspicions about the purpose of the experiment were reduced, and it is unlikely that the effects are attributable to the subject's prior knowledge of the experimenter's true purpose. However, the deception involved in this study raises ethical questions about the procedure. Consider whether you think that the deception was justified in this case. We will return to this issue at the end of the chapter.

In the next phase, the impact of this viewing experience was assessed. The subject was seated before a panel arrayed with two buttons labeled "Hurt" and "Help," which were connected to another child's panel in the adjoining room. The second child was playing a game that required turning a handle. The subject was informed that if he wanted to make the handle turning easier for the other boy, he could depress the "Help" button. On the other hand, if he pushed the "Hurt" button, the handle in the other room would feel hot and hurt the child. In fact, the "other" child was an accomplice of the experimenter and was not affected by the Help-Hurt buttons. The amount of time that children in the two viewing conditions depressed the Hurt button was employed as the main measure of aggression. For this experiment, the time spent in depressing the Hurt button is the *dependent variable*. In an experiment the dependent variable is the measure that is altered or affected by the manipulation, the *independent variable*. In our example, the independent variable was the type of TV program that the children watched. The results were clear. Children who viewed "The Untouchables" program showed reliably greater willingness to engage in interpersonal aggression than those who had observed the neutral program.

Exposure to TV violence does, in fact, *cause* increased interpersonal aggression. However, there are limitations to the study that make it difficult to generalize from this situation to the naturalistic environment. The test setting and the aggression index were artificially contrived and the TV program was edited; while it permits experimental control over the relevant variables the legitimacy of generalization from this type of laboratory study to the field is highly questionable. As one observer once noted, much of American developmental psychology is "the science of the strange behavior of a child in a strange situation with a strange adult for the shortest period of time" (Bronfenbrenner, 1979, p. 19).

An approach that overcomes some of the problems of artificiality of the traditional laboratory experiment involves a *laboratory analogue* of a natural situation in which the experimenter tries to duplicate many of the features of the natural context (for example, home) in the laboratory. In a recent study, children were observed while responding to any angry interchange between their mother and another adult—an event that could take place in everyday settings such as a store, park, or home (Cummings, Pelligrini, Notarius & Cummings, 1989). The laboratory context permits the experimenter to precisely videotape and later measure the child's reaction to this observed interchange while at the same time preserving some of the "naturalism" of real-life situations.

While this concern about "naturalism" may be valid for some types of studies, especially of social and emotional development, it should be recognized that the laboratory remains an important context for investigation of many aspects of development. As you will discover, important insights concerning infants' perceptual capacities, such as how well they see, smell, and hear are usually gained by the effective use of laboratory-based assessments. It is precisely the capacity to control the loudness, pitch, and other critical features of a sound in the laboratory that makes it possible to determine infants' perceptual capacities in an accurate fashion. In the case of perceptual development, many of the basic skills of interest, such as infants' responses to pitch or loudness, may not vary across contexts. Children's ability to detect differences in pitch, color, or brightness in the laboratory is unlikely to change when tested in everyday settings (Seitz, 1988). Research strategies need to be matched to the question being asked; different strategies serve different purposes. Laboratory experiments are useful and valid for some issues, but have limitations when used to examine other topics.

In the next section, we examine two alternative experimental strategies that overcome some of the limitations of the laboratory experiment.

Field and Natural Experiments

Experiments can sometimes be conducted outside the laboratory in the child's natural environment, and therefore some of the problems associated with the laboratory experiment, such as the artificiality of the setting, can be avoided. The clever investigator can arrange to introduce a change in the child's normal environment or even take advantage of a naturally occurring change in the child's everyday world. Let us examine each of these types of experiments.

The Field Experiment. In the field experiment, the investigator *deliberately* introduces a change in a nonlaboratory setting. An excellent example is the study by Friedrich and Stein (1973), who were interested in the impact of violent TV viewing on children's aggressive behavior. A field experiment differs from a laboratory experiment in a variety of ways. Unlike the laboratory study, where the child enters into a specially created world of the experimenter, the hallmark of the field experiment is the fact that the experimenter enters the child's world. In this case, the investigators moved into the nursery school and controlled the types of TV programs that the children watched. The observations of the impact of TV viewing were made during the daily play sessions at the nursery school; adult observers recorded the frequency of aggressive and prosocial behavior. The study was conducted during a nine-week summer nursery school session. For the first three weeks, they observed the children in order to achieve a baseline measure of their interaction patterns. For the next four weeks, the children watched a half-hour TV program each day. Some children always saw aggressive programs, such as "Batman" and "Superman" cartoons; other children watched a prosocial program, "Mister Rogers' Neighborhood"; the remaining children were put on a neutral TV fare of farm films, nature shows, and circus movies. In the last two weeks the long-term effects of the TV diets were assessed. To minimize bias, the adults did not know the type of programs that different children had been watching. The impact of the programs was determined by comparing the children's behavior during the first three weeks with their behavior during the next two periods. Exposure to aggressive cartoons did affect the children's behavior, but the amount of aggression exhibited in the pre-TV sessions was an important factor. Children who were initially high in aggression were more aggressive following exposure to the aggressive cartoons in comparison to subjects exposed to neutral or prosocial programs. However, the behavior of children who were less aggressive during the initial period did not differ across the TV diets. Exposure to TV violence does affect interpersonal aggressive behavior if a child is already likely to behave aggressively!

One advantage of the field experimental approach over the laboratory experiment is that the results can be generalized more readily to natural environments. The TV programs were unedited and typical of the kind of shows children are exposed to in their home environment. Moreover, the children's behavior was measured in a naturalistic setting. Any conclusion drawn from this type of study can be much more readily applied to children's daily behavior than studies conducted under more artificial circumstances. The study still retained the important feature of an *experiment.* The independent variable, namely, the type of TV program, was under the control of the experimenter. Hence, it is still possible to make causal statements: The TV diet, it appears, was the *cause* of the changes in aggressive behavior. If the children themselves had chosen the type of TV diet, we would never be sure that any changes were merely due to the possibility that aggressive children seek out aggressive programs. That may be the case, but through experimental control, this possibility was eliminated.

Sometimes, however, the field experiment is not feasible since changes cannot always be introduced by the experimenter for ethical or practical reasons. In the next section, we examine another alternative—the natural experiment.

The Natural Experiment. In this case, the investigator capitalizes upon a change in the child's world that occurs naturally and is not due to the investigator's intervention. Social policy may produce changes in school integration; or children may be adopted, hospitalized, or sent to camp. The investigator may take advantage of these happenings and measure their effect on the child's behavior. For example, Williams (1985) took advantage of a naturally occurring event, namely, the introduction of TV into a small town in Canada that previously did not have any TV reception. By measuring the children's aggressive play behavior in school and in the laboratory *before* and *after* the children's exposure to TV, these investigators were able to demonstrate that aggression increased after TV arrived in town. To the extent that it has not been arbitrarily introduced by the experimenter, the event may be more ecologically valid. In other words, it is part of the child's natural environment and therefore it is easier to make statements that can apply readily to children's real-life behavior. However, the specification of the exact nature and boundaries of the independent variable is often difficult. Children watch a variety of programs, and it is difficult to determine precisely whether violent TV programs are the cause of the increased aggressive behavior or if some other aspect of TV viewing is responsible for the change.

No research strategy is without its limitations. In our comparison of laboratory, field, and natural experiments, we see that there is often a trade-off between experimental control and generalizability of findings. Control is greatest in the laboratory experiment, but the extent to which the results can be applied to children in their natural environment is often limited. On the other hand, the results of field and natural experiments can be more readily generalized to real-life settings, but the clarity of the results may be less precise since the amount of control that the investigator can gain over important variables is less in field settings (see Table 2.1). No strategy is always best. It is important to remember that each method has a role in helping the investigator understand children's behavior. Often an investigator may start off in an unexplored area by using a correlational approach in order to establish some possible relationships. Finally, experiments may follow to more clearly isolate the causal links between the variables indicated by the earlier methods. Multiple methodological strategies are increasingly the preferred approach in studying children's development.

New Designs for Development: Combining Field and Laboratory Approaches

Field and laboratory approaches need not be used alone but can also be used in combination. By using field and laboratory-based strategies we can often achieve control that is needed for clear conclusions and at the same time

TABLE 2-1

ADVANTAGES AND LIMITATIONS OF THREE TYPES OF EXPERIMENTS

TYPE OF EXPERIMENT	DEGREE OF CONTROL OVER INDEPENDENT VARIABLE	DEGREE OF CONTROL OVER DEPENDENT VARIABLE	GENERALIZABILITY OF FINDINGS
Lab	High	High	Low
Field	Medium	Low	High
Natural	Low	Low	High

retain some degree of generalizability. Turn to Table 2-2 which shows four "combination" designs in which you vary between the field and laboratory settings where you manipulate or introduce the experimental variation (for example, the independent variable) or where you measure the effect (for example, the dependent variable). Cell number 1 describes the field experiment that we have just reviewed; in this case, the dependent and independent variables are located in the field. Similarly cell number 4 should be familiar as well. This is the traditional laboratory experiment in which both independent and dependent variables are located in the laboratory setting. Cells 2 and 3 are of greater interest here. In cell number 2, the design involves the manipulation of the independent variable in a naturalistic setting while measuring the dependent variable in a laboratory setting. For example, if you controlled children's TV viewing diet in their homes and then measured their aggressive and prosocial behavior in a controlled laboratory setting, this would be an illustration of this design. In cell number 3, the investigator may use the laboratory setting as a context for introducing the independent variable, while measuring the impact of the change in the child's natural environment. Consider this example. You wish to increase the social skills of a shy girl and teach her to be more sociable. In the laboratory, you expose the girl to a film (independent variable) designed to increase her level of social interaction. But then you measure the impact of the film by watching the child in her nursery school classroom to see if she becomes more outgoing and friendly. In both cases, there are advantages and disadvantages. In the case of cell number 2, the degree of control over the dependent variable is increased, while control is enhanced on the independent variable side in cell number 3. In each case, the degree of generalizability is enhanced. In one case (cell number 2) the generalizability of the independent variable is increased and in the other case (cell number 3) generalizability is enhanced for the dependent variable side. These designs represent useful compromises in a search for a balance between precision and control and the need to increase generalizability of our findings.

Case Study Method

Can we learn anything about development by studying a single case? Some of the earliest discoveries of developmental psychology have been based on case studies. In the 1800s Charles Darwin kept a detailed diary of his infant son's emotional expressions, which was the basis of his theory of emotional development in infants and children. This early work provided useful insights, hunches, and hypotheses for later investigators to pursue in a more systematic fashion with a larger number of cases. The chief limitation of the single-case approach is the inability to generalize from the single subject to a larger

TABLE 2-2 **TYPES OF DESIGNS INVOLVING COMBINATIONS OF FIELD AND LABORATORY**

LOCATION OF DEPENDENT VARIABLE	LOCATION OF INDEPENDENT VARIABLE	
	FIELD	LABORATORY
Field	No. 1 field experiment	No. 2 combined lab-field experiment
Laboratory	No. 3 combined field-lab experiment	No. 4 laboratory experiment

BOX 2-2 *PSYCHOLOGY IN ACTION* WHEN ALL ELSE FAILS: A CASE STUDY OF SHOCK AS A THERAPEUTIC TECHNIQUE

Is the use of electric shock in modifying harmful or undesirable behavior ever justified? Read the following case study and make your own judgment.

In this case, Lang and Melamed (1969) used electricity to suppress the chronic and life-endangering vomiting behavior of a 9-month-old infant. When these investigators first encountered their patient, he was in critical condition. From a 6-month weight of 17 pounds the infant had dropped to a skinny 12 pounds, and even though he was being fed through a nasogastric pump, he was continuing to deteriorate. The reason was obvious: He reliably regurgitated most of his food intake within ten minutes of each feeding and continued to bring up small amounts throughout the day. Before initiating treatment, Lang and Melamed did a careful evaluation of the pattern of the vomiting behavior. They reasoned that if they could detect some early signs that the child was beginning to regurgitate, they could arrange for a maximally effective presentation of the aversive event, electric shock. One of the principles derived from punishment research is that the earlier the punishment is administered, the more effective the suppression of the undesired behavior. By the use of electromyographic recordings, which detect changes in the muscle activity, they were able to determine when the child was about to vomit. At the first sign that the child was about to vomit, he received a one-second electric shock on the calf of his leg. The unpleasant shock continued at one-second intervals until vomiting was terminated. The treatment was relatively short and very effective; each session lasted less than one hour, and after two sessions shock was rarely required. By the sixth session the infant no longer vomited during the testing procedures. The number of shocks actually used was, in fact, quite low. After eight sessions, or three periods in which there was no evidence of the undesirable behavior, therapy was discontinued. A few days later there was a brief setback, but three additional sessions eliminated any further vomiting.

On the day of discharge from the hospital, the child had gained weight and was, in general, a healthy, smiling contrast to the anemic child who had entered the hospital thirteen days before (see the accompanying photos). After one year the infant continued to develop normally and no additional treatment was required. The remarkable success of this well-timed punishment procedure is highlighted further by the failure of all other therapeutic approaches to correct this illness.

In our view, the technique was justified since all else had failed and through this approach the infant's life was saved. Nevertheless, the use of potentially harmful procedures raises important ethical questions that we will address later in the chapter. Finally, this study clearly indicates that principles derived from laboratory studies can have important and practical application.

Source: Lang, P. J., & Melamed, B. B. (1969). Case report: Avoidance conditioning therapy of an infant with chronic ruminative vomiting. *Journal of Abnormal Psychology*, **74**, 1–8.

representative sample. You simply do not know whether the results are unique to this particular individual.

Sometimes a case study permits you to study a rare phenomenon such as feral children who have been reared without exposure to human language. Or consider the example of the treatment of a single sick child that illustrates the value of an unorthodox approach to healing (see Box 2-2). Due to the drastic nature of the intervention, it is unlikely that the procedure could be repeated on a large sample of children, and therefore the single case takes on increased value in helping us understand the impact of different procedures on children's behavior.

A variation in the case study theme is the experimental treatment of a single subject. In this case, the goal is to identify the environmental events that control a behavior. Consider this example. A 4-year-old called Joey was always hitting and teasing other children in the nursery school playground. Every time it happened, one or, on some days, two teachers would rush over and stop him. They often lingered with Joey and tried to tell him that he really shouldn't hit other kids. But Joey kept right on hitting! The experimenter thought that Joey hit other children, in part, as a way of gaining the teachers' attention and so instructed the teachers to ignore Joey whenever he was

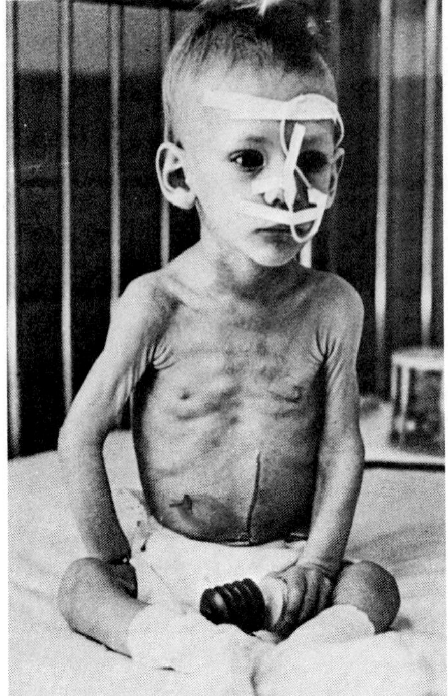

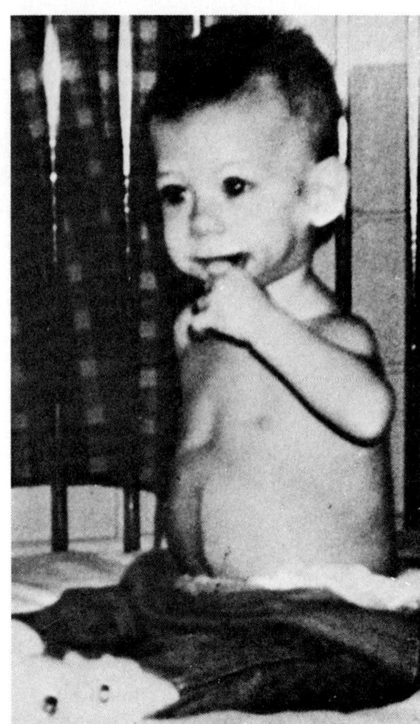

A 9-month-old infant before and after avoidance conditioning treatment using electric shock.

aggressive. At first Joey's aggressive attacks increased; however, after a few days of the "silent treatment" from his teachers, Joey's rate of hitting began to drop. In order to determine whether or not Joey's behavior was changing in response to the shift in teacher strategy, the teachers were instructed to go back to their normal routine—including paying attention to Joey when he hit. Again the hit rate increased, which suggests that the teacher attention was controlling Joey's deviant activity. The teachers were then again instructed to ignore Joey when he misbehaved, and again the hitting decreased. As this example suggests, the general strategy is to measure the child's behavior before intervening, then to experimentally modify or change the events that are suspected of controlling the behavior. As a next step, the situation is changed back to the way it was originally to see if the experimental treatments made any difference. Finally, as a further check, the change is introduced again. In a single-subject experiment, the subject serves as his or her own control and experimental condition. This set of procedures has been labeled a *reversal* design or an *ABAB* design, where A is the normal state and B represents the experimentally altered state.

RESEARCH DESIGNS FOR DEVELOPMENT

The study of development requires unique research designs. Child psychology has two main designs that help assess changes across development: a *cross-sectional* design and a *longitudinal* design.

The Cross-Sectional Design

Children not only learn to love their mothers but learn to leave them as well. To demonstrate how children's independence differs across development, you can use a cross-sectional design. This design involves selecting *different* groups of children at *different* age levels. Rheingold and Eckerman (1970) used a cross-sectional design in their investigation of this issue and recruited children at nine different ages. There were three boys and three girls at each half year of age between 12 and 60 months and, of course, their mothers. For their study, a seminaturalistic setting, a large untended lawn, was chosen. Mother and child were placed at one end of the lawn with the mother sitting in a chair and the child free to leave. Observers were stationed in nearby windows to track the path of the child's excursions. A clear relationship between age and distance traveled emerged. The average farthest distance for 1-year-olds was 6.9 meters; by 2 years of age children ventured 15.1 meters; 3-year-olds went 17.3 meters; and 4-year-olds ventured 20.6 meters. Stating the relationship differently, there was a linear increase in the distance traveled with increasing age. For each month of age the children went about a third of a meter farther.

The important feature of this cross-sectional design is that Rheingold and Eckerman were able to determine how independence differs over age by comparing the behavior of groups of different children at different ages in the same situation. One unique feature of this approach is that they collected their data across a wide age range in a very short time—a couple of months. They did not have to wait until the 12-month-old infant became a 4-year-old toddler to evaluate developmental advances. This advantage, of course, becomes very clear when the comparisons involve even wider age ranges. With only a little more time, they could easily have included 8-, 12-, and 16-year-olds and tracked how independence changes in adolescence.

However, the distinctive characteristic of this approach, namely, the examination of different children at each age level, has disadvantages. This approach yields no information about the possible historical or past determinants of the age-related changes that are observed because it is impossible to know what these children were like at earlier ages. Nor is there any information about the ways in which individual children develop. How stable is independence? Is the independent child at 1 year likely to be more independent at 5 years than a peer who exhibited little independence until 2 years of age? A cross-sectional approach cannot answer this question, but the longitudinal method is designed to tackle this kind of issue. In the next section, this alternative research method will be explored.

The Longitudinal Design

In 1929, a most ambitious project began: the Fels Longitudinal Study. By describing this undertaking, we can illustrate one of the strategies employed by child psychologists in their efforts to unravel some of the mysteries of development. When a parent enrolled a child in the study, there was a catch; the parent had to agree to have the child weighed, measured, observed, and tested for the next eighteen years. Such is the nature of longitudinal research; the subject is assessed repeatedly in order to determine the stability of the patterns of behavior of a particular individual over time.

Age-related or normative developmental differences in independence, for example, could be assessed just as they were in the cross-sectional study, reviewed above. In the case of the longitudinal study, however, the *same*—not *different*—individuals would be evaluated at each time point. This permits the evaluation not just of differences across age, but of *changes* across development as well. For the longitudinal approach, patience is a key since one has to wait until the infants mature in order to understand adolescence. However, a question of interest to child psychologists concerns the effects of early experience on later behavior; although there are a variety of ways to answer this question, the longitudinal method offers a particularly powerful technique. By tracking children over time, the psychologist can determine the impact of early events on later behavior.

Let us take a famous illustration, the Kagan and Moss study, *Birth to Maturity* (1962), to show how dependence and independence can be studied longitudinally. Kagan and Moss brought back seventy-one of the Fels longitudinal subjects, who were then between 20 and 29 years of age. A number of interviews and test procedures were employed in order to assess how dependent or independent these Fels subjects were as adults. Of course, these same individuals had been observed, measured, and tested throughout the first eighteen years. Kagan and Moss were able to use these early records as predictors of the adult behavior. Typically, a Fels child and mother were observed in the home, in nursery school, or at a summer day camp. In all these situations—home, school, and camp—ratings of each child's dependence were made. Kagan and Moss used this array of information about the children's behavior at different ages in their search for the patterns of behavior stability and change over time.

Kagan and Moss divided the childhood data into four age periods: birth to 3 years, 3 to 6 years, 6 to 10 years, and 10 to 14 years. For each age period the child's own behavior, as well as the mother's behavior, was rated. By relating these findings to the special adulthood assessments, these investigators sought to determine how early behavior patterns become established and the nature of the parental behaviors associated with later adult patterns. First, is behavior stable, or does it merely fluctuate randomly over time? While the first three years bore little clear relationship to adult behaviors, by the preschool years some behaviors began to stabilize. By the time that children were 6 to 10 years of age, one could predict how dependent the children would be as young adults. Children who were dependent at age 6 were likely to be passive and dependent in adulthood. However, the extent to which dependent behavior is stable between childhood and adulthood varies with the sex of the child. Girls show greater stability of passive-dependent behaviors than boys, while boys show greater stability of independent-assertive behaviors. Kagan and Moss argue that the sex-role appropriateness of the behavior determined the extent of stability; boys were expected and encouraged to behave in an independent, assertive fashion, while dependent behavior was more common for girls—or at least was more common when these children were growing up in the 1930s and 1940s!

What are the advantages and disadvantages of the longitudinal design? Some of the strengths are clear: The impact of earlier events on later behavior can be determined. Differences in behavior at different points in development can also be determined, just as in the case of a cross-sectional approach. The clear advantage over the cross-sectional approach, however, is that the same children are observed at each age point and so the stability of a behavior for an individual can be noted.

But there are disadvantages to the longitudinal approach, aside from the expense. There is a problem of subject loss: individuals move, become ill, or simply lose interest in being tested. The result is a shrinking sample, which not only reduces the reliability of the results but may bias the results. Can we assume that the sample dropouts are similar to those who continue in

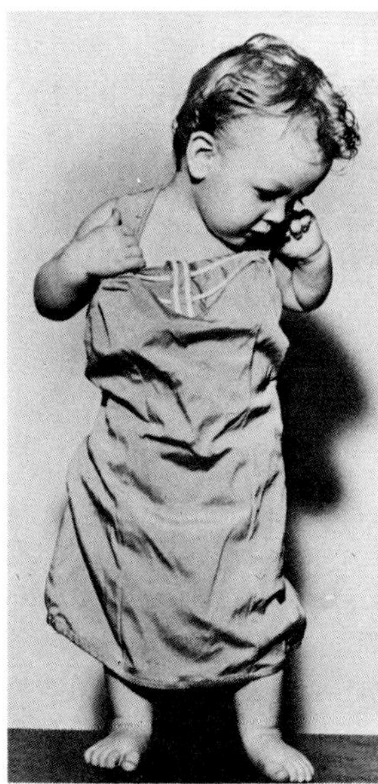
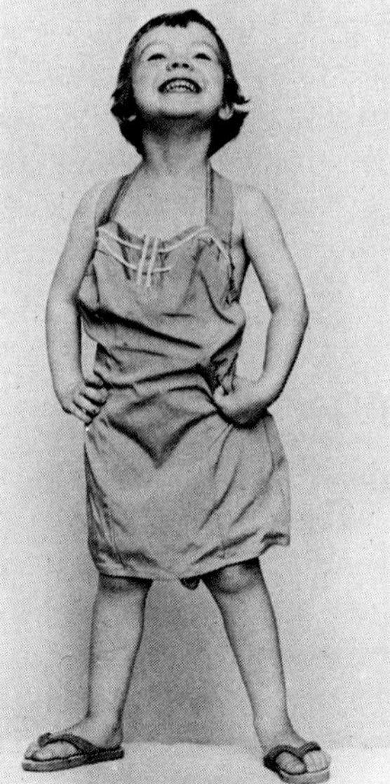
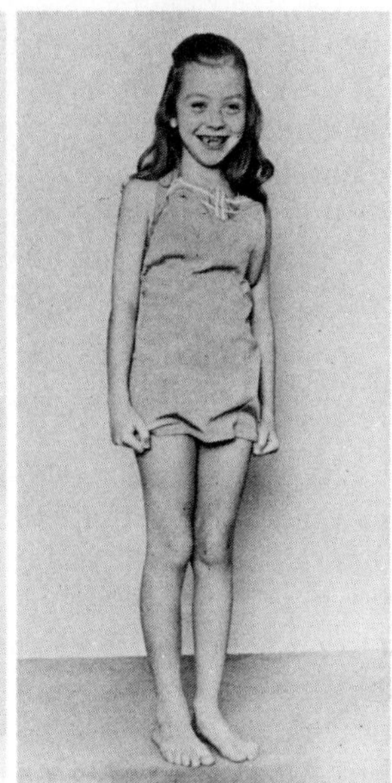
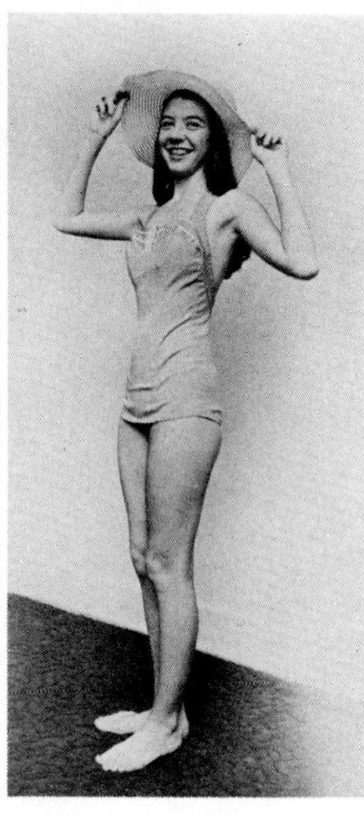

A girl wearing the same bathing suit at evenly spaced intervals for sixteen years.

the study? If not, the conclusions may be restricted to individuals who possess certain traits, such as immobility, scientific interest, and patience.

Another problem plagues the longitudinal approach: cross-generational change. Is the 4-year-old today similar to the 4-year-old of the 1930s? Times have changed: the family structure has shifted, more women work outside the home, and more children attend day-care centers. As a result, the experiences of the 4-year-old of sixty years ago and the typical experiences of a modern 4-year-old will be quite different. Therefore, it is difficult to conclude that the long-term effects of the experiences of our 1930s 4-year-old on later behavior can apply to our present 4-year-old. These changes in culture always date and limit the conclusions of longitudinal studies, particularly those which set out with a single large sample and track them over time. In the Fels study, which we discussed, this problem is less serious since it is a continuing study and a small sample of new children are enrolled each year. Thus it is possible to check directly on the differences between a 4-year-old of 1930 and a 4-year-old of 1990 to determine if, in fact, cultural shifts have produced changes in child behavior.

A final problem is inflexibility. It requires a rare wisdom and foresight to choose the measures that are likely to be important over a twenty-year period. Unlike a cross-sectional study, in which you can test your hunches and hypotheses until you find an appropriate measure to work with, in the longitudinal project you choose and hope. If you choose incorrectly, few interesting relationships may emerge. Moreover, the theory and research that are the source of hypotheses are constantly shifting, but in longitudinal research it is often not possible to take advantage of new insights and new methods. For example, in a longitudinal study of IQ, if a new test is discovered ten years after a study has begun, what can the longitudinal investigators do? Several options are available: They can start over with a new sample and the new test, or, alternatively, they can begin to give the new test to their

10-year-olds (the "old" sample). But then they lose the possibility of comparing the earlier results with the later findings, since the test instruments are not comparable. Here is a solution. You can give both the old test and the new test at the same time to the same subjects so you can judge the comparability of the two tests.

Table 2-3 summarizes the advantages and disadvantages of cross-sectional and longitudinal designs.

The Short-Term Longitudinal Design

As an alternative to extended longitudinal projects, investigators have chosen a new strategy: the short-term longitudinal project. This strategy involves the tracking of a group of individuals for a short time span of a few months to a few years. Unlike older approaches, the focus is usually more limited and restricted to a few key issues and questions that are more theoretically tied. For example, Roger Brown and his colleagues (Brown, 1973) at Harvard University tracked the language development of three children over a two- to five-year period. This project has yielded a wealth of detailed information concerning the natural development of language and grammar, and we will be discussing some of these findings in a later chapter. What are the advantages of this approach?

> The shorter the elapsed time of data collection, the less will be the attrition of the sample and the greater the ease of maintaining the same staff and measuring instruments and procedures. Annual increments can still be studied, and the effects of different life experiences can be canceled out or measured and statistically controlled. (Bayley, 1965, p. 1989)

Another advantage of this short-term approach is that the insights gained from this first project can now be utilized in designing another project. The interaction between knowledge gained from data and design can be more closely interwoven.

TABLE 2-3 **ADVANTAGES AND LIMITATIONS OF CROSS-SECTIONAL AND LONGITUDINAL DESIGNS**

	TYPE OF DESIGN	
RESEARCH CONSIDERATIONS	CROSS-SECTIONAL	LONGITUDINAL
Financial cost	Low	High
Time	Short	Long
Subject loss or selective dropout	Minimal problem	Serious problem
Flexibility in terms of use of new tests and measures	High	Low
Repeated testing effects	Low	High
Ability to assess research issues:		
Descriptive normative data about development at different ages	Excellent	Excellent
Impact of early events on later behavior	Poor	Excellent
Questions of stability vs. instability of behavior	Poor	Excellent
Developmental paths of individual children	Poor	Excellent

Cross-Sectional/Short-Term Longitudinal Design

Both cross-sectional and longitudinal designs have features that are helpful in answering developmental questions. A design that combines these two approaches is the cross-sectional/short-term longitudinal design.

You wish to investigate the question of how dependence and independence change between 6 and 14 years of age, but you have neither the time nor the money to run a longitudinal study in which you test the same children at different ages across childhood. You could use a cross-sectional design, but you are interested in the stability of the behavior of individual children. Since a cross-sectional study involves different children at each age, this type of study would not be satisfactory. A compromise approach—the cross-sectional/short-term longitudinal design—would be the most suitable alternative. According to this approach, one group would be tested at 6 years of age and again at 10 years of age, while a second sample of children would be tested for the first time at 10 years of age and later at age 14 years. Table 2-4 summarizes the design and contrasts this approach with the cross-sectional and longitudinal designs. There are distinct advantages to this combined cross-sectional/short-term longitudinal design. Information concerning the patterns of interaction at the three age points can be derived just as in a usual cross-sectional study. In addition, data concerning the developmental changes that occur for individual children between ages 6 and 10 and between 10 and 14 years can also be gathered. By testing both groups of children at age 10, one group for the second time and another group for the first time, one can determine the effects of repeated testing. Does testing the child at 6 years affect the child's response at 10 years? By testing another group for the first time at 10 years, it is possible to learn this effect. A final advantage of this approach is time: Approximately half the time would be required to execute this design in comparison with the complete longitudinal study.

It is clear that both cross-sectional and longitudinal studies are useful, and the choice of design will depend on the type of issue under investigation.

TABLE 2-4

COMPARISON OF THREE DEVELOPMENTAL DESIGNS

	LONGITUDINAL	CROSS-SECTIONAL	CROSS-SECTIONAL/ LONGITUDINAL
Main feature	Same group of children tested (group A) at several age points	Different groups of children tested (groups A, B, C) at each age point	Different groups of children (A, B), each tested at two points
	Age / *Group* 6 / A 10 / A 14 / A	*Age* / *Group* 6 / A 10 / B 14 / C	*Age* / *Group* 6 / A 10 / A, B 14 / B
Approximate time for data collection	Eight years	Time required to test each child once (typically less than one year)	Four years

THE ETHICS OF RESEARCH WITH CHILDREN

In the final analysis, a major consideration in deciding upon a particular research strategy is the effects of the procedure on the child. In recent years there has been an increasing awareness of the ethical issues involved in research with children. Various government review boards and professional organizations, such as the American Psychological Association and the Society for Research in Child Development, have suggested guidelines for child research projects. In addition, all projects are reviewed by institutional review boards, which are established in colleges and universities to ensure that proper ethical guidelines are being followed in research projects with children (and adults). These guidelines have been developed to protect children from harmful and dangerous procedures. Box 2-3 outlines a children's bill of research rights to illustrate the kinds of protection that are necessary for child research participants. In reading this list of children's rights, remember that, very often, children are too young to fully appreciate the complex issues that are involved in making informed decisions. Therefore, it is often parents who have to make decisions about their children's participation in research projects. In addition, institutions in which children are often contacted for research participation, such as schools, often provide another level of consent which, in turn, further protects the child participants. This is particularly critical since parents may not always pay close attention to activities at school or at a day-care center, or in some cases, such as maltreated children, parents may not necessarily always be in a position to represent their child's best interests (Thompson, 1990).

As a consequence of the increasing awareness of children's research rights, some types of investigations are becoming less frequent. Fewer child psychologists can be found looking into waiting rooms, watching behind one-way mirrors, or observing through the lens of a hidden camera. Laboratory research involving deception, in which the child is misled about the true purpose of the study, is becoming less frequent. Many investigators are increasingly accepting the view that this type of procedure is no longer acceptable. Of course, it should be stressed that most research has been executed safely and without deception of the children.

Before we leave our discussion of ethical issues in research, some of the types of difficulties that are occasionally encountered should be recognized. Sometimes the ethical course of action is not clear. Consider these dilemmas; you be the judge.

Is it unethical to study the long-term effects of being a premature or a full-term infant and not inform the families that they were selected because their infant was premature? Will informing these parents sensitize them to expect their premature offspring to be different and make them more anxious? Is deception or full disclosure of the aims of the study likely to have the most positive outcome?

Let us look at another study. In order to study children's persistence in the face of failure, children were given a very difficult task which guaranteed that they would not be able to master the task. An attempt to eliminate any negative effects of the failure experience was made by giving all children another task in which they succeeded before they finished the session. Since failure is a common experience in school, was its use justified in this case? Did the long-term goal of the study—to teach children to continue to work even after a failure experience—justify this experiment?

BOX 2-3 A CHILDREN'S BILL OF RESEARCH RIGHTS

1 *The right to be fully informed:* Each child participant has the right to full and truthful information about the purposes of the study and the procedures to be employed.

2 *The right to be informed and voluntary consent of participation:* Each child participant has the right either verbally or in written form to agree to participate in a research project. In the case of children who are too young to understand the aims and procedures and to make an informed decision about participation, parental consent should always be secured.

3 *The right to voluntary withdrawal:* Each child participant has the right to withdraw at any time from continued participation in any research project.

4 *The right to full compensation:* Each child participant has the right to be fully compensated for his or her time and effort as a research subject, even if he or she withdraws and does not complete participation in the project.

5 *The right to nonharmful treatment:* Each child participant has the right to expect that he or she will not experience any harmful or damage-producing events during the course of the research procedure.

6 *The right to knowledge of results:* Each child participant has the right to new information concerning the results of the research project. In the case of young children, their parents have the right to be provided this information. Often this information will take the form of the group scores on a task, rather than the individual participant's own score.

7 *The right to confidentiality of their research data:* Each child participant has the right to expect that personal information gathered as part of the research project will remain private and confidential. Nor will any information about individual research participants be available to any other individuals or agencies.

8 *The right to beneficial treatments:* Each child participant has the right to profit from the beneficial treatments provided to other participants in the research project. If experimental treatments are believed to be beneficial (for example, participation in a program to enhance reading or math skills), children in control groups, who do not originally receive this treatment, have the right to alternative beneficial treatments at some later time.

Sources: American Psychological Association, 1968; Society for Research on Child Development Committee on Ethical Conduct in Child Development Research, 1990.

Or consider this situation. You are an observer in a nursery school, and you are interested in the development of aggression and other forms of antisocial behavior in young children. When the teacher is out of the room, a child takes an expensive truck from the toy closet and puts it in his school bag. Do you score it and tell the teacher or just score it as antisocial behavior and forget it?

Finally, what about the case study that we discussed earlier, in which the infant was treated for his vomiting problem with electric shock? Do you think it was justified?

In the final analysis, a cost-benefit ratio is usually the guiding principle. Is the cost in terms of the child's time and effort warranted by the increase in information and understanding about children that will result from the research project? Research is a tool for increasing our knowledge about children, and through this knowledge, children will, it is hoped, benefit in the long run. The ethics of research in child psychology is a continuing debate, and the last word is yet to be heard. As you read research reports throughout the remainder of the book, think about these ethical issues.

SUMMARY

STEPS IN THE RESEARCH PROCESS: SELECTING A SAMPLE

- Choosing a sample is an important first step because it will determine the extent to which the researcher's conclusions can be applied or generalized to other types of people. As illustrated by the examples, investigators need to select multiple samples of children who vary in race, sex, and social class to be certain that their conclusions about development apply to a broad range of children.

METHODS OF GATHERING DATA ABOUT CHILDREN

- *Self-report measures* such as interviews and questionnaires are often used to understand development. Using this method, parents, teachers, peers, or the child are asked to report on the child's behavior.
- Parents often are asked to provide reports of their own or their children's behavior. However, such measures are criticized for being inaccurate, unreliable, and open to distortions. Improvement in parent reports is found by focusing on specific and current events rather than retrospective and more broadly defined attitudes. New strategies employed to increase accuracy include daily contact with the parent for behavioral reports, structured diaries, "beeping" parents at various times to prompt them to record ongoing activities, and training parents to record specific events.
- *Children's self-reports* are sometimes problematic because children are more difficult to interview, are slow to respond, may not understand questions, and may not be truthful.
- Self-reports have some unique advantages. They are the only way of collecting some kinds of information, such as the child's or parent's perceptions and feelings, and they are based on family members' observations of each other over time in a variety of situations. Some argue that knowing family members' perceptions may be just as important as knowing what really occurred.
- Peer and teacher reports or ratings are used in areas where parents are not likely to be good sources of information (for example, children's behavior in the classroom).
- To find out how people actually behave, researchers use *direct observation* of parents and children in a variety of situations, ranging from naturalistic home settings to highly structured tasks in the laboratory. When families know they are being observed, they act in more socially acceptable ways than the ways in which they ordinarily behave. To minimize such distortions researchers observe families in familiar situations, permit long periods of adaptation by conducting frequent or sustained observations, and try to use unobtrusive measures.
- There are many observational methods, including writing down everything the family does (specimen record), recording only particular events (event sampling), and checking off a list of behaviors that occur in a predetermined period of time (time sampling). If the question of interest is the ordering of behaviors, the order of events in the sequence in which they occur may be collected. If the research question involves infrequently occurring behaviors, situations in which the behavior is likely to occur may be structured by the investigator. Because of the limitations of all methods, multiple measures of the same behaviors are often used.

ESTABLISHING RELATIONSHIPS AND CAUSES: STEPS TOWARD UNDERSTANDING DEVELOPMENT

- *Correlational research approaches* involve examining the relationship between two events, such as children's aggressiveness and the amount of aggression they watch on TV. Correlations are expressed in terms of the direction (positive or negative) and size (-1.0 to $+1.0$) of their relationship. If two factors are correlated, they are systematically related to each other; however, it is impossible to determine if one factor caused the other.

- *Experimental research strategies* permit the researcher to establish cause-effect relationships by assessing behavior in a controlled laboratory setting in which an event (for example, a TV program) is introduced in order to determine it's effect on the child's behavior (for example, aggression). Using this strategy, the *dependent variable* is the measure that is affected by the manipulation, or the *independent variable*. One problem with experimental studies is that they may not be easily generalized to real-world settings.
- *The laboratory analogue experiment* is one in which the researcher duplicates many of the features of a natural setting in the laboratory. This approach allows the investigator to control the situation while preserving the "naturalism" of real situations.
- In the *field experiment*, the investigator deliberately produces a change and then measures the outcome in a naturally occurring context. By retaining control over the independent variable, the researcher can establish causality. This method has the advantage of greater generalizability due to being conducted in real-world settings.
- In the *natural experiment* the investigator measures the impact of a naturally occurring change on the child's behavior in a real setting. Although this strategy allows investigation of behaviors that cannot be manipulated, it is limited because interpreting the effects of the independent variable may be difficult due to a lack of control.
- There is always a trade-off between experimental control and generalizability of findings in the various research strategies. No single strategy is always best. Rather, multiple research strategies are increasingly preferred as a way to study development.
- Combination approaches for integrating field and laboratory settings allow greater control *and* generalizability. Table 2-2 describes possible combinations achieved by varying the contexts (field versus lab) in which the independent and dependent variables are introduced.
- The *case study approach* involves detailed examination of one child over a period of time. A special form of the case study is the *single subject design*, in which the subject's baseline behavior is measured, then change is introduced, withdrawn, and reintroduced to discover what controls a particular behavior.

RESEARCH DESIGNS FOR DEVELOPMENT

- *Cross-sectional designs* involve comparing different groups of children at different age levels in the same situation. This approach is economical and does not take much time; however a disadvantage is that it yields no information about past determinants of age-related change or change in individuals.
- A *longitudinal design* involves the examination of the same children at different age levels. The advantage of tracking children over time is that the impact of early events on later behavior can be determined as well as shifts in individuals. Disadvantages include cost, subject loss, cross-generational change, and limited flexibility in using new measures.
- The *short-term longitudinal design* involves tracking a group of individuals for a short time span (a few months to a few years) on key issues. The

approach eliminates many disadvantages of longer longitudinal studies.

- A *cross-sectional/short-term longitudinal design* combines the advantages of both of the other approaches. Using this design, the investigator collects longitudinal data at several ages on one sample (for example, 6 and 10 years) and at partially overlapping ages (for example, 10 and 14 years) in a second sample. This approach eliminates some of the problems inherent in traditional cross-sectional and longitudinal studies.

THE ETHICS OF RESEARCH WITH CHILDREN

- A major consideration when deciding on a research strategy is the effect of the procedure on the children. Various government and institutional review boards, in addition to professional organizations, are involved in setting and maintaining guidelines for the proper treatment of children as research subjects. Parents and schools are often the ones who make the decisions about allowing children to participate in a particular research project. To determine if certain practices are "ethical" in a given research project, the researchers and other decision-makers must weigh the cost in terms of the child's time and effort against the potential benefits in increased knowledge about child development.

CHAPTER 3

THE BIOLOGICAL BASES OF BEHAVIOR

If you look at newborn infants in the nursery of a maternity ward, one of the things that is most striking is their diversity. This diversity is found not only in their physical characteristics but also in their behavior. One infant may sleep most of the time, another may be squalling and irritable, and still another may be wakeful but contented and seem to scan and visually explore the room. What contributes to this individuality in such young children? Before birth and according to some researchers even before conception, the transactions among a vast array of genetic factors and environmental factors begin. These genetic-environmental transactions make the individual unique and continue to shape development throughout the entire life span, from conception until death. The infant may enter the world impaired by lack of oxygen because a genetic predisposition to be of large body size resulted in a difficult labor. The adult may exit from the world early because of a lifetime of gluttony and an inherited proclivity for heart disease.

Human development is the process by which the genotype comes to be expressed as a phenotype. An individual's *genotype* is the material inherited from ancestors which makes the individual genetically unique. With the exception of identical twins, no two individuals have the same genotype. An individual's *phenotype* is the way the genotype is expressed in observable or measurable characteristics.

The expression of the genotype is modified by a variety of experiences. Whether or not a child's genotype for high intellectual ability is manifested in school performance will depend in part upon whether or not the child's parents stimulate and encourage the child in intellectual pursuits. A child reared in a deprived slum environment may manifest a genotype for high intelligence by being a high school dropout and becoming the most devious, skillful con artist in the neighborhood. Similarly, although a child may appear to have his grandfather's temper, any inherited predisposition for impulsive and uncontrolled behavior will be considerably modified by how "cute" his parents think his rages are and whether he eventually gets his own way and finds it rewarding to have tantrums.

Some genotypes, such as eye or hair color, may be directly expressed in phenotypes, although as many people know, a visit to a skillful hairdresser can modify the direct phenotypical expression of hair color. However, most of the phenotypical motor, intellectual, social, emotional, and personality characteristics in which psychologists are interested are the result of extremely complex transactions between genetic and environmental factors during the course of development. In this chapter, some of the principles and processes which guide these transactions will be reviewed. The effects of transactions among genes and between genetic and environmental factors, and the importance of the timing of such transactions on the development of the child will be explored. Two approaches to the study of these transactions will be presented. One approach focuses on reproductive processes, genetic mechanisms, and the biochemical basis of development. The other approach, which is used by behavior geneticists, examines the relative contribution of genetic relatedness and environment to development. Behavior geneticists rarely study genes or biological processes directly; they study individuals with varying degrees of biological relatedness living in similar or different situations. These are called kinship studies. In such studies a comparison is made of the similarity on a characteristic such as intelligence test performance of unrelated strangers versus that of distantly related relatives, such as a child to his or her grandparents, cousins, aunts, and uncles, or of members of the immediate family, such as parents, children, and siblings. If the score on an intelligence test is strongly influenced by inheritance, it would be expected that there would be an increase in resemblance from strangers to distant relatives to immediate relatives. However, it could also be argued that immediate relatives are more likely to live in the same home and be exposed to the same environment and that it will be impossible to separate the effects of heredity and environment in these studies. Adoption studies and studies that compare twins reared together or apart are special types of kinship studies that attempt to separate these effects.

The critical question asked by behavior geneticists is "Why are people different?" (Plomin, 1990b). Why are some people physically active and others sedentary couch potatoes? Why are some ebullient and self-confident and others shy, depressed, or anxious? Why do some learn with ease and others with great effort and difficulty? We turn now to some of the processes that help explain such individual differences.

THE PROCESS OF GENETIC TRANSMISSION

Conception and the Beginnings of Life

At the time of conception, a *sperm* cell from the father penetrates and unites with the *ovum* (the egg cell) from the mother to form the *zygote,* or fertilized ovum. The cells of the zygote multiply rapidly by cell division and develop into the future child.

The human body is composed of two structurally and functionally different types of cells, the germ cells and the body cells. Within each cell nucleus are threadlike entities known as chromosomes on which genes are located. The genes contain the genetic code that will help to direct development. *Germ* cells (or gametes) are the female ovum and the male sperm cell. Sperm cells are continually produced in the testicles of males, however, at birth the female has the full complement of eggs that will be released during her reproductive life. All other cells in the body are *somatic* (or *body*) cells, which compose such things as the bones, muscles, organs, and digestive, respiratory, and nervous systems. Germ cells and body cells contain a different number of chromosomes and divide in a different manner.

The germ cells differ markedly in size. The ovum is the largest cell in the body and the sperm is the smallest. The relative size of these cells can be understood if it is noted that an ovum is about 90,000 times as heavy as a sperm. However, even an ovum is still smaller than the periods printed on this page.

Each germ cell contains 23 chromosomes. Each body cell of most normal men and women and the nucleus of the fertilized ovum (the zygote) contain 46 chromosomes (two sets of 23 chromosomes, 1 chromosome in each pair coming from the mother and 1 from the father).

Cell division in body cells occurs by *mitosis,* a process in which each of the 46 chromosomes in the nucleus of the parent cell duplicates itself. The resulting identical two sets of 46 chromosomes move to opposite sides of the parent cell. The parent cell then separates between the two clusters of 46 identical chromosomes and becomes two new cells, or daughter cells. These daughter cells and all the body cells formed by mitosis in the course of human development contain 46 chromosomes which are identical to those in the zygote. The process of mitosis is shown in Figure 3-1.

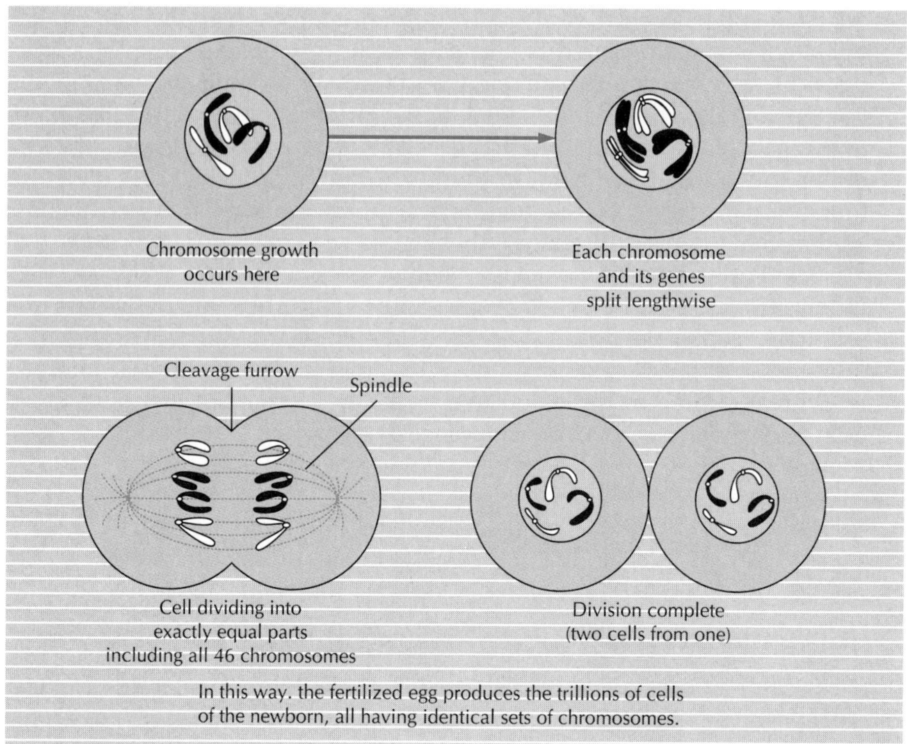

FIGURE 3-1
Mitosis: a process of cell replication in the zygote and body cells in which both pairs of each chromosome are reproduced. After cell division in humans, each cell contains the identical set of 46 chromosomes (that is, 23 pairs); only 4 chromosomes (2 pairs) are shown here for the sake of simplification. (Adapted from Rugh & Shettles, 1974, by permission of the publisher and the senior author).

Germ cells divide by a different process called *meiosis,* which is essentially a process of reduction division. In the testes and ovaries, a cell with 23 pairs of chromosomes divides in such a way that the daughter cells include only one member of each pair of chromosomes. This process is presented in Figure 3-2. Thus, mature sperm and egg cells contain only 23 single chromosomes rather then 23 chromosome pairs. When the sperm and egg cells with their 23 chromosomes unite, the zygote contains the 46 chromosomes, half contributed by each parent.

Since, at conception, any possible combination of chromosomes from the sperm and ovum may occur, the number of possible combinations in a zygote is immense. There are about 3.8 billion people alive today, but there are about 70 trillion potential human genotypes.

In addition, increasing this genetic variability is a phenomenon called *crossing-over,* which occurs during meiosis. In this process, equivalent sections of each chromosome break away and attach themselves to the adjacent chromosome. Thus, the chromosomes are actually altered because genes are exchanged between pairs of chromosomes and the genetic characteristics associated with those genes are now carried on different chromosomes. This process of crossing-over enlarges the already broad genetic array of possible combinations of characteristics that take place in reproduction and ensures the genetic uniqueness of individuals.

Chromosomes and Genes

Arranged along the length of a chromosome and for the most part occupying a specific location on it are thousands of segments called genes, which are the basic units of hereditary transmission and which specify the protein and

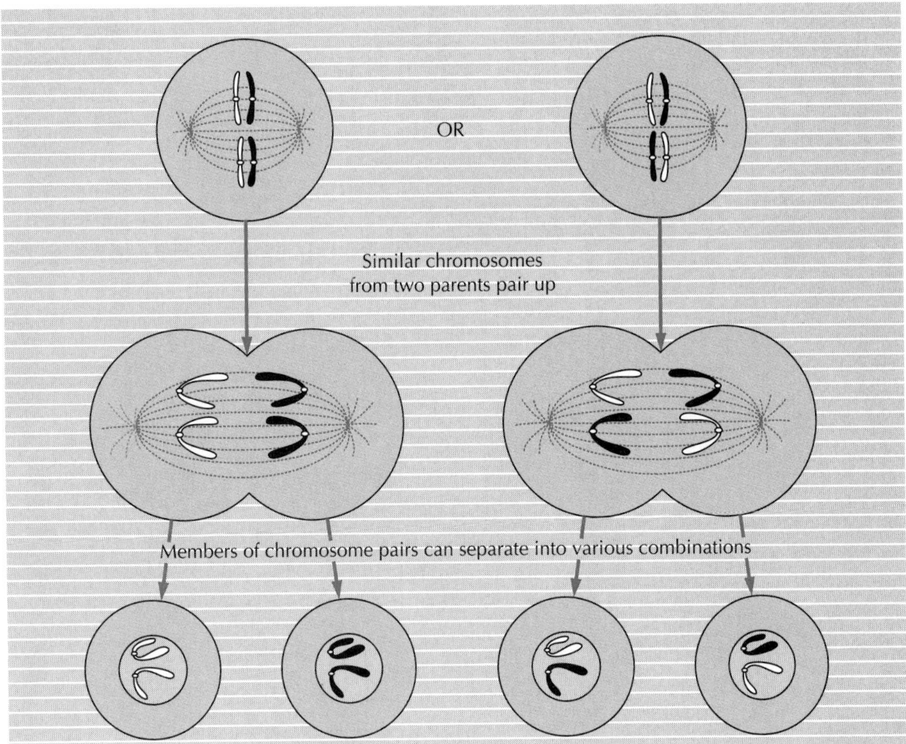
OR
Similar chromosomes from two parents pair up
Members of chromosome pairs can separate into various combinations

FIGURE 3-2
Meiosis: a process of reduction division in the germ cell (ovum and sperm). Following meiosis only one member of each pair of chromosomes, rather than 23 pairs of chromosomes, is present in each of the new germ cells. (Adapted from Rugh & Shettles, 1974, by permission of the publisher and the senior author.)

enzyme reactions to be activated during development. In the past few decades, great advances have been made in understanding the structure and processes associated with genetic transmission.

The gene is composed of *deoxyribonucleic acid,* or DNA. DNA is the template that directs the functioning of *ribonucleic acid,* RNA. RNA serves as a messenger in carrying the DNA-originated directions from the nucleus of a cell to its *cytoplasm,* which composes the rest of the cell, where the instructions are carried out. The environment of each cell, where it is located and what is around it, activates certain genes in that cell's chromosomes to send out their code. It is that message from the DNA to the RNA that determines what this cell will eventually become, such as skin, bone, nerve, muscle, and so forth. These directions lead to the synthesis of proteins from the amino acids in the cytoplasm. Since the body is composed of protein, instructions are being relayed as to how the newly formed organism is to develop. The DNA in each gene contains instructions for a specific type of protein chain. It has been found that genes of different types direct structural development and regulate cellular, chemical, and metabolic processes. Some of these protein chains control body processes, some are structural and form new tissues, and some regulate the functioning and turning off and on of structural genes. When even one of these genes is defective, marked developmental deviations may occur in the child.

The Double Helix

The now famous double-helix model of the structure and function of DNA proposed by James Watson and Francis Crick (1953) helps to explain how genes replicate themselves during cell division. Watson and Crick suggest

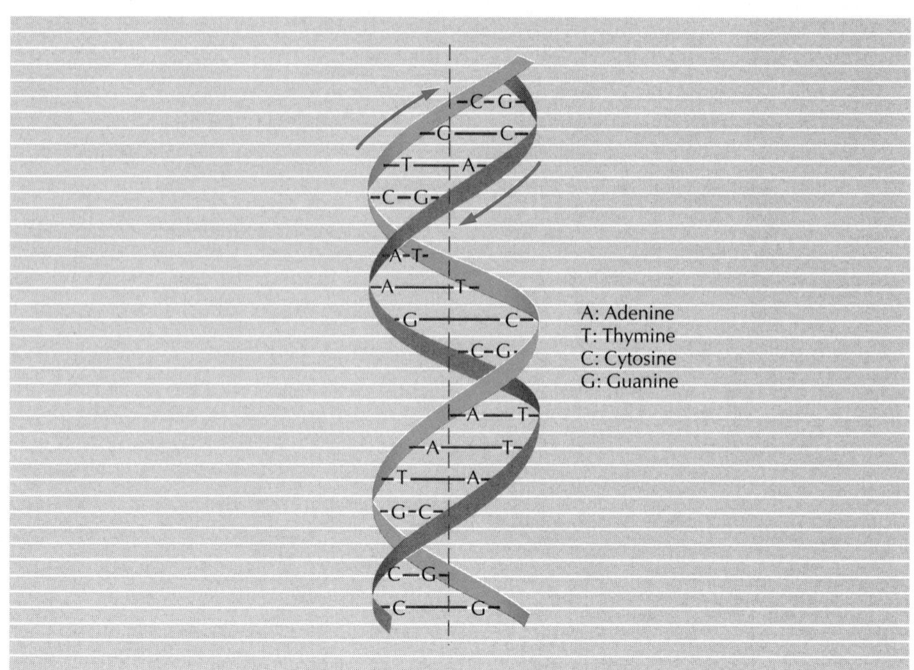

FIGURE 3-3
The alphabet of life: a model of DNA. (From Watson & Crick, 1953, by permission of the publisher and the senior author.)

that a molecule of DNA which is the core of each chromosome is like a spiral staircase, or a double helix or coil, with the side strips being composed of molecules of phosphate and sugar and the steps being composed of pairs of four chemical bases (see Figure 3-3). Genetic information is coded by the ordering, or arrangement, of these chemical steps at different locations on the chromosome. Only bases that are compatible with each other form pairs to make the steps (thus cytosine and guanine are paired and thymine and adenine appear together), but these pairs can follow each other in any order. A single gene on average involves over a thousand steps in the spiral staircase of DNA. It is the order of these steps that gives every gene its special character. This creates a kind of alphabet of life.

We have described the process of cell division, but what happens to our DNA molecules while cells are duplicating themselves? Watson and Crick speculate that during cell division this DNA ladder duplicates itself first by separating, or unzipping, down the middle of the structure—the bases separate from their mates, cytosine from guanine, and thymine from adenine. Think of the staircase being cut in half. Then each half of the DNA molecule serves as the framework to evolve a copy of the missing half from the materials of the surrounding cell and constructs a compatible half identical to the one from which it just separated. Thus, as a result of this unzipping and reconstruction of genes, every cell in the body carries the same genetic code or pattern as the original one.

Homozygotes and Heterozygotes

Much of the original work that served as the basis for modern genetics was done at the end of the nineteenth century by Gregor Mendel, who worked with rather simple hereditary characteristics, such as blossom color in hybridized plants. Many of the attributes he studied were ones in which a single pair of genes seemed largely responsible for the phenotypical appearance of the characteristic of the plant. It is now recognized that most phenotypical characteristics are determined by more than one gene. Although contemporary geneticists take a more complex approach in studying the transactions among a number of genetic factors and an array of environmental effects, some of Mendel's principles dealing with *dominant* and *recessive* genes are still accepted.

At each gene *locus,* or position on the chromosome, there may be two or more alternative forms of the gene, called *alleles,* one from the mother and one from the father. If the alleles from both parents are the same, a child is said to be *homozygous* at that locus; if they differ, the child is *heterozygous.* For example, if a child has alleles to have normal hearing from both parents, the child is homozygous; but if the child has an allele for normal hearing from one parent and an allele for congenital deafness from the other, the child is heterozygous. Using the code "A" to represent one allele and "a" another, it can be seen that three types of allelic combinations may result: AA, aa, or Aa (aA), depending on the parents' alleles. In our example of hearing, if "A" represents normal hearing and "a" congenital deafness, the child with an AA combination will hear normally and the child with aa alleles will be hearing impaired. But what happens with the heterozygous Aa child with different alleles from each parent? If a trait is determined by a single allelic pair, there are three main ways in which a heterozygous combination of alleles can be expressed in the phenotype. In the first case the heterozygous combination of alleles may be expressed in a phenotype intermediate between those carried by the individual alleles. For example, a light-skinned parent and a dark-skinned parent may produce a child of intermediate skin color. A second possible form in which the heterozygous combination of alleles may be expressed is by showing codominant or combined attributes carried by two alleles. In relation to some alleles that control chemical substances in the blood, the blood of the heterozygous child will contain both the blood substances which are contained singly in the blood of each parent. Finally, the characteristic associated with only one of the alleles may be expressed. One allele will be *dominant* over the other; that is, it is more likely to be expressed phenotypically than the less powerful *recessive* gene.

If the phenotype Aa is the same as the phenotype AA, the allele A is said to be dominant and the allele a is said to be recessive. As can be seen in Table 3-1 (p. 64) and Table 3-2, (pp. 68–70) however, most of the serious deleterious genes are recessive. This is fortunate since otherwise we would be confronted with an exploding rate of genetic abnormalities. One of the reasons that, historically, there have been prohibitions on close blood relatives marrying is that in the offspring of such unions there is a greater chance of the same harmful recessive allele being contributed by each parent.

Phenylketonuria: An Example of the Action of Recessive and Dominant Genes

Let us examine the development of phenylketonuria (PKU) as an example of the action of dominant and recessive genes. This example is important not only in order to illustrate the development of a recessive disorder but also to emphasize again the fact that "genetic" does not mean "unchangeable." The adverse outcome of this genetically based metabolic disorder can be effectively countered by dietetic intervention procedures.

Phenylketonuria is a disorder, caused by a recessive gene, that leads to the absence of an enzyme necessary to metabolize certain types of proteins,

TABLE 3-1 **SOME COMMON DOMINANT AND RECESSIVE CHARACTERISTICS**

DOMINANT TRAITS	RECESSIVE TRAITS
Curly hair	Straight hair
Normal hair	Baldness
Dark hair	Light or blond hair
Nonred hair (blond, brunette)	Red hair
Normal coloring	Albinism (lack of pigment)
Thick lips	Thin lips
Roman nose	Straight nose
Cheek dimples	No dimples
Extra, fused, or short digits	Normal digits
Double-jointedness	Normal joints
Normal color vision	Color blindness, red-green
Normal vision	Myopia, nearsightedness
Farsightedness	Normal vision
Immunity to poison ivy	Susceptibility to poison ivy
Normal hearing	Congenital deafness
Normal blood clotting	Hemophilia
Normal metabolism	Phenylketonuria
Normal blood cells	Sickle-cell anemia

some of which are found in milk, the basic diet for infants. Thus, an infant with two recessive genes for phenylketonuria is unable to convert the protein phenylalanine into tyrosine, which results in an accumulation of phenylpyruvic acid in the body. This has damaging effects on the developing nervous system of the child and usually results in mental retardation. The infant appears normal at birth, but with the gradual buildup of phenylpyruvic acid, increasing signs of mental retardation are shown.

The genetic transmission patterns for PKU are presented in Figure 3-4. Approximately 1 out of every 20 persons carries the recessive allele for phenylketonuria (p). If a heterozygote (Pp) marries an individual who carries two dominant alleles (PP) for normal metabolizing of phenylalanine, their children will be intellectually unaffected by phenylalanine. However, if two of these heterozygotes (Pp) marry, they will have 1 chance in 4 of producing a phenylketonuric child (pp). PKU is much less frequently found among blacks and Asians than among Caucasians.

Testing for PKU is now required in almost all states and the damage caused by PKU can be restricted if infants are fed an early diet of milk substitutes, which limits their intake of phenylalanine. There is controversy over whether, and when, this restricted diet can be discontinued. Some scientists argue that the special diet can be withdrawn in middle childhood when the brain and central nervous system are mature enough to be unlikely to be damaged by phenylpyruvic acid. Others cite evidence of declines in intelligence when school-aged children had their special diet terminated and recommend permanent dietary restrictions (Michals, Azen, Acosta, Koch, & Matalon, 1988; Pietz, Benninger, Schmidt, Scheffner, & Bickel, 1988). The importance of early dietary therapy is demonstrated graphically in Figure 3-5, which shows the relation between the start of treatment and eventual IQ of PKU patients. It can be seen that the effects of starting treatment decrease rapidly after the first few months of life, and that starting dietary remedies even as early as 7 months can do little to reverse the destructive

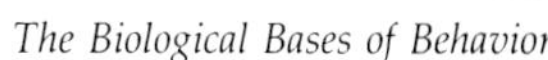

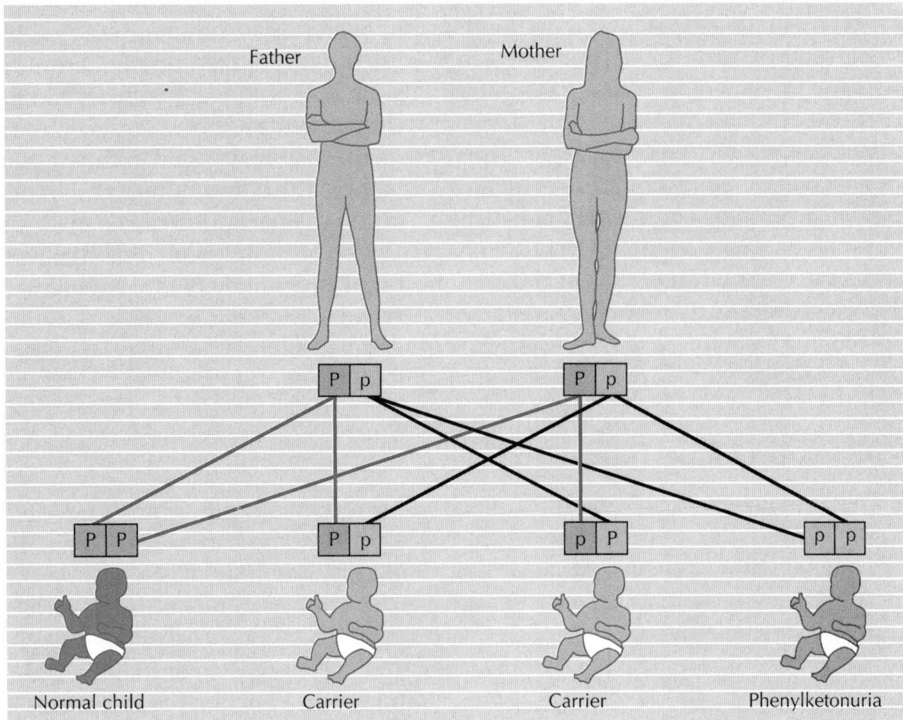

FIGURE 3-4
The genetic transmission of phenylketonuria in the children of two heterozygous parents carrying the recessive allele for phenylketonuria. (P is the dominant gene; p is the recessive gene.)

course of the disorder. This is an example of the point we emphasized earlier, that the timing of intervention is critical.

Although early imposed dietary restrictions interfere with the adverse effects related to the buildup of phenylpyruvic acid, treated children still may be more irritable and emotionally labile and have learning problems and lower IQs than their siblings without PKU (Kopp & Parmelee, 1979). Alterations in parent-child relations because of the guilt and anxiety experienced by parents of PKU children may contribute to these developmental deviations (Kopp & Parmelee, 1979). When phenylketonurics reproduce, the results can be disastrous. Male phenylketonurics pass on only one recessive

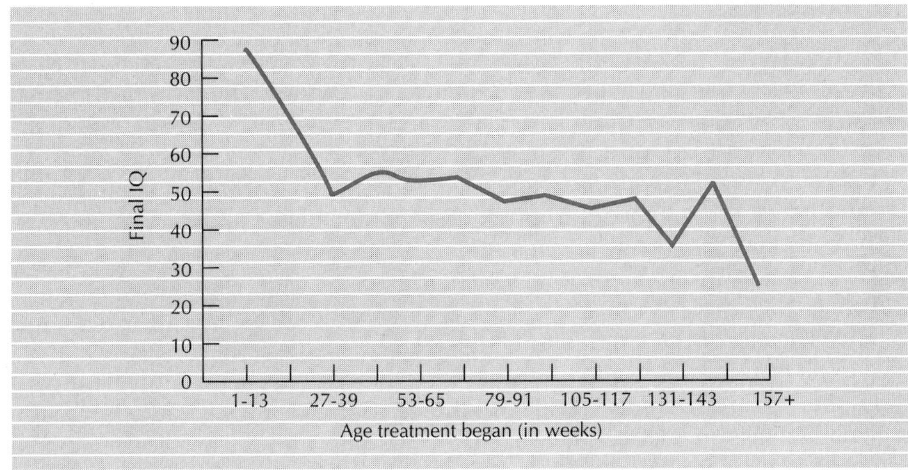

FIGURE 3-5
The relationship between age of starting dietary control and intelligence in phenylketonuria. (Adapted from Baumeister, 1967, by permission of the publisher and the author.)

gene for the disorder to their offspring, which may be counteracted by a normal gene in the women they marry. However, female phenylketonurics, even those who were on early dietary restrictions that were later terminated, present their children with a damaging prenatal intrauterine environment as well as a defective gene. The high levels of phenylpyruvic acid in the mother's bloodstream may enter the circulatory system of the baby in utero and damage the developing central nervous system. Although retardation can be prevented if the pregnant woman immediately resumes a low-phenylalanine diet, harm to the fetus often occurs in the first month of pregnancy before pregnancy is discovered and treatment is started (Howell & Stevenson, 1971; Lowitzer, 1987). This may be reason enough to recommend lifetime dietary restrictions for women with PKU.

Complex Gene Interaction

What has been presented thus far is a rather simple genetic model of one gene determining one characteristic. Although there are over 1000 characteristics transmitted according to laws of inheritance of dominant and recessive genes, many characteristics are determined not by a single gene but by a constellation of genes that act together. This is called *pleiotropism.* Furthermore a single pair of genes may influence more than one characteristic. Some genes, called *modifier genes,* influence the action or phenotypical expression of other genes. The action of a modifier gene is clearly demonstrated in the inheritance of early cataracts. The occurrence of cataracts is determined by a dominant gene; however, the type of opacity and the location on the lens of the cataract seem to be determined by modifier genes. Similarly, children with phenylketonuria have differing phenylalanine levels in spite of the fact that they have identical genes at the critical locus. This is because modifier genes at other loci determine the variation in phenylalanine levels and in intelligence levels in untreated cases.

Most of the characteristics in which psychologists are interested, such as intelligence, creativity, sociability, or emotionality, have not been demonstrated to be shaped by a single gene and it is likely that such attributes are the results of the interaction of multiple genes as well as environmental factors.

Sex Chromosomes and Sex-Linked Characteristics

Of the 23 pairs of chromosomes, 22 pairs are *autosomes,* that is, they are possessed equally by males and females. In contrast, the twenty-third pair, the *sex chromosomes,* differs in males and females. The female has two X chromosomes (XX), and the male has an X and a Y (XY) chromosome. The X chromosome is about five times as long as the Y chromosome and carries more genes on it. Since the mother is XX, her ovum always contains an X chromosome. However, sperms may carry either an X or a Y chromosome. If a sperm with an X chromosome fertilizes the egg, the offspring will be female (XX); if the sperm carries a Y chromosome, the offspring will be male (XY). The sex of the child is thus determined by the father.

The fact that some genes on the X chromosome have no equivalent genes on the Y chromosome results in the appearance of sex-linked recessive characteristics in males. Since a male has only one X chromosome, if the recessive allele for a defect is present on the X chromosome, the disorder will

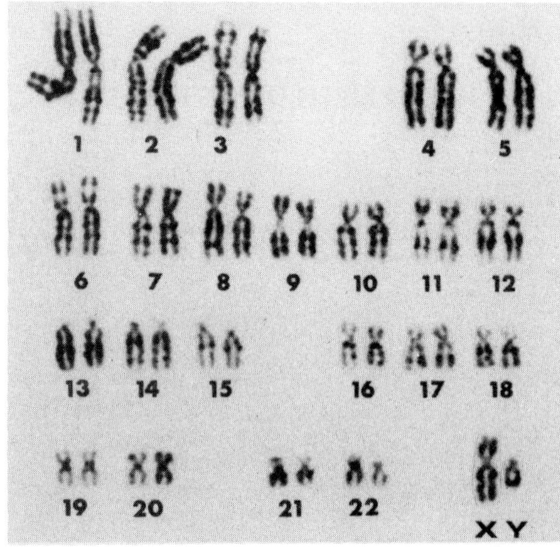

A karyotype or photograph of the chromosomes in a normal human female. The 22 pairs of autosomes or body cells are similar for both sexes, but the sex cells in females contain two X chromosomes whereas those in males contain an X and a Y chromosome.

be manifested since there is no equivalent allele on the Y chromosome to counteract this effect. In women the phenotypical expression of a recessive allele for a defect will be determined by its interaction with the matching allele on the other X chromosome. If the matching allele is a dominant one for normal development, it will overrule the effects of a damaging recessive allele.

For example, hemophilia, a disease in which the blood does not clot, is a sex-linked recessive trait carried on the X chromosome. Since it is recessive, if a female receives the deleterious recessive gene from one parent she will have blood which clots normally unless the matching gene from the other is also for hemophilia. Only if she is homozygous for the recessive gene will her blood clotting be impaired. In contrast, if a male receives the gene from the mother on the X chromosome, there can be no counteracting gene from the father and the son will be afflicted.

There are many X-linked characteristics in addition to hemophilia. These include color blindness, certain types of night blindness, one form of muscular dystrophy, diabetes, atrophy of the optic nerve, and a disorder resulting in an inability to produce antibodies to cope with certain bacterial infections. The high rate of miscarriage, infant mortality, and later deaths in males is partly attributable to their greater vulnerability to sex-linked disorders. Even resistance to certain childhood diseases appears to be sex-linked. Thus, although a ratio of 120 males to 100 females are conceived and a ratio of 106 males to 100 females are born, this numerical imbalance is rapidly eliminated over the course of development. It should be kept in mind that the high rate of mortality for males in later years may not be entirely due to their greater

TABLE 3-2

SELECTED BIRTH DEFECTS, USA

BIRTH DEFECT	TYPE	CAUSE	DETECTION	TREATMENT	PREVENTION
Down syndrome	Functional/ structural: retardation often associated with physical defects	Chromosomal abnormality	Amniocentesis, chromosome analysis	Corrective surgery, special physical training and schooling	Genetic services
Markedly low birthweight (prematurity)	Structural/ functional: organs often immature	Hereditary and/or environmental: maternal disorder or malnutrition	Prenatal monitoring, visual inspection at birth	Intensive care of newborn, high-nutrient diet	Proper prenatal care, genetic services, maternal nutrition
Muscular dystrophy	Functional: impaired voluntary muscular function	Hereditary: often recessive inheritance	Apparent at onset	Physical therapy	Genetic services
Congenital heart malformations	Structural	Hereditary and/or environmental	Examination at birth and later	Corrective surgery, medication	Genetic services
Clubfoot	Structural: misshapen foot	Hereditary and/or environmental	Examination at birth	Corrective surgery, corrective splints, physical training	Genetic services
Polydactyly	Structural: multiple fingers or toes	Hereditary: dominant inheritance	Visual inspection at birth	Corrective surgery, physical training	Genetic services
Spina bifida and/ or hydrocephalus	Structural/ functional: incompletely formed spinal canal; "water on the brain"	Hereditary and environmental	Amniocentesis, prenatal x-ray, ultrasound, maternal blood test, examination at birth	Corrective surgery, prostheses, physical training, special schooling for any mental impairment	Genetic services
Cleft lip and/or cleft palate	Structural	Hereditary and/or environmental	Visual inspection at birth	Corrective surgery	Genetic services
Diabetes mellitus	Metabolic: inability to metabolize carbohydrates	Hereditary and/or environmental	Appears in childhood or later; blood and urine tests	Oral medication, special diet, insulin injections	Genetic services

TABLE 3-2

SELECTED BIRTH DEFECTS, USA (*Continued*)

BIRTH DEFECT	TYPE	CAUSE	DETECTION	TREATMENT	PREVENTION
Cystic fibrosis	Functional: respiratory and digestive system malfunction	Hereditary: recessive inheritance	Sweat and blood tests	Treat respiratory and digestive complications	Genetic services
Sickle-cell anemia	Blood disease: malformed red blood cells	Hereditary: incomplete recessive—most frequent among blacks	Blood test	Transfusions	Genetic services
Hemophilia (classic)	Blood disease: poor clotting ability	Hereditary: sex-linked recessive inheritance	Blood test	Clotting factor	Genetic services
Congenital syphilis	Structural: multiple abnormalities	Environmental: acquired from infected mother	Blood test, examination at birth	Medication	Proper prenatal care
Phenylketonuria (PKU)	Metabolic: inability to metabolize a specific amino acid	Hereditary: recessive inheritance	Blood test at birth	Special diet	Carrier identification, genetic services
Tay Sachs disease	Metabolic: inability to metabolize fats in nervous system	Hereditary: recessive inheritance—most frequent among Ashkenazic Jews	Blood and tear tests, amniocentesis	None	Carrier identification, genetic services
Thalassemia	Blood disease: anemia	Hereditary: incomplete recessive inheritance	Blood test	Transfusions	Carrier identification, genetic services
Galactosemia	Metabolic: inability to metabolize milk sugar galactose	Hereditary: recessive inheritance	Blood and urine tests, amniocentesis	Special diet	Carrier identification, genetic services
Erythroblastosis	Blood disease: destruction of red blood cells	Hereditary and environmental: Rh − mother has Rh + child	Blood tests	Transfusion: intrauterine or postnatal	Rh vaccine, blood tests to identify women at risk, genetic services

TABLE 3-2

SELECTED BIRTH DEFECTS, USA (*Continued*)

BIRTH DEFECT	TYPE	CAUSE	DETECTION	TREATMENT	PREVENTION
Congenital Rubella syndrome	Structural/ functional: multiple defects	Environmental maternal infection	Antibody tests and viral culture	Corrective surgery, prostheses, physical therapy, and training	Rubella vaccine

Reproduced by permission of March of Dimes Birth Defects Foundation. (1985)

genetic vulnerability. It also may be attributable to greater participation by males in adventurous risk-taking activities, in hazardous occupations, rough sports, violent crimes, and war.

Chromosome Abnormalities

Developmental disorders sometimes appear because of defects or variations in chromosomes, or chromosome matching. Some of these deviations occur in the autosomes; others occur in the sex chromosomes. Almost 1 percent of all neonates have diagnosable chromosomal abnormalities. In addition, it is estimated that 60 percent of early spontaneous abortions and 5 percent of later abortions are attributable to chromosomal aberrations.

Down syndrome will be discussed as one example out of the many identifiable autosomal disorders, followed by a presentation of several of the more common disorders based on deviations in the sex chromosomes (see Table 3-2).

DOWN SYNDROME

A disorder known as *trisomy 21,* or *Down syndrome,* was for some time regarded as a nongenetic disorder attributable to the effects on the infant in utero of physiological and biological factors in the aging of the mother. As can be seen from Table 3-3, the incidence of Down syndrome does increase dramatically with maternal age, although it is less likely to occur with healthy older women than with those who have health problems.

In 1959, it was demonstrated that Down syndrome is related to a deviation in the twenty-first set of autosomes. This was an important genetic breakthrough, since it was the first identification of a chromosomal aberration as a cause of human disease. Down syndrome is usually attributable to the *nondisjunction* of chromosome 21 where the individual has an extra chromosome or part of a third chromosome on the twenty-first set of autosomes. This is thought to be a result of failure of the chromosomes to separate at meiosis in the egg, with the consequence that the individual has 47 rather than the usual 46 chromosomes. Why this occurs more frequently in older mothers is not known. It has been speculated that some deterioration of the ova produced by older women may occur or that older women may have been exposed to more environmental hazards during the course of their lifetimes, which could lead to increased chromosomal abnormalities. This

TABLE 3-3

RISK OF GIVING BIRTH TO A DOWN SYNDROME INFANT BY MATERNAL AGE

MATERNAL AGE	FREQUENCY OF DOWN SYNDROME INFANTS AMONG BIRTHS
30	1/885
31	1/826
32	1/725
33	1/592
34	1/465
35	1/365
36	1/287
37	1/225
38	1/176
39	1/139
40	1/109
41	1/85
42	1/67
43	1/53
44	1/41
45	1/32
46	1/25
47	1/20
48	1/16
49	1/12

Source: From Hook and Lindsjo (1978).

may be a factor contributing to some cases of Down syndrome; however, it has been shown that the sperm carries the extra chromosome in about one-quarter of Down syndrome conceptions (Magenis, Overton, Chamberlin, Brady, & Lorrien, 1977).

Over 10 percent of institutionalized retardates are persons with Down syndrome. The disorder is characterized by physical and mental retardation and a distinctive physical appearance. Children with Down syndrome have almond-shaped eyes with an Epicanthal eyelid fold, round heads often flattened on the back, short necks, protruding tongues, and small noses. In addition, they frequently have other unusual characteristics such as webbed fingers or toes, a rare long crease which extends across the palm of the hand, dental anomalies, and an awkward, flat-footed walk. Non-mentally retarded relatives of Down syndrome patients often show a few or muted symptoms of the disorder. The greater susceptibility of Down syndrome children to leukemia, heart disorders, and particularly to respiratory infections used to result in extremely early deaths. At one time it was unusual to see these individuals as adolescents or postadolescents; however, since advances have been made in the treatment of these disorders (such as the use of antibiotics for pneumonia), their life span has greatly increased.

Infants with Down syndrome appear to develop fairly normally for the first six months of life, but their rate of intellectual growth declines after the first year. Down syndrome children, in contrast to their normal peers, have difficulty attending to, discriminating, and interpreting complex or subtle information in their environment. This is reflected in problems in communication between Down syndrome children and their caretakers since these children are inattentive, have low levels of visual contact, verbalize little, give

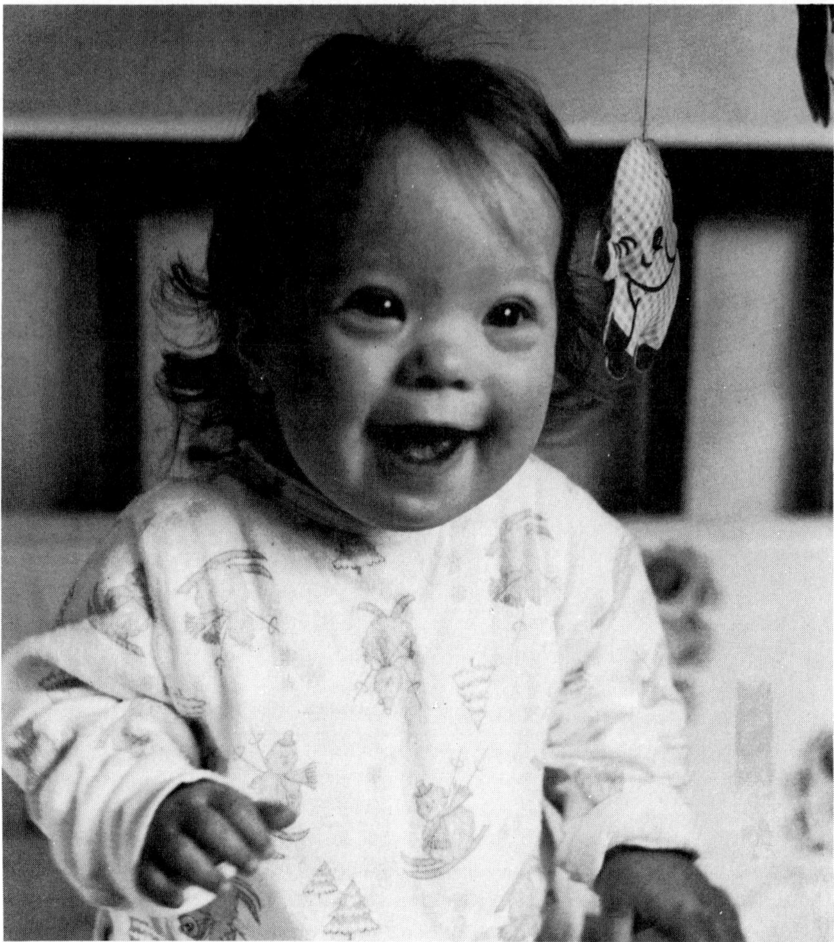

This Down syndrome baby has folds on the corner of the eyes and a flat profile typical of such children.

nonverbal signals that are difficult to interpret, and are low in emotional expressiveness. These behaviors on the part of Down syndrome children often induce their parents to talk more and be more directive than parents of normal children (Cardoso-Martins & Mervis, 1985; Kopp, 1983; Loveland, 1987; MacTurk, Vietze, McCarthy, McQuiston, & Yarrow, 1985). When mothers of Down syndrome children provide stimulation and encourage the children to attend and become involved in their environment, the children are more competent. However, such experiences are more likely to enhance emotional, social, and motor development than cognitive development in these children although with training some of these children are able to learn to read and write (Crawley & Spiker, 1983; Gibson & Harris, 1988).

SEX CHROMOSOME ABNORMALITIES

In addition to abnormalities in the autosomes, such as those found in Down syndrome, problems in sexual differentiation based on deviations in the number of sex chromosomes sometimes occur. Diagnosis of such individuals can be made on the basis of chromosome counts from cells that are drawn from samples of skin or mouth tissue and prenatally through amniocentesis.

Sex Chromosome Deviations in Females. One type of sex chromosome abnormality is *Turner syndrome.* Females having Turner syndrome, instead of having the customary XX combination of sex chromosomes, are missing the second X chromosome and are X0. They have only 45 chromosomes. Most cases of Turner syndrome result from an abnormal sperm containing neither an X nor a Y chromosome combining with a normal (X) ovum.

These girls remain small in stature, are usually of normal intelligence, and often have short fingers and webbed necks and unusually shaped mouths and ears. In personality they tend to be relaxed, docile, pleasant, and not easily upset. At puberty they remain infantile in the development of the mammary glands and other secondary sex characteristics because of the lack of female hormones. However, successful treatment is possible through the administration of estrogens (female hormones), which at puberty will lead to normal sexual development, although the girls will remain sterile. It should be noted that even when treated they are still short and have an eternally little-girlish appearance. Girls with Turner syndrome show feminine personality characteristics and interests even without hormone treatment, and it has been concluded that the normal female XX genetic pattern is not essential for the development of a feminine identity and behaviors. Girls with Turner syndrome do, however, have problems in social relationships. They are socially immature and lacking in assertiveness (McCauley, Ito, & Kay, 1986). These difficulties may be related not only to the responses of others to their physical appearance but also to their difficulty in discriminating and interpreting emotional cues and facial expressions in others, skills essential for appropriate social interactions (McCauley, Kay, Ito, & Treeler, 1987).

A second type of chromosomal abnormality found in females is the triple-X syndrome. In contrast to females with Turner syndrome, who have one less than the normal complement of two X chromosomes, triple-X girls have one more than the normal number. Triple-X girls appear normal physically and have normal secondary sexual development.

Although neither girls with Turner syndrome nor those with the triple-X syndrome are mentally retarded, they do show some specific cognitive deficits and learning disabilities, and the nature of the learning disability seems to be specific to the type of chromosomal pattern. Turner syndrome girls have marked difficulty in solving spatial tasks and have problems in handwriting, but have normal verbal skills (Pennington, Bender, Puck, Salenblatt, & Robinson, 1982). In contrast, the triple-X children have more global cognitive problems, with greater impairments in verbal skills and in short-term memory than in spatial abilities (Rovet & Netley, 1983). What happens to XXY males who also have an extra X chromosome? They too manifest verbal language deficits and more reading problems and some, but not all, are retarded (Netley, 1986).

Sex Chromosome Deviations in Males. Three types of abnormal sex chromosomal patterns in males have been extensively studied. The first, which we have mentioned, is known as *Klinefelter's syndrome* and involves an additional X chromosome, an XXY rather than the normal XY male chromosomal array. The second pattern involves an extra Y chromosome, yielding an XYY array. A third pattern, known as the *fragile-X syndrome,* has only recently been identified and is one of the most exciting new genetic discoveries.

XXY and XYY Males. Males with Klinefelter's syndrome (XXY) have testes, although they are sterile, and they have many female characteristics such as

BOX 3-1 THE INFLUENCE OF FAMILY DYSFUNCTION ON CHILDREN WITH SEX-CHROMOSOME ANOMALIES

Why is there such diversity in the phenotypic expression of sex-chromosome anomalies? A longitudinal study of children with sex-chromosome anomalies by Bender, Linden, and Robinson (1987) explores this question. Forty-six children with sex-chromosome anomalies, who were born between 1964 and 1974, were identified by screening 40,000 births in the Denver area. These children were compared to a control group comprised of their siblings who had normal complements of sex chromosomes. They were categorized as coming from competent nondysfunctional families or from dysfunctional families where parenting was ineffective and the family encountered multiple stresses, such as poverty, drug and alcohol abuse, or death of a family member. Children with sex-chromosome anomalies were more likely than their siblings to exhibit neuromotor, psychosocial, academic, and language problems. However, it can be seen in Figure 3-6 that for psychosocial and school problems these differences were obtained only if the children came from dysfunctional families, although even in well-functioning families differences in neuromotor and language impairment were found. Children with chromosomal anomalies are at greater risk for impaired development; however, psychosocial and school problems emerge only in a stressful dysfunctional family environment. Again the importance of environmental factors in the phenotypical expression of the genotype is seen.

Source: Bender, B. G., Linden, M. G., & Robinson, A. (1987). Environment and developmental risk in children with sex chromosome abnormalities. *Journal of the Academy of Child and Adolescent Psychiatry,* **26,** 499–503.

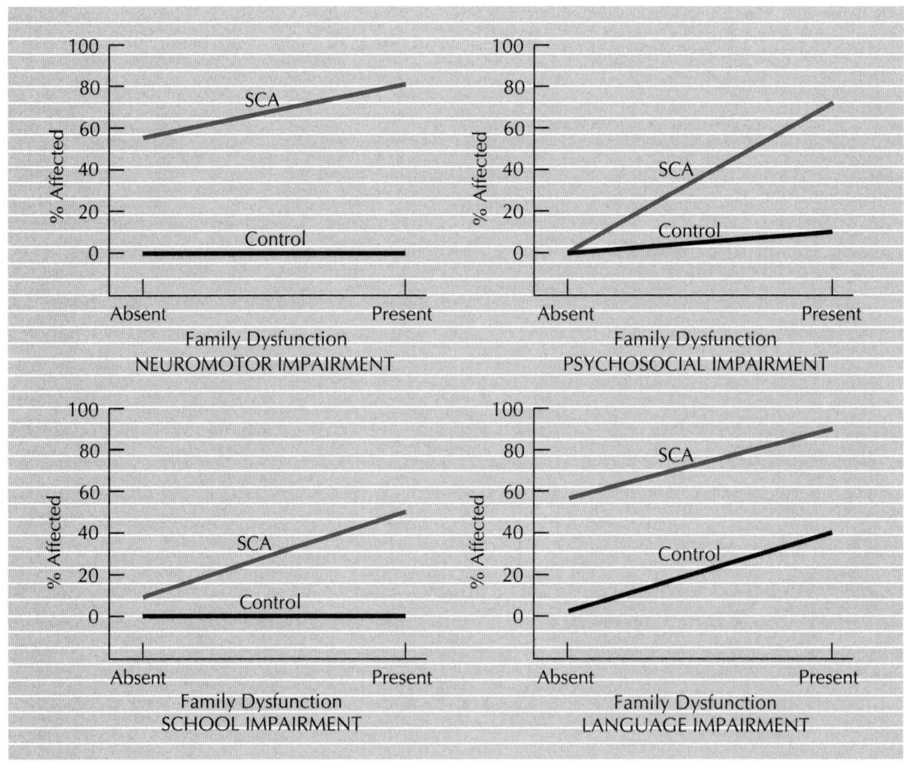

FIGURE 3-6
The influence of family dysfunction on children with sex chromosome anomalies.

breast development and a rounded, broad-hipped female figure. They share in common with XYY males a tendency to be significantly taller than normal XY males.

The psychological characteristics of males with these two types of chromosomal deviations have been a topic of considerable interest and controversy. XXY boys, perhaps because of the responses of others to their feminine appearance and awkwardness, are often shy and lacking in self-esteem and have problems with peer relations in adolescence. Furthermore, it was once believed that both XXY and XYY males were impulsive and antisocial and were likely to be involved in violent crimes (Forssman & Hambert, 1966; Hook, 1973). However, research indicates that although more XYY than XY males are likely to be in prison, they are more likely to be incarcerated for crimes against property than against people. The image of the XYY and XXY males as violent, assaultive, individuals is clearly not valid (Witkin et al., 1976; Schaivi, Thelgaard, Owen, & White, 1984).

The Fragile-X Syndrome. Some individuals carry an X chromosome that appears to be pinched or narrowed in some areas. These chromosomes are so fragile that the pinched areas may break and sections of the chromosome may separate off during preparations of cell cultures. Women who carry the abnormal gene on one of their X chromosomes transmit it to 50 percent of their sons but do not themselves have the clinical symptoms found in males except for occasional mild mental retardation (Opitz & Sutherland, 1984). The fragile-X syndrome is more frequent in males than females. It has been discovered that about 5 percent of retarded males with an IQ in the range of 30 to 55 have the fragile-X syndrome; however, fragile-X males show a wide range of intellectual functioning—ranging from normal intelligence to profound retardation (Barnes, 1989). It is estimated that the fragile-X syndrome may be the most frequent cause of mental retardation in males and that it is second only to Down syndrome in the association of chromosomal abnormality with mental retardation. In addition individuals with the fragile-X syndrome often show physical abnormalities and psychological and social problems. Cleft palate, seizures, abnormal EEGs, disorders of the eyes, and a characteristic facial appearance are associated with the fragile-X syndrome. The fragile-X chromosome may be related to autism, which is a mysterious childhood mental disorder characterized by severe disruptions in language development and social relationships. It is also associated with anxiety, hyperactivity, attentional deficits, abnormal communication patterns and deficits in social interactions in males, and to increased depression in females (Hagerman & Sobesky, 1989; Reiss & Freund, 1990). However, as many as one-quarter of fragile-X males are of normal intelligence (Barnes, 1989), which makes genetic counseling for women who are carriers of the defect problematic (Sherman, Jacobs, Morton, Froster-Iskenius, & Howard-Peebles, 1985).

As can be seen from the diverse symptoms listed above, there is wide variation in the characteristics and behavior of individuals having the same sex-chromosome abnormalities. The study reported in Box 3-1 suggests that the phenotypical expression of sex-chromosome anomalies may to some extent be moderated by environmental factors such as the quality of family life.

Mutation, Selection, and Evolution

Genetic variability results not only from the vast number of genetic combinations possible from the chromosomes in the gametes and the exchange of genetic material in the process of crossing-over during meiosis, but also from the development of *mutations.* Mutations are changes in the genes which may produce new phenotypes. In some cases a mutation occurs because of transformations in the gene; in other cases it may be the result of alterations in the arrangement of genes or the quantity of chromosomal material. The majority of mutations, however, consist of a deletion of one of the steps of the spiral staircase of DNA.

The reasons for spontaneous mutations in genes are not well understood and are of great concern to contemporary geneticists. Some mutations are controlled by special genes called *mutator genes,* which increase the rate of mutations in individuals who carry them. Other mutations occur because of external agents, or environmental toxins such as radiation.

The survival of a mutation depends upon a variety of factors; primarily, its survival depends upon its adaptability in relation to the environment in which it must develop. The vast majority of mutations are deleterious, or lethal, and do not survive. Others may be adaptive and enter the species gene pool. Theories of evolution are based on the notion of the selective survival of mutations with specific characteristics interacting with environmental factors. Survival involves the goodness of fit between characteristics of the individual and the environment.

SICKLE-CELL ANEMIA: AN EXAMPLE OF SELECTIVE SURVIVAL OF A MUTATION

One of the most dramatic examples of selective survival based on the interaction of genetic factors and environment is found in the history of a blood disease called sickle-cell anemia. A mutation appearing in the red blood cells proved adaptive in one environment and destructive in another. The history of the investigation of this disorder reads like a contemporary genetic detective story.

Under conditions of low oxygen, about 8 percent of American blacks exhibit a disorder where 40 percent of their red blood cells assume unusual crescent, sickle, or holly-leaf shapes. In most of these individuals the tendency of the blood to sickle is not associated with any deleterious symptoms, and these individuals are said to have the *sickle-cell trait.* However, 1 in 40 of these persons will be afflicted with a severe, chronic, often fatal form of anemia called *sickle-cell anemia.*

Two questions puzzled geneticists: What was the underlying genetic basis for the sickle-cell trait and for sickle-cell anemia? And why was the incidence of sickling relatively prevalent in blacks but rare in Caucasians? It was found (Neel, 1949) that a recessive sickling gene located on chromosome 11 exists which results in the sickle-cell trait in a heterozygous state and leads to sickle-cell anemia in a homozygous state. Thus both parents of a child having sickle-cell anemia will themselves have the sickle-cell trait. In the child, in its homozygous state, this sickling gene causes sickle-cell anemia and chemical changes in the hemoglobin molecule that makes transportation of oxygen by the sickle-shaped red blood cells ineffective, but only rarely do overt adverse symptoms appear in the heterozygotic parents who have the sickle-cell trait.

The high incidence of the sickle-cell trait in blacks and particularly in some African tribes, for example, the Baamba, where 39 percent of the population have this trait, was baffling to geneticists. The sickle-cell trait was found to be associated with a resistance to malarial infection. Thus, in malarial regions the heterozygous presence of the sickling gene actually has a selective advantage in survival. Heterozygotes, having a higher rate of survival, reproduce more frequently than noncarriers, and maintain the frequency of the gene in the population. This is not the case in nonmalarial areas where there is not a positive adaptive function served by the sickle-cell gene.

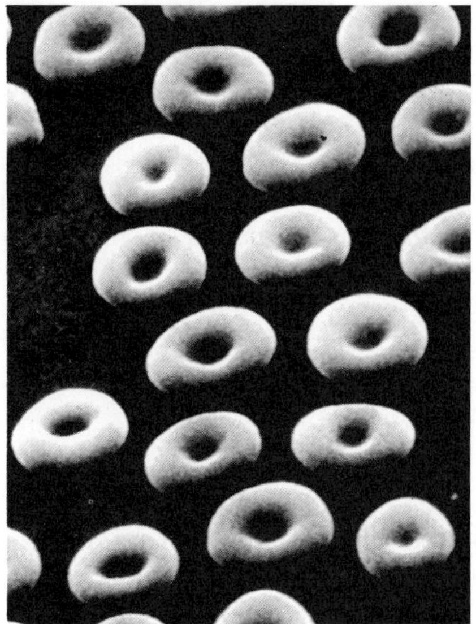

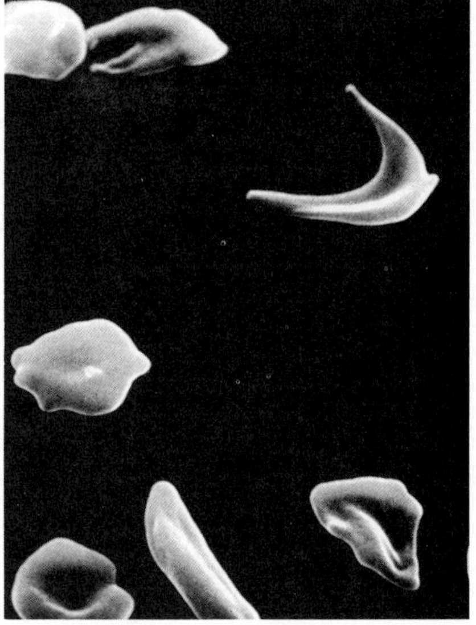

Normal blood cells on the left contrast with the sickle-shaped red blood cells of a person with sickle-cell anemia.

Although sickle-cell carriers have few adverse symptoms, under certain environmental circumstances such as extreme physical exertion at high altitudes or oxygen deprivation, they, too, can suffer from their genetic endowment (Sullivan, 1987). Under such conditions, these heterozygotes have 30 to 40 percent sickled cells, which can clog blood vessels and cause not only severe pain and tissue damage but death by blocking critical vessels in the brain and lungs.

GENETIC COUNSELING AND GENETIC ENGINEERING

Advances in biology and genetics have opened new opportunities for shaping and controlling some aspects of development. Through amniocentesis (which will be discussed in the next chapter) and chromosomal analysis in early pregnancy we can detect not only the sex of the child but also whether the child in utero has disorders such as sex-chromosome abnormalities, Down syndrome, sickle-cell anemia, or Tay-Sachs syndrome, a lethal genetic disorder leading to mental deficiency, blindness, and paralysis. Parents then have the option to abort or to prepare for the birth of a child with problems. But what kinds of ethical issues may arise from giving parents such information and from our growing genetic sophistication? Although XYY males are statistically more likely to become involved in crimes than are XY males, only a small percentage of males with the extra Y chromosome do so. Are children unfairly stigmatized by being labeled as XYY children? What does knowing this do to the parents' attitudes toward and relationship with the child? Research shows that parents frequently respond in terms of expectations, even false expectations, about their children. Such knowledge could initiate a destructive self-fulfilling prophecy.

If a fetus has no detectable genetic abnormalities, is sex of the child sufficient reason to abort? In this country almost all surveys show that, on the average, male children are preferred over female by expectant parents.

In some other countries this preference is even more extreme. In a survey of about 100 pregnant women in China who were screened to determine the sex of their unborn child it was found that over 60 percent of the mothers carrying girls wished to abort, where only 1 of the 53 women carrying a male child chose to abort (*China Medical Journal*, 1975).

Biologists have been able to transplant animal embryos from one uterus to another, to remove and transfer genes from one organism to another, and to artificially synthesize a gene in a test tube. However, the most important consequences of genetic engineering are in the development of babies through in vitro fertilization and in the development of recombinant DNA methods.

Test Tube Fertilization

The development of test tube babies through in vitro fertilization has permitted couples who are infertile or have anatomical problems that interfere with fertilization, such as obstructed or damaged fallopian tubes in the woman, and who otherwise would have little chance of conceiving, to have children. These procedures have raised complex challenges in terms of technology and in social and legal issues (see Box 3-2).

Recombinant DNA

Recombinant DNA techniques make it possible to extract a snippet of DNA from one organism and insert it into another organism, thus the name "recombinant" DNA. It has been found that a particular identifiable piece of DNA, called a *genetic marker,* may be present in people suffering from a specific hereditary disease. For example, the gene for cystic fibrosis has been located in the midsection of chromosome 7, and the gene for familial Alzheimer's disease is on the long arm of chromosome 21 (Martin, 1987). One of the more personal hunts for a genetic marker was led by neuropsychologist Nancy Wexler, whose mother had died of Huntington's disease, a painful, fatal disorder that afflicts young adults and one that Wexler would have a 50 percent chance of developing. Wexler charted patterns of Huntington's disease in a group of 5000 people in Venezuela who were all descendants of a woman who died of Huntington's disease over 100 years ago. By using DNA samples from the living family members in the clan who were affected with the disease, Wexler and geneticist James Gusella (Gusella et al., 1983) were able to identify a Huntington's marker which was located near one end of chromosome 4. Although this has permitted the development of a Huntington's gene test, many people are reluctant to take such a test since there is not yet a cure for the disease.

Although in the past decade genetic markers have made it possible to locate the chromosomal position for many single-gene diseases, most behavior geneticists believe that behavior disorders are determined by multiple genes and that a focus on single genes is unlikely to be fruitful in understanding most behavior problems (McGue & Gottesman, 1989; Plomin, 1990b; Gurling et al., 1989; Plomin & Rende, 1990).

Genetic Therapy

Scientists hope not only to identify and locate the genes responsible for inherited diseases but also eventually to use gene therapy to prevent or cure

BOX 3-2 TEST TUBE BABIES

On July 25, 1978, in England, a remarkable event occurred; Louise Joy Brown, the first baby conceived outside of her mother's fallopian tube was born. Since then, over 5000 such babies have been born in different countries around the world. In fact, the Browns now have a second test tube baby, Daniel. Among the babies born to parents going through in vitro fertilization—literally, fertilization in glass or in a glass dish—are unusually high numbers of quadruplets, triplets, and twins. This is due to two factors. First, some practitioners transfer more than one embryo at a time to the mother's uterus to increase the probability of a successful pregnancy. Second, at the same time that in vitro fertilization methods are being attempted mothers are often being given hormones to stimulate ovulation. This may result in the release of multiple ova which may be unexpectedly fertilized through a normal process of sexual intercourse.

Although the term test tube baby brings with it some "Brave New World" images of children being raised in laboratories in glass decanters, it is actually only fertilization that takes place outside of the mother's body in a glass dish. The prospective mother has her hormones monitored and is usually given hormones that stimulate the production of ova. These ova are harvested and removed from the ovary through a small incision in the woman's abdomen. An ovum is placed in a nourishing solution in a glass petri dish and is mixed with sperm. If fertilization is successful, the zygote begins to divide and when it is at the eight-cell stage, approximately two to four days later, it is picked up with another fine tube and flushed into the uterus through the woman's cervix. For the pregnancy to be successful the embryo must implant itself on the uterine wall. If the uterus is not at the optimum stage to facilitate implantation, seventeen to twenty-three days after menstruation, the embryo may be frozen and stored until the woman's uterus reaches the proper stage.

Although in vitro fertilization was a remarkable breakthrough, now, slightly over a decade later, some scientists are speaking of "old-fashioned" in vitro fertilization and point out the many combinations of mixes and matches of donors and recipients currently being used. A woman's egg may be fertilized with her husband's or another male donor's sperm, or the husband's sperm may be used to fertilize a female donor's egg, or the zygote from a husband's sperm and a wife's ova may be implanted in the uterus of another woman who serves as a human incubator. Recently a woman gave birth to a child who was the result of implantation of an in vitro zygote from her daughter and son-in-law. She became a mother and a grandmother at the same time.

Like many other medical breakthroughs, these new reproductive technologies have presented some ethical dilemmas. How should prospective parents be screened? What criteria should be used in selecting sperm donors in matching sperm to eggs? For example, does it lead to unrealistic expectations in parents to have the sperm donor be a Nobel Prize Laureate? There actually is a sperm bank of Nobel Prize winners. What legal rights does the male donor have? What should be done if one or both parents die while the zygote is frozen in storage, as happened in a recent Australian case? What legal rights to the child does a woman have who has accepted implantation of another couple's embryo? In spite of these difficult questions, the hope, joy, and prospect of parenthood for many couples unable to conceive or bear children that this procedure has given seems to outweigh other considerations.

Sources: Grobstein, C. (1979). External human fertilization. *Scientific American*, **240**(6), 57–68; Hubbard, R. (1980). Test tube babies: Solution or problem. *Technology Review*, **85**(5), 10–12; McGinty, J. J., & Zafran, E. I. (1988). *Surrogacy: Constitutional and legal issues*. Cleveland, OH: The Ohio Academy of Trial Lawyers; Ryan, K. J. (1988). Ethical issues in reproductive endocrinology and infertility. *American Journal of Obstetrics and Gynecology*, **160**, 1415–1417.

such disorders. By inserting good genes into their patients' cells, scientists hope to counter the effects of adverse genes. Viruses can be engineered to carry correctly functioning versions of the patient's deleterious genes. When bone marrow cells taken from the patient are exposed to these viruses, the virus inserts itself into the cellular DNA carrying the normal gene with it. These new healthy genes are then injected into the patient. The first attempt to use this procedure on humans was begun in treating a preschool girl with a deadly, previously incurable, genetic disease that shuts down the immune system. Children with this disorder are often raised in isolation or are involved in continuous drug treatment since they can be devastated in encountering any kind of infection, even ones such as the common cold that would be minor in a person with a normal immune system. A well-known case is that of David, the bubble boy raised in a glass isolation chamber. As an adolescent he finally left his glassed-in world but he could not survive because his immune system was unable to cope with a more open environment. The recombinant DNA treatment of the young girl thus far appears to be successful, to have activated her immune system and increased her resistance to disease. It was recently reported that she is now skating, taking dancing lessons, attending school, and enjoying interactions with friends and teachers.

In spite of the possible positive contributions of removal of deleterious genes and substitution of advantageous genes, the specter of engineered superbeings, the destruction of genetic uniqueness, and even the possibility of artificially producing a new bacteria or species destructive to human beings are now concerning not only the popular press and the public but the scientists themselves. The key issue is this: As greater genetic control becomes possible, how should it be used and how should it be limited for the good of human beings?

PROCESSES AND PRINCIPLES OF HEREDITY ENVIRONMENT INTERACTIONS

At one time, scientists were preoccupied with the question of the relative amounts contributed by genetic or environmental factors to different characteristics such as intelligence, motor skills, and personality. This resulted in what was called the nature-nurture controversy, with many psychologists assuming extreme positions on the issue. Those who were more biologically oriented emphasized the exclusive role of heredity and maturational factors in shaping development, while those who were more environmentally oriented often took an equally extreme and invalid position by denying any contribution of innate predispositions or capacities and emphasizing the exclusive role of learning and experience.

In the United States, with its political and social philosophy based on a belief in the equality of people and the importance of opportunity, education, and initiative, theories of biological determination fell on fallow ground. In contrast, the environmentalist position of John B. Watson and the behaviorists flourished. In 1926 in the heat of the nature-nurture controversy Watson expounded:

> Give me a dozen healthy infants, well-formed and my own specific world to bring them up in and I'll guarantee to take any one at random and train him to become any type of specialist I might select—a doctor, lawyer, artist, merchant-chief and, yes, even into beggar-man and thief, regardless of his talents, penchants, tendencies, abilities, vocations and race of his ancestors. (Watson, 1926, p. 10)

"Very interesting, Dr. Watson!" This expansively optimistic view of the total malleability of human behavior is no longer held by contemporary psychologists and some current concern has been expressed about a recent and equally untenable swing toward a position of extreme biological determinism (Baumrind, in press). Contemporary scientists are still interested in the contributions of environmental and genetic factors to the development of certain characteristics. However, they also want to know how and when the transactions between these factors affect development. The concepts of the range of reaction and canalization, and new theories about the ways in which genotypes shape experience help to explain some of the variations in the complex interactions which occur between heredity and environment.

Range of Reaction

Heredity does not rigidly fix behavior, but instead establishes a range of possible responses that the individual may make to different environments. Different children will vary in the array of possible responses they will make under different life experiences. These genetically based variations in an individual's responsiveness to environments are called the *range of reaction* (Gottesman, 1963). The genotype thus sets boundaries on the range of possible phenotypes within which individual characteristics may be expressed.

Let us take the example of the effect on intelligence test performance of the range of reaction as it interacts with environments with different degrees of stimulation or enrichment. Figure 3-7 presents the effects of varying degrees of environmental enrichment on the test performances of three children with different intellectual reaction ranges. It can be seen that under similar conditions of enrichment child C always performs better than the other two children. However, it is also apparent that child C has the widest range of reaction. The difference in child C's performance when raised in a stimulating versus a restricted environment is greater than that of the other two children. Child A has both a lower and a more limited range of reaction. The child not only scores below average in intelligence, whether raised in an enriched or restricted habitat, but also shows less variation in response to favorableness of the environment.

Canalization

Some kinds of genotypes are more difficult to deflect from their genetically programmed path of growth than others. These seem to have fewer possible alternative paths from genotype to phenotype, and it takes intense or more specific environmental pushes to deflect them. The term *canalization* is used

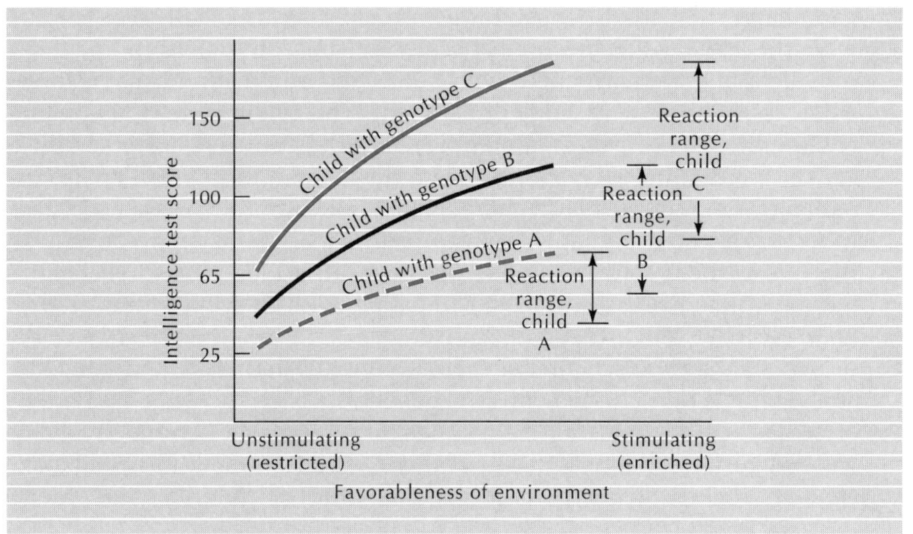

FIGURE 3-7
Hypothetical intellectual reaction ranges of children with three genotypes in stimulating and unstimulating environments. (Adapted from Gottesman, 1963.)

to describe the limiting of phenotypes to one or few developmental outcomes (Waddington, 1962, 1966). A characteristic that is strongly canalized is relatively difficult to modify even by what might be viewed as widely divergent or extreme experiences. For example, infant babbling is strongly canalized since babbling occurs even in infants who are born deaf and have never heard their own voices or the speech of others (Lenneberg, 1967). In contrast, intelligence is less highly canalized since it can be modified by a variety of physical, social, and educational experiences and will be manifested in a wide range of problem-solving and adaptive behaviors.

In addition to the effects of range of reactivity and canalization, the extent to which an individual's genotype is expressed in his or her phenotype depends on the timing, kind, and amount of environmental pressures, or pushes, to which he or she is exposed. Different experiences at different points in the course of development have different effects on the developing child. If a pregnant woman contracts German measles in the first three months of pregnancy, the child she is carrying, who may be genotypically predisposed to be of normal intelligence, may be born severely mentally retarded. However, if the mother contracts the disease later in pregnancy, it is unlikely to have an effect in modifying the expression of the child's intellectual genotype (Waddington, 1962, 1966).

Processes by Which Genotypes Shape Environments

It is widely accepted that children are influenced by their environments and the experiences they encounter. Most people would agree that children raised by punitive, rigid, rejecting parents would be likely to differ in their self-concept and their behavior from those reared by loving, responsive parents. The role of children's genotypes in shaping their environment is less commonly acknowledged.

It has been proposed that an individual's genotype may influence the environments which the person encounters in three ways (Plomin, DeFries, & Loehlin, 1977; Scarr & McCartney, 1983; Scarr, in press). The genotype may shape the environment passively. This occurs when, because of the genetic relatedness of the parent and child, parents provide the child with a home environment that is correlated with their own genotype. Since the parent and child share genes, this environment is also likely to be compatible with the child's genetic predispositions. Thus an intelligent parent may provide a home environment with books and stimulating conversation that enhances a child's heritability to be bright. The genotype may also shape the environment evocatively. Different genotypically based behaviors in the child evoke certain kinds of responses from the social and physical environment. Smiling, active infants elicit more stimulation from others than do passive, sober, unresponsive infants (Lytton, 1980). Finally, the genotype may shape the environment actively. Genotypes may cause individuals to actively seek out environments that are most compatible with their biological predispositions (Scarr & McCartney, 1983). This has been called *niche picking*. People may search for, select, or build environments that they find congenial or stimulating. Thus, children who are genetically predisposed to be extroverted or gregarious actively seek the company of others and become involved in a wide range of social activities and these experiences, in turn, enhance the expression of the genotype to be sociable. Since as children grow older their

Children may seek environments or pick niches that are compatible with their genetic predispositions.

environments are less in control of adults and they have greater freedom of choice in selecting activities, settings, and companions, it might be expected that the genotype would be more strongly manifested in behavior in adolescents than in younger children and this does seem to be the case. These constant transactions or feedback loops between the genotype and environment contribute to difficulties in identifying the relative contribution of heredity and environment to individual differences in development (Baumrind, 1991).

Influences of Heredity and Environment on Behavior

Biologists and geneticists have made great advances in understanding some of the processes and mechanisms related to development. However, their main contributions have been in identifying single genes and chromosomal errors that contribute to gross developmental deviations such as Down syndrome. Little knowledge is available of possible genetic processes involved in most of the important human attributes with which psychologists are concerned. Although biologists can point to the twenty-first chromosome as the basis of mental retardation in Down syndrome, they can't tell us why one normally developing child has an IQ of 90 and his or her sibling has an IQ of 150. They can't show what genetic material is transmitted or what biochemical or metabolic factors are involved in the development of aggression, altruism, sociability, or intelligence. Most of the advances in understanding the possible role of genetic factors in human behavior such as these have come from behavior geneticists.

It will become apparent that, in the questions they ask, in their research methods and in their focus on genetic contributions to *behavior,* behavior geneticists differ greatly from biologists interested in the study of heredity. Studies of behavior genetics can be conducted without mentioning chromosomes, genes, and DNA. In fact, behavior genetics was well under way before modern gene theory was developed. The central concern of behavior geneticists is in understanding genetic contributions to the wide range of individual differences observed in human behavior throughout the life span.

Studies of Family Resemblance

The study of similarities in characteristics of family members with varying degrees of biological relatedness is one of the most frequently used procedures in investigating the contributions of genetic and environmental factors to individual differences in human development. Adoption and twin studies are the most common types of family resemblance studies.

In adoption studies the similarity between the attributes of adopted children and their biological and adoptive parents is compared. There is no genetic similarity between the adoptive parents and adopted children, although they have shared environments. In contrast, the biological parent and adopted child have some shared genetic endowment, but they do not share environments since they are living apart. Thus, the child's similarity to the adoptive parents is assumed to reflect the effects of the environment, whereas the similarity with the biological parents is assumed to reflect genetic factors. A variation on the adoption study is one which examines the similarities between biological siblings and unrelated children who live in the same home.

Twin studies involve comparing the similarities in certain attributes of identical, or monozygotic twins and of fraternal, or dizygotic twins. Monozygotic twins are created by the separation of the zygote following fertilization of a single egg by a single sperm. This results in the development of two genetically identical embryos. In contrast dizygotic twins develop from two eggs that have been fertilized by two sperms and hence, although carried in utero at the same time, are no more genetically similar than other siblings. The degree of resemblance is usually measured either by a correlation coefficient or a concordance rate. Correlation coefficients, discussed in Chapter 1, are used on continuous variables that go from lower to higher, such as height, intelligence or sociability, to assess the relationship between how siblings vary along the scale. Concordance rates are used to assess the percent of times in which both siblings have an attribute or disorder if one of the siblings is identified as having that characteristic. This is used for discrete disorders where the individual is categorized or diagnosed as having something like Down syndrome, schizophrenia, or manic depressive psychosis. A concordance rate of 100 percent for schizophrenia would mean if one twin was schizophrenic the other was always schizophrenic. In twin studies the assumption is made that the environments of identical twins are no more similar than those of fraternal twins. If identical twins show more resemblance on a particular trait than fraternal twins, it is assumed that the appearance of the trait is strongly influenced by genetic factors. If sets of identical and fraternal twins who have shared the same home resemble each other almost equally on a characteristic, it is assumed that this characteristic is more strongly influenced by environmental than genetic factors.

Can we accept the assumption of similar environmental influences for both types of twins when they are raised in the same family? This assumption has been questioned by some investigators, who argue that the responses that identical twins evoke from others, the home environments provided by their parents, and the active selection by the identical twins of similar environmental niches that are compatible with their genotypes result in striking similarities in their experiences, social environments, and learning histories (Baumrind, in press; Lytton, 1976; Scarr & McCartney, 1983). Thus the genotypical similarity of identical twins promotes their exposure to similar environments and experiences, which, in turn, leads to more congruent phenotypes (Plomin, 1986).

Let us use twin and adoption studies to examine the proposal that individuals select niches or environments that are compatible with their genotypes and that this selectivity will become more marked with age as the freedom to choose activities, settings, and social groups increases.

Similarity between identical twins in such things as food preferences, hobbies, intelligence, academic achievement, vocational choice, friends, and characteristics of spouses are often found even when they are reared apart (Bouchard & McGue, 1990; Juel-Nielsen, 1980; Scarr & Carter-Saltzman, 1980). Identical twins evoke similar responses from others (Baumrind & Lytton, 1976; Scarr & McCartney, 1983), and given the opportunity to choose among diverse opportunities and experiences they choose similar ones. In contrast, the similarities between fraternal twins and biological siblings remains only moderately correlated. As they move outside the family and choose their niches, they select only moderately similar environments because their genotypes are only moderately correlated.

How similar are adopted siblings who are not related biologically to each other but are living in the same family? This is related to the age of the adopted siblings. They show some similarities to each other in early-to-middle childhood, probably promoted by sharing the same home environment provided by parents, but by late adolescence, when they have been increasingly choosing their own environmental niches, they do not resemble each other in personality, interests, intelligence, or other phenotypic attributes (Grotevant, Scarr, & Weinberg, 1977; Scarr, Webber, Weinberg, & Witting, 1981; Scarr & Weinberg, 1977).

These findings should not be taken to mean that environment is not important. The more dissimilar the environments of identical twins reared apart the less resemblance they show on various characteristics (Baumrind in press; Kamin, 1981; Rose and Kaprio, 1987). For example Bronfenbrenner (1975) found lower correlations between the I.Q.s of separated adopted twins living in dissimilar communities (.26) than in similar communities (.86). Furthermore, during adolescence adopted children become increasingly aware of their adoptive status and use it to justify resistance to other family members' values (Brodzinski, Singer, & Braff, 1984), which may be associated with their declining similarity to their adopted siblings and adoptive parents in this period. Finally access to various environmental niches may be restricted. Children genotypically predisposed to be of high intelligence may find themselves in settings where intellectually stimulating niches are unavailable, and unattractive children genotypically predisposed to be sociable may have difficulty gaining access to desired social niches. Freedom to pick niches may be limited for some children in some environments. The interpretation of twin and adoption studies is not as straightforward as was once believed, and these limitations should be kept in mind when we later review the results of these studies.

Nonshared Environment

Recently investigators have turned to studies of nonshared environment to examine why even biologically related siblings show only a modest similarity on most characteristics and this declines with age (Ross, Plomin, & Hetherington, 1991; Ross, Hetherington, & Plomin, in press).

It used to be assumed that children raised in the same families had the same environment. It is now recognized that children living in the same families and same home may share some aspects of their environment but not others. *Shared environment* would include common experiences shared by two siblings such as being poor, living in a crowded home or high-crime neighborhood, and having unemployed, alcoholic, mentally ill, or devoutly religious parents (Reiss, Plomin, & Hetherington, 1991). Children in the same family also have *nonshared* experiences; that is, experiences that differ in their homes, neighborhood, and schools with their parents, siblings, peers, and teachers. Some of the nonshared environmental differences may be due to characteristics of the child, such as temperament, handicap, illness, gender, or age; some to family composition, such as birth order or spacing between siblings; and still others to the timing or occurrence of factors external to the child, such as illness or unemployment of a parent or the timing of depression or war. It should be noted that sometimes a shared environmental factor may lead to nonshared experiences. For example, poverty, unemployment, or emotional problems in a parent may lead to that parent venting frustrations or anger on one child and not the other.

Even small differences in nonshared experiences may have effects on differences in sibling development. Furthermore, siblings' perceptions of differential parental treatment may affect their behavior, although these perceptions may not be accurate. Siblings are especially sensitive to real or imagined differences in treatment by parents.

There is substantial evidence to indicate that siblings, even twins, do encounter many aspects of their environment that are not shared (Plomin & Bergeman, 1991; Plomin & Daniels, 1987). One of the key challenges in explaining the lack of resemblance between siblings living in the same home, however, lies in demonstrating that these differences in experiences are related to differences in development. The study by Daniels and her colleagues presented in Box 3-3 clearly indicates that nonshared environment is associated with differences in the adjustment of adolescent siblings.

Physical and Physiological Characteristics

Monozygotic twins are more similar than dizygotic twins in a variety of traits associated with measures of both physical characteristics and biological functioning such as height, weight, rate of maturation, age of first menstruation, and longevity. However, of greater interest to psychologists is the similarity in identical twins in the functioning of the brain and of the *autonomic nervous system,* that system that is closely related to emotional arousal and responsiveness (Jost & Sontag, 1944; Lykken, Iacono, Harocan, McGue, & Bouchard, 1988). In recordings of electrical brain wave patterns, it has been found that monozygotic twins have highly similar patterns, whereas there is only a modest relationship between the brain wave recordings of fraternal twins. In habituation (a pattern of declining responsiveness to repeated stimuli) and in spontaneous fluctuations or lability of autonomic measures, identical twins are more similar than fraternal twins (Lader & Wing, 1966;

BOX 3-3 WHY PICK ON ME? DIFFERENTIAL TREATMENT OF SIBLINGS AND SIBLINGS' ADJUSTMENT

Why pick on me? How come he gets to stay up later than I do? You let him get away with murder! Mommy's baby! Children frequently complain about what they perceive as preferential treatment of their siblings by parents.

Observational studies support the fact that parents do treat children especially children of different ages or gender in a different manner. In a study of 348 families with two adolescent siblings, both siblings and the mother were interviewed separately about different aspects of family relations experienced by each sibling. These included such things as family cooperation, family stress, parental rules and chore expectations, closeness to mother and father, and the child's say in decisions. It was found that although parents perceived themselves as treating the siblings in a fairly similar fashion the siblings did not. The correlations between parents' reports of treatment of two siblings averaged about .53 in contrast to the sibling evaluation which averaged only .20. Other studies have found that trained observers, who might be assumed to be more objective in their evaluations, on the basis of watching the parents and children interact, usually rate the similarity of treatment of the two children midway between reports of parents and siblings. Do these perceived differences relate to children's adjustment? The results reported in Table 3-4 show that they do.

Both the parent and the sibling reports of parental treatment indicate that the sibling who experienced more maternal closeness, more power in family decision making, more parental chore expectations, and more sibling friendliness was better adjusted. Furthermore, when a composite measure combining parents', siblings', and teachers' reports of disobedience was used, this was related to both parents' and siblings' ratings of sibling differences in experience.

If relationships had been found only within the same person's report of environmental differences and of sibling adjustment, concern could be raised that there might be a response set to perceive things negatively or to justify one's behavior by critical evaluations of the other family member. Thus a mother who reported less closeness to one child might justify it by saying the child has more problems than that child's preferentially treated sibling. In this study, the correlations were larger and more

TABLE 3-4 RELATIONS BETWEEN DIFFERENCES IN SIBLING ADJUSTMENT AND DIFFERENCES IN SIBLING ENVIRONMENTS

ADJUSTMENT MEASURE	PARENTAL RATINGS OF SIBLING DIFFERENCES IN EXPERIENCE	SIBLING RATINGS OF SIBLING DIFFERENCES IN EXPERIENCE
Parental report of emotional distress	.38*	.25
Parental report of delinquency	.37*	.25
Parental report of disobedience	.37*	.26
Self-report of emotional distress	.12	.28
Self-report of delinquency	.29	.37*
Self-report of dissatisfaction	a	.35*
Teacher report of disobedience	a	.35*
Parent-sibling-teacher aggregate score of disobedience	.40*	.34

*$p < .05$. (This relationship could occur by chance less than 5 in 100 times.)
a = not available.
Source: Adapted from Daniels, Dunn, Furstenberg, & Plomin (1985).

(*Continued*)

BOX 3-3 WHY PICK ON ME? DIFFERENTIAL TREATMENT OF SIBLINGS AND SIBLINGS' ADJUSTMENT (Continued)

frequent within one person's report; however, some significant findings did emerge when different people rated the siblings' environment and the siblings' adjustment. For example, mothers' ratings of sibling differences in experiences were related to the siblings' reports of delinquency. In addition siblings' perceptions of environmental differences were associated with ratings of disobedience by teachers who probably had observed the child only in the school.

This study offers support for the association between differences in the siblings' life experiences and personality development, and evidence that children may be especially sensitive to differential treatment of siblings by parents.

Sources: Daniels, D. (1987). Differential experiences of siblings in the same family as predictors of adolescent sibling personality differences. *Journal of Personality and Social Psychology,* **51,** 339–346; Daniels, D., Dunn, J., Furstenberg, F. F., & Plomin, R. (1985). Environmental differences within the family and adjustment differences within pairs of adolescent siblings. *Child Development,* **56,** 764–774.

Stassen, Lykken, & Bomben, 1988). These variations in responses in the autonomic nervous system, even in infancy, have been related to the way individuals later adapt to stress and anxiety-arousing situations, control their impulses, and deal with emotional conflicts.

Intellectual Characteristics

The results of studies of similarities in intelligence test scores (IQ) of twins have been remarkably consistent. Performance on intelligence tests is heavily weighted by genetic factors. The closer the genetic kinship bonds, the more similar the IQ.

The results of an ambitious summary of 111 different investigations are presented in Table 3-5. In interpreting the correlations it should be remembered that a *correlation coefficient* is an estimate of how two measures vary together. As might be expected, the correlation of IQs for unrelated persons are extremely small. The correlation of IQs of unrelated children raised in the same home is about +.30. However, as genetic similarity increases, so does similarity in intelligence scores. It can be seen that there is a marked increase in the correlation of intelligence test scores as kinship bonds are closer. The correlation is lower in dizygotic twins than in monozygotic twins. Even monozygotic twins reared apart, and thus exposed to different home environments, have intelligence test scores more similar than those of dizygotic twins raised in the same home. Furthermore, although twin correlations of IQ decrease with age the decrease is greater for fraternal than for identical twins (McCartney, Harris, & Berniere, 1990).

In addition to the contribution of heredity to general intellectual performance, patterns of specific mental abilities are influenced by genetics, and some of these specific cognitive abilities show greater genetic influence than others. Spatial and verbal abilities are more influenced by genetic factors than are memory and perceptual speed. Even reading and spelling disabilities and vocational interests are influenced by heredity (Plomin, 1989). However, creativity, that aspect of cognition dealing with divergent thinking and scientific and artistic innovation, shows less genetic influence than any other specific cognitive ability.

Heredity affects the rates, not just the level, of mental development in different children. Just as children show spurts and plateaus in physical growth at different times, they show variations in the rate and timing of mental growth. Even in patterns of intellectual ability and in rates and timing of intellectual growth, monozygotic twins are more similar than are dizygotic

TABLE 3-5

STATISTICAL CORRELATIONS OF INTELLIGENCE AMONG FAMILY RELATIONS*

RELATIONSHIP	CORRELATION
Monozygotic twins:	
Reared together	.86
Reared apart	.79
Dizygotic twins:	
Reared together	.60
Siblings:	
Reared together	.47
Reared apart	.24
Parent/child	.40
Foster parent/child	.31
Cousins	.15

* These correlations are composited from 111 different studies from all parts of the world. In general, the closer the genetic relationship of two people, the higher the correlation between their IQs.
Source: From Bouchard & McGue (1981).

twins (Wilson, 1983). Infant intelligence test scores are notoriously unstable; however, as can be seen in Figure 3-8, even on such unreliable instruments the profile of successive test scores for identical twins over the first two years of life is remarkably similar (Wilson & Harpring, 1972).

Adoption studies also find significant genetic effects on intellectual development (Burks, 1928; Leahy, 1935; Plomin & DeFries, 1983; Scarr & Weinberg, 1977). Even if placement has been in the first year of life, the intellectual performance of school-age children correlates with those of their

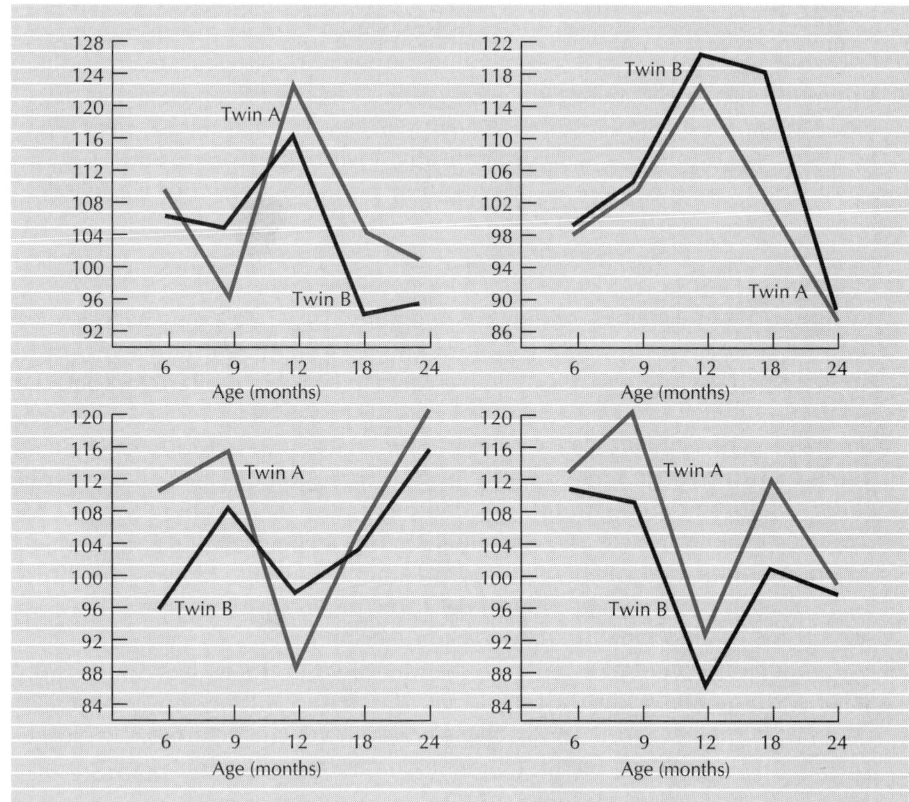

FIGURE 3-8
Infant intelligence test (Bayley Infant Intelligence Test) profiles for four pairs of twins over the first two years of life. (Adapted from Wilson & Harpring, 1972.)

biological parents more closely than those of their adoptive parents, and the correlation with foster or adoptive parents declines with age (Scarr & Weinberg, 1983).

The results of these studies of foster and adopted children cannot be assumed to indicate that the adoptive parents do not influence their children's IQs (Scarr-Salapatek, 1971; Schiff & Lewontin, 1986; Turkheimer, 1991). In one classic adoption study (Skodak & Skeels, 1949), it was found that adopted children often averaged 20 or more IQ points higher than their biological mothers. Since the adoptive parents tend to be more highly educated and more socially and economically advantaged than the biological parents, this may be due to the more stimulating environment provided by the brighter adoptive parents. The children's average IQs and the distribution of their IQs more closely resemble their adoptive (average IQ above 100) than biological parents (average IQ 85). However, the rank ordering of the children's IQs more closely resembles the rank ordering of their biological mothers' IQs, which is what a correlation coefficient measures. Adopted children scored higher on intelligence tests than did their biological mothers; the children who had the slowest biological mothers were likely to have lower IQs than those who had brighter biological mothers, even after years of living in an adoptive home. Although the *absolute* level of the adopted children's IQs was higher than might have been expected on the basis of their biological mothers' education or IQs, their performance *relative* to that of other adopted children was related to their biological mothers' intellectual level. It is this difference between absolute and relative levels that is critical to note. More recent studies (Capron & Duyme, 1989; Duyme, 1988) have given further evidence for the importance of the environment in the adoptive families. Adopted children in low socioeconomic adoptive homes have lower IQs and higher rates of school dropouts than those in high socioeconomic adoptive families.

Thus, although twin studies and adoptive studies are in agreement in showing that genetic factors make an important contribution to individual differences in performance on intelligence tests, environmental factors are also salient in such variations. As we will see in Chapter 11, very poor or stressful environments can dramatically lower IQ scores, and cognitively stimulating environments or intervention programs can raise IQ scores.

Temperament and Personality

Although genetic factors influence personality, the effects may be less marked than on intelligence (Loehlin, Willerman, & Horn, 1988). However, even in the earliest days of life marked differences can be seen in infant temperament.

Temperament. *Temperament* refers to biologically based differences among individuals in reactions to stimuli, in the expression of emotions, in arousal, and in self-regulation. Although temperament is initially thought to be biologically determined, it is modified by life experiences. Temperament in infants is often described in terms of whether a child is easy or difficult. Later, it is often discussed in terms of three personality traits that have some genetic basis: emotionality, activity, and sociability.

About 10 percent of infants can be identified in the earliest months of life as temperamentally difficult children (Graham, Rutter, & George, 1973; Thomas, Chess, & Korn, 1982). These children are characterized by biological irregularities in sleep, feeding, and elimination; inflexibility; avoidance or

Pictures showing mothers with easy and difficult babies.

distress in response to new experiences; slow adaptability to new situations; nonfastidiousness; and negative moods, including extremes of fussiness and crying. In contrast, some babies are described as easy babies, as friendly, happy, and adaptable. Even in the same family, children with dramatically different temperaments are born. One mother described her two sons as follows:

> Nothing was easy with Chris. Mealtimes, bedtimes, toilet training were all hell. It would take me an hour and a half to get part of a bottle into him and he'd be hungry two hours later. I can't remember once in the first two years when he didn't go to bed crying. I'd try to rock him to sleep but as soon as I'd tiptoe over to put him in his crib his head would lurch up and he'd start bellowing again. He didn't like any kind of changes in his routine. New people and places upset him so it was hard to take him anywhere.
>
> John was my touchy feely baby. From the first day in the hospital he cuddled and seemed so contented to be held I could hardly bear to put him down. He didn't cry unless something was wrong—he was wet, or hungry, or tired. We took him everywhere because he seemed to enjoy new things. You could always sit him in a corner and he'd entertain himself. Sometimes I'd forget he was there until he'd start laughing or prattling.

A higher rate of behavior disorders is found in later life in children described by their mothers as difficult children than is found in children who were not seen as difficult infants (Bates, Maslin, & Frankel, 1985; Pettit & Bates, 1989; Rutter, Quinton, & Yule, 1977; Thomas, Chess, & Korn, 1982).

This may be attributable to two factors. First, the less malleable child is likely to find adapting to environmental demands more difficult and be more prone to psychological damage. Second, the child with a difficult temperament will be more vulnerable to stress and will also be more likely to elicit different or adverse experiences. These children have been found to serve as targets for parental irritability, and their parents are more likely to take out their own stresses on these difficult children. Stressed mothers are especially likely to withdraw affection and be irritable toward temperamentally difficult boys (Hetherington, 1991). As can be seen in Box 3-4, if mothers are undergoing multiple stresses and do not have a supportive family or friendship network available to them, the problems in dealing with a difficult infant may disrupt the normal bonds of attachment between the mother and child. Thus the child's temperament does not lead directly to later deviant behavior, but it puts the child at a higher risk of encountering adverse experiences in interacting with his or her environment. Most research findings indicate that long-term outcomes of a difficult temperament occur only if the child encounters additional adversity, such as inept parenting, poverty, or divorce (Hetherington, 1991). Temperaments are not immutable. Many sensitive, responsive parents are able to moderate the behavior of difficult children (Beckwith, 1979; Dunn, 1980). Thus, although temperamental differences

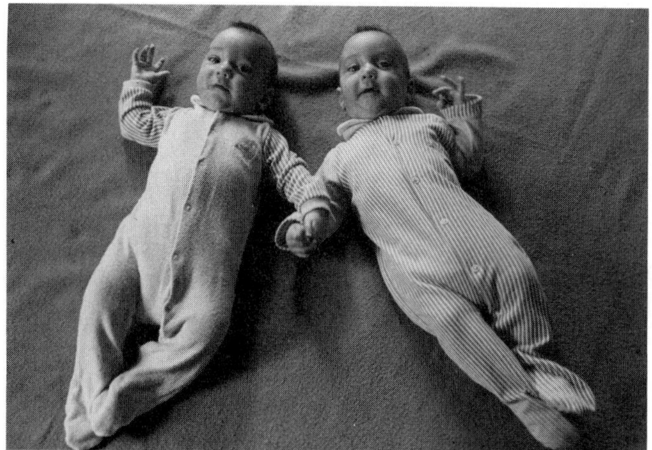

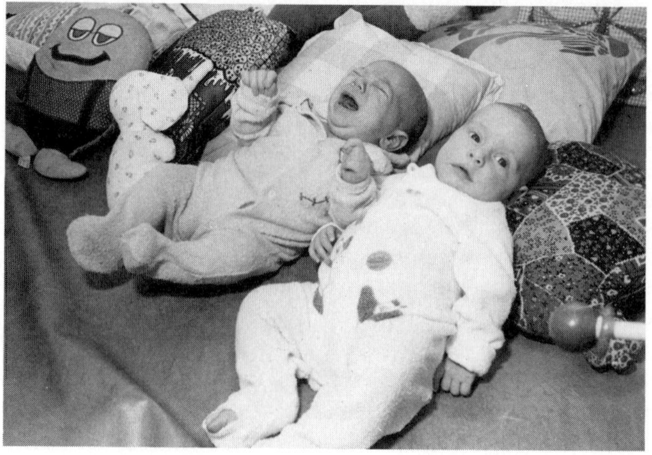

Pictures showing the similarity in social responses of identical twins, Michael and Peter (above), and the dissimilarity in social responses of fraternal twins, David and Jason (below) (names fictional).

BOX 3-4 THE PATH FROM INFANT IRRITABILITY TO PARENT-CHILD ATTACHMENT

Parents and infants form emotional bonds of attachment with each other, but the quality of these emotional relationships varies. Infants who are securely attached to their mothers are able to use their mothers as a source of comfort in times of stress and as a secure base from which to explore. They are confident of their mothers' responsiveness and availability. In contrast, insecurely attached infants do not trust or rely on their mothers' support and responsiveness and this is reflected in their responses to separation, the lack of solace they find in their mothers in strange situations, and the problems they have in later social relationships.

How do the different ways in which mothers respond to temperamentally irritable, difficult babies affect the attachment relationship? Does a supportive social network of friends, relatives, and an involved husband help the mother in dealing with her difficult baby?

In order to answer these questions Susan Crockenberg (1981) studied forty-eight mothers and their infants during the first year of the infants' lives.

Infant irritability was measured at 3 months through a standardized series of tests that assess irritability, intensity of excitement, and rapidity of buildup of excited irritable responses.

Maternal responsiveness was assessed when the infants were 3 months old through four one-hour home observations in which the length of delay of mothers in responding to their infants' distress signals was recorded.

Social support was assessed in an interview in which information was gathered about the number and types of stresses encountered by mothers and who helped them when support was needed.

Security of attachment was assessed in a frequently used laboratory procedure called "the strange situation," in which children's responses to departures and reunions with the mother and with a stranger are recorded. Proximity seeking, contact maintaining, avoidance, resistance, and crying were rated (see Chapter 7).

When mothers were encountering many stresses and had few supports available they were less responsive to their infants, who reciprocated with high resistance and avoidance and with anxious rather than secure attachment. Moreover, this differential effect of support on attachment was most marked in families with irritable babies. Less irritable babies seem somewhat impervious to the low-support environments which disrupted the bonds of attachment in their irritable peers. The finding that difficult infants exhibit later developmental difficulties only if their environments are deficient in meeting their special needs is one that will be found repeatedly in the studies reviewed in this book. In this case the infants were at risk because their irritable temperaments made them more demanding and less rewarding for their parents; however, in the next chapter we will find that similar outcomes occur with children who are at risk because of prenatal factors and traumatic births.

Source: Crockenberg, S. S. (1981). Infant irritability, mother responsiveness, and social support influences on the security of infant-mother attachment. *Child Development,* **52,** 857–865.

may have a hereditary basis, their specific manifestations are shaped through social interactions, particularly early interactions within the family.

There is some evidence that ethnic differences in personality may not be entirely culturally determined since ethnic differences in the temperament of newborns have been found. Chinese-American babies, in contrast to European-American infants, are calmer, easier to console, more able to quiet themselves after crying, and faster to adapt to external stimulation or changes (Freedman, 1974, 1976; Kagan, Kearsley, & Zelazo, 1978).

Emotionality, Activity, Sociability

Heredity has been found to play a role in the development of emotionality, sociability, wariness, activity level, specific fears and anxiety, anger, attention span and persistence, sensation seeking, and even in traditionalism, that is, the tendency to obey authority and rules and to support strict discipline and high moral standards (Campos, Barrett, Lamb, Goldsmith, & Stenberg, 1983; Goldsmith, 1983; Plomin, 1989; Tellegan et al., 1988). However, twins studies indicate that the most heritable dimensions of personality appear to be emotionality, activity, and sociability (Plomin, 1986), although a recent study of elderly twins reared apart suggests that the heritability plays a greater role in the expression of these personality traits in younger than in older individuals (Plomin, Pedersen, Nesselroade, McClearn, & Bergeman, 1988).

Emotionality is the tendency to be distressed, angry, or fearful. In infancy it is manifested in difficultness of temperament, and in later development it is associated with neuroticism and emotional instability. *Sociability* is related to gregariousness, lack of inhibition, extroversion, and the tendency to like to associate with others rather than to spend time alone, and at the other extreme to inhibition, shyness, and even fear in unfamiliar social situations. There is considerable stability across age in inhibited or uninhibited behavior in unfamiliar social situations, and inherited differences in physiological reactivity may underly this trait (Kagan, Reznick, & Gibbons, 1989). *Activity* involves vigor and tempo of movement. High activity level is predictive of such personality characteristics as noncompliance, low levels of inhibition, and greater outgoing, competitive, and manipulative behavior in older children.

Although genetically based temperamental and personality predispositions exist, the results of longitudinal studies indicate that depending on the individuals' experiences, the same temperamental genotype may be manifested in very different personality characteristics in children.

Deviant Behavior

Twin studies and adoption studies indicate that genetic factors may play a role in the development of a wide range of deviant behaviors such as neuroticism, depression, hysteria, suicide, manic-depressive psychosis, psychopathic personality, childhood behavior disorders, and crime. However, the form of psychopathology which has received the greatest attention is schizophrenia and, more recently, interest in the genetic basis of depression has increased. Schizophrenia is a severe mental disorder in which emotional and cognitive disruptions occur, often resulting in bizarre behavior and beliefs. Concordance rates for schizophrenia are about twice as high for identical (46 percent) as for fraternal twins (14 percent) or first-degree relatives (10 percent) (Gottesman & Shields, 1982). Similar rates of concordance are found for manic-depressive psychosis (Plomin, 1986). These findings suggest that, although genetic influence is important in the development of psychosis, nongenetic environmental factors play a major role in the development of these disorders.

Currently many studies are being conducted of children regarded as being vulnerable to the development of psychopathology because they have a parent who is emotionally disturbed. Studies of children with a schizophrenic mother show that such children have a greater-than-average probability of developing problems even if they are separated from their mothers at an early age (Mednick, Schulsinger, & Schulsinger, 1975). However, the psychiatric problems they develop are not necessarily schizophrenia. In a classic study by Heston (1966), a group of children of schizophrenic mothers, separated from their mothers at birth, were compared to offspring of nonschizophrenic mothers. About half of each group were placed in adoptive homes, and half remained in institutions. Both groups were compared on a

TABLE 3-6

COMPARISON OF SEPARATED OFFSPRING OF SCHIZOPHRENIC AND NORMAL MOTHERS

	OFFSPRING OF NORMAL MOTHERS (*N* = 50)	OFFSPRING OF SCHIZOPHRENIC MOTHERS (*N* = 47)
Age, mean	36.3	35.8
Adopted	19	22
Mental health ratings	80.1	65.2
Schizophrenia	0	5
Mental deficiency	0	4
Sociopathic	2	9
Neurotic disorder	7	13
More than one year in penal or psychiatric institution	2	11
Total years in institution	15	112
Felons	2	7
Number serving in armed forces	17	21
Discharged from armed forces	1	8
Mean IQ	103.7	94.0
Years in school	12.4	11.6
Divorces	7	6

Source: From Heston and Denny (1968).

variety of disorders at about age 35. The higher rates of deviant behavior in the offspring of schizophrenics, presented in Table 3-6, suggest that the genetic mechanisms involved may be manifested in a range of psychological anomalies, including schizophrenia, depending on the effects of life experiences. The results of this classic study have been confirmed in many more recent studies (Plomin, 1990b).

In an unusual variation of adoption studies, Wender, Rosenthal, Kety, Schulsinger, and Welner (1974) identified a rare sample of adults who had normal biological parents but as children had been adopted by schizophrenic parents. Having a normal biological parent was related to low rates of schizophrenia in the children with either schizophrenic or normal adoptive parents, an incidence of 11 percent in the children with schizophrenic adoptive parents, and 10 percent with normal adoptive parents. In contrast, almost twice as many children (19 percent) with a schizophrenic biological parent but normal adoptive parents later developed schizophrenia.

What happens with depressed mothers? Studies have suggested that schizophrenic mothers may provide children with a better environment than do depressed mothers. Schizophrenic mothers are at least responsive to their children, albeit in an erratic and sometimes strange fashion, whereas depressed parents are more likely to be unresponsive, irritable, tense, withdrawn, and disorganized (Sameroff, Seifer, & Zax, 1982; Cohn, Campbell, Matias, & Hopkins, 1990; Field, Healy, Goldstein, & Guthertz, 1990). The link between depression in mothers and in their children has been related to this inept parenting. The behaviors of depressed mothers also have been related to avoidant patterns of attachment (Radke-Yarrow, Cummings, Kuczynski, & Chapman, 1985), attention deficits, separation anxiety, conduct disorders, and lack of competence in school and in peer relations in their children (Baldwin, Cole, & Baldwin, 1982; Fendrich, Warner, & Weissman, 1990; Zahn-Waxler, Cummings, McKnew, & Radke-Yarrow, 1984; Zahn-Waxler, Kochanska, Krupnick, & McKnew, 1990). Again we see that a diverse array of pathological outcomes in children is associated with depression in parents and that these outcomes may be caused both by genetic and environmental factors.

SUMMARY

THE BIOLOGICAL BASES OF BEHAVIOR

- During development, the individual's *genotype,* or genetic make-up, comes to be expressed as a *phenotype,* or observable characteristics. The expression of the genotype is modified by the person's experiences, therefore the interactions between genetic and environmental factors are of interest to developmental psychologists. They have been studied by behavior geneticists, who study individuals with varying degrees of biological relatedness, living in particular situations, to determine the differential effects of biology and environment.

THE PROCESS OF GENETIC TRANSMISSION

- The human body contains *germ* cells and *body* cells, which are structurally and functionally different. Germ cells are the female ovum and the male sperm cells; all other cells are body cells. Within each cell nucleus are *chromosomes,* on which *genes* containing the genetic code are located. Genetic variability is due to the huge number of possible combinations of chromosomes, and to *crossing-over,* which alters chromosomes by exchanging genes during meiosis.
- *Genes* are the basic units of hereditary transmission. They contain DNA, which has instructions for protein chains about what and how to develop, and RNA, which acts as the messenger to carry the DNA instructions to the rest of the cell. When even one protein chain is defective, developmental problems may occur in the child. A molecule of DNA at the core of each chromosome is shaped like a double helix or spiral staircase. It duplicates itself by splitting down the middle, then evolving a copy of the missing half so that every cell in the body carries the same genetic code or pattern as the original one.
- Most phenotypical characteristics are determined by more than one gene, and there may be two or more alternative forms of the gene called *alleles,* one from the mother and one from the father. If the alleles are the same, the child is *homozygous* for the characteristic; if the alleles are different, the child is *heterozygous.* Heterozygous combinations may be expressed in the phenotype in three ways: (1) as a phenotype at an intermediate level between the two parent phenotypes; (2) as a combination of the parent phenotypes that contains characteristics of both; and (3) as a phenotype that is associated with only one of the parent characteristics when one allele is *dominant* over a *recessive* one. Additionally, many characteristics are determined by complex interactions among a set of genes acting together, called *pleiotropism,* rather than being determined by one gene.
- Phenylketonuria (PKU) is a disorder, caused by a recessive gene, that leads to the absence of an enzyme needed to metabolize certain types of

proteins including those found in milk. If unchecked, it can result in mental retardation; however if discovered early, the diet is restricted so that the intake of phenylalanine is limited and retardation can be avoided. PKU is an example of the action of dominant and recessive genes, and of the fact that genetically determined characteristics can sometimes be altered by environmental interventions.

- Sex-linked characteristics occur as the result of a recessive allele for a defect on the X chromosome. The fact that some genes on the X chromosome have no equivalent genes on the Y chromosome results in the more frequent appearance of sex-linked recessive characteristics in males. The disorder will be manifested in males because there is only one X chromosome, therefore there is no equivalent allele on the Y chromosome to counteract its effect. Hemophilia, a disease in which the blood does not clot, is an example of a sex-linked recessive trait carried on the X chromosome.
- Down syndrome is one example of the many identifiable chromosomal disorders. It is usually attributable to the fact that the individual has an extra chromosome or part of a third chromosome on the twenty-first set of autosomes. It is related to maternal age, possibly because some deterioration of the ova may occur in older women or because older women have been exposed to more environmental hazards during their lives. However, it has been shown that the sperm carries the extra chromosome in about one-quarter of Down syndrome cases. The disorder is characterized by physical and mental retardation and a distinctive physical appearance.
- In addition to abnormalities in the autosomes, such as those found in Down syndrome, problems in sexual differentiation sometimes occur based on deviations in the number of sex chromosomes. Examples are Turner syndrome (X0 pattern) and triple-X syndrome (XXX) in females, and Klinefelter's syndrome (XXY pattern) and Fragile X syndrome in males. Physical, psychological, and emotional characteristics of these individuals vary widely, depending on the specific chromosomal pattern and environmental factors.
- Genetic variability also may result from the development of *mutations,* or changes in the genes which may produce new phenotypes. The majority of mutations result from a deletion of one of the steps of the spiral staircase of DNA. The survival of a mutation depends upon its adaptability in relation to the environment in which it must develop. The vast majority of mutations are deleterious, or lethal, and do not survive. One of the most dramatic examples of selective survival based on the interaction of genetic factors and environment is the blood disease called sickle-cell anemia, a disorder found in about 8 percent of American blacks, in which their red blood cells assume unusual crescent, sickle, or holly-leaf shapes under conditions of low oxygen.
- Advances in biology and genetics have opened new opportunities for shaping and controlling some aspects of development. These advances include the ability to detect disorders in utero; progress in genetic engineering, including in vitro fertilization and recombinant DNA techniques used to pinpoint genetic markers; and genetic therapy used to prevent or cure genetic disorders. However, as greater genetic control becomes possible, ethical issues are raised concerning how such information is used.

PROCESSES AND PRINCIPLES OF HEREDITY/ENVIRONMENT INTERACTIONS

- Developmental psychologists are interested in the ways in which environmental and genetic factors interact to shape development. One description of the relationship is as a *range of reaction*, referring to the idea that heredity establishes a range of possible responses that an individual could make under varying circumstances rather than rigidly fixing behavior. However, some kinds of genotypes are more *canalized* than others, meaning that they have fewer possible alternative paths so that it takes stronger environmental influences to deflect them from their genotypic path. In addition, an individual's genotype may influence the environments that a person encounters in three ways: passively, evocatively, or actively.
- One of the most frequently used procedures in investigating the contributions of genetic and environmental factors to individual differences in human development is to study similarities in characteristics of family members of varying degrees of genetic relatedness, such as in adoption and twin studies. However, one problem with interpreting comparisons of monozygotic and dizygotic twins is that monozygotic twins may elicit similar responses from the environment, resulting in more similar environments as well as identical genotypes. Identical twins also are more likely to select similar niches or environments as they grow older and have the opportunity to make such choices.
- Studies by behavior geneticists indicate that most of the variation found in psychological disorders and behaviors is due to nongenetic or environmental factors. Even within families, environmental factors are not always the same for all family members. In addition to shared experiences such as poverty, housing, or neighborhood, siblings experience nonshared environments associated with different life experiences such as differences in parental treatment.
- Monozygotic twins are more similar than dizygotic twins on a variety of physical dimensions, including height, weight, body build, and facial characteristics. They also are more similar on physiological traits such as rate of maturation, longevity, brain functioning, and responsiveness of the autonomic nervous system.
- Twin studies of similarities in intelligence test scores have consistently shown that performance is related to genetic factors. In addition to overall intellectual performance, some patterns of specific cognitive abilities (e.g., spatial and verbal abilities) are more influenced by genetics than others, and the rate and timing of mental growth appears to be partially genetically determined. Adoption studies show similar findings of greater relationships between biological than adoptive parents and children. However, environmental factors also markedly influence cognitive development.
- Heredity has been found to play a role in the development of temperament and personality (e.g., emotionality, activity, and sociability). However, the effects of genetics are less marked than for intelligence and physical characteristics. Although genetic predispositions seem to exist, longitudinal studies indicate that the same genotypes may be manifested very differently depending on environmental and cultural influences.
- Studies by behavior geneticists indicate that a wide range of deviant behaviors such as depression, schizophrenia, and crime are related to genetic factors. In these studies, a *concordance rate,* or the percentage of

time in which the disorder is present in both members of a twin pair, is calculated. Although the concordance rates are typically higher for identical twins than for fraternal twins, the rates never approach 100 percent, indicating that environmental factors still play a large role in the development of these disorders.

- With current levels of methodological sophistication it is impossible to estimate exactly how much heredity and environment contribute to development. Both are important, and they are constantly interacting. Whether we are examining social, intellectual, or personality development, the transactions between genetic and experiential factors must be examined rather than either factor in isolation to form an accurate understanding of the emergence of individual differences.

CHAPTER

PRENATAL DEVELOPMENT AND BIRTH

Does the infant exist in a benign and protected intrauterine environment, impervious to external influences during prenatal development? Or do external factors and experiences of the mother modify the development of the young organism growing and changing so rapidly in utero? Few of us would accept old beliefs that if a pregnant woman listens to classical music throughout the course of her pregnancy she will have a child who appreciates fine music, or, that if she reads the Bible assiduously her child will exhibit high ethical standards, or that the presence on her newborn infant of a birthmark shaped like the head of a dog might be attributable to the mother being frightened by a dog in early pregnancy. However, it is now recognized that the prenatal organism is vulnerable to a variety of factors that can influence the course of its development. Some of these factors are genetic mechanisms, and some are variations in prenatal environment due to the physical and, possibly, the emotional condition of the mother. A variety of adverse agents such as maternal disease, x-rays, drugs, and dietary deficiencies can contribute to deviations in development. Surprisingly, some of these agents previously regarded as harmless, such as commonly prescribed drugs which may have no deleterious effects on the pregnant mother, can lead to abnormalities in her unborn child.

In this chapter the effects of these genetic and environmental factors on prenatal development will be discussed. First, what are the most important factors? Second, how does the timing of variations in the prenatal environment modify their impact on the developing fetus? Third, what are the effects of conditions of birth and the status of the child at birth on later development? Finally, what postnatal environmental factors sustain or modify the effects of prenatal and perinatal factors?

STAGES OF PRENATAL DEVELOPMENT

Over the period of the ten lunar months (usually about 280 days) of prenatal development, the new organism shows many varieties of change. Changes in the kinds, number, position, size, and shapes of cells, tissues, and somatic systems occur. Systems and structures usually increase in size and complexity. However, some prenatal structures actually decrease in size or disappear. For example, at the end of the third week gill arches appear, but by the middle of the second month they have been transformed into parts of the inner ear and neck and the cartilages of the larynx. Another example is the emergence and gradual disappearance of an external tail between the second and fourth months.

Prenatal development includes three periods: the period of the *zygote*, the period of the *embryo*, and the period of the *fetus*. These periods should be thought of as continuous phases of development, for from the moment the sperm penetrates the ovum, the development of the organism involves a systematic series of sequential changes by which the organism becomes increasingly complex and differentiated. It can be seen in Figure 4-1 that although many of the organ systems are present in the first three months of prenatal development, many also continue to evolve. The nervous system and brain continue to develop and differentiate even after birth.

The Period of the Zygote

The period of the zygote, which is sometimes called the germinal period, includes approximately the first two weeks of life, extending from fertilization

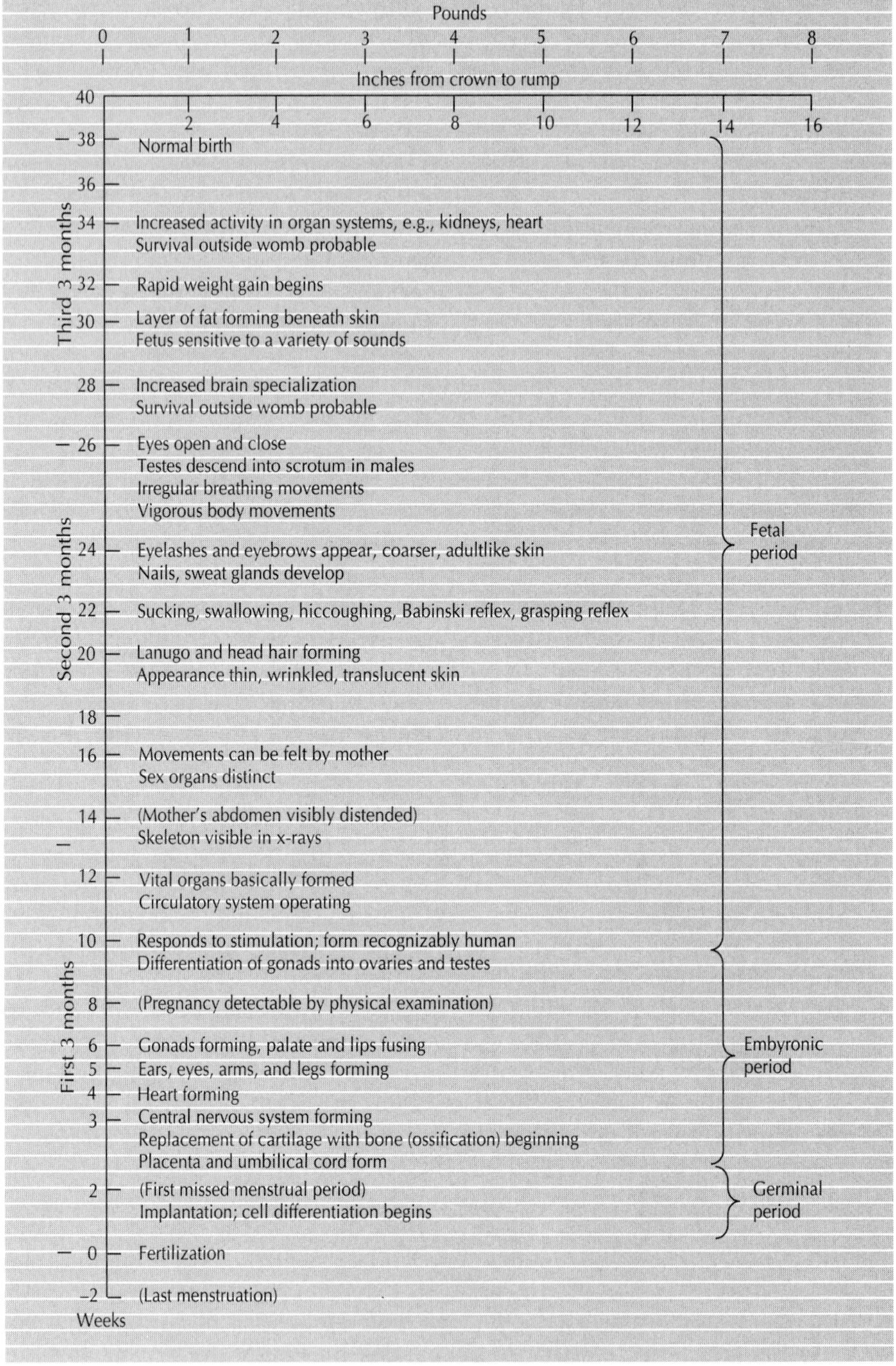

FIGURE 4-1
A summary of prenatal development. (Adapted from Fischer & Lazerson, 1984.)

until the fertilized ovum, or zygote, proceeds down the fallopian tube and becomes implanted on the wall of the uterus. It is estimated that it would take 100 to 200 zygotes placed side by side to equal an inch, or more than 5 million such cells to weigh an ounce (Meredith, 1975). Tendrils from the zygote penetrate the blood vessels in the wall of the uterus, and the zygote forms the physiologically dependent relationship with the mother that will continue throughout the course of prenatal development. The establishment of this relationship marks the beginning of the second period, the period of the embryo, a state of rapid growth that lasts until the end of the eighth week.

The Period of the Embryo

Differentiation of the most important organs and physiological systems occurs at this time, and by the end of this period, the embryo is recognizable as a partially functioning tiny human being. From the time of fertilization until the end of this period the infant increases 2 million percent in size. Because rapidly developing and differentiating organisms are most vulnerable to adverse environmental effects, the period of the embryo is the phase in which environmental intrusions caused by such things as maternal disease, faulty nutrition, and drugs may result in devastating, irreversible deviations in development.

In the period of the embryo the inner mass of the zygote differentiates into three layers: the *ectoderm,* the *mesoderm,* and the *endoderm.* From the ectoderm the hair, nails, and part of the teeth, the outer layer of the skin and skin glands, and the sensory cells and the nervous system develop. From the mesoderm the muscles, skeleton, excretory and circulatory systems, and inner skin layer evolve; and from the endoderm come the gastrointestinal tract, trachea, bronchia, eustachian tubes, glands, and vital organs such as the lungs, pancreas, and liver.

In addition, in this period, three other important auxiliary structures develop: the *amniotic sac,* the *placenta,* and the *umbilical cord.* The amniotic sac contains *amniotic fluid,* a watery liquid in which the developing embryo floats and which serves as a protective buffer against physical shocks and temperature changes. The tendrils which attach the embryo to the uterine wall increase in size and complexity to form a fleshy disc called the *placenta.* The embryo is joined at the abdomen to the placenta by the third accessory apparatus, the *umbilical cord,* which attains a final length slightly greater than that of the fetus and permits considerable fetal mobility. Although the umbilical cord is composed of blood vessels carrying blood to and from the infant and placenta, there is no direct connection between the bloodstream of the mother and child. The bloodstreams of the mother and child are separated in the placenta by semipermeable membranes, which permit transmission of chemicals with fine molecular structure, such as those found in nutrients and waste produces. In this way the placenta carries nourishment to the child and removes its waste products. Early in gestation the nutrients in the mother's bloodstream exceed the needs of the embryo and are stored by the placenta for later use. Certain drugs, hormones, viruses, and antibodies from the mother, which may have destructive effects on the embryo, are also transferred through the placental membranes. The rapid emergence and development of new organs and systems in this period make the embryo particularly vulnerable to environmental assault, and thus it is the period when most gross congenital anomalies occur.

> The neural folds appear about day 19 and begin to close 2 days later; if they fail to close, spina bifida results. The future lens of the eye is recognizable at 28 days. The limb buds appear in the 5th week; the hand is defined at the 30th day; the fingers and toes about the 35th. The lateral elements of the future lips and palate are fusing in the 5th and 6th weeks. In these same weeks, the heart and the great vessels are shifting toward their ultimate pattern. (Corner, 1961, p. 14)

By the end of the period of the embryo, the face and its features are delineated, and fingers, toes, and external genitalia are present. At 6 weeks the embryo can be recognized as a human being, although a rather strangely proportioned one in that the head is almost as large as the rest of the body. Primitive functioning of the heart and liver, as well as the peristaltic movement of ingestion, has been reported late in this period.

Most miscarriages, or spontaneous abortions, occur during this period; the embryo becomes detached from the wall of the uterus and is expelled. It has been estimated that the rate of spontaneous abortion is as high as 1 in 4 pregnancies but that many remain undetected because they occur in the first few weeks of pregnancy. This high rate of abortion may be advantageous to the species since the great majority of aborted embryos have gross chromosomal and genetic disorders. The most severely affected embryos are spontaneously eliminated.

The Period of the Fetus

The final stage of prenatal development, the period of the fetus, extends from the beginning of the third month until birth. During this time little further differentiation of the organs remains to be completed; however, muscular development is rapid, complete closure of the palate and reduction of the umbilical hernia occur, and differentiation of the external genitalia continues. The central nervous system develops rapidly in this period, although development of the central nervous system is not completed until several years after birth. By the end of the fourth month, mothers usually report movement of the fetus. At around 5 months reflexes such as sucking, swallowing, and hiccoughing usually appear. In addition, a Babinski reflex of a fanning of the toes in response to stroking of the foot occurs. After the fifth month, the fetus develops nails and sweat glands, a coarser, more adultlike skin, and a soft hair which covers the body. Most fetuses shed this hair in utero, but some continue to shed it after birth. By 6 months the eyes have developed, and opening and closing of the eyes occur. If an infant is born prematurely at 6 months, the regulatory processes and nervous and respiratory systems are usually not mature enough for survival without intensive intervention. One of the important shortcomings of the fetus at this time is an inability to produce and maintain an adequate amount of *surfactin,* a liquid which allows the lungs to transmit oxygen from the air to the blood. Without surfactin infants are often unable to breathe adequately, and they may develop *respiratory distress syndrome,* which can result in death. The age of 28 weeks, sometimes referred to as the *age of viability,* is an important point of fetal development, since at this time the physical systems of the fetus are sufficiently advanced so that if birth occurs, the child has a better probability of surviving. However, with the exceptional resources available in modern intensive care nurseries, infants as immature as 25 weeks can live. It is with these exceptionally small premature babies that later developmental deviations are likely to be found, especially if they encounter other adverse environmental conditions.

PRENATAL INFLUENCES ON DEVELOPMENT

During the course of prenatal development many agents may raise the incidence of deviations or produce malformations in the fetus. These agents are called *teratogens,* which derives from the Greek word *teras,* meaning "monster" or "marvel." Teratogens include maternal diseases and blood disorders, diet, irradiation, drugs, hormones, temperature, and oxygen level. In addition, maternal characteristics such as age, emotional state, and the number of children the mother has borne influence prenatal development.

In considering the effects of adverse prenatal and birth factors on development it is easy to concentrate on the resulting gross physical defects or mental impairments that sometimes result. However, an equally important issue to keep in mind is how these factors change the life experiences of the child and the responses of those around the child. How does a parent who views the child as at risk because of such things as Rh factors or prematurity treat the baby? Is the parent more anxious, more protective, more rejecting? What happens to parent-child interaction if the infant is lethargic and unresponsive because of drugs administered during delivery? How is the emotional bond that usually forms between parent and child affected by early separation necessitated by the use of isolettes for low-birthweight babies? It may be these experiential factors that are ultimately the most important in sustaining or in minimizing the long-term effects of early adversity.

Principles of the Effects of Teratogens

Certain general principles describe the effects of teratogens on prenatal development.

1 The effects of a teratogen vary with the developmental stage of the embryo (see Figure 4-2). Teratogens acting on newly differentiated cells may damage developing but yet unformed organ systems. Since the various organ systems begin and end their prenatal development at different times, their sensitivity to agents varies over time. The most vulnerable period for the brain is from 15 to 25 days, for the eye from 24 to 40 days, for the heart from 20 to 40 days, and for the legs from 24 to 36 days (Moore, 1989; Tuchmann-Deuplessis, 1965). Before implantation and after the beginning of the fetal stage the organism is less vulnerable than during the embryonic period. During the fetal stage, teratogen-induced abnormalities tend to occur only in locations or systems that are still maturing, such as the cerebellum, palate, and some cardiovascular and urogenital structures (Clegg, 1971). In addition, some damage can be done to the continuously developing nervous system, or the differentiation of the external genitalia can be impaired, resulting in pseudohermaphrodism (the appearance of both male and female sexual characteristics) (Clegg, 1971; Tuchmann-Deuplessis, 1975).

2 Since individual teratogens influence specific developmental processes, they produce specific patterns of developmental deviations. Rubella (German measles) affects mainly the heart, eyes, and brain; and the drug thalidomide results primarily in malformations of the limbs. This finding, in conjunction with the information on the critical vulnerable periods for these developing systems reported in the first principle, suggests that although the form of the deviations resulting from rubella and thalidomide varies, the organism's period of greatest vulnerability to them is in approximately the same time span during the embryonic period, that is, between the fourth and sixth weeks.

3 Both maternal and fetal genotypes can affect the developing organism's response to teratogenic agents and may play an important role in the appearance of abnormalities in offspring. Not all pregnant women who use the drug thalidomide or have German measles or poor diets produce

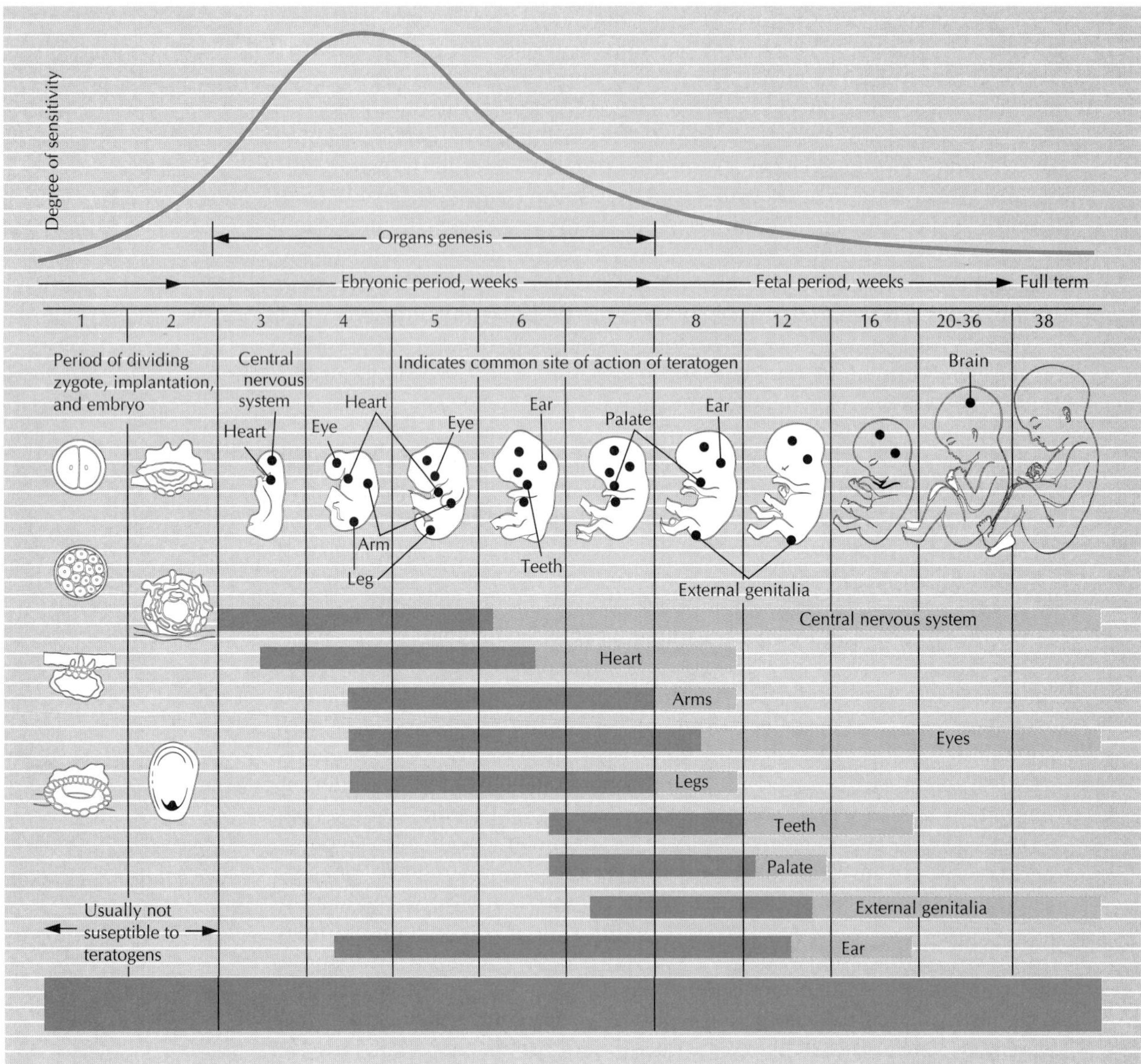

FIGURE 4-2

Critical periods in prenatal development and sensitivity to teratogens. Sensitivity to teratogens is greatest in the first two months and peaks at around four weeks after conception. The likelihood of a structural defect in an organ is greatest (dark color) early in the embryonic period since organs are being formed at that time. Thereafter susceptibility to anatomical defects diminishes (light color), and exposure to teratogens during the later fetal period is more likely to stunt growth or cause functional problems. (From Moore, 1974.)

defective infants. Those who do may themselves be genetically predisposed to being more vulnerable to those particular teratogens or may have fetuses who are so predisposed.

4 The physiological or pathological status of the mother will influence the action of a teratogen. Physiological factors, such as maternal nutritional and uterine condition and hormonal balance, will modify the impact of a teratogen. For example, not only will nutritional deficiencies themselves directly affect prenatal development, but they may intensify the adverse effects of the fetus of certain drugs ingested by the mother, such as cortisone (see Table 4-1).

5 Levels of teratogenic agents which will produce malformations in the offspring may show no, or mild, detrimental effects on the mother. With a variety of drugs, diseases, x-irradiation, and dietary deficiencies the mother may show no abnormalities, but gross deviations may appear in the child.

6 One teratogen may result in a variety of deviations, and several different teratogens may produce the same deviation. Rubella may lead to deafness, cataracts, mental retardation, or heart disorders in the early months of pregnancy, depending on the time at which the disease was contracted. However, deafness in infants can be caused not only by maternal rubella but also by drugs such as quinine or streptomycin taken by the mother.

Maternal Diseases and Disorders

A wide range of maternal diseases and disorders can affect prenatal development, and, in accord with the principles noted previously, the effects are correlated with the stage of fetal development. Maternal conditions, such as high blood pressure, diabetes, and blood incompatibilities between the mother and fetus, may increase rates of miscarriage, mortality, and fetal abnormalities. Even mild attacks of rubella may produce cardiac disorders, cataracts, deafness, and mental retardation in the infant (Cochi et al., 1989). The occurrence of deviations decreases from 50 percent if the mother contracts rubella in the first month to 17 percent if she contracts it in the third month; and there is almost no probability of abnormalities occurring if the mother contracts rubella after that time. Another maternal disease, mumps, also results in a higher incidence of malformations if contracted in the first trimester rather than later in pregnancy.

Chronic infections, such as venereal diseases, which invade the developing embryo and remain active, have their worst effects at later stages of development. The deleterious effects of the syphilis spirochete on the fetus do not occur before 18 weeks of age, and therefore early treatment of a syphilitic mother may avert abnormalities in the child. If the mother is untreated, invasion of the fetus by the syphilis spirochetes from the mother may result in abortion or miscarriage, mental retardation, blindness, or other physical abnormalities. In some cases the deleterious effects of syphilis are not apparent at birth but gradually emerge during the early years of development in the form of juvenile paresis, involving deterioration in thought processes, judgment, and speech, and in a decline in motor and mental abilities and eventual death.

In both gonorrhea and herpes simplex 2, babies may become infected during the birth process, with resulting damage to the eyes and central nervous system. Many women have gonorrhea without overt symptoms. If an active genital herpes infection is detected in a pregnant woman before

TABLE 4-1 **MATERNAL CONDITIONS THAT ADVERSELY AFFECT PRENATAL DEVELOPMENT**

AGENT OR CONDITION	POSSIBLE EFFECTS
Infectious diseases:	
Viruses:	
Rubella (German measles)	Deafness; cataracts; heart defects; mental retardation
Other viral infections; measles, mumps, hepatitis, chicken pox, influenza A, scarlet fever	Malformations; fetal death; heart disease
Venereal diseases:	
Syphilis	Death; blindness; deafness; mental retardation; miscarriage
Herpes simplex	Herpes infection; death; eye damage; mental retardation
Gonorrhea	Blindness; death
Cytomegalovirus	Mental retardation; deafness; blindness; seizures
Noninfectious diseases or disorders:	
Anemia (iron deficiency)	Stillbirth; death; brain damage
Diabetes mellitus	Miscarriage; stillbirth; fetal death; metabolic disturbances; respiratory difficulties
Environmental hazards:	
Lead	Anemia; miscarriage; hemorrhage
Radiation	Microcephaly; leukemia; stunted growth; cancer; cataracts; miscarriage; stillbirths
Methyl mercury	Cerebral palsy
Maternal condition:	
Stress	Pregnancy complications; higher rates of Down syndrome
Malnutrition	Prematurity; low birthweight; stillbirth; growth retardation; intellectual deficits
Maternal age	Older women have higher rates of delivery complications, Down syndrome, and difficulty in getting pregnant

labor, a cesarean delivery usually will prevent the infant from coming in contact with the disease in the birth canal and usually protects the infant from contagion. Herpes, less commonly, can be transmitted by exposure to the virus after birth. In infants less than 5 weeks of age who do not have a fully developed immune system, the disease can cause mental retardation, blindness, motor abnormalities, and a wide range of neurological disorders. Moreover, although treatment with antiviral agents has reduced the death rate of infected infants from 70 to 38 percent, half of the surviving babies are seriously disabled (Blough & Guintoli, 1979; Babson, Pernoll, Benda, & Simpson, 1980).

Although many viruses have been found to be damaging to the unborn child, cytomegalovirus (CMV), a herpes virus, is the single most important

PRENATAL DEVELOPMENT

The sequence of prenatal growth and differentiation, extending from the initial penetration of the ovum by a sperm to the birth of an infant. The rapid differentiation in the first four months can be noted.

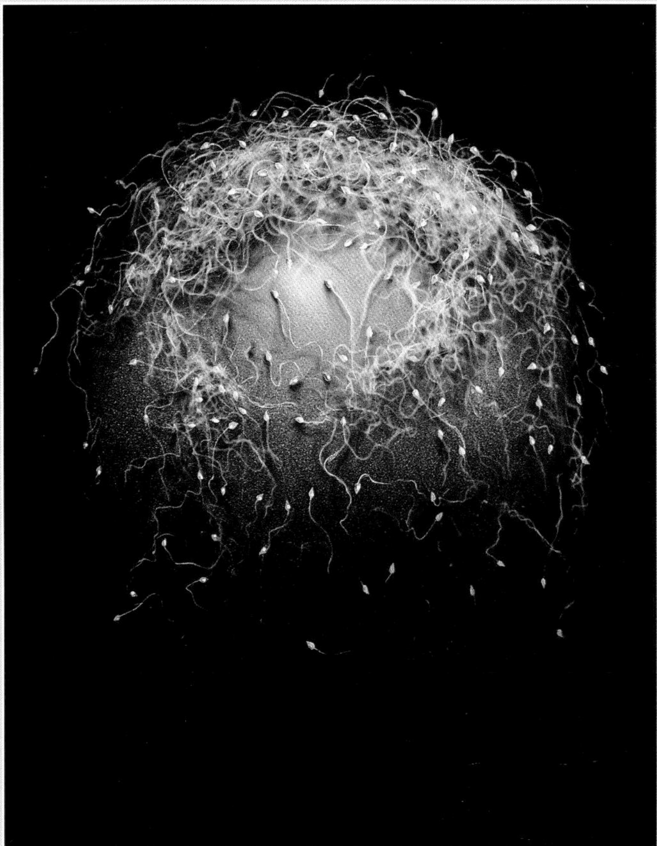

A human ovum surrounded by spermatazoa. Only a single sperm may successfully penetrate and fertilize the ovum.

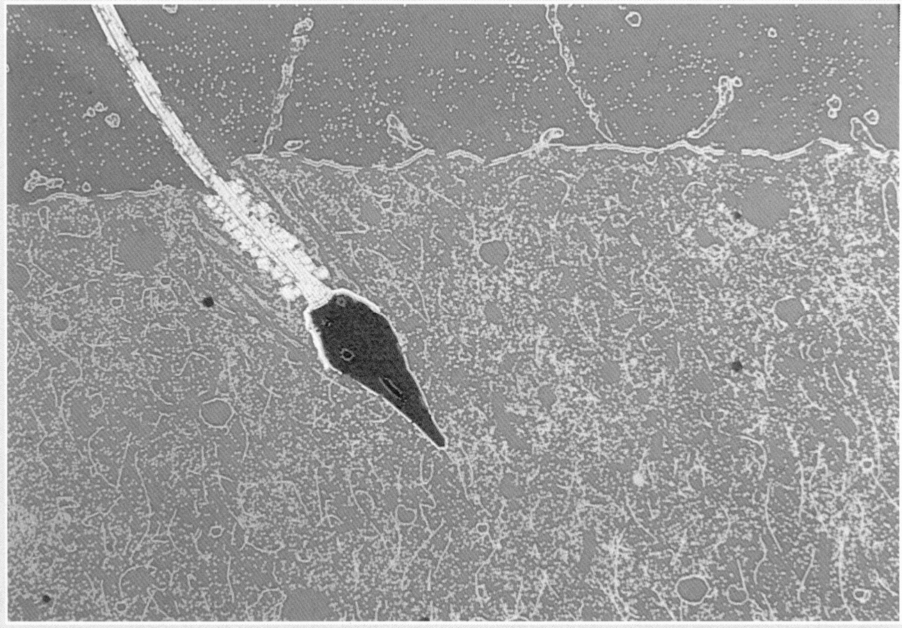

A sperm penetrates the ovum.

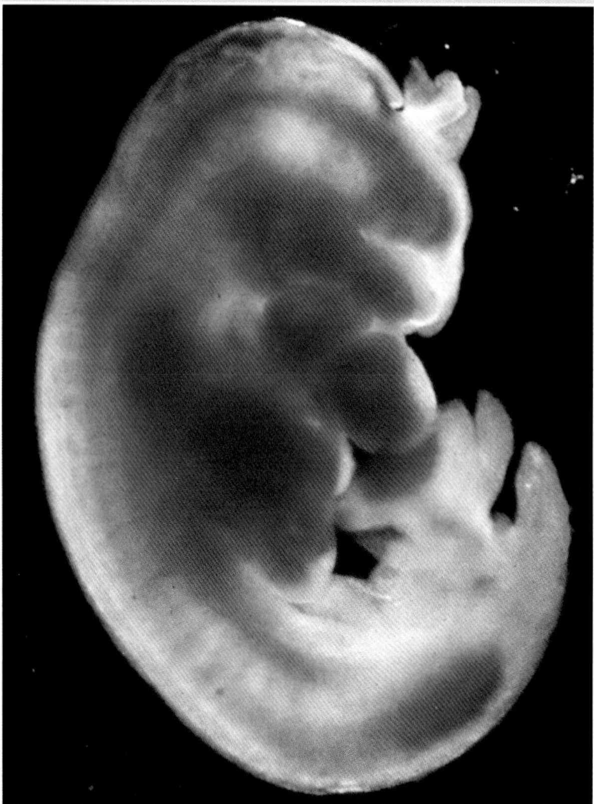
An embryo between the fourth and fifth week.

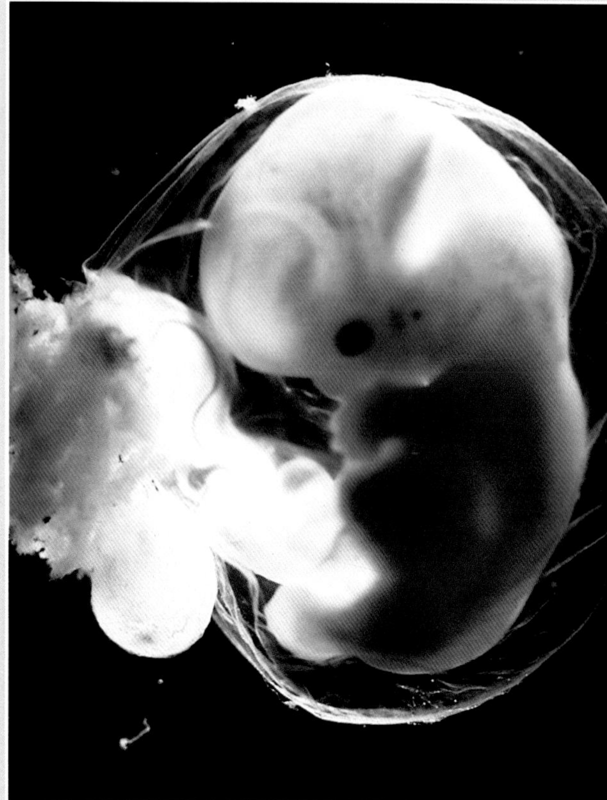
A fetus at 5 to 6 weeks.

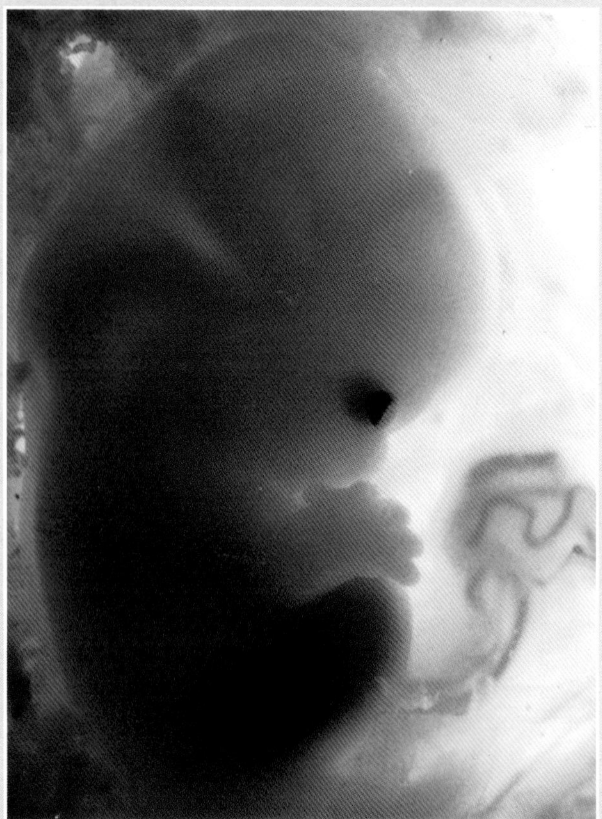
A fetus at 7 weeks; 2 centimeters long.

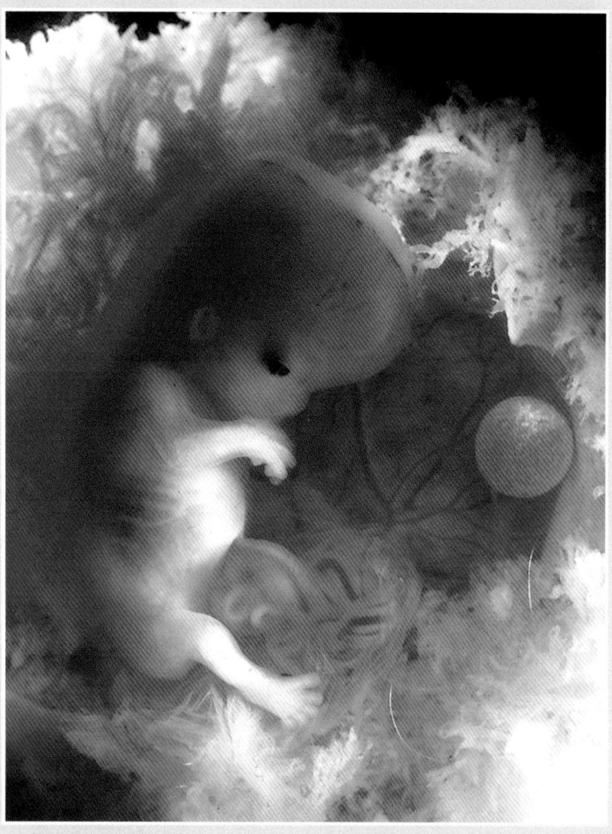
A fetus in the middle of the third month.

A 4-month-old fetus.

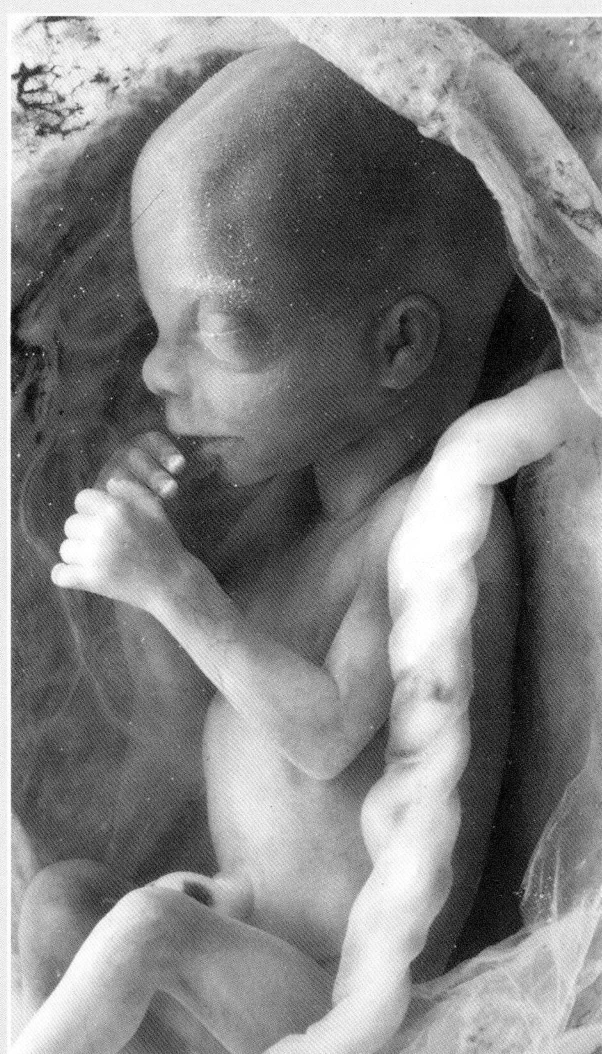

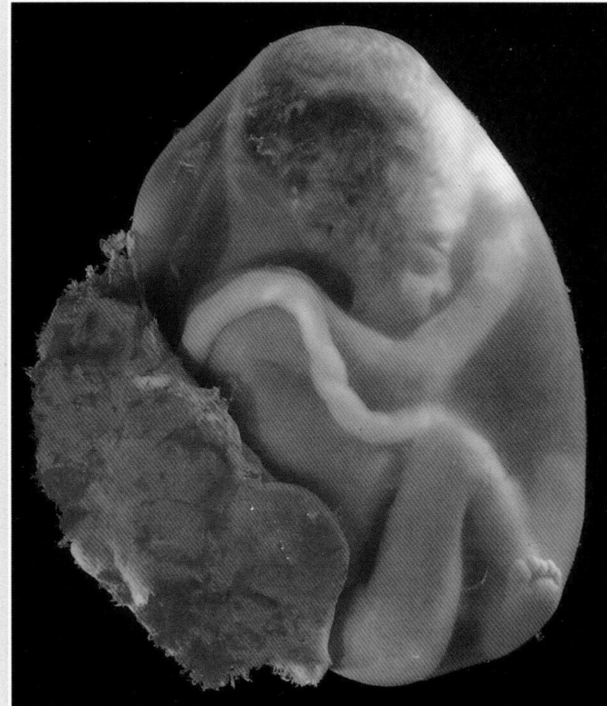

A fetus at 8 months.

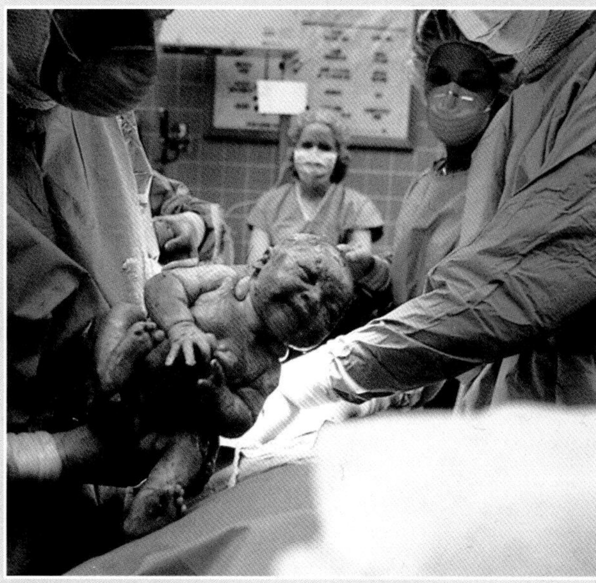

A newborn infant.

Pregnancy and birth involve not only physical changes, but changes in family relations as well.

PREGNANCY AND BIRTH AND FAMILY RELATIONS

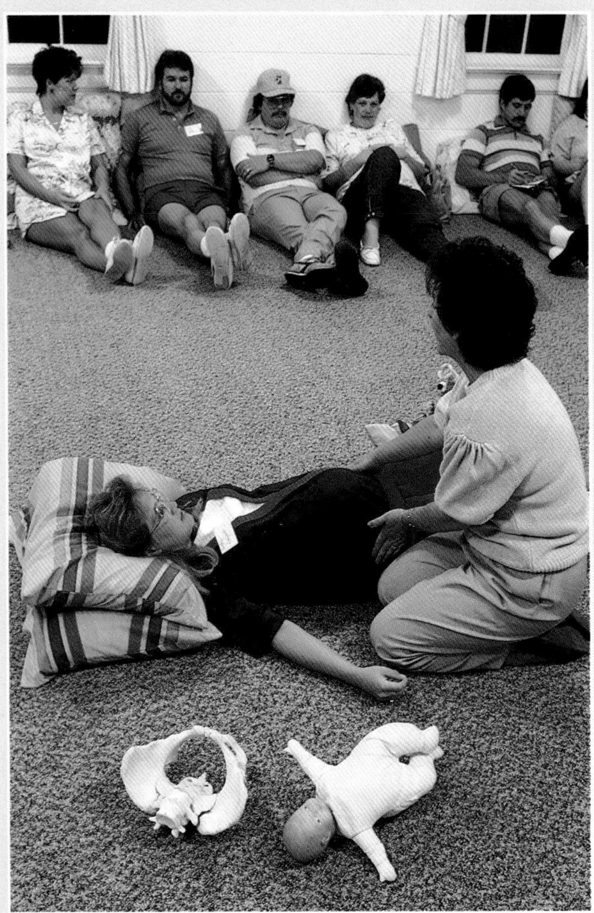

Many couples attend childbirth preparation classes together.

Children need to be actively involved in preparation for the arrival of a new sibling.

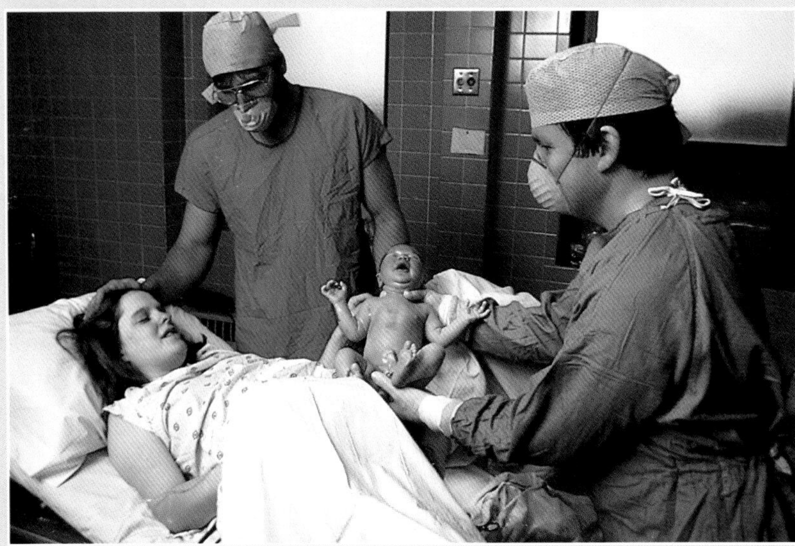

The support of the husband during childbirth has positive effects on the mother.

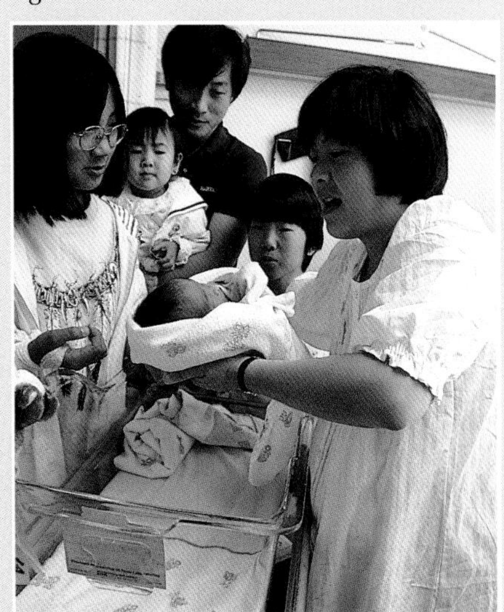

The birth of a child often draws family generations closer together.

MATERNAL CONDITIONS THAT ADVERSELY AFFECT PRENATAL DEVELOPMENT (*Continued*)

TABLE 4-1

AGENT OR CONDITION	POSSIBLE EFFECTS
High blood pressure, hypertension	Miscarriage
Incompatibility of maternal and fetal blood	Jaundice; anemia; death
Drugs/chemicals/hormones:	
Analgesics (painkillers)	Respiratory depression
Anesthetics or barbiturates	Respiratory depression
Aspirin in large quantities	Respiratory depression; bleeding; spontaneous abortion
Alcohol	Growth retardation; heart problems; developmental lag; microcephaly
Antihistamines	Fetal death; malformations
Diethylstilbestrol (DES)	Genital abnormalities in males and females; cancer of the vagina and cervix in females
Heroin, morphine	Newborn withdrawal symptoms; convulsions; tremors; respiratory depression; retarded growth; death
Quinine	Deafness
Isotretinoin (a vitamin A derivative for the treament of acne)	Abnormalities in heart, head, neck, and central nervous system; lack of ears; behavior problems; brain damage
Streptomycin	Hearing loss
Tetracycline	Discolored teeth; inhibition of bone growth
Tobacco	Spontaneous abortion; prematurity; low birth rate; convulsions; high heart rate; sudden infant death (SIDS); cleft lip and palate; reduced head circumference
Thalidomide	Deformed limbs; hearing defects; death

known infectious cause of congenital mental retardation and deafness. It is estimated that between 15 and 30 infants per 1000 live births are affected with this virus. Although experimental vaccines are being developed, there is, as yet, no known cure for this serious disease (Truss, 1981).

The viral infection that has caused the most recent alarm is the human immunodeficiency virus (HIV) infection and its expression in acquired immune deficiency syndrome (AIDS). Although AIDS was originally thought to be confined to homosexuals and bisexuals and to drug abusers who shared needles, it was later found in the heterosexual partners and offspring of these high-risk groups and in recipients of blood transfusions. The impact of AIDS on child development is discussed in Box 4-1.

BOX 4-1 CHILDREN WITH AIDS

More than 2000 cases of childhood AIDS were identified in the past decade and it is expected that this incidence will increase rapidly. The vast majority (77 percent) of these children were infected by their mothers prenatally or during the birth process. The remainder were infected by transfusions, especially for hemophilia. The chance that an infected pregnant mother will transmit the virus to her child is about 50 percent. Over 80 percent of children with AIDS are less than 5 years of age, since most of the children are congenitally infected and the progress of the disease from the time of infection to the appearance of clinical symptoms and death is more rapid in children than adults. Over half of the children infected are black, one-fifth are Hispanic, and one-fifth are white.

The average age of diagnosis for children congenitally infected with AIDS is 17 months. These children often show neurological impairment, delays in mental and physical development, and structural deformities characterized by microcephaly, thick lips, a square forehead, and widely spaced slanted eyes. It is, however, their vulnerability to disease and bacterial infections that is associated most closely with their early deaths. Children survive an average of nine months after diagnosis, three-quarters are dead within two years. Children diagnosed before the age of 1 have a shorter survival time.

Parents who have children with AIDS often have few resources; frequently, they are drug users and are ill and poor. In many cases, these parents are unable or unwilling to care for their HIV-infected child and foster care is difficult to obtain. Specialized care and support systems are needed for these children and their families. Many experts think that prevention through education and programs aimed at modifying high-risk sexual and drug-taking behavior may be the only effective means of dealing with AIDS since at this time there is no cure for the disease. The success of programs aimed at such high-risk behaviors is not well substantiated since most of these programs have not been evaluated. In addition, they are often school-based and do not serve the groups that are harder to reach but most vulnerable to AIDS—groups such as runaways, school dropouts, prostitutes, young people in prisons, and drug users (Brooks-Gunn, Boyer, & Hein, 1988). Since strategies for preventing AIDS are still in a relatively primitive and untested state much research is still needed on the prevention of high-risk behavior in adolescents and young adults.

Sources: Brooks-Gunn, J., Boyer, B., & Hein, K. (1988). Preventing HIV infection and AIDS in children and adolescents. *American Psychologist,* **43,** 958–964; Faloon, J., Eddy, J., Wiener, L., & Pizzo, P. (1989). Human immunodeficiency virus infection in children. *Journal of Pediatrics,* **114,** 1–30; Task Force on Pediatric AIDS. (1989). Pediatric AIDS and human immunodeficiency virus infection. *American Psychologist,* **44,** 258–264.

Drugs

Although most physicians and parents would probably agree that it is not good for pregnant women to take too many drugs during pregnancy, 60 to 80 percent of pregnant women take prescribed or over-the-counter drugs during pregnancy (Schnoll, 1986). The average pregnant American woman consumes about ten different drugs during pregnancy (Truss, 1981). Some drugs are prescribed for therapeutic reasons; others are taken by the mother for stimulation, tension release, or pleasure.

THALIDOMIDE

The *thalidomide* disaster in the late 1950s and early 1960s brought into public awareness the often unknown and potentially horrendous effects of the use of drugs by pregnant women. At this time an increasing number of children were born with an unusual group of abnormalities. The cluster of abnormalities included such things as eye defects, cleft palate, depressed bridge of the nose, small external ears, facial palsy, fusing of fingers and toes, dislocated hips, and malformations of the digestive and genitourinary tract and heart. However, the most unusual and characteristic deformity was *phocomelia,* an anomaly where limbs are missing and the feet and hands are attached directly to the torso like flippers (Karnofsky, 1965). It was partly the rarity of this anomaly that called attention to the fact that the mothers of these malformed infants had been prescribed thalidomide as a sedative or antinausea drug in the early months of pregnancy.

The problems in establishing the consequences of maternal intake of a drug during pregnancy on offspring are illustrated clearly in the case of thalidomide. The pregnant women showed no adverse effects of the thalidomide. Even in instances where adults have ingested massive quantities of thalidomide in suicide attempts, it has resulted in nothing more serious than deep sleep, headaches, and nausea. Only a small percentage of pregnant women who used thalidomide produced deviant children, and in some of the animal species studied no effects of thalidomide on offspring were obtained.

Although there is some controversy about the intelligence of thalidomide babies, the evidence suggests that among noninstitutionalized infants who are reared in a normal home situation and who do not suffer from gross sensory deficits (such as blindness, deafness, or paralysis, which might be expected to seriously handicap the development of a child), the intelligence quotients of thalidomide babies differ little from those of normal children.

Although the deleterious effects of thalidomide are the most widely known, other drugs ingested by the mother may also affect the fetus. For example, the use of quinine for the treatment of malaria in pregnant women can result in congenital deafness in the child. In addition, it has recently been found that other drugs which are commonly administered to pregnant women for therapeutic reasons may have deleterious effects. Maternal ingestion of reserpine, a tranquilizer, may lead to infant respiratory problems. Some of the drugs (such as the tetracyclines) used to combat maternal infections may depress infant skeletal growth. The intake of certain anticonvulsant drugs has been related to cleft lip and palate and problems in blood coagulation in the neonate. Even the common aspirin, if taken in high doses by pregnant women, may produce blood disorders in offspring (Schnoll, 1986; Vorhees & Mollnow, 1987).

HEROIN, METHADONE, LSD AND COCAINE

In this "turned-on" age, the prenatal effects of drugs such as heroin, morphine, methadone, cocaine, and LSD (lysergic acid diethylamide) are of increasing concern (see Box 4-2). Mothers who are heroin or morphine addicts or who use marijuana or cocaine have offspring who are also addicted or who have toxic effects from the drugs and are observed to go through withdrawal symptoms such as irritability, vomiting, trembling, shrill crying, rapid respiration, and hyperactivity, which may result in death in the first few days of life (Brazelton, 1970; Chasnoff, Griffith, MacGregor, Dirkes, & Burns, 1989; Householder, Hatcher, Burns, & Chasnoff, 1982; Lester & Dreher, 1989; Ostrea, Chavez, & Strauss, 1979; Vorhees & Mollnow, 1987; Zuckerman et al., 1989).

These symptoms may modify patterns of mother-infant interaction. Although these symptoms in addicted babies are likely to elicit increased attending from the caregiver, when these infants are held, they do not mold or cuddle readily. In addition, physically stimulating or placing the infant on an adult shoulder, which leads to alertness in normal babies, has little effect on addicted babies. Clinging, alerting, and eye contact are the main behaviors by which infants initiate and sustain social interactions with the caregiver (Field, 1990). The lack of these behaviors in addicted newborns may disrupt parenting and have long-term adverse outcomes for parent-child relationships. Moreover, these drug-using mothers may have difficulty in dealing with their stressful infants because they have so many problems of their own.

Female addicts seem to have reduced fertility; however, when they do

BOX 4-2 COCAINE BABIES

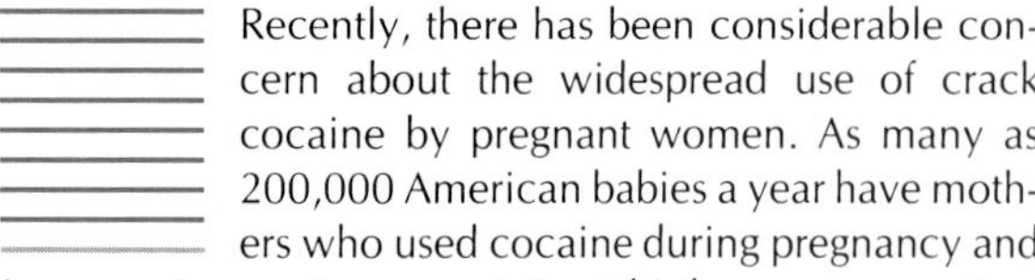

Recently, there has been considerable concern about the widespread use of crack cocaine by pregnant women. As many as 200,000 American babies a year have mothers who used cocaine during pregnancy and in some inner-city areas 1 in 4 births are to cocaine-addicted mothers (Atkins, 1988). Barry Lester reports that there are two common patterns found in the children of cocaine-using mothers. One pattern is characterized by excitable, irritable behavior, and high-pitched prolonged crying. This pattern seems to be associated with direct toxic effects of cocaine on the neurological system that speeds up response time and triggers the cry. It is also associated with irregular, accelerated heart beat, high blood pressure, and constriction in the upper airways. The second pattern is one of *depressed unresponsive behavior* with fewer and lower amplitude crying. This is an indirect result of the effects of cocaine use and is related to low birthweight and stunted growth.

Some children show a combination of both syndromes. These children appear lethargic and sleep a great deal but once they wake up they scream and are difficult to sooth. Although there are few studies of the long-term effects of cocaine use, some of these children appear to be impulsive, highly distractible, difficult to control, and to have problems in language development as they grow older. Communication problems are the most consistently identified deficit. It should be emphasized that not all mothers who take cocaine have babies with developmental delays or anomalies and that many symptoms in early infancy may be temporary.

Sources: Adler, A. (1990). Cocaine babies' reactions explored. *APA Monitor*, p. 8; Dixon, S. D. (1991). *Infants exposed perinatally to cocaine or methamphetamine demonstrate behavioral and neurophysiologic changes*. Paper presented at the meeting of the Society for Research in Child Development, Seattle, WA; Lester, B. M. (1991). *Neurobehavioral syndromes in cocaine exposed newborn infants*. Paper presented at the meeting of the Society for Research in Child Development, Seattle, WA.

conceive, their infants are often premature and of low birthweight, which makes them even less prepared to cope with the trauma of withdrawal symptoms (Eriksson, Catz, & Yaffe, 1973; Zuckerman et al., 1989). The severity of the neonate's symptoms are related to how sustained and intense the mother's addiction has been. If the mother stops taking drugs in the months preceding birth, the infant is usually not affected in this way (Chasnoff et al., 1989).

There has been a great controversy in the past two decades over the use of methadone as a less deleterious substitute for heroin. It has been found that the use of methadone by pregnant women leads to withdrawal symptoms in their infants that are believed by some experts to be even more severe than those resulting from heroin.

The evidence for the adverse effects of LSD during pregnancy is less conclusive than that for heroin and cocaine. Chromosomal breakages have been found in both humans and animals exposed to high and sustained doses of LSD. In animal studies some developmental anomalies have been associated with LSD, but in human studies no firm conclusions can be drawn about the relation between defects in children and maternal use of LSD (Eriksson et al., 1973). In studies of maternal use of LSD, as in those of other illegally used drugs, it is difficult to isolate the specific effects of the drugs. Frequently, these mothers have been multiple-drug users, are malnourished, and may have poor prenatal and delivery care, all of which could contribute to producing anomalies in their infants.

NICOTINE AND ALCOHOL

It is estimated that over 80 percent of pregnant women in the United States drink alcohol and over 30 percent smoke. Although many pregnant women might avoid using hallucinogens, others would be reluctant to consider giving up their evening glass of wine or cocktails or cutting down on cigarettes for the sake of their unborn children. How wise is this?

Both smoking and drinking are associated with disturbances in placental functioning and changes in maternal physiology that lead to oxygen deprivation and structural and functional changes in the brain of the fetus (Abel, 1982; Zuckerman, 1988).

The rate of abortions, prematurity, and low-birthweight babies is higher for mothers who smoke or drink than for those who do not (Aaronson & MacNee, 1989; Zuckerman, 1988). In addition, sudden infant death syndrome (SIDS), in which infants under the age of 6 months stop breathing and die, is more common in the offspring of mothers who smoke, drink, or take narcotics (Stechler & Halton, 1982). Women who are chronic smokers have premature infants almost twice as often as do nonsmokers; also, the rate of prematurity is directly related to the amount of maternal smoking. Even with full-term babies, infants of nonsmokers are heavier (Meredith, 1975) and less wakeful (Landesman-Dwyer & Sackett, 1983) than those of smokers. In observing such findings, Bernard (1962) has commented that "the choice between a desiccated weed and well cultivated seed often seems to be a quite difficult one" (p. 43).

Reports of abnormalities in the growth of children of alcoholic mothers can be found as early as 1800, when concern was expressed that the high consumption of gin, euphemistically known as "mother's ruin," in English women was leading to increased rates of dwarfism in their offspring. More recently, a malformation syndrome called the *fetal alcohol syndrome* has been discovered in one-third of infants of alcoholic mothers. These infants have a high incidence of facial, heart, and limb defects, are 20 percent shorter than average, and are often mentally retarded (Jones, Smith, Ulleland, & Streissguth, 1973; Aaronson & MacNee, 1989; Streissguth, Sampson, & Barr, 1989). The mental retardation may be related to apneic periods, that is, periods

Smoking and the consumption of alcohol by pregnant women may have adverse effects on the developing fetus.

where breathing movements cease in the fetus. It has been demonstrated that the intake of only an ounce of 80-proof vodka by women who were not heavy drinkers results in cessation of fetal breathing movements for over half an hour for many fetuses in the last trimester of pregnancy (Fox et al., 1978). In addition, many children with the fetal alcohol syndrome exhibit abnormal behaviors such as excessive irritability, hyperactivity, distractibility, tremulousness, and stereotyped motor behaviors such as head banging or body rocking, a failure to habituate to repeated stimuli, and deficits in the operant conditioning of head turning and sucking (Streissguth et al., 1989). The shaking, vomiting, and extreme irascibility of babies born to alcoholic mothers is caused by the withdrawal of alcohol from the addicted infant and is similar to the symptoms of delirium tremens found in adult alcoholics. It also has been suggested that heavy drinking in men may result in genetic damage that leads to birth defects in their offspring ("A man's drinking," 1975).

The fetal damage from alcohol appears to be greatest in the last trimester of pregnancy. If pregnant women who are heavy drinkers or smokers can cease drinking in this period, their babies are longer, weigh more, and have a larger head circumference than those of women who continue their heavy drinking (Rosett, Weiner, Zuckerman, McKinlay, & Edelin, 1980; Aaronson & MacNee, 1989).

It would be easy to minimize the implications of these studies by saying that disruptions in the behavior of infants occur only when the mother is an alcoholic rather than a moderate social drinker. However, abnormal behavior patterns have also been found in the infants of mothers who are social drinkers with a relatively modest maternal intake of alcohol, the equivalent of two-thirds of a drink of liquor or three-fourths of a drink of beer or wine per day (Streissguth et al., 1989). Furthermore, studies of older children indicate that cognitive deficits and lower IQs and academic achievement and attention problems are sustained in many children of mothers who smoke or drink (Barr, Streissguth, Darby, & Sampson, 1990; Streissguth et al., 1989). Finally, there seems to be an increased chance of developmental deviations if mothers both smoke and drink. Infants whose mothers use both alcohol and tobacco show greater prenatal growth deficiencies than do infants whose mothers use only alcohol or only tobacco (Little, 1975).

Recent studies have indicated that passive smoking effects found in the presence of a husband, friends, or coworkers who smoke can also contribute to low birthweight in the offspring of nonsmoking mothers (Martin & Bracken, 1986; Schwartz-Bickenbach, Sculte-Hobein, Abt, Plum, & Nau, 1987). Thus the hazards of smoking may be difficult even for a nonsmoking pregnant woman to avoid.

LABOR AND DELIVERY MEDICATION

Recently, concern has been focused on the administration of drugs to ease pain and sedate women during labor. Short-term effects of moderate-to-heavy obstetric medication on the newborn child have been demonstrated, although light levels of medication show few effects (Tronick et al., 1975). Genetic factors, the physiological condition of the mother, length of labor, birth order, size of the baby, and even maternal attitudes may modify the impact of obstetrical medications on the newborn (Horowitz et al., 1977; Lester, Als, & Brazelton, 1982). Offspring of mothers who received certain drugs during labor show a decrease in responsiveness and in cortical activity for several days after birth, disruptions in feeding responses, general neonatal depression, and behavioral disorganization (Brackbill, McManus, & Woodward, 1985). In fact, obstetrical medication results in impairment of attention and motor abilities that is still present at 1 month of age; however, longer-term effects are often not obtained.

How do mothers who receive a large amount of medication respond to the more lethargic, less adaptable, and less attentive behavior in their children? They attempt to stimulate and arouse their infants by touching and rocking and trying to get them to suck and attend (Brazelton, Nugent, & Lester, 1987; Parke, O'Leary, & West, 1972; Richards & Bernal, 1971). It can be imagined that this could be a rather frustrating experience with a sedated, unresponsive infant. These effects may be compounded since, although the neonate's deviant behavior may contribute to increased maternal anxiety, it may already have been the most anxious mothers who asked for or needed high levels of medication during labor and delivery.

What can we conclude from the research on maternal drug intake and fetal development? The effects of drugs are difficult to predict. Many of the drugs which produce unfortunate effects had been tested on animals and nonpregnant adults and found to be harmless. We cannot make valid generalizations from tests performed on animals and human adults to the rapidly developing fetus since teratogens may affect different species at different stages of development in diverse ways. The problems in prediction are increased by the wide individual differences in infants and mothers in vulnerability to drug effects. In addition, there is little research on the long-term effects of maternal drug intake. However, it is apparent that great caution should be used in the ingestion of drugs by women during pregnancy and labor.

Hormones

DIETHYLSTILBESTROL (DES)

An example of a hormone administered to pregnant women that had a tragic and delayed aftermath is the synthetic hormone diethylstilbestrol (DES). This hormone was frequently prescribed between 1947 and 1964 as an aid in preventing miscarriages. It is estimated that as many as 2 million women have taken DES. In the late 1960s it was found that many female offspring of women who had taken DES during pregnancy were developing vaginal abnormalities and cancer of the cervix (Nevin, 1988). This is notable for the delayed effects of the drug, which did not usually appear until the girls reached adolescence. It has been discovered that the adverse effects of DES are also manifested in a high rate of unfavorable outcomes of pregnancies, such as low birthweight, abortion, and prematurity, when these daughters who were exposed to DES in utero reach childbearing age (Linn et al., 1988). Although it was at first believed that the adverse effects of DES were confined to female offspring, it is now recognized that sons of women who ingested DES during pregnancy may have not only abnormalities of the reproductive tract but also seminal fluid abnormalities, fertility problems, and an increased risk of cancer of the testes (Herbst, 1981; Stillman, 1982).

Maternal Diet

It is difficult to separate the effects of maternal malnourishment from those of a variety of other deleterious factors. The mother who is malnourished often exists in an environment of poverty and disadvantage characterized by poor education, inferior sanitation and shelter, and inadequate medical care. In this country, malnutrition and high maternal and infant mortality are associated not only with socioeconomic factors but also with ethnicity. People who are both nonwhite and poor are exposed to more of these harmful environmental factors and experience more of their destructive effects. In the United States, nonwhites tend to be less affluent, begin childbearing early and end it later, have more births to unwed mothers, and have poorer diets and poorer prenatal and delivery care. Adverse prenatal conditions are followed by the environment of poverty, which sustains and compounds their effects.

Studies on a variety of populations have shown that gross dietary deficiencies, especially of some vitamins and protein, in the diets of pregnant women are related to increased rates of abortions, prematurity, stillbirths, infant mortality, physical and neural defects, and smaller size in their infants.

Studies of severely malnourished animals and infants suggest that early malnutrition may interfere with the development of the nervous system, and again we find that the specific form the damage takes depends on the age at which malnutrition occurs.

In the prenatal period and in the first 6 months of life the brain grows mainly by cell division; after that time it grows through the intake of fats and proteins, not by the formation of additional cells (Winick, 1970). Autopsies on malnourished animals and children suggest that early malnutrition leads to a decreased number of cells in the brain and disruption in myelination, the development of an insulating fatty sheath around nerves, which facilitates the speed of transmission of neural impulses (Davison & Dobbing, 1966).

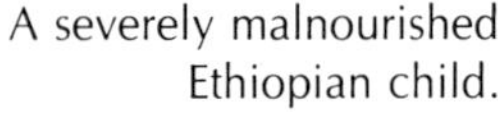

A severely malnourished Ethiopian child.

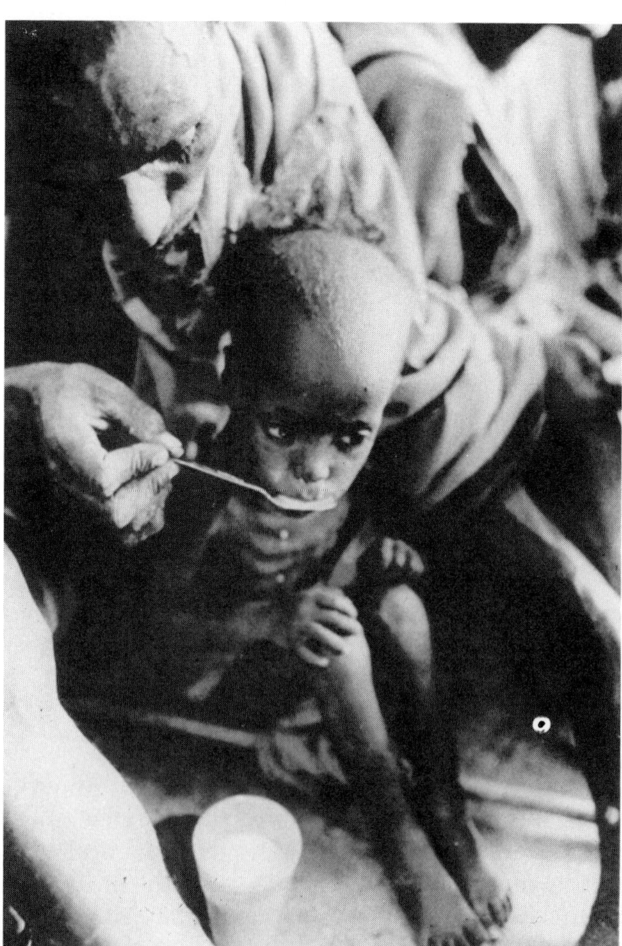

Later dietary deficiencies result in decreases in the size of the brain cells. Autopsies on the brains of malnourished children in other countries and on lower-class urban American infants who were stillborn or died within forty-eight hours of birth, found that the brains of malnourished children weighed 15 percent less than those of children from more affluent families (Naeye, Diener, & Dellinger, 1969). In addition to changes in brain structure and weight resulting from maternal malnutrition, chemical changes in the brain and abnormal electrical brainwave patterns have been found in the brains of malnourished infants. What really is not clearly understood is the relationship between these changes and mental development and how reversible these effects may be.

Impairment of intellectual development in children associated with prenatal malnutrition appears most marked when the mother has a history of dietary deprivation, when the malnutrition has been severe and long lasting, and when the effects are sustained by adverse nutritional, social, and economic factors following birth. It seems to be this network of deleterious factors associated with prenatal malnutrition that leads to continued ill effects on the child. Studies of short-term periods of famine attributable to such things as war suggest that there are no long-lasting intellectual deficits found in children if previously well-nourished mothers go through a temporary period of malnourishment during pregnancy and the child has a reasonably good diet and responsive caretakers following birth (Stein & Susser, 1976; Winick, Knarig, & Harris, 1975). The effects of malnutrition seem to be greatest on social and motor development (Barrett, Radke-Yarrow, & Klein, 1982; Joos, Pollitt, Mueller, & Albright, 1983). When apparent cognitive problems or school difficulties are encountered, they are often mediated by such factors as attention, responsiveness, motivation, emotionality, energy, and activity.

Although dietary supplements provided to severely malnourished women during pregnancy have been successful in reducing stillbirths, delivery problems, and mortality, and in increasing the birthweight of infants, their positive effects on marginally malnourished women and their offspring are less clear. Not all nutrients that are consumed are absorbed and utilized by the body. The placenta plays a remarkable role in adjusting maternal utilization of nutrients to assure better fetal support. Total iron needs in the last half of gestation are so high that if the standard rate of absorption of dietary iron were maintained it would require an impossible consumption of 50 mg per day of iron by a pregnant woman. Fortunately, iron absorption increases during pregnancy by as much as 30 percent, making a reasonable dietary supply of iron feasible. In addition, excretory loss of iron is reduced because the pregnant woman is not menstruating. There is some evidence that supplemental iron may pose a risk to an iron-sufficient, healthy, pregnant woman and her fetus. Until more is known about these changes in dietary absorption, dietary supplements of pregnant women who are not severely malnourished need to be approached with caution (Truss, 1981).

As was found in the effects of drugs, effects of prenatal malnutrition may be mediated by tired, malnourished parents being rejecting or nonsupportive and withdrawing from irritable or nonresponsive, malnourished infants (Lozoff, 1989). In addition to intervention programs for malnourished, low socioeconomic status children focusing on dietary supplements, many successful intervention programs have focused on training economically deprived parents to interact with their children in a more sensitive, involved, stimulating, and responsive manner (Grantham-McGregor, Schofield, & Powell, 1987; Zeskind, & Ramey, 1978, 1981).

Maternal Emotional State

The causal factors in the frequently cited finding that emotionally disturbed women produce disturbed children are difficult to isolate (Istvan, 1986). It might be attributable to genetic transmission of emotional characteristics or to the fact that emotionality in a pregnant woman induces metabolic or biochemical changes, such as alterations in adrenalin level, which affect the fetus. It also seems probable that the woman who is emotionally disturbed during pregnancy is also more likely to be an emotionally unstable and inadequate caretaker following pregnancy when she will be the main social influence on the infant. Emotional stress in women may therefore be a contributing factor to both problems in pregnancy and delivery and later intellectual and emotional deviations in offspring. Genetic or prenatal factors or early infant learning and experiences could all play a role in the findings of the following studies.

Maternal emotional disturbance has been related to complications during both pregnancy and delivery. High maternal anxiety has been associated with nausea during pregnancy, prematurity, abortion, prolonged labor, delivery complications, and higher use of anesthesia during childbirth. It might be expected that greater emotional stress would be found in women having psychiatrically diagnosed emotional disorders. Sameroff and Zax (1973) compared the difficulties during pregnancy and delivery of normal women and women diagnosed as schizophrenic, neurotic depressive, and personality disordered. Normal women had fewer difficulties during pregnancy and delivery than the women with severe emotional problems. However, there were no differences in the frequency of perinatal complications among the disturbed groups. The occurrence of obstetrical problems was related to the severity of disturbance rather than the psychiatric classification. Those who had the most prolonged history of emotional disturbance with the most frequent contacts with psychiatrists and hospitalization, regardless of diagnostic classification, had the most perinatal difficulties.

The effects of stress are likely to be moderated by the support available to the pregnant women. One study found that when pregnant women were going through severe life stresses, those with supportive relatives and friends had only a 33 percent rate of complications in pregnancy and birth in comparison to a 91 percent rate for those lacking in social support (Nickolls, Cassel, & Kaplan, 1972).

In a clever experimental study, the effects on labor and delivery of the presence of a supportive companion were shown (Sosa, Kennell, Klaus, Robertson, & Urrutia, 1980). The childbirth experiences of a group of healthy Guatemalan women in a hospital in which no relatives or friends were usually permitted to be present were studied. The women in the experimental group were assigned a supportive companion who talked to them, reassured them, rubbed their backs, and held their hands until delivery. The control group went through the normal hospital routine with no supportive person present. The mean length of labor was 19.3 hours for the control group and 8.7 hours for the women in the experimental group with a supportive companion. In addition, the mothers provided with emotional support had fewer problems, such as the need for cesarean sections, and their infants were less likely to experience fetal distress. One of the strengths of this study is the random assignment of mothers to the supportive or nonsupportive condition. It might be argued that it would be more valid to study deliveries in which the father chooses or does not choose to be present during labor and birth. However, fathers who choose to be present may have very different personalities, attitudes, and relationships with their wives than those who prefer to be absent.

Women who are anxious and emotionally disturbed during pregnancy have infants who are physically more active in utero. These infants also are hyperactive, irritable, cry more, and have feeding and sleep problems after birth. Such stresses during pregnancy as marital discord, fears about marriage, moving to a new locality, the woman's father becoming ill or dying, and unwanted pregnancy have been related to infant morbidity (Stott & Latchford, 1976). It has even been argued that stress in the first trimester of pregnancy may lead to biochemical changes that inhibit the normal spontaneous abortion of malformed fetuses (Stott, 1971). More frequent reports of intense emotional stress during pregnancy are made by women who subsequently bear children with Down syndrome, nonfamilial (thus unanticipated) cleft lip and palate, and infantile pyloric stenosis, a disorder involving a tightening of the stomach outlet (Drillien, Ingram, & Wilkinson, 1966; Drillien & Wilkinson, 1964; Revill & Dodge, 1978).

The disturbance and apprehension of women during pregnancy may just be selected symptoms in a broader continuing pattern of maladjustment, and this pattern of disturbance may be continued later in the handling of their infants. Women who have positive attitudes toward pregnancy have had happy childhoods and close family relationships and regard themselves as currently having satisfying marital, sexual, and social relationships; the reverse is true of women who have negative attitudes toward pregnancy.

Maternal Age and Parity

The development of offspring is related both to the age of the mother and to maternal parity, or the number of children she has borne, and these two factors interact. Women who have their first child when they are over age 35, or under 15, are likely to experience more problems during pregnancy and difficulties and complications during delivery than other women. It was thought that this was attributable to immaturity of the reproductive system in young teenagers and deterioration in the reproductive system in older mothers. It is now recognized that these risks in both groups are more closely associated with maternal health than with age. Since many teenaged mothers are of low socioeconomic status they often suffer from poor nutrition, a lack of prenatal care, and an environment with high rates of disease and environmental pollutants. They therefore encounter greater health risks. Teenaged mothers with adequate diets and prenatal care do not show higher rates of complications in birth or pregnancy than mothers in their twenties (Baker & Mednick, 1984; Robertson, 1981; Roosa, 1984). Similarly, in older mothers it is emerging health risks, such as the increase in hypertension, diabetes, alcoholism, and other health problems with age, that contribute to difficulties in pregnancy and birth. Healthy mothers over 35 are unlikely to have such complications (Spellacy, Miller, & Winegar, 1986).

ANTENATAL DIAGNOSIS

Parents concerned about genetic or developmental anomalies in their unborn child have several methods of antenatal diagnosis available to them. In amniocentesis, a needle is inserted into the amniotic sac, which surrounds the fetus, and fluid is removed. This fluid contains the cells that have been sloughed off by the fetus. In *chorionic villi biopsy* the sample is taken from the

BOX 4-3 THE CAT IN THE HAT IN THE UTERINE SAC: PRENATAL LEARNING

Thus far we have been emphasizing negative factors that affect prenatal development. However, recently a remarkable series of studies has been conducted by DeCasper indicating that children may be able to learn in utero. It all began when DeCasper asked himself why newborn human babies perceived sound so well. He wondered if they listened in the womb. A preposterous thought? If not, how would a good psychologist go about testing such a proposition? DeCasper and his colleague, Fifer (1980), designed a clever procedure where babies could suck to control what they heard on a tape recorder, either their mother's voice or the voice of a strange woman. As you will learn in the chapter on infancy, neonates are able to learn to vary their patterns of sucking. In this study, when infants sucked in a pattern of longer and shorter bursts, they activated their mother's voice on the tape recorder; a different sucking pattern activated the stranger's voice. It was found that infants sucked to hear their own mother's voice in preference to the voice of the stranger. Now it could be argued that the infants probably heard their mother's voice from the time of birth and could have learned to prefer it in the first few days or hours of life! In order to rule out this early postnatal familiarity hypothesis, DeCasper and Spence (1986) designed another study in which sixteen pregnant women were asked to read Dr. Seuss's famous children's book *The Cat in the Hat* to their fetuses twice a day for the last $6\frac{1}{2}$ weeks of pregnancy. The mothers might have felt a little foolish but some remarkable results occurred. After birth, when infants could suck in one distinctive pattern to hear their mother's tape-recorded voice read *The Cat in the Hat,* or another pattern to hear them read *The King, the Mice and the Cheese,* they sucked to hear *The Cat in the Hat*. Both books are long poems but with very different meters. In this study, since both poems were read by mothers in the postnatal test condition, it was not the mother's voice itself but the mother's voice reading the poem to which the infants had been prenatally exposed that they preferred. This is evidence that prenatal auditory experiences influence postnatal auditory preferences, although the exact mechanisms involved in the prenatal learning are not well understood. The sound in utero coming through the mother's body and the amniotic fluid must be qualitatively different from the mother's voice heard after birth. It seems likely that the component of maternal speech to which the fetus responds is *prosody*. Prosody includes the rhythm, intonation, and stress in speech and is carried by the frequencies that are least altered in the prenatal environment. There is accumulating evidence that newborns may exhibit a postnatal preference for a specific passage or melody experienced prenatally (DeCasper & Spence, 1986; DeCasper & Spence, 1992; Fifer & Moon, 1989). The results of these studies will probably precipitate a rush of pregnant women to their tape decks to serenade their unborn infants with their favorite music. A little Bach today, baby?

Sources: DeCasper, A. J., & Fifer, W. (1980). Of human bonding: Newborns prefer their mothers' voices. *Science,* **208,** 1174–1176; DeCasper, A. J., & Spence, M. (1986). Newborns prefer a familiar story over an unfamiliar one. *Infant Behavior and Development,* **9,** 133–150; DeCasper, A. J., & Spence, M. (1992). Auditorily mediated behavior during the perinatal period: A cognitive view. In *Newborn attention: Biological constraints and the influence of experience.* Norwood, NJ: Ablex; Fifer, W. P., & Moon, C. (1989). Auditory experience in the fetus. In W. P. Smotherman & S. R. Robinson (Eds.), *Behavior of the fetus* (pp. 175–187). Caldwell, NJ: Telford Press.

chorion, the outer wall of the membrane in which the fetus develops. Since each cell contains the genetic blueprint of the individual, these cells can be examined for the presence of certain chromosomal and metabolic disorders. The sixteenth week of pregnancy seems to be the best time to perform amniocentesis. At that time there are sufficient fetal cells in the amniotic fluid and the fetus is still small and unlikely to be injured. In addition it is still early enough in the pregnancy to permit safe abortion. Chorionic villi biopsy can be performed on the ninth to tenth week of pregnancy, considerably earlier than is possible with amniocentesis. This gives the parents the option of an earlier abortion if fetal abnormalities are detected.

Another form of prenatal diagnosis that is often used when a structural malformation is suspected is ultrasound sonography. In *ultrasound sonography* high-frequency sound waves are directed into the abdomen of the pregnant woman and the echo from these sounds is transformed into a visual representation of inner structures such as the uterus, placenta, and fetus. Such disorders as microcephaly, involving abnormal retardation in brain growth and skull size, and anencephaly, in which parts of the brain are

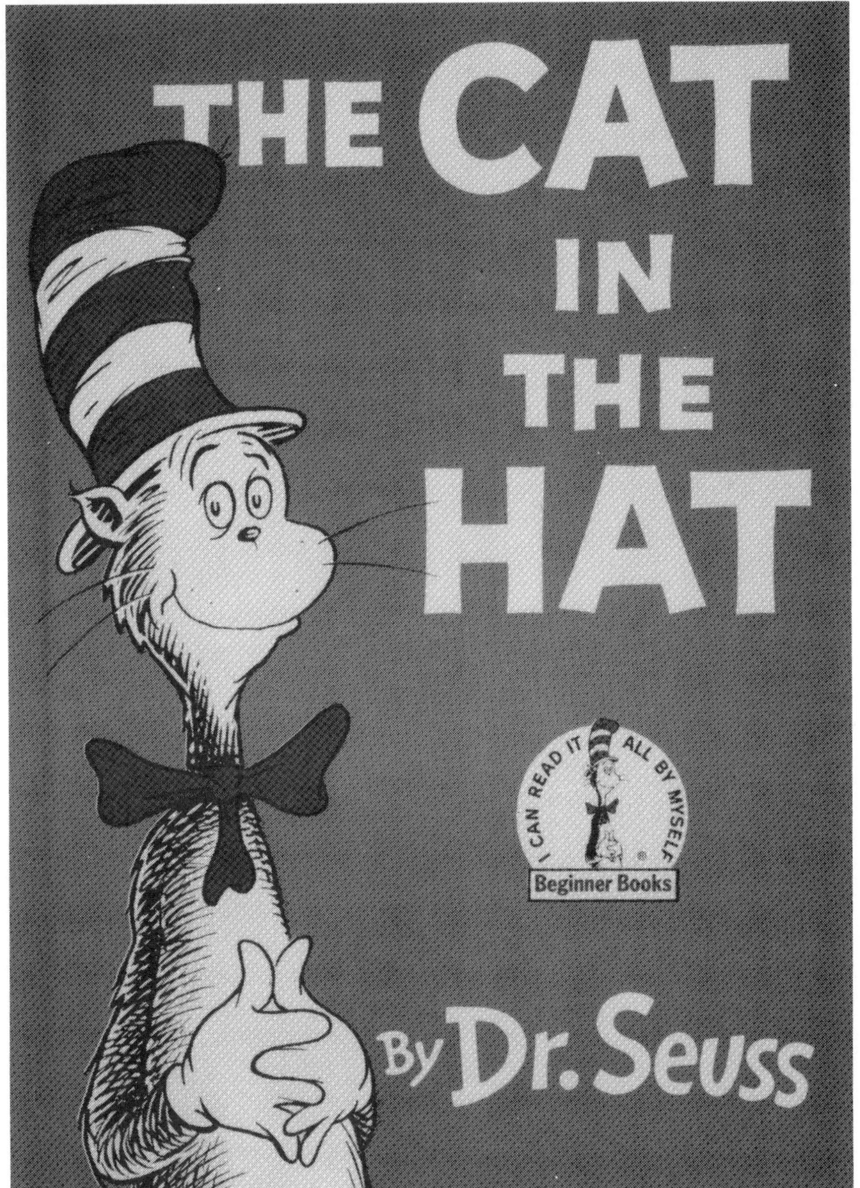

Infants who heard *The Cat in the Hat* prenatally preferred to hear it after birth.

missing, have been detected through sonography. This technique reduces the necessity for x-rays, is noninvasive, and produces no discomfort in the pregnant woman (National Institutes of Health, 1979).

BIRTH

Birth is one of the most dramatic and significant events in the lives of parents and children. The last few weeks of pregnancy are characterized in parents by joyous anticipation and especially in first births, also by apprehension about labor and childbirth, anxiety about whether the child will be normal, and concern about whether the mother will be permanently altered physically by pregnancy and delivery. Although both parents are exhausted by the process of birth, most are exhilarated, even awestruck in seeing and holding

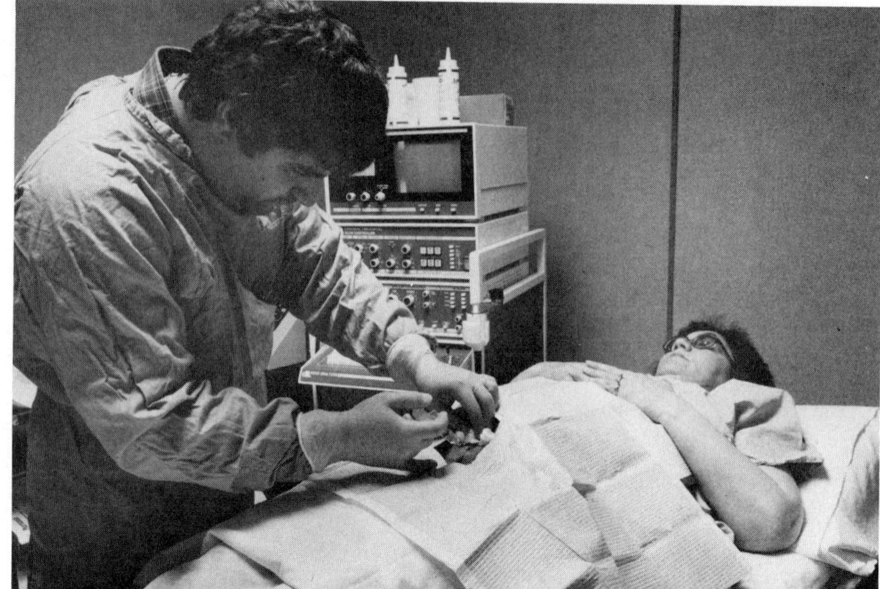

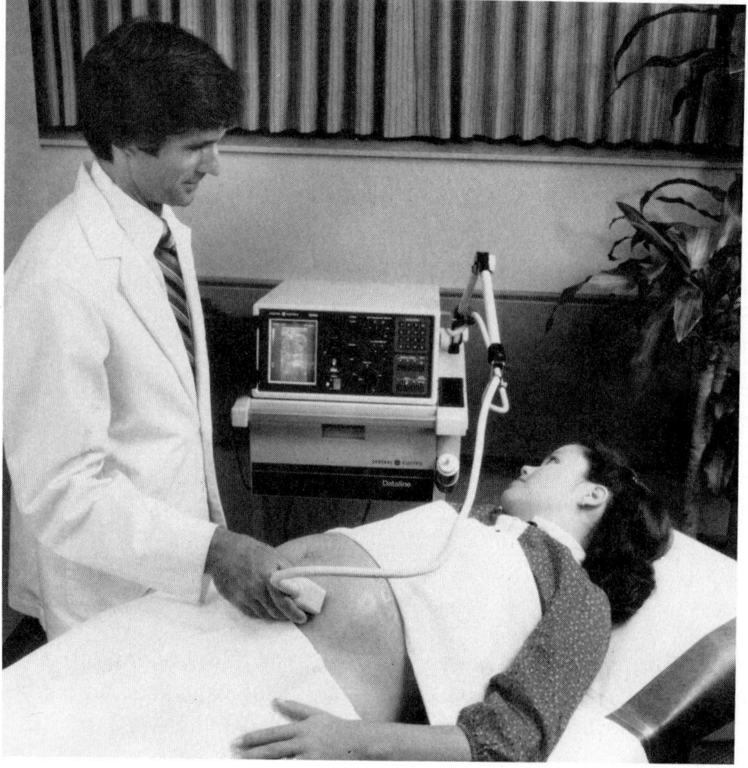

New diagnostic methods used to detect possible abnormalities in the developing fetus. The woman above is undergoing amniocentesis; the woman below is having an ultrasound examination.

their newborn for the first time. One new father said, "When I come up to see my wife . . . I go look at the kid and then I pick her up and put her down . . . I keep going back to the kid. It's like a magnet. That's what I can't get over, the fact that I feel like that" (Greenberg & Morris, 1974, p. 524).

Birth is also a momentous physical and social transition for the infant. The infant moves from the warm, wet, dark environment of the amniotic sac to the dry, cooler, bright environment of an external world full of changing lights, objects, movements, touches, voices, and faces. Even before birth, during pregnancy, the parents and child have established a relationship, and following birth the construction of this relationship becomes more intense and accelerated.

The Three Stages of Birth

Birth involves a series of changes in the mother that permits the child to move from the womb and be pushed out into the external world. There are three stages in the birth process.

The *first stage* of labor begins as the mother experiences regular uterine contractions usually spaced at ten- to fifteen-minute intervals and concludes when the cervix is dilated sufficiently to permit the movement of the infant's head out through the cervix into the vagina. Uterine contractions become more intense and frequent as labor progresses. This stage lasts about eight to fourteen hours for firstborn children and half of that for later-born children.

The *second stage* of labor occurs as the child descends through the birth canal and terminates at birth. This stage usually lasts less than an hour.

The *third and final stage* of birth involves expulsion of the placenta and takes only a few minutes.

Cesarean Births

The rate of cesarean deliveries, in which the baby is removed through an incision in the mother's abdomen and uterus, increased from 5 to 25 percent of births in the past three decades. Concern has been raised that the rate of cesarean deliveries is unnecessarily high and that there may be unforseen long-term adverse consequences of caesareans.

Cesarean births place mothers at greater risk of infection and involve longer hospital stays. In addition, cesarean babies are exposed to more maternal medication during delivery and have somewhat more trouble breathing and are less responsive and wakeful than other neonates (Trevarthan, 1987). However, short-term studies of the effects of cesarean births on infant development suggest that there are few effects on cognitive or neurological outcomes and that in the long run parents may have higher expectations for cesarean children (Entwisle & Alexander, 1987).

Although early mother-child interactions may be adversely affected, by the time the children are 1 year old these relationships are positive (Reilly, Entwisle, & Doering, 1987). One advantage of cesarean birth is that, because of the longer recovery period in mothers following a cesarean delivery, fathers are more involved with their infants in the first few months than are fathers whose wives have gone through a traditional delivery (Pedersen, Zaslow, Cain, & Anderson, 1981).

Natural Childbirth

Delivery in the relatively isolated unfamiliar setting of a hospital separated from relatives, often even from the husband, began as a response to the rise in health problems, and infant and maternal mortality associated with urbanization and industrialization in the nineteenth century. There has been a recent move to make pregnancy and birth a more shared family experience and even to have births occur in the home or in more homey birthing centers. Home deliveries by trained personnel or delivery in a birthing center are suitable for normal births; however, between 15 and 25 percent of women who begin labor in such settings are subsequently moved to a hospital because of birth complications (Baruffi, 1982).

Fathers are encouraged to participate with their wives in prepared childbirth classes involving relaxation techniques, and almost all hospitals now permit fathers in the delivery room. The presence of a supportive adult does reduce the incidence of labor and delivery problems and makes the mother feel more positively about birth (Entwisle & Doering, 1981; Lindell, 1988). The effects of being present at delivery on fathers are less clear and seem to depend on the quality of the birth experience and whether the father really wanted to be there. Although being present at the birth may improve the quality of the marital relationship, it is neither necessary nor sufficient to promote the closeness of fathers to their infants (Palkovitz, 1985).

One of the difficulties in interpreting many of these studies is that parents who go into natural childbirth classes, who want to avoid hospital deliveries and anesthetics, and who wish to have the father present at the birth may have very different attitudes, personalities, and relationships than those who do not. These characteristics and relationships, rather than the birth situation, may modify later behavior of both parents and children.

Complications of Birth

Although labor and birth are normal processes in human development and in the majority of cases occur with no lasting adverse influences, they sometimes do deleteriously affect the infant. More males than females are born with anomalies. This has been attributed in part to the role of the sex chromosomes (discussed in the previous chapter) and in part to the larger size of, and hence greater pressure on, a male's head during birth. The majority of infants do not suffer serious impairment at birth, however. Less than 10 percent have any type of abnormality, and many of these disappear during the subsequent course of development.

Important birth factors that are related to developmental deviations and infant mortality are anoxia (lack of oxygen in the brain) and prematurity and low birthweight. In early studies, an infant weighing less than 5½ pounds was classed as premature; however, the sole use of weight as an indicator of prematurity has been criticized, and some investigators are now considering criteria such as weight relative to stature of the parent, gestational age, nutritional condition of the mother, and a variety of skeletal, neurological, and biochemical indexes of maturity (Drillien, 1964; Mitchell & Farr, 1965).

One of the methods frequently used to assess the condition of the newborn infant is the Apgar scoring system (Table 4-2). At one minute and five minutes after birth, the obstetrician or nurse rates the heart rate, respiratory effort, reflex irritability, muscle tone, and body color of the infant. Each of the five signs is given a score of 0, 1, or 2. A high score indicates a more favorable condition. A total score of 7 to 10 indicates that the neonate is in good condition, a score below 5 indicates that there may be possible developmental difficulties, and a score of 3 or lower indicates that immediate emergency steps are necessary and that there may be a problem in survival.

Anoxia

All infants undergo some oxygen deprivation and retention of carbon dioxide during the birth process; however, infants born with no complications during

TABLE 4-2

APGAR EVALUATION OF THE NEWBORN INFANT

SIGN	SCORE 0	1	2
Heart rate	Absent	Less than 100 beats per minute	100 to 140 beats per minute
Respiratory effort	No breathing for more than one minute	Slow and irregular	Good respiration with normal crying
Muscle tone	Limp and flaccid	Some flexion of the extremities	Good flexion, active motion
Reflex irritability	No response	Some motion	Vigorous response to stimulation
Color	Blue or pale body and extremities	Body pink with blue extremities	Pink all over

Source: Adapted from Apgar (1953).

birth and with an average duration of labor of six to ten hours show fewest detrimental effects. Abnormalities in the mother and adverse conditions during labor and delivery can lead to severe anoxia, which results in brain damage, functional defects, or even death of the infant (Stechler & Halton, 1982). However, it has been suggested that anoxia may be a symptom, rather than a cause, of brain damage (Amiel-Tison, 1983). If an infant has a damaged brain because of either genetic factors or an adverse prenatal environment, difficulty in breathing immediately following birth may be just one consequence of the inadequacy of a malfunctioning brain to control a variety of body functions.

Longitudinal studies indicate that the effects of anoxia change or disappear with age. General intellectual and neurological impairments decrease over time. About 90 percent of black and 95 percent of white surviving children who, at birth, had an Apgar score of 3 or less, which is indicative of severe anoxia, have normal levels of intelligence seven years later. Moreover, with the small minority of anoxic children who do show later developmental deviations, such as distractibility, impulsivity, and lack of social adaptability, it is difficult to separate out the contributions of other factors, such as prenatal or genetic factors or low birthweight and low socioeconomic status which may be associated both with low Apgar scores and with developmental delays (National Institutes of Health, 1979).

Prematurity and Low Birthweight

Both extremely low and extremely high birthweights are associated with intellectual impairment. Examination of the findings on low-birthweight children shows that significant impairment in IQ occurs only among children with extremely low birthweights, that is, under $3\frac{1}{2}$ pounds (Kopp, 1983). Cognitive deficits associated with very low birthweights tend to be more enduring than those associated with anoxia. Although most low-birthweight babies catch up in motor and intellectual development by the time they are 4 years old, about 15 percent of those who weighed less than 3 pounds, 5 ounces (1500 grams) and about 30 percent of those weighing less than 2 pounds at birth continue to show some kind of cognitive deficit (Hoy, Bill, & Sykes, 1988; Kitchen, Ford, Richards, Lissenden, & Ryan, 1987; Kopp & Kaler, 1989). Problems in academic achievement, hyperactivity, motor skills, and speech and hearing disorders occur more often in very low-birthweight or premature babies than in maturely born infants. However, the long-term differences are small in most children (Aylward, Pfeiffer, Wright, & Verholst, 1989).

It has been pointed out that behavior associated with prematurity and low birthweight may also be the outcome of a number of related factors, such as delivery complications, the early period of isolation in an incubator, neonatal anomalies other than prematurity, the treatment by parents in response to infants' apparent frailty and small size, and early separation of mother and infant (Kopp & Krakow, 1983; Korner, 1989). Moreover, it should be remembered that many of the extremely low birthweight babies would not have survived fifteen years ago, before the introduction of neonatal intensive care units with specialized treatment procedures, equipment, and highly trained staff. More very sick, very low birthweight infants who require assistance are living, and it is when these high medical risks are compounded by adverse environmental circumstances that long-term developmental deviations may occur.

In attempting to identify the factors that may contribute to differences in development between premature or low weight for gestational-age children and full-term children, let us look at the early experiences of these children and their parents. Most parents look forward to holding, cuddling, and feeding their infants soon after birth and to leaving the hospital within three or four days to assume full care of a healthy, vigorous baby. Instead, in most hospitals, the premature baby is immediately taken from the parents and placed in an isolette where the infant is fed, cleansed, and changed through an opening in the isolette. Parents viewing their premature infants through the glass observation window in the nursery see a tiny, fragile-looking creature. Since the infant is not fully developed and has not formed the layer of subcutaneous fat found on full-term babies, the child appears thin, with wrinkled, transparent skin and a disproportionately large head. When the mother leaves to go home, she goes without her baby. The infant remains in the care of the hospital staff, often for several weeks until he or she is physically mature enough to leave the isolette.

Two aspects of these early experiences have concerned psychologists. The first is that the preterm infant in the early weeks of life in the isolette may be getting less and is certainly getting different sensory and social stimulation than the full-term baby. The second is that the early parent-child separation may disrupt the formation of an affectionate bond between parent and infant.

STIMULATION PROGRAMS FOR LOW-BIRTHWEIGHT BABIES

In order to study these factors, starting in the 1970s, experiments and programs were introduced where the development of preterm babies who received additional stimulation was compared to that of those who did not. Some experimenters have suggested that the stimulation used should approximate the conditions experienced by the infant in utero. Premature infants have been exposed to tape-recorded heartbeats with the sound intensity of that in the uterus of a pregnant woman (Barnard & Bee, 1983),

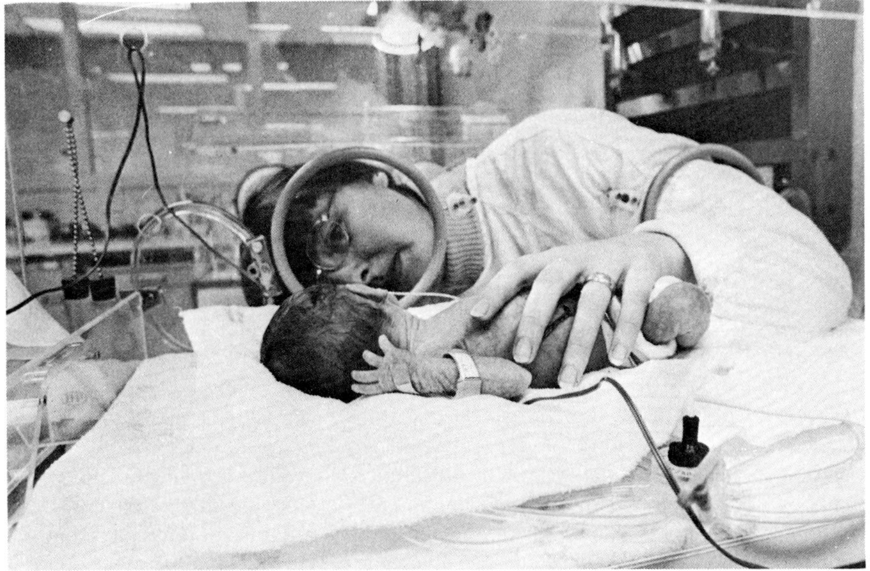

Mother handling premature baby in incubator. Although mother-child contact is established, it can be seen how awkward and atypical this mode of contact is.

or to rocking hammocks (Neal, 1968) or waterbeds within the isolettes (Burns, Deddish, Burns, & Hatcher, 1983; Korner, Kraemer, Hoffner, & Cosper, 1975) that permit rotation, movement, and rhythmical activity similar to the stimulation mediated through fetal flotation and movements in the amniotic fluid. Other investigators have used stimulation characteristic of the experiences of full-term infants such as mobiles, tape recordings of the mother's voice, manual rocking, talking and singing, and handling, cuddling, and stroking (Field et al., 1986; Powell, 1974; Rice, 1977; Scarr-Salapatek & Williams, 1972; Siqueland, 1970; Solkoff, Yaffe, Weintraub, & Blase, 1969). Both types of studies have found that additional stimulation can counteract some of the effects of the monotonous stimulation experienced by infants in isolettes (see Box 4-4). Stimulated premature infants have been found to be more advanced in mental development (Field et al., 1986), in neurological development, as measured by infant reflexes (Barnard & Bee, 1983; Rice, 1977), in sensorimotor and motor skills (Burns et al., 1983), in muscle tonus (Cornell & Gottfried, 1976), and in exploratory behavior, than are unstimulated premature infants. In addition, fewer incidents of apnea (temporary cessation of breathing which has been associated with later crib deaths) are found in stimulated infants (Korner, 1989). It is clear that stimulation has at least a short-term salutary effect on the development of premature infants, but long-term gains are rarely found (Korner, 1989).

Intervention programs facilitate not only the functioning of targeted systems but also of other systems that are about to develop. However, programs must be sensitive to individual differences; not all premature babies benefit from additional stimulation. Children who are ill, are being weaned from ventilators, or who have intensive medical care routines that disrupt their sleep may not respond positively or may actually be distressed by added stimulation (Oehler, Eckerman, & Wilson, 1988). In attending to the needs of different children "the question is no longer whether stimulation for preterm infants is indicated but also stimulation for whom, what kind, how much, at what intervals, at what post-conceptual age, and for what purposes" (Korner, 1989, p. 12).

BOX 4-4 *PSYCHOLOGY IN ACTION* SLEEPING WITH A BREATHING BLUE BEAR

Not everyone might want to sleep with a blue bear but it can have salutary effects for premature infants.

In most of the programs involving stimulation of premature infants the stimulation is imposed on the infant. The infant does not have the option of turning the stimulation on or of avoiding the stimulation. Evelyn Thoman (1987) designed a clever study to investigate whether premature infants can actively seek and regulate stimulation, rather than just being the passive recipients of stimulation, and whether stimulation instigated by the infant will facilitate the infant's developmental progress.

A breathing blue teddy bear was placed in the isolettes of one group of premature infants, a nonbreathing teddy bear in the isolettes of another group, and no bear in the isolettes of a third group. Infants were 32 weeks of conceptual age, or about eight weeks younger than full-term age at the time the study began. The intervention was carried on for three weeks until the infants were 35 weeks of conceptual age.

The breathing bear was designed through the use of a pneumatic pump to breath at a rate individualized for each infant. The bear's breathing was set to match half that of the infant during quiet sleep. Each infant controlled the amount and temporal distribution of stimulation since the infant could either make contact with the bear or not.

The investigator was interested in the amount of time the child spent in contact with the bear or, in the case of the group with no bear, in contact with the area in which the bear was placed in the breathing and nonbreathing bear groups. A second concern was whether contact with the breathing bear would cause the child's breathing to become more regular. Prematurely born infants show considerable respiratory irregularity and their respiration during quiet sleep is disrupted. The percent of available time spent in contact with the bear was 63.4 percent for the breathing bear, 13.3 percent for the nonbreathing bear, and 17.2 percent in the area of the nonbear condition. Even these very young premature babies were able to approach an available and attractive form of stimulation and clearly preferred the stimulation of the breathing bear over the nonbreathing bear. Furthermore, although most people might not think sleeping with a bear could be restful, the premature babies with the breathing bear showed more even respiration and increased quiet sleep than infants in the other two groups. The investigator speculates that this is because the additional stimulation may have influenced the organization of brain processes associated with mature sleep patterns. Structure and function are interactive. Physical and sensory maturity are associated with more advanced behavior; however, stimulating behavior and experiences may also advance physical and sensory development.

Source: Thoman, E. (1987). Self-regulation of stimulation by prematures with a breathing blue bear. In J. Gallagher & C. Ramey (Eds.), *The malleability of children*. Baltimore/London: Paul H. Brookes.

PARENTAL CONTACT AND THE DEVELOPMENT OF LOW-BIRTHWEIGHT INFANTS

It has been suggested that even with full-term babies contact between the mother and neonate in the first few hours of life may facilitate the formation of emotional attachment between mother and child (Klaus & Kennell, 1982). However, most research findings suggest that although early contact is potentially beneficial, it is not critical (Goldberg, 1983). There are many alternative routes or fail safes in the formation of the parent-infant relationship. The most marked effects of increased contact of mothers with their premature babies seems to be in building maternal self-confidence which leads to more sensitive parenting.

Even in modern neonatal intensive care units that encourage involvement between parents and their preterm infants, early contact is less than with full-term infants. Some mothers of premature babies report feelings of loss of self-esteem, guilt, failure, and alienation from their infants. In addition, mothers of premature babies who have been separated from their infants are apprehensive about handling and caring for their fragile-appearing infants. When mothers are eventually able to take their babies home from the hospital, they still show less emotional involvement with them than do mothers of full-term babies (Leifer, Leiderman, Barnett, & Williams, 1972; Lester, Hoffman, &

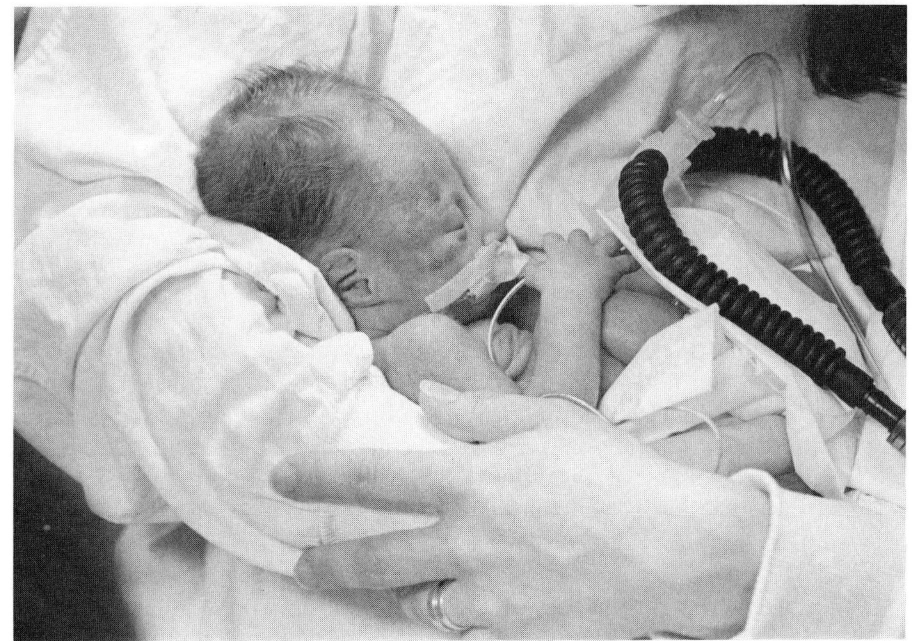

Premature babies whose birthweight is extremely low are most at risk for enduring developmental problems.

Brazelton, 1985; Quinn & Goldberg, 1977). This is especially true of mothers of premature babies who have been sick for over a month after birth (Corter & Minde, 1987). These effects have been found as long as nine months following hospital discharge with economically deprived black mothers and their preterm babies (Brown & Bakeman, 1977).

Suggested evidence of disruption in the affectional bond between mothers and premature infants comes from several sources. First, even when programs are set up to encourage mothers to return to the hospital to handle or care for their premature babies in the isolettes, mothers are sometimes reluctant to participate. Some mothers who have not previously had contact with their infants do not want to take the time required for such programs. In addition, when these mothers do visit their children, in spite of encouragement to touch their infants many will often just look at the child (Powell, 1974). Second, there is a higher incidence of premature babies among battered children and failure-to-thrive children who do not show normal weight and height gains in spite of no known organic impairments. In addition, in the case of twins, the twin who has been retained in the hospital, and separated the longest from the mother, is more likely to be abused or returned to the hospital as a failure-to-thrive child. These results could be attributed either to early separation and lack of emotional bonding or to characteristics of the low-birthweight child that make the infant more likely to elicit adverse parental responses. The unattractive physical appearance, small size, high-pitched cry, feeding difficulties, low responsivity, and late development of smiling in premature babies may not make them as appealing to their parents, and also may increase parental anxiety and frustration leading to abuse. However, it should be kept in mind that the highest rates of preterm birth are to mothers who are poor, young, uneducated, and members of a minority group. It is likely that circumstances surrounding poverty, stress, and lack of support contribute to child abuse rather than preterm birth alone.

How does increasing the amount of contact that mothers have with their premature infants affect mother-child relations? Mothers who are permitted early physical contact with their premature babies are initially more likely to feel self-confident and close to their babies and to cuddle and stimulate their infants than are mothers who were only able to look at their infants in the isolette (Barnett, Leiderman, Grobstein, & Klaus, 1970; Seashore, Leifer, Barnett, & Leiderman, 1973). However, unless continued support and training for the mother are available these effects disappear in a few months.

LONG-TERM EFFECTS OF PREMATURITY

What are the long-term effects of prematurity and early separation from the infant on the family? When disruptions in attachment, mother-child relations, or in the cognitive development of the child are sustained, they seem to be attributable to a variety of factors associated with individual differences in the responsiveness of the child, the general competence of the mother, environmental stresses encountered by the family, and supports from family members, nursing staff, and self-help groups available to the family (Bee et al., 1982; Crnic, Greenberg, Ragozin, Robinson, & Basham, 1983; Sameroff, 1977; Siegel, S., 1982). Disruptions are more marked and enduring for economically deprived families than for middle-income families (Leiderman, 1978; Resnick, Stralka, Carter, Ariet, Bucciarelli, Furlough, Evass, Curran, & Ausbon, 1990; Bradley, Caldwell, Rock, Casey, & Nelson, 1987).

The long-term effects of stresses associated with raising a premature baby have been found more consistently in the relations between the parents than between parent and child. A high incidence of marital discord has been reported in the first two years following the birth of a premature infant (Leiderman, 1983). These findings suggest that only by focusing on the entire family system will the effects of prematurity and early separation be understood.

Two Continuums: Reproductive Casualty and Caretaking Casualty

It has been proposed that there is a *continuum of reproductive casualty* (Pasamanick & Knoblock, 1966); that is, there are variations in the degree of reproductive complications which result in abnormalities in the child, ranging from relatively minor perceptual, attentional, intellectual, motor, and behavioral disabilities to extremely gross anomalies. However, in order to make predictions about the developmental course of such disorders, the transactions between the continuum of reproductive casualty and the *continuum of caretaking casualty* must be considered (Sameroff & Chandler, 1975; Sameroff & Seifer, 1983). The continuum of caretaking casualty ranges from an environment and family situation in which there are few adverse factors to one in which there are multiple, severe deleterious factors.

Although 10 percent of children are born with some kind of handicap or anomaly, many of these defects decrease or disappear with age. What factors contribute to the retention and increase of these handicaps or the gradual overcoming of these liabilities?

In order to predict later development from the neonatal condition the transactions between multiple measures of the infant condition and the environmental conditions in which the child will develop are necessary (Milham, Widmayer, Bauer, & Peterson, 1983; Siegel, 1981). This is vividly demonstrated in an outstanding longitudinal study of the effects of birth complications on the development of the entire population of 670 children born on the island of Kauai in the Hawaiian Islands in 1955 (Werner, Bierman, & French, 1971; Werner & Smith, 1977, 1982). At the time of birth 3 percent of the neonates showed severe complications, 13 percent showed moderate complications, 31 percent showed mild complications, and 53 percent showed no complications. Since all of the mothers participated in a prepaid health plan and had good prenatal care, a correlation between birth difficulties and socioeconomic status was not obtained. These children were examined at 2, 10 and 18 years of age.

When the children were reexamined at 2 years of age, 12 percent were rated as deficient in social development, 16 percent were deficient in intellectual functioning, and 14 percent were deficient in health. The more severe the complications of birth and the poorer the neonatal performance of the infants had been, the less adequate was the developmental level of children in these areas at the two-year follow-up. Of more interest was the relationship between perinatal difficulties and environmental factors, notably those associated with socioeconomic status. Infants living in unstable families of relatively low socioeconomic status with mothers of low intelligence showed a 19- to 37-point difference in the average IQ scores between the group with severe perinatal complications and the group with mild or no complications. In contrast, infants in stable, high socioeconomic family environments with mothers of high intelligence showed only a 5- to 7-point difference between the group with severe and the group with no perinatal complications.

By age 10 the effects of environmental variables had almost obliterated those of perinatal damage. No relationship was found between perinatal measures and a child's IQ at this age or at adolescence; instead the correlation between a child's intellectual performance and the parents' IQs and socioeconomic status increased with age, with lower-class children showing marked deficits on cognitive measures. The main effects of deviations caused by reproductive casualty occurred early in a child's development, and after that development was increasingly influenced by environmental circumstances such as chronic poverty, family instability, or mental health problems.

When the children were 18, Werner and Smith (1982) tried to differentiate between children who had developed problems and a group of "resilient children" who had been classified in infancy as high-risk children, but who had not developed problems. The resilient children in families of low socioeconomic status seem to have been buffered by a set of protective factors: good temperament, small family size, favorable parental attitudes, a relationship with a caring adult (not necessarily the parent), low levels of family conflict, a smaller load of stressful life experiences, and the availability of counseling and remedial assistance. The early assumption of responsibility in caring for another person—a sibling, aging grandparent, or ill or incompetent parent—was also associated with resiliency. This has been called *required helpfulness*. Thus both being cared for and caring for others were critical in buffering these high-risk children from adversity (Werner, 1989).

Although more high-risk girls than high-risk boys grew into resilient young adults, the periods of stress for males and females differed. In the first decade of life, boys were found to be vulnerable to both biological and environmental stresses, but girls had more difficulty in the second decade of life. By the late elementary school years, boys were more able to cope with problems that had troubled them earlier—the demands of school achievement and the control of aggression. However, in adolescence, girls were confronting social pressures and sexual expectations that led to an increasing rate of mental health problems. The complexity of these interactions demonstrates the difficulty of attempting to identify the contribution of prenatal and perinatal factors and experiential factors to long-term development. However, the investigators note that, at the conclusion of their study, ten times more children had problems related to the effects of poor environment than to the effects of perinatal stress.

SUMMARY

STAGES OF PRENATAL DEVELOPMENT

- Prenatal development is typically divided into three distinct periods (zygote, embryo, fetus). In reality, these periods represent continuous phases of development, during which the organism undergoes a systematic series of sequential changes to become increasingly complex and differentiated.
- The *period of the zygote* extends from fertilization until the zygote becomes implanted in the wall of the uterus, taking approximately two weeks. The *period of the embryo* begins at that point and lasts until about the eighth week. During this period of rapid growth most of the important organs and physiological systems develop, and the embryo is quite vulnerable to adverse environmental effects. By the end of the period, the embryo can be recognized as a human being.
- The *period of the fetus* extends from the beginning of the third month until birth. Although little further differentiation occurs during this period, the central nervous system develops rapidly, reflexes develop, and regulatory processes and the respiratory system continue to mature. If born before the *age of viability*, or 28 weeks, the fetus may not be developed enough to survive.

PRENATAL INFLUENCES ON DEVELOPMENT

- During prenatal development, *teratogens*, or malformation-producing agents, may affect development, resulting in physical and mental deviations. Six general principles summarize the effects of teratogens on prenatal development, indicating that the type, timing, and duration of the teratogen play a role in the outcome as well as the genotypes of the mother and child.
- A wide range of maternal diseases and disorders can affect prenatal development, including high blood pressure, diabetes, rubella, venereal diseases, and AIDS. The effects of maternal diseases are related to the stage of fetal development when they are contracted, and the length of time that they last, which may be related to a disease's amenability to treatment.
- Drugs taken by the mother during pregnancy, whether prescription or illicit, may have a negative impact on the developing fetus. Sometimes, as in the case of thalidomide and DES, the effects of the prescription drug on the infant are not known until much later. In the case of illicit drugs, such as cocaine or heroin, drug-addicted infants may exhibit symptoms that disrupt parenting and result in long-term adverse outcomes for

parent-child relationships. Drug-using mothers may have particular problems dealing with such infants because of their own troubles.

- The rate of premature and low-birthweight babies is higher for mothers who smoke cigarettes or drink alcohol. In addition, maternal drinking is related to *fetal alcohol syndrome,* which results in facial abnormalities, short stature, and mental retardation. Even modest amounts of alcohol and passive smoking have been related to negative effects in the offspring.
- Deficiencies in maternal diet are related to increased rates of prematurity, stillbirths, infant mortality, physical and neural defects, and small size. The specific effect is related to when the malnutrition occurs and its duration. Dietary supplements provided during pregnancy and after birth have been successful at reducing some of these effects, but the extent of the reversibility of such damage is not known. Continued ill effects seem to be related to the mother's history of dietary deprivation, the length and severity of the malnutrition, and continuing adverse nutritional, social, and economic factors following birth.
- Maternal emotional disturbance has been related to complications during pregnancy and delivery, and to infants who are physically more active in utero and who are hyperactive and irritable after birth. It is difficult to discover the causes underlying these relationships because women who are emotionally upset during pregnancy may be poorly adjusted in a variety of ways, affecting their care-taking and their infant's adjustment after the child's birth.
- Mothers who have their first child when they are over 35 or under 15 are likely to experience more problems during pregnancy and difficulties during delivery than women between these ages. In both groups, the risks are related to maternal health. Early adolescents are less likely to eat properly or to get prenatal care older women are more likely to have hypertension, diabetes, alcoholism, and other problems related to age.

ANTENATAL DIAGNOSIS

- Parents who are concerned about genetic or developmental problems in their unborn child may use several methods of antenatal diagnosis. These include *amniocentesis* and *chorionic villi biopsy,* from which certain chromosomal and metabolic disorders can be detected, and *ultrasound sonography,* from which structural disorders can be detected.

BIRTH

- Birth involves a series of changes in the mother that permit the child to move from the womb to the outside world. These include uterine contractions during the first stage of labor that allow the cervix to become large enough for the child's head; the child's descent into the birth canal and emergence out of the canal during the second stage; and the expulsion of the placenta during the third stage. If problems arise before or during the delivery, a cesarean delivery may be performed by removing the baby through an incision in the mother's abdomen.
- Birth complications occur in only about 10 percent of deliveries. Some important birth factors that are related to developmental deviations and mortality are *anoxia,* or lack of oxygen in the brain, prematurity, and low birthweight. All of these factors have been associated with physical, neurological, cognitive, and emotional deficits. Most of these negative

effects diminish with age, except in extreme cases. Stimulation programs have been successfully tried with low-birthweight babies to combat the effect of lack of stimulation and the infant-parent separation caused by spending the first weeks of life in an isolette.

- Two interacting continuums that affect the appearance and maintenance of problems in the child have been proposed: the *continuum of reproductive casualty* and the *continuum of caretaking casualty.* Most research indicates that, except in extreme cases, environmental or caretaking conditions play a major role in sustaining or eliminating early deficits in reproduction. It is clear that the attitudes and behaviors of parents toward children who have experienced prenatal or perinatal damage and the environmental supports that the child experiences are particularly important.

CHAPTER 5

INFANCY: THE EMERGENCE OF SENSATION, PERCEPTION, AND LEARNING

THE NEWBORN

INFANT STATES AND SOOTHABILITY

Classification of Infant States

Developmental Changes in States

Soothing Techniques

SENSORY AND PERCEPTUAL CAPACITIES OF THE INFANT

The Newborn's Repertoire of Reflexes

Problems of Investigation: Unlocking the Infant's Sensory Secrets

Evaluating the Newborn: The Brazelton Neonatal Assessment Scale

A Perspective on Emerging Infant Competencies

Listening: Development of Hearing

Looking: Visual Development

Smell and Taste

Putting the Pieces Together: Bimodal Perception in Infants

LEARNING IN INFANCY

Habituation

Classical and Operant Conditioning

Memory in Infancy

SUMMARY

Rebecca's mother started reading Shakespearean sonnets to her at 1 month; Joseph's dad played folk songs to him while he rocked him when he was only 3 days old; Jenny's grandma bought her picture books and brightly colored mobiles, but waited until she thought she was "ready" for them—at 6 months! Each of these caregivers assumes different things about exactly what babies are capable of doing. Babies can hear, see, and respond to interesting sights and sounds in their environment at a much earlier age than we might expect.

In this chapter we will examine the capacities of the infant. A variety of questions will be addressed. How alert is the newborn and how do the states of alertness change? What is in the newborn's repertoire of reflexes? What are the sensory and perceptual capacities of the neonate and how do these capacities improve as the infant develops? Many years ago William James suggested that the newborn's world is a "blooming, buzzing confusion." As you will see, very young infants have a wide range of available reflexes and capacities, and even their primitive abilities permit them to respond selectively and organize the information they are receiving. Recent methodological advances, particularly those in psychophysiology, have permitted developmental psychologists to gain a clearer understanding of the capabilities and response systems of the infant. Finally, can infants learn? And if they can learn, how early is learning possible? Both classical and operant conditioning in young infants will be examined, as well as studies on imitation and memory in early infancy. These are issues we shall explore in this chapter.

THE NEWBORN

Unlike the beautiful creatures in the advertisements for diapers, cribs, and toys, the newborn, is generally a homely organism. As one writer put it, "even a fond mother may experience a sense of shock at the first sight of the tiny, wizened, red creature that is her offspring" (Watson, 1962, p. 140). At birth the average baby weighs approximately 7½ pounds and is about 20 inches long; from birth on, boys are slightly larger and heavier than girls. Part of the newborn's unusual appearance is derived from odd bodily proportions, odd at least in comparison with adults (see Figure 5-1). For

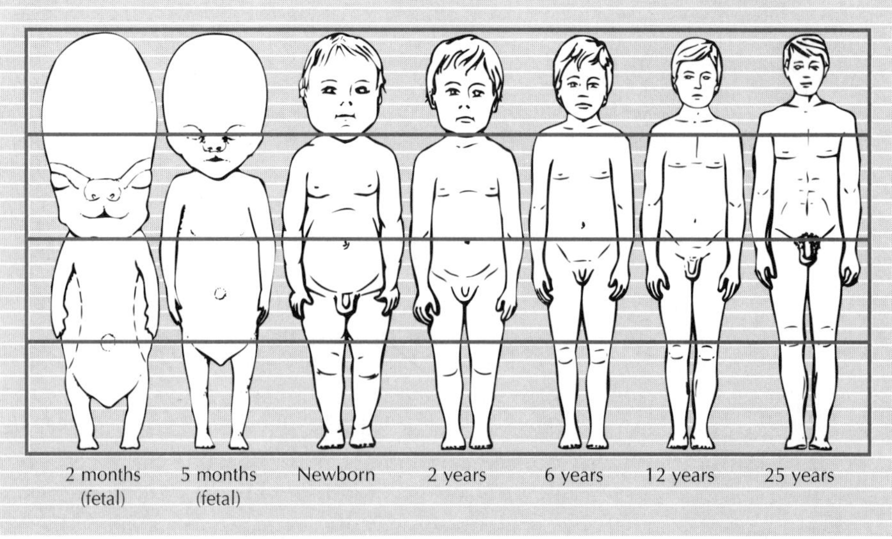

FIGURE 5-1
Changes in body form and proportion during prenatal and postnatal growth. (*From Jackson, 1933, by permission of McGraw-Hill.*)

example, the newborn seems to be "all head," and, in fact, the head represents one-half of the body length (the head is only one-eighth of the full-grown adult).

What is this odd-looking creature capable of doing? An understanding of how well equipped, behaviorally speaking, the new arrival is on entering the world is crucial for understanding the relative importance of genetic and experiential variables. Is the newborn the passive, nonreacting organism that scientists for many years had thought? Hardly! In fact, as we shall see, the newborn is a highly competent organism with a surprisingly well-developed set of reflexes and sensory responses, even at birth. Nor are the responses random and disorganized; rather, the newborn shows a capacity to respond in an organized, meaningful way from a much earlier time than was originally assumed. William James's claim that "the newborn baby's world is nothing more than a blooming, buzzing confusion" is clearly wrong.

INFANT STATES AND SOOTHABILITY

Watch a young infant for a few hours and one of your most obvious insights will be that infants go through cycles of alertness, activity, quietness, and sleep. Just as adults have organized shifts in their sleep-wake patterns, so do infants. In fact, one of the most fascinating aspects of the newborn infant's behavior is the periodic changes in his *state*. By state we mean the continuum of alertness or consciousness ranging from vigorous activity to regular sleep. Our exploration of the newborn begins with describing the baby's state for two reasons. First, it illustrates some important principles of early infant behavior, namely its spontaneity and its periodicity (Schaffer, 1977). As one observer notes:

> The infant is by no means inert and passive, stirred into action only by outside stimulation. On the contrary, it appears that there are internal forces that regulate much of his behavior and account for changes in his activity. . . . Periodicity is vividly illustrated by the cyclic alteration of states. There are, it appears, certain fixed rhythms that underlie the spontaneously occurring state changes. (Schaffer, 1977, pp. 30–31)

In addition, the state changes are not random, but are predictable and organized—another characteristic of newborn behavior.

A second reason for using the concept of state as a way to help understand the infant is that the impact of environmental stimulation will vary considerably with the baby's state. The presence, direction, and amount of the response to stimulation are dependent on the baby's state at the onset of stimulation. Even researchers have been frustrated when, after attaching a wide array of electrodes, wires, and recording equipment to an infant subject, the infant has burped and happily drifted off to sleep before the experimental procedures could be executed. In addition, at times some infants seem to sleep with their eyes open; although visually they appear to be awake, recordings of this physiological functioning suggest that they are really in a sleeplike state. In such cases, failure to attend or respond on the part of the infants may be due to their state rather than their capacities.

In light of the central role of state in determining infant responsiveness, many researchers view state not only as an obstacle to be controlled, but also as a phenomenon to be understood in its own right. It is clear that before the infant's reflex repertoire is examined and his sensory and perceptual capacities are probed, a look at the many states of the infant is necessary.

Classification of Infant States

How can infant states by classified? Wolff (1966, 1987) has offered the following criteria for infant states:

> *Regular sleep:* His eyes are closed and he is completely still; respirations are slow and regular; his face is relaxed—no grimace—and his eyelids are still.
>
> *Irregular sleep:* His eyes are closed; he engages in variable gentle limb movements, writhing, and stirring; grimaces and other facial expressions are frequent; respirations are irregular and faster than in regular sleep; there are interspersed and recurrent rapid eye movements.
>
> *Drowsiness:* He is relatively inactive; his eyes open and close intermittently; respirations are regular, though faster than in regular sleep; when eyes are open, they have a dull or glazed quality.
>
> *Alert inactivity:* His eyes are open and have a bright and shining quality; he can pursue moving objects and make conjugate eye movements in the horizontal and vertical plane; he is relatively inactive; his face is relaxed and he does not grimace.
>
> *Waking activity:* He frequently engages in diffuse motor activity involving his whole body; his eyes are open, but not alert, and his respirations are grossly irregular.
>
> *Crying:* He has crying vocalizations associated with vigorous diffuse motor activity.

Developmental Changes in States

To illustrate the state changes that occur as the infant develops, two extreme states are examined—sleep and crying.

SLEEP

The proportion of time that an infant spends in these various states not only differs for individual infants but also varies for each infant as he or she develops. As the infant develops, a larger proportion of time is spent in awake states; in turn, the proportion of time spent sleeping is reduced. The newborn sleeps about 70 percent of the time, and, of course, not continuously; rather, sleep time is distributed across the day in a series of short and long naps. By 4 weeks of age, fewer but longer periods of sleep than those of the newborn are typical, and by 8 weeks the infant is sleeping more during the night and less during the day (Sostek & Anders, 1981). By the end of the first year, most infants sleep through the night (see Figure 5-2). "Establishing a rhythm of diurnal waking and nocturnal sleep is in fact one of the more important developments in early infancy—it makes the baby so much easier to live with!" (Schaffer, 1977, p. 28). This shift to a culturally accepted pattern of sleep-wake cycles illustrates the way in which the infant's internal biorhythms become adapted to the demands of the external world.

The kind of sleep changes with age as well (Berg & Berg, 1987). By

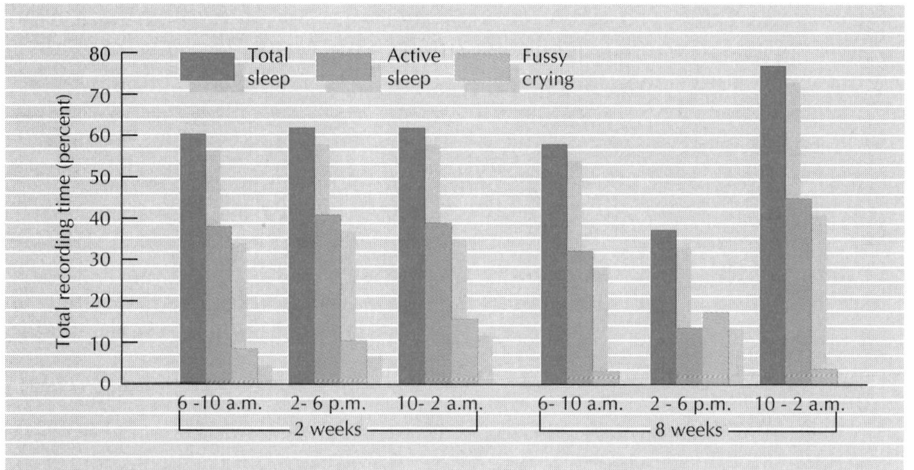

FIGURE 5-2

At birth, infants do not follow any day-night routine. They cry as much at night as during the day. After a few weeks, their behavior has been modified. Now, much less of their crying occurs in the late evening. (*From Sostek & Anders, 1981.*)

recording brain activity of infants and adults of different ages, investigators have distinguished different phases of sleep. The most important distinction is between REM (rapid eye movement) and non-REM sleep. Often termed *dream sleep,* REM sleep is a period characterized by rapid eye movements as well as fluctuations in heart rate and blood pressure. In adults, dreaming occurs in this period, and one might expect increased motor activity; but the body is wisely organized so that there is no physical acting-out of dreams during REM sleep. Apparently dreaming is not simply a pleasant nighttime entertainment. If people are wakened as soon as REM sleep begins, obtaining very little REM sleep, their subsequent waking behavior is irritable and disorganized.

Of particular interest is the change that takes place in the percentage of REM and non-REM sleep as the infant develops. In the newborn, 50 percent of sleep is REM sleep, but as the infant grows older, the percentage drops dramatically (see Figure 5-3). As yet there is no way of determining if infants

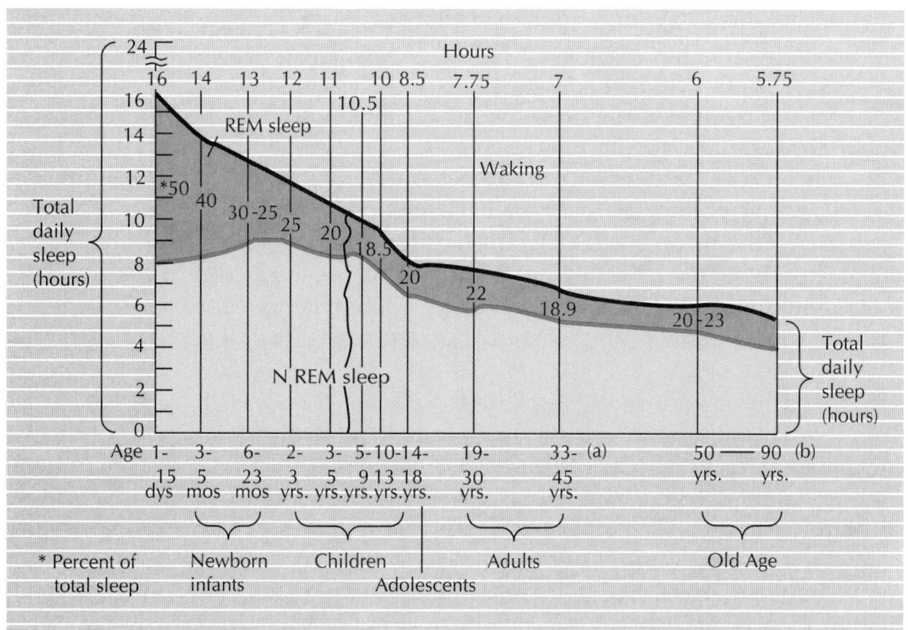

FIGURE 5-3

Age changes in the total amounts of daily sleep and daily REM sleep and in percentage of REM sleep. The percentage of REM sleep is indicated by the nonshaded area of the graph. The percentage of REM sleep drops from 50 percent in the newborn period to only 25 percent in the 2- to 3-year-old child. (*From Roffwarg, Muzio, & Dement, 1966. Revised since publication in* Science *by Dr. Roffwarg. By permission of the senior author.*)

dream and if this high amount of REM sleep is associated with dream activity. The organization and sequence of different phases of sleep also change from infancy to adulthood. For example, normal adults usually have an hour of non-REM sleep before drifting into REM sleep. In contrast, newborns enter REM sleep from almost any waking or sleeping state; only 25 percent of newborn REM sleep is preceded by non-REM sleep, and usually the babies go into REM sleep from a drowsy, crying, or waking state (Korner, 1972). By 6 months, infants begin to follow the adult pattern of non-REM sleep producing REM sleep (Kligman, Smyrl, & Emde, 1975).

An *autostimulation* theory has been proposed to account for the high level of REM sleep in newborns: The REM mechanism provides stimulation to higher brain centers, and the high degree of REM activity in infancy may therefore stimulate the development of the central nervous system of the young infant (Roffwarg, Muzio, & Dement, 1966). As the infant develops and becomes increasingly alert and capable of processing external stimulation, this type of built-in stimulation becomes less necessary. Possibly the speed with which infants reduce their percentage of REM sleep will depend on how much external stimulation the infant receives. In fact, it has been found that newborns who were circumcised and hence received intense stimulation spent less time in REM sleep than noncircumcised infants—a finding that is consistent with the autostimulation theory (Emde, et al., 1971). It would be interesting to determine whether shifts in REM/non-REM sleep fluctuate with the social and physical environment of the home. Although it is speculative, the autostimulation theory makes good sense. Before leaving this discussion of sleep, turn to Box 5-1 for a brief look at "crib death," a syndrome that may be related to sleep dysfunctions.

CRYING

At the other extreme of the continuum of infant states is crying, which, like sleep, is not a simple homogeneous state. Crying is considered important as one of the infant's earliest means of communicating his needs to his caretakers. In light of this communicative role, it is not surprising that different types of crying patterns can be distinguished. Three distinct patterns of crying have been identified:

1 A basic pattern, linked among other factors to hunger, which starts arrhythmically and at low intensity, but gradually becomes louder and more rhythmical.
2 The "mad" or angry cry, characterized by the same temporal sequence as the basic pattern (namely cry-rest-inspiration-rest) but distinguished from it by differences in the length of the various phase components.
3 The pain cry, which is sudden in onset, is loud from the start, and is made up of a long cry, followed by a long silence (during which there is breath holding), and then by a series of short gasping inhalations. (Schaffer, 1971, p. 61)

Most mothers can distinguish among different types of crying, such as pain and anger cries, but only when listening to the cries of their own infants (Wiesenfeld, Malatesta, & DeLoache, 1981). Although fathers can accurately identify the cries of their own infants, fathers are not as capable as mothers in distinguishing among types of cries. In trying to diagnose why an infant was crying, Holden (1988) found that women were more efficient and accurate than men in solving the problem, and nonparents, particularly males, had

BOX 5-1 SUDDEN INFANT DEATH SYNDROME (SIDS)

Each year 10,000 infants in the United States die in their sleep from unknown causes. These deaths are often classified as "crib death," or sudden infant death syndrome (SIDS). Some progress has been made in identifying who are to be victims and when crib death is likely to occur. Victims are more likely to be low-birth-weight male infants who have a prior history of neonatal respiratory difficulties, longer hospitalization, as well as abnormal heart-rate patterns and nighttime sleep disturbances (Rovee-Collier & Lipsitt, 1982; Shannan & Kelley, 1982; Sadeh et al., 1987). Their mothers are more likely to be anemic, smoke or use other narcotics, and have received little prenatal care, although it should be stressed that most infants with this history are not affected. Most often SIDS occurs during sleep in the winter months and often follows a minor respiratory ailment such as a cold. It occurs most commonly between 2 and 4 months of age and rarely after 6 months. It is not caused by suffocation, aspiration, or regurgitation, nor has there been any success in isolating a virus, although this is still a possibility. Another possibility is that apnea or the spontaneous interruption of respiration that occurs more often during REM sleep may be a factor in causing SIDS (Steinschneider, 1975), which is complicated by the fact that the brain stem which controls breathing may not be well enough developed to adequately overcome any interruptions (Shannon & Kelley, 1982). Currently researchers are investigating whether infants who have unusually long apnea periods during sleep may be more prone to crib death or if these infants have not developed adequate responses to nasal blockage and other threats to respiration (Lipsitt, 1979). Although newborns appear to have built-in defensive reactions to respiratory threats (for example, a cloth over the face) between 2 and 4 months of life, this reflex may undergo a change from an involuntary to a voluntary basis. It is during this transition period between reflexive and voluntary phases of different reflexes that crib death is most likely to occur. Failure to make this transition smoothly may put the infant at greater risk for SIDS.

One recent innovation is the use of monitors in the home which sound an alarm to alert parents when an infant's breathing is interrupted. Although controversial because of the stress and burden on parents, evidence suggests that it may save some potential victims.

In spite of recent advances, the possibilities far exceed firm knowledge concerning SIDS, but research on early development of infant states, reflexes, and sensory and learning capabilities will, it is hoped, contribute to an understanding of the causes of this tragedy.

Sources: Lipsitt, L. P. (1979). Critical conditions in infancy. *American Psychologist*, **34**, 973–980; Rovee-Collier, C. K., & Lipsitt, L. P. (1982). Learning, adaptation and memory in the newborn. In P. Stratton (Ed.), *Psychobiology of the human newborn*. New York: Wiley; Sadeh, D., Shannon, D. C., Abboud, S., Saul, J. P., Adselrod, S., & Cohen, R. J. (1987). Altered cardiac repolarization on some victims of sudden infant death syndrome. *New England Journal of Medicine*, **317**, 1501–1505; Shannon, D. C., & Kelley, D. H. (1982). SIDS & near-SIDS. *New England Journal of Medicine*, **306**, 959–964; Steinschneider, A. (1975). Implications of the sudden infant death syndrome for the study of sleep in infancy. In A. D. Pick (Ed.), *Minnesota Symposia on Child Psychology* (Vol. 9). Minneapolis: University of Minnesota.

more difficulty in solving the problem than parents. Probably, mothers' greater experience with infants as well as their increased caregiving responsibility accounts for these mother-father differences.

As the infant develops, the nature of cry patterns change and become part of the infant's emerging system of communication. Based on home observations of infants, Gustafson and Green (1988) found that simple crying—which occurred in the absence of other communicative behavior, such as looking at or gesturing—decreased over time and by their first birthday most babies used crying as a form of communication and as a way to control their caregivers. And crying as a way of eliciting a caregiver response works! In one study, 77 percent of the 2461 crying episodes they studied were followed by maternal intervention, but only 6 percent were preceded by contact with the mother (Moss, 1967). More recently, in a laboratory simulation study both mothers and nonmothers responded to a crying baby "doll" by holding, talking to, and stimulating the "baby" (Gustafson & Harris, 1990). "Holding and crying becomes an opportunity for social interaction and the parent is doubly rewarded: The crying stops and a mutually enjoyable interaction can occur" (Lester, 1988, p. 15).

Crying patterns can also be a sensitive diagnostic device that alerts pediatricians to possible abnormalities in early development (Lester, 1988). Brain-damaged infants and Down syndrome infants take longer to cry in response to a painful stimulus, require a more intense stimulus to elicit a cry, and produce a less sustained, more arrhythmical, and higher-pitched cry than normal infants (Lester, et al., 1988). Moreover, unusual cries—involving extreme variations in pitch—have been found in SIDS victims (Lester, et al., 1988). In summary, the infant cry is not only an important communicative signal for parents but is an early warning system for abnormality as well.

Soothing Techniques

Although general developmental changes from sleep to wakefulness and from agitation and crying to quieter states appear to follow a regular and preprogrammed course, there has been considerable interest in identifying specific techniques that are effective in shifting the infant's state. Of particular interest are soothing techniques, which can reduce agitation and distress in the baby.

The Caretaker as Soother. Soothing techniques are obviously of practical importance for salvaging the nerves of harried new parents. Korner and Thoman (1970) assessed the effectiveness of six different soothing techniques (see Figure 5-4), or in shifting newborn infants from either a crying or sleeping state into a state of alert inactivity. By far the most effective technique for eliciting visual alertness was putting the infant to the shoulder; this position evoked bright-eyed scanning in 77.5 percent of the infants. Figure 5-4 also clearly illustrates that the same type of stimulation will have either a strong or a minimal effect, depending on the infant's state at the time of intervention. For example, the same stimulation had a much greater impact on the infant who was crying than on the sleeping infant.

Of course, a variety of other techniques are effective in soothing infants, including rocking (Byrne & Horowitz, 1981) and swaddling, a technique in which the infant is tightly wrapped in a blanket or cloth (Campos, 1989). Neither of these appears to be dependent on learning or experience, but they are effective shortly after birth. Centuries of mothers can testify on behalf of their effectiveness.

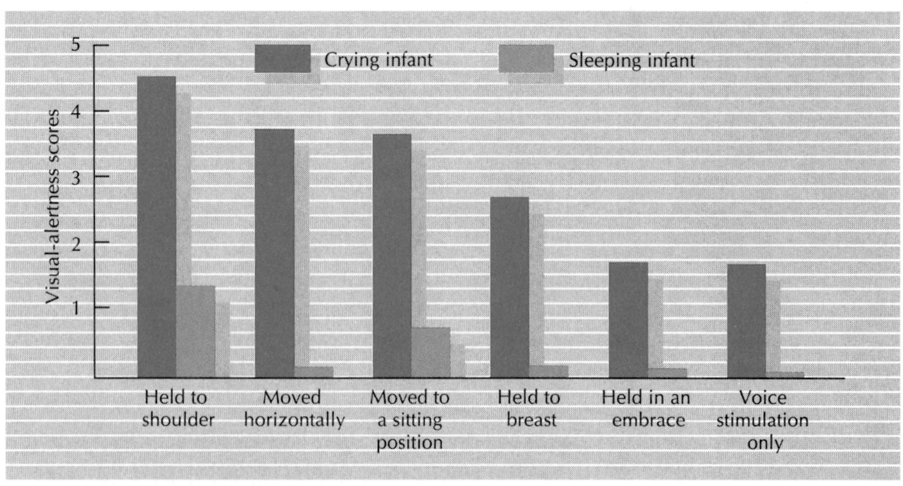

FIGURE 5-4
Effects of stimulation on visual alertness. (*From Korner & Thoman, 1970, with permission of the authors and publisher.*)

The Infant as a Self-Soother. To some extent, an infant is a self-sufficient soother and can shift from one state to another independently of outside stimulation. One way that an infant can often reduce distress is by sucking, a highly organized response pattern that is ready to operate at birth (Campos, 1989). In fact, pacifiers soothe infants more rapidly and completely than swaddling, according to a recent study of a 2-week-old infant; by 2 months, both pacifiers and swaddling were equally effective (Campos, 1989). Sucking as the principal means of feeding is important for infant survival, and for many years it was assumed that the pacifying effects of sucking were due to the association of sucking and feeding. However, sucking on a pacifier—without any accompanying food—is an effective means of reducing distress (Field & Goldson, 1984; Smith, Fillion, & Blass, 1990). In fact, sucking on a pacifier functions as a stress reducer immediately after birth—even before the first postnatal feeding (Kessen, et al., 1967). In short, sucking tends to reduce activity and movement in the newborn and may be viewed as a congenital stress reducer.

Individual and Cross-Cultural Differences in Soothability. There are wide and reliable individual differences in babies' ability to be soothed (Bates, 1987). As we saw in our earlier discussion of temperament in Chapter 4, some babies are easily calmed and others are really difficult to console. Boys are harder on parents than girls, since male infants are more difficult to pacify than female babies (Moss, 1967). And there are cross-cultural differences: In

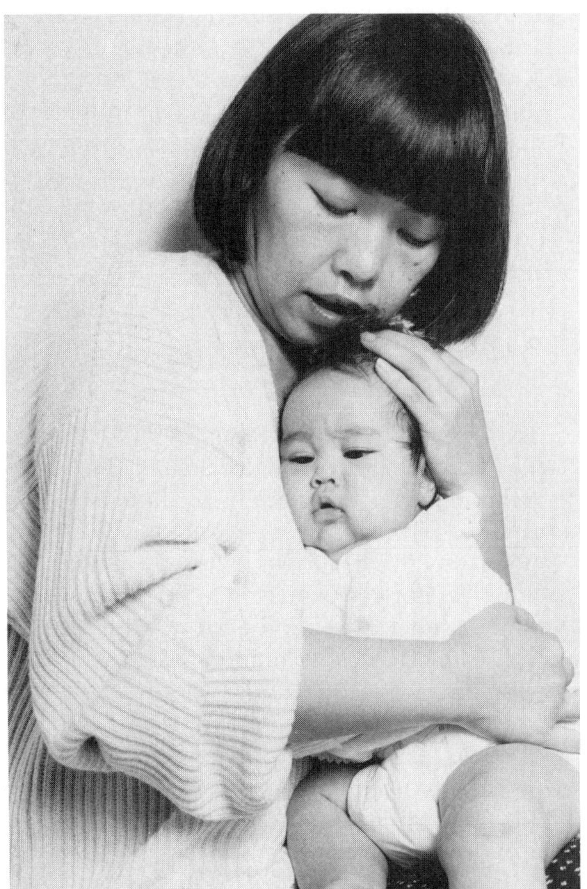

There are cultural differences in soothability; Asian infants tend to quiet more quickly than Caucasian infants.

assessing Chinese-American and European-American newborns, Freedman (1974) found that the European-American babies shifted between states of contentment and disturbance more frequently than the Chinese-American; Chinese-American babies tended to calm themselves more readily when upset and were more easily consoled by caretakers. These differences persist over the first few months of infancy and affect the ways in which infants are treated. Kuchner (1980) found that Chinese mothers allow their infants to cry for longer periods before intervening, but Chinese babies quieted quickly with minimal intervention (for example, hearing their mother's voice). Other groups, such as the Japanese, the Navajo, and Zinacanteco Indians of South Mexico show many of the same temperamental characteristics—including easier soothability—as Chinese babies (Nugent, Lester, & Brazelton, 1989).

SENSORY AND PERCEPTUAL CAPACITIES OF THE INFANT

The Newborn's Repertoire of Reflexes

In attempting to unravel the mysteries of infancy, it is becoming increasingly obvious how adaptively organized the young human organism really is. The confusion that psychologists traditionally have attributed to the newborn might be better attributed to the psychologists themselves. However, now that we are letting the organism speak for itself, even psychologists are becoming less confused. Consider the newborn's repertoire of *reflexes*, which are involuntary responses to external stimuli. These may be elicited at birth as a test for the soundness of the infant's central nervous system. Moreover, a neurological examination of the newborn has predictive value; signs of abnormality which may be evident in the first days or weeks may disappear during a "silent period" and not reappear as abnormal functions until months or even years later (Dubowitz & Dubowitz, 1981; Francis, Self, & Horowitz, 1987). In Table 5-1 (pages 148–149), some of the reflexes of the newborn are described. Note that some reflexes are permanent, while others may disappear after a few months.

Problems of Investigation: Unlocking the Infant's Sensory Secrets

Neonates and young infants are not easy organisms to understand; in fact, they guard the secrets about their abilities extremely well. Part of the difficulty is that many of the methods used to investigate the sensory and perceptual capacities of older children and adults cannot be used with infants. Infants' motor repertoires are limited: they cannot reach or point with any degree of accuracy, nor can they crawl. In addition, they cannot be asked whether one tone is louder than another or whether they prefer red to green. Thus, many well-defined adult techniques of investigation which depend on motor and verbal responses are useless in studying infants. There are other problems as well. How can you be sure that the standards defined by the adults (for example, as to what constitutes a sweet, pleasant taste) apply to infants? Perhaps subjective judgments change with age.

Techniques of investigation have been developed to capitalize on the responses that the infant can make. The autonomic nervous system, which controls such things as heart rate, muscle reactions, and respiration, has been receiving much attention in recent years, partly because we can use psychophysiological functions to probe the infant's sensory capacities. A change in respiration contingent upon a change in the pitch of a sound suggests that the infant is sensitive to changes in this auditory dimension. The neonate's motor responses, although limited, can give a clue to his sensory systems as well. In fact, one of the earliest means of detecting sensory capacities was the stabilimeter, an apparatus that monitors changes in an infant's movement. Recently, researchers have capitalized on the infant's well-developed sucking pattern as an index of the effect of sensory input.

The value of these different response measures is enhanced by the infants' ability to *habituate* or decrease their responding to a stimulus, such as a light or tone, which is repeatedly presented. This technique is widely used by researchers in exploring the infant's abilities. For example, if you shake a rattle near an infant's head, you may witness a startle response, including thrashing of the arms and legs and general body movement. If you repeat the noise, the infant responds less and may show only a brief kick. After a few more times, the infant appears to ignore the sound and shows no response at all. Now if you present a different sound (a bell), the infant will once again show a reaction until he adapts to the new noise. This reaction to the new sound tells you that the infant can distinguish between the rattle and the bell. Infants show the same habituation process for sights, smells, and tastes, as well as sounds. Therefore it is widely used to understand the sensory and perceptual capacities of babies.

Evaluating the Newborn: The Brazelton Neonatal Assessment Scale

A variety of assessment scales have been developed to assess the capacities and health status of young infants (Francis, Self, & Horowitz, 1987) that combine into a single assessment device our knowledge of infant reflexes and the babies' capacities to habituate, regulate their arousal level, and attend to social and nonsocial sights and sounds in their environment. One of the most widely used scales for assessing newborn babies is the Brazelton Neonatal Assessment Scale (Brazelton, 1984). The original goal was to attempt to describe autonomic, motor, state, and social attention systems—which were seen as integrative and interacting with each other in the normal healthy full-term infant (Brazelton, Nugent, & Lester, 1987, p. 780). Table 5-2 outlines the behavioral items on the scale. As you can see, the scale measures (1) habituation to a variety of stimuli, (2) the babies' ability to orient to social and inanimate objects, (3) motor development, (4) range of state, (5) the ability to regulate state and outcome, and (6) autonomic nervous system stability. In addition, the scale is supplemented by the assessement of a variety of reflexes of the type that you see in Table 5-1. The scale has been used for a variety of purposes. Performance on the scale helps distinguish infants at risk (due to prematurity and obstetric medication, for example) from healthy infants, and aids in the diagnosis of neurological impairment (Eldredge & Salamy, 1988). This newborn assessment is also useful in the prediction of later development. For example, infants who score high on the scale tend to score higher on later measures of cognitive, motor, or social development (Bakeman & Brown, 1980; Moss, Colombo, Mitchell, & Horowitz, 1988). In addition, there are clear relationships between infant behavior during the assessment and later parent-infant interaction during feeding and play. Since parental responsiveness is an important ingredient for optimal

Some examples of newborn reflexes. The moro reflex (a) is the infant's response to the sudden loss of support at the back of the head. The rooting reflex (b, c) occurs when a finger stimulates the infant's cheek causing the child to turn its head toward the stimulation, open its mouth, and try to suck the finger. The grasp reflex (d) occurs when stimulation against the infant's palm causes the infant to grasp object. The withdrawal reflex (e) occurs when stimulation of the soles of the feet causes the infant to flex legs.

(a)

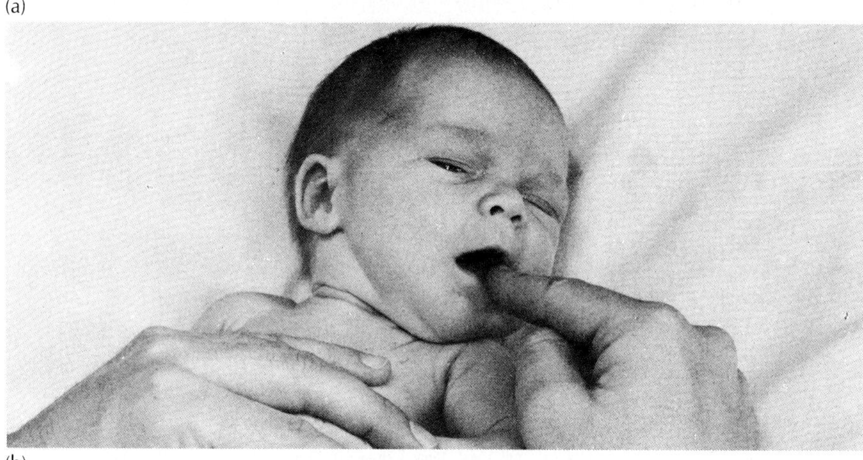

(b)

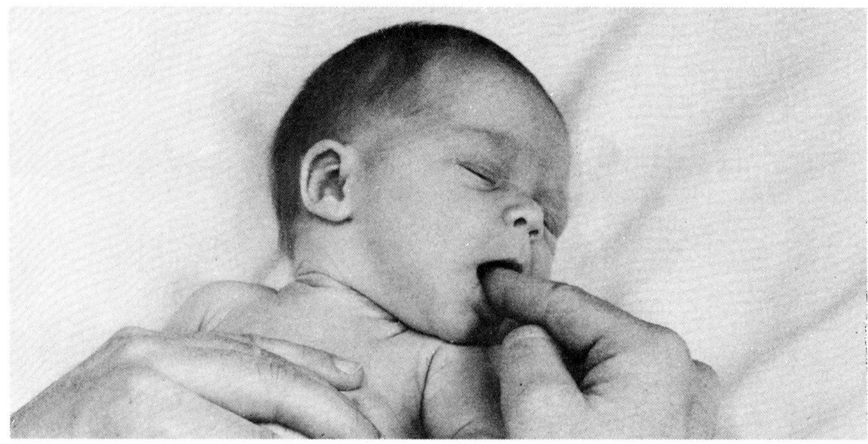

(c)

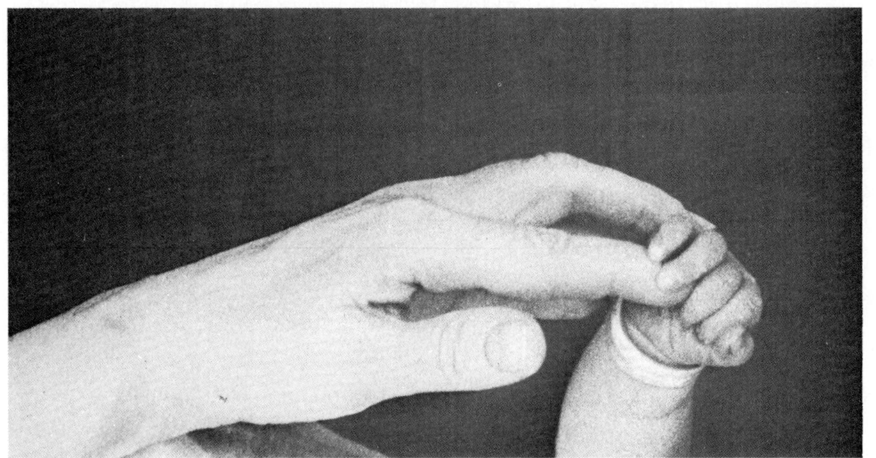

(d)

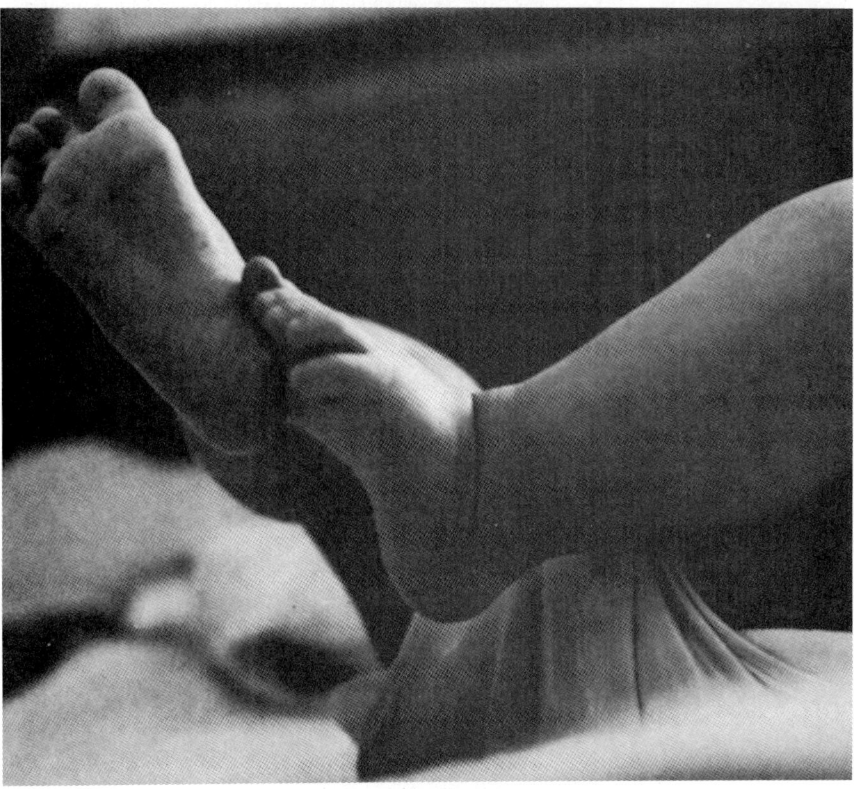

(e)

development, it is important to remember that the predictive value of the scale is probably due to the interaction of the babies' capacities and the type of parenting environment that is provided for the growing infant. Recall the earlier study by Crockenberg (1981) in Chapter 4, which suggested that both infant temperament and the child-care environment were important predictors of the infant's later social relationships.

Finally, the scale has revealed interesting cross-cultural differences among infants and illustrates the ways in which different environments encourage or shape distinctive styles of responding in infants that is consistent with the

TABLE 5-1

MAJOR NEWBORN REFLEXES

NAME	TESTING METHOD	RESPONSE	DEVELOPMENTAL COURSE	SIGNIFICANCE
Blink	Light flash	Closing of both eyelids	Permanent	Protection of eyes to strong stimuli
Biceps reflex	Tap on the tendon of the biceps muscle	Short contraction of the biceps muscle	In the first few days it is brisker than in later days	Absent in depressed infants or in cases of congenital muscular disease
Knee jerk or patellar tendon reflex	Tap on the tendon below the patella or kneecap	Quick extension or kick of the knee	More pronounced in the first 2 days than later	Absent or difficult to obtain in depressed infants or infants with muscular disease; exaggerated in hyperexcitable infants.
Babinski	Gentle stroking of the side of the infant's foot from heel to toes	Dorsal flexion of the big toe; extension of the other toes	Usually disappears near the end of the first year; replaced by plantar flexion of great toe as in the normal adult	Absent in defects of the lower spine
Withdrawal reflex	Pinprick is applied to the sole of the infant's foot	Leg flexion	Constantly present during the first 10 days, present but less intense later	Absent with sciatic nerve damage
Plantar or toe grasp	Pressure is applied with finger against the balls of the infant's feet	Plantar flexion of all toes	Disappears between 8 and 12 months	Absent in defects of the lower spinal cord
Palmar or automatic hand grasp	A rod or finger is pressed against the infant's palm	Infant grasps the object	Disappears at 3 to 4 months; increases during the first month and then gradually declines; replaced by voluntary grasp between 4 and 5 months	Response is weak or absent in depressed babies; sucking movements facilitate grasping

goals, values, and social organization of the culture (Nugent et al., 1989). Motor precocity is valued among the Gusu of Kenya and Zambian cultures and both provide high levels of visual and auditory stimulation, and physical contact that helps promote early motor development. As we saw earlier, Oriental and Navajo Indian cultures have quiet babies and appear to encourage these characteristics by caregiving practices that keep their babies calm. In short, newborn assessments such as the Brazelton scale can serve a variety of functions and are important tools in helping understand infant development.

TABLE 5-1

MAJOR NEWBORN REFLEXES (Continued)

NAME	TESTING METHOD	RESPONSE	DEVELOPMENTAL COURSE	SIGNIFICANCE
Moro reflex	(1) Sudden loud sound or jarring (for example, bang on the examination table); or (2) head drop—head is dropped a few inches; or (3) baby drop—baby is suspended horizontally and the examiner lowers hands rapidly about 6 inches and stops abruptly	Arms are thrown out in extension, and then brought toward each other in a convulsive manner; hands are fanned out at first and then clinched tightly; spine and lower extremities extend	Disappears in 6 to 7 months	Absent or constantly weak Moro indicates serious disturbance of the central nervous system
Stepping	Baby is supported in upright position; examiner moves the infant forward and tilts him or her slightly to one side	Rhythmic stepping movements	Disappears in 3 to 4 months	Absent in depressed infants
Rooting response	Cheek of infant is stimulated by light pressure of the finger	Baby turns head toward finger, opens mouth, and tries to suck finger	Disappears at approximately 3 to 4 months	Absent in depressed infants; appears in adults only in severe cerebral palsy diseases
Sucking response	Index finger is inserted about 3 to 4 centimeters into the mouth	Rhythmic sucking	Sucking is often less intensive and less regular during the first 3 to 4 days	Poor sucking (weak, slow, and short periods) is found in apathetic babies; maternal medication during childbirth may depress sucking
Babkin or palmar-mental reflex	Pressure is applied on both of baby's palms when lying on his or her back	Mouth opens, eyes close, and head returns to midline	Disappears in 3 to 4 months	General depression of central nervous system inhibits this response

A Perspective on Emerging Infant Competencies

The infant's sensory and perceptual skills do not emerge in a vacuum. Instead, these skills develop in a social and physical world and serve the important function of helping the developing infant understand and adapt to her environment. As you will see, as we explore various aspects of sensory and perceptual abilities, it appears that the infant is especially well equipped

TABLE 5-2 NEONATAL BEHAVIORAL ASSESSMENT SCALE

BEHAVIORAL ITEMS
Habituation:
1. Response decrement to light
2. Response decrement to rattle
3. Response decrement to bell
4. Response decrement to pinprick
Orientation to sights and sounds:
5. Inanimate visual orientation response—focusing and following an object
6. Inanimate auditory orientation response—reaction to an auditory stimulus
7. Animate visual orientation—focusing and following a person's face
8. Animate auditory orientation—reaction to a voice
9. Animate visual and auditory orientation—reaction to a person's face and voice
Motor development:
10. Pull to sit
11. Defensive movements
12. Degree of alertness
13. General tonus
14. Motor maturity
15. Activity
Range of state:
16. Peak of excitement
17. Rapidity of buildup
18. Irritability
19. Lability of state
Regulation of state:
20. Cuddliness
21. Consolability with intervention
22. Self-quieting
23. Hand to mouth
Autonomic stability:
24. Tremors
25. Startles
26. Skin

to respond to the social aspects of her world. Human voices, faces, and even smells are especially likely to be responded to by young infants, which suggests that the infant's sensory and perceptual systems may be biologically prepared or programmed to be sensitive to socially mediated events. This is clearly adaptive, since the baby's responsiveness to her caregivers may increase their interest in the infant and enhance the baby's well being and survival.

A second theme concerns the issue of interdependence of sensory and perceptual systems. To present the "facts" about the development of different sensory systems, such as vision, hearing, taste, and smell in an orderly way, we treat each system separately. However, in the real world, these systems develop together and advances in one system may trigger a change in another sensory or perceptual domain. Later in the chapter we will put the pieces together and show how these systems mutually influence each other and work in tandem to help the infant understand her world.

Finally, perception and action are not independent. Changes in the infant's developing capacity for motor action such as crawling or walking can have a profound impact on how she experiences the world. Although we will not discuss motor development until the next chapter, we will offer a few glimpses of how motor systems and the sensory and perceptual systems mutually influence each other. In short, the more we understand development, the more the principle of interdependence of systems becomes an important guide.

Listening: Development of Hearing

Can babies hear? There have been some exciting discoveries about the young infant's auditory capacities in the last decade. Just how soon after birth the neonate begins to hear is still a controversial issue since fluid in the inner ear may prevent proper assessment of the infant's hearing capacities until a few hours after birth. It is clear, however, that as soon as a fair (unobstructed) test can be made, the infant's hearing is remarkably well developed, but still not as good as adult hearing ability (Aslin, 1987). Several abilities are involved. Can infants detect sounds of different loudness and pitch? Can infants distinguish different sounds? Can infants locate sounds in space?

First, infants need a louder sound (10 to 17 decibels higher) than adults in order to detect a sound (Hecox & Deegan, 1985). A decibel is a measure of the loudness of a sound; normal conversation is generally about 60 decibels, a train is approximately 100 decibels, and a whisper is probably around 20 decibels. Infants are more sensitive to high-frequency than to low-frequency sounds (Aslin, 1987). Careful studies of infants indicate that babies rapidly improve over the first two years in terms of their abilities to discriminate sounds of different frequency or pitch.

Second, even newborn babies can distinguish among different sounds and will alter their sucking pattern to hear music and avoid noise (Butterfield & Siperstein, 1972). By 2 months, infants can distinguish among some types of musical sounds, such as the plucks and bows made on a violin (Jusczyk, et al., 1977). By 6 months infants can even distinguish changes in melodies (Chang & Trehub, 1977). Not only can they recognize melodies, they can even join in. Mothers were trained to sing at selected musical pitches and then tried to teach their babies to imitate. A later test in the laboratory revealed that 5-month-olds could imitate the three pitches (Kessen, et al., 1979). It is evident that babies are clearly biologically capable of not only appreciating the songs that caregivers sing but imitating them as well. Lullabies may be more important than we first thought! Finally, recent studies (Pick & Palmer, 1989) indicate that children's perception of musical events continues to develop well beyond infancy. Whether or not we can pick out babies who are budding Mozarts is not yet known.

Can babies locate sounds in space? Even newborn infants can detect a sound in space. Newborns turn their heads toward the sound of a rattle (Muir & Field, 1979; Muir & Clifton, 1985).

Evidence of the existence of a genetically based auditory mechanism comes from recent investigations of newborn responses to the human voice, which show that neonates respond to, and perhaps prefer, the human voice over other sounds (Aslin, 1987). Moreover, newborn infants appear to be differentially sensitive to the maternal voice. They changed their sucking responses more after the presentation of their mothers' voices than after the voice of another female (DeCasper & Fifer, 1980). Together these findings suggest that the human infant's auditory apparatus is organized to be particularly responsive to the characteristics of the human voice. In addition, babies are able to learn to discriminate among voices very rapidly and quickly learn to recognize their mothers' voices over other female voices. There are certain features of maternal speech to babies—high pitch and exaggerated pitch contours—that seem to make this type of speech attractive to babies. This pattern of exaggerated speech is called *motherese* (see Chapter 8). When 4-month-old babies are presented female voices containing either normal or motherese pitch contours, they turn to listen more to the motherese voice than the normal voice (Fernald, 1985).

Both a preparedness or predisposition to respond to certain kinds of sounds and an ability to learn are illustrated by these studies. The significance of this kind of preparedness and early learning ability stems from their role in the development of the affectional bond between parent and child (see Chapter 7). In addition, there is also evidence that the human infant may be particularly sensitive to certain aspects of language, such as consonants, from a very young age (Aslin, 1987) (see Chapter 8). In summary, it is becoming increasingly clear that the infant is capable of auditory discriminations that have functional significance for later social and language development.

Looking: Visual Development

Some animals, such as kittens, cannot see at all for many days after birth, but at birth the eye of the human newborn is physiologically ready to respond differentially to most aspects of its visual field.

Visual Sensitivity in Infants. Let us begin with some of the simplest dimensions. Newborn infants can detect changes in brightness, can distinguish movement in the visual field, and can follow or track a visual stimulus (Banks & Salapatek, 1983; Field, 1990).

In spite of the unexpected visual capacities found in newborns, visual acuity is not fully developed at birth. Visual acuity is the ability to detect separation in parts of a visual target. Recall your last visit to an eye specialist, where you read the letters of a Snellen Eye Chart. If you can read the big "E" at a distance no greater than 20 feet away but you should be able to read it at 200 feet, you have 20/200 vision. The optimal level, of course, is 20/20 vision. Infants under 1 month of age range from 20/200 to 20/800, although this may be a conservative estimate (Dobson & Teller, 1978). This ability improves rapidly during the first year and appears to be within the range of normal adult vision by 6 months to 1 year (Aslin, 1987).

Can the infant focus well at all distances? Of course, adults can accommodate or bring a distant object into sharp focus by changing the curvature of the lens. Very young infants cannot focus well, but considerable improvement occurs between birth and 3 months in the ability to focus both distant and near targets. Newborns and 1-month-olds display significant focusing errors (overaccommodation for distant targets and underaccommodation for near targets), whereas 3-month-olds display small errors. By 6 months the infant can focus as well as the average adult (Aslin, 1987; Banks & Salapatek, 1983).

Color vision. Are infants color-blind or can they distinguish colors? Not only can 3-month-old infants distinguish among different colors, but they can divide them into hue categories, such as red, blue, yellow, and green, just as adults do (Bornstein, 1978; Bornstein, Kessen, & Weiskopf, 1976; Teller & Bornstein, 1984). Some even argue that newborns can distinguish among certain colors including red and green but not among others (Adams, Mauer, & Davis, 1986; Mauer & Mauer, 1988). The evidence suggests that the ability to perceive color is probably universal and innate and may depend on specialized physiological sensors in the retina of the eye. The importance of this finding is far-reaching: It suggests that infants come equipped to make sense out of many of the colors in their visual world.

In summary, infants have a wide range of visual capacities that permit them to interact with their social and physical environment from a very early age.

Parts or Patterns: Development of Pattern Perception in Infancy. Is the visual world of the infant organized into patterns, images, and forms, or does the infant see merely lines, angles, and edges? Two radical positions regarding these issues can be distinguished: One view, the nativist position, suggests that the infant comes into the world capable of perceiving forms and patterns; the empiricists, on the other hand, argue that only through experience can the infant develop the ability to construct "forms" out of the pieces of visual information coming from the environment. Most of the evidence suggests that babies slowly develop the ability to see forms across the first few months of life. The complex developmental story on how the infant's perceptual world is organized is a fascinating one!

Generally this research shows that, as infants develop, they prefer increasingly complex stimuli. Complexity, however, is not the only factor that determines the kinds of visual stimuli infants prefer. As Olson and Sherman (1983) noted, infants prefer (1) curved over straight lines, (2) irregular over regular patterns, (3) concentric over nonconcentric stimuli, and (4) symmetrical over asymmetrical figures. Moreover, there are individual differences in infant visual preferences; some infants prefer to look at novel visual sights and others are content to look at familiar forms. As we will see in Chapter 11, these early individual differences may have important long-term implications for later development of the child, with infants who prefer novel events showing higher cognitive development at later ages.

Not only do infants prefer complexity, but the determinants of their attention are complex as well! To what parts of the visual target do the infants attend? In order to find out, Salapatek and Kessen (1966) substituted an infrared camera for the human observer. By this technique it was possible to determine not only that infants were looking at an object but precisely on what parts of the object their eyes were focused. When they photographed the exact position of infants' eye movements on a triangular target, they found that the infants' attention was concentrated on the angle and was *not* distributed over the whole form. This suggests that certain elements of complex patterns may elicit infant attention, but it is not fair to conclude that young infants perceive a pattern. Instead, they appear to be attracted to specific elements of a pattern, particularly a vertex or boundary. Later researchers have found a way of attracting infants to the inner parts of a figure: Make the inner elements move (Girton, 1979)!

Scanning of forms clearly improves with age. Although 4- to 6-week-old infants continue to show the fixation of the newborn on angles and edges, by 2 months of age there is visual tracing of both edges of the pattern and the center or internal areas (Salapatek, 1969; Aslin, 1987).

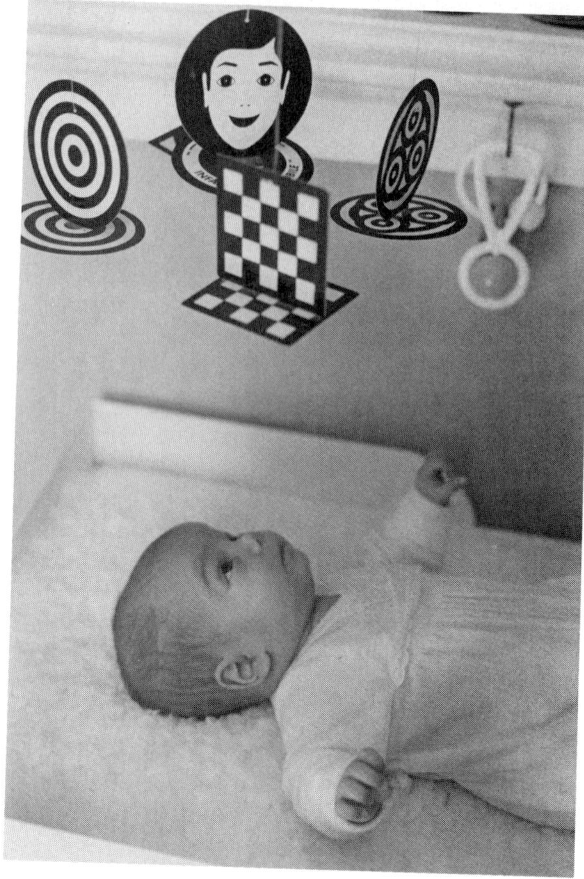

Babies prefer visual stimuli with high contrast such as faces and checkerboards. Toy manufacturers have been watching researchers as well as babies and designed mobiles that reflect the latest research on infant visual preferences.

Face Perception: The Beginnings of Social Responsiveness. Faces have attracted the attention of babies and researchers alike. How early can infants recognize faces? Does the recognition of social stimuli such as faces follow the same developmental course as recognition of checkerboards and colored squares? These are important questions since they provide some early clues concerning infants' social responsiveness and their ability to recognize familiar and unfamiliar people. Just as 1-month-old infants scan only a small section of the outermost contours of a triangle, they do the same when they look at a line drawing of a face. However, when 2-month-old infants are shown a drawing of a face, they do not stay fixated at the outer edge, but quickly move their eyes to the internal aspects of the figure (Maurer & Salapatek, 1976). Figure 5-5 illustrates these developmental changes in scanning patterns.

Other researchers have documented the developmental shifts in scanning of real faces (Haith, Bergman, & Moore, 1977). Using a technique that permitted them to determine which parts of the face were scanned, these investigators found that 3- to 5-week-old infants fixated on the face only 22 percent of the time, while 7-week-old and 9- to 11-week-old infants fixated 88 and 90 percent of the time. Figure 5-6 shows the parts of the face that the infants at different ages focused on. Not only did the older infants spend less time on the contours, but they looked at the eyes more than the younger infants did. "It is possible that between 5 and 7 weeks, the eyes have become meaningful to the infants as signals of social interaction. Whatever the case, it is highly likely that increased face looking, and especially eye contact,

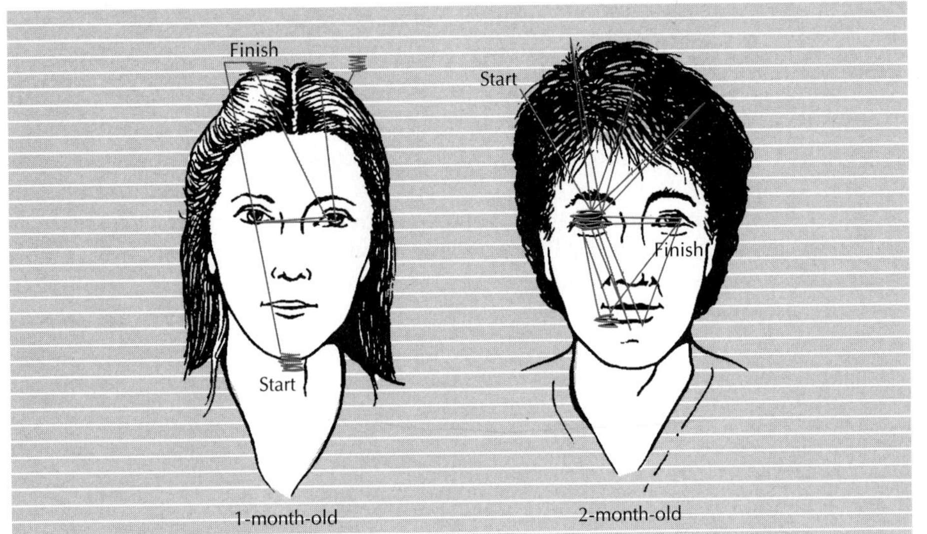

FIGURE 5-5
How 1- and 2-month-old infants scan the human face. (*From Maurer & Salapatek, 1976, with permission of the authors and the Society for Research in Child Development.*)

carries special social meaning for the infant's caretakers and plays an important role in the development of the social bond" (Haith et al., 1977, p. 8).

Faces are potent elicitors of infant interest, but this does not mean that infants have any innate preferences for faces or that young infants are even responding to faces or other objects as unified wholes. Faces may simply happen to possess an abundance of perceptual qualities, such as contour, contrast, and movement, which are intrinsically appealing to the infant. In fact, recent research has confirmed a general developmental sequence in the emergence of facial perception (Nelson, 1987). First, infants prior to 2 months of age cannot discriminate a schematic from a scrambled face. Second, by 3 months of age infants show a clear preference for schematic over scrambled faces. This suggests that instead of a face being a mere collection of interesting elements, such as eyes and nose, infants now perceive faces as distinct patterns and can even distinguish among dissimilar faces (Olson & Sherman, 1983; Mauer & Mauer, 1988). A recent experiment supports the argument that faces carry special meaning for babies by this age (Dannemiller &

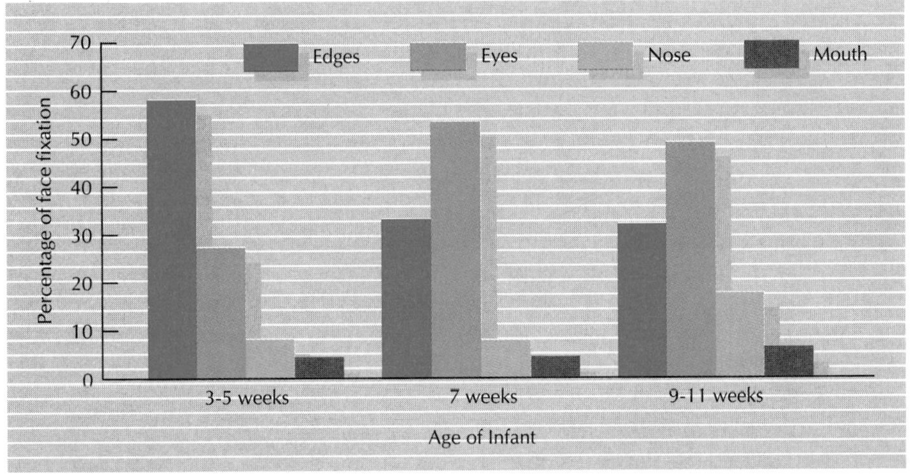

FIGURE 5-6
Shifts in face fixation of 3- to 11-week-old infants. (*Drawn from data of Haith, Bergman, & Moore, 1977.*)

Stephens, 1988). In this study, 6- and 12-week-old infants saw the computer-generated stimuli shown in Figure 5-7. Stimuli *a* and *b* are identical except that the black and white shading is reversed. Stimuli *c* and *d* are used to see if babies have a general preference for pictures with black borders and light interiors. At 6 weeks, babies showed no preference, while at 12 weeks, babies looked longer at Figure 5-7*a*—the picture that most adults view as more facelike! Babies showed no preference between *c* and *d*. These findings suggest that by 3 months babies seem to identify faces as faces and not just because of their perceptual features, such as symmetry or contrast. This shift from the perception of parts to the perception of patterns appears to be similar for both objects and faces. Finally, as Box 5-2 suggests, babies not only show a preference for schematic or patterned faces but a preference for attractive faces as well.

SEEING FORM FROM MOVEMENT

It is well known that moving objects attract greater visual attention from the infant than do stationary ones, but movement may also provide important information about the form of objects. Adults can perceive the form of a three-dimensional object even when all visual information except motion is reduced to a minimum. One of the most dramatic examples of this phenomenon involves the presentation of a two-dimensional stimulus array of ten to twelve point lights attached to the major joints and head of an unseen walking person (see Figure 5-8). Adults quickly and unequivocally recognize this moving display as depicting a person, but find it very difficult to organize any familiar form if the display is not moving. Are these findings a function of extended experience watching people move or do they reflect the presence of inborn motion-processing principles?

Bertenthal, Proffitt, and Cutting (1984) attempted to answer this question by testing the sensitivity of 3- and 5-month-old infants to three computer-generated versions of eleven point lights moving as if attached to a person walking (Figure 5-8). It was reasoned that infants might perceive one of three possibilities when viewing these displays: (1) an unorganized group of point lights moving across the screen like a swarm of fireflies, (2) the periodic motion paths of individual point lights, or (3) a connected form specified by the motions of the point lights. A series of different discrimination tests were conducted. Both age groups were found to discriminate between an upright (Figure 5-8*a*) and an inverted version of the point-light walker display (Figure 5-8*b*), suggesting that they perceived more than an unorganized swarm of lights. Furthermore, they discriminated the upright point-light walker display (Figure 5-8*a*) from a scrambled version (Figure 5-8*c*) in which the relative

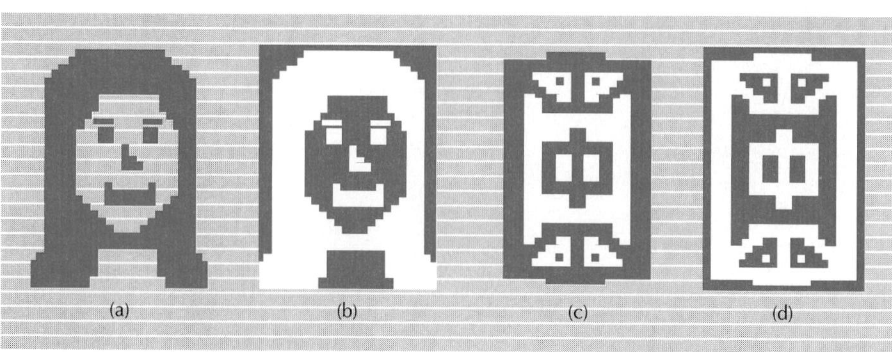

FIGURE 5-7
Stimuli used to evaluate infants' preference for facelike patterns. (*From Dannemiller & Stephens, 1988.*)

BOX 5-2 IS BEAUTY "IN THE EYE OF THE BEHOLDER"?

How early can babies distinguish attractive from unattractive faces? An answer to this question can help us discover whether infants learn over time what is beautiful or whether they possess an early and perhaps innate sense of beauty. To answer this question Judy Langlois and her colleagues (1987) showed 2- to 3-month-old and 6- to 8-month-old infants pairs of color slides of the faces of adult women previously rated by other adults for attractiveness. Both the older and younger babies looked longer at attractive faces when viewing pairs of faces in which one was attractive and one was unattractive. By 2 months of age, babies showed a visual preference for the attractive faces. In a further study, Langlois, Roggman, and Rieser-Danner (1989) found that babies respond differently not only to attractive and unattractive pictures but to attractive and unattractive strange adults as well. In a laboratory playroom, when the infants were exposed to a stranger who wore either an attractive or unattractive lifelike latex theater mask designed by a professional maskmaker, 12-month-old infants clearly preferred the "attractive" stranger; they showed more positive affect (smiling, laughing) and less withdrawal from the attractive stranger, and were more involved in play with the stranger in the attractive mask. Babies even preferred attractive dolls over less attractive ones. A new group of 1-year-olds were allowed to play with two 10-inch cloth dolls that were identical except for their faces and the color of their buttons. One doll had a face that had previously been rated as highly attractive and the other doll had a relatively unattractive face. The infants played with the doll with the attractive face more than the same doll that had less attractive facial features. Clearly babies prefer not only to look at attractive faces but to interact with people or dolls that have attractive faces.

Why do infants prefer attractive faces? Some argue that attractive faces are preferred because they contain more of the features that the infant's visual system is organized to react to. Infants prefer high contrast, contours, curves, and vertical symmetry, and attractive faces may be more curved and less angular or more vertically symmetrical than unattractive faces.

Others argue that attractive faces are more "facelike" or closer to a prototypic face. Moreover, it assumes that babies are organized to respond to social stimuli as a way of guiding their social behavior. If this is true, attractive faces provide better guides to social action and babies are more sensitive to these types of faces. No one knows the answer at this stage. However, these studies "seriously challenge the assumption that attractiveness is merely 'in the eye of the beholder' and that standards of attractiveness must be learned through gradual exposure to current cultural norms" (Langlois et al., 1987, pp. 367–368). Babies have a sharper eye for beauty than previously thought.

Sources: Langlois, J. H., Roggman, L. A., Casey, R. J., Ritter, J. M., Rieser-Donner, L. A., & Jenkins, V. Y. (1987). Infant preferences for attractive faces: Rudiments of a stereotype? *Developmental Psychology*, **23**, 363–369; Langlois, J. H., Roggman, L. A., & Rieser-Danner, L. A. (1989). Infants' differential social responses to attractive and unattractive faces. *Developmental Psychology*, **25**, 153–159.

locations of the lights were scrambled. Since the individual motions presented in these two displays were the same, discrimination must have been a function of extracting form information. Static images taken from these three displays were not discriminated. The results of this study show that infants can extract form from motion; however, they do not specify in any detail what particular form was seen. Later studies (Bertenthal, Proffitt, & Kramer, 1987) suggest that a form consistent with a person's body is probably not perceived in point-light walker displays until 9 months of age.

The clear conclusion emerging from these findings is that young infants can extract figural structure from motion information. Apparently, the infant must possess certain inborn motion-processing principles since it is unlikely that such complex processes could have been learned in a mere three months. There is more to movement than meets the eye!

DO INFANTS DEVELOP VISUAL EXPECTATIONS?

Not only do babies begin to "see" forms and figures at an early age, they are able to develop expectations about future events in their visual world by 3 months of age. To demonstrate this remarkable ability to anticipate future

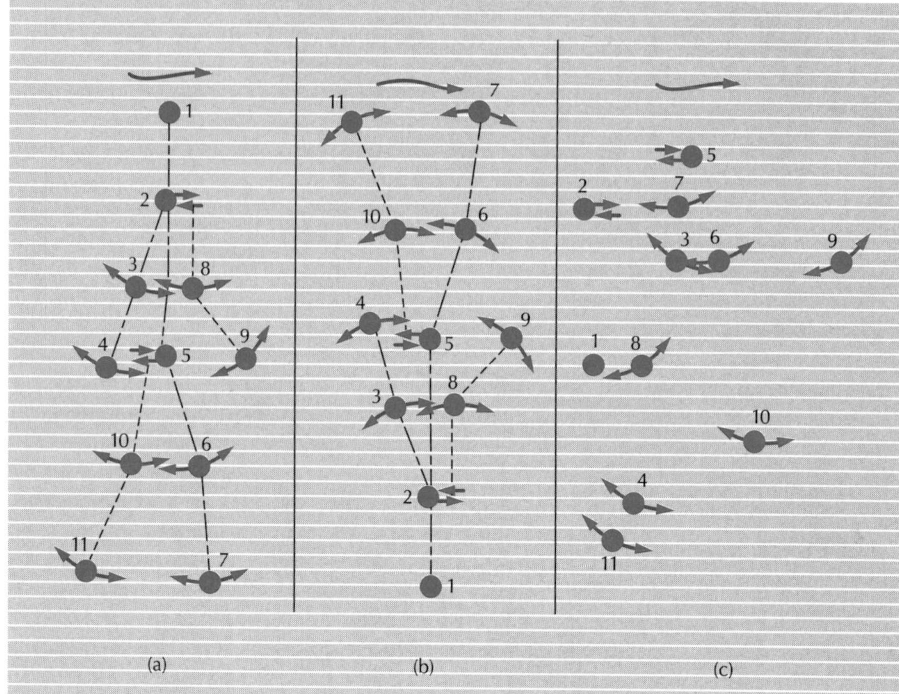

FIGURE 5-8
Seeing form from movement. (*From Bertenthal, Proffitt, & Cutting, 1984, with permission.*)

events in young infants, Haith and his coworkers (Haith, Hazen, & Goodman, 1988; Canfield & Haith, 1991) examined whether babies would form expectations about where an interesting picture would appear. Pictures were presented in either a regular alternating sequence (left, right, left, right) or in an unpredictable sequence (left, left, right, left, and so on). When the sequence was predictable, 3-month-olds began to anticipate the location of the picture by looking to the side on which it was likely to appear. And they showed this pattern of expectations in less than a minute! Younger infants did not show this pattern of future-oriented behavior, which suggests that cognitive or perhaps biological development is crucial for the emergence of this visual skill.

DEPTH PERCEPTION AND PERCEPTUAL CONSTANCIES

Our survey of the infant's visual capacities would not be complete without a discussion of two other aspects of visual behavior: depth perception and size and space constancy.

Depth Perception. How early can babies perceive depth or how far away an object is located? As early as 1 day of life infants can perceive which objects are closer and which are farther away (Granrud, 1991). However, the ability to judge this distance accurately improves across age, and depends on several kinds of cues or aids. Newborn infants' eyes do not work together; they move simultaneously in the same direction only half the time (Mauer & Mauer, 1988). Young infants then rely on cues that one eye can use, such as cues that involve the motion of objects. For example, as objects approach us they fill more of the visual field and when we move our heads the retinal images of close objects move faster than the images of distant objects. These kinds of changes associated with movement help the baby judge depth. By 4 to 5 months babies can coordinate their two eyes and use stereoscopic vision to help them perceive depth. In this case, the infant perceives depth based on the slight disparity between the two retinal images—in a way similar to adults (Mohn & van Hof-van Duin, 1986).

The ability to perceive depth has very real practical value; as adults it prevents us from routinely walking off cliffs and the edges of tall buildings. But how soon does the infant use this ability to avoid falling? To investigate this issue, Gibson and Walk (1960) developed an apparatus that they termed the *visual cliff* (see Figure 5-9). As you can see, it consists of an elevated glass platform divided into two sections. One section has a surface that is textured with a checkerboard pattern, while the other has a clear glass surface with a checkerboard pattern several feet below it. The investigators hypothesized that if infants can, in fact, perceive depth, they should remain on the "shallow" side of the platform and avoid the "cliff" side since it has the appearance of a chasm. In the natural world, of course, it is possible to misjudge the perception of depth; for example, the reflections from the surfaces of water may mislead a person to think that the water is not deep. However, in this visual-cliff apparatus, the glass surfaces are lighted in such a way as to eliminate any reflections. Thirty-six infants ranging in age from 6 to 14 months were tested. All infants eagerly approached their mothers when the mothers were on the "shallow" side of the platform but refused to cross the "deep" side in spite of the mothers' encouragements.

Later evidence suggests that the ability to avoid falling may occur even earlier than 6 months. In order to demonstrate that premotor infants do, in fact, have this capacity, Campos, Langer, and Krowitz (1970) developed a new strategy that did not require motor skills. Instead of indexing whether or not infants would crawl over the deep side of the visual cliff, they placed $1\frac{1}{2}$-month-old infants on both the deep and shallow sides of the visual cliff and measured changes in their heart rates. The infants showed a decrease in heart rate (an index of interest) when they went from the shallow to the deep

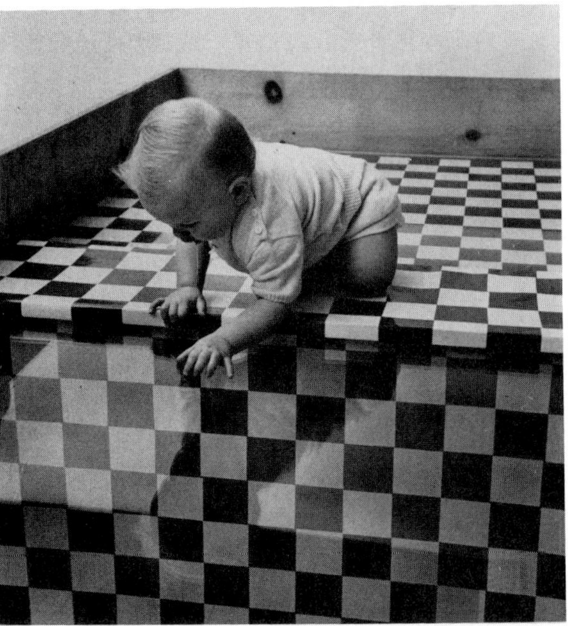

FIGURE 5-9
Picture of visual cliff. Infant is on the shallow side and is approaching the deep side.

side, which clearly suggests that infants as young as $1\frac{1}{2}$ months are able to use their depth detection skills to avoid falling.

However, later studies with older infants suggest that infants do not become *afraid* of height until they are able to crawl on their own (Campos, et al., 1978). In contrast to younger infants, older infants who can crawl show heart-rate accelerations (an index of fear arousal) when they are on the deep side—an indication that they had learned sometime between $1\frac{1}{2}$ and 7 months to be afraid of a ledge. Further evidence that locomotion is critical in the development of fear of heights comes from studies of artificially produced self-locomotion. When babies who were unable to crawl were provided walkers, they began to show fear of high places (Campos, et al., 1981).

> Why is self-produced locomotion important? One possibility is that crawling allows the infant to *calibrate* distances more accurately than before; that is, whereas the pre-locomotor infant may be able to tell that one object is closer than another, he or she may not be able to tell *how much* closer one is than another. If this is so, the human infant may be able to see depth, but not be able to gauge accurately how deep something is until he or she can move about. But there are other possibilities. Crawling may merely create the opportunity for the infant to experience more falls, and hence to appraise heights as dangerous. Or the mother may react to the infant's "near falls" with intense emotion, leading the infant to learn vicariously to fear heights, the way some infants learn to fear animals. (Lamb & Campos, 1982, p. 45)

Of course, all of these explanations may be valid; as in the case of many developmental phenomena, multiple determinants are often involved. The findings on the role of locomotion are consistent with experiments involving amimals with independent locomotion shortly after birth, which show that chicks, kids, and lambs avoid the deep side of the visual cliff when they are 1 day old. Together these studies illustrate the often intricate interplay between biology and experience. Human infants may be biologically prepared to learn to fear heights, but the experience of locomotion is a necessary triggering condition for the emergence of this fear.

The important role of the environment in maintaining and nurturing the development of binocular vision that helps us perceive depth comes from studies of children born with defects in their visual system. Children with a history of convergent strabismus (crossed eyes) may not develop normal binocular vision—an ability that helps us detect distance and depth (Banks, Aslin, & Letson, 1975). Studies of children who have experienced corrective surgery at different ages indicate that the period during which the cross-eye condition is most detrimental appears to begin several months after birth, reaches a maximum during the second year of life, and declines by 6 to 8 years of age (Salapatek & Banks, 1977). For children born with this condition, early corrective surgery before age 2 usually prevents long-term visual deficits. This research underlines the importance of the early environment for sustaining the proper development of the infant's perceptual systems.

Size and Shape Constancy. Next, we turn to the origins and development of size and shape constancy. As adults we are able to judge the size of an object, regardless of its distance from us; for example, even though a truck looks toylike at a great distance, we still recognize it as a truck with real-life proportions. This ability is called *size constancy* and is defined as the tendency of an object to retain its size in our perception regardless of changes in viewing distance, even though the size of the retinal image changes (see Figure 5-10). Again, the question arises: How early does the infant show size constancy? Infants show this ability by 6 months, but not at 4 months (McKenzie, Tootell, & Day, 1980). Moreover, unlike adults, even the older infants (8-month-olds) could manage size constancy up to a distance of only 70 centimeters. The data are consistent with an interactional view suggesting that both experience and neural developments in the visual system in the early months of life probably conspire in helping the infant achieve size constancy.

What about *shape constancy*? This refers to the ability to correctly see an object's shape in spite of change in its orientation. Even newborn infants are capable of shape constancy (Slater & Morison, 1985), which suggests that some perceptual abilities may even be present at birth. Perhaps as researchers improve their techniques for probing the infant's capacities we will find evidence of very early perceptual competence in other areas such as size constancy as well. Possibly "perceptual constancies in general are an inherent function of the visual system" (Yonas, Arterberry, & Granrud, 1987, p. 7). Keep an eye out for later advances!

A visual skill that is helpful is the ability to avoid impending collisions; as a result, most of us avoid crashing into each other as we drive our cars. As Yonas and his colleagues (Yonas et al. 1987) have found, infants show their sensitivity by blinking in response to an impending collision, such as an object that appears to be moving closer, by 3 months of age (Yonas et al., 1987) or even by 1 month of age (Manez, 1987).

Together these findings suggest that the infant is capable of a wide variety of visual feats and suggests a level of visual ability much greater than we had presumed only a few decades ago.

Smell and Taste

To conclude our excursion through the sensory world of the infant, we turn to two other senses—smell and taste. Just as we have seen in the case of vision and hearing, we will see that smell and taste are also well developed from a very early age. The infant's competence is not restricted to a few senses, but characterizes all sensory systems.

THE SENSE OF SMELL

Neonates can discriminate among a variety of odors. They even show different facial expressions to odors that adults rate as pleasant or aversive. Infants less than 12 hours old reacted to the odors of strawberry and banana with facial expressions of satisfaction while a whiff of fish or rotten eggs elicited expressions of rejection—just as these common food smells do in adults (Steiner, 1979). Since these young babies were strictly on a liquid diet and

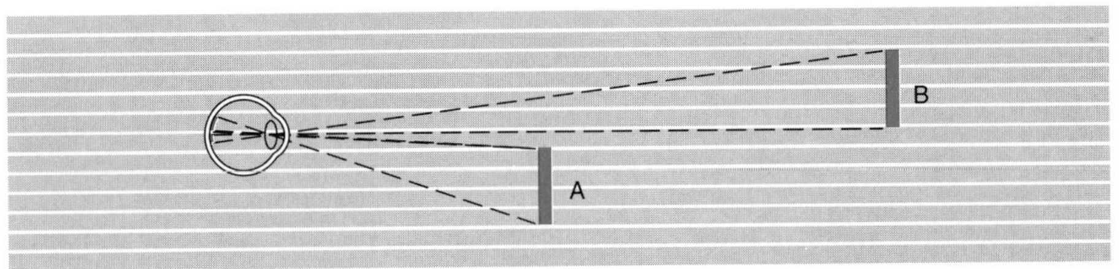

FIGURE 5-10
Size constancy. Two objects of the same physical size may produce very different retinal image sizes and yet be seen as the same size.

had not yet had the opportunity to learn through direct experience that strawberries are preferable to rotten eggs, the finding suggests that the capacity to discriminate odors may be innate. After a few days, smell may even play a role in early social interaction and provide one of the early means by which infants come to recognize their mothers. In a study in England, Macfarlane (1975) showed that 1-week-old infants can distinguish their mothers' odor from those of other people. In this clever demonstration, two used breast pads from nursing mothers were positioned above the infant's head. Infants turned to look at their mothers' breast pad more often than a stranger's pad. The preference was not evident in the first few days of life and seems to depend on the infants' learning to recognize their mothers' special smell. For young infants, smell provides another early guide to things and people in their world.

Nor is this rapid recognition limited to infants. Mothers can correctly identify shirts worn by their neonates compared to shirts worn by other neonates of either the same or different sex (Porter, Cernock, & McLaughlin, 1983). While rapid early learning is a likely explanation, other evidence suggests that an innate mechanism may be involved. The maternal-recognition effect held even in situations where the mothers had little postpartum contact with their neonates because of cesarean section deliveries (Porter et al., 1983). Although the exact mechanism remains unclear in view of the value of smell for infants and their mothers, maybe it is fortunate that our efforts to create an odorless environment have not yet reached early infancy! Once developed, our sense of smell is remarkably stable. There is a high degree of consistency in our smell sensitivity between 6 and 94 years of age, with little evidence of a decline even in the oldest subjects. This, of course, is in marked contrast to the decline in visual and auditory sensitivity that occurs in old age. In view of the fact that the olfactory sense is one of the earliest to be acquired prenatally, it has been suggested that "these sensitivities which develop the earliest will be those which are sustained longest in the lifetime of the individual, relative to those more recently acquired" (Rovee-Collier, Cohen, & Shlapack, 1975, p. 318).

A MATTER OF TASTE

Although controversy still exists concerning the exact taste preferences of the human newborn, there is little doubt that the neonate is selectively responsive to different tastes. Newborns reveal their ability to discriminate tastes in many ways. For example, they slow their rate of sucking and increase their heart beat when tasting a sweet liquid. Possibly infants are excited by pleasant tastes and just like adults try to savor a good taste (Lipsitt, 1986)! Another clue that babies can distinguish among tastes comes from their facial expressions. Steiner (1979) found that newborns showed different facial expressions when sour, sweet, and bitter substances were placed on their tongues. For example, sweet tastes were associated with an expression of satisfaction, sometimes a smile and smacking of the lips; in contrast, lip pursing and a wrinkled nose accompanied the sour taste, while bitter tastes led to a downturning of the edges of the mouth, a protruding tongue, and occasionally spitting! More recently, Rosenstein and Oster (1988) have confirmed that 2-hour-old infants show different facial expressions in response to sweet, sour, and bitter, as well as salty tastes. Since these characteristic expressions occurred even in infants who had never been fed anything but milk or milk substitutes, taste preferences appear to be innate. Evidence from studies of fetal lambs suggest that taste perception may be present even before birth, and lambs may prefer sweet rather than bitter substances in the prenatal period (Mistretta & Bradley, 1985). However, even in the earliest days of life, there are sex differences in taste: more females prefer sweet formula than males (Nisbett & Gurwitz, 1970).

In summary, the sensory and perceptual apparatus of infants is well developed very early in life, which suggests that infants are well prepared to profit from interactions with both their social and physical environments.

Putting the Pieces Together: Bimodal Perception in Infants

When a ball bounces, two kinds of information are available: the sound of the ball hitting the ground as well as the sight of the ball moving up and down. Do infants perceive one event—a bouncing ball—or separate visual and auditory events? This is an age-old philosophical question. In the seventeenth century, William Molyneux posed the question in perhaps its most celebrated form:

> He asked us to imagine a blind man who can recognize a sphere and a cube on the basis of touch. The objects are then placed in front of the blind man and he is suddenly made to see. The question is whether he can now recognize these objects on the basis of vision alone. . . . The answer was clear. A blind man who recovered his vision could not recognize these objects by sight alone, because visual and tactual sensations are not intrinsically related to one another. Only after the man gained some experience in simultaneously looking at and touching the objects, would he learn which visual impression corresponded to which tactual sensations. Put metaphorically, the view is that the visual tactual modalities do not at first "speak the same language" and that some experience is necessary to compile a dictionary which can be used to "translate" tactual impressions into visual ones and vice-versa. (Meltzoff, 1981, p. 85)

To find out whether infants can perceive bimodally specified events that require them to put together information from two separate modalities that are relevant to the event was the aim of the work of Elizabeth Spelke (1987). In one experiment (Spelke, 1979) 4-month-old infants watched films of a kangaroo and a donkey who were bouncing at different rates and producing different sounds. When one of the sound tracks alone was heard coming from between the two screens—to reduce the link between the sight and sound—the infants looked at the film that had previously accompanied the sound. Since these were novel sight-sound combinations, it is not due to prior opportunity to link these two events.

Infants not only have the ability to detect sight-sound relationships with inanimate objects but can associate particular faces and voices. In one study, 4-month-olds watched two films of unfamiliar women speaking. The voices were synchronized to the facial movements of the speaker (Spelke & Cortelyou, 1981). When a single voice was played through a central speaker, the infants looked more quickly and more often toward the film of the "speaking" woman. Infants can detect the invariant temporal relationship between the sight of a speaking person and the sound of his or her voice, even when they are spatially dissociated.

Finally, infants appear to be receptive to the common emotional tone of a visual and vocal communication. Walker (1980) showed 7-month-old babies a person telling a happy story in an upbeat voice and with an appropriate affective expression. Another person told a sad story using a sad voice. When tested with only the happy or sad voice, infants looked to the correct face that matched the emotional tone of the voice.

These studies suggest that people are perceived by infants as audible and visual objects from a very early age. This ability probably makes the task of learning to recognize familiar from unfamiliar people easier for infants. Finally, these findings challenge the commonly held view of early perceptual development—namely, that "humans begin life experiencing unrelated sensations in each sensory modality. They must learn to put together the separate experiences provided by each sense" (Spelke, 1979, p. 626). In contrast to this view, young babies do not appear to experience a world of unrelated visual and auditory sensations; instead they can perceive objects and people as unitary audible and visual events. How early this ability can be detected and the mechanisms that underlie this precocious ability of the very young infant still remain to be discovered. However, as Box 5-3 illustrates, very young infants can visually recognize objects that they have touched only with their mouths or hands!

These studies suggest that Molyneux may have answered his thought experiment about the blind man incorrectly. As Meltzoff suggests, "one can only wonder about possible differences in the history of philosophy and psychology had Molyneux framed his provocative philosophical question in terms of newborn infants instead of blind adults" (1981, p. 108).

LEARNING IN INFANCY

Can babies learn? As we have already seen in this chapter, babies have remarkably well-developed sensory and perceptual capacities. Now we turn to the issue of how soon infants can learn from their early encounters with the environment. Genetics sets the course for development, but learning principles and processes are important for shaping, molding, and directing the course of *genetically* based capacities. Principles of learning act together with the genetic, hereditary, and maturational factors discussed in earlier chapters. Learning refers to change in behavior that accrues over time as a result of experience. Learning covers many processes, but in infancy four approaches have been typically studied: habituation, classical conditioning, operant learning, and imitation. Although these processes continue to be important throughout the life span, as we will see in Chapters 10 and 11, studies of older children place more emphasis on problem solving, information-processing strategies, and abstract reasoning.

Habituation

One of the earliest forms of learning, and one that we have already discussed in our exploration of the infant's sensory and perceptual capacities, is habituation. Infants respond increasingly less to a stimulus, such as a tone or a light, that is repeatedly presented. Although the cortical mechanisms that may control this early form of inhibition are not well understood, the infant's capacity to cease responding is clearly well developed even for newborn infants (Rovee-Collier, 1987).

BOX 5-3 SEEING WITH THE MOUTH AND HANDS: THE TOUCH-VISION LINKAGE

Can infants recognize their pacifiers by sight or do they know them only by touch? To find out, Meltzoff and Borton (1979) designed two different pacifiers: both were round, but one was smooth while the other had a series of rubber nubs (see Figure 5-11). Sixty-four 29-day-old infants first sucked on one of the pacifiers and then had a chance to look at styrofoam replicas of the pacifiers. Seventy-two percent of the infants looked longer at the one that they had just sucked on than at the tactually unfamiliar one. Since infants of this age have had little opportunity to simultaneously touch and look at objects, the demonstration suggests that "human beings are able to recognize equivalences in information picked up by different modalities without the need of learned correlations" (Meltzoff, 1981, p. 107). Since the infants were already nearly a month old, experience cannot be completely ruled out.

Perhaps the mouth region that is so important for the infant's early feeding activities is particularly well developed at birth, which makes oral-visual transfer possible at an early age. Recently Streri and Spelke (1988) showed a similar phenomenon with 4-month-old infants, but instead of touching with the mouth, the infants explored objects with their hands. Infants were presented with either two rings connected by a stick or rings connected by a flexible band. A cloth cover prevented the infants from seeing the objects. After touching the rings until they habituated to the object (that is, they ceased exploring the rings), they were shown the two sets of rings. Since they were habituated to one set of rings, it was expected that they would look more at the unfamiliar or novel rings. And they did, which suggests that they were able to make the "link" between touch and vision. The specific features (edges, or information about the whole form) that are used by babies to make these links across sensory modalities are not yet clear, and the mechanisms by which infants are able to accomplish this feat are not specified. We do know that babies see more than meets the eye!

Sources: Meltzoff, A. N. (1981). Imitation, intermodal coordination and representation in early infancy. In G. Butterworth (Ed.), *Infancy and epistemology*. Brighton: Harvester Press; Meltzoff, A. N., & Barton., R. W. (1979). Intermodal matching by human neonates, *Nature*, **282**, 403–404; Streri, A. O., Spelke, E. S. (1988). Haptic perception of objects in infancy. *Cognitive Psychology*, **20**, 1–23.

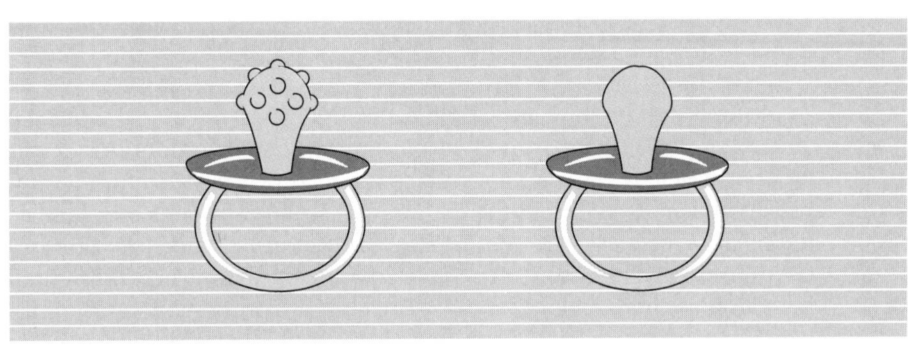

FIGURE 5-11
Pacifiers used to test infant cross-modal abilities. (*From Meltzoff & Borton, 1979.*)

Classical and Operant Conditioning

As we saw in Chapter 1, the first and most famous demonstration of the kind of learning termed *classical conditioning* was carried out by Ivan Pavlov over sixty years ago in his study of dogs. This type of conditioning can be found frequently in everyday life. Consider the child who cries when he sees a physician who gave him a painful injection on a previous visit. On the first visit, he did not cry when he saw the physician. It was only as a result of the pairing of the painful needle puncture (unconditioned stimulus) with the physician (conditioned stimulus) that the sight of the doctor alone elicited crying. Figure 5-12 illustrates this conditioning process.

For the past forty years there has been considerable controversy over the issue of how early children can be conditioned, and the controversy is not

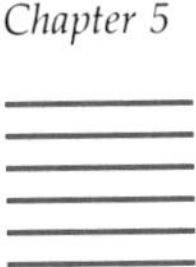

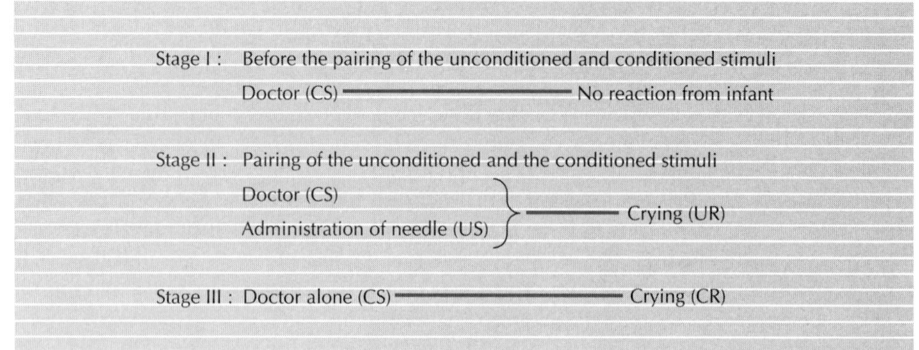

FIGURE 5-12
Three stages of classical conditioning.

yet over (Rovee-Collier, 1987). There is evidence that even newborns can be classically conditioned, especially in biologically meaningful contexts such as feeding. For example, human newborns as young as 2 hours of age learned to associate a tactile stimulus—stroking of the head with delivery of a sugar solution to the mouth. After classical conditioning the tactile stimulus alone elicited puckering and sucking responses (Blass, Ganchrow, & Steiner, 1984). While babies are clearly adept at learning relationships that make them more efficient at the important tasks of locating and ingesting food, they appear to lack the motor capacity to escape or avoid noxious events, such as pain and loud noises. As a result, babies have difficulty learning relationships associated with noxious or unpleasant events (Rovee-Collier, 1987). Human infants have parents to protect them, so it may be less critical to have this ability at birth. Moreover, neurological evidence suggests that the mechanisms that help infants form associations between aversive events and their consequences develop later than the mechanisms for positive events (Rovee-Collier, 1987).

Infants can learn from early life through operant conditioning. DeCasper and Fifer (1980) have shown successful operant conditioning of sucking in newborns using the mother's voice as a reinforcer—a reminder that these processes can help illuminate the infant's social capacities too. Just as we saw in the case of classical conditioning, successful demonstrations of operant conditioning in the newborn have involved existing organized patterns of behavior, such as sucking or head turning, as components of rooting-feeding behavior, which are of considerable biological importance to the infant's survival. Some responses are apparently more easily modified than others. Newborn infants, like members of any species, have certain response systems that are biologically prepared to operate efficiently very early in life. For the human newborn infant, these prepared responses, to use Seligman's (1970) term, are associated with feeding and through evolution have been selected as a result of their importance for survival. The infant is best organized in early life to perform behaviors that are functionally adaptive (Sameroff, 1972, 1983). Since the infant also has limited energy, learning is often guided by a principle of energy expenditure, with the well-adapted organism learning those responses which are most energy efficient (Rovee-Collier & Lipsitt, 1982). Failure to learn may sometimes be due to the fact that the response required costs too much to make it worthwhile for the infant!

As the studies in this section show, basic learning processes appear to be present very early in life; what changes over development seems to be the nature of the information that the infant is capable of learning and possibly the speed and efficiency with which learning proceeds.

In the next section, we turn to another type of learning—imitation, learning through observation.

Learning through Imitation. Although a great deal of learning takes place through direct contact with the environment, as we have seen in the cases of operant and classical conditioning, learning can occur vicariously as well. Merely observing the behavior of peers, parents, and teachers can significantly expand the behavioral repertoire of the observer. Research has clearly demonstrated that new responses can be acquired and old responses elicited and modified through imitation. Indeed, it would be extremely uneconomical in terms of time and energy if infants were forced to acquire all of their responses through either operant or classical conditioning.

Imitation begins early in life and provides another route for the acquisition and modification of developing behavior patterns. Imitation of at least some behaviors can occur in the first weeks of life. Meltzoff and Moore (1983) found that even newborns—7 to 72 hours old—imitated the mouth opening and tongue protrusions of an adult. There is evidence that imitation of lip movement can take place in the first hour of life (Reissland, 1988).

Infants as young as 9 months can imitate not only a series of modeled behaviors (for example, button pushing, egg rattling) immediately but, even more impressively, after a 24-hour delay (Meltzoff, 1988a). Babies who had no chance to imitate immediately did so accurately when they were given these same objects upon their return visit to the laboratory the next day! Related studies suggest that 14-month-old infants can delay or defer imitation over a period of one week (Meltzoff, 1988b). "Once seen, not soon forgotten" is clearly the implication of these findings.

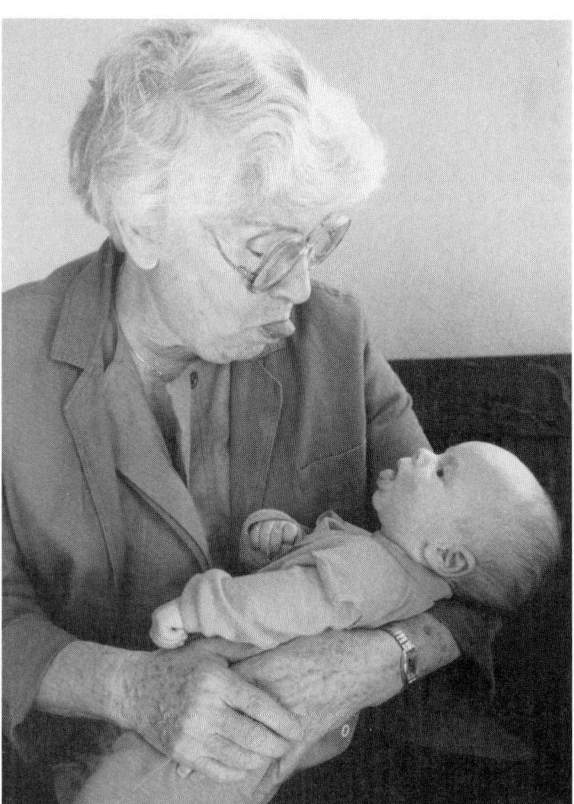

Infants can imitate adults from an early age, as this imitative exchange between a grandmother and her 5-week-old grandchild illustrates.

While the mechanisms underlying this extraordinary capacity of very young infants are still unclear, this could be viewed as a further illustration of the infant's ability to engage in active intermodal matching (Meltzoff, 1990). In this case, the newborn babies may form cognitive representations of the model's behavior, which they then translate into motor movements of a similar type. These findings suggest that infants may be ready for social interaction and learning by imitation at a much earlier age than previous theories thought possible.

Memory in Infancy

As the work on imitation suggests, even very young infants have memories of both visual and auditory events over relatively long time spans. In one remarkable demonstration, researchers (Werner & Siqueland, 1978) found that newborn infants could remember a visual event over a twenty-four hour period. The infants in this study altered their sucking patterns when the color and pattern of a visual reinforcer changed—even though they had not seen the visual stimulus for nearly a day! Babies can remember speech sounds as well (Ungerer, Brody, & Zelazo, 1978). Beginning at the ripe old age of 14 days, babies were exposed by their mothers to two words that are not generally typical vocabulary for 2-week-olds—*tinder* and *beguile*. The babies heard the new words sixty times a day for thirteen days—resulting in 780 exposures. At fourteen and twenty-eight hours after this marathon training session, the babies' memory for the words was tested. Not only could the babies remember the words but they recognized these novel words better than their own names. (Of course, few mothers repeat their babies' names quite so often as sixty times a day.) Even more remarkable is a recent demonstration that six 40-week-old babies can remember events and objects that they were exposed to during a visit to an infant researcher's laboratory after a two-year delay (Myers, Clifton, & Clarkson, 1987). On the first visit they saw pictures (a whale), touched objects (a clothespin), or heard sounds (a bell, a rattle). Upon returning two years later, when they were nearly 3 years old, the children were more likely to touch and grasp the objects and recognize the sounds that they were exposed to earlier than a control group of children who were seeing the objects for the first time. It's not only elephants who never forget!!

Can infants remember associations that they have learned? Three-month-old infants were first taught to kick in order to turn a mobile above their cribs (see Figure 5-13). Typically, babies forget the link between their kicks and the mobile after about eight days. This means that the effects of early learning may be short-lived if they are forgotten so quickly (Rovee-Collier, 1986). With the help of a reminder, infants could remember for as long as four weeks (Rovee-Collier, 1986). To remind the baby about the earlier learning, they let the baby have a brief three-minute look at the mobile about twenty-four hours before the memory test. During the reminder period, kicks did not turn the mobile, while during the memory test, kicks turned the mobile around. In comparison with babies who had earlier learned the links between kicking and mobile turning but had no reminder, the reminded babies kicked more often—an indication that they remembered the connection.

Sleep helps the reminder process since the longer the babies slept between the reminder and when they were tested, the better was their retention. It appears that "the reactivation of memory is a time-locked process; in other words it takes time to 'dredge them up' " (Rovee-Collier, 1986, p. 6). Clearly, infants can remember, but they may have more trouble retrieving the

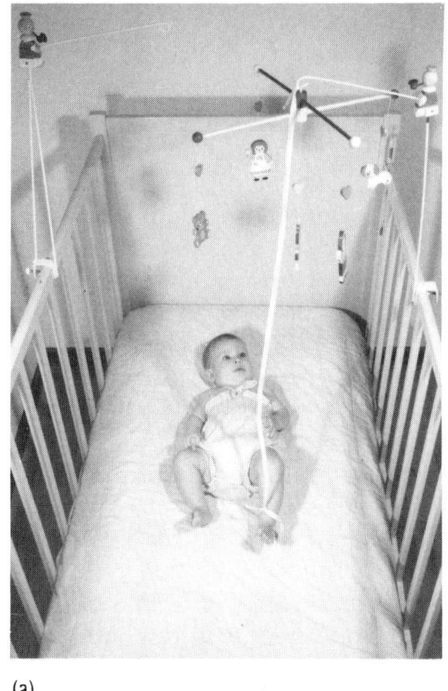

(a)

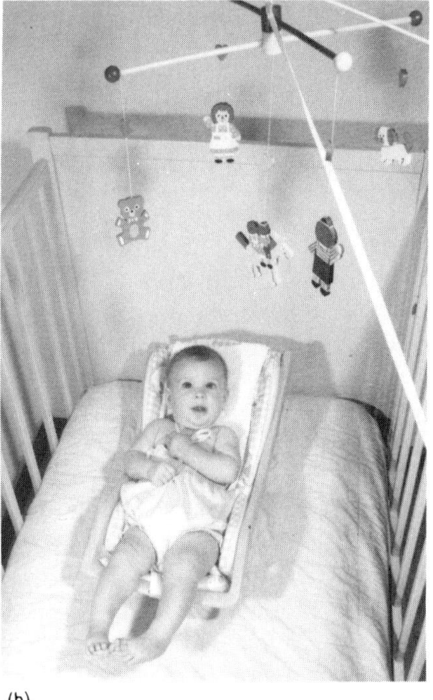

(b)

FIGURE 5-13

(*a*) An infant during a reinforcement phase with the ankle ribbon attached to the same suspension bar as that from which the mobile hangs. The empty mobile stand, clamped to the crib rail at the left, will hold the mobile during periods of reinforcement. (*b*) The same infant during a reactivation treatment. The mobile and ribbon are attached to the same suspension hook, but the ribbon is drawn and released by the experimenter (not shown), and concealed from the infant's view at the side of the crib. Also not shown is the empty stand, positioned as before. The infant will be exposed to the reinforcer (the moving mobile) for only three minutes, twenty-four hours before retention testing. (*Photograph by Breck P. Kent.*)

information from their memory banks. With a little help, they can remember over impressive lengths of time.

SUMMARY

INFANT STATES AND SOOTHABILITY

- Newborns experience predictable, periodic changes in *state,* ranging from vigorous activity to regular sleep. A state of alert inactivity is optimal for responding to external stimulation, thus a good time to assess the newborn's capacities.
- Two extreme states experienced by the infant are sleeping and crying. The amount, pattern, and kind of sleep shift during the first few months to more culturally accepted and adultlike patterns. Crying, an effective early means of communication, follows distinct patterns that also change with development.
- Although there are wide differences among individuals, sexes, and races in soothability, caregiver techniques of holding the baby on the shoulder and swaddling are effective. Sucking (on a pacifier or for food) is one way infants can soothe themselves.

THE ORGANIZED AND ORGANIZING NEWBORN

- Newborns come equipped with *reflexes*, or involuntary responses to external stimuli, that allow them to interact with the environment. Reflexes may be assessed to test the soundness of the infant's central nervous system.
- The auditory capabilities of the newborn are well developed. At birth infants are more sensitive to high-frequency than low-frequency sounds,

and they need a slightly louder sound than adults in order to detect it. These abilities improve rapidly during the first two years of life. Newborns also are capable of distinguishing among different sounds and of locating sounds in space. These early auditory discrimination abilities result in a predisposition or preparedness to respond to human voices, which may be related to later social and language development.

- Although visual capacities continue to develop throughout the first year, newborns are sensitive to brightness and movement, can distinguish colors, and can track a moving object. Newborns cannot focus well, but this ability increases during the first three months. In addition, babies slowly develop the ability to see forms and to scan all parts of a pattern, resulting in preferences for increasingly complex stimuli and greater attention to facial features over time. New research indicates that 3-month-olds also begin to anticipate future visual events.
- Two critical aspects of visual behavior are depth perception and size and space constancy. Although newborns can perceive which objects are closer and which are farther away, the ability to judge the distance accurately improves with age as babies begin to coordinate their two eyes and use stereoscopic vision. Even newborns are capable of shape constancy; however, size constancy does not develop until about 6 months of age. Newer research indicates that experience is needed to produce both size constancy and fear of heights in infants.
- Neonates can discriminate among a variety of odors, and by 1 week of age they have learned to distinguish their mothers' smells from those of other people. Neonates also are able to discriminate different tastes. Research using facial expressions and rate of sucking indicates that their preferences are for sweet rather than sour or bitter tastes.
- Research on bimodal perception in infants indicates that, from a very early age, they can put together information from two separate modalities. This is true for both inanimate objects and for human faces and voices, suggesting that babies perceive objects and people as unitary audible and visual events.

LEARNING IN INFANCY

- Four basic learning processes are present early in life, and have been studied in infants. They include *habituation*, *classical conditioning*, *operant conditioning*, and *imitation*.
- Habituation, or the infants' ability to decrease the degree of responding to a repeated stimulus, is well developed in newborns. Habituation to sounds, sights, or tastes is commonly used to study infants' sensory, perceptual, and memory abilities.
- Evidence suggests that even newborns can be classically conditioned by pairing pleasurable events, although they may not be able to form associations between negative events until later. However, operant conditioning, involving a modification in the infant's response following the consequences of a behavior, is evident in newborns.
- Although newborns are capable of imitation, the type and amount of obervational learning changes with development.
- Even newborns can remember things that they have learned over a period of weeks or months with the aid of retrieval cues. Thus, rather than having poor memories, it appears that infants just have trouble retrieving information from memory without help.

CHAPTER 6

BRAIN DEVELOPMENT, MOTOR SKILLS, AND PHYSICAL MATURATION

Tina's development always was rapid. She crawled and walked early, and by her first birthday she was forcing her parents to put their favorite vases on a high shelf out of her reach. Early in adolescence—at age 11—she reached sexual maturity well ahead of her sixth-grade classmates. In contrast, Jason was a leisurely baby and took his time about everything. The vases were safe in Jason's house until he was 14 months old. The pattern continued into childhood and Jason was nearly 16 years old when he had his pubescent growth spurt.

The differences between these two children are not unusual; they illustrate that the rates at which children develop vary enormously between the sexes and across individual children. In this chapter, we will examine the influence of biological and environmental factors on motor development and growth. First, we explore the development of the brain and examine how genetic and environmental forces work together in determining early brain growth. Next, we explore the motor and growth patterns that infants and children follow. What are the motor achievements of developing infants? When do they reach, crawl, and walk? What are the factors that speed up or slow down these emerging skills? In addition, we will explore the ways in which children grow. What determines how fast they grow? How do biological and environmental factors modify growth patterns? Have growth patterns changed over past generations? Are children growing taller or heavier, and if so, why? What are the consequences of reaching sexual maturity earlier or later than other adolescents? Finally, what happens when growth patterns go awry? What are the causes and consequences of being too thin or too fat? These are some of the questions we shall address in this chapter.

BRAIN GROWTH

The changes in brain growth during infancy are remarkable. While it is currently believed that the baby's brain has all its neurons or nerve cells at birth (Kolb, 1989), the brain has only about 25 percent of its adult weight at birth. Change occurs rapidly. By 6 months, it reaches 50 percent of adult size and reaches 75 percent by the end of the second year. Across development, changes take place in shape, in size, in density of connections among the neurons, and in the speed of transmission between neurons. By adulthood, there are approximately 1 trillion neurons, with each neuron engaging in 100 to 1000 synaptic contacts with other neurons. To put it differently, there are about 1 quadrillion synapses in the human brain (Huttenlocher, 1979; Lerner, 1984).

There is an orderly course to the development of the brain. As the infant moves from primarily reflexive behavior in the early stages of life to later voluntary control over motor movements, the primary motor area of the brain develops most rapidly. Lagging behind are the areas of the brain that control higher senses such as vision and hearing, with the visual area developing more rapidly than the auditory area.

Hemispheric Specialization

One of the most important features of the organization of the brain is its division into two halves or hemispheres. These two parts are connected by a set of nerve fibers called the *corpus callosum*. Not only are the hemispheres anatomically different but they control different functions (Best, 1988; Hahn,

MOTOR DEVELOPMENT

Infants and children show remarkable and rapid progress in their motor development. By the end of the first year most infants are able to crawl, sit up, stand up, and many are taking their first steps. They develop eye-hand coordination as well that allows them to explore and manipulate objects. Later they master practical skills such as buttoning their clothes and dressing themselves. Still later in the preschool years, children's motor coordination improves to allow them to play games and sports and to master complex skills such as jump rope and bike riding.

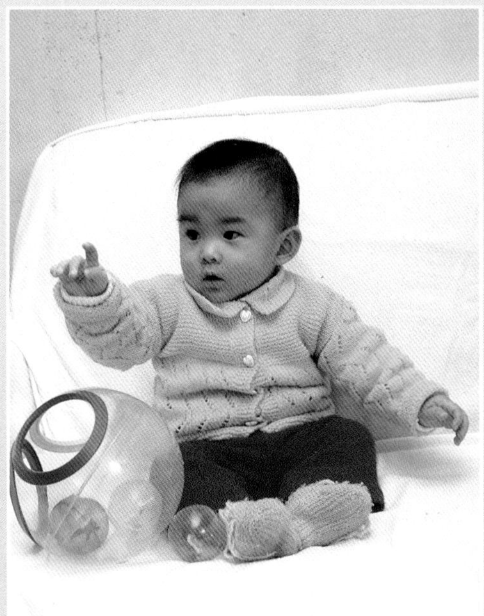

A 4-month-old in a sitting position.

A 4 1/2-month-old standing with the help of her father.

The joy of crawling.

A 7-month-old pulling a peg out of a hole—a demonstration of eye-hand coordination.

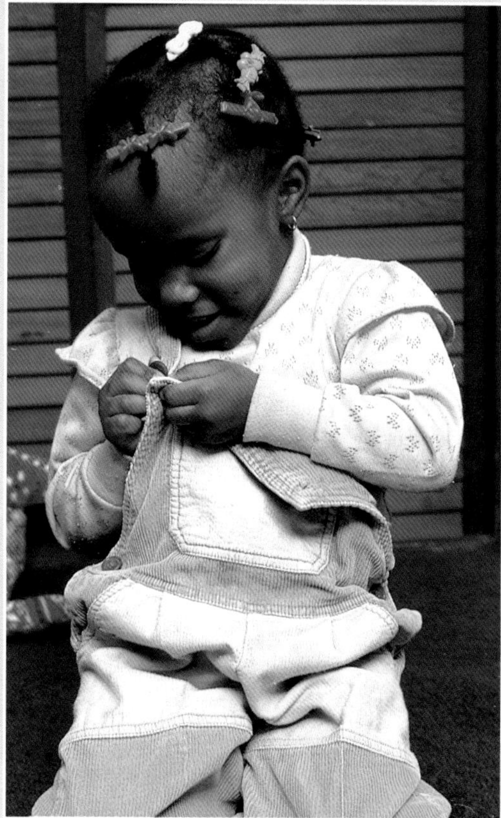

This 2 1/2-year-old is dressing herself.

Motor skills are important for social play with other children.

1987). Studies of patients who have suffered brain damage (for example, head injuries, tumors) give us important information about the functions controlled by the different halves of the brain. The left side controls the right side of the body, while the right half governs the left side of the body.

The right hemisphere is involved in the processing of visual-spatial information, nonspeech sounds such as music, and face recognition. For example, when brain damage is concentrated on the right side of the brain, people become spatially disoriented, their drawing skills are impaired, and they have trouble following a map (Bryden, 1982). Recently, researchers have found that the processing of emotional information is also under the control of the right hemisphere (Bryden & MacRae, 1989; Hahn, 1987). Five- to fourteen-year-old children distinguished angry, sad, and happy voices better when they heard them in their left ear (which is controlled by the right hemisphere) than when they heard the voices in the right ear (which is controlled by the left hemisphere) (Saxby & Bryden, 1984). Children recognized facial expressions representing different emotions better using the right than the left hemisphere (Saxby & Bryden, 1985), and individuals who have right hemisphere brain damage have trouble interpreting the emotional expressions of others. The implications of these findings are far-reaching. The inability to distinguish between an angry and a happy tone of voice or to know when someone is delighted or depressed can cause serious disturbances in social interaction patterns. Finally, recent evidence suggests that emotional production is lateralized as well, but not in a simple fashion. In contrast to recognition, the right side of the brain was activated during the expression of negative emotions while the left side was associated with production of positive emotions (Fox & Davidson, 1988).

The left hemisphere is dominant in the understanding of speech and language. Individuals who suffer left hemisphere brain damage can recognize a familiar song, and tell a stranger's face from an old friend's face, but they are unable to understand very well what is being spoken or to speak clearly. Normal children are better able to recognize letters or words that are presented to the right eye or the right ear than to the left eye or ear (Bryden, 1982; Bryden & Saxby, 1986).

How early does hemispheric specialization begin? Recent evidence suggests that lateralization of hemispheric function begins early in life (Hahn, 1987; Molfese & Segalowitz, 1988). For example, Molfese and Molfese (1979, 1980) recorded electrical potentials in newborn infants' brains evoked by spoken words, and learned that full-term newborns and even preterm infants process speech syllables faster in the left than in the right hemispheres. Moreover, the early measures of evoked potential from babies' brains were able to discriminate children who differed in language ability three years later (Molfese & Molfese, 1985). In infants who later exhibited better language performance, the left hemisphere differentiated among speech sounds and the right hemisphere discriminated among nonspeech sounds. However, the left hemisphere bias observable soon after birth is not as extreme as that seen in older children or adults. Only 70 percent of infants show anatomical or behavioral asymmetries favoring left hemisphere language processing. By 3 years of age, 90 percent of children show this kind of laterality effect. After this age, researchers find few developmental differences in children's reliance on the left hemisphere for processing verbal information or in children's superior ability to understand emotional cues through the right hemisphere (Bryden & Saxby, 1986; Saxby & Bryden, 1984, 1985).

A similar pattern of the emergence of lateralization is found in the development of handedness. About 90 percent of adults are right-handed, and this preference is evident in early infancy. A majority of infants show right-hand dominance. Infants use the right hand more than the left for reaching, touching, and grasping (Hawn & Harris, 1983; McCormick & Mauer, 1988). While young infants tend to shift from right to left hands and vice versa, handedness is generally fully established by 2 years of age (Bryden & Saxby, 1986). The establishment of right-footedness is slower, and it appears to continue to develop until 4 or 5 years of age or even longer (Porac & Coren, 1981).

Laterality and Reading

Cerebral lateralization may have important implications for everyday behavior. About 3 to 4 million, or 5 percent, of the children in the United States have serious problems in learning to read. These dyslexic children—as they are often called—have a fundamental difficulty in integrating visual and auditory information. They are unable to match the written letters or words to the sound of a word. Some children have difficulty breaking apart the letters that compose the words; they treat words as wholes (Liberman, Shankweiler, Liberman, Fowler, & Fischer, 1976). Another problem is that children either confuse or cannot remember the names of letters and call a "d" "b". While reading difficulties may have multiple origins and causes, one correlate of reading problems may be abnormal cerebral organization. Specifically, some researchers suggest that children who are poor readers do not show the normal pattern of lateralization. Instead they process spatial information not only on the right side of the brain but on the left or verbal side of the brain as well. In turn, the left side, which usually is restricted to understanding verbal information and language, may become overloaded, with resulting deficits in such language skills as reading (Witelson, 1977, 1983). This abnormal cerebral development may be genetically determined or may be caused by environmental factors in utero or in early childhood. Although the view that reading difficulties are caused by faulty development of lateralization is still controversial, there is a considerable body of evidence to support this hypothesis (Bryden, 1988; Corballis, 1983). At the same time, caution is advised, since the links between the brain and complex behaviors such as reading are only beginning to be understood.

The Environment and Early Brain Plasticity

The importance of the environment in brain development was demonstrated many years ago and continues to be an important concern. At the turn of the century, A. J. Carlson (1902) demonstrated that the physiological structures of the visual system of birds could be altered by variations in stimulation. However, Carlson was much ahead of his time, and a demonstration over forty years later would point the way to serious consideration of the effects of early experience. In 1947 Austin Riesen reported his classic experiments on the effects of reduced sensory stimulation on the development of the visual system of the chimpanzee. He found that the retinal structures of a chimp that had spent the first sixteen months of life in the dark failed to develop properly. Specifically, there was a loss of ganglion cells in the retina: those neurons whose axons form the optic nerve, which connects the retina with the rest of the nervous system. Moreover, even when the animals were returned to lighted conditions, their retinas failed to develop properly and they became permanently blind. Other studies (Hubel, 1988) have confirmed these original results. It is clear that even the anatomical structures of the central nervous system, the foundation blocks of maturation, require a certain amount of environmental stimulation for proper development.

Later research has shown that both brain size and function can be modified by experience (Greenough, Black, & Wallace, 1987). This is well illustrated in a series of pioneering studies by Rosenzweig, who "decided to set up two markedly different experimental situations, to put the rats in one or the other at an early age when their brains might be most plastic and to maintain the animals in these situations for a prolonged period. Animals were therefore assigned at weaning (about 25 days of age) and kept for 80 days in either an enriched environment—environmental complexity and training (ECT)—or in an impoverished condition (IC). . . . In the enriched situation, the animals are housed in groups of 10 to 12 in a large cage that is provided with 'toys' such as ladders, wheels boxes, platforms, etc. . . . The toys are selected each day from a larger group. To enrich the rats further, we gave them a daily half-hour exploratory session in groups of 5 or 6 . . . in a 3 × 3 foot field with a pattern of barriers that is changed daily. . . . After about 30 days, some formal training is given in a series of mazes. In contrast, the animals in the impoverished condition live in individual cages with solid side walls so that an animal cannot see or touch another. These cages are placed in a separate, quiet, dimly lighted room, while the ECT (enriched) cages are in a large, brightly lighted room with considerable incidental activity" (Rosenzweig, 1966, pp. 321–322).

What impact do these different rearing conditions have on brain weight and on brain chemistry? Brain weights were recorded, and it became apparent that their environmental manipulations were affecting the actual weight of the animal's brain. As Figure 6-1 indicates, separate analyses were performed for the cerebral cortex and the rest of the brain; this was fortunate, since not all areas, it turned out, were equally affected. The variations in early environment had their greatest impact on the cortex region, with the enriched animal's cortex weighing about 4 percent more than the cortex of the restricted littermates. Not only does the cerebral cortex differ from the rest of the brain in its response to the differential rearing experiences, but all regions of the cortex are not equally altered. The occipital region, which controls vision, shows the largest changes in weight, 6 percent; whereas the somesthetic area, the touch region, shows only 2 percent increase in weight. Other

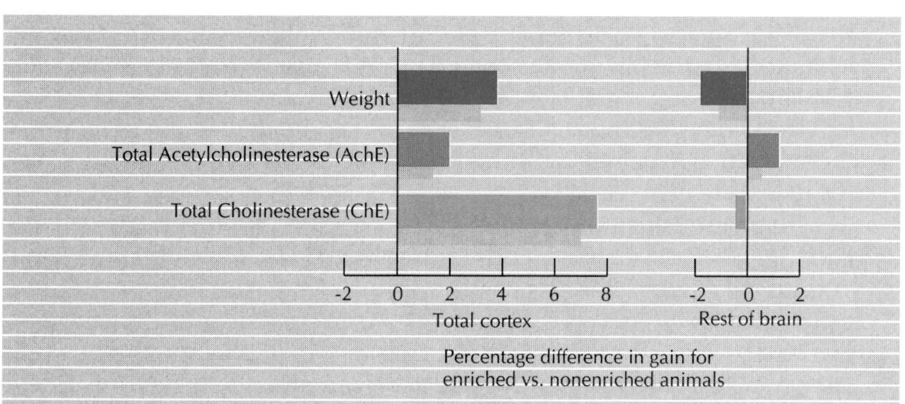

FIGURE 6-1
Effects of enriched rearing environment on brain chemistry and brain weight in rats. *(From Rosenzweig, 1966, with permission of the author and the American Psychological Association.)*

experiments indicate that there may be systematic relationships between the nature of the enrichment program and the particular region of the cortex that is affected. Rearing rats in darkness results in a shrinkage of the visual cortex. There is some suggestion of parallel effects at the human level. Donaldson in 1892 (cited by Rosenzweig, 1966) carried out a postmortem examination of the brain of a blind, deaf-mute human being and found deficient development of the cortical areas controlling speech and visual and auditory functions. The skin-sense region of the cortex, on the other hand, was apparently normally developed. Careful investigation may show that there is an anatomic as well as a behavioral basis for the overcompensation phenomenon wherein loss of one sense results in heightened sensitivity in the other sense organs.

Brain size may not be the only important factor; the biochemistry of the brain as well as the structure of neurons, or nerve cells, is affected by early experience. First, the neurons increase in complexity as a consequence of enriched environment, as measured by the number of branches and subbranches that develop from the neuron (Greenough & Green, 1981; Greenough et al., 1987). These branches, or dendrites, may, in part, account for the difference in brain size. In addition, these changes in neuron structure mean that there will be a considerably greater number of synapses per neuron in animals reared in complex environments (Turner & Greenough, 1985). Since synapses are junctions or switching stations between neurons, the amount of information that can be transmitted may be greater in these enriched animals. If all neurons in the human brain were equally plastic as the rat brain seems to be, the effect would be remarkable. "The difference of 2000 synapses per neuron in the rat (reared in enriched environments) would translate into many trillions of synapses on the 100–200 billion neutrons of the human brain" (Greenough et al., 1987, p. 547). Second, brain chemistry is affected. To assess these effects, Rosenzweig and Bennett (1970) measured the activity of two enzymes, acetylcholinesterase (AchE) and cholinesterase (ChE). These enzymes play an important role in synaptic transmission of nerve impulses between neurons. Specifically, they act on acetylcholine, the chemical transmitter that conveys messages from one neuron to the next. Examination of Figure 6-1 reveals that the total activity of both enzymes increases significantly as a result of the enriched rearing experience. As in the case of weight, the cortex is again the area most responsive to the rearing conditions.

The rats used in the original studies were young, and for good reasons: It was assumed that their brains would show their greatest plasticity prior to maturity. However, later studies showed that the weight and biochemical effects are not restricted to the immature brain. Adult rats exposed to the deprived or enriched experience after spending their early days under normal laboratory rearing conditions showed similar weight and biochemical effects (Greenough & Green, 1981). However, the effects of differential experience may be greater during the earlier periods of life and, as the organism ages, the impact of experience on the brain may be narrower and more specific (Greenough & Green, 1981).

Finally, the mechanisms that are involved in profiting from early experience in contrast to experience in adulthood may be different. In early development, a surplus of synapses appear, which are then pruned back by experience to a subset that is functionally valuable. Early development involves both gains and losses. In later development and adulthood, synapses appear to be generated in response to events that provide information to be encoded in the nervous system.

Do these changes in brain size, complexity, and biochemistry result in brighter rats? Although there is still debate, mounting evidence (Greenough et al., 1987) indicates that animals from a complex environment may be able to process and remember environmental information more rapidly or efficiently than animals reared under more impoverished conditions.

The implications of these findings for humans are clear: brain development is a lifelong process, and plasticity and malleability are not restricted to the early years of development. By studying plasticity over a wide span of ages, a better understanding of the reasons for decline in brain efficiency with aging and/or disease will be gained. Finally, intervention studies in animals involving neuronal cell transplants have yielded some success in correcting congenital defects in the central nervous system (Gash, Sladek, & Sladek, 1980). However, interventions of this type at the human level are promising, but highly controversial. In any case, these studies dramatically illustrate the impact of the environment on the development of the central nervous system.

MOTOR DEVELOPMENT

What course does the infant's motor development follow? How soon can an infant reach and grasp? How early do infants crawl and walk? One of the early achievements of infants is the ability to reach, grasp, and pick up objects. These skills are important, of course, because they provide another way, in addition to seeing and hearing, that infants can explore and learn about the objects in their new world. The schedule of these achievements is illustrated in Table 6-1 and Figure 6-2.

Until recently, most researchers accepted the classic description of Halverson (1931) who showed that grasping followed an orderly developmental sequence. It was further assumed that this sequence was governed

TABLE 6-1

DEVELOPMENT OF PREHENSION DURING THE FIRST YEAR OF LIFE

Age	Behavior
16 weeks	Scratches with fingers on tabletop Looks at and swipes at objects Retains toys put into hand Makes no contact with objects on table
20 weeks	Contacts toys on table Grasps block precariously
28 weeks	Bangs, shakes, and transfers toys from hand to hand Palmar grasp of block Whole hand contact of raisin
36 weeks	Finger grasp of block Scissors grasp of raisin
40 weeks	Holds one block in each hand Crude, voluntary release of block Index finger approach to raisin
48–52 weeks	Forefinger grasp of block Releases block into cup Neat pincer grasp of raisin

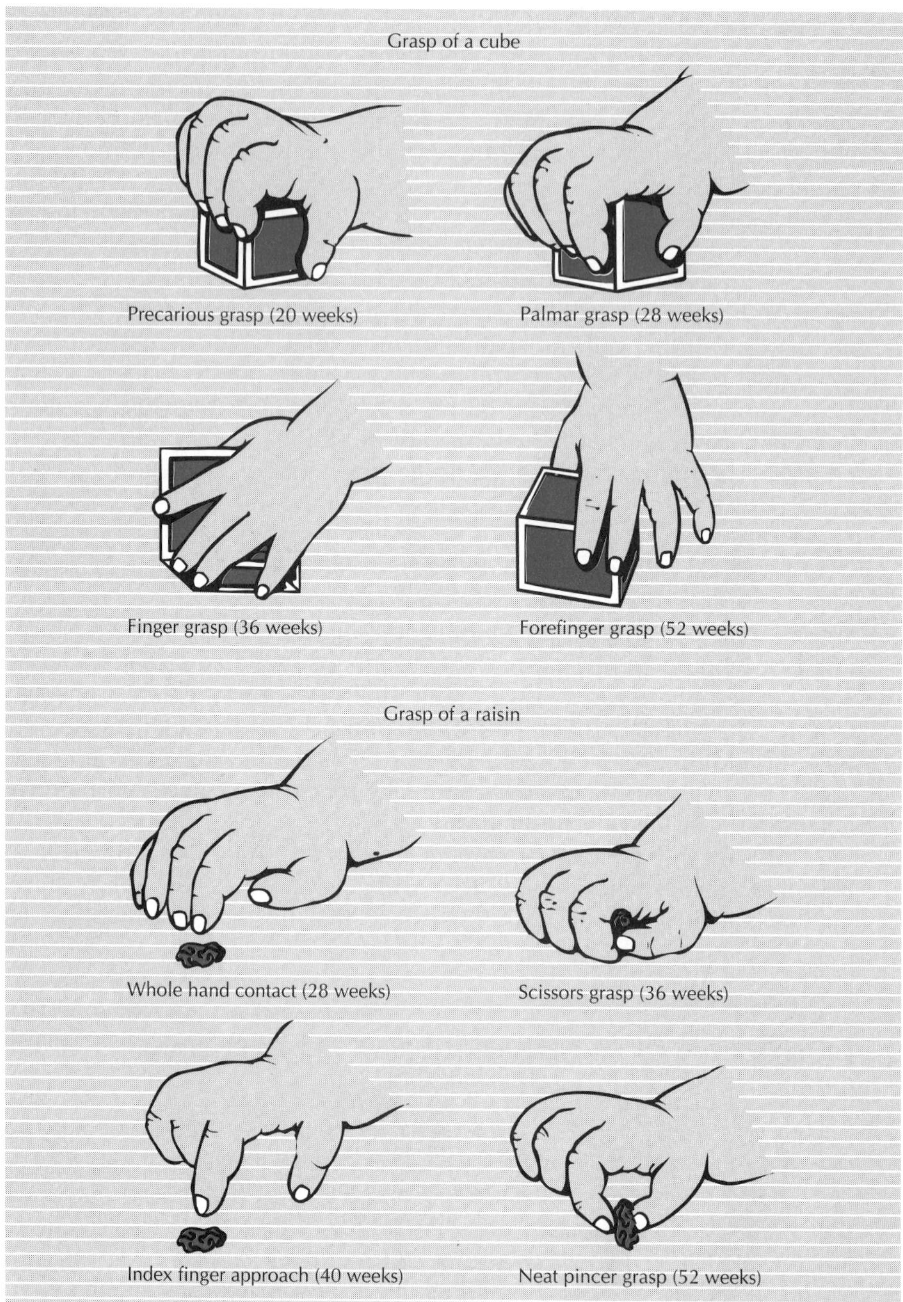

FIGURE 6-2
Prehension development during the first year of life.

by maturation of the brain and not influenced very greatly by environmental factors. However, recent research suggests that "the traditional estimates of the so-called milestones of the development of co-ordination are too conservative and inflexible" (Newell, Scully, McDonald, & Baillargeon, 1989). In the classic study, Halverson used a single object of a particular shape and size—a 1-inch cube. Newell and his colleagues have discovered that some of the early findings may have been due to the use of only a single object. By varying the size and shape of the objects presented to 4- and 8-month-old babies, they found that grasping is more complex and infants use a variety of different grips according to the size and shape of the object. For example, infants used a grip involving the thumb and index finger or thumb, index finger, and middle finger for small objects, while for large objects either all fingers of one hand or both hands were used. Of greatest interest is the fact that there were few developmental changes; both younger and older infants showed clear sensitivity to the size and shape of objects by modifying their grasping behavior in response to the object. Instead of a system that has only one way of doing things, the infant motor system is highly flexible and able to adapt to the demands of the situation. There is no doubt that neurological development sets limits on infants' abilities, but there is more room for change in response to the environment than we previously thought.

Developmental changes do occur in the way that infants decide how to grasp an object (Newell et al., 1989). Four-month-olds rely more on touch to determine grip configuration, while 8-month-olds use the visual system to guide their grasping activities. Age does have its advantages; picking up the relevant information from the visual system allows the older infant to "get ready" by shaping their hand to fit the object before they touch it. (For a further illustration of the development of visually directed reaching, see Box 6-1, which illustrates that learning to coordinate eye and hand depends not only on maturation but on experience as well.) In spite of the developmental change in visually directed reaching and grasping, the way that infants grasp an object at 4 and 8 months is similar. This suggests that grasping is a well-developed skill in early infancy—at least by 4 months and perhaps earlier.

Locomotor Development

The remarkable achievement of the development of posture and locomotion in infants was plotted by Shirley (1933), and her results are shown in Figure 6-3. One of the interesting aspects of locomotor development is that it follows a U-shaped course across the first year of life. The behavior appears early as newborn stepping, then disappears at about 2 months of age, and subsequently reappears in the last months of the first year in the form of walking.

Various accounts of how walking develops have appeared over the years. Some maturational theorists believe it is due to the development of the motor cortex (McGraw, 1940). Others view locomotor development as a response to cognitive plans or representations (Zelazo, 1983). Still others have suggested that a motor "program" in the spinal cord guides locomotor development (Forssberg, 1985). None of these explanations have been very successful in accounting for the disappearance and reappearance of stepping.

A recent alternative view—a systems approach—has been offered by Thelen (Thelen, 1988; Thelen & Ulrich, 1991). According to this view, locomotor skill is multiply determined and emerges from the interplay among a variety of developing components. She assumes that perceptual, affective, attentional, motivational, postural, and anatomic elements interact in particular contexts to determine the level of locomotor skill at any point in development. All the components have to be "ready" and at an appropriate maturational status and the context has to be appropriate before the behavior is evident. To illustrate, consider the issue of the case of the disappearing newborn stepping response. Thelen and Fisher (1982) suggested that the stepping didn't disappear at 2 months because of a central instruction that controlled the motor patterns but because of developmental changes in body size and composition. The baby's size and weight were too much load on the emerging motor system and therefore masked or hid the baby's capability.

BOX 6-1 EXPERIMENTAL MODIFICATION OF VISUALLY DIRECTED REACHING

Evidence of the plasticity of the human organism comes from a series of experimental studies of the modification of visual motor behavior. During the first half year of life, normal infants in average environments proceed through a rather remarkable set of landmarks that culminate in visually directed reaching for objects at about $5\frac{1}{2}$ months of age. Before this time, the hand and eye are simply not well coordinated. At first, the infant may attend to an object placed in her visual field, but only in the second month can any swiping action be seen. Gradually the young infant learns to use her eye and hand together, so that she not only swings at the target but, eventually, can accurately and consistently contact the object with her hand. Burton White and his colleagues (White, 1967; White & Held, 1966; White, Castle, & Held, 1964) have shown, however, that the speed of development of visual-motor coordination can be rather drastically altered by enriching the visual world of infants whose environments were deficient in opportunities and rewards for visually directed reaching. The subjects were institutionalized infants, whose visual-motor development generally lags behind the pace of normal home-reared infants because of the rather monotonous visual environment of the institution. In order to enrich the infants' surroundings, these investigators suspended a colorful stabile over the cribs, substituted printed multicolored sheets for the standard white ones, and adorned the sides of the baby beds with brightly colored bumpers. In addition, the infants were given extra handling by their caretakers and placed in a prone position for a short time each day to further enrich their visual input. These "treated" infants exhibited visually guided reaching by ninety-eight days, an advance of forty-five days over the control babies, who were given only routine institutional care. In another related experiment, visually enriched subjects reached this developmental milestone even earlier, at day eight-nine. Stating these findings somewhat differently, the experimental infants developed visually directed reaching in approximately 60 percent of the time required by the control-group children. The White study leaves little question that severely deprived environments can have delaying effects which, in turn, can be overcome by extra perceptual and sensory stimulation.

These data illustrate that timing of the enrichment is important, as the early studies of the effects of practice on the emergence of maturational skills clearly indicated (Gesell & Thompson, 1929). White's infants, who were given too large a dose of visual stimulation too early, tended to show less rather than more looking behavior during the first five weeks of the procedure. Once the infants began to engage in prehensory contacts with the stabile over their beds and the figured bumpers along the sides of their cribs, visual attention increased sharply. However, in the initial period they not only ignored the novel objects but showed much more crying than did the control subjects. Enrichment that comes too early and in too large a dose may slow down development. Stimulation can be helpful, but the dosage and timing must be carefully considered if maximal effectiveness is to be achieved. Probably the most effective enrichment provides a proper match of input to internally developing structures. Maturation, then, clearly limits the effect of externally imposed stimulation; the problem of producing maximal acceleration involves providing the child with new experiences that are paced just ahead of emerging capacities, but not so far ahead that with effort the child cannot incorporate these inputs into an emerging response repertoire. We will discuss this issue again in our consideration of Piaget's theory of cognitive development.

Sources: Gesell, A., & Thompson, H. (1929). Learning and growth in identical twin infants. *Genetic Psychology Monographs,* **6,** 1–124; White, B. L. (1967). An experimental approach to the effects of environment on early human behavior. In J. P. Hill (Ed.), *Minnesota Symposia on Child Psychology* (Vol. 1). Minneapolis: University of Minnesota Press; White, B. L., Castle, P., & Held, R. M. (1964). Observations on the development of visually directed reaching. *Child Development,* **35,** 349–364; White, B. L., & Held, R. (1966). Plasticity of sensorimotor development in the human infant. In J. Rosenblith & W. Allinsmith (Eds.), *The causes of behavior: Readings in child development and educational psychology* (pp. 60–70). Boston: Allyn and Bacon.

If this is true, by providing the baby with more support, walking may be possible at earlier ages. Stepping behavior may be possible well before actual locomotion, not because babies can't do it but because the baby is unable to provide the postural support and stability to stretch the legs backward. To solve the problem, Thelen (1986) provided nonstepping 7-month-olds with a motorized treadmill. When the babies were placed on a moving treadmill, they performed immediate alternating stepping movements that were remarkably similar to more mature walking. In a later study (Thelen, Ulrich, & Niles, 1987), they found that 7-month-olds could even adjust their walking speed when the treadmill moved at different rates for each leg. Babies are motorically

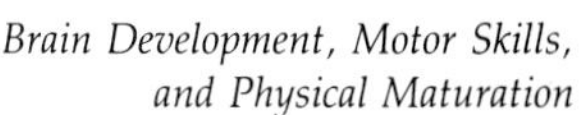

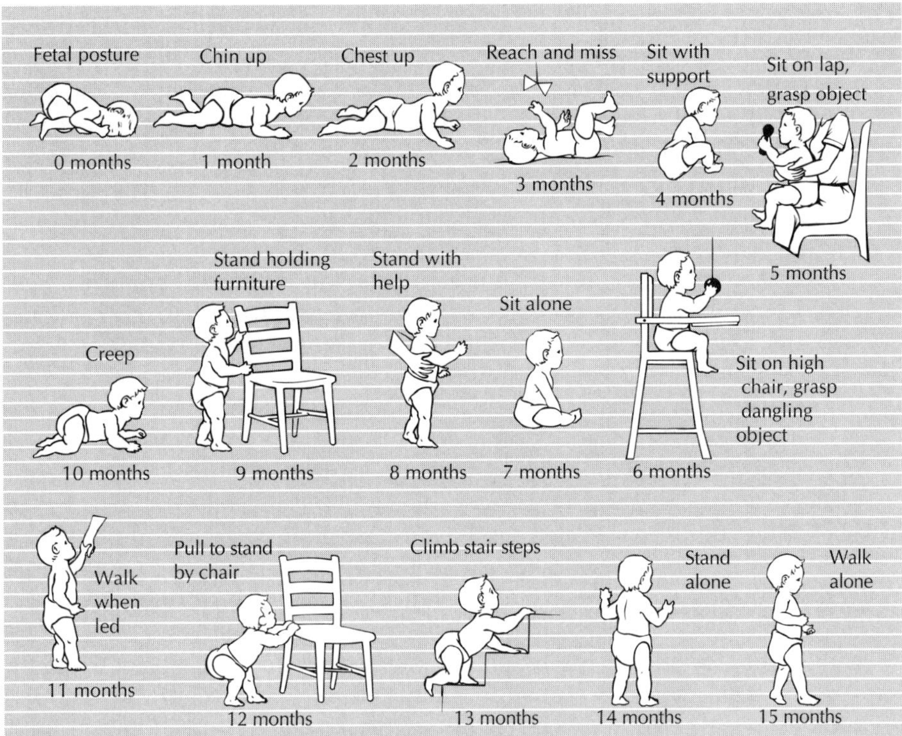

FIGURE 6-3
Sequence of motor development in locomotion. *(From Shirley, 1933. Reproduced by permission from Mary M. Shirley. Copyright renewed, 1961.)*

much more capable than we have previously thought; they just need the proper conditions to "strut their stuff"!

The Role of Experience and Culture

There are variations in the age at which walking begins. Some of these differences seem to be attributable to experiential or cultural factors, and some are based on biological factors. Children raised in different European

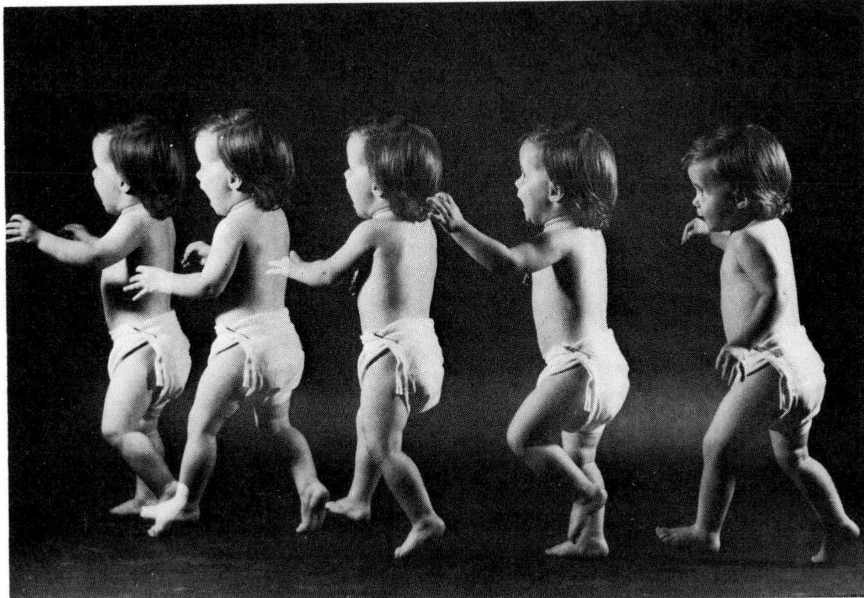

By 15 months of age, children are becoming proficient at walking and running. This picture shows the running steps of a 15-month-old baby photographed with a pulsating strobe.

cities, such as London, Paris, and Stockholm, show variations in the average age of onset of walking (Hindley, Filliozat, Klackenberg, Nicolet-Neister, & Sand, 1966). French children, for example, walk earlier than their peers in London or Stockholm. The differences in the cities are noteworthy, but even more striking is the wide range of differences in individual children. Although neither sex nor social class can account for these variations across cities, it is possible that nutritional and environmental factors may contribute to these differences.

Cross-cultural evidence indicates that variations in opportunities for practice can have an effect on emerging motor skills (Super, 1981). Consider two different cultures. In Zambian culture, infants are carried everywhere in a sling on the mother's back until the infant is able to sit. The infant receives a great deal of visual, auditory, and tactual-kinesthetic stimulation. After learning to sit, the infant is often left sitting alone for considerable periods of time; thus, the infant has plenty of opportunity to practice emerging motor skills. In another culture—the Zinacantecos of Mexico—the infants are carried, but always tightly swaddled, and even have their faces covered for the first 3 months of life. The mother's aim is a quiet infant, and so she tries to anticipate the infant's needs. The infants in these two cultures develop very differently. The Zambian infants, like many African and West Indian infants, show early development of motor behavior (Goldberg, 1966; Hopkins & Westra, 1988), while the Mexican infants show a lag in their development of motor skills (Brazelton, 1972). Together, these cross-cultural glimpses illustrate how early infant-rearing environments can alter patterns of motor development.

Rearing conditions in different cultures may affect motor development.

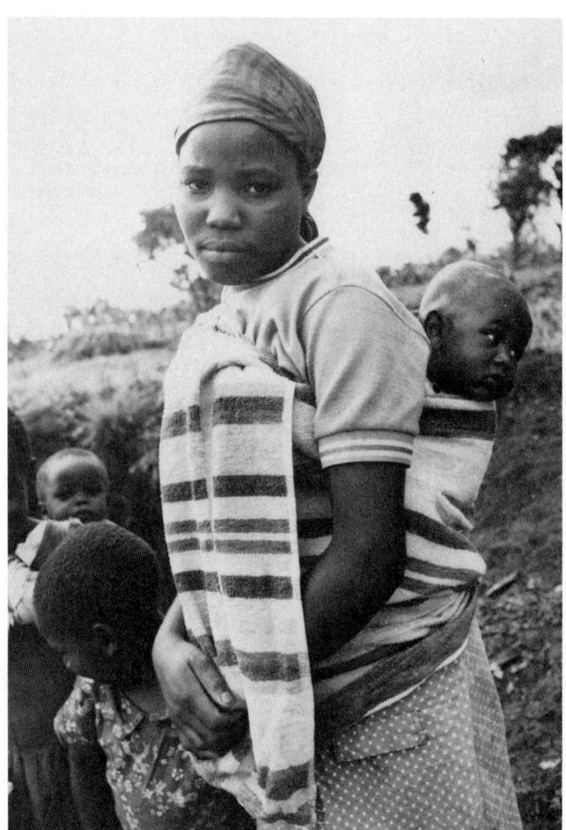

Zelazo, Zelazo, and Kolb (1972) have provided an experimental demonstration that walking can be elicited earlier by extra practice. As we noted earlier, stepping or walking is a reflexive pattern exhibited by newborn infants and these researchers sought to determine whether this reflex could be altered by exercise and whether this would affect voluntary and unaided walking. From 2 to 8 weeks of age, mothers provided walking practice for a few minutes a day for one group of infants, while another group received only passive exercise, which consisted of flexing the limbs, but not walking experience. Other groups received no training, but only periodic testing, and a final group received only the final test to evaluate the effect of the repeated testing. Figure 6-4 shows the results. The intervention increased the number of walking responses over the training period; mothers reported that the infants in the active exercise group walked sooner than infants who had not received this type of intervention. Experience does contribute to the age of onset of walking, but it is unlikely that walking at an early age confers a permanent advantage! Later work (Zelazo, Zelazo, Cohen, & Zelazo, 1988) replicated the effects of practice on stepping behavior in a group of 6-week-old infants. In addition, they found that practice can alter other motor patterns as well. Infants who were given practice sitting (three minutes a day for seven weeks) were able to sit upright longer than infants in a no-practice control group. However, the effects of practice are highly specific—practice in stepping did not affect sitting. Nor did sitting alter stepping.

Thus, available data indicate that although the general limits to motor development may be set by a maturational pattern, the timing of the emergence of motor skills may be either enhanced or slowed by particular environmental factors.

Psychological Implications of Locomotion

One of the important implications of these motor achievements is the increasing degree of independence that children gain. They can explore their environment more fully and initiate social contact with peers and caretakers. The new-found independence that is gained by learning to locomote by crawling, creeping, or walking also changes the way that others respond to infants.

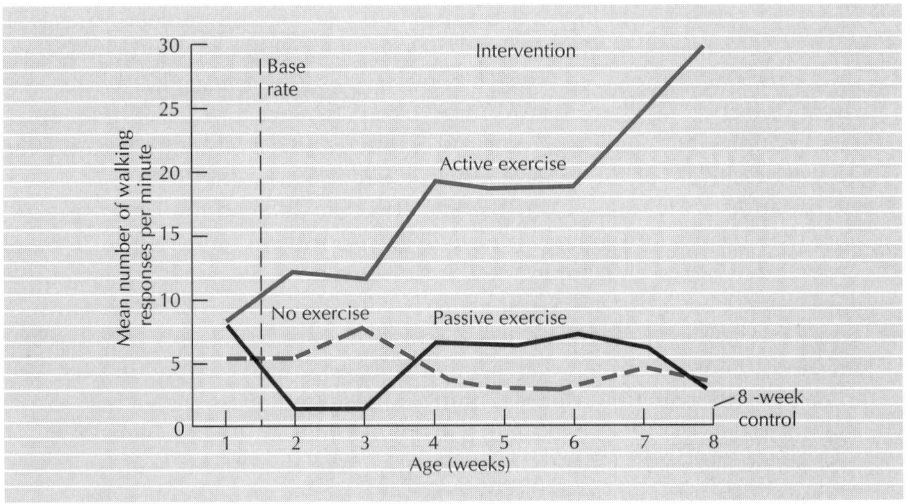

FIGURE 6-4
Newborn children given active exercise of the walking reflex showed an increase in this response and also walked earlier than newborn children in the controlled condition. *(From Zelazo, P. R., Zelazo, N. A., & Kolb. Copyright 1972 by the American Association for the Advancement of Science; reproduced by permission.)*

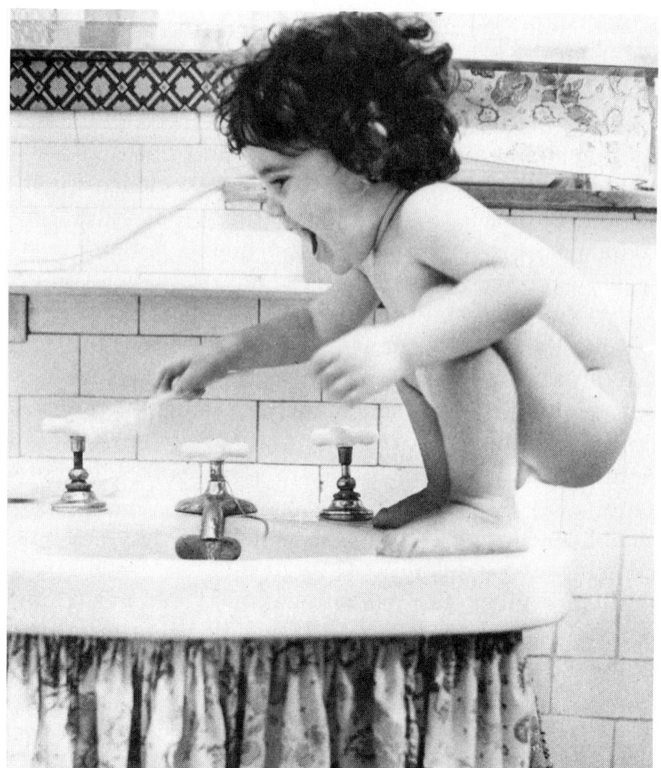

Improvement in motor skills can often lead to new adventures.

Parents feel relatively relaxed about monitoring their children's activities until the children attain self-propelled locomotion. Suddenly, parents can no longer place a child on a blanket in the middle of the room and proceed with their own activities. The child begins to crawl toward interesting objects, to totter to the brink of the stairs, to careen through her environment leaving what seems to the pursuing parent like a wake of mayhem in her passing—a package of half-eaten cigarettes, torn magazines, a dumped coffee cup, an overturned bowl of fruit with cherries squashed on the living room carpet.

Parents react differently to infants who can locomote and those who haven't yet gained this skill. Not surprisingly, after infants begin to locomote, parents are more likely to interrupt the infants' activity by relocating them, distracting them, setting up prohibitions, or making objects inaccessible (Green, Gustafson, & West, 1980). Even when infants' motor abilities are only artificially improved—when they are placed in a walker which allows them to locomote—parents are more likely to react to the infants' behavior. Locomotion clearly changes the way infants are treated by their caregivers—another example of the bidirectional nature of early development.

In addition to changes in the social world, locomotion onset affects the way that infants understand their perceptual and cognitive world. In the last chapter we noted that infants begin to develop a fear of heights only after crawling was established (Campos & Berthenthal, 1989). In addition, infants who have achieved self-produced locomotion are better able to solve spatial problems. For example, one group of researchers compared precrawling infants, belly-crawling infants, and babies who were proficient crawlers (hands and knees) for their ability to solve a hidden-toy problem. A toy was first located in one of two containers and then the infants were rotated 180 degrees. Crawlers were better able to solve the problem than noncrawlers or belly crawlers—a finding that supports the view that locomotion helps infants deal better with changes in spatial orientation. Other evidence (Kermonian & Campos, 1989) suggests similar results: locomotor infants perform significantly better on a memory for hidden objects task. In this case an infant sees an object covered by a cloth and then is given the chance to find it. The more experience infants have either with a walker or crawling, the better they are at locating the hidden object. You can fool a nonlocomoting baby, but it's harder to fool a locomoting infant! Together these studies suggest that motor development and perception should be viewed as mutually interdependent components of an "action system" (Campos & Bertenthal, 1987). As we see so often in development, changes in one domain of behavior have important implications for shifts in another area of development.

Motor Development in Blind Infants

Another way to discover what factors influence motor development is to examine the effects of various disabilities, such as blindness. As Figure 6-5 shows, the lack of light clearly slows motor development, especially reaching and independent walking (Adelson & Fraiberg, 1974). Limited mobility of the blind infant may have serious consequences: "It lessens his ability to explore independently, to discover by himself the objective rules that govern things and events in the external world" (Fraiberg, 1977, p. 270).

Can these blind infants be helped? On the assumption that the blind infants needed to learn to associate sound with touch activities, Fraiberg (1977) developed a program that maximizes the opportunities to use sound as a guide for touch. For example, parents are encouraged to talk to their blind infants when approaching them and during routine activities such as

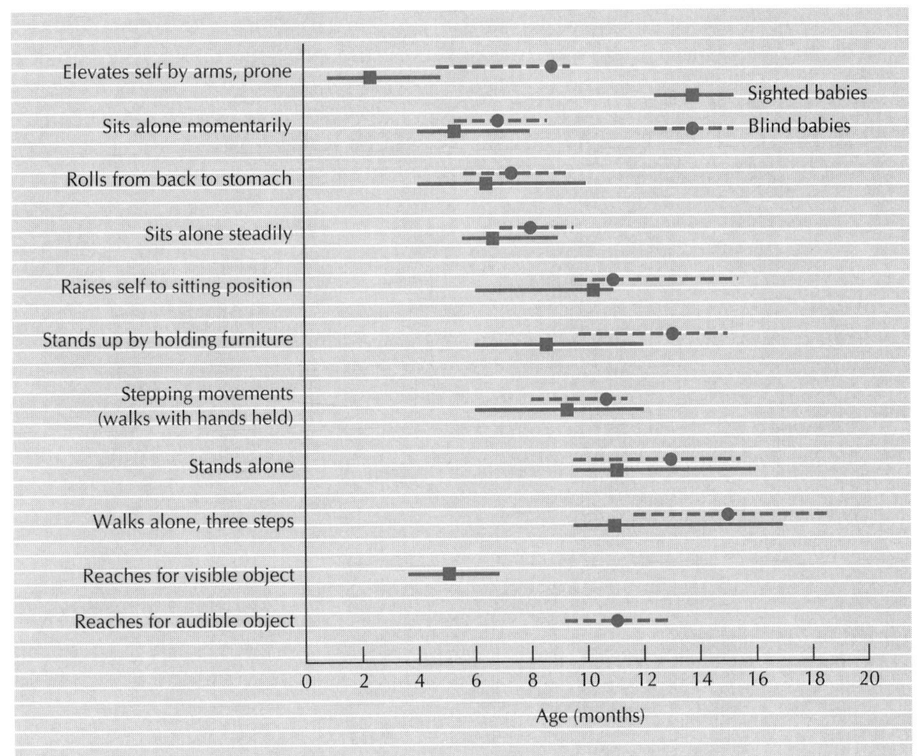

FIGURE 6-5

Comparative development of motor abilities of blind and sighted babies (means and ranges). *(Data from Adelson & Fraiberg, 1974; graph from Bower, 1977; with permission of authors and publisher.)*

feeding and dressing. Or they provide toys within easy reach to encourage coordinated two-hand activity and to increase exploration of objects that make sounds. Through these experiences, the infants learn to use a combination of sound and touch as a way of identifying people and things. And it does make a difference. In comparison to other blind children who do not receive such stimulation, delays these infants experience in standing and walking are lessened—although the stimulated blind children are still behind sighted infants in motor activities.

Moreover, other help may be on the way. Some experiments in Scotland suggest that an electronic device that produces echoes from objects may aid blind babies to "see." The echoes from objects can be used to judge distance and even size and texture. By outfitting blind infants with an echo-producing device, Bower (1979, 1982, 1989) successfully increased the reaching ability of young infants who wore the echo device for several months. Babies can do things with the aid of the echo-sounding device that are more typical of a sighted than a blind infant. Also, Aitken (1981) has found that the device works well for aiding sighted infants to "see" in the dark. These studies of the motor development of blind infants provide a further illustration of the interdependence among various sensory and motor systems.

Motor Skills and Sports Participation

Motor development, of course, does not stop in infancy and early childhood; as children develop, they continue to acquire new skills that permit more sophisticated and complex motor feats. Witness the basketball achievements of Michael Jordan or the tennis swing of Steffi Graf. Children learn a variety of motor skills such as hopping, jumping, riding a bicycle, throwing a baseball, or learning to swim (Clark, Phillips, & Petersen, 1989; Getchell & Robertson, 1989).

One of the arenas in which motor skills are most important is in children's sports. As Table 6-2 shows, during the period between 6 and 18 years of age,

TABLE 6-2 **ESTIMATE OF PARTICIPATION IN NONSCHOOL SPORTS AMONG CHILDREN AGES 6 TO 18 (IN MILLIONS)**

	BOYS		GIRLS		COMBINED	
SPORT	1977	1984	1977	1984	1977	1984
Baseball	4.20	3.91	0.79	0.62	4.99	4.53
Softball	1.97	2.10	2.41	2.62	4.38	4.72
Swimming	1.71	1.85	1.91	2.08	3.62	3.93
Bowling	2.07	2.07	1.51	1.50	3.58	3.57
Basketball	2.13	2.13	1.22	1.22	3.35	3.35
Football (tackle)	1.56	1.16	0.29	0.10	1.85	1.26
Tennis	0.88	1.35	0.95	1.24	1.83	2.59
Gymnastics	0.59	0.75	1.17	1.50	1.76	2.25
Football (flag)	1.11	1.20	0.36	0.45	1.47	1.65
Track and field	0.76	1.00	0.54	0.75	1.30	1.75
Soccer	0.72	2.20	0.52	1.70	1.24	3.90
Wrestling	—	0.25	—	0.0	—	0.25
Other	1.24	1.00	0.79	0.80	2.03	1.80
Totals	18.94	20.97	12.46	14.58	31.40	35.55
% by sex	60%	59%	40%	41%		

Source: Martens (1986).

Organized sports offer another outlet for developing motor skills.

girls, as well as boys, participate extensively in a wide range of sports. Estimates of the total number of children involved in competitive sports range up to 200 million worldwide. In one state in the United States there is even competitive wrestling for 4-year-olds (Roberts, 1987)! Participation in sports not only provides opportunities for refinement of motor skills but also provides a continuing opportunity to learn new social skills.

GROWTH

One of the most actively investigated areas of child development is physical growth. For many years, psychologists have tracked and plotted the manner in which the young infant grows.

Two classic principles guide infant children's body growth. First, growth follows a cephalocaudal principle, which means that development proceeds from the head downward. Second, growth follows a proximal-distal pattern; in other words, development occurs from the center outward. Therefore, the brain and neck develop earlier than the legs and trunk, while the internal organs develop sooner than the arms and hands. Growth proceeds at different rates in different stages of development. According to two infant watchers:

> Growth rate is faster in the first six months than it will ever be again. The human baby doubles in weight during the first three postnatal months, and triples within the first year. From birth to six months, babies increase in weight about 2 grams every 24 hours; from six months to 3 years, the increase averages about 0.35 grams; from 3 to 6 years, the increase is 0.15 grams per 24 hours. (Lipsitt & Werner, 1981, p. 101)

But it is just as well that the rate of growth slows down as the infant develops. "If growth continued at the rate typical of the first six months of life, the average ten-year-old would check in at approximately 100 feet tall and weigh roughly 240,000 tons. That is as tall as some fifteen-story office buildings and twenty times heavier" (McCall, 1979, p. 13).

As a culture, we are very concerned about how tall and heavy we are. Many parents still hope that their boys won't be too short or their girls too tall—even in the 1990s. Consider these interesting observations of our concern about height that appeared in a Sunday newspaper supplement:

> The Metropolitan Life Insurance Company reports that average life insurance coverage is twice as much for six-footers; bishops average 5′10½″, rural preachers 5′8¾″, presidents of major universities are 1″ taller than those of smaller colleges and high school principals; sales managers hit 5′10″, their salesmen average 1″ shorter; railroad presidents are 5′11″, station agents 5′9½″; in the depression of the 1930s, shorter men were first to be laid off; in 15 presidential elections, victory went to the taller candidate (Lincoln was the tallest at 6′4″, L.B.J. next at 6′3″). (Summarized by Krogman, 1972, pp. 28–29)

Although taller isn't necessarily better, it seems to help. It is not just height that we are concerned about. The monthly appearance of another new diet book or the announcement of a recently formed Weight Watchers club also testifies to our concern about weight.

Prediction of an adult's height and weight from birthweight is a very risky venture. In spite of parental beliefs that a baby's birthweight can predict later size and weight, this is generally untrue for infants considered in the normal range at birth. Part of the difficulty in predicting from birthweight is that the mother's size may determine the child's birthweight. Small mothers, of course, sometimes give birth to future linebackers, but to help the smaller mother during childbirth, the fetus may grow more slowly during the last

Doctor weighing and measuring a baby.

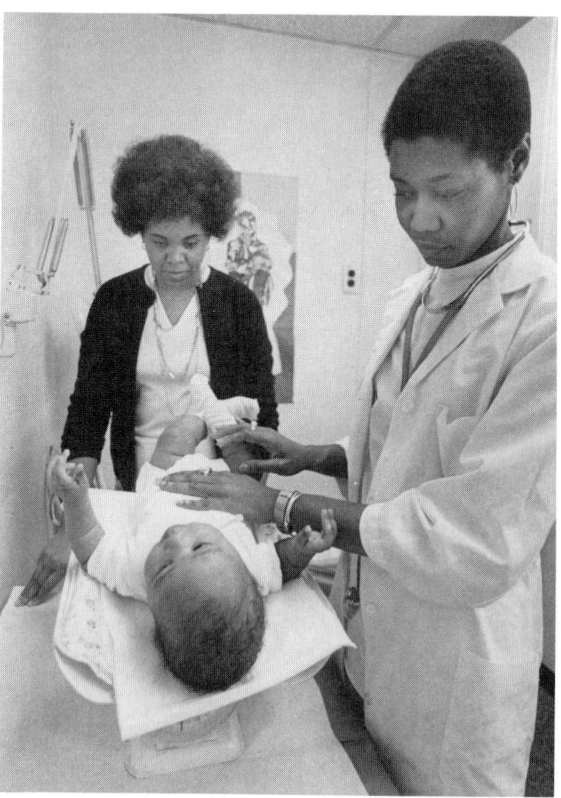

few weeks before birth. After birth, a slight growth spurt may put the baby who is destined to be tall and heavy back on track. Prediction to adulthood improves in later stages of childhood. In fact, you can successfully predict how tall a child will be in adulthood by knowing the child's height at age 9, his or her sex, and the mother's and father's heights (Roche, 1979).

Figure 6-6 summarizes curves for height and weight for boys and girls in the United States. Of interest are the sex differences; in height, the girls' curve crosses the boys' curve at about $9\frac{1}{2}$ years of age, and, until $13\frac{1}{2}$, girls are taller than boys on the average. Weight curves for boys and girls are similar. Girls are lighter than boys until nearly 9 years of age, and then are heavier than boys until about age 14. However, these curves do not tell the complete story; it is of interest not only to determine average height and weight at various age points, but to isolate periods of accelerated growth. The periods of peak growth occur at different ages for boys and girls. Between 7 and $10\frac{1}{2}$ for both boys and girls, the differences between successive age groups are relatively consistent. For boys the greatest mean change occurs at $13\frac{1}{4}$ years, while for girls the peak is earlier, at $11\frac{3}{4}$ years. Not only does their growth spurt occur earlier, but girls reach their mature height earlier than boys. Growth does not stop after the completion of the growth spurt, and additional slow growth may continue for several years. A similar pattern is evident for weight: boys start their spurt in weight gain at $12\frac{1}{4}$ years, while girls start their weight spurt about $1\frac{1}{2}$ years earlier, when they are $10\frac{3}{4}$ years old. Table 6-3 summarizes these growth-spurt data for boys and girls.

Moreover, there are wide individual differences in rate of maturation. Since these differences become obvious at adolescence, it is often assumed that they suddenly appear at adolescence. In fact, they are present at all ages, and early maturers are always ahead of their late-maturing peers. This tendency for development to be rapid or slow is named the "tempo of growth" by one of the early pioneers of physical growth. As Tanner (1978)

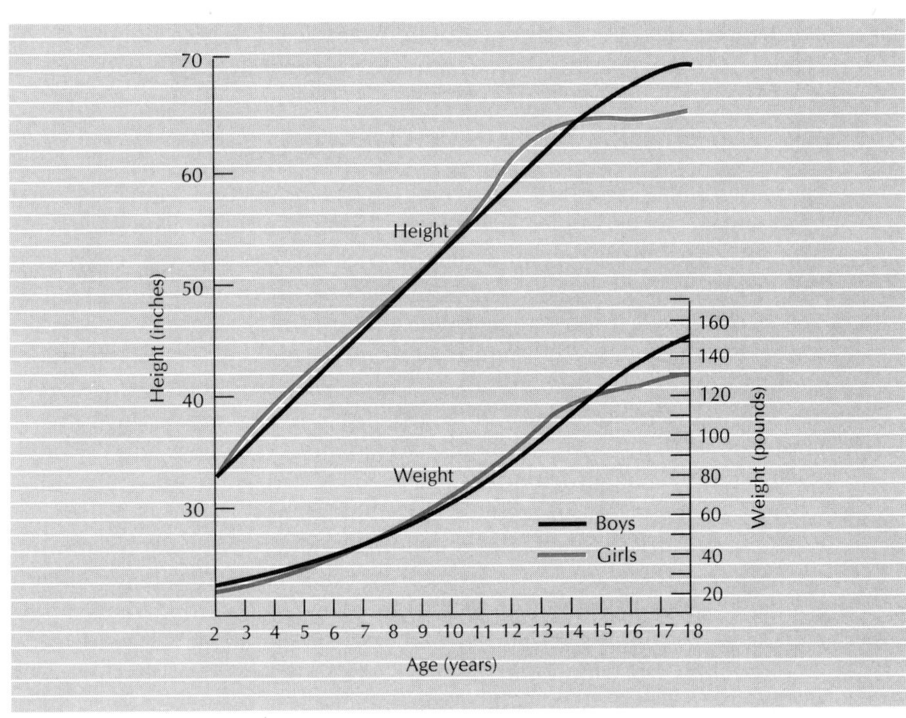

FIGURE 6-6
Growth in height and weight from 2 to 18 years. *(From National Center for Health Statistics, 1976.)*

TABLE 6-3 **PERIODS OF SPURT GROWTH FOR BOYS AND GIRLS**

	START	PEAK	END	DURATION
		HEIGHT		
Boys	$11\frac{3}{4}$	$13\frac{1}{4}$	$14\frac{1}{2}$	$2\frac{3}{4}$
Girls	$10\frac{1}{4}$	$11\frac{3}{4}$	$12\frac{1}{2}$	$2\frac{1}{4}$
		WEIGHT		
Boys	$12\frac{1}{4}$	$13\frac{3}{4}$	15	$2\frac{3}{4}$
Girls	$10\frac{3}{4}$	$12\frac{1}{4}$	$13\frac{1}{4}$	$2\frac{1}{2}$

Source: From Hamill, Johnston, and Lemeshow (1973). With permission.

observed, growth is like a musical score: "Some children play out their growth andante, others allegro, a few lentissimo. It seems that heredity plays a large part in setting the metronome, but we do not know the physiological mechanism" (Tanner, 1978, p. 78).

These differences have important implications for the social and emotional adjustment of boys and girls, and these issues will be discussed later in the chapter.

National Differences in Height and Weight

There are ethnic, class, and national differences in growth as well as age and sex differences. For example, there are income-level differences in height and weight across a wide variety of cultures—Brazil, India, Africa, and Central America. Children in upper-middle-class families are both taller and heavier than children of families living in poverty (Martorell, 1984). There are also variations across cultures. Northwestern and western Europeans, especially Scandinavians, are taller than southern Europeans, such as Italians. And, of course, there are even more extreme examples in Africa, where the Nicotics grow 7 feet tall and the Pygmies are approximately 4 feet tall.

Are We Growing Taller?

Estimates of the height of the average Englishman between the eleventh and fourteenth centuries have been made using careful measurements of bones exhumed from British cemeteries: he was approximately 5 feet 6 inches tall. In contrast, today, the average adult male is 3 inches taller, at 5 feet 9 inches tall. Serious measurement of these group trends in size has indicated that we need to be constantly updating our norms of height and weight. It should be noted, however, that these size increases are not occurring at every level of society. Indications are that in the upper 75 percent of the socioeconomic population of the United States, the majority of individuals—at least in our current social, nutritional, and medical environment—have apparently reached their maximum growth potential (Hamill, Drizd, Johnson, Reed, & Roche, 1976). Increases in the remaining segments of society continue.

National differences are evident as well. In Holland, for example, the secular trend (slow evolution of cultural change) toward increased height and weight is continuing regardless of socioeconomic level, while in Japan, England, and Norway the increase in stature has apparently stopped (Roche, 1979).

We are not only growing taller, but our feet are growing longer due to the fact that we are growing taller. Your grandfather probably wore a size 7A or 7B, while now the average American male wears a size 9 to 10B. This represents about a $\frac{1}{3}$-inch gain in length each generation. Krogman has spelled out the economic implications of this change: "About 650 million pairs of shoes are sold annually; add $\frac{1}{3}$-inch of leather needed per generation and you get about 6800 miles of additional shoe leather—diagonally from Maine to California" (Krogman, 1972, p. 42). If this demand continues, we may have a leather crisis in addition to an energy crisis.

Moreover, we are reaching our larger shoe size as well as our mature height at earlier ages than in the past. In contrast to 100 years ago when adult size was not attained until the early or mid-twenties, many 16- or 17-year-olds are often as tall as, or taller than, their parents. In turn, relationships between parents and children may be more competitive or parents may expect more independence—regardless of whether the physically mature adolescent is psychologically or socially ready.

There are several possible reasons for the historical trends toward greater height and weight. First, health and nutrition have been improved; specifically, there has been a decline in growth-retarding illness, particularly in the first five years of life. There has been an improvement in the amount and balance of nutritional intake. Medical care and personal health practices have improved. Second, socioeconomic conditions have improved; child labor is less frequent, and living conditions have improved. Third, changes in genetic factors have occurred, including interbreeding, which produces increases in height and weight in the offspring. An additional factor may be selective mating of tall individuals.

However, since secular trends are largely environmentally determined, should major changes occur in the environment, such as a famine or spectacular medical discoveries, the average height of the population could again undergo change. Both advances and reversals are possible. If the environment deteriorates, such as with a dramatic increase in pollution levels, these trends could be reversed; if the environment improves markedly, there could be further advances.

The Onset of Sexual Maturity

Height and weight are not the only significant changes in adolescence. Puberty, the attainment of sexual maturity, is another milestone in growth. Puberty is marked by a number of growth changes, such as the start of breast development in girls and the enlargement of the testes in boys. Table 6-4 summarizes the major changes in male and female pubertal development. Notice that this attainment of puberty is a gradual process, with menarche occurring in girls two to three years after the beginning of the sexual maturation process. In spite of its later occurrence, menarche is often viewed by many females as the "true" or real onset of puberty (Brooks-Gunn & Ruble, 1984). See Box 6-2 for a poignant account of this experience.

Are we reaching sexual maturity earlier? The onset of puberty is occurring earlier, especially in prosperous countries. A comparison of the age at which mothers and daughters reached puberty tells the tale: American mothers reached menarche at 14.38 years, while their daughters reached this developmental landmark nearly two years earlier—at 12.88 years (Damon, Damon, Reed, & Valadian, 1969). In fact, it is estimated that puberty is achieved $2\frac{1}{2}$ to $3\frac{1}{2}$ years earlier than it was a century ago (see Figure 6-7). However, this

TABLE 6-4 SEQUENCE OF CHANGES IN SEXUAL DEVELOPMENT WITH APPROXIMATE AGES OF ONSET

AGE OF ONSET	GIRLS	BOYS
10	Onset of breast development (breast bud)	
11	Pubic hair—sparse, slightly pigmented	Onset of growth of testes and scrotum
12	Between 12 and 13, underarm hair begins to appear	Appearance of pubic hair—lightly pigmented
13	Breast enlargement continues; areola and papilla project above the contour of the breast Onset of menarche	First ejaculation of semen
14	Increase in pubic hair, but area covered is smaller than in adult	Underarm and facial hair Voice deepens
15	Breasts and pubic hair are fully mature	Penis, testes, and pubic hair are fully developed Onset of growth of mustache and beard hair

Sources: Petersen and Taylor (1980); Tanner (1978).

trend to earlier menarche is slowing down among middle-class girls in the United States (Roche, 1979; Wyshak & Frisch, 1982). Just as in the shifts in height and weight, there are limits on the extent of change that is likely to occur. The reduction in age at menarche has not been uniform. There has been little change in Eskimos and changes for only some groups in India (Roche, 1979). Moreover, in certain underdeveloped countries, such as some parts of New Guinea, the median age is very late—17.5 to 18.4 years (Malcolm, 1970).

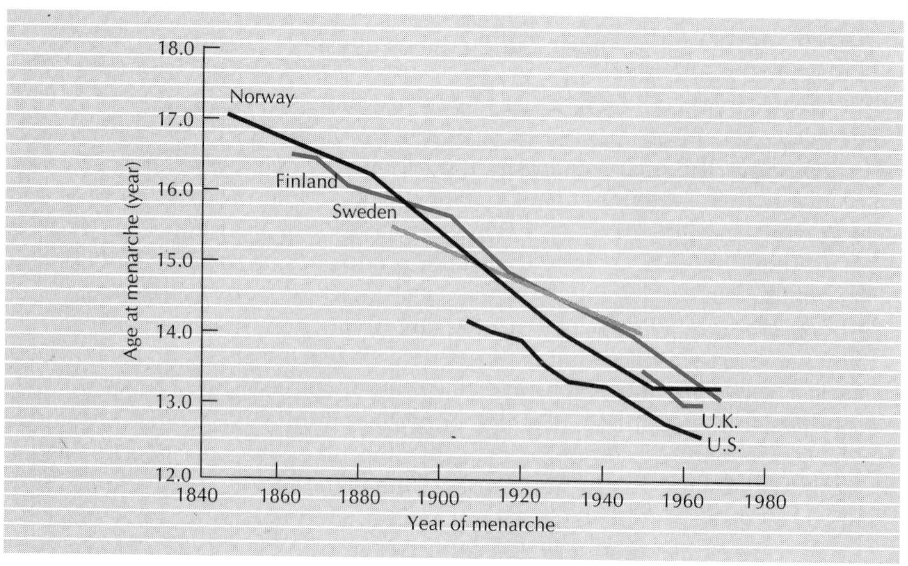

FIGURE 6-7 Median ages at menarche from 1845 to 1969 in selected European countries and the United States. *(From Roche, 1979, with permission of author and publisher.)*

BOX 6-2 THE EXPERIENCE OF MENARCHE

Researchers have begun to understand the experience of menarche and are beginning to catch up with some of the earlier literary accounts of this transition. Anne Frank made this entry in her diary.

Wednesday, 5 January 1944

Yesterday I read an article about blushing by Sis Heyster. This article might have been addressed to me personally. Although I don't blush very easily, the other things in it certainly all fit me. She writes roughly something like this—that a girl in the years of puberty becomes quiet within and begins to think about the wonders that are happening to her body.

I experience that, too, and that is why I get the feeling lately of being embarrassed about Margot, Mummy, and Daddy. Funnily enough, Margot, who is much more shy than I am, isn't at all embarrassed.

I think what is happening to me is so wonderful, and not only what can be seen on my body, but all that is taking place inside. I never discuss myself or any of these things with anybody; that is why I have to talk to myself about them.

Each time I have a period—and that has only been three times—I have the feeling that in spite of all the pain, unpleasantness, and nastiness, I have a sweet secret, and that is why, although it is nothing but a nuisance to me in a way, I always long for the time that I shall feel that secret within me again.

Anne Frank

The Diary of a Young Girl

Source: Katchadourian, H. (1977). *The biology of adolescence.* San Francisco: Freeman.

Even in the United States, there are still wide variations in the timing of the onset of menarche. Not all girls wish to reach puberty on schedule and lose their skinny, little-girl look. For example, ballet dancers who practice and diet to keep "dancer-fit" may delay the onset of menarche by as much as one year (Brooks-Gunn, 1988). Stated differently, only 30 percent of the dancers studied by Brooks-Gunn were defined as either early or "on time," in contrast to 80 percent of a comparison group of girls who were not dance

In early adolescence girls mature more rapidly than boys.

devotees. Figure skaters and gymnasts show delayed menarche as well (Brooks-Gunn & Warren, 1985). Nor do all girls keep on a regular menstrual schedule once they reach menarche; athletes who train hard and keep their weight low, such as runners and gymnasts, sometimes stop menstruating, or become amenorrheic. Firsch (1984) has found that such girls can turn their menstrual cycles on and off by stopping and restarting their training regime. As Box 6-3 shows, even family relationships may alter the timing of puberty and, in turn, be affected by the onset of these biological changes.

Early or Late Maturation: Does It Matter?

Do the normal differences in the rate of maturation make a difference? A set of classic studies carried out at the University of California indicate clearly that the timing of physical maturation can affect the child's social and emotional adjustment. However, not only do boys and girls differ in the age of reaching physical maturity, with girls ahead of boys, but the sex of the child determines the advantages and disadvantages of being an early or late maturer as well. For boys, it appears to be advantageous to peer acceptance to reach the developmental milestone of pubescence early, but for girls the advantages of early or late maturity are less clear.

Jones and Bayley (1950), in their pioneering study in this area, selected sixteen early-maturing and sixteen late-maturing boys from the extremes of a normal public school population and tracked their development over the six-year period of adolescence. Observations made in a number of free-play settings indicated that the boys who were slower in their physical development were rated lower in physical attractiveness, masculinity, and grooming than were their faster-developing peers. Behavioral ratings indicated that the late maturers were more childish, more eager, less relaxed, and generally higher in attention-seeking behaviors. Peer evaluations generally confirmed this profile; the late maturer is regarded as restless, bossy, talkative, attention seeking, and less likely to have older friends.

Moreover, later maturers as well as their parents have lower aspirations and expectations for educational achievement. On the basis of a national study of 493 boys, Duke and coworkers (1982) found that late maturers were less likely to want to complete college and that their parents agreed in not expecting them to graduate from college. Teachers, too, rated later maturers as lower in academic achievement than average or late maturers. And the boys' test scores indicated that these views were not without foundation, since the late maturers scored lower on IQ and achievement tests. Possibly, parents and teachers provide more opportunities for, and expect more from, early maturers because of their more adultlike physical appearance. However, this explanation was unlikely, since the boys who were destined to be late maturers had lower IQ scores at 8, 9, 10, and 11 years of age—well before the onset of puberty! It raises the intriguing possibility that there are either subtle biological differences between early and late maturers that may elicit differential treatment even before puberty or intrinsic genetic differences that affect not only rate of physical growth but also intellectual capacity. The question is clearly not settled.

In comparison to boys, early maturation is unlikely to be advantageous to girls. Early maturers may not be as prepared as later maturers since health classes typically occur after the onset of menarche for most early maturers. Moreover, mothers discuss changes less with their early maturing daughters

BOX 6-3 PARENT-CHILD RELATIONSHIPS AND THE ONSET OF PUBERTY: A TWO-WAY STREET?

Biological and social changes often mutually influence each other. No longer do we just assume that the timing of puberty leads to changes in social relationships and in sense of self, but the alternative view—namely, that social relationships may affect the timing of onset of puberty is gaining support as well. In a series of recent studies, Larry Steinberg has found support for this bidirectional view of puberty. In a longitudinal study of family relationships before and after the period that children entered puberty, Steinberg (1987) found that systematic changes occurred in the family system around the time of puberty. Among adolescent boys and girls alike, reports of closeness with their parents decreases, and reports of emotional autonomy from their parents increases with physical maturity. Among boys, these effects are accompanied by decreases in personal acceptance; among girls, physical maturity is accompanied by more negative descriptions of their mothers. Puberty also increases conflict between adolescents and their mothers. While father-child relationships showed less shift during this biological transition in this study, later studies (Steinberg, 1988) revealed that pubertal development leads to increases in father-child conflict for girls, and, for boys and girls, a decrease in closeness between adolescents and their fathers. Although these findings suggest that puberty *leads* to distance between adolescents and parents, the direction of influence may go the other way as well. Increased distance between parents and their children may accelerate pubertal maturation, whereas increased closeness between parents and their offspring may slow down the process of maturation. Evidence supports this possibility—at least in the case of girls. Whereas boys' rate of maturation was unaffected by their relations with their parents, girls' maturation appeared to be accelerated by parent-child distance, particularly in the mother-daughter dyad. Girls who report more intense conflict, fewer calm discussions, and more behavioral freedom matured biologically faster than their peers. These findings are consistent with other human studies as well as nonhuman primate studies (Belsky, Steinberg, & Draper, 1991; Paikoff & Brooks-Gunn, 1991). Sexual maturation among female cotton-top tamarinds was slower in the presence of their family and increased rapidly when they were removed from the family environment. Moreover the sensitivity of female reproductive development to environmental events and circumstances is consistent with other studies that show that females living in the same household often have synchronous menstrual cycles (McClintock, 1980; Warren, 1983). No evidence of such sensitivity to environmental factors is evident for males. Together these studies suggest that the onset of puberty may cause changes in relationships among family members but also may be caused by these same shifts in family ties. Clearly, biological and social development influence each other mutually; a two-way path of influence is evident.

Sources: Belsky, J., Steinberg, L., & Draper, P. (1991). Childhood experience, interpersonal development and reproductive strategy: An evolutionary theory of socialization. *Child Development,* **62,** 647–670; McClintock, M. K. (1980). Major gaps in menstrual cycle research: Biological and physiological controls in a biological context. In P. Komenich, M. McSweeney, J. Novack, & N. Elder (Eds.), *The menstrual cycle* (Vol. 7). New York: Springer; Paikoff, R. L., & Brooks-Gunn, J. (1991). Do parent-child relationships change across puberty? *Psychological Bulletin,* **110,** 47–66; Steinberg, L. (1987). Impact of puberty on family relations: Effects of pubertal status and pubertal timing. *Developmental Psychology,* **23,** 451–460; Steinberg, L. (1988). Reciprocal relation between parent-child distance and pubertal maturation. *Developmental Psychology,* **24,** 122–128: Warren, M. (1983). Physical and biological aspects of puberty. In J. Brooks-Gunn & A. Petersen (Eds.), *Girls at puberty* (pp. 3–28). New York: Plenum.

(Brooks-Gunn, 1988). Early maturers have a poorer body image than on-time or late maturers (see Figure 6-8), in part, due to the fact that the weight gains accompanying the onset of maturation violate the cultural ideal of thinness for girls (Brooks-Gunn, 1988). Moreover, they have a smaller network of close friends and are more likely to engage in "adult behaviors" (such as smoking, drinking, and intercourse) at a younger age than late maturers according to a recent longitudinal study in Sweden (Gustafson & Magnusson, 1991; Magnusson, 1988, 1989; Stattin & Magnusson, 1990). This seems to be due to the fact that earlier maturers tend to associate with older peers who are closer to them in terms of physical status and appearance. Finally, early maturing girls may have more adjustment problems. They have more difficulty inhibiting impulses and exhibit more depressive affect (Brooks-Gunn & Petersen, 1992; Crockett & Petersen, 1987).

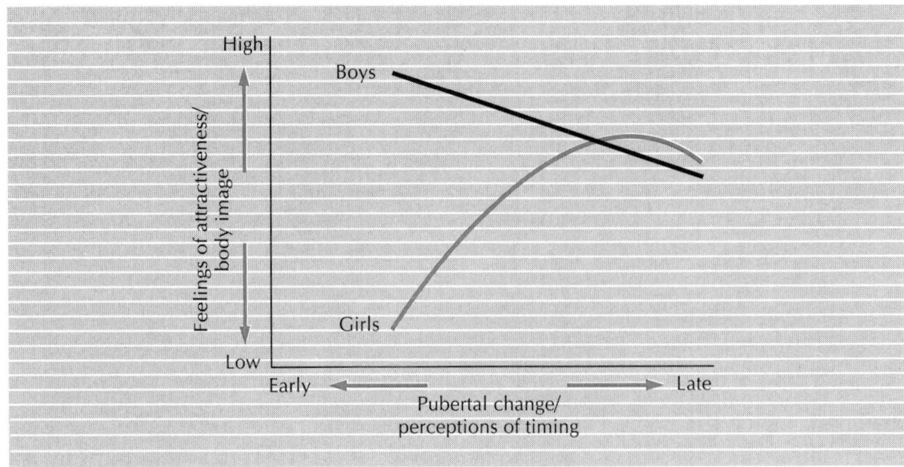

FIGURE 6-8
The model describing the relationship between indicators of pubertal change (except breast development) and body image of feelings of attractiveness. *(From Tobin-Richards, Boxer, & Petersen, 1983.)*

While early maturation for girls may entail some risks, experts suggest that caution is in order (Brooks-Gunn, 1988, 1990). First, there are individual differences and not all early maturers have a poor body image or will date, smoke, or drink earlier. Second, individuals differ in terms of whether they perceive early maturation as "on time" (that is, normal) or "off-time" (deviant for our culture), depending on a variety of factors such as one's reference group. Third, not all areas of development are equally affected.

"In the final analysis, a girl's adjustment to the changes of puberty will probably depend more on the kinds of support, encouragement, and guidance she receives from parents, and the values and expectations of her own particular peer group than it will on whether maturation is early, average, or late" (Conger & Petersen, 1984, p. 121).

The impact of transitions such as puberty cannot be fully appreciated in isolation from other changes in children's lives. Some adolescents attend junior high school after sixth grade, while others stay in their elementary school until high school. Similarly, some adolescents date early and others delay this step until later. Simmons, Blyth, and their colleagues (Simmons & Blyth, 1987; Simmons, Blyth, Van Cleave, & Bush, 1979) found that girls who entered puberty early, and at the same time changed schools and started to date, had lower self-esteem than other girls (see Figure 6-9). The effects were even more dramatic as the number of life transitions that accompanied puberty increased. Girls who moved their residence or experienced a major family disruption (divorce, death, remarriage) suffered even more loss in self-esteem, grades, and their participation in extracurricular activities decreased (Simmons, Burgeson, Carlton-Ford, & Blyth, 1987).

Moreover, the effects of coping with multiple life changes simultaneously is not limited to girls. Boys who experience a variety of life changes including puberty onset and school change as well as other shifts, such as moving to a new neighborhood or engaging in early dating, had poorer grades and participated less in extracurricular activities than boys who experienced fewer life transitions (Simmons et al., 1987). These findings underscore that the impact of the timing of puberty can best be understood in the context of other transitions and illustrate that environmental context (for example, school organization) can help or hinder children's abilities to cope with biological change.

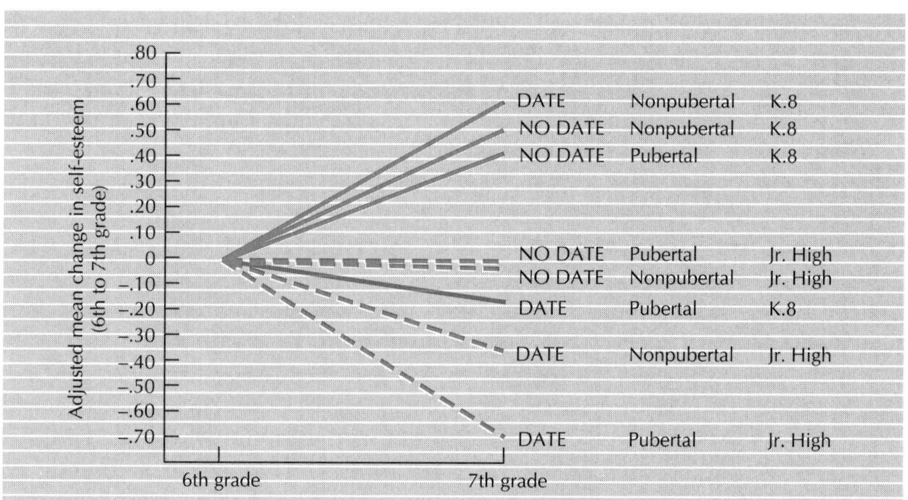

FIGURE 6-9

Changes in girls' self-esteem between sixth and seventh grades by dating behavior, puberty, and school type. *(From Simmons, Blyth, Van Cleave, & Bush, 1979, with permission of senior author and publisher.)*

Obesity in Childhood: Are We Growing Fatter?

As the proliferation of weight-reduction clubs, magazines devoted to weight and diet, and fad diets indicates, we are a weight-conscious society. In fact, as many as 70 to 80 percent of American girls have been on a diet by middle adolescence (Attie & Brooks-Gunn, 1989; Davis, Best, & Hawkins, 1981). Moreover, our conception of the ideal weight has changed in the last thirty years (Silverstein, Petersen, & Perdue, 1986). As one survey indicates, since 1969 the mean weight of Miss America Pageant participants has steadily dropped, and since 1970 the winners have been lighter than the losers. Another American cultural barometer tells the same story: *Playboy* magazine centerfolds are becoming lighter and taller (Garner, Garfinkel, Schwartz, & Thompson, 1980).

While the problem of obesity often begins in infancy and childhood, not all obesity is the same. Some people get fat early in infancy and childhood, while others become obese only after puberty. While most obese individuals—regardless of the timing of onset of their weight problem—have cells with a higher fat content, people with early-onset obesity have *more* fat cells than either the nonobese or those with late-onset obesity (Eichorn, 1979). Moreover, those who become overweight early may have more difficulty keeping weight off later, since weight loss in children and adolescents reduces only cell size but not the number of fat cells (Knittle, Timmers, Ginsberg-Fellner, Brown, & Katz, 1979).

Not all chubby infants will become obese adults. About one-quarter of obese infants will remain obese twenty years later. Predictions improve after infancy, in part, because recent evidence shows that there are at least two critical periods for the development of obesity, the first during infancy and the second during childhood at about 4 years of age. At age 4 those who will be obese later in life begin to gain weight at a faster rate than those who remain thin (Agras, 1988; Rolland-Cachera et al., 1984).

For example, one study found that 86 percent of overweight boys and 80 percent of overweight girls became overweight adults, in contrast to 42 percent of average-weight boys and 18 percent of average-weight girls who became overweight adults (Abraham, Collins, & Nordsieck, 1971). The odds against an overweight adolescent becoming an average-weight adult are 28 to 1 (Stunkard & Burt, 1967). Having fat parents doesn't help. If you have one fat parent, your chances of being a fat adult are 40 percent, and 80 percent if you have two fat parents (Winick, 1974).

Genetic factors may play a crucial role in determining who becomes overweight, but more for men than women, where environmental pressures may play a larger role. Recent studies (Stunkard, Sorenson, Hanis, Teasdale, Chakraborty, Schull, & Schulsinger, 1986) found a strong relationship between the weight of adopted children and their biological parents' weight, but no relationship for weight between adoptees and their adoptive parents. Similarly, concordance rates for obesity are twice as high for monozygotic than dyzygotic twins (Stunkard, Foch, & Hrubeck, 1986). Finally, findings in twins reared apart, where the effect of a common environment has been eliminated, showed marked similarity in weight—clear evidence of a genetic effect (Bouchard, Lykken, Segal, & Wilcox, 1986). Milstein (1980) found that newborn infants who had two overweight parents were more responsive to differences between the taste of a sweet-tasting solution and water than infants of two normal-weight parents. The presence of a sweet tooth early in life may increase the risk for obesity, as indicated by the fact that this behavior predicted relative weight at 3 years of age. Even individual differences in sucking patterns, which is probably genetically based, can help predict later weight. Two- to four-week-old infants who exhibited a more vigorous sucking pattern characterized by higher pressure and shorter breaks between bursts of sucking were found to be heavier at 2 years of age (Agras, 1988). However, parents may contribute as well. Among 2-year-olds, Klesges and his coworkers (1986) found that parents of obese children prompted 2.3 times as much eating as parents of normal-weight children. Even the common strategies that parents use to encourage their children to eat may, in the long run, be a factor in the development of overweight children (see Box 6-4).

Obese children and adolescents suffer from a variety of physical problems, including hypertension and diabetes. They suffer psychologically as well, as indicated by the fact that they have more body-image disturbances than their nonobese peers. In addition, overweight individuals, are discriminated against by both their peers and adults. They are teased more, excluded from peer groups, and picked last for athletic activities; in turn, chubby children will seek excuses to avoid gym class because of concerns about other children's ridicule about their bodies. Nor does it end in the locker room. Overweight children date less and are even less likely to be admitted to prestigious colleges than their thinner classmates. Clearly, being obese is a costly business (Buckmaster & Brownell, 1988).

TREATING OVERWEIGHT CHILDREN

Recently, a wide variety of treatments have been developed for helping overweight children "take it off and keep it off." Treatments range from straightforward dietary approaches, which usually involve less food and more exercise, to more exotic approaches, such as appetite-suppressant drugs, therapeutic starvation, and even bypass surgery. Unfortunately, the success rate to date has not been very striking.

"Most obese persons will not stay in treatment for obesity. Of those who stay in treatment, most will not lose weight, and of those who do lose weight, most will regain it" (Stunkard, 1958). But it's not simply lack of discipline. As Rodin (1981) reminded us,

BOX 6-4 "CLEAN UP YOUR PLATE AND THEN YOU CAN WATCH TV"

Eating is a social and cultural experience. Parents play a major role in teaching children about eating; they help children learn about what to eat, when to eat it, where to eat, and how much to eat (Rozin, 1990). Unfortunately, parents may often contribute to children's overreliance on external controls, such as feedback and instruction from parents in controlling their eating, especially in learning when to stop instead of learning to attend to internal biological cues that help indicate hunger or fullness. When a child says "I'm full" and the parent says "No, finish what's on your plate," the parent is giving a clear message that external cues and not internal ones are relevant in determining how much to eat.

Recently, Birch, McPhee, Shoba, Steinberg, & Krehbeil (1987) have shown that children can learn to rely on either internal or external feedback—depending on how adults respond to their eating. Twenty-two preschoolers attended a series of special snack sessions over a six-week period. For some children the adults helped the children focus on their sensations of hunger and fullness and stressed how these internal reminders tell us when to eat and when to stop eating. They felt their stomachs and discussed how eating changes our feelings of hunger. For other children, the context focused on external cues that signal eating. A bell rang to signal "snack time" and children were rewarded with toys and stickers for clearing their plates. To find out if children can rely on internal cues to control their eating, all children were given either a high- or low-calorie yogurt snack to eat to make them "feel full" or "feel hungry," then children were given a chance to eat another snack of cookies and granola bars. Children who had been taught to rely on their internal signals to determine how much they ate, consumed less of the second snack after the high-calorie yogurt. In contrast, children who had been taught to depend on external cues such as rewards and adult urgings to eat consumed the same amount of the cookies and granola snack—regardless of how full they were. Clearly, the social context can influence which cues—internal or external—children learn to rely upon in initiating, maintaining, and terminating eating.

Moreover, parental use of rewards for eating may not necessarily result in increased preferences. "Eat your spinach and then you can have dessert" may increase the amount of spinach consumed, but not necessarily how much kids like it. In a study by Birch, Marlin, and Rotter (1984), forty-five preschoolers were rewarded either by verbal praise ("That's very good, you drank your juice all the way down") or by a ticket to a ten-minute children's movie ("Okay, you drank it, you get a ticket to the movie") for drinking a juice that the child rated neutral in a prior taste-preference test or received no reward. Birch found that instead of liking the food more, the children liked it less well as a result of being rewarded for eating it. The findings are consistent with what has been called the overjustification hypothesis (Lepper, 1981), which suggests that sometimes the persistent use of a contingent reward may overjustify an activity. In this case praise overjustifies drinking of the juice, which leads the child to discount its value. As one child put it, "When Mom tells me that I can't have my dessert until I clean my plate, what's left on my plate is usually yucky" (Birch, et al., 1984, p. 438). Rewards often have a paradoxical effect and may decrease rather than increase preferences.

Together, these studies underscore the possibility that learning to eat as a way of gaining rewards can lead to inappropriate eating habits as well as an undue reliance on external cues, such as the time of the day and the amount of food remaining on the plate. Some theorists suggest that overreliance on external signals and insufficient attention to one's internal bodily messages can contribute to eating disorders, such as obesity.

Sources: Birch, L. L., Marlin, D. W., & Rotter, J. (1984). Eating as the "means" activity in a contingency: Effects on young children's food preference. *Child Development,* **55,** 431–439; Birch, L. L., McPhee, L., Shoba, B. C., Steinberg, L., & Krehbeil, R. (1987). "Clean up your plate": Effects of child feeding practices on the conditioning of meal size. *Learning and Motivation,* **18,** 301–317; Lepper, M. (1981). Intrinsic and extrinsic motivation in children: Detrimental effects of superfluous social controls. In W. A. Collins (Ed.), *Minnesota Symposia on child psychology* (Vol. 14). Hillsdale, NJ: Erlbaum; Rozin, P. (1990). Development in the food domain. *Developmental Psychology,* **26,** 555–562.

Obesity is unusual because being fat is one of the factors that may keep one fat. Indeed, we have all heard the familiar refrain of many an overweight person who complains, "But I eat so little." Despite the disbelieving and reproachful looks of their lean friends, the perverse fact is that it often does take fewer calories to keep people fat than it did to get them fat in the first place. This occurs because obesity itself changes the fat cells and body chemistry and alters levels of energy expenditure. Each of these factors operates to maintain obesity once it has developed. (1981, p. 361)

Behavioral approaches which recognize the important role that cues in the everyday environment play in regulating eating, appear to be promising.

> Individuals are instructed in methods for changing their personal, social, and physical environments to change their eating and exercise behaviors . . . typically these techniques include monitoring and recording the quality and circumstances of eating, restricting the range of cues associated with eating (e.g., eating only at certain times and places), altering the act of eating (e.g., eating more slowly), and changing physical and social cues associated with eating (e.g., food storage, stressful interaction with family members at mealtime). (Coates & Thoresen, 1976, p. 14)

Research findings show that these programs can be successful for some children (Israel, 1988). Recently, Epstein and his colleagues (1987) have found that some diet treatments are effective even five years after beginning treatment. All groups involved an obese parent and child who attended eight weekly meetings, which were gradually reduced to bimonthly sessions. Both diet and exercise were emphasized for all groups. However, the use of behavioral principles varied across different treatment groups. The most effective program includes the following components: (1) a focus on both the parent and child; (2) learning to self-monitor or keep track of your own diet and exercise regime; (3) learning to serve as models of good eating and exercise habits, and encouraging other family members to modify their dietary and exercise behavior; and (4) having a contract between parents and children, by which children earned rewards for weight loss. Similarly, parents earned refunds from the program for reaching weight-loss goals for themselves and their children. In a second group, only the children were targeted and were taught to self-monitor their progress, while in a third group, neither parents nor children engaged in self-monitoring activities. Although all groups showed a similar degree of weight loss at eight and twenty-one months, after five years, the children in group 1 maintained their weight loss while children in group 2 showed no change; children in group 3 were heavier (see Figure 6-10). Moreover, even obese siblings of children in group 1 had a significant weight loss, while siblings of children in the other treatment groups had an increase in weight. These findings suggest that some treatments may have

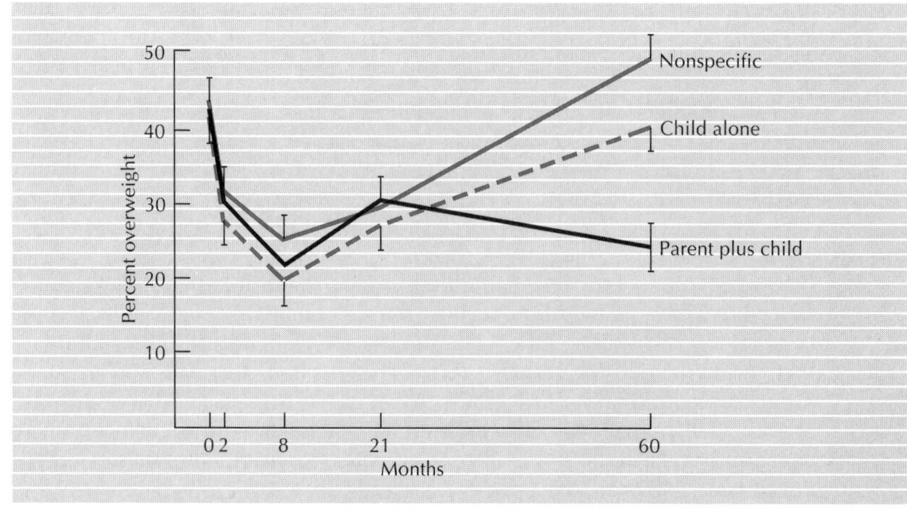

FIGURE 6-10
Average percentage overweight in obese children at 0.2, 8, 21, and 60 months for children in groups in which parent and child were both targeted and reinforced for weight loss, the child alone was targeted and reinforced for weight loss, or neither parent nor child was targeted or reinforced for weight loss. *(From Epstein, Wing, Koeske, & Valoski, 1987).*

"ripple effects" that spread to other members of the family who are not part of the treatment program.

School-based programs make the treatment available to a wider number of children than clinic-based approaches and have been successfully used for reducing weight in obese 5- to 15-year-old children as well (Epstein & Wing, 1987). In spite of these recent successes, it is still easier to put it on than take it off!

Finally, parents might be happier if children didn't eat quite so much. Eating, according to one estimate, is very expensive. A child in the United States runs up a rather formidable dining tab: food eaten at home—not taking into account the multiples of tacos and hamburgers eaten out—is estimated at $17,162 by age 18.

Dieting Disorders

Being underweight can cause psychological and physical problems just as much as being overweight can. Research shows that 1 out of every 200 American girls between 12 and 18 years of age will develop the eating disorder of self-starvation—*anorexia nervosa.* This syndrome is described in Box 6-5.

Another eating disorder, called *bulimia* may occur in individuals with anorexia nervosa or even among women of normal weight who do not have histories of weight disorders. In fact, as many as 50 percent of the patients with anorexia nervosa manifest bulimia as well (Fisher & Brone, 1991). However, the timing of onset for the two disorders differs. Most cases of bulimia emerge during the late teens and early twenties, in contrast to anorexia nervosa which may begin at a variety of points throughout adolescence, especially at puberty (Attie & Brooks-Gunn, 1989). Estimates of the incidence of bulimia among college populations are as high as 13 percent (Johnson & Berndt, 1983). Individuals with this illness indulge in "food binges" and then purge themselves through vomiting immediately after eating or through the use of laxatives or diuretics. The binge episodes typically occur in the evenings and last from one to four hours. Forbidden foods such as candy, pastries, and other carbohydrates are the usual targets. Binges range from 1000 to 55,000 estimated calories per episode and can be expensive—at an average cost of $8.30 per binge (Johnson, Stuckey, Lewis, & Schwartz, 1982). Different people are more likely to become anorexics and bulimics. In contrast to anorexic patients, who are usually not obese before the onset of illness and tend to be socially withdrawn, bulimics usually are extroverted, are inclined to be overweight, have voracious appetites, and engage in eating binges. Moreover, bulimics are more depressed and have a poorer body image than individuals who only occasionally engage in binge eating (Katzman & Wokhik, 1984). Their families may differ as well, with families of bulimic adolescents being more chaotic, conflict-ridden, stressed, and unable to openly communicate their feelings (Fisher & Brone, 1991). Even after being "cured," bulimics have a poorer chance of returning to normal weight than anorexics because their eating patterns have been altered for extended periods—often up to five years.

NUTRITION AND GROWTH

Growth is determined not only by genetic factors, which set limits to normal adult stature, but also by the environmental context. In a favorable

BOX 6-5 ANOREXIA NERVOSA: WHEN DIETING DOESN'T STOP

Fat and skinny had a race
All around the pillowcase
Fat fell down and broke her face
Skinny said, "ha-ha, I won the race."

With images of ballet dancers and fashion models bombarding teenagers, it is not surprising that "skinny is beautiful" is now accepted by many adolescents. Dieting can go awry, however. Anorexia nervosa, a disease that mainly affects females between ages 14 and 18, is one of the serious outcomes of too much dieting. Over the course of the disease, weight losses up to 25 percent of the body weight can occur, menstruation ceases, the skin dries out, and the hair becomes dull and may even fall out. Not a pretty sight. In spite of her skeletal appearance, the anorexic often sees herself as overweight and is in constant fear of gaining weight. Although food is taboo, there is, at the same time, a preoccupation with food. Girls may collect recipes, plan menus, put up calorie charts, and even hoard food.

Why does it happen? There is no simple answer, but many point to early family dynamics as a major contributor. These dynamics lead to the anorexic's low self-esteem and limited sense of control over her own fate. Bruch (1977) offers this description:

> Characteristically, patients with anorexia nervosa have been well cared for as children, were well fed and well dressed, and were exposed to the best educational and cultural opportunities. The parents may be described as overprotective, overconcerned, and overambitious. They overvalue their children and expect obedience and superior performance in return. As long as the children comply, they fulfill the parents' dreams of their own ideals by growing and behaving exactly as the parents had planned and expected. With approaching adolescence, conditions change and the child starts to make justified claims for independence; this is unacceptable to the parents and the illness begins as an expression of this struggle. (Bruch, 1977, pp. 2–3)

In short, taking control of weight is a way the anorexic gains control over at least one aspect of her life.

Biological and cultural factors may contribute as well. Genetic factors may predispose individuals for developing eating disorders (Scott, 1986), and the problem may run in families. About 50 percent of monozygotic twins have been found to be concordant for anorexia nervosa while only 7 percent of dyzygotic twins share the tendency to develop the disorder. It is higher than expected among sisters of anorexics and between parents and children (Fisher & Brone, 1991). Finally, the starvation associated with the disorder may help perpetuate the problem "For the anorectic, stringent dieting may become self-sustaining, fueled by a gain of control over eating, and the satisfaction of seeing one's weight go down to even lower numbers. Progressive weight loss is maintained by a phobic avoidance of body fat and of any weight gain" (Attie & Brooks-Gunn, 1989, p. 17). Nor can cultural ideals about thinness be ignored. For adolescent girls the addition of body fat with the onset of puberty may trigger increased efforts to diet (Attie & Brooks-Gunn, 1989).

Surveys of the long-term outcome of these women are not very encouraging. Less than half (49 percent) are cured of weight problems, while 26 percent continue to have fluctuating weight or become obese, 18 percent remain chronically anorexic, and another 7 percent die of anorexia or suicide (Schwartz & Thompson, 1981). What can be done to treat it? There is again no formula that has gained widespread acceptance. Some therapists use a behavior modification approach that focuses on the eating behaviors themselves, others treat the family as the "patient" and try to reestablish more satisfactory family interaction patterns as a way of treating the problem. Recently, multidimensional approaches that combine alternative therapeutic strategies have been advocated (Garner & Garfinkel, 1985). Perhaps a shift away from our preoccupation with thinness would help too!

Sources: Attie, I., & Brooks-Gunn, J. (1989). Development of eating problems in adolescent girls: A longitudinal study. *Developmental Psychology,* **25,** 70–79; Bruch, H. (1977). Psychological antecedents of anorexia nervosa. In R. A. Vigersky (Ed.), *Anorexia nervosa.* New York: Raven Press; Garner, D. M., & Garfinkel, P. E. (Eds.). (1985). *Handbook of psychotherapy for anorexia nervosa and bulimia.* New York: Guilford Press; Fisher, C. B., & Brone, R. J. (1991). Eating disorders in adolescence. In R. M. Lerner, A. C. Petersen, & J. Brooks-Gunn (Eds.), *Encyclopedia of Adolescence* (Vol. 1). New York: Garland; Schwartz, D., & Thompson, M. (1981). Do anorectics get well? Current research and future needs. *American Journal of Psychiatry,* **138,** 319–324; Scott, D. W. (1986). Anorexia nervosa: A review of possible genetic factors. *International Journal of Eating Disorders,* **5,** 1–20.

environment, there is a great deal of similarity in the growth curves; when nutrition is inadequate, however, growth rates are seriously depressed. Evidence of the controlling role of nutrition in physical growth comes from studies comparing growth before and during wartime periods in which nutritional intake was reduced. During World War I and World War II, there was a general growth retardation, while there was a general increase in growth during 1920 to 1940, the between-wars period. However, weight was affected more than height and boys more than girls. Age of puberty is affected by nutritional factors as well. During World War II, girls in occupied France did not achieve menarche until an average of 16 years, approximately three years later than the prewar norm (Howe & Schiller, 1952). In a recent study in Bogota, Columbia, Super and his colleagues (Super, Herrera, & Mora, 1990) demonstrated that the provision of food supplements for the entire family from midpregnancy until the child was 3 years old was effective in preventing severe growth retardation in children at risk for malnutrition. Moreover, the children who received the food supplements remained taller and heavier than control children at 6 years of age—three years after the intervention ceased.

A variety of other environmental factors affect growth as well, including illness, disease, climate, and psychological disturbance (Tanner, 1987). There is even a season of the year effect: growth in height is faster in the spring and growth in weight fastest in the fall.

Overcoming Environmental Deficiencies: Catch-Up Growth

As we have seen earlier in our discussions of the effects of prenatal deficiencies on later development, there is a strong corrective tendency to regain the normal course of development after an early setback. A similar corrective principle operates in the case of physical growth following environmental injury or deprivation. As Tanner notes:

> Children, no less than rockets, have their trajectories governed by control systems of their genetical constitution and powered by energy absorbed from the natural environment. Deflect the child from its growth trajectory by acute malnutrition or illness, and a restoring force develops so that as soon as the missing food is supplied or the illness terminated the child catches up toward its original curve. When it gets there, it slows down again to adjust its path onto the old trajectory once more. (Tanner, 1970, p. 125)

The degree of catch-up growth will depend on a variety of factors: duration, severity, and timing of the deprivation, and the nature of the subsequent treatment or therapy. A study of the effects of intervention following severe malnutrition will illustrate this phenomenon (Graham, 1966). When infants with varying degrees of malnutrition were treated, those with a 5-percent deficit in body length caught up; those with a 15-percent deficit benefited only somewhat, but remained significantly shorter. Similarly catch-up growth following severe malnutrition may be limited to only some aspects of growth. In a twenty-year longitudinal study of severely starved children, even a program of nutritional intervention produces only some catch-up height but a failure to develop fully in head circumference (Stoch, Smyth, Moodie, & Bradshaw, 1982). The impact of malnutrition on brain development may, in part, account for the intellectual and attentional deficits shown by malnourished children (Barrett, Radke-Yarrow, & Klein, 1982; Galler, Ramsey, & Solimano, 1985). Timing as well as severity is critical in determining the degree of catch-up growth. For example, pathology and undernutrition early in life can have serious consequences, and children starved early in utero through some placental imperfection usually show only partial catch-up (Pollitt, Gorman, & Metallinos-Katsaras, 1992; Tanner, 1978). In general, the earlier and more prolonged the malnutrition, the more difficult it is for regulation to be fully effective in achieving the normal level of growth.

SUMMARY

BRAIN GROWTH

- There is an orderly course in the development of the brain, with the motor area developing earliest, followed by the visual and auditory areas. Although all neurons are present at birth, changes take place in the shape, the size, and the density of connections among the neurons over the course of development.
- The brain is organized into halves, or *hemispheres*. The right hemisphere controls the left side of the body and is involved in the processing of visual-spatial information, face recognition, and interpreting emotional expressions. The left hemisphere controls the right side of the body and is important for speech and language development. Hemispheric specialization is evident early in infancy and is nearly complete by age 3. Some research suggests that an abnormal pattern of lateralization is related to dyslexia, a condition in which children have trouble learning to read because they have trouble integrating visual and auditory information.
- The environment plays a critical role in brain development, as illustrated by studies in which rats were reared in an enriched environment. A more stimulating early environment was related to increases in brain size, complexity of the neurons, and brain chemistry in the rats. Adult rats, exposed to similar enriching experiences, showed similar weight and biochemical effects. These studies illustrate the plasticity of the central nervous system and the importance of environment in biological development.

MOTOR DEVELOPMENT

- Earlier research described an orderly developmental sequence for grasping that was governed by maturational factors alone. New research suggests that infants use a variety of different grips according to the size and shape of the object, indicating that the infant motor system is highly flexible and able to adapt to the demands of the situation.
- Walking follows a U-shaped course in the first year of life, beginning with a stepping reflex at birth that disappears within two months and reappears as infants begin to walk near the end of the first year. A recent explanation for this developmental trend is a systems approach, which suggests that locomotor skill is multiply determined and will emerge when all of the biological, maturational, and contextual components are ready. Cross-cultural studies indicate that the timing of the emergence of motor skills may be either enhanced or slowed by particular environmental factors, such as the opportunity to practice the skill.
- One of the psychological implications of greater locomotion is increased independence for the infant. This results in more opportunities for the infant to initiate social contact with peers and caretakers and in clear changes in the way the infant is treated by others. Recent research suggests that, in addition to changes in the child's social world, locomotion is related to changes in perception and cognition.
- Motor development in blind infants typically progresses at a slower rate. However, programs that maximize sound and touch experiences or that use electronic echo-producing devices have successfully lessened the delays in motor development experienced by blind children.

- Participation in sports provides opportunities for the refinement of motor skills as children develop, as well as providing an opportunity to learn new social skills.

GROWTH

- Infants' and children's growth is guided by two principles. The *cephalocaudal* principle states that development proceeds from the head downward, and the *proximal distal* principle states that development occurs from the center outward. In addition, growth proceeds at different rates during different stages of development. The growth rate is the fastest during the first six months of life.
- Adult height and weight is difficult to predict from a baby's size, which tends to be more closely related to the size of the mother. Successful predictions can be made in later childhood based on the child's current height, gender, and parents' heights.
- There are wide individual differences in rates of maturation. However, in general, girls mature earlier than boys, with the greatest changes occurring two years earlier for girls.
- There are national differences in growth that appear to be related to income and nutrition as well as ethnic and cultural differences. *Secular trends,* or slow evolution of cultural changes, have been found for height. These appear to be related to (1) improvements in health and nutrition, (2) improvements in living conditions, and (3) changes in genetic factors. Recent indications are that in upper socioeconomic groups, the maximum growth potential has been reached.
- *Puberty,* the attainment of sexual maturity, is an important milestone in growth. It is marked by changes such as the start of breast development and menarche in girls, and the enlargement of the testes in boys. Although a secular trend has been found for the onset of puberty in prosperous countries, limits on this change are expected to occur.
- The timing of physical maturation can affect the child's social and emotional adjustment. Research indicates that the effects for late-maturing boys and early-maturing girls are largely negative. In general, the impact of the timing of puberty is best understood in the context of other transitions, such as school transitions and family disruptions, which may help or hinder the child's ability to cope with biological changes.
- Although the problem of obesity may begin in infancy and childhood, only about one-quarter of obese infants will remain obese 20 years later. The two critical periods for the development of obesity are during infancy and at about 4 years of age. Recent research indicates that genetic factors may play a role in determining later obesity; however, parents' strategies for getting their children to eat may contribute as well.
- In addition to physical problems, such as hypertension and diabetes, obese children and adolescents may experience body-image disturbances and discrimination from peers and adults. Effective diet programs for children have focused on changing the eating patterns and exercise behavior of both the child and other family members.
- Dieting disorders include *anorexia nervosa,* which may occur early in adolescence and results from reduced intake of calories, and *bulimia,* which typically occurs in later adolescence and is characterized by food binges and purging through vomiting.

- Inadequate nutrition may result in severely depressed growth rates. During World Wars I and II, height, weight, and age of puberty were affected by lack of adequate nutrition. Other environmental factors that may affect growth rates include illness, disease, and climate.
- Following environmental injury or deprivation, a strong corrective principle appears to operate in the case of physical growth. The degree of catch-up will depend on such things as the duration, severity, and timing of the deprivation, in addition to the nature of the subsequent treatment or therapy. In general, the earlier and more prolonged the malnutrition, the more difficult it is to regain a normal level of growth.

CHAPTER 7

EMOTIONAL DEVELOPMENT

THINKING ABOUT EMOTIONS

Children's Understanding of Complex Emotions: Pride, Guilt, and Shame

SUMMARY

Children show a wide range of emotional reactions. Sometimes they are elated and happy, at other times depressed and sullen, and on other occasions angry. What are the determinants of emotions? How do emotional responses originally develop, and how do they shift with age? When and how do children learn to recognize and label their own emotions and emotions in other people? In this chapter we will explore the origins and development of emotions and show how early emotional development and social development are related. Smiling, an early index of positive affect, will be examined. Next, we will explore the development of attachment, the process by which the infant develops a special affection for particular people. To illustrate the emergence of negative emotions, fear will be examined, with special attention to the development of social fears, particularly fear of strangers. Finally, we examine children's understanding of the meaning of emotions and the types of situations that evoke different kinds of feelings.

THE FUNCTIONS OF EMOTIONS

Children laugh and cry and show fear, anger, love, and affection. What functions do these emotional expressions serve? Emotions can be viewed as forms of communication by which the infant and child can communicate to others information about their current feelings, needs, and desires. By smiling, for example, an infant tells others that an event or object is pleasurable, while by frowning an infant can communicate displeasure. Second, emotions serve to regulate social distance. By smiling, the infant is more likely to maintain contact with the caregiver. Similarly, anger may help to keep a stranger at a distance, while sadness and crying cause adults to attend. Emotional signals such as smiles, frowns, and angry outbursts serve other social functions as well. Smiling can be viewed as a form of greeting behavior—a welcome sign to a person who enters a situation. Children often use emotional expressions to regulate conflict; expressions of anger and threat may deter a potential aggressor, while smiling may serve as a signal of appeasement in a losing-conflict situation. Through emotional displays, then, infants and young children can communicate their needs and desires. These displays provide one of the earliest means for gaining control over their social world. Emotions are a two-way process: Not only do children learn to regulate others by careful display of different emotions but, in turn, they learn to recognize or read the emotional messages of other people. Both processes—production as well as recognition of emotions—are important ways that children learn to regulate their exchanges with others in their environments. We begin our exploration of emotional development by examining the emergence of the abilities to produce and recognize emotional expressions in infancy and early childhood.

PRODUCTION AND RECOGNITION OF EMOTIONS

Production of Emotions

Recent theories of emotional development still disagree about this issue, but there is considerable recent evidence that facial expressions may be, at least in part, genetically determined—an assumption that gains support from the findings that similar facial expressions in adults are found in all cultures (Ekman & Oster, 1979; Izard & Malatesta, 1987; Izard, 1991). But what about babies?

According to mothers, infants display a wide range of emotions at a very early age (Johnson, Emde, Pannabecker, Stenberg, & Davis, 1982). Of the mothers in the study, 95 percent stated that their 1-month-old infants displayed joy, 85 percent reported anger, 74 percent surprise, 58 percent fear, and 34 percent sadness, and nearly all of the mothers (99 percent) thought their 1-month-old offspring expressed interest. These mothers were responding to the totality of their infants' behavior (that is, facial expression, vocalizations, body movement) as well as the situational context (for example, hunger, play). All of these clearly influence our perception of emotion in both infants and adults. However, even more objective observers report many of the emotions that mothers think they see. On the basis of videotapes of playful interactions of 3- to 6-month-old infants and their mothers, Malatesta and Haviland (1982, 1985) concluded that infants display specific facial patterns corresponding to adult expressions of anger, pain, interest, surprise, joy, and sadness. However, it is not clear that these expressions reflect exactly the same emotion in infants and adults (Sroufe, 1979). For example, anger and pain expressions in infants may reflect more generalized states of distress rather than specific adultlike emotions (Camras, Malatesta, & Izard, 1991). Just as adults are more emotional when they are interacting with someone else, babies show more emotional expression when they are playing with their mothers or another baby than when alone (Adamson & Bakeman, 1985).

Emotional expressions vary in terms of their order of appearance in the infant's repertoire. According to Izard and Malatesta (1987), pioneers in the art of watching infant emotions, some expressions, such as startle, distress (in response to pain), disgust, and a rudimentary smile, are evident at birth. Recall that newborn infants tell us that they can discriminate bitter from sweet tastes by displaying a disgust expression in response to bitter-tasting solutions (Rosenstein & Oster, 1988). These expressions are precursors of the social smile and the emotions of surprise and sadness that appear later. In contrast to the smile of the newborn, which appears to be unrelated to specific external elicitors, the social smile, which occurs in reaction to specific events such as voices or faces, appears at about 4 to 6 weeks. By 3 to 4 months facial expressions of anger, surprise, and sadness make their appearance. For example, recently Stenberg and Campos (1989) found that few 1-month-olds show anger expressions when their arms are gently restrained, while by 4 and 7 months, 56 percent of babies showed clear expressions of anger. Fear expressions enter the infant's emotional repertoire when the infant is 7 months old (Camras, et al., 1991), shyness comes slightly later at 6 to 8 months. According to Izard and Malatesta contempt and guilt do not appear until the second year of life.

(a)

(b)

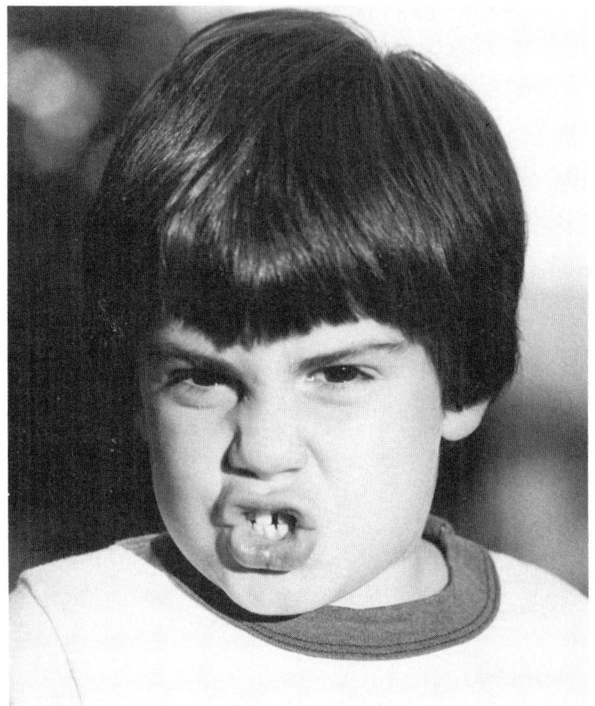

(c)

(d)

Children show a wide range of emotions, including (a) surprise, (b) distress, (c) anger, and (d) sadness.

Infant emotional expressions do not occur in a random fashion. There is increasing evidence that specific emotional displays occur in reaction to particular external events. For example, Stenberg, Campos, and Emde (1983) found that expressions of anger were reliably evoked in 7-month-olds when a biscuit was removed just before being placed in the baby's mouth. Others found that 2-month-old babies being inoculated registered a distinct distress expression, while older babies, 6 months and beyond, showed an anger expression (Izard, Hembree, Dougherty, & Coss, 1983; Izard, Hembree, & Huebner, 1987). Emotional expressions, in short, are highly specific in their pattern and closely tied to specific types of events.

Recognition of Emotions

It is interesting not only to understand the emergence of emotional displays but also to determine when infants learn to recognize the emotional states of others.

Well before the infant is capable of understanding verbal language, his caretakers communicate their feelings and wishes by a whole array of emotional expressions. As Darwin (1872) observed over a century ago, "Movements of expression in the face and body . . . serve as the first means of communication between the mother and her infant; she smiles approval and thus encourages her child on the right path or frowns disapproval" (p. 364). Moreover, mothers in the course of their interactions with their infants often display a variety of emotions, which provides infants with an opportunity to learn about emotional expressions. Malatesta (1982) estimated that between the ages of 3 months and 6 months, the peak time for face-to-face play, an infant is exposed to 32,000 examples of facial emotional expression.

As young as 4 months of age, infants can discriminate among different emotions. Infants from 4 to 6 months were shown slides of an adult face expressing joy or anger or a neutral expression. They looked longer at the joy expression than at either the anger expression or the neutral expression. (La Barbera, Izard, Vietze, & Parisi, 1976). This ability to distinguish joy before being able to recognize anger is consistent with the developmental course of the infant's own emotional expression. Smiling and laughter—positive emotions—develop before fear—a negative emotional state. (Camras et al., 1991). The findings are consistent with the view that

> Biological mechanisms underlying a particular discrete emotion become functional as that emotion becomes adaptive in the life of the infant. . . . Recognition of joy can provide rewarding and self-enhancing experiences for the infant. Such recognition can also strengthen the mother-infant bond and facilitate mutually rewarding experiences, particularly if the joy recognition leads to joy expression . . . anger recognition is not adaptive in the first half year of life. It seems reasonable that the threat of an anger expression would call for coping responses that are beyond the capacity of the 6 month old. (La Barbera, et al., 1976, p. 537)

Evidence indicates that both infants' and children's ability to accurately produce facial expressions is greater than their accuracy in recognizing them (Field, 1990; Field & Walden, 1982a, 1982b). Four-year-old children were asked to display different emotional expressions such as happiness, fear, and anger. The children then judged their own videotaped facial expressions, and adults did so as well. The adults were more accurate judges than the children of the same facial expressions—which supports the claim that children are better producers than recognizers of emotions. Just as we saw in infants, preschoolers were able to recognize positive emotions such as happiness more easily than anger or fear. Similarly, adults were more accurate in judging preschoolers' happy expressions than their displays of fear and anger (Field & Walden, 1982b).

Finally, production and recognition abilities are positively related: Preschoolers who send clear emotional signals are also skilled in judging emotional expressions (Malatesta, 1982). But children do improve over age in their ability to both discriminate and reproduce facial expressions. This developmental increase probably contributes to the more frequent and successful peer-group participation and increasingly more sustained and sophisticated social interactions of older children (Buck, 1984; Feldman & Rimé, 1991).

The Emergence of Emotional Display Rules

As a result of the development of self-regulatory processes through maturation and socialization, "the intense and unregulated expressions of infancy give way to expressions that are more modulated" (Malatesta, Culver, Tesman, & Shepard, 1989). A variety of aspects of emotional expression change with age. Emotional expressions become less frequent (Malatesta, Grigoryev, Lamb, Albin, & Culver, 1986), less variable and more conventionalized (Saarni, 1989), less discrete (Demos, 1982) and more miniaturized (Malatesta & Izard, 1984). Moreover, children learn to respond to cultural display rules which dictate what emotions to show and under what circumstances. This often means learning to separate emotional displays from emotional feelings. Children learn to smile even when they feel displeasure or to mimic distress that is not really felt. This can occur in a variety of ways according to Ekman (1977): intensification or exaggeration, deintensification or minimization, neutralization (putting on a poker face) and masking (concealing your true feeling by displaying a different expression).

Understanding "display rules" is evident as early as 2 years of age (Lewis & Michaelson, 1985). The earliest forms of deliberate or conscious expressive control involve intensification and deintensification of expressive behavior which may occur as early as the second year of life. Nondeliberate control over expressive behavior may occur even earlier when 3-month-old babies put their thumbs in their mouths to self-soothe.

By age 2 children have some understanding of display rules (Lewis & Michaelson, 1985). By preschool (age 3) children can display deadpan or neutralization. The most difficult developmental achievement is masking. While preschoolers can put on a happy face if you ask them to, they can only do it if there is no underlying competing negative state (Cole, 1985). However, even school-age children have difficulty simulating pleasure if they feel bad (Saarni, 1979, 1989).

With this general overview of emotions as a guide, let us turn to a closer look at the development of smiling and fear. As we will show, emotions serve important functions in organizing how babies learn to interact with others in their social worlds.

EARLY EMOTIONAL DEVELOPMENT: THE SMILE AS A SOCIAL SIGNAL

Infants are organized to emit a wide number of social responses—even from birth. One of the most interesting early social signals for both parents and researchers is the smile. When do infants begin to smile, and how does smiling change over development? Why do they smile? Let us try to answer these questions.

The Developmental Course of Smiling

Smiling begins early, and if you watch closely, you can see smiles even in the newborn infant. The earliest phase of smiling in the human infant has been termed spontaneous or reflex smiling (Wolff, 1987). An infant smile that is elicited by stroking the lips or cheek is an example of a reflex smile. Most early smiling is spontaneous and appears to depend on the infant's internal state. Early smiles have been attributed to "gas," but support for this theory has evaporated. The exact nature of the internal stimulus remains a mystery. In the first 3 or 4 weeks of age, infants are likely to smile when they are comfortable or in REM (rapid eye movement) periods of sleep (Emde, Gaensbauer, & Harmon, 1976; Wolff, 1987). However, it is not clear whether early smiles are due to fluctuations in arousal and excitability or whether they reflect enjoyment (Camras et al., 1991). Even in the newborn period there are sex differences in smiling. Girls show more spontaneous smiles than boys (Korner, 1974). Some have suggested that girls may be genetically better prepared for social interaction than boys because their higher frequency of smiling may more often engage others in interaction (Freedman, 1974).

Between 3 and 8 weeks of age, infants move to the next period of smiling, in which they are responsive not only to internal events but also to a wide range of external elicitors—including social stimuli such as faces and voices. A high-pitched human voice, or a combination of voice and face, particularly a moving face, are reliable elicitors of smiling in the first 6 months of life.

However, the critical aspects of the human face that are effective elicitors of smiling in normal infants change as the infant matures (Ahrens, 1954).

Infant and mother smiling at each other.

Figure 7-1 illustrates this developmental sequence; at first the configuration of the eyes is important, followed by the mouth, and finally the details of the face and expressions become important. Moreover, all social agents are not equally effective elicitors of smiles and by 12 weeks, infants begin to smile selectively to familiar persons (Camras et al., 1991). Three-month-old infants show greater increases in smiling when their smiles are reinforced by smiles and vocalizations of their mothers than when they are reinforced by equally responsive female strangers (Wahler, 1967). This evidence of differential responsiveness to different people suggests that by 3 months of age smiling signals enjoyment for infants rather than just arousal.

Further evidence of the fact that smiling signals joy comes from recent evidence that smiling was more frequent when 6-month-old babies were engaged in sustained social play than when they were not (Weinberg, Gianino, & Tronick, 1989). However, not all smiles are the same. Some are toothy grins, others sly; some are fleeting, while some smiles last a long time. Infants display different kinds of smiles to different kinds of environmental events (Dunkeld, 1978). Six- to twelve-week-old infants give brief smiles in response to a picture of large black dots while they give slower but longer-lasting smiles to their mothers' faces. Babies smile at a female stranger but only after an even longer delay. During play where the baby has to find out which behavior a stranger wants the baby to show (for example, head turn, tongue protrusion), the smiles are different again: quicker and shorter but larger than the other three kinds of smiles. Recent evidence confirms that

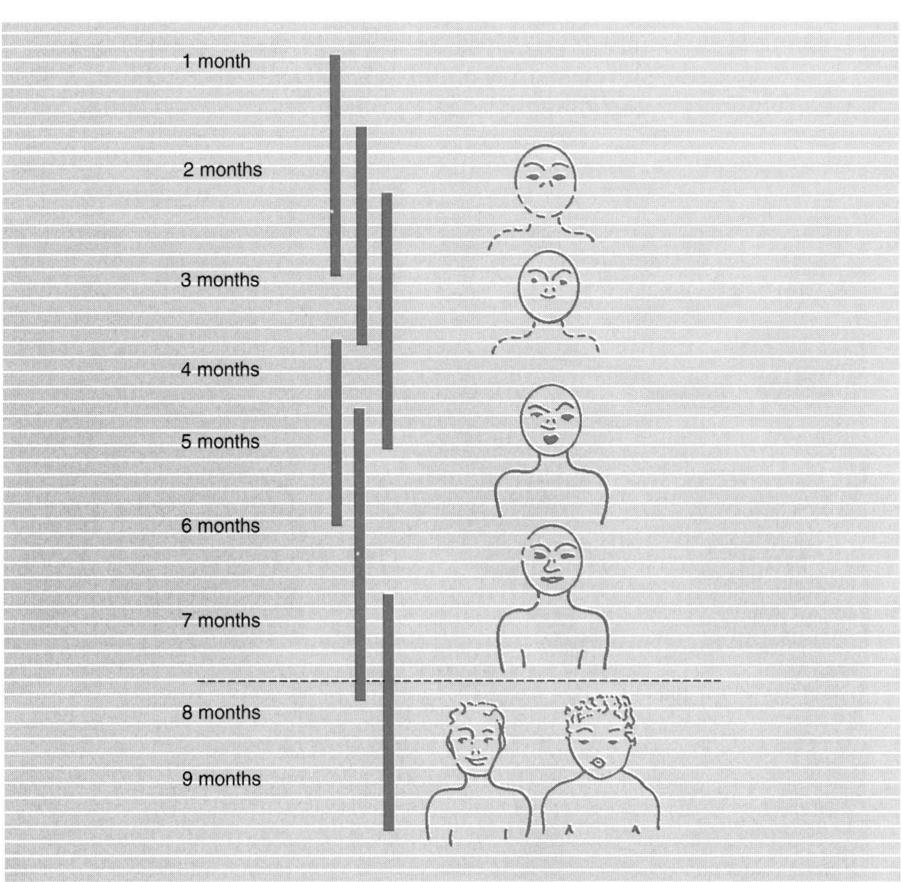

FIGURE 7-1
The stimulus features that elicit smiling in infants of different ages. (Adapted from Ahrens, 1954, with permission of the publisher.)

babies use a different kind of smile with their mothers than with strangers (Fox & Davidson, 1988). Smiles to mothers are more likely to be genuine smiles of happiness which involve not only an upturned mouth but also wrinkles around the eyes. These smiles are called Duchenne smiles after the Frenchman who noticed this pattern, over 100 years ago. In contrast, the 10-month-olds in the study showed fewer of these genuine or Duchenne smiles to strangers. A smile is not simply a smile but can convey different kinds of information and various types of reaction.

Not all environments are equally effective in promoting the development of smiling. As Gewirtz (1967) showed, Israeli children reared in a family environment exhibited more smiling than infants reared in either a kibbutz or an institution where the rate of stimulation was presumably lower (see Figure 7-2).

From Smiling to Laughter

By 4 months, infants not only are skilled smilers but begin to laugh (Sroufe, 1979). Laughter, like smiling, may play an important role in caretaker-infant interaction; specifically, the infant's laughter may serve to maintain the proximity of the mother or other caretaker and hence is a very adaptive response pattern.

Little was known about the early development of laughter until Sroufe and Wunsch (1972) helped fill this gap in our knowledge by their investigation of laughter in the first year of life. Using mothers as their experimental assistants, these investigators examined the amount of laughter elicited by a wide array of visual (human mask, disappearing object), tactile (bouncing on knee, blowing in hair), auditory (lip popping, whispering, a whinnying horse sound), and social (peek-a-boo, covering baby's face, and sticking out tongue) stimuli. Infants from 4 to 12 months participated, and Figure 7-3 shows their results.

After the onset of laughter at the age of 4 months, there is a clear increase with age in the number of situations eliciting laughter; the increase is most apparent between the fourth and ninth months of life. Moreover, the nature of the stimuli that elicit laughter changes as the child develops. While stimulation, such as tactile stimulation, may be effective for a 5-month-old,

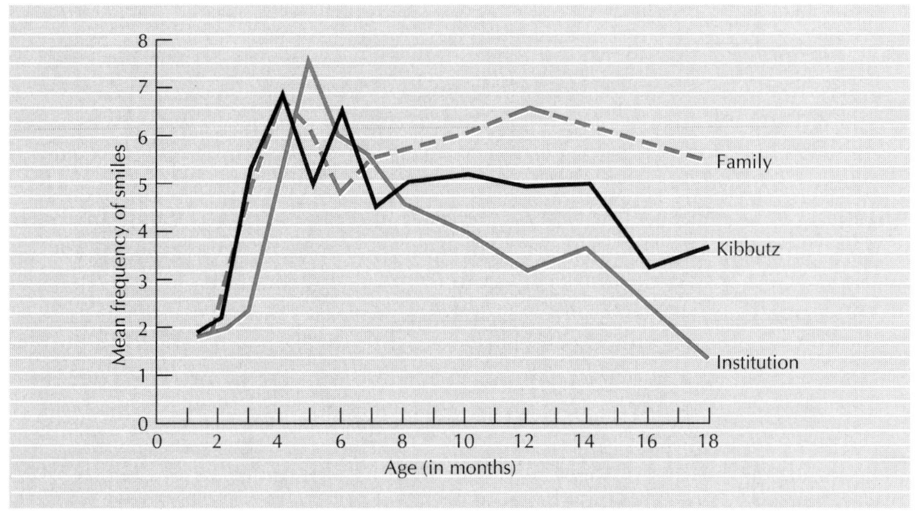

FIGURE 7-2
Frequency of smiling among infants raised in three different environments. (From Gewirtz, 1965, with permission of the author, the publisher, and the Tavistock Institute of Human Relations.)

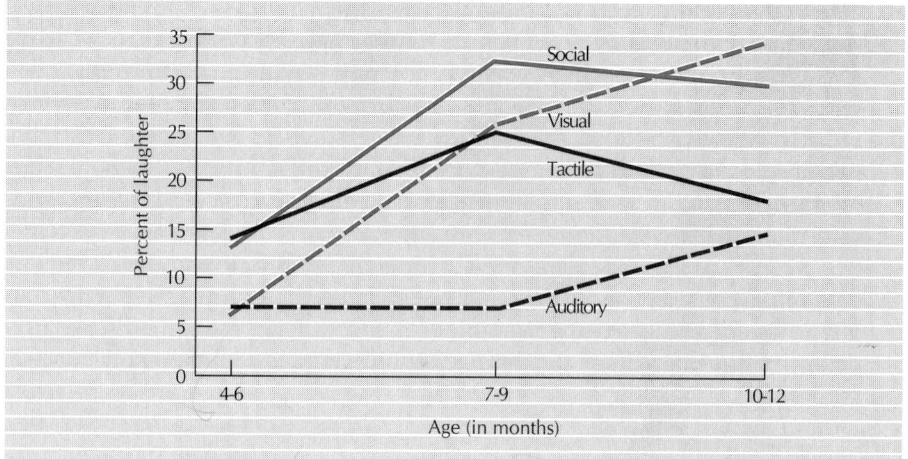

FIGURE 7-3
Laughter of infants in the first year of life in response to four different classes of stimuli. (From Sroufe & Wunsch, 1972, with permission of the authors and the Society for Research in Child Development.)

older infants lose interest in mere stimulation; in the third quarter of the first year, infants respond more to social games (peek-a-boo), visual spectacles, and other activities in which they can participate, such as covering and uncovering the mother's face with a cloth or playing tug-of-war with a blanket. By the end of the first year and throughout the second year of life, infants increasingly smile and laugh in response to activities that they create themselves. For example, an infant may repeatedly bat a mobile to make it turn and then laugh uproariously. Laughing increases as children develop and it becomes more of a social event. Nearly 95 percent of laughter occurred in the presence of other children and adults in one study of 3- to 5-year-olds (Bainum, Lounsbury, & Pollio, 1984). Acting silly and clowning was most often the elicitor of laughter among the nursery school set.

The Explanation of Smiling and Laughter

Few phenomena have a single explanation, and smiling and laughter are no exceptions. Some theorists regard smiling as innately determined (Spitz & Wolf, 1946), while others have emphasized the role of learning (Gerwirtz, 1967). Finally, some theorists have championed a perceptual-recognition hypothesis to explain smiling and laughter (Kagan, 1984).

Is smiling innate? Some support of the view that smiling and laughter have a strong maturational basis comes from twin studies and from investigations of premature infants. It has been found that identical twins exhibit greater concordance than fraternal twins in the time of onset and in the amount of social smiling (Plomin & DeFries, 1985). Studies of smiling in premature infants also point to the role of maturational factors in the onset of smiling. The normal conceptual age or period since conception for an infant at birth is 40 weeks. Most normal full-term infants begin to smile at 6 weeks, or at a conceptual age of 46 weeks. Premature infants who are born at 34 weeks often do not smile until 12 weeks after birth, or when they are 46 weeks since conception (Dittrichova, 1969). The fact that age based on the birth date is not the best predictor of the onset of smiling underlines the role that maturational factors play.

Although the timing of the beginning of smiling may be biologically determined, it is highly unlikely that genetic factors alone would be able to account for differences in the rate of development of smiling and laughter. As we have already seen, frequency of smiling seems to vary with the type of rearing environment. To account for these variations in smiling, learning-theory explanations have been suggested. Stimulation from adults, particularly familiar caregivers, that follows infant smiling can increase the rate of smiling (Brackbill, 1958).

An adequate explanation of smiling and laughter should account for the frequency of smiling and should explain why different events cause smiling and laughter at different ages. Why will young infants smile at simple toys while older children will be more likely to smile or laugh when playing interactive games? The perceptual-recognition viewpoint provides a better explanation of these aspects of smiling and laughter. According to this theory, development of smiling can best be understood by viewing the infant as an information-processing organism who is attempting to impose structure or meaning on incoming stimulation. One way in which the infant makes sense of the external world is by forming mental representations of external events; these internal pictures are called *schema*. This process of schema development will be discussed in detail in Chapter 9. Achieving a match between the schema and an incoming stimulus is the infant's means of understanding. This achievement, the creation of a schema for an event, is a source of pleasure that is signaled by a smile (Kagan, Kearsley, & Zelazo, 1978). Support for this hypothesis comes from Zelazo (1972), who found that infants who are presented a novel event, at first stay sober; later, after they begin to comprehend it, they smile; while later, after they become bored, the rate of smiling decreases. If one sees this phenomenon in real life, it is difficult to avoid the conclusions that the smile is produced following an act of perceptual recognition.

In summary, the onset of smiling and laughter may be biologically predetermined, but the developmental course of these behaviors is shaped by both shifts in cognitive abilities and the child's social experience.

FROM SMILING TO ATTACHMENT

A 3-month-old smiles more at his mother than at a stranger; three months later the infant may cry when his mother leaves; a few months after that he may crawl to his mother's side in an unfamiliar situation. These developments are part of a most remarkable achievement: the development of a specific social attachment, whereby the infant seeks to be near certain people—not just anyone. Few topics have generated as much interest as the process of attachment formation. It is of interest not only because it is a widespread and often extremely intense and dramatic phenomenon, but also because attachment is thought to enhance the parents' effectiveness in later socialization of the child. The child who has developed an attachment to his parent is more likely to be concerned about maintaining parental affection and approval through adopting socialized behaviors than is a child who has failed to develop this special social relationship with some adults in his environment.

The issues in attachment that have been the focus of greatest theorizing and research have been the parental characteristics and childrearing practices associated with attachment, the sequence and timing of attachment behaviors, and the consequences of attachment for later social and emotional development.

Theories of Attachment

A variety of theories have been offered to explain the development of attachment, including psychoanalytic theory, learning theory, and ethological theory. Each position makes different assumptions about the role of the infant in the development of attachment, the variables that are important for the development of attachment, and the processes underlying the development of attachment.

PSYCHOANALYTIC THEORY

Much of the work on the development of attachment has been directly or indirectly influenced by psychoanalytic theory. According to this viewpoint, parental caretaking activities, such as feeding, that are essential for the survival of the child are critical in attachment formation. Specifically, Freudians postulate that the infant has an innate need to suck, which interacts with, and is modified by, actual feeding experiences. The need for oral gratification through sucking and other forms of stimulation of the mouth results in the infant becoming attached to the satisfying mother's breast and ultimately to the mother herself.

LEARNING THEORY

Learning theorists as well as psychoanalytic theorists have stressed the importance of the feeding situation for the development of attachment (Sears, Maccoby, & Levin, 1957). According to a learning view, the caretaker acquires positive value through association with the satisfaction and reduction of hunger, a primary drive. The mother, as a result of being paired with drive-reducing feeding activity, acquires secondary reinforcement properties and consequently is valued in her own right. In other words, eventually, just the presence of the mother becomes satisfying and the child develops an acquired need for contact with the mother, which is referred to as attachment.

Few people accept the view that the feeding situation is the critical context for the development of social attachment. The most famous challenge to this traditional view came from the Harlow and Zimmerman (1959) study of cloth-and-wire surrogate mother monkeys, which showed that infants preferred cloth "mothers" even though they were fed on the wire "mother." Hunger reduction is clearly not necessary for the development of attachment.

Human studies tell a similar story: Variations in routine caretaking practices are poor predictors of infant attachment. For example, in one study of attachment in Scotland, it was found that infants formed attachments to some individuals, such as fathers and other relatives, who played little or no role in routine child care, such as feeding or diapering (Schaffer & Emerson, 1964).

Adults, however, do more than feed: They provide a wide variety of other types of stimulation for the infant. Some learning theorists suggest that the visual, auditory, and tactual stimulation that adults provide in the course of their daily interactions with the infant provides the basis for the development of attachment (Gewirtz, 1969). The infant is initially attracted to people because they are the most important and reliable sources of stimulation. As a result of *specific* individuals' regularly providing this satisfying stimulation, these individuals are valued by the infant and become the objects of attachment. The important feature of the learning-theory explanation, however, is that attachment is not an innate or instinctual process, but rather develops over time as a result of satisfying interaction with key people in the child's environment. Learning theorists, as well as others, view attachment as a two-way process with both the infant and the parent developing attachments to each other.

ETHOLOGICAL THEORY

Another theoretical view that has emphasized the reciprocal nature of the attachment process is John Bowlby's ethological theory (1958, 1969, 1973). Under the influence of both evolutionary theory and observational studies of animals, Bowlby has suggested that attachment is a result of a set of instinctual responses that are important for the protection and survival of the species. These infant behaviors—crying, smiling, sucking, clinging, and following—elicit necessary parental care and protection for the infant and promote contact between mother and infant. The mother is biologically prepared to respond to these infant elicitors, just as the infant is predisposed to respond to the sights, sounds, and nurturance provided by his human caretakers. It is as a result of these biologically programmed systems that both mother and infant develop a mutual attachment to each other. Bowlby, like other current theorists, minimizes the importance of the feeding situation. The value of this position lies in its explicit emphasis on the active role of the infant's early social signaling systems, such as smiling and crying, in the formation of attachment. Another attractive feature of the theory is its stress on the development of mutual attachment, whereby both partners, not just one, form attachments. Of some question, however, is the value of Bowlby's suggestion that these early behaviors are biologically preprogrammed. Less controversial than the theoretical viewpoints are the empirical findings concerning the developmental determinants and consequences of attachment. Next we turn to these issues.

The Developmental Course of Attachment

Attachment does not develop suddenly and unheralded, but emerges in a consistent series of steps in the first 6 to 8 months of life. Three general steps have been distinguished: First, at birth the infant is attracted to all social objects and prefers humans to inanimate objects. Second, the infant gradually learns to discriminate familiar and unfamiliar people. This second phase begins in the first few days after birth. Newborn infants can discriminate between their mothers' voices and those of other women (DeCasper & Fifer, 1980). Even after a total of four hours of exposure to their mothers' faces, 2-day-old infants could distinguish the mother's face from a stranger's face (Field, Cohen, Garcia, & Greenberg, 1984). As we saw earlier in Chapter 5, infants can recognize their mothers by smell by as early as 2 weeks of age.

Familiarization is not a unidirectional process with only infants learning about their parents. Parents too are becoming increasingly acquainted with the unique characteristics of their infants. They learn what makes them smile and laugh, and they learn how to calm and soothe their infants. In turn, the infants learn the unique features of their caretakers—their faces, their voices, their movements; however, during this period the infant does not protest the departure of familiar people.

The third phase, namely, the development of specific attachments, begins at about 6 to 8 months. Now the infant actively seeks contact with specific individuals and may protest when they depart. This general sequence is illustrated in Figure 7-4, where indiscriminate attachments precede the onset of specific attachment at about 7 months. In looking at Figure 7-4, it is

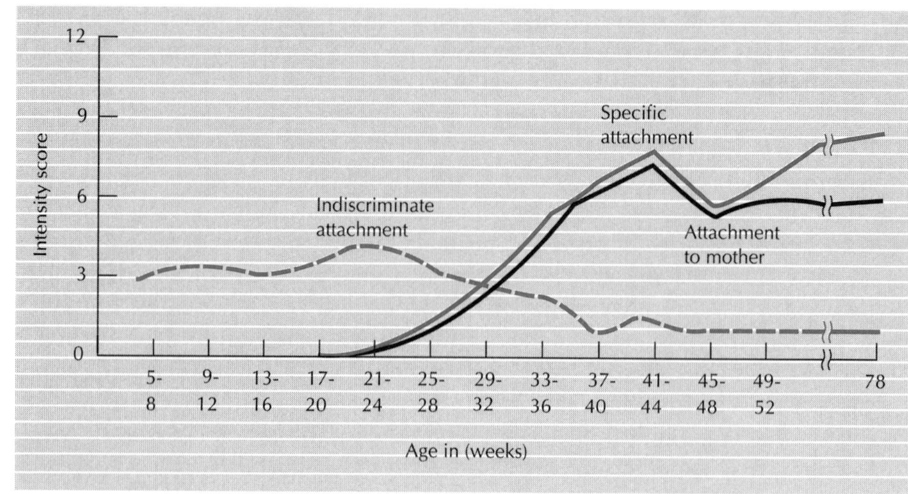

FIGURE 7-4
Developmental course of attachments. (From Schaffer & Emerson, 1964, with permission of the authors and the Society for Research in Child Development.)

important to remember that these ages represent averages and that there is considerable variation among babies in the timing of attachments.

The child's level of cognitive development plays an important role in the emergence of specific attachments. Before such responses can occur, the infant not only must be able to differentiate between mother and stranger, but must be aware that people still exist when they are not visible. The child must have developed object permanence, or the knowledge that objects, including humans, have a continuous existence. The child is unlikely to protest or call for a person who is out of sight if he is not aware that the person exists when he cannot see him.

Advances in the infant's cognitive development can also account, in part, for the gradual shift in the ways that attachment is expressed. Physical proximity becomes less important as the child develops, and hence, departures tend to result in less upset in the older child. Children also are better able to understand the reasons for separation and can appreciate that separations are temporary. With increasing understanding of verbal communication, parents are able to reduce the impact of separation by providing explanations for their departures. For example, when mothers informed their 2-year-old children of their departure ("I'm going out now for just a minute, but I'll be right back"), their children handled the separation better than when mothers just stepped out without explanation (Weinraub & Lewis, 1977). In general, as the child develops, reactions to separation lessen as the child learns that the mother will return.

Parental Behavior and the Development of Attachment

What determines the quality of the infant's attachment to his parents? What parent-child interactions in early infancy are important? In one study infants were attached to adults who responded quickly to their demands and cries and who spontaneously sought and initiated interactions with them (Schaffer & Emerson, 1964). Hence, when a relatively unstimulating mother, that is, one who tends to avoid contact with her infant except for routine physical care, is combined with an attentive, stimulating father, the child is more likely to form a paternal attachment despite the greater amount of routine contact with the mother. Stimulation and a sense of control over the environment seem to be critical factors in the development of early infant attachment.

In another study, Ainsworth (1973) observed a group of white middle-class mothers interacting with their infants for four-hour sessions every three weeks from birth until 54 weeks of age. Observations of the infants' attachment and exploratory behavior at about 1 year of age were made in a series of standard situations involving various combinations of the infant with the presence or absence of the mother and a stranger. This sequence is known as the "strange situation" (see Table 7-1). There are striking differences in the infants' responses to the strange situation, and through this test the quality of the infant-mother relationship can be assessed. The majority of the infants (60 to 65 percent) are clearly or "securely" attached to their mothers, as shown by occasional seeking to be close to and touching the mother when she is present and by intensified contact-maintaining behavior following being left alone in an unfamiliar situation. Ainsworth has labeled these patterns as the "B" attachment type. These infants feel secure enough to

TABLE 7-1

AINSWORTH "STRANGE SITUATION"

EPISODE NUMBER	PERSONS PRESENT	DURATION	BRIEF DESCRIPTION OF ACTIONS
1	Mother, baby, and observer	30 seconds	Observer introduces mother and baby to experimental room, then leaves. (Room contains many appealing toys scattered about.)
2	Mother and baby	3 minutes	Mother is nonparticipant while baby explores; if necessary, play is stimulated after 2 minutes.
3	Stranger, mother, and baby	3 minutes	Stranger enters. First minute: stranger silent. Second minute: stranger converses with mother. Third minute: stranger approaches baby. After 3 minutes mother leaves unobtrusively.
4	Stranger and baby	3 minutes or less	First separation episode. Stranger's behavior is geared to that of baby.
5	Mother and baby	3 minutes or more	First reunion episode. Mother greets and/or comforts baby, then tries to settle the baby again in play. Mother then leaves, saying "bye-bye."
6	Baby alone	3 minutes or less	Second separation episode.
7	Stranger and baby	3 minutes or less	Continuation of second separation. Stranger enters and gears behavior to that of baby.
8	Mother and baby	3 minutes	Second reunion episode. Mother enters, greets baby, then picks baby up. Meanwhile stranger leaves unobtrusively.

explore and manipulate a strange environment when their mothers are present. They do not cling and whine but are curious and manipulative in dealing with toys and other objects in the unfamiliar situation when their mothers are with them. In familiar situations, such as the home, these children are minimally disturbed by minor separations, although they greet the mother's return with enthusiasm. All children in this group had mothers who had permitted them to play an active role in determining the pacing, onset, and termination of feeding early in life. Note that it is not the particular child-care practice but the responsiveness and sensitivity to the infant's needs that are important in determining the quality of attachment.

Two other groups are viewed as insecurely attached to their parents. One group—the "avoidantly" attached infants or "A" pattern—that typically accounts for 20 percent of the infants in American samples shows little upset about the parent's absence. Upon reunion they avoid interaction with the parent and ignore the parent's bids for interaction. The mothers of these babies are insensitive to their infant's signals, rarely have close bodily contact, and instead of being affectionate, interact in an angry and irritable way.

A third group of infants, labeled "C," showed frequent intense distress

TABLE 7-2 **FOUR FORMS OF ATTACHMENT ORGANIZATION OBSERVED AT 12 MONTHS AND AT 6 YEARS OF AGE**

ATTACHMENT ORGANIZATION/AGE	DESCRIPTION
A. Insecure-avoidant:	
12 months*	Actively avoids and ignores parent on reunion, looking away, and remaining occupied with toys. At extremes, moves away from parent and ignores parent's efforts to communicate.
6 years	Minimizes and restricts opportunities for interaction with parent on reunion, looking and speaking only briefly and minimally as required and remaining occupied with toys or activities. At extremes, moves away, but subtly, with rationale such as retrieving a toy.
B. Secure:	
12 months	Seeks interaction, proximity, physical contact or any combination thereof, with the parent on reunion, often actively attempts to maintain physical contact. Readily soothed after distress by parent and returns to exploration and play.
6 years	Initiates conversation and pleasant interaction with the parent on reunion or is highly responsive to parent's own initiations. May subtly move into proximity or physical contact with parent, usually with rationale such as seeking a toy. Remains calm throughout episode.
C. Insecure-ambivalent:	
12 months	Distress because of separation is not effectively soothed by parent, although infant seems to want proximity and contact. Overt-to-subtle signs of anger

and crying when the mother was either present or absent, and either lacked interest in contact with the mother or showed ambivalence about contact by such things as intermittent proximity seeking accompanied by angry pushing away and rejection of the mother. These infants (about 10 to 15 percent) were termed "ambivalently" attached and had mothers who had been rated as being insensitive and awkward in their interactions with their infants, and low in affection but not as rejecting as the "avoidant" mothers.

More recently, a fourth group of infants has been identified, which are classified as "D" or disorganized (Main & Solomon, 1989). Infants identified as being in this group appeared disorganized and disoriented on reunion in the strange situation by showing "dazed" behavior, freezing or stilling movements, uncompleted or stereotypic movements (for example, rocking).

These attachment classifications reflect the quality of the relationship between the infant or child with the parent, and are not characteristic of either the parent or child; in short, they are not "traits" but rather relationships. As Table 7-2 shows, these same patterns can be detected at age 6 as well as in infancy in the "strange situation" (Main & Cassidy, 1988).

Other studies indicate that the antecedents of "securely" and "insecurely"

TABLE 7-2

FOUR FORMS OF ATTACHMENT ORGANIZATION OBSERVED AT 12 MONTHS AND AT 6 YEARS OF AGE *(Continued)*

ATTACHMENT ORGANIZATION/AGE	DESCRIPTION
	toward the parent are often present (for example, child may seek proximity and contact, then resist it).
6 years	In movements, posture, and tones of voice child appears to attempt to exaggerate intimacy with the parent as well as dependency on the parent. May seek proximity or contact, but shows some resistance or ambivalence (for example, lying on parent's lap while wriggling uncomfortably). Moderately avoidant, subtle signs of hostility are sometimes present.
D. Insecure-disorganized:†	
12 months	Child shows one or several signs of disorganization (for example, crying for parent at door, then moving sharply away when door opens; approaching parent with head averted) or disorientation (for example, stilling or freezing movement for a few seconds) during the "strange situation."
6 years	Seems partially to assume a parental role toward parent. Attempts to control and direct the parent's behavior, either through punitive behavior (directing, embarrassing, or humiliating the parent) or through overbright/caregiving behavior (exhibiting extreme enthusiasm for reunion, solicitous behavior to parent, or careful attempts to guide and direct parent).

* Descriptions of reunion behavior used to classify infant attachment organization at 12 months are taken from Ainsworth, Blehar, Waters, & Wall (1978).

† Sixth-year classification title is used for general title. There is no controlling category for infancy; in infancy, these children were identified as disorganized/disoriented.

Source: Adapted from Main & Cassidy (1988).

BOX 7-1 THE ROOTS OF ATTACHMENT: THE DEVELOPMENT OF CARETAKER-INFANT SYNCHRONY

Well before the infant shows evidence of a specific attachment, the early beginnings of mutual adaptation and regulation are evident. Just as sucking, sleeping, and other early behaviors are highly organized, so are interpersonal relationships. Only recently have we fully appreciated how early and how finely tuned the interaction patterns between infants and their caretakers actually are (Stern, 1985).

Let us take a close look at a mother and a 3-month-old infant playing together. To permit a detailed analysis, Stern (1977) filmed the face-to-face interactions between 3-month-old infants and their mothers. Rather than a disorganized pattern, the play behavior is a highly orchestrated interchange, with both mother and infant adjusting their behavior throughout the play period. Both mothers and infants show a pattern of mutual approach and withdrawal that permits the mutual regulation of stimulation of some optimal and presumably pleasurable level for the infant. Each partner makes a unique contribution to this early dialogue. Mothers constantly shift their behavior in order to elicit and maintain the baby's attention. One technique that mothers use to hold their infant's attention is to exaggerate their speech. For example, they talk louder and slower and use longer vowels. A mother might say, "Hi-swee-eet-ee, Hiii, Hi-i-iya, watcha looking at? Hu-u-uh? O-o-o-o-o-o, yeah, it's mommy ye-e-a-ah" (Stern, 1974, p. 192). Similarly, facial expressions are often exaggerated, slower to form, and longer in duration. The infant contributes to the regulation largely through the control of gaze, which allows him to regulate the amount of stimulation that he is receiving. When the amount of stimulation is too much, the infant turns away. In turn, the mother reduces her input. Stern has characterized the mutual regulatory actions of both partners who are constantly making readjustments in their behavior during play as a "waltz." The infant during this period is learning in a more precise way the features of his caretaker's face, the regulation of his attention, and an early lesson in social control. The caretaker is learning a variety of important lessons as well. Through this interaction, adults are learning to more sensitively and accurately "read" their baby's early social signals and to adjust their behavior to maintain the baby's attention and interest. It is out of these early dialogues that adults become increasingly more attached to their infants, and the infants' develop an attachment to their caregivers. Play, in short, is serious business.

Sources: Stern, D. N. (1974). Mother and infant at play: The dyadic interaction involving facial, vocal, and gaze behaviors. In M. Lewis & L. A. Rosenblum (Eds.), *The effect of the infant on its caregiver.* New York: Wiley; Stern, D. N. (1977). *The first relationship: Infant and mother.* Cambridge, MA: Harvard University Press; Stern, D. N. (1985). *The interpersonal world of the infant: A view from psychoanalysis and developmental psychology.* New York: Basic Books.

attached infants can be found in a variety of interaction contexts, including face-to-face play. During the first few months of life, the beginnings of later attachment can be seen in the playful frolic that often characterizes early parent-infant interaction. As described in Box 7-1, even 3-month-old infants and their mothers engage in highly involved, intricate, and delicately orchestrated play bouts. Not all infants and parents are able to adapt successfully to each other and achieve the interactive "waltz" described in Box 7-1.

Unfortunately, some of those parent-infant dyads that fail to achieve early interactive synchrony also fail to develop secure infant-parent attachment later. Maternal responsiveness to infant signals can play an important role in the emergence of attachment. In a longitudinal study, infants and their mothers were observed at 1, 3, and 9 months under naturalistic conditions in the home; at 12 months infant-mother attachment was assessed in the "strange situation" (Isabella, Belsky, & vonEye, 1989; Isabella & Belsky, 1991). Marked differences in the early patterns of interaction across the three attachment groups were found. As early as 1 and 3 months, mother and infant who later developed a secure relationship displayed more synchronous patterns of interaction, in which both mother and infant responded to one another in a reciprocal and mutually rewarding way than mother-infant dyads that later developed insecure relationships. Insecure dyads had more asynchronous interactions which were one-sided, unresponsive, and/or intrusive. Mothers of avoidant infants were verbally intrusive yet unresponsive to verbal signals, while mothers of ambivalent infants were generally unresponsive as well as underinvolved.

Relationships between parents and infants do not develop in a vacuum, but are affected by and affect other relationships among family members. A number of investigators have found a relationship between infant-parent attachment and marital adjustment. For example, Goldberg and Easterbrooks (1984) observed that secure infant attachments among 20-month-old infants and their parents were more likely when marital adjustment was high, whereas insecure attachments were more frequent when marital adjustment was low. Moreover, it appears to begin in early infancy. Although the birth of the child is associated with a decline in marital satisfaction (Cowan & Cowan, 1992), mothers who develop secure attachment patterns with their infants show less decline in their marital satisfaction (Belsky & Isabella, 1988). As we will see in Chapter 12 when we explore the family, marriage and parent-child relationships are often closely linked.

Finally, as Box 7-2 shows, parents' own relationships with their parents can potentially influence how they relate to their own infants. Intergenerational relationships are another possible influence on the development of attachments.

Infant Temperament and the Development of Attachment

In spite of the fact that the development of attachment is a process of mutual influence, most researchers have illuminated the mother's role and neglected the infant's contribution. Some babies may be more difficult to interact with and care for and, in turn, may develop less optimal infant-parent attachment. Newborn infants who are less skilled in orienting to objects and people are more likely to show insecure attachments (Waters, Vaughn, & Egeland, 1980). Similar findings were found for German newborns (Grossman, Grossman, Spangler, Suess, & Unzer, 1985). Perhaps early neonatal difficulties may reflect problems in integrative and adaptive mechanisms that continue to influence behavior, interaction, and later attachment relationships. Other studies suggest that babies with "difficult" temperaments or who are less sociable show greater distress during separations and reunions (Lewis & Fiering, 1989; Thompson, Connell, & Bridges, 1988). However, these findings of a link between infant temperament and later infant-parent attachment must be viewed with caution since many other studies have failed to find any relationships (Bates, 1987).

Other findings suggest that infant characteristics such as temperamental qualities may play a role in early social relationships but only when other features of the family context are taken into account. This suggests that difficult beginnings do not *necessarily* destine infants to a poor relationship with their parents. Parents who have difficult or irritable infants may be able to cope if they receive help and support such as child-care advice, social companionship, and physical assistance (babysitting) from spouses or people outside the family. As we saw in Chapter 4, Crockenberg (1981) found that irritable babies were more likely to develop insecure attachments to others than were nonirritable infants, but if the mothers of irritable infants received social support, their infants were just as likely as less irritable babies to be securely attached. Similarly, others (Levitt, Weber, & Clark, 1986) find support

BOX 7-2 ATTACHMENT ACROSS GENERATIONS: THE ROLE OF CHILDHOOD EXPERIENCE IN INFANT-PARENT ATTACHMENT

What determines the quality of care that a mother provides? There are many determinants of the quality of parenting, but one factor that has recently received attention is the kind of care that the parents themselves received when they were infants (Bretherton, Ridgeway, & Cassidy, 1989). As Bowlby (1973) argued as a consequence of the parent-infant relationships, *internal working models* of self and parents develop which, in turn, serve as guides or templates concerning how relationships work in other contexts.

> Because children tend unwittingly to identify with parents and therefore to adopt, when they become parents, the same patterns of behavior towards children that they themselves have experienced during their own childhood, patterns of interaction are transmitted, more or less faithfully, from one generation to another. (Bowlby, 1973, p. 323)

In support of this notion of intergenerational continuity, Main, Kaplan, and Cassidy (1985) interviewed 40 mothers about recollections of their own relationships with their mothers during infancy and childhood. Interestingly, the mothers' patterns of memories related to the quality of their current attachment relationships with their own infants. Parents who had developed secure attachment relationships with their infants revealed in their interviews that they valued close relationships with their parents and others, but at the same time were objective. They tended not to idealize their own parents but had a clear understanding of their own relationships with their parents—even if it was not always positive, and even if the relationship was sufficient to overcome this poor history. In contrast, parents of insecure-avoidant infants had a different set of memories; they dismissed and devalued attachment and frequently claimed that they couldn't recall incidents from their childhood. Recollections were often of idealized parents. "I had the world's greatest mom!" Parents of insecure-resistant infants, on the other hand, were preoccupied with earlier family attachments. They recalled many conflict-ridden incidents from childhood but couldn't organize them into a coherent pattern. Parents of infants classified as insecure-disorganized seemed to be struggling with unresolved issues over the loss of a parent in childhood; these adults seem to be still mourning the loss of a parent. Similar findings have been reported by others (Grossman, Fremmer-Bombik, Rudolph, & Grossman, 1989).

It is clear that early experience shapes later parental behavior, but the ways that adults come to terms with their own childhood experiences may be just as important as the events themselves.

Sources: Bowlby, J. (1973). *Separation and loss.* New York: Basic Books; Bretherton, I., Ridgeway, D., & Cassidy, J. (1989). The role of internal working models in the attachment relationship: Can it be studied in three-year-olds? In M. Greenberg, D. Cicchetti, & E. M. Cummings (Eds.), *Attachment during the preschool years: Theory, research and intervention.* Chicago: University of Chicago Press; Grossman, K., Fremmer-Bombik, D., Rudolph, J., & Grossman, K. E. (1989). Maternal attachment representations as related to patterns of infant-mother attachment and maternal care during the first year. In R. A. Hinde & J. Stevenson-Hinde (Eds.), *Relationships within families.* Oxford: Oxford University Press; Main, M., Kaplan, N., & Cassidy, J. (1985). Security in infancy, childhood and adulthood: A move to the level of representation. In I. Bretherton & E. Waters (Eds.), Growing points of attachment theory and research. *Monographs of the Society for Research in Child Development,* **50** (1–2, Serial No. 209).

for this view. In their study, temperamentally difficult 13-month-olds were more likely to be avoidant if their mothers had poor relationships with their own mothers. Together these findings remind us that a biological influence, such as infant temperament, may often be best understood in combination with an appreciation of the features of the social ecology in which the infant is developing (Bronfenbrenner, 1989; Mangelsdorf, Gunnar, Kestenbaum, Lang, & Andreas, 1990).

Stability of Attachment

Are the differences in patterning of attachment that we have discussed stable over time? Infants tested in the "strange situation" at 12 months with their mothers and again at 18 months are generally classified in the same way at the two time points. Infants who showed secure attachment at 12 months were rated as secure at 18 months just as the infants with avoidant and ambivalent attachment patterns showed stability over the six-month interval (Waters, 1978).

More recently, Main and Cassidy (1988) evaluated the stability of attachment classifications from 1 year to 6 years. (See Table 7-2 for a description of age 6 attachment classification.) One hundred percent of the infants rated as securely attached at 12 months were rated similarly at 6 years, while 75 percent of the children who had been judged to be insecurely attached to (avoidant) their mothers during infancy were judged avoidant five years later. Although not enough insecure ambivalent babies (C) were available to evaluate this group, 66 percent of the infants in the D or disorganized attachment category showed stability from infancy to age 6. A related study revealed that the C or insecure-ambivalent group is stable at 6 years over a brief time period of one month (Main & Cassidy, 1988). Moreover, a German study revealed that first-year ABCD attachment classifications predicted 78 percent of the sixth-year attachment classifications (Wartner & Grossman, 1987). Father-infant attachment classifications were stable as well, but the level of prediction was lower (61 percent) than in the case of mother-infant attachment classification. Again, note how the behaviors that reflect these different patterns of attachment relationships (described in Table 7-2) shift across development as the child matures.

However, does such stability in the attachment of infants occur only where there is little change in circumstances across the intervening time period? What happens to the attachment of infants who encounter stressful changes in their family circumstances such as divorce, job loss, or residence change? Will these infants show stability in attachment? Indeed some infants show a shift from secure to anxious attachment especially if the family's level of stress is high; other infants shift toward greater security of attachment over time if the change in family situation is associated with a relief from tension (Thompson, Lamb, & Estes, 1982). These findings illustrate the modifiability of attachment relationships. "Like any other affectional relationship, infant-mother attachments arise from interaction, they continue to develop even after an affective bond has formed and they are responsive to changes in the behavior of either partner" (Vaughn, Egeland, Waters, & Sroute, 1979, p. 975).

Multiple Attachments: Fathers and Peers as Attachment Figures

FATHERS AS ATTACHMENT FIGURES

Infants develop attachments not only to their mothers, but also to a variety of other persons—including their fathers. With changing cultural views, fathers often take a much more active role in early infancy, which makes it even more likely that they will develop an attachment to their infant, as well as serve as an attachment figure for their offspring (Bronstein & Cowan, 1988; Parke & Tinsley, 1987). Margaret Mead's famous claim that "fathers are a biological necessity, but a social accident" is no longer valid.

Even in the newborn period, fathers take an active interest in their infants. Although this is often through the looking glass of the newborn nursery, fathers who are given the opportunity to have contact with their infants hold, touch, vocalize, and kiss them just as much as mothers (Parke, 1981; Parke & O'Leary, 1976). This early father involvement is reciprocated by infants who show just as much attachment to their fathers as to their mothers later in the first year. This is well illustrated in an observational study by Lamb (1977), who studied 7- to 8-month-old and 12- to 13-month-old infants when both parents and a friendly but unfamiliar visitor were present in the home.

Although the infants were more attached to their parents than to the visitor, they showed no preference for either parent in terms of their attachment behaviors. They were just as likely to touch, fuss, approach, and be near their fathers as their mothers. "There was certainly no evidence to support the popular assumption that infants of this age should prefer—indeed be uniquely attached to—their mothers" (Lamb, 1977, p. 180). Infants form attachments not to a single individual, but to *both* mother and father in the first year of life.

Fathers and mothers, however, may play unique roles. Fathers are not merely substitute caretakers in their infant's social world, and in spite of current trends they are still less likely than mothers to be the primary caretaker. Similarly, grandfathers are less likely to play as active a role in direct child care as grandmothers (McGreal, 1985; Tinsley & Parke, 1988). Father involvement in caregiving increases under circumstances where mothers are less available due to employment (Gottfried, Gottfried, & Bathurst, 1988) or a cesarean section delivery (Pederson, Zaslow, Cain, & Anderson, 1980). Similarly father caregiving is greater when mothers are supportive of father involvement and view the father as a competent and capable caregiver (Bietel & Parke, 1990).

Nonetheless the father's special role is as a playmate, with fathers spending four to five times as much time playing with their infants as taking care of them. Nor is the father as playmate restricted to our American culture. A similar profile of the father engaging in more play than caregiving is found in a variety of other cultures including Australia, Israel, India, Italy, Japan, and even among the Aka Pygmies of Central Africa (Lamb, 1987; Roopnarine, 1992). Moreover, the quality of play is different. Fathers engage in more unusual and physically arousing games, such as rough-and-tumble play, while mothers verbally stimulate their babies and play more conventional games such as peek-a-boo (Parke, 1990; Power & Parke, 1982; Yogman, 1981). These stylistic differences continue well into early childhood, with mothers and fathers showing the same tendencies with their 3- and 4-year-olds (MacDonald & Parke, 1984, 1986). However, fathers are more likely to toss and bounce their sons than their daughters (Power & Parke, 1982).

These differences are very robust. Even when they stay home with their babies while their wives go to work, fathers are more physical than mothers, although fathers did adopt some aspects of the maternal style by imitating their babies' sounds in the same high-pitched way that mothers do (Field, 1978). Similarly, results from Sweden, where legislation allows fathers to stay home and participate in the care of their infants for a few months after birth, suggest that fathers and mothers still differ in their style of interaction (Hwang, 1986; Lamb, Frodi, Hwang, & Frodi, 1982). It is not yet established whether these mother-father differences are due to biology or experience. However, it is clear that infants react more positively to father play than to mother play (Field, 1990). If given a choice of play partners, 18-month-old infants in one study (Clarke-Stewart, 1978) chose their fathers more than their mothers, probably because a father is a more exciting and unpredictable play partner.

Fathers are not the preferred partner on all occasions. In times of stress, mothers are generally preferred. Infants who are introduced to a stranger in an unfamiliar situation when both parents are present show a clear preference for the mother over the father (Lamb, 1977). In view of the different roles often played by the mothers and fathers, with many mothers assuming primary caretaking responsibility, the infant's choice of mother in time of

a

b

Fathers and mothers have different styles of playing with infants. Fathers are more physical, and mothers are more verbal.

stress is sensible. The mother is presumably the parent who has most often served in this protective, anxiety-reducing capacity in other situations in the past.

Finally, fathers' roles can be changed by supportive interventions, such as educational programs that stress the importance of father involvement and teach ways of interacting effectively with their infants (Parke & Beitel, 1986; Levant, 1988).

In summary, fathers as well as mothers are important attachment figures and play an important role in the early social and emotional development of the infant. Moreover, the fact that fathers typically spend less time with the infant than mothers underscores a recurring theme: Quality of interaction is a more important determinant of social relationships than simply the amount of contact.

PEERS AS ATTACHMENT FIGURES

Although fathers and mothers are usually the most significant attachment objects, it should be stressed that a variety of other individuals are important in the infant's social world, including peers, siblings, and relatives, such as grandparents (Dunn, 1992; Tinsley & Parke, 1988). Peers can become important attachment figures—even for young children. In a preschool where some children were transferring to new schools, children who were leaving as well as those left behind experienced a variety of reactions including increased fussiness, activity level, negative effect, and illness, as well as changes in eating and sleeping patterns (Field, 1986). These reactions can be viewed as separation stress associated with the loss of familiar peers. For an even more dramatic illustration, see Box 7-3. Emotional development in early

BOX 7-3 PEERS AS ATTACHMENT FIGURES

A famous study (Freud & Dann, 1951) of six German-Jewish orphans, separated from their parents at an early age because of World War II and placed in an institution, tells how the children formed intense, protective attachments to each other while ignoring or being actively hostile to their adult caretakers. The children had lost their parents before the age of 1, most commonly in gas chambers. When they were in their fourth year of life, they arrived at Bulldog Banks, a small English country home that had been transformed into a nursery for war children. They had lived together in various concentration camps and institutions since their first year of life. Their stay at Bulldog Banks was their first experience in living in a small, intimate setting.

In their early days at Bulldog Banks these children were wild and uncontrollable. They destroyed or damaged much of the furniture and all of their toys within a few days. Usually they ignored adults, but when they were angry they would bite, spit, or swear at them, and often called them *bloder ochs* (stupid fools), which seemed to be their favorite epithet for their caretakers.

The contrast between their hostile behavior toward their caretakers and their solicitous, considerate behavior toward other children in their group was surprising. In one case, when a caretaker accidentally knocked over one of the children, two of the other children threw bricks at her and called her names. The children resisted being separated from each other even for special treats such as pony rides. When one child was ill, the others wanted to remain with her. They showed little envy, jealousy, rivalry, or competition with each other. The sharing and helping behavior the children showed was remarkable in children of this age.

The following are typical incidents in their first seven months at Bulldog Banks:

> The children were eating cake, and John began to cry when he saw there was no cake left for a second helping. Ruth and Miriam, who had not yet finished their portions, gave him the remainder of their cake and seemed happy just to pet him and comment on his eating the cake.
>
> On another occasion when one child lost his gloves, although it was very cold another child loaned his gloves without complaining about his own discomfort.

The investigators cited the following incidents when even in fearful situations children were able to overcome their trepidation to help the others in the group:

> A dog approaches the children, who are terrified. Ruth, though badly frightened herself, walks bravely to Peter who is screaming and gives him her toy rabbit to comfort him. She comforts John by lending him her necklace.
>
> On the beach in Brighton, Ruth throws pebbles into the water. Peter is afraid of waves and does not dare to approach them. In spite of his fear, he suddenly rushes to Ruth, calling out: "Water coming, water coming," and drags her back to safety. (Freud & Dann, 1951, pp. 150–168)

When, finally, positive relations with adults began to be formed, they were made on the basis of group feelings and had none of the demanding, possessive attitudes often shown by young children toward their own mothers. They began to include adults in their group and to treat them in some ways as they treated each other. This seemed to be a phase of general attachments that for some of the children was eventually followed by specific attachment toward an individual caretaker, with clinging and possessiveness appearing. During their year's stay at Bulldog Banks the intensity of the children's attachment to their surrogate mothers was never as intense as in normal mother-child relations and never as binding as those to their peers.

Source: Freud, A., & Dann, S. (1951). An experiment in group upbringing. In *The psychoanalytic study of the child* (Vol. 6). New York: International Universities Press.

life can best be understood by appreciating the complexity and diversity of the infant's social network.

Multiple Caretakers and Attachment: The Effects of Day Care

Is the development of attachment impaired if care is distributed among a number of caretakers as well as the parent? This question is frequently asked by researchers, parents, and policymakers since over 10.5 million children under age 6, including nearly 5 million infants and toddlers under age 3, have mothers in the labor force. Another 10 million children between the ages of 6 and 13 have working mothers and the numbers are continuing to rise (U.S. Bureau of Labor Statistics, 1988). While many children of working mothers are cared for by their parents, siblings, and other relatives, a growing proportion receive some form of day care, which involves leaving the child in the care of unrelated adults in their own homes, in their caretakers' homes, and in organized child-care facilities. In the 1990s, day care is a fact of everyday life for the majority of U.S. children and their families. What are the implications of day care for the development of children's attachment relationships with their parents? This is a very controversial question and at this point there is no simple answer. Some studies suggest that infants who are in day care as a result of their mothers' full-time employment are more likely to be classified as insecurely attached than infants of nonemployed or part-time working mothers, especially if children begin full-time care during the first year of life (Belsky & Rovine, 1988; Barglow, Vaughn, & Molitor, 1987). However, children who enter supplemental care after the first year of life do not generally show differences in security of attachment to their mothers. In a recent summary of all of these studies, Clarke-Stewart (1989) found that 36 percent of the infants of full-time working mothers are insecurely attached; while 29 percent of nonemployed or part-time working mothers were classified this way. Not only is this not a very large difference, but, what accounts for this difference is also not clear. Some have argued that infants of working mothers are at risk for emotional insecurity as reflected by insecure attachments because they interpret their mothers' absence as rejection or because repeated separations have disrupted their attachment relationships (Barglow et al., 1987; Belsky & Rovine, 1988). Others (Clarke-Stewart, 1989; Hayes & Palmer, 1989) argue that a variety of other factors may be involved as well, especially family factors. According to this view,

Day care continues to be both controversial and often expensive.

mothers who may behave insensitively or who dislike infants may opt to go to work. Or the stress associated with handling both babies and work may lessen their ability to develop a secure relationship with their infants. This suggests that day care has its effect on the baby because work has an impact on mothers. "The reason their infants might be insecurely attached is not that 40 hours of day care is hard on infants but that 40 hours of work is hard on mothers" (Clarke-Stewart, 1989, p. 270). In support of this possibility, it has been found that working mothers whose infants were insecure were more anxious and less competent, sensitive, empathetic, and happily married (Belsky & Rovine, 1988; Owen & Cox, 1988). In summary, there is little clear evidence that day care is likely to cause disruptions in the infant-parent attachment relationship. In fact, day care may have positive effects for some infants, especially if the day care is of good quality.

The day-care environment can sometimes offset or complement care received in the home by providing the child an opportunity to develop attachment relationships with caregivers in the day-care setting (Howes, Rodning, Galluzo, & Myers, 1988). Children with insecure attachments to their mothers, but secure attachments to caregivers in the day-care setting showed behaviors that indicated that the child-caregiver relationship was compensatory. These children were more socially competent than the children who failed to form compensatory secure relationships with alternative caregivers. Toddlers with insecure attachments to *both* mother and caregiver showed the least social competence as indexed by their ability to engage in interactions with caregivers in the child-care center. Children's behavior is clearly multiply determined and the kinds of relationships that children develop with a variety of social partners need to be considered.

Moreover, day care may even yield other beneficial effects: Infants with prior day-care experience adapt more quickly and explore more in an unfamiliar environment. They play more with peers, are more socially competent, exhibit more self-confidence and are less fearful of unfamiliar adults (Clarke-Stewart, 1987; Belsky, Steinberg, & Walker, 1983). On the other hand, day-care children are often reported to be more aggressive and noncompliant than their home-reared peers. However, the rates of aggression or noncompliance are within normal ranges and do not suggest that day-care children are, in any sense, socially maladjusted (Scarr, Phillips, & McCartney, 1990).

It is important to note that day care, like institutionalization, means many things and just as variations in the quality of home environments can either facilitate or slow the child's development, the *quality* of day care is an important determinant of the impact of this experience on the child (Phillips, 1991). More optimal social development as measured by better relationships with teachers and peers is more likely to be observed in high-quality day-care centers, where there are smaller groups, lower staff-to-child ratio, more interaction between staff and children, better caregiver training, more space, and better equipment than in poor-quality centers (Howes, Phillips, & Whitebook, 1992). Nor are the effects of quality short-lived. Howes (1988a, 1988b) found that higher child-care quality predicted less child hostility and more task orientation as rated by teachers during kindergarten. Children who entered day care before their first birthdays *and* experienced poor quality care were rated by their teachers in kindergarten as more destructive and less considerate. Other children in high-quality care four years earlier were friendlier, more competent, expressed more positive effect, and were better at resolving conflicts (Vandell, Henderson, & Wilson, 1988). Clearly, quality of day care that children experience in the preschool years is associated with their later social development. The debate continues and the definitive answers concerning the "best" kind of day care or even the long-term impact of day care are not yet available.

Consequences of Attachment

Now that we have examined the causes of attachment, we examine the consequences of attachment. Does the quality of early infant-parent attachment have implications for the child's later cognitive and social adaptation? Early social interactions with attachment figures do shape the child's later attitudes and behavior, including their sense of self, as well as cognitive and social development.

SENSE OF SELF

The developing sense of self may be affected by the nature of the children's quality of attachment with their parents. Cassidy (1988) assessed children's attachment relationships at age 6 and then determined whether children with different attachment relationships viewed themselves differently. To find out how the child thinks others view him or her, a puppet interview was conducted. A hand puppet, Bix, the frog, and Quax, the duck, asked the questions (for example, Bix, Do you like [child's name]? Do you like [child] the way he is or do you want to make him better? Tell me, Bix, do you want [child] to be your friend?) The child's answers to the puppet revealed how she thought others viewed her. Children who were securely attached tended to represent the self in a positive way but were still able to acknowledge less-than-perfect aspects of the self. Insecure-avoidant children tended to present themselves as completely perfect, while insecure-ambivalent children showed no clear pattern of responses. A final group—the insecure-controlling subjects (similar to the D, or disorganized, classification noted earlier) made excessively negative comments about themselves. Moreover, children who were more secure rated themselves as higher in overall self-esteem, as well as on ratings of cognitive competence and peer acceptance. Clearly, early attachment may foretell how the developing child's sense of self-worth will emerge.

COGNITIVE DEVELOPMENT

In cognitive development, the impact of earlier attachment relationships is most notable in exploratory behavior and problem-solving style. An early "secure" attachment promotes more complex exploratory behavior at 2 years of age (Main, 1973). As the child develops, this intellectual curiosity is reflected in a heightened involvement, persistence, and enjoyment in problem-solving situations seldom found in toddlers who have been insecurely attached infants (Matas, Arend, & Sroufe, 1978; Sroufe, 1983).

SOCIAL DEVELOPMENT

The quality of attachment in infancy is related to the child's peer relationships. To illustrate these links between attachment and peer relations, Sroufe (1983) followed forty children 12 months to 3½ years. Infants who were rated as securely and insecurely attached at 12 months developed very different social and emotional patterns. Teachers rated the securely attached children as higher in self-esteem, empathy, and positive affect and lower on negative affect. Specifically, securely attached infants more commonly initiated, responded to, and sustained interaction with others using positive affect.

Similarly, these children whined less, were less aggressive, and displayed fewer negative reactions to initiations. Not surprisingly, teachers rated the secure children as more socially competent, socially skilled, and higher in "number of friends." The children themselves apparently agreed: The securely attached children were rated by their peers as more popular than their insecurely attached classmates (Erickson, Sroufe, & Egeland, 1985; Suess, 1987). Finally, these children were higher in empathy as well (Kestenbaum, Farber, & Sroufe, 1989). Others have found similar links between early attachment patterns and later peer competence among preschool children (Erickson, et al., 1985; Suess, 1987) and elementary school children (Cohn, 1990).

A follow-up study of these children at age 11 when they attended a summer day camp suggests that the effects of attachment are not limited to the preschool years (Elicker, Englund, & Sroufe, 1992; Sroufe, Carlson, & Shulman, 1993). Counselors rated children with secure attachment histories as higher in social competence, self-esteem, and self-confidence, and lower in dependency on adults. The children with secure attachments spent more time with peers and less time either alone or only with adults. Moreover, these children were more likely to form close friendships than their anxiously attached peers. Finally, attachment history predicted friendship choices: Children with secure attachment histories are more likely to form friendships with other securely attached peers. Together, these studies provide impressive support for the importance of the quality of caregiver-infant relationships for later social development.

Nor are the effects limited to the preadolescent period. Just as we noted above that recollections of earlier experiences are related to patterns of infant-parent attachment (Main et al., 1985), childhood memories can provide clues about adolescent social relationships with others outside the family (Kobak & Sceery, 1988). Based on interviews about their working models of attachment, an index of how they think about earlier attachment relationships, college freshmen who were classified as secure in their attachments viewed themselves and were rated by their peers as better adjusted than freshmen who were insecure as indexed by either dismissing attachment as unimportant or by being preoccupied with attachment. These findings suggest that our working models of relationships may alter not only later parenting styles but also may color our relationships with peers in adolescence.

Finally, it is important to consider the relationships that the infants have developed with both mother and father in trying to understand children's later social behavior than either the mother-infant or father-infant relationship alone. In a study of 1-year-old infants, Main and Weston (1981) identified infants who were securely attached either to both parents or to neither parent. They observed two other types of relationships as well, in which babies were securely attached to mother and insecurely attached to father or vice versa. Even very young children often develop distinctly different relationships with their mothers and fathers. To determine whether the infants' relationships with their mothers and fathers affected their social responsiveness to others, Main and Weston also observed the infants' reactions to a friendly clown. The infants who were securely attached to both parents were more responsive to the clown than those who were securely attached to only one parent and insecurely attached to the other, and the babies who were insecurely attached to both parents were the least sociable with the clown. These results suggest that a less-than-optimal relationship with one parent can be compensated for by a better relationship with the other parent—and therefore, that it is not enough to study just mothers and fathers alone. Viewing the parents as part of a family system is the best way of understanding their role in child development.

In summary, a healthy attachment to parents facilitates rather than stifles exploration, curiosity, and mastery of the social and physical environment. At the same time, early attachment increases the child's trust in other social relationships and permits the later development of mature affectional relationships with peers. Longitudinal studies aimed at specifying the links between early parent-infant interaction and later relationships in adolescence and adulthood will help us determine the long-term stability of these positive cognitive and social effects of an early secure attachment. Clearly, developmental history leaves its mark (Sroufe, 1983).

THE OTHER SIDE OF EARLY EMOTIONS: THE DEVELOPMENT OF FEAR

At the same time that infants are developing a positive emotional relationship with a few special individuals, they are learning to be wary of strangers. In our continuing search for regularities in early development, few phenomena have captured as much time, effort, and interest as the following type of exchange between an infant and a stranger.

> Timothy, age 8 months, is exploring some toys in his playpen, looks up, and sees a strange woman standing beside his playpen. He turns back to his toys briefly, then again solemnly looks up at the stranger, whimpers, turns away, and begins to cry.

Fear of strangers, as this reaction to unfamiliar people is usually called, was at one time thought to be inevitable and universal and has become enshrined in the psychological literature as a developmental milestone. However, this reaction is neither inevitable nor universal. Instead, the appearance of fear is determined by a host of variables, including the identity and the behavior of the stranger, the setting, and the developmental status of the child. In fact, fear is not necessarily a typical reaction, and greeting and smiling may be a frequent reaction to strangers for some infants (Bretherton, Stolberg, & Kreye, 1981; Rheingold & Eckerman, 1973).

The Development of Fear of Strangers

In spite of this controversy, there is little doubt that some infants do show fear or at least wariness in reaction to unfamiliar people, but the timing of onset, the frequency of occurrence, and the intensity of the reaction are modified by a variety of factors. The emergence of fear, like the emergence of smiling, is gradual. In the early weeks of life, fear reactions depend on internal-biological factors, and only gradually does the infant become responsive to external events. In general, full-blown fear reactions develop more slowly than the emergence of positive emotional reactions such as smiling. In a longitudinal study, Emde and his colleagues (Emde et al., 1976) traced the development of fearful reactions in infants over the first year. By 4 months, infants smile less at unfamiliar adults than at their mothers. They are showing early signs of recognition, not by distress, but by less smiling to a stranger. However, infants show a great interest in novel people as well as novel objects, and a 4- or 5-month-old will often look longer at a stranger than at a familiar caretaker. In addition, these investigators found a comparison period in which the infant at 4 months looked back and forth between the mother's face and the stranger's face. A little later—at 5 to 7 months—the infant showed distress in the presence of the stranger. The sequence is summarized in Figure 7-5 and indicates that the development of fearful reactions to strangers is preceded by a series of less-intense emotional responses and does not make an abrupt appearance.

ARE ALL INFANTS EQUALLY FEARFUL?

There are wide individual differences among infants and young children in their reactions to strangers and other potentially fearful people and events. Support for the role of individual differences in the emergence of fear of strangers comes from the work of Kagan and his colleagues (Kagan, 1989; Kagan, Reznick, & Snidman, 1987). These researchers have identified a group of "behaviorally inhibited" children who tend to be shy, fearful, or introverted and are more anxious and distressed by mildly stressful events and tend to avoid even their age mates. These children show different psychological reactions as well; for example, the shy children show different patterns of heart rate. Of particular importance is the fact that these shy children show consistency in their fearful behaviors across time from 21 months to $5\frac{1}{2}$ years—further evidence that this may be a stable characteristic of some children (Kagan et al., 1987). Other evidence suggests that infants show considerable consistency in their reactions to a variety of eight different strangers, which suggests that individual differences among infants themselves may, in part, contribute to whether or not fear of strangers will occur (Smith & Sloboda, 1986). However, this does not mean that fear is an inevitable reaction to all strangers by all infants at this or other ages, or in all situations. Many factors will determine how an infant reacts to a stranger, and next we examine some of these determinants.

THE INFLUENCE OF CONTEXT

One determinant of children's reactions to strangers is the context or setting in which the assessment is conducted. Ten-month-old infants showed little fear of strangers when tested at home for their reactions to a stranger, but nearly 50 percent of the infants showed fear when tested in an unfamiliar

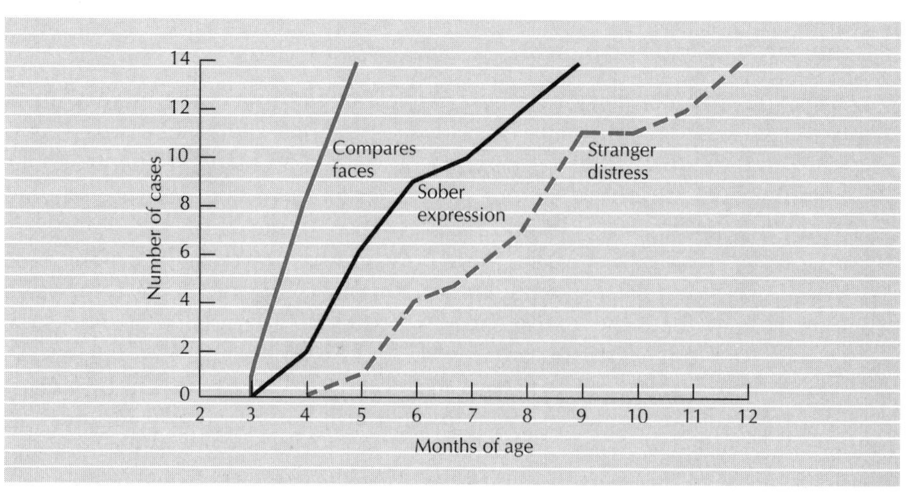

FIGURE 7-5

Onset of social fear. (From Emde, Gaensbauer, and Harmon, 1977, with permission of the authors and publisher.)

EMOTIONS

Infants and children display a wide range of emotions. As these photos illustrate, emotions are closely linked with the child's developing social relationships with family members and peers.

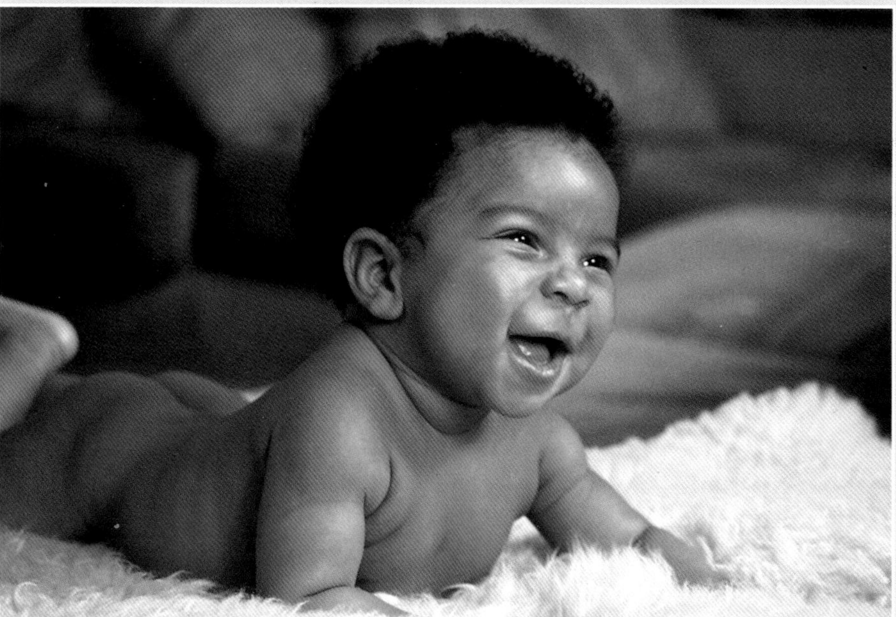

Smiling begins early in infancy.

Fear and apprehension develop in the last half of the first year.

▲ Emotions are often part of playful interchanges between parents and children or between peers. ►

▲ The self-conscious emotions such as pride and disappointment are later developing emotions. ◄

BOX 7-4 SOCIAL REFERENCING: USING MOTHER AS AN EMOTIONAL GUIDE

Eight-month-old Gillian was crawling along the floor and encountered a strange object—a rubber spider. She stopped short and looked at her nearby father, who smiled and reassured her. The journey continued as Gillian reached out and picked up the not-so-scary stranger.

Gregory, another 8-month-old, was sitting in his infant seat playing with a favorite rattle. His mother was sitting at a nearby table preparing dinner. A neighbor unexpectedly dropped by. The mother looked startled and a little upset. Gregory looked at the stranger and at his mother and began to cry.

These examples illustrate social referencing—the way infants systematically rely on emotional cues provided by significant others to help regulate their own behavior in uncertain settings.

Two studies illustrate this phenomenon. In one study, Feinman and Lewis (1983) instructed mothers of 10-month-olds to direct positive or neutral facial, vocal, and gestural messages about a female stranger to the stranger herself, or, in separate groups of infants, to the infants themselves. When the mother's communication was positive and directed at the infants, the babies showed much more positive behavior toward the stranger—smiling, approaching, and offering toys.

Nor is the effect evident only for strange people. As Klinnert (1981) has shown, mother's reactions can alter the way infants respond to strange objects as well. Twelve- to 18-month-old infants were exposed to three novel but frightening toys—a remote-controlled spider, a dinosaur, and a model of a human head (the "incredible Hulk"). Mothers looked alternately from the toy to the infant while posing joy, fear, or neutral expressions. Infants at both ages referenced the mother's face upon encountering the toy and used the mother's facial expression as a guide. If the mother reacted to the toy with fear, the infants moved closer to her. When she was happy and positive, the infants moved toward the toy and moved farther away from the mother. The infants remained at an intermediate distance when she appeared neutral. Social referencing clearly takes place in an ambiguous situation, as evidenced by the infant's active looking to the other for guidance. Moreover, maternal facial expressions serve to regulate the coping behavior of infants.

Furthermore, social referencing clearly undergoes changes across development (Walden, 1991; Walden & Ogan, 1988). As infants develop they are more likely to look at the mother's face than at other parts of the body; 14- to 22-month-olds in contrast to 6- to 9-month-olds were clearly more aware of the best source of information—the mother's face. Finally, infants are more likely to check with the mother first, before acting, as they get older. Younger infants often act first and look later—a strategy that could lead to trouble in a dangerous situation. As these studies suggest, infants learn to use others as a guide which underscores the importance of emotion for regulating social behavior—even in infancy.

Sources: Feinman, S., & Lewis, M. (1983). Social referencing and second order effects in 10-month-old infants. *Child Development,* **54,** 878–887; Klinnert, M. D. (1981, April). *Infants' use of mothers' facial expressions for regulating their own behavior.* Paper presented at the meeting of the Society for Research in Child Development, Boston; Walden, T. (1991). Infant social referencing. In J. Garber & K. Dodge (Eds.), *The development of emotional regulation and dysregulation.* New York: Cambridge University Press; Walden, T. A., & Ogan, T. A. (1988). The development of social referencing. *Child Development,* **59,** 1230–1240.

laboratory (Sroufe, Waters, & Matas, 1974). Infants who sit on their mothers' laps while a stranger approaches rarely show any fear reaction; but when placed in infant seats a few feet away from their mothers, they will gaze apprehensively, whimper, or cry if a stranger comes near (Morgan & Ricciuti, 1969). As Box 7-4 shows, it is not merely the presence or absence of a familiar person that matters, but emotional reactions of familiar caregivers to the strange person or event as well.

THE IMPORTANCE OF CONTROL

Some people are less "scary" because they allow the infant to control or dictate the pace of the interaction. Imagine a person who rushes at you and ignores your early signs of discomfort or uneasiness. Or consider a person who approaches slowly and waits to be invited before coming closer. To illustrate the role of control in the development of fear was the goal of a series of studies by Gunnar (1980). The stranger was a cymbal-clapping monkey—a frightening and scary sight for 12- and 13-month-olds. One group of infants learned how to make the monkey clap by hitting a panel—the "control" condition. For other infants the monkey clapped an equal number of times, but the infant had no control over the schedule of clapping episodes. When they could control the frightening monkey, babies showed less fear and more smiling and laughing. The boys, in particular, showed much less frequent fussing and crying in the control condition. As a later study showed, gaining control over fearful events does not reduce distress until 12 months of age (Gunnar, 1980). Finally, increasing the temporal predictability of a fearful event helps infants cope more effectively (Gunnar, Leighton, & Peleaux, 1984). Year-old babies responded less fearfully if the scary mechanical toy played on a fixed, predictable schedule (for example, four seconds on and four seconds off) than if it played on a variable schedule (for example, three seconds on and five seconds off). Both control and temporal predictability can help reduce infants' fear of frightening events.

Are All Kinds of Strangers Equal?

Do infants show fear reactions to all unfamiliar people—children as well as adults? To find out, Lewis and Brooks (1974) examined the reactions of infants between 7 and 19 months of age to strange male and female adults, a strange child (4-year-old girl), their mothers, and the self (as reflected in a mirror). The infants' responses were measured at four distances: 15 feet, 8 feet, and 3 feet away, and touching the infants. Figure 7-6 shows the results. First, it is not the mere *presence* of a stranger that elicits negative emotional reactions; distance matters too. As the strangers came closer, both positive and negative reactions were greater; the negative reaction to the strange adults became clear, while the positive reactions to the mother and mirror image of the self were more marked. How do babies react to an unfamiliar child? In contrast to their reaction to the adult, the infants showed a mild positive reaction. The characteristics of the stranger are an important determinant of whether or not a stranger will elicit fear. Infants do not show fear to all kinds of strangers. In a clever follow-up study, Brooks and Lewis (1976) evaluated a normal-sized adult, a child, and a midget as strangers in order to determine whether it is height or facial configuration that elicits fear. The 7- to 24-month-old infants showed more negative reactions to the adults—frowning

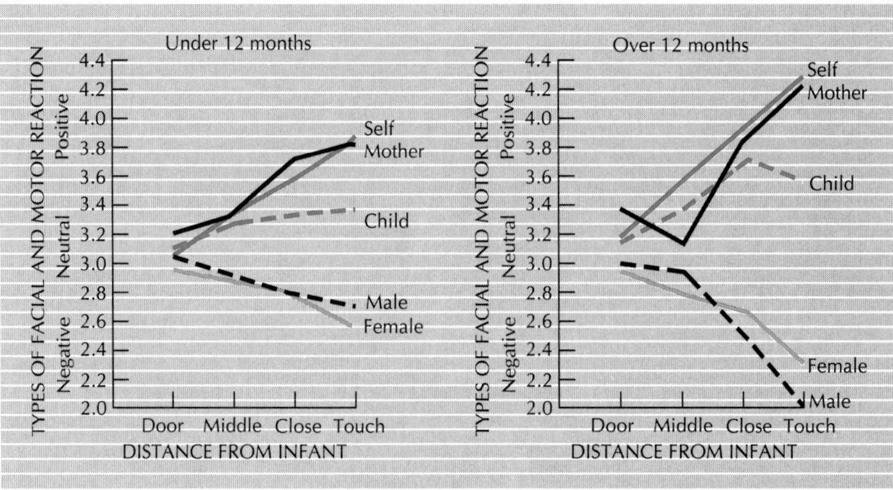

FIGURE 7-6
Amount of positive and negative facial and motor responses of human infants in reaction to self and to familiar and unfamiliar individuals. (From Lewis & Brooks, 1974, with permission of the senior author and the publisher.)

and moving away from both the normal-sized adult and midget—than to the child, which suggests that size alone is not a cue that infants use in evaluating strangers; facial configuration is also important. It is unfortunate that a "baby-faced" adult was not available for comparison purposes!

Physical characteristics, however, are not the only important factors: The *behavior* of the stranger makes a difference as well. As adults, we are more likely to respond positively if another person is friendly, outgoing, and active than if a person is quiet and passive. So, in infancy, the behaviors of the stranger determine how the infant will react (Bretherton et al., 1981; Ross & Goldman, 1977). When confronted by an active, friendly stranger who "talked, gestured, smiled, imitated and offered toys," 12-month-olds showed little fear. In fact, the infants were highly sociable with the stranger, and imitated him, and played games with him. In contrast, the infant touched and played less with the passive stranger than with the active stranger. A stranger is not just a stranger—it's the way the stranger behaves that makes the difference!

Developmental Changes in Specific Fears

It is likely that the specific objects and situations that evoke fear change as children develop. In fact, tracking the development of specific fears has been a favorite task of psychologists since the 1930s. Figure 7-7 illustrates age changes in particular fears, using a group of 228 girls, 7- to 12-year-olds (Barnett, 1969). Although the issues that evoke fear shift with age, the overall level of fear does not differ across development. As children grow older, fears concerning imaginary creatures and personal safety show a decline; probably this trend is due to the child's more sophisticated understanding of the laws governing physical reality. As adolescence approaches, there is another marked change: School and social concerns show a rapid rise. These developmental changes move the child closer to the adult fear profile, which is characterized by a higher degree of social fear and little concern for imaginary fears.

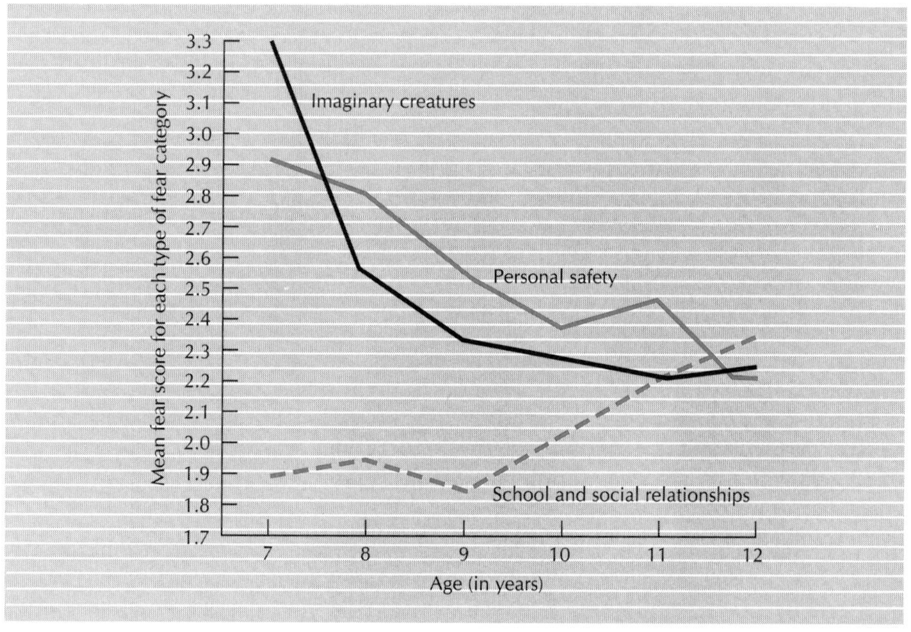

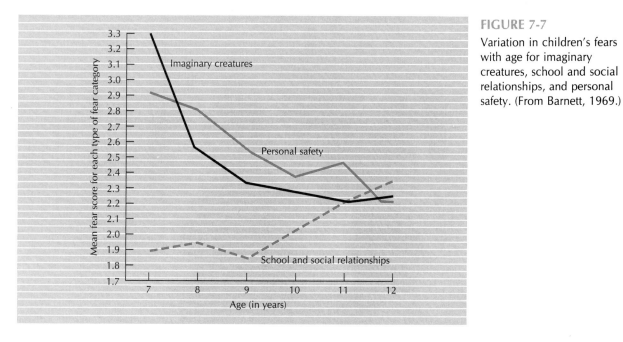

FIGURE 7-7
Variation in children's fears with age for imaginary creatures, school and social relationships, and personal safety. (From Barnett, 1969.)

Other studies confirm these trends. One of the most common fears reported by children in a recent national survey of school-age children and adolescents was fear of crime, violence, and personal injury (Zill, 1986). Two-thirds of the children were afraid "someone bad would get into my house," and 11-year-olds were just as fearful as 7-year-olds. Other types of crime-related fears drop with age; while 34 percent of the 7-year-olds were afraid that someone might hurt them when they played outside, only 10 percent of the 16-year-olds expressed this fear.

Moreover, boys report fewer crime-related fears than girls (Zill, 1986). This is consistent with other evidence that boys and girls differ in risk-taking, with boys being higher risk-takers than girls. This was the conclusion reached by Ginsburg and Miller (1982), who watched 480 children, 3- to 11-year-olds, in various risk-taking situations at a zoo. On the basis of their naturalistic observations, they found that boys rode elephants, patted a burro, and fed sheep and goats more than did girls. Whether boys are actually less fearful or whether they simply do not express their fears as openly is still an unresolved problem.

Explanation of Fear Development

Fear of strangers as well as fear of situations and objects may develop in a variety of different ways. Let us consider some alternative routes to the development of fear.

FEAR AS A GENETICALLY DETERMINED PHENOMENON

According to this viewpoint, fear has a constitutional basis and is not dependent on specific learning experiences. Plomin and DeFries (1985)

Separation anxiety is evident in all cultures.

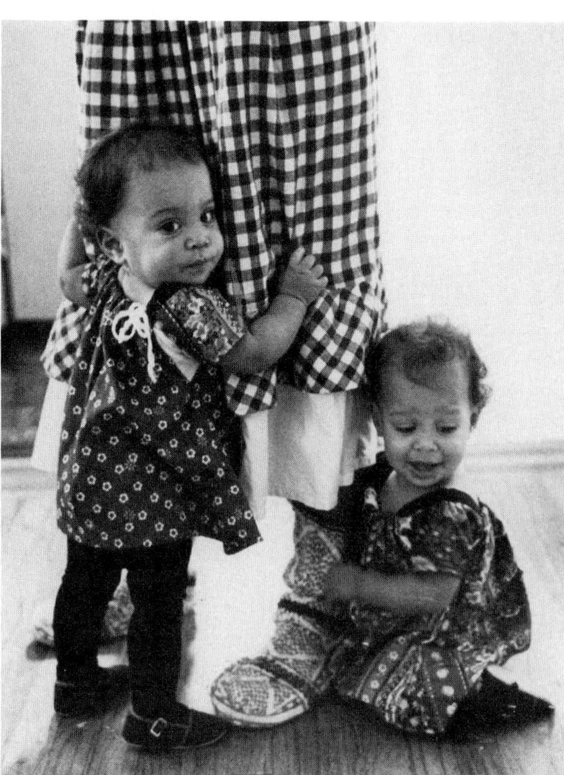

reported that monozygotic twins are more similar than dizygotic twins in their reactions to strangers. Similarly, wariness of unfamiliar people and situations is, in part, genetically based (Robinson, Kagan, Reznick, & Corley, 1993). Although it is possible that the experiences, such as frequency of exposure to strangers, may be more similar for identical than for fraternal twins, this is a rather weak and unlikely possibility.

Another kind of evidence in favor of a constitutional argument comes from cross-cultural and animal studies that show a high degree of similarity in the timing of fear reactions. If fear responses to certain events occur at similar times in different cultures where infants have experienced different backgrounds of child-care experiences, this would suggest a common maturational or biological basis for fear. In spite of childrearing practices that differ greatly from Western customs, both infants raised in Uganda (Ainsworth, 1963) and babies reared on a Hopi Indian reservation (Dennis, 1940) show the stranger-anxiety reaction at approximately 8 months, the same time as Western infants.

Somewhat later—at about 15 months—infants show a peak reaction to being separated from their mothers. As Figure 7-8 shows, there are many other cultures as diverse as African Kalahari bushmen and the Israeli kibbutzim in which infants display a markedly similar pattern of reaction to being separated from their mothers. Nor is the evidence for the emergence of specific fears according to a timetable restricted to maternal separation. Children show the greatest amount of distress in encounters with unfamiliar peers at approximately 20 months. In longitudinal studies of children seen at 13, 20, and 29 months, Kagan (1981, 1983) found that children played and vocalized less and stayed closer to their mothers at 20 months than at either the younger or older ages.

Still later, at 24 months, children become distressed by "performance anxiety" (Kagan, 1983). Children were exposed to an adult model who displayed a series of simple actions such as picking up some animals and taking them for a walk and having a doll talk on a toy telephone. Then the child was told: "Now it's your turn to play." Children from Vietnam, Fiji, and the United States showed similar reactions: They first showed signs of upset—clinging, crying, inhibition of play, protests, and requests to go

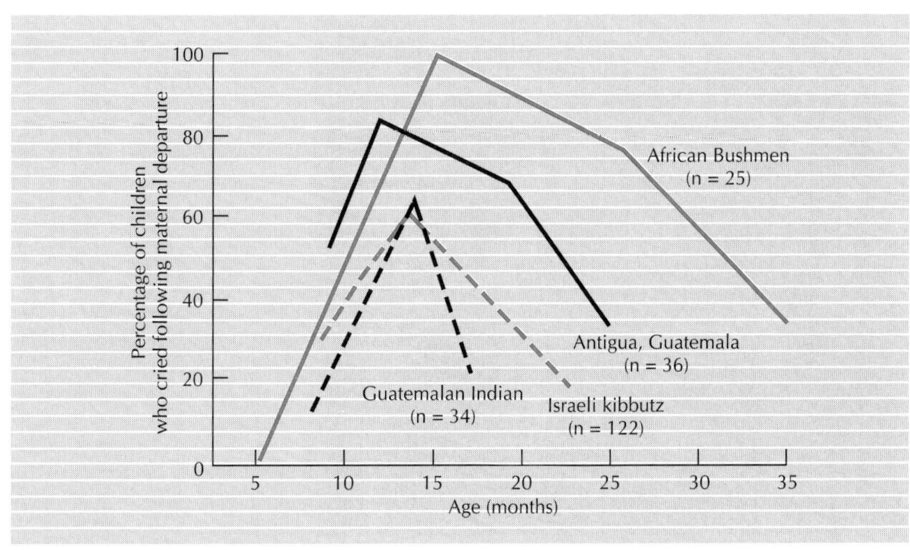

FIGURE 7-8
Separation protest seems to reach its peak at about the same age in a variety of cultures. (From Kagan, Kearsley & Zelazo, 1978.)

home—at 17 to 18 months and these reached a peak around 24 months. Kagan argues that children at this age are beginning to be aware of the possibility that they may be unable to meet the model's standards and perform correctly—the early beginnings of performance anxiety. All these examples suggest that the timing of the emergence of fear is closely tied to other aspects of development. The cross-cultural consistency in the emergence of fear supports a biological interpretation of fear development.

FEAR AS A LEARNED PHENOMENON

According to other theorists, fear is not innate or constitutionally determined; rather, children *learn* to fear certain aspects of their environment. Sometimes this can be accomplished in a very direct manner through either instrumental or classical conditioning, types of learning that were discussed in Chapter 1. A familiar example of instrumental fear conditioning is the young child who touches a hot stove; the consequence of touching the stove is pain, and as a result of this unpleasant outcome the child learns to fear the hot stove and avoids it on later occasions. Another approach is the classical conditioning position, which stresses not the outcomes but rather the events that are temporarily associated with a particular response. According to this viewpoint, young children learn to fear objects and even people in their environment by their association with an unlearned fearful stimulus. For example, children may not show any fear of doctors until they experience a polio or measles injection. As a result of the doctor being associated with the painful injection, many infants begin to scream even at the sight of the doctor.

Recent studies of children receiving chemotherapy (drug treatment) for childhood cancer vividly illustrate the power of conditioning (Redd, 1988). This type of treatment is often accompanied by a feeling of nausea and vomiting. After three or four treatments, patients begin feeling nauseated in anticipation of treatment. These anticipatory side effects are the result of

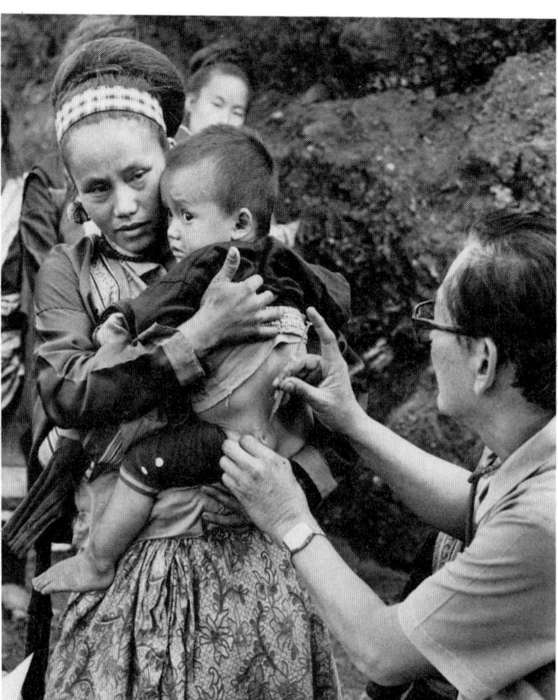

Children in all cultures show fear of injections.

conditioning: The repeated association of environmental cues, such as the sight of the hospital, the sound of the doctor's voice, and the smell of rubbing alcohol with the treatment and its aftereffects makes previously neutral stimuli come to elicit symptoms (for example, nausea and vomiting). Nor are the effects short-lived, but instead can last for years. In follow-up interviews with adults who were treated for and cured of cancer in childhood, they often report that they still feel nauseated whenever they enter a hospital or smell rubbing alcohol (Cella & Tross, 1986).

THE PERCEPTUAL-COGNITIVE VIEWPOINT

Just as smiling and laughter could be understood as a perceptual-recognition achievement, fear reactions also can be viewed this way. A classic experiment by Hebb in 1946 on the development of fear in the chimpanzee will illustrate. There were two critical conditions in this study. In the first condition, the chimps were given normal visual experiences, including the experience of seeing other chimpanzees. In the second condition, the animals were reared with a blindfold, which prevented them from seeing other chimps. Both groups were then exposed to a plaster replica of the head of a chimpanzee. For the animals who had been reared under normal conditions and allowed to interact with age-mates, the sight of the "chimpanzee head" caused extreme fear and flight; for the animals lacking this opportunity for visual learning, the sculpture caused either little fear reaction or even a mild curiosity. Why the difference? Hebb (1946, 1949) proposed that the normally reared chimps had learned a particular perceptual pattern that defined the concept of "chimpanzee." This familiar pattern included not only a head but, of course, a body, legs, and arms as well. It was the sight of the head alone, partially familiar but incomplete, that caused the animals' upset. Their expectation, based on past experience with the familiar object, the chimpanzee, was violated by this incomplete duplication of the familiar pattern. It was this violation of the expectation that evoked fear. It is now easy to see why the blindfolded animals failed to show any fear. They were deprived of the opportunity to build a standard of familiarity. Until the pattern has been learned or centrally coded, incongruous or violating events are meaningless.

At the human level, the phenomenon that most clearly resembles the reactions of Hebb's chimpanzees is a fear-of-strangers anxiety reaction. Part of the reason for this reaction may be due to the apparent discrepancy the infant notices between the familiar caretaker and the stranger. They share some similarities, just as the plaster head shared some similarities with the chimps' familiar experience, but there are some discrepancies as well. It may be that the discrepancy between the familiar and the partially familiar causes the anxiety. Since the central proposition involves the learning of a unique pattern—the characteristics of the mother, for example—the extent of the anxiety reaction should vary with the exclusiveness of the mother-infant relationship. The infant who sees only his mother is more likely to notice or detect the difference between the well-established pattern of mother and a strange female. On the other hand, a child who sees babysitters, grandmothers, day-care center aides, and the next-door neighbors, as well as the mother, will have a more diffuse concept of "mother" and will, therefore, be less likely to show a fear of strange adults. Using human infants, Schaffer (1966) found that fear of strangers was evident earlier in families with a small number of children and when the number of strangers typically seen by the child was small. These findings, then, are consistent with the perceptual-recognition approach to fear development.

However, there are problems too. Infants can usually discriminate between their parents and strangers *before* they show fear—a finding that is clearly inconsistent with this viewpoint. The view has survived, but with modifications. Kagan and associates (1978), for example, suggest that in the third quarter of the first year the infant develops the capacity to form hypotheses about the way things work in the world. Fear is the result not simply of noticing a difference but of the failure to understand. Fear results when the infant's hypothesis fails.

WHICH EXPLANATION IS CORRECT?

It should be obvious to the reader by now that no single viewpoint is correct; all views have some evidence in their favor. It is not unreasonable to assume that different types of fear may, in fact, develop according to different sets of principles. Moreover, it is possible that the contribution and importance of these viewpoints may vary with the developmental stage of the infant (Bronson, 1968; Campos, Barrett, Lamb, Goldsmith, & Stenberg, 1983; Izard, 1991). For example, in the first few months of life, the constitutional and classical conditioning positions are probably much more useful in explaining fear than is the perceptual-cognitive hypothesis. This viewpoint will be relevant only after the child is cognitively mature enough to generate hypotheses about how things in the environment ought to be organized. The task, then, is not to decide which explanation is correct, but to determine how each set of principles contributes to our understanding of the development of this complex emotional response pattern. Just as we saw in the case of smiling and attachment, different theoretical perspectives may be required at different developmental periods.

In summary, fear, like smiling, is a complex response that depends on a variety of factors including the type of stimulus, the infant's familiarity with the situation, the social agent, and the infant's developmental level. Only by considering these factors can the emergence of fear be understood. Without consideration of these factors, it is very unlikely that you would know when to expect a smile or a frown.

Next, we examine children's understanding of the meaning of emotional situations and emotional labels, as well as more complex emotions such as pride, guilt, and shame.

THINKING ABOUT EMOTIONS

A child is invited to a birthday party; another child's favorite pet dies; a third child heard a loud, unexpected bang. When are children aware of the emotional reactions that are likely to accompany these events?

Across development, children not only shift in their expressions of emotions but also develop a more complete understanding of the meaning of emotion terms and the situations that evoke different kinds of feelings. This knowledge can be referred to as emotional scripts—that is, a complex scheme involving the awareness of the type of emotional reaction that is likely to accompany different events (Lewis, 1989).

From a young age, children are able to indicate that they understand the types of situations that evoke different emotions. In an early classic study, Borke (1971) showed 3- and 4-year-old children simple stories involving getting lost in the woods or having a fight or going to a party and asked them to indicate the emotions that would be likely to be felt by the story characters. The children could easily identify situations that would lead to happiness and were reasonably good at identifying stories that were linked with sadness or anger. Later research (Stein & Trabasso, 1989; Trabasso, Stein, & Johnson, 1981) showed that 3- and 4-year-old children could describe situations that evoke emotions such as happy, excited, surprised, sad, angry, and scared. Young children are clearly aware of which emotions go with which situations.

Moreover, this knowledge is useful in helping children understand other people's emotions:

> Suppose that a child only knows what happened to another child but cannot see the child's emotional reaction. For example, the child is listening to a story in which the protagonist is lost in the woods or is given a present. The child should be able to anticipate the emotional reaction of the protagonist. Similarly, on learning that a story character or a playmate feels a particular emotion the child should be able to think of likely causes. . . . Children could use such information to guide their behavior toward other people; they will know what situations to create in order to provoke, amuse or confront another person. (Harris, 1989, p. 67)

However, young children's understanding of situations that accompany different emotions is still limited. Five-year-olds, for instance, understand situations that lead to emotions that have a recognizable facial display or kind of behavior such as angry, happy, or sad. By 7 years of age children can describe situations that elicit emotions with no obvious facial or behavioral expressions, such as pride, jealousy, worry, and guilt. By 10 and 14 years, children can describe situations that elicit relief and disappointment as well (Harris, Olthof, Meerum, Terwogt, & Hardman, 1987). A similar developmental sequence is found in a variety of cultures including Great Britain, the United States, the Netherlands and even in a remote Himalayan village in Nepal (Harris, 1989). Another aspect of emotional understanding that develops only gradually is the awareness that conflicting feeling can exist simultaneously (see Box 7-5).

As they develop, children are clearly learning to take into account a wider number of aspects of the situation, such as the goals and desires of the actors. Children realize that emotional expressions are produced by inner states and do not rely solely on the characteristics of the situation. A recent study by Harris and his colleagues (Harris, Johnson, Hutton, Andrews, & Cook, 1989) will illustrate how children learn to interpret the reaction to a particular event in terms of the story characters' own wishes, desires, and goals. Children were told about the taste preferences of a story character—a toy elephant—for either Coke or milk. According to this story a monkey tricked the elephant by replacing all of the Coke with milk. Children predicted how the elephant would feel when she found out the real contents by taking a drink from the can. Four- and 6-year-olds adjusted their prediction depending on the elephant's preference; if the elephant liked milk, they said she was happy to discover milk in the can. If she liked Coke, they correctly noted that she would be sad to find milk instead of Coke. In short, children can go beyond the situation to take into account the desires of another person in judging the emotions that will occur.

BOX 7-5 MIXED EMOTIONS: CHILDREN'S UNDERSTANDING OF MULTIPLE FEELINGS

Young infants often express ambivalence by seeking contact and also resisting being picked up. Or toddlers may call their new baby sibling "bad baby" and gently caress her. Clearly, children from a very early age are capable of experiencing conflicting feeling, but they are slower to develop an awareness that two conflicting emotions can be experienced simultaneously.

Susan Harter and her colleagues (Harter & Buddin, 1987; Harter & Whitesell, 1989) have found that children show a clear developmental sequence in their ability to understand conflicting emotions. They asked 4- to 12-year-olds to describe situations that would not only evoke different emotions (for example, sad, happy, angry, fearful), but would also provoke two emotions in succession and two emotions at the same time.

Five stages emerged from this procedure. The youngest children cannot coordinate two emotions simultaneously; the child assumes situations elicit only a single emotion ("You can't have two feelings at the same time").

By age 6, children in the second stage begin to show some evidence of an ability to conceive of two emotions occurring at once, but of the same type ("I was happy and proud that I hit a home run." "When my brother messed up my stuff, I was upset and mad").

In the third stage (about age 8 to 9), children are able to describe situations that cause two simultaneous emotions in response to different targets simultaneously (for example, "I was bored because there was nothing to do and mad because my mom punished me").

At none of these earlier stages can children recognize that opposite feelings exist simultaneously. Only by age 10 in stage 4 are children able to describe situations that involve opposite feelings like happy and sad. At first, they could only describe situations that involve two distinct targets ("I was sitting in school feeling worried about all the responsibilities of a new pet but I was happy that I got straight A's on my report card"). Or the two targets represent different aspects of the same situation (for example, "I was mad at my brother for hitting me and pleased that my father gave me permission to hit him back").

At 11 years, children are finally capable of understanding that two opposite emotions (for example, sad and happy) can be elicited by the same target (for example, "I was happy that I got a present but mad that it wasn't what I wanted").

Children, then, go through an interesting developmental progression from initially understanding that only single emotions are possible from an event to understanding that two feelings can occur, but in sequence to a final stage where two feelings can exist in reaction to the same event—and these can even be positive and negative emotions.

Clearly, children's ability to understand and express their knowledge of emotions emerges slowly over development and lags well behind children's capacity to experience ambivalence and mixed emotions. As in many aspects of development, the capacity to experience and the ability to articulate and acknowledge this experience may develop at different rates.

Sources: Harter, S., & Buddin, B. (1987). Children's understanding of the simultaneity of two emotions: A five-stage developmental acquisition sequence. *Developmental Psychology,* **23,** 388–399; Harter, S., & Whitesell, N. (1989). Developmental changes in children's emotion concepts. In C. Saarni & P. L. Harris (Eds.), *Children's understanding of emotions.* New York: Cambridge University Press.

Children's Understanding of Complex Emotions: Pride, Guilt, and Shame

As they develop, children begin to understand more complex emotions such as pride, guilt, and shame. An understanding of these emotions often depends on children's ability to appreciate the role of multiple factors and goes beyond the understanding of single factors that are sufficient for such basic emotions as happy, mad, or sad. Instead, an understanding of these complex kinds of emotions, such as pride or guilt, requires the differentiation and integration of several factors. In the case of guilt, a child combines a sense of self-directed anger or upset with an understanding of the role of personal responsibility. Unless you caused the outcome, you shouldn't feel guilty. Children develop this appreciation of the central role of personal responsibility in the development of guilt only gradually. In support of the view that the understanding of guilt emerges only in middle childhood is a study by Graham, Doubleday, and Guarino (1984). They asked children to describe a prior event when they felt guilty. Six-year-olds often described episodes that caused guilt even though they had little control over the outcome (for example, "I felt guilty when my brother and I had boxing gloves on and I hit him too hard . . . sometimes I don't know my own strength"). In contrast, 9-year-olds recognized that to feel guilty, it is critical to be responsible for the outcomes (for example, "I felt guilty when I didn't turn in my homework because I was too lazy to do it"). Later studies (Graham, 1988; Thompson, 1989) reach similar conclusions, namely, that young children focus on outcomes while older children understand the emotion of guilt better because they focus on the role of personal responsibility.

Similarly, children's understanding of pride depends on multiple factors, including pleasure over the task well done and happiness that others appreciate the accomplishment (Harter & Whitesell, 1989). To evaluate the role of effort in the understanding of pride, Thompson (1987, 1989) told stories to 7-, 10- and 18-year-olds involving accomplishments that individuals achieved by their own efforts or by luck. The 6-year-olds used the term proud in response to good outcomes—regardless of whether or not they had gained these successes through their own effort. Older children and adults were more discriminating and appreciated that "feeling proud" can only occur *both* when good outcomes occur and when these outcomes are due to their effort, not luck or chance.

Children's emerging sense of the differences between "easy" and "difficult" and between "success" and "failure" are important for distinguishing between pride and shame (Lewis, 1991). Pride is more likely to be felt when children succeed at difficult rather than easy tasks. Shame is a more likely emotion when children fail on an easy task, but little shame is experienced after failing a difficult task (Lewis, Alessandro, & Sullivan, 1991).

As these studies of the emergence of complex emotions show, children's cognitive understanding, such as their ability to understand causal sequences, are closely entwined with children's emotional development. Moreover, social influences such as variations in the family environment play a role in the emergence of children's understanding of emotions in others. For example, Dunn and her colleagues (Dunn & Brown, 1991; Dunn, Brown, & Beardsall, 1991) discovered a relation between 3-year-old children's conversations about feeling states with their mothers and siblings and their ability to understand others' emotions at 6 years of age. In families where there was more discussion of feelings, children were better able to recognize others' emotions than in families where feelings were less often discussed. Although we often explore development of different capacities (social, cognitive, emotional) separately, it is clear that different aspects of development are mutually interdependent.

SUMMARY

THE FUNCTIONS OF EMOTIONS

- Emotions serve as a way in which infants and children communicate their needs to others; and they serve to regulate social distance and conflict. Thus, emotions provide one of the earliest means for gaining control over the social world.

PRODUCTION AND RECOGNITION OF EMOTIONS

- Much recent evidence suggests that facial expressions may be, in part, genetically determined. Although some emotional expressions, such as distress, are evident at birth, others appear with development. However, they do not occur randomly; they are highly specific in their pattern of development and closely tied to particular types of events. Within the first half year of life, infants also can recognize emotional expressions in others. In general, children are more proficient at producing than at recognizing emotions, but the two abilities are positively related—children who are skilled at one are typically skilled at the other.

- As they develop, children begin to use *emotional display rules,* or strategies for separating emotional displays from internal emotional feelings. By age 2, children begin to understand the need to have deliberate control over the display of emotions; however, the ability to mask bad feelings by simulating pleasure does not occur until middle childhood.

EARLY EMOTIONAL DEVELOPMENT: THE SMILE AS A SOCIAL SIGNAL

- Smiling, an early positive emotional expression, follows a general developmental pattern, beginning with reflexive smiles and smiles that depend on the infant's internal state that appear at birth, progressing to smiles in response to external elicitors between 3 and 8 weeks of age. By 12 weeks, infants begin to smile selectively at familiar faces and voices, and their smiles differ depending upon the situation. By 4 months, infants begin to laugh, and the number and kinds of events that elicit laughter appear to change with development. Both laughter and smiling may play a critical role in maintaining the proximity of the caretaker to the infant.
- Alternative explanations have been offered to account for the origins and development of smiling and laughing. Evidence indicates that the timing of the beginning of smiling may be biologically determined, however, the developmental course of these behaviors appears to depend on infants' increasing cognitive capacities and on their particular social experiences.

FROM SMILING TO ATTACHMENT

- During the second half of the first year, infants begin to discriminate between familiar and unfamiliar caretakers, and to form *attachments* to the important people in their lives. Alternative theories of how attachment develops include psychoanalytic, learning, and ethological viewpoints. Each position makes different assumptions about the roles of the infant and caregiver and about the critical factors and processes that contribute to attachment.
- Attachment emerges during a consistent series of steps in the first six to eight months of life. Infants begin by preferring humans to inanimate objects at birth, then they learn to discriminate familiar people, and, finally, they begin to develop attachments to specific people. This is often seen when an infant protests the departure of a caregiver.
- The quality of an infant's attachment to parents is determined by early parent-child interactions. Parents who are responsive to infant's needs, giving their infant a sense of control over the environment, seem to have more securely attached infants. In addition to parents' contributions, recent findings suggest that infant characteristics, such as temperament, may play a role in the quality of early parent-child attachment. Other social relationships, such as the quality of the parents' marriage as well as the parents' recollections of their relationships with their own parents have also been related to the development of attachment.

- Attachment has usually been studied by using the *strange situation,* in which infants' reactions to a series of situations involving the presence or absence of the mother and a stranger have been rated. Using this paradigm, about 60 to 65 percent of infants are classified as securely attached to their mothers, while the rest fall into three other categories of less-than-ideal attachment patterns. Studies indicate that these classifications generally remain stable over time, unless major changes, like divorce or job loss, have occurred in the family.
- Recent research indicates that infants can be attached to more than one person. They are as attached to their fathers as to their mothers if the fathers are actively involved as interactive partners. However, fathers play the unique role of playmate with their infants while mothers are more often in the role of caregiver and comforter. Infants also may be attached to other caregivers and to their peers.
- Researchers, parents, and policymakers have been interested in the effects of day care on attachment. Although some studies indicate that infants of working mothers are slightly more likely to be classified as insecurely attached than those of nonworking mothers, the differences are not large. Moreover, the reasons for this are unclear. Some suggest that it is because the mother's absence disrupts the attachment relationship, but others suggest that it is because working is stressful for the mother, making her less sensitive to the attachment relationship. In addition, the quality of the day-care setting is clearly related to the quality of children's later social adjustment.
- Early attachments shape the child's later attitudes and behaviors, including their sense of self, and their cognitive and social development. Children who were securely attached as infants are more likely than those who were not to see themselves positively, to have a high self-esteem, to be intellectually curious and willing to explore, and to have positive social relationships with peers and others.

THE OTHER SIDE OF EARLY EMOTIONS: THE DEVELOPMENT OF FEAR

- At the same time that infants are becoming attached to significant others in their lives, they are learning to be wary or fearful of strangers. Although not all infants develop fear of strangers, in those who do, the emergence of fear is gradual. Like smiling, it begins as a reaction to internal events, then by 4 months infants smile less at strangers, and by 5 to 7 months they show distress in the presence of a stranger.
- There are wide individual differences among infants in their reactions to strangers. However, many factors will determine how an infant reacts to a particular stranger. Infants tend to be less fearful in a familiar context or setting and when they feel like they have some control over the situation. They also are less fearful of unfamiliar children than of unknown adults, and they are less likely to be afraid of friendly, outgoing strangers.
- Although the content of specific fears changes with development, the overall level of fear does not tend to change. Toddlers show fears about imaginary creatures and personal safety, but these give way to fears concerning school, social interactions, and crime during middle childhood and adolescence.
- Various explanations for the development of fear of strangers and other situations have been given, including genetics, learning, and perceptual-cognitive accomplishments. Although some support for all of these have

been found, none of them alone seems able to explain the phenomenon. It may be that all of the views are correct some of the time, depending on the developmental level of the child and the type of fear that is exhibited.

THINKING ABOUT EMOTIONS

- Not only do children's emotional reactions change with age, but their understanding of the meaning of emotions also changes. By ages 3 or 4, children understand the types of situations that evoke different emotions, but their understanding is limited to emotions that have a recognizable facial display. By age 7 they can describe more complex emotions, such as pride or jealousy, and by early adolescence they can describe even more complicated emotions, such as disappointment. As they develop, children are able to take a larger number of aspects of the situation into account when considering the emotional reactions of others.
- Understanding complex emotions requires the differentiation and integration of several different factors at the same time. For example, in the case of guilt, a sense of self-directed anger is combined with an understanding of the role of personal responsibility. Young children tend to focus on outcomes, saying they feel guilty even when they are not personally responsible, while older children are able to understand and integrate both factors. It is clear that children's cognitive ability to understand causal sequences is closely related to their emotional development.

CHAPTER

8

LANGUAGE AND COMMUNICATION

One of the most outstanding of the child's developmental achievements is the mastery of language. Language is one of the most complex systems of rules a person ever learns, but children in a wide range of different environments and cultures learn to understand and use language in a relatively short period.

WHY STUDY LANGUAGE DEVELOPMENT?

Language serves a wide range of purposes for the developing child. As Halliday (1975) discusses, language helps children interact with others; express their wishes; control others' behavior; express their unique views, feelings, and attitudes; explore and understand their environment by asking "why"; escape from reality through fantasy; and communicate new information. In this and other chapters we will see numerous examples of how language assists in organizing our perceptions, directing our thinking, controlling our actions, aiding our memory, and modifying our emotions. Without language you wouldn't be reading this page.

The study of language can also provide a window into cognitive and social-emotional development. Regularities in children's acquisition of word meanings can reflect their emerging ways of categorizing objects and events, providing a powerful method for exploring conceptual development. Other researchers (for example, Miller & Sperry, 1987; Dunn, 1988) have found that language is an important tool in understanding social-emotional development. For example, language encodes not only emotional states (for example, happiness) and overt actions (for example, laughter), but instigating events, reasons, plans, and consequences. Children's capacities to speak to these components of the emotion event reflects, in part, their emerging understanding of emotion (Huttenlocker, Smiley, & Ratner, 1989).

In this chapter we will try to unravel some of the fascinating complexities of language development and communication. We will begin with an overview of different domains in the study of language. Then, we will introduce some contrasting theoretical views on language development. We will see that most modern theorists account for the emergence of language through an interaction of genetic and environmental factors. With this background, we will begin our account of language development focusing on the "four faces of language."

How well prepared are infants for learning language? Is there any relationship between early infant vocal behavior and later language development? What types of words do children use first? How does the child's understanding of the meaning of words develop? Are there commonalities in young children's early sentences? Is there a systematic order in children's acquisition of more complex sentence forms? By tracing the child's development from one-word utterances to the mastery of complex sentences, we will explore how the child learns grammar. How similar is grammar in different cultures and in deaf children? What skills are necessary to be an effective speaker or listener? Children not only gain new language skills as they develop but gain insight into their own language behavior. How and when does this understanding develop?

THE FOUR FACES OF LANGUAGE: PHONOLOGY, SEMANTICS, GRAMMAR, AND PRAGMATICS

The study of language can be divided into four areas: phonology, semantics, syntax, and pragmatics. *Phonology* describes the system of sounds for a grammar, that is, how the basic sound units (phonemes) are put together to form words and how the intonation patterns of phrases and sentences are determined. A phoneme can be defined as the shortest speech unit in which a change produces a change in meaning; for example, the difference in meaning between "bat" and "cat" is accounted for by the different initial phonemes; "bat" and "bit" differ in their middle phonemes.

Although we will not emphasize phonology in this chapter, it is important to realize that phonological rules, like rules at other linguistic levels, are generative. That is, speakers and listeners know the proper stress and intonation patterns for novel sentences they have never heard before, as well as the sound relationships allowable in novel words. For example, a native speaker knows that the nonsense word "kib" is a possible sound pattern in the English phonological system, but that the nonsense word "bink" is not possible. Thus, even the rules of phonology form a system, and they are general rules in the sense that they are applicable beyond the cases from which they are derived.

Semantics is the study of the meaning of words and of sentences. Knowledge of the many aspects of meaning requires not only exposure to words themselves but also an understanding of the features and relationships encoded by the words and sentences. Thus, semantic knowledge continues to increase substantially throughout the school years as the child matures intellectually. Even as adults our vocabularies continue to expand to encompass our new knowledge. For example, the first-year medical student learns a whole new vocabulary of anatomic terms.

Grammar describes the structure of a language and consists of two major parts: morphology and syntax. Morphology describes the smallest units of meaning such as the prefixes and suffixes that modify the basic meaning of words. Rules for producing plurals, past tenses, inflections, and so forth, are all part of the morphological system. Syntax specifies the ways in which individual words are combined into sentences. Application of syntactic rules provides the greatest opportunity for linguistic creativity. Each language has specific syntactic rules for expressing grammatical relations such as negation, interrogation, possession, and juxtaposition of subject and object. These rules allow us to generate novel sentences to express particular meanings. Similarly, because we share the same syntactic knowledge of sentence structure, when someone says either "Bill hit John" or "Bill was hit by John," we know who did the hitting and who got hit. We can agree that the sentence "You didn't go, did you?" is an acceptable (grammatical) sentence, whereas "You didn't go, didn't you?" is unacceptable and ambiguous.

Pragmatics, the fourth face of language, can be defined as rules governing the use of language in context by real speakers and listeners in real situations (Bates, 1976; Shatz, 1983). For example, when do children learn to use polite forms, how do children adjust their speech for younger children, how do children learn to take turns, and why do children talk differently in classrooms and on playgrounds? This subfield of language has emerged out of the recognition that much of child (as well as adult) language cannot be understood without knowledge of the context and setting in which it occurs. Context refers to such things as information about the identity of the speaker and listener and the speaker's goal and the immediate physical setting. Finally, pragmatics concerns how children learn conversational rules and so provides a clear link between language development and one of the purposes of language—communication.

It is important to remember, however, that our "four faces of language" are categories constructed by scholars for the purposes of analysis. Children are involved simultaneously in learning about the sounds, meaning, structure, and use of language, and phonology, semantics, syntax, and pragmatics are not fully separable. For example, the meanings of relational terms such as verbs and spatial terms reside in part in how they combine with other words. Certain theorists concerned with vocabulary and grammatical development have proposed models whereby vocabulary and grammar are intimately related (Pinker, 1987).

Let us begin by briefly reviewing the major theoretical orientations that have helped to shape the current research in language development.

SOME CONTRASTING VIEWS ON LANGUAGE DEVELOPMENT

The field of language development has been influenced heavily by certain theoretical views. Some argue that the development of language is largely biologically determined, while others contend that learning accounts for the emergence of language. Most current theorists maintain a more middle ground and recognize the role that both genetic and environmental factors play in language development.

The Nurture View: Learning Theory Accounts of Language Development

Some theorists such as B. F. Skinner (1957) have adopted the extreme position that language can be accounted for by traditional learning principles. According to the operant or reinforcement view, the parent first selectively reinforces (that is, by approval, attention) those parts of the child's babbling sounds which are most like adult speech, thereby increasing the frequency of vocalization of these sounds by the baby. Parental reinforcement serves to gradually shape the child's verbal behavior through "successive approximations" until it becomes more and more like adult speech. Others (Bullock, 1983; Whitehurst, 1980) propose that the child learns through imitation. According to this view, the child picks up words, phrases, and sentences directly by imitation, and then through reinforcement and generalization the child learns when it is appropriate to use and combine these responses.

What's Wrong with Learning Theory Accounts?

Learning-theory accounts of language acquisition have not fared well. Critics have pointed out that the number of specific stimulus-response connections that would be necessary to even begin to explain language is so enormous that there would not be enough time to acquire these connections in a whole lifetime, not to mention a few short years. Moreover, naturalistic studies of parent-child interaction fail to support this account. Mothers are just as likely to reward their children for truthful but grammatically incorrect statements as they are to reinforce their children for grammatically correct utterances. It is ironic that people grow up to speak grammatically but not always truthfully! In short, parents often respond to the child's meaning and not to the grammar. Therefore, it is difficult to see how adult reinforcement can easily explain the child's learning of correct grammar (Brown, 1973). Furthermore, the vast majority of language utterances can in no way be directly predicted from specific "environmental eliciting cues." Utterances that are closely tied to environmental cues, such as "Hello," "Watch out!" or "You're welcome," are rare. For most sets of circumstances, language affords an enormous degree of creative latitude, which linguists argue is not accounted for by learning theories. Nor have learning-theory accounts explained the regular sequence in which language develops. Children in our culture and other cultures seem to learn the same types of grammatical rules and in the same order. For example, active constructions are learned before passive constructions. Finally, behavioral theories basically portray the child as playing a passive role in the language acquisition process; in contrast, linguists argue that the child plays an active and creative role in discovering and applying general rules of language.

Psychologists have thus far not been able to demonstrate that traditional learning principles play a *critical* role in the normal acquisition of language rules by the young speaking child. Nor do they seem to be critical for the deaf child who learns sign language (Goldin, Meadow, & Morford, 1985). Nevertheless, learning principles may play a very important and useful role in modifying language usage and in overcoming language deficits in some individuals (Whitehurst, Fischel, Caulfield, DeBaryshe, & Valdex-Menchaca, 1989). Lovaas (Lovaas, 1967; Lovaas & Smith, 1988), for example, has made remarkable demonstrations of the usefulness of imitation and reinforcement principles in overcoming, in part, the speech deficits in autistic children. However, due to neurological deficits these children still may not reach normal levels of communicative competence. Programs for parents based on learning principles have appeared. These programs are effective for helping children who are delayed in their language development catch up to their peers (Zelazo, Kearsley, & Ungerer, 1984).

The Nature View: Nativist Accounts of Language Development

The most influential advocate of the nativist position was the linguist Noam Chomsky (1968). He proposed that the human nervous system contains a mental structure that includes an innate concept of human language. Chomsky termed this innate structure a *Language Acquisition Device* or *LAD*. Nativists claim that certain "universal features" common to all languages (for example subject, verb, and object terms appear in sentences in all languages) are innate.

Another claim of nativist theory is that a set of innate "language hypotheses" are used by the child in deriving rules from the language "data" that s/he hears. Nativists also believe that the normal human child is biologically predisposed to learn any human language with ease.

Finally, in contrast to a nurture or learning view, language is viewed as an abstract system of rules that cannot be acquired by traditional learning principles.

Certain observations about language acquisition make the nativist position attractive (Maratsos, 1989). Consider the following observations: language is learned well by all normal children in many different cultures and language is acquired relatively quickly. Nativists point out that the input provided to children is so fragmented and incomplete that the environmental input alone cannot possibly account for the amazing feat of language. Children receive only a limited number of examples of the tremendous range of complex structures that language is capable of expressing; in turn, this requires children to go beyond the examples and figure out the patterns—a feat that they accomplish very successfully.

In light of these considerations, nativists argue that the child must be preset to acquire language. Some of the most striking evidence for the possibility of an innate predisposition for language comes from the work on children who speak a Creole language. See Box 8-1 for a surprising and innovative discovery.

Another source of support for specific biological involvement is evidence that humans learn language far more easily and quickly during a certain critical period of biological development, that is, from infancy to puberty. Before puberty, a child can achieve the fluency of a native speaker in any language (or even in two or more languages simultaneously) without special training. After puberty, it is extremely difficult to learn a first language. In cases of speech disruption due to brain damage, young children often recover their language capacity rapidly and completely; if the brain damage occurs after puberty, the prognosis for the recovery of language is poor (Lenneberg, 1967).

Lenneberg's theory, as well as our own cultural myths, predict that children will achieve fluency in a second language more readily than adults.

BOX 8-1 LEARNING CREOLE: EVIDENCE FOR A POSSIBLE UNIVERSAL FIRST LANGUAGE

The most striking evidence in support of the possibility of an innate program or template for grammar comes from the work of Derek Bickerton (1983). What happens when immigrants who all speak different languages are thrown together in a single culture? This happened around the turn of the century in Hawaii where Japanese, Chinese, Koreans, Portuguese, Filipinos, and Puerto Ricans immigrated to work the sugar cane fields. To communicate among themselves, these adults developed a pidgin language, which is a simplified linguistic system created when two languages come into contact. Pidgin is a hybrid language that adopts the vocabulary of the dominant language but lacks grammatical complexity and varies from speaker to speaker. Sentences are often no more than strings of nouns, verbs, and adjectives. What happens to the children of these pidgin speakers? Interestingly, the children do not speak pidgin, but they develop a different type of language—Creole. In contrast to pidgin, Creole is a highly developed linguistic system and the structure of the language is similar among all of the children in the community—*regardless of their parent's language*. Moreover, Creole languages, which develop in other places where people with different languages are congregated, such as the islands of Haiti or Mauritius, are very similar in their structure, even though the native language is Dutch, English, or French! Even more remarkable is the fact that the first generation of Creole-speaking children do not differ from later generations of speakers, which suggests that the acquisition of this new language happens very rapidly. Together, these pieces of evidence—the uniformity across speakers and geographical locales and the speed of acquisition—argue against any simple explanation that children who learn Creole are borrowing cafeteria style from one contact language or another. What are the implications of these observations for theories of language acquisition? According to Bickerton, "the evidence from creole languages suggests that first-language acquisition is mediated by an innate device . . . the device provides the child with a single and fairly specific grammatical model. It was only in pidgin-speaking communities, where there was no grammatical model that could compete with the child's innate grammar, that the innate grammatical model was not eventually suppressed. The innate grammar was then clothed in whatever vocabulary was locally available and gave rise to the creole languages heard today" (Bickerton, 1983, p. 121). Further support for this argument comes from evidence that the common errors that English-speaking toddlers make are perfectly acceptable Creole expressions. For example, between $3\frac{1}{2}$ and 4 years old, children often use double negatives (for example, "Nobody don't like me"). Creole is the only language that allows negative subjects with negative verbs. "Nothing not have value" is poor English but acceptable Creole. Similarly, when a feature of the local language matches the structure of Creole, children avoid making errors that would seem quite natural—further evidence that the structure of Creole may, in fact, be an innate language template. Whether or not the structure of Creole language can be firmly accepted as the basis of first-language acquisition requires much more research. If it turns out to be true, a biological basis of language would seem to be more than just a possibility.

Source: Bickerton, D. (1983). Creole languages. *Scientific American*, **249**, 116–122.

The evidence is mixed. In an early study of English-speaking families who moved to the Netherlands, adolescents and adults learned Dutch faster than young children—at least after a year (Snow & Hoefnagel-Hohle, 1978). More recent evidence that focused on how well children and adults could speak a second language after many years of exposure to this new language clearly support the view that there is a sensitive period for learning grammar. Johnson and Newport (1989) asked native Korean and Chinese speakers aged 3 to 39 years to judge the grammaticality of a variety of English sentences. There was a clear advantage for individuals whose first exposure to English occurred before puberty. (See Figure 8-1.) Moreover, children often come to sound like a native speaker, while adults do not. Accents are hard to modify after puberty—a finding that is consistent with the Lenneberg position. This accounts for the fact that an English-speaking adult who learns French still sounds like an Englishman speaking French. On the other hand, a child can learn a second language without any trace of a foreign accent (Krashen, 1975).

A second language is easier to learn in childhood.

If language ability is an inherited species-specific characteristic, all languages of the species must share common basic characteristics, or universal features. In examining features such as the sounds used in speaking, the way words are organized, and how meaning is determined in various languages, investigators have concluded that a set of common principles underlies all human languages (Slobin, 1979, 1982, 1985). For instance, speakers of all languages create a vast number of spoken words by combining a small set of meaningless sounds of a particular type. All languages use only a limited sample of vocal sounds of all the possible sounds humans can make; for example, no language makes use of snorting or clapping sounds. Words are always combined into structured sequences we call sentences. All languages have grammars, and linguists claim that these grammars share certain formal properties as well (for example, subject-predicate).

Although the organism is probably biologically prepared for learning language, it is unlikely that biological principles alone will account for all aspects of language development.

What's Wrong with Nativist Accounts?

As in the case of learning theory accounts, nativist accounts have limitations as well. First, few theorists agree about the exact nature of the types of grammatical rules that children learn. In fact, several theorists have offered alternative accounts of the nature of early transformational grammars that differ from Chomsky's original formulation (Maratsos, 1989; Slobin, 1985). Second, language learning is a gradual process and is not over as early as nativist accounts would predict. As we will see later in the chapter, specific aspects of grammar continue to develop into the elementary school years and beyond. Third, this perspective leaves little room for accounting for cross-cultural variations in language. Fourth, this view tells us little about the role of pragmatics and communication. Finally, the social context of language is

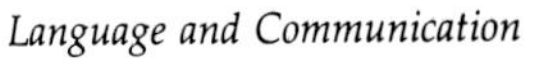

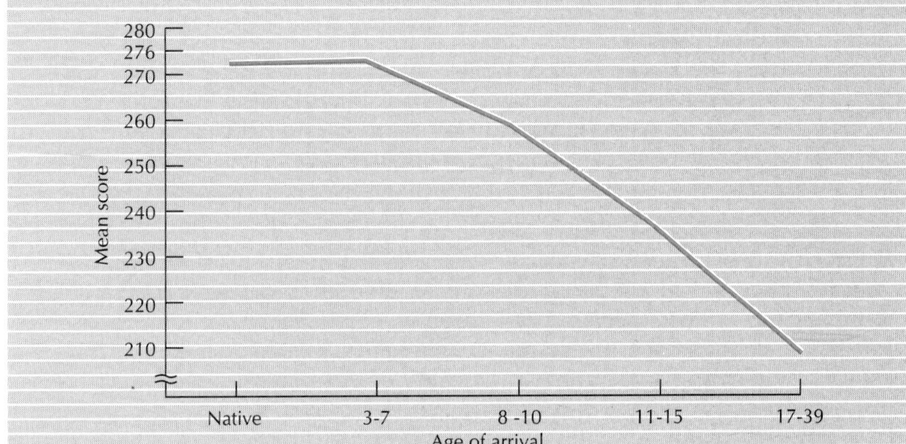

FIGURE 8-1
Total score on a test of English grammar in relation to age of arrival in the United States. (*From Newport, 1990; redrawn from Johnson & Newport, 1989.*)

given little recognition, but as we will see social influences play a much larger role in language development than previously thought.

An Interactionist Approach

Most modern theorists recognize that language is learned in the context of spoken language and that humans are biologically prepared for learning to speak. They are concerned with the interaction of biological and environmental factors in language development and view the child as playing an active role in acquiring language. "Children compile specific information from what they hear and formulate hypotheses concerning the nature of this language. Children are instrumental in the language development process. Not only do they formulate, test, and evaluate hypotheses concerning the rules of their languages, but they also actively compile linguistic information to use in the formulation of hypotheses" (Tagatz, 1976, p. 90).

Parents as Facilitators of Language Development

Not only has the child's role received increased emphasis, but the role of socializing agents as active facilitators of the child's language acquisition has been recognized. Parents and other adults use a variety of devices during the course of normal social interaction that may aid the child's learning of language. Language acquisition is no longer viewed as a purely linguistic or cognitive affair; it is recognized that language learning is best understood as a social activity as well. Normal language develops as a result of a delicate balance between parent and child understanding; if the parent speaks to the child in a way that recognizes how much the child already knows and understands, the child's chance of comprehending a message—even a novel one—is increased enormously (Swensen, 1983). Parents often introduce objects to provide a basis for their mutual play and speak about objects and events that are present and easily visible to the child. Parents do other helpful things as well. They closely monitor their child's apparent goals or intentions.

During most of their interactive turns, they attempt to modulate, correct, or elaborate their child's behavior rather than redirect it. "And they construct an internal model of their child's current preferences, skills, and world knowledge, which they continuously update and check" (Fischer & Bullock, 1984, pp. 75–76). These strategies make comprehension easier for children. It should be stressed that the tactics that parents use are usually not deliberate teaching techniques: instead, they follow naturally from simply trying to carry on conversation with a child.

Parental Strategies. One advocate of this social interaction view, Jerome Bruner, has termed the kinds of assets that the environment provides the language-learning child a "language acquisition support system" (Bruner, 1983). What does this support system consist of?

Nonverbal games: First, children learn about some of the structural features of language, such as turn-taking, from early nonlinguistic games. These games, such as peek-a-boo or patty cake, are regular, repetitive, and predictable—features that make them ideal for learning language. At first, young babies aren't capable of taking turns or engaging in a conversation. But parents help them learn this social skill by carrying more than their share of the conversation in early dialogues, by waiting for a pause in the infant's vocal or motor behavior and inserting an appropriate "answer." Well before the infant is capable of a full dialogue in the sense of being able to initiate or answer, the adults in his world provide opportunities to learn the essential ingredients of turn-taking. This supportive activity of the mother may contribute to social turn-taking in play, games, and conversation where the child is a full and equal partner (Garvey, 1990). A term used to describe this process by which infants and children with a little help from a friendly parent achieve more than they can on their own is *scaffolding* (Fischer & Bullock, 1984; Rogoff, 1990; Vygotsky, 1934). (See Chapters 1 and 10.)

Simplified speech: Another part of the language acquisition support system is the way that mothers and fathers modify their speech when they talk to infants and children. Parents' speech to children has been described as "language lessons in miniature" (Clark & Clark, 1977, p. 327). Sentences are typically short, well formed, simple in structure, repetitive, and refer to concrete objects and events. When talking to infants, adults talk slower, in higher-pitched voices, enunciate more clearly, and often end their sentences with rising intonation (Fernald, 1992). Moreover, they use these acoustical variations to help highlight the important words for their infants (Fernald & Mazzie, 1991). In reading a picture book to a 14-month-old, mothers consistently positioned the word that identified the picture (that's a *shirt* or that's a *boy*) at the end of the phrase and spoke the word in exaggerated pitch. When speaking to adults, mothers did not show this pattern. By using these tactics mothers may make "certain sounds much easier than others to detect, discriminate and remember" (Fernald & Mazzie, 1991, p. 218).

Adults adjust their speech according to the age of the child, and use a wider range of words and parts of speech as children develop (Shatz, 1983). It is assumed that there is some optimum level of language complexity. "Talking in baby talk to a child for the first 5 years of his life would surely hinder his learning, but so would speaking in the language of an encyclopedia or a diplomatic treaty" (Dale, 1976, p. 144). In fact, simplified speech is not always most helpful. In one study, children responded appropriately more frequently—if they were not in the one-word stage—to an adult form of a command ("Throw me the ball") than to a simplified form ("Throw ball").

Children learn about the structural features of language such as turn taking from early games such as peek-a-boo.

Just as we have seen in other areas of development, a level of complexity that is slightly ahead of the child may be the most effective elicitor of attention and provide the maximal opportunity for learning (Hoff-Ginsberg & Shatz, 1982). In addition to age, the child or infants' reactions play a role in the communication process. When children show signs that they are not comprehending, adults often simplify their speech further (Bohannon & Warren-Leubecker, 1988).

Children attend to simplified speech more than regular adult speech. Not only do words at the end of an utterance in a high-pitch manner gain infant attention more effectively (Fernald & Kuhl, 1987), they also elicit more positive affect, such as smiles, and may increase the chances that the child will understand the message (Werker & McLeod, 1989).

Does the use of a simplified code facilitate children's language learning? The fine tuning that adults engage in should help children learn. First, by listening to adults who speak slowly and exaggerate their pauses and who repeat phrases and words, the child learns some early segmentation rules, which indicate how utterances should be divided into words and phrases. Second, the child learns the relationship between words and objects. Indeed, Huttenlocher, Haight, Bryk, Seltzer, and Lyons (1991) found that a substantial portion of individual differences in toddlers' vocabulary growth is accounted for by differences in the amount particular mothers speak to their children. In addition, children learn to take turns, to know when they are being addressed, and learn clues concerning the right words for the right situation (Clark & Clark, 1977; deVilliers & deVilliers, 1992). Further, there is some evidence that certain language patterns are facilitated by parental speech (Newport, Gleitman, & Gleitman, 1977; Gleitman, Newport, & Gleitman, 1984), while other major kinds of developments are not. Nonessential language forms (for example, verb auxiliaries such as "are, can, will") are more likely to be acquired by children whose mothers frequently use these forms (that is, high use of yes/no questions), whereas children's advancement in terms of the number of basic sentence units (noun phrases per sentence) is unrelated to properties of maternal speech.

Other influence techniques: A variety of other tactics that parents use to facilitate early communication should be mentioned. Consider the following exchanges between a mother and her child:

Child: Baby highchair.

Adult: Baby is in the highchair.

Child: Throw daddy.

Adult: Throw it to daddy. (Brown & Bellugi, 1964)

These exchanges illustrate the technique of *expansion.* As you can see, the adult imitates and expands, or adds to, the child's statement. Brown (1973) has estimated that middle-class parents use this expansion technique about 30 percent of the time; lower-class parents use this tactic much less often. Parents are especially likely to use this expansion strategy after a child has made a grammatical error (Bohannon & Stanowicz, 1988).

Not only do parents expand on their children's utterances, but the children, in turn, may imitate the parent's expansions. Children are more likely to imitate adult recasts of their speech when they are wrong; when their speech is correct children rarely imitate the adult's speech (Bohannon & Stanowicz, 1988). Perhaps children are more aware of their own mistakes than we often recognize! Of particular interest is the fact that children's imitations of their parents' expansions are often grammatically more advanced than their free speech. Table 8-1 illustrates these types of exchanges between parent and child. Expansions have been shown to be an effective technique for increasing 2-year-old children's use of adjective-noun combinations (Hovell, Schumaker, & Sherman, 1978).

Although expansions sometimes help, a combination of expansion and "recasting" is more effective. In this case, the adult listener recasts the child's incomplete sentence into a modified grammatical form. For example, when a child says "kitty eta," the adult recasts the sentence as "What is the kitty eating?" Or a child's utterance "my ball" might become "Here is your ball." Children apparently profit from this type of experience, as evidenced by more complex grammatical speech during their spontaneous speech (Nelson, Carskadden, & Bonvillian, 1973). Other evidence (Nelson, 1977, 1989) suggests that the recasting approach can successfully increase children's language development; for example, they use questions and complex verbs such as verbal auxiliaries at an earlier age. Since we do not know how often mothers use recasting, how powerful a role recasting plays in normal language acquisition is still uncertain.

What are the implications of these influence techniques? Although the child is probably biologically prepared for learning language, it is increasingly necessary to formulate a more interactional theory—one that recognizes the role of both environmental input and biological predispositions as important determinants of language development.

Are Parental Modifications Necessary to Language Learning?

As much as social interaction is necessary to language acquisition, these specific devices may not be necessary. First, there is no universal pattern that

IMITATIONS OF EXPANSIONS

TABLE 8-1

TYPE OF IMITATION	EXAMPLE		RELATIVE FREQUENCY* ADAM	RELATIVE FREQUENCY* EVE
Unexpanded	Child:	Just like cowboy.	45	17
	Adult:	Oh, just like the cowboy's.		
	Child:	Just like cowboy.		
Reduced	Child:	Play piano.	7	29
	Adult:	Playing the piano.		
	Child:	Piano.		
Expanded	Child:	Pick-mato.	48	54
	Adult:	Picking tomatoes up?		
	Child:	Pick 'mato up.		

*These figures cover Adam from age 2;3 to age 2;10 and Eve from 1;6 to 2;2.
Source: From Slobin (1968). Reprinted by permission.

characterizes all parents within a cultural group; some use imitation and expansion, others do not. Indeed, there are impressive individual differences in the kinds of linguistic environments that parents within a cultural group provide their children (Shatz, 1983). But, parents tend to use their own favorite devices with a high degree of regularity, and the consistency in the style of interacting rather than what style a particular parent uses may be the most important factor.

In addition, not all cultures use the devices typical of the American middle class (Peters, 1983). Among the Kaluli of New Guinea or on American Samoa, "baby talk" is seldom heard; instead, children are spoken to as adults from a very early age (Ochs, 1980; Schieffelin & Ochs, 1987). In American Samoa, for example, Ochs (1980) found few instances of the use of expansion. In contrast to American middle-class mothers, Samoan caregivers assume that young children are not capable of communicating intentionally. Therefore, expanding children's utterances to help them express their intended meaning is obviously inappropriate! In spite of the fact that parents do not use these possible aids to language learning, their children do develop language. It is clear that social interaction is critical to language development, but there are varying forms that this interaction may take resulting in eventual competence in language.

THE ANTECEDENTS OF LANGUAGE DEVELOPMENT

Not By Word Alone: Preverbal Communication

Communication is not achieved by words alone and by restricting ourselves to verbal communication, we can easily misjudge how early communication begins. The first steps on the road to language are the early communicative behaviors of babies and their caregivers during the first few months of life (Uzgiris, 1989). However, careful observation of "conversations" between infants and adults indicates that these exchanges are more apparent than real. These interactions are best described as "pseudo-conversations" or "dialogues", because it is the parent who is responsible for maintaining the flow of the exchange (Schaffer, 1977). Babies still have limited control over the timing of their responses, but fortunately most parents do, and they use their skill to insert their behavior into the babies cycles of responsiveness and non-responsiveness. We have all watched a baby vocalize and then see the mother reply and then wait for the baby's response and if none is forthcoming, the mother may prompt the baby by changing her expressions, vocalizing, or gently touching the baby. These early lessons in conversation probably help the developing infant to become a "true" communicative partner, which they become by the end of the first year (Schaffer, 1977).

Between 3 and 12 months of age, infants improve in their ability to use gestures to communicate. From 3 or 4 months on, adults offer and show things to infants, and by six months infants reciprocate. By 7 or 8 months, adults begin to point in order to draw the infant's attention to an object or event. Within a few months, infants begin to actively use pointing gestures, and by a year of age, children become high skilled communicators. They can use gestures to bring an object to someone's attention, for example, by pointing to it or holding it up. Bates (1976) has termed this form of preverbal communication a "protodeclarative." Alternatively, they use gestures to gain help or assistance. For example, by pointing to their teddy bear that is on a high shelf, the child is "asking" for helping in rescuing their stranded toy. In Bates (1976) terminology, this is called a "protoimperative." Moreover, children use these early nonverbal tactics very effectively and often check and make sure that the partner is looking in the right direction. All of us have seen a child tug at the pant leg of a distracted father and then point. There are other common gestures such as reaching, grasping, or staring, and some children develop their own unique gesturing tactics.

As language develops, words and gestures are often used together for more effective communication. A child may point to an object and then verbally comment or gesture to emphasize the meaning of the words. However, children's ability to use and understand gestures may develop

Even before learning to talk, babies use pointing as a means of communication.

independently of verbal language. Only in the third year of life do children begin to recognize that gesture and language can be part of the same message and require an integrated response (Shatz, 1983). Across time, gestures decrease as children rely increasingly on their verbal skills to communicate their needs and wishes (Shatz, 1983).

Early Production and Comprehension of Language

Language involves both the production of sounds and the ability to understand speech. These two aspects of language are often referred to as *productive* and *receptive* language. Well before infants are able to speak, they are capable of selectively attending to certain features of speech sounds. In fact, newborns prefer listening to speech or vocal music rather than instrumental music or other rhythmic sounds (Butterfield & Siperstein, 1974). As we saw earlier in Chapter 5, infants very quickly become skilled listeners, even 2-day-old infants can distinguish their mother's voice from an unfamiliar voice. Moreover, just as in the case of adults, infants respond with different parts of their brain to speech and nonspeech sounds, such as music. Electrical activity increases in the left half of the infant's brain in response to speech, while the right side responds to music (Molfese, 1973). This does not exhaust the young infant's receptive abilities. One of the most remarkable discoveries of recent years is the finding that infants can discriminate among consonants such as "pah" and "bah" in the same way as adults. In an early study, Moffitt (1971) investigated whether 5-month-old infants could distinguish consonants. One group of babies heard sixty "bah" syllables and then ten "gah" trials; babies in a second group heard "gah" sixty times, followed by ten presentations of "bah"; a final group heard only "bah" throughout the series. Heart rate was monitored to determine if the infants' reactions changed with the presentation of the new consonant. The answer was positive; babies listening to repeated "bah" showed only limited cardiac reaction, but showed a marked recovery when the other consonant ("gah") was presented. A similar effect emerged for the "gah-bah" sequence; the control babies exhibited the same level of reaction throughout the series; after all, nothing changed. Very young infants, then, are able to perceive and discriminate speech sounds, in spite of no experience in producing these sounds, relatively limited exposure to speech, and certainly little, if any, differential reinforcement for this form of behavior. Research has shown that this ability is evident from 1 month of age and for a variety of other consonants such as "ma" and "na" or "dah" and "gah" (Aslin, Pisoni, & Jusczyk, 1983; Eimas, 1982).

These findings raise the question of whether infants are born with an innate device for verbal language perception. While recent evidence does suggest that infants have an innate tendency to look for the boundaries in sound patterns, this tendency is not unique to speech sounds. Speech, however, is more easily separable into perceptual categories than other sound stimuli (Aslin, Pisoni, & Jusczyk, 1983).

In spite of their precocity, young infants are unable to make all the distinctions that language requires; for example, 3-month-old infants cannot yet distinguish between "s" and "za" (Eilers, 1980). Moreover, by 8 to 10 months, infants lose the ability to make some discriminations that are not used in their particular language (Werker, 1989). For example, Japanese speakers cannot distinguish "rah" and "lah" (Miyawaki et al., 1975). Conversely, English speakers do not make some distinctions that are important in other languages (Sachs, 1985). These findings illustrate the dual role of innate as well as experimental factors in the early understanding of speech sounds.

In addition, the developing infant doesn't necessarily appreciate the importance of phonological differences for distinguishing between words in her native language. Not until the end of the second year can the child use differences in phonemes to distinguish words that label different objects. Consider this example (deVilliers & deVilliers, 1979):

> We can demonstrate this by presenting the child with two funny toys made up to look like people. Each object is given a nonsense-syllable name such as bok and pok, chosen so that they differ only by the initial consonant. The child is then invited to do things with each object, such as "Let pok take a ride on the wagon" or "Put the hat on bok." Although one-month-old infants can detect the sound differences between (b) and (p), children under eighteen months have little success in picking out the correct object in the bok-pok task. . . . The child must learn which of the many discriminable differences in speech sounds actually function to mark differences in reference to his native language. This requires considerable exposure to language and is not complete even at the end of the second year. (1979, pp. 18–19)

Thus, while even young infants demonstrate specialized language abilities, including selective attention, voice discrimination, and specialized phoneme perception, the abilities to distinguish and categorize phonemes continue to develop even beyond age 2.

Productive Abilities: Babbling and Other Early Sounds

It is not just receptive language abilities that are rapidly developing in infancy. The infant is actively producing sounds—even though not language—from birth onward. Anyone who has been awakened in the middle of the night by a crying 3-week-old baby knows that infants are neither quiet nor passive! But are the early sounds that an infant makes just random noise, or do they occur in some specific, meaningful sequence? And are early speech sounds related to later language development?

The production of sounds in the first year of life follows an orderly sequence. Four stages have been identified: (1) crying, which begins at birth. As we saw in Chapter 5, crying is important in detecting early signs of infant illness as well as serving as a rudimentary communicative system; (2) other vocalizations and cooing which start at the end of the first month. According to Sacks (1985): "The sounds are called cooing from their vowel-like "oo" quality resembling the sounds made by pigeons" (p. 46). These often occur during social interchanges between the infant and caregiver. (3) Babbling, which begins at the middle of the first year; and finally (4) patterned speech at the close of the first year. However, even as early signs of speech appear, babbling and speech often occur together.

Not only does early sound production follow an orderly sequence, these early sound scenarios, such as babbling, are similar across different linguistic communities; only the intonations are similar to their cultural language (Thevenin, Eilers, Oller, & La Voie, 1985). Most examinations of babbling in infants across cultures have failed to find differences, but a recent review (Ingram, 1989) suggests that in some languages, such as French and Arabic

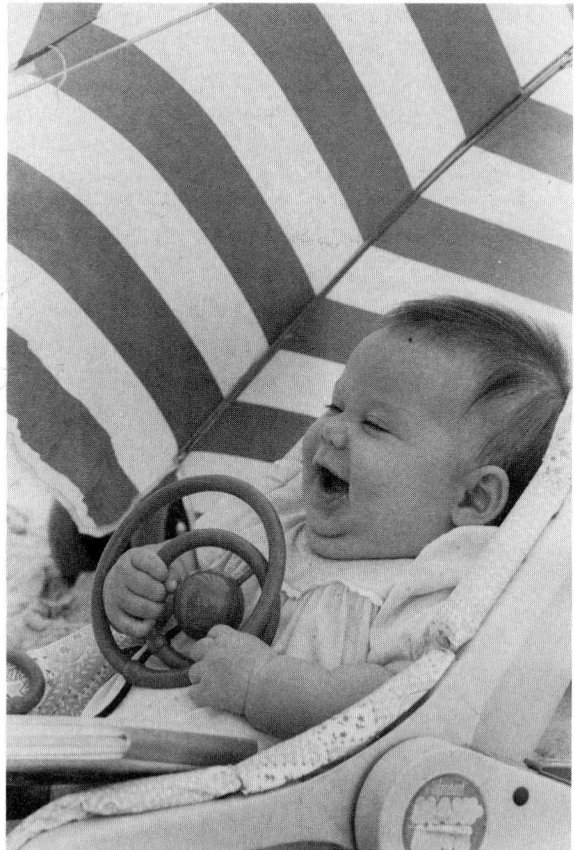

Babbling is more complex and meaningful than earlier theorists thought.

which differ in voice quality and pitch, listeners can reliably detect differences in infant babbling of 8 and 10 month old infants but not in younger babies.

The pattern of development of early sounds suggests that maturational changes in both the articulatory structure and the central nervous system probably underlie these shifts. However, a maturational view may not be totally correct and the environment may play a role in the emergence of babbling and early vocalization. Do deaf babies who receive little or no auditory stimulation from the environment babble? A classic study (Lennenberg, Rebelsky, & Nichols, 1965) suggested that even deaf babies display early signs of babbling, but later work found that more complex babbling that begins to resemble speech is not found in deaf infants (Oller & Eilers, 1988). Together this work leads to the view that maturational factors may be responsible for early infant sounds, but exposure to normal speech may be required for later and more advanced forms of babbling.

Infants also are capable of modifying their babbling to suit the physical and social setting. Their babbling is different in different situations—in the crib, looking at a mobile, or sitting on mother's lap (Delack, 1976). Infants under 1 year of age modify their own babbling according to the pitch levels and intonation of patterns of their adult caretakers. For example, compared to the babbling of American babies, the babbling of 6-month-old Chinese babies show much more pitch variation, reflecting the Chinese language they hear (Weir, 1966). Even in the first years of life, infants are sensitive to variations in context and tell us by shifts in their vocalizations.

The toughest question still remains. Is there any relationship between babbling and later meaningful speech? Although, historically, linguists have favored a discontinuity view (Jakobson, 1968) which susggests that there is no relationship between early vocalizations and later speech, more recent evidence has challenged this view. Specifically studies of early babblings of infants over the first year have found that babbled syllables resemble the child's first meaningful words in a variety of ways (Elbers & Ton, 1985; Oller, Wieman, Doyle, & Ross, 1976). As one language expert notes: "Late babbling contains sounds very much like those that are used in early attempts to pronounce words, independent of the language to which the child is exposed. . . . . babbling is indeed relevant to the child's developing linguistic skills" (Sachs, 1985, p. 49)

In summary, the child's early productions not only are orderly, but related to later speech. In both production and receptivity, the infant is surprisingly well prepared for learning to talk.

SEMANTIC DEVELOPMENT

As we noted earlier, the remarkable growth of vocabulary in early childhood is a dramatic example of the human capacity for language. To learn words children must acquire the relevant phonemes, form appropriate concepts, and then link sound and meaning. Imagine that you are in a foreign country. Your first task is to learn the language. A native points to a dog sitting on a rug and says, "xitf." How do you know whether "xitf" refers to the dog, the dog's twitching ear, the dog's fur, the dog sleeping on the rug, or indeed, the rug? Philosophers have proposed that the acquisition of object names is potentially a difficult problem for the word learner, since the words used to refer to objects could instead refer to parts of those objects, to the material the objects are made of, or a variety of other features of the dog, the rug, or both. Despite the complexity of this task, recall that the average child knows approximately 900 root words by 2 years and 8000 root words by 6 years (Carey, 1978). Rice (1989) has described the process by which children learn new words so quickly as follows: "Obviously children manage to do this without explicit word-by-word tutoring. Instead they seem to absorb or 'map' new meanings as they encounter them in conversational interactions" (Rice, 1989, p. 152). Carey (1978) has termed this process "fast-mapping", whereby children learn to link up a new word with a concept that is already understood. Several studies support this concept of fast mapping (deVilliers & deVilliers, 1992). For example, Dockrell & Campbell (1986) found that 3–4 year-olds learned a nonsense name for a new animal after only one exposure to the word. Similarly, Rice (1990) found that children could learn meanings for unknown words, especially objects, from a single exposure to these words presented in the context of a video display.

How do children build up large vocabularies with such speed? Recent evidence suggests that rather than considering the vast majority of logically possible hypotheses about word meanings, young children's hypotheses are constrained in such a way that they focus on the most likely alternative. Ellen Markman (1989) identified two constraints especially important for learning word meanings. The first key constraint posited by Markman—the taxonomic constraint—involves the assumption, made by children as young as 18 months, that a new object word refers to the class of objects, not a part or property of the object. For example, upon hearing the word "anteater" for the first time while visiting the zoo, the young child will assume that "anteater" refers to the animals, not its nose, body, and so on. The taxonomic assumption, together with context and linguistic cues considerably narrows the possible meanings the word may have. Indeed, Markman (in press) speculated that "the emergence of the taxonomic constraint may be what accounts for the very young child's sudden ability to acquire words rapidly."

The other key constraint posited by Markman—the mutual exclusivity constraint—involves the assumption that words refer to nonoverlapping sets of referents. That is, children assume that each object has one and only one name (Markman, 1989). As early as 2½ years, when children encounter an unfamiliar word in a context in which the word might refer to one of two objects, they assume that the unfamiliar word refers to the unfamiliar object. For example, if a 3-year-old already knows the word "spoon" and not the word "tong," and is asked "Show me the tongs," she will very likely choose the tongs rather than the spoon.

The Meaning of First Words

Examination of the kinds of words children acquire and how they use them provide important information about semantic development, the way in which children attach meaning to words. In a study of the first fifty words, Nelson (1973) classified words into six categories. Figure 8-2 illustrates the different kinds of words used by young children. Children show considerable uniformity in their early vocabulary. Object labels comprise 60 to 70 percent of children's first 50 to 100 words, while action terms make up only 10 to 30 percent (Gentner, 1982). Children's first words primarily represent objects that they can act on and that produce a change or movement. For example, the words "shoes," "socks," and "toys" are more common than words denoting objects that are just "there," such as "tables," "stove," and "trees," or words that refer to actions (Clark, 1983).

Furthermore, research using novel words to control the child's prior experience with specific words, found that object words were easier to learn than action words (Schwartz & Leonard, 1984). One explanation for this finding is that the concepts encoded by object words are conceptually simpler than those encoded by action words (Huttenlocher & Smiley, 1987). To learn

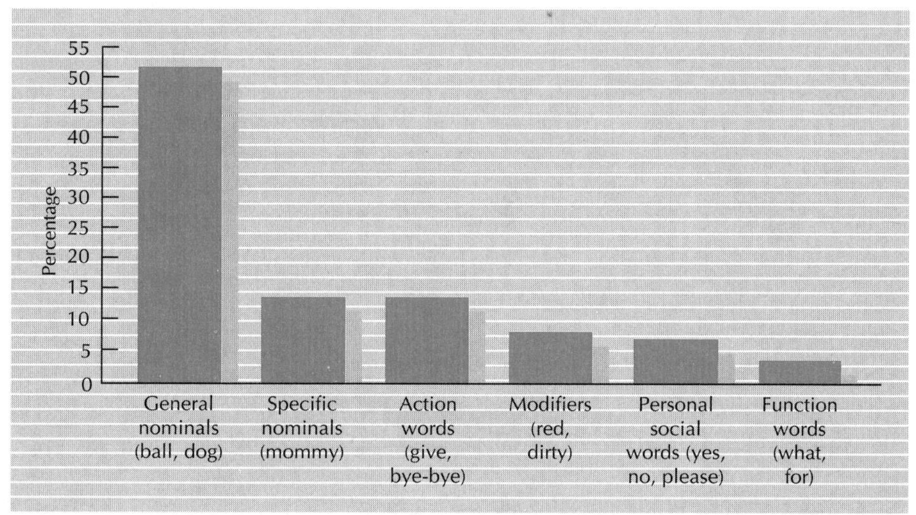

FIGURE 8-2
Types of first words used by young infants and children. (*Based on data from Nelson, 1973.*)

BOX 8-2 WHAT WORD MEANINGS REVEAL ABOUT CONCEPTUAL DEVELOPMENT: THE CASE OF PERSON CATEGORIES

Children's early word use may differ from adults' because of limitations in children's conceptual development. For example, children may apply the word "sad" only to the self because they have not yet recognized the similarities between the inner state of self and others. As their understanding of emotion develops their use of "sad" becomes more conventional. Alternatively, children's word use may differ from adults' not because their underlying concepts differ, but because they have only heard the word used in a restricted way. For example, children's underlying concept of "sad" may be similar to adults', but because, when addressing children, adults use "sad" primarily to describe children's experiences, children assume that the word "sad" refers only to this subcategory of the larger "sad" category. Huttenlocher and her colleagues consider both children's and parents' word use when studying children's emerging concepts of persons. They focus on the question of when children understand that others have inner states such as intentions and emotions similar to their own.

Smiley and Huttenlocher (1989) examined children's emotion concepts through the emergence of emotion state words (for example, sad, happy). The child's first use of emotion state words emerge at around 2 years and initially apply to the self primarily. The few instances of children's use of emotion words refer to others' habitual behavioral expressions of emotion—crying, smiling, stomping around. By 6 months to a year later, however, children begin to use emotion words, not just for observable aspects of others' experiences, but apparently for their inner states as well. An examination of parent speech, however, revealed that children's usage corresponds to parent's usage: parent uses for the child referred to emotion states while uses for others were restricted to expressive behavior (for example, crying). Such correspondences between parents and children suggest that *both* parental input *and* children's conceptual development may influence children's understanding of the meaning of emotion words.

An even stronger case for the role of conceptual development in the emergence of meaning comes from a study of action words (Huttenlocher, Smiley, & Charney, 1983). Like emotion words, intentional action verbs characterize inner states. Intentional action verbs such as "open" and "get" do not describe regular movements but are defined by changes caused by the actor and hence required inferences about intentionality. In contrast, verbs such as "walk," "jump," and "wave" describe simple actions and that are directly observable. Huttenlocher and associates found that children first applied intentional action verbs to their own actions and only later extended them to the actions of others. Parents, however, do not show a similar bias in their use of verbs when addressing their children. Thus, the pattern of development most likely reflects conceptual development; probably this pattern of acquisition reflects both the accessibility of their own intentions to the self and the conceptual problem of inferring intentions in others.

Sources: Huttenlocher, J., Smiley, P., & Charnery, R. (1983). Emergence of action categories in the child: Evidence from verb meanings. *Psychological Review*, **90**, 72–93; Smiley, P., & Huttenlocher, J. (1989). Young children's acquisition of emotion concepts. In C. Saarni & P. Harris (Eds.), *Children's understanding of emotion*, pp. 27–49. New York: Cambridge University Press.

object words, children need to match objects with their appropriate linguistic referents (Gertner, 1982). In contrast, verbs require an understanding of the connections between objects and actions (Huttenlocher & Lui, 1979). Recent cross-cultural evidence shows that higher proportions of nouns are found in the vocabularies of children learning several non-English languages even when, in those languages, object words are not as perceptually salient in the spoken sentences (Gentner, 1982; Slobin, 1985). This evidence, as well as the work presented in Box 8-2, suggests that children's acquisition of word meanings reflects children's conceptual development rather than solely the ways in which adults use words with children.

Errors in Children's Early Word Use

There are characteristic errors in children's early word use and these errors can help illuminate the learning process. First, children overextend and use a single word to cover many different things. For example, everyone has heard a young child use the word "doggie" for horses, cows, giraffes, and other four legged animals. This is a common practice among young language-learning children—about one-third of the child's words are overextended at one time or another (Nelson, 1977). Some overextensions can be easily understood in terms of perceptual similarities of different objects. For example, a child may call all round objects "ball" including cakes, the sun and moon, pancakes, and oranges.

As deVilliers & deVilliers (1992) note, observations of their son, Nicholas, revealed that sometimes children's overextensions can be complex. Consider this overextension of the word "turtle" (a wind up toy that swam in the bath). "Within days of its first production, 'turtle' was used to refer to other turtles, including ones with wheels, to a real turtle, and to pictured turtles. But other objects were also called 'turtle': several toys that shared his bath, including a plastic walrus and a wind-up frog. . . and a pinecone with a stem that stuck out like a turtle's head. . . . finally, Nicholas's big toe stuck out through a hole (in his pajamas) . . . and he said with delight 'turtle' (deVilliers & deVilliers, 1992, p. 352).

Clearly children show creativity and ingenuity in their overextensions. However, with development comes improvement and as their vocabularies increase; children become more selective in their use of overextended words (deVilliers & deVilliers, 1992).

Children may also *underextend* the use of a single word in a highly restricted and individualistic way. A child may only use the word "car" when she sees her father's yellow Chevy. All other automobiles including her mother's green Ford are called trucks.

There are several explanations for children's early word errors. Children probably learn to overextend from their parents who may not label every type of vehicle such as cars, trucks, and tractors by the correct names at first. For example, Mervis & Mervis (1982) found that mothers use basic nouns to label toys and objects. They called both lions and leopards "kitty cats". While this may be helpful to the child in everyday life, such as successfully having her parent pick out the stuffed animal rather than the fire engine from the array of toys on a shelf, this same strategy may contribute to overextending categories.

Others argue that overextensions and underextensions may reflect children's gradual development from immature to mature adult conceptual

In the early stages of language acquisition, children overextend and use the same word for different objects. This child may call the deer a "doggie."

BOX 8-3 SPEECH SAMPLES TEN MONTHS APART

These samples of speech are from the records of Brown and Bellugi (1964). The first is from a boy at 28 months of age, and the second is from the same boy at at 38 months of age.

Child—28 months	**Adult**
What dat . . .	Whose pencils are they?
somebody pencil	
Floor	Floor?
Where birdie go?	
Birdie	
Birdie up dere	
Birdie	
Read dat?	
Read dat?	Will you read it to me?
What innere?	Is that a hammer, Adam?
Hammer	
Hit Hammer, Mommy,	
No Cromer——,	
mommy?	
Hurt	Poor Adam. Did you hurt yourself? What happened, Adam?
Screw (did) happen	Screw happened? You didn't even have a screw.
have screw	
——no down	
there . . . table	
. . . get broom	Does that one fit?
Yep, it fit	
Yep, it fit	Does it fit?
No . . . fit	

Child—38 months	**Adult**
I like a racing car	
D'you like some?	
I broke my racing car	Oh, did you used to have one?
Yes	
Look at dat one	
Like dis part broke	What part broke?
Dis part broke, like that	
It's got a flat tire	
What is dat?	
It's a what?	
He . . . his mouth is open	
What shall we shall have?	
Why he going to have some seeds?	
Why it's not working?	
You got some beads?	Yes
Just like me?	
I got bead 'round myself	
Hit my knee	Hit my knee
Hit your knee	
What dat teacher will do?	
Why you pull out?	
Who put dust on my hair?	Dust in your hair Can you tell Ursula what the lesson is . . . on the blackboard?
On the black which board?	
We going see another one	
We can read 'bout dis	
You wanto read?	
What is dat?	
What is dat got?	
It's got a flat tire	
When it's got flat tire, it's need to go the . . . to the station.	
The station will fix it.	

Source: Cited in McNeill, D. (1970). *The acquisition of language: The study of developmental psycholinguistics* (pp. 16–19). New York: Harper & Row. Brown, R., & Bellugi, U. (1964). Three processes in the acquisition of syntax. In E. G. Lenneberg (Ed.), *New directions in the study of language*. Cambridge, MA: M.I.T. Press.

categories (Huttenlocher & Smiley, 1987). For example, the distinction between "dog" and "cow" may not be relevant to a very young child with extremely limited experience with cows and dogs. Recent evidence indicates, however, that even very young children's use of words is more accurate than previously assumed. Indeed, children's use of object words is remarkably adultlike from the onset of speech.

An alternative explanation for overextension is that they are a special communication technique that young children use as long as their vocabularies are limited. The child is not just making an error; she is trying to find the relationship between linguistic form and an element of experience. As Bloom notes, "It seems entirely reasonable for the child to use an available word to represent different but related objects—it is almost as if the child were reasoning, "I know about dogs, that thing is not a dog. I don't know what to call it, but it is like a dog' " (1976, p. 23). For the child, applying words in different contexts is a type of hypothesis testing, a process that will continue throughout childhood. This process manifests itself particularly in the first three years when the process of relating the word form with the object begins (Kuczaj, 1982). Gradually as the child's discriminations improve and her conceptual categories become more stable, the child's accuracy in the use of words increases.

THE ACQUISITION OF GRAMMAR: FROM WORDS TO SENTENCES

Read over the passages in Box 8-3 of the speech of the same child at 28 months and again at 38 months. It will be clear that a great deal has happened in this short time. Both the length and the complexity of the utterances have increased. These speech samples come from a longitudinal study of children's spontaneous speech; the strategy of studying a few children over an extended period of time has provided a wealth of information about children's speech development. As we argued in Chapter 2, its main advantage over the manipulative experimental approach is that only by studying the same child extensively over a period of time is it possible to analyze in detail how the individual child's language system changes and develops.

First Words: An Early Grammar?

Are first words just single words? Or are they early attempts to express sentences? When a young child points to a toy airplane on a high shelf and says "down" or when he takes a spoon from his mother and says "me", is there more than meets the ear? In the first case, the child may be requesting that the toy be taken down off the shelf, or in our second example, the child may be saying "I want to do it myself". As Dale notes, "First words seem to be more than single words. They appear to be attempts to express complex ideas—ideas that would be expressed in sentences by an adult" (1976, p. 13).

One investigator, Dore (1979, 1985), has termed these one-word expressions "speech acts" because they refer to situations, events, or sequences rather than simply to a single object or action. Whether or not children are really expressing sentences in a word remains more an intriguing idea than a proven fact at this point.

Beyond Single Words

The next important step in language development is the use of not just a single word but two words together. Children generally take this step around 18 to 20 months of age. At this point, language is still simpler than adult language, and more selective, since, although nouns, verbs, and adjectives are generally present, other forms such as articles and prepositions are often absent. However, the child's speech is still novel and creative and not merely a copy of adult language. Table 8-2 shows some of the kinds of two-word sentences used by young children not only in English but in other cultures

TABLE 8-2

FUNCTIONS OF TWO-WORD SENTENCES IN CHILD SPEECH, WITH EXAMPLES FROM SEVERAL LANGUAGES*

FUNCTION OF UTTERANCE	LANGUAGE					
	ENGLISH	GERMAN	RUSSIAN	FINNISH	LUO	SAMOAN
LOCATE, NAME	*there book*	*buch da* [book there]	*Tosya tam* [Tosya there]	*tuossa Rina* [there Rina]	*en saa* [it clock]	*Keith lea* [Keith there]
DEMAND, DESIRE	*more milk*	*mehr milch* [more milk]	*yeshchë moloko* [more milk]	*anna Rina* [give Rina]	*miya tamtam* [give-me candy]	*mai pepe* [give doll]
NEGATE	*no wet*	*nicht blasen* [not blow]	*vody net* [water no]	*ei susi* [not wolf]	*beda onge* [my-slasher absent]	*le 'ai* [not eat]
DESCRIBE EVENT OR SITUATION	*Bambi go*	*puppe kommt* [doll comes]	*mam prua* [mama walk]	*Seppo putoo* [Seppo fall]	*odhi skul* [he-went school]	*pa'u pepe* [fall doll]
INDICATE POSSESSION	*my shoe*	*mein ball* [my ball]	*mami chashka* [mama's cup]	*täti auto* [aunt car]	*kom baba* [chair father]	*lole a'u* [candy my]
MODIFY, QUALIFY (attributive)	*pretty dress*	*milch heiss* [milk hot]	*mama khoroshaya* [mama good]	*rikki auto* [broken car]	*piypiy kech* [pepper hot]	*fa'ali'i pepe* [headstrong baby]
QUESTION	*where ball*	*wo ball* [where ball]	*gde papa* [where papa]	*missä pallo* [where ball]		*fea Punafu* [where Punafu]

*The examples come from a variety of studies, published and unpublished. Data from the three non-Indo-European languages are drawn from the doctoral dissertations of Melissa Bowerman (Harvard, 1973; Finnish), Ben Blount (Berkeley, 1969; Luo), and Keith Kernan (Berkeley, 1969; Samoan). (Luo is spoken in Kenya.) The examples given here are representative of many more utterances of the same type in each language. The order of the two words in the utterance is generally fixed in all of the languages except Finnish, where both orders can be used freely for some utterance types by some children.
Source: Adapted from Slobin (1979).

as well (Slobin, 1985). Notice the high degree of similarity of the semantic relation of the two-word phrases used by children in language as different as Finnish, English, and Samoan. If you ignore word order, the two-word utterances read like direct translations of one another.

Nor are these patterns limited to oral language. As Box 8-4 shows, children acquire sign language in the same way as oral language, but there are differences in how quickly children learn spoken and oral language.

These early utterances of children cannot be understood easily by an examination of the syntax or grammatical relations alone. A knowledge of the context in which early speech occurs is critical for capturing the child's meaning. For instance, 21-month-old Kathryn, as studied by Bloom (1970), was observed to say, "Mommy sock," in two separate contexts: when Kathryn picked up her mother's sock, and when mother was putting Kathryn's sock on Kathryn. In the first context, Kathryn was probably describing the sock as belonging to Mommy, whereas in the second context, she probably meant that Mommy was doing something involving a sock. Theoretically, "Mommy sock," might express many things, including "Mommy, is that a sock?" "Mommy, give me the sock," or perhaps even "Mommy, go sock Daddy!" As another example, Bloom (1970) has pointed out that the observed negative sentence "No dirty soap" could be interpreted in at least four ways: There is not dirty soap; the soap isn't dirty; that isn't dirty soap; and I don't want the dirty soap.

This young child and her mother communicating by sign language. Signing follows the same developmental course as spoken language.

Since the meaning is ambiguous from word order alone, Bloom and others (Clark, 1983; Garvey, 1990) recorded and evaluated the child's immediate behavior and the context in which the language occurs as a clue to the meaning. This is necessary in studying the child's progress in expressing meaning syntactically. Even as children move from words to sentences, in order to understand language, the context in which it occurs must be considered.

Why are the early utterances of children similar? Language can be viewed as a way of expressing what one understands about the world at a particular age. The content of what children say is closely related to their general level of intellectual functioning at any given stage in development. Children who are beginning to speak are also beginning to understand various environmental relationships, such as self-other distinctions, primitive concepts of causality, and notions about the permanence of objects. Therefore, beginning speakers all over the world use similar types of relations in their early speech, such as agent-action relations, possessives, disappearance, and reappearance. This is presumably because these particular relations are significant in the children's cognitive processes at that time. That is, semantic development and cognitive intellectual development are probably closely related (Clark, 1983).

The Emergence of Meaning Modifiers

One of the interesting achievements during the early phases of grammar acquisition is the way in which children learn to qualify the meaning of their utterances. This accomplishment also illustrates the close ties between semantic and grammar development. Roger Brown (1973) has provided the most complete description of the course of this type of grammatical development in children. In his longitudinal study of three children, Adam, Eve, and Sarah, he noted that children acquire certain morphemes in remarkably regular order. For example, during this period, children acquire

BOX 8-4 LANGUAGE LEARNING IN THE DEAF: SIGN LANGUAGE

Sign language, the system used by most prelinguistically deaf individuals, has been of interest to students of language. A central question concerns the similarity in the child's acquisition of oral language and sign language (Meier & Newport, 1990). Just as there are cross-cultural similarities in two-word phrases, the same semantic relations that occur in oral language appear in the first two sign strings in sign language. Compare the following examples observed in a child using sign language with the examples in Figure 8-3:

1 Daddy work (Daddy is at work).

2 Barry train (her brother's train).

3 Bed shoes (referring to slippers).

4 Daddy shoe (trying to persuade her father to take off his shoes and play in the sand).

We can see instances of (1) locative, (2) possessive, (3) attributive, and (4) agent-object strings that are remarkably similar to those observed in the language of speaking children (see Table 8-2). Similarly, the length of strings increases in a steady fashion, and just as in spoken language, children who use sign language tend to overgeneralize. Nor are young signing children always accurate; as with the early language of their speaking peers, early signs are not always perfect. Instead of pointing to their mouths, they may miss and point to their chins! Although the steps that children follow in learning language—either gestural or spoken—are similar, recent evidence suggests that learning sign language may occur faster and earlier than spoken language. In a longitudinal study of thirteen infants being reared by deaf parents, Bonvillian and his colleagues (Bonvillan, Orlansky, Novack, & Folven, 1983) found that these children learned "signs" several months earlier than children learning to speak. Most infants do not utter their first recognizable word before the end of the first year. The signing infants produced their first recognizable sign by 9 months. By 17 months, the children began to combine two or more signs—again two to three months ahead of speaking

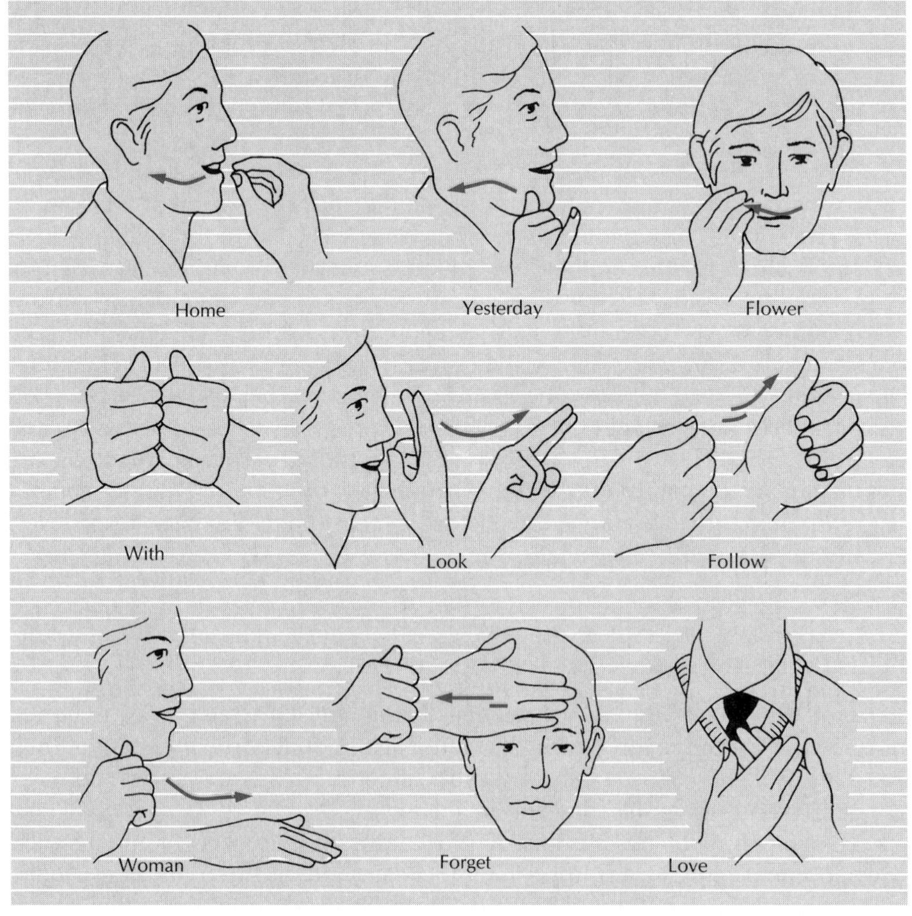

FIGURE 8-3
Some signs of American sign language. (*From Riekehof, 1963. Reprinted by permission.*)

BOX 8-4 LANGUAGE LEARNING IN THE DEAF: SIGN LANGUAGE (*Continued*)

children. However, the advantage doesn't appear to last. After 2 years of age, where cognitive development plays an increasingly important role in language acquisition, the differences between signers and speakers disappear (Bonvillian, Orlansky, & Folven, 1990). Nevertheless, these studies do suggest that some kinds of languages are more easily acquired—at least in the early stages—than others. Why? The most plausible explanation is that the motor centers of the brain are more fully developed than the speech centers and the rate of development of the speech centers during the first year proceeds more slowly.

In spite of the differences in rate of acquisition, the really important aspects of language and the really important abilities the child brings to the problem of language learning are independent of the modality in which the linguistic system operates. Language is a central process, not a peripheral one. The abilities that children have are so general and so powerful that they proceed through the same milestones of development as do hearing children (Dale, 1976, p. 59).

Sources: Bonvillian, J. D., Orlansky, M. D., & Folven, R. J. (1990). Early acquisition: Implications for theories of language acquisition. In V. Volterra & C. J. Erting (Eds.), *From gesture to language in hearing and deaf children*. Heidelberg: Springer-Verlag; Bonvillian, J. D., Orlansky, M. D., Novack, L. L., & Folven, R. J. (1983). Early sign language acquisition and cognitive development. In D. R. Rogers & J. A. Sloboda (Eds.), *The acquisition of symbolic skills*. New York: Plenum; Dale, P. S. (1976). *Language development: Structure and function* (2nd ed., pp. 54–59). New York: Holt; Meier, R. P., & Newport, E. L. (1990). Out of the hands of babes: On a possible sign advantage in language acquisition. *Language*, **66**(1), 1–23.

qualifiers to indicate plurality or to indicate a possessive. Table 8-3 lists the fourteen morphemes that Brown studied and the order in which they occur in English. Although the rate at which Adam, Eve, and Sarah acquired these morphemes varied, the order for each child was the same. Can we generalize from these children? Fortunately, we don't have to rely on this evidence alone. In a cross-sectional study, deVilliers and deVilliers (1973) studied not just three but twenty-one children and provided confirmation of Brown's

TABLE 8-3

SUFFIXES AND FUNCTION WORDS
Fourteen suffixes and function words in English

FORM	MEANING	EXAMPLE
1. Present progressive: -ing	Ongoing process	He is sitt*ing* down.
2. Preposition: in	Containment	The mouse is *in* the box.
3. Preposition: on	Support	The book is *on* the table.
4. Plural: -s	Number	The dog*s* ran away.
5. Past irregular: e.g., went	Earlier in time relative to time of speaking	The boy *went* home.
6. Possessive: -'s	Possession	The girl*'s* dog is big.
7. Uncontractible copula be: e.g., are, was	Number; earlier in time	*Are* they boys or girls? *Was* that a dog?
8. Articles: the, a	Definite/indefinite	He has *a* book.
9. Past regular: -ed	Earlier in time	He jump*ed* the stream.
10. Third person regular: -s	Number; earlier in time	She run*s* fast.
11. Third person irregular: e.g., has, does	Number; earlier in time	*Does* the dog bark?
12. Uncontractible auxiliary be: e.g., is, were	Number; earlier in time; ongoing process	*Were* they at home? *Is* he running?
13. Contractible copula be: e.g., -'s, -'re	Number; earlier in time	That*'s* a spaniel.
14. Contractible auxiliary be: e.g., -'s, -'re	Number; earlier in time; ongoing process	They*'re* running very slowly.

Source: Based on Brown (1973).

order of acquisition of morphemes. In general, Brown's claims have been confirmed by later investigators (Maratsos, 1989). Notice that the order is a sensible one. In terms of complexity, simpler morphemes are acquired earlier than more complex ones. For example, plurals, such as "s," are learned before the copula "be." We will see that this same general principle of development from simple to complex characterizes children's cognitive development as well. This parallel in the development of language and cognition has led some theorists to suggest that language development is dependent on the child's prior level of cognitive development (Clark, 1983).

Slobin (1985) suggests that children go through four phases in their application of grammatical rules such as the learning of plurals. First, they can't do it, of course. In phase two, they learn some of the irregular verbs such as "broke" and "went," but they memorize them. At this point, they haven't yet achieved a grammatical rule. However, without some general rules, language learning would be a very inefficient process. Imagine how long it would take children to learn to talk if they had to learn specific rules for each new set of words that they encountered. It would be very time-consuming if a child could learn that two dogs was dogs, but had to have a separate lesson to learn how to pluralize other words such as cat or house. In the third phase, children learn general grammatical rules, which can be used with new as well as familiar words. Only in the fourth stage, when the child is 7 to 8 years old, does the child finally begin to approach the full adult usage and recognize when to apply the general rule and when it is inappropriate to do so. When *not* to apply a rule is just as much a part of the acquisition process as when to do so!

Unfortunately, adult language does not always follow the rules and is full of exceptions and irregularities. When first learning a language, children ignore these irregularities and apply the rules in a rigid way. In other words, children show *overregularization* of rules they acquire. They apply a rule to form regularities in cases where the adult form is irregular and does not follow the rule. For instance, a young child may use the words "went" and "came" correctly. But after learning that "-ed" forms the past tense for many verbs, the child will use this ending on *all* verbs and will switch to saying "goed" and "comed" (Slobin, 1985). Similarly, a child often uses the word "feet" until the regular plural ending "-s" is learned; at that time, she switches to "foots" (or sometimes "feets"). In some cases, it has been reported that after learning that some plurals are formed by adding "-es" (such as "boxes"), the child may then say "footses" for a time.

Children also sometimes "create" regularized singular words from an irregular plural. For example, a child the authors knew used the word "clothes" and insisted on calling one piece of clothing a "clo." A different type of overregularization was demonstrated by a child who said, "I'm magic, amn't I?" It has been observed that young children in the Soviet Union and other countries also broadly apply the rules they learn to form novel "regularized" words and phrases that do not occur in adult speech (Slobin, 1982).

Further Steps on the Road to Formal Grammar

In the third year of life, "there is a grammatical flowering" (deVilliers & deVilliers, 1992, p. 378). Children's simple sentences start to become more subtle and complex, as children show early signs of understanding the rules of adult grammar (Valian, 1986). "The missing function words and inflections make their first appearance, although it is many months (sometimes even years) before they consistently appear in every context in which an adult would use them" (deVilliers & deVilliers, 1992, pp. 378–379).

Consider these achievements (deVilliers & deVilliers, 1992): (1) children start to use auxiliary and modal verbs: Daddy can run. I will run; (2) children begin to use questions: Can you run?; (3) children can negate simple sentences: No run; and (4) use simple tenses: I kicked it; and (5) children begin to use pronouns, articles, and even complex phrases: The teddy and doll are gonna play (deVilliers & deVilliers, 1992, p. 379).

Let us take a closer look at two of these grammar milestones: questions and negatives.

The Development of Questions and Negatives

Around the age of 3 to 3½ years children begin to use forms of the auxiliary verb "to be" which opens up the possibility of new forms of expressions, such as questions and negatives. In English, auxiliary verbs are central in many sentence structures including questions and negatives.

QUESTIONS

To express a question, young children first may simply use an assertion such as "sit chair" or "see hole," but raise their voice at the end to indicate that it is a question and not merely a statement.

I have some?

You like dis? (deVilliers & deVilliers, 1979)

Children's acquisition of "wh" questions begins in the latter part of the third year. Examples of "wh" questions are what, when, who, why, and which. In addition, children begin to use the question "how." The child's first such question is usually some variant of "whatsat," "whasit," "whatsit," "whaddes," "whatisdes" (deVilliers & deVilliers, 1979, 1992). In some cases, children learn these constructions early. Consider the following anecdote, which linguists Peter and Jill deVilliers tell about their son:

> At the age of 11 months, Nicholas picked up a whatisdat as one of his first "words" and pronounced it very accurately. We were trying in vain to keep him under control in a restaurant when he lunged over a neighboring diner's shoulder and demanded loudly, "Whatisdat?" to which the startled woman answered, "Fish!" (1979, p. 61)

Between 2 and 3, children's "wh" constructions may fail to include the auxiliary verb. They can be heard to say things like, "Where you going?" A little later they include the auxiliary without inverting it, for example, "Where you are going?" Finally, they incorporate all the rules for producing a "wh" question, for example, "Where are you going?"

One of the important features of "wh" questions is that they are an early way for children to begin to exercise their curiosity and ask "Why?" Again, we see that language and cognitive progress are closely tied, with each serving the other system and mutually promoting the child's overall development.

NEGATIVES

Many of the same stages found for children's question development hold for the development of negatives as well. Research indicates that children use different rules to form different kinds of negatives. Over 20 years ago Lois Bloom (1970) argued that there are three types of negation and they appear in a particular developmental order. "These categories include (1) non-existence: when the child remarks on the absence of something, for example, "no cake" or "all gone cookie" (2) rejection: when a child opposes something, for example, "no wash hair" and (3) denial: when the child denies the truth of a statement made or implied by someone else, for example, "that not daddy" (Tajer-Flusberg, 1985, p. 156). Language researchers have found that not only do these types of negations appear in this order in English (Bloom, 1970) but in Japanese (Clancy, 1985; McNeil & McNeil, 1968) as well.

The development of these two systems—negatives and questions—is only a sample of a wide range of grammatical accomplishments during the preschool years. By 3 years of age, children begin to use complex sentences "that drive nonlinguists to their descriptive grammar books" (deVilliers & deVilliers, 1991, p. 379). Again, progress is gradual but orderly. At first they tack on relative clauses, for example, "See the ball that I got", and only later do they interrupt a main clause with a subordinate clause, "The owl who eats the candy runs fast" (Slobin, 1985). And they ask and answer complex questions; "Where did you say you put my doll?", "These are punk rockers, aren't they?" (deVilliers & deVilliers, 1992, p. 379).

Although most fundamental forms of grammar are acquired by 4½ to 5 years, the process of grammar acquisition is not over during the preschool years. Specific aspects of syntax continue to develop through the elementary school years as children experience exceptions and try to understand them. In fact, mastering the intricacies of grammar, for most of us, is a life-long process!

Integrating Semantic and Grammatical Knowledge

Not only do children need to know how to speak grammatically correct sentences, they need to learn to *understand* the meaning of sentences. Knowledge of single words alone is insufficient. Children use a variety of types of information to make sense of sentences. Consider this situation:

> Imagine listening to a conversation on a noisy telephone line. Parts of words are obliterated by the noise. Often a word cannot be completely identified on the basis of the acoustic signal alone, but identification is generally easy because we have heard other words in the sentence and can narrow down the range of possibilities. For example, after *the boy* a verb is extremely likely; after *the red* a noun is very probable. If the conversation is a sensible one and if we know something about the topic, stronger predictions can be made on semantic grounds. After *the boy* the verb *lectured* is unlikely, though grammatically correct. (Dale, 1976, p. 189)

Can children use syntactic and semantic cues to help them understand sentences, and does the ability to use these kinds of information improve with age? Entwisle and Frasure (1974) utilized the "noisy telephone" technique with 6- to 9-year-old children. The children heard the following sentences with superimposed noise and were required to repeat the sentences. Since the noise blocked out part of the sentence, the children had to rely on their prior knowledge of how sentences are generally formed to fill in the missing words.

Meaningful: Bears steal honey from the hive.

Anomalous: Trains steal elephants around the house.

Scrambled: From shoot highways the passengers mothers.

The meaningful sentence was correct in terms of both syntax and semantics and therefore should be the easiest for the listener. Both grammar and meaning could serve as guidelines. The anomalous sentence doesn't make much sense, but it is syntactically correct. Grammar, not meaning, is the only guide. In the last type of sentence, neither syntax nor semantics is in order, and therefore this should be the most difficult for children to reproduce. Figure 8-4 confirms these predictions and indicates that as children develop, they are better able to use the syntactic and semantic information that is available.

Recent evidence indicates even 1½- to 3½-year-old children use semantic and syntactic cues to identify spoken words (Goodman, 1989). In a sentence completion task, children were presented with spoken sentences and filled in a final missing noun. For example, when presented with the utterance "Mommy feeds the ———," children said "baby." In a word identification task, children listened to complete sentences and pointed to pictures to identify the final word. In one condition, the sentence meaning constrained the final noun, but the noun actually spoken was *not* a member of the expected category. For example, when presented with the sentence, "Ann drives the duck" and pictures of a duck, truck, dog, and book, children chose the truck picture. When presented with the sentence, "The man sees the duck," however, children chose the duck picture. Even when given very complex sentence types, children understood semantic constraints. For example, "The boy put on his ———" elicited responses such as "shirt," but "Before bed, the boy put on his ———" elicited "pajamas." This is striking because children can use much more sophisticated syntactic and semantic contexts to understand sentences more complex than they can produce. They have a great deal of linguistic knowledge and they can use it to set up expectations about the identity of possible words.

In order to make sense of a number of English sentences, children must learn to violate some of the rules they have previously acquired. These semantically complex sentences may resemble simpler forms at the surface level. For example, in the two sentences, "John is eager to please" and "John is easy to please," the subject, John, takes on two very different functions. In "John is eager to please," John is doing the pleasing. But in "John is easy to please," John is the logical object, the one being pleased. This sentence is unusual in that the subject of a sentence is more often the actor than the

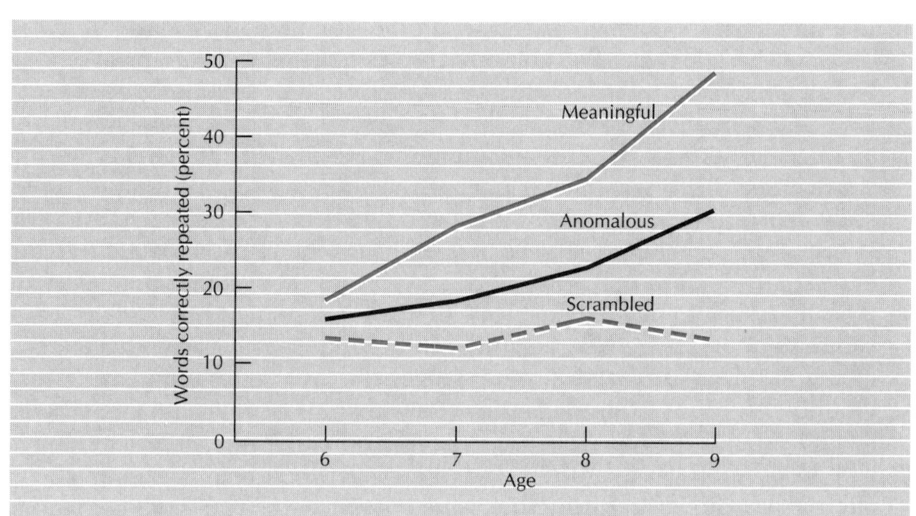

FIGURE 8-4
Percent of words repeated at four age levels as a function of syntactic and semantic structure. (*From Entwisle & Frasure, 1974. Reprinted by permission of the senior author and the American Psychological Association.*)

recipient of action. Most children younger than 8 or 9 years old are not able to understand this type of sentence in which the subject is also the logical object.

This phenomenon was investigated by Carol Chomsky (1969). In one of her experiments, she used a sentence with the same form as "John is easy to please." Her subjects were individually presented with a blindfolded doll and asked, "Is the doll easy to see or hard to see?" Finally, children were asked to make the doll easy or hard to see (opposite to their previous responses). Most of the youngest children (the 5-year-olds) misinterpreted the sentence. They initially said the blindfolded doll was "hard to see," and then took off the doll's blindfold in an effort to make her "easy to see." In contrast, all the 9-year-olds said the doll was "easy to see," and then hid the doll or covered their own eyes in an effort to make her "hard to see," thus demonstrating the correct interpretation of the sentence. The 6-, 7-, and 8-year-olds showed intermediate levels of correct interpretations. This is one of several experiments demonstrating that children's use of specific aspects of syntax continues to develop well into the school years, although the basic syntactic system is acquired in the preschool years (deVilliers & deVilliers, 1992; Marastsos, 1989).

Children's comprehension of many complex constructions remains poorly understood. We still don't know when children understand "John was thought by Mary to have been scratched by Sam" or "Whom do you think Mary could ask Sam to talk to about that?" (Maratsos, 1983). In summary, it is clear that children continue to develop in both their production and understanding of complex syntax well beyond the early school years. A comparison of children's speech at the first- and eighth-grade levels testifies to these developments in production. Listening to a third-grade English lesson and a college lecture on Shakespearean sonnets clearly indicates that comprehension continues to develop as well.

PRAGMATIC DEVELOPMENT: SPEAKING AND LISTENING

Pragmatic development refers to the appropriate use of language to accomplish various ends in differing social situations. Speakers have a variety of pragmatic intentions, such as getting people to do things for them, thanking or blaming people, and so forth, and they also need to know how to express their intentions appropriately, depending on the situation and speakers involved. Thus, even with syntax solvable and meaning meaningful, you still wouldn't be fully equipped to be an effective communicator. You must learn another set of rules, namely, when to use what language in which situations. To be an effective speaker requires a complicated set of skills. A number of things are required. First, you have to engage the attention of your listeners so they know that you want to address them and that they should listen. In addition, effective speakers have to be sensitive to listeners' feedback. If children don't know that they are not being understood, and don't know how to change their messages to make them clear, they are not going to be very successful communicators. Moreover, you must adjust your speech to the characteristics of the listeners—such the listener's age, sex and cultural and social background. You don't address visitors from Russia in English and expect them to understand. Nor do you use unique landmarks (the Trevi Fountain) to help lost visitors on their first trip to Rome. It won't help to talk to a 2-year-old in a day care center using the same vocabulary as you would to students in a college lecture hall. Being a good communicator requires that you adapt your message to take into account "who the listener is, what the listener already knows, and what the listener needs to know" (Glucksberg, Krauss & Higgins, 1975, p. 329). Finally, children must learn to adjust their speech to suit the situation. Children and adults learn to talk differently on a playground or street than in a church or a classroom.

Communication is a two-way process—an effective speaker is not enough. To have a conversation, for example, requires not only a competent speaker but a skilled listener as well. For effective communication, learning to listen is just as important as learning to speak.

> Listeners can do at least three things within a communicative interaction. First, they can judge or estimate their confidence or certainty of understanding. That is, they can recognize ambiguous or noninformative messages as such. Second, if they recognize that a message or communication is inadequate, they can make this known to the speaker. Finally, they can specify the additional information that is needed in order to clarify the message. (Glucksberg, Krauss, & Higgins, 1975, p. 331)

Children's understanding of the effectiveness of their own communicator or listener skills is another important determinant of their effectiveness in communication situations. In other words, when do children know that their own messages are clear and helpful and when do they know when someone else's message to them is unclear and inadequate?

To summarize, consider Garvey's (1990) characterization of the requirements for successful talk:

> Talking with another person requires the simultaneous engagement of several interconnected systems—a transmission system, a tracking and guidance system, and what might be called a facilitation system. The first system operates to assure the sending and reception of messages, the second to identify meanings, and the third to assure that the messages are acceptable and appropriate to the participants. . . . Many kinds of talk also require a fuel system, the motive force for talk, which includes meanings, intentions, and actions to be communicated. (Garvey, 1990, p. 31)

How early do children acquire these various communication skills? How do they develop? How do they shift across different types of communicative situations? We will explore these questions next.

Learning to Communicate

Speaker skills develop rapidly, and by 2 years of age, children are remarkably adept at engaging the attention of the listener and responding to listener feedback. Wellman and Lempers (1977) videotaped the interactions of ten 2-year-olds in their day-to-day interaction in a nursery school. They scored 300 referential communicative interactions where the communicator's intent was to point out, show, or display a particular object or referent to another child. The results were striking in their demonstration of the competence of 2-year-olds as speakers. These toddlers addressed their listeners when the two were either interacting or playing together (82 percent) or when the listeners were at least not involved with someone else (88 percent), when they could see each other (97 percent), when they were physically close to each other (91 percent), and to a lesser extent when the listeners were looking at them (41 percent). Similarly, the children made sure that they—as speakers—were close to the referent (92 percent) and so was the receiver (84 percent), to make it more likely that the receiver would understand the message. In light

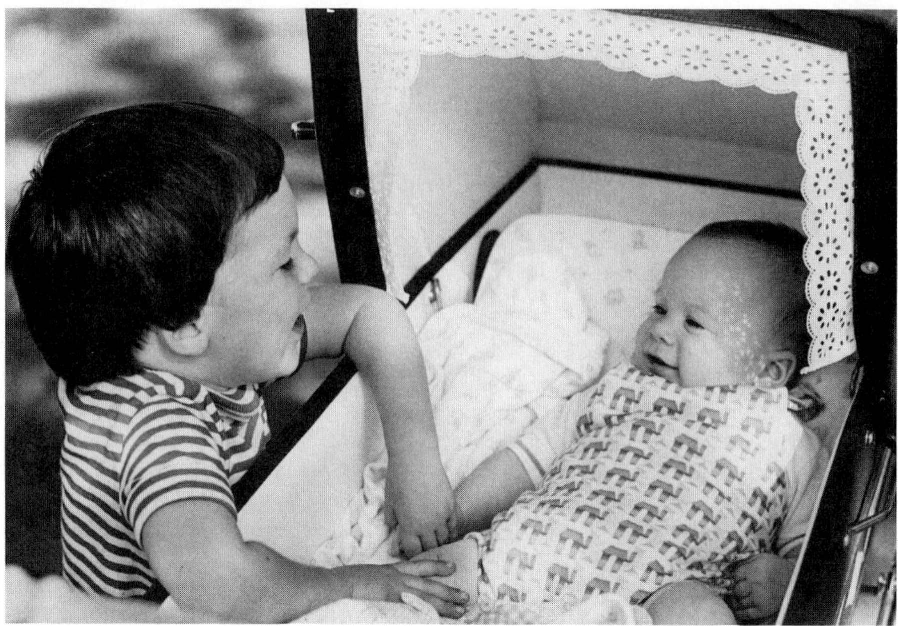

Children adjust their speech when talking to infants.

of these precautions on the part of our young speakers, it is not surprising that they were effectively able to engage their receivers. In fact, 79 percent of the messages met with an adequate response from the listener. Moreover, the children showed an awareness of the difficulty of the situation and adjusted their communications accordingly; they communicated more in difficult situations (for example, where there might be a visual obstacle or where the object is hard to locate, such as a single toy in a toy box) and used shorter messages in easy situations. Finally, these children were responsive to feedback from their partners. For example, in 54 percent of the cases where the speakers received no response, they repeated their message in some form; in only 3 percent of the cases where they received an adequate response did they repeat. Or if the listener either just looked or gave a negative verbal reaction—an indication that the listener didn't understand—the children always recommunicated. In sum, these 2-year-olds were surprisingly sophisticated speakers.

Children adjust their speech when talking to children of different ages. Children as young as 2 years of age show these adjustments. Two and 3-year-olds adjusted their speech when talking to 14-month-old siblings. In contrast to speech addressed to their mothers, these toddlers used more repetitions and more attention-eliciting words ("hey," "hello," "look") when talking to their baby brothers and sisters (Dunn, 1988; Dunn & Kendrick, 1982). These adjustments are not limited to the family. Four-year-olds switch their speech when talking to unfamiliar adults and unfamiliar 2-year-olds (Gelman & Shatz, 1977; Shatz, 1983). When speaking to a 2-year-old, they used shorter utterances than when speaking to adults. Consider these contrasting utterances to an adult and a 2-year-old listener:

> AM (to adult) . . . You're supposed to put one of these persons in, see? Then, one goes with the other little girl. And then the little boy. He's the little boy and he drives. And then they back up. And then the little girl has marbles. . . .
> AM (to younger child) . . . Watch Perry. Watch this. He backing in here. Now he drives up. Look, Perry, look here. Those are marbles, Perry. Put the men in here. Now, I'll do it" (Shatz & Gelman, 1973).

In spite of their sophistication as communicators, there are limitations. Preschoolers are better in a one-to-one conversation and do less well when they have to compete for their turn with adults and other children. Before $4\frac{1}{2}$ years of age, according to Ervin-Tripp (1979), children interrupt and are interrupted more often when in a group of other speakers than when talking to another child alone. Moreover, children have trouble tracking the conversations of two or more people and have trouble gauging when to enter the conversation or to judge competently when it is their turn. On the other hand, all of us know adults who seem not to have learned these lessons very well either! Children are more competent when speaking about single familiar objects that are present in their immediate environment than speaking about absent objects (in time or space), internal referents (one's own feelings, motivations, thoughts), and relationships of one or more referents (relationships over space and time, the functions of referents) (Dunn, 1988; Shatz, 1983). Clearly, speaking does improve as the child develops. However, in combination with the other evidence that we have reviewed, it is clear that speaker skills develop at different rates for different kinds of communication tasks.

How do children acquire such sophisticated sociolinguistic skills? Just as in the case of many forms of social behavior, direct instruction and observational learning clearly play important roles (Bandura, 1989; Dunn, 1988). In addition, children learn these skills by listening to stories or narratives about earlier events that help them acquire rules of how to communicate with others (Miller & Sperry, 1987). Much of what children learn from parents about the culturally appropriate use of language involves the acquisition of subtle and complex social conventions and moral rules (we will examine this issue in detail in Chapter 16). Box 8-5 illustrates how children learn the appropriate rules governing the expression of anger. When, where, and to whom it is appropriate to express anger, is a clear example of a cultural norm. On the other side, children learn how to use positive or politeness scripts, such as hello and goodbye, and please and thank-you. These simple social routines are often children's first formal communicative acts (Grief & Gleason, 1980) and are present in all cultures, not just our own (Schieffelin & Ochs, 1987). In short, children in all cultures learn a variety of social rules about language use that help make their normal social encounters with others easier and more predictable.

Learning to Listen

Being a good listener requires that you know when a message is clear. Young children are often unaware that they do not understand a message. In one experiment, Markman (1977) gave first and third graders instructions for a game that left out critical information which made it impossible to play the game. The younger children were unaware of the inadequacy of the communicator's message and often had to be urged to try to play the game before becoming aware of the problems. In contrast, the third graders noticed the inadequacy of the message more readily. Others (Flavell, Speer, Green, & August, 1981) find a similar developmental trend: Kindergarten children were less likely than second graders to recognize that a communication—in this case, about how to build a toy house—was defective.

Again, the difficulty of the task makes a difference. As Revelle, Wellman, & Karabenick (1985) have found, even 3-year-olds recognize an ambiguous message when they hear one and can act in appropriate ways to resolve the communication gap if the task is simplified. During a play session, an adult made a variety of requests of 3- and 4-year-olds. In some cases, the requests

BOX 8-5 THE ROLE OF LANGUAGE IN THE SOCIALIZATION OF ANGER AND AGGRESSION

Cultures and subcultures vary in the ways in which particular emotions are expressed and their intensity, and the contexts in which these emotions are expressed. A major question for developmentalists is how children are socialized into the culturally appropriate expression of emotion. During intensive home observations and parent interviews, Peggy Miller and Linda Sperry (1987) observed the early socialization of anger and aggression in three young children from an urban, working-class community in South Baltimore. They found that language plays a central role in this process. First, talk was a major method through which children learned when and how to express and respond to anger and aggression. Second, talk was a major tool through which anger and aggression was expressed. Language encodes not only emotion states (for example, anger) but also instigating events, reasons, plans, overt actions, and consequences. A person may choose to speak of any of these aspects, but cultures may favor the verbal expression of some aspects rather than others.

In South Baltimore, justification of anger by reference to social and moral standards was central, while discussions of emotion states was discouraged. Children learned these cultural norms in a variety of contexts. First, mothers told numerous informal narratives in the presence of their young children about events in which someone got mad or responded with verbal or nonverbal aggression. Explicit reference to the state of anger was not an essential element in these stories. What was essential was to justify the retaliative responses (for example, a silencing put-down) by linking it to the transgression that caused it (for example, an unprovoked insult).

> I was walkin' on Charles St.—and the girl happens to be my girlfriend now. She big and fat, boy. She could sit on me and flatten me out, but I stuck up to her. Her name was Janie. And she hung with the bad people too, boy. And she says, "Look at that big-nosed B-I-T-C-H." And I turned around and I says, "Uh, you talkin' to me?" I said, "ARE YOU TALKIN' TO ME?" I says, "Well, you fat slob you, I put you in a skillet and strip you down to normal size, if you mess with me." (p. 13)

Children also learned about anger and aggression through playful interactions initiated by mothers as a way of preparing them for real-life encounters. All of the mothers were concerned that children be able to defend themselves, and all were observed to initiate playful teasing with their children. Two mothers volunteered that they even initiated playful fighting as a way of preparing the child for real-life encounters.

> That's why a lot of times when we used to play little games together, I'd take my fist and like punch her in the chest. You know, not hard enough to hurt her, but you know, to knock her down. She'd get back up. She'd think it was funny, right? Or I'd take my fist and I'd hit her in the arm and then she'd hit me back. I'd pretend it hurt and I'd (say) "Oh, you know," but it toughened her up. When she got out there to where somebody really meant it, then she realized, you know, "Hey, this is it, they're really pickin' on me." And she just, you know, punch back. (p. 18)

Children also learned about anger and aggression through their mothers' direct responses to their own anger and aggression. While each mother encouraged their children to defend themselves against other's aggression, if a child was at fault, the anger/aggression was viewed as inappropriate and required an apology.

By the age of 2 to $2\frac{1}{2}$ years, children controlled a variety of verbal resources for communicating anger and aggression and showed rudimentary ability to justify their anger. All children formulated accusations signifying that they recognized breaches in moral rules and had learned something about the rules for when to respond with anger/aggression, namely, when one has been wronged. Children also learned how to communicate anger and aggression. Children did not use anger labels. Rather, they learned to refer to acts of aggression rather than to feelings of anger. Children also learned to defend themselves verbally. Their talk was not emotion talk but moral talk, embodying rules and standards. These responses were consistent with mothers' childrearing ideology (self-protection and defense) and mothers' disproportionate use of verbs of aggression rather than anger labels.

In sum, social and moral standards are critically implicated in the socialization of anger and aggression. Language is both a central medium through which these rules are conveyed, and a potent tool for expression of anger. Children in South Baltimore learned to distinguish justified from unjustified anger. This distinction was conveyed through mothers' direct responses to their children's anger and through talk about personal experiences occurring in the child's presence. By $2\frac{1}{2}$ children understood the rule that they need to justify anger and aggression by reference to another's instigating act.

Source: Miller, P., & Sperry, L. (1987). The socialization of anger and aggression. *Merrill-Palmer Quarterly*, **33**, 1–31.

were ambiguous, such as asking for the cup without specifying which of four different ones was correct. Or the adult might yawn in the middle of the request, making it difficult to hear clearly. In other cases, the request was either impossible—"Bring me the refrigerator" (only a real one was available)—or the object was unavailable—"Bring me your mother's slippers." Even the 3-year-olds showed clear evidence that they could recognize when a request was problematic. Moreover, preschoolers knew how to remedy the communication problem by requesting more information. For example, even 3-year-olds said, "How? It's too heavy," when asked to bring the refrigerator. As Revelle and associates (1985) suggest, "Essential skills involved in monitoring communication are realizing that problems can occur, recognizing when they do and knowing how to remediate them" (p. 22). Three- and four-year-olds seem to possess all of these fundamental monitoring skills.

It has been shown that 6- to 10-year-old children can be taught to be better listeners; children who were encouraged to ask the speaker clarifying questions performed more effectively than children who were not given this lesson in listening (Cosgrove & Patterson, 1977; Patterson & Kister, 1981). Four-year-olds, however, did not benefit from the instruction, which suggests that this type of listener strategy may be a moderately advanced communication skill.

OTHER ASPECTS OF LANGUAGE

Figurative Language

Figurative expressions such as "Clouds are like pillows," "A seed is like a pregnant woman," and "The rose is out of town," are powerful imaginative communications. These expressions communicate something about a concept by comparing it to a similar concept from a different conventional category. When do children begin to produce and comprehend metaphor and other forms of figurative speech? Almost as soon as they start to talk, children produce utterances that have the superficial appearance of a metaphor. According to Winner, McCarthy, Kleinman, and Gardner (1979), a 26-month-old child exclaimed "Corn, corn!" while pointing to a yellow plastic baseball bat, and an 18-month-old called a toy car a snake while twisting it up his mother's arm. Utterances such as these are known as "child metaphors" because they violate the conventions of naming (they refer to things by a name different from their literal names) or because they involve a comparison between two objects that belong to different conventional categories.

The comprehension of metaphor is conceptualized as a continuous process that starts very early and develops gradually to encompass a greater variety of figurative linguistic inputs (Gentner & Stuart, 1983; Vosniadou, 1987; Winner, 1988). What develops is the ability to understand more complex metaphorical inputs in a variety of linguistic and situational contexts. The development of metaphor comprehension is constrained primarily by limitations in children's conceptual knowledge and linguistic skill (Vosniadou, 1987). Even adults would find it difficult to compare items they know little about. In addition, metaphoric expressions can take a variety of linguistic forms, and some of these forms appear to be easier to understand than others. For example, similes are based on nonliteral similarity but unlike predicative metaphors are explicit comparisons. As such, they are easier for children to understand (Vosniadou, 1987). One can find evidence of the comprehension of figurative speech in very young children if the metaphors used are simple, and if they occur in the appropriate context (Winner, 1988). While the beginnings of metaphor comprehension emerge during the preschool years, this development is not complete until the late childhood years when the child's conceptual and linguistic knowledge approximates that of the adult. Although children's ability to produce and comprehend metaphoric language depends critically on what they already know, metaphors may advance and enrich conceptual development itself. Metaphoric competence is based on children's ability to see similarities among objects and events in the world around them. This ability not only plays a fundamental role in categorization, it also allows children to use existing knowledge to understand new things. Metaphors reflect the transfer of knowledge from well-known to less familiar domains and, as such, may serve as important mechanisms in the acquisition of new knowledge (Vosniadou, 1987).

METALINGUISTIC AWARENESS, OR KNOWING ABOUT LANGUAGE

One of the crowning achievements in language development and one of the latest to develop is the ability not merely to know language in the sense of being able to speak and understand it, but to know *about* language. By this we mean that children know that they know language and can think and talk about language.

Do children understand that words are made up of discrete sounds? Can children tell you what a word is? When can children distinguish between grammatically correct and incorrect sentences? This ability—or *metalinguistic awareness*—emerges well after children are proficient producers of sounds and sentences (Bullinger & Chatillon, 1983). Before age 5, children have trouble recognizing that words are groups of sounds and are baffled if you ask them to tell you the first sound in their names. Reflecting on sounds is a lot tougher than making them for children! Nor are words any easier to talk about. Instead, before age 8, children confuse words with the object that they describe. Words are cats, toys, and cars, but children have trouble articulating the concept that words are language parts that are independent of the objects or events to which they refer (Wetstone, 1977). Only from age 10 onward do children define words as "meaning something" (Berthoud-Papandropoulou, 1978).

To determine children's understanding of grammar, ask children to judge between grammatical and ungrammatical sentences and acceptable and unacceptable word order. Here is one example. In this investigation, deVilliers and deVilliers (1972) tested children's ability to judge and correct word order in active sentences. Using the clever technique of asking children to teach a puppet to talk correctly, they were required to correct the puppet's language. Sometimes the puppet spoke in correct word order (for example, "Eat the cake"), while at other times the puppet spoke in reversed order ("Dog the pat") or in a semantically anomalous fashion ("Drink the chair"). The children both indicated whether the puppet was right or wrong and were required to help the puppet say it the "right way." There was a clear relationship between the children's level of language development and their metalinguistic awareness; as their ability to produce and comprehend sentences increased, their awareness increased (deVilliers & deVilliers, 1992). But insight lags behind production and comprehension:

> A child may "know" a particular linguistic rule, in the sense of following the rule in producing sentences and understanding sentences when the only cue is the structure described by the rule long before he can consciously state the rule or use it to make judgments of grammatical or ungrammatical sentences . . . The process of becoming aware of language is one that continues throughout

development. In its highest form, it becomes the basis of aesthetic pleasure in poetry and prose. (Dale, 1976. p. 128)

SUMMARY

WHY STUDY LANGUAGE DEVELOPMENT?

- Language serves a variety of purposes for the developing child. It facilitates interpersonal communication, helps organize thinking, and aids in learning. The study of language acquisition can provide a window into children's cognitive and social-emotional development.

THE FOUR FACES OF LANGUAGE

- The study of language can be divided into four areas. *Phonology* describes the system of sounds for a language, or how the basic sound units, called phonemes, are connected to form words. *Semantics* is the study of the meaning of words and sentences. *Grammar* describes the structure of a language, and includes syntax and morphology. Finally, *pragmatics* is defined as the rules that govern the use of language in different social contexts for various purposes.

SOME CONTRASTING VIEWS ON LANGUAGE DEVELOPMENT

- One view of language development, proposed by B. F. Skinner, is that language is acquired through imitation and the principles of classical and operant conditioning set forth in traditional *learning theory*. Although learning principles seem to be important in modifying language usage, they do not explain the regular sequence of language development, the creative utterances children come up with, or the fact that children learn to speak grammatically when parents rarely reinforce grammar.
- Noam Chomsky proposed a *nativist* position to account for language development. According to this view, children have an innate language acquisition device (LAD) that enables them to learn language early and quickly. Support for this position comes from evidence that there may be a critical period for learning language and that children in a wide variety of cultures master language in a predictable and similar way. Critics point out that the first word combinations of young children are not based on the consistent use of formal grammatical rules and that language acquisition is not accomplished as quickly as nativists once thought.
- Most modern theorists take an *interactionist* position which recognizes that children are biologically prepared for language, but require extensive experience with expressed language for adequate development. According to this view, children play an active role in acquiring language by formulating, testing, and evaluating hypotheses concerning the rules of their languages.
- Parents and other adults play a critical role as facilitators of a child's language acquisition by using a variety of devices that may aid the child's learning. American middle-class mothers support a child's beginning language by using tactics such as nonverbal games, simplified speech, expansion of a child's statements, and recasting a child's incomplete sentence into a grammatical form. However, not all cultures provide these supports, indicating that such devices are not necessary for learning language.

THE ANTECEDENTS OF LANGUAGE DEVELOPMENT

- Preverbal communication begins by about 3 months of age when the beginnings of conversational turn-taking are observed in *pseudodialogues* between infants and caregivers. By the end of the first year babies know a lot about communication, shown by their use of gestures and verbalizations aimed at getting someone to do or look at something.
- Even young infants demonstrate specialized language abilities, including selective attention, voice discrimination, and specific phoneme perception. As children are exposed to their native languages, their abilities to distinguish and categorize phonemes continue to be refined and specialized for the sounds within their language.
- The child's early production follow an orderly sequence, beginning with crying, then cooing, babbling, and ending with patterned speech by the end of the first year. By 12 months, babbling includes a broad range of vowels and consonants and a variety of stress and intonation patterns that sound much like conversational speech. The expansion of babbled sounds results from the maturation of the vocal structures and from hearing language in the environment.

SEMANTIC DEVELOPMENT

- In early childhood children use *fast mapping* to connect a new word with an underlying concept in order to build large vocabularies with great speed. Recent evidence suggests that this feat is possible because young children's hypotheses about word meanings are limited by taxonomic and mutual exclusivity constraints which allow them to focus on the most likely object for the new word. Object words appear to be easier to learn than action words, thus most of children's first words are objects that they can act on to produce a change or movement. Typical errors in children's early word use include *overextension*, or using a single word to mean different things, and *underextension*, using a word to mean only a particular instance rather than the more general category.

THE ACQUISITION OF GRAMMAR: FROM WORDS TO SENTENCES

- Between the ages of 1 and 2, children are speaking their first words and building their vocabularies. During this period, single-word utterances are typically combined with gestures and intonation which seem to express thoughts that are larger than one word.
- Around 18-20 months of age, children usually begin to put two words together. Although nouns, verbs, and adjectives are generally present, other forms such as articles and prepositions are often absent. A knowledge of the context in which these utterances occur is typically needed in order to understand the child's meaning. There is a high degree of similarity in the semantic relations found in two-word combinations for different languages. They also may be beginning to formulate restricted word-based rules that will form the basis for later grammatical structures.
- During the early phases of grammar acquisition, children learn to alter the meaning of their utterances by using qualifiers (e.g., adding "-s" for possessive). They typically learn simpler morphemes first and add more complex ones later. As children begin to learn the rules of grammar, they ignore irregularities and exceptions, and *overregularize* the rules by applying them to all cases.

- By age $3\frac{1}{2}$, children's use of particular kinds of words, such as adjective, article, and nouns, is highly consistent, suggesting that they understand adult grammatical categories to use. Children begin to ask "Wh" questions and negatives, which require the use of auxiliary verbs and inversion of subject and verb. More complex aspects of syntax continue to be acquired through the preschool and elementary school years.
- Children use both syntactic and semantic cues to understand the meaning of sentences. Although these cues are used by toddlers to identify missing words, children's comprehension of complex sentence structures continues to develop throughout the elementary school years.

PRAGMATIC DEVELOPMENT: SPEAKING AND LISTENING

- Pragmatic development is the ability to use language appropriately to accomplish various communication goals in differing social situations. To be effective communicators children need to be able to send and receive messages, to be able to identify meanings, and to make sure that their messages are appropriate for the listeners.
- During the preschool years, children are surprisingly sophisticated speakers. They adjust their communications depending on the situation, feedback from the partner, and the age and status of the listener. However, they are not as adept at talking in groups as in pairs because they are not good judges of when it is their turn and have trouble tracking the conversation. Children probably learn sociolinguistic skills from observation of others and from direct instruction about some social forms.
- A major skill required of a good listener is knowing when a message has not been understood. Young children often are unaware that they do not understand a message. Although 3- and 4-year-olds seem to possess fundamental monitoring skills, as children develop they become better discriminators of good and poor messages.

FIGURATIVE LANGUAGE

- Understanding figurative expressions, such as metaphors, begins during the preschool years. However, development of the ability to produce and comprehend metaphoric language is not complete until the late childhood years because it is based on the child's ability to see similarities among objects and events.

METALINGUISTIC AWARENESS OR KNOWING ABOUT LANGUAGE

- *Metalinguistic awareness*, the ability to think and talk about language, emerges well after children are able to produce complex communications. They do not understand the concept of "words" until after age 10, and they may use a grammatical rule long before they understand it. Thus, knowledge about language is a late-developing achievement.

CHAPTER 9

THEORIES OF COGNITIVE DEVELOPMENT

One of the main tasks confronting children is understanding the world in which they live. As adults we take for granted that objects exist when we can see them and continue to exist when we cannot. Further, we assume that these objects will behave in a stable and predictable manner. We know how objects appear and what attributes they can possess: objects can be both red and big, but they cannot be both big and small. We know that because of gravity an object will fall down, not up. We understand time and space and realize that two objects cannot occupy the same space at the same time. Based on this knowledge, we form expectations about people, objects, and situations. Although the sun is slipping down behind the western horizon, we expect it to reappear tomorrow morning in the east. If we drop a fragile glass, we expect it to fall to the floor and break. We expect children to run and shout in the playground but not in the classroom. We even comprehend the significance of symbols—of language, the written word, music, art, and social gestures.

The study of cognitive development is concerned with describing and understanding the ways in which children's intellectual abilities and their knowledge of the world change through the course of development. Cognition refers to mental activity and behavior through which knowledge of the world is attained and processed, including learning, perception, memory, and thinking. The concept of cognition is such a broadly integrative one that most of the topics covered in the previous chapters of this book have relevance for cognitive development. Biological factors, environmental and experiential factors, social factors, emotions, and motivation all play a role in cognitive development.

The next three chapters in this book examine different aspects of cognitive development. In this chapter we will examine different theories proposed to explain the course of cognitive development. Each of these theories offers a different explanation for the pattern of children's developing intellectual abilities; however they must all explain the same basic abilities in children. These basic abilities will be covered in Chapter 10. We will also relate children's performance in a variety of cognitive tasks to the theories covered in this chapter. Chapter 11 will focus on individual differences in mental abilities and the factors that contribute to these differences, particularly in the area of intelligence and intelligence testing.

Several different models of the psychological processes and intellectual structures that underlie cognitive development will be presented in this chapter. The first model is one that emphasizes developmental changes in the organization or structure of children's thinking processes, and how differences in these structures are reflected in the way children learn at different ages. In this chapter, Piaget's monumental theory of cognitive development, which evolved from his own interest in natural science and from observations of his own children, will be presented as an example of this approach.

A second model of cognitive development, the information processing approach, will also be examined. This view emerged from a comparison between the workings of the human mind and the computer. Information processing theorists view children as having an array of cognitive processes and strategies which help them to process information. Consequently, rather than focusing on structural changes which occur with age, this model explores the role of cognitive operations used to learn about objects and events in the world.

We will discuss a third model of cognitive development which merges aspects of Piaget's theory and information processing, the neo-Piagetians. The synthesis of these two theories produces a model which proposes structural changes brought about by changes in strategy use. Finally, we will discuss the influential theory proposed by Lev Vygotsky, a Russian psychologist who proposes that cultural influences and children's level of cognitive competence interact to cause development.

PIAGET'S COGNITIVE DEVELOPMENTAL THEORY OF INTELLIGENCE

One of the most important, detailed, and controversial theories of intellectual development is that of the Swiss scientist Jean Piaget (Beilin, 1992). Piaget began his career at a very early age. In 1907, at the age of 10, he published his first article on a rare albino sparrow in a natural history journal. His later writing on mollusks led to the offer, sight unseen, of the position of curator of the mollusk collection in the Geneva Museum of Natural History. The chagrined director of the museum hastily withdrew his offer when he discovered that the creative young biologist was still a schoolboy. Piaget continued to be interested in biology and by 1920 began to integrate into his work the relationship between biology and psychology, particularly in the area of development. Piaget was a prolific writer. In the two decades to follow he published a remarkable series of books on the intellectual development of children and by the time of his death in 1980 (at the age of 84) he had produced over 40 books and more than 200 articles.

Despite this massive amount of published work, Piaget's influence on developmental psychology in America did not begin until the early 1960s. One factor leading to this delay was the climate of American psychology at the time of Piaget's writing. Child psychology in the 1930s and 1940s was largely a descriptive field without a theoretical focus. The topic of interest to most psychologists of the day was the measurement and description of

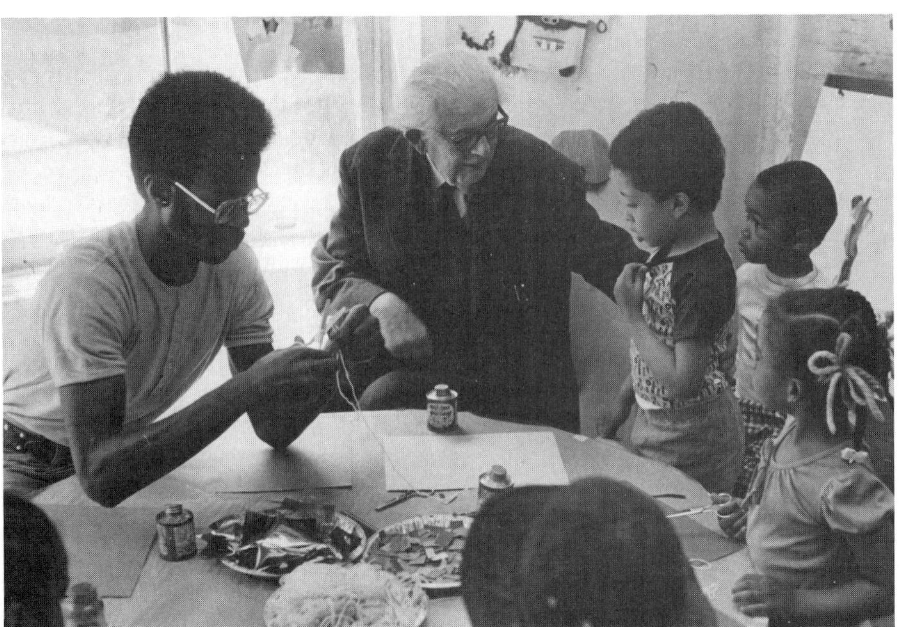

Jean Piaget—a pioneer in cognitive development.

intelligence rather than explanation of its development. When theory did impinge on child psychology in the late 1940s, it was predominantly in the form of stimulus-response theories—derived from the behaviorism of John B. Watson—which had dominated the mainstream of psychology for twenty years. Stimulus-response theorists emphasized the role of learning rather than any innate predispositions, processes, or structures in intellectual development. They were not concerned with differences in learning in terms of age; rather, their goal was to discover the unifying principles of learning which would hold across all ages. Standard laws of conditioning, reinforcement, generalization, and extinction were invoked to explain the behavior of both children and adults. A theory such as Piaget's, which proposed radically different mechanisms applied at different points in development, was contrary to their view of psychology.

By the end of the 1950s, however, the influence of behaviorism began to wane. Despite the attempts of the learning theorists, no completely satisfying developmental theory existed and, further, disenchantment with learning theory itself had set in. Some psychologists claimed it was not a real developmental theory since it did not allow for the different capacities of children at different ages. Piaget's theory presented an attractive alternative; it was a genuinely developmental theory derived from direct observations of children. Thus, when in 1963 John Flavell published *The Developmental Theory of Jean Piaget,* a lucid, comprehensive summary and analysis of Jean Piaget's work, the Piagetian perspective began to be widely cited and researched.

Piaget's unique perspective on development took shape during his work in the Binet laboratory in Paris with Theophile Simon, one of the developers of the first intelligence tests. While working with Simon, Piaget participated in the design of standardized intelligence tests. He found, however, that the children's incorrect responses were often more enlightening than their correct responses. Further, he noticed that children of the same age made similar errors, and that these errors differed from those of older or younger children. These differences in the type of errors made by children of different ages seemed to reveal varying developmental strategies or processes in thinking. For Piaget, the study of *what* children know was only an avenue to understanding changes in *how* children think.

In order to attain this goal Piaget used an unstructured method of questioning children. During these unstructured interview sessions it was the child's responses and not a standardized procedure which directed the questioning. Many of his conclusions were derived from detailed observations and question sessions with his own three children, Laurent, Lucienne, and Jacqueline. This looseness in Piaget's methodology is frequently criticized by more rigorously oriented psychologists, a criticism which still remains despite Piaget's later attempts to test some of his hypotheses with more controlled experiments.

Structures and Processes of Piaget's Theory

The goal of Piaget's theory of cognitive development (Piaget, 1952) is to explain how children adapt to and interpret objects and events in the world. How do children learn about the functions of objects such as toys, furniture, clouds, and food? How do they learn to group objects based on similar characteristics? To understand how and why things change and to form expectations based on these changes? Organizing all this knowledge is a formidable task; one which Piaget felt children played an active role in accomplishing. According to Piaget, children do not passively wait to take in information from their environment. On the contrary, although children's thought processes and conceptions of reality are modified by their encounters with the world about them, they actively seek out information and adapt it to the knowledge and conceptions of the world which they already have, thus constructing their knowledge of reality from their own experiences.

COGNITIVE STRUCTURES

Piaget places great emphasis on children's organization of their behaviors and knowledge into increasingly more complex structures. He builds much of his theory around *schemata,* or cognitive structures which form a basis for organizing behavior in order to respond to the environment. Schemata differ qualitatively among children in different developmental stages. These cognitive structures are not physical entities in the brain; rather, they are an interrelated and organized group of memories, thoughts, actions, and strategies that the child uses when attempting to understand a particular situation. Children possess many different schemata and these schemata change as the children develop.

Even infants' behavior reflects some organized pattern of relating to, or "knowing," their environment. It is not the same kind of process used by older children and adults; we "know" our world through the use of internal mental representations, such as intentions, expectations, plans, and goals, and through the use of symbol systems, such as language and mental imagery. Rather, in the newborn the schemata take the form of innate reflexes and "reaction patterns." For example, newborns will suck anything that touches their lips. In adapting to their environment, they carry out organized sucking behaviors in response to a wide range of suckable objects. Thus, they may be said to possess a sucking *schema.* They possess many other schemata, such as grasping, kicking, looking, and hitting, that are manifested in organized patterns of activities. These early schemata are rapidly modified as infants interact with the world around them. Although these early schemata are primitive in their reliance on sensory input and physical activity, the infant is responding to objects in an organized way.

As the child grows and gains experience, there is a gradual shift from schemata based on overt physical activities (such as the sucking example above) to schemata based on internal mental activities. Piaget calls these mental equivalents of behavioral schemata *operations.* Operations are formed when the physically based schemata of younger children are internalized and become part of an organized structure. Operations can become quite complex and can include strategies, plans, rules for problem solving and for classification. Thus, previously acquired kicking, reaching, and grasping schemata can become part of a complex plan for possessing a favorite toy which has been taken from the child. Note that while operations may eventually be put into overt physical action, they are formed by organizing a set of mental structures. These internal structures used by older children become increasingly more similar to those used in adult thought, and less similar to the mental operations of younger children.

COGNITIVE PROCESSES

Piaget proposed that even young infants form schemata. However, the schemata formed by infants' motoric interactions with their environment must undergo some transformations to be appropriate for older children and adults. Piaget proposes that certain unlearned principles of processing and responding to experience result in the continuous modification of schemata. The most important of these inherited principles are *organization* and *adaptation*.

Organization is the predisposition to combine simple physical or psychological structures into more complex systems. In the previously cited example of the sucking schema, the infant may initially have a sucking reflex, a looking reflex, and a grasping reflex that function independently. These separate simple behaviors are gradually organized into a high-order system involving the coordination of all these activities. After organizing these three reflexes into a schema the infant can look at an object, grasp it, and then place it in his mouth to suck on it.

The second principle, that of *adaptation,* involves two processes: *assimilation* and *accommodation.* These two processes interact to modify children's existing schemata. When a child has a new experience he *assimilates* it into his existing schemata. That is, he molds the new information to fit into his current cognitive structures and level of understanding. Based on this new information he alters his response to the experience. For example, a young child who has never seen a spinning top might assimilate this new toy into a familiar schema, perhaps that of "round toys." The child may then assimilate the top into this schema and respond accordingly—bouncing and rolling the top around his playroom. Thus, assimilation allows children to use previously acquired knowledge to understand new experiences, to form predictions about new events, and to come to conclusions about new objects, people, and situations.

Accommodation is a complementary process to that of assimilation. When accommodating, rather than adjusting his response to new experiences based on schemata he possesses, the child adjusts his schemata to fit the new experience. This coping with the environment results in the continuous modification of schemata. If an adult shows the child the appropriate function of the top, the child will modify his schema and begin to spin the top in the proper manner. Thus, schemata can be continually modified and updated to include new information.

Most environmental encounters involve both assimilation and accommodation. Take, for example, the simple schema of sucking. Infants may try their sucking schema on many objects. They may suck their bottles, their thumbs, their pacifier, the ears of their teddy bears, or the plastic birds on their mobiles. Some of these objects, such as bottles, thumbs, and pacifiers, fit more easily into the infant's schema of "suckable" objects than others and thus may involve more assimilation than accommodation. Thus, the child's schema of "suckable" objects remains unchanged and the child will relate, or assimilate, the new objects in his existing sucking scheme. In response to objects such as the plastic birds, the child's sucking schema, as it exists, may not be appropriate. The wings may be sharp and the plastic distasteful and the plastic bird may not fit easily into the child's mouth. Consequently, the child will have to modify, or accommodate, the schema to fit the characteristics of the new object. Thus, in adapting to the bird mobile, the child may accommodate by changing his sucking schema to include merely sucking on the soft body rather than the entire object, or he may give up his sucking schema and entertain himself by using a hitting or kicking response to make the birds move.

Cognitive development therefore is based on alterations in intellectual structures resulting from innate predispositions to organize and to adapt experience in certain ways. These processes are found in all normal children and continue to operate throughout the life span.

Piaget's Developmental Stages

Piaget viewed the course of intellectual growth in terms of progressive changes in children's cognitive structures. These changes manifest themselves in stages of development, each one different from the previous stage. All children do not go through these stages at exactly the same age; however, all children pass through the stages in the same order. The attainments of earlier stages are essential for those in later periods of development. The changes in children's cognitive abilities across the stages can sometimes be quite abrupt, but the picture of development as a whole involves gradual and continuous change.

Piaget divides intellectual development into four main periods (presented in Table 9-1): the sensorimotor period, the preoperational period, the period of concrete operations, and the period of formal operations. As children pass through these periods they change from organisms incapable of thought, dependent on their senses and motor activities to know the world about them, to individuals capable of great flexibility of thought and abstract reasoning.

SENSORIMOTOR PERIOD

During the first period, the *sensorimotor period,* which encompasses approximately the first two years of life, the child makes a dramatic transition from

TABLE 9-1 **CHARACTERISTICS AND ACHIEVEMENTS IN STAGES OF INTELLECTUAL DEVELOPMENT ACCORDING TO PIAGET**

STAGE	APPROXIMATE AGE RANGE, YEARS	MAJOR CHARACTERISTICS AND ACHIEVEMENTS
Sensorimotor period	0–2	Infant differentiates himself from other objects; seeks stimulation and prolongs interesting spectacles; attainment of object permanence; primitive understanding of causality, time, and space; means-end relationships; beginnings of imitation of absent, complex behavior; imaginative play and symbolic thought
Preoperational period	2–6	Development of the symbolic function; symbolic use of language; intuitive problem solving; thinking characterized by irreversibility, centration, and egocentricity; beginnings of attainment of conservation of number and ability to think in classes and see relationships
Period of concrete operations	6 or 7 through 11 or 12	Conservation of mass, length, weight, and volume; reversibility, decentration, ability to take role of others; logical thinking involving concrete operations of the immediate world, classification (organizing objects into hierarchies of classes), and seriation (organizing objects into ordered series, such as increasing height)
Period of formal operations	11 or 12 on	Flexibility, abstraction, mental hypotheses testing, and consideration of possible alternatives in complex reasoning and problem solving

being a reflexive organism to one possessing rudimentary symbolic thought, that is, from a *reflexive* to a *reflective* organism. Piaget divides the sensorimotor period into six substages, each of which is characterized by an increase in complexity of the child's thought processes.

Stage 1: Reflex Activity. In the first month of life, the stage of *reflex activity*, infants refine their innate responses. They become more proficient in the use of reflexes, such as the sucking reflex, and in finding stimulation that will allow them to use these responses.

Stage 2: Primary Circular Reactions. In the stage of *primary circular reactions* (1 to 4 months) the infant repeats and modifies actions which may have initially occurred by chance and which the child finds to be satisfying or pleasurable. The infant may have accidentally sucked his fingers when they were near his mouth; later, since the experience was pleasing, he seeks his fingers to repeat the sucking, but has difficulty coordinating the visual and manual schemata required for the act. These behaviors are *primary* in that they are basic reflexive or motoric functions of his own body; they are *circular* in that they are repeated again and again. Notice that primary circular reactions are focused on the infant's activities and body rather than on objects around him.

Stage 3: Secondary Circular Reactions. It is not until the stage of *secondary circular reactions* (4 to 8 months) that the infant's attention becomes centered on the manipulation of objects. Unlike the stage of primary circular reactions, the infant is now interested in outcomes which occur outside the reach of his body. In common with the previous stage, the reactions are still circular; the infant will repeat the pleasurable action again and again. For instance, the child will now grasp and shake a rattle in order to hear the interesting sound it makes. Notice that the infant is already beginning to combine simple schemata to produce relatively more complex patterns of behavior; the

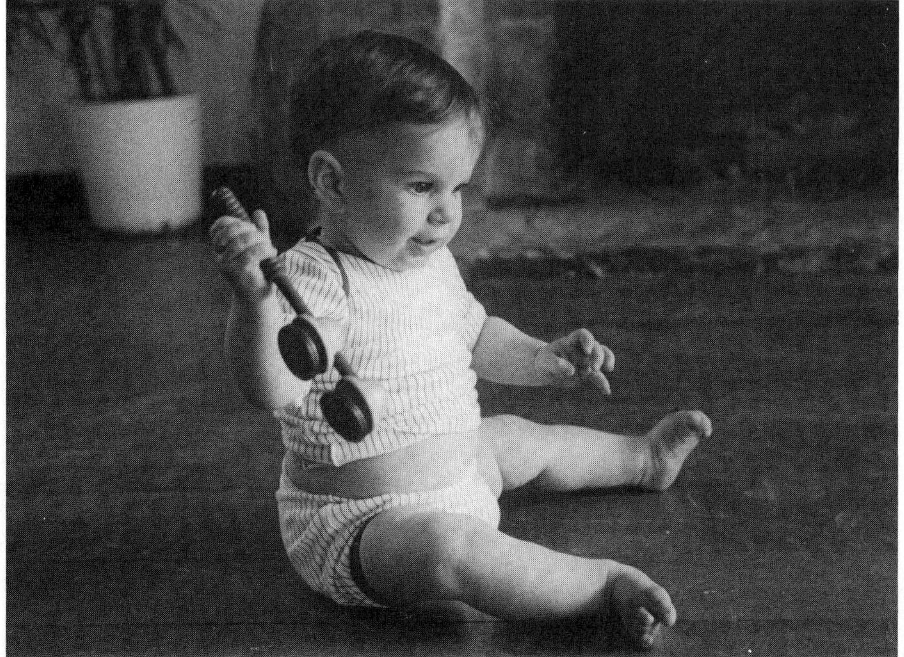

During the stage of secondary circular reactions, the infant will often repeat a simple motor action, such as shaking a rattle.

reaching, grasping, and shaking motions necessary for the movement of the rattle are simple schemata that the child possessed in the stage of primary circular reactions.

It is tempting to say that at this stage the infant's behavior is *intentional;* that is, the child mentally formed the goal of shaking the rattle in order to hear the pleasant sound. At this stage, however, Piaget would not attribute intentionality to the child. The child's goal of shaking the rattle is generated by the objects in his environment; if the rattle were out of the child's grasp he would not form the intention of finding and shaking it. It is not until later in development that Piaget attributes the ability to generate goals to infants.

Stage 4: Coordination of Secondary Reactions. In the stage of *coordination of secondary reactions* (8 to 12 months) the child begins to use or combine two or more secondary schemata as a means of attaining a goal. The infant intentionally uses schemata from a previous situation to solve problems in a new situation. In the previous stages schemata were tied to the environment in which they occurred. Now, schemata which had previously been used only in particular circumstances will be used in a variety of situations. Further, the infant can now combine several schemata into complex patterns of behavior. For example, a previously acquired hitting schema, initially developed as a means of moving a mobile, will now be used to strike away a barrier in front of a toy. Notice also that a schema may now be used as an intermediate step—as a means of attaining a desired goal. Only now would Piaget attribute intentionality to the developing infant. His use of a schema as an intermediate step to a goal shows a planfulness on the part of the child that Piaget requires of intentional thought.

Stage 5: Tertiary Circular Reactions. In the stage of *tertiary circular reactions* (12 to 18 months) children's curiosity leads them to experiment with objects. They will actively use trial-and-error methods to learn more about object properties and how they react to various actions. For example, children become fascinated by the properties of falling objects and will often experiment with any object that happens to be in the vicinity. They will drop different toys, vary the way the toy is dropped, the position and the distance of the drop, the place from which the object is dropped, and the characteristics of the surface on which it lands. This exploration is a kind of early problem solving that leads children to accommodate to new aspects of their environment and assimilate them into their constantly changing schemata. Additionally, through experimentation they learn about characteristics of objects around them and new ways to attain a desired goal.

Stage 6: The Invention of New Means through Mental Combination. It is not until the sixth and last stage of the sensorimotor period, the stage of *invention of new means through mental combination,* that the beginnings of symbolic thought occur. Although the use of symbolic-representational systems is the foundation for the ability to understand language and to speak, it is also reflected in a variety of other cognitive activities that appear in this last stage of the sensorimotor period and are refined in later stages of development. These include deferred imitation, drawing, fantasy play, and abstract problem solving.

This ability to use internal representation facilitates problem solving. The child can now invent new ways to attain a goal by mentally combining several schemata, rather than by physically exploring, manipulating, and

COGNITIVE DEVELOPMENT

Infants and children demonstrate their cognitive abilities in a wide variety of ways. There are dramatic shifts in cognitive development from infancy to adolescence as children move from perceptual-motor modes to increasingly abstract representational ways of understanding their cognitive world.

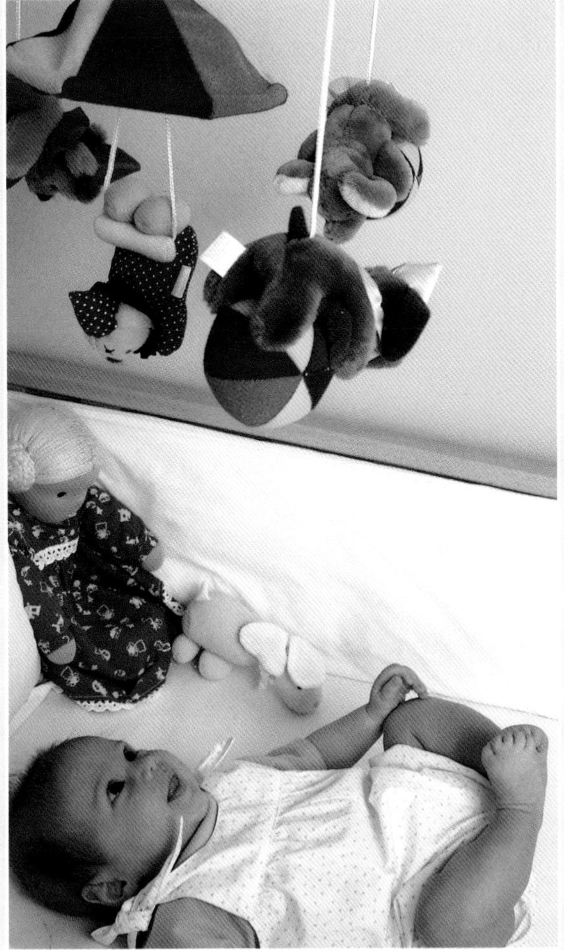

Attention to objects is a commonly used index of cognitive understanding. Some researchers argue that early attentional abilities are related to later intelligence.

Object permanence is clearly demonstrated in this 10-month-old, but researchers now maintain that this cognitive landmark may come even earlier.

Counting is an important skill in learning about numbers.

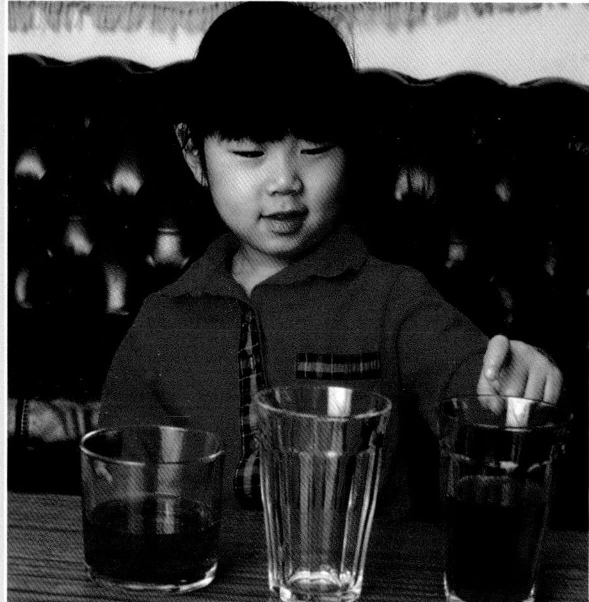

This child is trying to decide whether the two glasses of liquid are equal as part of a test for her understanding of conservation of volume.

This preoperational child is puzzling over a classic conservation-of-matter problem.

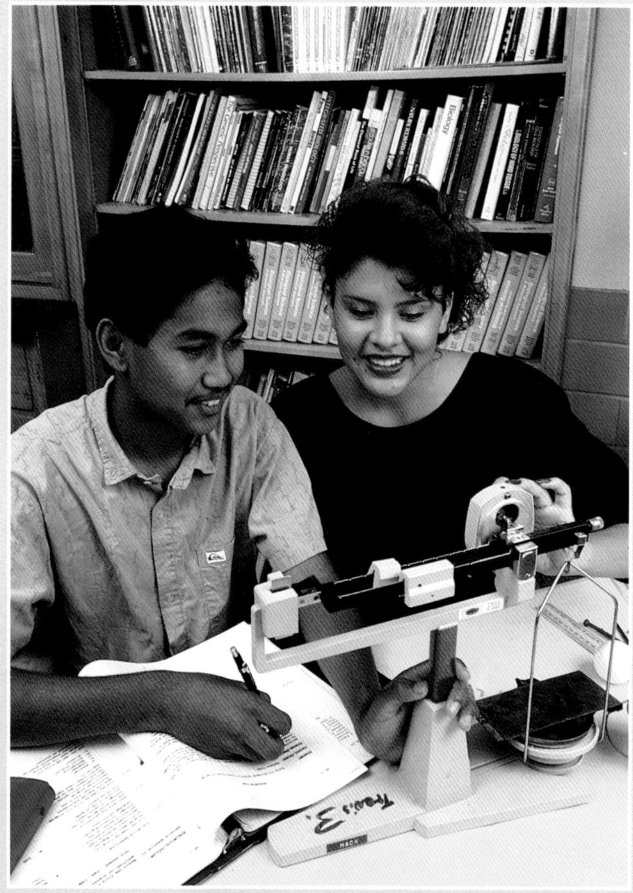

Balance-beam problems require a sophisticated skill that is generally not evident until adolescence and the period of formal operations.

In the stage of tertiary circular reactions, children begin to experiment with objects, by dropping them to see the results.

experimenting as in the previous stage. This primitive ability to think through problems leads to the emergence of sudden solutions to problems with little or no overt trial-and-error behavior. The child is now able to think without acting.

The emergence of the ability to mentally represent objects which are not present is manifested in the occurrence of deferred imitation. The child is now able to imitate complex behavior exhibited by a model at a previous time—without the presence of the model. Piaget cites an occasion when his daughter Jacqueline, who did not have temper tantrums, watched in amazement as a visiting child threw a wild tantrum in her playpen. The next day when Jacqueline was placed in her playpen she exhibited the same pattern of behavior, complete with the screaming, foot stamping, and pen rattling, that she had observed in her visitor. Piaget reasoned that in order to replicate the child's behavior in the same circumstances Jacqueline must have stored a representation of the previous day's events and then used it when placed in the same environment.

The child's conception of his world undergoes massive change during these six stages. Nowhere is this more apparent than in the child's changing conception of object permanence. We will now examine how this understanding of the permanence of objects develops.

THE CONSTRUCTION OF A WORLD OF PERMANENT OBJECTS

It is difficult to conceive of a world in which objects cease to exist when we are not perceiving them. As adults, when we can no longer see, hear, or touch an object we do not assume that it no longer exists. We accept the existence of objects and people as being independent of our own interaction with them. Piaget proposes, however, that young infants do not have this ability to conceive of the permanence of objects. For the very young child, when mother goes out of the room or when a favorite toy drops over the edge of the crib, it is not only "out of sight, out of mind" but "out of sight, out of existence" (Flavell, 1985).

Piaget believes that the process of learning that objects exist when the child is not in direct contact with them is one that occurs gradually and in a predicted sequence over the course of the sensorimotor period. Table 9-2 summarizes the progression of the concept of *object permanence.* In the first two stages of the sensorimotor period the child shows no comprehension that objects have an existence of their own. When a toy vanishes the infant does not actively seek to find the lost object. In fact, if the toy drops from a child's hand he will stare at his hand rather than follow the path of the falling object to the floor. When an object is not being perceived, the infant behaves as though it does not exist.

It is not until about 4 months of age, in the stage of secondary circular reaction, that some increased awareness of the permanence of objects is found. If the loss of the object is associated with interruption of the child's own movements, the child is more likely to visually search for the object than if it has been hidden by another person. Additionally, children will now anticipate the path of moving objects and look for them there. However, the child's concept of object permanence is not robust at this point. If the infant watches as an object is covered he will not attempt to retrieve it. For example, if an adult hides a desired toy under a blanket the infant will not search for the toy, even though he watched as the toy was hidden.

Although marked improvement in the development of object permanence occurs in subsequent stages, these transitions are gradual. In the stage of coordination of secondary schemata, the child's concept of object permanence continues to evolve. Early in this stage a child will be surprised to see a toy clown disappear behind a screen and then reappear as a brightly colored plastic doughnut, while a child in the previous stage will accept the magical transformation (Gratch, 1982; Meicler & Gratch, 1980).

In the period of tertiary circular reactions (about 12 months), the infant is finally able to recognize the permanence of an invisible object. The child will now track an object visually and search for it in the position where it disappeared. Despite this new knowledge of object permanence, however, children in this stage still have difficulty with invisible sequential displacement of objects. Piaget describes an incident with his son Laurent, which illustrates children's difficulties during this stage. While playing a hiding game with Laurent, Piaget hid his watch behind one of two cushions, alternating the hiding spot between the two cushions. Laurent consistently searched for the watch under the correct cushion, regardless of where he had last seen it hidden. However, obtaining the watch was not to be that simple for Laurent. Piaget next placed the watch in a box, put the box behind the cushion, and surreptitiously removed the watch, leaving it behind the cushion. Laurent

TABLE 9-2 **STAGES IN THE ATTAINMENT OF OBJECT PERMANENCE**

APPROXIMATE AGES	SEARCH BEHAVIOR
0–4 months	No visual or manual searching
4–8 months	Searches for partially concealed objects
8–12 months	Searches for completely concealed objects
12–18 months	Searches after visible displacements of objects
18 months and older	Searches after hidden displacements of objects

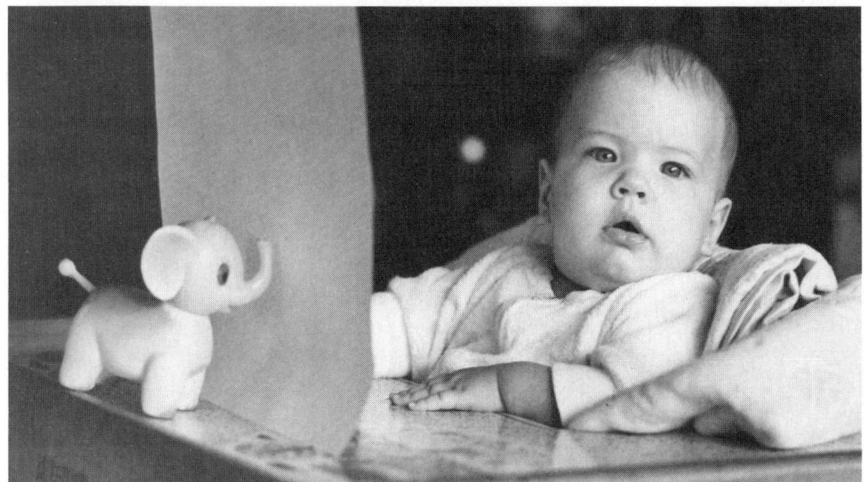

This child, who has not yet attained object permanence, shows no interest in searching for the concealed object.

was then handed the box, only to find that it was empty. Despite having seen his father place the box behind the cushion, Laurent did not search for the watch. Laurent manifested object permanence only when he could observe the sequential displacement of the watch. Thus, it is not until the last stage of the sensorimotor period that true object permanence is attained. The child is finally able to make inferences about the position of unseen objects and can overcome sequential displacements.

Understanding object permanence is a milestone in Piaget's account of the developing child; consequently his claims regarding its acquisition have undergone a great deal of scrutiny. One common criticism is that in all of Piaget's tasks used to track the development of object permanence, the child's search behavior is used as a measure of his knowledge of the object concept. Many development psychologists have wondered whether the child may have attained object permanence, but may not be able to reveal it in search activities because of other developmental limitations. For example, could it be that the child is aware that the object that has disappeared still exists, but that his hand-eye coordination (that is, coordination of reaching movements with visual regard) is not yet developed enough to permit effective searching? If this is the case, then a task which requires manual search is not a true evaluation of the child's knowledge of object permanence. An example of a nonmotor task which shows that young infants' knowledge of object permanence has been underestimated by Piaget can be seen in the research of Renée Baillargeon, which is described in Box 9-1.

SUMMARY OF PROGRESS IN THE SENSORIMOTOR PERIOD

The child's intellectual development in the first two years of life is a monumental attainment. Through active interaction with the environment the child has changed from being focused on reflex activity and sensory and motor experiences into an organism with considerable understanding of realities in the environment and an ability to adapt to them. The child has now developed new behaviors and strategies to attain goals and has begun to use symbolic thought processes to help solve problems. It is the increasingly efficient use of these symbolic processes that leads to the rapid changes in thought that occur in the next period, the *preoperational period.*

PREOPERATIONAL PERIOD

Piaget divides the preoperational phase into two subperiods: the preconceptual period (2 to 4 years) and the intuitive period (4 to 7 years).

The Symbolic Function. The major characteristic of the preoperational period is the development of systems of representation, or the *symbolic function,* which means that the child can now use symbols, such as words, images, and gestures, to represent objects and events. The elaboration of the symbolic function can be traced through both periods of the preoperational stage. In the preconceptual period the emergence of the symbolic functions are shown in the rapid development of language, in imaginative play, and in the increase in deferred imitation. In the intuitive phase it is manifested in changes in thought processes involving such things as new understanding of relationships, numbers, and classifications. All these behaviors suggest that the child is able to produce mental symbols that mediate his performance.

One major accomplishment of the preoperational child is the rapid acquisition of language during the preconceptual period. Piaget regards the rapid increase in the use of language as an *outcome* of the child's developing ability to use symbols, rather than its cause. The use of the symbolic function leads to the child's ability to acquire language. Once the use of language symbols begins, it greatly broadens the child's problem-solving abilities and also permits learning from the verbalizations of others. The symbolic process is also apparent in imaginative play. The child who has seen a train going down the track may push a series of blocks and say "toot toot"; the blocks are now the symbol for a real train.

The Preconceptual Period. Two marked limitations of thought characterize the preconceptual period: *animistic thinking* and *egocentricity.* Animistic thinking occurs when children attribute life to inanimate objects. For example, the child may believe that plants feel pain when they are picked or that the wind is talking to his friends, the trees. Consider the animistic conception of the sun revealed in the following interchange between Piaget and a preconceptual child.

Piaget: Does the sun move?
Child: Yes, when one walks it follows. When one turns around it turns around too. Doesn't it ever follow you too?
Piaget: Why does it move?
Child: Because when one walks, it goes too.
Piaget: Why does it go?
Child: To hear what we say.
Piaget: Is it alive?
Child: Of course, otherwise it wouldn't follow us, it couldn't shine. (Piaget, 1960, p. 215)

The lifelike characteristics attributed to the sun are clear. In addition, this dialogue reveals another characteristic of preconceptual thought: *egocentrism.* The sun follows the child, imitates the child's turning, and listens to the child. The child believes that the universe is organized and created for him and is centered around him. He has difficulty seeing any point of view but his own. Although egocentrism is most marked in the preconceptual period, Piaget feels that it continues throughout the entire preoperational stage and into the concrete operational stage.

Egocentrism also manifests itself in the preoperational child's inability to see things from the perspective of others. This inability is apparent in children's performance on the three-mountain task, which was designed by Piaget to test children's perspective-taking skills. Three mountains of varying sizes are set on a square table with one chair at each side of the table. The child is seated in one chair, and a doll is placed sequentially in the other chairs. The child is asked to identify what the doll sees from each of the three positions, either by selecting from a set of drawings or by using cardboard cutouts of the mountain to construct the doll's views (see Figure 9-2). It is not until age 9 or 10 that children can consistently choose the picture showing what the doll would see from each of the other locations.

Just as Piaget's claims about the limitations on children's knowledge of object permanence have been questioned, so too have his hypotheses regarding animistic and egocentric thought. One criticism of Piaget's position on animistic thought is that the objects used to test the limits of children's animistic thought, such as the sun, the moon, and the wind, are often open to magical interpretations (Bullock, 1985). When simple and familiar objects are used, children as young as 4 years are quite good at determining whether animate objects, such as mammals, or inanimate objects, such as statues, can initiate their own movement (Massey & Gelman, 1988). Similarly, Dolgin and Behrend (1984) found that very few 3-year-olds would attribute animate characteristics to vehicles (which can move like animate beings) or to dead, stuffed animals (which look like animate beings).

Piaget's three-mountain task is also open to criticism. The three mountains used in his task did not contain any salient characteristics which would be used to differentiate one view of the mountains from the next. Additionally, the task of reconstructing the display, or even of choosing the appropriate photos, may be beyond the ability of a young child. Two simple changes in Piaget's original task led to very different results: (1) familiar objects were placed on the side of the mountains in order to make them more distinctive and (2) the children were asked to rotate a small model of the display to the appropriate view rather than reconstruct the model or choose from photos. When these simple steps were taken, children as young as 3 years were able to accurately indicate the correct perspective from each of the different positions (Borke, 1975).

BOX 9-1 OBJECT PERMANENCE IN YOUNG INFANTS

What do infants expect to happen when a moving object hits a stationary object? Do they expect the same thing to happen if just moments before impact the stationary object is hidden by a screen? This is the question addressed in a series of studies performed by Renée Baillargeon. Addressing several of Piaget's claims regarding an infant's knowledge of object permanence, she designed a clever task which allowed her to investigate young infants' knowledge of the object concept.

Baillargeon presented 6- and 8-month-old infants with an impossible event in which one solid object appeared to move through the space occupied by another solid object. In these experiments, infants sat in front of a large stage. On the left side of the stage there was a long inclined ramp (see Figure 9-1a). At the bottom of the ramp, directly in front of the infant, was a small screen. The infant watched as the screen was raised and then lowered. After the screen had been lowered a small car rolled down the ramp along a track set in the stage, disappearing at one end of the screen and reappearing at the other end. This event was repeated until the infant became habituated to the display.

After habituation the infant saw one of two test events (Figures 9-1*b* and *c*). Both of these events were identical to the habituation event in all but one respect: When the screen was raised the infant saw that there was a box placed behind it so that the box was hidden by the screen when it was lowered. After the screen was lowered the car again rolled down the ramp and across the stage. In the *possible event,* the box was placed in the back of the stage, *behind* the tracks, and well out of the car's trajectory. In the *impossible event,* the box was placed in the front of the stage, on *top* of the tracks and directly in the car's path. Thus, in the possible event the car rolls safely in front of the box, while in the impossible event the car rolls through the box! (During the impossible event, the car was actually removed through a door in the back of the stage.) Baillargeon measured the infant's reaction to these two events through the infant's looking time—infants look longer at surprising events compared to events that they expected.

According to Piaget, infants of this age do not have the concept of object permanence. Consequently, as soon as the screen covers the box it ceases to exist for the child. Thus, if Piaget is correct in his assessment of infants' abilities there should be no difference in the infant's response to either the possible or the impossible event—the box no longer exists, therefore it cannot stop the trajectory of the car. If, however, infants do represent the existence of the box even when it is out of sight, they should look longer at the impossible event than the

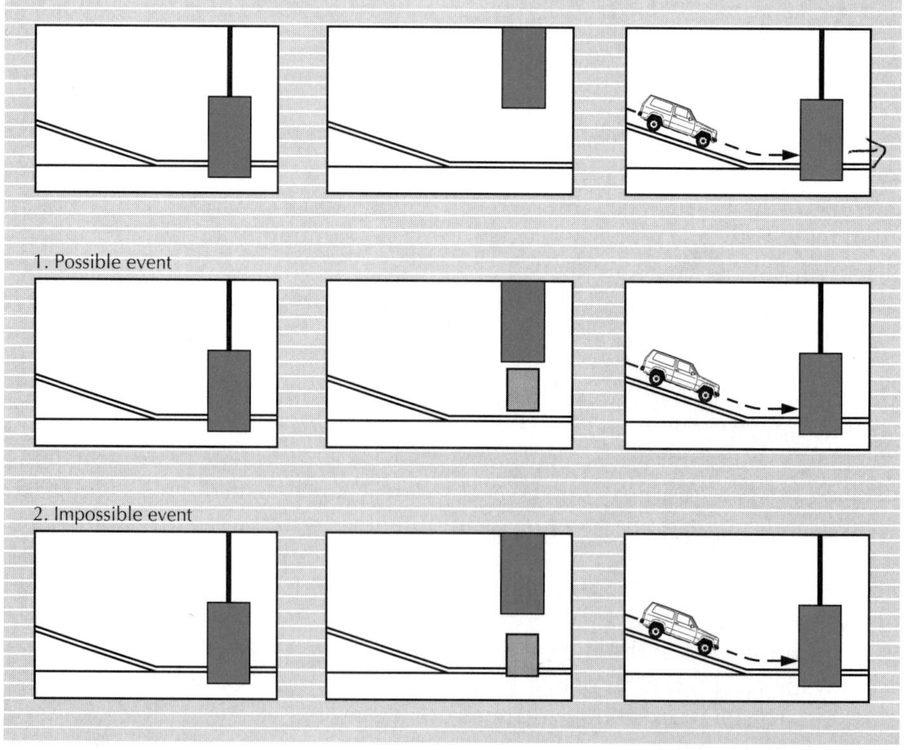

FIGURE 9-1
Schematic representation of the habituation and test events used in Experiment 1: (A: top panel) habituation event; (B: middle and bottom panels) test events.

BOX 9-1 OBJECT PERFORMANCE IN YOUNG INFANTS (*Continued*)

possible event. This is in fact what Baillargeon found. The infants looked reliably longer when the box was placed on the track compared to when the box was placed behind the tracks. In later studies, $3\frac{1}{2}$ month-old infants have demonstrated a similar awareness of object permanence (Baillargeon, 1987, 1992).

From infants' performance on this task, Baillargeon concluded that not only do infants represent the existence of hidden objects, they also represent their location. Both of these results run counter to Piaget's claims regarding infants' understanding of the object concept and have led to further research which has shown that infants know a great deal more than Piaget ever imagined.

Source: Baillargeon, R. (1986). Representing the existence and the location of hidden objects: Object permanence in 6- and 8-month-old infants. *Cognition*, 23, 21–41. Baillargeon, R. (1992). The object concept revisited: New investigations in the investigation of infants' physical knowledge. In C. E. Granrud (Ed.), *Carnegie-Mellon symposia on cognition*: vol. 23. *Visual perception and cognition in infancy*. Hillside, NJ: Erlbaum.

Piaget's views on egocentrism have stimulated interest in social aspects of cognition, such as role taking. We turn to this topic briefly.

Egocentric Perspectives and Role Taking

As children grow older, they are better able to decenter from their own perspectives, motives, and feelings and understand the perceptions, intentions, thoughts, and emotions of others. It has been suggested this shift away from an early, egocentric orientation underlies improved communication skills, the development of moral standards involving concern for the feelings and welfare of others, and the development of empathic understanding, which are basic in socialization (Harter, 1983; Shantz, 1983). The development of these abilities is described in detail in other chapters in the book.

Selman and his colleagues have proposed that this decentering process involves a developmental sequence of role-taking ability in learning how to differentiate between perspectives of the self and others and the relationship between these perspectives (Selman, 1980; Selman & Byrne, 1974; Selman & Jacquette, 1978). These role-taking stages are presented in Table 9-3. Selman and his colleagues have described the developmental progression of these

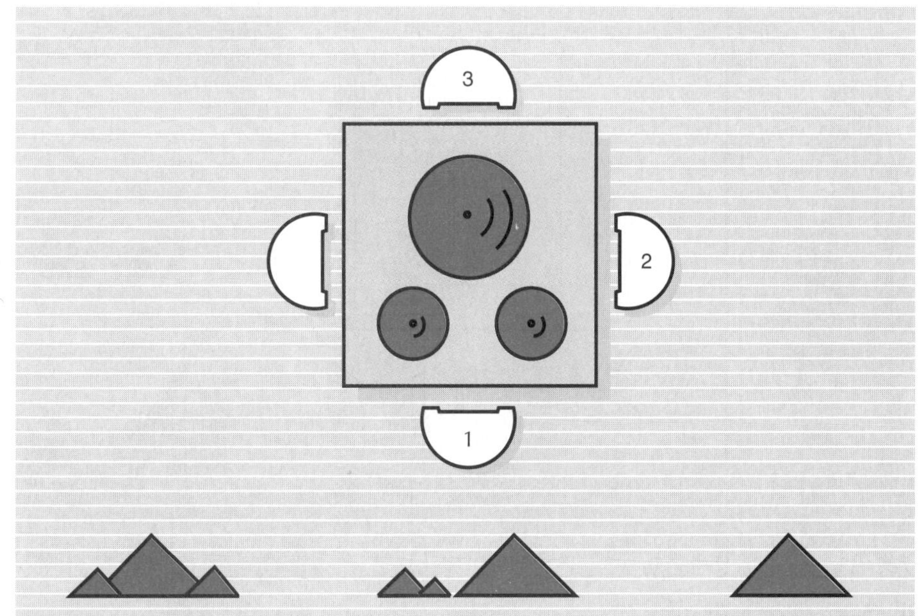

FIGURE 9-2
The three-mountain problem. *(From Phillips, 1969.)*

stages. The study presented in Box 9-2 clearly shows that with increasing age children are more likely to attain higher levels of perspective taking. Other studies have confirmed Selman's general progression (Taylor, 1988).

Some individuals reach higher levels of social role-taking abilities than others, or may attain them earlier. What kinds of factors contribute, or are related to, individual differences in role-taking abilities? Performance on standard intelligence tests shows a modest relation to social role-taking ability (Shantz, 1983). In addition, as we will discuss in detail in Chapter 16, some studies have found positive relations between prosocial behavior, such as helping and sharing, and role-taking skills. For example, children's offers of help, offers of support, and responsible suggestions to other children on the playground and in classrooms were observed and recorded. The frequency with which altruistic behaviors occurred correlated with laboratory measures of role taking (Eisenberg, 1992; Eisenberg & Mussen, 1989).

Intuitive Period. The term *intuitive* is applied to the child in the period from 4 to 7 years; this term is appropriate because although certain mental operations (such as ways of classifying, quantifying, or relating objects) occur, the child does not seem to be aware of the principles he has used in the performance of these operations; he can solve problems involving these operations but he cannot explain why he solved them in a certain way.

Although the child's symbols are becoming increasingly complex, reasoning and thinking processes have certain characteristic limitations which are manifested in a variety of tasks. Some of these limitations are reflected in the

(Peanuts reprinted by permission of UFS, Inc.)

TABLE 9-3

PERSPECTIVE TAKING (RELATION BETWEEN PERSPECTIVES OF SELF AND OTHERS)

STAGE 0—EGOCENTRIC OR UNDIFFERENTIATED PERSPECTIVES
The child does not distinguish his own perspective from that of others. The child does not recognize that another person may interpret experiences differently than he does.
STAGE 1—SUBJECTIVE OR DIFFERENTIATED PERSPECTIVES
The child realizes that the self and others may have the same or different perspectives. The child is concerned with the uniqueness of the cognitions of each person. However, although he recognizes that different people may have different perspectives he can't accurately judge what the other person's perspectives will be.
STAGE 2—SELF-REFLECTIVE OR RECIPROCAL PERSPECTIVES
The child is able to see himself from another's perspective and is aware that the other person can do the same thing. This permits him to anticipate and consider the thoughts and feelings of others.
STAGE 3—MUTUAL PERSPECTIVES
In this stage not only is the child able to understand his own perspective and that of another person and be aware that the other person can do the same thing simultaneously, but he can view this mutual perspective from the position of a third person. He can think of how some member of another group (parents, teachers, the other kids on the team) might view both persons' perspectives.
STAGE 4—SOCIETAL OR IN-DEPTH PERSPECTIVES
People are able to see networks or systems of perspectives, such as society's perspectives, or the Republican point of view, or the black perspective. These systems of perspectives among people are seen not only to exist on the plane of common expectations or awareness, but also to involve deeper levels of communications such as unverbalized feelings or values.

Source: Selman, and Jacquette. (1978). By permission of the University of Nebraska Press. Copyright © 1978 by the University of Nebraska Press.

preoperational child's inability to perform a *seriation task* in which he is asked to order objects on the basis of particular dimension, for example, to order a group of sticks in a series from shortest to longest. Limitations are also found in problems of *part-whole relations* (often called *class-inclusion* problems). This is vividly illustrated in the child's response on a task where he is given seven toy dogs and three toy cats, for a total of ten animals. If the child is asked if there are more dogs or more cats he can answer correctly. However, if the child is asked if there are more dogs than there are animals, the child responds that there are more dogs. Piaget proposes that the child is responding incorrectly because he is unable to focus simultaneously on a part of the set of animals (the set of dogs), as well as on the whole set of animals, and so interprets the question to mean are there more dogs than cats.

This particular task has been criticized because of the confusing manner in which the question is posed. By using simpler questions which still address the children's ability to use part-whole relations, such as "A pug is a kind of dog, but not a shepherd. Is a pug an animal?" children as young as 4 years displayed knowledge of the part-whole relation between dogs and animals (Smith, 1979). Additional work has shown that the use of *collective terms,* such as "family" and "forest," when used to describe the whole set (for example, "Who would have more pets, someone who owned the baby dogs or someone

BOX 9-2 HOW DO I SEE YOU? HOW DO YOU SEE ME?

Is there a systematic developmental progression in role-taking skills? The results of this study by Selman and Byrne suggest that there is.

Groups of 4-, 6-, 8-, and 10-year-old children were presented with filmed stories and questioned about the perspectives and thoughts of the characters in the story. A sample story is as follows:

> Holly is an 8-year-old girl who likes to climb trees. She is the best tree climber in the neighborhood. One day while climbing down from a tall tree she falls off the bottom branch but does not hurt herself. Her father sees her fall. He is upset and asks her to promise not to climb trees any more. Holly promises.
>
> Later that day, Holly and her friends meet Sean. Sean's kitten is caught up in a tree and cannot get down. Something has to be done right away or the kitten may fall. Holly is the only one who climbs trees well enough to reach the kitten and get it down, but she remembers her promise to her father. (Selman & Byrne, 1974, p. 805)

The questions were structured to assess the levels of role taking attained by the child. These are levels 1, 2, and 3 in Table 9-4. The questions were as follows.

Level 1—Subjective Role Taking

(a) Does Holly know how Sean feels about the kitten? Why?

(b) Does Sean know why Holly cannot decide whether or not to climb the tree? Why or why not?

(c) Why might Sean think Holly will not climb the tree if Holly does not tell him about her promise?

Level 2—Self-Reflective Role Taking

(a) What does Holly think her father will think of her if he finds out?

(b) Does Holly think her father will understand why she climbed the tree? Why is that?

Level 3—Mutual Role Taking

(a) What does Holly think most people would do in this situation?

(b) If Holly and her father discussed this situation, what might they decide together? Why is that?

(c) Do you know what the Golden Rule is (explain if the child says no)? What would the Golden Rule say to do in this situation? Why? (Selman & Byrne, 1974, p. 805).

The percentage of children in each age group reaching a given role-taking level is presented in Table 9-4.

A steady progression can be seen through these role-taking stages. No 4- or 6-year-old children have attained stage 2 or 3 role taking, whereas most 8- and 10-year-old children have reached at least stage 2 and some have attained level 3.

Later longitudinal research confirmed the original findings and demonstrated that these skills emerge in an invariant sequence as the child develops (Gurucharri & Selman, 1982).

Source: Gurucharri, C., & Selman, R. L. (1982). The development of interpersonal understanding during childhood, preadolescence, and adolescence: A longitudinal follow-up study. *Child Development*, **53**, 924–927. Selman, R. L., & Byrne, D. F. (1974). A structural-developmental analysis of levels of role taking in middle childhood. *Child Development*, **45**, 803–806.

TABLE 9-4 PERCENTAGE OF CHILDREN IN DIFFERENT AGES REACHING A GIVEN ROLE-TAKING LEVEL

STAGE	AGE 4	AGE 6	AGE 8	AGE 10
0	80	10	0	0
1	20	90	40	20
2	0	0	50	60
3	0	0	10	20
Total	100	100	100	100

Source: Selman and Byrne (1974).

who owned the whole family?") highlighted the part-whole relations between the objects and improved the performance of preschool children (Markman, 1973; Markman & Siebert, 1976).

THE ACQUISITION OF CONSERVATION

Just as acquisition of the object concept is considered the primary accomplishment of the sensorimotor period, the crucial acquisition of the preoperational period is the ability to *conserve.* When certain attributes of an object remain the same despite changes in the object or the situation, these attributes have been conserved. During the preoperational stage, children gradually acquire the skills necessary to make conservation judgments. Conservation applies to many different types of attributes of objects, for example, mass, length, and quantity.

In a liquid conservation task, a child is shown two short, wide, cylinders which contain equal amounts of water. The child then watches as the experimenter pours the water from one of the two containers into a tall, thin cylinder. When the child is asked whether the tall cylinder contains *more, less,* or *the same* amount of water as the short cylinder, the child usually answers that the tall cylinder contains more. Asked if anything was added or taken away from each cylinder the child will say no, but will still insist that they now contain different amounts of water. The child has failed to conserve the amount of liquid—he focused on the changes in the height and width of the water rather than on the constant amount. What processes are at work that lead to this remarkable error in judgment, this lack of conservation, even though the child has viewed the entire procedure?

LIMITS ON PREOPERATIONAL THOUGHT

Piaget proposes that there are three characteristics of preoperational thought which lead to limitations on children's cognitive functioning. These limitations manifest themselves in all aspects of children's preoperational thought: in their egocentric behavior, their inability to perform a seriation task, as well as in their ability to conserve. The most important characteristic of

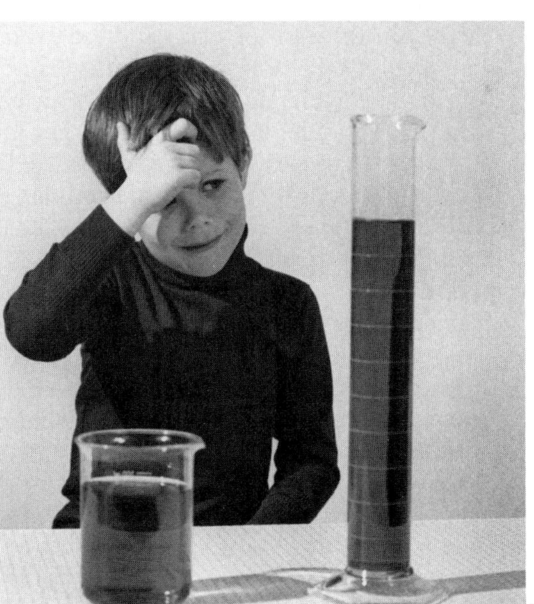

A child, in the period of concrete operations, solving a conservation problem.

preoperational reasoning is *irreversibility.* Children do not see that every logical operation is reversible; for instance, in the conservation task they do not reason that if the water is poured back into the short cylinder it will reach the same depth. Irreversibility manifests itself in many other responses of the preoperational child. For example, a 4-year-old subject is asked:

> "Do you have a brother?" He says, "Yes."
>
> "What's his name" "Jim."
>
> "Does Jim have a brother?" "No." (Phillips, 1969, p. 61)

A second characteristic, which is associated with irreversibility, is the focusing on the end state of a changing event rather than on the process or *transformations* by which the change occurs. In the liquid conservation task described previously, the preoperational child ignores the experimenter's action of pouring the water from one cylinder to the other, and the subsequent rise in water level. Instead, he focuses on the end state of the process; the high water level in the tall container which now differs from the water level in the short container.

Finally, our example of the lack of conservation of liquid demonstrates the third characteristic of preoperational thought, *centration* in thinking. The child focuses on one dimension of the object, that is, on either the height of the water or the width of the cylinder, in giving his reasons for why he thinks the amount of water in the containers is no longer equal. One child may say the tall cylinder contains more because the water level is higher; another child that the short cylinder contains more because it is wider. This attention to only one attribute of the objects and not to reciprocal changes between dimensions (that is, the height of the cylinder compensates for the lack of width—thus the amount of water is still equal) contributes to the child's inability to conserve.

The conservation of many attributes and materials other than liquid have also been studied, and the age of attainment of conservation varies for different characteristics. Some of the problems used to test conservation are illustrated in Figure 9-3. Conservation of number is usually achieved by about age 6, conservation of mass and length between 6 and 7, weight around 9, and finally volume sometime after 11. Cross-cultural studies have found considerable variation in the age at which conservation is attained in different societies, but only moderate differences in the order in which different types of conservation occur (Newman, Riel, & Martin, 1983; Rogoff, 1990).

The differences in age of conservation in these different tasks is a problem for Piaget's theory of development. If children have developed the logical abilities to perform one type of conservation task, they should be able to perform all conservation tasks. Piaget attributes differences in the age of acquisition of different kinds of conservation to a phenomenon he calls *horizontal decalage.* Horizontal decalage refers to the fact that children may be able to perform tasks requiring similar operations at different ages. Piaget believes that conservation of mass, weight, and volume differs in the degree of abstractness of the specific operations necessary to perform the task. He proposes that mass requires the least abstract operations and volume the most, consequently conservation of mass is acquired first. Further, the attainment of the earlier concept is essential for the development of the one of greater abstraction, and that increasing age is essential for progress from one concept to the next.

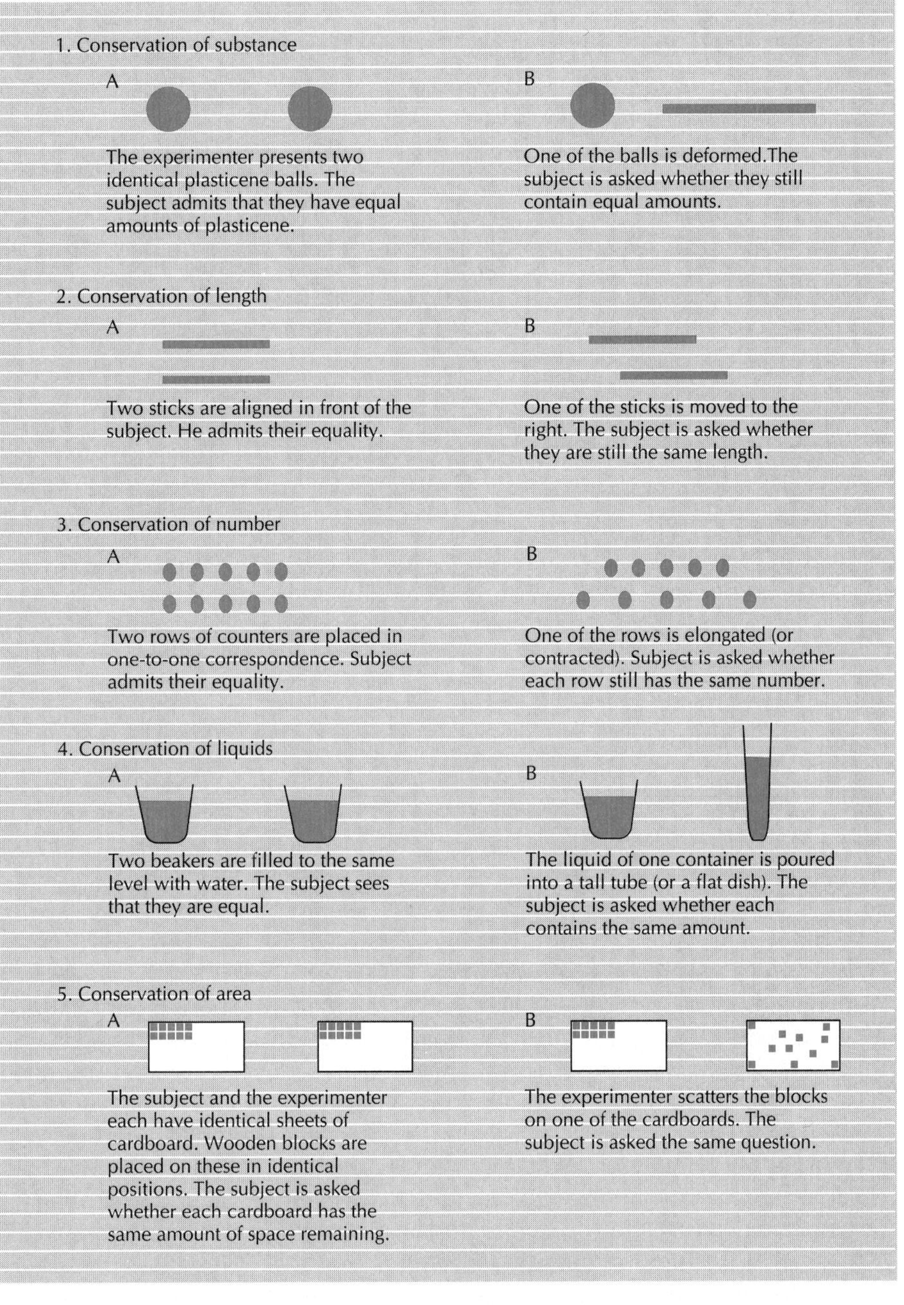

1. Conservation of substance
A
B
The experimenter presents two identical plasticene balls. The subject admits that they have equal amounts of plasticene.
One of the balls is deformed.The subject is asked whether they still contain equal amounts.
2. Conservation of length
A
B
Two sticks are aligned in front of the subject. He admits their equality.
One of the sticks is moved to the right. The subject is asked whether they are still the same length.
3. Conservation of number
A
B
Two rows of counters are placed in one-to-one correspondence. Subject admits their equality.
One of the rows is elongated (or contracted). Subject is asked whether each row still has the same number.
4. Conservation of liquids
A
B
Two beakers are filled to the same level with water. The subject sees that they are equal.
The liquid of one container is poured into a tall tube (or a flat dish). The subject is asked whether each contains the same amount.
5. Conservation of area
A
B
The subject and the experimenter each have identical sheets of cardboard. Wooden blocks are placed on these in identical positions. The subject is asked whether each cardboard has the same amount of space remaining.
The experimenter scatters the blocks on one of the cardboards. The subject is asked the same question.

FIGURE 9-3
Some simple tests for conservation. *(From Lefrancois, 1973.)*

Many researchers have been dissatisfied with Piaget's description of the evolution of conservation in young children. The concepts underlying conservation seem so basic to many different aspects of daily life that Piaget's proposal that children acquire them only late in the preoperational stage has been questioned. Consequently, developmental psychologists have attempted to test children's ability to conserve prior to the end of the preoperational stage. A classic series of studies performed by Rochel Gelman examining children's ability to conserve number is presented in Box 9-3.

A wide variety of studies (Halford, 1990; Sugarman, 1987) have consistently found that Piaget underestimated the capacities of the young child. When children are presented with simpler tasks or taught to attend to the

BOX 9-3 YOUNG CHILDREN'S ABILITY TO CONSERVE NUMBER: THE MAGIC MICE

To test their knowledge of number conservation, Piaget presented children with two rows of objects, each row containing the same number of objects spaced at equal intervals. After the children responded that both rows contained the same number of objects, Piaget lengthened or shortened one of the rows of objects and asked the children again. After this transformation, preoperational children would respond that the transformed row contained more (or fewer) objects than the other row of objects. Based on this, Piaget concluded that the ability to conserve number does not develop until children reach 6 years of age.

Rochel Gelman questioned Piaget's conclusions regarding young children's ability to conserve number. She designed a simpler conservation task, and tested children prior to the age at which Piaget hypothesized the ability to conserve number developed. In Gelman's task, a 3-year-old child was shown two plates; one contained three toy mice, the other contained two. Both plates were covered and the child was asked to pick one of the two plates and identify it as either the "winner" or the "loser." Across a number of trials, the plate with the three mice was consistently the "winner." During these trials no mention was made of number and every time the child correctly identified the winner or the loser, he was given a prize.

Once the child had come to recognize the three-mice plate as the winner, the experimenter surreptitiously altered the winning plate by either decreasing the number of mice on the plate to two, or changed the spacing of the mice to match the two-mice plate (that is, the three mice were pushed closer together). When the child uncovered the altered "winner" plate, he found that the mice had magically changed!

Piaget's theory would predict that these children would now be unable to decide which plate was the winner; instead the children would choose purely on the basis of row length or density. Gelman's results directly contradicted this prediction. She found that on those trials where the mice had merely been pushed together the children could still correctly identify the "winning" plate. Not only could children as young as 3 years of age correctly choose the winner, on the trials where one of the mice had magically disappeared, the children could tell the experimenter that one of the mice was missing and how this plate could be made like the previous "winning" plate, showing that young children can conserve number far younger than Piaget had hypothesized.

Source: Gelman, R. (1972). The nature and development of early number concepts. In H. W. Reese (Ed.), *Advances in child development and behavior* (Vol. 7). New York: Academic.

relevant aspects of the stimuli being presented they are often able to show their understanding of conservation at earlier ages than Piaget originally predicted. Consider these illustrations. To test the notion that failure to conserve may occur because the child attends to irrelevant aspects of the stimulus, such as shape, length, height, color, and so on, Jerome Bruner (1966) presented preoperational children with Piaget's liquid conservation task. In this experiment, however, as the experimenter poured the water from the short cylinder to the tall cylinder a screen was placed in front of the tall cylinder so that the child could not see the water level. When the distracting changes in the height and width of the water were removed, the majority of the children conserved.

Training procedures that modify children's attentional processes have been effective in facilitating conservation in children who were previous nonconservers (Field, 1987). For example, nonconservers were trained to attend to the relevant dimensions of the stimuli and their ability to conserve increased (Gelman, 1969). Not only have such attentional training procedures improved the children's conservation on the task on which they were trained, but the effects have also generalized to other forms of conservation. Thus, if a child was given attentional training involving conservation of number, the effects of the training would also generalize to improved conservation of mass, on which the child had had no training (Gelman, 1969). Nonconserving children have also improved their performance on conservation tasks through observational learning by watching children or adults who were able to solve conservation problems or by discussing their solutions with them (Murray, 1981).

In summary, under the right conditions, preoperational children are better conservers than Piaget thought! However, it is important to remember that children clearly improve in their conservation skills across development and are able to solve more difficult problems and with less aid from others as they grow older.

THE CONCRETE OPERATIONS PERIOD

Dramatic changes in the characteristics of thought occur in the concrete operations period, which extends from about age 7 to about age 11. In this period, an increased understanding of reversibility, and a decrease in centration and egocentrism, lead to an increased flexibility of thinking. Logic and objectivity increase and children begin to think deductively. Children are able to conserve quantity and number, to form concepts of space and time, and to classify or group objects *if the objects are things that the child experiences in everyday life.* However, they are still tied to operations performed on objects in the immediate world. Frequently, they are able to solve problems only if the objects necessary for the solution of the problem are physically present. For example, if three children of varying heights are presented in pairs so that in pair 1 a child sees that Joan is taller than Sandra, and in pair 2 Sandra is taller than Mary, without seeing Joan and Mary together the child can reason that Joan is taller than both Sandra and Mary. However, if the visual stimuli are not present and the problem is presented verbally as "Joan is taller than Sandra and Sandra is taller than Mary; who is the tallest of the three?" the concrete operational child will have difficulty with its solution.

Marked changes in classification abilities and the understanding of concepts also occur in the concrete operations phase. In dealing with classification tasks the concrete operational child can sort objects according to complicated combinations of the attributes of the objects. For example, the concrete operational child will sort a group of flowers into classes of yellow roses, yellow tulips, yellow daisies, red roses, red tulips, and red daisies. Concrete operational children become able to understand these multiple classifications even when they involve subtle distinctions on the relevant dimensions, such as different shades of yellow or different types of daisies. Moreover, they are able to ignore irrelevant features such as number of petals or size (Fischer & Roberts, 1986; Frith & Frith, 1978).

Again it has been questioned whether the solution of such problems is based on the underlying changes in mental operations proposed by Piaget. Some investigators have suggested that in tests of inference, such as the one previously cited dealing with the height of the three girls, the concrete operational child is not being thwarted by the lack of physical stimuli, but by the lack of memory capacity. If children could be trained to remember the rather complicated components of the problem, perhaps they could solve it in the absence of the three girls. Bryant and Trabasso (1971), in a study involving a similar problem using sticks of differing lengths, demonstrated that when procedures are used to assure that the information is retained, even very young children can make logical inferences. The difference in memory capacity of younger and older children, therefore, is one of the critical factors in difference in performance on tests of logical inference (Harris & Basset, 1975).

THE FORMAL OPERATIONS PERIOD

In the period of concrete operations the child was beginning to utilize symbolic thought and was building the foundation of logical thinking that characterizes the adolescent child. How do thought processes in the formal operations period, which begins at around age 12, differ from those in the concrete operations period?

The adolescent is able to think about fanciful problems not based in reality. He realizes that logical rules can be applied to ideas that violate reality. For example, take the problem "If all blue people live in red houses, are all people who live in red houses blue?" The concrete operational child would have difficulty getting beyond the fact that there is no such thing as blue people. In contrast, the child in the formal operations period would focus on applying logical solutions to the problem regardless of the unrealistic content.

During adolescence the child's thought becomes increasingly flexible and abstract. To solve problems, the child uses logical processes in which all the possibilities in a situation are considered. In contrast to the concrete operational child, who, under most circumstances, can only solve problems when the objects are actually present, the adolescent can solve mentally represented problems. Children in this stage will also consider a number of possible alternatives or hypotheses in a problem-solving situation. It is in flexibility of thought, the use of mental hypotheses testing, and appreciation of the many possibilities that the adolescent differs from the concrete operational child.

An example from a task used by Inhelder and Piaget (1958) will serve to illustrate the differences between children in the two stages. In this task, children are asked to arrive at a law to explain why some objects float and others do not by experimenting with an assortment of objects and water. The children are being asked to derive Archimedes law of floating bodies, which states that an object will float if its weight per unit (density) is less than that of water. Thus, if two objects are of equal weight, the larger object is more likely to float than the smaller. Concrete operational children may focus on weight (because it is heavy) or on size (because it is bigger) as a reason why things float or sink. They may even arrive at a double classification that involves the categories large and heavy, large and light, small and heavy, or small and light. However, they always base their solutions on the observable characteristics of size and weight. They are perplexed when their rules do not fit contradictory observations. For example, a large piece of wood may be heavier than a small lead weight, but will float while the weight sinks. They are still unable to consider alternatives not directly observable in the physical world. In contrast, the child in the formal operations period is able to free himself from the obvious cues of weight and size and conceptualize a variety of possible alternatives and arrive at the concept of density. Piaget describes the comments of a formal operational child grappling with this problem: "It sinks because it is small, it isn't stretched enough. You would have to have something larger to stay at the surface, something of the same weight and which would have a greater extension" (Inhelder and Piaget, 1958, p. 38).

As in the case of other Piagetian stages, there is continuing debate about the best ways to describe this type of thinking (Byrnes, 1988; Kuhn, 1991; Keating, 1990; Overton & Byrnes, 1991). The stage of formal operations and the flexible problem solving associated with it are not attained by all adolescents, nor for that matter by all adults or in all societies (Kuhn, 1984, 1991; Niemark, 1981). This is attributable partly to cultural and educational factors and partly to general intellectual level. Unlike concrete operational thought, which seems to be attained to some degree in all societies, the attainment of formal operations is influenced by culture (Dasen & Heron, 1981; Greenfield, 1976; Rogoff, 1990). In groups that do not emphasize symbolic skills or in which educational experiences are limited, the stage of formal operations may occur late in development or may even be absent. Additionally, logical abstract reasoning is more likely to occur in adolescents' or adults' own areas of interest or expertise rather than in other domains (DeLisi & Staudt, 1980; Falmagne, 1980). Scientific training in such subjects as physics, chemistry, or logic has been found to be associated with greater ability to use formal operations.

Evaluation of Piaget's Theory

Piaget attempted to describe and explain the cognitive growth of the child using several basic cognitive structures and processes; specifically, Piaget proposes that through the processes of assimilation and accommodation the basic cognitive structures of the child are modified. Further, he proposes that the child goes through an invariant sequence of four stages of growth in which the attainments of one period depend on those of the preceding period. Key to this growth is the attainment of symbolic thought, which begins to develop during the sensorimotor period and continues to develop until the period of formal operations.

As we have seen, Piaget's theory and observations have received considerable criticism on the basis of recent evidence. Many children seem to be more cognitively advanced for their age than Piaget's theory would suggest. This is particularly true of the abilities of infants. The current findings in infant conditionability and perceptual ability presented in the chapter on infancy (Chapter 5) suggest that the infant may know more than Piaget discerned (Flavell, 1985; Sugarman, 1987). The cognitive abilities in preoperational and concrete operational children also appear to have been underestimated by Piaget (Gelman & Baillargeon, 1983; Halford, 1990).

Further, the sequence of intellectual growth that Piaget proposes may not be as unvarying as he suggests. The results of cross-cultural studies suggest that growth may be modified by cultural and experiential factors (Rogoff, 1990) as well as by training in problem-solving strategies (Gelman & Baillargeon, 1983). In addition, there is some question of whether the underlying operations regarded by Piaget as necessary in solving certain problems are really essential in those tasks.

Although his theory has recently been questioned, and in some cases, supplanted by more recent hypotheses, the current concern with cognitive factors in development and the establishment of many centers for the study of cognitive psychology throughout the world are largely attributable to the impact and influence of Jean Piaget (Beilin, 1992). In spite of the frequently noted limitations and lack of objectivity of his methodology, he has asked and answered important questions in an innovative way, and his provocative theory has stimulated a vast amount of research and theorizing by other behavioral scientists. It is inconceivable that our understanding of the intellectual development of children could have advanced to its present stage without the monumental work of Jean Piaget.

THE INFORMATION PROCESSING APPROACH

The information processing approach to the study of cognitive development emerged from the American experimental tradition in psychology. Psychologists taking this approach are interested in many of the same phenomena that concerned Piaget and his followers, but tend to use the computer as a metaphor, or model, of human thought. They propose that, like the computer, the human mind is a system that processes information through the application of logical rules and strategies. Also, like the computer, the human mind is limited in the amount and nature of information it can process. Finally, just as the computer can be made into a better information processor by changes in the hardware (the circuit boards and microchips) and software (programming), so does the child become a more sophisticated thinker through the changes in hardware (the brain and sensory system) and software (strategies and rules that the child has learned) that occur during development.

The use of the computer as an analogue leads information processors to be interested in the role of input, or registering, of information, how information is stored, and how it is retrieved when it is needed. Thus, information processors are interested in the cognitive processes and strategies used by children of different ages to process information in different situations. These situations are often set up as problems that the children have to solve, and through their solutions modify and refine their mental abilities. Thus, information processors view their task as describing and explaining the changes that occur in children's mental systems which lead to changes in competence.

Characteristics of the Information Processing Approach

Robert Siegler (1991) has described four main characteristics of a psychologist studying development from the information processing approach. First, information processors believe that "thinking *is* information processing" (Siegler, 1991). Cognitive processing occurs when information is perceived, encoded, and represented in the mind. Further, thinking entails the storage and retrieval of information, strategies which can be applied to the information, and constraints or limitations on these processes.

The second characteristic of an information processor is a focus on change mechanisms and their role in development. These mechanisms work together to bring about change in children's cognitive abilities. Siegler discusses four critical mechanisms: encoding, strategy construction, automatization, and generalization. Siegler states:

> To solve problems effectively, children must encode the critical information within the problem. They must then use this encoded information and relevant previous knowledge to construct a strategy for dealing with the problem. To gain the full benefit from the newly-constructed strategy, they must generalize it to other problems where it is also applicable. Finally, new strategies are almost always slow and effortful: practice is needed to automatize the strategy's execution and thus to maximize its effectiveness. (Siegler, 1991, p. 61)

The third characteristic is the assumption that development is driven by the process of *self-modification.* Through self-modification the child uses knowledge and strategies he has acquired from previous problem solutions to modify his responses to a new situation or problem. In this way, newer and more sophisticated responses are built from prior knowledge. Like Piaget's theory of cognitive development, the information processing approach allows the child to play an active role in his own development; through the process of self-modification the child can shape and mold his own development.

The final characteristic of an information processor is the use of careful task analysis. In addition to the effect of the child's own level of development, psychologists in the information processing tradition believe that the nature of the task itself constrains the child's performance. In this view, a child may possess the basic ability necessary to perform a particular task when the task is presented in a simple form, without any extraneous complexities added. However, if the same task is presented with the addition of extra or misleading information, the child may become confused and be unable to perform the task.

STRUCTURES OF THE INFORMATION PROCESSING SYSTEM

Because the flow of information is the primary focus of the information processing approach, the basic structures proposed by this view center around the processing of information—how it is acquired, stored, and retrieved. One view of the human information processing system is a model proposed by Atkinson and Shiffrin (1968) (which can be seen in Figure 1-2). According to this model, information from our senses enters the system through the *sensory registers*. The sensory registers store the information in its original form. This storage is fleeting, however; storage of information in the visual sensory register lasts for only one second (Sperling, 1960).

From the sensory registers specific aspects of the stimulus are *encoded*, or transformed into mental representations, and placed into *short-term* memory. The information cannot stay in short-term memory indefinitely; in order to be permanently retained it must be transferred from short-term memory to permanent, *long-term* memory. While the information is in short-term memory, strategies are used to transfer the incoming information to long-term memory. Thus, short-term memory can best be thought of as work space of the mind, while long-term memory can be thought of as the mind's encyclopedia, housing memories of other problems, rules, and techniques for problem solving, and more general knowledge about the world. The path between short-term memory and long-term memory is not one way; the strategies used to transfer information from short-term memory are stored in long-term memory. Additionally, knowledge gained through encoding and representing this information will then be added to the store of knowledge in long-term memory.

An alternative to this basic model of the human information processing system has also been proposed. This theory proposes that differences in the type of memory displayed by humans is not due to different memory stores; rather, the *level of processing* applied to the information determines the length of time it will be retained (Craik & Lockhart, 1972). If shallow processing is performed on the incoming information, that is, the information is processed at a superficial level, it will be retained for only a short period of time. An example of shallow processing of information is looking at a sample of text and noting the appearance of the words, whether they are uppercase or lowercase, printed in black or red, and so forth. If, in contrast, deep processing is applied to the information, it will be retained indefinitely. Deep processing occurs when we think about and reflect upon what the words mean, what images they produce, and so on. These two examples reflect extremes of the continuum—different levels of processing, for example, sounding out the words in the text, exist in between.

PROCESSES OF THE INFORMATION PROCESSING SYSTEM

The basic structures of the information processing system do not change with development; rather, the developmental changes occur in the processes which are applied to information. Thus, with development, children become more expert with the processes necessary for the information processing system to function. Children's thought processes do not qualitatively change with development, they simply become more efficient. Although there are many different processes hypothesized to be important in development, we will concentrate on the processes of *encoding and representation*, *strategy construction*, *automatization*, and *generalization*.

ENCODING AND REPRESENTATION

The human processing system is not capable of managing the massive amount of information taken in by our senses. Consequently, not all the information that reaches the senses is retained and stored. Instead we attend to and *encode,* or change into mental representations, what we judge to be the relevant features of the environment. Sometimes the encoding process is efficient and the crucial aspects of the stimulus are encoded, and sometimes the process is inefficient and critical information is lost. Often, what determines which information is retained and what information is lost is *attention*. The ability to attend to relevant information is one that improves with development.

Representation, or the form in which information is stored, is a crucial part of the flow of information through the system. Knowledge can be represented in many different ways: words, pictures, images, and actions, to name just a few. It is the change in type and complexity of representations that some developmental psychologists hypothesize underlie some aspects of development. One type of representation that is of particular interest to psychologists is *scripts*. Scripts are conceptual frameworks that center around an event or series of events. These events are stored in temporal order and are based on common experiences of daily life. A common example of the use of a script is a trip to a restaurant. Children know that during a visit to a restaurant you cannot eat your food before you order it, and that after you receive the food you must pay for it. Scripts are used to understand new events and to generate predictions about how those events will unfold.

Encoding and representation are particularly important in the levels of the processing model of human cognition. Efficiency of encoding the information will affect the type of processing which can be applied to the information, while the complexity of the representation will determine whether an object is processed at a deep or shallow level.

STRATEGIES

Strategy use is one of the most important processes hypothesized by the information processing approach. Strategies are conscious cognitive or behavioral activities that are used to enhance mental performance. Strategies can be applied at all levels of the information processing system; there are strategies for optimal storage and retrieval of information, strategies which

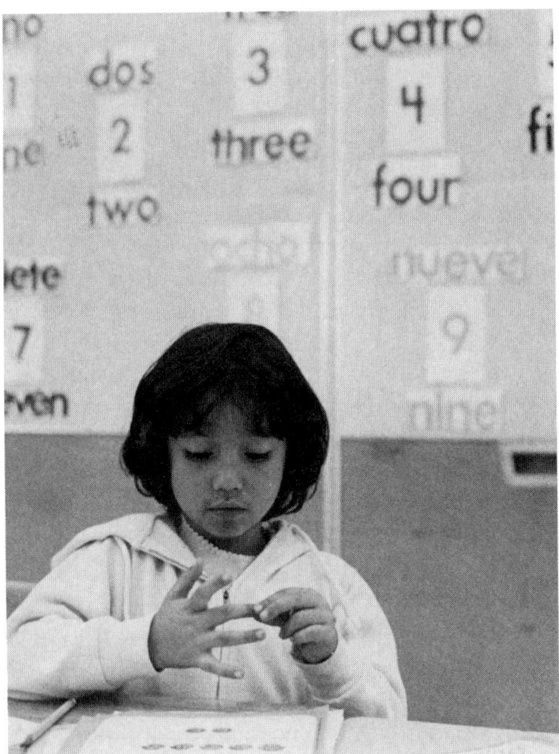

Children use a variety of strategies in solving math problems.

produce deep processing of information, and strategies for logical problem solving. An example of strategy use can be found in children's counting. When presented with an addition problem, such as "3 + 14," young children will use the "count-all" strategy, and will count from 1 up to the first term of the problem (that is, 3) and then continue counting the number of the second term (that is, 14 more) until they arrive at the answer of 17. Older children, in contrast, will use a more efficient strategy for addition, the "min rule." Using this strategy, the child will begin counting from the larger of the two addends (14 in the previous example), and continue upwards, adding the amount of the smaller number, counting "15, 16, 17" until he arrives at the answer (Siegler, 1987).

Thus, the main purpose of a strategy is to decrease the load on the child's information processing system by increasing the efficiency of each process, thus freeing up space for other tasks. Another way to increase the efficiency of the information processing system is to *automatize* certain aspects of the solution process.

AUTOMATIZATION

Automatization occurs when behaviors which were once conscious and controlled become unconscious and automatic. The most common example of automatization occurs in adults who are learning to drive a car with a stick shift. At first, every shifting of the gears is slow and strained, with the driver concentrating on each aspect of shifting in order to do it right. With practice, however, the driver can shift gears quickly and efficiently, unaware of the individual steps involved and often unaware of shifting altogether. This same process can occur with mental strategies developed during problem solving. Mathematics again provides a good example. When calculating multiplication problems, 7-year-old children use a variety of strategies to arrive at the answer. With development, the use of memorization strategy (one of the simpler strategies used) becomes automatic (Miller & Paredes, 1990).

GENERALIZATION

The strategies developed by children are often quite specific to the task at hand. For instance, our previous examples with the min rule could have taken place during the performance of mathematical problems in a school situation. Through the process of *generalization* children come to apply strategies learned while solving a previous problem to new situations. Initially, a child may be presented with an addition problem in a school setting and may apply the min rule correctly. However, the same child, when presented with a set of real objects, may insist upon counting up from 1. As the child becomes more familiar with the min rule, he will begin to generalize it to new situations. Thus, the strategy learned while trying to solve a mathematical problem in school can be generalized to counting objects such as jelly beans at home—a useful skill to make sure that you and your brother have the same number of candies!

THE ROLE OF EXECUTIVE CONTROL STRUCTURES

All of the processes—encoding and representation, strategy use, automatization, generalization—enable the child to increase his efficiency in processing information. One aspect of development, which is crucial to the efficient use of these skills, is the ability to know *when* to use them. Thus, an executive function must be added to any model of human information processing to reflect the child's role in selecting problems and strategies, as well as monitoring the success of his problem solving. Additionally, the child approaches intellectual problems with goals, purposes, and motivations, and these factors will also have a major influence on the child's performance.

In short, children have to monitor their cognitive functions and act as executives in selecting, organizing, and interpreting the information available to them. Thus, most theorists feel it necessary to add an *executive control structure* to the model of human information processing. The executive function directs the intake of information (perception and attention), and selects the strategies applied to the problem and monitors the success of the strategies as well. The child can then choose what problem he will work on, decide how much effort he will direct to the solution, select the strategies he will apply, avoid distractions and interruptions that hamper his efforts, and evaluate the quality of his solution. Between the ages of 3 and 12, the child's executive control function shows dramatic development. Whereas the preschooler often seems to have his actions dominated by the task and applies a single ineffective strategy to a variety of tasks until he is overwhelmed by frustration, the 12-year-old is able to master a wide range of intellectual tasks, orchestrating his strategies to find the best solution to the problem at hand.

Effects of Knowledge on the Information Processing System

One aspect of children's development which plays a major role in the ability to encode and represent information, as well as the use of appropriate strategies, is the amount of knowledge the child possesses about the problem he is trying to solve. It would be impossible for a child to display appropriate

Expertise plays an important role in problem solving according to information processing theory. Even a young experienced chess player can surpass the performance of an older but less expert adult.

problem-solving strategies on a math problem if he knows nothing about math!

The role of children's knowledge base has recently become of great interest to developmental psychologists. Recall that the information processing approach proposes the same structures throughout the life span—what changes with development is the efficiency of the mental processes the child applies to the information. One determinant of the efficiency of problem solving is the child's familiarity with the domain of the problem. For example, one strategy often used by adults to aid in recall is to group similar items together. This is a strategy that is not often used by children when they are placed in a standard recall task. If, however, children are asked to recall the names of their classmates, a subject they know a great deal about, 6-year-olds will display sophisticated groupings based on seating arrangements, reading groups, and gender (Ornstein & Naus, 1985). Other research has shown that when children are given problems in an area in which they have a great deal of knowledge, they will equal, and even surpass, the performance of less knowledgeable adults (Bédard & Chi, 1992; Chi, 1978). One example of the phenomenon is presented in Box 9-4.

Example of an Information Processing Task Analysis

Using an information processing model, the goal of the developmental psychologist is to discover how the information processing system changes as the child matures. Typically, the information processing model assumes that the capabilities of the child are different from, and more limited than, those of an adult. The child cannot take in and encode as much information, is less systematic about what information is encoded, has fewer strategies to apply to a problem, and has less knowledge about the world with which to understand the problem. An analysis similar to those performed by information processors can be applied to children's performances in a very simple task: counting out pennies. Imagine that a preschool child has been asked to count out a pile of pennies and is having difficulty counting past ten. There are many possible reasons why the child is unable to perform this task: he may not be able to remember the appropriate number terms, suggesting a

BOX 9-4 TURNING THE TABLES: CHILDREN'S MEMORY IN AN AREA OF EXPERTISE

Why do adults remember information better than children? While many theorists argue that adults have a larger memory capacity, Michelene Chi believes that much of adult's superiority can be attributed to their greater knowledge and understanding of the information to be memorized. To test this notion, Chi recruited children from the third through the eighth grades who were well versed in the game of chess to participate in a memory study. The children were asked to view either a sequence of ten numbers or a chessboard in a midgame position for a ten-second interval. The number of times the child could recall (either numbers or chess piece positions) was assessed, as was the number of ten-second viewings needed to correctly recall the entire number sequence or chessboard. The children's performance was then compared to that of adults who had a basic understanding of the game of chess, but no special expertise.

As can be seen in Figure 9-4, adults were better than children on the digit recall task; they remembered more numbers after a single viewing (immediate recall), and required fewer viewings to reach perfect recall (repeated recall). This replicated previous studies that had examined children's and adults' memory capabilities.

However, the opposite trend was found for the recall of chess positions. Here, children who were more experienced in chess performed much better than the adult novices on both the immediate recall and repeated recall measures. Chi concluded from her findings that knowledge plays an important role in memory performance. The superiority of adults' performance on traditional recall tasks (like the digit task) may reflect the adults' greater familiarity with number systems, rather than any difference in basic memory capacity between children and adults.

Source: Chi, M. T. H. (1978). Knowledge structures and memory development. In R. S. Siegler (Ed.), *Children's thinking: What develops?* Hillsdale, NJ: Erlbaum.

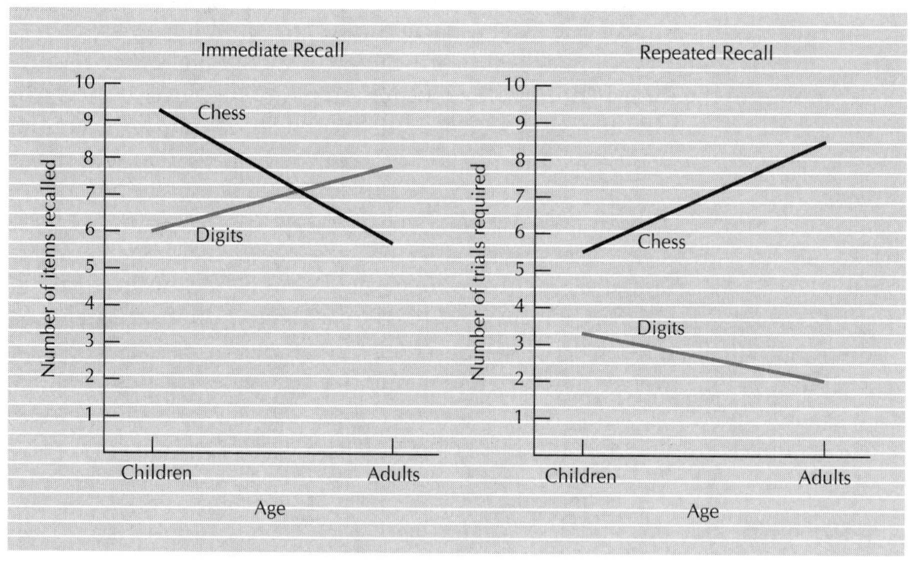

FIGURE 9-4

Two measures of recall: the number of chess pieces or numbers recalled after a ten-second viewing (left) and the number of ten-second viewings needed to achieve perfect recall (right). *(From Chi, 1978.)*

lack of memory access or possibly a failure to correctly encode the numbers 1 through 10 during learning. Also, he may be unable to match the number with the pennies in the correct manner, exhibiting a lack of counting strategies. Additionally, he simply may not be able to count twenty pennies because he only knows how to count to ten, displaying a lack of domain knowledge.

Of course, the different components are interdependent and so it is often the case that decreasing the demands placed on one component improves the performance of another component. Thus, if the child can complete the task when there are only five pennies to be counted, he may be doing better because he now knows all the numbers. His improved performance may also be due to a decrease in the memory load; remembering five numbers is easier than remembering ten and thus more effort can be placed on matching the numbers to the pennies. Nonetheless, in many situations it is possible to trace failure to a shortcoming in one particular component.

The situation of having more pennies than the child can count suggests a second major concern of the developmental psychologist within the information processing approach: What can we learn about the child's cognitive processes and capabilities from problems that he fails to solve (Roberts, 1981)? Although this concern is similar to the one voiced by Piaget, the way the information processing approach analyzes children's failure is very different. Piaget would probably conclude from the child's failure that he lacked a firm grasp of the number concept. In contrast, an information processor would conclude that the child understands part of the problem and then would set out to discover just what aspects of numbers and counting the child does or does not understand.

However, in common with Piaget, the information processing approach also finds children's errors enlightening. For example, in the twenty pennies problem above, our preschooler might commit some interesting errors that tell us what he does understand. The child might count out ten pennies and then tell us that there are "ten and a bunch more." If the child is very clever, he might count out ten, then repeat the process and conclude that there are "ten and ten more." The child certainly knows that there are more than five pennies, and is likely to know that there are fewer than, say, a million. Obviously much can be learned from the child's "incorrect" answers. The information processing approach is very much concerned with this form of error analysis, that is, examining incorrect answers for evidence of less sophisticated, yet systematic, strategies children apply to problems. What such analyses can tell us about children's thinking is illustrated in the work Robert Siegler has done on children's solutions to the balance beam problem and other logical problems (Siegler, 1983; 1991). (His balance beam work is described in Box 9-5.)

Summary

The information processing approach to cognitive development is an attempt to provide a more systematic and quantitative description than is provided by Piagetian theory. Researchers within the information processing framework are concerned with the demands different intellectual tasks place on the child's perceptual, attentional, memory, and problem-solving capabilities. Development is viewed as improvements in these capabilities, either through increasing the amount of information that can be handled, or by streamlining the manner in which the information is processed.

A Comparison between the Piagetian and Information Processing Approaches

One of the most troublesome aspects of Piaget's theory is the concept of horizontal decalage, that is, why children are able to solve some concrete operational problems but not others. For example, why are children able to solve conservation of length problems before they can solve conservation of volume problems? Piaget's argument that conservation of volume requires a greater degree of abstraction is, in itself, too abstract to be a useful explanation. In contrast to the difficulty that Piagetian theory has in accounting for horizontal decalage, the information processing approach can account for

BOX 9-5 AN INFORMATION PROCESSING APPROACH TO CHILDREN'S PERFORMANCE ON A LOGICAL PROBLEM: THE IMPORTANCE OF BEING IN ERROR

One of the problems Piaget used to assess whether a child had achieved formal operational thought was the balance beam problem. Here, in a teeter-totter problem, the child must predict which way a beam balanced on a fulcrum will tilt. In Piaget's framework, formal operations are necessary to correctly integrate the two dimensions relevant to the solution of the problem (the number of weights on each side, and the distance of the weights from the fulcrum). Siegler reanalyzed the problem in order to derive simpler strategies that children might use to yield correct solutions in at least some cases. Siegler actually used Piaget's research findings to formulate three of the four rules listed below (rules I, II, and IV). His analysis suggested that there are four levels of sophistication for children's strategies:

Level 1: Rule I—The side with more weights is heavier.
Level 2: Rule II—Use rule I, but if weights are equal, the

FIGURE 9-5

Proportion of correct responses expected on each of the six types of problems for children using different response rules.

Type of problem	Rule employed: I	II	III	IV
1. Balance problems. There are the same number and configuration of weights on each side of the fulcrum. 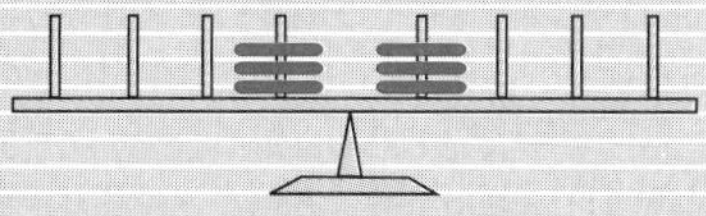	100	100	100	100
2. Weight problems. There are unequal amounts of weight at the same distance from the fulcrum on each side. 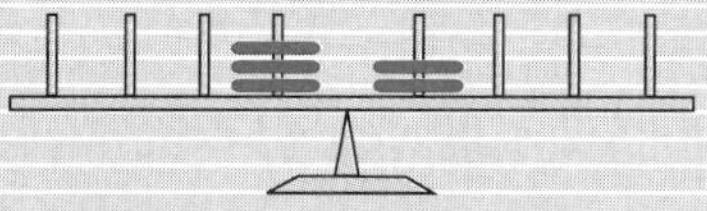	100	100	100	100
3. Distance problems. There are equal amounts of weight on each side but at different distances from the fulcrum. 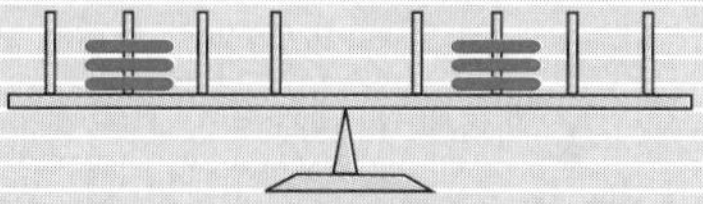	0 (Should say "balance")	100	100	100
4. Conflict-weight problems. One side has more weights; the other side has weights at a greater distance from the fulcrum. The side with more weights goes down. 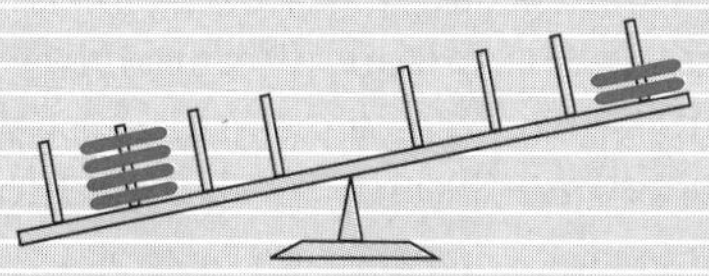	100	100	33 (Chance responding)	100
5. Conflict-distance problems. Same as 4, but the side having weights at a greater distance goes down. 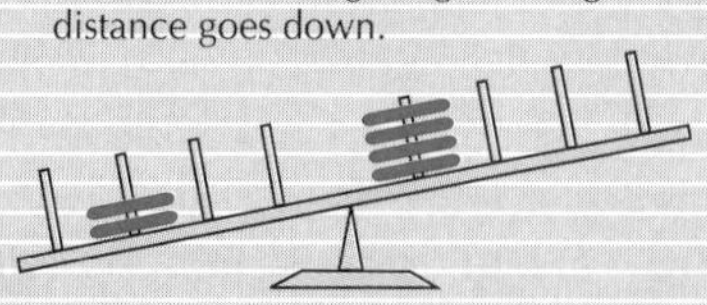	0 (Should say "right down")	0 (Should say "right down")	33 (Chance responding)	100
6. Conflict-equal problem. Like 4 and 5, but the two sides balance.	0 (Should say "right down")	0 (Should say "right down")	33 (Chance responding)	100

BOX 9-5 AN INFORMATION PROCESSING APPROACH TO CHILDREN'S PERFORMANCE ON A LOGICAL PROBLEM: THE IMPORTANCE OF BEING IN ERROR (*Continued*)

side whose weights are farther from the fulcrum is heavier. Level 3: Rule III—Weight and distance are both considered, but when there is a conflict where one side has more weights but the other side's weights are farther from the fulcrum, the child must "muddle through" and guess. Level 4: Rule IV—Weight and distance are combined in the proper manner, that is, weights x distance equals torque; the side with greater torque will go down (equivalent to Piaget's formal operations).

Siegler then constructed six types of problems that would differentiate children at the different levels of sophistication as shown in Figure 9-5. Thus, in the conflict-distance problem, the right side has three weights one distance unit from the fulcrum; hence, the beam will tilt to the left. Children at level 1 and level 2 will answer incorrectly, children at level 3 will respond correctly some of the time (that is, at a chance level), and children at level 4 will consistently answer correctly. Other problems produce different patterns of responses. Thus, by examining the child's responses to all types of problems, Siegler could infer the child's level of cognitive sophistication.

Siegler found marked developmental differences in children's use of the various rules. Three-year-olds appeared not to use rules. About 50 percent of 4-year-olds use rule I. All 5-year-olds use rule I. Nine-year-olds are usually equally divided between rules II and III, and 13- and 17-year-olds almost always use rule III. Even among college students, only a minority use the complex reasoning entailed in rule IV.

Then, using a research strategy common to information processors, Siegler began to break down the task to see why young children had such difficulties in their attempts to solve the balance beam problem. These children seemed to have difficulty using the information about weight and distance given to them. Why? Two possible explanations seemed reasonable. First, young children might have limited memory; they might not be able to remember all of the information about the balance task. Second, they might not have sufficient knowledge; they might need more information or more precise directions to solve the task. Siegler and his colleagues used a situation in which they allowed the original balance scale arrangement to remain visible so that the child was not required to remember it. Thus the child could check the arrangement of weights as often as desired. In addition, information was increased by giving the children repetitive, detailed, direct instructions. The combination of low memory demands and detailed instructions resulted in children as young as 5 years old encoding or using the information about distance and weight effectively. When only one of the conditions, of either low memory demands or detailed instructions, was presented separately, no improvement was shown. Apparently both memory and information deficits play a role in the difficulty young children have in solving the balance scale task.

Notice that what characterizes this approach is the use of a detailed analysis of the processes and behavior involved in solving the task, an emphasis on the child's existing knowledge base, and refined models of behavior that parallel computer simulations.

Source: Siegler, R. S. (1978). The origins of scientific reasoning. In R. S. Siegler (Ed.), *Children's thinking: What develops?* Hillsdale, NJ: Erlbaum.

differences in children's behavior. By employing a more precise task analysis, researchers attempt to identify just what demands a given problem places on the child's attention, memory, and problem-solving abilities. Such precise analyses lead to more accurate predictions of children's successes and a more complete understanding of their failures.

Thus, in the case of conservation tasks, an information processing task analysis would show that the conservation of length is logically less complex than the conservation of volume. If you look at Figure 9-3, it can be seen that to solve the conservation of length task, the child need only compare the two items on one dimension: length. To conserve volume, however, it is necessary for the child to consider both the height of the container and its width. Further, these two dimensions must be combined in the proper way; that is, width times height equals volume. This added complexity increased the processing load on the information processing system, thus preventing the child from displaying the ability to conserve even though he may have the concept of "conservation." Hence, this analysis shows us why conservation of volume is more complex than conservation of length and should, therefore, be a later-developing skill.

THE NEO-PIAGETIAN APPROACH

As we have said previously, Piaget's theory of cognitive development and the information processing view approach the study of cognitive development from very different perspectives. However, a group of developmental psychologists called the neo-Piagetians have attempted to integrate these two very disparate viewpoints. One neo-Piagetian, Robbie Case, has developed a theory of cognitive development which draws heavily on features of both the Piagetian and the information processing theories (Case, 1984, 1985). Drawing from Piaget's theory, Case proposes that development occurs in stages in which children's underlying mental structures become increasingly more sophisticated. This increasing sophistication of thought is brought about by a set of basic cognitive functions which do not change with development. In Piaget's theory these functions are assimilation and accommodation; Case, however, proposes a different set of invariants which includes the ability to set goals, the ability to solve problems, the need to explore, and the use of observation and imitation to acquire new knowledge. Another difference between these two theories is the proposed basis for children's thought structures. Piaget modeled children's thought structures on symbolic logic, while Case proposes that concepts developed within the information processing tradition, such as encoding, strategies, and in particular executive control structures, are more appropriate models of children's thought processes. Specifically, he proposes that children form *executive control structures* in order to solve problems and also that improvements in memory capacity contribute to the stagelike development of children's abilities.

Executive Control Structures

Case (1984, 1985) proposes that one major change which occurs during development is the ability to form and combine executive control structures. An executive control structure is a "mental blueprint or plan for solving a class of problems" and is composed of three distinct components (Case, 1984). First, the executive control structure must contain a *representation of the problem situation,* which includes the conditions under which it is appropriate to use this particular plan. Second, it must contain a *representation of the problem objectives,* which state the desired end state, or solution, to this problem. Finally, the executive control structure must contain a *representation of the appropriate problem strategy,* which contains the actual procedure for moving from the present situation to the desired solution of the problem. Examples of each of these components of an executive control structure can be seen in Box 9-6.

Executive Processing Space

Case proposes that the more efficient use of *executive processing space,* or the space available for cognitive functioning, serves as a major mechanism for development. Executive processing space is divided into two distinct components: *operating space* and *short-term storage space (STSS).* Operating space is the amount of space necessary for a particular operation or control structure to operate. Short-term storage space refers to working memory, or the amount of space being devoted to short-term memory storage. Case proposes that, with development, children become more efficient in their execution of operations, consequently they need less operating space to perform a control structure. This decrease in the amount of operating space necessary for cognitive functioning, in turn, frees up more of the child's executive processing space, thus causing an increase in available short-term storage space. With this increase in short-term storage space, children can now attempt to solve complex problems which may contain a great deal of information to be remembered.

Notice that Case does not propose that, with development, children have an increase in basic capacity; instead, with development, children become more efficient in the use of the limited space they possess. As the processes children use when performing a task become more efficient, capacity is made available for other short-term storage. Case attributes children's increased efficiency to two factors: streamlining of executive control structures and biological maturation. The biological aspect of Case's theory involves the maturation of neurons as children grow. He proposes that, as children develop, myelinization (insulation of neurons) increases. The presence of myelin (a substance which covers the axons of neurons) increases the efficiency of neuronal firing, thus increasing the efficiency of brain functions.

Similar to Piaget, Case proposes that development can be divided into four structurally different stages. Each stage is characterized by a different set of executive control structures. During development these executive control structures are combined and integrated to form new, qualitatively different structures. The formation of these new executive control structures marks the boundaries between the four stages. Thus, just as in Piaget's theory, abilities acquired during the lower stages are necessary for the acquisition of the higher stages.

The four different stages of Case's theory differ in the "mental elements," or type of representations, which make up the child's executive control structures. Case uses a children's performance on a balance beam task (similar to Siegler's task described in Box 9-5) to derive examples of control structures at the different stages.

Sensorimotor Control Structures (Birth to $1\frac{1}{2}$ years). In this stage, infants mental representations are linked to their physical movement. Their executive control structures are combinations of physical objects and motor actions which the infant can perform. For example, "move hand to balance beam at point *x*."

Relational Control Structures ($1\frac{1}{2}$ to 5 Years). Children's representations include knowledge of relationships among objects, people, and events. Their executive control structures now include cause-and-effect statements, and explicit goal structures. For example, "move far end down by moving this end up."

Dimensional Control Structures (5 to 11 Years). Children begin to extract the significant dimensions from the physical world. Children become able to compare two dimensions, such as distance, number, and weight, in a logical way. For example, "determine side with weight at greater distance."

Abstract Control Structures (11 to $18\frac{1}{2}$ Years). Building upon the dimensional control structures of the previous stage, children begin to use abstract systems of thought which allow them to perform higher-order reasoning tasks. For example, "determine torque."

The unique synthesis of Piaget's stage view and the information processing view can be used to account for many different aspects of development that neither theory can adequately explain. In fact, Case and his colleagues

BOX 9-6 HOW TO MAKE JUICIER ORANGE JUICE: CHILDREN'S ABILITY TO FORM EXECUTIVE CONTROL STRUCTURES

One of the tasks used by Case to demonstrate the formation of executive control structures is the *juice-mixing task* developed by Noelting (1980). In this task, children are presented with two sets of beakers, set A and set B. The beakers in these two sets contain either orange juice or water. The children are then told that the contents of these beakers are going to be poured into two different pitchers and are asked "When the beakers are poured into a pitcher, which mixture will taste more strongly of juice, pitcher A or pitcher B? Or will they taste the same?" As seen in Figure 9-6*a*, by varying the number of beakers which contain orange juice or water, several different task situations can be formed.

Case proposes that young children ($3\frac{1}{2}$ to 5 years) will begin by assuming that the set of beakers which contains the most juice will result in the "juiciest" pitcher. Consequently, they should pick the set of beakers which contains the most orange juice. The executive structure involved in this reasoning is pictured in Figure 9-6*b*. Note that the child begins by representing the problem situation: there are two pitchers which will be filled with liquid from the beakers. Next, the child represents the objective of the task, which is to decide which pitcher will be "juicier." Finally, the child represents the appropriate strategy to apply to this situation; pick the set of beakers which contains the most juice. This executive control structure will enable the child to choose easily the correct

FIGURE 9-6
Juice-mixing task used to demonstrate executive control strategies. (*From Case, 1985.*)

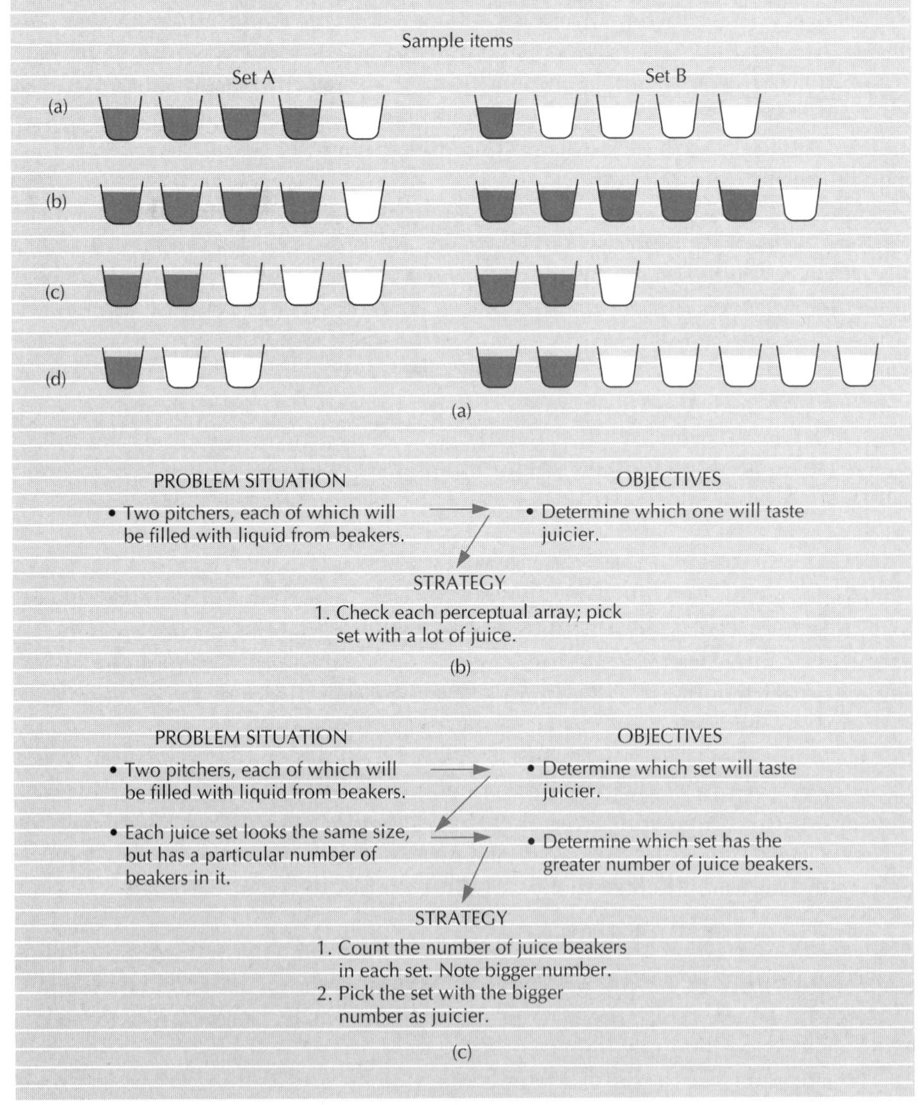
Sample items
Set A
Set B
(a)
(b)
(c)
(d)
(a)
PROBLEM SITUATION
• Two pitchers, each of which will be filled with liquid from beakers.
OBJECTIVES
• Determine which one will taste juicier.
STRATEGY
1. Check each perceptual array; pick set with a lot of juice.
(b)
PROBLEM SITUATION
• Two pitchers, each of which will be filled with liquid from beakers.
• Each juice set looks the same size, but has a particular number of beakers in it.
OBJECTIVES
• Determine which set will taste juicier.
• Determine which set has the greater number of juice beakers.
STRATEGY
1. Count the number of juice beakers in each set. Note bigger number.
2. Pick the set with the bigger number as juicier.
(c)

BOX 8-4 HOW TO MAKE JUICIER ORANGE JUICE: CHILDREN'S ABILITY TO FORM EXECUTIVE CONTROL STRUCTURES (*Continued*)

set of beakers (set A) in problem *a* of Figure 9-6a. However, this rudimentary control structure will not help the child when the amount of juice in the two sets is about equal, as in problem *b*. In this case, the child must count the number of juice beakers and choose the set which has the greater number of juice beakers. This new knowledge is represented in the modified control structure found in Figure 9-6c. Note that the knowledge to count the number of juice beakers in each set has been represented in the strategy portion of this control structure. This knowledge will enable the child to solve problem *b*.

During the course of development the child will continue to modify the basic executive control structure for this task and will consequently be able to solve more complex problems. For example, in order to solve problem c, the child's control structure will expand to include consideration of the number of water beakers in each set. With this new information the child will be able to accurately report that set B will result in the juicier juice. Finally, the relationship between the number of water beakers and the number of juice beakers will be represented; specifically the notion that the juice-to-water ratio will determine the juiciness of the liquid in the pitcher, thus, solving problem *d*.

Notice how the stagelike modification of the child's control structures is similar to Piaget's view of development, while the use of executive control structures is derived from an information processing viewpoint. It is in this way that Case combines aspects of both approaches into a coherent theory of children's cognitive development.

Sources: Case, R. (1985). *Intellectual development: Birth to adulthood.* New York: Academic; Noelting, G. (1980). The development of proportional reasoning and the ratio concept. *Educational Studies in Mathematics,* 11, 217–253 (I), 331–363 (II).

have applied this theory to a variety of different tasks and domains (Case, Sandieson, & Dennis, 1986; Case & Griffin, 1990; Marini & Case, 1989). However, it has been noted that Case's position on the role of myelinization in cognitive development is still to be fully tested (Siegler, 1991), and further, that the role of short-term memory capacity in the execution of procedures has not been fully explicated (Flavell, 1984). Despite these problems, the neo-Piagetian perspective offers a detailed and rich account of children's developing abilities.

VYGOTSKY'S SOCIOCULTURAL THEORY

None of the theories we have discussed have addressed the impact of the children's social and cultural worlds on their cognitive development. One theory which places a great deal of emphasis on those factors is Lev Vygotsky's sociocultural theory. Vygotsky was born in Russia in 1896—a fine year for cognitive development, since Piaget was born this same year. Unlike Piaget who lived a long and productive life, Vygotsky died at the relatively young age of 38 in 1934. In spite of his brief career, he has had a major influence on our thinking about cognitive development, not only in Russia and Eastern Europe, but in recent years in Western developmental psychology as well. At the time of his writing, the Communist Revolution had just come into full bloom in the Soviet Union, and much of Vygotsky's theory reflects the philosophy of the times. When Stalin came to power, however, much of the philosophy of the revolution was either subverted to fit his ends or repressed. Consequently, Vygotsky's work was banned in the early 1940s. Because of this, good translations of Vygotsky's work have only recently become available to psychologists in the west, and his theory has begun to receive the attention it deserves (Belmont, 1989; Rogoff, 1990; Wertsch, 1985; Wertsch & Tulviste, 1992).

Vygotsky's theory of development proposes an interaction between the child's social world and his cognitive development. He places great emphasis on the culture in which the child develops, and in particular, on the effect of learning a language on the child's intellectual development. Vygotsky's position is in marked contrast to Piaget's theory of development. Piaget and most Western theories of development focus on the individual as the unit of study. In contrast, Vygotsky focuses on the social nature of cognitive development, and emphasizes the critical role that the social world plays in facilitating children's development. For Vygotsky, development is best understood as a product of social interaction between partners who jointly solve problems together. The focus is between people rather than on individuals. Through the assistance provided by others in his social environment, the child gradually learns to function intellectually on his own—as an individual. According to Vygotsky, each child is given a set of innate abilities, such as attention, perception, and memory. Input from the child's society, in the form of interactions with more skilled adults and peers, then molds these basic abilities into more complex, higher-order cognitive functions.

Vygotsky was a proponent of the "genetic or developmental method" of analyzing human mental processes. He proposed that only by studying the development of an organism can you fully understand it and this means a focus on the processes involved in development rather than simply observing the end point or product of development. As in the case of Piaget and in contrast to information processing views, Vygotsky defined development in terms of "revolutionary" or abrupt shifts rather than steady quantitative increments. He was a stage theorist, since the qualitative nature of development changes at these transition points. In addition he accounted for shifts in development by the types of mediation that children rely upon to understand their world. Mediators can take a variety of forms but generally refer to tools or signs. Of particular interest to Vygotsky were psychological tools such as language, counting, mnemonic devices, algebraic symbols, art, or writing. Across development, the emergence of different types of signs or tools permit the child to function more effectively in solving problems and understanding his cognitive world.

Elementary and Higher Mental Functions

One transition in children's thinking occurs between *elementary* and *higher mental functions.* Elementary mental functions are those endowed to the child by nature: for instance, memory, attention, and perception. The "natural" forms of mental functioning are transformed by the child's culture into higher mental functions. These higher mental functions are assumed to be a new level of psychological processing for the child. An example of the difference between elementary and higher mental functions is provided by Vygotsky's discussion of memory. He proposes that the elementary form of memory is constructed of images and impressions of events. This type of memory is very close to perception; it is unanalyzed and is under the direct influence of the environment. An example of a higher form of memory is provided by the use of *signs* to mediate memory functions; for instance, the use of a writing system to form a list. In this example, the writing system is used as a sign, or mental tool, to elaborate upon the natural functioning of memory. Further, the writing system is provided by the child's society, revealing the social origins of higher mental functions.

Zone of Proximal Development

As part of his emphasis on the genetic approach to studying human development, Vygotsky was not interested in children's intellectual abilities at a particular point, but in the child's *potential* for intellectual growth (Cole, 1985; Wertsch, 1985; Wertsch & Tulviste, 1992). Thus, Vygotsky proposed the notion of the *zone of proximal development.* He defined this zone as the difference between a child's "actual developmental level as determined by independent problem solving" and the "potential development as determined through problem solving under adult guidance or in collaboration with more capable peers" (Vygotsky, 1978, p. 86). Thus, a child's potential level of development was determined by the level of competence he displayed under the tutelage of either adults or more capable children through the use of instruction.

This concept is a twofold one. On the one hand, it represents an alternative approach to *assessment* of intelligence by examining the child's intellectual potential under optimal social conditions. On the other hand, the zone of proximal development represents a way of understanding how children's intellectual development occurs, namely, through social interaction with more sophisticated partners.

Recently, researchers (Ferrara, Brown, & Campione, 1986; Belmont, 1989; Rogoff, 1990) have illustrated the value of this approach in studies of children's learning, by showing that children's planning, problem solving, and memory can be improved when guidance is provided by more skilled partners. Consider the example of adult-assisted planning in Box 9-7. We will see more applications of this type of approach in the next chapter. According to Vygotsky, working within a child's zone of proximal development allows him to respond to his environment in more complex and competent ways.

One form of instruction that was inspired by Vygotskian thinking that has received attention in recent years is termed *scaffolding.* Scaffolding is an instructional process by which the teacher adjusts or modifies the amount and type of support offered to the child that is best suited to his level of development. In an early classic demonstration, Wood, Bruner, and Ross (1976) taught 3- and 5-year-olds to build a pyramid out of interlocking wooden blocks through verbal and physical scaffolding. This involved modeling the steps, encouraging the child to put the blocks in the right slots, helping the child by segmenting the task and, in general, leading the child through the process. By careful monitoring of the child's progress, the tutor was able to constantly adjust the task to make it manageable and provide assistance when needed. As the child becomes more skilled, the amount of support is gradually reduced so that, eventually, the child is able to execute the task in a skilled fashion independently of adult help. Scaffolding has been demonstrated in a variety of tasks by later researchers (Pratt, Kerig, Cowan, and Cowan, 1988; Rogoff, 1990).

THE ROLE OF CULTURE

Another important feature of Vygotsky's approach is his recognition of the significance of culture in our accounts of development. There are two messages about culture that are evident in Vygotsky's theory. First, cultures vary in terms of the institutions and settings they provide to facilitate children's cognitive development. Schooling, or the introduction of new economic or occupational activities, can transform the ways in which we

BOX 9-7 BECOMING A MORE EFFICIENT PLANNER: VYGOTSKY IN ACTION

Do children solve a planning problem more efficiently when given guidance from a more skilled partner? According to Vygotsky, children should do better under these conditions. To find out, Radziszewska and Rogoff (1988) asked 9-year-olds to plan an errand either in collaboration with a 9-year-old partner or a parent.

Partners were given a map of an imaginary town (see Figure 9-7) and two lists of errands and were asked to plan a trip to get materials for a school play (for example, uniforms from the theatrical supplies store, paint brushes from the paint shop or the shopping center, and so on). They were asked to plan an efficient route to save gas, which required that the subjects develop a plan incorporating the stores to be visited and decide from which of two stores to purchase the needed supplies.

Adult-child dyads were better planners than peer-child dyads. The adult-child dyads planned longer sequences of moves (average of 4.9 stores per move) than the peer-child dyads (average of 1.3 stores per move). Nearly half of the adult-child dyads planned the whole route at the onset, while none of the child-child dyads showed this kind of careful planning. Children learned other helpful strategies when they worked with an adult—such as exploring the map of the town before making any moves and even marking stores that they wished or did not wish to shop at with different colors. Of great importance was the fact that the children were actively involved in the planning decisions, which the adults often verbalized to help the children's understanding. In contrast, the peer partners often dominated the decision-making process, ignored their coworkers, and communicated very little.

Not only did children profit more from participation with an adult, but they were able to transfer their learning to later planning tasks that they executed by themselves. In an independent planning test, children in adult-child dyads produced more efficient routes (20 percent shorter) than children in peer-child dyads.

As Vygotsky would have expected, "children appear to benefit from participation in problem-solving with the guidance of partners who are skilled in accomplishing the task at hand" (Rogoff, 1990, p. 169).

Sources: Radziszewska, B., & Rogoff, B. (1988). Influence of adult and peer collaborators on children's planning skills. *Developmental Psychology*, **24**, 840–848; Rogoff, B. (1990). *Apprenticeship in thinking.* New York: Oxford University Press.

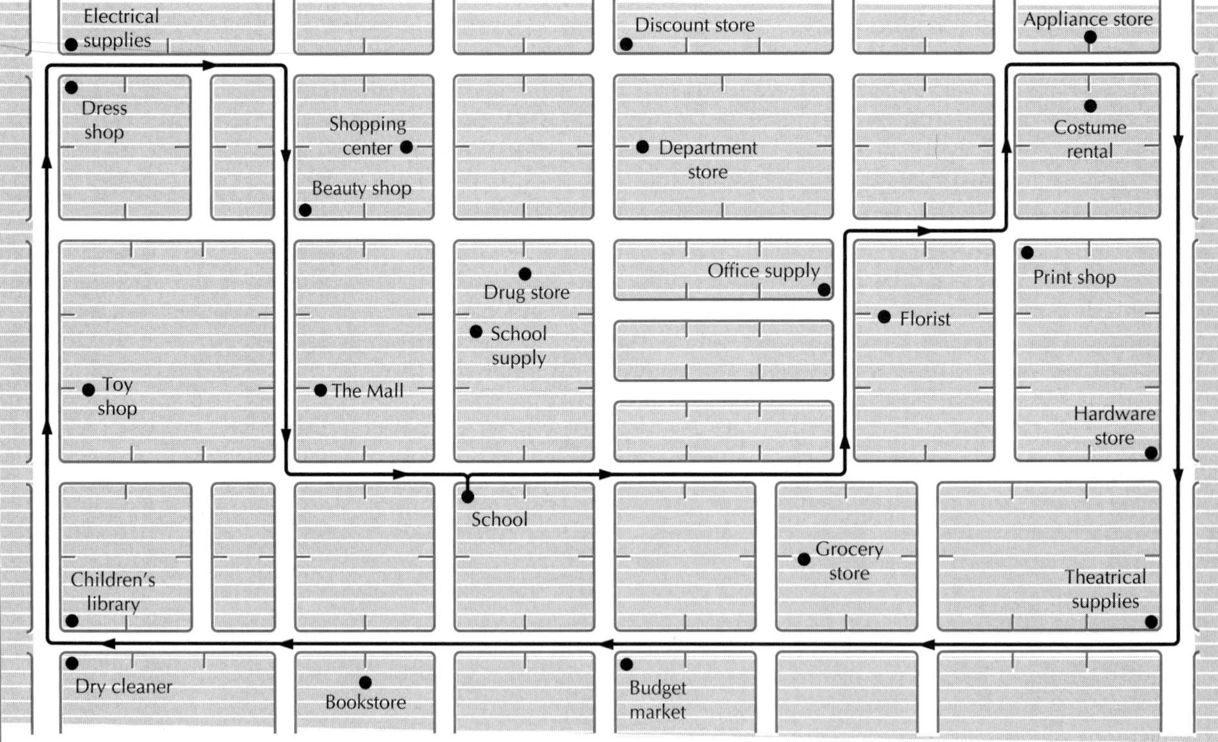

FIGURE 9-7

Map of imaginary downtown for errand-planning task, showing an optimal route. *(Reprinted by permission of the publisher, from Radziszewska & Rogoff, 1988, copyright 1988 by the American Psychological Association)* think. Luria (1971), an early collaborator of Vygotsky, showed that the Uzbekis of central Asia who learned to read and write began to approach reasoning problems in different ways. Traditional Uzbekis responded to reasoning problems using concrete examples based on their own experience, while more literate individuals treated the reasoning problems (for example, syllogisms) as logical puzzles (Scribner, 1985). Similarly, the Oksapmim people of Papua, New Guinea, rely on a rudimentary number system based on body parts to help them deal with the demands of daily life. However, the system is changing as a result of new occupational and trading activities, and paper and pencil notations as well as calculators are transforming the traditional counting methods (Saxe, 1982). Culture, in short, has a profound influence on how our thinking is organized.

A second reminder is the importance of considering cultural contexts in our assessments of children's cognitive development. Cognitive tasks should be embedded in their appropriate cultural context and serious underestimates of children's development can occur if the culturally specific nature of children's learning is ignored (Rogoff, 1990). A wide variety of cross-cultural studies have documented that children learn highly sophisticated and complex culturally important skills through social guidance, including weaving among the Zinacantecans of Mexico (Childs & Greenfield, 1982) and tailoring in Liberia (Lave, 1977). For example, children learn to weave through a series of steps that initially involve watching, then intensive adult guidance, and finally independent mastery.

> In the earliest stages of learning the girls spend a bit more than half their time watching the teacher perform the weaving task. As they get more proficient, more and more of their interaction with the teacher is of a cooperative participatory variety. Teacher intervention changes from taking over the weaving from the learner to participating cooperatively as learners gain more experience. . . . The amount of time the learner spends weaving independently goes from 7% for first time weavers to 52% if the girl has already made one garment to 58% if she has made two to four items to 100% independent work for the expert. (Greenfield & Lave, 1982, p. 202)

Several teaching skills are involved here, including developmentally guided scaffolding whereby the teacher provides just the amount of help required for successful task completion by the apprentice weaver. The concept of scaffolding also means that teachers intervene more at the tougher parts, so that task difficulty is always within the ability range of the learner. Finally tasks are developmentally sequenced from easier to harder aspects of the weaving process. As this example illustrates, the Vygotskian notions of the zone of proximal development and social guidance are useful in understanding the transmission of culturally important skills.

THE ROLE OF LANGUAGE

Language plays a special role in Vygotsky's social-cognitive theory. He believes that the acquisition and use of language is a primary component of children's developing intellectual abilities and he proposes three stages in children's use of speech: *social, egocentric,* and *inner speech.*

The first stage of the language of thought proposed by Vygotsky is *social speech.* During this time language is used primarily for communicative purposes and has no relationship with the child's thought processes. Thus, the communicative function of speech is separate from the intellectual function of speech. The second stage, *egocentric speech,* occurs when children begin to use speech to form thoughts and regulate intellectual functions. At this point in development, however, the children cannot use language internally; they must talk to themselves, using language as a way to guide thought and behavior. Finally, the child internalizes egocentric speech, changing it to *inner speech.* Language still plays its regulatory function; however, the child can now use language internally.

Evaluation of Vygotsky's Theory

This approach offers a fresh perspective from which to view cognitive development, by emphasizing the socially mediated nature of cognitive processes. Second, the theory has made us more aware of the importance of the immediate social contexts of learning and cognition and pointed the way to new ways of assessing children's cognitive potential through his use of the zone of proximal development and new ways of teaching reading, mathematics, and writing (Belmont, 1989; Brown & Campione, 1990). Moreover, Vygotsky has increased our appreciation of the profound importance of cultural variation in development and made us appreciate the uniqueness of cultural domains. It is currently leading to a great deal of research activity in Western countries, but the theory has not yet received the full scrutiny that other cognitive theories, such as Piaget's have received. It does, however, hold great promise as a new way of thinking about cognitive development in context.

SUMMARY

THEORIES OF COGNITIVE DEVELOPMENT

- *Cognition* refers to the mental activity and behavior that allows us to understand the world. It includes concepts such as learning, perception, memory, and thinking; and it is influenced by biological, environmental, experiential, social, and motivational factors. A variety of theories have been proposed to explain the pattern of cognitive development seen in children.

PIAGET'S COGNITIVE DEVELOPMENTAL THEORY OF INTELLIGENCE

- By the end of the 1950s, Piaget's theory began to replace behaviorism in America. Unlike behaviorism, it was seen as a truly developmental theory because it allowed for the different capacities of children of different ages. Piaget based his theory on observations of his own and other children as they answered questions during an unstructured interview.
- According to Piaget, children actively seek out information and adapt it to the knowledge and conceptions of the world that they already have. Thus, children construct their understanding of reality from their own experiences. Children organize their knowledge into increasingly complex structures called *schemata.*
- Children possess many different *schemata,* and these change as the children develop. In the newborn the schemata take the form of innate reflexes and reaction patterns, like sucking. As the child grows and gains experience, the schemata shift from motor activities to mental activities called *operations.* These operations become increasingly complex with age.

- Piaget suggested that schemata are modified according to the principles of *organization* and *adaptation* which continue to operate throughout the life span. Organization is the predisposition to combine simple physical or psychological structures into more complex systems. Adaptation involves the two complementary processes of *assimilating,* or fitting new experiences into current cognitive schemata, and *accommodating,* or adjusting current schemata to fit the new experiences. Most encounters involve both processes.
- Piaget divided intellectual development into four unique periods or stages which are indicative of the changes in children's cognitive structures. The attainments of earlier stages are essential for those in later periods of development. All children go through the stages in the same order, although not necessarily at the same ages.
- During the first two years of life, called the *sensorimotor period,* a child makes the transition from relying on reflexes to using internal representation, which is the cornerstone of symbolic thought. Piaget divided this period into six substages, during which the child physically explores the environment to developing abilities such as deferred imitation, and mentally representing objects that are not present.
- The major developmental milestone during the *preoperational period* is the development of the *symbolic function,* or the ability to use symbols such as words, images, and gestures to represent objects and events. This can be seen in the rapid development of language, in imaginative play, and in an increase in deferred imitation. Piaget divided this stage into the *preconceptual period* (2–4 years) and the *intuitive period* (4–7 years).
- During the preconceptual period children's thinking is limited by *animistic thinking,* the tendency to attribute life-like characteristics to inanimate objects, and by *egocentricity,* an inability to see things from the perspective of anyone else. Recent researchers have suggested that the shift away from egocentrism is related to the development of role-taking abilities.
- During the intuitive period, children are able to use certain mental operations, but they do not seem to be aware of the principles used because they cannot explain them. Limitations in their thinking are still found in problems involving seriation, part-whole relations, and conservation.
- Piaget believed that there were three characteristics of preoperational thought which limit children's thinking. The first is *irreversibility,* or the inability to understand that all logical operations are reversible. The second is the tendency to focus on the end states of a change rather than on the process of *transformation.* Finally, the third characteristic is *centration,* or focusing on only one dimension of a problem.
- During the *concrete operational period* (ages 7 to 11) children are able to use most operations on objects or experiences in their immediate world. This allows them to do most of the tasks that they were unable to do in the previous stage, including conservation, classification, and seriation.
- Children in the *formal operations period* (beginning around age 12) are able to use flexible and abstract reasoning, can test mental hypotheses, and are able to consider multiple possibilities for the solution to a problem. This stage is not attained by all people or by adults in all cultures. It is more likely to occur in groups with higher educational experiences and in areas in which adults have some expertise.
- Piaget's theory and observations have received criticism based on newer research. Recent studies indicate that Piaget may have underestimated

the ages at which certain abilities develop, that the sequence of development may not be invariant and may be modified by cultural experiences, and that the underlying operations specified by Piaget may not always be needed to explain the behaviors. However, his influence is clearly evident in our current understanding of cognitive development.

THE INFORMATION PROCESSING APPROACH

- The *information processing approach* views the human mind as a system that processes information according to a set of logical rules and limitations, similar to those of a computer. Research using this perspective tries to describe and explain changes in the processes and strategies that lead to greater cognitive competence as children develop.
- One view of the human information processing is a model in which information enters the system through our senses and is encoded and stored in long-term memory. A second model proposes that memory is based on the *level of processing* applied to the information rather than on the way in which it is stored.
- The basic structures of the information processing system do not change with development; instead, development is due to changes in the efficiency of the processes which are applied to the information. Four important processes considered to be important in development are *encoding and representation, strategy construction, automatization,* and *generalization.* Most theorists also add *executive control structures* that develop to monitor, select, and organize the processes that are applied to the information. In addition, knowledge plays a critical role in children's abilities to encode and represent information.
- Researchers using the information processing perspective often use task analysis to examine children's incorrect answers for evidence of systematic errors. Although the interest in error analysis is similar to Piaget's approach, more fine-grained task analyses lead to a more complete understanding of cognitive development.

THE NEO-PIAGETIAN APPROACH

- Case has developed a neo-Piagetian theory of cognitive development that integrates information processing theory and Piagetian theory. He proposes that the more efficient use of *executive processing space,* or the space available for cognitive functioning, is the major mechanism for development. As efficiency increases, children progress through four stages during which their underlying mental structures become increasingly sophisticated. Each stage is characterized by a different set of executive control structures which are combined and integrated to form new, qualitatively different structures.

VYGOTSKY'S SOCIOCULTURAL THEORY

- Vygotsky's theory emphasizes the critical role played by the social world in facilitating the child's development. According to his theory, children generally internalize thought processes that first occur through interaction with others in the social environment. Qualitative transitions between elementary and higher mental functions occur because of shifts in the use of mediators such as language and other symbols. The acquisition and use of language plays a primary role in children's developing intellectual abilities.

- Vygotsky's interest in the child's potential for intellectual growth led him to develop the concept of the *zone of proximal development* to study the level of competence shown while working with an adult or more capable peer. In recent years this concept has led to the use of *scaffolding*, an instructional process in which the teacher adjusts the amount and type of support offered to the child to suit the child's abilities, withdrawing support as the child becomes more skilled.
- In this theory, culture is important because it determines the available institutions that ultimately influence the ways in which we think, and because it provides the context in which cognitive development is assessed. This theory is important because it emphasizes the immediate social contexts of learning and cognition, as well as the role of culture in development.

CHAPTER

10

PROCESSES OF COGNITIVE DEVELOPMENT

Everyday of their lives children are presented with a series of challenges: figuring out a math problem, remembering to bring their homework to school, learning to tie their shoes, and many others throughout the day. The focus of this chapter is the cognitive processes children bring to bear upon these daily challenges and how these abilities change and grow through development. We will begin by describing changes in attention and memory; or children's developing ability to take in and store information. We will then discuss children's increasing ability to solve problems and their understanding of numbers and numerical concepts. Finally, we will discuss children's knowledge of their own mental capabilities and how their abilities are affected by the type of tasks being performed and the strategies they apply.

Each of these abilities plays a crucial role in children's daily problem solving. Because much of the more recent research in this area of child development has been motivated by the information processing approach, this chapter is loosely based on abilities thought to be crucial to development from this approach. Keep in mind, however, that each of these abilities is also a component of both the Piagetian and the neo-Piagetian perspectives. Further, these abilities are constantly being affected by the society in which the child develops, and thus can be studied from a sociocultural, or Vygotskian, perspective.

PERCEPTION AND ATTENTION

When a group of childen are in the same situation and are exposed to the same sensory stimulation, they do not necessarily gain the same amount and kind of information. Their *perception,* or intake of information from the surrounding environment, may be the same, but their *attention* may be focused on different aspects of the environment. In the same classroom, one child focusing on the teacher will hear and understand the lesson, while another child, more interested in a whispered message from a neighboring peer, may regard the teacher's voice as no more than an annoying buzz. The effects of the sights, sounds, smells, touches, and sense of movement provided by their surroundings will depend on what aspects of the situation the children attend to and what meaning these features have for them.

Changes in what information can be gained from a situation is due to development of both the child's perceptual capabilities and her attentional strategies. These two processes are tightly intermeshed; perception presupposes some attentional abilities, and attention would be meaningless if the person were unable to glean meaning from what she was observing.

How Perception Develops

There are two main theories of the way in which experience affects perceptual learning and development. An enrichment theory, such as that of Piaget discussed in the previous chapter, proposes that each time a child perceives an object she learns a little more about that object. The first time a child sees a cat, it may be viewed as little more than another fuzzy, four-footed animal. The next time she sees the cat, it may be drinking milk and purring. She elaborates her cat schema to include "purrs and likes milk." Finally, the child may attempt to pick the cat up but discovers that the cat is too heavy. Cats then become fuzzy, four-footed animals that drink milk, purr, and are heavy. With experience, information is added to the existing schema of an object, and the schema becomes more detailed and elaborated. The sensations that are received from the stimulus are meaningless until they are modified and enriched by information from other schemata. Meager sensory information is reorganized and elaborated by the child. As this enrichment of schemata occurs for many different objects, the child is better able to discriminate among objects (Bruner, 1957; Vernon, 1955).

In contrast to the enrichment theory, the differentiation theory of Eleanor Gibson (1969, 1991, 1992) proposes that sensory input is a rich source of information. The sensory information is not an impoverished information base that must be enriched through schemata or associations as is proposed in the enrichment theory. Instead, the task of the child is to gradually learn to attend to, identify, and discriminate the important features of objects and relationships from the vast flow of sensory information. Through experience, the child learns to make increasingly finer discriminations among objects and events and to attend to the relevant attributes of objects. These attributes are termed invariants, that is, characteristics of objects, or relationships among objects that do not change under different conditions. Often, these invariants define relational characteristics of an object rather than any absolute quality. Thus, a gray cat may appear nearly black in dim light (for example, by a table lamp in the den), but nearly white in bright light (for example, in the yard on a sunny day). If, however, the cat has a black collar on, the fur will always appear lighter than the collar, regardless of the amount of light. The relationship between the brightness of the cat and the collar remains constant (invariant); that is, the cat is always four times as bright as the collar. Thus, an object's brightness relative to other objects in its surroundings is a perceptual invariant.

According to Gibson's theory, it is these higher-order relationships, or invariants, which the perceptual system attends to and which uniquely describe objects and relationships despite any changes (transformations) in distance or orientation (Gibson, 1991; 1992). What perceptual development entails is learning to attend to the relevant invariants of objects and finding new differences among similar stimuli. Over time, the child will learn to distinguish the friendly neighborhood cat from the king of the jungle.

Gibson's theory has had a major impact on research and has underscored the importance of understanding perceptual processing and its impact on attention (Pick, 1992). For the infant, attention tends to be controlled primarily by the physical properties of stimuli. However, as children mature, their needs and goals come to direct attention to a greater degree. What is attended to in a particular situation becomes determined by the demands of the task and the goals and strategies the child brings to the situation.

Attention: Choosing What Is Perceived

When a topic is interesting to us, it often feels as though attention is simple and effortless. In fact, attention is a very complex process; one that is affected by the type of information being presented, how it is being presented, and the sophistication of the perceiver. One aspect of attention that is often difficult for children is controlling their attentional capabilities.

Control of Attention. Very young children can sustain their attention for only short periods of time, but this ability increases across development. Between ages 1 and $3\frac{1}{2}$ years, children show a steady increase in the amount of time that they attend to objects, such as toys. (Ruff & Lawson, 1990). While 1-year-olds attend to a toy for only $3\frac{1}{2}$ seconds, by age $3\frac{1}{2}$ children

Selective attention is an important ingredient for reading.

spend over 8 seconds attending to a single toy. No teacher or parent expects a young preschool child to show the persistence in play or in task-oriented activities that is found in older children. Even when they are watching television, young children are more easily distracted than older children and adults. Two- and three-year-old children will often talk to others, play with toys, and wander around the room in between glances at the television (Anderson, Lorch, Field, Collins, & Nathan, 1986). In contrast, the older children are less distractible and spend more time with their attention directed toward the television program. Once their attention has been fully engaged by the television program, however, young children (3- and 5-year-olds) are less likely to attend to an external audiovisual distractor (Anderson, Choi, & Lorch, 1987).

The type of information being perceived also has an effect on children's attention. Children are more likely to attend to programs that are appropriate to their intellectual level as well (Anderson, Lorch, Field, & Sanders, 1981). Programs that are too complex are of little interest. Children are also quite sensitive to the importance of the information being presented for the flow of the program. When questioned about a program they had previously viewed, 4- and 6-year-old children were more likely to recall important facts from the program rather than unimportant facts (Lorch, Bellack, & Augsbach, 1987). Further, children younger than 6 are more interested in the visual content of programs than the audio content (Hayes, Chemelski, & Bernbaum, 1981). Thus, when watching *Sesame Street*, they are more likely to be interested in Big Bird's funny appearance, big feet, awkward movements, and wry facial expressions, than in what he is saying.

Adaptability. In learning situations, it is not enough merely to attend to the task at hand. It is critical that the child is able to focus on the relevant aspects of the task and ignore the irrelevant features. As children mature, they are better able to selectively attend to the crucial aspects of a situation and are less likely to be distracted by irrelevant features. For example, Miller and Wiess (1981) presented 7-, 10- and 13-year-old children with an *incidental learning* task. In this task the children were asked to remember the location of a number of small animals, each of which was hidden behind a different cloth cover. When the children were shown each of the hidden animals they also saw a different household item, either above or below the animal. The goal of this task is to remember the location of the target object (the animal) while rejecting the irrelevant object (the household object). When the children's memory of the location of animals was tested, the older children performed much better than the younger children. In contrast, when the children's knowledge of the irrelevant knowledge was tested, the opposite pattern was found; the younger children often remembered where the household objects were hidden, unlike the older children. In fact, the younger children remembered as much about the location of the household objects as they did about the location of the animals. A similar methodology has also been used to assess children's attentional capabilities in pictures containing relevant and irrelevant information (Day, 1975; Hagen & Hale, 1973), as well as in listening to information coming through either ear (Cherry, 1981; Maccoby, 1967, 1969). The young children in these tasks failed to filter out the irrelevant aspects of the situation and, instead, attended to both the relevant and irrelevant information.

Studies also find that older children are more flexible than younger children in modifying their attention in accordance with the requirements of the task (Hale & Taweel, 1974; Pick & Frankel, 1974). For example, if children are shown pictures of dogs and cats and are instructed to remember the color and number of spots for dogs, but only the color of cats, older children perform better; that is, they remember both color and spots for dogs and only color for cats. Younger children are likely to remember both features for both cats and dogs and/or forget the number of spots on the dogs. Thus, older children are better able to broaden or narrow their attentional range depending on the demands of the task. Since no single strategy is most effective on all tasks, this adaptability is quite advantageous. Being able to use different strategies for different tasks is the most effective approach to learning.

As can be seen in Figure 10-1, the general pattern of the findings from these studies is that processing of the relevant information increases during

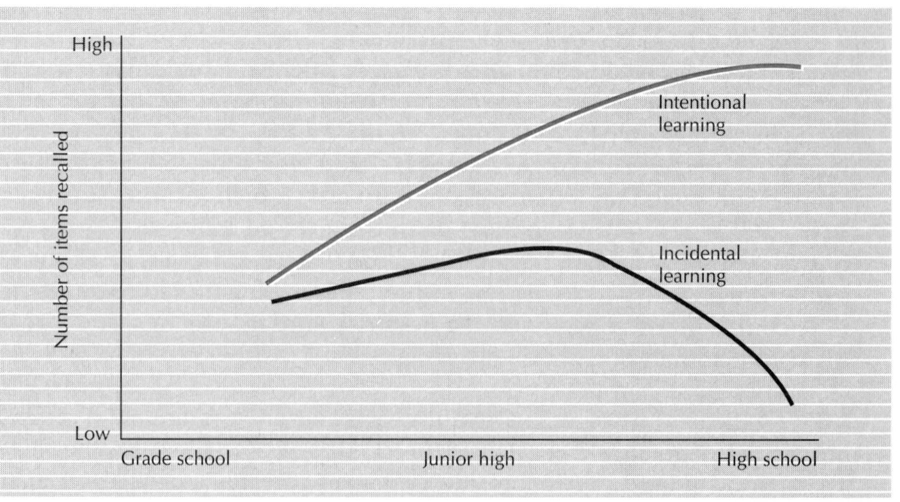

FIGURE 10-1
Pattern of children's performance on selected attention tasks.

the elementary and high school years. At the same time, processing of the irrelevant information remains constant or increases until the age of 11 or 12 and then decreases. This suggests that the older children are devoting more of the attention to the relevant materials than are the younger children. This view of children's developing attentional focus fits well with the predictions of the information processing view of development. You will recall that in the information processing approach, development is caused by the increased efficiency of the child's cognitive processing. The increase in the ability to attend to relevant aspects of a situation is just one example of one of the cognitive processes proposed by this approach affecting the child's ability to deal with her environment.

Planfulness. One of the most striking changes in the child's attention strategies is the development of more organized plans or systematic strategies in gathering and filtering information relevant to the solution of problems. Imagine that you have before you drawings of two houses. Each house has six windows, like those in Figure 10-2. Your task is to determine whether the two houses are identical. How might you approach this problem? Probably, you would compare the six pairs of corresponding windows in the house,

FIGURE 10-2
Sample of the stimuli: A pair of identical houses on top and a pair of different houses on the bottom. (*From Vurpillot, 1968.*)

one pair at a time, until you found a pair that did not match. If all the pairs match, you would conclude that the houses were identical. In an early classic study Vurpillot (1968) administered this task to young children, as is described in Box 10-1. Her findings demonstrated that the younger child is far less systematic in her comparisons of the stimuli. She is more likely to make a judgment based on inadequate or incomplete samplings of the pertinent information than is an older child. The young child fails to apply a systematic plan to extract the information necessary to make a meaningful comparison.

Can we conclude from this research that the young child is unable to plan an efficient strategy for attention? Further research by Miller and Weiss (1981) suggests that this is not the case. They modified the incidental learning task described previously to include information relevant to the location of either the animals or the household items. (The animals were hidden behind pictures of cages, while the appliances were hidden behind pictures of houses.) When this information was made available to the child, 7- and 10-year-old children consistently looked behind the cages when told that they would be tested on the animals and looked behind the houses when told they would be tested on the household items. Further research revealed that when additional cues (for example, a story which united all the animals pictured) were provided, children as young as 6 years performed quite well (Woody-Ramsey & Miller, 1988). Thus, it appears that young children can utilize a strategy to focus their attention on relevant aspects of their environment when that strategy is simple and easily available (DeMarie-Dreblow & Miller, 1988).

MEMORY

In the next two sections we will discuss what is known about developmental changes in children's memory and problem-solving ability. Sometimes the distinction between these two areas of cognitive processing becomes rather blurred. In fact, researchers often emphasize the similarities of the processes involved in memory and problem solving rather than the differences. It could even be said that to remember is a problem that must be solved by utilizing various types of cognitive processes. Perhaps the best perspective to take is to consider that there exists a whole range of cognitive tasks that vary in the extent to which they tap pure memory ability versus more general problem-solving strategies. The division employed in this chapter exists more for organizational convenience than to capture any fundamental conceptual distinction.

What do we mean when we talk about memory? In fact, we mean many things. We mean the ability to remember a phone number from the time we look it up in the directory until we dial the phone. We also mean the ability to remember more general information we have gained in our lifetime. This kind of memory would include an understanding of what a phone is, how one uses it, and why one uses it to call that attractive person whose name we just looked up in the directory.

There does seem to be a difference between the two kinds of memory just described. The first seems to involve short-term memory for specific events and information, and the second type, long-term memory, involves the more general knowledge store that results from our experiences. As we discussed previously in the information processing section of Chapter 9, there are differing hypotheses to explain this difference in memory types. However,

BOX 10-1 LOOKING WITHOUT SEEING: A CLASSIC STUDY OF CHILDREN'S VISUAL SCANNING STRATEGIES

Many problem-solving situations require that the child make a systematic comparison of two sets of stimuli to determine whether they are identical or different. Elaine Vurpillot's studies of children's eye movements while performing these tasks indicated that development occurs in the systematicity of their scanning strategies.

Vurpillot showed children pairs of houses. The children were asked to decide whether or not the houses were identical. Half of the houses were identical; the other half differed by displaying various things in one, three, or five of the houses' six windows. For example, in the pairs shown in Figure 10-2 the top pair are identical but the bottom pair differ in that the house on the left has a bird cage in its top right window whereas the one on the right has plants in that window. Vurpillot filmed the children's eye movements as they made their comparisons, then plotted the path of their eye movements and where their gazes stopped and fixated.

This analysis revealed that younger children tended to make unsystematic comparisons of the houses. They would look at several of the windows in a random fashion, then respond (often incorrectly) that the houses were alike or different. For example, they would never even look at the windows that differentiated the two houses before responding that the houses were identical. Older children, on the other hand, would take a much more logical approach, comparing each pair of windows until they found a difference. These findings illustrate that between the ages of 4 and 9, children develop much more organized and systematic strategies with which to process visual information.

Source: Vurpillot, E. (1968). The development of scanning strategies and their relation to visual differentiation. *Journal of Experimental Child Psychology*, **6**, 632–650.

regardless of whether differences in memory are due to separate storages for long-term and short-term information or are due to different levels of processing, the development of these abilities is a major accomplishment in children's cognitive development.

The three areas of memory that have been considered to show improvement with development are (1) basic capacity, the amount of information that can be held in short-term memory; (2) strategies, actions performed to enhance the transfer of information to long-term memory; and (3) world knowledge, the larger context of information into which the child can fit new information. Let us consider each of these aspects in turn.

Basic Capacities

Suppose you are given the task of repeating a sequence of numbers that I recite. I begin with three digits, then progressively add more. Eventually, you will not be able to repeat all the numbers correctly. I will have exceeded your memory span for this kind of information. The digit span is about eight units for college students, six or seven units for 12-year-olds, and four units for 5-year-olds (Brener, 1940; Starr, 1923). Pascual-Leone (1980, 1989) uses evidence of this sort to argue that an increase in the capacity or working memory must occur during this time (Carroll, 1976; Case, 1984). That is, there is an improvement in the child's basic memory capability partly based on brain changes; she simply has more "room" in which to remember things. Others argue that there is no solid evidence for changes in the basic capacity of memory as children develop (Dempster, 1985); in fact, it has been found that the young children show an impressive ability to retain more about lists of children's items that adults do (Lindberg, 1980).

Another possibility is that even on a simple task such as memory for a series of numbers the older child or adult may perform better on the task because she applies a different method or *strategy* to the task (Chi, 1976). For example, the older person may "chunk" the information into smaller numbers of units (Miller, 1956). Thus the young children may not be able to remember the sequence 1 7 7 6 1 4 9 2 1 9 2 9 because it is too long, but the adult can recall the sequence because she groups the numbers into three chunks (1776, 1492, 1929) she finds meaningful and hence easy to remember. Every cognitive step or strategy the child uses in solving a problem takes some space to store in working memory as the child moves on to the next step. Finally, it has been argued that working memory increases because the child's application of strategies becomes more automatic. This *automaticity* frees space in working memory to cope with other problems or strategies. Because the role of memory is so crucial to the model of cognitive development proposed by the information processing approach, the role of memory capacity and the use of memory strategies has been widely studied from this perspective. In particular, the increasingly important role of strategies is an area of interest which has been widely researched by information processors. While most memory is based on past events, sometimes we have to remember a future event. For an example, see Box 10-2.

Strategies

Since even performance on the most straightforward memory tasks cannot be evaluated without considering what strategies the person applies to the task, we will now examine what developmental changes occur in children's employment of various memory strategies.

Unless information is processed in some fashion it is quickly forgotten. If you doubt this, just try to repeat the last sentence of the previous section. People employ a wide range of cognitive activities that increase the likelihood that they will be able to remember needed information at a later time. Some of these strategies involve external supports such as taking notes in lectures or writing appointments on calendars. Even 2-year-olds have been observed to use external memory supports, for example, using furniture as landmarks to find hidden toys (DeLoache, 1989; DeLoache & Brown, 1983). Other memory supports are purely mental (for example, repeating that attractive person's name several times so you can look up his or her phone number later). Three of these mental strategies that adults frequently employ have been studied in children. These are *rehearsal, semantic organization,* and *elaboration.*

Rehearsal. One of the most simple strategies that can be used to aid later recall is to repeat, either verbally or "in one's head," the information to be remembered. Thus, to remember a phone number from the time we look it up until we dial the phone, it is helpful to repeat, or rehearse, the number several times. Research has shown (Flavell, Beach, & Chinsky, 1966) that there is a clear increase with age in the *spontaneous* use of verbal rehearsal as a memory strategy. That is, in contrast to older children, young children tend not to rehearse unless explicitly told to do so. Moreover, young children are less efficient than older children when they do spontaneously rehearse. Thus, they will repeat the items to be remembered only once or twice when more repetitions are needed and they are less likely to repeat earlier items (Naus, 1982). However, even young children can employ and benefit from rehearsal strategies if instructed to use them (Keeney, Cannizzo, & Flavell, 1967).

Why do young children fail to use strategies that older children and adults find so useful? Two different explanations have been proposed to

BOX 10-2 "DON'T FORGET TO TAKE THE CUPCAKES OUT OF THE OVEN": THE USE OF PROSPECTIVE MEMORY STRATEGIES BY CHILDREN

Researchers often study how well children use strategies to recall previous events, that is, their *retrospective* memory. Another aspect of memory performance in which children utilize strategies is their *prospective* memory, or remembering to attend to a future event. Urie Bronfenbrenner and Stephen Ceci (1985) investigated the effects of age, task and location of testing on 10- and 14-year-old children's ability to efficiently use their retrospective memory. Bronfenbrenner and Ceci were specifically interested in children's ability to use *strategic time monitoring* when asked to perform a task at some time in the future. There are three distinct phases to strategic time monitoring: First, an early calibration phase when a child checks the clock frequently in order to "synchronize their psychological clocks" to the actual passing of time. Second, there is an intermediate phase of clock checking in which a child pursues some other activity and checks the clock quite infrequently. Last, in the final phase, a child checks the clock with great frequency as the deadline approaches. This pattern of behavior leads to the most efficient use of time and also the most accuracy in completing the task at the appropriate time.

In order to study children's use of this strategy, Bronfenbrenner and Ceci offered a group of children $5 to either bake cupcakes or charge a motorcycle battery. The children were told that they would have to take the cupcakes out of the oven (or disconnect the battery from the charger) after half an hour, but until that time they were allowed to go to an adjoining room and play with a video game. Experimental observers were in the room with the child and recorded how often the child looked to the clock in the room in order to monitor the passing of time.

Bronfenbrenner and Ceci had several different hypotheses they wanted to test using this basic method. These researchers hypothesized that the location of the testing would also have an effect on children's use of strategic time monitoring. They proposed that if the children were tested in a familiar environment, specifically their own home, they would engage in the strategy more often than if they were tested in a stressful laboratory situation. Second, they hypothesized that there would be an age difference in the use of this strategy, with older children using strategic time monitoring more than younger children.

Overall, the results of this experiment supported the hypotheses of Bronfenbrenner and Ceci. There was an effect of age on children's use of strategic time monitoring; older children were more likely to use the strategy than younger children. Most important, they found an effect of location—children of both ages used strategic time monitoring in their homes more often than in the laboratory.

Clearly, children are able to perform more optimally under familiar and relaxed testing conditions. This finding that context influences cognitive performance is consistent with both Bronfenbrenner's ecological viewpoint that we discussed in Chapter 1 and Vygotsky's sociocultural theory that we examined in the last chapter. In the future, don't forget that context is critical for cognition!

Source: Bronfenbrenner, U., & Ceci, S. J. (1985). "Don't forget to take the cupcakes out of the oven": Prospective memory, strategic time-monitoring and context. *Child Development*, **56**, 152–164.

account for these findings: First, that children possess a *mediational deficiency*, that is, strategies used as tools to incorporate information into long-term storage will not help children to remember information. This suggests that strategies such as rehearsal will not help children even if they are taught to use them (Reese, 1962). A *production deficiency*, in contrast, proposes that strategies will help children, but they simply cannot spontaneously produce them.

Research performed by John Flavell and his colleagues (Flavell et al., 1966) has helped to determine which of these deficiencies is leading to children's poor strategy use. They showed children ranging in age from kindergarten to fifth grade a series of pictures and asked them to recall the sequence in which the experimenter pointed to a subset of the pictures. The younger children in this experiment exhibited very different behavior than the older children. Observing the children's lip movements for a sign that they were rehearsing by naming the pictures as a memory aid, Flavell found that the children who used spontaneous verbal rehearsal demonstrated better memory for the pictures. In addition, the use of spontaneous verbal rehearsal increased dramatically with age. Only about 10 percent of kindergarten children spontaneously named the common objects in the pictures, whereas over 60 percent of second graders and about 85 percent of fifth graders did so. Does this mean that the younger children had a mediational deficiency, that they were unable to benefit from a particular strategy such as verbal rehearsal even when it was available to them? No! The evidence suggests that the problem with the kindergarten children was that of production deficiency; that is, they did not spontaneously produce verbal mediators. When verbal labeling occurred, either by the experimenter's naming the objects in the pictures or by instructing the child to name the pictures, the young child's memory was greatly improved. In fact, in a study of first graders, when children who had not spontaneously named the pictures were required to do so, memory performance differences between children who did and did not spontaneously rehearse were eliminated. Since older children already spontaneously rehearse, it was found that training and induced rehearsal in the use of verbal mediators were of less benefit to them than to their younger peers.

Although the young children's performance in a memory task improved with the use of rehearsal, further studies revealed that children will not generalize their new strategy knowledge. Unless given explicit instructions to do so, young children will not use previously successful strategies in new situations (Keeney et al., 1967). This lack of generalization poses a problem for the hypothesized production deficiency; if children possess a useful strategy, why wouldn't they use it in new situations? Rather than being solely due to a production deficiency, it appears that children's ability to use memory strategies is based upon an interaction between the costs and benefits of using that particular strategy (Siegler, 1991). For example, the cost of simply rehearsing a set of numbers is quite high for young children. When asked to perform a simple manual task (such as tapping their finger on the table as quickly as possible) while also rehearsing a set of numbers, the young children's ability to perform the simple manual task decreased (Guttentag, 1984, 1985; Kee & Howell, 1988). In accord with these findings, young children's ability to use strategies increases when the cost of using that strategy is decreased. For example, young children will rehearse more often when given the opportunity to view previously presented words. Ornstein, Medlin, Stone, and Naus (1985) presented second-grade children with a set of words to memorize. The words were presented to the children on white index cards; for half the children each word was presented for five seconds only, while for the other half of the subjects each word was left on display for the child to refer to while performing the task. Given this situation, Ornstein and his colleagues found that the incidence of rehearsal was greater in the group of children given visual access to the words than the group not given visual access. The young children in this task were more likely to use the rehearsal strategy when the presence of the stimulus words made it easier to rehearse. Thus the use of strategies seems to be related to both the costs and benefits of their use. As children become more adept at strategy use, the costs decrease while the benefits increase.

Semantic Organization. The information the child receives is not processed or stored in a fragmentary or random fashion but is reorganized and reconstructed in a way to make it more meaningful and, hence, easier to remember. How does the process of actively altering and rebuilding information vary for children of different ages? One of the main ways is through the use of *semantic organization*, or organizing information to be remembered using categories and hierarchical relationships. Semantic organization is an example of *deep processing*, which according to the levels of processing model of human information processing leads to long-term memory storage. The use of semantic organization is one way that information is processed at a deep level by the information processing system.

One aspect of the use of semantic organization which changes during development is the increasing use of categories and verbal labels. If children were asked to remember a series of cards containing pictures of a sweater, hat, apple, orange, jeans, sandwich, gloves, coat, milk, and dress, they could form the cards into two groups of similar objects (apple, orange, sandwich, and milk); the other would include items of clothing (sweater, hat, jeans, gloves, coat, and dress). It has been found that older children are more likely than younger ones to physically group the cards into categories (Moely, Olson, Halwes, & Flavell, 1969; Neimark, Slotnick, & Ulrich, 1971) and that those children who utilize this strategy are better able to recall the items in a subsequent test (Best & Ornstein, 1986). Further, older children and adults are more likely to form categories that are useful in later retrieval (Ford & Keating, 1981), while younger children group things together haphazardly. As with the rehearsal strategies, children as young as 7 years old can employ and benefit from an organizational strategy if instructed to use one (Cox, Ornstein, Naus, Maxfield, & Zimmler, 1989).

The increasing use of categorical structures and verbal labels as a strategy for memory storage by young children fits well within the information processing approach to child development. However, children's use of categories at a young age runs counter to the pattern of development proposed by Piaget. Recall that Piaget hypothesized that children are still unable to use class-inclusion relationships during the intuitive period of the preoperational stage (ages 4 to 7). According to this theory, even when given the appropriate category information to use in these retrieval tasks, young children should not be able to take advantage of the categorical structure present in the stimuli. Just as with other criticisms, the findings in the area of strategy use do not disprove Piaget's theory, but they do suggest that Piaget greatly underestimated young children's cognitive abilities.

Another perspective on memory is offered by Vygotsky, who suggests that memory skills develop, in part, through the guidance and instruction offered by other more skilled social partners, such as parents and teachers. By including adult partners in the learning process, children are often able to perform at higher levels than when attempting to memorize items on their own. As Box 10-3 illustrates, a skilled partner can help children use strategies more appropriately and effectively and thereby improve their performance on memory tasks.

Elaboration. *Elaboration* as a strategy entails adding to the information to be remembered in order to make it more meaningful and, hence, easier to place in long-term memory. It is interesting that elaboration is an effective aid to memory, since one is actually increasing the amount of information to be recalled by providing a common context into which several to-be-remembered items can fit. Nevertheless, elaboration strategies usually do aid children's retention (Pressley, Heisel, McCormick, & Nakamura, 1982). The "Peanuts" cartoon in Figure 10-3 shows how Charlie Brown elaborates the numbers of his locker combination to provide a meaningful context (Major Leaguers' jersey numbers) for three seemingly random numbers. Research

BOX 10-3 WITH A LITTLE HELP FROM A PARTNER: IMPROVING MEMORY BY GUIDED PARTICIPATION

Do children do better in memory tasks when they are provided support and guidance from a more sophisticated partner? According to the Vygotskian perspective, children should be able to perform at a higher level under these circumstances. In a series of studies, Rogoff and her colleagues have tested this proposition to see if memory improves when assisted by an adult or a peer teacher. In one study (Ellis & Rogoff, 1986) 6-year-old children were presented two classification tasks resembling home and school activities. One task involved putting eighteen grocery items on six shelves (for example, condiments, sandwich spreads, fruits, baking goods, and dry goods). The second task placed photographs of kitchen items into compartments (for example, machines, cutting tools, table settings, hygiene articles, baking utensils, and cleaning tools). After a short delay, the child was asked to place some old and new items in their proper slots. Children performed better when assisted by adults than 8-year-old children. The adults helped the children learn the classification system in a variety of ways. They explained the tasks before placing the items into slots, referred to the need to categorize and provided a rationale for the groupings of items. Less than half of the child teachers provided this kind of assistance.

To prepare for the learner's memory test, teachers provided four types of help, including (1) mnemonics or hints to assist in the memory of items, for example "you can remember that the snacks go down on this bottom shelf because that's where they are easiest to reach"; (2) rehearsal-replacement, which involved removing all of the items from their slots and replacing them; (3) rehearsal-verbal, which involved reciting the names of category labels (for example, fruits or cleaning tools) out loud; (4) *remind about test* involved reference to the upcoming test, including admonishments to study. Adult teachers were more successful, in part, because they used these strategies, especially rehearsal and mnenomics, much more than child teachers.

It is important to remember that this is a joint process between adult and child. Consider how the mother in a related study (Rogoff & Gardner, 1984) jointly developed a mnemonic strategy for remembering locations of categories. "The mother created a temporal mnemonic for the locations of the first group of objects, thinking aloud as she suggested making up a little story according to a daily routine. Then she reviewed the categories and enlisted the child's help in creating the story for the remaining groups. She provided guidance and invention in suggesting the mnemonic and getting the child started on it and she and the child collaborated on the level of the child's participation in producing the mnemonic. Once the child showed some grasp of the mnemonic, the mother turned it over to the child to manage further review" (Rogoff, 1990, p. 165).

Few child teachers were skilled in these ways, and did not offer the guided participation that the more competent adult teachers provided. These results suggest that memory can be improved through interaction with a skilled partner who provides guided participation. As Vygotsky argued, learning can often be improved if the social nature of instruction is recognized.

Sources: Ellis, S., & Rogoff, B. (1982). The strategies of efficacy of child vs. adult teachers. *Child Development*, 53, 730–735; Ellis, S., & Rogoff, B. (1986). Problem solving in children's management of instruction. In E. C. Mueller and C. R. Cooper (Eds.), *Process and outcomes in peer relationships*, New York: Academic Press; Rogoff, B. (1990). *Apprenticeship in thinking*. New York: Oxford University Press; Rogoff, B., & Gardner, W. P. (1984). Guidance in cognitive development: an examination of mother-child instruction. In B. Rogoff and J. Lave (Eds.), *Everyday cognition: Its development in social context*. Cambridge MA: Harvard University Press.

performed by Michael Pressley and his colleagues provide an example of an elaboration strategy in action (O'Sullivan & Pressley, 1984; Pressley, Cariglia-Bull, Deane, & Schneider, 1987). They trained fifth- and sixth-grade children to use an elaboration technique called the *keyword strategy*. In order to use this strategy children were shown a list of fifteen names of real cities in the United States and were taught the major product of that city. These names were not chosen at random; instead, a portion of each of these names sounded like a concrete object that a fifth- or sixth-grade child would know (for example. Lock Haven contains the word "lock"). During instruction in the keyword method, children were told to notice the object which appeared in the name of the town. They were then told to construct an interactive image between the object and the major product of the town. In the case of Lock Haven, the major product of the town is paper; children were shown a picture of a lock attached to a newspaper. Children taught this keyword strategy

FIGURE 10-3
(Peanuts reprinted by permission of UFS, Inc.).

recalled many more city-product pairs than a comparable group of children who had not received the keyword training.

The fact that elaboration can improve recall despite the increase in informational load points to the importance of meaning in memory. We are more likely to remember that which is meaningful to us. Further, what we understand about an event will influence what we will recall about it later. This leads us to the next major aspect of memory development: the role of knowledge in memory.

World Knowledge

What a person knows about the world, what she has learned from past experiences, influences what she understands about a present event and what she will recall about it later. Consider what happens when a real fan and a novice attend a basketball game together. In contrast to the novice, the fan will understand more about the game and be able to relate more about the game to her roommates who could not attend the game because they had to study for a child psychology exam. The differences between novices and experts have been documented in both adults and children (Bédard & Chi, 1992; Chi, 1978; Chi & Koeske, 1983; Chase & Simon, 1973). We saw an example of the effects of knowledge on children's memory in our discussion of Michelene Chi's work with the child chess experts in Chapter 9.

Just as factual knowledge acquired through instruction or interaction with the environment has an effect on memory processes, so too does information the child learns from her society and family. In accord with Vygotsky's sociocultural view of development, research of children's memory processes has focused on the role of their society on children's use of strategies and their overall memory performance. A great deal of the cross-cultural research investigating children's memory processes has transferred the commonly used experimental techniques of Western society to the new population to be tested. Thus, members of nonliterate societies are often tested using tasks such as free recall, memory span, or paired associates. Research using lists of unrelated objects to be memorized has found that children in non-Western cultures often find these tasks quite difficult and do not spontaneously apply memory strategies (Cole & Scribner, 1977; Rogoff & Mistry, 1985; Rogoff, 1990).

When memory tasks are presented in culturally familiar contexts, however, children in non-Western cultures perform as well as, or better than, children tested in the United States. Rogoff and Waddell (1982) presented a group of 9-year-old Mayan children growing up in Guatemala and a group of 9-year-old children growing up in the United States with a memory reconstruction task. These children watched as twenty familiar objects were placed into a panorama model of a town that contained familiar landmarks (each model was appropriate for the culture of the group being tested). These objects were placed in their culturally appropriate location, for example, boats on lakes, furniture in houses, and so forth. The objects were then removed from the display, and after a short delay the children were asked to recreate the display they had seen previously. Rogoff and Waddell found that not only did the Mayan children perform as well as the American children, they actually performed slightly better! When the information to be memorized is placed in a culturally appropriate task and context, Mayan children display abilities equal to, or better than, their American counterparts. What led to the advantage of the Mayan children? Rogoff speculates that the performance of the American children is due in part to the attempts of approximately one-third of the American children to apply a rehearsal strategy to these organized displays. Because rehearsal is a strategy best suited for unrelated lists of objects, the use of this strategy was only minimally effective in this spatial reconstruction task. The Mayan children, in contrast, appeared to be relying on the look of the display; they used the spatial relationships of the objects to organize their memory and consequently their performance was enhanced (Rogoff, 1990). The use of the effective strategy of rehearsal, which is often taught in schools, actually led to a decrease in performance in the American children.

Children As Witnesses

We have been discussing the improvements in children's memory as they develop. However, many of the studies cited display the limitations on children's memory capabilities. Given these limitations, one logical question is how accurate are children when asked to give testimony in a court of law? In particular, how suggestible are children to the introduction of false information into their testimony? Recent research (Doris, 1991; Ornstein, Laras, & Clubb, 1992) suggests that children may be quite susceptible to having their memory distorted by the suggestions of others. In these studies, young children are told brief stories which are followed by the introduction of inaccurate information. Children's memory for the original story is then tested. Using this type of experiment, researchers have found that young children (3-year-olds) are more often affected by the inaccurate information than adults and older children (Ceci, Ross, & Toglia, 1987).

Children do not always change their testimony in the face of suggestions from others, however. Their suggestibility to inaccurate information is affected

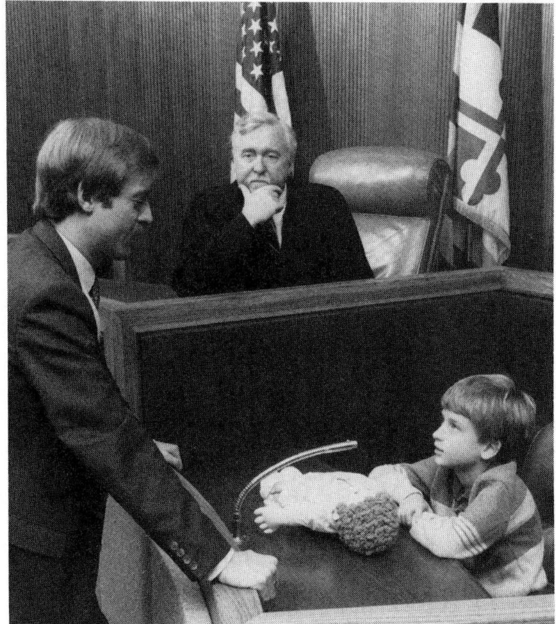

Children's effectiveness as witnesses depends on many factors.

by many different factors. Goodman, Bottoms, Schwartz-Kenney, and Rudy (1991) found that the attitude of the interviewer had an effect on children's accuracy; when the interviewer was intimidating and forceful the children were less accurate than when the interviewer was kind and supportive. An additional factor in children's ability to accurately recall information is whether the child was an active participant in the event being recalled (Rudy & Goodman, 1991). When a child is an active participant in the event, rather than merely a spectator, she is less likely to be susceptible to misleading suggestions.

Regardless of whether the children's testimony is accurate or has been altered by suggestions from others, the jury's perception of children as witnesses is usually not favorable. Both average people and legal scholars believe that children make poor witnesses (Yarmey & Jones, 1983), while people serving on mock juries perceive children as inferior to adults in terms of recall memory. In fact, these jurors believe that children cannot provide accurate testimony until after the age of 11 (Leippe & Romanczyck, 1987). Although these adults had a low opinion of children's ability to be accurate witnesses, they did believe that children make more honest witnesses than adults! Overall, this research provides an uncertain picture of children's ability to accurately relate previous events. As with many other cognitive functions of the child, accuracy of memory in children is affected by many different factors, from the type of event witnessed to the person questioning the child.

PROBLEM SOLVING

Problem solving involves a higher level of information processing than the other functions that have been considered. In fact, problem solving mobilizes perception, attention, and memory in a concerted effort to reach a higher goal: the correct solution to a logical puzzle. As children develop, their

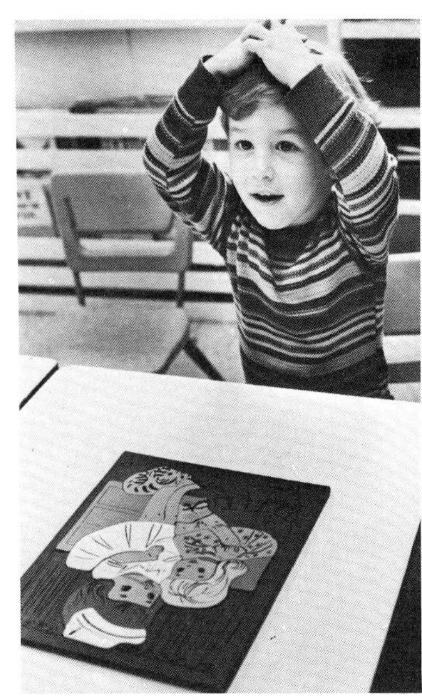

The joy of problem solving.

problem solving abilities become more sophisticated as the strategies they possess become better developed and as they acquire new strategies. In order to illustrate the impact these changes have on children's problem-solving abilities, we will examine development in three areas of problem solving. The first of these is the use of information from one problem to solve another problem, or solving problems by *analogy*. The second is children's use of day-to-day routines, or *scripts* to solve problems they encounter in their daily life. The third area we will examine is children's ability to use forms of *deductive reasoning* to solve problems.

Solving Problems by Analogy

Suppose that you are trying to learn how to use a personal computer and are having difficulty understanding the maze of directories, subdirectories, computer disks, and drives which are part of a personal computer. In this situation an analogy between the workings of the computer and that of a filing system in an office may be helpful: files on the computers are the same as documents in an office, directories are filing cabinets, and subdirectories are drawers in the filing cabinets. This simple analogy can help make a confusing task quite easy.

The use of analogy, or solving one problem based on its similarity to another problem, is a powerful problem-solving strategy. Despite its usefulness, however, both children and adults often find it difficult to notice and use analogies (Gick & Holyoak, 1980, 1983). Children's difficulty in noticing and using analogical similarity can be seen in a study performed by Brown, Kane, and Echols (1986). They asked 3- to 5-year-old children to help the Easter Bunny move the Easter eggs across a river and into a basket on the opposite bank by using the materials provided by the experimenter: a flat piece of paper, a rolled up tube, a walking cane, tape, scissors, string, and a few other objects. The children had previously been told a story in which a genie was faced with the problem of transporting jewels from one bottle to another. The genie solved the problem by rolling the magic carpet into a tube and sliding the jewels from one bottle to another through this tube. The children found it quite difficult to help the Easter Bunny with the problem; very few of the 3-year-olds were able to solve the problem, and even some of the 5-year-olds failed. However, the children's difficulties with this task were not due to an inability to reason by analogy; when the children were given a hint to help them recall the genie story their rate of solution of the Easter egg problem increased dramatically. Other researchers have found that highlighting the goals of the protagonists of the story aids in analogical transfer (Chen & Daehler, 1989), as does multiple examples of the problem solution (Crisafi & Brown, 1986). A further determinant of the ability of both children and adults to notice an analogy is the presence of surface similarity between the objects in the two problems (Gentner & Toupin, 1986; Gentner & Rattermann, 1992). For instance, children found it easier to reenact a story about a jealous friend with new characters if the new hero looked similar to the original one (Gentner & Toupin, 1986). Finally, analogies are often most useful when children know a great deal about the topic of the original problem (Inagaki & Hatano, 1987).

Scripts and Mental Maps

Scripts. From a very early age, children seem to be competent in many routine situations. The 2-year-old participates in many activities during the day: dressing, eating, shopping, and bathing, to name just a few. Moreover, the child seems to have a good understanding of her "role" in these situations. If you doubt this, just try to deprive the 2-year-old of the piece of candy she usually gets in the grocery store checkout line. How do children structure information from past experiences in order to achieve an understanding of the present situation and develop a plan for appropriate behavior? It has been suggested that children and adults form scripts for many routine activities. The scripts provide a basic outline in terms of what is to be expected and what should be done, thus allowing for many behaviors to become rather automatic (Schank & Ableson, 1977). Just as you were able to get up, shower, dress, and eat breakfast this morning without thinking about it very much, so can the child deal with many routine situations in an effective and efficient fashion.

The development of script structure in children has received attention recently (Hudson, 1990; Mandler, 1984). Children as young as 3 years know about, and rely on, the sequence of familiar events (Nelson & Greundel, 1981). Eating always comes before throwing out the wrappers when the family has dinner at McDonald's. To change the sequence is very confusing and disconcerting for the child; young children are more rigid in their applications of scripts than older children and adults (Wimmer, 1980). In fact, when asked to recall stories, young children will eliminate inconsistent elements of the story in order to preserve the expected sequence of events (Hudson & Nelson, 1983) or replace missing events that they were expecting to happen in the story (Myles-Worsley, Cromer, & Dodd, 1986).

Maps. Just as the child needs to be able to negotiate her way through the routine events of the day, so too she must find her way through the spatial environment. Even very young children manage to maneuver their way through familiar places, avoiding obstacles and barriers in their paths (Heth & Cornell, 1980). But it requires more cognitively complex skills to form mental maps of familiar places. For instance, if you were asked to draw the route you take to your psychology classroom, could you provide a reasonably accurate map. Young children find such a task difficult, even when they are perfectly able to find their way to the destination (Liben & Downs, 1989; Siegel & White, 1975). Young children often misconstrue the symbols used on maps and take them to be accurate descriptions of actual objects and places. Thus, the outline of an airplane on a map signifies the presence of a real airplane at that location, rather than the presence of an airport (Downs & Liben, 1986). (Children's inability to use replica representations as tools for finding the location of objects is discussed in Box 10-4.) As children mature, they become more skillful at constructing mental and physical maps of places they know (home, school, and neighborhood) and routes they have traveled. Table 10-1 provides a map for the reader concerning the developmental progression that children follow in their understanding of how to find their way in spatial environments, such as neighborhoods. Similarly, as the child grows, she is better able to utilize information provided by maps and landmarks to negotiate new surroundings (Anooshian & Siegel, 1985; Scholnick, Fein & Campbell, 1990).

Deductive Reasoning

In our discussion of Piaget's cognitive development theory we noticed that Piaget placed great emphasis on children's ability to perform tasks based on logical reasoning: conservation, class inclusion. All of these skills rely on children's ability to use logic and deductive reasoning. Although we have seen that children's cognitive abilities are far greater than Piaget had initially predicted, children do often find tasks based on deductive reasoning quite difficult.

Transitive Reasoning. One of Piaget's classic reasoning tasks is transitive inference. He found that children below the age of 6 or 7 years could not deduce that Jim was taller than Bob when given the information "Jeff is taller than Bob" and "Jim is taller than Jeff." Piaget attributed their failure to an inability to use logic of transitive inference. An alternative hypothesis, proposed by Halford (1990), is that children do understand transitive inference but are simply using an incorrect strategy to solve these problems. For instance, one alternative strategy used by young children is to assume that the most recently mentioned object is also the largest, and they form their inferences based on this assumption. Another strategy is to assume, often erroneously, that one of the given objects is longer that the others, regardless of what the experimenter actually said (Brainerd & Reyna, 1990). Both of these strategies serve the purpose of reducing the child's memory load, which has been shown to be crucial in this type of transitive inference task (Bryant & Trabasso, 1971), but often lead to erroneous conclusions.

Hierarchical Categorization. Another crucial logical ability is the use of hierarchical categorizations. It is one thing to know that there are dogs and collies and much more sophisticated to understand that collies are a kind of dog, such that all collies are dogs but not all dogs are collies. Although some studies have suggested that children do not view such class-inclusion problems in the same way as adults and older children (Klahr & Wallace, 1976; Trabasso et al. 1978), recent evidence suggests that even very young children are capable of forming categories based on hierarchical relationships. Mandler and Bauer (1988) studied 12-, 15-, and 20-month-old infants' knowl-

BOX 10-4 WHEN A PICTURE IS WORTH MORE THAN A THOUSAND WORDS: THE USE OF REPRESENTATIONS AS A TOOL FOR PROBLEM SOLVING

How well do children use models as representations of actual objects? This was the question addressed in a series of studies performed by Judy DeLoache. In the first of several studies to use the same basic paradigm, 31-month-old and 39-month-old children were shown a living room with a couch, a table, rug, and so forth, and then were shown a small model of that room which duplicated the objects and the position of the objects. Then they were shown a large doll and a miniature replica of that doll. While the children watched, the miniature doll was hidden in the model room. The children were told that the large doll was hiding in the same place in the original room as the miniature doll was hiding in the model room. The children were then asked to find the large doll in the original room. When given this task 39-month-old children had little problem retrieving the large doll from the original room. Surprisingly, the 31-month-old children were unable to find the large doll hidden in the original room. (Yet, like the older children, they had no trouble retrieving the miniature doll from the model room, showing that they remembered the location of the miniature doll.) It should be stressed that these two rooms were identical except for size—they contained the same furniture, the same colors, and so on.

DeLoache proposes that the young children's difficulty with tasks lies in their inability to form a *dual representation*. That is, they cannot conceive of the model room as both an object in its own right as well as a representation of the original room. To test this hypothesis, DeLoache repeated this experiment, but instead of showing the children the miniature doll's location using the model room, DeLoache used a picture of a line drawing of the original room. Since pictures and drawings are forms of representations that children are very familiar with, DeLoache reasoned that they would be more willing to treat them as a representation of the original room, and consequently, their ability to find the large toy in the original room would increase. This is in fact what she found. When the small toy's hiding place was pointed out using a picture of the room, young children were able to find the large toy with no difficulty.

Source: DeLoache, J. S. (1987). Rapid change in the symbolic functioning of young children. *Science*, 238, 1556–1557.

edge of categories using a method called *sequential touching*. This methodology takes advantage of young children's tendency to touch and manipulate objects within their grasp. These experimenters recorded the order in which an infant reached for and grasped objects which were placed, as a group, within the child's reach. They presented the infants with objects from the basic level (dogs and cars), superordinate level (animals and vehicles), and also contextual

TABLE 10-1

DEVELOPMENTAL STEPS IN UNDERSTANDING SPACE AND MAPS

STEP 1: THE USE OF LANDMARKS
At this step, children use landmarks to help orient themselves in space. For example, children may use the yellow house or the red fire hydrant as landmarks.
STEP 2: THE USE OF ROUTE KNOWLEDGE
At this step children are able to integrate different landmarks (for example, the yellow house, the post box, and the red hydrant) into a sequence that forms a route through space. In turn, this allows the child to successfully reach the baseball diamond or the neighborhood candy store.
STEP 3: THE DEVELOPMENT OF COGNITIVE MAPS
This is the last step and is a major accomplishment and represents an overall cognitive map of a familiar area and incorporates the different routes that were learned in the earlier stages.

Sources: Anooshian & Siegel, 1985; Siegel & White, 1975.

categories (for example, bathroom things). Mandler and Bauer found that the children in their study would consecutively touch objects which belonged to the same hierarchical category (for example, all the dogs). This pattern of sequential touch was strongest at the basic level and, to a lesser extent, at the superordinate and contextual level. Thus, even infants have some knowledge of class-inclusion relationships and, further, they are able to use this information to form categories for familiar objects.

What could infants as young as 12-months-old use as a basis to form categories? Their knowledge of dogs and cars is quite limited at this point in their lives. There are two factors which have been hypothesized to affect children's ability to form hierarchical categories. The first factor is the *similarity* between the objects which form a category. Most dogs resemble each other in some way; they all have four legs, a furry coat, and a tail. It has been proposed that young children take advantage of this similarity when forming their categories of the world (Rosch, Mervis, Gray, Johnson, & Boyes-Braem, 1976; Rosch & Mervis, 1975).

The second factor which has an effect on children's formation of hierarchical categories is the use of labels to denote category membership (Gelman & Markman, 1987; Waxman & Gelman, 1986). Markman and Hutchinson (1984) gave 2- to 3-year-old children a set of three objects and asked the children to sort the objects, for example, by putting a police car where it belongs, either with another car (an object from the same category) or with a policeman (an object which is thematically related). When no label was used to describe the object the children would put the police car with either object indiscriminately. When a label was used to denote the police car, the children shifted from sorting randomly and placed the police car with the object that shared the same category membership. This finding is even more remarkable when you consider that Markman and Hutchinson used a nonsense word (the syllable "daz") to label the police car, rather than the common word "car." Similar findings have been found using Japanese words instead of nonsense syllables (Waxman & Gelman, 1986). Children also use the category information provided by labels to determine whether objects share common internal structure (Gelman & O'Reilly, 1988). For example, preschool and second-grade children were taught new information about an apple ("It has auxin inside"), and were asked whether other objects would also contain "auxin." These objects were either from the same category as the orignal object (that is, other fruit) or were unrelated. The children were quite good at generalizing the possession of "auxin" to other fruit and were unlikely to propose that an unrelated object contained "auxin." Children will also extend common behavioral characteristics based on category membership (Gelman & Markman, 1987). When told that a particular black and white cat can see in the dark, 3- and 4-year-old children will say that a brown cat can see in the dark, but that a skunk cannot. In summary, children's ability to form hierarchical categories is evident from a very young age.

NUMERICAL REASONING

Most students reading this text take for granted their sophistication about number systems. They do not view it as much of an achievement that they can count the number of books on their desks, the number of students in their class, or the amount of money they have left for their weekend dates. However, in order to do this they must have mastered some critical principles

This kindergarten teacher uses a magic trick to demonstrate that 100 pennies equal one dollar.

of counting, principles that began to be acquired at an astonishingly early age.

Rochel Gelman has studied extensively what preschool children do and do not understand about number systems. As we noted in our discussion of Piaget's conservation task in the previous chapter, work has shown that children as young as 3 years of age are able to perform a simple version of a number conservation task (Gelman, 1972). The fact that children learn to master some aspects of counting at such an early age led Gelman and Gallistel (1978) to conclude that there are several basic principles of counting which lead to children's competence with numbers. These principles are:

1 *The one-one principle:* Each object should be counted once and only once.
2 *The stable-order principle:* Always assign the numbers in the same order.
3 *The cardinal principle:* A single number can be used to describe the total of a set.
4 *The abstraction principle:* The other principles apply to any set of objects.
5 *The order-irrelevance principle:* The order in which objects are counted is irrelevant.

A simple example will show these principles in action. Imagine that a child is shown ten pennies placed in a row and asked to count them. Pointing to each one she proceeds to count them aloud, "1, 2, 3, 5, a, b, c, 10, 15, 12." After finishing she is asked to count them again, starting from the other end. Again she counts all ten of the pennies, counting each one once and only once. "How many pennies are there?" she is asked. "Twelve" is her sure reply. She is then asked to count twelve gumballs. She repeats: "1, 2, 3, 5, a, b, c, 10, 15, 12." Again, she is asked, "How many?" "Twelve." Can it be said that this child understands numbering and counting? Based on the principles outlined above, the answer is yes. Despite her use of an unconventional number sequence, she does seem to understand the critical principles of counting. She assigned only one number to each of the objects and always assigned the numbers in the same order, showing that she understood the one-one and stable-order principles. She had no problem switching the order in which she counted the objects, nor did she mind counting both pennies and gumballs, demonstrating her command of the order-irrelevance and abstraction principles. Finally, when asked how many objects there were she replied "Twelve," showing that she understood the cardinal principle.

Children may be competent in some or all of these principles at different points in their development. For example, a 3-year-old may grasp the one-one principle and the cardinal principle. However, she may only be able to apply the stable-order principle to sets with five or fewer members since her numbering becomes unstable after five (for example, she counts 1, 2, 3, 4, 5, 10, 18, 7 on one occasion and 1, 2, 3, 4, 5, 7, 18, 10 on another). Such a child would be able to solve Gelman's mouse task that we saw in the last chapter (Box 9-3) but would fail on more complex number conservation tasks. Through such a careful analysis of the component skills involved. Gelman has provided a detailed and accurate description of young children's number skills (Gelman, 1978, 1979; Gelman & Gallistel, 1978).

In addition to these five basic principles of counting, there are also many different strategies which are often useful when trying to count efficiently. Examples of these strategies are sequentially counting adjacent objects, or starting at the end of a linear array, as opposed to starting in the middle. Unlike the five principles discussed above, these strategies are optional when counting objects. Children often overlook the distinction between optional and necessary features of counting (Gelman & Meck, 1983). Briars and Siegler (1984) presented 3- to 5-year-old children with puppets, which, when counting, made two different types of errors. In the first type of error the puppet counted correctly, but did not count adjacent objects sequentially and did not start at the end of an array. In the second type of error the puppet counted incorrectly, violating the one-one principle. Three- and four-year-old children did not distinguish between the optional adjacency and start-at-end strategies and the necessary one-one principle. The 5-year-olds, however, were aware of which were necessary and which were optional features of counting.

Children also show a sensitivity to the arbitrariness of the actual symbols used to denote each number. When asked to use the alphabet to count a set of objects, children as young as 6 years of age were willing to use this new method of counting. Children are not entirely comfortable using nonstandard sets of symbols in a counting task; they still consider the usual set of numbers a better system for counting (Saxe, Becker, Sadeghpour, & Sicilian, 1989).

Mathematics and Culture

The acquisition and use of counting systems often takes place before children begin attending school; by early elementary school, children have mastered the principles underlying counting (Saxe, Guberman, & Gearhart, 1987; Wilkinson, 1984). However, the acquisition of more complex numerical concepts usually takes place within a school setting. How do children without the benefit of a formal education acquire the ability to solve mathematical problems?

Geoffrey Saxe (Saxe, 1988) has studied the acquisition of mathematical

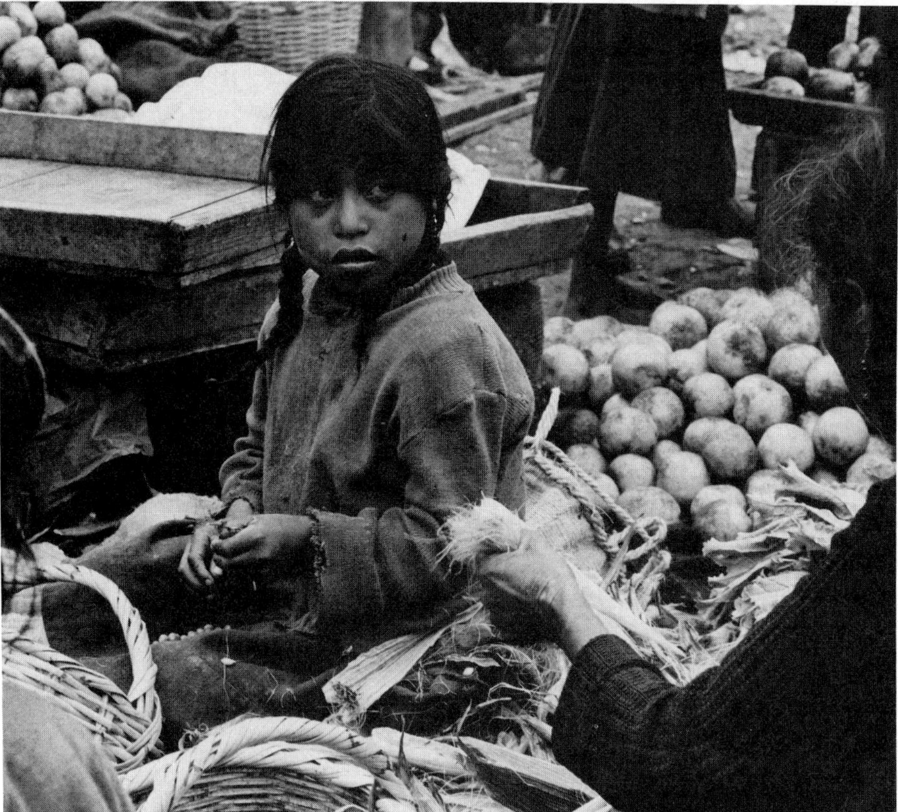

Child street vendors often show a high degree of mathematical skill.

concepts by uneducated children living in developing countries, in particular, the young street vendors (10 to 12 years old) in the cities of Brazil. These children make their living by selling candy and fruit to the people riding on buses or walking through the downtown area of Brazil's major cities. Because of the severe inflation affecting Brazil's economy, these children often deal with large numerical values in the course of their everyday activities. Saxe found several interesting effects of the children's occupation on their mathematical abilities. Despite dealing with large denominations daily in their everyday lives, the children performed quite poorly when asked to read multidigit numerical values when they were in written form. In contrast, the children performed quite well when asked to identify and compare multidigit numbers based on bills and coins. Further, Saxe found that the children found small-number comparisons more difficult than comparisons based on large numbers; a finding that he attributes to the fact that the young vendors often deal with numbers in the thousands in their daily sales. Their everyday interaction with addition and subtraction, as well as their lack of formal schooling, has also led to differences in the manner in which these children perform mathematical functions. These differences are discussed in Box 10-5.

Together these studies underscore the importance of considering context, especially the cultural context, in our evaluations of children's competence (Rogoff, 1990). Everyday demands often lead to the development of much more sophisticated levels of competence than we have previously thought. This focus on cultural context is consistent with Vygotsky's sociocultural approach to cognitive development.

BOX 10-5 MATHEMATICS IN THE STREETS AND IN THE SCHOOLS: A STUDY OF CHILDREN'S ACQUISITION OF MATHEMATICAL CONCEPTS

We use mathematics and numerical reasoning throughout our daily lives; we balance our checkbooks, calculate the cost of the items in a trip to the grocery store, or equally divide the pizza among all our friends. Often, the skills we use in these situations are learned during grade school. Not all children and adults have the opportunity to receive a formal education; how do they perform the same tasks in which we utilize our knowledge of mathematics? In a study of young street vendors of Brazil, Carraher, Schliemann, and Carraher have examined these young children's ability to solve common mathematical problems. These experimenters tested five street vendors (ranging in age from 9 to 15 years) using either a common commercial transaction between a vendor and a customer, or computation exercises presented in a school-like setting.

Carraher, Schliemann, and Carraher found striking differences in the children's ability to perform these different tasks. When tested using the familiar commercial transaction the children were correct 98 percent of the time. When the same problems were presented in the form of school exercises, the percent correct dropped to 37. The experimenters noticed striking differences in the way that the children represented the problems in the street or in the school. When presented with a problem in the street, the children solved it mentally, as opposed to the school-like situation in which the children resorted to pencil and paper to solve the problem. Most striking, however, are the differences in the strategies used to solve the math problems in the two situations. The following protocol from one of the children illustrates the difference.

Street Condition

Customer: I'll take two coconuts (each coconut costs 40 cruzados and the customer pays with a 500 cruzado bill). What do I get back?

Child (before reaching for the customer's change): Eighty, ninety, one hundred, four hundred and twenty.

School Condition

Test item: What is 420 + 80? The child writes 420 plus 80 and obtains 130 as a result. (The child lowers the 0 and then apparently proceeds as follows: adds the 8 + 2, carries the 1, and then adds the 8 + 5, obtaining 13. The result is 130. Note that the child is applying steps from the multiplication algorithm to an addition problem.)

In this example, the child approaches the same problem (420 + 80) in two distinctly different ways. In the street an "add-on" strategy is efficiently used to arrive at the correct answer, while in the school setting strategies learned in school are incorrectly applied. This study underscores again the importance of context for understanding cognitive development.

Source: Carraher, T. N., Schliemann, A. D. & Carraher, D. W. (1988). Mathematical concepts in everyday life. *New Directions for Child Development,* **41,** 71–87.

METACOGNITION

Metacognition refers to the individual's knowledge and control of cognitive activities. These two aspects of metacognition are interrelated and act upon each other. The child's understanding of her cognitive abilities and processes, of the abilities of others, and of the task situation will influence the strategies she uses in overseeing and monitoring learning. In turn, her experience and ability to act as an executive in planning, monitoring, checking, and modifying strategies will contribute to her knowledge about cognition and what contributes to success or failure on intellectual tasks. Three types of metacognitive knowledge have been studied: knowledge about the self, about the task, and about strategies.

Knowledge about the Self

Every student burning the midnight oil and studying for a critical test has asked the question "Do I need to go through these notes once more in order to ace the exam?" Younger children are less able to assess whether they have studied material well enough to remember it than are older children (Flavell, Friedricks, & Hoyt, 1970).

It has been shown that older children have a more realistic and accurate picture of their own memory abilities and those of others than younger ones do (Flavell, 1985; Flavell et al., 1970; Yussen & Berman, 1981). Younger children, for example, will greatly overestimate the number of items they can remember from a brief viewing. Further, older children are more likely to appreciate that memory ability varies from occasion to occasion for any individual and may vary among individuals in any age group. They recognize that they do not learn well when they are tired or anxious, and that their sister may be a whiz at math, but they are better at learning French vocabulary. Still, even young children recognize that older children can recall better than younger children (Wellman, 1978), although they fail to attribute these differences to study strategies as older children do (Kreutzer, Leonard, & Flavell, 1975).

Children's Theory of Mind. What do young children understand about their own minds? Henry Wellman (1990) proposes that from the age of 3 years children have a belief-desire theory regarding the functioning of their minds; children believe that internal beliefs and desires of a person lead that person to action. Although this may appear to be a fairly simple theory of how the human mind works, in fact, it leads to very rich and complex expectations regarding the beliefs of others, their actions, and the outcome of these actions. Additionally, the child must also understand the relationship between her beliefs and desires and those of other people. If any aspect of this relationship is misunderstood, the child's ability to correctly distinguish their own and other people's actions and desires will suffer. For example, Wellman and Bartsch (1988) presented 3- and 4-year-old children with a story depicting a character's beliefs and desires. In this story the character, Jane, wanted to find her kitten. Her kitten was really in the playroom, but Jane thought it was in the kitchen. The children were then asked where Jane would look for her kitten. The majority of the 3-year-olds asked this question responded that Jane would look for her kitten in the playroom, disregarding Jane's belief that the kitten was in the kitchen. Wellman (1990) suggests that the young children in this task are finding it difficult to separate their own beliefs regarding the location of the kitten (that it is in the playroom) from the discrepant beliefs of the character in the story.

Despite some early difficulties understanding the beliefs and actions of others, children's knowledge of the distinction between thought and reality is actually quite sophisticated. For instance, young children know that it is impossible to touch thoughts, showing that they understand the distinction between objects of the mind and objects of the world (Wellman, 1990). They understand that a person must see an object in order to know about it, and that merely standing by an object without seeing it will not result in being knowledgeable about that object (Pillow, 1989). Finally, they understand, that their mental image of an object is a representation of something that exists in the world.

Knowledge about the Task

The ability to monitor one's comprehension is critical for a wide range of problem-solving and communication tasks. Do you understand the directions to get to the party Saturday night? Do you understand the instructions for this week's chemistry experiment? What is the professor saying about the balance beam problem? In order to be an effective processor of information, the child has to be sensitive to her present state of knowledge to seek out the appropriate information from the environment to further her understanding.

Markman (1977, 1979) assessed children's ability to monitor their comprehension of task instructions. In one study (Markman, 1977), first, second, and third graders were given blatantly inadequate instructions concerning a card game. Children were dealt four cards and given the following explanation:

> We each put our cards in a pile. We both turn over the top card in our pile. We look at cards to see who has the special card. Then we turn over the next card in our pile to see who has the special card this time. In the end, the person with the most cards wins the game. How would you like to try to play this game with these instructions?

There was no mention of what the "special card" might be (the cards had letters on them), or how one acquired more cards. The first graders were far less likely to realize the inadequacy of the instructions than the second and third graders, who asked for more instructions before attempting to play the game. One-quarter of the first graders never asked a question, and most only recognized that a problem existed when they were asked to repeat the instructions or began to flounder in playing the game. The younger children failed to execute the instructions mentally and hence did not notice the problem.

Do children realize that some things are harder to learn than others? Apparently, yes. Even 4-year-olds know that a long list of objects is harder to remember than a very short list and that success on the harder task is more likely if a greater effort is put forth (Wellman, 1978; Wellman, Collins, & Glieberman, 1981). Many kindergartners and first graders know that it would be easier to relearn information (for example, a list of birds) that one had forgotten than to learn it for the first time. Further, even young children realize that it is easier to recognize items than recall them (Speer & Flavell, 1979). Of course, there are some aspects of memory of which younger children are not aware; for example, only older children appreciate that it is easier to retell a story in their own words than to repeat it verbatim (Kurtz & Borkowski, 1987).

Knowledge about Strategies

Finally, there is much the child can know concerning strategies which are useful in memorizing. Children seem particularly sensitive to the value of external aids to memory: leaving your books where you will see them in the morning, writing notes to yourself (this was suggested even by children who were not yet literate). Children are also aware of the value of associations in memory (for example, remembering your mother's age by adding thirty to your own) and develop an understanding of the use of "mental searches" for information (Wellman, 1977). Sometimes children reveal a rather sophisticated understanding of memory strategies. When asked how she would remember a phone number, a third grader responded:

> Say the number is 633-8854. Then what I'd do is—say that my number is 633, so I won't have to remember that, really. And then I would think, now I've got to remember 88. Now I'm 8 years old, so I can remember, say, my age two times. Then I say how old my brother is, and how old he was last year. And that's how I'd usually remember that phone number.

"Is that how you would most often remember a phone number?" the experimenter asked.

'Well, usually I write it down." (Kreutzer et al., 1975, p. 11)

What, however, is the relationship between metacognition and performance on cognitive tasks? If children understand that a strategy like rehearsal is useful, do they necessarily employ it to help them remember things? Conversely, are children able to articulate all the cognitive strategies and techniques they employ? Can they tell how they solved an arithmetic problem and why they did it that way? Unfortunately, the relationship between metacognition and cognitive performance is not straightforward (Miller & Weiss, 1981). Some situations are more likely to engage the child's metacognitive activity than others. Even adults do not apply strategies they "know" to be effective in all relevant situations. It would be unrealistic to expect the child always to act at an optimal level of cognitive functioning.

Metacognition and School Performance

One reason that many investigators are currently interested in metacognition is because of its relevance for educational problems such as reading. Poor readers have been shown to have metacognitive deficits in a wide variety of aspects of reading (Baker, 1982). They are less likely than better readers to expend more time on difficult passages, to review the passages least well learned, and to adapt their reading activities to the demands and goals of the reading task (Brown, Bransford, Ferrara, & Campione, 1983). They do not redeploy their efforts in a task-adaptive manner over time.

If many children are lacking the metacognitive skills necessary for effective school learning, perhaps the school curriculum can be modified to train them

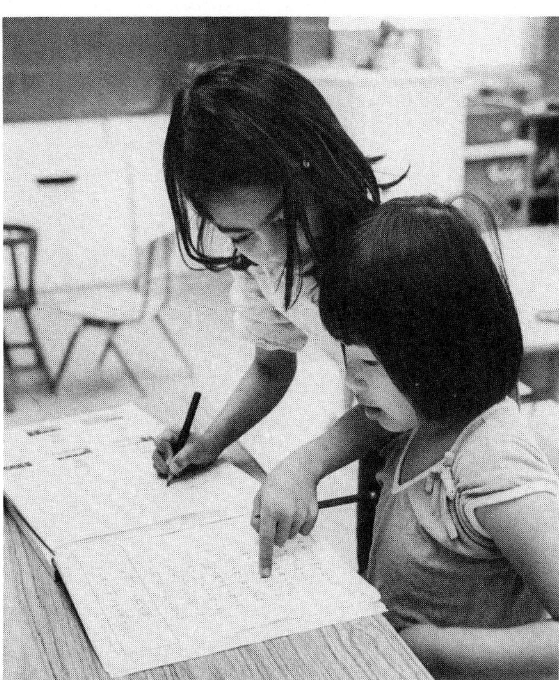

Skilled classmates can act as tutors to guide less competent students, according to Vygotskian theory.

in these skills. Several investigators have initiated school-based programs to train children in metacognitive skills involved in effective reading comprehension (Brown & Campione, 1990; Palincsar & Brown, 1984, 1987). These involve what has been called reciprocal teaching, where children are taught to use comprehension and monitoring techniques to aid in their reading. Four activities were taught to these students: summarizing, self-directed questioning, clarifying, and predicting. Using more skilled fellow students to act as tutors or specially trained classroom teachers the reading ability of seventh-grade remedial readers improved over the course of the training. These tutors instructed the delayed readers in the proper ways to summarize and clarify text. Understanding the benefits of these strategies makes students more likely to use them when they are not being prompted and this has resulted in improved reading, studying, and academic problem-solving skills. In fact, three months after the intervention, the reciprocal teaching group showed an average gain of fifteen months in reading comprehension grade level. These results provide an impressive demonstration that children's reading can be enhanced by the application of principles derived from Vygotsky's sociocognitive approach to learning (Belmont, 1989).

SUMMARY

PERCEPTION AND ATTENTION

- Changes in what information can be gained from a situation are due to the development of *perception*, the intake of information from the environment; and the development of *attention*, focusing on a particular aspect of the environment. These two processes are tightly interwoven, so that perception is dependent on what is attended to in a particular situation.
- There are two main theories that describe the way in which experience affects perceptual learning. Piaget proposed an *enrichment theory*, in which information is added to the existing schema of an object over repeated contacts with the object, thus elaborating or enriching the schema over time until the child is able to distinguish among objects. In contrast, Gibson proposed a *differentiation theory*, in which the child gradually learns to attend to, identify, and discriminate the relevant information about objects.
- As children mature they can control and focus their attention for greater periods of time. In addition, older children are better than younger children at modifying their attention to fit the requirements of the task. Older children also implement more systematic plans to focus their attention when gathering needed information, although younger children can utilize a strategy to focus attention when the strategy is provided for them.

MEMORY

- Memory includes remembering short-term specific events and long-term memory that involves general knowledge that accumulates because of our experiences. The three areas of memory that appear to improve with age are basic capacity, strategies, and world knowledge.

- Short-term memory improves between infancy and adulthood as evidenced by increases in the ability to recall a list of digits. Some researchers suggest that this is due to the development of increased capacity based on changes in the brain. Others suggest that the difference is due to better strategies for organizing or "chunking" the information. Still others suggest that the increase is due to the fact that the use of strategies becomes more automatic over time, freeing space to remember more.
- People employ a wide range of *strategies,* or cognitive activities that increase the likelihood that they will remember information at a later time. Some of these are external (e.g., taking notes), but many of them are mental strategies, such as rehearsal, semantic organization, and elaboration.
- There is a clear increase with age in the spontaneous use of verbal *rehearsal* as a memory strategy, however even young children can use rehearsal as a strategy if instructed to do so. Although their memory performance improves when they use rehearsal, they fail to generalize the strategy to new tasks. Research indicates that this lack of generalization is due to both the costs and benefits of strategy use for young children; as they become more adept at strategy use, the costs decrease while the benefits increase.
- Another strategy that improves with age is the use of *semantic organization* to process and store information in a meaningful way. Two such strategies that increase with age are the use of categories and verbal labels; however, as with rehearsal, young children can successfully use these strategies if instructed to use them.
- *Elaboration,* a strategy that involves adding to the to-be-remembered information in order to make it more meaningful, appears to aid children's retention. The fact that elaboration improves recall despite the increased informational load points to the importance of meaning in memory.
- *World knowledge,* or what a person has learned about the world from past experiences, influences what the person will understand and remember about a present event. Evidence for the role of world knowledge comes from studies indicating that experts remember more than novices, and that when memory tasks are presented in culturally familiar contexts children in non-western cultures perform as well as or better than children tested in the United States.
- One important application of the research on children's memories is in the area of eyewitness testimony. Recent studies suggest that children may not be reliable witnesses because they are susceptible to suggestions by others. However, they are more resistant to misleading questions when the interviewer is supportive, and when they are actively involved in the recalled event.

PROBLEM SOLVING

- Problem solving involves a high level of information processing because it mobilizes perception, attention, and memory to reach a solution. Changes in children's use of analogies, scripts, and deductive reasoning have been studied in order to understand the development of problem solving.
- Young children have trouble using *analogy* to solve problems unless they are given hints by the experimenter. Other factors that make analogies

more useful to children are multiple examples of the solution, surface similarity between the problems, and experience with the topic of the problem.

- *Scripts* of routine activities provide a basic outline of what happens in many situations so that behaviors in those situations are automatic. Children as young as age 3 know about and use the sequence of familiar events available in scripts to guide their actions. Children also use mental and physical *maps* to negotiate their way through their surroundings. Although even young children are good at finding their way through familiar territory, they are unable to draw a reasonable map of the same.
- Children use *deductive reasoning* skills, such as transitive inference and hierarchical classification to solve problems. Recent research suggests that even young children may understand transitive inference, but that they employ poor strategies when using it. Studies also indicate that even 1-year-olds can form categories based on the similarity between objects, and that slightly older children can use labels to form hierarchical categories.

NUMERICAL REASONING

- Children's competence with numbers is related to five basic principles of counting that develop during the preschool years. In addition, they learn the difference between optional (e.g., starting to count at the end of a row) and necessary (e.g., counting each object only once) features of counting. Recent research with child street vendors in Brazil highlights the importance of cultural context when assessing children's math competence with numbers.

METACOGNITION

- Metacognition refers to the individual's knowledge and control of cognitive activities. Metacognitive knowledge includes knowledge about the self, the task, and strategies. Metacognitive control involves using strategies to plan, monitor, check, and modify current strategies to maximize performance.
- Metacognitive knowledge improves with age. Young children are aware of the importance of memory strategies, and they are particularly sensitive to the use of external memory cues. However, older children have a more accurate and realistic view of their own memory abilities, and they are able to separate their own beliefs and desires from reality. Although young children understand the importance of some task parameters for memory, even first graders are not good at monitoring their comprehension of information about a task.
- The relationship between metacognition and cognitive performance is not always strong. Researchers who have applied the concept of metacognition to reading performance, however, have found that better readers have more metacognitive knowledge. Some school-based interventions aimed at teaching metacognitive skills have resulted in improved reading, studying, and academic problem solving.

CHAPTER 11

COGNITIVE DEVELOPMENT: INDIVIDUAL DIFFERENCES IN INTELLIGENCE AND ACHIEVEMENT

In the last two chapters we discussed processes and structures that underlie developmental changes in cognition. The views of cognitive development presented in those chapters emphasized common processes involved in the development of cognition along with the ways these processes change with age. In this chapter we will take a very different perspective. We will examine individual differences in intelligence. We will ask how these differences can be measured, what contributes to these differences, and what these individual differences predict about performance in other situations. Many psychologists are interested in the *processes* that contribute to intellectual differences, such as information processing styles and contexts of learning. The more traditional focus, however, has been upon the *products* of intellectual differences, that is, upon intellectual performance. The most common approach to assessing cognitive products is by administering a standardized intelligence test that yields a score, whereby an individual's performance can be compared to the performance of others. This score often takes the form of an *intelligence quotient*, or IQ. Much of the research on the development of intellectual abilities comes from the IQ testing tradition.

Many of the students reading this book probably had never heard of cognitive schemata or information processing strategies until they read the last two chapters. However, all will have heard of the IQ, or intelligence quotient. Many will confess their own IQ at the slightest provocation, and many who do not know their IQ often wish they did. IQ is a term that is widely used and often misconstrued by a great many people. It is frequently regarded as some kind of innate, fixed endowment, like a baritone voice, big ears, or "your father's family's nose." It sometimes comes as a shock to find that the IQs vary over age, can be modified by experience, and depend to some extent on the type of test administered and the circumstances under which the test is taken. In this chapter, we are going to present individual differences in intellectual performance, not as some kind of stable internal trait of the individual, but as an outcome of genetic, experiential, and situational factors.

We will begin by discussing prominent views of intelligence and describing the cognitive products—or IQ testing—approach. Next we will consider some alternative approaches to the assessment of intelligence, including an information processing approach as well as an approach that emphasizes different types of intelligence. Next, we will ask about the many factors that contribute to intellectual abilities, including environmental variables as well as some of the factors highlighted by the process approach. This will include an examination of children's emotions, anxieties, and achievement beliefs. Finally, after describing the factors that contribute to intelligence, we will ask whether it is possible to improve the IQs of children at risk for intellectual difficulties.

An important point should be emphasized at the start of this chapter. What is measured on an intelligence test is intellectual performance, not intellectual capacity. Although intellectual capacity and performance may be correlated, intellectual capacity always remains only an inference on the basis of the child's responses to test items. Capacity cannot be directly measured. Even the type of intellectual performance measured on any given test is limited by the criteria used to select items and validate the test. In addition, situational, emotional, and experiential factors will influence the child's performance in any given test situation. This distinction between capacity and performance is important for understanding much of the controversy about IQ.

DEFINITIONS OF INTELLIGENCE

Few topics in psychology have generated a more voluminous literature than that of intelligence, and yet, strange though it may seem, there is no widely accepted definition of intelligence. Before asking how psychologists have attempted to understand this concept, a good starting point is to ask how lay people define intelligence. People regularly make judgments about the intelligence of others in social situations, the workplace, and the classroom. Most of us think we know who is smart and who is not, and how to judge intelligence. In fact, our everyday assessments of intelligence take place much more frequently than formal IQ tests, and probably have important influences on our dealings with other people (Weinberg, 1989).

Robert Sternberg and his colleagues (Sternberg, Conway, Ketron, & Bernstein, 1981) examined ordinary people's beliefs about the nature of intelligence. They asked laypeople in New Haven, Connecticut, including commuters waiting in a train station, people in supermarkets, and college students studying in the Yale library, to list the behaviors they saw as characteristic of intelligence. There is widespread agreement among people that intelligence has three aspects: *practical problem-solving ability* (for example, reasoning logically, identifying connections among ideas, and seeing all aspects of a problem), *verbal ability* (for example, speaking articulately, reading widely, and writing well), and *social competence* (for example, admitting mistakes, making fair judgments, and showing sensitivity to other people's needs). The researchers also asked whether psychologists in the field of intelligence agreed with laypeople's definitions. These experts were sent a questionnaire listing the typical responses of laypeople, and were asked to rate the extent to which they saw the behaviors listed as characteristic of intelligence. The experts, like the laypeople, saw problem-solving ability, verbal ability, and social competence as central to intelligence.

In spite of the agreement among both experts and laypeople about the most general characteristics of intelligence, a great deal of controversy arises when psychologists attempt to define the nature of intelligence in more detail. This controversy has important ramifications, because psychologists' conceptions of intelligence influence their views of the methods most appropriate for its assessment, as well as their beliefs about its usefulness in predicting other behaviors. Alternative views of intelligence have centered on three questions. First, is intelligence a unitary, generalized function, or is it composed of a group of relatively separate abilities? If it is a generalized function, an intelligent child should perform well across a variety of intellectual tasks; if it is composed of independent factors or skills, an individual could excel on some cognitive tasks or in certain domains and perform poorly on others. Second, how does intelligence develop, and to what extent can it be modified? Is its development determined primarily by genetic factors, or is it more dependent upon learning experiences in environments with varying degrees of stimulation or deprivation? Finally, is intelligence an underlying construct, trait, ability, or capacity that can never be directly assessed, or should it be defined only in terms of performance on specific cognitive tests? If the latter position is accepted, the most appropriate definition of a child's intelligence might be his score on a particular intelligence test under particular circumstances. However, if the former position is taken, as suggested in the introduction, intelligence test scores must be regarded as an inference about underlying capacity.

Differing positions on these issues are reflected in the frequently cited definitions of intelligence that follow: Intelligence is "innate, general cognitive ability" (Burt, 1955, p. 162). Intelligence is "the aggregate or global capacity of the individual to act purposefully, to think rationally and to deal effectively with his environment" (Wechsler, 1958, p. 7). "Manifest intelligence is nothing more than an accumulation of learned facts and skills . . . innate intellectual potential consists of tendencies to engage in activities conducive to learning, rather than inherited capacities as such" (Hayes, 1962, p. 337). Some psychologists have even gone to the empirical extreme and defined intelligence as being what intelligence tests test. Clearly even the experts are by no means in full agreement concerning the definition of intelligence or the uses and interpretations of scores on intelligence tests. We turn now to an examination of some alternative models of intelligence and their implications for the construction of intelligence tests.

THE ASSESSMENT OF INTELLIGENCE

The strategies used in constructing intelligence tests will depend to some extent on the model of intelligence held by the test constructor. Psychologists who believe in a factor of general intellectual ability may select items that intercorrelate with each other. Others who believe in relatively independent factors of intellectual abilities may select items to measure these postulated abilities and would not expect these items to be interrelated.

In spite of the fact that different views of intelligence influence the selection of test items, certain common goals or principles are utilized in the construction of all intelligence tests.

Norm-Referenced Assessment and Standardization

The performance of an individual on an intelligence test is always described in terms of the individual's position relative to the performance of other members in a group. The individual may be described as being above average, average, or below average in relation to the comparison group. *Norms* are established through administering the test items to groups having particular characteristics. One of the important issues in establishing norms is the determination of critical similarities between the subject and the members of the comparison group. Age is always one of the critical factors to be considered in setting up norms for children. Actual performance on the test items generally improves throughout childhood. When a child is 10, he is usually able to answer more items than when he was 6. However, it is the maintenance of his position relative to other children his age that is regarded as significant in evaluating his intellectual development. Although most psychometricians would agree that age should be considered in establishing norms, there is less consensus on whether comparison groups should be further broken down on the basis of factors such as education, socioeconomic class, ethnic group, and sex. In evaluating test performance, it is always important to consider how similar the attributes and experiences of the individual being tested are to those of the normative group. It would be inappropriate to use the same set of norms in evaluating the performance of children raised in an isolated New Guinea tribe with no access to formal schooling as is used in evaluating the performance of middle-class American children. Less extreme cultural variations such as those found among American children may also make application of the same norms to different subcultural groups inappropriate.

It is also important to consider the similarity in the administration of the test from one test session to another. For this reason the stimuli, instructions, and scoring of test items are carefully *standardized* so that the test procedures will be identical when they are administered by different examiners.

Test Validity

The *validity* of a test refers to whether it measures what it claims to measure. In the case of an intelligence test, does it measure problem-solving skills, the ability to learn, or whatever other definition of intelligence the test constructor might subscribe to? In evaluating the validity of a test, performance on the test is usually correlated with a criterion measure or measures that are assumed to reflect the attribute being assessed. Achievement test scores, grades in school, teachers' ratings of cognitive ability, and performance on other intelligence tests are the most frequently used criteria in establishing the validity of intelligence tests. A very restricted range of problem-solving and adaptive skills is being sampled with such criteria and a limited view of what constitutes intelligent behavior is held by psychometricians using such criteria. That is probably why intelligence tests are much more successful in predicting school performance than in predicting unusual creativity, adaptive ability in social situations, or performance in some skilled occupations. Even within school performance, intelligence test scores have more relation to mathematical problem solving and reading comprehension than to drama, art, or music.

Test Reliability

Reliability refers to the consistency or stability of a test. If an individual's test scores fluctuate unpredictably, they are not very useful measures of intellectual functioning. The most frequently used method of assessing test reliability is to correlate the scores of the same individuals on repeated administrations of the test. However, sometimes the individual's performance on alternative forms of the same test is correlated. Alternatively, internal consistency within a single administration may be assessed by correlating scores on the odd-numbered items with those on the even-numbered items. The most widely used intelligence tests are fairly reliable when internal consistency measures are used or when repeated test intervals are not too widely spaced. Let us move on now and look at how some of these factors were handled in the development of the most frequently used intelligence scales of children.

INTELLIGENCE TESTS

The Binet-Simon Tests

In 1904, the Parisian school system was overcrowded because of newly instituted compulsory education laws. Poor, uneducated families were sending their children to school, often for the first time. Some of these children (as well as children of wealthier families) would require special assistance if they were to benefit from their school experience. The administrators of the Paris schools presented Alfred Binet and Theophile Simon the challenging task of devising a means of identifying children who were mentally retarded and unable to learn in traditional classroom settings, in order to give these children the opportunity for special education. The administrators wanted such an instrument because they were afraid that teachers' prejudices against the lower classes might cause them to judge some children unfairly.

Binet and Simon were remarkably successful in developing a measure to serve their original goal of an academic screening device. It is a tribute to these testing pioneers that the modern version of the Binet-Simon intelligence test remains one of the best predictors of academic success. Their approach to their task was particularly notable in three ways: they took an empirical approach to item selection; they attempted to measure higher mental processes rather than simple functions; and they were sensitive to the chronology of intelligence, that is, to the fact that older children are able to solve a greater number of, and more complex, problems than are younger children (Siegler, 1992). Binet and Simon were critical of earlier psychologists who had attempted to assess intelligence through simple sensory or motor responses that had failed to correlate with school achievement or with each other. They argued that in order to differentiate among individuals, higher mental functions involving judgment, comprehension, and reasoning must be examined. They developed an array of intellectual tasks varying in difficulty, including such things as the ability to recognize logical absurdities, memory for digits, attentional tests, and also some skills that were taught in school, such as counting coins, naming the days of the week, and recalling details of a story after reading it. To some extent, a sample of academic achievement was being used to predict future achievement in school settings.

Thus Binet and Simon assessed two of the three aspects of intelligence seen as important by ordinary people in the Sternberg et al. (1981) study—verbal ability and problem-solving ability. They did not assess social competence. Moreover, they focused on those aspects of verbal and problem-solving ability related to school learning. Binet and Simon believed that the items on their test that were selected to predict academic success may have little relation to what they called "good sense" or intelligent behavior outside the classroom. They did not emphasize a general factor of intellectual ability, although they did refer to the "faculty of reasoning" as being a pervasive factor in intelligence. In constructing their scales, they selected items to sample cognitive abilities they thought might be unrelated. However, the fact that their tests yielded a single score led many people to view this as support for a unitary model of intelligence. They also believed that intelligence was malleable, and that children who performed poorly on their test should be given special programs of "mental orthopedics" to improve their capacity to learn (Binet, 1909/1973; Siegler, 1992).

In refining their tests, Binet and Simon administered large numbers of items to children who had been labeled by their teachers as having bright or dull characteristics, and they retained items that discriminated among these children. In later revisions of their tests, they used the criterion that if items were to be included in the test, they must be effective in sorting children by their ages. Items were selected to reflect the competence of children at different age levels. Items that were passed by about 60 percent of 6-year-olds and were passed by fewer 5-year-olds and significantly more 7-year-olds were assumed to reflect the performance of the average 6-year-old.

Binet originated the concept of *mental age*. Mental age is based on the number of items the child gets correct relative to the number of items the average child of various chronological ages gets correct. Thus, if a 6-year-old child has a mental age of 7, he is performing as well as the average child whose actual chronological age is 7. Later, William Stern, a German psychologist, conceived of the intelligence quotient, which is a ratio of the child's mental age (MA) divided by his chronological age (CA) and multiplied by 100.

$$IQ = \frac{MA}{CA} \times 100$$

It can be seen that if a child had an IQ of 100, his performance would be average for a child of his age. As the IQ rises above 100, his performance is increasingly superior to other children his age; as it drops below 100, he is doing relatively less well than his peers.

Subsequent revisions of the Binet-Simon scale and many other contemporary intelligence tests are designed to include items that are less directly influenced by academic experience. It is clear that items such as vocabulary questions involving definitions of words or mathematical problem solving are heavily weighted by different experiences. However, the extent to which learning and education affect form-board tasks, building designs out of blocks, or assembling a jigsaw puzzle is less clear. These items that appear less dependent on academic learning are often referred to as *performance* items. Since language and mathematics are heavily culturally and educationally influenced, much effort has been put into attempting to design tests that do not solely emphasize skills in these areas.

The Wechsler Scales

David Wechsler (1952, 1958) developed a series of intelligence tests that were influenced by Binet's test but placed less emphasis on verbal items. In fact, the Wechsler scales yield separate verbal and performance IQs as well as a full-scale IQ based on the combination of these two scores. The student can look at the type of items included under the verbal and performance scales presented in Table 11-1 and see that the performance items are less likely to be influenced by formal education or cultural factors. It is important to realize, though, that even the performance items may be influenced by nonability factors such as anxiety or a child's prior experience in working with similar kinds of tasks. The Wechsler IQ test is widely used in American schools, in part because educators find the distinction between the performance and verbal scales valuable. For example, imagine a child who performs poorly on the verbal subscales but does quite well on the performance items. This pattern suggests that a child may have a specific learning problem (for example, a difficulty with language) rather than overall low intelligence.

Wechsler does not use mental age to estimate intelligence; rather, he uses a score called a deviation IQ, which is determined by the relation of a person's score to the distribution curve of scores for people his age. The deviation score indicates how far above or below the mean the individual's score lies relative to children of the same age in the standardization group. In the most recent revision of the Binet scale, a shift to the use of deviation scores has also occurred.

Many other types of intelligence tests that differ from both the Binet and Wechsler scales have been designed since Binet and Simon's ingenious first

TABLE 11-1 **THE WECHSLER INTELLIGENCE SCALE FOR CHILDREN***

VERBAL SCALE	PERFORMANCE SCALE
1. General information: A series of questions involving a sample of information that most children will have been exposed to. (For example, Where does the sun rise? How many weeks are there in a year?)	1. Picture completion: The child is asked which part is missing in each picture in a series of twelve pictures of common objects. (For example, a car with a wheel missing, a rabbit with an ear missing)
2. General comprehension: Items in which the child must explain why certain practices are desirable or what course of action is preferred under certain circumstances. (For example, Why should people not waste fuel? What is the thing to do if you lose a friend's toy?)	2. Picture arrangement: A series of sets of pictures in which the pictures will tell a story if they are arranged in the correct order. These are rather like wordless comic-strip pictures.
3. Arithmetic: A series of arithmetic questions ranging from easy ones involving simple counting to more difficult ones involving mental computations and reasoning.	3. Block design: The child receives a set of small blocks having some white, some red, and some half-red and half-white sides. The child is shown a series of red and white designs that he or she must reproduce with the blocks.
4. Similarities: The child is asked to tell in what way a series of paired words are alike. (For example, In what way are a shoe and a slipper alike? In what way are a boat and a car alike?)	4. Object assembly: The child must assemble jigsawlike parts of common objects into the whole puzzle. (For example, a chair, a foot)
5. Vocabulary: A series of increasingly difficult words are presented and the child is asked what each word means.	5. Coding: A task in which symbols are to be matched with numbers on the basis of a code given to the child.
6. Digit span: A series of numbers of increasing length are presented orally and the child is asked to repeat them either in the same order or in a reverse order.	6. Mazes: The child must trace the correct route from a starting point to home on a series of mazes.

*The examples given are similar, but not identical, to items on the Wechsler Intelligence Scale for Children.

scale. A frequently administered test in the United States is the Stanford-Binet, which is an American adaptation and revision (produced at Stanford University) of Binet and Simon's IQ test. In addition, scales based on Piagetian constructs have been devised. Tests that can be administered in groups rather than individually often are used. In addition, tests for infants have been devised in the last two decades (Bayley, 1969; Rosenblith, 1992a, b). Performance on all these tests is influenced to varying degrees by cultural factors, although these cultural differences and influences are less marked with children under 18 months of age (Golden & Birns, 1983).

We will now examine two other influential perspectives in the study of intelligence and intelligence testing. The first perspective is derived from research and theory in information processing, and the second perspective looks specifically at different domains of skill. Both perspectives emphasize the relationship between intelligence and the environments in which children learn and perform.

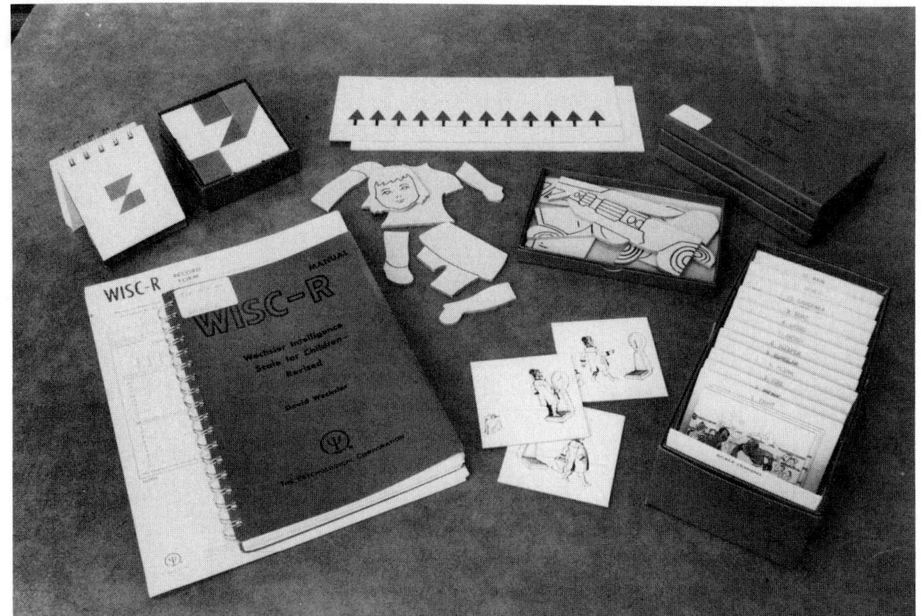

Examples of items from the Wechsler Intelligence Scale for Children.

ALTERNATIVE APPROACHES TO INTELLIGENCE

Information Processing Approaches

Many of the tasks and cognitive skills involved in the research on information processing presented in the previous chapter are similar to those found on intelligence tests, such as memory, classification, analogies, knowledge or expertise, and comprehension. Recently, information processors have suggested that, in order to really understand intelligence, we need to supplement traditional intelligence tests with procedures that assess the information processing components, mental representations, and strategies people use in performing intellectual tasks (Sternberg & Powell, 1983). This *componential analysis* of intellectual functioning involves an assessment of both the *components,* or steps, the individual goes through in solving a problem and the *metacomponents,* or strategies and metacognitive processes, that the individual uses in deciding how to solve the problem. This componential analysis then involves assessing the steps in processing information we described earlier—how children search for, monitor, receive, encode, or interpret information; store and retrieve knowledge; and decide on which strategies to use. Rather than focusing solely on the *product*—that is, on whether the child has or has not solved the problem—a componential analysis would focus on exactly where in the problem-solving *process* the child had difficulties. Did the child misinterpret the instructions? Did the child not attend to relevant information? Did he use inappropriate strategies?

Sternberg's (1985, 1989) triarchic theory of intelligence is an influential example of the information processing approach. According to Sternberg, there are three major components of intelligent behavior, specifically *information processing skills, experience,* and *context.* The first component of intelligence behavior in this model is the information processing skills involved in encoding, combining, and comparing various types of information as central aspects of intelligence. These skills involve a wide range of cognitive processes, ranging from memory and attention to metacognition and analogical reasoning, that may be brought to bear on a variety of tasks.

The second aspect of intelligence involves people's experiences. Intelligent individuals have two skills related to experience: They can learn by means of experience and perform familiar tasks effortlessly, and yet they can also deal effectively with novel tasks. In asking whether a person performs intelligently on a task, the questions will be very different if that person is encountering the task for the first time, in which case persistence, creativity, and comprehension would be important, or if he has done this task a hundred times before, in which case smooth, effortless completion of the task would be evidence of intelligence. If a 12-year-old must be carefully coached about the steps in long division every time she encounters a division problem, her intellectual performance would be considered poor. If, however, this same child wrestles effectively with a long-division problem the first time she ever encounters such a problem, this would suggest that she is quite intelligent. In order to understand intelligence fully, we must take individuals' prior experience into consideration.

Finally, intelligence is exercised in a sociocultural *context* and cannot be separated from that context. In Sternberg's words, "intelligence [is] mental activity directed toward purposive adaptation to, and selection and shaping of, real-world environments relevant to one's life" Sternberg, 1985, p. 45). What is adaptive in one environment may be less adaptive or even maladaptive in another environment, and intelligent persons must be able to function effectively in the environment in which they live. The professor's ability to give lengthy explanations of various concepts may be highly intelligent in the classroom, but might be considered unintelligent in a business cocktail party. Thus, in order to understand whether behavior is intelligent, we need to examine *the context in which that behavior is exercised.* Others (Ceci, 1990, 1991); Vygotsky, 1978) stress the importance of context in defining and assessing intelligence. For example, Ceci suggests that many people who perform poorly on traditional IQ tests may perform sophisticated cognitive operations in other, more familiar domains. Imagine, for instance, an auto mechanic who has difficulty with verbal analogy problems on traditional tests of intelligence. The same mechanic may use highly complex reasoning to diagnose the problems in malfunctioning cars; his or her intelligence is exercised in a setting other than the academic context of IQ tests.

An intelligent person according to Sternberg is one who is able to use these cognitive skills effectively in the environment in which he is working, and to adjust the ways he processes information with experience. Sternberg's information processing approach differs from Binet's in several respects. First, it emphasizes the question of how children process information, rather than asking whether or not they can answer specific items. Second, this approach takes into account the child's own characteristics, especially prior experience, in evaluating performance. Third, the approach addresses more than academic intelligence; it views school as one context in which intelligence may be exercised, but recognizes that children adapt to a variety of contexts and may function very intelligently in contexts outside the classroom.

Sternberg's model has not been specifically applied to the creation of intelligence tests. However, a recently developed intelligence test, the Kaufman Assessment Battery for Children (K-ABC) (Kaufman & Kaufman, 1983), is directly based on research in cognitive development and measures several types of information processing skills. The skills are grouped into two categories, sequential processing (solving problems in a step-by-step fashion) and simultaneous processing (examining and integrating a wide variety of material). In addition, achievement in tasks related to school, such as vocabulary and arithmetic, is assessed. The test designers tried to choose test items that are not culturally biased (many items are nonverbal) and to establish norms using a wide and representative sample of many American cultural and socioeconomic groups. Most remarkably, testers are instructed to teach children who fail early items how to complete these items before administering the rest of the subscale. In other words, children who do not have the requisite experience to complete certain types of problems will be taught to do so, so that their performance when they do have experience can be assessed. While this test has received some criticism, it represents an innovative approach to the assessment of intelligence that incorporates important insights from the information processing approach. At this point the information processing approach is seen as providing a promising new direction in the study of intelligence and intelligence testing.

Multiple Factor Approaches

One of the main questions in this area is whether intelligence is unitary, or whether different kinds of intellectual abilities might vary within the same individual. Can people be described accurately in general terms such as very intelligent or below average? Or is it more accurate to describe people in terms of specific intellectual skills—for example, "He's very articulate and verbally fluent, but is a bit of a dolt at arithmetic"? Our discussion of expertise and domains of knowledge in the previous chapter would suggest that some unevenness in areas of intellectual ability might be expected. We turn now to an approach that explores different domains of intellectual skill.

Over 60 years ago, Charles Spearman (1927) concluded that intelligence comprises a "g," or general, factor and a number of "s," or specific, factors. He regarded "g" as general mental energy or ability that would be involved in all cognitive tasks, and "s" factors as factors unique to a particular task. Thus, someone with a high "g" would be expected to do well on all intellectual tasks. Variations in performance among tasks would be attributable to differential amounts of "s." Later approaches increased their emphasis on specific factors and paid less attention to the idea of general ability. Thurstone (1938) suggested that intelligence was composed of seven separate, primary skills, including perceptual speed, numerical ability, word fluency, verbal comprehension, space visualization, associative memory, and reasoning. He constructed tests to measure each of these mental abilities. Later, Guilford (1966) argued that intelligence consists of 120 separate factors, and he has devised tests for about 75 of these. Interestingly, some of the factors identified by Thurstone and Guilford are similar to those emphasized by the information processing approach. In multiple-factor approaches, though, these abilities are seen as representing independent and potentially measurable aspects of intelligence, rather than as processes contributing to cognitive performance.

The debate about whether there is one general ability that constitutes intelligence or an array of separate abilities remains unresolved even today. The most recent approach to this problem is Howard Gardner's (1983) theory of multiple intelligences, which proposes that at least seven separate types

Nigerian children (Anang tribe) demonstrating *musical intelligence*: boys playing Ibo xylophone.

American child displaying spatial intelligence: model airplane builder.

of intelligence can be found in humans. His theory differs from traditional multiple-factor approaches in many respects, but may be seen stemming from this tradition.

The seven intelligences are described in Table 11-2. The linguistic, logical-mathematical, and spatial intelligences are related to the types of intelligence assessed in traditional IQ tests. The musical, bodily-kinesthetic, interpersonal, and intrapersonal intelligences, however, are equally important to human functioning, yet much less widely studied. According to Gardner, each type of intelligence has its own developmental path and is guided by its own form of perception, learning, and memory. For example, linguistic intelligence may take years of educational experience before it is developed, whereas bodily-kinesthetic intelligence may manifest itself quite early. Various well-known individuals exemplify different combinations of intelligences. Einstein possessed high levels of both logical-mathematical intelligence—used in the mathematical formulations in his theory—and spatial intelligence—seen in the intensely visual *gedanken* experiments (experiments carried out in the mind) that led to many of his greatest insights. The poet T. S. Eliot used both linguistic intelligence and interpersonal intelligence—the understanding of a range of human emotions and experiences—to write his poetry. In addition, Gardner argues that different cultures place different relative values on the various intelligences. Americans, among other cultural groups, give special

GARDNER'S THEORY OF MULTIPLE INTELLIGENCES TABLE 11-2

TYPE OF INTELLIGENCE	DESCRIPTION	EXAMPLES
Linguistic intelligence	Sensitivity to the meanings and sounds of words; mastery of syntax; appreciation of the ways language can be used	Poet Political speaker Teacher
Musical intelligence	Sensitivity to individual tones and phrases of music; an understanding of ways to combine tones and phrases into larger musical rhythms and structures; awareness of emotional aspects of music	Musician Composer
Logical-mathematical intelligence	Understanding of objects and symbols, of the actions that can be performed on them and of the relations between these actions; ability for abstraction; ability to identify problems and seek explanations	Mathematician Scientist
Spatial intelligence	Capacity to perceive the visual world accurately, to perform transformations upon perceptions, and to recreate aspects of visual experience in the absence of physical stimuli; sensitivity to tension, balance, and composition; ability to detect similar patterns	Artist Engineer Chess master
Bodily-kinesthetic intelligence	Use of one's body in highly skilled ways for expressive or goal-directed purposes; capacity to handle objects skillfully	Dancer Athlete Actor
Intrapersonal intelligence	Access to one's own feeling life; ability to draw on one's emotions to guide and understand one's behavior	Novelist Therapist Patient
Interpersonal intelligence	Ability to notice and make distinctions among the moods, temperaments, motivations, and intentions of other people and potentially to act on this knowledge	Political leader Religious leader Parent Teacher Therapist

Source: Gardner, H. (1983). *Frames of mind: The theory of multiple intelligences*. New York: Basic Books.

emphasis to logical-mathematical intelligence. In contrast, the Anang of Nigeria emphasize musical intelligence and infants are introduced to music and dancing in the first weeks of life. By the age of 5, an Anang child is expected to be able to sing hundreds of songs as well as play several instruments and perform intricate dances. Other cultures emphasize still other types of intelligence.

In contrast to Binet's approach, Gardner gives equal attention to a variety of domains of skill, not just those addressed in school. His perspective is broader than that of information processing theorists, who focus on more traditional types of cognitive skill.

Gardner's theory of multiple intelligences has been criticized for several reasons. Some argue that the theory does not take into consideration a great deal of evidence suggesting that many intellectual skills are hierarchically organized (Weinberg, 1989). In other words, Gardner's intelligences may not truly separate, but rather some intelligences are subsets of other types of intelligence. Others dispute the particular types of evidence Gardner uses to support his theory, and suggest that his evidence can be interpreted differently. He argues, for instance, that the existence of *idiots savants* supports the theory of multiple intelligences. *Idiots savants* are mentally retarded individuals who show a remarkable talent in one area that is especially surprising in light of their low overall levels of performance. For example, Raymond, the fictitious *idiot savant* played by Dustin Hoffman in the 1988 film *Rainman*, was quite limited in his general intellectual skills, but possessed astonishing mathematical abilities that permitted him to count items extraordinarily quickly and to keep track of all the cards in a casino blackjack game. Other *idiots savants* possess remarkable drawing or musical skills. According to Gardner, the isolated pockets of intelligence seen in *idiots savants* suggest that humans possess many separate types of intelligence. However, critics note that *idiots savants* often function at much lower levels than did Raymond, and their isolated skills, while surprising, are still more limited than those of true geniuses in an area (Hill, 1978; Gleitman, 1991). Perhaps these pockets of skill do not represent truly independent intelligences but are constrained by overall level of ability.

Although Gardner's theory has been criticized, it is causing psychologists and educators to broaden their definitions of intelligence and give more attention to types of skill that have not been traditionally recognized. At

Idiots savants display unusual intellectual feats as illustrated by actor Dustin Hoffman's character Raymond in the film *Rainman*.

present, Gardner is developing both tests to measure his seven intelligence types and educational programs that train children in all areas of intelligence (Winn, 1990).

This trend toward broadening our understanding of intelligence and recognizing that IQ tests tap a limited set of abilities in one particular context represents a promising new direction in intelligence research.

We turn now to the question of how stable IQ is over time. Note that most of the research described in the following pages involves traditional IQ tests, not the more recent approaches to intelligence and intelligence testing just described.

STABILITY OF IQ

If it is assumed that intelligence tests measure a capacity to learn, it might be expected that the IQ would remain stable over time. However, when one keeps in mind that intelligence tests measure current performance rather than underlying ability, it may not be surprising to find out that IQ scores can, and do, fluctuate. Most of the information on the consistency of performance on intelligence tests over age has been obtained from longitudinal studies in which the same children were repeatedly tested over long periods of time, in particular the Fels Longitudinal Study, the Berkeley Guidance Study, and Berkeley Growth Study described in Chapter 2. In some cases these multiple testings have extended from the first month of life until adulthood.

Investigators who have collected and analyzed the results of a large number of these longitudinal studies conclude that infant intelligence tests in the first year of life do not accurately predict IQ performance later in childhood, although they may be useful in identifying neuromotor abnormalities or extreme intellectual deficits (McCall, Hogarty, & Hurlburt, 1972; Honzik, 1983; Lewis, 1983). The types of tasks used in the first year of life are largely sensorimotor tasks involving such things as reaching and grasping an object or visually following a moving object. These tasks differ considerably from the type of task used with older children that frequently taps problem-solving ability and verbal skills. After about 18 months, when items of the latter type are included in intelligence tests, the prediction of later test performance from early IQ scores improves (Golden & Birns, 1983; Honzik, 1983). In general, it has been found that the shorter the period is between repeated test sessions and the older the child is at the time of the initial testing, the more stable are the IQ scores. This is clearly illustrated in Figure 11-1, in which the correlations between infant and preschool test scores and IQ at age 8 derived from three different studies are presented. Although different infant tests were used in the Stockholm studies and in the two Berkeley studies, it can be seen that none of the studies were able to effectively predict IQ at age 8 from tests in the first few years of life. However, as the child gets older and the interval between the earlier test and the test at age 8 is relatively shorter, prediction becomes very efficient.

Several studies in the last decade have attempted to devise new ways of predicting ability from infancy. In particular, these studies have moved away from the use of the traditional sensorimotor tests of infant ability. Instead, these studies show the influence of the information processing approach in that they examine infant attentional processes. They have focused on two indexes of attention—*decrements of attention* and *recovery of attention*. These

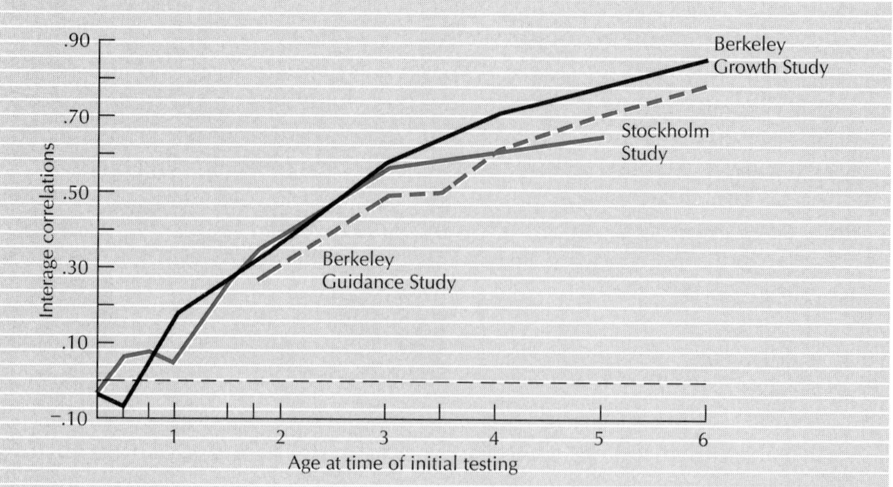

FIGURE 11-1
Prediction of the IQs on the Stanford-Binet at 8 years from earlier scores on the Berkeley Growth Study and the Berkeley Guidance Study and from earlier scores on the Brunel-Lezine scale in the Stockholm study. (From Honzik, 1976.)

processes involve the concepts of habituation and recovery described in Chapter 5. That is, two early hallmarks of intellectual ability may be the ability to quickly familiarize oneself with new material and also the tendency to recognize and prefer novel stimuli. Researchers in this area have asked whether infants who habituate quickly (that is, stop attending to repeated stimuli) or show a strong recovery of attention for a novel stimulus are likely to perform at higher levels on intellectual tasks in later childhood. These studies indicate that there are moderate correlations between attentional measures at 2 to 7 months of age and scores on traditional intelligence tests at ages 3 to 6 years (Bornstein & Sigman, 1986). (See Box 11-1).

While these correlations are not as strong as those obtained between tests administered in middle and later childhood (see Figure 11-1), they are substantially higher than the correlations between traditional measures of infant intelligence and later IQ. These relationships suggest that there is some continuity in the development of intelligence from infancy to childhood. Early patterns of attending to familiar and new information may be related to the ways the child learns and processes information later in life. However, the correlations between infant measures of attention and later IQ are far from perfect, and there is much room for change as a child develops (Bornstein & Sigman, 1986). Moreover, although it may be tempting to conclude that early individual differences in habituation and response to novelty reflect genetic predispositions, there have already been several months in which the environment could affect the child's attentional processes. In fact, children's attentional processes are related to mothers' responsitivity in 5-month-olds (Bornstein & Tamis, 1986) and to mothers' encouragement of attention to the environment in 4-month-olds (Bornstein, 1985), suggesting that parental behavior may have an early influence on attention.

What happens as children grow older? Do IQ tests in the early school years predict IQ scores in later childhood? How much change in IQ is likely to occur within the individual child? Most research suggests that IQ tests from the middle childhood years onward are reasonably good predictors of adult intelligence test performance. For example, one study found a correlation of .70 between IQs at age 8 and at age 18 (Honzik, MacFarlane, & Allen, 1948). Figures such as these are based on analyses of large groups of children

BOX 11-1 *PSYCHOLOGY IN ACTION* PREFERENCE FOR NOVELTY IN INFANCY: ARE SOME BABIES JUST MORE CURIOUS OR SMARTER TOO?

One of the questions that researchers have posed is whether or not infant visual preferences are predictive of later cognitive development. To find out, Joseph Fagan and his colleagues (Fagan, 1984) tested a group of thirty-six 7-month-old infants for their preference for viewing a novel or a familiar visual stimulus. The infants were later tested at 3 years and again at 5 years for their intellectual functioning. At this age the children were given a picture vocabulary test—a standard method of assessing intelligence for children of these ages. Of course, the persons administering the tests at these later ages were unaware of the children's earlier performances. The results were striking: The relationship between 7-month novelty preference and 3-year and 5-year intelligence test scores was similar and indicated that the more the infants indicated a preference for novel stimuli, the higher their IQ scores at later ages.

These findings suggest that infant visual attention may be a useful screening device to detect children who may develop cognitive developmental problems at later points in time. In fact, Fagan, Montie, and Shephard (1988) have recently found that infants who were at risk for later cognitive developmental problems because of such conditions as prematurity, failure to thrive, or maternal diabetes can be diagnosed remarkably accurately, based on measures of infant attention. In one study they found that they could correctly detect 75 percent (21 out of 28 infants) of children with an IQ below normal at age 3, based on the infant screening test. Similarly they correctly identified 85 percent (127 out of 149 infants) who at 3 years were in the normal range of IQ. Later work (Rose, Feldman, Wallace, & McCarton, 1989) found that infant preference for novelty was a better predictor of later intelligence scores than standard infant tests of intelligence (for example, Bayley test) at 5 years of age. Finally, evidence suggests that infant novelty preferences as well as other measures of visual processing are related to estimates of adult intelligence (DiLalla et al., 1990). Together these findings suggest that infant visual attention can provide a useful diagnostic tool for detecting children who may later develop cognitive deficits.

Sources: DiLalla, L. F., Thompson, L.A., Plomin, R., Phillips, K., Fagan, J. F., Haith, M. M., Cyphers, L. H., & Fulker, D. W. (1990). Infant predictors of preschool and adult IQ: A study of infant twins and their parents. *Developmental Psychology,* 26, 759–779; Fagan, J. F. (1984). The relationship between novelty preferences during infancy to later intelligence and later recognition memory. *Intelligence,* 8, 339–346; Fagan, J. F., Montie, J. E., & Shephard, P. A. (1988, April). *Research on infant intelligence: Preference for novel applications.* Paper presented at the Sixth International Conference on Infant Studies. Washington, DC; Rose, S. A., Feldman, J. F., Wallace, I. F., & McCarton, C. (1989). Infant visual attention: Relation to birth status and developmental outcome during the first 5 years. *Developmental Psychology,* 25, 500–576.

(250 children in this particular study). Another way to ask this question is whether and how much the IQs of individual children change over the course of development. This type of analysis indicates that there is still considerable variability in the IQs of some children. An investigation of the stability of test IQs of 140 children in the longitudinal Fels Institute Study was summarized as follows:

> Normal home-reared middle-class children change in IQ performance during childhood, some a substantial amount. In the present sample, the average individual's range of IQ between 2½ and 17 years of age was 28.51 IQ points, one of every three children displayed a progressive change of more than 30 points, and one in seven shifted more than 40 points. Rare individuals may alter their performance as much as 74 points. High-IQ children are likely to show greater amounts of change than low-IQ children. (McCall, Appelbaum, & Hogarty, 1973, p. 70)

The rate of mental growth varies among different children. Just as different children may experience a spurt or a plateau in physical growth at different ages, the ages at which sudden accelerations or leveling in cognitive development occur vary among children. These variations in rate of growth will obviously affect the reliability of IQ scores. When changes in IQ over age are examined, it is found that the changes are most likely to occur at ages

6 and 10. It has been proposed that the 6-year change may be associated with a shift to higher levels of abstract reasoning and conceptual process that Piaget and other investigators have discussed. The reason for the variability at age 10 is less clear.

It is known that stressful life events such as parental divorce or death, or a geographical move or shift in schools, can cause at least temporary disruptions in cognitive performance. Indeed, children who show the most dramatic increases or decreases in IQ over time are often the same children who have experienced major changes in their life circumstances—for example, they may have been placed in a foster home or may have had a serious illness (Honzik, 1983). One study (McCall, 1983) showed that the birth of a baby can lead to marked declines in the IQs of older siblings that may last several years. Eventually, however, the intellectual performance of older siblings recovers and may surpass that of their younger brothers and sisters (Zajonc & Marcus, 1975).

CORRELATES OF INTELLECTUAL PERFORMANCE

The preceding sections have presented various approaches to understanding and assessing intelligence, and have suggested that IQs show moderate stability over time. We turn now to the complex question of how individual differences in intelligence develop. We consider "nature" first—the relationship between genetics and IQ—and then discuss the role of "nurture," or environment, in intelligence.

Genetic and Constitutional Correlates of Intellectual Performance

The role of genetic factors in intellectual development is clearly supported by the studies reported in Chapter 3 on the greater similarity of IQs of monozygotic than of dizygotic twins, and in studies involving comparisons among children raised by natural parents or by adoptive or foster parents. Most estimates of the *heritability* of intelligence, that is, of the proportion of population variance in intelligence which is attributable to genetic factors, center on a figure of about .50 for middle-class white Americans (McGue & Bouchard, 1987; Plomin, 1986, 1989, 1990). This means that about 50 percent of the variability in intelligence *among individuals in this group* is due to genetic factors, whereas the remaining 50 percent of the variability is due to other sources such as environmental influences. (Recall from Chapter 3 that these estimates apply to *entire groups,* not to individual people.) Many psychologists disagree with these figures, with some arguing that these heritability estimates are far too high (Ceci, 1990; Scarr & Kidd, 1983) and others arguing that they are too low (Jensen, 1969, 1980). Nonetheless, even the most extreme environmentalist would not deny that heredity has some influence on cognitive development. The question is how these genetic factors are manifested in intellectual performance and what environmental factors interact with, shape, and modify the effects of genetic and constitutional predispositions.

Some intellectual abilities are more influenced by experience than are others, and that there may be individual differences in vulnerability to environmental influences. Bayley (1970) speculated that genetically determined nonintellective behaviors associated with temperament or personality factors may shape the expression of inherited intellectual capacities. Thus, characteristics such as social orientation, thresholds of physiological arousal, activity, fearfulness, and attention span may retard or enhance cognitive development or performance. Support for the relationship between such temperamental characteristics, which are probably genetically based, and mental development was obtained in a longitudinal study in which neonatal physiological activity was compared with differences in intellectual and personality measures at age 2½ (Bell, Weller, & Waldrop, 1971). Infants who were categorized as "low-intensity" neonates because they showed low respiration rates, low tactile sensitivity, and little response to interrupted sucking were described at 2½ years as being advanced in speech development, manipulative skills, geographic orientation, and modeling of adults. These associations were more marked for boys than for girls. Similar relationships between temperament and intellectual development have since been found in a number of studies. However, temperament alone is less predictive of intellectual development than is the goodness-of-fit between the child's temperament and parents' and teachers' needs and expectations (Lerner & Lerner, 1983; Wachs, 1992). In addition to the influence of these genetically based influences on intellectual performance, physiological effects of such things as conditions of pregnancy and birth, nutrition, drugs, disease, and physical injury shape the cognitive skills of the child. While it is true that genetic and physiological factors influence the development of intelligence, however, it is equally true that various aspects of the environment make a major contribution to IQ and intelligence.

Environmental Impoverishment and Stimulation

It has been suggested that "Trying to predict what a person's IQ will be at 20 on the basis of his IQ at age one or two is like trying to predict how heavy a two-week-old calf will be when he is a two-year-old without knowing whether he will be reared in a dry pasture, in an irrigated pasture or in a feed lot" (Hunt, 1972, p. 41). It is apparent that the quality, amount, and patterning of stimulation received by children in different environments vary greatly. In this section we address the impact of these variations on the development of intelligence.

Community Influences on Intellectual Performance

Many studies have dealt with the intelligence test performance of children living in isolated conditions, which are frequently associated with both educational and economic deprivation. An increasing intellectual deficit with age is found among rural children and other children living in isolated circumstances. For example, the IQs of children living in lonely hollows of the Blue Ridge Mountains of Virginia were significantly lower than those of children in nearby villages, and the IQ scores of the isolated children decreased with age (Sherman & Key, 1932). Others find an average IQ difference of 5 points between children in metropolitan and in rural areas (Kennedy, 1969).

Children living in poor rural environments often do not perform as well on intelligence tests as do urban children.

It may be that different environments stimulate and facilitate the development of different cognitive abilities and that standard intelligence tests do not measure a wide enough array of these abilities. Children living in remote Newfoundland outpost communities, for example, had highly developed motor and perceptual abilities that might be considered adaptive in that setting, whereas their verbal and reasoning skills, which might be less necessary for survival, were below average (Burnett, Beach, & Sullivan, 1963).

The Pulawat islanders, who live an isolated, seafaring existence in a society with little technology or formal education, have developed an amazing navigational system. This system reveals an understanding of navigational rules and the relationship among winds, tides, currents, and direction, and permits the islanders to navigate over long distances out of the sight of land. These remarkable navigators would not perform well on a standard test of intelligence or even on Piagetian tasks of formal operations, although on problems that are culturally relevant they are clearly demonstrating very advanced deductive reasoning. On navigational tasks they have certainly attained the stage of formal operations. Such observations show the importance of analyzing intellectual performance within the naturalistic, cultural context in which it occurs (Ceci, 1990; Christenson, Abery, & Weinberg, 1986). This is an important issue not only in cross-cultural studies and studies of isolated communities but also in studies of social class, race, and ethnicity in the United States.

Family Influences on Intellectual Performance

To understand IQ development, it is necessary to look not only at the child's community, but also within the home. Specific aspects of family interaction have been found to relate to IQ differences across social classes. A supportive, warm home environment that encourages exploration, curiosity, and self-reliance leads to high achievement (Gottfried & Gottfried, 1984; Estrada, Arsenio, Hess, & Holloway, 1987). In homes characterized by extreme punitiveness and rejection, or in homes where the father is overly authoritarian and enmeshes the child in rigid rules and regulations, low achievement results (Bradley, Caldwell, & Elardo, 1977; Radin, 1976). Such restrictiveness may inhibit early exploration and curiosity in children. It also seems probable that such parental behaviors lead to insecurity and high anxiety in children, factors that play an increasingly salient role in the school years (Hill & Eaton, 1977). Parents who are emotionally and verbally responsive to their children, who provide appropriate play and reading materials, who stimulate their children's educational abilities, and who provide a variety of experiences tend to have children with higher IQ scores (Gottfried & Gottfried, 1984; Bradley et al., 1989; Wachs, 1992).

The student should keep in mind that although parental behaviors and characteristics are related to intelligence and achievement in children, other factors such as social class, education, and social opportunities set important limits on the attainments of children.

Social Class, Race, and Intellectual Performance

Social class, race, and ethnicity are important factors that are correlated with intellectual performance. We examine these factors together because they are difficult to separate. Social class and racial or ethnic background frequently go together in our society. Members of several minority groups such as African-Americans and Latinos, for example, are overrepresented in lower socioeconomic groups. Thus it is difficult to untangle the effects of membership in certain minority groups from the effects of poverty. Unfortunately, the distinction between social class and race or ethnicity has not always been made clear in research on this topic. Interpretations of social-class and racial differences in intellectual performance cover a variety of hypothesized causes already discussed, including genetics and parent-child interaction. We address these and other interpretations of racial and social-class differences in IQ in this section.

Differences in performance on standardized intelligence tests among children from various ethnic and racial groups and social classes frequently have been noted (Brody, 1985; Golden & Birns, 1983; Jensen, 1980; Mackenzie, 1984). However, the views on which groups are disadvantaged change with historical times, current political and social values, and the situation involved. In 1912, an eminent psychologist who saw IQ as a fixed measure of innate intelligence sounded the alarm about "feeblemindedness" in the new waves of immigrants entering the United States (Goddard, 1912). Until that time, immigrants had been mainly northern Europeans, many from Great Britain, who came from cultures more closely resembling the mainstream culture in the United States than did the new immigrants who came from eastern and southern Europe. On the basis of intelligence tests administered to immigrants newly arrived on Ellis Island, Goddard announced that 83 percent of the Jews, 80 percent of the Hungarians, 70 percent of the Italians, and 85 percent of the Russians were feebleminded and would have difficulty being assimilated in their new country. Fortunately his dire predictions were unwarranted. At the present time, many studies are focusing on African-Americans, and more recently on other ethnic minorities such as Asians, Hispanics, and Native Americans.

Currently, children of low socioeconomic class score 10 to 15 IQ points below middle-class children, and black children score on the average 15 to

Children with different ethnic backgrounds show different profiles of mental abilities.

20 IQ points below white children (Hall & Kaye, 1980). These differences are present by first grade and are sustained throughout the school years (Kennedy, 1969). It has been found that in poor environmental circumstances, such as those in the rural south, deficits on both verbal and performance IQ in blacks increase with age from 5 to 18 years (Jensen, 1973). However, in better environmental circumstances, a deficit is found for verbal but not performance IQ, and this verbal difference between blacks and whites increases with age. Some analyses of more recent trends in reading achievement tests and SAT verbal and mathematics scores indicate that the gap in performance between blacks and whites on these measures has been narrowing in the last two decades (Jones, 1984). This narrowing is due more to increases in blacks' scores than to decreases in whites' scores, and may be related to the increasing numbers of black families entering the middle class in recent decades. Not all recent studies, however, have found the gap in academic achievement to be narrowing in recent years (Norman, 1988); differences in these studies may be due to the specific populations involved as well as to the measures employed.

In many studies the effects of race and social class have not been clearly separated, since in our country a disproportionate number of black Americans are found in the lower classes. However, when these factors are controlled, a consistent finding emerges that social-class differences are found on cognitive measures that involve language as early as 18 months of age, and that starting around 2 years of age these measures are highly correlated with performance on standardized intelligence tests (Golden & Birns, 1983). In trying to understand these data, keep in mind that the average IQ figures are obtained from *distributions* of people. To put it simply, although the mean IQ of minority and disadvantaged children is lower than the mean IQ of white middle-class children, there are many children in both groups who fall on either side of their respective group averages. The two distributions overlap to a large extent; many individual black and lower-class children have higher IQs than many individual white and middle- or upper-class children.

Some investigators have argued that a more fruitful approach to racial and socioeconomic differences is to look at differences in the patterns of cognitive skills rather than at overall levels of IQs. On what kinds of intellectual dimensions do members of different groups show the greatest relative strengths or weaknesses? Such an approach leads to construction of a profile of patterns of abilities. One classic study investigated the relative standing on tests of verbal, reasoning, number, and spatial abilities of middle- and lower-class Chinese-American, Jewish-American, Puerto Rican-American, and African-American children from New York City (Lesser, Fifer, & Clark, 1965). The children were between the ages of 6 years, 2 months, and 7 years, 5 months. A careful, systematic attempt was made to develop measures that were culture-fair and to administer the test in a way that minimized anxiety. As illustrated in Figure 11-2, distinctive profiles of mental-ability scores emerged for the four ethnic groups: Puerto Ricans and Chinese showed higher spatial abilities relative to their verbal abilities, whereas the pattern was reversed for African-Americans and Jews. It was found that social class influenced the elevation, but not the pattern, of scores, whereas ethnicity influenced both pattern and level. When the groups were separated on the basis of socioeconomic class, the profiles of abilities for lower-class ethnic groups were parallel to the middle-class profiles but they were lower on all abilities. The difference between the levels for the lower- and middle-class children was greatest for blacks, which suggests relatively greater socioeconomic disadvantages for lower-class blacks. The findings of this study are even more impressive when one realizes that it has been replicated and similar ethnic patterns of ability were found with a different sample of children.

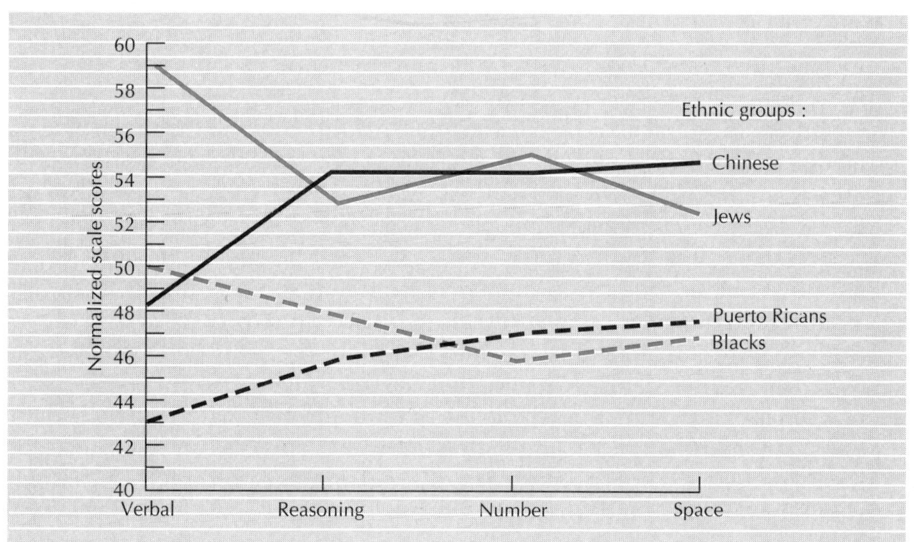

FIGURE 11-2
Pattern of verbal, reasoning, number, and spatial mental ability scores for 6- and 7-year-old children of different ethnic groups. (Reproduced from Lesser, Fifer, & Clark, 1965.)

INTERPRETATIONS OF RACIAL, ETHNIC, AND SOCIAL-CLASS DIFFERENCES IN COGNITIVE PERFORMANCE

Three main types of explanations have been advanced to explain the widely reported ethnic and social-class differences in intellectual performance: a position that emphasizes the inappropriateness of the tests for lower-class and minority children, a genetic position, and an environmental position.

Test Bias and Group Differences in IQ. Advocates of the first position argue that the most widely used intelligence tests have not been standardized on minority groups, and that the items contained on these tests are not a true measure of adaptive or problem-solving ability for the circumstances within which lower-class children and some ethnic groups live. The content of the usual intelligence test draws to some extent on white middle-class language, vocabulary, experience, and values. Here is an example of cultural bias on a recent version of the Stanford-Binet scale. Correct responses to the item "What's the thing for you to do if another boy hits you without meaning to do it?" are such statements as "I'd say 'That's alright. I know it was an accident,' and walk away." In some black communities, a child must fight back as a means of survival and to walk away would mean suicide (Williams, 1970).

Similarly, the vocabulary used in standard intelligence tests may not reflect the dialect or language that children use in their everyday lives. This may result in lower scores for minority children not because they are less intelligent, but due to the cultural bias of the tests. Culture-fair tests have been developed that aim to minimize cultural bias, such as the Kaufman Assessment Battery (Kaufman, Kamphaus, & Kaufman, 1985). On this test there is less difference between African-American and Caucasian children than on standard IQ tests. Other culture-free tests focus on nonverbal items, which involve discriminating patterns from one another. However, even on nonverbal tests, such as the Raven Progressive Matrices Test, more highly educated individuals perform better than their less well educated peers (Anastasi, 1988). This raises a critical problem in the development of culture-free tests. As long as one of the aims of intelligence tests is to predict academic performance in schools whose goals are largely defined by white middle-class values, and as long as school grades or other intelligence tests are used as validating criteria, differences among subcultures at least partly attributable to experience are likely to occur.

In addition to bias in the test content, testing conditions themselves may be deleterious to the performance of low socioeconomic status and minority-group children. As we saw earlier, many modern alternative approaches to intelligence emphasize the effects of context on children's intellectual performance. The context of IQ testing may not be one that enables minority and lower-class children to display their abilities to the fullest. Such factors as unfamiliarity with testing situations, discomfort with white middle-class testers, and motivational issues may contribute to poor performance (Zigler & Seitz, 1982). Attempts to elicit the best possible performance in children by familiarizing them with the test situation and test materials, by providing encouragement, and by using material rewards such as candy for motivation have been successful in improving the performance on intelligence tests of some lower-class and minority-group children (Golden & Birns, 1971). Moreover, optimal supportive testing conditions enhance the performance of economically deprived children more than middle-class children (Zigler, Abelson, Trickett, & Seitz, 1982). Thus there is some support for the position that intelligence tests do not measure the *competencies* of lower-class black children as well as they do for middle-class white children. Note that the distinction between capacity and performance is involved here; performance on IQ tests may reflect the intellectual capacities of some groups more accurately than others.

A study by Mercer (1971) asked whether intelligence tests tap into the actual competencies of minority and white children and young adults equally well. Mercer was especially concerned with the relationship between IQ and adaptive behavior outside the classroom. She focused on a large group of children who received low IQ scores in the range considered mentally retarded. She devised a test of adaptive ability involving persons' increasing ability to cope with more complex roles and practical problems as they mature. The scale consisted of age-graded skills ranging from such things in younger children as self-care items (dressing, feeding) to more complex items in adults, such as being able to travel alone, hold a job, shop, and so on. The results of the study were clear and somewhat disturbing. Ninety percent of the black children and 60 percent of the Chicano children with IQs in the bottom 3 percent (below 70) actually passed the test of adaptive functioning. That is, despite an IQ score which would classify them as mentally retarded, they were able to shop, to travel alone, and to hold jobs. In contrast, every white child with an IQ below 70 also failed the test of adaptive functioning. For these children, low IQ scores appeared to be reliable indicators of mental retardation. These results suggest that minority children are far more likely than white children to be inappropriately classified as retarded based on IQ tests, and that, for minority groups, standard intelligence tests do not accurately distinguish individuals who function well in the community from those who cannot cope with practical problems in their environment. Mercer's findings support the argument that IQ tests are biased in that they do not adequately measure the competencies of minority children. This problem is likely to lead to dire consequences, especially for children receiving very low IQ scores. Once children have been labeled retarded, the label follows them and plays a pervasive role in shaping their life experiences and others' expectancies about them.

Heredity and Group Differences in IQ. The second position that has been advanced to explain variations among social and racial groups in IQ is that these differences are based on genetic factors. One variant on this theme is that in a mobile society the brighter members of the lower class move upward and become middle class, and also that there is a tendency for people to marry within their class. This selective migration and assortative mating will tend to increase the difference between average IQ scores of the lower and middle classes over time (Herrenstein, 1971).

The most articulate exponent of the genetic position is Arthur Jensen (1969, 1973). He proposes that there are two genetically independent types of learning: *associative learning,* or level I learning, involving short-term memory, rote learning, attention, and simple associative skills; and *cognitive learning,* or level II learning, which involves abstract thinking, symbolic processes, conceptual learning, and the use of language in problem solving. The latter is clearly manifested in the ability to see relationships in such problems as:

Which number goes in the following series?

2, 3, 5, 8, 12, 17, . . .

How are an apple and a banana alike?

Most intelligence tests measure predominantly level II abilities. Some simple experimental tests, such as recalling a group of familiar objects or memory for numbers, measure level I abilities. According to Jensen, level I associative intelligence does not correlate with school performance and is not very important in academic learning, whereas level II intelligence as measured by IQ tests is predictive of achievement in school. Jensen suggests that level I abilities are equally distributed across social class and ethnic groups but that level II abilities are more concentrated in middle-class and Anglo-American than in lower-class or African-American groups. He sees this pattern arising, in part, because of selective mating and social mobility and, in part, because of different heritability patterns for level I and level II abilities. Jensen argues further on the basis of twin studies that 70 to 80 percent of the contribution to intelligence is due to heredity and the remainder to environment.

Prominent psychologists specializing in intelligence, including behavior geneticists, believe that Jensen's estimate of a 70 to 80 percent heritability factor in IQ is far too high and believe that the environment contributes to *at least* 50 percent of the variation in IQ among individuals (Weinberg, 1989; Plomin, 1989); some suggest that the contribution of the environment is even higher.

A slightly different kind of argument against Jensen's position concerns a logical flaw in Jensen's use of heritability estimates. Specifically, these estimates may describe the extent of genetic influence *within the group on which they were calculated*, especially if people's environments across that group are fairly similar. The contribution of genetic factors to intelligence will vary with the population being studied and the environmental conditions under which they develop. The example of stature illustrates this point (Kagan, 1965). In the United States under conditions of reasonable nutrition and immunization against disease, height is largely genetically determined. Because the majority of Americans are well nourished, the genes associated with height express themselves fairly directly in actual height. However, the differences in height between these well-nourished American children and children suffering from disease and malnutrition in another, less affluent culture are not mainly genetically determined. Extremely adverse health and nutritional factors overwhelm and minimize genetic contributions to stature. Most starving children remain small in stature. Since the contribution of heritability to height in the two cultures is not the same, it is inappropriate to use heritability indexes calculated on the basis of studies in one population and generalize these findings to different populations. Similarly, it is *not* appropriate to use estimates of the heritability of intelligence, which were obtained from and apply to middle-class white families with reasonably similar backgrounds and life circumstances, to explain differences *between* this group and minority or lower-class groups whose circumstances often differ dramatically from those of America's white middle class. Because their circumstances are so different, and one environment presents greater economic deprivation than the other, genetic contributions to intelligence are probably expressed more directly among middle-class Euro-American families than among lower-class minority group families. The heritability estimates calculated for middle-class Euro-American families simply do not apply to individuals from other groups.

In a twin study, Sandra Scarr-Salapatek investigated this problem directly by looking at the relationship between heritability and IQ in black and white lower- and middle-class children (Scarr-Salapatek, 1971). The investigator assumed that lower-class children and most blacks have limited experiences with environmental factors relevant to the development of academic skills or performance on intelligence tests. Therefore, just as the range of stature is smaller under conditions of extreme malnutrition, variability in scores on cognitive tests will be less for these groups than for white middle- or upper-class children. This was found to be the case. Genetic intellectual variations are more directly expressed in the performance on cognitive tests of white middle- or upper-class children than in lower-class or black children.

Many who read arguments such as Jensen's, psychologists and laypeople alike, conclude that if socioeconomic and ethnic differences in IQ scores are genetic, social programs aimed at improving cognitive development are futile. Even if these group differences in IQ are due to genetic factors (and as we have seen, there are several serious problems with this argument), the environment is still contributing to some significant portion of developmental outcomes. Many other differences in development are influenced by genetic factors—for example, certain types of blindness and deafness. The fact that these conditions may be genetically influenced does not mean that special educational programs will be useless for these children (Goldstein, 1990). On the contrary, special educational opportunities and changes in environmental circumstances can still enhance genetically influenced abilities. In particular, if psychologists achieve an understanding of precisely how nature and nurture interact with one another, they can design intervention programs that are likely to be more effective (Scarr & Weinberg, 1983).

Many disagree with Jensen, and next we turn to the environmental viewpoint.

Environment and Group Differences in IQ. Psychologists who emphasize environmental factors point to the fact that the conditions of physical and cultural deprivation imposed by poverty are adequate to explain the social-class differences in cognitive performance without invoking genetic factors. Deprivation may overwhelm the effects of genetic contributions to IQ. Poor nutrition, inadequate living conditions, poor health, and limited education may all contribute to lower IQ scores (Garcia Coll, 1990; Goldstein, 1990).

Perhaps the best way to understand the effects of these factors is to use the concept of *cumulative risk.* In other words, one of the many factors associated with poverty may lower a child's IQ; alternatively, many strong points in that child's environment may easily outweigh the risk associated with that one factor. However, as more and more of the factors associated with poverty are present in the life of a given child, that child's risk of poor academic performance increases substantially. Researchers identified ten specific factors that were likely to present risks to children's cognitive development (Sameroff, Seifer, Barocas, Zax, & Greenspan, 1987), including poor maternal mental health, high maternal anxiety, low maternal education, unemployed or unskilled occupational status of the head of the household, father absence, minority-group status, presence of more than four children in one family, and high incidence of stressful life events such as illness, job loss, or death in the family. In a sample of 215 4-year-old black, white, and Puerto Rican children, they examined the links between risk and IQ.

The findings, illustrated in Figure 11-3, were striking. Children with only one risk factor had IQs approximately equivalent to children who had no risk factors at all. As the number of environmental risk factors increased, however, children performed more poorly on the IQ test. Children in the sample who had the most risk factors (seven to eight) also had IQs 30 points lower than children with no risk factors. This study indicates that environmental risk to IQ increases as the number of risk factors present in the lives of the children increases. Moreover, the study found that the presence of several risk factors was associated with low IQs in both low and high socioeconomic status families, although the factors were more likely to be present in low socioeconomic status families.

These arguments suggest that there are factors in the lives of poor and minority children that contribute to declines in intelligence test performance, and that if these factors were not present, the children would achieve higher test scores. Psychologists who believe that IQ tests are biased argue that the tests assess something related to experience with white middle-class culture, that many children do not have access to the same body of knowledge assumed by the test, and that these children therefore cannot perform as well on the tests. One way to test these ideas is to ask what happens if black children are adopted by white parents and raised in economically advantaged families that have an intellectual climate similar to that of white middle-class children. These adopted black children, thus, are being reared in environments relevant to the culture of schools and IQ tests. If the racial and social-class differences usually obtained on IQ are attributable to such experiential differences, the IQs of these adopted black children should more closely resemble those of white middle-class children. In Box 11-2 a study that examines these effects is presented.

Social-Class, Ethnic, and Racial Differences in Parent-Child Interactions. The Scarr and Weinberg study in Box 11-3 speaks not only to the effects of social class and economic deprivation on IQ, but also to the issue of group

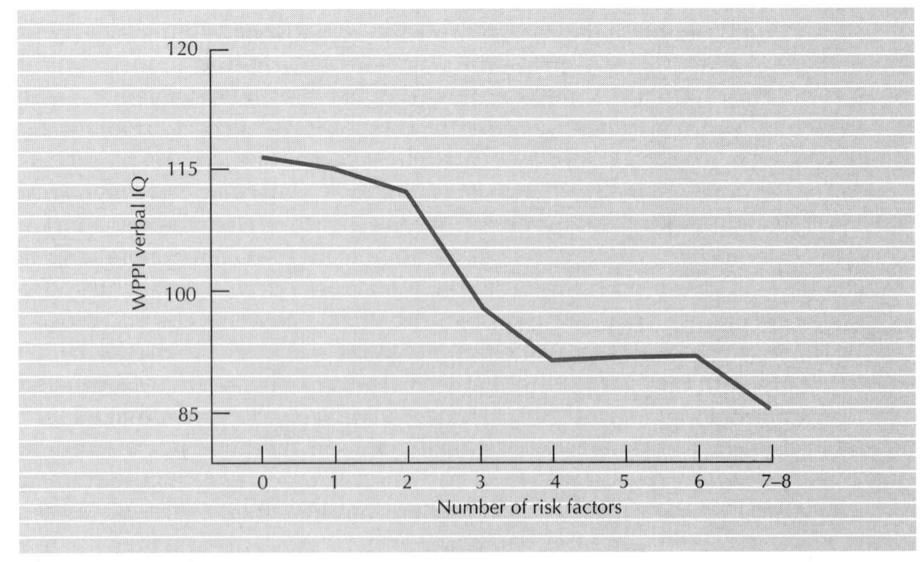

FIGURE 11-3
Means of 4-year-old children's verbal IQ scores for each cumulative-risk score. Cumulative risk scores are totals of high-risk factors present in each child's family. WPPSI, Wechsler Primary and Preschool Scales of Intelligence.

differences in parent-child interaction. Some psychologists suggest that differences in parental beliefs and behavior may mediate some of the relationships among IQ, social class, and ethnicity.

Many investigators have studied differences in middle- and lower-class parent-child interactions that may influence the development of verbal and cognitive skills. Social-class differences in parent-child interaction have been found even in infancy. Many of these social-class differences in family interaction are found within races and are not attributable to racial differences. The greatest differences between middle- and lower-class mothers are in their use of language. Middle-class mothers are more likely than lower-class mothers to talk in response to vocalizations by their infants. However, lower-class mothers touch and hold their infants more (Lewis & Wilson, 1972; Tulkin & Kagan, 1972). In addition, there are differences in the ways lower- and middle-class babies respond to their mothers' vocalizations. Lower-class children are more likely to continue vocalizing when their mothers are speaking, whereas middle-class babies tend to cease vocalizing and listen (Lewis & Freedle, 1973). It has been suggested that these early social-class differences in the way infants attend to their mothers' speech may be related to later social-class differences in the ease with which children use verbal information for learning (Golden & Birns, 1983). Barnard, Bee, and Hammond (1984) found a similar pattern of differences between mothers with more than a high school education and mothers with less than a high school education: Highly educated mothers were more emotionally and verbally responsive to their infants, were more likely to avoid restriction and punishment, and were more highly involved with their infants. These differences, measured at several intervals before children reached age 2, were significantly related to children's IQ scores at age 4. Goldstein (1990) argues that lower-class parents often experience higher levels of stress than do middle-class parents, and that stress may directly influence parents' styles of interaction. Parents' style of interacting—for example, whether parents are more concerned with discipline (which may easily be the case under stressful circumstances) or with positive emotional communication—may in turn have different effects on children's intellectual development.

Robert Hess and Virginia Shipman (1967) studied the interaction among maternal control techniques, teaching styles, language, and the child's cognitive development. The individualistic control approach used by middle-class mothers emphasizes the child's feelings, characteristics, and reasons for actions and orients the child toward attending to relevant cues in problem-solving situations in the environment. The mother makes the child aware of the complexities of his social and physical environment. She organizes information for her child and uses a more complex linguistic code to do so. In contrast, the lower-class mother uses status-oriented control, characterized by fewer individualized responses and a simplistic stereotyped restrictive form of language. This type of maternal communication is less likely to facilitate the kinds of discriminations and classifications necessary for later problem-solving skills in the child, but may enhance the likelihood that children will behave well while working.

Moreover, middle-class and lower-class parents appear to orient their children to school in a manner consistent with their styles of interaction. This is illustrated in a classic study by these same researchers (Hess & Shipman, 1967), who examined the ways in which black middle- and lower-class mothers introduced their children to school. Mothers indicated what they would tell their children on the first day of school before they left the house.

BOX 11-2 WHEN BLACK CHILDREN GROW UP IN WHITE HOMES

What happens to the IQs of black children who are adopted and raised by white parents? Scarr and Weinberg studied 101 white families who adopted black children. The parents in these families were above average in intelligence, education, and socioeconomic status. All members over age 4 of the adoptive families, including the parents, adopted child, and biological offspring of the adoptive parents, were given age-appropriate IQ tests. The parents also were interviewed about experiences associated with the adoption, about being an interracial family, and about their life-style. The study involved 145 biological offspring of the adoptive parents, 130 adopted black children, and a small group of adopted white, Asian, and Native American children. Two-thirds of the adopted children were in the adoptive homes before their first birthday.

Figure 11-4 presents the IQ scores of the black and white adopted children. As shown in the graph, these children tend to score above the national average IQ of

FIGURE 11-4

IQ scores for adopted children of different races. (Adapted from Scarr & Weinberg, 1976, p. 732.)

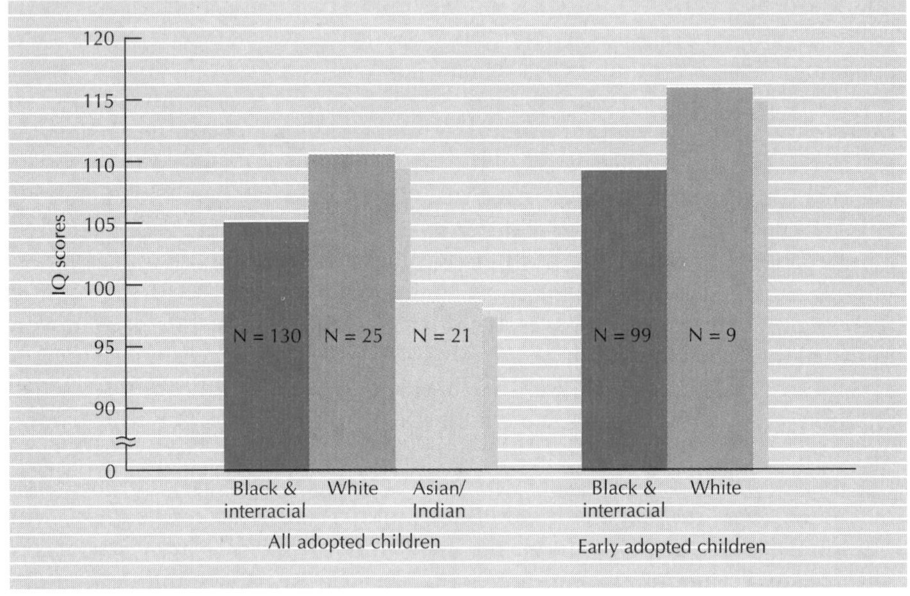

The lower-class mothers tended to give their children unqualified commands concerning how to behave in school. Little or no rationale for their directives was provided: "sit down," "don't holler," and "mind the teacher" were typical answers. In contrast, the middle-class mothers tended to use a more cognitive, rational orientation that provided the children with some explanation for the rules that the school would impose on their behavior. For example, a middle-class mother might instruct her child: "You shouldn't talk in school because the teacher can't teach so well and you won't learn your lessons properly." These mothers encouraged their children to ask for explanations if they didn't understand.

The lower-class child who is given the imperative orientation is likely to view the school as a rigid authoritarian institution governed by inflexible and unexplained rules and regulations. This attitude may lead to overzealous acceptance of absolute answers and less likelihood of inquiry, interest, and involvement. In contrast, the child given the rational, cognitive orientation will be more likely to expect that answers should have reasons underlying them. A spirit of inquiry is kindled in the middle-class child, which probably delights the teachers and, in turn, aids the child's progress. In fact, Hess and

BOX 11-2 WHEN BLACK CHILDREN GROW UP IN WHITE HOMES (*Continued*)

100. Moreover, the earlier children are placed, the more they benefit from their home experiences. The white adopted children tended to be placed at a younger age than were other children and had the highest IQs, averaging 111. The Asian and Native American children, who had endured longer periods of institutionalization and were the latest group to be placed, had IQs at the national average of 100. In fact only three Asian and Native American children were adopted early, and therefore they are not included in the early adopted groups in Figure 11-4. The black children, who were intermediate in age of placement, are also intermediate in terms of test scores with an IQ of 106. It should be noted that these black adopted children, especially the early placed children, score about 20 points above the national averages for black children and are performing much better than would have been predicted on the basis of the educational level and occupations of their natural parents. In addition, the range of scores for black and white adopted children was similar. That is, the top-scoring black children scored as high as the top-scoring white children, and this similarity was also found for the lowest-scoring children. The effects of the adoptive environment enhanced not only the IQ scores of the black children but also their performance at school and scores on standardized achievement tests, which were again above the national average. The natural children who have lived in these middle-class educated environments since birth scored higher than any of the adopted children. It is unfortunate that the race of a child is confounded with the time of placement. However, there is a trend for early adoption to increase the scores of white as well as nonwhite children. The results of this study certainly show that social environment plays an important role in determining IQ scores and that the deficits in performance on IQ tests by black children can be reduced with placement in educated middle-class environments. A large part of these effects may be due to social class rather than to race per se. The results suggest that middle-class Euro-American environments facilitate the development of the skills necessary for good performance on intelligence tests, rather than that there are innate racial differences in intellectual ability.

Before we rush off and start placing black children in white adoptive homes, let us keep in mind a precautionary note advanced by the investigators.

> Our emphasis on IQ scores in this study is not an endorsement of IQ as the ultimate human value. Although important for functioning in middle-class educational environments, IQ tests do not sample a huge spectrum of human characteristics that are requisite for social adjustment. Empathy, sociability, and altruism, to name a few, are important human attributes that are not guaranteed by a high IQ. Furthermore, successful adaptation within ethnic subgroups may be less dependent on the intellectual skills tapped by IQ measures than is adaptation in middle-class white settings.
>
> . . . The major findings of the study support the view that the social environment plays a dominant role in determining the average IQ level of black children and that both social and genetic variables contribute to individual variation among them. (Scarr & Weinberg, 1976, p. 739)

Source: Scarr, S., & Weinberg, R. A. (1976). IQ test performance of black children adopted by white families. *American Psychologist,* 31, 725–739.

Shipman found a clear relationship between the mother's orientation and the child's mental performance: The use of an imperative approach was associated with low performance in several areas, including lower IQ scores among children of imperative mothers. However, it is unlikely that these roles are always closely linked with social class; children in any social class can play an active or passive role and, in turn, be differently treated by their teachers (Kedar-Viovodas, 1983).

It is important to note that these differences in parent-child interaction do not imply that minority or lower-class parents do not place importance on their children's education and intellectual development. In a recent study of black, Hispanic, and white first-, third-, and fifth-grade children and their mothers, Stevenson, Chen, and Uttal (1990) found that black and Hispanic mothers placed a higher value on their children's education than white mothers and saw homework as more important for improving children's education than white mothers. Nor are these effects limited to young children. In a study of nearly 8,000 San Francisco Bay Area adolescents and 3,000 parents, Ritter, Mont-Reynaud, and Dornbush (1990) found that black parents were concerned about and involved in their children's education. Hispanic

BOX 11-3 MAKING THE GRADE: SCHOOL ACHIEVEMENT IN JAPAN, TAIWAN, AND THE UNITED STATES

The popular press has abounded with stories of declining achievement in children in the United States, and it is fashionable to blame these academic woes on the school system. However, a recent study conducted by Harold Stevenson and his colleagues on schoolchildren in the first and fifth grades in Japan, Taiwan, and the United States found that children in the United States already lag behind other children in academic achievement in the earliest months of first grade, when they have as yet had little exposure to formal education. Although differences in the educational system may contribute to later differences in achievement, these early achievement deficits suggest that more is involved than inadequate educational practices.

In this study, over 4000 first and fifth graders in 120 classrooms in the cities of Minneapolis (U.S.), Taipei (Taiwan), and Sendai (Japan) were given individually administered achievement tests. In addition, 1440 children (equal numbers in each city) were tested and studied intensively and were observed in school for twenty randomly selected forty-minute periods. The children's mothers were also interviewed and their teachers filled out an extensive questionnaire. Finally, the first graders were studied again when they had reached fifth grade.

In first grade, Americans tended to be overrepresented among both the best and worst readers; however, by fifth grade the number of poor readers increased markedly. The deficits in mathematics shown by children in the United States were more startling. Among 100 students from the three countries who received the lowest scores, there were 58 American children in first grade and 67 in fifth grade. Among the 100 highest scores in first grade there were 15 American children, and this had declined to only 1 in the 100 high scores by fifth grade.

What might be contributing to these dire findings? There was no evidence that American children had lower intellectual levels or more poorly educated parents. However, there were marked differences in the beliefs of these parents, their reported activities with their children, and the evaluations they made of their children and the educational system. Mothers in all three countries viewed their children's academic performance as above average; however (as can be seen in Figure 11-5), American mothers voiced the most positive views about their children's scholastic achievement and experience. This unrealistically optimistic evaluation of their children's attainment and the educational system occurred in spite of the fact that American children had the lowest levels of academic achievement. In addition, American mothers had very different beliefs about what led to successful performance in school. American mothers put more emphasis on the role of ability and less on effort as an important requisite of success. Parents who emphasize ability more than effort may be less likely to require that their children work hard on academic tasks. This was the case! American children spend significantly less time on homework and in reading for pleasure and more time playing and doing chores than did Japanese or Taiwanese children. The differences with the Taiwanese families were especially notable. Only 17 percent of first-grade and 28 percent of fifth-grade Taiwanese children did chores, in contrast to 90 percent and 95 percent of American first and fifth graders. When one Taiwanese mother was asked why she did not assign her children chores she replied, "It would break my heart. Doing chores would consume time that the child should devote to studying." Moreover, American mothers were less likely to be actively involved in helping their children with homework and participating in the learning experience than were the other two groups of mothers. Japanese mothers in particular were likely to see themselves as *kyoiku mamas,* that is, the "education mom" who is responsible for assisting, directing, and supervising the child's learning. In the authors' words,

> Whereas children's academic achievement did not appear to be a central concern of American mothers, Chinese and Japanese mothers viewed this as the child's most important pursuit. Once the child entered elementary school, Chinese and Japanese families mobilized themselves to assist the child

parents were also concerned about their children's education, but were less directly involved, perhaps because of language barriers. The frustration experienced by many parents in trying to comprehend the "new math" and computer courses for example, suggests that the problem of helping children with school work is not limited to either lower-class parents or parents in minority cultures. With increasing specialization and curriculum innovation it may be necessary to teach the parents as well! Nonetheless, cultural differences in styles of interacting and approaching cognitive tasks may influence children's academic achievement, as well as their comfort in schools that largely promote white middle-class values.

BOX 11-3 MAKING THE GRADE: SCHOOL ACHIEVEMENT IN JAPAN, TAIWAN, AND THE UNITED STATES (*Continued*)

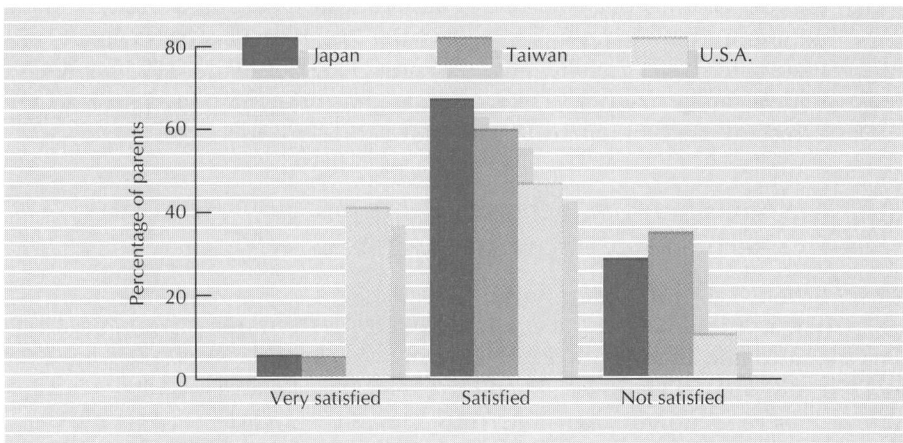

FIGURE 11-5
Mother's attitude toward child's academic performance. (From Stevenson, 1983.)

> and to provide an environment conducive to achievement. American mothers appeared to be less interested in their child's academic achievement than in the child's general cognitive development; they attempted to provide experiences that fostered cognitive growth rather than academic excellence. (Stevenson et al., 1990, pp. v–vi)

In addition to these family differences, there were some differences in the schools. However, even some of these seem attributable to factors in the home. First, American teachers felt they had to spend too much time in roles irrelevant to the goal of teaching (such as counselor, family therapist, and surrogate parent). Second, American children spent much more time in inappropriate, uncontrolled, inattentive activities than did their Japanese and Taiwanese peers. Teachers had to devote more time to controlling the class and less to teaching because the children had not been trained to be attentive and to restrain inappropriate behaviors. There were other differences in the schools not directly attributable to parents. American children spend fewer hours in school, have a shorter academic year, and have less instruction in mathematics. The investigators present some specific questions that need to be addressed if we are going to modify practices and policies that are hindering our children's academic progress:

> Should we not recruit parents as partners in the educational process, so that the parents participate directly in their children's education, especially during the elementary school years?
> Should we not give parents information that will allow them to make a more realistic appraisal of their children's cognitive abilities and levels of scholastic achievement? Should we not ask the children to spend more time at home working on homework? Should we not increase the number of days our children attend school each year, and the amount of time they spend in school each day?
> Should we not ask for modifications in school policies and teaching practices so that the time children spend in school is spent on productive activities? (Stevenson, 1983, p. 51)

Sources: Stevenson, H. W. (1983, April). *Making the grade: School achievement in Japan, Taiwan, and the United States.* Report to Bush Center's Board of Trustees (pp. 41–51). Stevenson, H. W., Lee, S., Chen, C., Stigler, J. W., Hsu, C., & Kitamura, S. (1990). Contexts of achievement. *Monographs of the Society for Research in Child Development,* 55 (No. 221).

For a cross-cultural perspective on achievement, see Box 11-3, which reports an extensive study of family influences on cognitive development in families in the United States, Taiwan, and Japan. That American children, as a whole, perform less well than Japanese and Chinese school children raises a number of provocative questions about American education practices and policies (Stevenson & Stigler, 1992).

In addition, these cross-cultural studies have raised the question of whether patterns of interaction in Asian-American families can explain the high levels of achievement frequently shown by Asian-American Children. Just as Afro-American and Hispanic-American parents, Asian-American families appear to strongly support their children's academic achievement. They hold high expectations for their children's education and also tend to convey the idea that achievement is part of children's duty to parents. Asian-American families often strictly monitor children's free time and homework time. In addition, they frequently profess the belief that effort will be rewarded (Slaughter-Defoe, Nakagawa, Takanishi, & Johnson, 1990). However, the critical family factors that determine the different patterns of achievement across diverse ethnic groups are not yet fully understood.

Beyond Families: Schools, Peers and Intellectual Development

Schools, Ethnicity and Social Class

The fact that the school is a middle-class institution, espousing middle-class values and often staffed by white middle-class teachers, puts the child from a different social-class or cultural background at a disadvantage from the outset. The lower-class child experiences the middle-class-oriented school as discontinuous with his home environment (Comer, 1988; Lightfoot, 1978).

Support for the claim that middle-class teachers fail to understand and appreciate the differences in background, experience, and values of lower-class children comes from a study by Gottlieb (1966). When the attitudes of white middle-class teachers and Afro-American teachers were compared, they differed in their perceptions of their lower-class students. White teachers described these pupils as "talkative," "lazy," "fun-loving," "high-strung," and "rebellious." Afro-American teachers, however, saw these pupils in a much more positive light and described them as "happy," "cooperative," "energetic," and "ambitious."

These attitudes may translate in differential treatment, which, in turn may lead to the lower-class child's lack of achievement. For example, Cadmus (1974), in his study of a racially integrated first-grade classroom, found that low-income Afro-American children received about 75 percent of all the negative teacher comments, while the affluent white students garnered about 75 percent of all positive teacher remarks! Similar effects are evident even among preschoolers; as Quay and Jarrett (1986) found, teachers were more likely to be negative to lower-class children than to middle-class preschool children.

Moreover, it is not restricted to negative comments. Black students are 2.3 times as likely as white students—and all minority students are 1.6 times as likely as white students—to be placed in a special-education class for mentally retarded or emotionally disturbed children. Minority students are suspended more often as well—at nearly twice the rate of their white classmates. Afro-American students are suspended at nearly three times the rate of their white peers (Bates, 1990).

Moreover, this differential treatment has consequences. As Soar and Soar (1979) found, the lower-income students learn less in classrooms where large numbers of negative messages emanate from teachers and classmates. "If pupils of low socioeconomic status come to school with patterns of behavior that the teacher dislikes and responds to with negative affect, a *vicious circle* is created that makes it difficult for such pupils to learn" (Soar & Soar, 1979, p. 105). It is not surprising that nearly twice as many lower-class as middle-class students drop out before completing high school.

It is clear that any program aimed at improving the academic progress of lower-class children should not be restricted to content and curriculum innovations. Alterations in teacher preparation and teacher attitudes are necessary, including extensive exposure to lower-class life and lower-class values. While modifying teachers' attitudes alone is obviously not sufficient to help children from impoverished backgrounds learn, it is an important starting point.

Peers, Ethnicity and Intellectual Attainment

Peer culture plays a role in determining children's academic achievement. Often the orientation of peer groups is antiacademic, with ridicule and isolation being imposed on those who try to succeed academically (Ogbu, 1988). Many low-income black children face a tough choice between school success or maintaining their peer group status. Often, children who succeed in school consciously choose strategies to hide or camouflage their real academic attitudes and efforts (Fordham & Ogbu, 1986). These techniques, such as athletic participation or assuming the role of the comedian or jester, helps them both pursue academic work and avoid peer criticism.

A Word of Caution

There are many limitations in studies of ethnicity, social class and intellectual achievement. Studies of ethnic group differences are frequently confounded with social class; moreover, many minority groups have received little or no research attention. In addition, researchers frequently lump many diverse groups together into one ethnic group. For example, many studies of Asian-Americans include groups of Chinese, Japanese, Korean, Filipino, or Vietnamese descent, but these studies typically do not examine potential differences among these groups. Whereas many studies of Asian-Americans are designed to ask why these groups are successful, studies of blacks frequently ask why these groups perform poorly. The cultural assumptions underlying this distinction is troublesome and research on all minority groups might benefit by looking for the strengths that the various cultures provide (Slaughter-Defoe et al., 1990). Finally, some scholars see the focus on family interaction patterns as a factor in academic achievement as overly narrow; greater emphasis needs to be given to educational, societal and economic factors that influence the options and patterns of adaptation available to these families (Ogbu, 1988).

In summary, environmental factors, including family, school, and peers, play a large role in understanding differences in IQ among social classes and racial and ethnic groups. Next we address the question of the role of motivational, emotional, and personality variables in achievement.

The Effects of Emotion, Motivation, and Beliefs on Achievement

We turn now to an area sometimes called *hot cognition* because it involves emotion rather than cognitive processing strategies per se. Children's intellectual performance is affected not only by their external environment, but also by their motivation to achieve, the emotions they associate with learning tasks, the ways they view themselves and their ability, and their responses to success and failure.

"Achievement motivation is an overall tendency to evaluate one's performance against standards of excellence, to strive for successful performance, and to experience pleasure contingent on successful performance" (Feld, Ruhland, & Gold, 1979, p. 45). Achievement motivation varies among children and for the same child across tasks, situations, and times. Variations in achievement motivation and performance are often related to emotions and opinions about oneself as a learner. Some children have negative feelings about certain learning tasks and may be convinced of their inability to learn in certain areas. Mathematics is a particularly troublesome area for some people, especially females. How many times have you heard people describe themselves as a "math phobic"? Negative emotions can serve as a block to effective learning by directing a considerable amount of cognitive effort to making anxiety-producing, self-defeating self-evaluations. "I'm going to fail, again"; "I can't do this"; "I can't pass multiple-choice exams." Such negative thoughts distract the learner from the details of the task and can have an immobilizing effect on learning (Brown, Bransford, Ferrara, & Campione, 1983). Moreover, people tend to avoid situations about which they have negative feelings and may therefore obtain less practice in the areas in which they most need it.

Two different response patterns in achievement settings have been identified (Dweck & Leggett, 1988; Nicholls, 1984). These differences are particularly likely to appear when children are working on a challenging achievement task, one that holds the possibility of failure. Fifth- and sixth-grade children attempted to solve a series of difficult hypothesis-testing problems that somewhat resembled a complex game of twenty questions (Diener & Dweck, 1978). At first, they were able to solve the problems, but then the experimenter presented several problems that the children failed. Some children, referred to as *helpless,* tended to give up easily or to show marked performance deterioration when working on the difficult problems. Although they were fully capable of completing the task earlier, helpless children often used inefficient strategies more commonly seen in kindergartners after exposure to failure. In contrast, other children, referred to as *mastery-oriented,* maintained or even improved their level of performance during the failure problems. Helpless children expressed negative emotions such as frustration and blamed their ability for their performance ("I know I can't do this.") and had low expectations for their future performance. Mastery-oriented children were strikingly different. They expressed neutral or even positive affect; one boy, upon working on a problem and failing to solve it, leaned forward, smacked his lips, and said, "You know, I was hoping this would be informative." In addition, they attributed their poor performance to lack of sufficient effort rather than ability and maintained high expectations for future success. (Note the similarity to the research on Asian-American, Japanese, and Chinese families discussed earlier; these groups, too, often stated that effort was an extremely important factor in achievement.)

What would cause children to react so differently to the same task? Helpless and mastery-oriented children do not differ in their ability levels; instead, these children think about ability and achievement in very different ways (Dweck & Leggett, 1988; Nicholls, 1984). Children who show the helpless pattern tend to have *performance goals* in achievement situations—that is, they are concerned with "looking smart," with obtaining positive judgments, and avoiding negative judgments of their ability. Mastery-oriented children are much more likely to have *learning goals.* In other words, they are more concerned with *improving* their skills and learning new things than they are with judgments of their ability. These different goals are associated with different beliefs about the nature of ability itself. Helpless children tend to hold an *entity theory of intelligence.* This is an implicit belief that intelligence is a fixed quantity, an unchangeable entity that people possess in varying degrees. Mastery-oriented children, on the other hand, tend to hold an *incremental theory of intelligence*. That is, they view intelligence as a malleable body of skills and knowledge that can be increased by means of effort.

Dweck suggests that the two theories of intelligence and the two goals orient children to react very differently to achievement tasks. The entire set of relationships is illustrated in Table 11-3. When children are highly confident in their abilities, differences between the two groups are not apparent; even children with an entity theory and performance goals are likely to show the mastery-oriented pattern. Possibly, they believe, in these cases, that their good performance is indicative of high ability. However, when children lack confidence in their abilities, an entity theory and performance goals make children especially vulnerable to the helpless pattern. Under these circumstances of failure and low confidence, their poor performance may seem diagnostic of low ability and lead them to give up easily. In contrast, when children have learning goals and an incremental theory of intelligence, poor performance may simply indicate to them that they have more to learn, and that different strategies may even lead to improvements in ability. For these reasons, effort may be seen as especially important, and the mastery-oriented response pattern of performance enhancement and high expectations is more likely to occur. The following responses of children with entity and incremental theories illustrate their different perspectives about achievement.

> **Question:** Sometimes kids feel smart in school, sometimes not. When do you feel smart?
>
> **Answers:**
> Incremental: When I don't know how to do it and it's pretty hard and I figure it out without anybody telling me.
>
> Incremental: When I'm doing school work because I want to learn how to get smart.
>
> Incremental: When I'm reading a hard book.
>
> Entity: When I don't do mistakes.
>
> Entity: When I turn in my papers first.
>
> Entity: When I get easy work. (Dweck & Bempechat, 1983, p. 249)

TABLE 11-3

THEORIES, GOALS AND BEHAVIOR PATTERNS IN ACHIEVEMENT SITUATIONS

THEORY OF INTELLIGENCE	GOAL ORIENTATION	PERCEIVED PRESENT ABILITY	BEHAVIOR PATTERN
Entity (intelligence is fixed)	Performance (goal is to gain positive judgments/avoid negative judgments of competence)	High	Mastery oriented (seek challenge; high persistence)
		Low	Helpless (avoid challenge; low persistence)
Incremental (intelligence is malleable)	Learning (goal is to increase competence)	High or low	Mastery oriented (seek challenge that fosters learning; high persistence)

Source: Dweck & Leggett (1988).

Different situations can elicit different responses, and most mastery-oriented children may occasionally show helpless responses when performance goals are made very salient (Dweck & Leggett, 1988).

Although an incremental theory is usually more advantageous than an entity theory, there may be situations in which this is not the case. Many teachers may foster a classroom "entity" environment where the emphasis is on success and evaluation and little other encouragement is given for engaging in learning activities. In such a setting, lessons are learned to please the teacher, not for their own value or interest. However, as the academic and professional environment changes to encourage independent choice, perseverance, and long-term outcomes, the incremental theorist will be at an advantage. For example, many children with entity theories start to receive lower grades upon entering junior high school, perhaps because the new school and the more challenging course materials make them feel doubtful about their abilities (Henderson & Dweck, 1990). Research on high school students (Boyum, Dweck, & Hill, 1990) suggests that children with entity theories may be less likely to seek out challenging courses when they are allowed to select their own classes.

How early do children's achievement motivation patterns develop? One set of answers to this question looks at developmental changes within the child. Many researchers in this field (for example, Nicholls & Miller, 1983; Stipek & MacIver, 1989) argued that children younger than 9 or 10 do not fully understand the concept of ability, do not view achievement tasks in the same ways as older children, and therefore cannot show the helpless pattern of performance deterioration and blaming one's ability. However, recent research suggests that this picture of development is not entirely accurate. Several studies have found that some 4-, 5-, and 6-year-old children show a response pattern that closely resembles the helpless pattern found in older children (Cain, 1990; Heyman, Dweck, & Cain, 1992). For example, Patricia Smiley (1989) asked 4- and 5-year-old preschoolers to complete four wooden puzzles, three of which could not be solved by the children. Afterward, children were asked which puzzle they would like to do again. Children who chose to repeat the easy puzzle rather than try to solve one of the difficult puzzles were classified as nonpersisters (42 percent of the sample). In comparison to other children, the nonpersisters expressed more negative emotion and self-doubts about their abilities during the puzzle task, were less likely to believe their performance would improve if they had another chance, and had lower expectations for success on an entirely different task (building with blocks). Finally, see Box 11-4 for another example. These developmental data suggest that striking differences in children's achievement orientations are present early, probably before children enter formal schooling.

Academic Context and Achievement

Changes in the contexts in which children perform intellectual tasks as well as changes in children's ability to interpret their performance are important in achievement. As children grow older, schools increasingly emphasize competition and provide less praise and individual support. These contextual changes should make it increasingly likely that some children will worry about their abilities and show motivational difficulties (Eccles & Midgley, 1989).

Recent research has examined the changes that occur in children's environments when they enter junior high school (Eccles & Midgley, 1989;

BOX 11-4 SELF-BELIEFS AND CHILDREN'S REACTIONS TO CRITICISM

Young children may not encounter failure in school as often as do older children, and they also may not be quite as quick as older children to recognize failure when it occurs. However, it is likely that most children are exposed to criticism—sometimes mild, sometimes more serious—when they are young. How do they react to criticism? Do some young children see criticism as an indictment of their abilities? Are they able to say that some criticisms are unfair, or do they always believe the critic and conclude that their work is flawed? Are there individual differences among children in the ways they react to criticism of their work?

Heyman, Dweck, and Cain (1992) conducted a study with 107 kindergarteners. They asked the children to imagine themselves in a series of three situations in which they worked on an age-appropriate project for their teacher, namely painting a family, building a house with blocks, or writing numbers. At the same time, they acted out the story using toy people, one of whom represented the child. Each story involved careful work on the task, but in each, the child made a small mistake. For example, one story was as follows:

> You spend a lot of time painting a picture of a family to give to your teacher. You pick out colors you think are nice and carefully draw each person. As you are about to give it to your teacher you say to yourself, "Uh oh, one of the kids has no feet." But you worked really hard on the picture and want to give it to her. You say, "Teacher, here's a picture for you."

Some of the stories ended here, but some continued with a critical response from the teacher doll: "There are no feet on that child. That's not what I call drawing people the right way. I'm disappointed in you." After acting out the story with the toys, children were asked a number of questions concerning their feelings about themselves and their work. For example, they chose how many smiley faces or frowns they felt they deserved for the work, and they used pictures of faces to show the extent to which they felt happy, sad, and mad. They also answered questions about whether they were good at the task and whether they thought they were a good person, a nice person, and a smart person. Finally, they used the toy people to act out what they thought their parents might say and what their teacher might do next.

Children found the imaginary situations very realistic and were able to recall all the main parts of the stories. When there was no criticism from the "teacher," the children evaluated their work positively, despite the small mistake. In contrast, when the "teacher" criticized their work, children tended to respond in different ways. First, some children continued to believe their work deserved lots of smiley faces, but others (39 percent of the sample) now began to criticize their work and said they deserved frowns. Those children who gave their work a low rating (low-product raters) went on to report more sadness about what had happened. They also were likely to say that they were not good at the task and, more disturbing, that they were not smart, not nice, and not a good person. When they acted out imagined parental responses, many involved criticism. For example, one child thought his parents would say, "How could you do this? This is not a very good building. I don't like it." Another imagined parental response was "You are very bad." Finally, when asked to act out what would happen next with the teacher, they were not very likely to envision constructive solutions. For example, one boy enacted himself throwing away the page of numbers he had written.

The children who maintained their positive ratings despite the criticism presented a striking contrast. They tended to report feeling happy, or if they felt negative, they were more likely to report anger at the teacher than sadness. They believed that they were good at the task, and they did not cast doubt on their smartness, niceness, or basic goodness. Many of them believed that their parents would praise them despite the small mistake. One child, for example, imagined her parents saying, "You did a good job. I'm proud of you." Moreover, when asked how the story would end, over half of these children spontaneously acted out constructive solutions to the problem. For example, "One girl acted out her teacher telling her, 'You are a good girl but you missed the 8.' In response she said, "That's o.k. because I didn't have time,' and said she would finish it for homework. She then brought the completed homework to a pleased teacher" (Heyman et al., 1992, p. 410).

The different responses by the children in the study provide a vivid illustration of young children's reactions to criticism. While some kindergarteners appear to take criticism in stride, to continue to think highly of themselves and their work, and to envision constructive ways to correct mistakes, others rate their work negatively, feel quite badly about themselves, and do not enact constructive solutions. This study illustrates first that there are important individual differences in children's motivational response when they are first entering school, and second that even young children can have very compelling concerns about achievements. The question of how these different orientations arise presents a challenging task for future research.

Source: Heyman, G. D., Dweck, C. S., & Cain, K. M. (1992). Young children's vulnerability to self-blame and helplessness: Relationship to beliefs about goodness. *Child Development*, **63**, 401–415.

Eccles, Lord, & Midgley, 1991; Henderson & Dweck, 1990). Children frequently experience motivational declines after entering junior high school; declines are reported in adolescents' school interest, self-confidence, and grades. At the same time, children become more likely to worry about performance rather than learning, to show test anxiety, and to stay away from school (truancy). Eccles and colleagues believe that there is a developmental mismatch between the characteristics of junior high schools and young adolescents' needs. They conducted a two-year longitudinal study of 1350 students making the transition from elementary school (sixth grade) to junior high school (seventh grade). Questionnaires were completed by the children's teachers; in addition, survey results were supplemented by systematic classroom observations. The study revealed that seventh-grade junior high school teachers are more likely than sixth-grade teachers to emphasize classroom control and discipline, and to see children as untrustworthy. Teachers in seventh grade also feel less efficacious about influencing learning. Observers and students saw seventh-grade teachers as less supportive, friendly, and fair than sixth-grade teachers. Moreover, classroom ability grouping and social comparison of grades increased in seventh grade; individualized instruction declined.

How did these contextual changes affect students? After children moved from a sixth-grade teacher who felt effective to a seventh-grade teacher who felt less efficacious, they had lower expectancies for their own performance and evaluated their performance more negatively. When junior high school teachers were less supportive and more controlling than elementary school teachers, the students' interest in the subject matter declined. Unfortunately, both sets of effects were more pronounced for low-achieving students. Finally, when seventh-grade teachers exerted more classroom control than sixth-grade teachers and allowed children less freedom in decision making, student interest in the subject area declined. Eccles and her colleagues argue that adolescence is a time when children need emotional support and opportunities to make independent decisions, and many junior high schools are less likely to meet these needs than are elementary schools. This mismatch between children's needs and the contexts in which they must perform appears to contribute to declines in achievement motivation.

To summarize, research on achievement motivation suggests that emotions and beliefs can play an important role in academic achievement from the preschool years onward. Moreover, changes in the contexts of achievement are likely to have a negative impact on children's interest in academic tasks as well as their performance. Intellectual performance depends on far more than ability; a variety of emotional and motivational factors affect children's performance on academic tasks throughout development. Sex differences in motivation and self-beliefs may also affect achievement; this issue is taken up in Chapter 15.

The major question remaining in our discussion of intelligence and achievement involves intervention and prevention. Given that many environmental and motivational factors such as poverty, family interaction, and self-beliefs contribute to a child's intellectual functioning, is it possible to alter these factors and improve intellectual functioning in children? Cognitive intervention studies are designed to address this question.

COGNITIVE INTERVENTION STUDIES

In the past three decades a great many compensatory education programs aimed at modifying the development of learning-disabled or economically deprived children have been initiated. Some of these programs were intended to prevent cognitive declines in preschool children; others were remedial and focused on school-age children who already had learning problems. Moreover, some programs emphasized the teaching of specific skills such as number skills or vocabulary, and others focused on teaching general problem-solving strategies, communication patterns, and principles of logical thought that would be helpful in a variety of domains. Still others tried to alter emotions, self-concepts, attributions, and achievement motivation. One of the most well-known cognitive intervention programs is Head Start, a federally funded program for severely economically deprived preschoolers begun in 1965. The program provides these children with an intensive preschool experience, combined with social services and medical and nutritional interventions, for one or two years before they enter kindergarten.

Almost all intervention and prevention programs were able to produce at least short-term gains in children's academic performance. In kindergarten, the children who had attended Head Start were more advanced than the others on several measures of cognitive and social development and in the first grade, children who had attended Head Start continued to show cognitive gains (Lee, Brooks-Gunn, & Schnur, 1988; Lee, Brooks-Gunn, Schnur, & Liaw, 1990). The long-term effects have been examined as well. A survey of fourteen long-term follow-up studies of children who were involved in preschool intervention projects in the 1960s indicates that there may be positive, but delayed, effects of intervention (Lazar & Darlington, 1982). When these children were in later elementary grades or junior high school, in contrast to children from similar backgrounds who did not participate in intervention projects, they scored higher on arithmetic and reading achievement tests and on IQ tests. In addition, they were less likely to have been retained in a grade or to have been assigned to special education classes. Moreover, these children felt more competent when they were adolescents. Fewer of them dropped out of school and more went to college. Several recent long-term follow-up studies continue to support this pattern of findings (Seitz, Rosenbaum, & Apfel, 1985; Seitz, 1990).

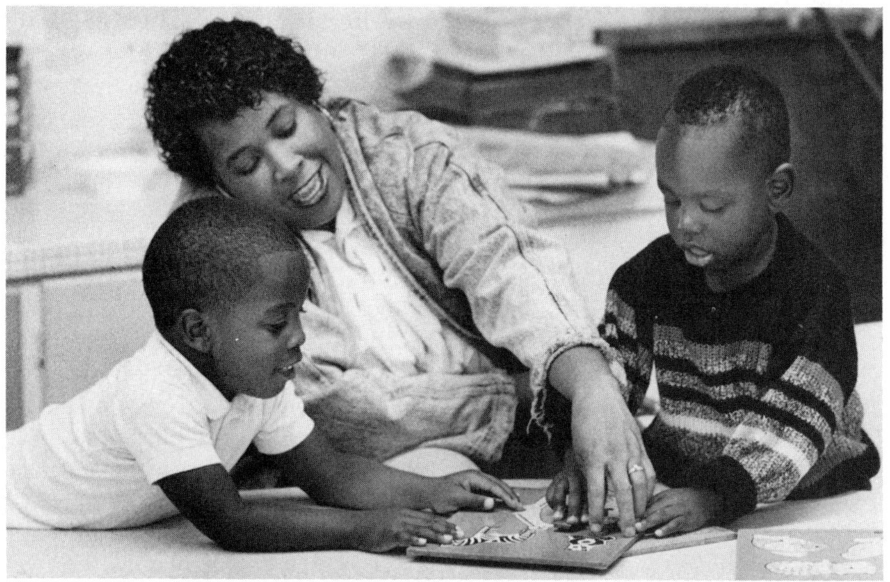

Head Start programs have long-term benefits for young children.

Programs in which the focus is on the parent-child relationship and on improving the natural support systems of the family as well as on placing the child in an educationally stimulating program are the most successful (Slaughter, 1988). Equally successful programs seem to be those in which low-income parents are actively involved in the education of their children. In some cases the mothers are employed as teaching aides in the preschool centers; in other studies mothers are visited in their homes and instructed and supported in their educational activities with the child. Moreover, the family ecology may need to be altered. Families whose children are at the greatest risk for cognitive problems are often unable to benefit from parent-training interventions. Severely stressed and economically disadvantaged families may be expending all of their time and energy just surviving. There are too many adverse reality factors in their lives, such as crowded or inadequate housing, lack of money, or unemployment, to make concerns like improving child-care practices seem important (Horowitz & Paden, 1973; Stipek & McCroskey, 1989). Thus, the most successful programs have also altered the family-life situation through helping families utilize resources available in their community, through encouraging further education or providing job training opportunities, and through efforts to strengthen family relationships and family functioning (Slaughter, 1988). Placing young children in a nursery school setting may be an extremely effective way not only of offering the child additional cognitive and social stimulation but also of relieving some parental stress and allowing the parent to take advantage of opportunities for such things as employment, education, or supportive social relationships.

A highly successful intervention program, the Carolina Early Intervention Program, involves day care and parent education. (Ramey, Lee, & Burchinal, 1989) This is a structured, cognitively and socially stimulating day-care program that emphasizes the development of communication skills as well as intensive parent education. In a study of the effectiveness of this project, one group of high-risk children participated in the project, and a second (control) group received no intervention. In most cases, children in the day-care group began attending the preschool center by 3 months of age, which is substantially earlier than most intervention programs. As can be seen in Figure 11-6, by 12 months of age the groups' cognitive performances had begun to diverge. The IQ scores of children in the combined day-care plus parent-education group were higher than the scores of those in the nontreated high-risk group. This difference in favor of the intervention group was maintained through age 4, to date the most recent follow-up. The children in the intervention condition, although showing some decline, were still well above the control group and well above average (IQ 100). Whereas 39.6 percent of children in the control group were classified as mentally retarded (IQ 84 or below) between ages 2 and 4, only 8.3 percent of the children receiving the intervention had IQs this low. The combined treatment program had prevented the deterioration in intellectual skills that ordinarily occurs by this age in such economically deprived high-risk populations. The investigators compared their results to those of other major preschool intervention programs and concluded, "Programs that have many hours and years of contact with the families and particularly many hours of contact with the children, are likely to have the most positive effect on children's intellectual outcomes" (Ramey, Bryant, Sparling, & Wasik, 1985, p. 84). In 1988, they stated, "Our data suggest that the 15 point IQ difference typically reported between Blacks and Whites in the United States (Jensen, 1969) can be

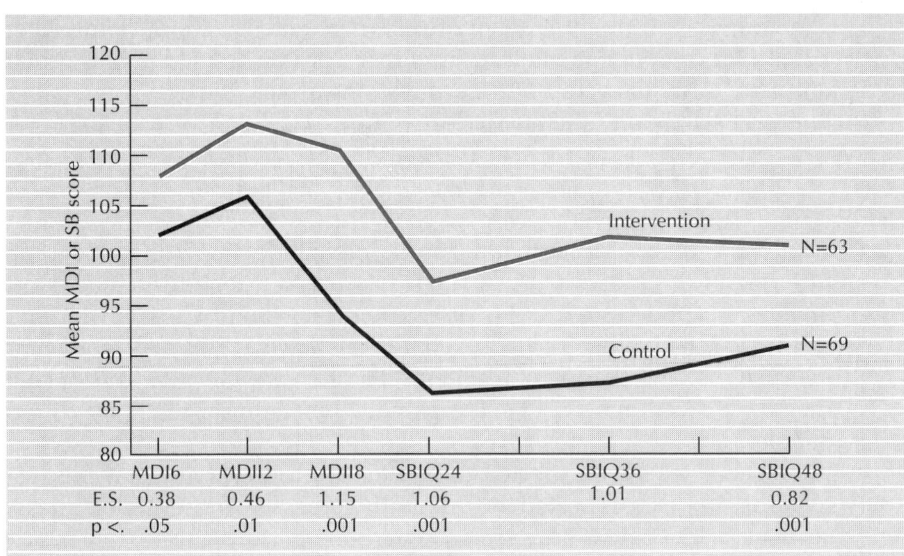

FIGURE 11-6
Carolina Early Intervention Program. Mean MDI (Mental Development Index) and IQ scores for preschool control and intervention from 6 to 48 months.

effectively eliminated during the preschool years and that high-risk, socially disadvantaged children can perform at least at the national average on standardized tests of intelligence if they and their families are provided additional educational and family support services" (Ramey, Bryant, Campbell, Sparling, & Wasik, 1988, p. 17).

We have been discussing intervention programs as if they were appropriate only for the poor. However, in the few studies in which middle-class children were included, these children and their mothers also benefited from the experience of early intervention. One investigator comments, "Middle-class children respond beautifully . . . most of them literally soar in it" (Caldwell, 1973, p. 31). Although middle-class homes may be more likely than lower-class homes to provide children with a milieu that promotes positive academic attitudes and achievement in school, it is the rare family that provides an *ideal* environment for cognitive development. Perhaps many families would benefit from the training and instruction found to be effective with disadvantaged groups.

SUMMARY

DEFINITIONS OF INTELLIGENCE

- Interest in intelligence has centered on the *products* of intellectual differences, rather than on the *processes* discussed in the previous chapter. Intelligence has typically been measured by constructing an *intelligence quotient* or IQ. However, it is important to remember that what is measured on an IQ test is intellectual performance because capacity cannot be directly measured.
- Experts and laypeople agree that intelligence has three aspects: practical problem-solving ability, verbal ability, and social competence. However, controversy concerning the underlying nature of intelligence focuses on three questions. First, is intelligence a single, general construct, or is it a collection of abilities? Second, is intelligence determined primarily by

genetics, or is it more dependent on environment? Third, is intelligence a trait that can only be inferred from tests, or is it defined by performance on tests? The answers to these questions shape the ways we use and interpret scores on intelligence tests.

THE ASSESSMENT OF INTELLIGENCE

- The performance of an individual on an intelligence test is always described in terms of the individual's position relative to the performance of other members of the same group. *Norms* are established by administering the test to groups having particular characteristics, such as age. The stimuli, instructions, and scoring of test items also are carefully *standardized* so that the test procedures will be the same when administered by different people.
- Intelligence tests are expected to be *valid*, or to measure what they claim to measure. This is tested by comparing results to a criterion measure such as achievement test scores or school performance. They also are expected to be *reliable*, meaning that the results are stable or consistent over repeated administrations of the test.

INTELLIGENCE TESTS

- Around the turn of the century Binet and Simon developed a measure to screen children who would not be successful in the Paris schools. Their measure focused on verbal and problem-solving abilities, and was normed by age. Binet developed the concept of *mental age*, based on the numbers of items correctly answered by the average child of the same chronological age, which was later combined with mental age to create an intelligence quotient by Stern. The Binet-Simon scale was revised to include performance items that depend less on academic learning, and an American adaptation, the Stanford-Binet, is still used in this country. However, the Wechsler IQ scales, based on a deviation IQ, or the relation between a person's score to the distribution of scores for the group, is more commonly used now because it includes more performance items that are less likely to be influenced by schooling.

ALTERNATIVE APPROACHES TO INTELLIGENCE

- The information processing approach suggests that traditional intelligence tests need to be supplemented with assessments of the components and metacomponents of problem solving. Sternberg has developed a *triarchic theory* of intelligence which includes information processing skills, experience, and context. This differs from Binet's approach by emphasizing how children process information, by taking the children's characteristics into account, and by considering intelligence in contexts outside of school.
- Another approach to intelligence is to consider more than one type of intelligence. Examples of the multifactor approach include Spearman's suggestion that we all have a general, or "g," factor and a number of specific, or "s," factors, and Gardner's theory of seven types of intelligence that each have its own developmental path and is guided by different forms of perception, learning, and memory. Such theories have broadened our understanding of intelligence to include contexts besides the ones tested in traditional IQ tests.

STABILITY OF IQ

- IQ scores can and do fluctuate because they measure current performance rather than underlying ability. Longitudinal studies indicate that scores on intelligence tests during infancy do not predict to later childhood or adulthood; however recent research suggests that measures of infant attention may be related to IQ scores during early childhood. After about age 8, prediction becomes more accurate, although the rate of mental growth varies among children so that IQ scores are more stable for some than others.

CORRELATES OF INTELLECTUAL PERFORMANCE

- Most estimates of *heritability* of intelligence indicate that about 50 percent of the variability in intelligence among middle-class white Americans is due to genetic factors. In addition, other genetically determined behaviors such as temperament or personality may affect intellectual performance.
- If half of the variability in intelligence is due to inheritance, the other half is due to environment, and a number of environmental factors have been indicated, such as the child's community and home. For example, intellectual deficits have been found in children who live in isolated areas compared to those who do not. It may be that different environments stimulate and facilitate the development of different cognitive abilities and that standard intelligence tests do not measure abilities that are considered adaptive for a particular setting. Specific family characteristics also have been found to relate to IQ across social classes. Higher intellectual performance has been related to supportive, warm home environments and to parents who are responsive to their children's needs and provide a variety of educational experiences.
- Differences in performance on standardized intelligence tests among children from various racial and ethnic groups and social classes have commonly been noted. Generally, the average IQ of minority and economically disadvantaged children is lower than for white, middle-class children. Four main explanations have been advanced to explain these differences: test bias, heredity, environment, and parent-child interactions.
- According to the test-bias explanation, the content of standard IQ tests is drawn from white middle-class language, vocabulary, experience, and values so that it is inappropriate for other groups. In addition, testing conditions may be deleterious to the performance of low SES and minority children. One study showed that minority children are more likely than white children to be inappropriately classified as retarded based on IQ tests.
- The second position is that IQ differences are based on genetic factors. This is derived from the idea that in a mobile society the brighter members of the lower class move up and become middle class, and people tend to marry within their class, so that differences between average IQ scores of the two groups will increase over time. Jenson calculated that up to 70 percent of the variance was due to genetics. Most agree that this calculation is too high and that his estimates were inaccurate because it is not appropriate to use heritability estimates calculated on one group as a basis of comparison between groups.
- The third perspective emphasizes the fact that the physical and cultural deprivation imposed by poverty can explain the differences in intellectual

performance found between groups. Studies indicate that children who experience more risk factors, such as unemployment or poor nutrition, are more likely to perform poorly than those children who had experienced less risk.

- A final perspective is that social-class differences in parent-child interactions may influence the development of verbal and cognitive skills. Studies indicate that early differences in mothers' use of language and infants' attention to their mothers' speech may account for later differences in the use of verbal information. Finally, research indicates that there are ethnic and cross-cultural differences in parents' attitudes and enthusiasm for education that may affect children's performance on academic tasks.
- Children's intellectual performance is affected by more than their external environment and inherited abilities; it is affected by their motivation to achieve, the emotions they associate with learning tasks, the ways they view themselves and their abilities, and their responses to success and failure. Some children, referred to as *helpless,* tend to give up easily or show deterioration when working on hard problems. Others, referred to as *mastery-oriented,* use failure feedback to maintain or improve their performance. Dweck and colleagues suggest that these two groups of children have different learning goals and different theories of intelligence. Recent research indicates that some of these differences are present before children enter formal schooling.
- Changes in the contexts in which children perform are just as important as the other factors discussed. For example, the change in school context that occurs during the transition from elementary school to junior high tends to result in motivational declines for most students. This may be due to a mismatch between children's needs and the contexts in which they need to perform.

COGNITIVE INTERVENTION STUDIES

- In recent years many programs aimed at modifying the development of learning-disabled or economically deprived children have been launched. One of the most well known and successful is Head Start, a federally funded program for severely economically deprived preschool children. Most of these interventions have produced short-term gains in academic performance, and recent long-term follow-up studies indicate that other positive, although delayed, effects exist. Programs that focus on involving parents in their children's education have been particularly successful.

CHAPTER 12

THE FAMILY

THE FAMILY AS AN AGENT OF SOCIALIZATION

THE FAMILY: AN ECOLOGICAL, FAMILY SYSTEMS PERSPECTIVE

FAMILY FUNCTIONING AND THE FAMILY SYSTEM

The Marital System

The Parent-Child System

Dimensions of Parental Behavior

CHILD ABUSE: A BREAKDOWN IN THE FAMILY SYSTEM

Abused Children and Their Parents

The Ecology of Child Abuse

Consequences of Abuse

THE SIBLING SYSTEM

Family Size

Parent-Child Interactions and Birth Order

Sibling Interaction and Birth Order

Characteristics of Firstborn Children

SOCIAL CLASS, ETHNICITY, AND SOCIALIZATION

Powerlessness and Poverty

Social Class and Childrearing

Ethnicity and Childrearing

THE CHANGING AMERICAN FAMILY

Marital Transitions

Maternal Employment and Child Development

CHILDREN, FAMILIES, AND WAR

SUMMARY

Socialization is the process whereby an individual's standards, skills, motives, attitudes, and behaviors are influenced to conform to those regarded as desirable and appropriate for his or her present or future role in society. "From the moment of birth when the child is wrapped in a pink or blue blanket, swaddled and placed on a cradleboard, or nestled in a mobile-festooned bassinet, indulged by a tender mother or left to cry it out by a mother who fears spoiling the child, socialization has begun" (Hetherington & Morris, 1978, p. 3).

Certain groups and organizations within society play key roles in socialization. Parents, siblings, peers, and teachers spend a great deal of their time communicating values and directing and modifying children's behavior. Some organizations, such as the school, the church, and legal institutions, have evolved with the specific mission of transmitting the culture's knowledge and its social and ethical standards and maintaining culturally valued behaviors. In addition, the mass media, particularly television, constitute a relatively new and potent force in modifying the attitudes, wants, and behaviors of the developing child.

In the following chapters there will be a discussion of some of the processes involved as families, peers, and teachers participate in the intricate task of socialization. Although these groups may seem to play very different roles in their relationship to the child, they share common processes in modifying the child's values, beliefs, and behavior. Each group influences the child through direct tuition, that is, by putting forth rules or standards of behavior and trying to maintain them through rewards and punishments. Each group exhibits behavior that the child may acquire through observational learning. Each group makes attributions about the child's behavior that shape the child's view of himself or herself and the social environment. Finally, the home, school, and peer group provide settings in which children have the

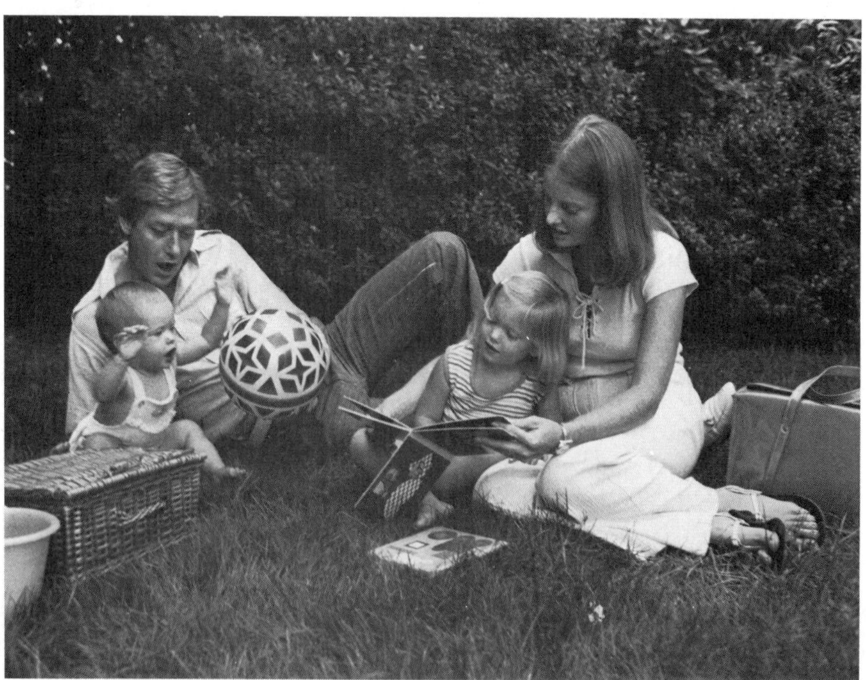

It is said that the typical American family consists of a mother, a father, two children, a dog, and two cars. Here is an almost typical American family.

opportunity to test and compare their beliefs and behavior with those of others and to practice and modify their new-found social skills.

In our presentation, the impact of these groups on the development of morality and self-control, on the inhibition of aggression and encouragement of positive social behavior, on achievement, and on behaviors regarded as appropriate for males or females within our culture will be emphasized particularly.

Although many social factors and groups affect the process of socialization, the family is frequently regarded as the most influential agency in the socialization of the child. This chapter will deal with the processes and problems of socialization within the family. Socialization has frequently been viewed as a process by which parents modify the behavior of children. However, it would be more accurate to think of it as a process of mutual shaping. The family is best conceived of as a complex system involving interdependent functioning among members. This functioning of the family system may be modified by changes in structure or by the behavior of a single family member. We will examine some of the changes in contemporary families, such as the increases in divorce, in single-parent families, and in maternal employment, that may modify the functioning of the family system.

In addition, families do not function in isolation; they are influenced by the larger physical, cultural, social, and historical settings and events in which they are embedded. The extent to which the social environment is supportive or stressful will modify family relations.

Finally, families are not static; they change over time. Although most people recognize that alterations in the age and capacities of the child influence family functioning, few consider that every member of the family is changing and that these changes will be reflected in family relationships. Alterations in the marital relationship, the economic security of the family as parents gain more work experience, are promoted, or move in and out of the marketplace, and the changes in parents' relationships with friends and relatives all have an impact on the family.

Bushman family.

THE FAMILY AS AN AGENT OF SOCIALIZATION

Among the many social influences that contribute to the socialization of the child, the family is clearly of central importance. Why is this the case?

The family is both the earliest and most sustained source of social contact for the child. In the early years the sole relationships available to the child may be those with parents. The interaction and emotional relationship between infant and parents will influence the child's expectancies and responses in subsequent social relations. The beliefs, values, and attitudes of the culture are filtered through the parents and presented to the child in a highly personalized, selective fashion. The personality, attitudes, socioeconomic class, religious affiliation, education, and sex of the parents will influence their presentation of cultural values and standards to their offspring. The social standards, beliefs, and role behavior valued and exhibited by a child of a lower-class, Baptist, authoritarian father would be quite different from those presented by a child of an educated, middle-class, atheistic, feminist mother.

Although rearrangements in family ties are becoming increasingly common, family relationships remain the most intense and enduring bonds. Families have histories of shared experiences and expectations of future relationships over time. It is, in part, the continuity of this history that makes the family qualitatively different from shorter-lived relationships with friends, teachers, neighbors, or coworkers. The memories of past interactions are carried forward in standards, expectations, perceptions, and feelings about other family members.

Family relationships persist and there is an expectation of support and availability in times of stress. In the words of Robert Frost (1959):

Home is the place where,
when you have to go there,
they have to take you in.
I should have called it
Something you somehow haven't to deserve.

Divorced women often return with their children to their family of origin; family members may aid each other in times of unemployment or of financial need; parents may turn to their adult children for assistance in old age or infirmity.

THE FAMILY: AN ECOLOGICAL, FAMILY SYSTEMS PERSPECTIVE

It is only recently that socialization has been thought of as a complex process of family members influencing each other rather than as a process whereby parents shape the behavior of children. Children play an active role in their own socialization (Bell & Harper, 1977). They elicit, interpret, and respond to the behavior of others in a unique fashion on the basis of their abilities, temperament, personality, and past experience. The frequently reported finding of a correlation between physical punishment, rejection, and inconsistent discipline in parents and aggression or delinquency in children does not necessarily mean that these discipline practices led to the deviant behavior in the child. Temperamentally difficult, noncompliant, antisocial behaviors in children also tend to evoke these punitive responses in parents. It is an interaction involving a feedback loop of mutual coercion. Parental punishment leads to antisocial behavior in children and antisocial behavior in children leads to rejecting, punitive responses from parents.

The view of the family as an interdependent system that functions as a whole comes out of the work of therapists who found that it was often impossible to change the behavior of a troubled child without changing the family system (Steinglass, 1987; Reiss & Klein, 1987), and from the work of ecological psychologists concerned about the larger social setting and systems in which families are embedded (Bronfenbrenner, 1986). There are seven basic principles of family processes in this ecological family systems perspective.

1 *Wholism.* The whole of the family system is different than the sum of its parts. In order to understand family functioning it is not enough to know about the characteristics of individual family members or even the relationship between two family members; the organization of family relationships and the whole family as an interacting unit need to be studied.
2 *Organization.* Families are organized into patterns of relationships and functional roles. Often these roles are organized by age or gender where adults have more power and responsibility than children and where, in traditional homes, mothers assume the role of caretaker and father of economic providers. However, with the great contemporary variation in family forms has come greater diversity in family organization and roles.
3 *Interdependency.* Each family member and family subsystem influences and is influenced by each other family member and the relationships among other family members. Parents involved in unhappy, acrimonious marriages become more inept and irritable in relations with their children, which leads to more antisocial behavior in children. This resistant antisocial behavior in the children may, in turn, intensify the problems in the marital relationship. It is both a cause and an effect of marital conflict.
4 *Boundaries.* Families have boundaries which vary in their permeability and vulnerability to outside influences. In families which are too rigidly bounded, family members may have difficulty in disengaging from the family at appropriate times such as in adolescence, going away to college, or moving into a new marriage, and in utilizing resources outside of the family. Parents who are *insular*, that is who have few positive community contacts and social supports, are more likely than less insular parents to be punitive and inconsistent in dealing with their children and to perceive their children negatively (Dumas & Wahler, 1985; Wahler & Dumas, 1987). However, families with too permeable boundaries can be disorganized and vulnerable to disruptions by external forces such as intrusive in-laws, friends who undermine a marriage, or peer groups who deviate from family standards for acceptable behavior.
5 *Homeostasis.* Families attain a certain balance or equilibrium in their pattern of functioning and are resistant to forces that might change this balance. Many interaction patterns become highly rigid and ritualized. Family routines and rituals may serve to establish a sense of family history and identity and to make family relations easier to anticipate and negotiate; however, they also may sustain maladaptive family relations. In unhappily married couples (Gottman, 1989) or in families with an exceptionally aggressive child (Patterson, 1982) a characteristic and predictable pattern is one of hostile, coercive exchanges of escalating intensity. There is no attempt to communicate rationally and solve problems, to defuse anger,

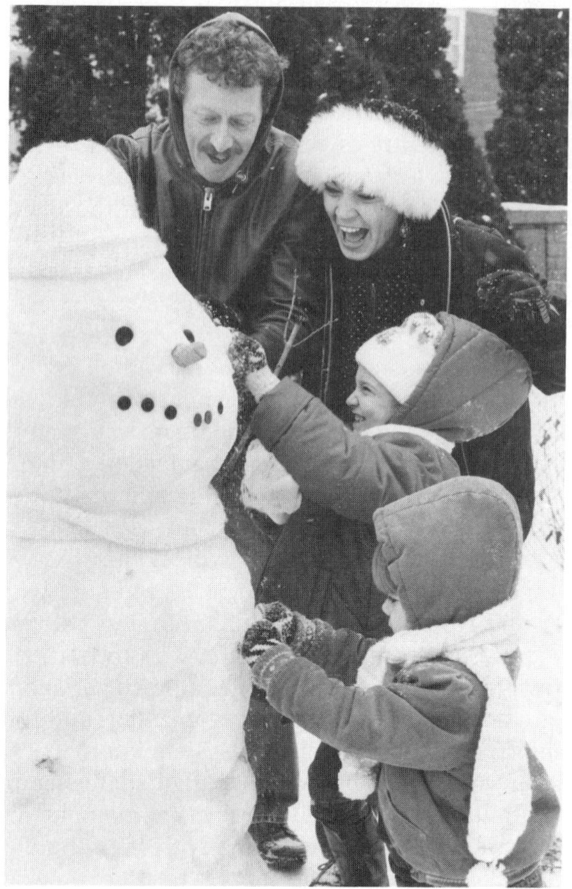

Families must be considered as systems where the behavior and relationships among all family members are interdependent.

and to protect feelings of the other person as there is in nondistressed families. No one knows better than family therapists that even when family members acknowledge discomfort in their relationship they can be highly resistant to change and even after successful therapy families may gradually lapse back into old dysfunctional patterns of interaction. Families can become locked into a pattern of interactions that promotes or sustains psychopathology in one or more family members. Patterns that induce deviance in one family member or in a subsystem in the family such as the marital, parent-child, or sibling subsystem may protect another. Parents may avoid confronting problems in a troubled marriage or in recognizing deficiencies in one child by blaming all family difficulties on the behavior of another child who serves as a family scapegoat.

6 *Morphogenesis.* Morphogenesis is a counterforce to homeostasis. Morphogenesis refers to the growth and adaptation of families to changes both within and outside of the family. Family members and the situations in which they function change. Children go to school, become teenagers, leave home, get jobs, marry, and go on to establish new families of their own. Parents raise children, may have midlife crises, change jobs, retire, and may grow old and dependent on their children. Family members must adapt not only to changes in family members and different developmental tasks confronted throughout the family life cycle but also to historical change, to sometimes unexpected events, and to changes in social values and institutions—to wars; depressions; changing attitudes toward women, minorities, and education; escalating rates of crime, substance abuse, maternal employment, divorce, remarriage, cohabitation, and children born to unmarried mothers. Adaptability is the central criterion of a well-functioning family. A well-functioning family does not necessarily have fewer problems than a distressed family, but it is better able to adapt to the problems, challenges, and changes it encounters.

7 *Ecological relativism.* Families exist within larger social, cultural, and physical milieus. An ecology of poverty, starvation, social disorder, and disease will influence the functioning of families in a different way than one characterized by affluence and social privilege. The same family will function differently in different situations and under varied circumstances.

FAMILY FUNCTIONING AND THE FAMILY SYSTEM

We turn now to an examination of how different subsystems within the family—the marital system, the parent-child system, and the sibling system interact to produce different developmental outcomes in children, and how the behavior of children impacts on the functioning of these systems.

The Marital System

A satisfying marital relationship is often regarded as the cornerstone of good family functioning which directly or indirectly facilitates effective parenting, positive sibling relationships, and the development of competent, adaptive children.

THE IMPACT OF THE MARITAL RELATIONSHIP ON PARENTS AND CHILDREN

It is important to remember that parents have a relationship with each other as well as with their children. Parents serve as sources of mutual emotional and physical support and comfort and such support is especially important in their role as caretakers. Increased parent-child involvement and sensitive, competent, affectionate parent-child relationships have been found when spouses are mutually supportive (Cowan, Cowan, Heming, & Miller, 1991; Cox et al., 1989; Crnic, Greenberg, Ragozin, Robinson, & Basham, 1983; Feldman, Nash, & Aschenbrenner, 1983). Dual participation in household chores and caretaking can free both parents for more playful and pleasurable interactions with their children and relieve some of the burdens often experienced by parents, especially mothers with young children. Dirty diapers, 2 A.M. feedings, and the crying of a sick child are more tolerable, and developmental milestones such as the child's first words or staggering steps, and academic, social, or athletic successes are more fun if they are shared with an involved spouse.

A home environment that is characterized by quarreling, nagging, and disagreement has deleterious effects on both parents and children (Dix, 1991). High conflict between parents is associated with negative feelings and behavior directed toward their children and in turn with disruptions in social and cognitive competence and increased antisocial behavior in children (Emery, 1982; Hetherington, Cox, & Cox, 1982; Cowan et al., 1991; Hetherington & Clingempeel, 1992).

Boys are much more susceptible to the negative effects of family disharmony than are girls (Block, Block, & Morrison, 1981; Hetherington et al., 1982; Rutter, 1977). Why should this be so? Boys are more likely to be directly exposed to parental bickering and physical abuse than are girls (Hetherington et al., 1982). Parents quarrel more often and their quarrels are longer in the presence of their sons. If parental disagreements arise in the presence of girls they are more likely to be rapidly terminated with a quizzical expression, raised eyebrows, or a nod of the head indicating the presence of the daughter, or a terse "we'll talk about this later." Parents are more protective of daughters and this protectiveness extends to protection from parental conflict.

THE IMPACT OF THE BIRTH OF A CHILD ON THE MARITAL RELATIONSHIP

As is true in considering the role and functioning of any family subsystem, we must view these marital relations in terms of the total family system. At the same time as the relationship between the parents is affecting how they respond to their children, the presence and behavior of the child is influencing the marital relationship. Pregnancy and the birth of a first child, in particular, are associated with a shift toward a more traditional-type division of family roles (Cowan et al., 1991; Entwisle & Doering, 1981). This shift toward more stereotyped masculine and feminine roles occurs whether or not the initial role division in the family before having children was traditional or egalitarian. In spite of the rhetoric concerning equality of roles for men and women, even in relatively untraditional homes, there seems to be an implicit assumption that the role of the mother with young children is in the home and that of the father is to provide. Although in rare cases a father takes time from his work to be with his wife and newborn, that time rarely exceeds two weeks, and then even in families where both parents have worked, it is the wife who is most likely to give up her occupation. It is thus not surprising to find that the most marked immediate decline in marital satisfaction following the birth of the first child is found in mothers (Belsky, Long, & Rovine, 1985; Cowan et al., 1991). Declines in marital satisfaction also occur in fathers but emerge more slowly as men become increasingly aware of the restrictions imposed on their lives by a baby and no longer being the focus of their wives' attention, and sometimes because the mother and child form a close relationship from which the father is excluded. Mothers not only get more of the responsibilities but often also more of the pleasures in raising a child (Wilkie & Ames, 1986).

Children have an impact on the relationship between their parents in other ways. Temperamentally difficult, deviant, or handicapped children impose additional stresses on parents that may be reflected in marital conflict. The presence of a demanding, recalcitrant child may be enough to fragment a fragile marriage (Wilkie & Ames, 1986; Wright, Henggler, & Craig, 1986). However, couples who were satisfied with their relationship before the birth of a child show fewer disruptions in the marital relationship than those who were previously distressed. Thus, the birth of a child usually neither salvages a bad marriage, nor destroys a good marriage.

Since the transition to parenthood is a time of heightened risk to the marital relationship and subsequent parent-child relationships, preventative interventions are being designed that are aimed at strengthening couple relationships and reducing the adverse consequences of the transition to parenthood. One of the most successful of these interventions is presented in Box 12-1.

BOX 12-1 *PSYCHOLOGY IN ACTION* HELPING PARENTS COPE WITH BECOMING A FAMILY

The Becoming a Family Project involved seventy-two couples expecting their first baby and twenty-four comparable couples who had not yet decided whether to become parents. One-third of the expectant couples participated in a six-month-long couples group intervention that lasted until three months after the birth of the child. The others did not. The sessions were directed by a clinically trained married couple and the participants were encouraged to raise issues and concerns that were on their minds. They talked about their dreams of creating an ideal family, about the families they grew up in, and the impending birth. Everyone had trouble imagining what would follow after birth. When the pregnant couples began to have babies their infants were brought to the group. Then, couples began to try to find their way in the common problems, conflicts, and changes encountered in becoming a family. Who could give up what? Who would take responsibility for what? How to keep the marital relationship fulfilling while dealing with the incessant demands of the child? Assessments of family functioning, the marital relationship, parenting, and parents' and children's adjustment were performed in late pregnancy, 6 months, 18 months, $3\frac{1}{2}$ years, and $5\frac{1}{2}$ years after birth. The effects of the intervention early on at the 18-month follow-up were encouraging. Fathers in the intervention group in comparison with those in the nonintervention group were more involved and satisfied in parenting and reported less negative change in sexual relations, in marital satisfaction, and in social supports. Mothers also benefited from the intervention. Mothers in the intervention group, in comparison to those in the nonintervention group, viewed aspects of themselves outside of the family as workers and students as more important; they were more satisfied with the couple's division of labor, their sexual relations, and their marriage, and seemed better able to balance life stresses and social supports. In addition, significantly more of the nonintervention groups were separated or divorced at the time of the 18-month and $3\frac{1}{2}$-year follow-up. On other measures, however, by the time the children were in kindergarten, at age $5\frac{1}{2}$, positive effects of the early intervention had waned. Marital satisfaction was beginning to decline and few differences between the intervention and nonintervention groups were found in parenting style or children's adaptation. Clearly, early interventions do not last forever. They do not immunize families from later adversity. Subsequent findings from this research project indicated that a "booster shot" intervention when the child was 2 could address some of the issues that led to later declines in marital satisfaction, to disruptions in family functioning, and to children's behavior problems. It seems however that as new changes and challenges arise over the family life cycle, continued intermittent intervention focusing on new issues may be necessary to sustain good family functioning. Some therapists have even suggested that just as we go for regular medical checkups we should go for regular checkups of family well-being in order to identify family problems and prevent them from escalating.

Source: Cowan, C. P., Cowan, P. A., Heming, G., & Miller, N. B. (1991). Becoming a family: Marriage, parenting and child development. In P. A. Cowan & E. M. Hetherington (Eds.), *Family transitions* (pp. 79–110). Hillsdale, NJ: Erlbaum.

The Parent-Child System

Most parents have some beliefs about the kinds of characteristics they would like to see in their children and the childrearing methods that should be used to attain them. However, it should be remembered that there are many paths to the development of positive social behaviors, just as there are many paths to the development of antisocial behaviors. There is no magically effective childrearing formula. Parental practices must be adapted to the temperament and needs of the individual child and the demands of the culture. Often, very similar family situations are associated with divergent development in different children, and some children seem to be relatively resilient in the face of adverse environments (Hetherington, 1989, 1991b; Masten & Garmezy, 1985; Werner, 1991; Cowan & Work, 1988).

PROCESSES OF SOCIALIZATION IN THE PARENT-CHILD RELATIONSHIP

Early attachment of the parent to the child and the child to the parent in infancy serves as the foundation for later family relationships. Although

Modeling is an important process in the learning of social roles and the acquisition of skills.

socialization is certainly occurring in the first year of life, it seems to become more conscious and systematic with the occurrence of greater mobility and the beginning of language in the second year. Behaviors that previously were accepted, indulged, or regarded as "cute" start to be limited. Feet are no longer permitted on the high-chair tray, smearing food is frowned on, exploration is restrained by playpen bars, and serious attempts at toilet training begin. As children are practicing their new-found motor skills and exploring the world about them, climbing out of their crib, tottering to the head of the stairs, discovering the delights of the pot-and-pan cupboard, or eating cigarette butts, the air may be ringing with "No!" "Don't!" and "Stop!". The child will also be cuddled, petted, and praised for achievements, for learning to use a spoon, for naming objects, for repeating words, for dry diapers, for the many behaviors that parents and society regard as desirable. The process of socialization has begun in earnest.

Parents teach children social rules and roles by telling them what the rules are and by praising them or disciplining them when they conform to or violate acceptable standards of behavior. Reinforcement both provides information about behaviors viewed as desirable or undesirable and motivates the child to behave in some ways and not in others. Parents also influence the child's self-concept through attributions they make about the child's behavior. In addition, parents modify their children's behavior by serving as models whom the child can identify with or imitate.

An important distinction should be noted between observational learning versus tuition, reward, and punishment as processes of socialization. Parents in verbalizing standards and trying to enforce them through rewards and punishment usually are knowingly trying to shape the child's behavior. In contrast, imitation and identification often occur without the parent's having intended to influence the child. Many parents verbalize one set of values and exhibit quite another.

> A "do as I say, not as I do" approach to socialization is ineffective. If the child sees a church-going, platitude-spouting, moralizing parent lie about his golf score, cheat on his income tax, bully his children, and pay substandard wages to his help, the child may emulate his parent's behavior rather than his hypocritical words (Hetherington & Morris, 1978, p. 2).

Finally, parents manage aspects of their children's environment and social life that will influence their development. They choose the neighborhoods and home in which the child lives, decorate the child's room in a masculine or feminine style, provide the child with toys and books, expose the child to television viewing, and promote the social life and activities of the child by arranging social occasions—inviting other children over to play or enrolling the child in sports and in skill enhancement or social programs (Parke, MacDonald, Beitel, & Bhavnagri, 1988).

Dimensions of Parental Behavior

Parents' relationships with their children have frequently been conceptualized in terms of the interaction between two dimensions of parental behavior. The first deals with the emotional relationship with the child and ranges from warm, responsive, child-centered behavior to rejecting, unresponsive behavior focused on the needs and wishes of the parents. The second dimension deals with parental control and varies from restrictive, demanding behavior to a permissive, undemanding parental style in which few restraints are placed on the child's behavior.

PARENTAL WARMTH AND RESPONSIVENESS OR HOSTILITY

Parental warmth is regarded as important in the socialization process for several reasons. First, the child is likely to wish to maintain the approval, and be distressed at any prospect of the loss of love of a warm parent, and, therefore, the need for harsh forms of discipline to gain compliance is often unnecessary (Baumrind, 1991; Maccoby & Martin, 1983). In contrast, the threat of withdrawal of love is unlikely to be an effective mechanism of socialization when used by hostile parents who have little demonstrable affection to rescind. What has the child to lose? Even on those occasions when physical punishment is utilized by warm parents, they find it more effective in limiting their child's behavior than do hostile parents. Again, this is probably both because the child wishes to conform to the standards of warm parents and because these parents are more likely to provide information about alternative socially desirable responses available to the child.

Second, the frequent use by warm parents of reasoning and explanation permits the child to internalize social rules and to identify and discriminate situations in which a given behavior is appropriate. It is easier to learn the rules of the game if someone tells you what they are and why you should play that way.

Third, warmth and nurturance by parents are likely to be associated with responsiveness to the child's needs. Loving, responsive parents make children

The use of reasoning and explanation in discipline has positive effects on the social development of children.

feel good about themselves and this leads to security, low anxiety, and high self-esteem in the children. Such attitudes and emotions are more likely to be conducive to learning and lead to acceptance and internalization of parental standards than the high anxiety and tension associated with hostility or physical punishment by rejecting parents (Crockenberg & Litman, 1990; Lipscomb, McAllister, & Bregman, 1985). The high stress associated with a hostile, unresponsive family situation may interfere with the child's learning the rules of the "socialization game" that the parent is attempting to teach.

PARENTAL CONTROL

Parental love alone is not enough to lead to positive social development in children. Some degree of parental control is necessary if children are to develop into socially and intellectually competent individuals. However, it should be kept in mind that the goal of socialization is socially responsible self-regulation by the child, not control externally based on the behavior of the parent. Although we have emphasized that socialization involves a process of mutual influence between parents and children, the parent usually has more control than the child in their interactions. If parents are not in charge, the family is likely to be dysfunctional (Baumrind, in press). Parents' beliefs about their children's behavior will influence their discipline practices. Parents who think that the child's behavior is largely shaped by experience in contrast to those who think problems in the child are due to the child's disposition, are more likely to try to change the child's negative behavior (Bugental, Blue, & Cruzcosa, 1989; Lin & Fu, 1990). However, it is not surprising that most parents accept greater responsibility for desired than undesired behaviors in their children (Himelstein, Graham, & Weiner, 1991).

When parents use suggestions and reasoning, and, when they present possible alternative courses of action the child is more likely to comply with

FAMILIES AROUND THE WORLD

In all cultures parents teach children appropriate social roles, skills, and traditions.

Nomadic Somalian father and son caring for camels.

Egyptian father and son praying in a mosque.

Japanese mother teaching her daughter the traditional tea ceremony.

Inupiat mother from Kotzebue, Alaska, teaching her daughter to mend fishnets.

Native Americans from Taos Pueblo, New Mexico, during a ceremonial dance.

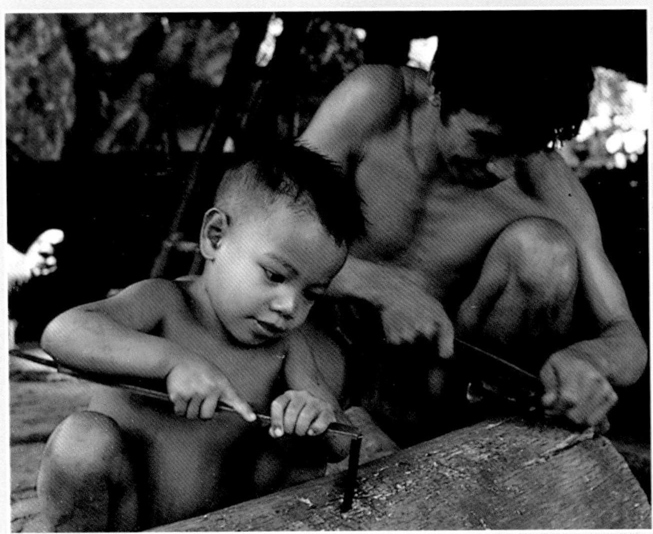

A blacksmith father from the Ifugao tribe in the Philippines teaching his son to use a file.

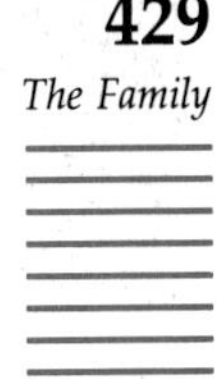

the parents' wishes. If parents are consistent in their discipline, use the minimum amount of pressure necessary to change the child's behavior, and encourage the child to view this compliance as self-initiated, children are more likely to cooperate and to adopt or internalize the standards of the parents (Crockenberg & Litman, 1990; Lepper, 1982; Perry & Perry, 1983).

Attributions made by the parent about the child are important in the development of the child's self-esteem, self-concept, and sense of personal control. To a large extent, these characteristics develop from attributions made by people who play a significant role in the child's life. Consider the difference in the implications for the child of the following maternal statements:

> "Share with your brother or I'll shut you in your room." (You are helpless.)
>
> "You're a selfish little brat." (You are worthless.)
>
> "You're the kind of person who enjoys sharing." (You do positive things because you are a good person who enjoys helping others.)

If parents use methods of discipline such as physical punishment, threats, or humiliation that are heavily reliant on the superior power of the parent or are demeaning to the child, children may come to view themselves as helpless or unworthy. Furthermore, although power-assertive techniques may be effective in gaining immediate control of the child's behavior, in the long run they are likely to be deleterious. When power-assertive methods such as physical punishment are used to control aggression, the hostile parent is also in the anomalous situation both of frustrating the child, which may lead to arousal of anger, and of offering an aggressive model to the child. In addition, the child may attempt to avoid contact with the punishing parent, which gives the parent less opportunity to socialize the child. As might be expected under such circumstances, the child often exhibits little overt aggression in the home toward the threatening parents, but displaces it to others outside the home where the child is less fearful of retaliation.

Children's age plays an important role in their responses to discipline. As children grow older they resist being externlly controlled ard manipulated, and self-reinforcement for appropriate social behavior becomes increasingly important. Older preschool children try to negotiate with their parents ("I'll do it after I finish my painting. Alright?" "How about if you and I do it together?") Both a parental shift to using increased reasoning and the child's active bargaining are based on the child's increasing social and cognitive competence and autonomy (Kuczynski et al., 1987). This gradual shift of control from the parents and other adults to self-control in the child becomes critical as the child moves out of the home and the parent is increasingly less able to directly monitor and control the child's activities in the elementary school years and most notably in adolescence (Steinberg, 1990). It is fortunate that over the school years children become more able to delay immediate gratification for long-term rewards and become oriented toward the welfare of others rather than toward self-gratification. Moreover, the advanced information processing abilities of older children improve their ability to interpret events, to consider the motives of themselves and others, and to weigh alternative outcomes. This suggests that the relationship between a particular behavior and an immediate contingent reward or punishment will be more important in altering the behavior of younger children than of older children or adults (Maccoby & Martin, 1983). At any age, however, the effectiveness of parents as agents of socialization depends on their emotional relationship with the child, the type of controls they attempt to exert, and the appropriateness of the controls to the age and personality of the child and the demand of the situations.

PARENT TYPOLOGIES

Family systems theorists would argue that it is not the sum of individual dimensions of parenting but the configuration or combinations of dimensions that are important. Table 12-1 presents a classification of four types of parenting based on combinations of the warm/responsive, unresponsive/rejecting dimension and the restrictive/demanding, permissive/undemanding dimension. This yields a classification of four types of parenting: authoritative, authoritarian, indulgent, and neglecting. A critical question is whether these variations in parenting style relate in any systematic way to differences in social, emotional, and cognitive development in children.

A classic study by Baumrind (1967) was one of the earliest systematic studies attempting to relate parenting typologies to children's behavior. On the basis of fourteen weeks of behavioral observation in the nursery school, Baumrind identified three groups of children who had widely varying patterns of behavior. She called these three groups *energetic-friendly children, conflicted-irritable children*, and *impulsive-aggressive children*. She then interviewed the parents of these children and observed the parents interacting with their children in the home and the laboratory. As can be seen in Table 12-2, distinctive patterns of parental behavior were related to the patterns of child behavior. She found that *authoritative* but not *authoritarian* or overly *permissive* behavior by parents led to positive emotional, social, and cognitive development in children. *Authoritative parents* were not intrusive and did permit their children considerable freedom within reasonable limits, but were firm and willing to impose restrictions in areas in which they had greater knowledge or insight. They did not yield to their children's attempts to coerce them into acquiescing to their demands. Such discipline gives children the opportunity to explore their environment and gain interpersonal competence without the anxiety and neurotic inhibition associated with hostile, restrictive, power-assertive discipline practices, or the inexperience in conforming to the demands and needs of others associated with extreme permissiveness. In general, high warmth and moderate restrictiveness, with the parents expecting

TABLE 12-1 A TWO-DIMENSIONAL CLASSIFICATION OF PARENTING PATTERNS

	ACCEPTING, RESPONSIVE, CHILD-CENTERED	REJECTING, UNRESPONSIVE, PARENT-CENTERED
DEMANDING CONTROLLING RESTRICTIVE	Authoritative-reciprocal High in bidirectional communication	Authoritarian Power-assertive
UNDEMANDING LOW IN CONTROL ATTEMPTS PERMISSIVE	Indulgent	Neglecting, ignoring, indifferent, uninvolved

Source: Adapted from Maccoby and Martin (1983).

PARENTING STYLES AND CHILDREN'S BEHAVIOR TABLE 12-2

PARENTAL TYPE	CHILDREN'S BEHAVIOR
Permissive-indulgent parent	Impulsive-aggressive children
Rules not enforced	Resistive, noncompliant to adults
Rules not clearly communicated	Low in self-reliance
Yields to coercion, whining,nagging, crying by the child	Low in achievement orientation
Inconsistent discipline	Lacking in self-control
Few demands or expectations for mature, independent behavior	Aggressive
Ignores or accepts bad behavior	Quick to anger but fast to recover cheerful mood
Hides impatience, anger, and annoyance	Impulsive
Moderate warmth	Aimless, low in goal-directed activities
Glorification of importance of free expression of impulses and desires	Domineering
Authoritarian parent	Conflicted-irritable children
Rigid enforcement of rules	Fearful, apprehensive
Confronts and punishes bad behavior	Moody, unhappy
Shows anger and displeasure	Easily annoyed
Rules not clearly explained	Passively hostile and guileful
View of child as dominated by uncontrolled antisocial impulses	Vulnerable to stress
Child's desires and opinions not considered or solicited	Alternates between aggressive unfriendly behavior and sulky withdrawal
Persistent in enforcement of rules in the face of opposition and coercion	Aimless
Harsh, punitive discipline	
Low in warmth and positive involvement	
No cultural events or mutual activities planned	
No educational demands or standards	
Authoritative Parent	Energetic-friendly children
Firm enforcement of rules	Self-reliant
Does not yield to child coercion	Self-controlled
Confronts disobedient child	High energy level
Shows displeasure and annoyance in response to child's bad behavior	Cheerful
Shows pleasure and support of child's constructive behavior	Friendly relations with peers
Rules clearly communicated	Copes well with stress
Considers child's wishes and solicits child's opinions	Interest and curiosity in novel situations
Alternatives offered	Cooperative with adults
Warm, involved, responsive	Tractable
Expects mature, independent behavior appropriate for the child's age	Purposive
Cultural events and joint activities planned	Achievement-oriented
Educational standards set and enforced	

Source: Baumrind (1967).

appropriately mature behavior from their children and setting reasonable limits but being responsive and attentive to their children's needs, are associated with the development of self-esteem, adaptability, competence, internalized control, popularity with peers, and low levels of antisocial behavior.

In contrast, the *authoritarian parents* of the conflicted-irritable children were rigid, power-assertive, harsh, and unresponsive to the children's needs. In such families, children have little control over their environment and receive few gratifications. They may feel trapped and angry but fearful of asserting themselves in a hostile environment. This results in the unhappy, conflicted, neurotic behavior often found in these children.

Finally, in spite of the *permissive parents'* reasonably affectionate relationship with their children, their excessively lax and inconsistent discipline and encouragement of the free expression of their children's impulses were associated with the development of uncontrolled, impulsive behavior in their children. Both authoritarian and permissive parents viewed their children as being dominated by primitive self-centered impulses over which they have little control. However, the permissive parents thought that free expression of these impulses was healthy and desirable, whereas the authoritarian parents perceived them as something to be suppressed or stamped out (see Figure 12-1).

Baumrind has followed her authoritarian, authoritative, and permissive parents and their children from the preschool period through adolescence in a longitudinal study (Baumrind, 1991). She found that authoritative parenting continued to be associated with positive outcomes for adolescents as with younger children and that responsive, firm parent-child relationships were especially important in the development of competence in sons. Moreover, authoritarian childrearing had more negative long-term outcomes for boys than for girls. Sons of authoritarian parents were low in both cognitive and social competence. Their academic and intellectual performance was poor. In

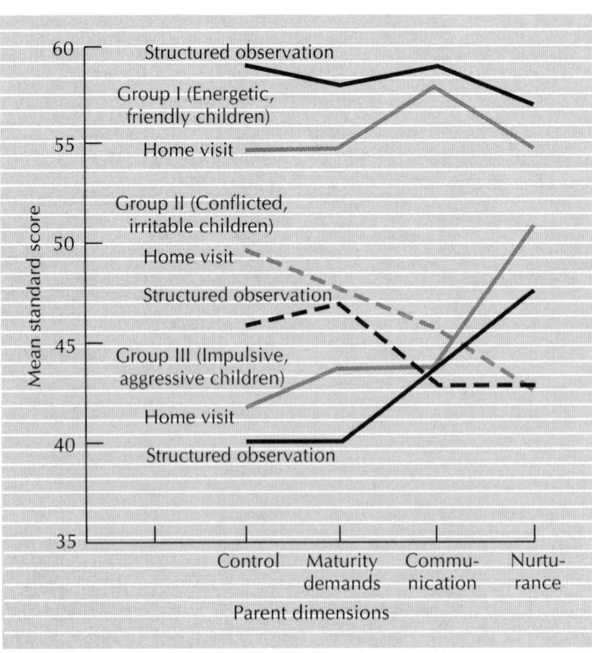

FIGURE 12-1
Profile of composited parent dimension scores from the summary ratings for the structured observation and the home visit sequence analysis for each pattern. (From Baumrind, 1967, p. 73.)

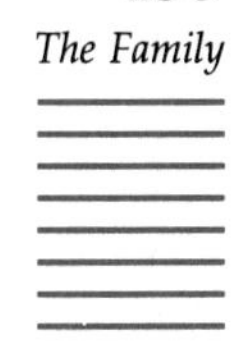

addition, they were unfriendly and lacking in initiative, leadership, and self-confidence in their relations with their peers.

It can be seen that only three of the parenting types presented in Table 12-1 were identified by Baumrind in her preschool children. We are missing the fourth parenting style, in the lower right-hand quadrant, which is characterized by neglect and lack of involvement. These are disengaged parents who are "motivated to do whatever is necessary to minimize the costs in time and effort of interaction with the child" (Maccoby & Martin, 1983). Such parents are motivated to keep the child at a distance and focus on their own needs rather than the needs of the child. They are parent-centered rather than child-centered. With older children this is associated with the parents' failure to monitor the child's activity, to know where the child is, what the child is doing, and who the child's companions are. This pattern of parenting has been related to several different types of personality characteristics in parents and to social change and stressful life events. Parental detachment is often found in depressed mothers (Egeland & Sroufe, 1981a, 1981b). Depressed mothers have difficulty in mobilizing themselves to be responsive to their children's needs and are more likely to be influenced by their own emotional state than to respond contingently to their children's behavior (Kochanska, 1991). Moreover, in times of stress such as during marital discord or divorce, because of their own anxiety and emotional neediness, some parents may relentlessly pursue self-gratification at the expense and neglect of their children's welfare (Hetherington et al., 1982; Patterson & Capaldi, 1991).

In infants such a lack of parental involvement is associated with disruptions in attachment (Egeland & Sroufe, 1981a, 1981b); in older children it is associated with impulsivity, aggression, noncompliance, moodiness, and low self-esteem (Baumrind, 1991; Block, 1971; Loeb, Horst, & Horton, 1980; Martin, 1981). Adolescents and young adults from neglecting homes are more likely to have drinking problems, be truant, spend time on the streets with friends who are disliked by the parents, be precociously sexually active, and have a record of arrests (Baumrind, 1991; Pulkkinen, 1982). Lack of parental monitoring is strongly associated with the risk of delinquent behavior (Baumrind, 1991; Patterson, DeBarsyshe, & Ramsey, 1989; Patterson & Capaldi, 1991; Patterson, Reid, & Dishion, 1992). It is not just that children with disengaged parents are socially incompetent, irresponsible, immature, and alienated from their families. They also show disruptions in peer relations and in cognitive development, achievement, and school performance (Baumrind, 1991; Hetherington & Clingempeel, 1992; Patterson et al., 1989; Patterson et al., 1992; Pulkkinen, 1982). It is this "double whammy" of not having the skills to be able to gain gratification in either social or academic pursuits that frequently leads to delinquency in children with neglecting parents (Patterson, DeBarsyshe, & Ramsey, 1989; Patterson et al., 1992). Parental involvement plays an important role in the development of both social and cognitive competence in children.

CHILD ABUSE: A BREAKDOWN IN THE FAMILY SYSTEM

In some cases family functioning breaks down and severe abuse of children may occur. Although it is difficult to obtain precise figures on how many children in the United States are abused, it is estimated that over 2.5 million children are maltreated each year. Many of these children have been sexually molested, starved, burned, beaten, cut, chained to furniture, or kept in isolation.

What circumstances contribute to this disastrous treatment of children? Some of the contributing risk factors lie in the characteristics of parents and their abused children, some are attributable to ecological factors such as the quality of the neighborhood and available support systems, while still others are related to the life experiences and stresses encountered by family members. Abuse is unlikely to occur when only one risk factor is present. It is the occurrence and interaction among multiple risk factors, especially in the face of few protective factors such as a supportive marital relationship, social network, and community resources, high intelligence and education, good health and adaptability, that is likely to lead to abuse (Cicchetti & Olsen, 1990).

Abused Children and Their Parents

Most students reading this book probably think that no one they know would ever abuse a child or that only someone who is really mentally ill would inflict grievous physical harm on defenseless children. However, although chronic maltreatment is most likely to occur in economically deprived, poorly educated families, child abusers are found in all social classes and all religious, racial, and ethnic groups. In addition, there is little evidence of severe mental illness or specific personality traits that consistently distinguish abusive from nonabusive parents. Rather, abusive parents are enmeshed in a multiproblem family with deficits that include a wide range of dysfunction in family members and in their relationships with each other. Differences between maltreating and nonmaltreating parents are most likely to be found in their self-involvement, their inability to take the role of others and to understand the needs, capabilities, and responses of the child in relation to the specific situation or demands made by the parent (Pianta, Egeland, & Erickson, 1989). Furthermore, abusive parents are less concerned about social conformity than are nonabusive parents (Egeland, Jacobitz, & Sroufe, 1988; Egeland, Breitenbucher, & Rosenberg, 1980).

Two of the factors most commonly associated with abusive parents are a distressed often sexually unsatisfying marriage and a history of a disturbed or abusive relationship with their own parents. There is accumulating evidence that both competent, loving parenting and incompetent abusive parenting may to some extent be transmitted across generations (Grusec, Covell, & Paucha, 1991). This does not mean that young parents are locked into their own parents' style of parenting. Only about one-third of parents who were abused when they were young abuse their own children (Kaufman & Zigler, 1987). Mothers who break this intergenerational cycle are more likely to have had a warm, caring adult in their background, to have established a close marital relationship, and at sometime to have received therapy. (Egeland et al., 1988).

Certain characteristics of the child and family also are associated with maltreatment of children. Child abuse is more likely to occur in large families and to children under the age of 3. A higher-than-normal incidence of birth anomalies, physical and intellectual deviations, irritability, negativism, and other behaviors that exasperate the parents are found in many of these children. These factors may all contribute to the parents' feeling antagonistic to the child and feeling that the child is different. Abusive parents frequently feel that the child is abusing them. It should not be thought that these characteristics are found in all abused children; it is just that they are found more often in abused than nonabused children. These factors alone do not lead to abuse; however, such problems in children may be enough to tip the balance in already stressed or dysfunctional families.

Parents in these families often have conflicts with each other and are socially isolated (Trickett & Susman, 1988). They seem to have fewer friends, relatives, or neighbors they can turn to in times of stress. The isolation may contribute, in part, to the fact that these parents frequently do not seem to recognize the seriousness of their behavior and blame the child rather than themselves for what is occurring. They may even justify their behavior by saying they are doing it for the child's good or that harsh discipline is necessary if children are to be taught what is right. It is not surprising that mothers are often the persons who abuse the child. They are locked into a stressful family situation and spend more time with the child than do other family members (Martin, 1976; Cicchetti & Lynch, in press).

In addition, abusive parents seem to have unrealistic beliefs about parent-child relationships and respond less appropriately to their children's behavior than do nonabusive parents. They often expect their children to perform in an impossibly developmentally advanced way or to exhibit levels of independence and self-control that would be unlikely in children of that age (Trickett, Aber, Carlson, & Cicchetti, 1991). Abusive parents frequently think that their child should act as a caregiver for the parent, and role reversals where the child appears to be the more nurturant member of the dyad often occur in these families (Dean, Malik, Richards, & Stringer, 1986).

Physical violence does not suddenly emerge in usually well-controlled parents. Child abuse is preceded by an escalating cycle of other forms of verbal and physical aggression. Abusive mothers show fewer positive behaviors (Burgess & Conger, 1978) and more severe negative behaviors, such as threatening commands, criticism, and physical punishment toward their children, than do nonabusive mothers (Reid, Taplin, & Loeber, 1981; Trickett & Kuczynski, 1986). In addition, in comparison to nonabusive parents, the behavior of abusive parents is unpredictable and is less contingent on the type of behavior the child is exhibiting (Mash, Johnson, & Kovitz, 1982; Reid et al., 1981). A tantrum or a task well done may elicit the same response from the mother. This failure of maltreating mothers to discriminate between desirable and undesirable children's behavior is also reflected in physiological measures. Abusive mothers, in contrast to nonabusive mothers, show a similar pattern of autonomic arousal in response to either a smiling or a crying baby (Frodi & Lamb, 1980). They seem to be experiencing both the crying baby and the pleasant, happy baby as emotionally aversive. We have spoken earlier of the importance of parents' accurately reading and responding to children's cues. This distorted perception of the child's behavior must greatly increase the stress and confusion in already disturbed parent-child relationships. Intervention programs which have been successful in lowering rates of abuse have focused on educating parents about child development and childrearing and in providing support networks and raising parents' self-esteem (Garbarino, 1989; Sedlack, 1989).

The Ecology of Child Abuse

Parents who abuse their children are frequently unemployed (Steinberg, Catalano, & Dooley, 1981), poorly educated, and economically deprived (Garbarino & Grouter, 1978). However, it is obvious that most parents of low socioeconomic status do not maltreat their children. What environmental factors might be associated with child abuse? In order to answer this question, James Garbarino and Deborah Sherman (1980) identified two neighborhoods that were similar in racial and socioeconomic composition but had markedly different rates of child maltreatment. The high-risk neighborhood had a rate of 130 cases of child abuse per thousand families, compared to only 15 cases in the low-risk neighborhood. In the study presented in Box 12-2, it can be seen that the neighborhoods had very different characteristics that affected the well-being of families and children. In addition, parents in the high-risk neighborhood utilized social relationships and resources in a different way than did those in the low-risk neighborhood. This again suggests that it is the interaction between family characteristics and neighborhood characteristics, rather than either alone, that produces abuse.

It has been suggested that the high incidence of child abuse also may be supported by the general acceptance of physical punishment of children in the American culture (Christoffel, 1990). In groups in which physical punishment of children is not accepted, such as among the Chinese, battered children are rarely found. Thus, the cultural approval of violence such as spanking in childrearing may combine with the lack of social, economic, and emotional resources of caretakers to produce child abuse.

In summary, no single factor leads to child abuse. It involves complex interactions among dysfunctional family relationships, multiple stressful experiences, a disorganized or nonsupportive environment, and cultural values that tolerate or justify aggression and physical punishment.

Consequences of Abuse

Even as infants, abused children show less secure attachment and more noncompliant, resistant, and avoidant behavior toward their mothers (Crittenden, 1988; Egeland & Sroufe, 1981a, 1981b). Moreover, problems in emotional regulation and the transmission of aggressive behavior can be seen in the social interactions of abused children outside of their homes (Cicchetti & Lynch, in press). Carol George and Mary Main (1979) observed that abused toddlers in a day-care center not only were more aggressive with their peers but also were more ambivalent toward their caregivers. They threatened to attack or did attack caregivers, behaviors that never occurred in nonabused children. In addition, they showed great wariness in response to friendly behavior by the caregivers. They seemed both to have learned not to trust adults and to have acquired their parents' aggressive responses. Such attitudes and behaviors would seem likely to lead to difficulties in childrearing when the abused children themselves become parents. Furthermore, as these abused children advanced through the school year they not only continued to show problems in relations with peers, teachers, and caregivers, they also had academic problems and low self-esteem, exhibited behavior problems, and, not surprisingly, were depressed and withdrawn (Toth, Manly, & Cicchetti, in press). Long-term effects of abuse are most likely to be found if children remain in low socioeconomic environments with multiple stresses and few supports available (Cicchetti & Lynch, in press).

THE SIBLING SYSTEM

Over 80 percent of the families in the United States have more than one child. The functioning of the family is influenced by the number, sex, and

BOX 12-2 THE ECOLOGY OF CHILD ABUSE

Can the quality of the neighborhood increase or decrease the incidence of child abuse? In order to answer this question, James Garbarino and his colleagues interviewed "expert informants" in neighborhoods that were at high risk and low risk for child abuse about the neighborhood as a setting for families and children. These expert informants included such people as school principals, public health nurses, mailmen, policemen, clergy, scout leaders, and others who had firsthand knowledge of life in the two areas. In addition, mothers were interviewed to gain information about the experiences and attitudes of individual families, the stresses they encountered, and the social supports available to them.

The expert informants and the mothers were in agreement in seeing the high-risk neighborhoods as less desirable areas in which to live and raise a family. It was not just that the high-risk neighborhoods were more unstable, physically run down, and uncared for in spite of the fact that the two areas were equally economically deprived, but that the social ambience of the neighborhoods differed. In the high-risk area there was less adequate provision of child care, less self-sufficiency, and less exchange of such things as child supervision or the use of neighborhood children as playmates. In addition, in the high-risk area there were more "latchkey children," that is, children who came from school to arrive at a home with no caretaker present. In 86 percent of the low-risk families a parent was present when the child returned from school, whereas a parent was present in only 25 percent of the high-risk families.

The families in the high-risk neighborhoods perceived themselves as more stressed and in more need of support but as having fewer supports available to them. In addition, they seemed to use the supports that were available less effectively than did parents in low-risk neighborhoods. They were less likely to use the type of preventive and recreational community services such as Boy Scouts or social and athletic groups that improve the quality of life, and they were more likely to resort to treatment and rehabilitative services such as family service associations when a family crisis arose. They did not utilize their neighborhood resources until they were in desperate straits. In contrast to families in the low-risk area, parents in high-risk families were described as being

> inclined to seek an advantage by getting all they can from others while giving as little as they can get away with. There is ambivalence about neighborly exchanges and a recognition that, overall, the neighborhood exerts a negative effect on families. Family life is threatened from without and within. A family's own problems seem to be compounded rather than ameliorated by the neighborhood context dominated as it is by other needy families (Garbarino & Sherman, 1980, pp. 194–195).

Garbarino and Sherman conclude that not only do neighborhood characteristics influence family functioning, but also there is a tendency for poorly functioning families to cluster in high-risk neighborhoods. This drift into adverse neighborhoods compounds the difficult problems of high-risk families.

Source: Garbarino, J., & Sherman, D. (1980). High-risk neighborhoods and high-risk families: Human ecology of child maltreatment. *Child Development,* 51, 188–198.

spacing of children. These factors must be considered not only in view of their effects on parent-child interaction but also in terms of the influence siblings—that is, brothers and sisters—have on each other.

Family Size

As family size increases, opportunities for extensive contact between the parents and the individual child decrease, but opportunities for a variety of interactions with siblings expand.

A parent's attitude toward childrearing and the circumstances under which a child is reared will change as more children are added to the family. Parents become increasingly dissatisfied with both their marital relationship and their parenting as families expand (Rutter & Madge, 1976). With a large number of children, particularly in families with over six children, family roles tend to become more precisely defined, chores are assigned, and discipline is more authoritarian and severe, particularly in mothers' control of daughters.

Frequently, older siblings are assigned the supervisory and disciplinary roles maintained by parents in smaller families (Wagner, Schubert, & Schubert, 1985). Girls are more likely than boys to play an active caretaking and helping role with their siblings (Cicirelli, 1982). A firstborn 12-year-old girl in a large family may warm bottles, burp babies, change diapers, and soothe a squalling infant with the alacrity and skill of a young mother.

Because the parents in large families cannot interact as closely with their children as those in smaller families, there is less opportunity for overprotection, infantalization, constant harassing, or close supervision of children. The results of this relationship are reflected in the greater independence, antisocial behavior, and delinquency, but lower self-esteem and academic achievement of children from large families (Blake, 1989; Wagner et al., 1985). It should be noted that larger families are poorer than smaller families and many of the adverse outcomes found in children in large families may be related to factors associated with economic duress—from living in high-crime neighborhoods and crowded inadequate housing, to malnutrition, unemployment, and parental stress (Rutter & Madge, 1976).

Parent-Child Interactions and Birth Order

In cases where differences related to birth order have been revealed, they are usually attributed to variations in interaction with parents and siblings associated with the unique life experiences found in children with that position in the family.

This is particularly true in the unusual role of the firstborn child. Eldest children are the only ones who, until they are dethroned by the birth of a subsequent child, do not have to share their parents' love and attention with other siblings. How distressing the dethroning of the firstborn child will be depends to a large extent on the responses of the parents. The birth of a new baby usually decreases the amount of interaction between spouses and between mothers and older children (Dunn, 1983; Taylor & Kogan, 1973). Following the birth of a sibling many firstborn children, especially boys, show emotional and behavioral problems (Nadelman & Begun, 1982). These problems are related to the temperament of the child and to the emotional state of the mother, with children of depressed mothers and children with difficult temperaments having more difficulty adjusting to changes in the family situation (Brody, Stoneman, & Burke, 1987; Stocker, Dunn, & Plomin, 1989). These outcomes seem to be mediated to a large extent by changes in mother-child interaction. Mothers become more negative, coercive, and restraining and engage in less playful interactions with the firstborn following the birth of a second child (Dunn & Kendrick, 1980, 1982). If mothers continue to be responsive to the needs of the elder child and discuss the feelings of the younger child with the older child, intense sibling rivalry is unlikely to occur (Bryant & Crockenberg, 1980; Howe & Ross, 1990). However, increased involvement of the father with the firstborn child also can counter to some extent the child's feelings of displacement and jealousy of the younger sibling (Legg, Sherick, & Wadland, 1974). In fact, since the demands of parents are increased by the birth of second or subsequent children, it has been found that a positive effect of the second birth may be that it requires greater participation in child care by fathers (Lamb, 1979; Stewart, Mobley, Van Tuyl, & Salvador, 1987).

In spite of the fact that a new infant or younger child necessitates more attention and care from parents than does an older child, there seems to be an especially intense and concerned involvement of parents and firstborn children that is maintained throughout life. Parents interfere more with the activities of firstborn than secondborn children. They have higher expectations of firstborns and exert greater pressures on them for achievement and the acceptance of responsibility (Baskett, 1985; Cushna, 1966; Hilton, 1967; Lasko, 1954; Rothbart, 1971). Firstborn children also have greater disciplinary friction with their parents. At any age, more physical punishment is likely to be administered to a firstborn than to a later-born child. In contrast, parents are more consistent and relaxed in disciplinary functions with later-born children, perhaps as a result of self-confidence gained from practice in childrearing. In a sense, the firstborn is the "practice baby" on which the parent, through trial and error, learns parenting skills.

Sibling Interaction and Birth Order

In addition to being associated with differences in parent-child relations, birth order is associated with variations in sibling relations. Eldest children are frequently expected to assume some responsibility and self-control toward the younger sibling who has displaced them. When eldest children feel jealousy or hostility, they are likely to be restrained or punished by their parents, whereas the younger child is likely to be protected and defended. On the other hand, the eldest child is more dominant, competent, and able to bully or, conversely, to assist and teach the younger offspring. Thus, it is not surprising that older children have been found to show both more antagonistic behavior, such as hitting, kicking, and biting, and more nurturant

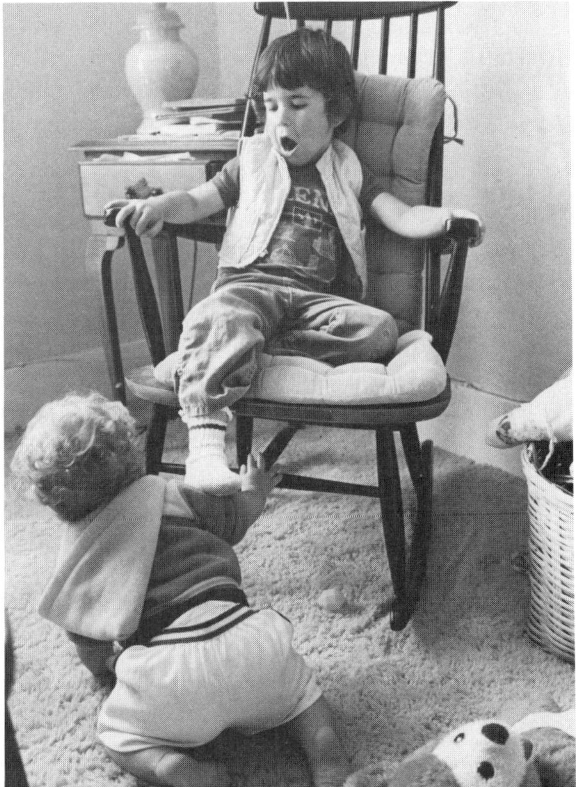

Although sibling conflict is high in toddlers, it tends to decrease with age.

prosocial behavior toward their younger siblings (Abramovitch, Pepler, & Corter, 1982; Abramovitch, Corter, Pepler, & Stanhope, 1986; Berndt & Bulleit, 1985). It has been remarked that "siblings show considerable pragmatic understanding of how to annoy and how to console the other" (Dunn & Kendrick, 1982, p. 42). Although the annoying rivalrous aspects of the sibling relationship often seems to be emphasized more than the consoling, positive aspects, recent research suggests that both have significant effects on development (Buhrmeister & Furman, 1987).

Eldest children focus on parents as their main sources of social learning within the family, whereas younger children use both parents and siblings as models and teachers (Summers, 1987). Direct observational studies of the social interaction of siblings have confirmed that younger siblings, even infants as young as 12 months, tend to watch, follow, and imitate their older siblings (Lamb, 1977; Samuels, 1977). The fact that they take over toys recently abandoned by their older brothers and sisters and imitate their behavior suggests that older siblings may play an important role in facilitating the younger child's mastery over the inanimate environment (Lamb, 1977; Pepler, Corter, & Abramovitch, 1982). It is noteworthy that no such reciprocal behavior or imitation by the older sibling toward the younger is found. When children enter school the teaching role of older children may become more formalized; 70 percent of children report getting help with homework from siblings, especially from older sisters who seem to be somewhat more effective academic instructors than older brothers (Cicirelli, 1976).

Siblings may also serve as resources when children are confronting stress (Conger, 1992; Hetherington, 1988; Hetherington & Clingempeel, 1992; MacKinnon, 1989). Children are most likely to turn to each other as buffers in the face of stress when a supportive adult is not available. Males are less likely to obtain support from their siblings than are females. Males often have to "go it alone" in times of family crises, whereas female siblings may become mutually protective.

Sibling relationships change with age. In adolescence some of the early overt sibling rivalry and ambivalence may diminish and a special intimacy may arise between sibling pairs where the sibling serves as the most trusted confidant and source of emotional support. In concerns about appearance, peer relations, social problems, and sexual feelings and activities, siblings may be able to communicate more openly with each other than with peers or parents (Cicirelli, 1976). Female siblings often become increasingly close over the life span.

In addition, what is learned in the sibling relationship may carry over into other situations outside of the family such as those with peers and teachers (Buhrmeister & Furman, 1987). Since a sibling is a less threatening target of aggression than a parent, the sibling relationship may provide an important situation in which to practice aggressive behavior, and conflictual sibling relationships are associated with the development of antisocial behavior in children; however, supportive relationships may also be associated with increased social skills especially in younger children (Buhrmeister & Furman, 1987; Hetherington, 1988; Hetherington & Clingempeel, 1992; Patterson, 1982; Richman, Graham, & Stevenson, 1982).

Characteristics of Firstborn Children

In view of the marked differences in family dynamics related to birth order, it is not surprising that different characteristics are associated with firstborn and later-born children. Firstborn children remain more adult-oriented, helpful, self-controlled, conforming, and anxious than their siblings. The parental demands and high standards imposed on firstborns result in eldest children being more studious, conscientious, and serious (Baskett, 1985). These children excel in academic and professional achievement (Zajonc, Marcus, & Marcus, 1979; Sutton-Smith & Rosenberg, 1970). This is supported by their overrepresentation in *Who's Who* and among Rhodes scholars and eminent Americans in the fields of letters and science. However, it has been found that in major scientific controversies related to such issues as evolution, it is the secondborn sons who support innovative theories and the firstborn sons who support the status quo.

It may be that some of the same pressures on firstborns that lead to high achievement are also associated with their greater guilt, anxiety, and fear, their inability to cope alone with stressful situations, their higher rate of admission to child guidance clinics, and their lowered self-confidence and social poise.

The only child has frequently been regarded as a "spoiled brat," combining undersirable symptoms such as dependency, egotism, lack of self-control, and emotional disorders. However, research findings suggest that in many ways the only child has advantages over other children, especially children in families with three or more children. Although exposed to the same high level of parental demands and intrusiveness as other firstborns, an only child does not have to adapt to ultimate displacement and competition with siblings. As was the case with firstborns, this sustained close relationship with the parents is associated with high achievement; however, an only child is lower in anxiety and shows more personal control, maturity, and leadership (Falbo & Polit, 1986). In social relations both outside and inside the home, only children seem to make more positive adjustments than children distressed by sibling rivalry.

SOCIAL CLASS, ETHNICITY, AND SOCIALIZATION

No culture is entirely homogeneous. Subgroups within a culture may have different problems to cope with as well as divergent values. These may be reflected in different goals and methods in socialization.

Powerlessness and Poverty

Considerable concern has been focused on differences between the life situations of low socioeconomic class families and middle-class families in the American culture. Although the most obvious differences between these social groups are related to income, education, occupation, and prestige, other related pervasive features of their life may be more directly relevant to the process of socialization.

Powerlessness is a basic problem of the poor. They have less influence over the society in which they live and are likely to be less adequately treated by social organizations than are members of the middle class. They receive poorer health and public services, and they are more likely to have their individual rights violated by agents of the law, social workers, educators, or the medical profession. Their lack of power and prestige and lack of educational and economic resources restrict the availability of options in most areas of their lives. They have little control or choice of occupations or housing and little contact with other social groups; they are tragically vulnerable to disasters such as job loss, financial stress, and illness; and they are subject to impersonal bureaucratic decisions in the legal system and in social institutions, such as welfare agencies. In addition, the low educational level, restricted experience, and lack of information of the poor make it difficult for them to understand and avail themselves of the limited resources that are open to them. It is not surprising in view of the multiple stresses, few resources, and little social power of poor parents, that many of them experience considerable psychological stress and feel helpless, insecure, and controlled by external forces (Hess, 1970; McLoyd, 1990).

However, it may be that the very stresses that engender an awareness of lack of social power in working-class families also result in the formation of extensive support networks of kin, friends, and neighbors by these families, particularly by economically deprived black families (McAdoo, 1978; McQueen, 1979; Stack, 1974; Wilson, 1989). These systems, which involve not only emotional support but tendering of unpaid services, cannot be purchased. Mutual assistance is rendered in fulfilling not only emergency needs of the family in times of unemployment, childbirth, illness, and death, but also the day-to-day needs of family life (McLoyd, 1990; Pearson, Hunter, Ensminger, & Kellam, 1990).

CYCLES OF DISADVANTAGE

The poor get involved in cycles of disadvantage. There is a higher probability of encountering sequences of events which make childrearing difficult and which lead to adverse outcomes occurring in poor families. For example, family disorganization, unemployment, divorce, and birth to unwed and teenaged mothers are more common in poor and less educated families. If

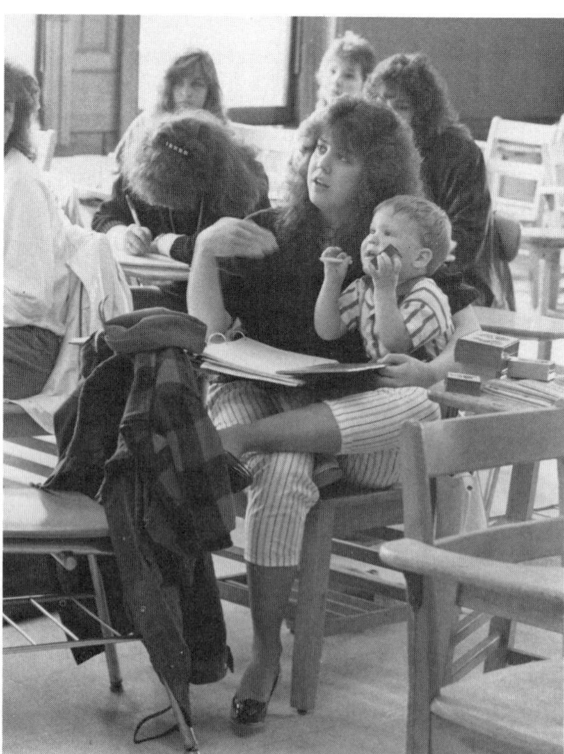

Continued education is an important factor in avoiding downward economic mobility for teenaged mothers.

we take the example of teenage pregnancy we find that women who have their first child as teenagers tend to drop out of school and subsequently do not catch up educationally; those already out of school at the time of birth tend not to return to school (Furstenberg, Brooks-Gunn, & Chase-Lansdale, 1989; McLuskey, Killarney, & Papini, 1983). In addition, young mothers have more children over time and this in turn limits their freedom to work. The lack of education, work skills, and available work time tends to be associated with continued poverty. With economic need comes a dependence on public assistance. Furstenberg (1976) found that one-third of his sample of teenaged mothers were on welfare, whereas only 4 percent of their peers were. In the United States it is estimated that well over half of all payments of aid for dependent children go to mothers who had their first child as teenagers. Thus teenage pregnancy may initiate a cycle of low educational attainment, economic dependence, and poverty. There is new evidence, however, that over the long run the effects of early childbearing on mothers may not be as marked as those found in the short run. Based on his follow-up study of 300 teen mothers and their children, Frank Furstenberg has noted that if teen mothers continue in school, control the number of subsequent births, and have a successful marriage, in the long run they resemble mothers who bore their first child after the teen years (Furstenberg et al., 1989).

Although the consequences of teenaged birth tend to moderate somewhat for mothers, they remain or become greater over time for their children, and these effects are greater for sons than daughters. The children of teenaged mothers show deficits in cognitive development and school achievement and higher rates of school dropouts. In addition they show less self-control and more antisocial behavior such as drug abuse and delinquency (Nord, Moore, Morrison, Brown, & Myers, 1991). The effects are likely to be related to the environment of economic disadvantage, family instability, and high stress encountered both by the teenaged mothers and their children.

Social Class and Childrearing

In view of the wide discrepancy in life situations between the poor and the more economically privileged, it is surprising that more differences are not found in values and childrearing. What few there are can best be conceptualized in terms of a dimension of power and self-direction versus helplessness and obedience to the demands of others. Lower-class parents place more emphasis on respectability and obedience to authority; middle-class parents put more emphasis on the development of curiosity, internal control, the ability to delay gratification and work for distant goals, and sensitivity in relations with others.

Social-class differences are found in the kind and timing of restrictions placed on children (Bronfenbrenner, 1961; Clausen & Williams, 1963; Hess, 1970; Hoffman, 1984; Laosa, 1981). Kagan and his colleagues (Kagan, Kearsley, & Zelazo, 1978) found that in interactions with their preschool children in the home, working-class mothers uttered a prohibition—a "no," "don't," or "stop"—every five minutes, in contrast with middle-class mothers, who restrained their children only once every ten minutes. In addition to intruding more on their children's activities, lower-class mothers are less likely to offer reasons for their punishments or restrictions. The investigators associated this pattern of behavior with the lesser sense of personal internalized control found in lower-class children. Although there is less restrictiveness among middle-class parents toward the infant and young child, there is greater parental supervision and control in adolescence.

It has been proposed that the experiences of parents outside of the home, particularly in the world of work, are reflected in their childrearing practices. There is a relationship between the amount of occupational self-direction a father experiences in his work situation and his relationship with his children. Working-class fathers, in jobs with little self-determination, emphasize the importance of obedience, conformity, and service from their wives and children and are more willing to use physical punishment to attain these goals. Middle-class fathers, whose work is more likely to be self-directed, value and promote self-control, initiative, and independence in their children. It could be argued that if children are going to remain in the same social status as their fathers, such discipline is adaptive to their future role in the marketplace; however, in a mobile society this may not enhance their prospects for improving their status (Kohn, 1979; Kohn & Schooler, 1978). Again, we see that family functioning can be understood only in terms of its broader ecological relations. In addition, we see that parents, as well as children, continue to develop and change in response to their experiences.

Ethnicity and Childrearing

In general, social-class differences in family relations have been found to be more marked than variations based on race or ethnicity (Laosa, 1981; Zill, 1986). Since race and social class tend to be related, with an overrepresentation of minorities in poorer and less educated families, it often has been difficult to separate these factors. In addition, investigators often treat ethnic groups as if they are homogeneous rather than recognizing the great variability within groups. For example, there are many distinct Hispanic groups in the United States, such as Chicanos, Puerto Ricans, Cuban-Americans, and Spanish-Americans. These groups often have quite different socioeconomic, cultural, and linguistic characteristics, as well as considerable variability in attributes within each subgroup; therefore, generalizations about ethnic groups such as Hispanics become difficult.

The behavior of parents and children must always be understood in the context of the meanings and values of the individual's particular socioculture (Harrison, Wilson, Pine, Chon, & Buriel, 1990; Laosa, 1981; McLoyd, 1990). Many ethnic minorities in contrast to the white majority place greater emphasis in socialization, on continuity of ethnic values and world views, and on social interdependence (Harrison et al., 1990), as seen in the importance of the extended family in many minority groups. It is also reflected in a greater emphasis on cooperation, obligation, sharing, and reciprocity in some minority families that contrasts with Western ideals of self-reliance and competition. However, again we need to underscore the diversity in minority groups. This emphasis on cooperation is more likely to be found in Hispanic-American, Native-American, and African-American than many Asian-American groups. Chinese-American parents are even more encouraging of self-sufficiency and achievement than are Caucasian-American parents although they also place greater emphasis on parental control (Lin & Fu, 1990).

Ogbu (1981) has argued that childrearing within subcultures is oriented toward the development of competencies required for adult political, economic, and social roles. These competencies and the childrearing practices necessary to develop them differ for the white middle class and for minority groups such as urban ghetto blacks. Ogbu speculates that for ghetto blacks, although adult categories of success include conventional jobs, they also include "survival strategies" such as sports, entertainment, collective struggle, hustling, pimping, and preaching, among others. The ghetto theory of success does not differ from that of the white middle class in the goals of attaining money, power, social credit, and self-esteem, but it differs in views of the means to attain these goals.

> Having experienced a long history of racial barriers, ghetto blacks believe less in the sufficiency of schooling and tend to approve the use of other alternatives. . . . Some techniques used by ghetto parents may not receive white middle-class approval, but seem to be adapted to produce ghetto functional competencies. Among such techniques are the contrasting treatment of the infant with abundant nurturance, warmth, and affection and their scarcity in postinfancy; establishment of a child-adult contest relationship in the postinfancy period; inconsistent demands for obedience in sanctions and in other ways of relating to the child; and the use of verbal rebuffs and physical punishment. These techniques probably promote functional competencies like self-reliance, resourcefulness, ability to manipulate people and situations, mistrust of people in authority, ability to "fight back" or to ward off attacks, etc. . . . (Ogbu, 1981).

In spite of Ogbu's generalizations about ghetto blacks, it has been found that there are wide variations in values and behavior among poor urban blacks. McQueen (1979) studied two groups of poor black families in Washington, DC. They were identified as the *troubled poor,* who had difficulty dealing with the economic necessities of food, clothing, and rent, and the *future-oriented poor,* who were able to cope with their financial needs. Although both groups of families wanted to have good family relationships, raise their children well, and improve their financial situation, they differed in some significant ways. In contrast to the troubled poor, the future-oriented poor families were more likely to be headed by fathers, with the mothers having higher educational and occupational goals for their sons. These families had strong links with the church, and they neither loaned money to kin nor borrowed from them. In spite of their economic stresses they were self-sufficient. They went without rather than going into debt. Moreover, one-quarter had savings and one-third were buying their own homes. The investigator speculates that the tendency of the troubled poor to get involved in sequences of borrowing and lending with relatives keeps them insolvent, which adversely affects their children's experiences and attitudes. The strong kin network of black families offers resources and emotional support that can be of great assistance in raising children, especially for mother-headed families (Kellam, Ensminger, & Turner, 1977; McAdoo, 1978; Wilson, 1989). However, accepting support, especially financial support, often involves an indebtedness that inhibits poor families from moving out of a state of chronic poverty (Stack, 1974).

Finally there is some evidence that regardless of ethnicity, class, or parents' marital status authoritative parenting is associated with psychosocial maturity, and low depression, anxiety, and behavior problems. The relations between authoritative parenting and school performance, however, is less consistent for African-American and Asian-American adolescents than for white- and Hispanic-American adolescents (Steinberg, Mounts, Lamborn, & Dornbusch, 1991). In high school, peer-group values and differential access to peer groups may modify the effects of parenting styles on the achievement of Asian-American and African-American adolescents as can be seen in Box 12-3.

The move toward a less ethnocentric perspective in the study of families and socialization is just beginning; however, as it increases in the next decade it is likely to make great contributions to our understanding of human development in a cross-cultural context.

BOX 12-3 DIFFERENCES IN ADOLESCENT ACHIEVEMENT: AN ETHNOLOGICAL PERSPECTIVE

African-American and Hispanic-American students usually earn lower grades, drop out more often, and attain less education than do non-Hispanic white students, whereas the academic performance of Asian-American students exceeds that of the other three groups (Mickelson, 1990; Sue & Okazaki, 1990). Even when the role of such factors as socioeconomic status and family structure are controlled for, these ethnic differences in achievement are found.

In a longitudinal study of adolescent adjustment and achievement in a multiethnic, multiclass, multiregional sample of over 20,000 high school students, Steinberg, Dornbusch, and Brown (in press) examined the contribution of family and peer contexts to ethnic differences in adjustment and achievement. They found that in European-American, African-American, and Asian-American families authoritative parenting has similar benefits in promoting better psychosocial adjustment and less depression and delinquency in adolescents. On school performance, however, European and Hispanic-American adolescents were more likely to benefit from authoritative parenting than were African- or Asian-American adolescents. Within African- and Asian-American groups, adolescents with authoritative parents did not show greater academic achievement than those with nonauthoritative parents. How can these findings be explained?

As children grow older, extrafamilial settings such as the school, neighborhood, and peer group become more salient in development. The investigators mapped the social structure of the peer groups in each school by interviewing children about the crowd characteristics of their school and the position of their classmates in these peer niches. Similar peer crowds (for example, populars, brains, jocks, nerds, druggies, and so on) were identified across schools, although they sometimes were called different names. Three striking results emerged. First, students from one ethnic group rarely knew or associated with students from other ethnic groups. Second, across all ethnic groups, children performed best when they had both parents and peers who supported achievement, less well with support from only one source, and least well when neither their parents nor peers supported achievement. White adolescents raised in authoritative families were more likely to belong to peer groups that encouraged engagement in school activities and academic achievement. Both Hispanic-American and Asian-American parents were likely to be authoritarian, a parenting style often associated with low achievement. However, the effects of this authoritarianism in Asian-Americans was countered by the fact that these children were almost invariably found in peer groups that value and reward achievement. In contrast, such peer groups were less available to African-American adolescents. African-American adolescents, even with authoritative parents, were seldom found in achievement-oriented peer groups. Afro-American children often view achievement as giving in to the system or as "white" behavior and find themselves in a conflict between being popular and performing well in school (Fordham & Ogbu, 1986). Consequently, high-achieving African-American students frequently associate with students from other ethnic groups (Liederman, Landsman, & Clark, 1990). Although we talk of niche picking as if different niches are freely available to children, this clearly is not the case in ethnic choices in peer niches.

This study is only one piece in the puzzle of explaining ethnic differences in achievement. The influence of the family on child development can only be understood by taking the ecological approach of examining the interaction of the child and family with the multiple contexts in which children live.

Sources: Fordham, S., & Ogbu, J. V. (1986). Black students' school success: Coping with the burden of acting white. *Urban Review*, **18**, 176–206: Liederman, P. H., Landsman,, M., & Clark, C. (1990, March). *Making it or blowing it: Coping strategies and academic performance in a multiethnic high school population.* Paper presented at the biennial meeting of the Society for Research on Adolescence, Atlanta; Mickelson, R. (1990). The attitude-achievement paradox among black adolescents. *Sociology of Education*, **63**, 44–61; Steinberg, L., & Darling, N. (in press). The broader context of social influence in adolescence. In R. Silberstein & E. Todt (Eds.), *Adolescence in context*. New York: Springer; Steinberg, L., Dornbusch, S. M., & Brown, B. B. (1992). Ethnic differences in adolescent achievement: An ecological perspective. *American Psychologist,* **47,** 723–729; & Okazaki, S. (1990). Asian-American educational achievements: A phenomenon in search of an explanation. *American Psychologist*, **45**, 913–920.

THE CHANGING AMERICAN FAMILY

It is difficult to escape from modern prophets of doom predicting the demise of the nuclear family. Their gloomy prognostications often begin with "We view with alarm" and end with dire references to affirmative action, working mothers, teenage pregnancies, abortion, the rising divorce rate, or the ominous threat of state-supported day-care centers. The American family is

changing just as society is changing, but is it dying? It seems more accurate to say that family roles and forms are becoming more varied.

Most children (60 percent) still live in families with two parents who have only been married once. However, the proportion of traditional nuclear families composed of two parents and children, with the father as the sole breadwinner, is declining as other family forms are increasing. What are some of the main changes in family structure and functioning that are occurring?

There is a decrease in the average size of households to 2.6 people per household and slightly less than an average of two children per family and an increased number of single-adult households. This is, in part, attributable to delays in marriage, declines in birth rates and in remarriage, and an increase in the number of elderly living alone.

There has been an increase in single-parent households largely because of the rising divorce rate and to a lesser extent because of a rise in pregnancies to unwed women. One out of every five children under the age of 18 is living with a single parent. The divorce rate doubled between 1960 and 1985, and it is now estimated that 40 to 50 percent of marriages will end in divorce and 60 percent of these divorces involve children. Furthermore, one-third of children will experience their parents' remarriage and 62 percent of remarriages end in divorce. Thus more parents and children are undergoing multiple marital transitions and rearrangements in family relationships.

There also has been a marked increase in out-of-wedlock births. In 1950, 4 percent of children were born to unmarried mothers in contrast to almost one-quarter in 1988. These rates vary by race and age of the mother with 60 percent of births occurring to unmarried black mothers, one-third to Hispanics, and one-sixth to white non-Hispanics. Although unmarried mothers are often thought to be teenagers, almost two-thirds are women over the age of 20. However 91 percent of current births to black teenagers are to an unmarried mother compared to 54 percent to white unmarried teens.

The number of working mothers also has increased. Sixty percent of mothers with children under the age of 18 now are employed and more than a third of mothers with children under the age of 3 work. Young mothers, poor mothers, and mothers from single-parent families are most likely to enter the labor force because of economic need. Two-thirds of mothers in single-parent families work and another 20 percent are seeking employment. This is to a large extent attributable to their deprived financial situation and has led some social scientists to point to the "feminization of poverty" (Harrison, Serafica, & McAdoo, 1984). Eighty-six percent of black mother-headed households and 38 percent of white mother-headed households fall below the poverty line, in contrast to 46 percent and 16 percent, respectively, of two-parent households.

We will turn now to a closer examination of two of the most notable changes in the American family: those associated with the transition involving divorce, life in a single-parent household, and remarriage, and those associated with maternal employment. Most of our discussion of divorce will involve mother-custody families since about 85 percent of children reside with their mothers following divorce.

Marital Transitions

Divorce and remarriage should not be viewed as single discrete events but as part of a series of transitions that modify the lives and development of parents and children. Children's experiences in earlier family situations will modify their response to the current transition. The response to divorce and life in a single-parent family will be influenced by the quality of family life preceding the separation and divorce, and the response to remarriage will be shaped by experiences in the earlier marriage and in the single-parent household. Both divorce and remarriage involve the restructuring of the household and changes in family roles and relationships; however, they differ in several important ways. Divorce usually involves high levels of family conflict and a decrease or lack of contact with a parent, whereas remarriage involves the addition of a member to the family.

In spite of the fact that divorce may be a positive solution to destructive conflictual family functioning and the eventual outcome may be a constructive one, for many family members the transition period following separation and divorce is stressful. In fact, there is some evidence that feelings of distress and unhappiness in parents, poor parent-child relationships, and the social and emotional adjustment of children actually get worse during the first year following divorce. However, for many parents there is a dramatic improvement in the sense of personal well-being, interpersonal functioning, and family relations in the second year following divorce, when families are adapting to their new single-parent status. In the long run, children in stable, well-functioning single-parent households are better adjusted than children in conflict-ridden nuclear families. In the short run, in the first year following divorce, the children in single-parent households are more disturbed (Hetherington et al., 1982). There are however some provocative recent findings that children whose parents later divorce in contrast to those children of parents who remain in their marriage show more behavior problems long before the divorce occurs (Block, Block, & Gjerde, 1986; Cherlin et al., 1991). This could be because children are responding adversely to the acrimony and conflict often found in stressed marriages or because behavior problems in children exacerbate difficulties in a troubled marriage and help to precipitate a divorce.

Stresses in Single-Parent Households

How do the life-style and functioning of parents and children in single-parent households differ from those in nuclear families? What stresses and patterns of coping and adjustment are more likely to be encountered in single-parent households?

First, parents in single-parent households suffer from task overload. The single parent is dealing with family tasks and needs that are regarded as a full-time job for two adults in a nuclear family (Hetherington et al., 1982; Hetherington, Stanley-Hagan, & Anderson, 1989).

Second, custodial mothers, but not custodial fathers, suffer marked declines in income following divorce (Zill, 1991). Custodial fathers, because of their greater economic resources, are more able to hire someone to assist in child care and housekeeping tasks and also are more likely to receive help from friends.

Third, mothers in single-parent households are often socially isolated and lacking in social and emotional support. A divorced mother's main source of support is her family, especially her mother. About one-third of mothers spend some time living in their family of origin following divorce.

Fourth, mothers in single-parent households who are lacking support in childrearing may confront problems in raising their children. Children view fathers as more powerful and threatening than mothers. In nuclear families, children exhibit less noncompliant and deviant behavior toward their fathers than toward their mothers, and when undesirable behavior occurs, the father can terminate it more readily than the mother can (Hetherington et al., 1982). It has been proposed that the presence of the same-sex parent may be especially important in the development of children, and research findings suggest that preadolescent sons may adapt better in father-custody homes whereas preadolescent daughters may develop better in mother-custody homes (Santrock & Warshak, 1979; Zill, 1988). There is, however, some evidence that there are higher rates of deviant acts and antisocial behavior in adolescent children in father-custody families, perhaps because fathers are less persistent in monitoring their children's activities, friends, and whereabouts (Buchanan, Maccoby, & Dornbusch, 1992).

Finally, in a one-parent household the custodial parent is likely to become more salient in the development of the child. There is not a spouse to serve as a buffer if acrimonious relationships develop between parent and child in a single-parent family or if the custodial parent is incompetent or dysfunctional. This is often a problem in divorced families since both mothers and fathers immediately following divorce are at greater risk for psychological and health problems (Dura & Kiecolt-Glaser, 1991). A depressed, preoccupied, or ill parent and a confused, angry, demanding child may be able to give each other little support and may actually exacerbate each other's problems (Hetherington, 1989).

If divorced parents and their children do not experience additional stresses following divorce, most are coping reasonably well two to three years after the divorce. However, one-parent mother-headed households are at increased risk of encountering multiple stresses that may combine to create a home situation in which it is difficult to raise children successfully.

Family Interaction in Divorced Families

A period of diminished parenting is often found following divorce (Hetherington et al., 1982). Custodial mothers may become self-involved, erratic, uncommunicative, nonsupportive, and inconsistently punitive in dealing with their children. They also show a lack of effective control and monitoring of their children's behavior. Their children reciprocate in the immediate aftermath of divorce by being demanding, noncompliant, and aggressive but also whining and dependent. Not a very winning combination! Divorced mothers and sons are particularly likely to engage in escalating, mutually coercive exchanges. Some desperate divorced mothers describe their relationship with their children one year after divorce as "declared war," a "struggle for survival," "the old Chinese water torture," or "like getting bitten to death by ducks." Although this inept parenting is most marked in the first year following divorce and improves markedly in the second year, it is more likely to be sustained with sons especially with temperamentally difficult sons, than with daughters. Divorced mothers and their daughters often eventually form exceptionally close congenial relationships; however, this is sometimes disrupted by conflict as the divorced mothers attempt to control their daughters' acting-out behavior in adolescence (Hetherington, 1991a; Hetherington & Clingempeel, 1992).

In most single-parent households, particularly where the father has custody, parents expect older children to be more autonomous, to participate more actively in family decision making, and to assume greater household and child-care responsibilities than children in two-parent households. Some

This remarrying family will face the challenge of establishing new roles and relationships in a blended family.

parents may make inappropriate emotional demands and elevate the older child to the level of a confidant. For many children the increased practical and emotional responsibilities accelerate the development of self-sufficiency and maturity. These children do tend to "grow up faster". If, however, the parent makes excessive maturity demands, the child is likely to experience feeling of incompetence and resentment.

Although we have emphasized the increasing salience of the custodial parent in the development of children following divorce or separation, noncustodial parents can continue to play a significant role in their children's development. When there is agreement in childrearing, a positive attitude toward the spouse, and low conflict between parents, and when the noncustodial parent is emotionally stable, frequent visitation by the noncustodial parent is associated with more positive adjustment and self-control in children. Continued contact with a noncustodial father is especially beneficial for sons. When there is continued conflict between parents, especially conflict where the child feels caught in the middle or when the parent is a nonauthoritative parent or is poorly adjusted, frequent contact between the parent and the child may be associated with disruptions in the child's behavior (Buchanan, Maccoby, & Dornbusch, 1991; Camara & Resnick, 1988). It is not a simple matter of the availability of the noncustodial father or mother, but the quality of the parental contact and exposure and involvement of the child in conflict that counts.

Family Interaction in Remarried Families

The family's response to remarriage must be considered in the light of their previous family experience. Remarriage is the most common route out of poverty for divorced women, and a new spouse may give a custodial parent emotional support and help in childrearing as well as economic support. However the resistant behavior of children to the entry of a stepparent sometimes places considerable stress on the marital relationship.

Boys who often have been involved in coercive relationships with their custodial mothers may have little to lose and much to gain from the addition of a caring stepfather. Daughters on the other hand may feel the intrusion of stepfathers into their close relationship with their mothers as more threatening and disruptive. In preadolescent children, it does seem to be the case that divorce has more adverse consequences for boys and remarriage for girls (Hetherington, 1989). In adolescence such sex differences are rarely found (Hetherington, 1991; Hetherington & Clingempeel, 1992).

Both stepmothers and stepfathers take a less active role in parenting than do biological parents (Bray, 1988; Hetherington, 1991a; Hetherington & Clingempeel, 1992; Santrock & Sitterle, 1987). Even after two years, disengagement is the most common parenting style in stepfathers. Many stepfathers tend to be like polite strangers with their stepchildren. They hesitate to become involved in controlling or disciplining their stepchildren. Biological fathers are both more likely to praise the children for good behavior, be affectionate and interested in their children's activities, and set limits on their children and criticize them for undesirable behavior—for not cleaning up their room, not getting their homework done, or for fighting with a younger sibling. Stepmothers, because of the demands of the maternal role, are forced to take a more active role in discipline than are stepfathers (Santrock & Sitterle, 1987), which may in part explain the finding that the children are more resistant and have poorer adjustment in stepmother families (Brand, Clingempeel, & Bowen-Woodward, 1988; Furstenberg, 1988; Santrock & Sitterle, 1987). Furthermore, the age of the child at the time of remarriage is associated with acceptance of the remarriage and behavior problems in children. Early adolescence is a particularly difficult time in which to have a remarriage occur (Hetherington, 1991a; Hetherington & Clingempeel, 1992).

Although we have been focusing on the effects of divorce and remarriage on parent-child relations, sibling relations also are often disrupted. More antagonistic nonsupportive relations are found among siblings in divorced and remarried families than those in nondivorced families (Hetherington, 1988; Hetherington & Clingempeel, 1992; MacKinnon, 1989). These adverse effects are most marked for male siblings, whereas some pairs of female siblings serve as mutual supports in coping with their parents' marital transitions.

The Adjustment of Children in Divorced and Remarried Families

There is great diversity in children's responses to their parents' marital transitions. Many children manifest some behavioral disruptions and emotional upheavals immediately following their parents' divorce or remarriage. Anger, resentment, anxiety, and depression are common at this time. Following their initial response to their parents' divorce and remarriage, some children exhibit remarkable resiliency and, in the long term, may actually be enhanced by coping with these transitions; others suffer sustained developmental delays or disruptions; still others appear to adapt well in the early stages of family reorganization but show delayed effects that emerge at a later time, especially adolescence. The most commonly reported sustained problem behaviors found in children from divorced and remarried families are aggressive, noncompliant, antisocial behavior; decrements in prosocial behavior and disruptions in peer relations (Bray, 1988; Hetherington, 1991; Hetherington & Clingempeel, 1992; Zill, 1988). In adolescence, substance abuse and precocious sexual activity are found in both boys and girls in mother-headed one-parent families (Hetherington, 1991a; Hetherington & Clingempeel, 1992; Newcomer & Udry, 1987). Problems in academic achievement, school adjustment, and school dropout are greater for boys than girls in divorced families. In adolescence, more depression may emerge in children in divorced and remarried families. In preadolescence, boys show the most marked and sustained responses to divorce and girls more lasting resistance to remarriage. However, adolescence seems to trigger behavior problems in both boys and girls in divorced and remarried families, even in some who have previously been functioning well. It should be noted that most boys and girls adjust reasonably well following the initial crisis period after their parents' marital transitions. Only about one-quarter have long-term problems. Authoritative parenting is associated with more positive adjustment in children in divorced and remarried families just as it is in nondivorced families. If divorce reduces stress and conflict and leads to better functioning on the part of the custodial parent or if the child's loss of an uninvolved or incompetent father eventually results in the acquisition of a more accessible, responsive father figure, the child often benefits in the long run from divorce and remarriage. Preadolescent boys in particular may benefit from a close, caring relationship with a stepfather.

Maternal Employment and Child Development

Over the past decade there has been a steady increase in the number of mothers who are employed. This increase has been most marked in the mothers of preschool children. Mothers no longer feel compelled to remain in the home when their children are infants or toddlers. It seems likely that as mothers spend more time in their places of employment and less time in the home, family roles and patterns of family functioning will change. What are some of these changes in family roles and interaction that have already occurred and how do they influence children's behavior?

Role Models

When both parents work outside of the home, the role of the mother may be perceived as similar to the role of the father, not only because the mother works but also because the father participates more actively in family and childrearing tasks, often regarded as part of the maternal role (Pleck, 1979, 1984). Children with employed mothers therefore are exposed to less stereotypical models of the father as breadwinner and the mother a housekeeper and caregiver. It should be noted that, in dual-career families, although father participation increases the mother continues to do most of the child care and housework. Working mothers report that time is their scarcest and most valued resource. Both working mothers and their school-age children complain that the employed mothers have too little time to spend with their children. However, greater involvement of the father in dual-earner families may compensate for some of these problems. In both dual-earner and single-earner families high father involvement is associated with high IQ scores and achievement test scores and with social maturity in both sons and daughters (Gottfried, Gottfried, & Bathurst, 1988).

It is not surprising that maternal employment is associated with more egalitarian views of sex roles by their children, particularly by daughters (Gold & Andres, 1978; Hoffman, 1989). In middle-class families, maternal employment is related to higher educational and occupational goals in children. Maternal employment also is associated with fewer traditional feminine interests and characteristics in daughters. Daughters of working, as compared to nonworking, mothers more often perceive the woman's role as involving freedom of choice, satisfaction, and competence, and they themselves are career- and achievement-oriented, independent and assertive, and high in self-esteem (Hoffman, 1989). Sons of working mothers, in contrast to sons of unemployed mothers, not only perceive females as more competent, but also view men as warmer and more expressive.

Attitudes

The attitudes of both parents toward dual work status and the mother's satisfaction with the work will modify the effects of maternal employment on children. If the working mother obtains personal satisfaction from employment, if she does not experience excessive guilt about being away from her children, and if she has adequate household arrangements to prevent her from being stressed by dual-role demands, she is likely to perform as well as, or better than, the nonworking mother as a parent (Greenberg & Goldberg, 1989).

Nonworking mothers who have a sense of satisfaction and competence in their homemaking role and working mothers who enjoy their employment both show more positive relations with their husbands and with their children than do unhappy nonworking mothers who would like to be employed (Hoffman, 1989; Schultz, 1991). However, mothers and fathers both display more negative feelings and behavior toward their children when their attitudes toward maternal employment and the wife's work status are not congruent (Stucky, McGhee, & Bell, 1982).

Parent-Child Relations

There is some evidence that the childrearing practices of working mothers may differ from those of nonemployed mothers, particularly in the area of independence training. Except in cases where mothers feel guilty about leaving their children in order to work, employed mothers encourage their children to become self-sufficient and independent, and to assume responsibility for household tasks at an earlier age (Hock, 1978). This early independence training may be beneficial in leading to high achievement motivation, achievement behavior, and competence (Woods, 1972). However, maternal employment in some families is also associated with less supervision and monitoring of school-aged children (Crouter & MacDermid, 1991). Lack of monitoring is associated with especially adverse consequences for boys—lower school performance, more behavior problems, and an increase in mother-child conflict (Crouter & MacDermid, 1991). For both boys and girls, lack of supervision is associated with earlier dating behavior, precocious sexuality, and greater peer involvement (Dornbusch et al., 1983).

In summary, in spite of predictions to the contrary, the results of studies of maternal employment suggest that with adequate alternate child care it does not usually have detrimental effects on children; in fact, positive consequences usually have been obtained, especially for girls. However, the effects of maternal employment can be evaluated only in relation to other factors, such as the reason why the mother is working, the mother's satisfaction with her role, the demands placed on other family members, the attitudes of the other family members toward the mother's employment, and the quality of substitute care and supervision provided for the children.

CHILDREN, FAMILIES, AND WAR

We have been discussing recent changes in American society and families that affect the psychological well-being of children. However, one of the notable events that modify the experiences of many families and the adjustment of their children is one that has not been directly experienced in the United States for over 100 years, and that is war. Armed combat is associated with the witnessing, experiencing, or participation in violent acts by children; the destruction of social networks and social institutions; hunger and homelessness; and the disruption or loss of families. Children comprise three-quarters of the population in refugee camps in warring third-world nations (Green, Asrat, Maurs, & Morgan, 1989).

Research on the effects of war on families and children began in World War II. Much of this research indicated that the long-term psychological effects of war and air-raids on children were less severe than might have been expected and that continuity in social networks and support from family, friends, and neighbors played a major role in buffering children from the adverse consequences of war. If children were separated from their parents or if parents showed anxiety, the children exhibited more psychological disturbance than those who remained with their families or who had parents who were able to maintain a responsive, stable caretaking regime (Freud & Burlingham, 1943; Burbury, 1941). When separations from parents did occur, continuity of contact with other family members or familiar adults and neighbors were a benefit to the children. Many children in Lebanon, Kuwait, Iraq, Ireland, South Africa, and Cambodia experience violence and deprivation

In war-torn countries, children often become participants in armed combat.

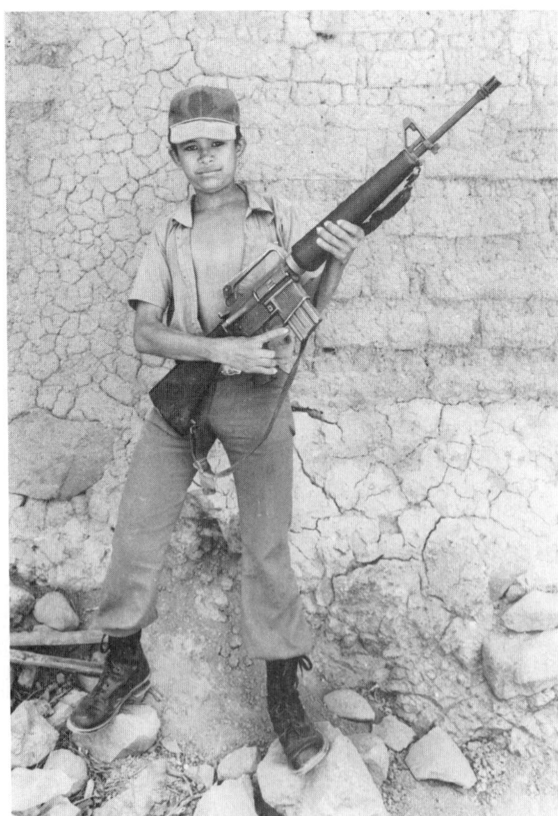

BOX 12-4 CHILDREN OF MOZAMBIQUE

Thousands of children involved in the civil war in Mozambique have been exposed to violence, physical and sexual abuse, torture, and abduction as victims, observers, and as instigators. Neil Boothby describes the experience of 6-year-old Franisse who was kidnapped by the Renamo (the Mozambique National Resistance). He was forced to set his family's hut ablaze, watch as his parents were decapitated and dismembered, and their heads impaled on stakes. He was then taken back to a Renamo camp where he went through a brutal and systematic indoctrination program to transform the kidnapped children into combat soldiers and cold-blooded killers. What happens to children who go through such a dehumanizing experience where violence is required and approved of? Is their sense of social and moral values permanently damaged or behavior pattern irreversibly altered?

Boothby studied the adjustment of forty-two kidnapped boys between the ages of 6 and 16 when they were retaken and returned to a government refugee center where staff attempted to establish regular daily routines and safe codes of behavior. He found that the length of time spent in the Renamo base camp rather than the amount of direct involvement in violence was related to their later ability to behave in a socially responsible fashion. Boys who had been in Renamo camps less than six months tended to define themselves as victims rather than members of Renamo. Although they were unusually aggressive and distrustful of adults they rapidly showed appropriate feelings of remorse over previous acts of violence and decreases in antisocial behavior. In contrast, the longer-retained children had crossed some kind of identity threshold in which they identified with their captors and viewed themselves as members of Renamo. Remorse and control over aggression occurred slowly in these boys and were accompanied by a gradual positive attachment to their new adult caretakers.

An intensive search for the boys' surviving family members was initiated. Most boys derived satisfaction from, and were able to identify with, parents, extended family members, and other members of their village or group. Only four boys who had been in Renamo for longer than a year were unable to adapt to their new family situation and continued to exhibit hostility, socially deviant behaviors, and a desire for revenge. For these boys the struggle to leave an environment in which killing was encouraged and to reenter one in which killing was condemned was a difficult one.

The acceptance, the recognition that these boys were victims, and the forgiveness of families, teachers, and community members played a major role in the remarkable recovery and resiliency of most of these boys.

Source: Boothby, N. (1991). *Children of war: Survival as a collective act.* Paper presented at the meeting on vulnerability and resiliency in children and families: Focus on children with disabilities. Baltimore, MD.

and yet demonstrate considerable resiliency following such traumatic experiences. Even children exposed to sustained conflict in Belfast and the violence generated by the "troubles" in Northern Ireland maintain conventional moral standards and show no increases in juvenile delinquency, antisocial behavior, or school absenteeism (Cairns, 1991). Repeatedly, resiliency is related to family support and to the continuity and availability of social networks (Garmezy, 1983; Garbarino, 1990). This is vividly demonstrated in the study by Neil Boothby presented in Box 12-4 of children involved in the civil war in Mozambique. In circumstances of peace or war, of tranquility or stress, of poverty or affluence, of transition or stability, but especially in adversity, a well-functioning family and a supportive social environment can serve to protect children and promote children's psychological well-being.

SUMMARY

THE FAMILY

- Socialization is the process by which an individual's standards, skills, motives, attitudes, and behaviors are shaped to conform to those regarded as appropriate for the society. Parents, siblings, peers, and teachers are major agents of socialization. They may influence the child by directly teaching standards, rules, and values; by providing role models; by making attributions about the child; and by creating the environment in which the child lives.

- The family is a complex system involving interdependent members whose functioning may be altered by changes in the behavior of one member, or relationships among family members, and by changes over time. In addition, family functioning is influenced by the larger physical, cultural, and social setting in which the family lives.

THE FAMILY AS AN AGENT OF SOCIALIZATION

- The family is both the earliest and most sustained source of social contact for the child. The beliefs and values of the culture are filtered through the parents, and their interpretation is influenced by the parents' personalities, religion, social class, education, and sex. Although rearrangements in family ties are increasingly common, family relationships remain the most intense and enduring bonds.

THE FAMILY: AN ECOLOGICAL, FAMILY SYSTEMS PERSPECTIVE

- Family processes involve mutual influences among family members and adaptation to changes in family members and their relationships as well as to circumstances external to the family. Seven basic principles of family processes have been identified in the ecological family systems perspective: wholism, organization, interdependency, boundaries, homeostasis, morphogenesis, and ecological relativism.
- The functioning of the marital system, parent-child system, and sibling system are interrelated and impact on children's adjustment. A satisfying marital relationship is often regarded as the basis of good family functioning which directly or indirectly affects the interactions with the children. Increased parent-child involvement and positive parent-child relationships have been found when spouses are mutually supportive; however, high conflict between parents is associated with negative feelings and behavior directed toward the children and disruptions in social and cognitive competence in the children. Boys are more susceptible to the negative effects of family disharmony than girls because they are more likely to be directly exposed to family conflict while girls are more likely to be protected from it.
- Children have an impact on the marital relationship. Pregnancy and the birth of a first child are associated with a shift toward more traditional masculine and feminine roles, so that the woman does more of the child care. Both mothers and fathers report declines in marital satisfaction following the birth of the first child, but they emerge more slowly in fathers. In addition, temperamentally difficult, deviant, or handicapped children place additional strain on the marriage, and may be enough to destroy an already fragile marriage.
- Parents typically begin to consciously and systematically socialize their child during the second year by saying "no" to some behaviors and by praising other behaviors. They also teach social rules directly, serve as models with whom the child may identify or imitate, and choose the environment and social life that their child will experience.
- Parents' relationships with their children have frequently been categorized along the dimensions of warmth-hostility and permissiveness-control.

Parental warmth is regarded as important to socialization because (1) the child is likely to try to maintain the approval of a warm parent, (2) the use of reasoning and explanation by warm parents permits the child to internalize social rules, and (3) warmth is associated with responsiveness to the child's needs. Some degree of parental control also is necessary for positive social development, however the goal is the child's self-regulation rather than external control by the parents. Thus, discipline strategies that present alternatives and rely on reasoning, and attributions about the child's positive intentions are the most effective.

- The interaction of the two dimensions of warmth-hostility and permissiveness-control forms a typology of four types of parenting: authoritative, authoritarian, indulgent, and neglecting. In a classic study Baumrind found that distinctive types of parental behavior were related to specific patterns of child behavior. She found that authoritative parenting involving high-warmth responsiveness and communication, but also consistent and firm control and high-maturity demands, led to the most positive emotional, social, and cognitive development in children and adolescents.

CHILD ABUSE: A BREAKDOWN IN THE FAMILY SYSTEM

- When family functioning breaks down, severe abuse of children may occur. It is most likely to occur when multiple risk factors are present without protective factors such as community resources, good health, high intelligence and education, and a social network.
- Child abuse is more likely to occur in large families, to children under age 3, and to children with physical and intellectual deficits or excessive fussiness and crying. Parents in abusive families often are socially isolated and have unrealistic beliefs about young children's abilities and about the parent-child relationship. Child abuse is preceded by escalating verbal and physical aggression that is often unpredictable and not contingent on the child's actual behaviors.
- Parents who abuse their children are frequently involved in a distressed marriage, have been abused by their own parents, are unemployed, poorly educated, and economically deprived. No single factor leads to abuse. It is a product of the interactions between family characteristics, nonsupportive environments, and cultural values that tolerate aggression and physical punishment. The consequences of abuse are less secure attachment in infants; problems with emotional regulation and aggressive behavior in toddlers; poor relations with peers and adults, academic problems, and low self-esteem as children get older.

THE SIBLING SYSTEM

- Most families in the United States have more than one child. The functioning of the family is affected by the number, sex, and spacing of the children. These factors influence both parent-child interaction and sibling interaction. As family size increases, parents and children have less opportunity for extensive contact, but siblings experience more contact. This results in greater independence, but lower self-esteem and academic achievement in children from large families.
- Variations in interactions with parents and siblings have been associated with birth order. Firstborn children often show emotional and behavioral

problems after the birth of a sibling, but the outcome is mediated by the mother's reaction and efforts to include the first-born and by the father's involvement. In general, parents tend to stay highly involved with firstborn children throughout their lives, often having higher expectations, exerting greater pressure for achievement, and requiring the acceptance of more responsibility.

- Birth order is associated with variations in sibling relations. Eldest children are typically expected to assume some responsibility for and self-control toward the younger children. This leads to both antagonistic behavior (e.g., biting, kicking) and more nurturant behavior toward younger siblings. Eldest children tend to focus on parents as sources of social learning, while younger children use both parents and older siblings as models and teachers.
- Different characteristics have been related to firstborn and later-born children. Firstborns are more adult-oriented, helpful, self-controlled, conforming, and anxious than their siblings, and they tend to excel in academic and professional achievement. Although only-children experience many of the same parental demands of firstborns, they do not have to compete with siblings. Thus, they tend to be high in achievement, but lower in anxiety, and make more positive adjustments in social relations both within and outside of the home.

SOCIAL CLASS, ETHNICITY, AND SOCIALIZATION

- Subgroups within our culture have both divergent values and different problems with which to cope. These may have an impact on the goals and methods of socialization parents choose. In addition to obvious differences in income, education, and occupation, lower-class and middle-class families may differ in other ways. Poor families generally experience little power within all of the systems (e.g., education, health, legal) that they encounter, leading them to feel helpless, insecure, and controlled by external forces. In addition, they may be involved in cycles of disadvantage, associated with accumulating risk factors that make childrearing difficult (e.g., teenage parenthood) and lead to adverse outcomes in the next generation. However, the stresses experienced by poor families often result in the formation of extensive support networks which involve both emotional support and services that cannot be purchased.
- Social class and ethnicity have been related to differences in childrearing. The specific differences in styles of childrearing and their effect on children are influenced by other systems—the workplace, the neighborhood, peers, and the school.

THE CHANGING AMERICAN FAMILY

- In recent years family roles and forms have become more varied as the number of working mothers has increased, the average size of households has decreased, and single-parent households have increased due to divorce and an increase in out-of-wedlock births.
- Divorce, life in a one-parent family, and remarriage should be viewed as part of a series of transitions that modify family roles and relationships and the lives of parents and children. In the first year following divorce, the children in single-parent households tend to be more disturbed, but in the long run most are able to adapt to their parents' divorce. However,

single, custodial mothers suffer from task overload, a marked decline in income, and a lack of social support.

- Family interactions immediately following divorce are characterized by inept parenting on the part of mothers and distressed, demanding, noncompliant behavior on the part of children. These effects seem to last longer and to be more negative for preadolescent sons than for daughters.
- Responses to remarriage vary depending on the previous family experience, but, in general, boys adjust more easily to a stepfather than do girls. However, the age at which the remarriage occurs is associated with the child's acceptance of the new parent. Adolescence is a particularly difficult time in which to have a remarriage occur. Antisocial behavior, depression and anxiety, school problems, and disruptions in peer relations have been associated with divorce and remarriage. In preadolescence, boys show the most negative responses to divorce and girls the most lasting resistance to remarriage; however, gender differences are rarely found in adolescence.
- The effects of maternal employment have been related to the mother's reason for working, the mother's satisfaction with her role, the demands placed on other family members, the attitudes of the other family members, and the quality of substitute care provided for the children. If each of these is positive, maternal employment does not have detrimental effects on children. Instead, positive effects, especially for girls, have been found.

CHILDREN, FAMILIES, AND WAR

- Research indicates that many children are able to survive the disruptions and violence associated with war without long-term adverse psychological effects. Resiliency is associated with continuity in social networks and social support but especially with sustained supportive family relationships.

CHAPTER

13

PEERS AND FRIENDS

In recent years, observers have begun to recognize the importance of individuals outside the family in the socialization process. With the rise in maternal employment and the increase in the availability of preschool education, the role of peers and teachers has been brought into sharp focus. The purpose of this chapter and the next will be to examine the contribution of the peer group and the school to childhood socialization.

Peers play a different role in children's development than do families. Although the child's relationship with parents is more intense and enduring than with peers, interactions among age-mates is more free and egalitarian. This quality of relationship with peers permits a new kind of interpersonal experimentation and exploration, and most particularly a new kind of sensitivity, which will serve as one of the cornerstones for the development of social competence, social justice, and the capacity to love (Piaget, 1951; Sullivan, 1953).

We will see that interactions with peers begin to shape children's behavior at an early age. These peer interactions are important factors in the development of social and cognitive competence in children. We will explore the development of friendships and some of the new techniques for helping children without friends. Finally we will examine group formation and cross-cultural differences in peer relations.

DEVELOPMENTAL TRENDS IN PEER INTERACTION

As early as the first year of life, infants are responsive to their peers. Babies in the first 6 months of life touch and look at each other and even cry in response to the other's crying. However, it is unlikely that these early responses are really social in the sense of the infant's seeking and expecting a social response from the other child. It is not until the second half of the first year that truly social behaviors begin to appear and infants begin to recognize the peer as a social partner (Brownell, 1990; Howes, 1987). Between 6 and 12 months they begin to attempt to influence their partner, by vocalizing, looking, touching, and waving at the other baby. Although they may engage in a little hitting or pushing as well (Bronson, 1981), a surprisingly high amount of social behavior among the baby crowd is friendly (Eckerman & Didow, 1988). Here is an example of a simple interchange:

> Larry sits on the floor and Bernie turns and looks toward him. Bernie waves his hand and says "da," still looking at Larry. He repeats the vocalization three more times before Larry laughs. Bernie vocalizes again and Larry laughs again. Then, the same sequence of one child saying "da" and other laughing is repeated twelve more times before Bernie turns away from Larry and walks off. Bernie and Larry become distracted at times during the interchange. Yet, when this happens, the partner reattracts attention either by repeating his socially directed action or by modifying it, as when Bernie both waves and says "da," reengaging Larry. (Mueller & Lucas, 1975, p. 241)

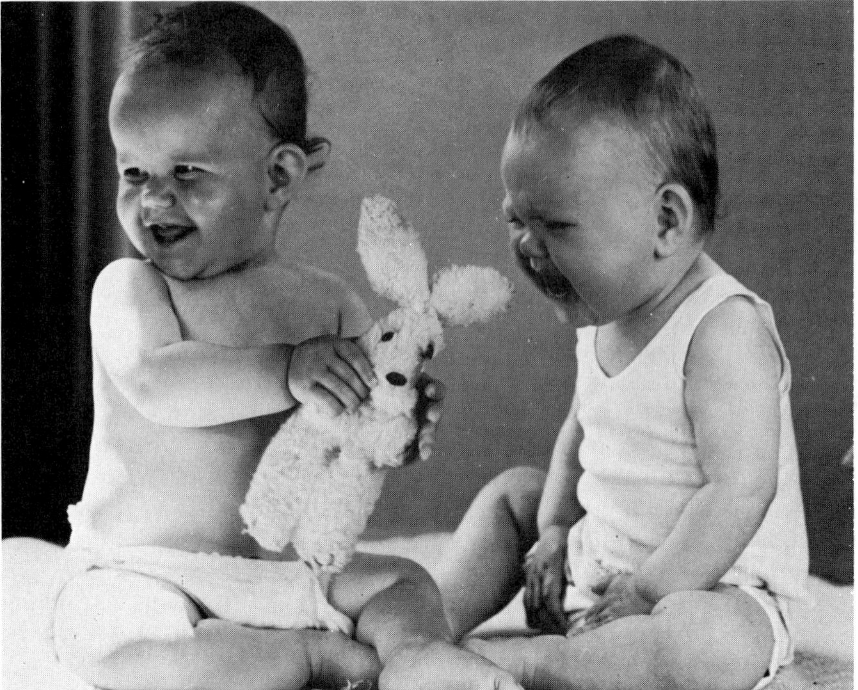

As infants grow older, positive as well as negative exchanges increase.

In the early toddler period (13 to 24 months), peers develop the capacity to engage in social interaction with a complementary structure (Howes, 1987). Partners exchange both turns and roles in action. Complementary role relationships are seen, such as "chaser" and "chased," "hider" and "seeker," or "giver" and "receiver." Now, when positive social interactions occur, they are more likely to be accompanied by a smile or a laugh or other displays of appropriate positive affect (Mueller & Brenner, 1977).

In the late toddler period (25 to 36 months), the main social achievement is the ability to share meaning with a social partner (Mueller, 1989). "When children communicate meanings, they know how to play a particular game, for example, being pulled in or pulling a wagon, the signal or invitation to begin the game (eye gaze, plus run to wagon), the signal to switch roles ('my turn' plus a tug) and how to communicate that they share this knowledge . . . children's communication of meaning makes possible a wider range of games and variations on the themes of games, as well as early forms of pretend play" (Howes, 1987, p.260).

As children's competence with peers develops, they shift toward increased social play and a greater preference for playing with peers rather than adults. This is clearly illustrated in the classic study by Eckerman and her colleagues, presented in Box 13-1.

Nevertheless, the social exchanges are different with mothers than with other infants (Vandell & Wilson, 1987). Mothers are more reliable and respond more often than infant peers. Exchanges with mothers are longer and more sustained, but the interchanges may be a bit one-sided, with mothers bearing the larger share of maintaining the interaction. In exchanges between infant peers, the two partners contribute more equally. Mothers make it easy; peers make you work for your social life!

Trends toward increased peer interactions continue throughout the preschool and elementary school years. In one investigation, over 400 children

BOX 13-1 I LOVE MY MOM, BUT OH YOU KID

We know that children enjoy playing with their parents, but given a choice would they rather play with their mothers, a peer, or a strange adult? In order to answer this question, children of three different age groups (10 to 12, 16 to 18, and 22 to 24 months) and their mothers were observed for twenty minutes in a playroom with another mother-child pair. As can be seen in Figure 13-1, older children, in contrast to the younger children, spent more time in social than in solitary play, and with increasing age children showed a marked preference for playing with each other, rather than with their mothers. At no time did children prefer to play with the unfamiliar adults, that is, the other mother.

Source: Eckerman, C. O., Whatley, J. L., & Kutz, S. L. (1975). Growth of social play with peers during the second year of life. *Developmental Psychology*, 11, 42–49.

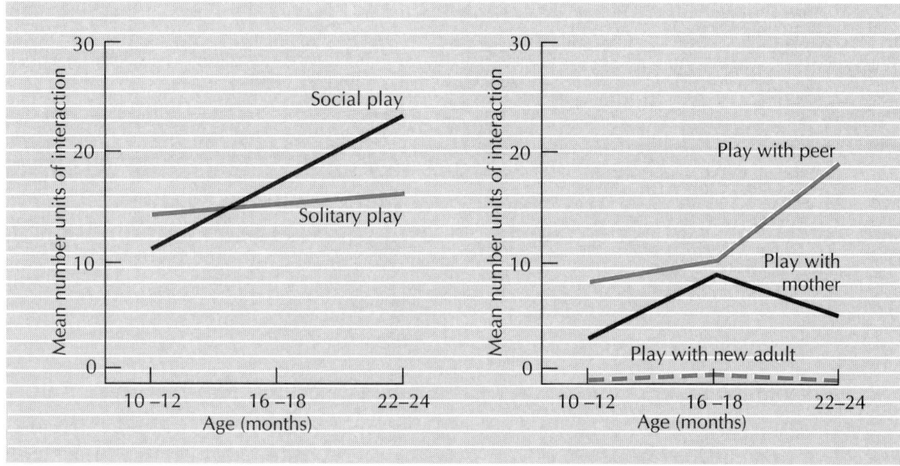

FIGURE 13-1

The development of social play. In social play, the child involves others—peer, mother, or new adult—in his activities with nonsocial objects. (From Eckerman, Whatley, & Kutz, 1975).

ranging from 1 to 12 years of age were observed at home or outdoors in a middle-class neighborhood (Ellis, Rogoff, & Cromer, 1981). Whom do children of various ages spend time with? Children were alone 26 percent of the time, solely with other children in 46 percent of the observations, and with both adults and peers 15 percent of the time. As Figure 13-2 shows, across development, time with adults decreases while time with child companions increases. These trends continue into adolescence with decreases in time with family and increases in time alone and time with friends (Larson & Richards, 1991). However, the kinds of peers that children choose change over age as well. Companionship with same-age peers increases with age. Up to age 7, children are just as likely to choose an opposite-sex companion, but after this age, boys are with boys and girls associate with girls more than with opposite-sex play partners. Adolescence, of course, heralds a reversal as cross-sex friendships begin to blossom once again (Parker & Gottman, 1989).

THE FUNCTIONS OF PEERS

We have spoken of socialization as learning to play by the rules of the social game. Peers are a source of information about these rules, and about how well the child is playing the game, from a different perspective than that of the family. It is the perspective of equals with common problems, goals,

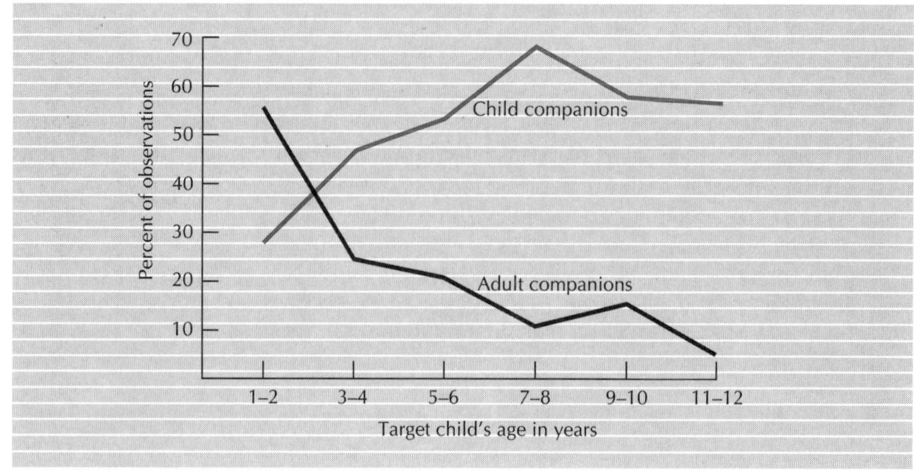

FIGURE 13-2
Developmental changes in children's companionship with adults and other children. (From Ellis, Rogoff, & Cromer, 1981.)

status, and abilities. How does the peer group influence the development of the child? In many of the same ways that parents do, through reinforcement, modeling, and social comparison and by providing opportunities for socializing and learning.

Peers as Reinforcers

As children grow older, the salience of peers as reinforcing agents and as models increases. Many parents, particularly of adolescents, bemoan the fact that their children ignore their wise advice while listening to, and emulating, their peers. Even throughout the preschool years, the frequency with which peers reinforce each other increases. Four-year-olds praise, attend to, or share with their peers more than 3-year-olds (Charlesworth & Hartup, 1967). Even among nursery schoolers, reciprocity is common: children tend to reinforce the same peers who reinforce them (Hartup, 1983). There is no doubt that peer reinforcement in the form of attention and approval affects the behavior patterns of the peer recipient. Numerous studies (Furman & Masters, 1980; Furman & Gavin, 1989) have documented that when peers are instructed to attend only to certain behaviors of a classmate (for example, helpful, cooperative ones) and to ignore other behaviors (for example, nasty, aggressive ones) significant behavioral change can be produced.

Peers as Models

Peers influence each other by serving not only as reinforcers but also as social models. Children acquire a wide range of knowledge and a variety of responses by observing the behavior of their peers. Imagine the situation of the new child at school. Through observation, he may rapidly learn that the children are expected to stand when the teacher enters the room, that it is risky to shoot spitballs, that the game of marbles is played with different rules in this school, and that contact with the big redheaded kid in the corner should be avoided because he is the class bully. Children also learn new social skills through imitation by modeling the dominant and (presumably socially skilled) member of the group (Grusec & Abramovitch, 1982). As children develop and internalize the rules, the need to rely on others decreases and they imitate others less often (Grusec & Abramovitch, 1982). However, rule learning may not be the only function of imitation. Since a majority of imitations are followed by positive outcomes in the form of maintained or increased social interaction, imitation may be an important way of maintaining such social interaction. As Eckerman (1989) has shown, even in 2-year-olds imitation sustains joint play between partners and leads to more sophisticated forms of play, such as social games.

It is interesting to speculate on how the rigid age grading of organizations and activities dealing with children, such as schools and team sports, may be limiting, or at least altering, their opportunities to learn from peers of different status.

Peers and the Social Comparison Process

There is another way in which peers may play an important role, and that is through serving as standards against which children evaluate themselves. Since there are few objective ways in which children can rate their characteristics, values, and abilities, they turn to other people, particularly to peers. They use others as a yardstick with which to measure themselves. This process of social comparison is one basis of the child's self-image and self-esteem.

> To whom do we turn when we engage in social comparison? Festinger (1954) persuasively claims that we seek people who are similar to ourselves as the comparison group. If a child wants to know how good a fighter he is, he doesn't dwell on how he'd do against Muhammad Ali but, instead, is more likely to take into account the outcomes of neighborhood scuffles he's been in, together with his impression of how tough his peers see him as being. How good a reader the child thinks he is is affected little by the fact that his mother can read many more words faster than he can, but much by his opportunity to observe other children in his class. Thus, the answer to the question of whom we turn to is the peer group. In matters of self-definition, the peer group has no peer. . . . (Hetherington & Morris, 1978, p. 60)

It has been found that the use of social comparison with the peer group as a means of self-evaluation in children increases markedly in the early elementary school years (Harter, 1983, 1990; Ruble, 1987; Zarbatany, Hartmann, & Rankin, 1990). The child's self-image and self-acceptance are closely associated with how he is received by peers.

Peers as Providers of Opportunities for Socializing and Learning

Peers provide opportunities for socializing and developing relationships, as well as the development of a sense of belonging (Zarbatany et al., 1990). These functions increase in importance as the child develops and spends increasing amounts of time with peers than family (Larson & Richards, 1991). Peers also offer a context for instructions and learning (Zarbatany et al., 1990). This is evident in Western cultures where children acquire skills in games and sports with peers or in tutorial relationships in schools (see Chapter 14). Peer-based learning is even more dramatically evident in other cultures, such as India and Africa where young children are cared for and instructed by older siblings and peers (Whiting & Edwards, 1988).

PLAY

Most of the social interchanges of peers occur in the setting of play, and children spend more of their time outside of school playing with friends than they do in any other activity. What is play? We would all agree that when children are chasing each other around the school grounds, swinging on swings, climbing trees, or engaging in a game of chess, Monopoly, or baseball, they are playing. What distinguishes play from other types of activity? It seems to be intrinsically motivated rather than imposed or directed by others, it is concerned with means not ends, it is free from external rules, and it is nonserious and highly engaging (Rubin, Fein, & Vandenberg, 1983).

The Functions of Play

What are the functions that play serves in the development of competence in children? First, play facilitates the cognitive development of children. It permits them to explore their environment, to learn about objects, and to solve problems (Garvey, 1990; Rubin et al., 1983). Second, play advances the social development of the child. Particularly in fantasy play, through acting out roles, children learn to understand others and to practice roles they will assume as they grow older (Haight & Miller, 1993). Finally, play permits children to solve some of their emotional problems, to learn to cope with anxiety and inner conflicts in a nonthreatening situation.

PLAY AND SOCIAL COMPETENCE

> Within the context of play, children are granted opportunities for discovery without risk. For example, in make-believe play, children can experiment with dominant and submissive roles with few adverse consequences. The child learns to recognize, and to act in, his or her own fantasies, as well as those of others. One play session may find the child taking a variety of roles, ranging from cowhand to lion to baby. Children can learn behaviors appropriate to each play situation in a relatively risk-free setting. They can test without fear the outer limits of what is acceptable. Later on in life, failure to abide by social conventions may prove more costly. (Fein, 1978, p. 269)

Fantasy play teaches children important social and cognitive lessons.

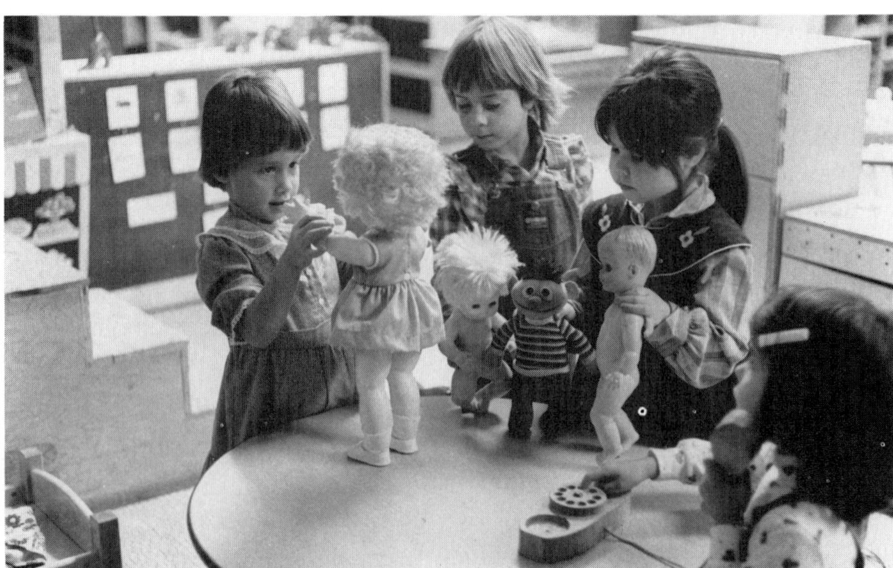

Imaginative play seems particularly important in the development of social competence. It permits children to practice their own future roles as well as to playfully experience the roles and feelings of others. It teaches children to function as part of the social group and to coordinate their activities and roles with those of other children.

Imaginative play initially appears about halfway through the second year although some children begin as early as 12 months of age (Haight & Miller, 1992). While it was often thought that pretend play was initially solitary, recent research suggests that it is often social. In the early years, pretend play is usually with the mother or siblings and as the child develops and gains opportunities to meet peers, other age-mates become common pretend-play partners (Dunn, 1988; Haight & Miller, 1993). Pretend-play partners vary across cultures as well. While mothers are most often the most frequent play partners in the United States, in Mexican villages mother-child pretend play is rare; instead, siblings and other young relatives are the child's primary partners for pretend play (Farver, 1992; Zukow, 1989). Pretend play usually involves symbolic activities such as feeding a doll with make-believe food in the United States. Often in rural agrarian Mexican communities pretend play focuses on functional roles such as routine adult activities like cooking or going to the market rather than fantasy themes (Zukow, 1989). By age 3, not only is make-believe play occurring but complex cooperative dramatic play is emerging (Fein, 1989; Garvey, 1990). This often takes a fanciful, exaggerated, roughhousing form that has been called "galumphing" (Miller, 1973). In aggressive play, children may have slow-motion fistfights and gun battles or prolonged, staggering, agonized death throes that would do credit to a diva at the Metropolitan Opera. The gestures are broad caricatures. The mock blows are telegraphed. Imaginative play peaks around 6 years of age when it involves highly coordinated fantasies, rapid transitions between multiple roles, and unique transformations of objects and situations.

Domestic fantasy play begins to decline in the school years as children play more structured games (Fein, 1981). Other types of fantasy, such as adventure fantasies, actually increase through preadolescence (Gottman & Parker, 1986) and even adults daydream, read, and enjoy space-adventure movies. Fantasy doesn't disappear but is expressed in different ways as children develop.

FANTASY AND THE CONTROL OF FEARS

Fantasy play also may be a way in which children learn to master fear. In their pretend play, they select something to be afraid of, rehearse the fear in a milder form, and then master the fear, often pretending to be or to conquer the feared object.

> A 4-year-old girl who was afraid of the dark and slept with a night-light often played a game involving dolls being afraid of the dark. With the lights off, the little girl would pretend to be the doll, would scream, and then, as mommy, would comfort the doll. After a few months, she announced to her parents that she no longer needed the night-light, and the theme of being afraid of the dark disappeared from her fantasy play. Both the girl and the doll were cured. (Gottman, 1986, pp. 26–27)

Moreover, boys and girls may differ in how they cope with fear (Gottman, 1986). Girls overcome fears by the use of emotional support and love to comfort, soothe, and ease the fear. Boys use humor or a strategy of mastery and involvement in which they pretend to be the thing they are afraid of or pretend to conquer it.

PLAY, PEERS, AND PATHOLOGY

Children's peer interactions and play not only provide a critical opportunity to acquire certain social competencies but also have been found to play an important role in the development of self-control and in working through or modifying problem behavior in children (Berndt & Ladd, 1989; Hartup, 1983).

Disruptions and rigidity in the play patterns of emotionally disturbed children frequently have been noted. Age-inappropriate play, deviations in play, and unpopularity with peers have consistently been found to be related to anxiety and emotional disturbance in children (Singer, 1977). Processes in imaginative play seem to be particularly vulnerable to the effects of psychological stress. It has been suggested that the failure to develop imaginative play is indicative of serious pathology, particularly of an aggressive, acting-out, impulsive type in children. Children who are undergoing psychological stress, such as those whose parents have recently gone through a divorce, show a marked rigidity in imaginative play (Hetherington, Cox, & Cox, 1979). They have fewer different characters involved in their fantasies, less frequently make different uses of the same objects in play, and are more bound to objects in play. They are less able to free themselves from reality. They need a stick to be a sword or a chair to be a castle. They rarely fantasize completely imaginary objects or people. They also show less reversibility in play. Once a stick is a sword, it is not subsequently transformed into a witch's broomstick or a magic wand or a horse. In addition, they show less diversity in both themes and affect. Another characteristic that is revealed in their play is one that is frequently reported in disturbed children: a preoccupation with aggression and an inability to assume the role of providing or caring for others in imaginative play. In addition, they seem to have great difficulty in moving from "I" to the assumption of another's role in fantasy play, in moving out of the self. Gould (1972) has remarked that the transition from the consistent use of "I" in play to play in which the child is able to assume or alternate in playing another's role ("I'm R2 D2" or "I'll play Batman") occurs between the ages of 3½ and 4. She notes that continued focusing on the "I" in fantasy play in children beyond this age tends to be associated with psychopathology and a lack of self-control.

Imaginativeness in play is associated not only with self-control, low impulsivity, and low aggression, but also with sharing, cooperativeness, independence, and social maturity (Rubin et al., 1983). In addition, children who show spontaneous imaginativeness in play are likely to show a broader range of emotions and more positive emotions than less imaginative children. They are more likely to smile, be curious and interested in new experiences, and express joy in play and in peer relations (Singer & Singer, 1980).

DETERMINANTS AND EFFECTS OF PEER ACCEPTANCE

Assessing Peer Status

A common approach to assessing peer status is the use of the *sociometric* technique. On this measure, children are asked to identify a number of peers "you especially like" and "don't like very much." Various measures of social status are derived from these simple procedures. On the basis of the number of nominations received from peers, *popular* children are those who receive the greatest "most like" scores and the fewest "like least" scores. *Rejected* children tend to elicit many "like least" nominations, in contrast to *neglected* or isolated peers, who are friendless but not necessarily disliked by their classmates. *Average* children have some friends but are not as well liked as popular peers. However, rejection can occur for a variety of reasons and researchers have recently distinguished different types of rejected children—aggressive and nonaggressive (French, 1988; Parkhurst & Asher, 1992; Williams & Asher, 1987). Based on a variety of measures, including sociometrics, teacher ratings and observations, French (1988) identified two subgroups of rejected boys; one group of rejected boys exhibited high aggression, low self-control, behavior problems, and withdrawn behavior. Boys in a second group were withdrawn but had no problems with aggression, self-control, and behavior problems. Similar subgroups of rejected children have recently been found for older children and girls as well as boys. Aggressive and submissive young adolescents who were low in their prosocial behavior were rejected by their peers (Parkhurst & Asher, 1992). Clearly children are rejected for different reasons.

Children have expectations about how other children should behave, but are these expectations the main basis for acceptance or rejection by the peer group? Let us examine some of the personal characteristics and social skills associated with being well received by peers. It would be pleasant to believe that children accept or reject one another on the basis of desirable personal attributes such as altruism, honesty, and sensitivity. However, a number of characteristics associated with peer acceptance are enduring, are difficult to change, and have little to do with the personal merits of the individual child. Children cannot readily modify their appearance, race, sex, age, or name, but these attributes are correlated with how well they are accepted by their peers.

First Impressions: Names and Appearance

Children often form first impressions of others based on surface characteristics, such as names and appearance. Children seem to respond adversely to unfamiliar or strange names. Sam, Karen, Michael, and Steven are going to be greeted more cordially by the peer group than are Dwayne, Darcy, Lana, and Abigail (McDavid & Harari, 1966). However, a cautionary note is in order.

> It is important not to overestimate the importance of names. It is only one of the many variables that influence social acceptance. United States presidents in the twentieth century have included a Theodore, Woodrow, Warren, Calvin, Herbert, Franklin, Dwight, Lyndon, and Gerald. Vice-presidents have included an Alben, Hubert, and Spiro. It may be that many Americans will vote for a man they wouldn't want as a friend; a more plausible interpretation is that names are not everything. (Asher, Oden, & Gottman, 1976, p. 3)

Although everyone has heard the maxim "Beauty is only skin deep," most people don't respond as if beauty were such a negligible attribute. Physical attractiveness plays an important role in the responses and evaluations of children and adults. Children as young as 3 to 5 years old can differentiate attractive from unattractive children and seem to judge these children on the basis of the same physical attributes as adults do (Langlois, 1985). (As we saw in Chapter 5, this ability to distinguish attractive and unattractive faces may even be evident in infancy.)

More desirable characteristics are attributed by both children and adults to attractive than to unattractive children. Aggressive, antisocial behavior and meanness are regarded as more characteristic of unattractive children, while behaviors such as independence, fearlessness, friendliness, sharing, and self-sufficiency are attributed to attractive children. Peers prefer pretty partners and view unattractive ones as unacceptable (Langlois & Stephan, 1981). Moreover, being good-looking is more important for girls' acceptance than for boys' acceptance (Vaughn & Langlois, 1983). Thus, the prevailing perception appears to be that what is beautiful is good.

Are these negative views of unattractive children all in the eye of the beholder, or are they based on behavioral reality? Langlois and Downs (1979) found no difference in the social behavior of attractive or unattractive 3-year-olds. However, unattractive, in contrast to attractive, 5-year-olds were more likely to be aggressive, to hit peers, to play in an active, boisterous manner, and to play with masculine toys. This age trend suggests that the aggressive behavior may be a response to being perceived negatively by others. Perhaps the negative expectations and perceptions peers and adults have of unattractive children foster the emergence of the very characteristics attributed to these children. Individuals do behave to some extent in a manner consistent with others' expectations. A self-fulfilling prophecy may be occurring.

Age and Peer Acceptance

To some extent the relation between age and playmate choice may be attributed to the fact that for small children, groups in Western societies tend to be age-graded. In many cultures such as India and Africa, for example, particularly those where older children are responsible for the care of younger children, multiage play groups are more common (Whiting & Edwards, 1988). However, in American culture, children play less than one-third of the time

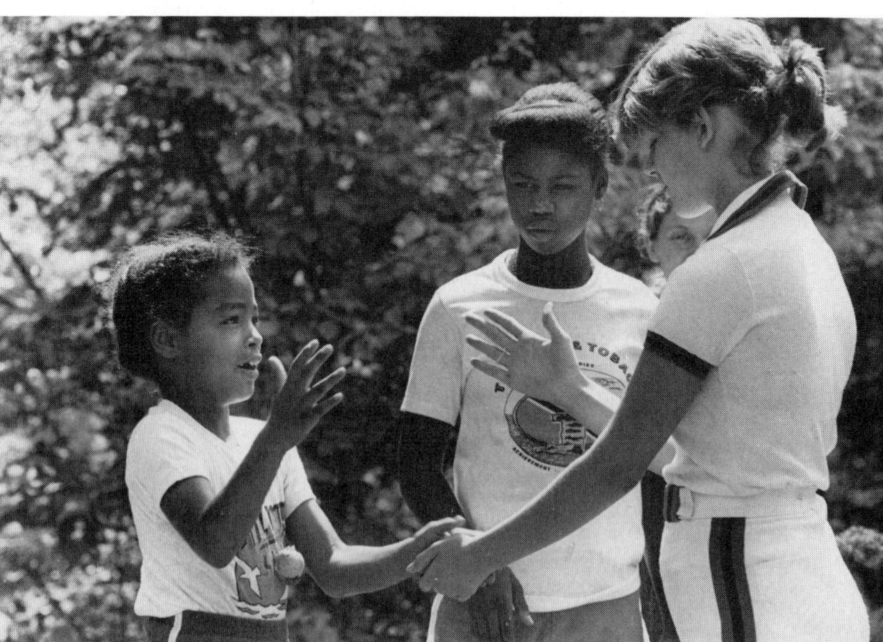

Cross-age friendships are common in some cultures.

with cross-age companions who are 2 or more years older; most of the time is spent with same-age peers (Ellis et al., 1981).

Older and younger peers serve different functions, and even young children seem to understand the various roles of peers of differing ages. Children attribute helping, assisting functions to older peers and play to age-mates and younger peers (Edwards & Lewis, 1979). Cross-cultural observations of children across three continents indicate that all children, in fact, generally understand the different functions of peers of various ages (Whiting & Edwards, 1988).

For children who are socially isolated or poorly adjusted, younger peers may provide an opportunity to acquire caretaking or social skills. Children with emotional or social problems may actually be driven out of their same-age peer groups and find acceptance easier to gain with younger children (Hetherington et al., 1979). In addition, younger children may be less threatening and exhibit social skills at a level more comparable to that of a disturbed or socially immature child. Interaction with younger peers may actually play a therapeutic role. In Harlow's famous studies, the adverse social effects of prolonged isolation on rhesus monkeys were reversed by a program of sustained contact with younger monkeys (Suomi & Harlow, 1972). Moreover, Furman, Rahe, and Hartup (1979) found that the sociability of socially withdrawn 4- and 5-year-old children could be improved by providing contact with younger peers.

In spite of the contributions of older and younger peers, the preference for same-age peers serves a very special role in social development.

> Age-grading would occur even if our schools were not age-graded and children were left alone to determine the composition of their own societies. After all, one can only learn to be a good fighter among agemates: the bigger guys will kill you, and the little ones are no challenge. Sexual experience at pubescence with bigger people is too anxiety-laden and sexual experience with littler ones is really not very interesting. (Hartup, 1976, p. 10)

Sex and Peer Acceptance

Sex of a child has a marked effect on playmate choices. Even in the preschool years, same-sex peers prefer to play together, a tendency that increases throughout the elementary school years (Maccoby, 1988). It is not until early adolescence, when dating begins, that this pattern changes. Often sex segregation begins early. Listen to these preschoolers:

> (Jake and Danny are on the big swing together.)
> **Laura** (running up, excited): Can I get on?
> **Jake** (emphatically): No!
> **Danny** (even more emphatically): No!!
> **Jake:** We don't want you on here. We only want boys on here. (After Laura leaves, I ask Jake why he said that.)
> **Jake:** Because we like boys—we like to have boys.
> (Rubin, 1980, p. 102)

Nor does it get any better. Consider this exchange at a junior high school:

> The chairs in Mr. Socker's room are arranged in the shape of a wide, shallow U. As the first few kids come into the room, Harry says to John, who is starting to

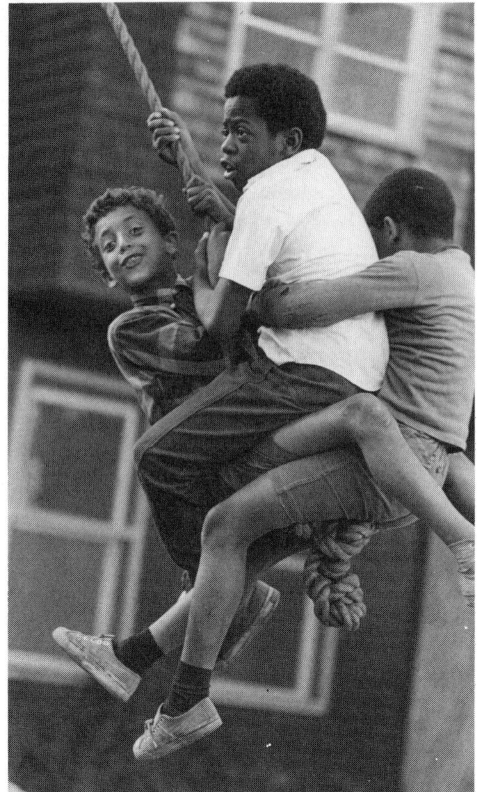

In the elementary school years, same-sex play groups are common.

sit down in an empty section of the room along one side of the U, "Don't sit there, that's where all the girls sit." Harry and John sit elsewhere. . . . (Schofield, 1981, p. 62)

There are exceptions, of course, but cross-sex friendships across the elementary school years often operate underground. A boy and girl might remain friends outside of school; for example, they may associate at church or in their neighborhood but generally keep their friendship a secret from their classmates (Gottman, 1986; Thorne, 1986). Some commentators see this low level of cross-sex interaction as unfortunate, since "cross-sex play can expose boys and girls to a wider range of behavioral styles and activities, expand their pool of potential friends and help to give them a fuller appreciation of the qualities that are in fact shared by the two sexes" (Rubin, 1980, p. 104)

What might be causing this self-imposed segregation and lack of acceptance between boys and girls? It seems to be related to differences in the interests and play patterns of girls and boys. In a study of boys and girls in elementary school, Thorne (1986) found marked differences in the play styles of the two sexes. Girls tend to play in low-energy games in small groups near the school building and close to adult supervision. Boys occupy nearly ten times the space of girls and play high-energy run-and-chase games when they are young and organized rule-oriented games when they become older. As they develop, older girls prefer unstructured, unorganized activities such as talking and walking in contrast to structured group activities (Savin-Williams, 1987). Moreover, young boys are involved in boisterous, rough-and-tumble play or play with blocks and cars (DiPietro, 1981; MacDonald &

Parke, 1984), while girls prefer art, books and dolls (Eisenberg, Murray, & Hite, 1982). Even the nature of pretend play differs, with boys more likely to enact superhero roles while girls portray familial characters (Connolly, 1980; Garvey, 1990). Play doesn't go well when Batman and Robin meet Mom and her little baby! It seems possible that as traditional sex roles break down, more shared interests will emerge and boys and girls will accept and interact with each other more. We will return to this issue when we explore gender roles in Chapter 14.

Social Skills and Peer Social Acceptance

Children of various social status differ in their *goals, strategies,* and *behaviors* in social encounters with their peers. First, not all children have the same goals. Renshaw and Asher (1983) presented third to sixth graders with a hypothetical social situation and then asked the children to choose an appropriate goal. Here are two examples

> Your parents have moved to a new town. This is your first day at a new school. As recess begins, the children go out to play.

or

> You ask a child who is new to the neighborhood to watch cartoons one Saturday morning. After about ten minutes, the child changes the channel without asking.

Children of high status, in contrast to low-status children, focused on wanting to be outgoing, sociable, and sympathetic toward other children (for example, "I'd want to start making friends with them"). Similarly, older children, in contrast to younger children, were more likely to suggest these types of positive, outgoing goals as well as more positive, accommodating goals, which focus on wanting to be friendly but in a more cautious manner ("I just like making friends slowly"). On the other hand, younger children suggested more hostile goals ("I'd want to get back at that kid").

Similarly, when children indicated what they would do in these situations, it was clear that children differed in their strategies as well. High-status children offered more direct and friendly strategies (for example, "I'd say, 'Can you play with me?' ") than low-status peers. Moreover, older low-status children were likely to avoid the situation ("I'd probably just go play outside by myself"), in contrast to their higher-status peers. As this study suggests, both the goals and the strategies of children of different social status vary.

In addition, social skills, such as reinforcing others and being able to initiate interactions effectively and communicate well, play an important role in social acceptance (Coie, Dodge, & Kupersmidt, 1990). The new child in school who tries to initiate a relationship by hovering silently or making aggressive or inappropriate responses is behind before he gets started. In contrast, the young child who asks for information (for example, "Where do you live?"), gives information (for example, "My favorite sport is basketball"), or tries to include the other child in a mutual activity (for example, "Wanna help me build this sand castle?") is well on the way to being accepted by the group (Putallaz & Gottman, 1981).

Persistence and flexibility help too. Many children are rebuffed or ignored when they first attempt to initiate interaction with their peers, but most children eventually succeed in being accepted. The ability to adopt alternative strategies when initial attempts fail is important in successful peer interaction. Variations in children's willingness to persist is due, in part, to their differing perceptions of "what happened" when their initial tries failed. Goetz and Dweck (1980) examined the explanations of elementary school children when their attempts to begin a new relationship with a peer were rebuffed. Some thought the problem was due to lack of effort or misunderstanding—a temporary problem that can be remedied. Others saw their failure as due to their own lack of ability ("It happened because it is hard for me to make friends"). In contrast to the former children, the latter children were less likely to continue to try to make friends. This is the same issue that we saw in our discussion of children's achievement behavior (Chapter 11). Children who believed they failed to solve a math problem because they were "bad at math" gave up trying sooner than their classmates who thought they simply didn't try hard enough.

Recent studies (Coie et al., 1990) have identified behaviors associated with peer social status. They compared children of four different social statuses: popular, average, rejected, or neglected. Each social status is associated with distinctive social behaviors. Popular boys who are engaged in more prosocial behavior are rarely aggressive, and they help set the rules and norms for the group. Rejected boys are aversive, aggressive, and active, while neglected boys are less aggressive, less talkative, and more withdrawn.

Often children who are unpopular have multiple cognitive and behavioral deficits and it is the combination of problems that leads them to be unsuccessful with their peers. Box 13-2 illustrates how a variety of shortcomings among rejected or aggressive children often work together to lead to poor peer relations. Although single factors are important, in reality, these deficits often operate together to produce these social outcomes.

Next we turn to the consequences of being unpopular with peers.

Consequences of Being Unpopular

Being unpopular among your peers can lead to both short-term and long-term problems. First, you feel differently if you have friends than if you are not accepted by your peers. Unpopular children report feeling lonely and socially dissatisfied (Asher, Hymel, & Renshaw, 1984; Asher, Parkhurst, Hymel, & Williams, 1990; Cassidy & Asher, 1992). Turn to Table 13-1 for some moving examples of children's descriptions of how it feels to be lonely. As Figure 13-3 shows, rejected children are especially likely to feel lonely, while neglected children are no more lonely than average-status children. Children who are rejected as a result of their submissiveness feel lonelier than aggressive rejected children (Parkhurst & Asher, 1992). It is being actively disliked by many of one's peers, not simply the lack of friends in a class, that leads to strong feelings of social isolation and alienation. However, having a friend helps. Rejected children who have a stable friendship with at least one other child feel less lonely than rejected and friendless children (Sanderson & Siegal, 1991; Parker & Asher, 1992).

What are the long-term consequences of being a low-accepted child? Poor peer relationships in childhood do have implications for later adjustment. In their recent review, Parker and Asher (1987) found that children who were poorly accepted by their peers were more likely to drop out of school and be more likely to develop patterns of criminal activity than well-accepted children. As Box 13-3 shows, even children who are shy and withdrawn follow a different life-course pattern than less shy children.

TABLE 13-1

EXAMPLES OF CHILDREN'S LONELINESS NARRATIVES

The following are examples of children's stories about their own loneliness experiences and reflect the variety of contexts and relational provisions cited by children in describing loneliness.

Female, Grade 6

"Today everybody's going to Mary Ann's party in the group. I'm sort of the one that gets left behind. I'm not invited to the party so I won't do anything on the weekend. Anywhere the whole group goes, I don't."

(Why did that make you feel lonely?) "I'm just the person that gets left back. Maybe they don't realize that I get left, that I'm there, but it happens all the time."

Male, Grade 5

"I was living in Greenvalley. It was a Sunday. All the stores were closed, I had no money. Jason, a friend, had to go to his aunt's. I decided to call on Jamie, but no one was home. I went to turn on the TV and only church stuff was on. I went upstairs to play with my toys, but it was so boring. The dog was behind the couch so I didn't want to bother him. Mom was sleeping. My sister was babysitting. It wasn't my day."

(Why did that make you feel lonely?) "There was no one to talk to or play with, nothing to listen to."

Female, Grade 8

"Last year, at the beginning of the year, I had a friend, Sandy. Then she went with another group of people who didn't like me. They would walk away when I'd go over to Sandy. They started spreading rumors about me to make everyone hate me. Sandy also didn't hang around me 'cause her other friends didn't like me."

(Why did that make you feel lonely?) "I didn't have any friends. They didn't want to be near me."

Source: Hayden, Turulli, & Hymel (1988).

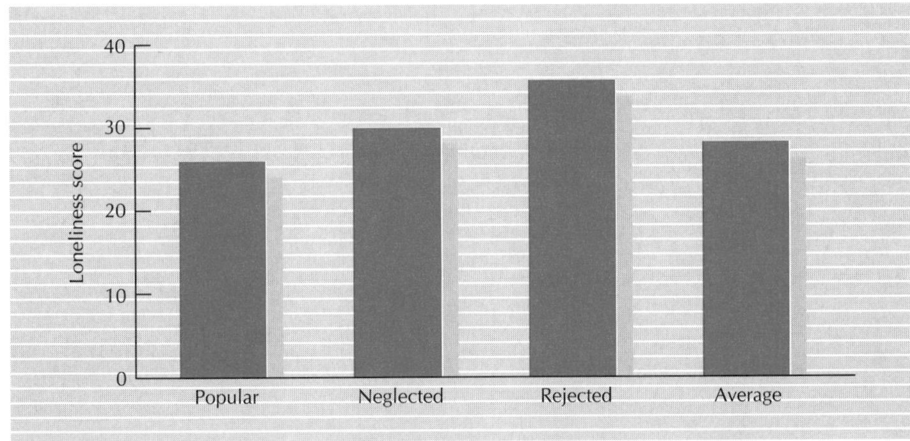

FIGURE 13-3

Loneliness and status. (From: Asher et al., 1984)

Unfortunately for socially unpopular children, social standing tends to remain stable across time and in different situations. Across a five-year span, Coie and Dodge (1983) found modest stability for popular children and neglected children. While popular children might lose their high status and neglected children might become more socially accepted, children who were once rejected have a higher chance of staying rejected across a wide time span. In part, the stability is due to "reputational bias," which means that

BOX 13-2 MISREADING THE SOCIAL WORLD: AN INFORMATION PROCESSING APPROACH TO UNDERSTANDING PEER RELATIONS

To succeed in forming and maintaining good relationships with other children requires that the child understand the behavior of the other child and make the appropriate responses to the partners' behavior. This is not a simple task, but requires that the child make a series of decisions in order to evaluate the situation and respond according to his assessment. Kenneth Dodge and his colleagues believe that how well children make these decisions plays a central role in how likely they are to be successful with their peers. These investigators suggest that the child goes through the five decision-making steps that are outlined in Table 13-2.

At each stage of the decision-making chain, the child can make a decision that will be either helpful or misleading. Consider Marianne—a socially competent 7-year-old who encounters two children playing a board game. She carefully surveyed the situation and noticed that one of the children smiled at her (step 1—encoding of cues). Next she interpreted this cue to mean that the girl wanted her to play too (step 2—interpretation). In the third step, she thought about what she could do (smile back, ask to join in, make a positive comment, leave, and so on). Next she considered the likely reaction that each of these actions would elicit from the girls and decided to make a friendly comment about the game. Finally, when the smiling girl looked up again, she smiled and said, "Looks like fun." The pair of girls subsequently invited her to play the next game.

Or consider Anne—a not very socially competent 8-year-old. When she surveyed the two girls playing, she failed to notice the smile from one of the girls and instead noticed their clothes. At the next step, because she failed to see the smile she thought that they were unfriendly. At the third step she thought about what she might do, but could only think of mean things ("Why are you so unfriendly?" "It's not nice not to let me play"). She decided that these strategies would work and finally blurted out "You two are really selfish not to let me play." And it is no great surprise that they didn't invite her to play!

Dodge and his coworkers tested this model by comparing 5- to 7-year-old children who were rated as either socially competent or socially incompetent by their

TABLE 13-2 A SOCIAL INFORMATION PROCESSING MODEL OF COMPETENCE

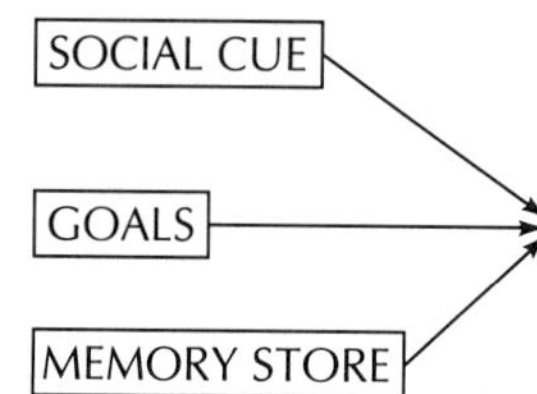

1. Encoding process
    - A. Perception of social cues
    - B. Search for cues
    - C. Focus (attention to cues)
2. Interpretation process
    - A. Integration of memory store, goals, and new data
    - B. Search for interpretations
    - C. Match of data to programmed rule structure
3. Response search process
    - A. Search for responses
    - B. Generation of potential responses
4. Response decision process
    - A. Assessment of consequences of potential responses
    - B. Evaluation of adequacy of potential responses
    - C. Decision of optimal response
5. Enactment process
    - A. Behavior repertoire search
    - B. Emission of response

teachers and peers. Children were presented with a videotape of a situation similar to the one described above where the child is trying to join the play of two other children. They were then asked about each of the five steps in the model to see if children of different levels of competence respond differently. Just as the two girls in our example differed, so did the children in Dodge's study; the incompetent children were less likely to correctly notice and interpret the cues, generated less competent responses, chose less appropriate responses, and were less skilled at actually enacting or carrying out the behavior. Moreover, children were then asked to participate in an *actual* peer-group entry task with two peers from their classroom. Measures of each of the five steps in the model predicted children's competence and success at this task; children who understood what to do were better at the real task of gaining entry into the peer group (see Figure 13-4). In a related study, well-adjusted children as well as aggressive 8- to 10-year-olds were presented with a situation involving their response to a provocation by a peer (for example, a peer knocks over your block tower—in an ambiguous way so you can't tell if it was accidental or not). Figure 13-5 shows that aggressive children showed more deficits at each of the processing steps. In addition, the child's processing ability successfully predicted how children responded when actually provoked by another child. These studies provide strong support for the role of cognitive factors in understanding children's social relationships with peers. Deficits in social understanding can lead to poor social relationships. In this case, thought and action are clearly linked.

Sources: Dodge, K. A. (1986). A social information processing model of social competence in children. In M. Perlmutter (Ed.), *Minnesota Symposium on Child Psychology* (Vol. 18). Hillsdale, NJ: Erlbaum; Dodge, K. A., & Feldman, E. (1990). Issues in social cognition and sociometric status. In S. R. Asher & J. D. Coie (Eds.), *Peer rejection: Origins, consequences and intervention*. New York: Cambridge University Press; Dodge, K. A., Pettit, G. S., McClaskey, C. L., & Brown, M. M. (1987). Social competence in children. *Monographs of the Society for Research in Child Development,* 51 (2, Serial No. 213).

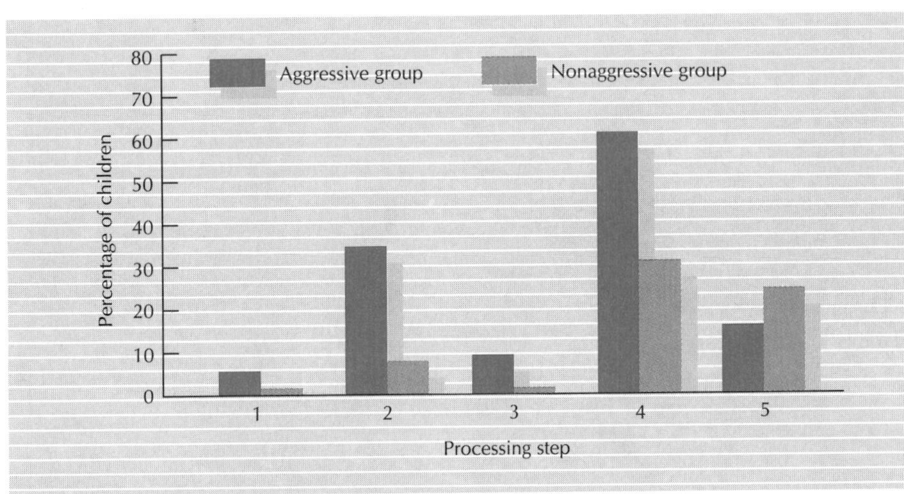

FIGURE 13-4

Percentages of children displaying processing deficits in the group entry domain. (From: Dodge et al., 1986.)

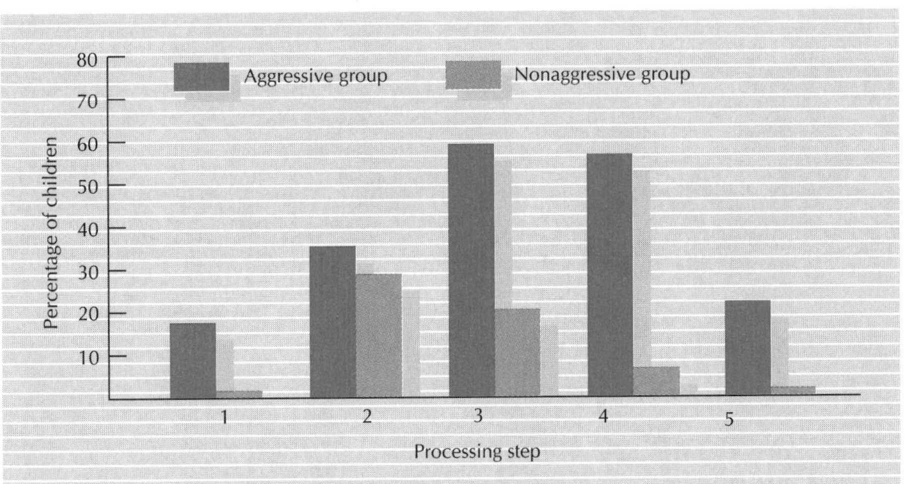

FIGURE 13-5

Percentages of children displaying processing deficits in the provocation domain. (From: Dodge et al., 1986.)

children interpret the behavior of their peers based on their past encounters and feeling about these children (Hymel, Wagner, & Butler, 1990). When judging the negative behavior of previously disliked or liked peers, children are more likely to deny or minimize actor responsibility for the negative behavior in the case of a liked than a disliked peer. Liked peers are given the "benefit of the doubt;" disliked peers are not. Reputations color how children interpret peer actions and help account for the stability of behavior across time (Hymel, 1986). However, it is not reputation alone that accounts for the stability of peer ratings of rejected children; behavior matters too.

Nor is the stability due simply to the fact that the composition of the examined peer groups remained the same over time. Even in new groups with unfamiliar peers, children tend to retain their social rank (Coie et al., 1990). When unfamiliar boys of differing social status were brought together in play groups once a week for six weeks, within three weeks their social status in these new groups was very similar to their social status in their classrooms. Boys who were rejected in school were similarly shunned by their peers in the new group, just as the popular boys in school retained their high social rank in the new setting (Coie & Kupersmidt, 1983). In view

When they are left out or rejected by their peers, children may experience feelings of loneliness.

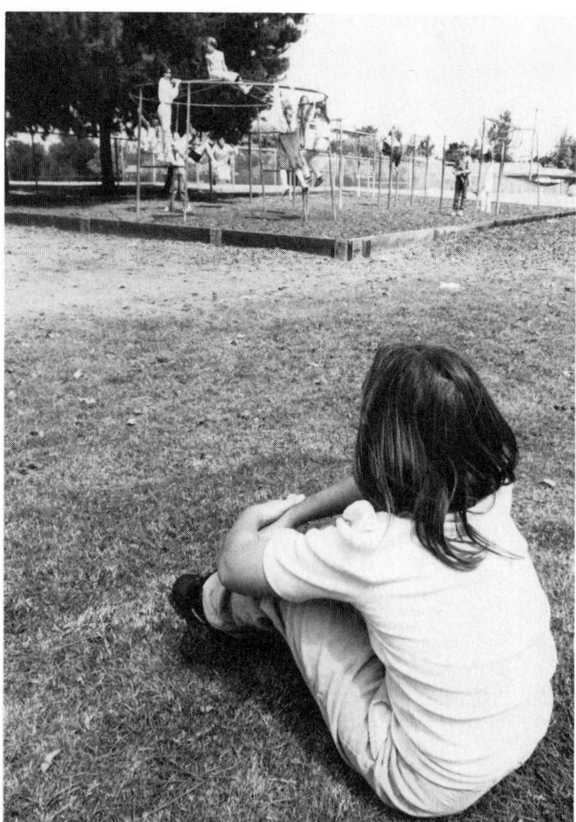

BOX 13-3 WHAT HAPPENS TO SHY CHILDREN—THIRTY YEARS LATER?

What happens to shy children as they grow up. To find out, Caspi, Elder, and Bem (1988) traced the developmental patterns of children who had been rated in terms of their shyness between 8 and 10 years of age. Shyness was indexed two ways. First, a shyness scale ranged from high (acute discomfort to the point of panic in social situations) to low (enjoys meeting new people). In addition, children were rated on a measure of social reserve; children who were high on the scale were "emotionally inhibited that leads to feelings of strain and awkwardness in others" while children who were low were "spontaneous and uninhibited in their expression of feelings." Shyness, then, consisted of both social anxiety and inhibited social behavior. Teachers rated these children when they were 10 to 12 years old and found the shy boys and girls to be less friendly, less sociable, more reserved, more withdrawn, and to be followers rather than leaders. These children were reinterviewed twenty and thirty years later in adulthood. Boys who were rated as shy in childhood were delayed in marrying, becoming fathers, and establishing stable careers (see Figure 13-6). Moreover, as adults these shy boys achieved less occupationally than their less shy peers. "Men who were reluctant to enter social settings as children appear to have become adults who are more generally reluctant to enter the new and unfamiliar social settings required by the important life course transitions into marriage, parenthood and career" (Caspi et al., 1988, p. 827).

Shy girls, on the other hand, were more likely than their peers to follow a conventional pattern of marriage, childbearing, and homemaking. The majority (56 percent) of women with a childhood history of shyness were more likely either to have no history of outside employment or to terminate employment at marriage or childbirth with no later reentry into the labor force. In contrast only 36 percent of their more outgoing peers followed this more traditional pattern. In addition, women with a history of childhood shyness were married to men who had higher occupational status at midlife than husbands of other women. Clearly the life course of men and women is shaped, in part, by the cultures' sex-role prescriptions. "The women who as children moved 'away from the world' were dispositionally suited to adhere to the female social clock" (Caspi et al., 1988, p. 829).

Shyness does have consequences for later development, but whether you are male or female is a significant determinant of the form that early shyness will eventually assume. Note, however, that these patterns are "normal" and do not imply that shy children are at risk for later problems. The life-course patterns may differ, but they should not be viewed as maladaptive.

Source: Caspi, A., Elder, G., & Bem, D. (1988). Moving against the world: Life course patterns of shy children. *Developmental Psychology*, **24**, 824–831.

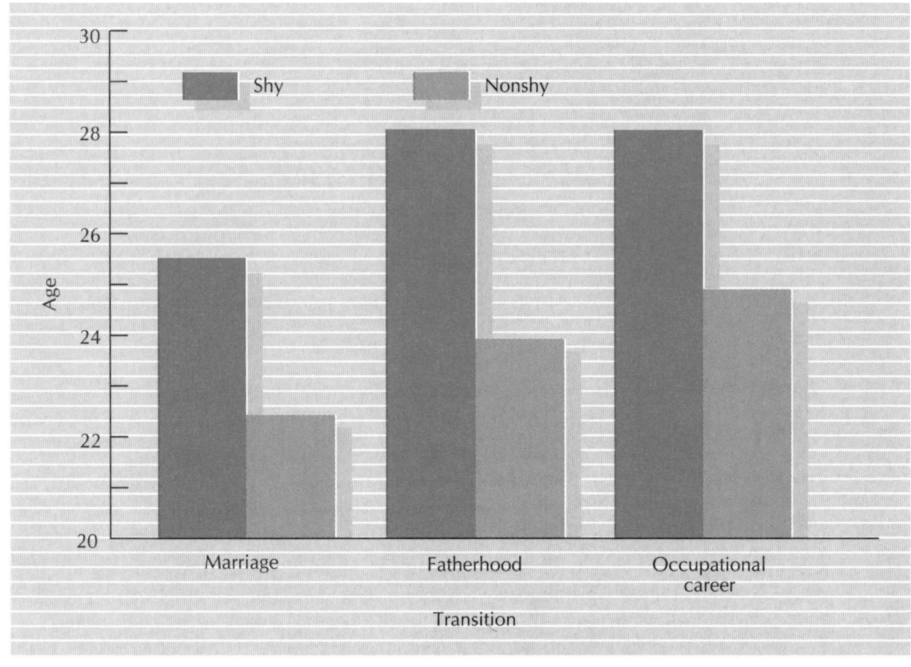

FIGURE 13-6
Timing of life transitions as a function of shyness in late childhood. (From: Caspi et al., 1988.)

of the difficulties that rejected children encounter, it is important to find ways to help them.

Helping Children with Peer Problems

What can we do to help socially isolated and rejected children become more accepted and perhaps less lonely? Social acceptance can be increased by shaping socially desirable behavior through reinforcement or modeling and by directly coaching social skills (Mize & Ladd, 1990). Coaching involves teaching a general concept or strategy, usually through providing examples of successful approaches (see Table 13-3). Ladd (1981) coached unpopular third graders on three communication skills: asking positive questions, offering useful suggestions or directions, and offering supportive statements. Children participated in eight forty- to fifty-minute sessions over a three-week period. During these sessions, the adult "coach" verbally instructed children in the concepts, guided them through rehearsals of the ideas, letting the children practice on their own while playing with a classmate, and

TABLE 13-3 SAMPLE OF COACHING SCRIPT: CONCEPT OF PARTICIPATION

Coach:	Okay, I have some ideas about what makes a game fun to play with another person. There are a couple of things that are important to do. You should *cooperate* with the other person. Do you know what cooperation is? Can you tell me in your own words?
Child:	Ahh . . . sharing.
Coach:	Yes, sharing. Okay, let's say you and I are playing the game you played last time. What was it again?
Child:	Drawing a picture.
Coach:	Okay, tell me then, what would be an example of sharing when playing the picture-drawing game?
Child:	I'd let you use some pens too.
Coach:	Right. You would share the pens with me. That's an example of cooperation. Now let's say you and I are doing the picture-drawing game. Can you also give me an example of what would *not* be cooperating?
Child:	Taking all the pens.
Coach:	Would taking all the pens make the game fun to play?
Child:	No.
Coach:	So you wouldn't take all the pens. Instead, you'd *cooperate* by sharing them with me. Can you think of some more examples of cooperation? (The coach waited for a response.) Okay, how about taking turns. . . . Let's say you and I . . . (etc.). Okay, I'd like you to try out some of these ideas when you play (name of new game) with (other child). Let's go and get (other child), and after you play, I'll talk to you again for a minute or so and you can tell me if these things seem to be good ideas for having fun at a game with someone.

Source: Oden & Asher (1977).

reviewed the concepts following the practice session. The review phase involved teaching the children to evaluate their own behavior in relation to what they had learned about successful social interaction. Assessments immediately after the training program and again four weeks later indicated that the coached children's classroom behavior improved and their popularity increased. The control group, which received no coaching, showed no improvement. Even young children can be helped. Mize and Ladd (1990) were able to improve the social relationships of neglected and rejected preschool children with similar types of interventions.

A WORD OF CAUTION

Do all unpopular children need help? As we noted earlier, unpopularity can assume a variety of forms—and not all kinds of unpopular children need to be changed. Rejected children who appear to retain their outcast status are at the most risk for later problems of social adjustment and clearly could benefit from intervention. On the other hand, neglected children, who have often been the focus of intervention, probably are not at such high risk for later problems; moreover, as Coie and Dodge (1983) found in their five-year longitudinal study, many neglected children are quite likely to become more socially accepted and competent. Besides, there may be nothing wrong with being preoccupied with puzzles and play dough rather than peers. The preschooler with a passion for puzzles may be the later college computer whiz! Rubin (1982; Rubin & LeMare, 1990) has found that preschoolers who play simple repetitive games such as banging on the table either alone or close to other children tend to be less socially competent. Similarly, children who engage in dramatic play and pretend to be Mr. Batman by themselves are not very socially skilled. But there are other kinds of lone play that are not related to indices of social competence, such as solitary constructive play—artwork, puzzles, block construction—a frequent kind of play among preschoolers. Moreover, some forms of solitary activity, such as constructive play in which children sit around a table and individually put together Lego sets or practice their artistic skills as budding Picassos, are highly predictive of social competence. In summary, doing things alone may not be necessarily bad. Only some kinds of solitary activity are indicators of later social problems.

Parents as Peer Promoters

Parents influence their children's peer relationships in a variety of ways. Figure 13-7 illustrates three common ways in which parents contribute to their children's developing peer relationships. First, they serve as partners with whom the child may acquire skills that help her to successfully interact with other children. This first pathway can take several forms. As we saw in Chapter 7, infants who developed secure attachments to their mothers became socially competent preadolescents (Elicker, Egeland, & Sroufe, 1992). In addition, the ways that parents are currently interacting with their children is related to their social behavior with peers. Mothers of higher-status first graders were found to interact in a more positive and agreeable manner with their children and to be more concerned with feelings, both their own and those of their children, than mothers of lower-status first-grade children; in contrast, mothers of lower-status children were found to exhibit more negative and controlling behavior with their children than did mothers of higher-status children (Puttalaz, 1987; Puttalaz & Heflin, 1990). Similar findings are evident for fathers as well (Parke, Cassidy, Burks, Carson, & Boyum, 1992).

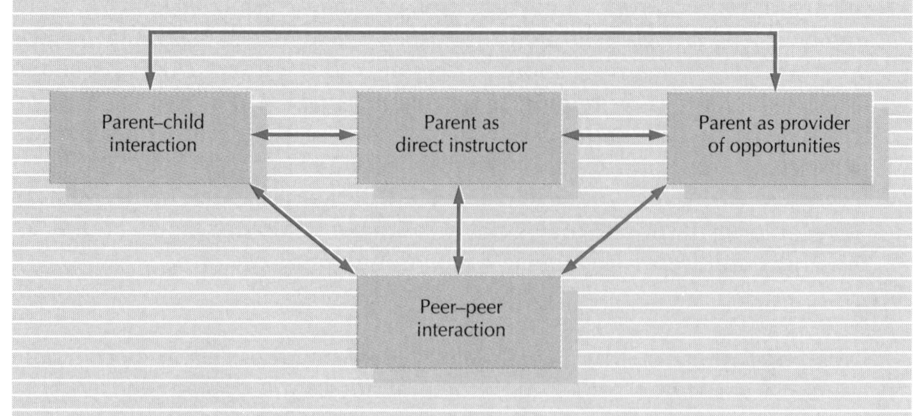

FIGURE 13-7
Family-peer relationships: Three modes of linkage.

A second way in which parents influence their children's peer relationships is through their roles as coaches or educators (Bhavnagri & Parke, 1985; 1991; Lollis & Ross, 1992). They can give advice, support, and directions about the most helpful strategies for their children's conduct with their peers. In a comparison of parents of popular and unpopular children, Australian researchers (Finnie & Russell, 1988; Russell & Finnie, 1990) found differences in the advice and guidance that mothers would give when their children encountered a problem with a peer (for example, how can the child reduce conflict after having sand thrown at him or her during play in the sand box or how should the child gain entry to a group after being told to go away). Mothers of children of high social status suggested more positive-direct approaches (for example, a positive alternative action) and more rule-oriented strategies (tell the other child that they can take turns). In contrast, mothers of low-status children used more avoidance strategies (not bother about it if another throws sand) or vague-unspecific tactics (for example, the child should "look friendly" or "get to know the children"). Not only did the mothers differ in knowledge, but they behaved differently when assisting their children in joining in and playing with two unfamiliar peers. Mothers of high-social-status children used more skillful strategies (for example, encouraged communications, helped their own child join conversation of the dyad), whereas mothers of low-social-status children used less skillful strategies (took control of the game, disrupted play patterns of the children) or avoided active supervision of her child. Parents can clearly be helpful but some ways seem more effective than others.

A third way in which parents influence their children's peer relationships is through their role as providers of opportunities for peer interaction (Ladd, Muth, & Hart, 1992; Parke et al., 1989). This can assume a variety of forms. Parents can set the stage through their choice of a neighborhood that may increase or limit the children's opportunities to find suitable playmates. As one parent put it: "Just look at this street—kids, swing sets, swimming pools everywhere. It's a kid's paradise. That's one of the main reasons we moved. Before, we were in another section of town. We had a beautiful house, but there weren't many kids to play with" (Rubin & Sloman, 1984, p. 231). As Box 13-4 shows, research supports parental views that neighborhoods make a difference to children's peer relations.

Especially in the case of young children, parents play an important role as "social arrangers." Two-year-olds generally have trouble finding age-mates

BOX 13-4 SOME NEIGHBORHOODS MAKE FRIENDSHIPS EASIER THAN OTHERS

Choosing a neighborhood in which to live can have a serious impact on the nature of children's friendships. In a study of 12-year-olds' social relationships, Medrich and his colleagues (Berg & Medrich, 1980; Medrich, 1981) discovered wide variations in friendship patterns across neighborhoods. One neighborhood in Oakland, California, "Monterey," is white and affluent, with large homes on oversized lots and plenty of space between houses. Friends often live far apart. The steep hills and lack of sidewalks make it hard for friends to see each other on their own. Instead of spontaneous meetings and unplanned play, parents often chauffeur children to preplanned social events. In contrast, "Yuba" is a low-income black inner-city neighborhood. Houses are close together, friends are abundant and nearby, and play tends to be more extensive and spontaneous and less organized and planned. Friendship patterns in the two areas differ also. In Monterey, children are unusually selective in their friendships; many have only one or two friends whom they choose because they have "something in common." In contrast, children of Yuba typically have four or five close friends, are less exclusive in their selections, and move in large groups. Clearly, ethnic and economic factors may account for some of these differences, but the physical environment of the two neighborhoods is probably responsible as well. Of course, both settings have advantages and drawbacks. The affluent children complain that there are not enough children around and miss the freedom to control their social activities, but enjoy the abundance of play spaces. The poor children gain more freedom and a wider network of friends, but are often crowded and have fewer places to play. Neighborhoods do make a difference in the ways in which friendships develop.

Source: Berg, M., & Medrich, E. A. (1980). Children in four neighborhoods: The physical environment and its effects on play and play patterns. *Environment and Behavior,* 12, 320–348; Medrich, E. A. (1981). *The serious business of growing up: A study of children's lives outside the school.* Berkeley: University of California Press.

without help from a parent. Parents facilitate their children's peer contacts by scheduling visits between young friends, enrolling children in organized activities, and of course fetching, carrying, and chauffeuring them from one house or social event to another (Rubin & Sloman, 1984). And arranging makes a difference. Children of parents who tended to arrange peer contacts had a larger range of playmates and more frequent play companions outside of school than children of parents who were less active in initiating peer contacts. In the school context, boys with parents who initiated peer contacts were better liked and less rejected by their classmates than were boys with noninitiating parents; girls did not differ in their acceptance by their classmates as a function of parental initiation activities (Ladd & Golter, 1988; Ladd et al., 1992).

In summary, parents play an important role in promoting children's peer relations. It is important to remember that children's peer relations may influence parents as well. For example, the parents of children's playmates may serve as a source of friends for adults. As in most domains of development, bidirectional influences are common.

BEYOND PEER ACCEPTANCE: THE DEVELOPMENT OF CHILDREN'S FRIENDSHIPS

In our exploration of peers, we have focused largely on how well children are accepted by their classmates or peer group. Although this group perspective is an important one, children also develop close dyadic relationships with a few peers that we commonly refer to as *friendships*. "The essentials of friendship are reciprocity and commitment between individuals who see themselves more or less as equals" (Hartup, 1989, p. 124).

However, as the following exchange indicates, young children may not necessarily be able to define a friend very easily. What is a friend? Here is one child's answer:

> **Interviewer:** Why is Caleb your friend?
>
> **Tony:** Because I like him.
>
> **Interviewer:** And why do you like him?
>
> **Tony:** Because he's my friend.
>
> **Interviewer:** And why is he your friend?
>
> **Tony** (with mild disgust): Because—I—choosed—him—for—my—friend. (Rubin, 1980)

Children seem to have certain expectations about relationships with friends that appear across different kinds of peer groups (Keller & Wood, 1989). In addition, these expectations about friends seem to progress in three stages (Bigelow, 1977; Bigelow & LaGaipa, 1975).

1. A *reward-cost stage.* This stage emerges at about grades 2 or 3 and is characterized by similar expectations, common activities, and propinquity (nearness).
2. A *normative stage.* At about grades 4 and 5, similar values and attitudes toward rules and sanctions appear.
3. An *emphatic stage.* In this stage, which emerges at about grades 6 and 7, self-disclosure, understanding, and shared interests occur. This is the relationship that Sullivan (1953) has so poignantly described as "chumship" and which represents a unique kind of intimacy in the development of children.

The progression of these stages and attributes associated with them are presented in more detail in Table 13-4. The expectations about friendship that emerge at each stage do not disappear with the next stage; in fact, those marked with asterisks tend to increase with age. The obligations of friendship change as well. Youniss and his colleagues (Youniss, 1980; Smollar & Youniss, 1982) have examined 10- to 17-year-olds and find that friendship obligations undergo marked shifts over adolescence. While 80 percent of the 10- to 11-year-olds thought friends should "be nice to one another and help each other" only 11 percent of the 16- to 17-year-olds indicated that this was a central obligation. In contrast, 62 percent of the 16- to 17-year-olds thought that providing emotional support was important, but only 5 percent of the 10- to 11-year-olds agreed. The reasons change also. Young children view obligations as important "so he'll be nice to you too" or "to keep the relation going good." Obligations are important to older children because they would benefit the other person ("because she'll be happier if you do") or because it defines the relationship ("That's what friends are supposed to do"). Sex of the person matters: Females at all ages are more likely than males to be concerned with emotional assistance and to stress reasons based on benefiting the other person.

Unfortunately, there is no clear evidence that these expectations translate into action! What children say and expect and what they do are not always highly related. Nor are friendships always smooth and everlasting. Fights

TABLE 13-4

ONSET GRADES FOR FRIENDSHIP EXPECTATIONS

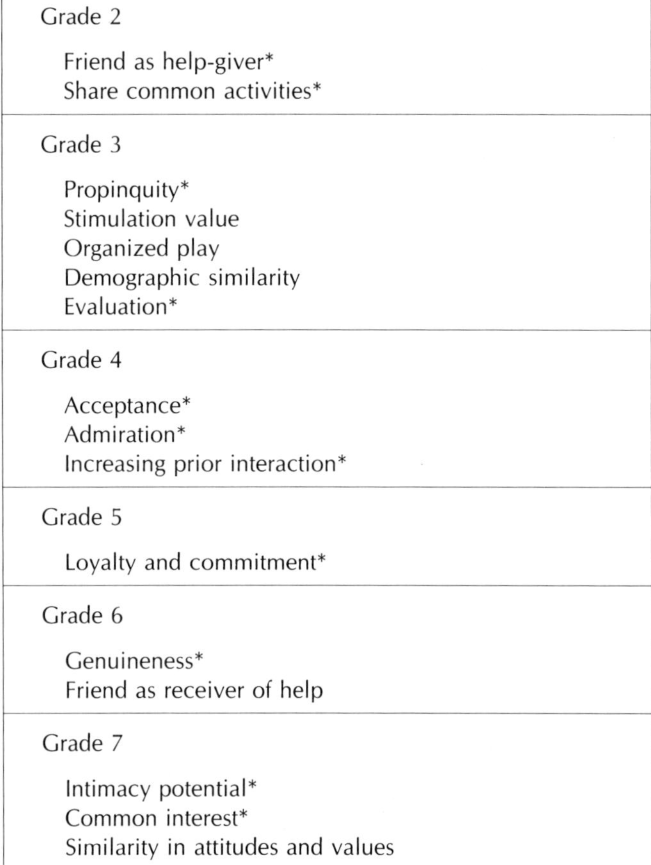

Grade 2	Friend as help-giver* Share common activities*
Grade 3	Propinquity* Stimulation value Organized play Demographic similarity Evaluation*
Grade 4	Acceptance* Admiration* Increasing prior interaction*
Grade 5	Loyalty and commitment*
Grade 6	Genuineness* Friend as receiver of help
Grade 7	Intimacy potential* Common interest* Similarity in attitudes and values

* These friendship expectations tend to increase with age.
Source: Adapted from Bigelow and LaGaipa (1975).

often occur, friends can and do hurt each other, and friendships do end. In the next section, we explore how children make friends and how they behave with friends.

How Children Become Friends

In spite of many decades of studying children's peer relations, it is still difficult to answer a simple question, "How do children become friends?" Gottman and his colleagues (Gottman, 1983; Gottman & Parker, 1986; Parker & Gottman, 1989) have set out to try to provide an answer. Children ranging in age from 3 to 9 years participated in a series of studies. Gottman sent a tape recorder into the children's homes and listened to children while they played together. Some children played with their best friends; others played with strangers. Eighteen unacquainted peers played in their homes for three sessions, with the researchers tracking how much children progressed toward being friends as they became more familiar with each other. One of the accomplishments was the discovery of a set of social processes that successfully distinguished between the play patterns of friends and strangers. Table 13-5 provides a detailed summary of these processes. Friends communicated more clearly, self-disclosed more, had more positive exchanges, established

TABLE 13-5 THE SOCIAL PROCESSES OF FRIENDSHIP FORMATION

PROCESS	DEFINITION	EXAMPLE
1. Communication clarity and connectedness	Request for message clarification followed by appropriate clarification of the message.	Child A: Give it to me. Child B: Which one? Child A: The purple one with yellow ears.
2. Information exchange	Asking questions and eliciting revelant information.	Where do you live? What color is your crayon?
3. Establishing common ground	Finding something to do together and/or exploring their similarities and differences.	Let's play trucks. I like tea parties, do you?
4. Self-disclosure of feelings	Questions about feelings by one child are followed by expression of feeling by the partner.	I'm really scared of the dark and snakes, too.
5. Positive reciprocity	One partner responds to another's positive behavior or serves to extend or lengthen a positive exchange: usually involves joking, gossip, or fantasy.	Child A: Did you hear what happened to Mary's sister? Child B: No, tell me and then I'll tell you another thing about Mary.
6. Conflict resolution	The extent to which play partners resolve disputes and disagreements successfully.	Child A: I want the blue truck. Child B: No, I'm playing with it. Child A: I want it. Child B: OK let's play with it together.

Source: Adapted from Gottman (1983).

common ground more easily, exchanged more information, and were able to resolve conflict more effectively than strangers. Moreover, unacquainted children who got along well and who were rated as more likely to become friends scored higher on these dimensions.

Other studies confirm many of these findings with other samples of children at different ages. Not surprisingly, children spend more time with friends and express more positive affect than with nonfriends (Hartup, 1989). They share more with their friends (Jones, 1985) although friends are sometimes tough competitors, which may decrease their sharing with each other (Berndt, 1986). Being friends does not mean never disagreeing (Hartup, 1992). In fact, friends disagree more than nonfriends, but engage in less heated conflicts and are more likely to stay in contact after the disagreement than nonfriends (Hartup, Laursen, Stewart, & Eastenson, 1988). And friends, of course, are more intimate and self-disclosing with each other than acquaintances (Berndt & Perry, 1990). In turn, they are more knowledgeable about each other than nonfriends—they know each other's strengths and secrets as well as their wishes and weaknesses (Ladd & Emerson, 1984). As someone once said, "A friend is one who knows our faults but doesn't give a damn!"

How do friendship patterns change across development? Parker and Gottman (1989) suggest that the goals and central processes involved in successful friendship formation shift across age. For young children (age 3 to 7 years), the goal of peer interaction is coordinated play with all of the social processes organized to promote successful play. In the second developmental phase—the 8- to 12-year period—the goal changes from playful interaction to a concern with being accepted by one's same-sex peers. Children are concerned with the norms of the group, figuring out what actions will lead to acceptance and inclusion, and which to exclusion and rejection. The most salient social process in middle childhood is *negative gossip,* which involves sharing some negative nugget about another child: When it works well the partner responds with interest, more negative gossip, and even feelings of solidarity. Both boys and girls engage in gossip, ritual insults, and teasing during this period. It reaches organized levels in some cases. One study found, for example, that in some schools girls kept "slam books" in which nasty things were written by each girl about other girls (Giese-Davis, cited by Gottman, 1986). Here is an example of two children, Erica and Mikaila, gossiping about another girl, Katie.

Erica: Katie does lots of weird things. Like every time she, we make a mistake, she says, "Well, *sorry.*" (sarcastic)

Mikaila: I know.

Erica: And stuff like that.

Mikaila: She's mean. She beat me up once. (laugh) I could hardly breathe she hit me in the stomach so hard.

Erica: She acts like . . .

Mikaila: She's the boss. (Gottman, 1986)

Negative gossip is a salient aspect of social friendships in middle childhood.

Often gossip is used as a way of establishing the norms for the group; in this case it is important not to be too aggressive or bossy.

In the third developmental period (age 13 to 17 years), the focus shifts to the understanding of self. The salient social processes are gossip and self-disclosure, with a heavy emphasis on problem solving and intense honesty, and with *self-disclosure* being the most central process. Table 13-6 summarizes these developmental periods.

Confirmation that the focus of friendship changes across age comes from recent work by Gottman and Mettetal (1986), who listened to the conversations of friends at three age levels; 6- to 7-year-olds, 11- to 12-year olds, and 16- to 17-year olds. As expected, coordinated play is highest for the youngest group and declines rapidly for the middle and adolescent groups. Similarly, gossip shifts across age and first becomes important in middle childhood and remains important into adolescence. Negative gossip about a person they know was especially important beginning in middle childhood. Finally, self-disclosure, a vehicle for self-exploration, increases across age and is most important and frequent during adolescence.

GROUP FORMATION

Children not only develop friendships across age but they also form groups that possess common goals and aims and rules of conduct. In addition, groups usually develop a hierarchical organization or structure which identifies each member's relationship to other members of the group and which facilitates the interaction among its members. Some group members are identified as dominant or as leaders, and their roles are quite different from those of the less dominant children in the group.

Group Hierarchies

Groups are not organized in a random fashion; instead, children form "pecking orders," or hierarchies, even in the preschool years. Children very

TABLE 13-6

CHARACTERISTICS OF THE HYPOTHESIZED DEVELOPMENTAL PERIODS OF FRIENDSHIP

	DEVELOPMENTAL PERIOD		
CHARACTERISTIC	EARLY CHILDHOOD	MIDDLE CHILDHOOD	ADOLESCENCE
Underlying theme of concern	Maximization of excitement, entertainment, and affect levels in play	Inclusion by peers, avoidance of rejection: self-presentaton	Self-exploration: self-definition
Salient conversational processes in friendship	Processes of play coordination: activity talk, play escalation, play deescalation, conflict resolution	Negative evaluation gossip	Self-disclosure: problem-solving
Affective developments	Management of arousal in interaction	Acquisition of affect display and feeling rules: rejection of sentiment	Fusion of logic and emotion: understanding of implications of affect for relationships

Note: Adapted from Gottman & Mettetal (1986).

early become aware of group hierarchies. Although preschool children's perception of their own position of relative dominance may be somewhat aggrandized, their accuracy in perceiving their own status increases rapidly in the early school years (Strayer, 1984). Preschool children, when asked "Who is the toughest?" often respond "me." In contrast, by second grade there is over 70 percent agreement on the relative toughness of students in their class (Edelman & Omark, 1973). Although preschool children's dominance hierarchies are simpler and more loosely differentiated than those of older children, older preschool children show considerable agreement in identifying group status structures (Sluckin & Smith, 1977; Strayer & Strayer, 1976). Moreover, recent evidence (Pettit, Bakshi, Dodge, & Coie, 1990) suggests that dominance hierarchies emerge very quickly. In the first forty-five minutes of contact, unacquainted first- and third-grade boys began to develop a coherently organized social structure. Children's ability to order their peers from highest to lowest in dominance seems to be related to their ability to perform cognitive seriation tasks. Children who are able to do such things as order a series of sticks of varying length from the shortest to the longest are also able to order peers in terms of dominance (Omark, Strayer, & Freedman, 1980). Again, we see the close relationship between the child's cognitive and social development. Moreover, dominance ratings among children who stay together are surprisingly stable across time. Children who were rated by their classmates as high in toughness in first and second grade are viewed as high in dominance, athletic ability, popularity, leadership, and self-confidence in the twelfth grade (Weisfeld, Muczenski, Weisfeld, & Omark, 1989).

As this view of stability suggests, the criteria for determining dominance changes across age. Young children seem to differentiate the status of peers on the basis of toughness, the ability to direct the behavior of others, leadership in play, and physical coercion. In contrast, in older children such status structures are more likely to be based on appearance, leadership skills, pubertal development, athletic prowess, and academic performance (Savin-Williams, 1987).

Dominance and status affect social interaction as well. A number of researchers, observing nursery school children in free play, found that dominant children are looked at and imitated more than nondominant children (Strayer, 1980; Vaughn & Waters, 1981). In addition, children are more likely to conform to the opinions and behavior of high-status peers (Hartup, 1983).

What functions do hierarchies serve? First, they reduce aggression among members of the group, who establish nonaggressive means of resolving conflict. For example, a high-ranking member may use a threat gesture in order to keep a lower-ranking group member in line. In fact, aggression is rarely seen in a group with a well-established hierarchy (Strayer, 1984). A second purpose is to help divide up the tasks and labor of the group, with worker roles being assumed by the lower-status members and leadership roles going to the more dominant members. Third, dominance hierarchies determine the allocation of resources—especially limited resources (Charlesworth, 1988). Whether it is among the nursery school set (Charlesworth & Dzur, 1987) or among adolescent summer campers (Savin-Williams, 1987), rank has its privileges. In a study of adolescents at a summer camp, Savin-Williams (1987) found that the dominant campers "frequently ate the bigger piece of cake at mealtimes, sat where they wanted to during discussions and slept in the preferred sleeping sites during camp-outs (near the fire)—all scarce resources at summer camp" (p. 934). Clearly, dominance hierarchies play important roles in regulating interaction, but as is often the case, the ones at the top of the hierarchy seem to benefit most.

PEER VERSUS ADULT INFLUENCES ON THE CHILD

Many behavioral scientists view preadolescence and adolescence as particularly stressful periods during which the child is being pulled and buffeted by the often conflicting standards of parents and peers. However, other authors have argued that the conflict between these two sets of standards is not as extreme as is believed and that there is often remarkable agreement between the values of peers and adults (Cooper & Cooper, 1992; Douvan & Adelson, 1966). A better question than whether peers or adults are more influential is, "Under what conditions and with what behaviors are peers or adults influential?" Peers and parents each have their own areas of expertise; while peers may not be the best source of advice about occupational choices, parents are not the best oracle for the latest word on video music. Peers exert more influence in friendship choices, interpersonal behavior, entertainment, and fashion standards, while parents are more influential in job preferences, academic choices, and future aspirations (Hartup, 1983). Moreover, when adolescents are with parents and peers they engage in very different types of activities—work and task activities with parents and recreation and conversation with peers (Larson & Richards, 1991). Finally, peer relations offer more opportunities to practice certain behaviors. For example, aggression against a parent is likely to have more adverse consequences than aggression against a peer. Sexual behavior can be discussed with parents but is practiced with peers. Nor do peers always lead adolescents astray and into deviant activities. As Brown, Lohr, and McClenahan (1986) found, peer influence

Peers can influence children's habits—good and bad.

isn't necessarily evil. Figure 13-8 clearly shows that peers are more likely to influence your choice of hairstyle than convince you to smoke crack!

In most cases, a child's behavior is a result of both peer and parental influence (Simons, Conger, & Whitbeck, 1988). Kandel (1973) studied marijuana use by adolescents whose parents either used or did not use psychoactive drugs and whose best friends either used or did not use marijuana. Among teenagers whose best friends were nonusers but whose parents were users, only 17 percent smoked marijuana. If only friends used drugs, 56 percent of the adolescents reported using marijuana. However, 67 percent of the subjects used marijuana when both parents and peers were users. Thus, there was a combined impact of drug usage by parents and peers on marijuana use by adolescents. Age makes a difference. Krosnick and Judd (1982), in their study of the impact of parents and peers on smoking, found that the two sources were equally influential among 11-year-olds. But among 14-year-olds, children's smoking was more strongly determined by whether or not their friends smoked than by parental influences.

Family relations play an important part in children's susceptibility to peer pressure. When families are warm and supportive and neither highly punitive nor highly permissive, what we have called "authoritative parenting" (see Chapter 12), their children are less likely to succumb to peer influence. Steinberg (1986) recently studied 865 adolescents who varied in their types of after-school supervision. Some were at home after school or at a friend's house, while others described themselves as "hanging out" with little adult supervision. As Figure 13-9 shows, supervision matters and children are more likely to be open to peer pressure when "hanging out" than at home. However, being reared authoritatively can buffer children and make them less susceptible to peer influence even when adult supervision is lax. Parenting style clearly carries over to peer settings and can help children avoid being swayed by their peers.

THE PEER GROUP IN CROSS-CULTURAL PERSPECTIVE

Are peers equally important in all cultures or in all parts of one culture? Is America a uniquely peer-oriented culture? Even within cultures, patterns of

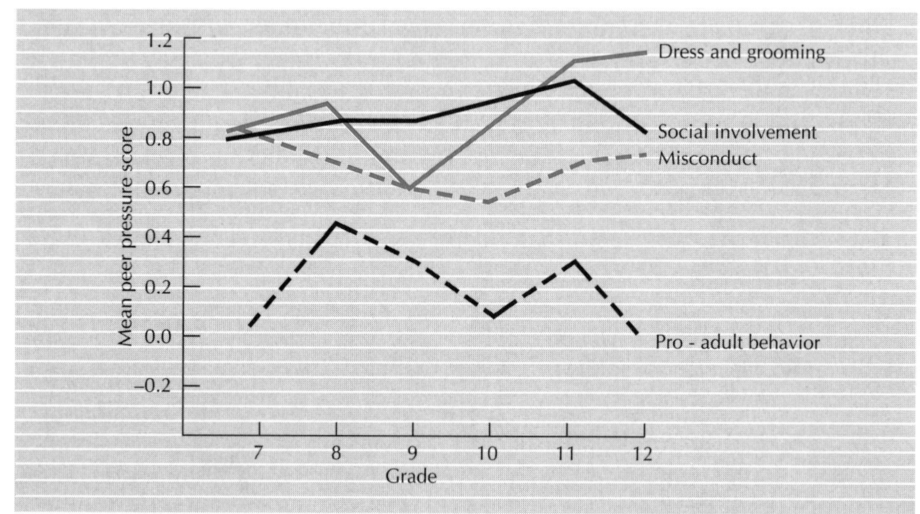

FIGURE 13-8
Grade differences for four areas of behavior (From: Brown, Lohr, & McClenahan, 1986).

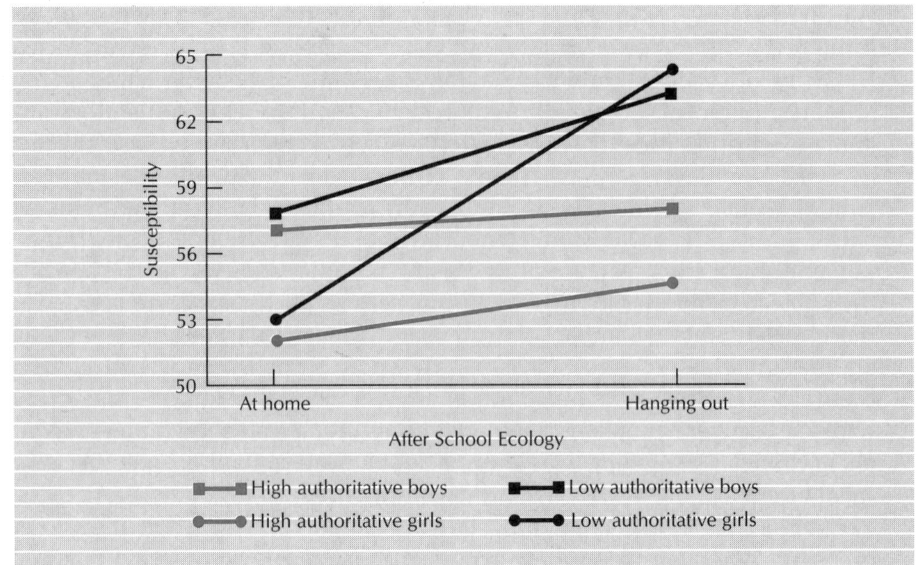

FIGURE 13-9
Susceptibility to peer pressure of latchkey boys and girls who are at home or "hanging out" after school as a function of parental authoritativeness (high or low). (From: Steinberg, 1986.)

peer interaction may differ; for example, comparison of urban and rural peers indicates that Israeli children reared in rural kibbutzim are more cooperative and supportive than city-reared children (Auger, Bronfenbrenner, & Henderson, 1977). Therefore, it is not surprising that there are cross-cultural variations that deviate in both directions from the American pattern; in some countries, peers play an even more influential role, while in others the family and adult agents are more important. For example, in Hispanic cultures children are more family-oriented and less under the influence of peers (DeRosier & Kupersmidt, 1991). In Mexico and Central America, for example, this family orientation often is maintained by the parents' direct discouragement of peer interaction (Holtzman, Diaz-Guerrero, & Schwartz, 1975).

Russian children are particularly resistant to peer pressures that conflict with adult societal values in comparison to German, English, or American children (Bronfenbrenner, 1970). This cross-national difference is due to Russian socialization practices. From the earliest years in school the peer group is employed to help adult authorities teach and enforce the dominant social values of the society. The social group, or collective, rather than the individual, is the main unit of concern; evaluation of the individual's behavior is mainly in terms of its relevance to the goals and aims of the collective. In Russia the peer group is a mechanism for maintaining the adult system. In America, at least in adolescence, the peer group is often in the vanguard of efforts to alter the existing system. In summary, there are clear differences in peer relationship across different cultures as well as within our own culture.

SUMMARY

DEVELOPMENTAL TRENDS IN PEER INTERACTION

- Peers play a different role in children's development than do families. Although the child's relationship with parents is more enduring than that with peers, interactions among age-mates are more free and egalitarian, engendering a new kind of interpersonal sensitivity to the needs of others.

EXTRA-FAMILIAL INFLUENCES ON DEVELOPMENT

A wide range of influences outside the family play an important role in the child's development. Extended family members, day care, school, clubs, organizations and teams, as well as peers and TV, all play significantly larger roles in development than we previously recognized.

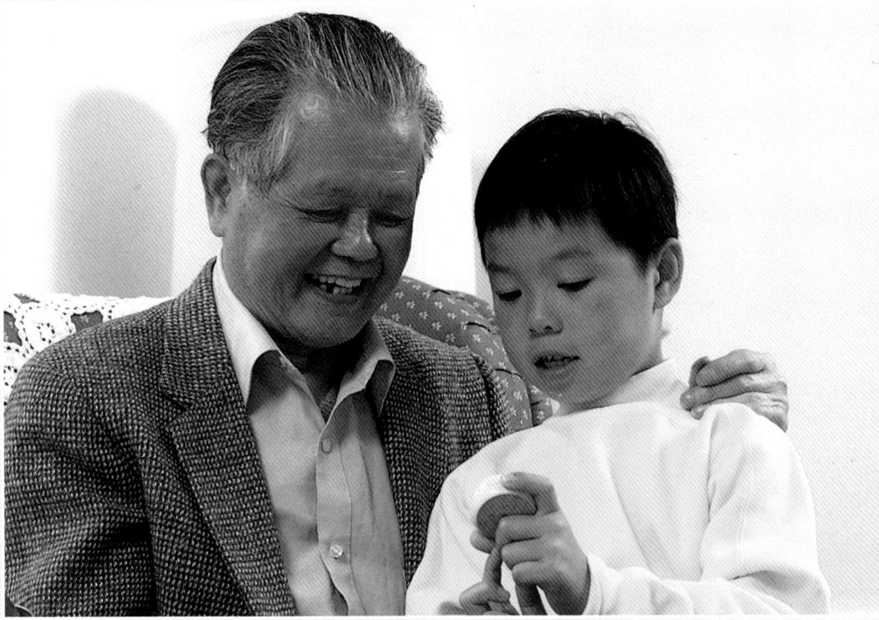

Grandparents play important roles in children's lives.

Day care and preschools are significant parts of the lives of young children in the 1990s. Out-of-home care can take a variety of forms from informal play groups to structured educational programs.

Clubs and teams provide important opportunities to learn and improve social skills such as cooperation and sharing.

Children spend many hours during childhood and adolescence watching television—a potent influence in their lives.

Peers are an important part of children's lives. Partners and activities change dramatically from childhood through adolescence.

- During the second half of the first year, infants begin to recognize peers as social partners and attempt to influence one another by vocalizing, looking, touching, and waving. In the early toddler period, peers begin to exchange both turns and roles during social interactions; in the late toddler period, a major achievement is the ability to share meaning with a social partner. As children's competence with peers develops, they shift toward increased social play and a preference for playing with peers rather than adults, a trend that continues throughout the preschool and elementary years. After about age 7 children are more likely to choose same-sex rather than opposite-sex play partners; this remains the case until adolescence, when interest in the opposite sex begins

THE FUNCTIONS OF PEERS

- The peer group influences the development of the child in many of the same ways that parents do, including reinforcement and modeling. Peers reinforce one another with increasing frequency throughout the preschool years, with reinforcement commonly reciprocated by those who receive it. In addition to the effects of reinforcement, children acquire a wide range of knowledge and a variety of responses by observing and imitating the behavior of their peers. Imitation may serve as a way both to learn social rules and maintain social interaction.
- Peers also serve as standards against which children evaluate themselves. Research indicates that the use of social comparison with the peer group as a means of self-evaluation increases dramatically in the early elementary school years. The process of self-comparison is one basis of the child's self-image and self-esteem. In addition, peers provide opportunities for socializing and forming relationships as well as the development of a sense of belonging.

PLAY

- Play is an activity that is intrinsically motivated rather than imposed or directed by others; that is concerned with means, not ends; that is free from external rules; and that is nonserious and highly engaging. The functions of play are to facilitate cognitive development, advance social development, and provide a nonthreatening situation for coping with emotional problems.
- Make-believe or pretend play appears as early as 12 months, usually involving symbolic activities about routine events (e.g., cooking, shopping). By age 3, pretend play has become complex, cooperative dramatic play with partners; peaking around age 6, pretend play involves highly coordinated fantasies, multiple roles, and transformations of objects and situations. Domestic fantasy play declines in the school years and is replaced by more structured games, but adventure fantasies continue into preadolescence. Imaginative play allows the child to experiment with multiple roles and learn to coordinate activities with other children in relatively risk-free situations. Fantasy play also may be used to master fears when children practice conquering the fear, comforting someone who is fearful, or even becoming the feared object.
- Disruptions and rigidity in the play patterns of emotionally disturbed children have been noted. Failure to develop imaginative play is indicative of serious pathology, and children who are undergoing stress show less

reversibility, less diversity, and more aggression in play. Imaginativeness in play is associated with self-control, less impulsivity, independence, and social maturity.

DETERMINANTS AND EFFECTS OF PEER ACCEPTANCE

- Peer status is typically assessed in research by using *sociometric* techniques, in which children identify peers whom they "especially like" and those whom they "don't like very much." On the basis of these nominations, children have been classified as *popular* (those who receive many positive but few negative nominations), *rejected* (those who receive many negative but few positive nominations), *neglected* (those who receive few nominations in either direction), and *average* (those who have some friends but not as many as the popular group). Rejection occurs for a variety of reasons, including lack of social skills as well as withdrawn and aggressive behaviors.
- Children often form first impressions based on names and appearance. Children respond adversely to unfamiliar names and to unattractive children. By age 3, children distinguish attractive from unattractive children on the same basis that adults do, and they attribute more negative characteristics to children judged to be unattractive. Some evidence indicates that unattractive children tend to behave in more aggressive ways than other children, but this may be a result of being perceived more negatively by others.
- In general, children prefer spending time with peers of the same age and the same sex. Although age preferences may be due to the age-grading of many institutions in our society, some research suggests that children would choose same-age playmates on their own. Segregation by gender is clearly self-imposed, and it seems to be related to differences in the interests and play patterns of girls and boys.
- Although children may have different goals, strategies, and behaviors when playing with peers, social skills such as reinforcing others, being able to initiate interactions effectively, and communicating well play important roles in achieving social acceptance. Popular children engage in more prosocial behavior and help set the norms for a group, while rejected children are often aggressive, aversive, and socially unskilled. Neglected children are less talkative and more withdrawn.
- Being unpopular among peers can lead to both short-term and long-term problems. Unpopular children (especially rejected ones) feel lonely and socially dissatisfied, and they are more likely to drop out of school and develop criminal behavior patterns. Social standing tends to remain stable across time and situations, showing the most stability for rejected children. Some programs to help these children by shaping socially desirable behavior through reinforcement and coaching in social skills have proved beneficial.
- Parents play an important role in promoting a child's peer relations. They serve as partners with whom the child acquires social skills that help them interact with other children. They also act as coaches or educators by giving advice and support and by modeling strategies for conduct with peers. Finally, they provide opportunities for peer interaction through their choice of neighborhood and their willingness to schedule visits with friends (especially for preschoolers).

THE DEVELOPMENT OF CHILDREN'S FRIENDSHIPS

- Children develop close relationships that we think of as *friendships* with only a few peers. Expectations about what a friend is change during the elementary school years from simply someone who shares activities to someone who can also be told secrets and will be understanding. Studies indicate that friends interact differently with each other than do unacquainted peers and that the goals of friendship appear to change with development. For young children (ages 3 to 7) the goal is coordinated play, while for older children (ages 8 to 12) the goal is establishing group norms and being accepted by peers. By adolescence (ages 13 to 17) the focus shifts to understanding the self, making self-disclosure a critical component of friendship.

GROUP FORMATION

- In addition to friendships, children form groups that possess common goals and rules of conduct. Such groups are usually hierarchically organized in such a way as to identify members' relationships with one another and to facilitate interaction. Dominance hierarchies within groups are apparent even among preschoolers, and a "pecking order" appears to develop within a short time of first contact. The criteria for establishing dominance changes with age from physical toughness to leadership abilities and academic performance. Within groups of children, hierarchies serve the purposes of resolving conflict, dividing up tasks, and allocating resources.

PEERS VERSUS ADULT INFLUENCES ON THE CHILD

- Peers and parents both exert some influence on children, with peers exerting more influence during the preadolescent and adolescent periods. However, peers and parents each have their own areas of expertise. Parents are more likely to be consulted about academic and career decisions, while peers are more likely to influence entertainment, fashion, and friendship choices. In most cases, both parents and peers influence adolescents' choices. Children from homes with authoritative parents are less susceptible to negative peer pressure.

THE PEER GROUP IN CROSS-CULTURAL PERSPECTIVE

- Within and between cultures, patterns of peer interaction differ. Due to different socialization practices, peers have more or less influence. In Mexico, for example, family influences remain strong throughout adolescence, while in Russia peers are seen as sources of information about what is good for the collective. In the United States, the adolescent peer group often advocates change in the existing system.

CHAPTER

14 SCHOOLS, TECHNOLOGY, AND TELEVISION

The family and the peer group are not the only major forces in the socialization process. From an early age, the mass media, especially television, is also a central part of the everyday lives of children in many parts of the world. Another significant socialization agent in much of the world is schooling. Between TV and school, a very significant portion of the child's waking hours are consumed. Both exert a strong influence over children's emotional, social, and cognitive development. From early infancy onward, television is part of the lives of most children, and by age 4 or 5, an increasingly large proportion of the child's life will be dominated by the school. Even outside of school hours, the demands of the school through homework assignments, the social obligations and ties of school clubs and activities, and the ways in which school structures children's social networks make the school a salient force in the child's daily existence.

In this chapter, we will focus on the ways in which these two extrafamilial socialization agents influence children's development. The importance of school as a socialization agent will be discussed, and then some of the structural features of schools will be considered, such as school size, classroom size, and seating arrangement. Second, we will examine the effects of open- versus traditional-classroom organization on children's development. Next, the effects of the central character in the school drama, the teacher, will be investigated. Do variations in teaching styles affect the child's progress in school? Next, we examine one of the major technological innovations in the classroom—the computer. How do computers change learning and social interaction? How important are textbooks? Do they mislead and misinform young children, as some experts claim, or has the influence of texts been exaggerated? In addition, the issue of special classes for special children such as the retarded and the gifted will be explored. We will also consider the relationship between socioeconomic class and the school system. Finally, the effects of desegregation on social academic outcomes will be discussed.

When we turn to the issue of television, several issues will be explored. First, how do viewing patterns change with age? Second, the programming features that help attract and maintain children's attention will be examined.

Next, we will look at the impact of TV on children's social, emotional, and cognitive development. Then, we will explore children's understanding of TV's messages, including commercials. Finally, we will ask how parents can modify the effects of television viewing.

THE IMPORTANCE OF THE SCHOOL

Children in the United States today attend school for more hours each day and more days each year than preceding generations. Children go to school an average of five hours a day, 180 days a year. In 1880 the average pupil attended school about eighty days each year. Not only are children attending school more often and for longer periods of time, but a larger proportion of the population goes to school. And they start school earlier and stay in school longer.

Although impressive, the increasingly large amount of time children spend in the classroom is hardly convincing evidence that the school has a benefit on the child's development. One influential kind of evidence concerning the importance of the school as a socializing force has come from studies of the effect of schools on children's values and aspirations. These studies show that schools, along with the family and the peer group, can influence children's moral-value orientation and political views as well as their achievement and occupational aspirations (Hess & Holloway, 1984; Minuchin & Shapiro, 1983).

More controversial is the issue of whether schools make a difference in children's cognitive development—independently of family and socioeconomic background. Some school critics, such as Coleman and associates (1966) and Jencks and coworkers (1972), have argued that schools have little influence. More recent evidence indicates that these early critics were wrong, and in contrast, suggests that schooling does influence pupil achievement—even when differences in levels of achievement at the time of school entry

Schooling is one way of broadening our cross-cultural perspective; these children are studying a globe in a geography lesson.

are taken into account (Minuchin & Shapiro, 1983; Rutter, 1983). Moreover, as cross-cultural studies have demonstrated, schooling has a major influence on the way in which children organize their thoughts and cognitions (Farnham-Diggory, 1990; Rogoff, 1990). Schooling exposes children to an abstract symbolic orientation to the world, an orientation that allows children to develop the capacity to think in terms of general concepts, rules, and hypothetical events. Schools do not simply teach children more knowledge; schools teach children to think about the world in different ways. These diverse impacts of schooling underline the important and unique role that the school plays in modifying children's social and cognitive development.

THE PHYSICAL STRUCTURE AND ORGANIZATION OF THE SCHOOL ENVIRONMENT

Although most discussions of the school concentrate on teachers, tactics, and texts, the structural features of the school environment merit consideration. Does the size of the school that a child attends make any difference? Similarly, do such factors as seating arrangements, class size, wall color, and ventilation affect the child's scholastic achievement, her attitudes toward school, or the degree to which she actively participates in class and in extracurricular functions? Although it is impossible to answer all these questions, recent research has given us the answers to at least some of them.

Big School, Small School: The Effect of School Size

> The large school has authority: its grand exterior dimensions, its long halls and myriad rooms and its tides of students all carry an implication of power and rightness. The small school lacks such certainty; its modest building, its short halls and few rooms and its students, who move more in trickles than in tides, give an impression of a casual or not quite decisive educational environment. (Barker & Gump, 1964, p. 195)

But that is only an outsider's view. And appearances are often deceiving. How do schools of different sizes look from the standpoint of the students? Does the extent of student participation in extracurricular functions vary in small and large schools? It is clear that much of the schools' influence in transmitting social and cultural values comes through these extracurricular functions—a reminder that much of the learning taking place in school is not in the classroom. Barker and Gump (1964) set out to answer these questions. They wanted to learn whether or not large schools offer more, and more varied, activities for their students than smaller schools and whether this meant that the student in the large school has a richer experience. High schools ranging in size from 35 to 2287 students participated in the study; all were located in an economically, culturally, and politically homogeneous region of eastern Kansas. The results were surprising. Although the largest school had twenty times as many students as a small school in a nearby county, there were only five times as many extracurricular activities. More important, the large and small schools did not differ greatly in terms of the variety of activities they offer. The small school was small in enrollment but not necessarily limited in opportunities for activity and participation. It can be compared to a small engine in that "it possessed the essential parts of a large entity but had fewer replications and differentiations of some of the parts" (Barker & Gump, 1964, p. 195). Given fewer students but nearly as many participation opportunities, one would expect that more students would be more involved in more activities in more important ways in the smaller setting. In fact, the proportion of students who participated in music festivals and dramatic, journalistic, and student government competitions was three to twenty times as great in the small, as contrasted with the large, institution. Figure 14-1 presents a graphic picture of this relationship. Students at a small school participated in twice as many activities over their high school career. Moreover, there was greater variety in their activities at a small school.

There is one other way in which the two types of institutions differed. In the small-school setting students felt more obligation and responsibility to play an active role in the their school functions, and they felt that their peers expected them to participate more. One outcome is that there are fewer "outsiders" in the smaller schools; that is, students who were left out of most extracurricular activities. This greater sense of identification and involvement of the marginal students in the smaller school may be part of the reason that dropout rates are lower in small schools. Recent evidence confirms these findings: Children at risk for such problems as dropping out of school, substance abuse, teenage pregnancy, suicide, and depression are less likely to be involved in school and extracurricular activities (Steinberg, 1985).

Although it is difficult to change school size, educators have argued for greater flexibility and design in the organization of schools (Farnham-Diggory, 1990; Sizer, 1984). Some recommend an organizational structure in which smaller units designed to match more closely the needs of students would function simultaneously within the large unit. These "schools within schools result in the creation of additional behavior settings or niches in which students can develop a sense of identity and belonging that may prevent them from dropping out of school and enhance the likelihood of positive academic and socioemotional outcomes" (Linney & Seidman, 1989, p. 338). "What size should a school be? . . . Sufficiently small that all of its students are needed for its enterprises. A school should be small enough that students are not redundant" (Barker & Gump, 1964, p. 202).

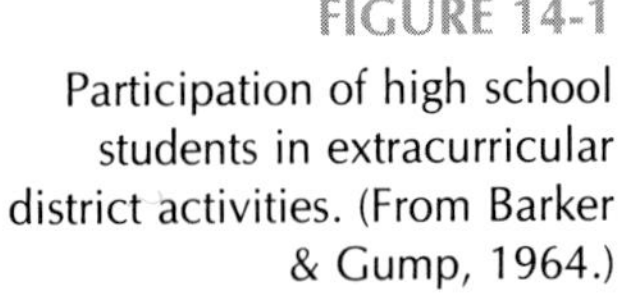

FIGURE 14-1

Participation of high school students in extracurricular district activities. (From Barker & Gump, 1964.)

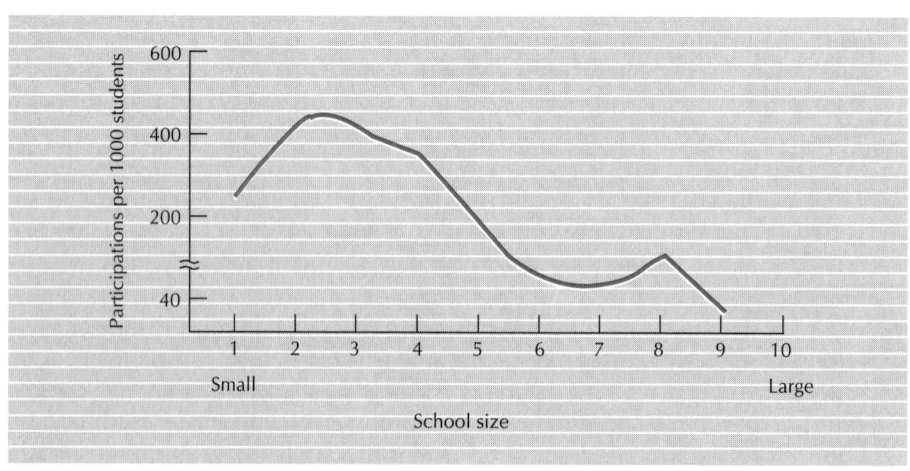

Age Groupings of Schools: Junior High or No Junior High?

Size is not the only factor that affects children's sense of self and sense of identification with their school and its activities. The division of the school years from kindergarten through grade 12 matters as well (Gump, 1980). While a common pattern is eight years of elementary school and four years of high school, other divisions have emerged in recent years. The most common alternative is six years of elementary school and three years of junior high (or "middle school"), followed by three years of high school. Recent research suggests that organization makes a difference in students' behavior. Simmons, Blyth, and McKinney (1984) compared students moving from the sixth to the seventh grade either in a regular eight-year elementary school or in a junior high school, where this transition involved moving to a new school. For adolescents who may also be undergoing other transitions, such as puberty, the added burden of shifting to a new school has a negative impact. In comparison to the seventh graders who stayed in elementary school, the junior high schoolers had lower self-concepts, were less involved in activities and clubs, and perceived themselves as less integrated into their school and peer groups.

For adolescents who may be undergoing many transitions, such as puberty, the onset of dating, residence change, or family disruption, the added burden of shifting to a new school may be especially difficult (Simmons, Burgeson, & Carlton-Ford, 1987). Not only was self-esteem lower for children, especially girls, who were undergoing three or more transitions, but their degree of participation in extracurricular activities and their grade-point average were lower as well. The implications are clear:

> If change comes too suddenly or if change is too early given children's cognitive and emotional states or if it occurs in too many areas of life at once, then individuals may experience considerable discomfort. . . . Individuals do better both in terms of self-esteem and behavioral coping if there is some "arena of comfort" in their lives. (Simmons et al., 1987, p. 1231)

On the other hand, it is clear that no particular age grouping will be ideal for all children especially in view of the range of individual differences in the timing of puberty for boys and girls that we saw in Chapter 6.

THE CLASSROOM: SPACE AND ORGANIZATION

The Spatial Arrangement of the Classroom

One of the most obvious features of the learning environment is the rectangular classroom. Why not a round class or a square one? Or does it matter anyway? According to one design expert:

> The present rectangular room with its straight rows of chairs and wide windows was intended to provide for ventilation, light, quick departure, ease of surveillance and a host of other legitimate needs as they existed in the early 1900s. . . . The typical long narrow shape resulted from a desire to get light across the room. . . . Despite new developments in lighting, acoustics and structures,

most schools are still boxes filled with cubes each containing a specified number of chairs in straight rows. There have been attempts to break away from this rigid pattern, but experimental schools are the exception rather than the rule. (Sommer, 1969, pp. 98–99)

Maria Montessori once described the children who have to exist in these traditional classrooms as "butterflies mounted on pins, fastened each to a desk, spreading the useless wings of barren and meaningless knowledge they have acquired" (Montessori, 1964, p. 81).

Does a pupil's location within the classroom make a difference? Are individuals in front more active than those in the rear? Are those in the center more active than those on the aisles, regardless of the type of room? Location does make a difference, and participation is highest among pupils seated across the front and down the middle of the room. This action zone of the classroom (Gump & Ross, 1977) is illustrated in Figure 14-2. However, the reasons for the effect are unclear. Do interested students sit closer to the teacher, or do students take a greater interest if they do sit closer to the teacher?

Finally, what about class size? Is there an optimal class size for maximal achievement? This has been debated for over half a century and the debate continues. In an early study, Dawe (1934) examined the effects of kindergarten size on pupil participation. In classes ranging in size from fifteen to forty-six children, the number of comments made by each child during a controlled discussion period was recorded. As class size increased, not only did the total amount of discussion decrease, but a smaller percent of the children participated; when they did talk, their average amount of participation was

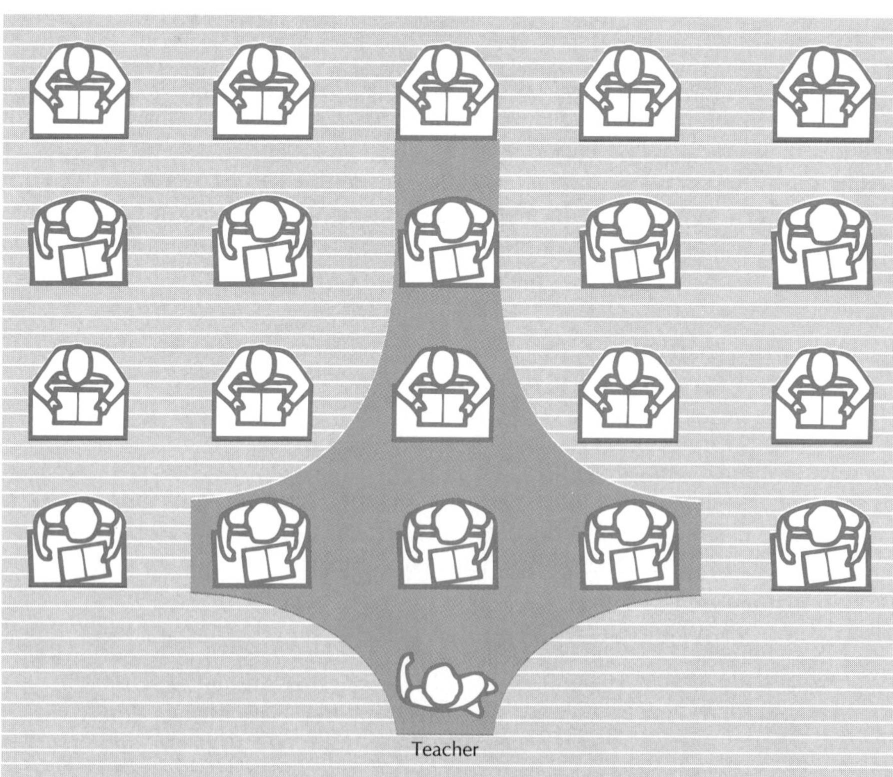

FIGURE 14-2
Area of maximum amount of teacher-pupil interaction (shaded area) in classroom. (From Adams & Biddle, 1970.)

likely to be less. Evidence suggesting that the educational experience is different in small and large classes continues to accumulate. In small classes there is more individualization, greater group activity, more positive student attitudes, and less misbehavior: not surprisingly, teachers are more satisfied in smaller classes (Minuchin & Shapiro, 1983). However, class size makes little difference to achievement within the usual range of twenty to forty pupils, although a smaller class may be advantageous to the learning of reading and mathematics in the early grades and may aid the academic progress of handicapped or disadvantaged pupils (Rutter, 1983). Moreover, interpretation of the impact of class size is often difficult since the effects depend on whether teachers structure small classes differently from large ones (Minuchin & Shapiro, 1983).

The Organization and Structure of the Classroom

The teacher can organize the classroom in a multitude of ways. For example, she can arrange to have students participate in the decision making, she can organize the class into small groups, she can arrange for students to help each other, or she can organize classroom activities in the traditional manner. In this section we will focus on the consequences of different types of classroom organization.

Originally developed in Great Britain, the open-classroom philosophy is based on the assumption that children learn best by actively participating and becoming involved in their own learning rather than being passive recipients of knowledge. Here is a description of the open classroom:

> In the open classroom it is rare for all the children to be engaged in the same activity at the same time. . . . A typical view of an open classroom might show us two youngsters stretched out on a rug reading books they have chosen from the classroom library. The teacher is at the math table, showing a small group of children how to use a set of scales to learn about relative weights. Two children in the writing corner are playing a word game. And one child is taking notes on the nursing behavior of the class guinea pig. Other children are working individually or in small groups at desks or tables. A sense of purpose pervades the room, attesting to the children's interest in their various learning activities. (Papalia & Olds, 1975, p. 463)

But, do children benefit from the open-classroom arrangement? Socially there are clear benefits: "children (elementary school) in open environments have more varied social contacts, positive attitudes toward school and show both self-reliant and cooperative behavior in learning situations. Students in less authoritatively organized high schools participate more in school activities, have more varied social relationships and create fewer disciplinary problems than students in traditionally organized schools" (Minuchin & Shapiro, 1983, p. 67).

The academic benefits are less clear. Some investigators find no differences in the achievement test scores of children in open and conventional classrooms, while others report that children learn more math and read better in structured classes (Minuchin & Shapiro, 1983). Part of the answer to this puzzle lies in the fact that some kinds of children do best in a traditional structured classroom and others fare better in an alternative classroom organization (see Box 14-1).

BOX 14-1 *PSYCHOLOGY IN ACTION* SOCIAL ORGANIZATION OF THE CLASSROOM: DIFFERENT CULTURES, DIFFERENT ORGANIZATIONS

Some cultures stress individual learning while other cultures encourage cooperative and collaborative approaches to learning. Awareness of the cultural background of the students is critical in designing a classroom organization, because students learn best when the social structure matches their cultural orientation and values.

> The typical North American classroom uses primarily whole class organization, with rank and file seating and a teacher-leader who instructs and demonstrates to the whole group. This instruction is then followed by some form of individual practice and then teacher-organized individual assessment. (Tharp, 1989)

But does this social structure work well for students from all cultures? For some, such as Euro-American cultures which stress individual learning, the system works fine. For others, such as Hawaiian cultures who value cooperative approaches to learning, it works less well. Among Hawaiian children, this type of structure produces a low level of attention to teachers and classwork and a high level of seeking attention from peers (Tharp, 1989). Teachers tend to view the problem as lack of motivation and interest on the part of the students rather than as due to an alien social organization. By providing a culturally compatible social structure, Hawaiian children do better. An innovative project in Hawaii, called the Kamehameha Early Education Program (KEEP) has developed a culturally compatible program for kindergarten through third grade children of Hawaiian ancestry. In recognition of the emphasis on collaboration, cooperation, and assisted performance, as well as sibling caretaking in traditional Hawaiian culture, the KEEP program designed an alternative social organization for the classroom. Hawaiian children do much better academically in this culturally compatible system—a small group classroom organization in which the children work in independent groups of four to five students and the teacher moves from group to group to offer intensive instruction. By shifting the organization to better suit the cultural backgrounds of the students, the children learned more! Classroom social organization needs to match the cultural experiences of the pupils.

Sources: Tharp, R. G. (1989). Psychocultural variables and constants: Effects on teaching and learning in school. *American Psychologist,* **44** (2), 349–359;

In summary, the open classroom is a mixed success. The arrangement seems to help children socially, but for some children this arrangement is not the most efficient way to learn. While it is unlikely that American public schools will convert to the open classroom model, many schools already offer both types of classroom, the traditional and the open, attempting to assign students and teachers to the one that seems best suited to their own needs, predispositions, and abilities.

In the final analysis, "the physical context of the school is not a given. It is created and mediated by people, who largely determine the effects of the setting" (Minuchin & Shapiro, 1983, p. 210). Since teachers are the central organizers in schools, we turn now to their impact on children's social and academic progress.

THE TEACHER

By far the most important figures in the school are the teachers. In this section we will examine who they are, what they do, and what effects they have on their pupils' academic progress and social and emotional adjustment. As we will see in our later discussion of sex roles (Chapter 15), teachers tend to treat boys and girls differently in their classroom interactions. In this section, we focus on other aspects of the teacher's behavior. Do teachers' early impressions of a child's abilities make a difference? The teacher plays a variety of roles in the classroom as evaluator, disciplinarian, and social model. The way that each of these roles is managed can affect the pupils in a variety of ways.

(King Features Syndicate.)

(Peanuts reprinted by permission of UFS, Inc.)

Teacher Expectation and Academic Success

Although many teachers would probably deny it, most of them form impressions early in the school year concerning the probable performance of the incoming group of students. These expectations come from a variety of sources, such as the pupil's past academic record, achievement test scores, family background, appearance, and classroom conduct history. Do these prejudgments of the child's performance have an impact on the child's actual scholastic success or failure? It is possible to investigate the effect of these naturally developed expectations on the child's performance by soliciting predictions from teachers early in the year and then determining how closely the child's output conforms to the teacher's prediction. A more powerful technique involves experimentally planting an expectation concerning certain children in a classroom and then assessing to what degree the expectation is fulfilled. Rosenthal and Jacobsen of Harvard University (1968) have carried out such an experiment, "Pygmalion in the Classroom." In a number of elementary school classes, teachers were informed that 20 percent of their students—who were in fact, randomly chosen—were "intellectual bloomers who would show unusual intellectual gains during the academic year" (Rosenthal & Jacobsen, 1968, p. 66). In order to assess the impact of teacher expectations, the children were administered an IQ test before the experiment commenced and again after eight months of additional classroom experience with the "expectant" teacher. Would the children labeled as academic bloomers show a larger improvement than nonlabeled control children in the same classroom? For the school as a whole, those children for whom the teachers had been led to expect greater intellectual gain showed a significantly greater increase in IQ scores than did the remaining students. Moreover, the "intellectual bloomers" did better than their classmates in reading and were rated as higher in "intellectual curiosity" than the control children. Apparently it is easier to modify teacher expectations early, since the gains were most marked in the lower grades. In fact, the lower the grade level, the greater the effect.

Even though Rosenthal's tests to reveal a self-fulfilling prophecy in the classroom have met with severe methodological criticism and in spite of some failures to find a Pygmalion effect, other investigators have corroborated the central finding in the case of Head Start children, retarded children, and institutionalized adolescent female offenders, as well as children in regular classrooms (Raudenbusch, 1984).

How can we explain the Pygmalion or teacher-expectation effect? Since teachers expect certain kinds of behavior from high and low achievers, they treat them differently and thereby sustain the patterns (Brophy, 1986). Not only do higher achievers receive more teaching, they are given more chances to participate in class and more time to answer. They receive more praise for correct answers and less criticism for wrong ones. In contrast, low achievers are not expected to know and to participate and are provided less opportunity and encouragement for doing so (Minuchin & Shapiro, 1983). The case is not closed and the questions raised by the original study still remain: "How much of the improvement in intellectual performance attributed to the contemporary educational programs is due to the context and methods of the programs and how much is due to the favorable expectancies of the teachers?" (Rosenthal & Jacobsen, 1966, p. 188).

The Teacher as a Disciplinarian

Teachers not only act as evaluators but spend a good deal of their time as disciplinarians. How effective are different teacher-control techniques for achieving and maintaining classroom order, and what effect do teacher tactics have on children's motivation? Although it might be intuitively predicted that praise is more effective than disapproval, systematic analysis of the use of praise is necessary before any conclusions concerning its effectiveness can be legitimately drawn. Other questions also require consideration. How important are classmates in achieving classroom control? Can the power of the peer group be effectively harnessed by the teacher to achieve more effective discipline?

OPERANT REINFORCEMENT IN THE CLASSROOM

Recent attempts to apply operant reinforcement principles to classroom control have been very successful (Kazdin, 1982). In some cases, social reinforcement in the form of verbal approval is used whereby teachers are taught to praise appropriate behavior and ignore disruptive behavior in a systematic manner. Another technique that has proved effective in establishing classroom control is the combination of material or token rewards and social reinforcements. This approach was not used routinely until the 1960s, but it is certainly not new.

> In 610 A.D., a monk formed the ends of leftover bread dough into strips, which he folded into a twisted loop to represent the folded arms of children in prayer. The baked treat, called a *pretiola* (Latin for "little reward"), was then offered to children as a reward for learning their prayers. (O'Leary & O'Leary, 1977, p. 257)

In the modern version of this program, children accumulate points or tokens for good behavior, which they can then exchange for material rewards such as candy, peanuts, comics, or toys. Numerous studies have demonstrated the effectiveness of this approach for controlling children in classrooms (Kazdin, 1982). In addition, all of the children may pool their rewards for special treats such as parties or trips to museums or the zoo. Such group rewards exert considerable pressure on deviant students to improve their behavior. Woe betide the classroom cutup who deprives his peers of a Halloween party because of his antics.

But token rewards may not always be necessary and, in fact, they may undermine children's interest in their school activities—under some circumstances. As the study in Box 14-2 illustrates, activities that are intrinsically interesting may lose their appeal if rewards are provided. While this study implies that token rewards should be introduced in classrooms only

BOX 14-2 WHEN TOKENS FAIL: LOSS OF INTEREST THROUGH UNNECESSARY REWARD

Token rewards in classrooms are neither always necessary nor always desirable. There are many activities in school that are intrinsically interesting for children; solving math problems can be fun for a high school student, just as making a paper hat can be interesting for a preschooler. What happens if children are rewarded for already interesting activities? Will they simply become more interested, or will interest lag? To find out, Lepper, Greene, and Nisbett (1973) rewarded one group of preschoolers with a "Good Player Award"—a big gold star and a bright red ribbon—for drawing pictures with felt pens, an activity that these children already enjoyed a great deal. Other children, who also enjoyed using the pens, were asked to draw pictures but received no reward for their products. The amount of time that the children spent drawing during their free-play periods in the nursery school was recorded by observers before and after the special drawing and reward sessions. The results were dramatic: The children who were rewarded for drawing spent less time during free-play periods in this activity after the reward than they had displayed prior to the experience, while the children who did not receive an "award" maintained their interest in drawing at the same level as before. Moreover, rewards can undermine artistic creativity as well; when anticipating prizes for the most creative work, individuals tend to do less creative work than when no prize is anticipated (Amabile & Hennessey, 1988). These basic findings have been replicated by a number of other investigators and some of the conditions under which the effect "works" have been uncovered (Lepper & Hodell, 1988). For example, if children think that they are being rewarded for performing well on the task, interest will not necessarily decrease (Boggiano & Ruble, 1979). Receipt of a reward that is contingent on a superior performance tells a person how well he is doing at an activity, and this information is likely to enhance later intrinsic interest. In contrast, receipt of a reward only for engaging in a task—regardless of how good or poor the performance—decreases later intrinsic interest. Age matters as well. If children are too young to be able to compare their performance to other children's skills, focus on performance doesn't matter.

These findings suggest that token reinforcers may sometimes undermine the intrinsic interest in activities. Reinforcers can be effective in the classroom but should be used in situations where intrinsic interest in the activity is low. Once the merits of the activity become clear to the child, tangible rewards may become unnecessary or even undesirable.

Sources: Amabile, T. M., & Hennessey, B. A. (1988). The motivation for creativity in children. In A. K. Boggiani & T. Pittman (Eds.), *Achievement and motivation: A social developmental perspective.* New York: Cambridge University Press; Boggiano, A. K., & Ruble, D. N. (1979). Perception of competence and the overjustification effect: A developmental study. *Journal of Personality and Social Psychology, 37,* 1462–1468; Lepper, M. R., Greene, D., & Nisbett, R. (1973). Test of the "overjustification hypothesis." *Journal of Personality and Social Psychology,* **28**, 129–137; Lepper, M. R. & Hodell, M. (1988). Intrinsic motivation in the classroom. In C. Ames & R. Ames (Eds.), *Research on motivation in education* (Vol. 3, pp. 73–107). New York: Academic.

when necessary and not as a routine practice, there are many classroom activities, such as learning multiplication tables, that may be unappealing. In such cases, tokens, or extrinsic rewards can often increase children's interest in these classroom activities (Lepper & Hoddell, 1988). Token programs have a place in the classroom, but care needs to be exercised in choosing the target activities. Finally, using rewards in a consistent, immediate, and clear manner will increase their effectiveness—not an easy task for a teacher with thirty or forty children in the class!

Peers as Teachers

Not only can peers aid in controlling their classmates, but they can function as peer-teachers as well. Older children are sometimes cast in the role of assistant teachers and given responsibility for teaching younger children. Although the details of different programs vary, most involve some kind of instruction session for the "helpers" in which they learn the techniques of relating to and teaching younger children. In addition, to coordinate the tutoring program with the younger child's regular classroom experience, assistants often meet with the teacher of the child they are aiding. The results

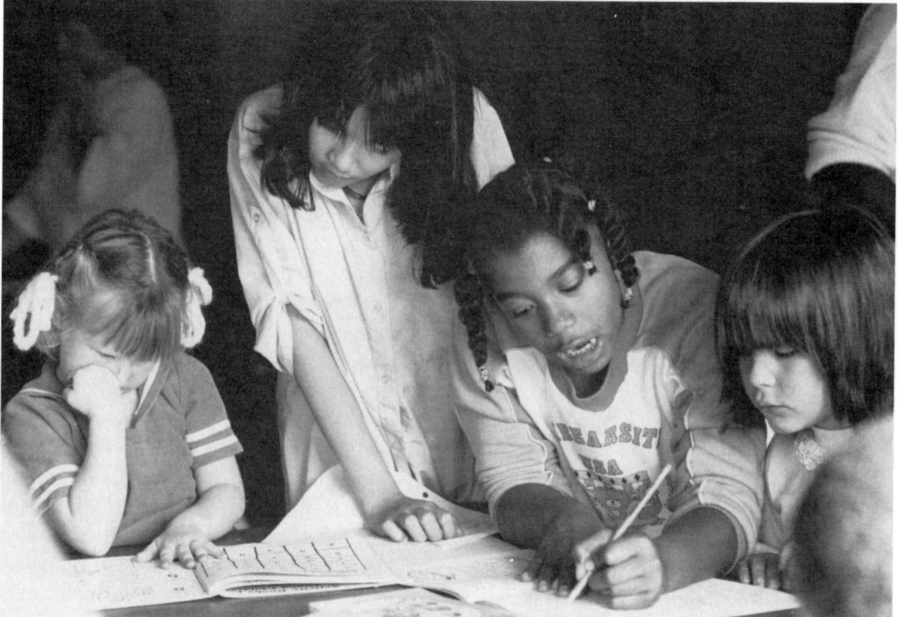

Older children, in tutoring younger children, can benefit both children's learning.

indicate that both tutor and pupil benefit in a variety of ways, although the tutor benefits more (Dansereau, 1987).

The experience of being a tutor can even benefit low-achieving children (Allen & Feldman, 1976). Low-achieving fifth graders whose reading scores were at least one year below average grade level taught a third grader for twenty minutes a day or studied the material alone. By the end of the two-week period, tutoring resulted in a significantly better performance than studying alone for the low-achieving fifth-grade children. These gains were made in spite of the fact that the third graders learned equally with the tutor or studying alone. The tutoring effect had more impact on the tutors than on the tutees. More recent studies show a similar effect of the tutor gaining even more than the student being taught (Lambiotte et al., 1987). Clearly, children can serve as effective helpers for their classmates and for younger pupils and may, in the process, help themselves.

Cooperative Learning

Many variations of peer tutoring have sprung up in recent years, and often peer tutoring is combined with other approaches such as cooperative learning environments. Cooperative environments involve small groups of students who work together to master learning material. Often the group is heterogeneous, with children of different sexes, abilities, and ethnic backgrounds working together on common problems. However, cooperative learning groups differ from peer tutoring arrangements in that no one is obviously more knowledgeable from the outset or singled out to lead the group. "The goal is to maximize the learning of all students and to increase the mutuality of their relationships with children different from themselves" (Minuchin & Shapiro, 1983, p. 114). One example that uses peer tutoring as part of the cooperative learning format is the "jigsaw method" developed by Aronson and his colleagues (Aronson, Stephan, Sikes, Blaney, & Snapp, 1978). The material is divided into parts and each member of a small group is responsible for one part. Pupils work with other group participants on a segment and then "teach" the other members of the team the material they have mastered. They also learn to work independently as well as to rely on other team members. Most studies of cooperative learning environments have demonstrated a positive impact on self-esteem, helping behavior, interpersonal liking, mutual concern among peers, cooperation, and attitudes toward school and learning (Minuchin & Shapiro, 1983). Moreover, Slavin and his colleagues (Slavin, 1983, 1987) report greater increases in math skills in cooperative classrooms in comparison with control classes.

Another form of cooperative learning is *peer collaboration* in which a pair of novices work together to solve tasks that neither could do previously. Even though no adult instruction was provided, the children in these programs made substantial progress in solving math problems in comparison to control children (Damon & Phelps, 1989). However, there are drawbacks. As Crockenberg (1979) has shown in an experimental study of third and fourth graders, cooperative learning experiences can lead to greater conformity and susceptibility to peer influence, as well as to an unwillingness to risk disagreement. While helpfulness and mutual respect are important and desirable outcomes, blind conformity is not.

We have examined teachers, tutors, and tactics. Now we turn to technology and explore the impact of introducing computers into classrooms.

INNOVATIONS IN TEACHING: COMPUTERS IN THE CLASSROOM

Antiquated

Mr. Edison says
that the radio will supplant the teacher.
Already one may learn languages by means of Victrola records.
The moving picture will visualize
What radio fails to get across.
Teachers will be relegated to the backwoods . . .
Or, perhaps, shown in museums.
Education will become a matter of pressing the button.
Perhaps I can get a position at the switchboard.

Virginia Woodson Church (1925, p. 59).

Every decade brings forth a new technological innovation that holds promise of revolutionizing teaching and learning. Television and teaching machines held sway for a time, and computers are currently in the forefront of educational change. Although technological advances have not replaced teachers, computers are becoming an important aid to learning (Greenfield, 1984; Lepper & Gurtner, 1989). Recent evidence suggests that microcomputers may help children learn more and learn more rapidly. Moreover, they may change the ways that classrooms are organized and may even alter how children relate to each other.

There are three major ways in which computers are used in the classroom (Lepper & Gurtner, 1989). One of the first and oldest ways uses the *computer as a personal tutor.* In this case, learning is individualized and tailored to the needs and capabilities of the learner. Students proceed at their own pace and receive immediate and personal feedback, and help if they need it. One

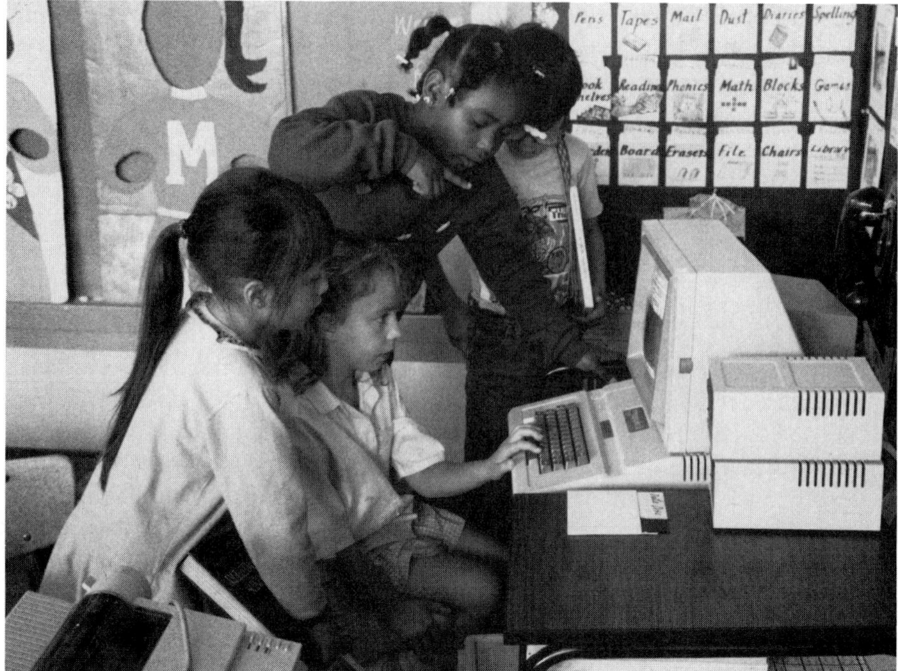

Computers are becoming common in classrooms—even in early elementary school.

of the simplest applications are drill-and-practice programs—often called computer-assisted instruction—question-and-answer programs in which the computer poses the problem, gives the student a chance to respond, and then tells her if she is correct. These are useful as supplements to traditional instruction and often free the teacher to do other tasks. In one study, children who used the computer for drill and practice did better in a variety of subjects than other children who did not use the computer (Niemiec & Walberg, 1987). This approach is especially helpful with math and vocabulary and with younger or lower ability or remedial students. And children like it! "As a seven-year-old put it, 'The computer doesn't yell.' Nor does it have favorites. Indeed computer technology lowers both the real and psychological cost of error in all areas it touches, not just in drill-and-practice software. This is important because many negative patterns of behavior in school grow out of fear of error and fear of failure" (Greenfield, 1984, pp. 131–132).

A second use of computers is the *computer as a medium for experiential learning*. According to this view, "the computer is seen as offering a uniquely appropriate medium for the creation of more open ended, exploratory learning environments" (Lepper & Gurtner, 1989, p. 171). For example, computer simulations of scientific laboratories allow children the rare opportunity to perform experiments that would be too complex or dangerous to try in the real world. Or they can experiment with the laws of physical systems such as varying the law of gravity and observing the results. A trip in a spaceship would probably accomplish the same thing, but is unlikely to be a common classroom exercise any time soon! Transfer to noncomputer tasks is sometimes limited (Salomon & Perkins, 1987), although more recent studies appear to be more successful in achieving successful transfer or generalization to regular classroom environments.

Third, the computer can be used as *a multi-purpose tool* in the classroom.

> Computers with appropriate software are powerful tools for creative expression. Word processing programs remove much of the tedium of writing and editing, thereby encouraging more and better writing. Graphics creation programs facilitate the creation of pictures, animations and special visual effects. Music composition programs open new possibilities for exploring music, even for people who do not know how to play an instrument. (Kleiman, 1984, p. 27)

Can children learn to write better with the help of a good word processor? Since revision is a key element in the composing process, it is not surprising that word processing does improve children's writing skills (Collins, Brown, & Newman, 1990). For example, Kleiman and Humphrey (1982) reported that learning-disabled children 7 to 16 years of age, many of whom had refused to do any kind of writing, began writing more, editing more, and producing better compositions when permitted to use a word processor.

The value of computers as learning aids is clearly very great, but there are social consequences of computers as well. As Box 14-3 suggests, the introduction of computers in schools and homes may unintentionally increase the gender gap. Many educators fear that computers will lead to social isolation: Children will choose to work away at their keyboards and ignore each other. Recent research suggests that the opposite is true. Observers watched children both when they were working with computers and when they were engaged in the more traditional classroom activities. In both cases, the children were free to interact with each other. The children talked more and interacted more—verbally and physically—when they worked with computers than when they engaged in noncomputer activities (Hawkins, Sheingold, Gearhart, & Berger, 1982). Computers seem to promote rather than reduce social interaction. A word of caution, however: In the final

"Short day at school. The computers are down."

(Chon Day; © 1985 The New Yorker Magazine, Inc.)

BOX 14-3 ARE COMPUTERS WIDENING THE GENDER GAP?

Computers are becoming commonplace in classrooms, but do boys and girls benefit equally from this technological revolution? Recent research by Mark Lepper has found large sex differences in children's participation in optional computer activities of many kinds—elective courses, summer camps, after-school clubs, and home use. There are as many as five to ten boys for each girl in these programs. Moreover, this difference in participation rates increases as the activity becomes more costly and more effortful. In California schools, boys outnumber girls in introductory programming classes by a 2 to 1 ratio. In contrast, the ratio is 10 to 15 boys for each girl in advanced programming classes.

Why is there a gender gap? Since the computer field is dominated by males, as in other areas of math and science, there are few female role models for girls. Moreover, parents are more likely to buy a computer for their sons than their daughters. In his California study, Lepper has found that families with only boys were twice as likely to own a home computer as families with only girls. Computer labs in schools are often competitive, noisy, and high-activity environments in which boys may feel more comfortable than girls. Moreover, the kinds of programs which are often used to introduce students to computers seem to have been written for boys. The two most common themes of educational games involve war and violence and male sex-typed sports such as baseball, basketball, and football. Even the titles of the games may turn girls off: Alien Addition, Demolition Division, Spelling Baseball. Finally, in spite of the fact that computers have many varied uses—such as graphic design and word processing—schools typically present computers as mathematical instruments. Computer labs are usually found in the math department, run by math teachers; and credits for computer courses often count toward math requirements. As Lepper notes, "Such an identification—of course—feeds into the historically widespread attitudinal and attributional influences that have served in the past to keep girls away from careers in math and science" (1985, p. 17).

Clearly, computers can be effective learning aids; but with the early indications suggesting boys may benefit more from them than girls, computers may even contribute to widening the gender gap.

Sources: Lepper, M. R. (1985). Microcomputers in education: Motivation and social issues. *American Psychologist,* 40, 1–18.

analysis, computers are only tools and, like any technological aids, can help or hinder, depending on how they are used. Their potential is clear; their ultimate role in the classroom is still being determined. Now we turn from technology to textbooks.

TEXTBOOKS

What's Wrong with Primary Readers?

In the past two decades there has been a reawakening of interest in, and concern about, children's readers. Educators have recognized that children are influenced not only by their teachers and peers but also by the reading material to which they are exposed. Primers serve an important socializing function. Many of the attitudes and cultural values that are slowly emerging during the early school years are directly shaped by the content and themes of these textbooks. In addition, these readers play an important role in determining the child's attitudes toward the task of reading itself. Particularly from children who have had little encouragement to read before entering school and therefore have little appreciation of the value of books and the rewards of reading, primers with lively, interesting, and relevant content would seem to be necessary to interest them in books and reading.

One would expect that children would be much more involved and motivated if the content of the reading material were relevant to their own background, interests, and experience (Tharp, 1989). Cross-cultural studies suggest that Navajo and Hawaiian children show higher levels of interest and participation when textual material is related to the children's own personal experiences (Au, 1979; Tharp, 1989). One would also expect differences between reading ability of children exposed to the "Dick and Jane" stories and of those taught to read with more realistic, and culturally relevant materials. In fact, children do comprehend more when reading high-interest rather than low-interest material (Asher, 1980). The reading scores of boys, even more than girls, are affected by the interest value of stories (Asher & Markell, 1974). Fifth graders were given passages to read that were of either high or low interest. When boys had the chance to read stories about astronauts and airplanes, they read much better than when they read low-interest stories and the typical difference in reading level between boys and girls disappeared when the material was interesting. Girls, on the other hand, tended to be less affected by the interest level of the stories (see Figure 14-3). Although there is no single solution to the problem of lower reading achievement of boys in elementary school, this study suggests that more attention should be paid to motivational factors. Boys can read better if the material turns them on. It probably comes as no surprise to the readers of this book that the effects are not restricted to children; even college students learn better when they read interesting material than dull and boring passages (Shirley & Reynolds, 1988)!

Moreover textbooks carry hidden agendas to the young about sex-role mythologies in our society (Stockard et al., 1980). An analysis of first-, second-, and third-grade readers revealed evidence of a stereotypic portrayal of male and female roles (Saario, Jacklin, & Tittle, 1973). Boys are compliant, self-disclosing, and engage in fantasy. In view of the importance of attributions for success and failure in children's achievement (see Chapter 11), it is unfortunate that boys in stories receive positive outcomes as a result of their own actions, while girls receive rewards because of circumstance. Texts in school may inadvertently be contributing to sex differences in achievement.

Perhaps the most appropriate way to close this section is to offer the following plea that texts not only need to recognize differences in sex and race, but should be generally more aware

> that the real world is more varied than the one depicted in elementary readers. Boys and girls, and men and women, are fat and skinny, short and tall. Boys and men are sometimes gentle, sometimes dreamers. Artists, doctors, lawyers,

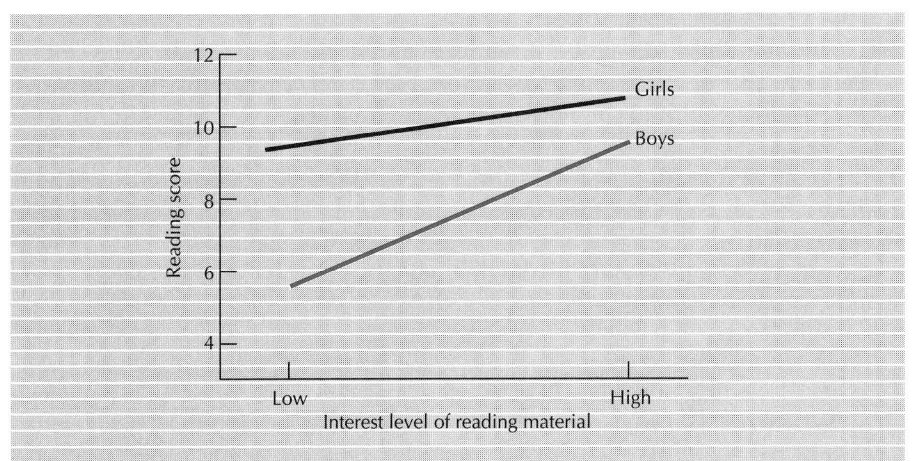

FIGURE 14-3
Reading level of boys and girls with low- and high-interest material. (From Asher & Markell, 1974.)

> and college professors are sometimes mothers as well. Rather than limiting possibilities, elementary texts should seek to maximize individual development and self-esteem by displaying a wide range of models and activities. If the average is the only model presented to a child and therefore assumed to be the child's goal, most children—and most adults—would probably be unable to match the model. (Saario et al., 1973, p. 399)

SPECIAL CHILDREN, SPECIAL NEEDS?

Mainstreaming

Not all children learn at the same pace or in the same way. Some are slower to learn; others learn faster than their classmates; some are blind or deaf or in a wheelchair. A major issue of the last two decades was the question of whether these "special" children should be placed in separate classes or whether they should be integrated into regular classrooms. In the world of special education, this shift toward including children of all abilities in regular classrooms is known as "mainstreaming," and in the 1970s it became a law. Supporters of this legislation cite some powerful arguments but few hard facts. First, they argue that mainstreaming will result in higher levels of achievement, both academically and socially. Second, they suggest that this move away from special isolated classes to a regular school setting "does a better job than a segregated setting of helping children adjust to and cope with the real world when they grow up" (Brenton, 1974, p. 23). Third, they assume that exposure to a wide range of children will help more normally functioning children understand individual differences in people and that it will also help to diminish the stereotyping of children with various types of handicaps or disabilities (Brenton, 1974). In spite of the legal fact of mainstreaming, there are skeptics. Part of the skepticism stems from the fact that the academic and social gains of mainstreaming has not always been realized. First, there are relatively small differences in academic achievement between mainstreamed students and pupils in self-contained classrooms (MacMillan, Keogh, & Jones, 1986). Second, integration of mildly retarded children may lead to increased social rejection (Taylor, Asher, & Williams, 1987) by their nonretarded peers. Recent evidence suggests that the basis for the rejection varies; some mildly retarded children are shy and avoidant while others are aggressive and disruptive. In spite of the basis for rejection, it doesn't go unnoticed, and the mildly retarded rejectees are more lonely and more dissatisfied and anxious about their peer relationships than nonretarded children (Taylor et al., 1987).

Interventions designed to improve the social acceptance of retarded children in mainstreamed classrooms are successful in achieving some improvement, although even after intervention the retarded children are not as well accepted as their nonretarded classmates (Gottlieb & Leyser, 1981; Gresham & Reschly, 1988). As long as people judge others by their abilities, increased contact with those who are relatively less expert may lead to less, rather than more, acceptance (Asher, Oden, & Gottman, 1977, p. 42). Perhaps the most reasonable view is one that encourages flexibility in response to the individual needs of the children in the schools.

> In schools that are most responsive to individual differences in abilities, interests, and learning styles of children, the mainstream is actually many streams, sometimes as many streams as there are individual children, sometimes several streams as groups are formed for special purpose, sometimes one stream only as concerns of all converge. (Hobbs, 1975, p. 197)

> What number is that which, being divided by the product of its digits, the quotient is 3, and if 18 be added, the digits will be inverted? He flew out of his chair, whirled around, rolled up his eyes, and said in about a minute, 24. Multiply in your head 365, 365 365, 365, 365, 365 by 365, 365, 365, 365, 365, 365 . . . in not more than one minute said he, 133, 492, 850, 208, 566, 925, 016, 658, 299, 583, 255! (mid-nineteenth century child prodigy, Barlow, 1952, p. 43)

> I was standing at the front of the room explaining how the earth revolves and how, because of its huge size, it is difficult for us to realize that it is actually round. All of a sudden, Spencer blurted out, "The earth isn't round," I curtly replied, "Ha, do you think it's flat?" He matter-of-factly said, "No, it's a truncated sphere." I quickly changed the subject. Spencer said the darndest things. (Payne, Kauffman, Brown, & DeMott, 1974, p. 94)

Just as there are special problems in organizing the best type of education of retarded and handicapped children, similar problems exist for exceptionally talented children (Sternberg, 1988; Tomlinson-Keasey, 1990). Should these extremely bright children be accelerated and be permitted to begin school early, skip grades, and graduate ahead of their age-mates? These are controversial issues. Some argue that acceleration is necessary to maintain interest and motivation. Critics retort that the accelerated child's intellectual needs may be met at the expense of the child's social and emotional development. Since accelerated children are with older peers, they may be socially isolated. However, this is probably another myth, since very bright children often seek out the company of older children and adults. As Terman (1954), one of the earliest leaders in the study of the gifted child noted, bright children are usually far ahead of their age-mates, not just intellectually, but socially and physically as well. Recent evidence suggests that Terman was probably right! Instead of being viewed as "nerds" who are rejected by their peers, there is little evidence that acceleration leads to social adjustment problems.

Richardson and Benbow (1990) evaluated the social development of 1247 gifted children who accelerated their education and a comparison group of gifted but nonaccelerated peers. Children were identified at ages 12 to 14 and evaluated in terms of their social-emotional adjustment at 18 and 23 years of age. At age 18, there was little evidence that acceleration altered their sense of self-esteem; only 5 percent felt that being moved ahead had a negative effect. By age 23 only 3.3 percent of the students felt that their socioemotional adjustment had been hindered by being accelerated in school.

Further support for acceleration comes from a program at Johns Hopkins University called "Study of Mathematically Precocious Youth" (Stanley & Benbow, 1983; Brody & Benbow, 1987). In the program, seventh and eighth graders with exceptional talent for mathematics are identified. These children are helped through a variety of special programs to move ahead at an accelerated pace in mathematics. The results have been spectacular. By 1982 approximately 35,000 mathematically talented youth had been identified, and the program continues to identify about 2200 per year. These students either take college courses or enter college early. A number have graduated before their eighteenth birthdays. To cite one example: "A young man graduated from Johns Hopkins at barely age 17 with a BA in mathematical sciences after only 5 semesters there, one year in senior high school and one year in junior high school. . . . Nor was he narrow in his interests. . . . His list of extracurricular activities is long, including a high school letter in wrestling and a varsity spot for two years on the college golf team (Stanley, 1976, p. 41). As the program so dramatically shows, talented children can be accelerated and succeed extremely well. One wonders how much talent has been wasted by our reluctance to accelerate precocious pupils in the past.

Stanley makes an eloquent plea for acceleration:

> A well-known quotation from Thomas Gray's famous elegy sums up the case for seeking talent and nurturing it:
>
> *Full many a gem of purest ray serene,*
> *The dark unfathom'd caves of ocean bear;*
> *Full many a flower is born to blush unseen,*
> *And waste its sweetness on the desert air.*
> *another poet (Browning) tells us that ". . . a man's reach should*
> *exceed his grasp, Or what's a heaven for?"*
>
> *It is our responsibility and opportunity to help prevent the potential Miltons, Einsteins, and Wieners from coming to the "mute inglorious" ends Gray viewed in that country churchyard long ago. The problem has changed little, but the prospects are much better now. Surely we can greatly extend both the reach and the grasp of our brilliant youths, or what's an education system for (Stanley, 1976, p. 41)?*

Other education alternatives for gifted children include enrichment programs, which avoid accelerating the child's grade level. These include extra work on the same level of difficulty, but more of it. One critic termed this form of enrichment "busywork" (Stanley, 1976). A second type involves "irrelevant academic enrichment," which consists of setting up a special subject or activity meant to enrich the educational lives of some group of intellectually talented students. For example, a special class in science or social studies might be arranged as a supplement and diversion for the bored high-IQ students. Another form of enrichment is "cultural," which involves supplying opportunities in the performing arts such as music, art, drama, dance, and creative writing, or offering instruction in a foreign language. Critics argue that these opportunities are often unrelated to the area of the child's talent and do not provide full opportunity for the development of these areas of unique talent. Clearly, the case for acceleration needs to be more fully evaluated before any final conclusions about the best way to treat the gifted child can be drawn.

CULTURE, CLASS, AND RACE

It has been estimated that the school has a cumulative effect on the lower-class child such that "by the third grade he is approximately one year behind academically, by the sixth grade two years behind, by grade eight two and one half to three years retarded academically and by the ninth grade a top candidate for dropping out" (Rioux, 1968, p. 92). For the middle-class child the picture is very different; rather than dropping out, he is much more likely than his lower-class peers to go to college (Comer, 1988).

Why the social-class difference? In Chapter 11, we discussed the differential effects of such factors as parent-interaction styles, peer contexts, and teacher behavior on the cognitive development of children from lower- and middle-class homes and children of differing ethnic backgrounds. In this discussion, it was noted that those differences are present and detectable before the child even reaches the schoolroom. So it may not be entirely the schools' fault; children of lower-class backgrounds may simply not be well prepared to fit into the middle-class culture of the classroom. But it is the aim of education presumably to teach children regardless of their background. Various societal strategies have been developed to achieve these aims. Some of these issues were explored earlier in Chapter 11. One solution to the problem of making education equally accessible and relevant to all children, regardless of demographic or cultural background, is desegregation. We now turn to an examination of the extent to which this strategy achieves its goals.

School Desegregation

Few topics have generated as much public concern in the last four decades as the desegregation of American schools. In 1954 the United States Supreme Court mandated an end to segregated education in the classic case of *Brown v. Board of Education.* Here is part of that landmark decision:

> Does segregation of children in public schools solely on the basis of race, even though the physical facilities and other "tangible" factors may be equal, deprive the children of the minority group of equal educational opportunities? We believe that it does. . . . To separate them from others of similar age and qualifications solely because of their race generates a feeling of inferiority as to their status in the community that may affect their hearts and minds in a way unlikely ever to be undone. . . . We conclude that in the field of public education the doctrine "separate but equal" has no place. Separate educational facilities are inherently unequal. *(Brown v. Board of Education,* 1954)

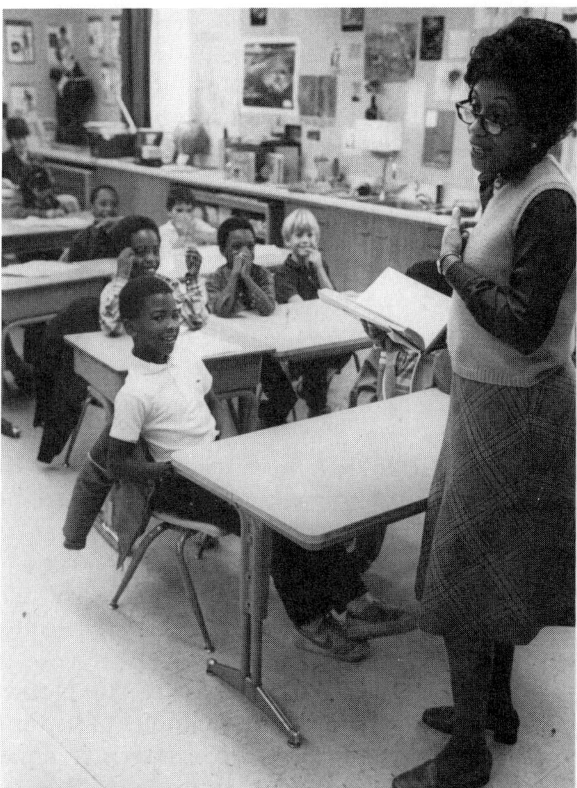

Integrated classrooms provide opportunities to learn about students of other ethnic and racial backgrounds.

Desegregation was expected to correct these ills, and recently there has been an evaluation of how successful desegregation efforts have been in achieving these goals. Here are the main expectations that emerged from the 1954 decision:

1 For whites, desegregation will lead to more positive attitudes toward blacks.
2 For blacks, desegregation will lead to more positive attitudes toward whites.
3 For blacks, desegregation will lead to increases in self-esteem.
4 For blacks, desegregation will lead to increases in achievement. (Stephan, 1978, p. 221)

First, are Caucasians and African-Americans less prejudiced toward each other after going to school together? The evidence is mixed. Some studies (Singer, 1976) find that black and white children in *naturally* integrated schools are more accepting of each other than those in segregated schools. Other investigations indicate that blacks and whites had more negative attitudes toward the other group in integrated schools—particularly if integration is forced rather than voluntary (St. John, 1975). The manner in which integration is reached makes a difference as well. Modifying racial attitudes is complex, and merely placing black and white children in the same school does not mean that they will necessarily interact with each other or that attitudes will change (Grant, 1990). In their extensive four-year longitudinal study of the effects of desegregation in Riverside, California, Gerard and Miller (1975) concluded that the "data we have examined point unmistakably to the conclusion that with the exception of playground interaction, little or no real integration occurred during the relatively long-term contact situation represented by Riverside's desegregation program. If anything, we found some evidence that ethnic cleavages became somewhat more pronounced over time" (p. 243). Other studies agree and as Box 14-4 suggests, cross-race friendships decrease across grades in integrated schools.

What does help to improve interracial relations in integrated schools? A national study by Forehand, Ragosta, and Rock (1976) of ninety elementary schools and seventy-two high schools provides some clues about what strategies are most effective at different ages. For elementary school children, active learning programs, curricula embracing concepts of equal racial status, and integrated work groups promote positive interracial attitudes (Epstein, 1980), and even interracial friendships (Hallinan & Teixeira, 1987).

At the high school levels, the picture is different. Multiethnic texts, minority history courses, multiracial grouping, and discussion of race relations do not improve race relations. However, when high school students are assigned to work together or participate in multiethnic sports teams, race relations improve (Minuchin & Shapiro, 1983; Slavin & Madden, 1979). Another factor that affects cross-race acceptance is the extent to which the numbers of black and white children in a school are equal. In the final analysis "contact that is intimate, equal status, cooperative and sanctioned by authority promotes favorable relations between groups" (Stephan & Rosenfield, 1982). Note how this takes more ongoing effort than just putting children with different backgrounds together and expecting changes to happen on their own.

How is self-esteem affected? Some report increased self-esteem among black students, while others report either no effect or decreases in self-esteem, especially in academic self-concept (St. John, 1975). One difficulty with this area is the underlying assumption that the black child has low self-esteem

BOX 14-4 *PSYCHOLOGY IN ACTION* DESEGREGATION AND CROSS-RACE FRIENDSHIP

What happens to children's friendship choices as a result of integration? To find out, Asher and his colleagues have tracked children in racially integrated schools over a seven-year period. They asked black and white third graders to indicate how much they would like to play with each of their classmates. The children completed similar ratings in the sixth and tenth grades. Figure 14-4 presents a rather positive picture of cross-race acceptance among third-grade children who have been in desegregated schools from the onset of their school careers. However, a marked increase in own-race preference took place between third and sixth grade, and remained evident in the tenth grade. Moreover, if a more stringent measure of social acceptance is used—best friends—the developmental shift is even more dramatic. In the third grade, 24 percent of white children's friendship choices were of blacks, while 37 percent of black children's choices were of whites. In contrast, by tenth grade only 8 percent of white children's best-friend nominations were black, while only 4 percent of the black children's friendship choices were cross-race. Asher and his associates suggest that cross-race acceptance and friendship may decrease, in part, because of organizational features of the school, which may reduce the opportunities for white and black students to become acquainted.

> Different curricular and extra-curricular emphases as well as relatively little time in any particular class together may conspire against black and white students getting to know each other very well. This is especially important since black and white students come from different neighborhoods and to a large extent different social classes, thereby reducing the possibility of after-school contact.
>
> Still, organizational features of the school do not tell the whole story. Even in seventh grade when the students knew nearly everyone else well enough to do the ratings, own-race preference was stronger in third grade. Our guess is that the phenomenon of increasing race cleavage over age can be partly understood in terms of the personal identities that each group projects and interprets of the other as they work, play, and converse together in school. Schofield (1981) has written insightfully about the way identities get played out in desegregated schools. Black children often come to interpret the white children's behavior as aloof, conceited, and academically "show-offish." Whites often perceive blacks as aggressive and threatening. Increasing racial cleavage over age may also be mediated by the growing gap in school achievement that develops between whites and blacks over the school years. (Asher, Singleton, & Taylor, 1982)

Finally, in recent years, the rise of ethnic pride has meant that spontaneous cross-race mixing is less likely, and integration may foster this type of in-group orientation. To illustrate, black children in one city who were bused to achieve integration increased in black separatist ideology more than did nontransferred siblings (Armor, 1972). Even in schools where children have never been in a racially segregated classroom, longitudinal comparisons indicate that as children progress in school, cross-race acceptance decreases.

Sources: Armor, D. J. (1972). The evidence on busing. *Public Interest,* 28, 90–126; Asher, S. R., Singleton, L. C., & Taylor, A. R. (1982). *Acceptance versus friendship: A longitudinal study of racial integration.* Paper presented at the American Educational Research Association Meeting, New York; Schofield, J. W. (1981). Complementary and conflicting identities: Images and interaction in an interracial school. In S. R Asher & J. M. Gottman (Eds.), *The development of children's friendships* New York: Cambridge University Press.

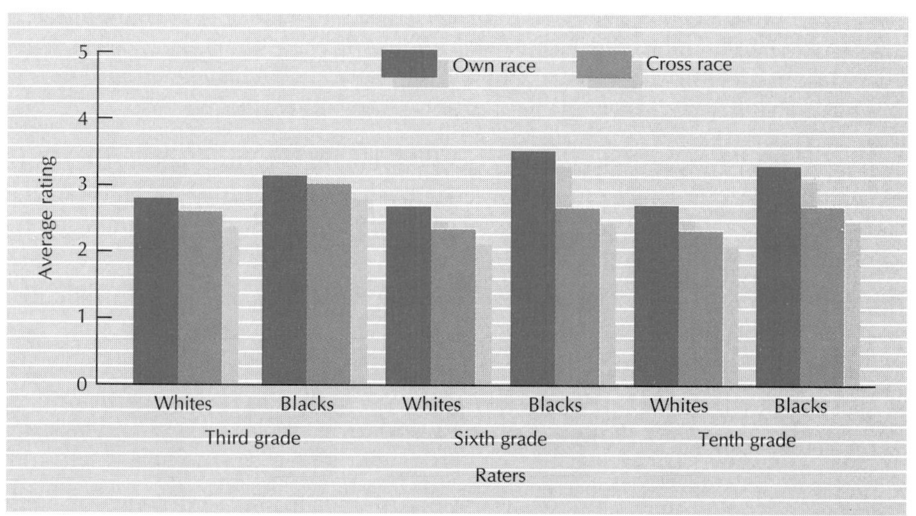

FIGURE 14-4

Sociometric ratings: own-race versus cross-race comparison.

and that desegregation will improve the black child's self-image. However, the assumption of the black child's low self-image has been challenged by studies (Spencer & Markstrom-Adams, 1990) which have shown that black children's self-image is at least as positive as that of white students. Even when a gain in self-esteem is clear, the factors that account for this change are uncertain. Possibly such changes are "a by-product of improved achievement, increased attention by faculty to black educational needs, a greater sense of black unity, or still other factors" (Evans & McCandless, 1978, p. 485).

There is some support for the final prediction concerning increases in the achievement of black students in integrated schools. In only 3 percent of the studies does desegregation lead to a decrease in achievement, while in 29 percent of the studies, an increase occurs (Stephan, 1978). This means that in 68 percent of the studies, the achievement of black children was unaffected by integration. Moreover, even when there are changes, not all academic areas are equally affected: increases in verbal test scores are more likely than in math test scores (Miller, 1983). Moreover, there are historical effects, with greater achievement gains for black children in the 1960s than in the 1970s and 1980s (Stephan, 1983). The most consistent effects concern the age of the child at the time of integration. In general, the earlier the desegregation occurs, the more beneficial it is for students in terms of achievement-test performance. In spite of modest gains, the achievement gap between black and white children remains after integration (Miller, 1983).

In the 1990s, disenchantment with desegregation as a solution to education for minorities is, in fact, on the rise because of conservative Supreme Court decisions, the withdrawal of federal involvement in education, continuing segregation in housing patterns, and growing opposition among middle-class whites as well as decreasing consensus among blacks about the value of desegregated schools (Bates, 1990; Tauber, 1990). It is also important to remember that desegregation is a multiethnic issue. While the original Supreme Court decision was inspired and led by African-Americans, a wide range of ethnic groups—Hispanic, Asian, Native Americans, as well as African-Americans—are all seeking to secure their rights in schools and other social institutions. In California, for example, it is estimated that Hispanic-Americans will constitute 27 percent of the population in 2000, and Asian-Americans 12 percent by the turn of the century.

> Desegregation policy and practice need to take into account these varying concentrations of Hispanic and Asian-American students as well as the cultural characteristics that the different Hispanic and Asian-American ethnic groups bring to the desegregation process. (Grant, 1990, p. 26)

The complexities of desegregation remain to be unraveled. Understanding desegregation will require investigation of a multitude of factors, including busing, voluntary and mandatory integration, attitudes and values of teachers and families, and ethnic ratios. Once we have considered these issues, we may begin to ask not whether desegregation works but under what conditions it can work.

TELEVISION: A HARMFUL OR HELPFUL SOCIALIZATION INFLUENCE

Schools are an undoubtedly important socialization influence on children's development. An even earlier and perhaps more persuasive influence on children's development is television. By the age of 16 the average child has spent more time watching TV than attending school.

How much time do children spend on a daily basis watching TV? Do viewing patterns change with age? What kinds of programs do children watch? How much of the content of TV programs do children actually understand? Do they read fewer books? And does it affect children's behavior for better or worse? Are TV viewers more aggressive? Or do they learn more? Finally, are children affected by advertisements as well as programs?

Development of TV Viewing Patterns

TV viewing starts early in life. Even infants are consumers of TV and a typical 6-month-old is in front of a TV set almost 1½ hours a day (Hollenbeck & Slaby, 1982). However, it is probably not until about 2½ to 3 years of age that children become consistent viewers. Even then, watching is not constant. When 3- to 5-year-olds were monitored while watching "Sesame Street," they looked away about 215 times an hour. When they did look, nearly 75 percent of their glances at the TV were brief—six seconds (Anderson & Levin, 1976)! TV viewing patterns are affected not only by program content, but by the "formal features" of television such as animation, high action, loud music, and visual and auditory special effects. These formal features help to elicit or recruit as well as maintain children's attention to TV. Moreover, these effects are, in part, independent of the program content and are important for younger and older children alike (Huston et al., 1992; Huston & Wright, 1989). Viewing time increases gradually until adolescence, when TV is watched almost four hours per day (See Figure 14-5). It is important to point out that children are not the heaviest consumers of TV. Adults watch even more TV than children, especially the retirement set—those over 65 years old (Gunter & McAleer, 1990). This pattern of TV viewing may be universal and similar trends are found across Europe, Canada, and Australia (Liebert & Spratkin, 1988).

What Do Children Watch?

Children watch a variety of programs including cartoons, situation comedies, family-oriented programs, and educational shows such as "Sesame Street."

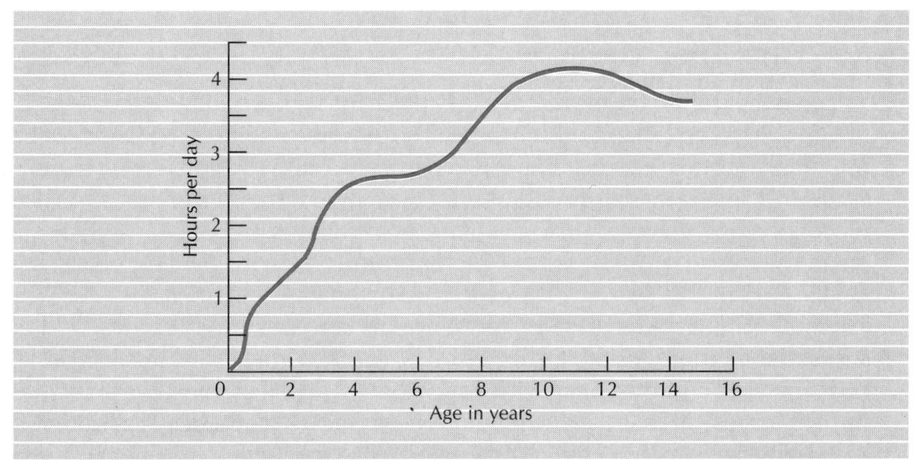

FIGURE 14-5
Estimated average hours of TV viewing by age in the United States in 1987.

Boys and girls differ in their TV tastes. Boys watch more action-adventure and sports while girls prefer human social dramas, such as soap operas. As children develop, they watch fewer children's programs and more general-adult audience fare (Weber, 1988).

In spite of the variety of TV shows that children watch, by late adolescence the average American child has witnessed 13,000 violent murders on TV (Waters & Malamud, 1975). This figure is easy to understand since much of American TV programming contains violence. Over 80 percent of all programs sampled from 1967 through 1985 contained violence, with violent acts being beamed at viewers at a rate of 8.4 per hour. Weekend cartoons that are typically designed for children had an even higher rate: 95 percent of these programs contained violence and violent acts were presented at a rate of 21 per hour. In spite of popular claims to the contrary, these rates have remained remarkably stable from the late 1960s to the mid-1980s (Gerbner, Gross, Signorielli, & Morgan, 1986).

Do Children Understand TV Programs?

As children's cognitive skills develop, they are better able to understand the relationships between action and consequence and, in turn, may be less affected by TV viewing. Early studies of the effects of aggressive models indicated that punishing a model for his or her aggressive acts decreased viewer imitation (Parke & Slaby, 1983). However, TV plots are often complex and involve considerable separation of the action and the subsequent punishment, which may make it more difficult for young viewers to make the link between crime and punishment (Collins, 1983). In a study evaluating this hypothesis, third-, sixth-, and tenth-grade children watched an aggressive sequence that was followed by punishment either immediately before or immediately after a commercial (Collins, 1973). When the commercial was inserted between the crime and the punishment, the third-grade children indicated that they would behave more aggressively than when they saw the violent sequence followed by the punishment without a break. The insertion of the commercial did not affect the subsequent aggression of sixth and tenth graders. This inability of young children to make links between actions and outcomes in regular TV programming may contribute to the heightened effect of TV on young viewers.

Television and Children's Time Use (or "Something Has to Go")

TV viewing takes time and may displace other activities, such as sports, reading, or even talking with others. To find out whether TV displaces other pursuits is not easy, since nearly 99 percent of households have a TV set. A study in Canada helps provide an answer by comparing towns with no TV reception, one channel or four channels (Williams & Handford, 1986). The results were clear. Involvement in community activities was greatest in the no-TV town, and least in the town with four TV channels. After TV was available, children decreased attendance at dances, supper parties, and even sports (see Figure 14-6). Other studies confirm these findings: Heavy TV consumers spend less time with friends, get less sleep, and were less likely to play a musical instrument. Although we may lose the next Mozart to TV, it is important to remember that many children learn to watch TV while

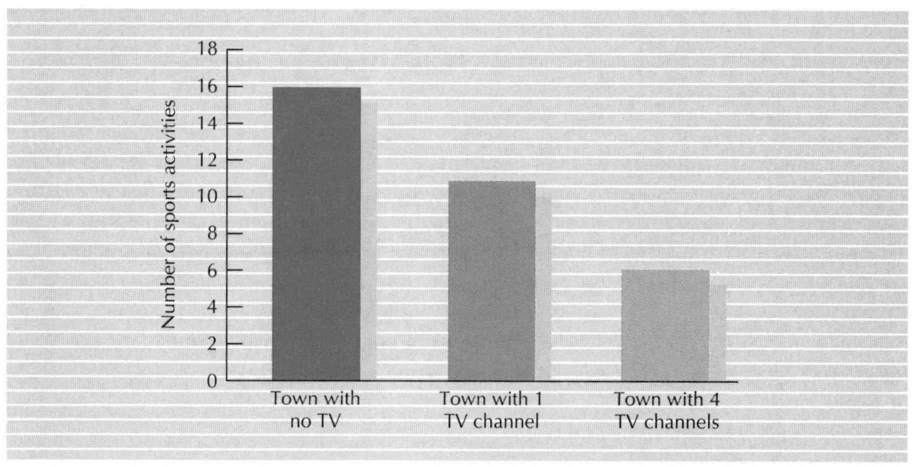

FIGURE 14-6

Average number of sports activities participated in by youths (Grades 7-12) in three Canadian towns. (From data reported in "Television and Other Leisure Activities" by T. H. Williams and A. G. Handford, in *The Impact of Television: A Natural Experiment in Three Communities* (pp. 143–213) edited by T. H. Williams, 1986. Orlando, FL: Academic Press, Inc. Copyright 1986 by Academic Press, Inc. Reprinted by permission.)

doing other things—such as eating dinner or even doing homework (Kubey & Csikszentmihalyi, 1990).

The Harmful Effects of TV Viewing

As indicated throughout this book, exposure to aggressive models on TV can increase children's subsequent aggressive behavior (Parke & Slaby, 1983; Perry, 1990). Heavy doses of TV violence can affect children's attitudes as well and can lead them to view violence as an acceptable and effective way to solve interpersonal conflict (Thomas & Drabman, 1977). Children learn a lesson from TV that "violence works, for both the good guys and the bad guys; it gets things done" (Dominick & Greenberg, 1972, p. 331). Moreover, the effect of TV violence on aggression is not a strictly American phenomenon. Cross-cultural studies indicate that children in Australia, Finland, Great Britain, and Poland show similar reactions to violent TV fare (Huesmann, Lagerspetz, & Eron, 1984).

There are other outcomes: Frequent viewers show less emotional reaction when viewing televised aggression (Cline, Croft, & Courier, 1973). Children who watch televised violence may become indifferent to real-life violence (Drabman & Thomas, 1976). However, exposure to TV violence affects children differently at different ages, due to shifts in children's cognitive abilities. Children who can distinguish between fantasy and reality may react differently from those who are unable to make this distinction. Children who were told that a violent film clip was real (a newsreel of an actual riot) reacted more aggressively later than children who believed that the film was a Hollywood production (Atkin, 1983). As children develop and are able to make this fantasy-reality distinction, many of the fictional TV programs may have less impact. As Box 14-5 illustrates, teaching children to make the distinction can lessen the impact of TV violence.

Aggressive behavior is not the only aspect of children's development that is affected by TV viewing. The level of TV viewing matters, especially in combination with other parental practices. When parents use physical punishment and fail to control children's viewing in terms of hours and content, children tend to be not only more aggressive, but to display more restlessness and motor activity, have less imagination, and do not accurately comprehend television plots despite their heavy viewing (Singer & Singer, 1981; Singer & Benton, 1989).

BOX 14-5 *PSYCHOLOGY IN ACTION* TELEVISION AND REALITY: TEACHING THE DIFFERENCE

Can the impact of violent TV viewing be reduced by helping children distinguish between fantasy and reality? To find out, Rowell Huesmann and his colleagues conducted a two-year treatment study with over 170 children, 6 to 8 years old, who were heavy consumers of TV violence.

Children in the treatment group participated in small groups for five sessions over a two-year period. Three lessons were taught: (1) that television is an unrealistic portrayal of the real world, (2) that aggressive behaviors are not as universal and acceptable in the real world as they appear on television, and (3) that it is just not good to behave like the aggressive characters on TV. Children in the control group met in groups but discussed neutral topics in their sessions. After two years, the children in the experimental group were rated as less aggressive by their peers than those in the control group. Moreover, while there continued to be a positive relation between television violence viewing and aggression in the control group, there was no link between TV violence and aggression for the children who had been taught to interpret media aggression differently. Some of the negative effects of watching TV may be reduced by a program of helping children understand that the world of TV and the everyday world are different.

Sources: Eron, L. D., & Huesmann, L. R. (1984). The control of aggressive behavior by changes in attitudes, values and the conditions of learning. In R. J. Blanchard & C. Blanchard (Eds.), *Advances in the study of aggression* (Vol. 2). New York: Academic; Huesmann, L. R., Eron, L. D., Klein, R., Brice, P., & Fischer, P. 1983). Mitigating the initiation of aggressive behaviors by changing children's attitudes about media violence. *Journal of Personality and Social Psychology*, **44**, 899–910.

Heavy viewing has an adverse impact on reading as well. Beginning at age 3, before the children were reading, the investigators traced viewing patterns and reading scores until age 8. Children's viewing habits were stable with the early heavy viewers remaining high-TV consumers at age 8. Unfortunately, their reading scores were significantly lower than lighter-TV viewing children (Singer & Singer, 1981).

TV AND CHILDREN'S SOCIAL ATTITUDES

Since children spend so much time watching TV, it would be surprising if their attitudes were not altered as well as their behavior. TV is a powerful source of children's knowledge of other groups. As George Gerbner—a prominent TV researcher—notes "the more time one spends 'living' in the world of television, the more likely one is to report perceptions of social reality which can be traced to television's representations of life and society" (Gerbner, Gross, Morgan, & Signorielli, 1980, p. 14). In support of his theory that TV cultivates and shapes viewer attitudes, Gerbner found that heavy TV viewers overestimated the degree of danger and crime in the world and underestimated the trustworthiness and helpfulness of others. Attitudes toward racial groups, gender roles, and sexual relationships are affected by the way in which TV represents these issues as well.

Stereotyping of Minorities on TV. Children's attitudes toward minority groups may be influenced by the portrayals of these individuals on TV. For many years, African-Americans rarely appeared on TV; since the 1970s African-Americans have appeared on TV programs, but still not in proportions that reflect their representation in the population (Greenberg, 1986). Moreover, the roles represent a range of characters in a variety of occupations. Witness the popular Bill Cosby series where the lead character is a successful physician in a upper-middle-class environment. This represents a significant improvement over earlier distorted pictures of blacks as poor, dangerous, or silly. However, the change may be deceptive (Liebert & Sprafkin, 1988), since blacks and whites are still often segregated on TV. Even children's programs

Television shows such as *The Cosby Show* help break down stereotypes of African-American families.

and cartoons are segregated; in 82 percent of the programs white and African-American children didn't appear together (Barcus, 1983).

Moreover, not all groups are even making progress. Hispanic-Americans and Native Americans are not only underrepresented on television, but often are depicted unfavorably as either villains or victims of violence (Gerbner et al., 1986; Greenberg, 1986).

Do these portrayals affect children's racial attitudes? The evidence is mixed. Some evidence (Graves, 1975) suggests that white children who watched a cartoon depicting blacks in a poor light (inept, destructive, lazy, and powerless) developed more negative attitudes toward blacks. In contrast, positive portrayals of blacks as competent, trustworthy, and hard working had a positive impact on white children's racial attitudes. Other long-term studies of the impact of TV viewing on racial attitudes (Atkin, Greenberg, & McDermott, 1978) suggest that prior attitudes influence the way that TV depictions impact our views. Rather than producing dramatic changes, TV may, instead, strengthen existing attitudes. However, even if TV only reinforces existing bigotry and doesn't necessarily produce it, there is still plenty of reason for concern.

Stereotyping Older People. Nor are the elderly depicted fairly on TV. In spite of their growing numbers, old people are underrepresented on TV, especially older women (Liebert & Sprafkin, 1988), and their portrayals are not very flattering either. They are depicted as unhappy, negative, helpless, and rarely romantic. The recent TV program "The Golden Girls," in which older women are depicted more positively as fun loving and capable, may help overcome these distortions.

The Beneficial Sides of TV Viewing

TV has a positive side, as well as a negative one, and it is important to underscore the benefits of TV for the developing child.

THE EDUCATIONAL IMPACT OF TV

As you recall from the opening chapter of the book, "Sesame Street" is a vivid illustration of the educational potential of TV viewing. Other programs such as "Electric Company" which ran from 1971 to 1985 on American TV were designed to help second graders learn to read. Evaluations indicate that first through fourth graders who watched the program in school achieved higher reading scores than children who did not watch the "Electric Company" (Ball & Bogatz, 1973). However, later studies confirm that the "Electric Company" is effective, but only when combined with teacher guidance (Corder-Bolz, 1980).

Other new educational TV ventures include "3-2-1 Contact"—a program designed to help 8- to 12-year-olds "experience the joy of scientific exploration, to become familiar with various styles of scientific thinking and to recognize science and technology as open to their participation" (Children's Television Workshop, 1980, cited by Liebert & Sprafkin, 1988). Topics include oceans, tropics, space, electricity, senses, communication, and babies. Nearly 5 percent of U.S. TV households have watched the program on a weekly basis. Another recent show, "Square One TV" opened in 1987 to increase children's interest and knowledge about mathematics. The show has reached 20 million or 23 percent of U.S. TV households (Liebert & Sprafkin, 1988). To date it is unclear whether these programs have achieved their educational goals; however, the availability of these educational TV offerings means that children have increased viewing options. Clearly, children's development is probably better served when there is more to watch than cartoons and comedies or soaps and shoot-outs!

Finally, as we will explore in Chapter 17, television can have a positive impact on children's social and emotional development as well. Programs such as "Mr. Rogers' Neighborhood" can have beneficial effects on children's helping and sharing activities.

Not through Programs Alone: The Impact of TV Advertising on Children

TV affects children not only through the programs that they watch but also by the commercials and advertising that accompany TV programs (Huston et al., 1992). On average, children watch nearly 20,000 TV commercials each year. The issue is of concern to parents and developmental psychologists because the ads often advocate foods and fads that may not be desirable for children (Tinsley, 1992). Sugary cereals, fast food snacks, and expensive toys are often the main fare of TV ads directed at children.

But do kids pay attention to these ads? Probably not as much as advertisers would like. Children's attention drops when commercials appear and this drop increases with age. Even though there is an attention drop, 90 percent of 4- and 5-year-olds and 100 percent of 6- to 8-year-olds can correctly distinguish a commercial from the program itself (Gaines & Esserman, 1981). However, only 1 percent of 4- to 5-year-olds and 28 percent of 6- to 8-year-olds realize that the goal of the ad is "to try to make you buy things" (Gains & Esserman, 1981).

In spite of children's limited understanding of the purpose of commercials, TV ads are effective in influencing children's preferences. Gorn and Goldberg (1982) exposed 5- to 8-year-olds to one of a variety of different commercials. Some saw sweetened snack food commercials (that is, candy bars, Cracker-

Television can influence children's food preferences.

jacks, Kool-Aid), while others saw fruit ads (orange juice, grape juice) or a public service message emphasizing a balanced diet. Children in the control group saw no commercials. To find out if the ads affected children's food choices, children were allowed to select a snack from orange juice, Kool-Aid, two fruits, and two candy bars. The children who watched the sweetened snacks ad selected the least orange juice and the least fruit of the four groups. In short, children's diet and subsequent health may be affected by the kinds of commercials on TV. In view of one finding that 34 percent of commercials were for sweetened cereals, 29 percent for candies and sweets, and 15 percent for fast food chains, parents have reason to be alarmed! Although few 5-year-olds make an independent trip to the supermarket, children often try to influence their parents' consumer choices. Eighty-five percent of children indicated that they had asked their parents to buy them something that they had seen on a TV ad (Greenberg, Fazel, & Weber, 1986) and a majority of children indicated that they were successful in influencing their parents. Parents beware!

Parents' Role in Modifying the Effects of TV

Parents can help diminish the negative impact of TV by helping children interpret and evaluate more adequately the programs that they are watching. Family members frequently talk to each other while watching television; adults might use such conversation to alter children's reactions to TV by helping the younger ones make the connection between actions and consequences. When an adult helps young viewers make this connection, their subsequent understanding of TV plots is just as good as that of older children (Collins, Sobol, & Westby, 1981). Moreover, parents who use a mediational style (explanation of events, clarifying information), especially if their children are lighter television viewers, are more imaginative, less aggressive, less hyperactive, and understand the TV plots better (Singer, Singer, Desmond, Hirsch, & Nicol, 1988).

Here is one example: To assess the impact of adult reactions to a violent TV show, an adult either approved ("Boy, he really landed a good one." "Terrific") or disapproved ("That's awful; he's really hurting him") of the program. Children who heard the disapproving remarks were less likely to behave aggressively than the children who watched with an adult who condoned the televised violence (Grusec, 1973).

However, it is not clear that parents are active managers of their children's television viewing (Wright, St. Peters, & Huston, 1990). When approximately 5000 parents were asked if they control the kinds of programs that their children watched on TV, 85 percent reported that the children themselves control the channel selector. Only 10 percent reported that they engaged in "positive guidance" whereby they indicate what their children "should" or "must" watch on TV (Mohr, 1979).

Although programming changes may be hard to achieve, adults can serve as mediators of the impact of TV and reduce the negative effects of TV programs on their children.

A Final Frame

There is no doubt that TV is a pervasive influence on children and will probably continue to be a major pastime of children (Huston et al., 1992; Liebert & Sprafkin, 1988). Whether or not we will harness this potential for the good of children remains an unanswered question. TV can be educational and beneficial but, to date, the negative side of TV has received higher billing in the homes of American children and children across the world.

SUMMARY

THE IMPORTANCE OF THE SCHOOL

- Schools alter values, and aspirations, as well as moral and political views. Achievement and occupational aspirations are influenced by schools. Schools expose children to an abstract, symbolic orientation to the world.

THE PHYSICAL STRUCTURE AND ORGANIZATION OF THE SCHOOL ENVIRONMENT

- School size determines the extent of involvement in extracurricular activities; students in small high schools are more likely to participate. Although there are fewer dropouts from small schools, academic achievement is unaffected by school size.

THE CLASSROOM: SPACE AND ORGANIZATION

- Both class size and pupils' location in the class determine the extent to which they participate in classroom activities. Participation is higher in smaller classrooms, and children located in the front and center of the class, the action zone, participate more than children seated in other parts of the room.
- Studies of different classroom organizations found that students generally prefer a group-centered or open classroom in which they are allowed some opportunity to participate in the decision making. Children in open

classrooms are more cooperative, more self-reliant, and better behaved. The academic benefits are less clear. Classroom organization works best when it matches the cultural experiences of the students.

THE TEACHER

- Teachers' early impressions and expectations concerning a pupil's probable success can affect the child's academic progress. A self-fulfilling prophecy is evident: children succeed when teachers believe they will do well and perform poorly when teachers expect them to fail. Applications of behavior modification techniques were found to be successful in controlling children's classroom behavior especially when they used material or token reinforcers for shaping appropriate behavior. Caution in the use of external rewards is necessary, since children's intrinsic interest in school activities may, under some conditions, be undermined by external reinforcers.
- Studies of peer tutoring indicate that both the tutor and the child who is assisted benefit from this arrangement. Collaborative activities seem to enhance certain cognitive skills.

INNOVATIONS IN TEACHING: COMPUTERS IN THE CLASSROOM

- Computers are entering classrooms at a high rate. Children benefit by being able to practice previously learned material with computer-assisted instruction. Word processors aid children's writing skills. Contrary to expectations, computers increase rather than decrease social interaction among children in the classroom.

TEXTBOOKS

- Textbooks are important vehicles for learning and for reinforcing attitudes and social values. Unfortunately, some current primers are inadequate and present unrealistic and culturally insensitive views of children and families. Evidence indicates that children provided with more reality-oriented, interesting readers scored higher on a variety of reading and language measures. Many white middle-class, suburban biases still persist in more recent "new look" primers.

SPECIAL CHILDREN, SPECIAL NEEDS?

- Special children, such as the retarded, often require special treatment. The controversy over mainstreaming, which involves placing children of varying abilities in regular classrooms rather than segregating low-ability children in special classes, remains unresolved.
- Acceleration does not harm the social adjustment of gifted children and may enhance their learning.

CULTURE, CLASS, AND RACE

- A number of factors mitigate against the success of the lower-class child in school, including parental attitudes and behavior, peer contexts, and teacher attitudes and behavior.

- Race relations are not necessarily improved by desegregation, and ethnic cleavages increase across grades. Multiethnic activities such as team sports may have a modest positive impact. Nor is there any evidence that the self-esteem of black children is significantly altered by school integration. While some evidence suggests that black achievement may increase, especially in verbal test scores, fewer achievement gains are being registered today than in the previous decades.
- Desegregation is a multicultural issue; a wide range of ethnic groups need to be considered.

TELEVISION: A HARMFUL OR HELPFUL SOCIALIZATION INFLUENCE?

- The role of television as a socialization force was examined. TV viewing starts early in life and viewing time gradually increases until adolescence.
- Children watch a variety of programs, with boys preferring action-adventure and sports programs, and girls preferring human social dramas. However, many TV programs (80%), especially children's cartoons, contain violence.
- As children's cognitive skills develop, they are better able to understand television programs and distinguish fantasy from reality.
- TV viewing often displaces other activities and decreases social and community participation.
- Television viewing has a multitude of effects, including increases in aggression and negative effects on the development of imagination and reading.
- Social attitudes are altered as well, with heavy TV consumers viewing the world as more dangerous and less trustworthy. Minorities are only beginning to be fairly represented on TV, but TV programs often serve to strengthen existing racial stereotypes. Older people are often misrepresented as well.
- TV has beneficial effects as well, as indicated by the positive impact of educational programs such as "Sesame Street" or "The Electric Company" on children's cognitive development; this is especially true when viewing such programs is combined with a supportive home or school environment.
- Advertising impacts on children's preferences; in view of the high percentage of non-nutritional food ads and toy-oriented ads, these effects are not necessarily positive.
- Parents can modify the effects of TV by serving as interpreters of TV messages and managers of program selection.

CHAPTER 15

THE DEVELOPMENT OF GENDER ROLES AND GENDER DIFFERENCES

In all societies, males and females are treated differently, act differently, and play distinctive roles. At the same time, there are many ways in which the two sexes are highly similar in roles, behaviors, and treatment. One of the challenges for developmental psychology is to determine the nature of these differences and similarities and to understand the processes that help promote the patterns of similarities and differences between children of different gender.

The process by which children acquire the values, motives, and behaviors viewed as appropriate to either males or females in a specific culture is called gender-role typing. Systematic attempts to communicate gender-role standards and to shape different behaviors in boys and girls begin in earliest infancy and have been described as follows:

> Sex-role differentiation usually commences immediately after birth, when the baby is named and both the infant and the nursery are given the blue or pink treatment depending upon the sex of the child. Thereafter, indoctrination into masculinity and femininity is diligently promulgated by adorning children with distinctive clothes and hair styles, selecting sex-appropriate play materials and recreational activities, promoting association with same-sex playmates, and through non-permissive parental reactions to deviant gender-role behavior. (Bandura, 1969, p. 215)

One investigator who was studying sex differences in infancy and did not want her observers to know whether they were watching boys or girls complained that, even in the first few days of life, some infant girls were brought to the laboratory with pink bows tied to their wisps of hair or taped to their little bald heads. Later, when another attempt at concealment of sex was made by asking mothers to dress their infants in overalls, girls appeared in pink and boys in blue overalls, and as the frustrated experimenter said, "Would you believe overalls with ruffles?"

The topics of gender roles and gender differences are controversial. The women's movement in Western cultures as well as the rise of feminist thinking have led to a revision in our ways of thinking about gender differences and gender roles. Two major changes permeate our discussion. First, many of the gender differences that we once viewed as fixed characteristics of males and females are being challenged, such as female verbal superiority and male mathematical superiority. Second, our current theories of gender roles focus on the multiple factors that shape our gender roles, such as cognitive, social, and biological determinants.

To help orient the reader to this topic, it is important to distinguish among several different distinctions that guide research and thinking in this domain. *Gender* and *sex* both refer to biological maleness or femaleness. *Gender stereotypes* are the beliefs that are held by members of a culture about the behaviors and attitudes appropriate to the two sexes in a culture. *Gender roles* are the behaviors that are typically exhibited by males and females in a culture. *Gender typing* is a process by which children acquire the values, motives, and behaviors viewed as appropriate to either males or females in a specific culture.

In this chapter, several questions will be addressed. What is the nature of gender stereotypes in our culture and other cultures? Are there differences between males and females in social, cognitive, and physical abilities? Are there differences in gender roles? How do biological, cognitive, and social factors influence gender roles? These are some of the issues that will be covered this chapter.

GENDER-ROLE STANDARDS AND STEREOTYPES

Considerable consistency in standards of "appropriate" gender-role behavior exists within and between cultures. In this chapter, when we talk about culturally defined behavior as masculine or feminine, we will be talking about behavior viewed as more characteristic of males or females in our culture. The term *appropriate* is in no way meant to imply desirable. The male role is stereotypically oriented toward controlling and manipulating the environment. Males are expected to be independent, assertive, dominant, and competitive in social and sexual relations. Females are expected to be more passive, loving, sensitive, and supportive in social relationships, especially in their family role as wife and mother. Expression of warmth in personal relationships, anxiety under pressure, and suppression of overt aggression and sexuality are regarded as more appropriate for women than for men (Broverman, Vogel, Broverman, Clarkson, & Rosenkrantz, 1972). Although this may appear to be a rather outdated presentation of gender-role standards, studies have indicated that there has been little change in the stereotypes between the 1970s and the present—despite the increased concern with equality of the sexes (Liben & Bigler, 1987; McHale, Bartko, Crouter, & Perry-Jenkins, 1990). In a recent comparison of gender stereotypes among college students assessed in 1972 and again in 1988, Bergen and Williams (1991) found no evidence of shifts in gender stereotypes. Cross-cultural studies also find these stereotyped roles widespread not only in the American culture but in the majority of societies (Williams & Best, 1990; Whiting & Edwards, 1988). In their study of gender stereotypes in twenty-five countries from the Americas, Europe, Africa, Asia, and Oceania, Williams and Best (1990) found a similar pattern of gender stereotypes across most cultures.

There is, however, some variation in culturally accepted gender-role standards both within the United States and across cultures. Within the United States, gender-role standards vary with ethnicity, age, education, and occupation. For example, black American families are more likely to socialize children without strict gender-role distinctions across boys and girls. Early independence is valued for boys as well as girls and there is less differentiation in roles and family tasks across the sexes (Peters, 1981; Gibbs, 1989). Similarly, girls are encouraged to be aggressive and assertive, while boys are encouraged to express emotion and nurturance (Lewis, 1975; Allen & Majidi-Abi, 1989). In contrast, gender-role socialization standards for boys and girls are much more clearly differentiated among Mexican-American children (Ramirez, 1989). Boys are expected to show independence earlier than females in this culture.

Age and education alters gender-role expectations as well. In the United States, female students and college-educated women between the ages of 18 and 35 are more likely than older or less educated females to perceive the feminine role as involving greater independence and achievement striving. Children with mothers who are employed in skilled occupations and professions also regard female educational and professional aspirations and the assumption of housekeeping and child-care tasks by males as more appropriate than do children whose mothers are not employed. However, men, even young educated men, maintain more stereotyped gender-role standards than do women (T. L. Ruble, 1983). Moreover, single-earner fathers are more traditional in their gender-typed attitudes than fathers from dual-earner families, while mothers, whether working or not employed outside the home, did not differ in their gender-typed stereotypes (McHale et al., 1990). Although adults regard gender-role standards in preschool children as less clearly delineated than those in older children, more men than women rate the behaviors of toddlers as young as 18 months as gender-typed (Fagot, 1973). This clearer differentiation of gender roles by men is probably related to the frequently reported finding that fathers are more concerned than mothers about their children maintaining sexually appropriate behaviors, and that the father plays a more important role in the gender-role typing of children than does the mother (Block, 1983; Siegel, 1987). However, recently, researchers (Fagot & Hagan, 1991; Lytton & Romney, 1991) have challenged this view and, in light of shifts in male and female roles in the 1990s, mothers and fathers may play more similar roles in gender typing than previously thought. It is interesting that in spite of some variations in gender-role standards among groups in the United States, almost all groups regardless of sex, social class, and education still view aggression as more characteristic of men and interpersonal sensitivity as more frequent in women (T. L. Ruble, 1983). A word of caution: Even within groups there are important individual differences in the strength of their endorsement of gender stereotypes (Signorella, 1987).

One of the most frequently cited reports of divergence among cultures in gender-role standards and behavior is Margaret Mead's study of social roles in three primitive tribes: the Arapesh, the Mundugumor, and the Tchambuli (Mead, 1935). Little gender-role differentiation was prescribed by the Mundugumor and the Arapesh. However, the Arapesh men and women exhibited behaviors that in many societies would be regarded as feminine and the Mundugumor, those traditionally thought of as masculine. The Arapesh were passive, cooperative, and unassertive, whereas both men and women in the Mundugumor tribe were hostile, aggressive, cruel, and restrictive. Both Arapesh mothers and fathers were actively involved in raising infants. In fact, Mead remarks, "If one comments upon a middle-aged Arapesh man as good-looking, the people answer: Good looking? Ye-e-e-s? But you should have seen him before he bore all those children?" (Mead, 1935, p. 56).

In the Tchambuli a reversal of traditional sex roles was found. The men were socially sensitive and concerned with the feelings of others, dependent, and interested in arts and crafts. The women were independent and aggressive and played the controlling role in decision making. Thus, although the traditional gender roles are most common, there is enough variability within and across cultures to indicate that there is a great deal of plasticity in the development of masculine and feminine behaviors. If constitutionally based social and cognitive differences between males and females exist, they can be considerably modified by cultural forces.

GENDER DIFFERENCES IN DEVELOPMENT

How accurately do gender-role stereotypes reflect differences in the actual behaviors of males and females (Fagot, Leinbach & Hagan, 1986; Caldera, Huston, & O'Brien, 1989)? Table 15-1 presents some characteristics in which sex differences have been found, some that are commonly assumed but are not true, and some attributes where evidence for sex differences is equivocal. That is, these are suggestive findings, but more research needs to be done before definite conclusions can be drawn. Moreover, as children develop into adulthood there are many differences among adult men and women in terms of employment and work opportunities, power and status in the workplace, household child-care and family obligations, sexual experiences and concerns, and, of course, reproductive experiences that shape and regulate our lives as adults (Tavris, 1992). In examining this table and in our discussion of gender differences, one should keep in mind that there is *considerable overlap* in the characteristics of males and females. Some males are more compliant, verbal, and interested in the arts than are some females. Similarly, although males seem constitutionally predisposed to be stronger and better adapted to successful aggressive interactions, some women are pretty hardy types, as witnessed by women's greater health and longevity and their success as rugby players! In addition, in the area of intellectual and occupational achievement there are outstanding female architects, mathematicians, engineers, and scientists, although males receive more encouragement in these areas.

DEVELOPMENTAL PATTERNS OF GENDER TYPING

Not only are there differences in adult stereotypes and in actual behavior between the sexes, but children develop gender-typed behavior patterns at an early age (Fagot, Leinbach, & Hagan, 1986; Caldera, Huston, & O'Brien, 1989). As Figure 15-1 shows, even 15- to 36-month-old toddlers in a day-care center had already developed clear preferences for gender-role-appropriate toys (O'Brien, Huston, & Risley, 1983). This observational study revealed another common finding: girls conform less strictly than boys to gender-appropriate behaviors. Girls are more likely to play with a truck than boys are to cuddle a doll. There are many reasons for this sex difference in adherence to gender-role stereotypes. Our culture is basically a male-oriented culture, with greater esteem, privileges, and status accorded to the masculine role. The male role is more clearly defined, and there is greater pressure for boys than for girls to conform to narrower gender-appropriate standards. Tomboys are tolerated, but sissies are rejected. Parents and peers condemn boys for crying, retreating in the face of aggression, wearing feminine apparel, or playing with dolls. In contrast, an occasional temper tantrum, rough-and-tumble play, wearing of jeans, or playing with trucks is at least moderately acceptable for girls. Mothers and fathers and other adults respond more negatively to opposite-sex behaviors by boys than by girls and are quick to discourage such behaviors in boys (Fagot, 1977b; Fagot & Leinbach, 1987; Langlois & Downs, 1980). Studies have suggested that fathers tend to respond more negatively to feminine behaviors in boys than do mothers. Such intense concern about inappropriate gender-typed behavior as is revealed by fathers may be a manifestation of their anxieties about their own masculinity (Goodenough, 1957) or may be due to a pervasive masculine concern in our culture (Seavey, Katz, & Zalk, 1975).

Nevertheless, boys and girls do develop distinctive patterns of interest that are consistent with gender-role stereotypes. In a national survey of over 2000 children from 7 to 11 years old, Zill (1985) found that boys like guns,

TABLE 15-1 ACTUAL, EQUIVOCAL, AND MYTHICAL GENDER DIFFERENCES

ACTUAL GENDER DIFFERENCES	
Physical, motor, and sensory development	Girls are physically and neurologically more advanced at birth and earlier in walking and attaining puberty. Boys have more mature muscular development, larger lungs and heart, and lower sensitivity to pain at birth. With increasing age, boys become superior at activities involving strength and gross motor skills. Boys are miscarried more, have a higher rate of infant mortality, and are more vulnerable to disease, malnutrition, and many hereditary anomalies. Females are definitely not the weaker sex in terms of physical vulnerability.
Cognitive development	In infancy to early school years, girls are superior in verbal abilities, including vocabulary, reading comprehension, and verbal creativity. During middle childhood and adolescence, sex differences are very small or nonexistent. From about age 10, boys excel in visual-spatial ability, which is involved in such tasks as manipulating objects in two- or three-dimensional space, reading maps, or aiming at a target. Boys excel in mathematics beginning at about age 12, especially in mathematical reasoning. Almost all children labeled as exceptionally talented in mathematics by the junior high school level are male.
Social and emotional development	Boys are more often the aggressors and the victims of aggression, particularly of physical aggression, even in early social play. Girls are more compliant to the demands of parents and other adults as early as 2 years of age. Boys are more variable in their responses to adult directions. Sex differences in compliance are not consistently found in peer relations, although preschool boys are less compliant to the demands of girls than they are to boys, or than girls are with partners of either sex. Girls are more nurturant toward younger children than boys are.
Atypical development	Boys are more likely to have school problems, reading disabilities, speech defects, and emotional problems. Genetic defects, physical disabilities, and mental retardation are higher among boys than girls.
EQUIVOCAL GENDER DIFFERENCES	
Activity level	When differences in activity level are found, it is usually boys who are more active than girls. Many studies find no differences in activity level.
Dependency	There is no difference in dependency in younger children. However, older girls and adult females tend to rate themselves as more dependent. This is probably changing in the 1990s.
Fear, timidity, and anxiety	In young children, consistent differences in timidity between boys and girls are not found. However, older girls and women report themselves as being more fearful, and

ACTUAL, EQUIVOCAL, AND MYTHICAL GENDER DIFFERENCES (Continued)

TABLE 15-1

EQUIVOCAL GENDER DIFFERENCES	
	males are more likely to involve themselves in physically risky recreations and occupations.
Exploratory activity	A number of studies of early exploratory activity have found boys to be more venturesome and curious and likely to attack barriers intervening between themselves and a desirable object. However, differences on these behaviors are not consistently found.
Vulnerability to stress	Recent findings suggest that males are more vulnerable to family disharmony and interpersonal stress. This is supported by the overrepresentation of boys in child guidance clinics. However, further research needs to be done before conclusions can be firmly drawn.
Orientation to social stimuli	There is some evidence that infant girls may orient to faces more than boys, and may recognize their mother's face at an earlier age.

MYTHICAL GENDER DIFFERENCES	
Sociability	Boys are not less social than girls. Boys and girls spend as much time with others and are equally responsive to others.
	The need for love and attachment does not differ across the sexes. Nurturance is similar as a capacity, although girls and women do more of the actual care of children, relatives, and friends.
Suggestibility and conformity	Girls are not more suggestible. Girls are not more likely to conform to standards of a peer group or to imitate the responses of others.
Learning style	Girls are not better at rote learning and simple repetitive tasks. Boys are not better at tasks involving the inhibition of previously learned responses or complex cognitive tasks. Boys are not more responsive to visual stimuli and girls to auditory stimuli.
Achievement	Boys do not have more achievement motivation than do girls. Differences in achievement motivation and behavior vary with the type of task and conditions involved. Under neutral conditions, girls are often more achievement-oriented than boys. However, competition is more likely to increase the achievement motivation of boys than of girls.
Self-esteem	Girls do not have lower self-esteem than boys. There are few sex differences in self-satisfaction. However, girls rate themselves as more competent in social skills, and boys view themselves as stronger and more powerful.
Verbal aggressiveness and hostility	Boys and girls do not differ in verbal aggression.

Sources: Maccoby and Jacklin (1974); Tavris (1992); Hyde and Linn (1988); Linn and Hyde (1989).

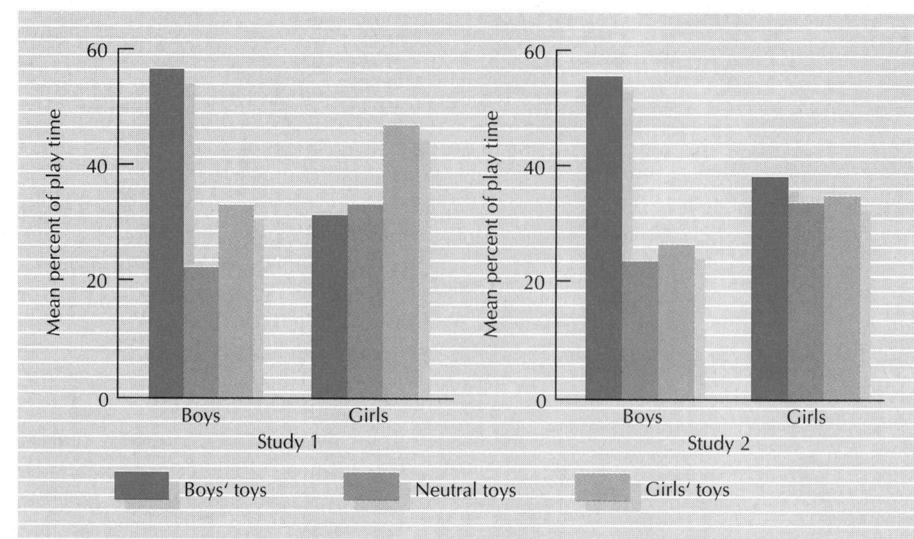

FIGURE 15-1

Boys' and girls' choices of masculine, feminine, and neutral toys. (From O'Brien, Huston, & Risley, 1983; by permission of the author and publisher.)

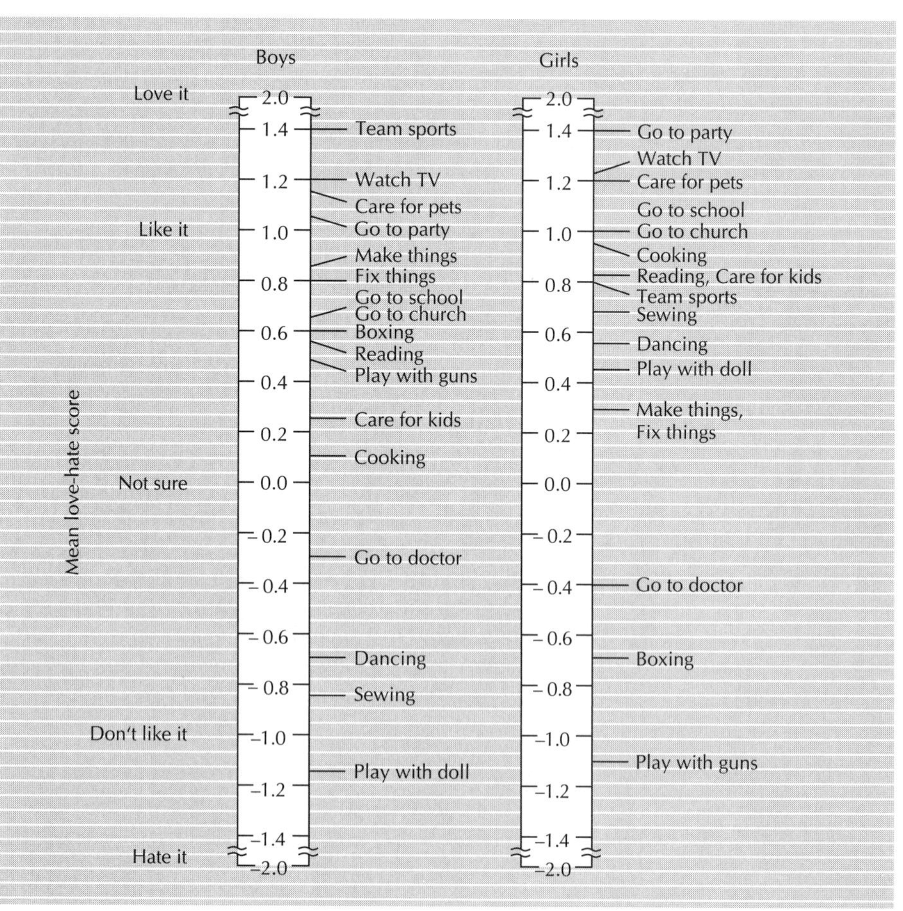

FIGURE 15-2

Average "love-hate" ratings of various activities by boys and girls. (Zill, 1985).

boxing, wrestling and karate, team sports, and fixing and making things more than do girls. In contrast, girls prefer dolls, sewing, cooking, dancing, and looking after younger children more than do boys (see Figure 15-2). These patterns of interest are encouraged in a variety of ways—even in the assignment of household tasks for boys and girls. Even in the 1990s, girls are more likely to make beds, houseclean, make meals, wash dishes, and do laundry. Boys are more likely to get involved in fixing things, taking out the garbage, and mowing lawns (Goodnow, 1988; McHale et al., 1990).

Again, remember that there are individual differences across families and some boys are assigned dish-washing duties and girls can be found fixing the car! In spite of this cautionary note, there are a great many "old" stereotypes still persisting in contemporary roles for boys and girls.

STABILITY OF GENDER TYPING

Masculinity or femininity appears to be developed remarkably early and is a stable personality characteristic. The longitudinal Fels Institute Study (Kagan & Moss, 1962), which examined the development of a group of middle-class children from birth to adulthood, found that adult heterosexual behavior could be predicted from gender-typed interests in elementary school. Figure 15-3 presents a summary of the relationship between some selected child behaviors and similar adult behaviors. Boys who were interested in competitive games, gross motor skills, and such things as mechanics, and girls who were interested in cooking, sewing, reading, and noncompetitive games were involved in gender-typed activities in adulthood. The earlier gender typing of boys is again demonstrated since childhood sexuality and masculine play even in the preschool years are associated with adult gender-role interests and heterosexual activities in boys and not in girls. The stability of many of the personality characteristics investigated was related to their similarity to

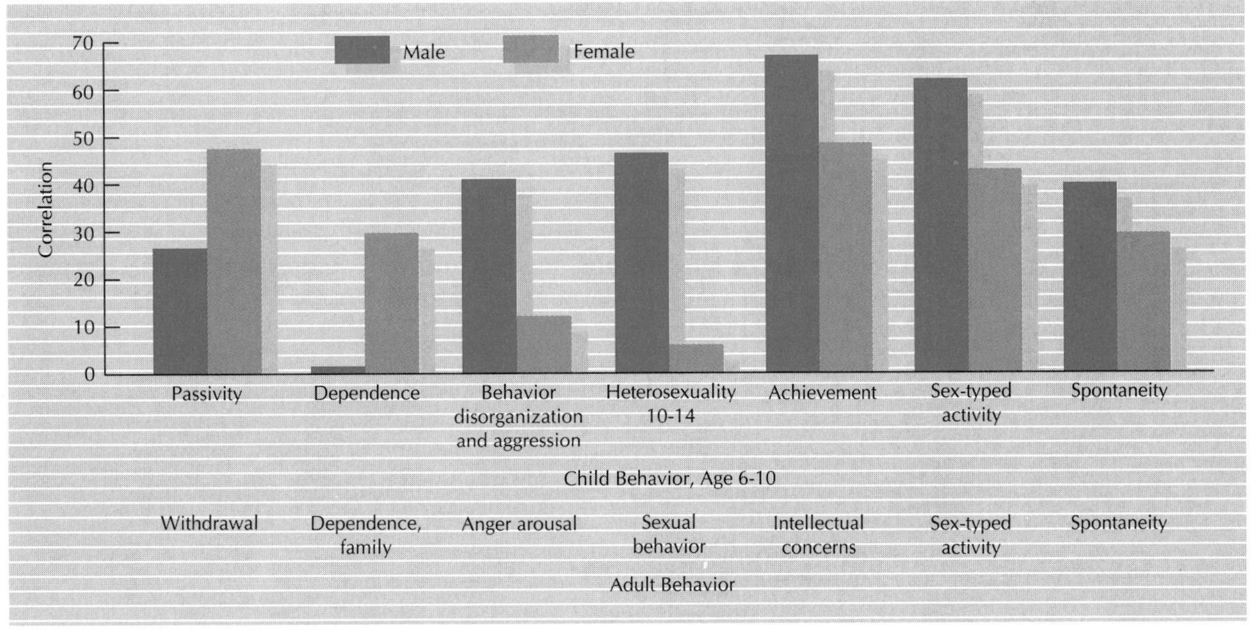

FIGURE 15-3
Summary of relationship between selected child behaviors and functionally similar adult behaviors. (From Kagan & Moss, 1962).

culturally accepted gender-role standards. When a characteristic conflicted with gender-role standards, it led to some form of more socially acceptable substitute or derivative behavior in adulthood. When it was congruent with such standards, it tended to remain stable from childhood to maturity. Thus gender-typed interests, which are encouraged in both sexes, tend to remain stable in both males and females. In contrast, childhood sexuality and aggression are predictive of adult sexuality and anger arousal in males but not in females, and childhood passivity and dependency are predictive of these adult behaviors in females but not in males. However, this study was conducted several decades ago and less stability may be evident in the 1990s.

The culturally nontraditional behaviors, which it may be assumed are eliminated through socialization practices, do emerge in derivative forms of behavior in adulthood. Anger and tantrums in girls are associated with intellectual competitiveness, masculine interests, and dependency conflict in women. Passivity in boys is related to social apprehension, noncompetitiveness, and sexual anxiety in men. Even in adulthood there is evidence of stability; 54 percent of adults were rated similarly in terms of their masculinity or femininity across a ten-year period (Hyde, Krajnik, & Skuldt-Neiderberger, 1991).

However, not *all* adults stay the same in terms of their gender roles. Gender roles fluctuate across the life course as adults change to meet the demands of new situations and circumstances. One of the most important traditions—parenthood—is associated with a sharp divergence of gender roles. Even in egalitarian couples who are committed to equal sharing of household tasks, the onset of parenthood heralds a return to traditional sex roles (Cowan & Cowan, 1992). Women become more nurturant and child-oriented while men become more occupation-oriented. In comparison to childless women, young mothers of infants are more responsive to babies (Nash & Feldman, 1981). Moreover, self-perceptions of gender roles shift as well. Across age, men tend to become more expressive and nurturant, especially in old age. Women tend to become more autonomous as they develop, but return to a more feminine gender-role orientation in old age (Hyde et al., 1991). In light of these findings, gender typing is best viewed as an ongoing and changing process; development, in this case, clearly continues across the years of adulthood.

FACTORS THAT INFLUENCE GENDER DIFFERENCES AND THE DEVELOPMENT OF GENDER ROLES

Biological, cognitive, and social factors interact to shape the development of gender roles and gender differences in behavior.

Biological Factors in Gender-Role Typing

Most of the interest in the influence of biological factors on gender-role typing has focused on two areas. The first is that of the effects of hormones on gender typing. The second is the relationship between gender differences in development and lateralization of brain function, that is, the relatively greater specialization of the two hemispheres of the brain in determining various behaviors.

THE EFFECTS OF HORMONES ON GENDER DIFFERENCES IN SOCIAL BEHAVIOR

Hormones are powerful and highly specialized chemical substances that interact with cells that are able to receive the hormonal message and respond to it. Androgens are male hormones, and testosterone, which has been involved in many studies of sex differences, is a special type of androgen. Estrogens and progesterones are female hormones. However, both male and female hormones are found in differing concentrations in male and female infants, adolescents, and adults. The differences are less marked in preschool and elementary-school-age children. It has been suggested that the prenatal and pubertal periods are critical periods in terms of the response of the organism to hormones (Hines, 1982). Hormones *organize* the psychological and biological predisposition to be masculine or feminine in the prenatal period, and the increase in hormones during puberty activates these early predispositions determined in the organization phase.

Hormonal differences experienced prenatally or during the subsequent course of development may contribute to differences in social behavior between sexes and within the same sex. Young, Goy, and Phoenix (1967) injected pregnant monkeys with testosterone (a male hormone) during the second quarter of pregnancy. This resulted in pseudohermaphroditic female offspring who exhibited not only genital alterations but also social behavior patterns that are characteristic of male monkeys. These infant female monkeys manifested masculine behaviors such as more threatening gestures, less withdrawal from approach or threat by other animals, more mounting behavior, and more rough-and-tumble play.

Subsequent studies have found that if male hormones are injected into normal female monkeys after birth but preceding puberty, the females also become more assertive, sometimes even attaining the prime dominance status in the monkey troop. The female restricts sexual and rough-and-tumble play between males and demands more restrained and docile behavior from her followers.

The relation between testosterone and aggression is a good one for demonstrating the complexities of interactions between biological and environmental factors. Not only are testosterone levels in young adult males associated with aggression, but stress in humans and repeated defeats in fights, or placement of animals in situations in which they cannot be dominant, cause drops in testosterone (Hood, Draper, Crockett, & Petersen, 1987). Thus testosterone may be causing social responses, but social experiences are altering testosterone levels as well.

Another example of modification of the effects of hormonal factors by social experiences is dramatically demonstrated in the studies of Money and his colleagues (Money & Annecillo, 1987; Money, 1987; Ehrhardt, 1987; Money & Ehrhardt, 1972). These investigators studied prenatal hormonal anomalies, such as high levels of androgen, which result in masculinizing the female child and in the subsequent mistaken sexual identity of the child. Many of the subjects in these studies were female infants who had the normal internal female reproduction system but an enlarged clitoris, which resembled a penis, and labial folds often fused and resembling a scrotum.

John Money's studies of androgenized girls found that if the reassignment of the child to her correct feminine gender role occurred after the first few years of life, inadequate gender typing and poor psychological adjustment occurred. If early reassignment occurred, normal psychosexual development in most of the subjects followed. This finding led the authors to conclude that there is a "critical period" for the establishment of gender role between 18 months and 3 years.

A study of twenty-five fetally androgenized girls who were raised as girls, and given corrective surgery if it was necessary, found that these girls were characterized by tomboyishness. Such girls enjoy vigorous athletic activities such as ball games. There is little rehearsal of the maternal role early in life in such things as doll play, or at adolescence in baby-sitting or caring for younger children. These girls also prefer simple utilitarian clothing, such as slacks and shorts, and show little concern with cosmetics, jewelry, or hairstyles.

In addition to the play and grooming interests of these girls more closely resembling those of boys, their assertiveness and attitudes toward sexuality and achievement are similar to those more often found in males in our culture. These girls are assertive enough to be successful in establishing themselves in the dominance hierarchy of their male friends, although they do not compete for the top position in the hierarchy. They show little concern in establishing a position in the dominance hierarchy of groups of girls, perhaps because of a lack of interest in traditional feminine games and activities.

Even in childhood the fantasies of these girls show a preference for success through achievement rather than marriage. They do show some interest in marriage and children but think in terms of a late marriage in conjunction with a career and few children. It should be noted that there is not an unusual incidence of lesbianism in these girls. Although their dating behavior tends to begin late and although their sexual fantasies tend to resemble those of males in specifically portraying the imagined sexual partner, they choose a male sexual partner in real life and in fantasy. Moreover, follow-up studies of these children as adults show them to be successful mothers (Money, 1985, 1987).

Finally, the issue of prenatal hormones and gender-role development is far from settled and continues to be controversial. Although Money has stressed the importance of very early gender assignment, some other work has brought the issue of critical periods into question. Imperto-McGinley, Peterson, Gautier, and Sturla (1979) studied a group of male pseudohermaphrodites in the Dominican Republic. These boys, due to a genetic disorder, were born with ambiguous external genitalia. Although these children had normal male hormone levels, they were reared as females. In spite of their rearing for female roles, at puberty, when physical virilization occurred, these children assumed masculine orientations. These findings suggest that either prenatal or pubertal hormones may alone or in combination outweigh socialization in determining sexual orientation.

However, others raise questions concerning how strictly these boys were treated as females during their childhood, especially in view of their ambiguous appearance (Rubin, Reinisch, & Haskett, 1981; Ruble, 1984).

> Perhaps the culture provided an atmosphere of acceptance that made these transitions possible. Indeed, after a time, the culture developed three gender labels: *quevedoce* ("eggs at 12"), *quevote* ("penis at 12") and *maehihembra* ("first woman, then man"). (D. N. Ruble, 1984, p. 343)

The final answer to this issue of hormones, critical periods, and gender-role development has not yet been found. Clearly, biology alone does not determine sex roles; instead, it is probably the interplay between biological factors and environmental influences that shapes gender roles (Ruble, 1988).

HORMONES, CEREBRAL LATERALIZATION, AND GENDER DIFFERENCES IN COGNITION

Cerebral Lateralization. Behavior is determined to some extent by how the two cerebral hemispheres are organized. As we discussed in Chapter 6, the right hemisphere is more involved in processing spatial information and the left hemisphere in processing verbal information. The functioning of the brain becomes increasingly more specialized and lateralized with age. There is some evidence that men are more lateralized than women in brain function (Witelson & Swallow, 1987; Springer & Deutsch, 1989). Women who suffer damage to the left hemisphere are less likely than men to have verbal deficits, and right-hemisphere-damaged women show fewer spatial deficits than do men (Witelson & Swallow, 1987). The greater bilaterality of brain functioning in girls can be seen in the following study of form perception. Recall from Chapter 6 that information from each side of the body is mainly transmitted to the opposite hemisphere. Since the right hemisphere is better at perceiving form and space, it would be expected that form information to the left hand or eye would be more accurately perceived than form information to the right hand or eye. In a study of 6- to 13-year-olds, boys were more accurate in recognizing shapes with their left hands. In contrast, girls were equally accurate in shape perception with their right and left hands, which supports the view of greater bilaterality in girls than in boys (Witelson, 1978).

Missing X Chromosome. Other evidence concerning the role of hormonal levels in determining hemisphere specialization comes from studies of individuals who have abnormal levels of sex hormones. Individuals with a genetic disorder called Turner syndrome have a missing X chromosome and reduced levels of sex hormones compared to normal females. In contrast, individuals with Klinefelter syndrome have an extra Y chromosome and reduced testosterone levels compared to normal males. Both of these groups exhibit more hemispheric bilaterality than normal females and males in processing verbal information. In short, there is more overlap in the functioning of their right and left hemispheres—an indication that hormones may play an important role in the process of hemispheric specialization that differentiates males and females (Witelson & Swallow, 1987). Again, controversy is high and any definite conclusions about gender differences in lateralization of brain function await further research.

Hormones and Verbal-Spatial Skills. It has been suggested that at a critical period in prenatal development sex hormones may determine the potentials for hemispheric lateralization and brain organization. This brain organization may, in turn, extend not only to differences in lateralization but to gender differences in the effectiveness with which males and females develop verbal and spatial skills. That is, prenatal hormones may sensitize the brains of females to be more effective processors of verbal information and those of males to be more effective processors of spatial information. Recent evidence suggests that intellectual abilities are related to hormonal levels assessed at birth (Jacklin, Wilcox, & Maccoby, 1988). Girls with higher levels of androgens (testosterone and androsteindione) in their blood at birth had lower scores on tests of spatial ability when they entered school than did girls with low

BOX 15-1 BOYS AND GIRLS: DIFFERENCE RULES FOR THE SPATIAL WORLD?

Evidence of differences in the spatial abilities of boys and girls comes from studies of children's understanding of horizontals and verticals in the physical world (Liben & Golbeck, 1980). Consider the following situations. A glass of water is tipped from an upright position to an angle of 50 degrees. What would the water level in the glass look like? Or how would a light bulb on a cord hanging from the ceiling of a van look if the van drove up a hill inclined at 50 degrees? Boys and girls in grades 3 to 11 answer differently, with boys better able to correctly judge the horizontal levels for the water or the vertical position of the hanging light bulb. Children of both sexes improve as they become older, but the sex difference remains at all ages. Figure 15-4 illustrates this sex difference in spatial ability. Possibly girls have less adequate knowledge of physical phenomena or, at least, are unable to apply such knowledge to these kinds of tasks.

Source: Liben, L. S., & Golbeck, S. L. (1980). Sex differences in performance on Piagetian spatial tasks: Differences in competence or performance. *Child Development,* **51,** 594–597.

levels of androgens at birth. There were no effects for boys. Since hormone measures were not available at age 6, it is unclear whether prenatal hormones actually sensitized the brain resulting in differential cognitive abilities or whether the hormonal levels at birth are related to hormonal levels at later points in development. In this latter case, the hormones themselves may influence cognitive development. At this point, we are simply unsure how hormones influence behavior (Jacklin, 1989). For an example of the gender differences in spatial ability, see Box 15-1.

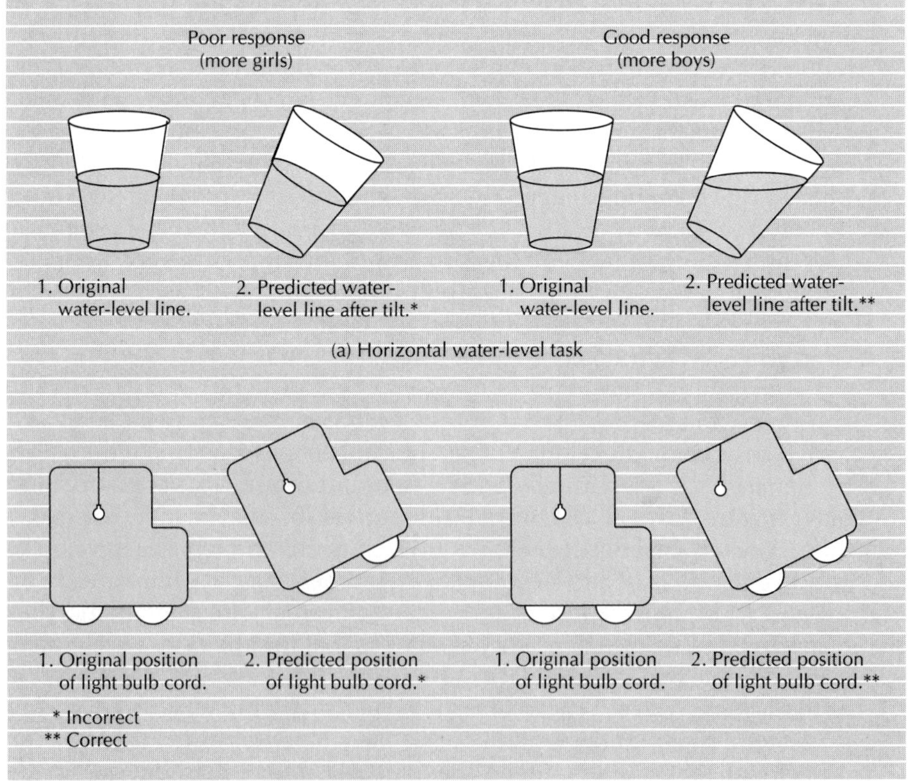

FIGURE 15-4
Gender differences in children's understanding of horizontal and vertical relations.

Boys often have more opportunities to develop their spatial skills than girls do.

This more effective spatial processing of males may be associated with their superiority in mathematics (Benbow & Stanley, 1980; Benbow, 1988). Why should spatial ability be associated with mathematical ability? The marked superiority of males over females is found in geometry, which requires spatial visualization (Hyde, Fennema, & Lamon, 1990). In fact, girls do better in computational skills than boys and there are no sex differences in tests of basic math knowledge and algebra—which is less reliant on spatial ability than geometry (Hyde et al., 1990).

A word of caution, it is important to note that this difference between males and females in spatial ability is relatively small (Linn & Hyde, 1989). Even if definitive evidence of a biological basis for sex differences in spatial abilities were established, it would not mean that these differences are not culturally influenced or modifiable (Petersen & Gitelson, 1984). It has been suggested that boys are encouraged more often to play with toys such as models or motors that involve spatial abilities (Sherman, 1980), and are encouraged in mathematical and scientific endeavors (Kimball, 1989). Moreover, mothers as early as the first grade believe that boys are better at mathematics and girls at reading. Nor is the effect limited to the United States; similar differences were found in Taiwan and Japan (Lummis & Stevenson, 1990). Whatever the reason may be, girls enroll in increasingly fewer mathematics and science courses over the high school and college years, and it becomes more difficult to interest even girls with superior mathematical abilities to remain involved in the subject (Eccles, 1985). For example, in a study of California schools between 1983 and 1987, girls made up only about 38 percent of physics classes, 34 percent of advanced physics classes, and 42 percent of chemistry classes (Linn & Hyde, 1991). However, a national study involving over 400,000 children compared the cognitive skills of high school children in 1960 and 1975 and found a great improvement in the mechanical and spatial performance of girls (Flanagan, 1978). Others suggest that the gap is continuing to lessen (Feingold, 1988; Hyde et al., 1990), which may mean that changing gender-role standards are having some effects on the cognitive interests and abilities of girls.

LIVING IN A MALE OR FEMALE BODY

Finally, it has been proposed that the difference between living in a male or female body in terms of such things as physical strength and the necessary roles in sexual intercourse, pregnancy, and the breast feeding of infants may have an important effect in shaping gender-role standards and in gender typing. Particular interest has focused on whether females are in some way biologically programmed to be more responsive to the sight and signals of infants and children. By age 4 or 5, girls interact more with babies than boys and do so in a more active way than boys. When asked to care for a baby, boys are more inclined to watch the baby passively, while girls are more likely to actively engage in caretaking the baby (Berman, 1987; Reid, Tate, & Berman, 1989). However these differences could easily be due to cultural expectations and training, not just biological differences. These sex differences in adolescents and adults are less apparent under private conditions than in situations where the subjects are aware that they are being observed (Berman, 1987). When subtle measures of responsiveness to an infant's crying are used, such as changes in autonomic nervous system responses, blood pressure, or electrical skin conductance, no differences are found in the autonomic responses of mothers and fathers (Frodi, Lamb, Leavitt, & Donovan, 1978). Moreover, young mothers are more responsive to babies than are childless women (Nash & Feldman, 1981). Together these findings suggest that culturally proscribed gender roles rather than biological preprogramming, have considerable impact on overt responses to babies.

Cognitive Factors in Gender-Role Typing

Biology and social influences are not the only determinants of gender typing. Children's own understanding of gender roles and rules may contribute to the development process of gender-role acquisition. Two related questions are central to understanding the role of cognition. First, when do children acquire different types of gender information? Second, does knowledge modify children's gender-role activities and behavior? Two cognitive approaches to gender typing will be examined: (1) Kohlberg's cognitive developmental theory and (2) gender-schema theory.

> Both theories share the assumption that individuals take an active role in perceiving and interpreting information from their environments. Rather than assuming that people are passively shaped by environmental forces, cognitively-oriented scientists assume that individuals use implicit "theories" to interpret environmental information and that in so doing create environments supportive of their theories. (Martin, 1992, p. 4—5)

COGNITIVE DEVELOPMENTAL THEORY

Lawrence Kohlberg (1966) has presented a provocative cognitive theory of the development of gender typing. In contrast to the social learning position that gender typing is a result of reinforcement and modeling, he argues that children's differentiation of gender roles and their perception of themselves as more similar to same-sex models precedes, not follows, identification.

When the child, on the basis of physical and gender-role differences such as clothing, hairstyle, or occupation, categorizes himself or herself as male or female, it then becomes rewarding to behave in a gender-appropriate manner and imitate same-sex models. Thus the girl says, "I am a girl since I am more like my mother and other girls than boys; therefore I want to dress like a girl, play girl games, and feel and think like a girl." Consistency between the child's gender, self-categorization, and appropriate behaviors and values is critical in sustaining self-esteem.

Kohlberg thinks all children go through the following stages in gaining an understanding of gender:

1 *Basic gender identity.* In this stage the child recognizes that he or she is a boy or a girl.
2 *Gender stability.* In this stage the child accepts that males remain male and females remain female. Little boys no longer think they might grow up to be a mommy, and little girls give up their heady hopes of becoming Batman.
3 *Gender constancy.* In this stage children recognize that superficial changes in appearance or activities do not alter gender. Even when a girl wears jeans or plays football, or when a boy has long hair or a burning interest in needlepoint, the child's gender remains constant.

What is the evidence concerning this developmental progression outlined by Kohlberg? The process by which infants come to recognize males and females as distinct categories probably has its origins in early infancy—well before infants can understand labels and language. Recent evidence suggests that 75 percent of infants at 12 months can recognize male and female faces as belonging to distinctive categories (Leinbach & Fagot, 1992). Of course, this differs from being able to recognize that you belong to a male or female group, but it suggests that the process of acquiring an understanding of gender begins earlier than Kohlberg originally thought. The ability to

"How old do babies hafta get to start bein' boys and girls?"

Children develop cognitive theories about gender roles, although their early versions may be incorrect. (© 1984, Cowles Syndicate, Inc. Reprinted with permission.)

understand gender-typed labels such as boy and girl is not far behind. By 24 months of age, children can correctly label their own sex but still have a very limited understanding of gender identity (Thompson, 1975; Fagot & Leinbach, 1992). They have some understanding of gender words such as "man" and "woman" and recognize that some activities and objects are associated with each sex. They recognize that men wear neckties and women wear skirts, but fail to understand that they themselves belong to a gender class, such as boys or girls, along with other children. Only by age 3 do they achieve this concept of gender class. As in many spheres of cognitive development, children acquire stereotypes about concrete objects and activities before the more abstract aspects of gender roles, such as traits. When children were asked which of two pictures (male or female) was best characterized by each of several traits (for example, who gets into fights, who cries a lot) few 5-year-olds showed any trait knowledge, while 75 percent of the 8-year-olds and nearly 100 percent of the 11-year-olds exhibited clear knowledge of the gender-typed traits (Best et al., 1977).

Identity is only the first step in the attainment of gender-role knowledge. In direct tests of Kohlberg's theory, researchers have found that identity occurred first, followed by an understanding of stability, and finally by an appreciation of constancy—an order of appearance that is consistent with Kohlberg's prediction for both boys and girls (Martin & Little, 1990; Slaby & Frey, 1975). Moreover, children in other cultures (Belize, Kenya, Nepal, and American Samoa) show a similar progression in their understanding of gender stages (Munroe, Shimmin, & Munroe, 1984). While identity occurs relatively early, children begin to grasp stability and constancy only around age 5, and not until age 7 do they fully appreciate the meaning of these concepts. To illustrate, consider the following exchange between two 4-year-old boys. A boy named Jeremy who wore a barrette to nursery school was accused by another boy of being a girl because "only girls wear barrettes." Jeremy pulled down his pants to show that he really was a boy. His young classmate replied, "Everyone has a penis; only girls wear barrettes" (Bem, 1983, p. 607). Clearly he did not yet understand gender constancy.

Recently, Bem (1989) has shown that genital knowledge is an important determinant of gender constancy. Nursery schoolers were first shown anatomically correct photos of a nude boy and girl. These same children were then seen dressed in same- or opposite-sexed clothing. Even when boys were seen in dresses, or girls in trousers, nearly 40 percent of the children correctly identified the sex of the child in spite of the opposite-sex clothing. To determine if genital knowledge was a factor, Bem tested children's understanding of genital differences between the sexes. Nearly 60 percent of the preschoolers who had already acquired genital knowledge showed gender constancy while only 10 percent of those without this understanding exhibited gender constancy. Clearly, modesty comes at a price—a delay in children's understanding of gender constancy!

Moreover, children seem to understand gender constancy earlier when it applies to themselves than when it is applied to others (Eaton & VonBargen, 1981; Wehren & DeLisi, 1983). They are certain at an earlier age that no matter how much they might want to be transformed into a member of the opposite sex, it could not happen. But they are not so sure about that kid down the street. In addition, in support of a cognitive position, gender constancy is related to cognitive level and to performance on Piagetian tasks of physical conservation, which, of course, requires the recognition of constancy of physical objects in spite of the appearance of superficial transformations (Marcus & Overton, 1978).

GENDER-SCHEMA THEORY

Another cognitive approach to sex typing, gender-schema theory, derives from modern information processing perspectives (Bem, 1981, 1985, 1991; Martin & Halverson, 1981, 1983). According to this viewpoint, children develop schema, or naive theories, that help to organize and structure experience. They tell the child the kinds of information to look for in the environment and how to interpret such information. In the chapter on individual differences in cognition (Chapter 11), we discussed how children's theories about intelligence caused them to perceive and respond to achievement situations and success and failure in different ways. In a similar way, according to Martin and Halverson (1981), beliefs about gender stereotypes are important for children because they are relevant to their emerging self-concept and are highly salient in the everyday world of children. Do gender-role schema affect the way children see things? To find out, Martin and Halverson (1983) showed 5- and 6-year-olds pictures of males and females performing gender-consistent (for example, a boy playing with a train) or gender-inconsistent (for example, a girl sawing wood) activities. A week later they asked the children to recall the pictures. Children tended to distort information by changing the sex of the actor in the gender-inconsistent pictures. Children were also more confident of their recall of gender-consistent pictures. A variety of studies (Bigler & Liben, 1990; Martin & Little, 1990; Stangor & Ruble, 1989) report similar findings; for example, girls remember feminine toys and objects more easily than masculine toys and objects, while the reverse is true for boys (Bradbard & Endsley, 1984).

There are developmental and individual differences in how strongly children rely on gender schemas in interpreting their social world. Young children (4 years or younger) appear to rely relatively more on gender schemas than older children (5 years or older), in part, because older children not only have more complete and elaborate knowledge of gender roles but attach less importance and rigidity in applying their knowledge (Levy, 1989). Similarly, children vary in the extent to which they have well-formed gender schemas (Carter & Levy, 1988). Some children are "gender schematic" and are highly sensitive to gender notions while other children are "gender aschematic" and focus more on nongender aspects of information in their environment. Not surprisingly, gender-schematic children display better memories for gender-consistent information and are more likely to distort gender-inconsistent information (for example, remember a boy with a doll as a *girl* with a doll) than less gender-schematic children (Levy, 1989). These studies remind us that individual as well as developmental differences are important to consider in understanding cognitive approaches to gender typing. In short, gender-role schema clearly alter the ways in which children process social information and tend to distort it to suit their prior concepts.

COGNITION-BEHAVIOR RELATIONSHIPS

Does increasingly sophisticated gender-typed knowledge influence children's gender-role activities and behavior? The two theories—Kohlberg and gender-schema—provide different answers (Martin, 1992). Kohlberg's theory predicts that the achievement of gender constancy should influence children's gender-typed choices. Therefore, prior to the 5- to 7-year age period, there should be little preference for gender-appropriate activities. Gender-schema theory, on the other hand, suggests that children may need only basic information about gender such as identification of the sexes (Martin, 1992). Merely labeling the sexes is sufficient for children to begin to form rules concerning gender. The schema theorists are apparently correct. Contrary to Kohlberg, gender labeling is sufficient to affect gender-typed activity preferences—an achievement that occurs well before the child develops a stable concept of gender constancy (Martin & Little, 1990; Martin, 1992). As Fagot and Leinbach (1989) found, children who developed gender identity early (before 27 months) engaged in more gender-typed play than children who gained gender identity later in development. In short, the early boys were more likely to be playing with trucks and trains, while the early girls were more likely to be found in the doll corner! Moreover, at age 4, the early gender-role identifiers possessed greater knowledge of gender-role stereotypes as well.

Another kind of basic gender category information that is important in organizing gender-typed preferences is children's recognition of their membership in a gender group (Maccoby, 1988). Recognition of their gender membership as male or female is related to children's gender-typed preferences and to their gender-role knowledge (Martin & Little, 1990).

Sex-typed play such as choosing trucks or dolls as the appropriate gender-role choices does not seem to depend on the achievement of gender stability or gender constancy. Instead, the first stage—the acquisition of basic gender identity—seems sufficient for the emergence of gender-typed play. However, in contrast to choice of toys, choice of playmate may depend on the level of gender understanding according to Smetana and Letourneau (1984). In their study, girls who had acquired gender stability chose to play with other girls more than did girls who had acquired only gender identity. "Lacking the certainty that gender is invariant across contexts and situations, females may actively seek the presence of same sex peers to affirm their conceptions of themselves as females" (1984, p. 695). Once girls reach gender constancy and their gender concepts are firmly established, they are less rigid in their choice of playmates and play with both boys and girls. Girls at the highest level of gender understanding are confident that play with boys will not alter their gender. Cognitive understanding, in this case, brings increased freedom of social choices. Possibly the same pattern is evident for boys also, but only girls participated in this study. Together, these studies suggest that the link between the acquisition of gender concepts and behavior varies across both the stage of gender understanding and the kind of behavior.

Social and Situational Factors in Gender-Role Typing

Gender-role standards and pressure to adopt gender-typed behavior patterns converge on the developing child from a variety of sources—from family, teachers, friends, television, and children's books.

The Family and Gender-Role Typing

PARENTS AS ORGANIZERS OF THEIR CHILDREN'S GENDER-TYPED CHOICES

Well before children are making lists of toys for their birthdays, parents are actively shaping their children's tastes and preferences. Take a close look at the bedrooms of boys and girls. This is exactly what several researchers (Rheingold & Cook, 1975; Pomerleau, Bolduc, Malcuit, & Cossette, 1990) systematically did: They carefully recorded the kinds of toys, decorations, furniture, and even the curtains and bedspreads that were in the bedrooms of boys and girls between the ages of 1 month and 6 years. Boys' rooms contained more vehicles, depots, machines, army equipment, soldiers, and

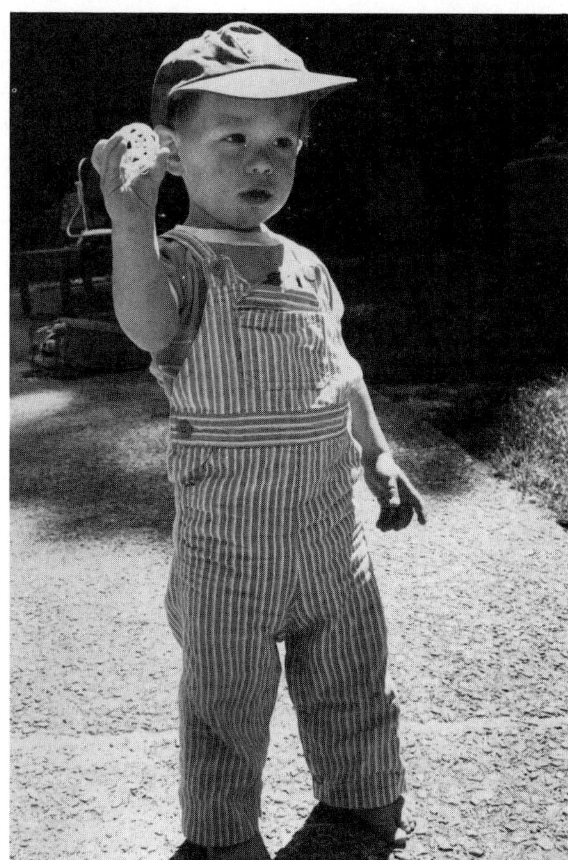

Parents' clothing choices are another way in which gender-role typing occurs.

sports equipment. In contrast, girls' rooms were more likely to house dolls and floral-patterned and ruffled furnishings (for example, floral curtains with lace). The toys of boys were more action-oriented; girls' toys were less action-oriented and more family-focussed. Of interest is the fact that there was little change between the studies conducted in 1975 and 1990; the times may be changing but not children's rooms! Parents announce the sex of their offspring by how they dress their children as well; children are subtly being shaped toward "appropriate" sex roles. When a group of researchers watched 1- to 13-month-olds in a shopping center, they found baby girls in pink, puffed sleeves, ruffles, and lace. Boys wore blue or maybe red, but few bows, barrettes, or ribbons (Shakin, Shakin, & Sternglanz, 1985). "Sex-typed clothing serves very well to announce the child's sex and thereby ensures sex appropriate treatment even from strangers" (Fagot & Leinbach, 1987, p. 93).

PARENTS' TREATMENT OF MALES AND FEMALES

Infants and Toddlers. From earliest infancy, parents are likely to view their sons and daughters differently. Parents are more likely to describe their newborn daughters as smaller, softer, less attentive, cuter, more delicate, and finer featured than their sons. And fathers, even if they have seen but not yet handled their infants, are more extreme than mothers in emphasizing

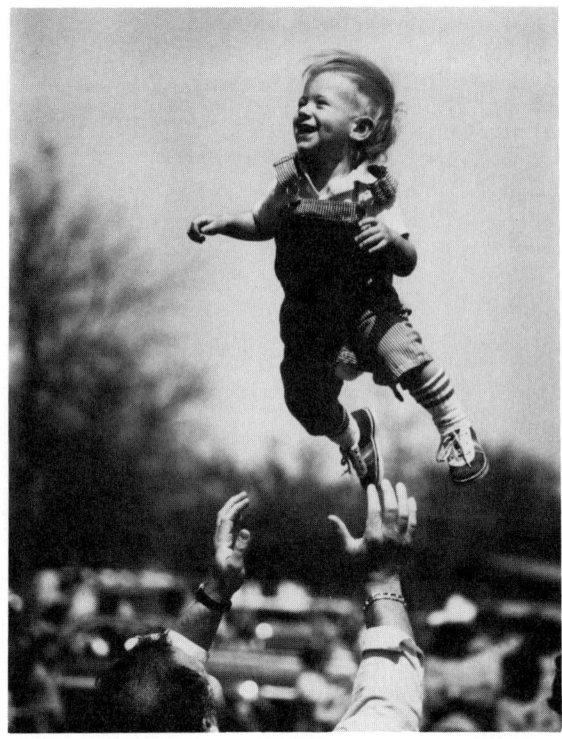

Fathers engage in more rough and tumble play with sons than with daughters.

the size, strength, coordination, and alertness of their sons versus the fragility and beauty of daughters (Rubin, Provenzano, & Luria, 1974; Stern & Karraker, 1989). In view of such differences in parents' perceptions of their male and female infants, it is not surprising that, from the earliest days of life, boys and girls are treated differently and that this differential treatment of boys and girls is most marked for fathers (Stern & Karraker, 1989). These researchers found that adults play in more masculine ways with a baby that they think is a boy and in a gentler and more nurturant fashion with a "girl" infant—regardless of the infant's actual sex. Moreover, by 18 months, parents are more involved with toys culturally appropriate for the sex of their child (Caldera et al., 1989). Gender-role stereotypes clearly serve to shape our treatment of children—even in infancy.

Even before their child is born, fathers show a strong preference to have a son (Hoffman, 1977). After birth, especially with firstborn children, they are more likely to stimulate and talk to their sons (Parke & Tinsley, 1987). As children grow older, fathers with male toddlers spend more time in play and watch and touch their infants more. They indulge in rough-and-tumble antics or talk in a sort of "hail-baby-well-met" style, saying such things as "Hello, Tiger!" or "Come here, Dingbat" more than do fathers with daughters (Jacklin, DiPietro, & Maccoby, 1984; Carson, Burks, & Parke, 1992). Fathers are more likely to gently cuddle than actively stimulate their infant daughters. In contrast, mothers' differential treatment of sons and daughters is less extreme and less consistently found (Siegel, 1987). However, mothers are more verbally responsive to girls and talk to them and imitate their vocalizations more than those of their sons.

This pattern of differences in mothers' and fathers' interactions with sons and daughters suggests that the social forces involved in gender-role typing may begin as early as the newborn period and that fathers, through their

BOX 15-2 MOTHERS AND FATHERS, SONS AND DAUGHTERS

Do mothers and fathers encourage different types of behavior in their sons and daughters? To find out, Langlois and Downs (1980) studied how mothers and fathers reacted to the gender-typed play of 3- and 5-year-old girls and boys. Both masculine gender-typed toys, such as soldiers or a gas station, and feminine gender-typed toys, such as a dollhouse or pots, dishes, and utensils, were available, and to ensure that boys and girls played with both masculine and feminine toys, the experimenter instructed the child to play with either kind of toy. On separate sessions, mothers' and fathers' reactions to their children's toy choices were recorded. Socialization pressure for gender-typed behaviors came more consistently from fathers than from mothers. Girls were rewarded by their mothers for playing with same-sex toys and were punished by mothers for playing with cross-sex toys. In contrast, boys encountered a different and inconsistent pattern of treatment. Boys were both punished and rewarded by their mothers for playing with cross-sex toys. Fathers differentially rewarded play with same-sex toys and punished play with cross-sex toys for both sons and daughters. Fathers rewarded their daughters for playing with dolls and their sons for playing with toy soldiers; they punished their girls for playing with trucks and their boys for playing with pots and dishes. The findings are consistent with other evidence that men are more likely to sex type toys than women and more likely to purchase gender-typed toys, especially for boys (Fisher-Thompson, 1990; Thompson, Molison, & Elliott, 1988). These findings are consistent with the view that fathers are the principal agent of gender-role socialization while mothers play a less influential role in this process.

Source: Fisher-Thompson, D. (1990). Adult gender typing of children's toys. *Sex Roles,* **23,** 291–303; Langlois, J. H., & Downs, A. C. (1980). Mothers, fathers and peers as socialization agents of gender-typed play behaviors in young children. *Child Development,* **51,** 1237–1247; Thompson, D. F., Molison, K. L., & Elliott, M. (1988, April). *Adult selection of children's toys.* Paper presented at the annual meeting of the Eastern Psychological Association, Buffalo, NY.

more differential treatment of boys and girls, may play a more important role in the gender-typing process than do mothers. However, as noted earlier in this chapter, some (Lytton & Romney, 1991) have questioned whether this differential role of fathers and mothers is correct. Perhaps the 1990s may see more equal roles for moms and dads in the gender-typing process.

Older children. As children grow older, do parents actively encourage and reinforce them for behaving in a gender-stereotypic manner? According to social learning approaches, reinforcement and modeling ought to play an important role in shaping gender roles (Bandura, 1989). It can be seen in the study presented in Box 15-2 that such processes begin very early.

In general, it has been found that parents are more apprehensive and protective about their daughters' physical well-being. This is associated with more encouragement of dependency and close family ties in girls and more emphasis on early exploration, achievement, independence, and competition in boys. While parents show few sex differences in their expectations for independence and maturity in such safe activities as tidying up rooms, putting away toys or clothes, or getting dressed, parents treat boys and girls differently in areas where there are greater risks. Parents think boys should be able to play away from home without telling parents where they are, run errands in the neighborhood, cross the street alone, use sharp scissors, and indulge in other venturesome activities at an earlier age than should girls. Boys are more likely to be left unsupervised after school and less likely to be picked up at school (Hoffman, 1977; Huston, 1983). This differential treatment may limit the development of feelings of effectance, risk-taking, and free exploration in girls, and may promote greater conformity to cultural norms and values (Ruble, 1988). However, recall that this differential treatment of boys and girls is not evident among all groups in our culture; African-

American boys and girls are treated more similarly than white male and female children in the United States (Allen & Majidi-Abi, 1989).

Many of the parents' sex-differentiated behaviors seem to be associated with achievement, particularly in the attitudes and behavior of fathers. Parents, especially fathers, are more likely to stress the importance of a career or occupational success for sons than for daughters (Block, 1983; Hoffman, 1977). Differences in treatment of boys and girls is particularly marked in the area of mathematical achievement (Eccles, 1985). In a variety of cultures (for example, United States, Taiwan, Japan) parents believe boys are better in math than girls, while girls are superior readers (Lummis & Stevenson, 1990). In teaching and problem-solving situations, fathers of boys are more attuned to achievement and the cognitive aspects of the situation. Fathers of girls seem to be less concerned with performance and more concerned with interpersonal interactions with their daughters (Block, Block, & Harrington, 1974). In addition, fathers, but not mothers, will respond to appropriate task-oriented questions and requests for help from boys, but are more likely to reinforce inappropriate dependency bids from daughters (Cantor, Wood, & Gelfand, 1977).

Before we leap to the conclusion that differential reinforcement of gender-typed behavior can explain all observable sex differences in behavior, it should be noted that boys do not get more reinforcement for aggressive behavior than girls. Physical aggression is the most consistently reported difference between boys and girls, and neither sex is encouraged to be aggressive (Parke & Slaby, 1983; Perry, Perry, & Boldizar, 1990).

Gender-role typing begins early, and many believe that fathers are particularly important.

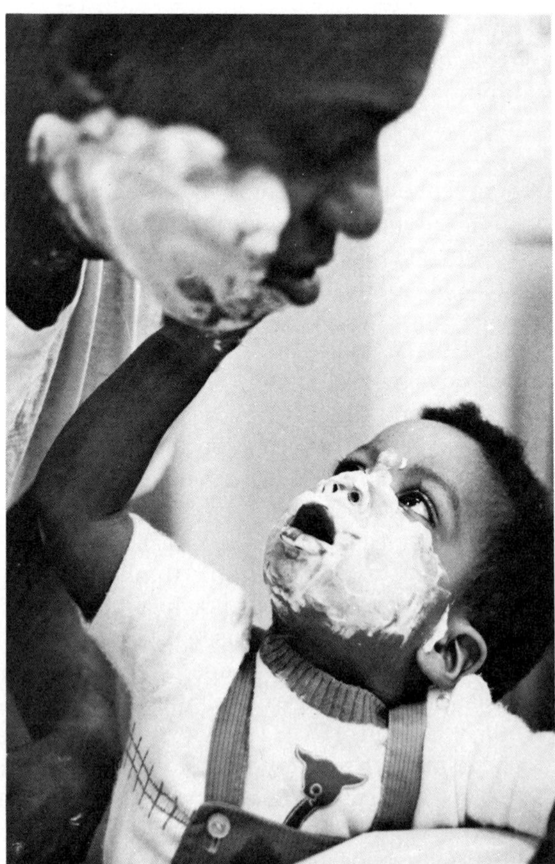

PARENTAL CHARACTERISTICS, MODELING, AND GENDER TYPING

Let us now turn to the role of parental characteristics and the possibility of imitation of the same-sex parent as an explanation for the development of gender typing. Although warm and nurturant parents increase appropriate gender-role learning for their same-sex children, parental power has an even greater impact on gender typing, especially in boys. Dominant mothers and passive fathers are particularly destructive in the identification of boys, although they have no effect on femininity in girls. If a boy has a weak father and a powerful mother, he is likely to exhibit feminine characteristics. Highly masculine boys have fathers who are decisive and dominant in setting limits and dispensing both rewards and punishments. In contrast to its strong relationship with the development of masculinity in boys, parental power has little effect on the development of femininity in girls (Hetherington, 1965, 1967).

Does the parents' own degree of masculinity or femininity matter in children's gender typing? Boys' masculinity is unrelated to either gender typing of parents or parental encouragement of gender-typed activities. In girls we see the importance of the father in gender typing; femininity in daughters is related to father's masculinity, father's approval of the mother as a model, and father's reinforcement for participation in feminine activities. It is interesting that it is not related to femininity in mothers. More feminine mothers do not have more feminine daughters (Hetherington, 1967).

Even in adulthood, sexual adjustment and marital relations are more influenced by earlier relations with fathers than those with mothers. A lack of involvement in family life and ineffectuality or hostility in fathers have been related to problems in forming lasting heterosexual relationships. A woman's desire to get married and have children and even her sexual responsiveness and orgasmic satisfaction in intercourse are related to an affectionate, attentive, supportive relationship with her father (Fisher, 1973). The studies underscore the critical role of the father in gender typing.

FATHER UNAVAILABILITY, SINGLE-PARENT FAMILIES, AND GENDER TYPING

Since the father plays such an important role in gender typing, it might be expected that children from homes in which the father is either permanently absent or away for long periods of time would show disruptions in gender typing. In some ways, the home in which no father is present may resemble a mother-dominated nuclear family since the mother must, of necessity, assume a more decisive role in rearing her children alone. The absence of a male model and lack of opportunity for interaction with a father may also contribute to difficulty in gender typing in such homes (Hetherington, 1989).

Permanent father absence because of death or divorce, temporary separation from, or unavailability of, a father due to war or occupational demands, and lack of paternal interest have all been shown to disrupt gender typing in young boys (Huston, 1983). Disruptions in gender typing are most apparent in preadolescent boys. These effects are most severe if the separation has occurred before age 5 (Hetherington, 1966). With increasing age and wider social contacts, other models such as teachers, peers, siblings, surrogate fathers, and those in the mass media serve to partially mitigate the effects of father absence on gender-role adoption (Huston, 1983).

The effects of parental absence on preadolescent girls appear to be minimal. However, studies of adolescents suggest that parental absence may have a delayed effect on the gender typing of girls. The father's absence is associated with disruptions in relating to other males by adolescent daughters; the form of this disruption differs for daughters of widows and divorcees. Adolescent girls from divorced homes were found to be more sexually precocious and assertive with males, while those from widowed families were characterized as excessively anxious about sexuality as well as shy and uncomfortable around males (Hetherington, 1972, 1991; Newcomer & Udry, 1987).

The studies of paternal absence again indicate the important role of the father in the social development of girls. Daughters learn to feel competent and to value and acquire the social skills necessary for effective heterosexual interactions by interacting with a warm, masculine, instrumental father who rewards and enjoys her femininity. However, the severity of the effects of father absence is moderated by maternal behavior. Mothers who present their husbands and their previous relationships with them in a positive manner and who are themselves stable lessen the deleterious effects of father absence.

A follow-up study indicated how long-lasting the effects of father absence on daughters' relationships with men are, as reflected in the girls' subsequent marital relationships. Not only did daughters of divorcees marry younger, but more of them were pregnant at the time of marriage and several were already separated or divorced. No differences in frequency of marital sexual intercourse were reported for the three groups, but orgasmic satisfaction was less in girls from single-parent families (Hetherington, 1980). Moreover, the husbands of the daughters of divorced parents were less educated, had less stable employment records, and were more frequently involved in problems with the law than were the other two groups of husbands. In addition, they felt more ambivalent or hostile toward their wives and infants and were less emotionally mature and more impulsive and self-centered. In contrast, daughters of widows tended to marry husbands with more education or a higher vocational status than their parents had. These men were self-controlled, nurturant, ambitious, concerned about social approval, and conventional, and they maintained stereotyped views of male and female roles. One interviewer characterized them as "repulsively straight." In summary, the effects of fathers' absence on their daughters' interactions with males were long-lasting and extended even into their marital choices.

Extrafamilial Influences on Gender-Role Typing

As children grow older, influences outside the family become increasingly important in shaping gender-role typing.

TELEVISION, BOOKS, AND GENDER ROLES

Male and female roles are portrayed in similarly gender-stereotyped ways on television and in children's stories. Males on television are more likely than females to be depicted as aggressive, decisive, professionally competent, rational, stable, powerful, and tolerant. In contrast, females are more often portrayed as unemployed or involved in housework and child care, warmer, more sociable, more emotional, and happier. When women on television are aggressive, they are usually inept or unsuccessful aggressors, and women are more likely to be shown as victims than as initiators of violence. Females are less likely to be leading characters and are more likely to be in comedy roles, to be married or about to be married, and to be younger than males

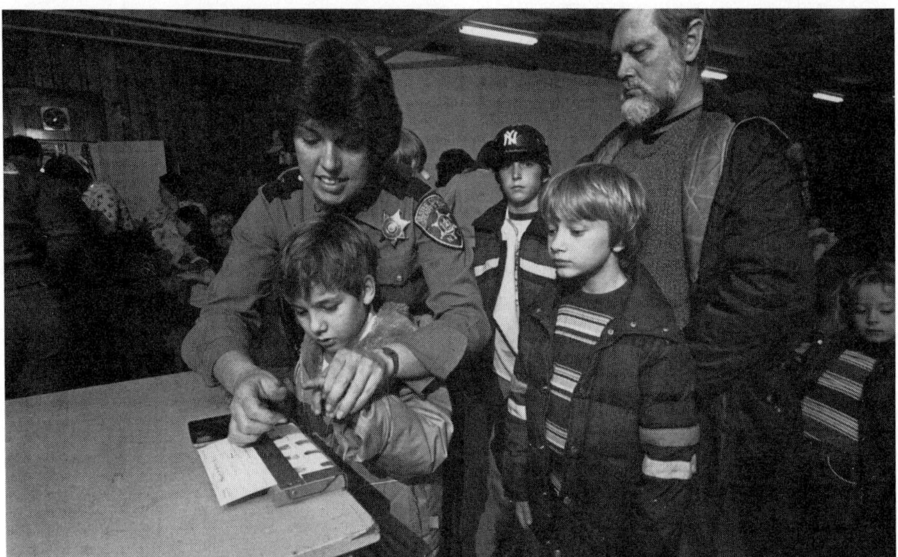

Women in nontraditional roles, such as fire fighter, doctor, or law enforcement officer, provide alternative role models for children. TV programs often fail to provide these alternatives for viewers.

(Calvert & Huston, 1987; Signorielli, 1989). Even in television commercials, males are more often portrayed as the authorities and are used in the voice-over comments about the merits of products, and women are usually the ones who are shown as believing demonstrations of a product's superiority (Loudal, 1989). When women are shown as experts, it is likely to be in food products, laundry, soap, or beauty aids. These trends are found in the United States and other countries as well (Williams, Baron, Phillips, Travis, & Jackson, 1986).

Children's books often provide the same gender-role stereotypes as TV. Just as in the case of TV, females are more passive and dependent, while males are more action-oriented. However, a shift to more egalitarian treatment of males and females is evident in a comparative study of elementary school children's readers in 1975 and 1989 (Purcell & Stewart, 1990). Girls appear as often in 1989 as boys and in a wider range of activities than in 1975. However, women are still depicted in a narrower range of occupations than men and continue to be depicted as more dependent and helpless. As in the case of television, more change is still needed to close the gender gap!

The impact of such stereotypical presentations of male and female roles is suggested by findings that children who are heavy TV viewers are more likely to have stereotypical notions of sex and race and are more likely to show conformity to culturally appropriate gender-role preferences (Leary, Greer, & Huston, 1982).

Television can also be used to change children's gender-role stereotypes. In one study, 5- and 6-year-olds who were shown a cartoon in which the characters played nontraditional roles (girls helping boys build a clubhouse) developed less conventional gender-role attitudes (Davidson, Yasuna, & Tower, 1979). Similarly, "Freestyle," a television series that tries to counteract children's sex and ethnic stereotypes, has been moderately successful in increasing acceptance of boys and girls who exhibit nontraditional gender-typed behaviors. For example, the 9- to 12-year-old viewers were more accepting of girls who participated in athletics and mechanical activities and boys who engaged in nurturant activities (Johnston & Ettema, 1982). However, as Liben and Bigler (1987) caution, the effects of most TV-based interventions have been relatively modest and short-lived. Perhaps, television can help change gender-role stereotypes, but it is unlikely that television alone can produce long-lasting shifts in gender-role attitudes.

PEERS AND GENDER ROLES

Peers often serve as enforcers of society's gender-role standards. Fagot (1977a) watched over 200 preschoolers at play and found marked reactions from peers when children violated appropriate sex-typical behavior patterns. Boys who play with dolls rather than trucks have a tough time; they are criticized five to six times more often by their classmates than are more conforming children. On the other hand, girls who would rather play firefighter than nurse are not treated as harshly; instead they are ignored and not criticized. Moreover, this kind of feedback makes a difference to children's behavior. Lamb and his colleagues (Lamb, Easterbrooks, & Holden, 1980; Lamb & Roopnarine, 1979) found that peer punishment was an effective way to stop children's cross-gender activity. In addition, children who were rewarded by their peers for gender-role-appropriate behavior persisted longer in this type of activity. However, the source of the reinforcement makes a difference. Fagot (1985a), for example, found that children respond more to feedback from a same-sexed child. Boys respond to feedback from boys, but not from girls, while girls, in turn, are more receptive to feedback from other girls than they are to boys. As Maccoby shows in Box 15-3, this pattern of increased responsiveness may lead to gender segregation which, in turn, may provide opportunities to learn appropriate gender roles. Clearly, peers serve as important influences on gender roles.

TEACHERS AND GENDER ROLES

When children move out of the home and into the school, boys and girls continue to be treated differently. In many ways schools are feminine: They value quiet, obedience, and passivity, and these are many of the qualities, unfortunately, that the culture dictates as gender-role-appropriate for girls. The boisterous, assertive, competitive, and independent qualities that are encouraged in boys are often frowned upon in school. It is not surprising that in the early grades, at least, girls tend to like school more and perform better in their academic work than do boys. For boys, on the other hand, school may not be a happy place. They view themselves as being less well liked than girls by their teachers (Dweck & Goetz, 1977). They have more difficulty in adjusting to school routines, create more problems for their teachers, are criticized more (Ben Tsvi-Mayer, Hertz-Lazarowitz, & Safir, 1989; Fagot, 1981), and generally perform not only at a lower level than their female classmates but often well below their abilities.

Even in the preschool years, boys and girls are responded to differently by teachers. Although boys are encouraged to engage in quiet activities rather than aggression and rough-and-tumble play, they receive more criticism from teachers and peers for cross-gender behaviors such as dress up and doll play (Fagot, 1977a, 1985a). Girls are less likely to receive criticism from teachers and peers for engaging in cross-sex play. Fagot (1985a) found that teachers often react to boys and girls in gender-stereotypic ways. Teachers respond to girls' social initiatives, such as talking and gesturing, more than to these same displays on the part of boys. In contrast, teachers respond to boys' assertive behavior more than girls' pushing and shoving. Not surprisingly, the differential teacher attention has an impact: Nine months later there were

BOX 15-3 GENDER SEGREGATION: ANOTHER ROUTE TO GENDER ROLES

A visit to any school playground reveals one striking fact: Children have a very strong tendency to segregate themselves according to their gender. In spite of efforts to equalize the sexes, boys and girls seem to have ignored the message and show a marked preference for playing with a playmate of their own gender.

In preschool, when children are $4\frac{1}{2}$ years old, children spend nearly three times as much time with same-sex play partners as with children of the other sex. By age $6\frac{1}{2}$, the effect is even stronger and children spend eleven times as much time with same-sex as with opposite-sex partners (Maccoby & Jacklin, 1987).

Moreover, this is not restricted to one culture; rather, this phenomenon is evident across a wide range of cultures, including India, Africa, and the United States. Nor is the segregation a result of adult pressure; children spontaneously choose same-sex partners even though there is no adult guidance or encouragement to do so. In spite of individual differences in measures of masculinity and femininity or to indices of gender schema, children show the same preference for same-sexed playmates (Powlishta, 1989).

What goes on in same-sexed peer groups? Maccoby (1990) summarizes the difference:

> The two sexes engage in fairly different kinds of activities and games. . . . Boys play in somewhat larger groups on the average and their play is rougher . . . and takes up more space. Boys more often play in the streets and other public places; girls more often congregate in private homes and yards. Girls tend to form close, intimate friendships with one or two other girls and these friendships are marked by sharing of confidences. . . . Boys' friendships, on the other hand, are more oriented around mutual interests in activities. . . . The breakup of girls' friendships is usually attended by more intense emotional reactions than in the case of boys. . . . In male groups there is more concern with issues of dominance. (Maccoby, 1990, p. 516)

These stylistic differences in boys' and girls' groups has led Maccoby to suggest several reasons for this sex segregation. First, the rough-and-tumble play style of boys and their competitive-dominance orientation is viewed as aversive by girls and therefore they avoid interactions with boys. Second, girls find it difficult to influence boys. Girls are successful in influencing each other using their preferred form of influence—polite suggestions. These same tactics are not very effective with boys, who use more direct demands. "Girls find it aversive to try to interact with someone who is unresponsive and they begin to avoid such partners" (Maccoby, 1990, p. 515).

The result is that children from preschool onward choose to live in segregated play worlds that, in turn, nurture and encourage separate styles of interaction that are distinctly male and female. This suggests that self-socialization in the form of children's spontaneous adoption of gender-appropriate behavior may be another powerful way in which gender roles are learned and maintained. Children themselves and children's peer groups may play an important role in children's gender-role socialization.

Sources: Maccoby, E. E. (1988). Gender as a social category. *Developmental Psychology,* **26,** 755–765; Maccoby, E. E. (1990). Gender and relationships: A developmental account, *American Psychologist,* **45,** 513–521; Maccoby, E. E., & Jacklin, C. N. (1987). Gender segregation in childhood. In H. W. Reese (Ed.), *Advances in child development and behavior* (Vol. 20, pp. 239–288). New York: Academic; Powlishta, K. K. (1989). *Salience of group membership: The case of gender.* Unpublished doctoral dissertation, Stanford University, Stanford, CA.

clear sex differences with girls talking to the teacher more and boys exhibiting a higher level of assertiveness. Although increasing the number of male teachers was once viewed as the answer to the differential treatment of boys and girls by female teachers, both male and female teachers react more positively to children of either sex who are involved in female-typical behaviors such as art activities and helping behaviors (Fagot, 1985b).

There are a clear set of relationships between children's perception of the gender-role appropriateness of different activities (for example, mechanical, artistic, reading, math) and their motivation to achieve in these tasks (Huston, 1983). Sixth and ninth graders rated how "boyish" or "girlish" a variety of activities were and then indicated the importance of accomplishment in each of these areas. In addition, the children indicated how well they thought they would perform and what minimum standard of performance they would be satisfied with. For activities that were viewed as gender-appropriate, the children attached more importance to achievement, set higher minimum standards, and expected to do better than on gender-role-inappropriate activities. As Box 15-4 shows, other factors may affect course and career choices as well.

What are the implications of the young boys' perception of school as a gender-inappropriate institution? One of the obvious effects is that he is less likely to be as motivated and interested in school-related activities as girls, who, of course, view school as consistent with their own gender-role identity. It is not surprising, therefore, to find that girls outperform their opposite-sex peers in the early grades, especially in reading skills (Lummins & Stevenson, 1990). Sex ratios in reading problems range from three boys to one girl to as high as six boys to one girl in some surveys (Halpern, 1992). Although this difference in reading achievement may be due in part to the fact that boys' cognitive development is slower than that of girls, it is possible that boys simply fail to excel in the feminine environment of the early elementary school years.

However, there is an apparent paradox that must be resolved. The school situation we have been describing certainly is not adequate to explain the greater eventual achievement of males in the late high school and college years. Up to this point, the argument has centered almost exclusively on the detrimental effects of the school environment on boys. What are the effects on girls? Girls may have an advantage in the early grades, but the advantage is short-lived. Girls' achievement levels decrease as they grow older, and by college, the proportion of female underachievers exceeds the proportion of male underachievers (Licht & Dweck, 1983). The kinds of passive and dependent behaviors that teachers accept and encourage in girls may, in the long run, be detrimental for later academic success. Intellectual achievement is negatively related to dependency. Independence, assertiveness, and nonconformity are much more likely to lead to creative problem solving and high levels of achievement in both boys and girls (Dweck & Leggett, 1988).

In addition, some work on how the type of teacher feedback is related to sex differences in response to failure may cast light on this issue (Dweck & Elliott, 1983; Dweck, Goetz, & Strauss, 1980). We previously noted that when girls have difficulty on a task, they are more likely to attribute their failure to lack of ability, whereas boys attribute failure to external factors or lack of motivation. In response to these attributions, girls are more likely than boys to show decreased persistence or poor performance under failure or increasing task difficulty. What might be contributing to these differences in response to failure? Teachers' negative criticism of boys is more often for conduct and nonintellectual aspects of work such as neatness, sloppy writing, or lack of motivation. In contrast, girls are more often graded on the accuracy and intellectual quality of their work. It has been proposed that boys see that teachers' responses are unrelated to their intellectual performance and begin to discount them, attribute them to external circumstances, and become less concerned about feedback from teachers and adults. Girls, in contrast, feel that the evaluation is a valid indicator of their intellectual ability and become more distressed and disrupted by failure.

Finally, public achievement, particularly in competitive activities, is often threatening to females. Some girls cope with their conflict about achievement by concealing their ability, particularly from males (Huston, 1983). For example, they may tell male peers that they received lower grades than they actually did. Another coping response is to decrease their efforts and intentionally perform less adequately. A competent woman may counteract her achievement striving by being superfeminine in appearance and behavior. She may be warm, flirtatious, and submissive. She may even try to be

BOX 15-4 MATHEMATICS AND ENGLISH, BOYS AND GIRLS, OR WHY ELLEN DOESN'T WANT TO BE AN ENGINEER

Boys and girls differ in their performance on verbal and quantitative tasks, with boys doing better in mathematics and girls in English. These differences are reflected in enrollments in school courses, selection of a college major, and adult career choices. Women receive only 6 percent of the degrees in engineering, 23 percent in architecture, and 26 percent in computer science. In contrast, 73 percent of the degrees in education, 76 percent in foreign languages, and 88 percent in library science are awarded to women (Eccles, 1985). Why are women underrepresented in mathematics-related endeavors? Various explanations have been offered. Some suggest that males receive more encouragement for their mathematical pursuits. Others argue that males perceive themselves as more competent in learning mathematics than do females. It has also been proposed that, perhaps, mathematics is viewed by women as a male-achievement domain, which makes math study inconsistent with their gender-role identity. In a recent comprehensive study of 668 children in the fifth to twelfth grades, Eccles (1985) asked children about their attitudes toward mathematics and English. In addition, she assessed whether the students planned to take further mathematics and English courses. Boys and girls differed in a variety of ways. Boys rated their mathematics ability higher, felt they had to exert less effort to do well in mathematics, and expected to do better in future mathematics courses than did girls. Both boys and girls rated mathematics as more useful for boys than for girls. In spite of these differences, there were no sex differences in mathematics performance! Across development, females liked mathematics less and enjoyed English more, while boys' attitudes toward both subjects remained fairly stable over time. Not surprisingly, more females than males were likely to drop mathematics prior to high school graduation. Why? For girls, the best predictor of this sex difference in continuing to take mathematics courses was the value they attached to mathematics. Girls saw mathematics as less important, less enjoyable, and less useful to them in the future. Boys, on the other hand, were less influenced by these factors in making their course choices. Males' enrollment decisions were influenced primarily by their performance history; boys continue to do what they have done well in the past. However, girls' avoidance of mathematics courses and careers is not inevitable, and other studies have found that the value students attached to various school subjects can be changed with appropriate role models, information, school programs, and career guidance (Eccles & Midgely, 1988).

Sources: Eccles, J. S. (1985). Sex differences in achievement patterns. In T. Sonderregger (Ed.), *Nebraska Symposium on Motivation.* Lincoln: University of Nebraska Press; Eccles, J. S., & Midgely, C. (1988). Stage environment fit: Developmentally appropriate classrooms for early adolescents. In R. E. Ames & C. Ames (Eds.), *Research on Motivation in Education* (Vol. 3). Orlando, FL: Academic.

supermother, superwife, and super career woman by fulfilling all the demands of a conventional domestic role in addition to having a career. Clearly, no single factor is likely to account for gender differences in achievement.

ANDROGYNY

Many psychologists believe that traditional ideas of masculinity and femininity have been socially and psychologically destructive. We have been speaking almost as if people are either masculine or feminine in their interests, attitudes, and behaviors when we know in reality that most people possess a combination of characteristics viewed as masculine or feminine. Any person, male or female, can be tender and nurturant with children, a competitive terror on the tennis court, professionally successful, and a good cook. Many people are *androgynous;* that is, they possess both masculine and feminine psychological characteristics (Bem, 1974, 1981, 1985, 1991; Spence, 1985). Children, as well as adults, can be androgynous; children who are androgynous are less likely to make stereotyped play and activity choices (Boldizar, 1991). Moreover, androgyny tends to change across the life span, with women becoming more feminine and men more androgynous in old age (which suggests that each gender may become more feminine with age). "The

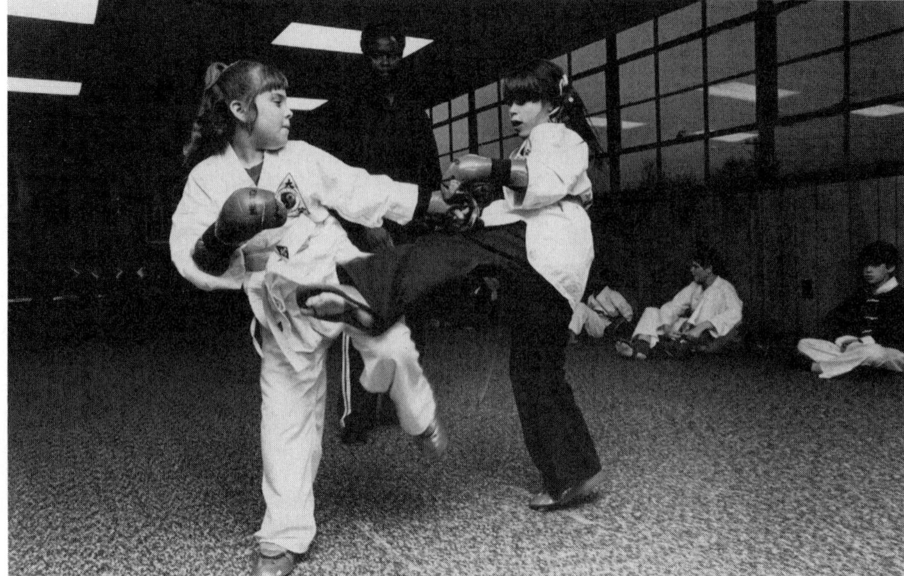

Children who are taught to be androgynous show less gender-stereotyped behavior.

increase in femininity in later life may reflect the increased dependency of old age that affects both sexes because of postretirement lack of employment and disadvantaged financial position" (Hyde et al., 1991, p. 517). However, it is important to recognize that not only do gender-related traits such as expressiveness, nurturance, instrumentality, or assertiveness vary across individual males and females but individuals will vary across situations, settings, and tasks in the extent to which they display these characteristics (Spence, 1985). It would seem constructive to facilitate the development of desirable characteristics such as social sensitivity, nurturance, open expression of positive feelings, appropriate assertiveness, and independence in both males and females.

Can children's gender-role stereotypes be modified? Can children be taught to be more androgynous? Can children learn that a fashion model or a firefighter can be either a male or a female?

The following exchange nicely illustrates the issue:

> A psychologist overheard her 4-year-old son trying to explain her occupation to a young friend.
> **Son:** My mother helps people. She's a doctor.
>
> **Friend:** You mean a nurse.
>
> **Son:** No. She's not that kind of doctor. She's a psychologist. She's a doctor of psychology.
>
> **Friend:** I see. She's a nurse of psychology.

Recent work by Bigler and Liben (1990) suggests that children can be taught to reduce traditional stereotypes. These investigators used ten occupations that children view as typically masculine (for example, dentist, farmer, construction worker) or feminine (for example, beautician, flight attendant, librarian) and tried to reduce children's stereotyping of these occupations. Children were taught that gender is irrelevant and instead focused on two other ways of conceptualizing these jobs, namely, a person's liking of some part of their job (for example, construction workers must like to build things) and the skills they need to learn to do the job (for example, construction workers must learn to drive big machines). Children were given practice problems and received corrective feedback when they relied on gender for their answers. In contrast, children in a control group participated in a group discussion about the role of specific occupations within the community, with no emphasis on gender stereotyping. Children in the experimental group later gave more nonstereotyped answers (that is, when asked, "Who can do various activities?" gave more "Both men and women" responses) not only for the occupations involved in the "lessons" but for a range of other occupations as well (for example, police officer, nurse). Children in the control group still argued that "girls can't be firefighters!"

Consistent with the theory of gender schemas that was discussed earlier, these investigators found that children in the experimental intervention showed better recall of counterstereotypic information in a later memory test. While children in both groups remembered stories about Frank the firefighter and Betty the beautician, children who were in the experimental intervention remembered stories about Larry the librarian and Ann the astronaut far better than did children who were given the control intervention. These findings suggest that even children's ways of thinking about gender roles can be modified.

Some contemporary parents and schools are working toward the goal of reducing the degree of gender typing. In open preschools, where the staff consciously attempts to minimize gender stereotyping, children spend more time in mixed-sex groups and less time in conventional gender-typed activities than children in traditional schools. Children of both sexes are likely to be playing house and gassing up their toy trucks in nontraditional preschools (Bianchi & Bakeman, 1983).

One of the most powerful tests of the plasticity or modifiability of gender roles comes from families who deliberately choose to organize their life-style in order to enhance gender-role equality. These countercultural families often show a high commitment to questioning of conventional culture and institutions, including gender roles. Often a product of the 1960s cultural rebellion, these parents frequently endorse more egalitarian attitudes toward gender roles. Weisner and Wilson-Mitchell (1990) recently examined the gender roles, beliefs, and attitudes of 6-year-old children who were reared by nonconventional parents. In comparison to children reared by conventionally married couples, these countercultural children were less gender-typed in a variety of ways. The countercultural children were more androgynous in terms of activities and interests and gave more non-sex-typed answers concerning questions about appropriate occupations for boys and girls. These children were more likely to assume that girls could be engineers and firefighters and boys could be librarians or nursery school teachers. Over 70 percent of the countercultural children gave non-sex-typed answers compared to only 40 percent of the children in the conventionally married comparison group. It is important to note that these countercultural children did not differ in a variety of ways: Their play preferences and their basic knowledge of the cultural sex typing of familiar objects (for example, dishes, trucks, dolls) were similar to conventionally reared children. All children acquired the normative cultural schemas for sex typing—regardless of family type. This suggests that even children who grow up in nonconventional families are not rigidly stereotyped in terms of sex typing. Instead, these children tend to be *multischematic:* They displayed conventional and more egalitarian sex-typing schemas depending on the situation or domain. "These children have more than one cultural schema available for responding to their world and have developed selective criteria for when to recognize and use either conventional or egalitarian schema" (Weisner & Wilson-Mitchell, 1990, p. 19).

This capacity to be flexible and multischematic is part of a more general pattern that characterizes these families. These families regularly "engage in negotiations and conversation regarding all kinds of cultural standards, reflexively debate and question these standards and include children in these negotiations. When focused on sex typing schemas and sex roles, this process encourages children to think about and question beliefs rather than to always adopt either conventional or alternative beliefs. . . . Overall they have acquired the ability to think about situations, and to purposively select the type of schema best suited for that situation" (Weisner & Wilson-Mitchell, 1990, p. 20).

Finally, some family styles can make children even more rigidly sex-typed. Children reared in devotional communes, for example, that strongly emphasize culturally conventional gender typing were even less androgynous than children in conventionally married families (Weisner & Wilson-Mitchell, 1990). Socializing institutions such as families and schools can modify children's gender roles, but the form that these shifts assume clearly depends on the value system of these social agents. One message is clear: Gender roles and attitudes are modifiable.

Attitudes toward gender roles and acceptable behavior for males and females are slowly changing, but it is clear that there is no single formula for the appropriate behaviors for males and females. Individuals, families, and cultures vary widely and no single script for gender roles will suit these many variations.

SUMMARY

- The process by which children acquire the values, motives, and behaviors viewed as appropriate for males and females within a culture is called *gender typing*. This process includes learning both *gender roles*, or the behaviors typically exhibited by males and females within the culture, and *gender stereotypes*, or the beliefs held by members of the culture regarding behaviors and attitudes appropriate to each sex.

GENDER-ROLE STANDARDS AND STEREOTYPES

- Great consistency in standards of desirable gender-role behavior exists both within and between cultures. Males are expected to be independent, assertive, and competitive; females are expected to be more passive, sensitive, and supportive. These beliefs have changed little over the past twenty years within the United States, and one study has shown them to be held by people in twenty-five other countries around the world.
- Some variation in cultural gender-role standards exists both within the United States and across cultures, however. Within the United States, standards vary depending on ethnicity, age, education, and occupation. For example, black American families are less likely to adhere to strict gender-role distinctions when socializing their children, while Mexican-American families are more likely to highlight gender differences. Diver-

gence between cultures is also clearly seen in Margaret Mead's study of differences between three primitive tribes in which whole tribes took on female- or male-typed characteristics or reversed roles. However, even within groups, individual differences in the strength of stereotypes often outweigh group characteristics.

GENDER DIFFERENCES IN DEVELOPMENT

- Differences in the actual behaviors and attributes of males and females are reported in Table 15-1. Real, equivocal, and mythical differences in behaviors and attributes of males and females can be distinguished. Real gender differences exist in physical, cognitive, social, and atypical development.
- Girls are more physically and neurologically advanced at birth. Boys have more mature muscular development but are more vulnerable to disease and hereditary anomalies. Girls excel early in verbal skills, but boys excel in visual-spatial and math skills. These differences may be decreasing in recent years. Boys are more aggressive, and girls more nurturant. Boys have more reading, speech, and emotional problems than girls.
- More equivocal are gender differences in activity level, dependency, timidity, exploratory activity, and vulnerability to stress. There are no gender differences in sociability, conformity, achievement, self-esteem, or verbal hostility.
- Although differences exist, it is important to remember that the overlap between the distributions is always greater than the differences between them. In addition, noting the existence of the differences does not tell us why they exist. It is clear that girls and boys have many different experiences and opportunities as they develop, which may lead to divergent outcomes or highlight existing differences.

DEVELOPMENTAL PATTERNS OF GENDER TYPING

- Children develop gender-typed patterns of behavior and preferences as early as age 15 to 36 months. Girls tend to conform less strictly to gender-role stereotypes than do boys, possibly because there is greater pressure from parents and teachers for boys to adhere to the masculine role or because the male role has greater status and privilege in our culture. Although some boys and girls receive support for cross-gender behavior, most are encouraged to behave according to traditional stereotypes.

STABILITY OF GENDER TYPING

- A longitudinal study conducted by the Fels Institute found that adult heterosexual behavior could be predicted from gender-typed interests in elementary school. Greater stability was found when a characteristic was related to culturally accepted standards; culturally nontraditional childhood behaviors tended to emerge in divergent forms in adulthood. Thus gender-typed interests tended to remain stable from childhood to maturity. However, newer research indicates that gender roles fluctuate across the life course as adults change to meet the demands of new situations and circumstances, such as childrearing.

FACTORS THAT INFLUENCE GENDER DIFFERENCES AND THE DEVELOPMENT OF GENDER ROLES

- Biological factors that are thought to shape gender differences include hormones and lateralization of brain function. Hormones may organize a biological predisposition to be masculine or feminine during the prenatal period, and the increase in hormones during puberty may activate that predisposition. In addition, social experiences may alter the levels of hormones, such as testosterone. Gender differences in the organization of the brain may be reflected in the greater lateralization of brain functioning in males, possibly leading to better spatial and math skills. However, great controversy exists over whether this difference exists and what effect it has if it does.
- It has been suggested that the difference between living in a male or female body in terms of physical strength, sexual intercourse, pregnancy, and breast-feeding may be another biologically based difference leading to gender standards and gender typing. However, little evidence to support this view exists, because most of these differences could be due to cultural expectations rather than biology.
- Cognitive factors in children's understanding of gender and gender stereotypes may contribute to their acquisition of gender roles. Two theories have looked at when children acquire different types of gender information and how such information modifies their gender-role activities and behaviors. Kohlberg's three-stage *cognitive developmental theory* suggests that children begin by categorizing themselves as male or female, then feel rewarded by behaving in gender-consistent ways. To do this, they must develop gender identity, stability, and constancy. Another approach, *gender-schema theory,* suggests that children develop naive mental schemas that help them organize their experiences in such a way that they will know what to attend to and how to interpret new information. Individual differences in how *gender-schematic* children will be are expected according to this theory. According to cognitive developmental theory, gender-typed behavior should not be seen until after gender constancy is reached (around age 6). However, gender-typed toy and activity preferences are seen much earlier, while same-sex playmates are not preferred until later. These findings suggest that the link between the acquisition of gender concepts and behavior varies depending on gender understanding and kind of behavior.

SOCIAL AND SITUATIONAL FACTORS IN THE DEVELOPMENT OF GENDER-ROLE TYPING

- Families actively play a role in gender-role socialization by the ways in which they organize the environment for their child. Boys and girls are dressed differently, receive different toys to play with, and sleep in bedrooms that are furnished differently. In addition, girls and boys are viewed and treated differently by their parents, particularly their fathers. Boys are thought to be stronger and are treated more roughly and played with more actively than girls as early as birth. As children get older, girls are protected more and allowed less autonomy than boys, and girls are not expected to achieve as much in the areas of mathematics and careers as are boys.

- Parental characteristics influence gender typing in terms of the role models that are available for the child to imitate. Parental power has a great impact on sex typing in boys, but not in girls; femininity in girls is related to the father's masculinity, his approval of the mother as a model, and his reinforcement of participation in feminine activities, but boys' masculinity is not related to parents' gender typing. Because the father plays such a critical role in the development of children's gender roles, his absence has been related to disruptions in gender typing in preadolescent boys and to problems in relationships with peers of the opposite sex for adolescent females. Studies show that the effects of a father's absence on his daughter's interactions with men are long-lasting, extending to marital choices.
- Many extrafamilial influences affect gender-role typing. Male and female roles are portrayed in gender-stereotypic ways in television and many childrens' books. Males are more likely than females to be portrayed as aggressive, competent, rational, and powerful in the work force. Females are more often portrayed as involved primarily in housework or caring for children. In addition, females are less likely to be leading characters on TV, and male characters are overrepresented in children's books—although some change toward more equal treatment has occurred in recent years. Children who are heavy TV viewers hold more stereotyped views; however, this may be due to their interpretations of what they see based on previously held stereotypes. A few attempts to use television to change gender stereotypes have been successful, but the effects typically have been modest and short-lived.
- Peers also serve as an important source of gender-role standards. They are likely to react when other children violate gender-typical behaviors, and boys' cross-gender behaviors are more likely to meet with negative reactions from peers. Reactions from peers typically result in changes in behavior, particularly if the feedback is from a child of the same sex. This pattern of responsiveness may lead to gender segregation, which, in turn, provides opportunities to learn gender-typical roles.
- Teachers also treat girls and boys differently. Due to the emphasis in school on typically feminine characteristics such as quietness, obedience, and passivity, girls tend to like school better and perform better than boys in the early grades. Even in preschool, boys receive more criticism from teachers, who often react to children in gender-stereotypic ways. The implication of young boys' perception of school as gender-inappropriate may be lowered motivation and interest in school activities, leading to the higher rate of learning problems found in boys during the early grades. However, the kinds of passive and dependent behaviors encouraged in girls may be detrimental for their later academic success. This may be because boys learn to discount teachers' criticisms as unrelated to their intellectual abilities, thus persisting in the face of negative feedback while girls give up, or because public achievement is not consistent with female gender-role stereotypes.

ANDROGYNY

- Most people are not strictly feminine or masculine but *androgynous*, that is, they possess both masculine and feminine characteristics. Children who are more androgynous make less stereotyped play and activity choices. Recent research interventions and the experience of nontraditional preschools indicate that children's gender stereotypes can be reduced. Similarly, children of nonconventional parents who place a high value on gender egalitarianism are less gender-typed in their beliefs about possible occupations for males and females, although they are no different from other children on play preferences and knowledge of cultural sex typing. In other words, they are *multischematic,* holding more than one gender schema for responding to the world.

CHAPTER 16

MORALITY, ALTRUISM, AND AGGRESSION

All sensitive observers who have spent time watching children in the classroom or on the playground are impressed by the diversity of children's behaviors. Some children are involved in one altercation after another—successive bouts of name calling, quarreling, shoving, and pushing, with occasional bursts of more violent physical fighting. Other children spend more of their time in cooperative play, in helping or sharing with others, or in soothing a crying classmate who has a broken toy or a scraped knee. Watch children during an exam—some are whispering or straining to catch surreptitious glances at a neighbor's exam or stealthily slipping out crib notes concealed in their desks. Others sit with their brows furrowed in focused attention, trying to solve the problems on the exam. What contributes to the marked variations we observe in such social behavior in children? How do moral values and behaviors develop? How does the child become capable of self-control, resistance to temptation, and personal sacrifices for the welfare of others? This chapter will trace the course of moral development. Theories of the development of moral judgment will be presented. The relationship of moral judgment and moral behavior, and their consistency across situations and over time, will be discussed. In addition, the development of altruism and prosocial behavior will be examined. How early does altruism begin, how does it change, and what role do parents play in the emergence of prosocial behavior? Finally, aggression will be explored. How does aggression change in form and frequency? What are the ways in which biological factors and environmental factors, such as the family, contribute to aggression? How can aggression be effectively controlled?

AN OVERVIEW OF MORAL DEVELOPMENT

A basic task of socialization in every culture is that of communicating ethical standards and shaping and enforcing the practice of "good" behaviors in the developing child. Although the specific values and behaviors regarded as desirable vary among cultures, all societies have a system of rules about the rightness and wrongness of certain behaviors. The child is expected to learn these rules and to experience emotional discomfort or guilt when violating them and satisfaction when conforming to them.

Initial control over the young child's behavior is maintained largely through immediate external social factors, such as the presence of authority figures or fear of punishment. However, with age, the child's behavior seems to be increasingly maintained by internalized standards of conduct that lead to self-control in the absence of external restraints. This shift from external factors to personal feelings and ethical beliefs as the basis of moral behavior is called *internalization.* Many psychologists believe internalization to be the basic process in the development of morality.

Psychological research has focused on the development of three basic components of morality—the cognitive component, the behavioral component, and the emotional component—and the relationships among these three factors and their roles in the process of internalization. The cognitive factor involves the knowledge of ethical rules and the judgments of the "goodness" or "badness" of various acts. The behavioral factor has to do with actual behavior in a variety of situations involving ethical considerations. Most studies have investigated disapproved-of aspects of children's behaviors, such as cheating, lying, and the inability to delay gratification, resist temptation, or control aggression. However, recent studies of moral development

(Miss Peach by Mell Lazarus. Courtesy of Mell Lazarus and Field Newspaper Syndicate.)

have also included positive behaviors, such as sharing, cooperation, altruism, and helping. Studies of the emotional dimension of morality have traditionally focused on negative aspects, such as feelings of guilt, often measured by confession or reparation following transgression. Recent work has focused on positive emotions such as empathy—in response to others' misfortunes or distress (Eisenberg, 1992; Zahn-Waxler & Kochanska, 1990). Again we find that different psychological theories have focused on different aspects of moral development. Cognitive theories have emphasized moral judgments; psychoanalytic theories have emphasized affective components of morality, particularly those of guilt and anxiety; and learning theories have emphasized ethical behavior. Both analytic and behavior theory have been greatly concerned with internalization, although they invoke different mechanisms to explain its development.

Freud believed that moral behavior and the guilt experienced when violating moral standards were the result of the formation of the superego through identification, when children take on the ethical standards as they perceive them in their parents. Social learning theorists use the same learning principles of classical and operant conditioning and imitation as the foundation for the acquisition of all social behaviors including moral conduct and self-control.

In spite of the convenience of dividing the world of morality into separate parts, in real life these different aspects often operate together in determining how a child will act when faced with a moral decision. One solution has been offered by Rest (1983), who proposes a four-step process in executing a moral action. When faced with a situation, the child first interprets the situation in terms of how people's welfare could be affected by the child's possible actions. Then the child must figure out what the ideally moral course of action would be. Step 3 involves the child's deciding what she or he actually intends to do, and finally, the child must actually perform the act. In this chapter we will focus on each of these steps. First, we turn to steps 1 and 2—the study of how children judge the appropriate course of moral action.

COGNITIVE THEORIES OF MORAL DEVELOPMENT

Alternative explanations for the acceptance and development of moral standards are presented by the cognitive theorists Jean Piaget and Lawrence Kohlberg. Piaget's theory of moral development involves many of the same principles and processes of cognitive growth that were encountered in the earlier presentation of his theory of intellectual development. In fact, the key thing to remember is that for these theorists the study of moral development is just an approach to the study of intellectual development as it bears on the specific topic of ethical cognition. Since intellectual growth proceeds through a specific sequence of stages, moral judgments will also advance in stages related to the changes in the child's general cognitive development.

Jean Piaget's Cognitive Theory of Moral Development

Piaget proposes a cognitive developmental theory of moral development in which the moral concepts of the child evolve in an unvarying sequence from an early stage, which is often called the *stage of moral realism,* to a more mature stage, referred to as the *morality of reciprocity or autonomous morality.* No one could reach the stage of moral reciprocity without first having passed through the stage of moral realism. According to Piaget, mature morality includes both children's understanding and acceptance of social rules and their concern for equality and reciprocity in human relationships, which is the basis of justice. He investigated changing moral judgments in two main ways, namely by shifts with age in children's attitudes toward rules in such common games as marbles and by changes in children's judgments of the seriousness of transgressions.

The preschool child shows little concern for, or awareness of, rules. In children's games, such as marbles, the child does not try to play a systematic game with the intention of winning, but seems to gain satisfaction from the manipulation and multiple uses of the marbles. By age 5, however, the child begins to develop great concern and respect for rules. Rules are regarded as coming from external authority, usually the parents; rules are immutable, unchanging through time, and never to be questioned. What Piaget calls *moral absolutism* prevails. If children of this age are asked if children in other countries could play marbles with different rules, they will assure the interviewer that they could not. This is reflected in the rigidity with which children approach social interactions, frequently falling back on a "my mommy says ———" ploy to solve disputes. In addition, any deviation from

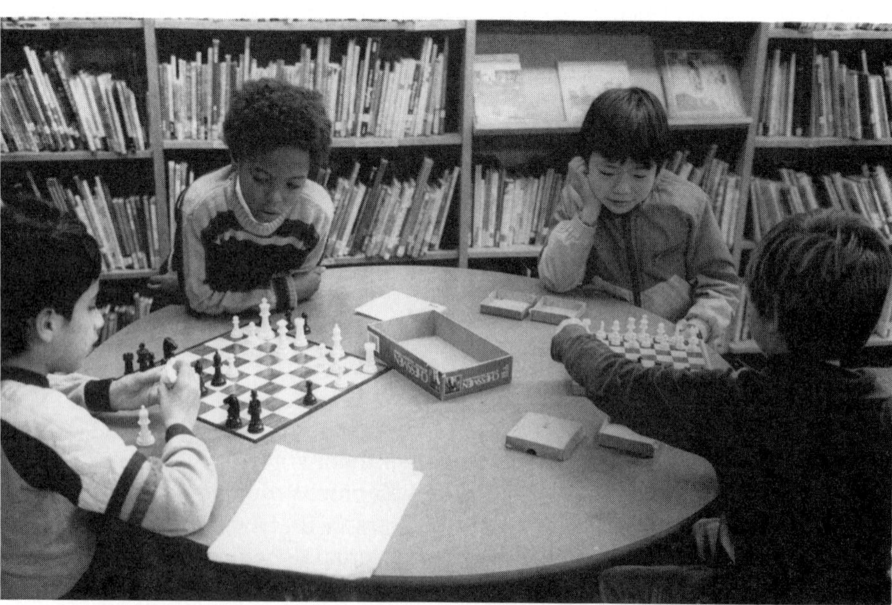

Learning to follow the rules of the game is an important part of moral development according to Piaget.

the rules is seen as inevitably resulting in punishment by *immanent justice.* Someone or something is going to get you one way or another! Such retribution might take the form of accidents or mishaps controlled by inanimate objects or by God. A child who has lied to his mother may later fall off his bike and skin his knees and will think, "That's what I get for lying to mother." In this stage, children also evaluate the seriousness of an act in terms of its consequences rather than according to the good or bad intentions of the actor. Behavior is assessed in terms of *objective responsibility* rather than intentionality. The two factors that contribute to young children's moral realism are their *egocentrism,* that is, their inability to subordinate their own experiences and perceive situations as others would, and their *realistic thinking,* which leads them to confuse external reality with their own thought processes and subjective experiences.

Piaget believes that a *morality of reciprocity* begins to emerge in older children at about age 9 to 11. Moral judgments are now characterized by the recognition that social rules are arbitrary agreements that can be questioned and changed. Obedience to authority is neither necessary nor always desirable. Violations of rules are not always wrong, nor inevitably punished. The child considers the feelings and viewpoints of others in judging their behavior. When there is to be punishment, reciprocity in relating the punishment to the intentions of the wrongdoer and the nature of the transgression should be considered; the punishment should be in the form of restitution that will make up for harm done or help teach the culprit to behave better if the situation should arise again. Finally, there should be "equalitarianism" in the form of equal justice for all.

Some of these shifts in attitude from the stage of moral realism to that of moral reciprocity are vividly illustrated in the children's responses to stories reported by Piaget in *The Moral Judgment of the Child* (1932). Piaget would present the child with pairs of stories such as the following ones and ask the child if the children in each are equally guilty, and which child was the naughtiest and why.

> Story I. A little boy who is called John is in his room. He is called to dinner. He goes into the dining room. But behind the door there was a chair, and on the chair there was a tray with 15 cups on it. John couldn't have known that there was all this behind the door. He goes in, the door knocks against the tray, "bang" to the 15 cups and they all get broken!
>
> Story II. Once there was a little boy whose name was Henry. One day when his mother was out he tried to get some jam out of the cupboard. He climbed up on a chair and stretched out his arm. But the jam was too high up and he couldn't reach it and have any. But while he was trying to get it, he knocked over a cup. The cup fell down and broke. (Piaget, 1932, p. 122)

A characteristic response for a child in the stage of moral realism is given by a 6-year-old:

> "What did the first boy do?"
> "He broke 15 cups."
> "And the second one?"
> "He broke a cup by moving roughly."
> "Is one of the boys naughtier than the other?"
> "The first one is because he knocked over 15 cups."
> "If you were the daddy, which one would you punish most?"
> "The one who broke 15 cups."

"Why did he break them?"
"The door shut too hard and knocked them over. He didn't do it on purpose."
"And why did the other boy break a cup?"
"Because he was clumsy. When he was getting the jam the cup fell down."
"Why did he want to get the jam?"
"Because he was alone. Because his mother wasn't there." (Piaget, 1932, p. 129)

In spite of the fact that Henry was clumsy while trying to deceive his mother, John is regarded by the child in the stage of moral realism as behaving less ethically since he destroyed more cups, although it was unintentional. In contrast, Russ, a 10-year-old, shows advances to the stage of moral reciprocity when he responds that the one who wanted to take the jam was naughtiest. He is considering intentions. When asked if it makes any difference that the other child broke more cups, he replies: "No, because the one who broke 15 cups didn't do it on purpose" (Piaget, 1932, p. 130).

Evaluation of Piaget's Theory of Moral Development

How well had Piaget's theory fared after sixty years of evaluation? One of the central arguments of cognitive theories of moral development suggests that people progress from one level of moral judgment to another in a fixed and invariant sequence. In Piaget's theory, the general developmental progression from moral realism to moral reciprocity has frequently been replicated (Ferguson & Rule, 1982). In industrialized Western countries such as the United States, Great Britain, France, and Switzerland, across a wide range of populations and social classes and for both sexes, there are regular age trends of development in moral judgment. However, the findings in cross-cultural studies are less consistent. A study by Havinghurst and Neugarten (1955) of ten Native American tribes found developmental increase rather than the predicted decrease in belief in immanent justice in six tribes. Also, only two of the ten groups showed the expected shift in the conception of rules toward greater flexibility with age. It seems that cultural factors can alter the sequence of Piaget's moral judgments.

Although there is support for the general developmental sequence, recent research in moral development suggest that Piaget underestimated the cognitive capacities of young children. In judging the behavior of others, even 6-year-old children are able to consider other people's intentions when the situation is described in a way that they can comprehend. When the format of the moral stories is changed from a verbal presentation, which young children may have trouble processing, to videotaped presentations, 6-year-olds respond to the intentions of the actor as well as older children do (Chandler, Greenspan, & Barenboim, 1973). As the authors note, "The medium is the message!" A further methodological shortcoming of Piaget's early studies may be another reason for the underestimation of the moral judgment abilities of young children. In the original Piaget stories, children were always required to judge whether a child who causes a small amount of damage in the service of bad intentions was any "worse" than one who caused a large amount of damage in the pursuit of good intentions. The intent of the child in the story was confounded with the consequences of his or her behavior. When stories are presented where good and bad intentions can be evaluated separately from good and bad outcomes, even young elementary-school-age children are able to use intentions as the basis for their judgments (Feldman, Klosson, Parsons, Rholes, & Ruble, 1976; Yuill & Perner, 1988).

Moreover, researchers continue to isolate factors that affect the outcome of moral development studies using Piagetian stories (Grueneich, 1982). For example, "Instead of having only two factors (intentions and consequences), some studies have shown the influence of a multitude of factors: (1) whether the consequences are negative or positive, (2) the extent or degree of the consequences, (3) whether the object of the consequence is an inanimate object, animal or person, and if a person, (4) whether the effects of the action were physical or psychological, (5) whether the consequences were intended, or happened accidentally or through carelessness or recklessness, and if intended, (6) whether the person was provoked, forced or pressured, or whether the consequences were willful and premeditated, (7) whether the specific activity was part of an overall plan to be helpful, or malicious and selfish, or part of no plan at all . . . and so on" (Rest, 1983, p. 119). The "simple" tasks that Piaget devised over half a century ago have become much more complicated by the 1990s! It is clear that there are many more factors to consider in understanding moral reasoning than simply intentions and consequences. A more complex approach to the study of moral judgments has been offered by Lawrence Kohlberg. We turn to his theory next.

Lawrence Kohlberg's Cognitive Theory of Moral Development

Kohlberg (1963a, 1963b, 1969, 1985) has extended, modified, and refined Piaget's theory on the basis of his analysis of interviews of 10- to 16-year-old boys who were confronted with a series of moral dilemmas in which they had to choose either acts of obedience to rules and authority or to the needs and welfare of others that conflicted with the regulations.

A representative dilemma is one in which a man needs a particular expensive drug to help his dying wife. The pharmacist who discovered and controls the supply of the drug has refused the husband's offer to give him all the money he now has, which would be about half the necessary sum, and to pay the rest later. The man must now decide whether or not to steal the drug to save his wife; that is, whether to obey the rules and laws of society or violate them to respond to the needs of his wife. What should the man do, and why?

Kohlberg formulated a series of three broad levels of moral development subdivided into six stages; each stage was based not only upon whether the boys chose an obedient or need-served act but also on the reasons and justification for their choices. Kohlberg believes that the order of the stages is fixed, but that stages do not occur at the same age in all people. Many people never attain the highest level of moral judgment, and some adults continue to think in immature preconventional terms of conforming only to avoid punishment and gain rewards.

Kohlberg would agree with Piaget in noting that the young child is oriented toward obedience, but for different reasons. Whereas Piaget regarded this early conformity as being based on the young child's dependency and respect for authority, in level 1, the *preconventional level,* Kohlberg regards it as based on the desire to avoid punishment and gain rewards. At level 1 there is no internalization of moral standards. At level 2, the *conventional level,* although the child identifies with his parents and conforms to what they regard as right and wrong, it is the motive to conform rather than ethical standards that have been internalized. It is only at level 3, the *postconventional level,* that moral judgment is rational and internalized and that conduct is controlled by an internalized ethical code and is relatively independent of the approval or castigation of others. At this level, moral conflict is resolved in terms of broad ethical principles, and violating these principles results in guilt and self-condemnation.

The levels and stages of moral development as conceptualized by Kohlberg (1963a) are as follows:

Level 1 Preconventional morality

Stage 1 Obedience and punishment orientation
This orientation involves deference to prestigious or powerful people, usually the parents, in order to avoid punishment. The morality of an act is defined in terms of its physical consequences.

Stage 2 Naive hedonistic and instrumental orientation
In this stage the child is conforming to gain rewards. Although there is evidence of reciprocity and sharing, it is a manipulative, self-serving reciprocity rather than one based on a true sense of justice, generosity, sympathy, or compassion. It is a kind of bartering: "I'll lend you my bike if I can play with your wagon." "I'll do my homework now if I can watch the late night movie."

Level 2 Conventional level: morality of conventional rules and conformity

Stage 3 Good boy morality
In this stage good behavior is that which maintains approval and good relations with others. Although the child is still basing his judgments of right and wrong on the responses of others, he is concerned with their approval and disapproval rather than their physical power. He is concerned about conforming to his friends' and families' standards to maintain goodwill. He is, however, starting to accept the social regulations of others and is judging the goodness or badness of behavior in terms of a person's intent to violate these rules.

Stage 4 Authority and social-order-maintaining morality
In this stage the individual blindly accepts social conventions and rules and believes that if society accepts the rules they should be maintained to avoid censure. It is no longer just conformity to other individuals' standards but conformity to the social order. This is the epitome of "law and order" morality involving unquestioning acceptance of social regulations. Behavior is judged as good in terms of its conformity to a rigid set of rules. It is unfortunate that most individuals in our culture do not pass beyond the conventional level of morality.

Level 3 Postconventional level: Morality of self-accepted moral principles.

Stage 5 Morality of contract, individual rights, and democratically accepted law.
There is a flexibility of moral beliefs in this stage that was lacking in earlier stages. Morality is based upon an agreement among individuals to conform to norms which appear necessary to maintain the social order and the rights of others. However, since it is a social contract, it can be modified when the people within the society rationally discuss alternatives which might be more advantageous to a larger number of the members of the group.

Stage 6 Morality of individual principles and conscience.
In this stage individuals conform both to social standards and to internalized ideals to avoid self-condemnation, rather than criticism by others. Decisions are based upon abstract principles involving justice, compassion, and equality. It is a morality based upon a respect for others. People who have attained this level of development will have highly individualistic moral beliefs which may at times conflict with the social order accepted by the majority. A greater number of

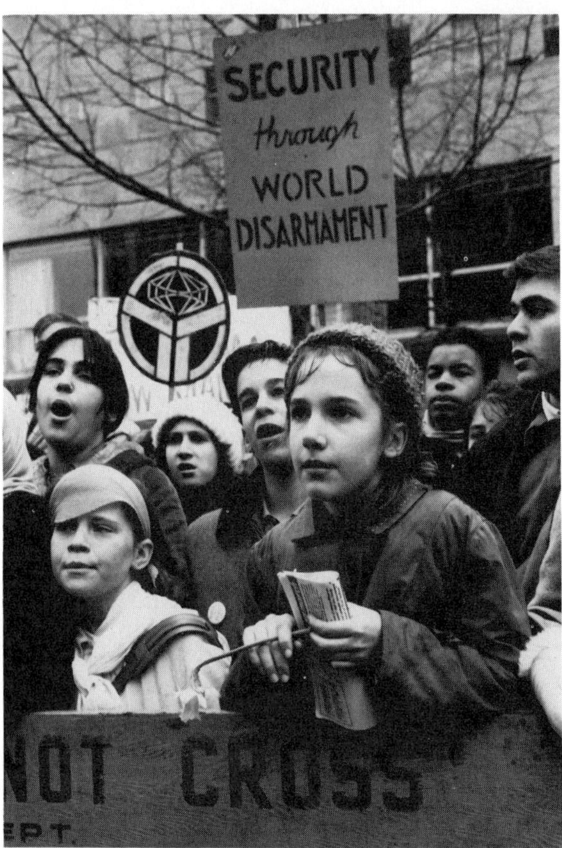

Moral beliefs are expressed in many types of social and political action.

nonviolent, activist students taking part in the anti-Vietnam war demonstrations had attained the postconventional level of morality than had nonactivist students.

Kohlberg, like Piaget, believes that stages of moral development are determined by the cognitive capabilities of the individuals. Like the orderly progression of Piaget's general cognitive theory of development with the attainments of one stage building on the achievements of earlier stages, moral development builds on the moral concepts in previous stages. Figure 16-1 presents the percent of moral statements of different types or stages of development at four ages (Kohlberg, 1963a). Although Kohlberg predicts no direct relations between age and moral maturity, it can be seen that more preconventional responses are made by young children and more postconventional responses by the older children in the study. The sequence should be invariant across cultures, although the ultimate level attained may vary among cultures and for individuals within the same society. Once an individual has attained a high level of moral cognition, especially stage 6, she will not regress and go back to earlier stages of moral judgment.

Evaluation of Kohlberg's Theory of Moral Development

Kohlberg's more complex theory of moral judgment maintains more current support than Piaget's, but, again, there are critics as well as defenders (Snarey, 1987). There is general support for the assumptions that children

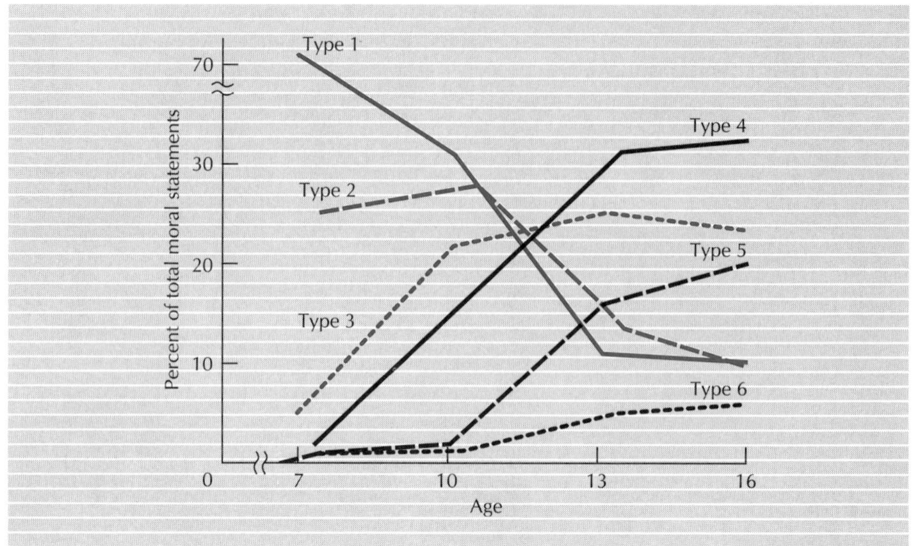

FIGURE 16-1
Use of six types of moral judgments at four ages. (From Kohlberg, 1963a.)

proceed through Kohlberg's stages of moral judgment in a fixed and invariant fashion (Walker, 1988, 1989; Rest, 1983). Cross-cultural confirmation of this general pattern of movement from the lower to higher stages has been found in a three-year longitudinal study of 8- to 17-year-old children in the Bahamas (White, Bushnell, & Regnemer, 1978). Studies in Turkey (Nisan & Kohlberg, 1982), Taiwan (Lei & Cheng, 1989), and Israel (Snarey, Reimer, & Kohlberg, 1985) all support the expectation that individuals, regardless of their cultural background develop through the sequence of stages in the same manner. Few individuals either regress to lower stages or skip stages as they develop.

In spite of some support, other evidence suggests the possibility of cultural bias. For example, some cultures, such as New Guinea, emphasize community obligations over individual rights while others, such as India, emphasize the sacredness of all forms of life in their belief systems. Kohlberg's focus on individual rights and obligations may lead to either underestimates of moral development in other cultures or exclude some domains of morality that are culturally unique (Snarey, 1987; Shweder & Much, 1987).

Can moral judgments be changed? Studies have used role-playing and modeling techniques to determine whether moral judgments can be successfully modified. Although some studies report that shifts to less mature levels of moral judgment can be induced by modeling (Bandura & MacDonald, 1963), the majority of studies indicate that it is generally easier to advance an individual's moral judgment to a higher stage than to shift it to a lower stage (Rest, 1979, 1983; Turiel, 1966). Moreover, subjects who are exposed to a model's reasoning about a moral dilemma at a stage above or a stage below their own stage of moral development prefer the more advanced to the less advanced stage (Rest, 1983). This short-term laboratory evidence is generally consistent with both Piaget's and Kohlberg's views that progress should be toward higher rather than lower stages.

The most impressive evidence substantiating his theories comes from a twenty-year longitudinal study of fifty-eight boys (Colby, Kohlberg, Gibbs, & Lieberman, 1983). Subjects were 10, 13, and 16 at the start of the study and were interviewed five times at three- and four-year intervals. At each point, the boys were individually interviewed for their judgments about nine hypothetical moral dilemmas. All, except two of the subjects, showed upward movement toward higher stages, and no one skipped stages. While the vast majority of the subjects stopped at stage 4, a few individuals continued to develop their moral reasoning in their twenties, reaching stage 5 levels in young adulthood. This suggests that moral development does not cease in midadolescence, as many previously assumed, but continues into adulthood (see Figure 16-2).

However, these findings also underscore a major fact: The dominant pattern of moral reasoning in most adults is conventional (stages 3 and 4). Notice that there were *no* adults who reached stage 6, and a meager 5 percent were at stage 5. Recently, Kohlberg has expressed doubts about the practical value of scoring stories for stage 6 responses and this final stage has been dropped from the most recent form of the scoring system for moral judgments (Colby & Kohlberg, 1987). There may be fewer Ghandis among us than Kohlberg originally imagined!

Another criticism comes from the feminist front; it is contended that there is a sex bias against females in Kohlberg's theory (see Box 16-1).

Finally, historical events that individuals encounter as they develop may contribute to their views of morality, just as the life span theorists that we discussed in Chapter 1 would predict

> Consider the subjects tested in Kohlberg's twenty-year longitudinal study, initiated in the mid-1950s. Over the period in which these subjects have been assessed for moral judgment, Americans have experienced the civil rights struggle, student protests, the Vietnamese war, Watergate, and the women's movement. All of these events have raised issues of justice and have focused attention on moral concerns. It seems highly likely that these social events have had a general impact on people's concepts of fairness, and would cause them to have differing concepts of moral and social justice from those of other generations developing during different social times such as the Depression in the 1930s or World War II in the 1940s. Changes in moral judgment scores over the past twenty years, therefore, may reflect cultural change as well as individual ontogenesis (Rest, Davison, & Robbins, 1978, p. 272).

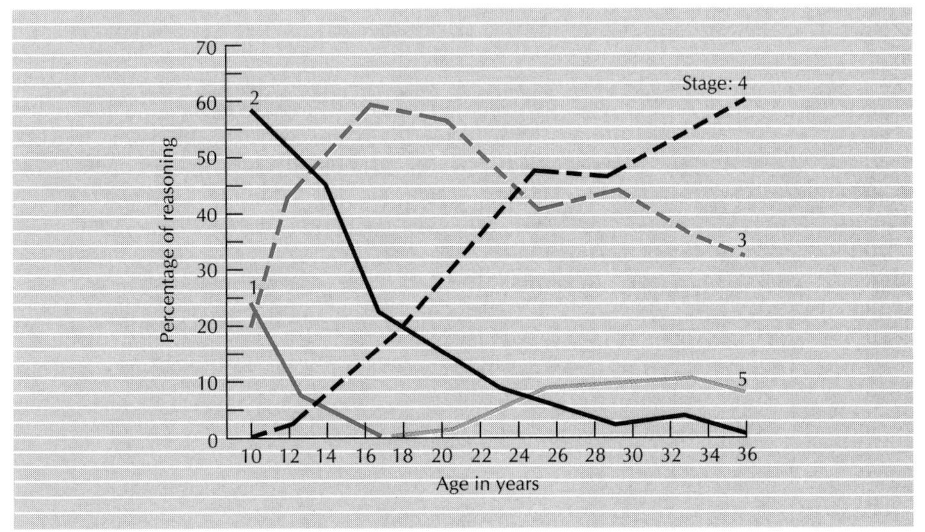

FIGURE 16-2
Moral reasoning from preadolescence to adulthood. (From Colby, Kohlberg, Gibbs, & Lieberman, 1983.)

BOX 16-1 ARE COGNITIVE THEORIES OF MORAL DEVELOPMENT UNFAIR TO WOMEN?

Some critics have argued that women have been unfairly treated by the Kohlberg tests for moral development, which tend to indicate that women score lower than men. The foremost spokeswoman has been Carol Gilligan, who has eloquently argued in her book *In a Different Voice* that the Kohlberg scoring scheme is biased against women. Specifically, it is alleged that women usually score lower than men on the moral stages. Most women's judgments seem to be given stage 3 ratings—a stage in which morality is conceived in interpersonal terms and goodness is equated with helping and pleasing others. As Gilligan notes, "the very traits that traditionally have defined the 'goodness' of women are those that mark them as deficient in moral development" (Gilligan, 1982, p. 18).

In contrast to this caring and interpersonal orientation to moral issues that is common among women, men's moral orientation emphasizes masculine values such as rights, individuality, and principles of justice. Since the main body of work out of which Kohlberg's stages were derived was based largely on the study of men's lives, Gilligan argues that women may appear to score lower on moral reasoning when, in fact, they are not lower but merely have a different moral orientation than males.

Consider how two children—a boy and a girl respond to a Kohlbergian dilemma concerning Heinz and the drug.

Jake, age 11, responds in the following way when asked whether Heinz should steal the drug:

> For one thing, a human life is worth more than money, and if the druggist only makes $1,000, he is still going to live, but if Heinz doesn't steal the drug, his wife is going to die. (*Why is life worth more than money?*) Because the druggist can get a thousand dollars from rich people with cancer, but Heinz can't get his wife again. (*Why not?*) Because people are all different and so you couldn't get Heinz's wife again. (Gilligan, 1982, p. 26)

The response emphasizes logic and the balance between life and property rights—a clearly masculine orientation.

In contrast, consider the response of Amy, age 11, to the same dilemma. When asked whether or not Heinz should steal the drug to save his wife's life, she said:

> Well, I don't think so. I think there might be other ways besides stealing it, like if he could borrow the money or make a loan or something, but he really shouldn't steal the drug—but his wife shouldn't die either.

Asked why he should not steal the drug, she considers neither property nor law but rather the effect that theft could have on the relationship between Heinz and his wife.

> If he stole the drug, he might save his wife then, but if he did, he might have to go to jail, and then his wife might get sicker again, and he couldn't get more of the drug, and it might not be good. So, they should really just talk it out and find some other way to make the money. (Gilligan, 1982, p. 28)

Instead of focusing on the issues of property or law, Amy focused on the impact of the theft on the relationship between Heinz and his wife—an interpersonal focus or orientation.

Others have found support for Gilligan's claim of separate moral orientations for males and females. When asked to recall real-life dilemmas (for example, abortion, life preservation, birth control, inequitable wills), Walker, deVries, and Trevethan (1987) found that adult women were more likely to focus on a caring orientation while adult men more often adopted a "rights" orientation. Boys and girls on the other hand, did not differ in their moral orientation. However, women are more likely to recall dilemmas that concern personal relationships, while males recall prior dilemmas in their lives that are more impersonal. When males and females respond to *similar* real-life dilemmas, the sex differences disappear.

While there is some basis for Gilligan's contention that there may be different orientations to morality, there does not appear to be a great deal of support for the claim of a sex bias in moral reasoning. Walker (1988) has reviewed data from over 10,000 subjects and found little evidence that females and males differ in the levels of their moral judgments. While the case for sex bias in moral judgments has not found strong support, Gilligan (1991) suggests that the *care prospective* ought to be considered as an aspect of moral reasoning in both males and females.

The case is not yet closed and the debate continues!

Sources: Gilligan, C. (1982). *In a different voice*. Cambridge, MA: Harvard University Press; Gilligan, C. (1991, April). Psychology and the good: How should we talk about development. *Symposium at the biennial meeting of the Society for Research in Child Development;* Walker, L. J. (1988). The development of moral reasoning. *Annals of Child Development*, 5, 33–78; Walker, L. J., deVries, B., & Trevethan, J. D. (1987). Moral stages and moral orientations in real-life and hypothetical dilemmas. *Child Development*, **58**, 842–858.

RELATION OF MORAL JUDGMENTS TO OTHER COGNITIVE MEASURES

It is not surprising that general cognitive maturity has been found to be related to moral maturity. A high level of abstract thinking is required in the development of evaluation of intent, generalized rational ethical standards, and sensitivity to the roles, perceptions, and feelings of others. In one study (Tomlinson-Keasey & Keasey, 1974), college females who reasoned at the postconventional level (stages 5 and 6) also showed formal operational thinking. However, not all who reasoned at the formal operations level reached the postconventional levels of moral development. This evidence suggests that formal operations is a necessary, but not sufficient, condition for advanced levels of moral judgment. In addition, measures of role-taking skills correlate with Kohlberg's levels of moral judgment, and shifts to higher levels of moral development are preceded by increases in role-taking ability (Rest, 1983).

EFFECTS OF SOCIAL INTERACTIONS ON MORAL DEVELOPMENT

Kohlberg has emphasized the importance of social interactions involving role-taking opportunities for moral development. Not only are children who participate in more social activities rated by their peers and teachers as more popular and as group leaders, but also these socially active children have been found to be more mature in moral judgments (Enright & Sutterfield, 1980).

Further support for Kohlberg's emphasis on the importance of social role-taking experience in moral development is found in studies showing that restricted social environments—such as isolated communities or large, impersonal, diffuse school environments where there is a lack of opportunity for intense and varied role-taking experiences—are related to undifferentiated simplistic descriptions of social roles (Rest, 1983). This might be expected to restrict the role-taking abilities basic to moral judgment.

The educational programs established in recent years to foster the development of moral judgments provide another way of evaluating Kohlberg's theory, as well as the relationship between social interactions and moral development. These programs are designed for classroom use and usually focus on peer discussion of controversial moral problems. Practice in solving moral dilemmas, mutual probing of each other's solutions, and accommodating and negotiating with others are the key ingredients in these programs. While there is some evidence that the opportunity to discuss controversial moral dilemmas with peers fosters moral judgment (Higgins, Power, & Kohlberg, 1984), these educational interventions are still controversial. Not only do the programs sometimes fail, but it is still unclear what specific teaching tactics or curriculum materials are most effective in changing children's moral judgments.

Although Kohlberg argues that parents do not play a crucial role in moral development, the cognitive structuring involved in parental discipline does affect moral judgments. When parents use consistent disciplinary techniques that involve reasoning and explanation (Aronfreed, 1976; Parke, 1977), initiate discussion of the feelings of others (Hoffman, 1984), and promote a democratic family-discussion style (Edwards, 1980), more mature moral judgments in addition to more self-controlled behavior occur. Further evidence of the role of family factors in moral development comes from Dunn (1989), who shows that moral understanding may occur at a much earlier age than previously thought (see Box 16-2).

Another Kind of Social Violation: Social Conventions

Are all types of social violations the same? Children learn not only moral rules concerned with the inappropriateness of cheating, lying, and stealing, but many other nonmoral rules about everyday conduct. Learning table manners, correct ways of dress, forms of address and modes of greeting, and other rules of etiquette can be distinguished from morality. Elliot Turiel (1983) has argued that reasoning about moral issues and reasoning about those types of behavior which he calls *social conventions* are different. Moreover, children's understanding of social conventions may follow a different developmental course than the stages for morality offered by Kohlberg. In one study of nursery-school-age children (Nucci & Turiel, 1978) children were asked how wrong it would be to commit certain acts such as hitting someone, lying, or stealing (example of violating moral rules), in contrast to addressing a teacher by a first name, a boy entering a girl's bathroom, or eating lunch with one's fingers (examples of violating rules of social convention). In support of Turiel's argument that morality and social conventions represent independent domains, children and adolescents from second grade to college consistently viewed the moral violations as more wrong than violations of social convention. Even children as young as 3 years of age can make these distinctions between these two domains of social judgments (Smetana & Braeges, 1987). Children view moral violations as more wrong because they result in harm to another, violate rights, and "never should be committed." In contrast, children view deviations from social conventions as merely impolite, disruptive, or messy.

While moral issues are often viewed as fixed, absolute, and invariant across cultures, conventions more often are viewed as arbitrary and relative and as varying across communities and cultures (Turiel, Killen, & Helwig, 1988). Children agree with these distinctions. When asked if it would be acceptable to steal in a country that had no laws against stealing, children as young as 6 thought it was wrong to steal. On the other hand, children thought that people in different countries could play games by different rules. Clearly, children distinguish violations of social conventions and morality in terms of their wrongness and relativity.

How do children learn to distinguish moral and conventional transgressions? Probably parents and other family members play an influential role in helping children learn these distinctions among moral categories. Children learn from their parents at a very early age that eating your spaghetti with your hands or spilling your milk (conventional violations) leads to different consequences than taking your brother's toy and pulling your kid sister's pigtails (moral transgressions). Mothers of 24- to 26-month-olds responded to conventional violations with rules about social order and social regulation that focused on the disorder that the act created ("Look at the mess that you made!"). In contrast, maternal responses to moral transgressors focused on the consequences of the acts for other's rights and welfare or by perspective-taking requests ("Think about how you would feel if you were hit") (Smetana, 1989). Other socializing agents, including teachers and peers, play a part in helping children learn as well. In day-care centers, adults respond differently to the moral and conventional transgressions of 12- to 36-month-old toddlers

BOX 16-2 EARLY SIGNS OF MORAL UNDERSTANDING: FAMILY DISPUTES

Children's understanding of moral rules begins at a very early age. This is well illustrated in studies by Judy Dunn and her colleagues in which they observed the natural interactions among 2- and 3-year-olds and members of their family. Between 2 and 3 years, children showed not only the beginnings of moral understanding but rapid increases as well. In incidents involving conflicts and disputes (for example, over a toy) between siblings, or between mother and child, the children showed clear awareness of rules, for example, by looking at their mothers and laughing when carrying out a forbidden act or by pointing out to their mothers the consequences of the rule violation (for example, a broken object). In fact, children as early as 14 months showed an interest in broken objects, which they brought to their mother's attention and this increased steadily over the succeeding seven months.

As early as 16 months, mothers and children engaged in "moral dialogues" about rules with children often nodding, shaking their heads, or providing verbal answers to their mothers' inquiries about rules. Even more interesting is that children at a young age commented on their own responsibility for transgressions.

> **Ella** (21 months): At table, throws toy to floor (previously forbidden). Looks at mother.
>
> **Mother:** No! What's Ella?
>
> **Child:** Bad bad baba.
>
> **Mother:** A bad bad baba.

Children also joined in conversations between mother and siblings to comment on the transgressions of others.

> **Child** (24 months): Sibling shows mother that she has drawn on a piece of jigsaw puzzle.
>
> **Sibling** (to mother): Look
>
> **Mother** (to sibling): You're not supposed to draw on them, Caroline. You should know better. You only draw on pieces of paper. You don't draw on puzzles.
>
> **Child** (to mother): Why
>
> **Mother** (to child): Because they aren't pieces of paper.
>
> **Child:** Naughty.
>
> **Mother:** Yes, that is a naughty thing to do.

As children develop, more sophisticated forms of moral understanding begin to emerge—the use of justifications. By 36 months, children produce justifications in nearly a third of their disputes with mothers and siblings. The justifications were often in terms of their own wants, needs, or feelings (for example, "But, I need that" as sibling tries to take a child's spoon), but also in reference to social rules (for example, "That doesn't belong to you"), to the feelings of others (for example, "Rachel will be cross if you do that"), or to the material consequences of actions (for example, "You'll break it if you do that"). At an early age children are emerging as young moral philosophers.

There are wide individual differences and mothers seem to contribute to their children's understanding of moral rules. Children who show high levels of reference to rules and justifications come from families in which the mothers, in their interventions in sibling conflict, frequently referred to social rules and to the feelings of the siblings.

These studies also show the important interplay between emotion and the development of social and moral understanding. It is often in the context of highly emotionally charged interchanges—family disputes and conflicts—that early clues about children's awareness of rules first emerge. Perhaps emotions—both positive and negative—serve "to heighten the children's awareness of others, of the feelings, the relationships, the rules and roles of the family world . . ." (Dunn, 1987, p. 102).

By looking at natural interchanges among family members, we are reminded that moral understanding not only begins at home, but at a surprisingly early phase of development.

Sources: Dunn, J. (1987). The beginning of moral understanding. In J. Kagan and S. Lamb (Eds.), *The emergence of morality in young children.* Chicago: University of Chicago Press; Dunn, J. (1989). *The beginnings of social understanding.* Cambridge, MA: Harvard University Press.

(Smetana, 1984). Even other children react differently to conventional and moral violations; 2- and 3-year-olds react more emotionally and retaliate more often in response to moral than conventional transgressions. Not surprisingly, children become more sophisticated in their responses as they develop, with the 3-year-olds displaying more adultlike responses than 2-year-olds. The older children were more likely to make statements about rights (for example, that's not fair or the rules say that you can't do that), a major accomplishment for a 3-year-old!

In summary, children are able to distinguish different kinds of violations and can do so at a surprisingly early point in development. As we have seen in other realms of development—perception, cognition, language, emotion—children are more competent at earlier ages than previous generations of developmental psychologists ever imagined.

Moral Judgments and Moral Behavior

Does knowledge of the maturity of a child's moral judgments help us predict how a child will actually behave when in a situation involving personal choices between ethically desirable and undesirable behavior? Moral judgments and moral behavior such as cheating are often unrelated, especially in young children (Blasi, 1983; Straughtan, 1986). Much behavior is impulsive and not always guided by rational and deliberate thought (Burton, 1984). A child may have reached stage 3, the level of "good girl morality," where she is concerned with maintaining parental approval. However, when her younger brother breaks her favorite toys, she may kick him even if the parent is present to disapprove of his action. The child may later even be able to offer mature reasoning that it is wrong to hit young children because they do not really know what they are doing. Thought, in short, does not always guide action.

However, there is some evidence of closer relationships between moral judgments and moral behavior among older subjects. Individuals who are in the two most advanced stages of Kohlberg's classifications of moral development (stage 5 and stage 6) are less likely to cheat than those at earlier levels (Leming, 1978), less likely to inflict pain (Kohlberg & Candee, 1984); and they are more likely to endorse free speech and due process and to oppose capital punishment (Rest, 1986).

In summary, the evidence suggests that moral judgments *may* relate to behavior among older children, but the link between moral cognition and action among young children is very weak. In the next section, we explore some of the factors that *do* affect children's moral conduct.

THE BEHAVIORAL SIDE OF MORAL DEVELOPMENT: THE EMERGENCE OF SELF-CONTROL

Self-control is the ability to inhibit or direct one's actions to conform to social or moral rules. Life is full of temptations, traps, and tugs that try to pull the young child away from socially acceptable courses of action. The child's ability to resist these detours is a consequence of both the child's own emerging cognitive and representational capacities as well as the guidance provided by parents, siblings, and other socializing agents.

What develops in the emergence of self-control or self-regulation? According to Kopp (1982, 1987) the child proceeds through several phases leading to self-regulation. In the *control phase* (12 to 18 months) "children show awareness of social and task demands that have been defined by caregivers and initiate, maintain, modulate or cease acts accordingly upon demand. . . . In the control phase, children are highly dependent upon the caregiver for reminder signals about acceptable behaviors" (Kopp, 1987, p. 38). And, in fact, children do begin to show compliance to caregiver demands during this period (Kaler & Kopp, 1990). In the next phase—*self-control*—the child gains the ability to comply with caregiver expectations in the absence of external monitors. Kopp suggests that development of representational thinking and recall memory permits the child to remember family rules and routines involved in common activities such as eating, dressing, and playing. In the final phase *self-regulation* emerges, which involves children's use of strategies and plans to direct their behavior and aid them in resisting temptation and delaying gratification.

Support for this developmental progression comes from a study by Vaughn, Kopp, and Krakow (1984). When presented with attractive objects (for example, toy telephone, an attractively wrapped gift, or a raisin under a cup) that the adult told them not to touch, 18-, 24- and 30-month-olds are clearly different in how well they complied. While the 18-month-olds were able to wait only 20 seconds, the 24-months-olds waited 70 seconds, and the 30-month-olds waited nearly 100 seconds before touching the attractive but forbidden objects.

Other research confirms this progression that self-control increases markedly over the preschool period (Kopp, 1992; Kuczynski & Kochanska, 1990). As Box 16-3 shows, children actively contribute to this process and help themselves to not violate rules by developing strategies and plans that direct and guide their behavior. Children use a range of techniques including self-distraction (for example, looking away, sitting on their hands), self-instructions (for example, No, no; don't touch), or redefinition of the object (for example, thinking about marshmallows as puffy clouds to reduce their appeal) (Kopp, 1987; Mischel & Mischel, 1983).

The development of self-control is influenced not only by the child's own efforts, but by the actions of parents and other caregivers as well. Various kinds of parental disciplinary practices, such as consistent and carefully timed punishment as well as the provision of a rationale for compliance, help increase resistance to temptation (Kuczynski, 1983; Parke, 1977). Moreover, mothers shift their control strategies from physical to verbal modalities with age; explanations, bargaining, and reprimands increase with age and distraction decreases with age (Kuczynski, Kochanska, Radke-Yarrow, & Girnius-Brown, 1987). This suggests that parents shift their strategies to match the increasingly sophisticated quality of the child's cognitive and language capacities. In turn, these types of parental input aid the child's own abilities to use verbally based control strategies (Kopp, 1987, 1992).

Similarly, models who follow the rules are often effective in reducing cheating (Grusec, Kuczynski, Rushton, & Simutis, 1979). Models are particularly effective if they display alternative acceptable behavior at the same time that they resist breaking the rules (Bussey & Perry, 1977).

Consistency across Situations and Time

Are children consistent in their moral behavior across situations? To answer this question, we turn to the most extensive investigation of moral behavior ever attempted. In their project, Hartshorne and May (1928) studied the responses of 11,000 school-age children who were given the opportunity to cheat, steal, and lie in a wide variety of situations: athletics, social events, the school, the home, alone, or with peers. Burton (1963, 1984) took only the measures that were reliable from the original Hartshorne and May (1928) studies in deceit, and found strong evidence for a general factor of moral behavior. Burton concludes that each child does have a different general

BOX 16-3 PLANS FOR RESISTING TEMPTATION

Children's self-control can be enhanced by teaching them to instruct themselves not to cheat. Charlotte Patterson and Walter Mischel demonstrated the value of self-instructions for preschoolers. Children were promised attractive prizes for completing the boring task of copying letters of the alphabet onto a page, but the experimenters made the children's task harder by attempting to distract them with a nearby talking clown who invited the children to look at him and play with him. Some children were provided with a plan to help them resist the distracting clown ("No, I can't. I'm working"). while others were given no verbal plan for resisting the clown's invitation. The preschoolers who were provided with a verbal plan were less distracted by the clown than were the classmates without a plan.

Some plans are better than others. Providing the child with a verbal plan that focuses specifically on resisting the temptation (When Mr. Clown says to look at him . . . you can just not look at him and say, "I'm not going to look at Mr. Clown") is more effective than a task-formulating plan (You can just look at your work and say, "I'm going to look at my work"). Children who were provided with the temptation-inhibiting plan spent less time attending to the clown, worked longer, and completed more work than did either the children with the task-oriented plan or those with no plan. Moreover, a nonspecific plan doesn't help young children very much. When preschool children were offered plans that specified the general nature but not the specific contents of the verbalizations to be used, they were just as distracted as children with no plan at all. Older children, who are capable of filling in the appropriate details at the time when the plan is needed, are capable of using generalized plans to help achieve self-control. Why do young children, who are clearly capable of using verbal plans offered to them, fail to come up with their own? Some young children do spontaneously generate their own helpful plans, but most do not. Part of the reason seems to be that preschoolers' knowledge about the effectiveness of different strategies is limited. In contrast to third and sixth graders, preschoolers are unaware, even when directly asked, that some strategies are more effective than others in helping them resist temptation. As they develop, children not only learn to use self-control strategies more efficiently but also become more aware of the best strategies to use.

Sources: Mischel, W., & Patterson, C. J. (1978). Effective plans for self-control. Patterson, C. J. (1982). Self-control and self-regulation in childhood. In T. M. Field et al. In W. A. Collins (Ed.), *Minnesota Symposia on Child Psychology* (vol. 2). Hillsdale, NJ Erlbaum; (Eds.), *Review of human development*. New York: Wiley.

predisposition to behave morally or immorally in a variety of situations. The more similar the situations, the greater the consistency in self-control; the less the situations resemble each other, the less generality of moral behavior is obtained. Measures of cheating on different achievement tests in the classroom are going to correlate more highly with each other than with measures of cheating on games in the home. Such findings do not minimize the importance of the situational variables, such as fear of detection, peer support for deviant behavior, and the instigation of other powerful motivational factors, such as achievement needs in moral conduct. However, they do suggest that some children are more likely than others to yield to such demands.

Finally, does knowledge of early moral behavior predict later behavior? Recent evidence suggests that children who are able to delay gratification in early life are able to cope better socially and academically as adolescents (Mischel, Shoda, & Peake, 1988; Shoda, Mischel, & Peake, 1990). Four-year-olds were given a simple test of self-control in which children's ability to wait for an attractive reward (a toy or candy) was evaluated. Children were given the option of obtaining a small reward immediately or a much larger and more attractive one later. Some children were very poor at waiting and others were able to delay taking their prize for a considerable period. Ten years later, when these children were adolescents, Mischel asked the parents to rate their children on a variety of traits. Children who were able to delay in nursery school were rated during adolescence as more socially and cognitively competent. They were playful, resourceful, skillful, attentive, and able to deal with frustration and stress—a cluster of traits that are important ingredients for successful coping with the academic and social demands of adolescence. In summary, the early ability to inhibit impulses and delay gratification may be an important antecedent of later competence.

THE DEVELOPMENT OF ALTRUISM

Although there has been a voluminous amount of research done on antisocial behavior, it has been only within the past two decades that psychologists have become involved in the study of more positive, altruistic aspects of social behavior, such as cooperation, helping, and sharing. Therefore, much less is known about why and when prosocial behavior occurs.

The Developmental Course of Prosocial Behavior

Altruism begins very early in life and is evident in a number of different ways (see Table 16-1). Some of the earliest instances of prosocial behavior can be seen in children's pointing, playing, showing, and sharing. As we noted in our earlier discussion of communication (Chapter 8), children learn to "share" interesting sights and objects with others by pointing and gesturing even before the end of the first year. In a study of early sharing, Rheingold and her colleagues (Rheingold, Hay, & West, 1976) found that showing and giving toys to a variety of adults (mothers, fathers, and strangers) are very

TABLE 16-1

MILESTONES OF EARLY PROSOCIAL DEVELOPMENT

YEAR 1: BIRTH TO 6 MONTHS
Responds positively to others (smiles, laughs with others) Participates in social games (peek-a-boo) Reacts emotionally to distress (others' cries or upsets)
YEAR 1: 6 TO 12 MONTHS
Takes an active role in social games Exhibits sharing behaviors Displays affection to familiar persons
YEAR 2
Refines ability to point with index finger Complies with simple requests Indicates knowledge of rules of cooperative games Shows knowledge of caregiving skills Comforts persons in distress Participates in the work of adults
YEAR 3
Draws person's attention to objects with words as well as gestures Exhibits increasingly planful caregiving and helping sequences Expresses own intentions to help and knowledge to task objects

Source: From Hay and Rheingold (1983).

Helping and comforting occur at an early age.

frequent behaviors among 18-month-old children or even earlier—at 12 months (Hay, 1979). Moreover, these early sharing activities occur without prompting, direction, or praise.

The authors propose that "the sharing behaviors, from the first holding up of an object for others to see, the first offering of an object to another . . . qualify as developmental milestones. That children so young share contradicts the egocentricity so often ascribed to them and reveals them instead as already contributors to social life" (Rheingold et al., 1976, p. 1157).

Sharing and showing are not the only ways in which young children reveal their capacity for prosocial action. From an early age, children engage in a variety of other behaviors such as caregiving, helping adults with housework, or comforting another in distress—striking evidence that altruism begins very early in life (Rheingold, 1982). Even by the end of the first year, young children begin to show reactions to the distress of others. Researchers (Zahn-Waxler, Radke-Yarrow, Wagner, & Chapman, 1992) have explored the issues by training mothers to observe and report emotional distress that is either caused by or witnessed by their children during everyday interactions. In addition, mothers simulated distress; they pretended to be sad (sobbing for five to ten seconds), to be in pain (bumping their feet or heads, saying "Ouch," and rubbing the injured parts), or to feign respiratory distress (coughing/choking), and then recorded their children's reactions. Between 10 and 12 months, children become agitated or may cry in response to another child's distress, but there is little attempt to help. By 13 or 14 months, however, children often approach and comfort another in distress. Although these early approaches involve comforting, it is often general and not specific to the source of distress. By 1½ years, children not only approach a distressed person but offer specific kinds of help. A child with a broken toy may be offered another one with which to play or a mother with a cut finger may be given a Band-Aid. Moreover, children, by age 2, engage in a wide range of prosocial actions, including verbal advice ("Be careful") indirect helping (gets mother to retrieve infant's rattle), sharing (gives food to sister), distraction (for example, closes picture book that makes mother sad), and protection/defense (for example, tries to prevent another from being injured, distressed, or attacked). However, children do not always show prosocial reactions to anothers' distress. Children sometimes laugh or behave aggressively or even become distressed themselves (Radke-Yarrow & Zahn-Waxler, 1983; Zahn-Waxler, et al., 1992). The studies suggest that children's altruistic behavior not only begins very early in life, but that altruistic behavior changes in form and expression as children develop.

Moreover, the nature of the cues by which children recognize that help is needed changes over time. One of the significant modifications is in the subtlety of distress cues to which children react. As Pearl (1985) has shown, using a series of vignettes in which the explicitness of the distress cues is varied (from a slight frown to a full-blown cry), 4- and 8-year-olds are equally likely to note distress when the cues are explicit. Conversely, 4-year-olds are less likely to see a problem or suggest help when the cues are subtle. Naturalistic studies show similar results. For children at 2 and 7 years of age there are clear developmental trends in the effects of the subtlety of the elicitors of concern. The 7-year-olds, in contrast to younger children, are better able to deal with more abstract kinds of distress and subtle cues and to take into account feelings other than those expressed in the immediate situation, as illustrated by a child's response after viewing a TV report of a family killed in a fire: "I hope that those children weren't so young so they had a chance to have some life before having to die" (Radke-Yarrow, Zahn-Waxler, & Chapman, 1983). As Box 16-4 shows, it is not just the form of altruistic *behavior* that shifts across development; changes in the ways that children reason about prosocial issues are evident as well.

Does knowledge of children's early altruistic tendencies help predict children's helpful behavior at later ages? For an answer to this question, children's nurturance and sympathy to their peers, thoughtfulness, and understanding of the viewpoints of other children were assessed in the nursery school and again in elementary school five or six years later (Baumrind, 1971). There was modest stability between the two age points. Other evidence tells a similar story; in a longitudinal study of children's tendencies to donate to needy children and to assist an adult (for example, by helping pick up paper clips) were assessed over a period of years. Both donating and helping behavior were consistent between 10 and 12 years of age; children who were high on altruism at one age were likely to remain high at later ages (Eisenberg, Shell, Pasternack, Lennon, Beller, & Mathy, 1987). Together these studies suggest that there is consistency or stability in children's altruistic behavior across time.

Examining *how much* the same children share and care at different ages is not the only way to answer the stability question. Children differ in *how they show* their prosocial tendencies. There are individual differences in both the frequency and the quality or style of children's prosocial responses. Consider how Sarah, Jenny, Tami, and Joanne—all 2-year-olds—react when their mothers cry after reading a sad story in the newspaper. Sarah begins to tense up and fights back her tears. Jenny shows little emotion, but asks, "What's wrong, Mommy?" In contrast, Tami tears up the newspaper that makes her mother cry. Joanne covers her ears and turns the other way. As these very different reactions illustrate, infants and children develop their own style of dealing with the distress of others. Some children are very

BOX 16-4 PROSOCIAL DEVELOPMENT: A COGNITIVE DEVELOPMENTAL PERSPECTIVE

Not only do children change in how they behave prosocially, but they shift in their judgments about prosocial issues. Nancy Eisenberg and her colleagues have developed a set of prosocial dilemmas that they have used to determine how children's thinking about prosocial activities changes across development. Here is a sample story:

> One day a girl (boy) named Mary (Eric) was going to a friend's birthday party. On her/his way she/he saw a girl (boy) who had fallen down and hurt her/his leg. The girl (boy) asked Mary (Eric) to go to her/his house and tell her/his parents so the parents could come and take her/him to the doctor. But if Mary (Eric) did run and get the child's parents, she/he would be late to the birthday party and miss the ice cream, cake, and all the games. What should Mary (Eric) do? Why?

Table 16-2 illustrates the levels of prosocial reasoning.

Children were tested at $4\frac{1}{2}$ and $11\frac{1}{2}$ years of age. As children develop they become less egocentric and more other-oriented, as well as more abstract in their reasoning about prosocial dilemmas. Specifically, hedonistic reasoning decreased with age whereas needs-oriented reasoning, a relatively simple type of reasoning peaked in midchildhood and then leveled off. Moreover, the other more sophisticated modes of reasoning increased with age including approval-oriented stereotypic, empathic forms of reasoning. Sex differences emerged as well, with girls increasing their rate of empathic reasoning in early adolescence more than boys. Moreover, sharing was negatively related to hedonistic reasoning; and empathy was positively related to a general level of reasoning and negatively related to hedonistic reasoning.

Relationships between children's prosocial reasoning and children's moral judgments (Kohlberg) were only modestly related, which suggests that the reasoning in these two types of domains may be following parallel but independent developmental paths. These findings support a multifaceted view of prosocial development that includes cognitive as well as behavioral components. The ways in which these cognitive changes relate to behavioral outcomes is not yet fully understood.

Sources: Eisenberg, N., Lennon, R., & Roth, K. (1983). Prosocial development: A longitudinal study. *Developmental Psychology,* 19, 846–855; Eisenberg, N., Shell, R., Pasternack, J., Lennon, R., Beller, R., & Mathy, R. M. (1987). Prosocial development in middle childhood: A longitudinal study. *Developmental Psychology,* 23, 712–718.

TABLE 16-2 LEVELS OF PROSOCIAL REASONING

LEVEL	ORIENTATION	DESCRIPTION	GROUP
1	Hedonistic, self-focused	The individual is concerned with self-oriented consequences rather than moral considerations. Reasons for assisting or not assisting another include consideration of direct gain to self, future reciprocity, and concern for others whom the individual needs and/or likes (due to the affectional tie).	Preschoolers and younger elementary school children
2	Needs of others	The individual expresses concern for the physical, material, and psychological needs of others even though the other's needs conflict with one's own needs. This concern is expressed in the simplest terms, without	Preschoolers and elementary school children

LEVELS OF PROSOCIAL REASONING (Continued)

TABLE 16-2

LEVEL	ORIENTATION	DESCRIPTION	GROUP
		clear evidence of self-reflective role taking, verbal expressions of sympathy, or reference to internalized affect such as guilt.	
3	Approval and interpersonal and/or stereotyped	Stereotyped images of good and bad persons and behaviors and/or considerations of others' approval and acceptance are used in justifying prosocial or nonhelping behaviors.	Elementary and high school students
4	(a) Empathic	The individual's judgments include evidence of sympathetic responding, self-reflective role taking, concern with the other's humanness, and/or guilt or positive affect related to the consequences of one's actions.	Older elementary school and high school students
	(b) Transitional (empathic and internalized)	Justifications for helping or not helping involve internalized values, norms, duties, or responsibilities, or refer to the necessity of protecting the rights and dignity of other persons; these ideas, however, are not clearly stated.	Minority of people high school age
5	Strongly internalized	Justifications for helping or not helping are based on internalized values, norms, or responsibilities, the desire to maintain individual and societal contractual obligations, and the belief in the dignity, rights, and equality of all individuals. Positive or negative affect related to the maintenance of self-respect for living up to one's own values and accepted norms also characterizes this stage.	Only a small minority of high school students and virtually no elementary school children.

Source: Eisenberg, Lennon, and Roth (1983).

BOX 16-5 THE MOTHER'S ROLE IN LEARNING TO REACT TO ANOTHER'S DISTRESS

How do children learn to react in helpful ways when they have caused distress in another person or when they see another person suffering? To find out, Carolyn Zahn-Waxler and her colleagues devised a clever scheme: They trained mothers of 18-month-olds to tape record incidents of distress occurring in a normal home situation that the child either caused or witnessed. The mothers recorded both their own reactions and the child's behavior over a nine-month period. In addition, observers visited the home for a few hours every three weeks in order to check on the accuracy of the mother's records. During the home visits, the mother simulated (that is, acted out) certain common distress situations, such as bumping her ankle and crying, as a further assessment of her routine recordings. Mothers were found to be accurate and reliable reporters of their own and their children's reactions.

Even 18-month-old children are active responders to another person's distress. On the average, children reacted in a helpful fashion about 30 percent of the time, either when they hurt someone else or when they merely witnessed another person's distress. However, children differed greatly in their responsiveness—some failed to respond at all, while others responded in the majority of distress situations (60 to 70 percent).

Mothers' reactions to their own children doing harm and mothers' reactions when they witness another person's distress can influence their children's development of helpful behavior in distress situations. Mothers who frequently used explanations linking the child's behavior with its consequences for the victim had children who were more likely to respond in a helpful way when they caused harm to someone. These mothers might say, "Tom's crying because you pushed him"—a clear but neutral explanation. Even more effective are explanations accompanied by strong emotional overtones, such as "You must never poke anyone's eyes" or "When you hurt me, I don't want to be near you. I am going away from you." Children of mothers who used these affective explanations were also more likely to intervene in bystander situations where they did not cause any harm but saw that someone else was upset. Some maternal tactics such as physical restraint ("I just moved away from him"), physical punishment ("I swatted him a good one"), or unexplained prohibitions ("Stop that") are not effective and may even interfere with the development of altruism.

Altruism begins at an early age. Parents play an important role in facilitating the development of the child's emerging altruistic behaviors by helping children make connections between their own actions and other people's emotional states. Altruism appears to begin at home!

Source: Zahn-Waxler, C., Radke-Yarrow, M., & King, R. A. (1979). Child-rearing and children's prosocial initiations toward victims of distress. *Child Development*, 50, 319–330.

emotional and show a great deal of upset when faced with another's distress. Other youngsters are cool and reflective and appear to be approaching the distress "cognitively"—by inspecting, exploring, asking questions. Still others, like Tami, have an aggressive, defensive flavor to their prosocial style (for example, "hit the person who made the baby cry"). Finally, some children try to "shut out" signals of distress and turn or run away. Radke-Yarrow and Zahn-Waxler (1983) observed their subjects at 2 years and again at 7 years of age. In about two-thirds of the children, the same style of reaction to others' upset and discomfort was evident in infancy as well as five years later. The pattern of intense, empathic, affective prosocial attempts by certain toddlers was still evident at age 7. Likewise, the combative responders, the problem solvers, and the anxious-guilty types were still exhibiting their characteristic style at the later age. Of course, not all children respond similarly across time and for some, "development meant change" (Radke-Yarrow & Zahn-Waxler, 1983, p. 16).

Determinants of Prosocial Development

What determines the course of altruistic development? Some have argued that individual differences in prosocial behavior may have a genetic basis. Identical twins are closer in their levels of altruistic behavior than fraternal twins

(Rushton, Fulker, Neale, Nias, & Eysenck, 1986). Other researchers (Zahn-Waxler, Robinson, & Emde, 1992) found only limited support for the heritability of prosocial behavior. In this study of 2-year-olds, identical and nonidentical twins do not differ in their observed prosocial behaviors. However, these researchers found modest evidence for hereditability of empathy or expressions of concern for the victim. In spite of the possible genetic contribution, there is clear evidence that experience in the family makes a difference as well.

Parents may directly encourage, elicit, and shape these behaviors or act as models from which children can learn new prosocial acts (Eisenberg, 1992; Grusec & Dix, 1986). As the study in Box 16-5 shows, mothers' childrearing practices contribute to children's reactions to distress in others; however, much of the early acquisition of altruistic behavior is probably not the result of direct teaching. "For example, parents may show any given objects to their infants, thus modeling these actions: at other times parents may request objects or the infants' possessions. . . . Such experiences inform infants about situations in which certain actions are socially appropriate and offer them opportunities for practicing and refining the actions" (Hay & Rheingold, 1983, pp. 28–29).

It would be expected that parents who explicitly model prosocial behavior and at the same time provide opportunities for children to perform these actions may be particularly successful in promoting altruism. Hay and Murray (1982) observed four groups of 12-month-old infants who observed an adult either offer them objects (model the target action), request objects from them (perform the complementary action), both offer and request objects (try to induce a game of give-and-take), or merely chat with their mothers while displaying neither action. Merely seeing the adult in a prosocial manner wasn't enough to increase the infants' altruistic behavior. Only the infants who observed the model request objects and those who played give-and-take were reliably more likely than those in the control condition to offer objects to the model. Furthermore, the give-and-take experience facilitated infants' later sharing with their own mothers.

Models of prosocial behavior are not confined to the family. Television is another source for learning prosocial behaviors. A variety of studies have assessed the impact on young children's prosocial behavior of watching segments from "Mister Rogers' Neighborhood," a program focusing on understanding the feelings of others, expressing sympathy, and helping. The children who watched "Mister Rogers' Neighborhood" not only *learned* the specific prosocial content of the program but also were able to apply that learning to other situations involving children. In comparison to those who saw the neutral TV shows, then, the children who saw the prosocial programs learned some generalized rules about prosocial behavior (Huston et al., 1992; Friedrich & Stein, 1992).

In summary, exposure to prosocial TV not only increases knowledge about prosocial behavior but can increase helping behavior in a situation that is very different and far removed from the television program. TV is clearly an important learning medium for prosocial behavior.

Responsibility Taking and Prosocial Behavior: Cross-Cultural Perspectives

A common way that parents provide opportunities for learning prosocial behavior is by assigning children responsibility for household tasks. Even children as young as 2 years old will spontaneously assist adults in a variety of household tasks such as sweeping, cleaning, and setting tables (Rheingold, 1982). Moreover, providing children with these opportunities to assist may be important for their prosocial development. As Rheingold wryly notes, "Their [parents'] efficient execution of chores makes for inefficient teaching of the young" (1982, p. 124). Children in other cultures, in contrast to those in the United States, often are assigned responsibility for taking care of siblings and other children, as well as for household tasks (Eisenberg & Mussen, 1989). What effect does this have? Cross-cultural evidence of children from a wide range of cultures—Mexico, the Philippines, Okinawa, India, and Africa—suggests that "children who perform more domestic chores, help more with economic tasks and spend more time caring for their infant brothers, sisters, and cousins, score high on the altruistic dimension" (Whiting & Whiting, 1975; Whiting & Edwards, 1988). Laboratory research confirms these findings. In studies in which children were given responsibility for teaching other children to make puzzles for hospitalized youngsters, while some children made puzzles but were not given any teaching responsibility, those who had been assigned teaching responsibility were subsequently more willing to share their prizes with needy children and made more puzzles for hospitalized children than did the boys and girls in the control condition (Staub, 1975). Finally, just as we saw in other areas of moral development, role taking and empathy also play an important part in the development of prosocial behavior.

Empathy, Role Taking, and Altruism

Two important determinants of altruism are empathy, or the ability to *feel* the same emotion that someone else is experiencing, and role-taking ability, which refers to the capability of *knowing* how others are feeling (Eisenberg, 1992; Hoffman, 1987). According to Hoffman, children have the capacity to feel or empathize with another person's emotional states. Another child's distress can elicit a similar emotion in an observer, just as a child can experience another person's joy or happiness. This empathetic ability often motivates children to engage in prosocial actions which relieve not only another person's distress but also their own emotional upset. In turn, prosocial acts that result in positive affective feelings can vicariously produce similar positive emotions in the helping child. Evidence supports the expectation that children who are higher on empathy behave in a more prosocial manner (Eisenberg & Miller, 1987; Eisenberg & Fabes, 1991; Eisenberg, Fabes, Miller, Shell, Shea, & May-Plumee, 1990). Clear links between role taking and altruism have also been found (Iannotti, 1985; Strayer & Roberts, 1988). In one study, 6-year-old children who received role-taking training were more likely to share with a needy child than children who did not receive this type of training (Iannotti, 1978). This direct experimental evidence demonstrates that increasing role-taking skills can heighten altruistic behavior in children.

In summary, altruistic behavior is a complex and multiply determined set of behaviors. While clues concerning the puzzle of prosocial action are slowly emerging, developmental psychologists are not yet able to write any simple prescription for raising a helpful and caring child.

Now that we have examined moral development and altruism, we turn to another important and troublesome aspect of social development—aggression.

THE DEVELOPMENT OF AGGRESSION

Altruism is a behavior that is viewed positively by parents, peers, and teachers; aggression, on the other hand, is seen as an unwelcome but common occurrence. For decades, psychologists have puzzled over the knotty problem of aggression. Why do some children attack others? How do these patterns change over age? What role do families, peers, and the mass media play in the development of aggression? Finally, how can aggression be reduced?

What is Aggression?

Aggression is usually defined as behavior that intentionally inflicts harm or injury on another person. By focusing on "intentions," this definition helps us avoid labeling dentists, surgeons, or even parents as aggressive since these individuals may, in fact, inflict pain on others, but this is not the intent or goal of their actions.

Developmental Changes in Aggression

A visit to a nursery school and a stopover at an elementary school playground reveal some striking age differences in the form and frequency of aggressive behavior. The nursery school children not only display more aggression but are more likely to quarrel and fight over toys and possessions; in other words, their aggression is instrumental. In contrast, the older children (6- and 7-year-olds) use more person-oriented or hostile aggression, such as criticism, ridicule, tattling, name calling, or verbal disapproval (Hartup, 1974). This shift from *instrumental* to *hostile aggression* may be due, in part, to older children's ability to infer the intention and motives of their attackers (Ferguson & Rule, 1980). When children recognize that another person wants to hurt them, they are more likely to retaliate by a direct assault on the tormentor rather than by an indirect attack on the aggressor's possessions.

Although there are clear improvements with age in children's ability to infer intent, children differ in how well they can correctly "read" another person's intentions. Some children, especially those who are highly aggressive, have more difficulty in judging the intentions of their peers. According to Dodge (1985), this is especially true in ambiguous situations, where the intentions are not clearly either aggressive or beneficial. In such a situation, boys who are rated by their classmates as aggressive are likely to react in a hostile way—as if the other person intended to be aggressive. Aggressive boys see the world as a threatening and hostile place. They perceive the actions of others differently and see more anger and aggression in others than do less aggressive boys. As Dodge and Frame (1982) found, the biased views of aggressive boys may have some basis in reality, since they not only initiate more unprovoked aggressive acts but also receive more aggressive attacks than do nonaggressive boys. This suggests that "the biased attributions of aggressive boys may have a basis in their experience. Their collective expectancy that peers will be biased in aggressing toward them is consistent with their experience" (1982, p. 28).

A second distinction between types of aggression has been made. Some children act aggressively only in response to being attacked, threatened, or frustrated. These children display *reactive aggression.* In contrast, other children show *proactive aggression;* these children use force to dominate another person or bully or threaten them in order to gain a prized possession or object. As in the case of instrumental aggression, proactive aggression decreases across development.

Moreover, misinterpretations of others' intentions are most likely to occur among boys who display reactive aggression in their interactions with peers, while proactively aggressive children—like the playground bully—are less likely to misread a partner's intentions (Dodge & Coie, 1987).

The mode of aggression also changes over development. While toddlers rely more on physical attacks, older children, with their improved language and communication skills, are more likely to aggress verbally rather than physically (Parke & Slaby, 1983). These developmental shifts in the style of expressing aggression are due not only to increased verbal skills but also to changes in adult expectations and rules. Most parents and teachers become less tolerant of physical aggression as children mature, while they are more likely to ignore a "battle of words" even among older children.

Finally, how stable is aggression over age? Does the level of aggression fluctuate across development? For both males and females, aggression appears to be moderately stable (Olweus, 1979, 1982). In fact, aggression is as stable as intelligence. For both sexes, the stability is higher across shorter spans of time; as the time between assessment points increases, the degree of stability decreases. Earlier reports such as the famous Fels Longitudinal Study (Kagan & Moss, 1962) had found greater stability of aggression for boys; perhaps due to changing societal values, girls are beginning to show greater stability in assertive and aggressive behaviors. Even across a twenty-two-year span aggression shows a moderate degree of consistency. In a follow-up study of over 600 individuals who were originally seen at 8 years of age, Huesmann and his colleagues (Huesmann, Eron, Lefkowitz, & Walder, 1984) found that the more aggressive 8-year-olds were still more aggressive than their peers at age 30. The boys who were rated by their peers in childhood as aggressive were more likely to be higher in criminal convictions, spouse abuse, moving traffic violations, and drunk driving as adults (see Figure 16-3).

However, early aggression may have different long-term consequences for males and females. 40-year-old men who were rated as ill-tempered at 8 to 10 years of age experienced erratic work lives, held poorer jobs than their parents, and were more likely to divorce than their even-tempered peers (Caspi, Elder, & Bem, 1987). On the other hand, ill-tempered girls married

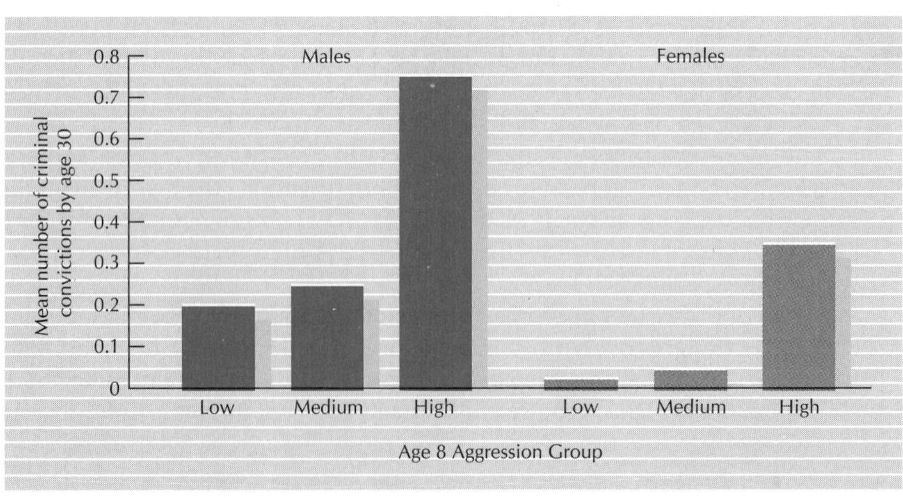

FIGURE 16-3
Relationship between childhood aggression and criminal behavior in adulthood. (From Huesmann, Eron, Lefkowitz, & Walder, 1984.)

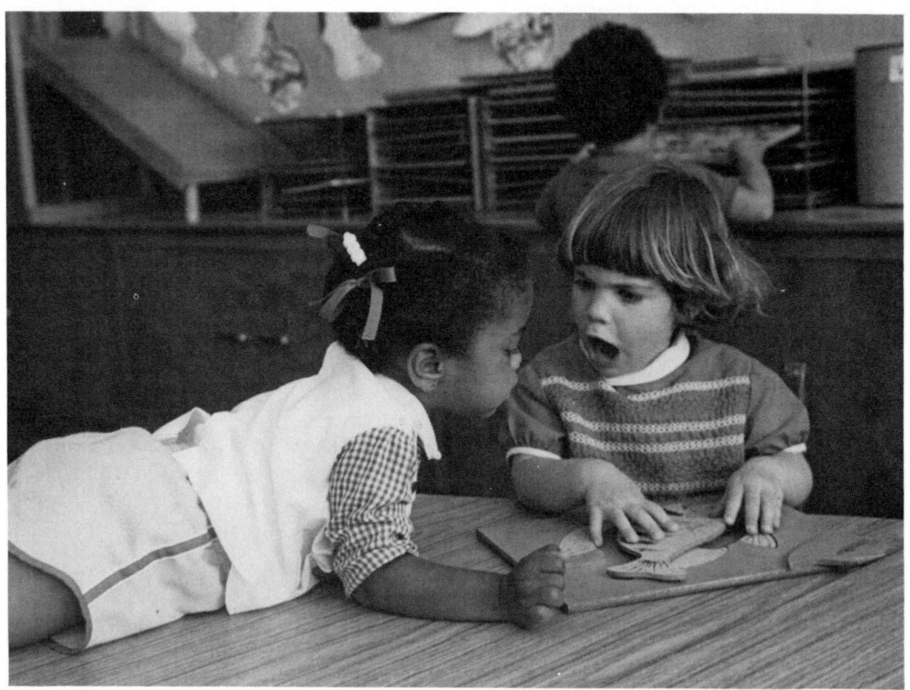

Boys and girls differ in their usual ways of expressing aggression; girls are less likely than boys to be physically aggressive.

men with lower occupational mobility, were more likely to divorce, and were less adequate, more ill-tempered mothers (Caspi et al., 1987). Clearly, a history of aggression and ill-tempered behavior affects males as well as females, but the domains (work versus parenting) that are affected vary across the sexes.

Sex Differences in Aggression

One of the most striking aspects of these developmental trends is the markedly divergent courses followed by boys and girls: nursery school boys more often instigate, and are more often involved in, aggressive incidents than are girls (Maccoby & Jacklin, 1980; Perry, Perry, & Boldizar, 1990). The aggressive patterns of boys and girls differ in other important ways: Boys are more likely to retaliate after being attacked than are girls (Darvill & Cheyne, 1981), and aggression is more likely to occur when a male rather than a female partner is involved (Barrett, 1979). Moreover, boys approve of aggression more than girls (Huesmann, Guerra, Zelli, & Miller, 1992). They anticipate less negative self-evaluation and parental disapproval for acting aggressively than girls (Perry, Perry, & Weiss, 1989). However, girls may use different aggressive strategies than boys. Seventh-grade girls, but not boys, used social ostracism, as opposed to direct confrontation. The exclusion of individuals from social cliques as an aggressive strategy increased as girls entered adolescence (Cairns, Cairns, Neckerman, Ferguson, & Gariepy, 1989). Marked differences between males and females in aggression remain in adolescence and adulthood. Using violent crime as a measure, there are approximately five times as many adolescent boys as girls arrested for violent crimes (for example, criminal homicide, robberies, aggravated assaults), although there has been a gradual increase in the amount of violent crime reported for females (Cairns & Cairns, 1985; Schlossman & Cairns, 1993) (see Figure 16-4).

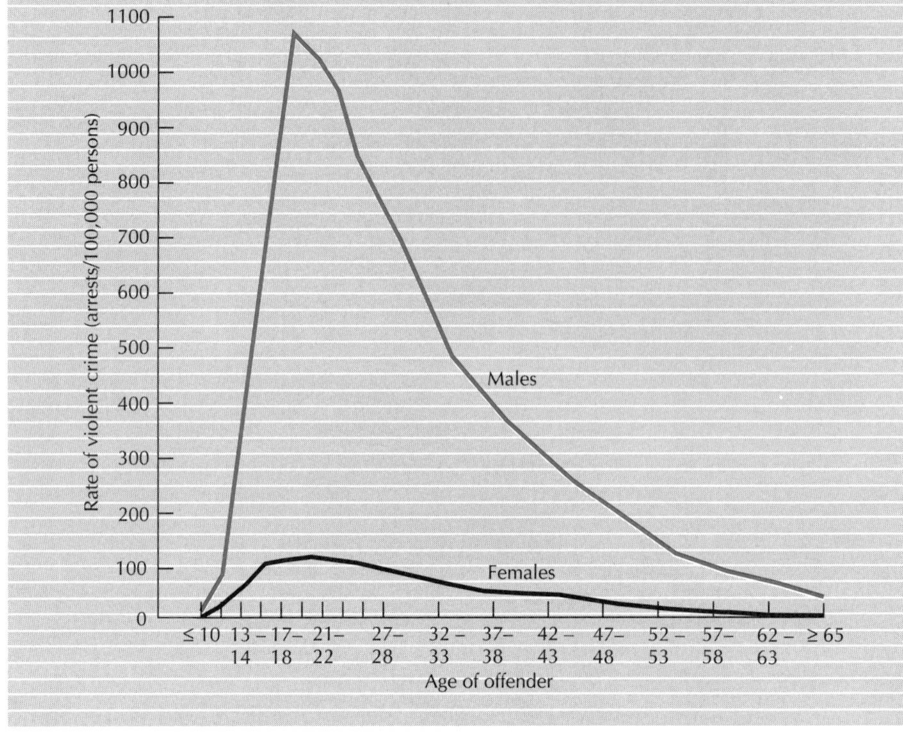

FIGURE 16-4
Arrest rates for violent crime by males and females as function of age. (From *Crime in the United States, 1982,* and *United States Census Report, 1980.*)

A number of factors—environmental as well as biological—play an influential role in shaping the development of aggression. Next, we examine the impact of these factors.

Determinants of Aggression

THE FAMILY AS A TRAINING CENTER FOR AGGRESSION

Do parents contribute to their children's aggression? Although some parents may set out deliberately to teach aggression in order to "defend oneself" or "be a man," most parents do not view themselves as giving aggression tutorials. The parents' typical control tactics, however, may contribute to their children's aggression. Whether with juvenile delinquents or playground bullies, the answer is similar: Parents who use physical punishment, especially on an inconsistent and erratic basis, are likely to have aggressive, hostile children (Eron & Huesmann, 1984; Patterson, Reid, & Dishion, 1989).

Patterson's work (Patterson, 1982; Patterson et al., 1989) is of particular importance since his conclusions are based on actual observations of families of aggressive and nonaggressive children in their home environments. The aggressive children were referred to the Patterson project by schools and clinical agencies for treatment of their excessive antisocial, aggressive behavior. The family environments of aggressive and nonaggressive children were strikingly different. The families tend to be erratic and inconsistent in their use of punishment for deviant behaviors and ineffective in rewarding their children for prosocial behaviors. Not only did the parents of aggressive boys punish more often, they punished more often even when the child was behaving appropriately! As a result of the inept parenting practices, coercive patterns develop by which children learn to use aversive behavior to force or coerce parents to give them what they want. The child learns the lesson that coercive behaviors, such as whining or even hitting, is an effective way to control other family members. (Recall that we discussed a similar development of a coercive interaction cycle between a child and parent in Chapter 12, where we examined the single-parent family.)

As Patterson notes, however, children are not passive victims in this process, but often actively elicit punitive reactions from their parents by their misbehavior. The most appropriate model of punishment is a bidirectional one, which recognizes that parent and child influence each other, and that both contribute to the development of aggressive behavior patterns.

Families not only directly shape the development of aggression through their control tactics, but also indirectly contribute to their children's aggressive behavior. Parental monitoring of their children's whereabouts, activities, and social contacts is another important determinant of children's aggression. Some parents can report accurately what their children are doing, whom they are with, and where they are. They are aware of their children's activities, problems, and successes. Other parents are largely oblivious to their children's experiences. They don't know if their children are hanging around on street corners or are at a school dance, whether they are habitual truants or involved students, or whether one of them is the friendly neighborhood drug dealer. Lack of parental monitoring has been found to be associated with high rates of delinquency, attacks against property, and poorer relations with peers and teachers among seventh and tenth graders (Patterson & Stouthamer-Loeber, 1984; Patterson, 1990). To understand the development of aggression in the home, the family must be viewed not only as a social system in which all the interrelations among family members are recognized but also as a buffer or gatekeeper for outside influences. Parental awareness and control over activities in the community may be just as important in determining aggression as direct childrearing practices. Finally, as Box 16-6 shows, parental management of their own marital conflicts may contribute to the development of aggression as well.

The outcome of poor parental disciplinary practices and lack of monitoring results in a child who is aggressive and antisocial but also a child who is socially unskilled. As Figure 16-5 shows, Patterson, De Baryshe, and Ramsey (1989) have outlined a developmental sequence that flows from these early experiences in the family. When these antisocial children enter school, two outcomes follow—they are rejected by their peer group and they experience academic failure. A final stage in the sequence occurs in late childhood and adolescence when these antisocial children seek out deviant peers, who, in turn, provide further training in antisocial behavior and opportunities for

Lack of parental monitoring of a child's activities is associated with aggression and delinquency. *(Calvin & Hobbes by Bill Waterson. Universal Press Syndicate.)*

BOX 16-6 WHEN PARENTS ARGUE: THE IMPACT OF WITNESSED ANGER BETWEEN ADULTS

Even in the happiest of families, parents may argue. What effect does the observation of anger between others have on children's behavior? Cummings and his colleagues (Cummings & Cummings, 1988) have explored this issue in a series of studies in which children watched real or videotaped interactions between adult actors who behaved in ways that are similar to two parents in a home setting. Of interest was the differential impact of watching the actors express different kinds of emotion toward each other. For example, the actors might *verbally disagree* about which movie to see or start to argue over sharing the task of washing dishes. In one study (Cummings, Iannotti, & Zahn-Waxler, 1985), 2-year-olds who witnessed these angry interchanges were more aggressive in their play with another same-aged peer, while exposure to prosocial adult interactions reduced aggression. Moreover, unresolved anger, where the partners fail to settle their dispute, leads to greater feelings of anger and distress in children than witnessing conflict which is settled (Cummings, Vogel, Cummings, & El-Sheikh, 1989). Children with problem behaviors or those with a history of exposure to marital distress and interparent physical hostility were more distressed than others by conflicts involving the mother (Cummings, Pelligrini, Notarius, & Cummings, 1989). Finally, boys reacted with more angry feelings than girls. These studies demonstrate that children often learn to be aggressive and angry by witnessing conflict between parents. Fighting in front of the kids may not be such a great idea!

Sources: Cummings, E. M., & Cummings, J. L. (1988). A process-oriented approach to children's coping with adults' angry behavior. *Developmental Review,* 8, 296–321; Cummings, E. M., Iannotti, R. J., & Zahn-Waxler, C. (1985). Influence of conflict between adults on the emotions and aggression of young children. *Developmental Psychology,* 21, 495–507; Cummings, E. M., Vogel, D., Cummings, J. S., & El-Sheikh, (1989). Children's responses to different forms of expression of anger between adults. *Child Development,* 60, 1392–1404; Cummings, J. S., Pelligrini, D. S., Notarius, C. I., & Cummings, E. M. (1989). Children's responses to angry adult behavior as a function of marital distress and history of interparent hostility. *Child Development,* 60,

delinquent activities. Antisocial youth are more likely to be school dropouts, have uneven employment, marital problems, and end up in jail. Recently, Patterson and Bank (1989) have provided support for this sequence. Interestingly, it matters a great deal whether the child starts along a deviant path early or later in development. If the family environment is already encouraging antisocial behavior before age 5 or 6, the child is more likely to develop serious and persistent delinquent behavior than if the child starts on the deviancy road at a later age—in middle to later adolescence (Patterson & Bank, 1989). The late starter may have avoided the social rejection and school failure that is common for the early starter. Clearly, the developmental timing of earlier experience makes an important difference in determining whether childhood aggression results in serious delinquent behaviors.

The Role of Biology in the Development of Aggression

Environmental forces are not the only determinants of aggression; biology also contributes to the development of aggressive behavior patterns. Does

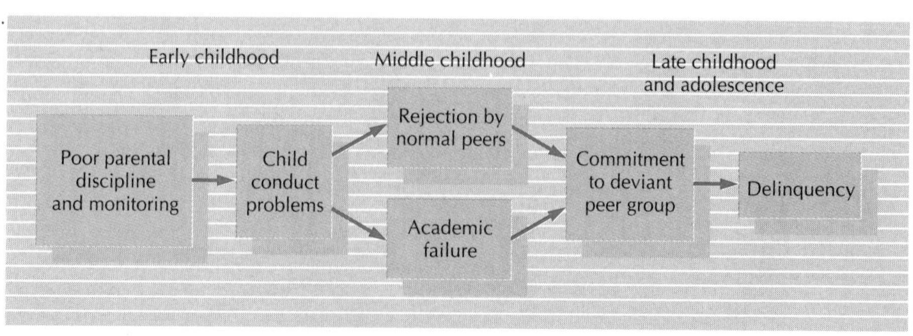

FIGURE 16-5
A developmental progression for antisocial behavior. (From Patterson, De Baryshe, & Ramsey, 1989.)

aggression have a genetic basis? Recent evidence (Rushton et al., 1986) suggests that genetics clearly plays a role in the emergence of individual differences in aggressive behavior. Identical twins of the same sex rated themselves as being more similar on a questionnaire concerning aggression (for example, some people think that I have a violent temper) than nonidentical twins. This suggests that genetic factors should not be ignored in our attempts to understand aggression.

As you recall from Chapters 3 and 5, infants differ in their temperaments, with some babies being whiny and difficult and others more easygoing and adaptable. Recent evidence suggests that difficult infants—those who are irritable, unpredictable, and hard to soothe—may be more likely to develop aggressive behavior patterns at later ages. Infants who were rated as difficult at 6, 13, and 24 months were rated as higher in anxiety, hyperactivity, and—of greatest relevance—hostility at 3 years of age (Bates, 1987).

Nor does the impact of biology on aggression end in infancy. Recent work suggests that adolescence may be another development period in which the role of biology in aggression can be seen. A recent study of 15- to 17-year-old boys in Sweden (Olweus, Mattson, Schalling, & Low, 1988) found a link between hormone levels (testosterone) and aggression. Boys with higher levels of testosterone in the blood rated themselves as more likely to respond aggressively to provocations and threats from others. In this case the testosterone had a *direct effect* on the aggressive behavior. Second, the boys with high levels of testosterone were more impatient or irritable, which, in turn, increased their readiness to engage in unprovoked and destructive kinds of aggression (for example, start fights and say nasty things without being provoked). In this case, the effect was *indirect* since the hormone affected levels of irritation which then, in turn, altered the level of aggression. The hormonal effects were present even after they eliminated other factors that may have caused aggression, such as child-rearing practices and the boy's temperament. These factors are, of course, important, but hormones contribute to aggression as well. Nor are the effects limited to boys. In a recent study (Inoff-Germain, Arnold, Nottleman, Susman, Culter, & Chrouses, 1988), levels of hormones, especially estradiol, that increase during puberty were positively linked with expressions of anger and aggression when adolescent girls were interacting with their parents.

These findings do not mean that biological factors such as hormones act independently of the social environment; instead, they suggest that hormones may be more influential at certain points in development, such as adolescence, and under certain conditions, such as provoking and threatening situations. Some individuals may be more likely than others to be aggressive as a result of their biological makeup, but especially if they live in a provoking and conflict-ridden environment.

Control of Aggression

How can aggression be controlled? A variety of solutions have been offered, but few are put forth as often as the recommendation that children be offered safe outlets for their aggression. Let us examine this alternative first.

THE CATHARSIS MYTH

One of the most persistent beliefs about aggression is that opportunities for acting aggressively will reduce hostile aggressive tendencies. The commonly accepted term for this process is *catharsis.* The catharsis doctrine asserts that aggressive urges build up in an individual and unless this accumulating reservoir of aggressive energies is drained, a violent outburst will occur. The implications are clear: Provide people with a safe opportunity to behave aggressively and the likelihood of antisocial aggression will be lessened. This dictum is expressed as "blowing off steam." In clinical circles there is widespread belief in catharsis. People are often encouraged to express aggression in group-therapy sessions. There are punching bags on many wards in mental hospitals, and Bobo dolls, pounding boards, toy guns, and knives in many play-therapy rooms.

In her popular advice column, Ann Landers has propagated a similar view, as illustrated in her suggestion for dealing with a 3-year-old child's temper tantrums:

> Hostile feelings must be released. If children could be taught to vent their anger against furniture and not other people, they would grow up to be healthier and happier adults and we could close some of our reform schools and penitentiaries.
>
> Ann Landers

In spite of its apparent popularity, the research evidence in favor of this position is neither voluminous nor convincing. The findings from most studies have indicated that aggressive experiences may promote rather than "drain off" aggressive behaviors. Here is a classic test of the catharsis issue (Mallick & McCandless, 1966): Third-grade children were allowed to shoot a toy gun after being frustrated by a peer who interfered with a task they were working on. Others were allowed to work on arithmetic problems after being upset by the peer. When children were allowed to express their aggression toward the peer who had upset them, using a "rigged" procedure in which the child thought he was delivering a shock to the other child (in reality no shocks were administered), there was no support for the catharsis theory, since the intervening activity made little difference. Target shooting did not lower the aggressive behavior of the angered children any more than a passive session of arithmetic problems did. Merely acting aggressively toward an alternative target appears to be insufficient. Nor are opportunities to pound rubber mallets or vigorously pedal an exercise bicycle effective ways of reducing aggression (Parke & Slaby, 1983). Given these findings, it is not surprising that public faith in catharsis theory is on the wane. Consider the following reader's reaction to Ann Landers's "catharsis" advice:

> Dear Ann: I was shocked at your advice to the mother whose 3 year old had temper tantrums. You suggested that the child be taught to kick the furniture and get the anger out of his system. I always thought you were a little cuckoo. Now I'm sure.
>
> My younger brother used to kick the furniture when he got mad. Mother called it letting off steam. Well, he's 32 years old now and still kicking the furniture—what's left of it, that is. He is also kicking his wife, the cat, the kids, and anything else that gets in his way. Last October, he threw the T. V. set out the window when his favorite football team failed to score and lost the game. (The window was closed at the time.)
>
> Why don't you tell mothers that children must be taught to control their anger? This is what separates civilized human beings from savages, Dummy.
>
> Star Witness

In summary, the opportunity to behave aggressively is unlikely to reduce hostile tendencies.

TEACHING CHILDREN EFFECTIVE CONFLICT-REDUCING STRATEGIES

Aggressive children may behave in a hostile and inappropriate fashion because they are not very skilled at solving interpersonal problems. Several studies (Richard & Dodge, 1982; Slaby & Guerra, 1988) found that aggressive children and adolescents gave fewer solutions to social conflict situations than their nonaggressive peers. Moreover, their proposals for resolving social disputes were generally less effective than the solutions offered by less aggressive individuals. Making aggressive children and adolescents aware of the negative consequences of aggression for themselves and others through modeling and explanations, and through the encouragement or teaching of alternative problem-solving behaviors such as cooperation or turn taking, has been found to reduce aggression (Chittenden, 1942; Guerra & Slaby, 1990).

Another approach to aggression control is to elicit alternative responses that are incompatible with the expression of aggression, such as cooperative behaviors. This is well illustrated by Brown and Elliot (1965), who decreased aggression by teaching nursery school teachers to ignore aggression and reward cooperative and peaceful behaviors. Making someone laugh is an effective way to control aggression. Humor, of course, is a reaction that is incompatible with aggression. Watching a humorous cartoon can decrease aggression in angered college students (Parke & Slaby, 1983). Some psychologists are putting these findings into practical use. Curricula have been developed to improve the social problem-solving skills of aggressive children, and some success has been reported in studies in both the United States and Sweden (Guerra & Slaby, 1990; Weissberg, Caplan, & Sivs, 1989). Turn to Box 16-7 for a description of a Swedish example of a successful school-based intervention program.

INCREASING AWARENESS OF HARMFUL EFFECTS OF AGGRESSION

Aggression can often be reduced by increasing the attacker's awareness of the harmful consequences for the victim of his aggression. Baron (1977) found that adults who heard expressions of pain and anguish from their victims were less aggressive than subjects not exposed to this type of feedback. Similar kinds of effects have been found in film studies, where the anguish of the victim is graphically displayed (Parke & Slaby, 1983). The development of empathy during socialization is probably responsible for these effects (Hoffman, 1984).

However, socialization is not always successful—as a glance at any daily newspaper will show. Some individuals seem to take great pleasure in other people's suffering, and many street crimes—such as purse snatchings—are often accompanied by much higher levels of violence than is necessary to successfully steal a purse. Seeing the anguish and pain of their victims seems to be the only motive behind these crimes of unnecessary violence. There is no doubt that pain cues increase rather than inhibit aggression in some individuals.

Even normal youngsters who are rated as aggressive by their peers appear to enjoy making others suffer. This is dramatically demonstrated in a study of 12-year-old aggressive boys (Perry & Perry, 1974). Using a "rigged" procedure in which the boys thought that they were administering loud, noxious noises to another child, the experimenters varied the victim's reaction. The victim either signaled that the noise "hurt a lot" or denied he was in any discomfort. When the victim denied that an aggressive attack caused any

BOX 16-7 *PSYCHOLOGY IN ACTION* REDUCING AGGRESSION IN SCANDINAVIAN SCHOOLS

Aggression is a worldwide problem. In Norway and Sweden nearly 9 percent of the children in the first nine grades of school are victims of aggression. To help these 150,000 students, Dan Olweus, in cooperation with the Ministry of Education, launched a nationwide campaign to reduce the amount of aggression in the schools.

The goals of the program were:

1 To increase awareness of the problem and knowledge about aggression in the schools
2 To achieve active involvement of teachers and parents
3 To develop clear classroom rules against aggressive behavior such as
(*a*) We shall not bully others, (*b*) we shall try to help students who are bullied, (*c*) we shall help include students who are left out
4 To provide support and protection for the victims of aggression

Since it is well known that parents, teachers, and children themselves can contribute to the level of aggression, a program was designed to target all of these individuals. The main components were as follows:

1 A booklet for school personnel describing the nature and scope of aggression in schools and giving practical suggestions about what teachers and other school personnel can do. These steps include increasing adult awareness of their responsibility to control interpersonal aggression in school and providing more adequate supervision during recess, encouraging teachers to intervene in bullying situations, and giving a clear message to the students: "Aggression is not accepted in our school." In addition, teachers are advised to initiate serious talks with victims and their aggressors and their parents if the aggressive attacks persist.
2 A four-page folder designed to inform and help parents of both victims and aggressors and ordinary children.
3 A videocassette showing episodes from the everyday lives of two children who were victims of aggressive attacks.
4 A short inventory for students to provide anonymous information on the frequency of aggressor/victim problems in the school and the reactions of teachers and parents, including their awareness of the problem and their readiness to interfere.

While the program was made available to all schools in Norway and Sweden, detailed evaluation of the effectiveness of the program was based on about 2500 students in 112 grade 4 to 7 classes in 42 primary and junior high schools in Bergen, Norway. Did this multilevel national campaign aimed at reducing aggression work? The answer was clearly positive. There were marked reductions in the levels of aggression problems both eight and twenty months after the initiation of the intervention program. Fewer children reported being attacked by others and fewer children reported that they acted aggressively. Peer ratings told a similar story; classmates reported that both the "number of students being bullied in the class" and "the number of students bullying others" showed a marked drop. There was also a reduction in general antisocial behavior such as vandalism, theft, and truancy, and a rise in student satisfaction with school life.

While it is not clear which aspect of the program (class rules, teacher awareness, parental intervention) was most important in achieving these effects, it is clear that *intervention* can make a difference!

Source: Olweus, D. (1989). Bully/victim problems among school children: Basic facts and effects of a school-based intervention program. In K. Rubin & D. Pepler (Eds.), *The development and treatment of childhood aggression*. Hillsdale, NJ: Erlbaum.

pain, high-aggressive boys escalated the intensity of their attacks. In the case of the low-aggressive boys, this denial of suffering did not increase the level of aggression. For the aggressive child, signs of pain and suffering are an indication that the aggression is successful. Moreover, aggressive individuals often show little or no remorse after behaving aggressively, while low-aggressive boys show self-disapproval after harming another person (Perry & Bussey, 1977). Possibly, highly aggressive children have a poorly developed empathic reaction to other people's distress and suffering. Training children and adolescents to be more empathic and sensitive to the views and feelings of other individuals can be an effective way of controlling aggression (Chandler, 1973; Guerra & Slaby, 1990). Empathy clearly plays an important role in the development of aggression.

Playing with guns can increase aggression.

REORGANIZING ENVIRONMENTS AS A WAY OF CONTROLLING AGGRESSION

Aggression is to some extent under environmental control, and alterations in how children's social and physical worlds are organized often can affect the level of aggression. Stress, crowding, and competition for inadequate resources can increase aggression. If the population of a nursery school with a modest amount of playground equipment and toys suddenly doubles, aggression is likely to increase as well. On the other hand, even though more children are added there may be no increase in aggression if the number of slides, swings, and toys available to the children also increases (Smith & Connolly, 1980).

Moreover, it is not only the number of toys available, but the kind of toys, that may alter the amount of aggression. Another way to control aggression is to reduce exposure to aggressive toys. For example, it has been found that preschoolers behave less aggressively toward other children in the presence of nonaggressive toys such as airplanes than when aggressive playthings such as toy guns are available (Turner & Goldsmith, 1976). Although research has demonstrated that aggression can be controlled in multiple ways, it is still unclear which tactics are most effective for children with varying personalities, and how these factors interact with the wide range of situations children encounter in their everyday experiences.

SUMMARY

AN OVERVIEW OF MORAL DEVELOPMENT

- The socialization of moral beliefs and behavior is one of the main tasks in all cultures. Different theorists have focused on different aspects of moral development. Psychoanalytic theorists have focused relatively more on affective components of morality, such as guilt and remorse; social learning theorists, on moral conduct; and cognitive theorists, on moral judgments.

COGNITIVE THEORIES OF MORAL DEVELOPMENT

- Jean Piaget and Lawrence Kohlberg have both proposed theories involving invariant sequences of stages of moral development related to the increasing cognitive complexity of the child.
- Piaget proposed a two-stage approach—a stage of moral realism followed by one of autonomous morality. Moral absolutism, a belief in immanent justice and objective responsibility, characterizes moral realism. In contrast, children in the stage of autonomous morality recognize the arbitrariness of social rules and intentionality in their moral judgments. In spite of research support for the general developmental sequence, recent studies suggest that Piaget underestimated the cognitive capacities of children. While the inability to distinguish between intentions and consequences was once thought to be a key factor in the development of moral judgments, subsequent research has found that many other factors affect children's judgments.
- Kohlberg proposed a six-stage theory of the development of moral judgment. The order of development is fixed and invariant, and movement is generally toward higher stages. Moral judgments continue to develop into adulthood, but few individuals reach the most advanced levels (stages 5 and 6).
- Criticisms of Kohlberg include possible sex and cultural biases. Gilligan has proposed a care orientation that may describe women's moral judgments more adequately.
- Piaget emphasized the role of peers and Kohlberg, the importance of varied opportunities for role taking in the development of moral judgments. Both views tend to minimize the influence of parents in the development of moral judgments. There is evidence that consistent discipline involving reasoning and explanation and concern with the feelings of others leads to both more mature moral judgments and more self-control.
- Social conventions, such as table manners and forms of address, are distinct from moral rules and follow a different developmental course, according to Turiel, who views conventions as arbitrary and relative and as varying cross-culturally.

THE BEHAVIORAL SIDE OF MORAL DEVELOPMENT: THE EMERGENCE OF SELF-CONTROL

- Self-control, the ability to behave in accord with social or moral rules, proceeds through three stages—(1) external control, (2) self-control, and (3) self-regulation.
- Self-control or moral behavior is strongly influenced by situational factors. As the elements of situations and types of behavior assessed become more similar, more consistency of moral conduct occurs. Individual differences in self-control are evident as well. Early self-control ability is related to later social and cognitive competence.

- Contrary to prior beliefs, it has been found that altruistic behavior begins very early, and helping, sharing, and exhibiting emotional reactions to the distress of others occur in the first and second years of life.
- Developmental changes occur both in the cues that elicit altruistic behaviors and in the ways in which prosocial actions are expressed.
- Reasoning about prosocial situations undergoes a developmental progression that is only modestly related to the development of moral judgment.
- Parents influence the emergence of altruistic behavior by their direct teaching in "distress" situations, by providing models, and by arranging for opportunities to behave in prosocial ways.
- Opportunities for responsibility taking appear to lead to increased altruistic behavior. Similarly, role playing and empathy both contribute to the development of altruism and helping behavior.

THE DEVELOPMENT OF AGGRESSION

- Aggression is behavior that intentionally inflicts harm or injury on another person.
- Aggression undergoes important developmental shifts: Younger children show more instrumental aggression, while older children display more hostile or person-oriented aggression. Children's ability to correctly infer intent in others may account, in part, for these shifts. Proactive aggressive, which is used to dominate another person, decreases across development more than reactive aggression, which occurs in response to being attacked.
- Clear sex differences in aggression are evident, with boys instigating and retaliating more than girls. Aggression is moderately stable over age for both sexes.
- Certain parental disciplinary practices, especially ineffectual and erratic physical punishment, contribute to high levels of aggression in children. Lack of parental monitoring of children is another contributor.
- Biological influences on aggression include genetic, temperamental, and hormonal factors.
- Catharsis theory, the belief that aggression can be reduced by behaving aggressively against a safe target, has been seriously challenged by research evidence. Encouraging alternative prosocial behaviors, presenting humorous material, and increasing a child's awareness of the harmful effects of aggression are more effective control techniques.

CHAPTER 17

DEVELOPMENTAL PSYCHOPATHOLOGY

DEVELOPMENTAL APPROACHES TO PSYCHOPATHOLOGY

Risk and Resiliency

WHAT IS ABNORMAL?

The Medical Model

Abnormality as Deviation from the Average

Abnormality as Deviation from the Ideal

The Social Judgment of Child Psychopathology

Problem Behaviors

CLASSIFICATION OF CHILD PSYCHOPATHOLOGY

Undercontrolled Disorders

Overcontrolled Disorders

Pervasive Developmental Disorders

THE TREATMENT OF DEVELOPMENTAL PSYCHOPATHOLOGIES

Medication

Play Therapy

Behavior Therapy

Family Therapy

Community Psychology

SUMMARY

The issues, topics, and processes that have been discussed throughout this book have generally referred to normal development. In this chapter, we turn to a particularly intriguing, often painful, and poorly understood area of child development—developmental psychopathology. The focus is on the abnormal or deviant, and the goal of this chapter is to attempt to understand why some children develop problems or difficulties that require special treatment and intervention. A number of questions will be addressed. What is abnormal, and how have psychologists defined abnormality? What is unique about a developmental approach to psychopathology? How do risk factors, vulnerabilities, and protective processes interact to promote or protect against the development of abnormal behavior? How are the disorders of childhood best classified? We will consider different types of problems that are illustrative of the types of difficulties found in children. Some problems involve lack of control, as in hyperaggressive or hyperactive children. Others involve inner-oriented problems or overcontrol, such as depression or anxiety disorders. Other disorders are extreme, occur infrequently, and represent profound disturbances across many spheres of functioning, as in the case of autistic children. Finally, what are the causes and treatments of these different kinds of problems? We will try to answer some of these questions in this chapter. To introduce the chapter and to illustrate the range of problems that children can exhibit, consider these case studies.

> Billy had always been a "handful" in his parents' eyes. As an infant, he cried frequently, woke up at all hours, and soon gave up his afternoon nap in favor of exploring tabletops and other forbidden territories. As a toddler, he raced around from dawn until dark, always seeming to run when others walked. When he was 4, one of his favorite games was scrambling onto the roof of the family car and fearlessly diving off into his father's tired arms.
>
> During times like these, his parents would try to discipline Billy by reasoning with him, but that tactic rarely worked. Instead, they would tolerate—and often secretly enjoy—his antics until they reached their limit, at which point they found it necessary to simply force Billy to comply. Although exhausted by him, Billy's parents never considered him to have a real problem—until he started school. At the end of first grade, Billy's principal called his parents in for a conference. The principal told them that Billy wasn't paying attention in class, was consequently falling behind in his work, and required more supervision than his teacher said she could give. In addition, his antics in the classroom were distracting other children and disrupting the entire class. It was suggested that Billy's parents talk to their pediatrician about how to do something to change his behavior before he started the second grade. If not, the school was going to consider placing Billy in their "resource room" next year—a special class for "emotionally disturbed" children.
>
> Jennifer was beginning to worry her mother. She was a very well-behaved and helpful 12-year-old, but to her mother Jennifer seemed unhappy. She really didn't have any close friends and her mother wondered why the phone wasn't constantly ringing for Jennifer as it had for her when she was Jennifer's age. To her mother, Jennifer seemed to be spending too much of her time alone in her room and not enough time socializing. More than that, her mother was concerned about Jennifer's schoolwork. Her straight A's in sixth grade had slipped down

to mostly B's and even one C for the first term in her new junior high school, and Jennifer had dropped out of the one thing that her mother thought she really seemed to enjoy—orchestra. Her mother tried to talk with Jennifer about how she was feeling, but both times she tried to approach her, Jennifer first got angry at her mother's "bugging her" and then ended up running to her room in tears. Her mother blamed Jennifer's unhappiness on her father and their divorce six years earlier. But what could she so about that now?

Peter was becoming a source of grave concern to his parents. At age 3, he had not yet spoken his first word, and his unusual behavior could not be ignored. He spent hours every day sitting and spinning a top that he had played with since he was 2, and he became violently upset if the toy was taken away from him. Peter showed no interest in other children and would jerk away from his mother or father if they tried to give him a hug. Even as an infant Peter had resisted being held and stiffened at physical contact, and his mother could not remember a time when they had really cuddled. She commented that holding Peter was more like holding a log than a baby since he did not mold or cling to her shoulder the way most babies do. His rejection of his parents didn't seem to be one of anger; rather it almost seemed as if it were physically painful for Peter to be touched by someone.

Although he had been an exceptionally good baby. Peter's absence of speech and endless repetitive play gradually became more distressing to his parents. The pediatrician's calm reassurances when Peter was younger had now ceased, and he suggested that Peter be taken for an evaluation at a special hospital for exceptional children in a city 200 miles away. Peter's parents were frightened by this possibility. Would they be asked to leave him at the hospital, and, if so, for how long?

It is difficult for parents to determine when children are becoming seriously disturbed or when they are coping with normal life transitions.

All the children described in these brief case histories are exhibiting some behavior that is a cause of concern to their parents. Billy's energy could be tolerated and even appreciated by his loving and indefatigable parents, but his uncontrolled activity is causing trouble for him, his teacher, and his classmates in school. Does Billy have a special problem that differentiates him from his peers and may require special attention? Should he be placed in a special classroom? His teacher seems to think so. As for Jennifer, her apparent unhappiness may be a problem, but we don't really know how she feels about herself and her life. Is she feeling depressed, helpless, and angry at her mother and father for getting divorced? Or is she going through a "stage," feeling confused and lonely as she enters puberty? Perhaps Jennifer is simply experiencing the normal feelings of a quiet girl who is going through a transition to a new school. Of the three children, Peter is exhibiting the most disturbing behavior. But why is he behaving in this unusual manner? Is Peter suffering from some sort of an emotional problem or is he perhaps mentally retarded?

We will discuss Billy, Jennifer, and Peter again as we explore the complexities of developmental psychopathology.

DEVELOPMENTAL APPROACHES TO PSYCHOPATHOLOGY

Developmental psychopathology combines the study of psychopathology with the study of development. It involves the investigation of the origins, course, changes, and continuities in maladaptive behavior over the life span.

Four basic themes or principles of developmental psychopathology have been proposed (Cicchetti, 1990; Masten & Braswell, 1990). First, psychopathology occurs in a developing organism. The role of development must be considered in the origins of symptoms and course of behavior disorders. The frequency and patterns of symptoms in behavior disorders will vary across the course of development. For example, depression increases from preschool to adolescence, with a notable increase in depression in adolescent girls. Gender differences in depression are not found in preadolescents. Depression in young children is characterized by social withdrawal and dysphoric mood; however it is often masked by other symptoms including hyperactivity, bed wetting, learning problems, and antisocial behavior. Furthermore children in third to sixth grades do not have the psychomotor retardation or motivational deficits present in depressed adults (Kazdin, 1989; Leon, Kendall, & Garber, 1980). In depressed adolescents, suicidal thoughts, which are quite uncharacteristic for younger children, begin to appear and the pattern of symptoms involving low self-worth, guilt, depressed mood, negative self-attributions, and inactivity found in depressed adults also emerge, (Cantwell, 1990). The increase in depression and suicidal behavior at adolescence is probably associated with puberty, advances in cognitive development, and the many stresses and adaptive challenges encountered in this developmental period (Masten, 1988).

Second, developmental psychopathology should be viewed in relation to normal development and the major developmental tasks and changes that occur across the life span. Psychopathology is defined in terms of deviations from normal behavior and normal attainments for a person that age. A critical issue is how to distinguish between developmental disruptions that are within the normal range and those that reflect more serious disordered behavior. As we will see, all children have some problems at some time in their lives and at some points in development certain problems occur with such frequency as to be regarded as normal. Although temper tantrums are common in 2-year-olds they would be viewed as more deviant in adolescents.

Third, the earliest precursors of disordered behavior must be studied. Although psychopathology is less clearly defined and less stable in younger children than in adults there are early behaviors that often are associated with later problem behavior. Two of these early behavioral warning signs are noncompliant behaviors and rejection by peers. These two precursors of later antisocial behavior may actually be related in young children. Young children who are resistant, coercive, nonconforming, and confrontational with parents are also likely to be insensitive, unskilled, aggressive, and hence unaccepted in peer relations. Peer rejection eventually may drive children to associate with a deviant peer group and to become involved in antisocial behavior. Thus, although neither early noncompliance and coercion with parents nor rejection by peers would be labeled as pathological they are associated with more serious later conduct disorders such as stealing, drug and alcohol abuse, physical violence, and fire setting (Cairns, Cairns, Neckerman, Fergusen, & Gariepy, 1989; Patterson, DeBarshyshe, & Ramsey, 1989; Patterson, Capaldi, & Banks, in press).

Finally, there are multiple pathways to both normal and abnormal adjustment over the course of development. Multiple factors, some genetic and some environmental or experiential, interact and may deflect a child into a deviant trajectory or from a deviant trajectory into a normal developmental pathway.

Risk and Resiliency

A broad array of factors may place children at risk for developing psychological problems. They may be at risk because of genetic or biological factors such as a psychotic parent or serious illness; or because of demographic factors

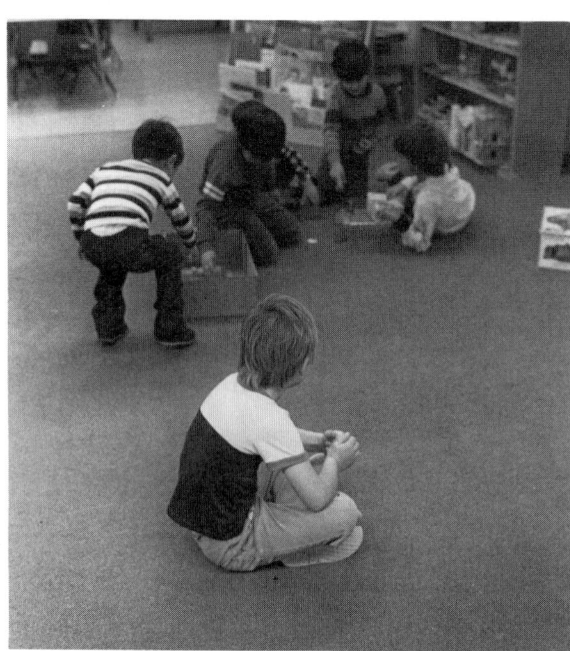

Early rejection by peers is often predictive of later problem behavior.

such as parents' income or education, family size and structure, or minority status. They also may be at risk because of adverse social relationships within and outside of the home or because of stressful life events such as divorce, death or remarriage of a parent, accidents, multiple shifts in homes or caretakers, institutionalization or repeated hospitalization. There is great variability in response to such risks. Many children exhibit resiliency under extremely difficult circumstances. Some children, however, seem to suffer permanent developmental delays or disruptions. Others show "sleeper" effects, seeming to cope well initially but having problems emerge later in development. Still others adapt well and for the most part function competently but at a cost. Children who are resilient in the face of adversity sometimes not only exhibit social and academic competence but also more depression and anxiety than competent children from less stressful backgrounds (Luthar, 1991). Finally, some children not only are able to cope with stress, they actually seem to be enhanced by it. On confronting stresses later in life they have learned from their experiences and seem better able to adapt to new challenges than are children who have experienced little or no stress. This has been called a "steeling" or "inoculation" effect, (Rutter, 1987; Hetherington, 1991). Such a "steeling" effect is most likely to occur when stress levels are moderate rather than excessively low or high, when unresolved stresses have not accumulated over time, and when supportive or protective factors are available.

Protective factors are factors that buffer the individual from the effects of stress and promote coping and good adjustment in the face of adversity. Three types of protective factors have frequently been identified. The first of these are positive individual attributes. Children who have easy temperaments, high self-esteem, an internal locus of control, are intelligent, independent, and, in some circumstances, children who are female are more adaptable in the face of stressful life experiences (Garmezy, 1983; Hetherington, 1991; Rutter 1987; Werner, 1988). The second set of protective factors involve a supportive family environment. For example the presence of one warm supportive parent can help to buffer the adverse effects of poverty, divorce, family discord, and child abuse (Luthar & Zigler, 1991). The final set of protective factors involves extrafamilial individuals or societal agencies, such as the school system, peer group, or church, that support the child's coping efforts. The effects of these protective factors are not automatic; protection does not lie in the availability of potentially supportive resources but in the use made of them. Furthermore, when stressful life events are intense and massed they may overwhelm the available protective factors and then even the most resilient child can develop problems (Hetherington, 1991; Werner, 1988).

WHAT IS ABNORMAL?

The Medical Model

It might be thought that the term *developmental psychopathology* implies that children who display abnormal behaviors suffer from some form of disease of the "psyche" or mind analogous to a physical illness. Many who have studied abnormal behavior have attempted to further our knowledge of the psychological problems that children experience by borrowing from medical science some of the ideas about the cause and treatment of emotional problems. According to the medical model, it is assumed that the psychological disorder—like a physical disease—resides within the individual and results from abnormal physiological or intrapsychic processes.

Most researchers and clinicians feel that the medical model is an inappropriate, or at least insufficient, means of explaining much of what is called abnormal child behavior. Rather, these critics argue that what is called psychopathology is better thought of as *problems in living*. Such problems are said to be pathological or abnormal on the basis of a *social judgment*, not on some objective medical test. Our view of abnormal is dependent upon our individual and cultural values. What is abnormal are those behaviors, thoughts, and feelings that a group of individuals agree upon as being deviant. While this view may be preferable to the physical illness analogy, the reader should readily see that there are problems in this definition. There are many different criteria that various groups of individuals use to define abnormality, and these criteria can conflict with one another. Gaining an awareness and an understanding of the diverse views on defining abnormal child behavior is the first step that must be taken in the understanding of developmental psychopathology.

Abnormality as Deviation from the Average

The term *abnormal* literally means "departing from the normal"; therefore, one way of defining abnormality is to view as being abnormal any behaviors or feelings that differ from the average by some set amount. This method of defining abnormality is referred to as the statistical model. While there are problems with the statistical definition of abnormality, this model is often used as a guide to what constitutes deviance. In the well-accepted definition of mental retardation offered by the American Association of Mental Deficiency (AAMD) for example, a child whose individual IQ test score is 2 standard deviations below the mean (that is, below 70 on the Wechsler Intelligence Scale for Children–Revised) is said to be mentally retarded.

However, the model is not as straightforward as it would appear at first glance. Abnormality is defined as deviation from the average, but this implies that deviation from the mean in *either* direction is abnormal. Do we want to define as abnormal a score of 2 standard deviations *above* the mean IQ? Most people are understandably reluctant to call superior functioning a sign of psychopathology! Another problem with the statistical model is that it doesn't serve as a guide in deciding *how much* of a difference is abnormal and under which circumstance differences matter. Why not define mental retardation as being an IQ score that is 1 or 3 standard deviations from the average IQ rather than 2? Indeed, the arbitrariness of setting some fixed amount of deviation on the standard intelligence test to distinguish normality from abnormality has been noted in the case of mental retardation, and the AAMD now states that to be classified as retarded children must not only have a low IQ but also show deficits in adaptive behavior, that is, in their ability to function in the real world. Young children who can dress themselves, find their way around the neighborhood, and use the telephone are less likely to be identified as retarded than children with the same IQ who do not exhibit these practical competencies.

Abnormality as Deviation from the Ideal

One alternative to the statistical model is to define abnormality as a *deviation from the ideal*. Rather than defining the average as normal or healthy, this model identifies an ideal healthy personality and claims that deviations from this ideal state are abnormal. The main problem with this alternative concept comes in defining the ideal healthy personality. Several personality theorists such as Freud and Maslow have suggested guidelines for what they believe to be the ideal personality, but who is to say they are right? What do you consider to be ideal adjustment? Are you willing to say that anyone who falls short of this ideal is abnormal? Are you prepared to accept someone else's judgment of what ideal functioning is? Your parents' definition perhaps? It seems doubtful. This seems to be too big a task for anyone, no matter how highly regarded, to assume.

Elements of this concept of abnormality are seen in Western definitions of psychopathology, however. In Western culture, people are expected to work hard, to love forever, and further, to be happy in achieving these two goals. When someone falls short of these cultural criteria (for example, a high school dropout), we, as a society, become concerned. Some differences in cultural norms between the perception of childhood behavior problems by adults in the United States and Thailand can be seen in the study in Box 17-1. Although no one will accept one definition of the ideal adjustment, it can be seen in the study that there are *implicit* ideals that affect cultural definitions of abnormality.

The Social Judgment of Child Psychopathology

Consider for a moment the information conveyed by the following brief excerpt from the case history of Tom. Tom is a boy who is living with his aunt and cousin; he often skips school, which he hates, and he sneaks out of the house at night. Tom had the following thoughts just before running away from home:

> Tom's mind was made up now. He was gloomy and desperate. He was a forsaken, friendless boy, he said; nobody loved him; when they found out what they had driven him to do, perhaps they would be sorry; he had tried to do right and get along, but they would not let him; since nothing would do them but to be rid of him, let it be so; and let them blame *him* for the consequences—why shouldn't they? What right had the friendless to complain? Yes, they had forced him to it at last; he would lead a life of crime. There was no choice.

What can you conclude about the normality or abnormality of Tom's behavior on the basis of this admittedly brief excerpt? Does Tom differ sufficiently from the average to be considered abnormal according to the statistical model? Certainly he deviates from many people's ideal, including, we might presume, the ideal of some of those people who frequently must deal with Tom. Put yourself in the position of a psychologist who has been asked to evaluate Tom's psychological adjustment. Are your suspicions raised that he is exhibiting some form of developmental psychopathology or would you be more inclined to dismiss his activity as nothing to worry about? Let us provide you with some help in weighing your decision. The case of Tom is actually an excerpt from Mark Twain's *The Adventure of Tom Sawyer* (Twain, 1976, p. 493). Is Tom Sawyer abnormal? Why, just the opposite: Tom represents the prototype of the ideal all-American boy. He is hardly a

BOX 17-1 CHILDHOOD PSYCHOPATHOLOGY IN THE EYE OF THE BEHOLDER: THAI AND AMERICAN PERSPECTIVES ON OVERCONTROLLED AND UNDERCONTROLLED CHILD-BEHAVIOR PROBLEMS

Cultural values may determine whether adults consider a child's psychological problems to be serious and whether they think the child is in need of professional help. In order to study this relationship John Weiss and his colleagues investigated adults' concern about overcontrolled and undercontrolled child behavior problems in Thailand and the United States.

The teachings of Thai Buddhism propose that some unhappiness is inevitable, that all things change for the better, and that an individual's behavior is not reflective of an enduring personality. In contrast, Americans are exposed to child psychology, deviant behavior, and childrearing theory in academic courses, popular literature, and the media so that they may be sensitized to view child problems as being more serious than members of other cultures do. In this study, parents, teachers, and psychologists in the United States and Thailand read vignettes describing two children, one with overcontrol (such as shyness, fearfulness, depression, worrying, and dependency), the other with problems in under control (such as aggression, cruelty, disobedience, and lying). The adults were asked to rate each child on the seriousness of the problem, their level of concern about the problems, whether the child's behavior would improve over time, and which child had a greater need for professional help.

As can be seen in Figure 17-1, consistent with their beliefs, Thais, compared with Americans, rated both overcontrolled and undercontrolled behaviors as less serious and worrisome and more likely to improve.

Cross-national differences were less extreme in psychologists' responses than in the responses of parents and teachers, perhaps because their professional training sensitized them to children's problems.

Childhood psychopathology is to some extent in the eye of the beholder and the beholder's perspective will be modified by his or her cultural context.

Source: Weisz, J. R., Suwanlert, S., Chaiyasit, W., Weiss, B, Walter, B. R., & Anderson, W. W. (1988). Thai and American perspectives on over and undercontrolled behavior problems: Exploring the threshold model among parents, teachers, and psychologists. *Journal of Consulting and Clinical Psychology*, **53**, 601–609.

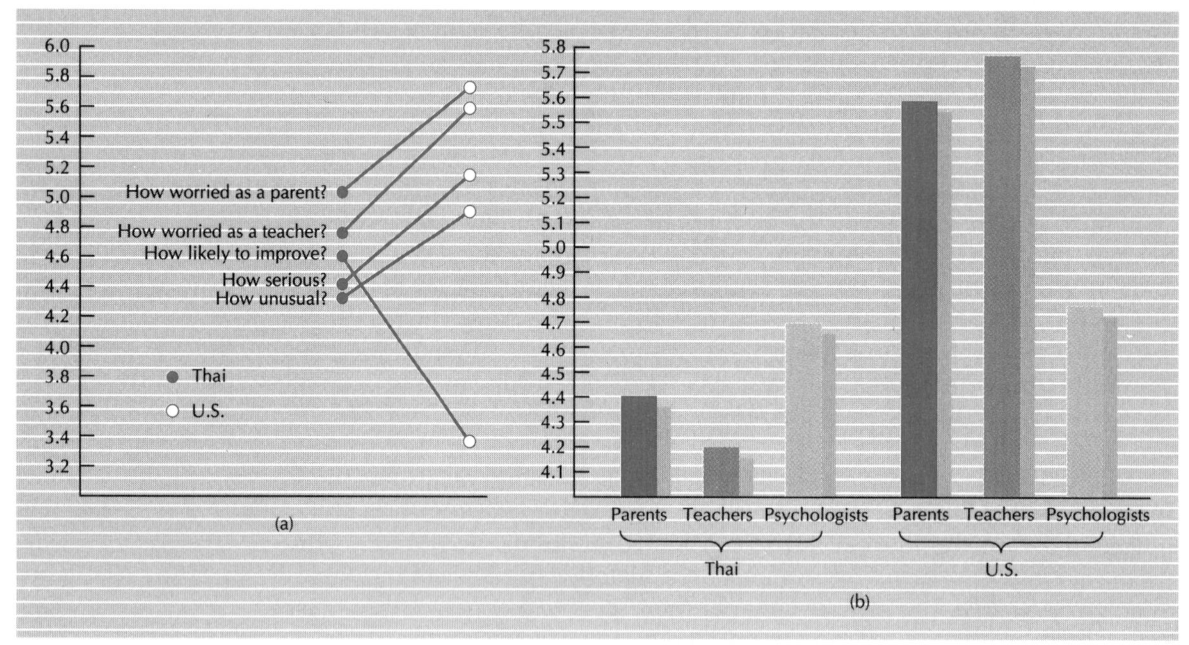

FIGURE 17-1

(a) Thai and American adults' answers to five questions about child problems (problem types combined). The numbers reflect mean ratings on Likert scales ranging from 1 to 7.

(b) Mean responses to the question, "How serious is this child's problem?" (Ratings ranged from 1 ["not serious at all"] to 7 ["very serious].

candidate for psychotherapy! But taken out of context, Tom's behavior doesn't seem quite so fun-filled, does it? Obviously, therefore, something other than a child's behavior in any given situation affects people's social judgments as to what constitutes abnormal behavior.

Since children are usually not self-referred but are identified by an adult as being disturbed and in need of the attention of mental health professionals, psychologists must constantly be alert to factors other than the child's behavior itself that might influence the referring adult's judgments about the child. That is, therapists must always ask themselves: Is this child really having a problem or does this adult have a distorted view of the child for some reason? Three sets of factors that may subtly influence the adult's perception are the characteristics of the child, the characteristics of the adult, and contextual influences.

CHILD CHARACTERISTICS

Parents and other adults are more likely to perceive and respond to a behavior as deviant if it occurs in boys, in children who have been temperamentally difficult infants, in unattractive children, or in children with a history of other forms of deviancy (Chess & Thomas, 1972; Hetherington, 1991; Huston, 1983; Emery, Binkoff, Houts, & Carr, 1983; Serbin & O'Leary, 1975; Werner et al., 1975). In addition, a behavior displayed by a socially skilled child is less likely to be judged abnormal than the same behavior displayed by an unskilled child (Emery et al., 1983; Werner et al., 1975). Social judgments of abnormality are influenced by behaviors other than the ones that are being judged directly.

One reason you probably are inclined not to view Tom Sawyer as having a psychological problem, even when he misbehaves, is that you know other things about Tom. He's cute, he's clever, he loves Becky. Not even his Aunt Polly can get *really* mad at him.

CHARACTERISTICS OF THE REFERRING ADULT

Certain characteristics of the adult who has identified a child as being disturbed also can distort the judgment as to whether a child's behavior is normal or abnormal. That is, a parent's, teacher's, or even a health professional's view that a given child has a psychological problem not only reveals something about the child's behavior but also often says something about the adult. Various teachers, for example, have different standards as to what they consider acceptable behavior, as you can easily recall by thinking back through your own experiences with some of your different elementary and high school teachers. Huck Finn also could tell you that different adults have contrasting views of the same children. The Widow Douglas apparently saw some potential for good in Huck that was somehow missed by the rest of the townspeople. Much to Huck's chagrin, the widow was determined to make the good she saw in Huck more apparent to all as she went to great lengths to "civilize" the free-spirited boy. Thus some parents' perceptions of disturbance in their child only partially reflect the child's behavior; their views also appear to reflect characteristics about themselves.

Parents too may have a distorted view of their children's behavior and their children's need for psychological help. Parents who are depressed, are abusive, or who refer their children to a clinic for help report their children's behavior to be much more negative and deviant than the child's actual behavior is observed to be in the clinic and home (Griest, Wells, & Forehand, 1980; Lobitz & Johnson, 1975). Some differences in perceptions and attributions of abusive and nonabusive mothers are seen in the study by Larrance and Twentyman (1983) presented in Box 17-2. Finally, it has been found that two different adults, whether they are mother and father or parent and teacher, frequently disagree about whether a given child has a problem or not. Trained professionals often cannot even agree with each other very reliably as to what constitutes developmental psychopathology (see below); thus it is not surprising that parents or teachers frequently disagree.

CONTEXTUAL CONSIDERATIONS

The third general category of extraneous influences on adults' judgments of developmental psychopathology is the context in which the child is observed. The same behavior may be judged differently according to the demands of different situations. Think back to the behavior of Billy in the case history presented at the beginning of this chapter. His inattentive and overactive behavior was determined to be tiresome, although still acceptable, as long as he was at home. But stricter standards are set in school, and Billy's behavior was judged to be abnormal according to the demands of the classroom context. Billy's behavior did not change, but the setting in which it occurred did.

Contextual influences on the evaluation of children's psychological adjustment include, but are not limited to, the demands of the setting in which the child is observed. Factors such as a child's social background, race, and prior behavior can create contexts that influence how a current behavior is judged. Such factors lead to the tagging of children with value-laden labels—retarded, a child from a broken home, delinquent, high-risk. Labels do not change a child's behavior, initially; rather, they provide a context that alters the way in which a behavior is perceived and responded to by others and this eventually may have adverse consequences for the child's development. Consider once again the differences between Tom Sawyer and Huck Finn. It seems quite possible that our contrasting views of these two boys' behavior were influenced by the fact that Huck's father had been the town drunk, while Tom's Aunt Polly was a churchgoer. Do people still view the behavior of children in lower status families as more problematic than that of children in mainstream families who do the same thing? Some police officers apparently do: More lower-class minorities than middle-class whites are sent on to court when arrested for similar offenses (Gibbons, 1970). Such treatment may lead to detrimental self-labeling and exposes the child to additional risks that push the child toward more deviant behavior.

Problem Behaviors

While it is important to recognize that adults' views about what constitutes developmental psychopathology comprise potentially distorted social judgments, the potential for distortion should not be overstated. Adults' judgments *are* influenced by the child's behavior! There are children with psychological problems whose behavior is abnormal according to statistical, ideal, and social standards. The remainder of this chapter is devoted to the discussion of examples of some of the more important behavior disorders of childhood.

Whether or not a particular behavior problem is to be viewed as normal or not depends greatly on the child's age and the probability that it will continue over time or be manifested in some form of adult disorder. Some problems, such as bed-wetting, thumb-sucking, temper tantrums, and tics,

BOX 17-2 PARENTAL PERCEPTIONS AND ATTRIBUTIONS

As was discussed in the chapter on the family, evidence suggests that abusive mothers tend to be biased toward having negative views of their children's behavior, a finding clearly relevant to the present discussion of parents' perceptions of normal and abnormal behavior in children. A study by Larrance and Twentyman (1983) has carried this observation one step further in examining abusive parents' attributions about the cause of their children's positive and negative behavior.

In this study, abusive and nonabusive mothers were shown a series of photographs of either their own child or an unfamiliar child acting in a variety of social situations in which children were either (1) transgressing against each other, (2) in a play situation with a destructive outcome, or (3) in a competitive situation that had an ambiguous outcome. After being shown the photographs, the mothers were asked a series of questions evaluating the children and also were asked to provide explanations of why they thought the children acted as they did.

Consistent with other research, abusive mothers, in comparison to nonabusive mothers, were found to have negative expectations of their children. Furthermore, the two groups of mothers gave very different explanations for why the children acted as they did. Abusive mothers gave stable, internal attributions for their children's transgressions or failures, suggesting that they viewed this behavior as traitlike and would expect it to happen again. When their children succeeded or when another child transgressed, on the other hand, abusive mothers attributed this to external and unstable causes, suggesting that they thought this behavior was situation-specific. Nonabusive mothers, in direct contrast, gave almost the exact opposite pattern of causal explanations. They emphasized their children's positive attributes as leading to success, and adverse circumstances or atypical behaviors that were unlikely to recur as responsible for transgressions.

This study indicates that adults' judgments of children's behavior involve more complex processes than simply a positive or a negative bias alone. It is not enough for therapists to help a parent see a child as behaving in a more positive way; the parent also must attribute the child's behavior to internal, stable causes. For example, if a parent who has referred a child to a psychologist concludes that the child is doing better "only because he is in therapy," the parent is unlikely to maintain a positive view of the child. Ultimately, the goal must be for the parent to see the child as doing better as a result of internal, stable causes. "Because he's basically a good kid" is one such attribution.

Source: Larrance, D. T., & Twentyman, C. T. (1983). Maternal attributions and child abuse. *Journal of Abnormal Psychology* **92**, 449–457.

decline with age; others, such as nail-biting, increase from early childhood to adolescence; still others, such as disturbing dreams and nightmares, peak in preadolescence at about age 10 and then decline (MacFarlane, Allen, & Honzik, 1954). However some childhood disorders such as hyperactivity (Weiss & Hechtman, 1986), autism (Hertzog & Shapiro, 1990), aggression, and antisocial behavior (Eron & Heusmann, 1990) are more likely to be associated with later adult dysfunction.

Many investigators are interested in the differences over age in the behavioral manifestations of particular disorders and in processes and factors that sustain or maintain problem behaviors. Caspi, Elder, and Bem (1987) studied the stability of behavior in children who at age 8 had been identified as having an irritable social interactional style manifested in temper tantrums, explosiveness, and verbal abuse. Boys who were irritable school-age children, thirty years later, as adults, were undercontrolled, moody, and unsociable. They also were less dependable, ambitious, and productive, and this was reflected in erratic work patterns and downward occupational mobility. For both males and females, early explosive, ill-tempered behavior was associated with marital problems and divorce, and for women, with marriage to a man of low socioeconomic status and with irritable inept parenting. The investigators propose that continuity in maladaptive behaviors is sustained by two related processes: *cumulative continuity* and *interactional continuity*.

Cumulative continuity is similar to niche picking which was discussed in Chapter 3, where the child promotes experiences or selects environments that support or reinforce maladaptive predispositions. However, it also involves the notion of transactional stressors, where being irritable increases the chance that stressful life experiences such as school dropout and job loss will also occur, leading to increased frustration and irascibility. Interactional continuity involves the interaction with others and is related to the evocative processes described in Chapter 3. Irritable persons are likely to evoke and to be the targets of hostile, rejecting responses from the people with whom they interact. It seems likely that genetic and experiential factors contribute to continuities and discontinuities in problem behavior.

As an aid in helping clinicians determine when a problem behavior is likely to prove to be only a passing concern and when it signifies the need for treatment, psychologists have developed classification systems that take into account variations in behavior problems. Two of the most important systems are examined next.

CLASSIFICATION OF CHILD PSYCHOPATHOLOGY

Given the many problems in defining what abnormal child behavior is, it should not be surprising to find that there is much disagreement over the proper assessment and classification of developmental psychopathology. Until quite recently, in fact, the psychological disorders of childhood were most commonly classified in much the same way as adult psychopathologies. Childhood psychological problems were viewed as downward extensions of the recognized adult disorders, and the diagnostic categories that were developed for adults were said to apply to children as well (Achenbach, 1990). Disturbed children were viewed as munchkins with adult problems. The irony of this is striking. Most theories view psychological functioning during adult life as a product of child development. It is during the early years that the seeds of abnormal development are thought to be sown, but abnormal behavior in children has been much more rarely studied than adult psychological disorders. This narrow view reminds us of the portraits painted in the Middle Ages where children were physically portrayed—in their dress and body proportions—as little adults. As should be quite clear by now, children are not simply little adults either physically or psychologically, and recent years have seen an increased interest in the psychological problems that are unique to childhood. In discussing some of the most recent developments, two important means of assessing and classifying childhood psychopathology are examined: the diagnostic approach and the rating scale method.

The diagnostic approach to assessing and classifying psychopathology is rooted in the medical tradition. In medicine, a diagnosis is useful or valid if it either conveys information about the *etiology* (cause) of a disorder or helps to pinpoint some specific method of *treatment*. Given that the classification of childhood psychopathology is still in its infancy, few categories of psychological disorders are sufficiently valid to suggest many firm implications for etiology or treatment. At present, diagnostic classification systems are based primarily on description. That is, problems characterized by similar patterns of behavior, disturbing thoughts, or feelings are classified together into various *diagnostic categories*.

The best known and most widely used diagnostic classification system has been compiled by the American Psychiatric Association (APA). The current *Diagnostic and Statistical Manual* (American Psychiatric Association, 1987) is the third classification scheme that APA has developed (it is often referred to as DSM-III or DSM-III-R for revision). The childhood disorders section of this third version of the DSM can be seen in Table 17-1; it differs radically from the taxonomies offered in earlier forms. Whereas DSM-I, published in 1952, had only two diagnostic categories that were to be applied exclusively to children, and DSM-II, published in 1968, contained seven general categories applied to children, the current version contains over thirty different diagnoses for developmental psychopathology.

The change in the DSM over the past thirty years is an important indication of the recent increased interest in psychological disorders that are particularly relevant to childhood. Inasmuch as this change reflects a trend away from merely viewing children as little adults, it is to be applauded. DSM-III-R is not without its problems, however. Perhaps the biggest problem with the classification system is that many of the diagnostic categories it contains are unreliable. *Diagnostic reliability* is a measure of how often two or more different clinicians will independently arrive at the same diagnosis of a child. Reliability is the first test of any classification system; without reliability no system can be valid. If two psychologists cannot reliably agree, for example, whether or not a child is clinically depressed, very little can be learned about depression in childhood. Should psychologist Smith consistently decide that someone like Jennifer, the girl portrayed in the case study at the beginning of the chapter, suffers from depression, but psychologist Jones determines that Jennifer is merely experiencing normal ups and downs, when Smith and Jones talk about "depression," they are talking about two different things. As a matter of fact, research suggests that clinicians agree only about 40 percent of the time that a child is depressed (Cantwell et al., 1979). This is well below what is considered to be an acceptable level of diagnostic reliability. To illustrate the importance of reliability: Would it be acceptable if two physicians disagreed six times out of ten as to whether a tumor was cancerous or not?

While the reliability of many of DSM-III-R's diagnostic categories is quite low, it is acceptably high for others such as attention deficit disorder with hyperactivity, or what is more commonly known simply as *hyperactivity*. For reliable categories like hyperactivity, the next test is whether the diagnosis is *valid*—that is, does the diagnosis yield information about either etiology or treatment? If a diagnosis is both reliable and valid, it is useful; if not, the diagnosis has little value. While some of the DSM-III-R childhood diagnoses are both reliable and valid, the great expansion of the diagnostic system has led, unfortunately, to the development of many diagnoses that meet neither of these scientific criteria (Rutter & Tuma, 1988).

An alternative to the traditional diagnostic methods of classification is the empirical approach (Achenbach & Edelbrock, 1978; Achenbach, 1990). In applying this method, a large number of problem behaviors are rated by an adult familiar with the child, usually a parent or teacher, and then statistical techniques are used to determine which problem behaviors are associated with one another. While there is considerable overlap among the classifications that are arrived at by both the diagnostic and the empirical methods, there are also many disparities (Achenbach, 1990).

There is one area where the two systems closely overlap in the classification of developmental psychopathology. Whereas there is considerable disagreement on specific, or *narrow-band*, diagnoses such as *depression, identity disorder, avoidant disorder*, the two systems generally agree on *broad-band* diagnoses. Broad-band diagnoses are classifications that combine several narrow, specific categories into a single, more general, category (DSM-III-R's broad- and narrow-band diagnoses are indicated in Table 17-1). A comparison with the botanical classification of fruits may help to clarify this point. The broad-band category, for example, apples, can be subdivided into many narrow-band categories, such as McIntosh and Delicious as can the broad-band category, oranges. It is much easier for us to make broad- than narrow-band classification decisions in the case of psychopathology as well.

Not only is there more general agreement as to what are appropriate broad-band classifications of developmental psychopathology, but these categories are also more reliable and valid (Achenbach & Edelbrock, 1978; Cantwell et al., 1979; Werry, Methuen, Fitzpatrick, & Dixon, 1983). Thus, the remainder of the chapter is devoted to the discussion of three well-accepted broad-band categories of childhood psychopathology and to the review of at least one narrow-band disorder within each general category. The three broad-band disorders that are discussed are (1) undercontrolled behavior disorders, (2) overcontrolled disorders, and (3) pervasive developmental disorders.

Undercontrolled Disorders

Undercontrolled behavior disorders can be discriminated from other broad-band categories in that the child's problem behavior has an impact on, and is most disturbing to, those people in the child's environment. Thus, the term *undercontrol* refers to the fact that the child's behavior is not sufficiently controlled according to the demands of a given environment. Aggression, disobedience, rule violation, and noncompliance are examples of specific undercontrolled behaviors. Since undercontrolled behavior is defined by its negative impact on others, and since most childhood psychopathologies are defined by adults' social judgments, it is not surprising that undercontrolled behavior disorders are the most frequently reported of all the psychological problems of childhood. Over three times as many boys as girls are reported to exhibit conduct disorders (Martin & Hoffman, 1990).

While different researchers have divided the broad-band category of undercontrolled disorders into a variety of narrow-band subcategories, the two most commonly used narrow-band diagnoses have been *conduct disorders* and *hyperactivity*.

CONDUCT DISORDERS

Conduct disorders are defined by a repetitive and persistent pattern of rule violations (American Psychiatric Association, 1987). When these rule violations occur in the company of peers, the problem is called a *socialized conduct disorder*, whereas when the children violate rules primarily when alone, the disorder is said to be *unsocialized*. Some of the problems that are considered to be conduct disorders were included in Chapter 16 in the discussion of aggression.

When the rule breaking that is a part of conduct disorder involves a violation of the law, the youth is said to be *delinquent*. Delinquency is not a psychological term; rather, it is a legal designation indicating that a juvenile

TABLE 17-1

DSM-III-R CATEGORIES FOR DISORDERS USUALLY FIRST EVIDENT IN INFANCY, CHILDHOOD, OR ADOLESCENCE

AXIS I

- Disruptive behavior disorders:
  - Attention-deficit hyperactivity disorder
  - Conduct disorder
  - Oppositional defiant disorder
- Anxiety disorders of childhood or adolescence:
  - Separation anxiety disorder
  - Avoidant disorder
  - Overanxious disorder
- Eating disorders:
  - Anorexia nervosa
  - Bulimia nervosa
  - Pica
  - Rumination disorder of infancy
  - Eating disorder NOS*
- Gender identity disorders:
  - Gender identity disorder of childhood
  - Transsexualism
  - Gender identity disorder of adolescence or adulthood, nontranssexual type
  - Gender identity disorder NOS*
- Elimination disorders:
  - Functional encopresis
  - Functional enuresis
- Speech disorders not elsewhere classified:
  - Cluttering
  - Stuttering
- Other disorders of infancy, childhood, or adolescence:
  - Elective mutism
  - Identity disorder
  - Reactive attachment disorder
  - Stereotype/habit disorder
  - Undifferentiated attention-deficit disorder

Axis II—Developmental Disorder

- Mental retardation
- Pervasive developmental disorders:
  - Autistic disorder
  - Pervasive developmental disorder NOS*
- Specific developmental disorders:
  - Academic skills disorders
  - Language and speech disorders
  - Motor skills disorder
- Other developmental disorders

*The abbreviation NOS stands for not otherwise specified. The term is used to indicate cases that do not fit well into other specific subcategories.

Source: Reprinted with permission from American Psychiatric Association (1987).

has been found to have violated the law. Juveniles can be judged delinquent for two types of offenses. *Status offenses,* such as possession of alcohol, are illegal only because of the youth's age, whereas *criminal offenses* are illegal regardless of the age of the individual. Criminal offenses committed by juveniles are no small matter. They account for 38 percent of the eight major

Juveniles commit 38 percent of all major criminal offenses, and they are involved in a disproportionate number of violent crimes.

offenses listed in the FBI's Crime Index (U.S. Department of Justice, 1989). Furthermore, adolescent self-reports of delinquent activity are higher than those found in official records with 80 to 90 percent of adolescents reporting having participated in delinquent activity (Moore & Arthur, 1989).

Substance abuse among children and adolescents is one conduct problem that has been the cause of much concern. Drug use among youths rose dramatically in the late 1960s and early 1970s; fortunately, however, surveys suggest that the prevalence of the use of most drugs may be leveling off. Still, although the number of children using drugs may be stabilizing, evidence suggests that those who do use drugs have been doing so at younger ages. Table 17-2 presents the percent of children in grades 4 to 12 who have ever sampled various substances. It can be seen that there is a sharp increase in substance use between the sixth and seventh grades when many children move into junior high school. It has been found that almost 10 percent of 14-year-olds are already drinking excessively. In addition, over 6 percent of high school seniors use marijuana every day, and some smoke and remain stoned while in school. Whereas adolescent boys are almost twice as likely as girls to be daily marijuana users, the use of tobacco by girls has increased in the past decade, until teenage girls are now heavier smokers than are their male peers.

A number of surveys, notably those school-based surveys involving high school seniors, indicate that Native Americans show the highest drug-use rates, particularly those living on reservations. Mexican-American and white American youths are the next highest and Asians and blacks have the lowest rates of use (Oetting & Beauvais, 1990). These findings seem incompatible with reports of crack epidemics in inner-city black areas and heavy use of some types of drugs in barrio Hispanic youths and of higher urban emergency room admissions for drug overdoses in blacks and Hispanics. It should be

TABLE 17-2

1988–1989 AMERICAN DRUG AND ALCOHOL SURVEY: PERCENTAGE OF LIFETIME PREVALENCE BY GRADE

	GRADE								
SUBSTANCE	4th (*n* = 791)	5th (*n* = 1,531)	6th (*n* = 800)	7th (*n* = 11,175)	8th (*n* = 26,587)	9th (*n* = 13,693)	10th (*n* = 14,529)	11th (*n* = 10,369)	12th (*n* = 26,720)
Alcohol	22.8	33.6	39.5	65.8	77.2	83.3	87.4	91.7	93.4
Got drunk	3.3	4.2	10.2	19.5	32.6	44.7	57.3	67.7	75.0
Marijuana	1.8	2.8	6.6	10.4	16.9	24.9	32.9	41.0	48.2
Cocaine				2.9	4.1	5.3	7.1	9.2	12.5
Crack	1.2	1.2	1.4	2.9	3.8	4.3	4.7	5.1	5.6
Inhalants	5.4	6.9	11.1	14.9	18.8	18.0	16.9	15.9	14.9
Stimulants				5.7	8.7	12.6	15.6	17.9	19.0
Downers				3.0	4.6	6.3	6.5	6.6	5.8
Hallucinogens				4.1	6.2	8.1	9.3	12.5	14.7
PCP				3.1	3.4	3.9	3.7	4.3	3.4
Heroin				3.3	3.5	3.6	3.0	3.1	2.3
Cigarettes	12.9	19.6	33.3	40.8	50.9	55.4	58.7	61.5	63.9
Smokeless tobacco	8.0	9.6	12.4	20.7	26.2	30.0	34.0	36.2	36.4

Source: Oetting and Beauvais (1990).

kept in mind that the emergency room studies have been done mainly in urban settings, where such facilities are more likely to be used by lower socioeconomic populations. Two possible explanations have been offered for these apparently discrepant findings (Oetting & Beauvais, 1990). First, school-based surveys may underestimate substance use of some minorities because minority drug users have high dropout rates and are unlikely to be in school to be surveyed. Rates of drug use in alternative schools, often attended by dropouts, have been found to be exceptionally high. Such results suggest that drug-use rates for minorities with high dropout rates might be more similar to, or even higher than, nonminorities.

Second the highest rates of drug involvement appear in places where economically disadvantaged minorities live in separate enclaves in ghettos, barrios, and Native American reservations. In such settings, unemployment, poverty, poor school situations, isolation, deviant role models, prejudice, and sometimes gang influence may interact to promote substance abuse. After a careful review of the survey literature on drug abuse, Oetting and Beauvais (1990) concluded that these pockets of high-minority drug use are probably not well represented in general surveys of substance abuse especially those involving high school students, and are not typical of other American minority youth (p. 391).

Some of the factors associated with drug use or abstinence are listed in Table 17-3, although the salience of different factors varies with the abuse of different drugs. Children who are undercontrolled and impulsive, moody, easily irritated, and overreactive to minor frustrations are more likely to become frequent drug users (Block, Block, & Keyes, 1988; Shedler & Block, 1990). Heavy drug use by parents and peers is related to the use of both

TABLE 17-3 **CHARACTERISTICS OF YOUTHFUL DRUG USERS AND ABSTAINERS**

CHARACTERISTIC	USERS	ABSTAINERS
1. Family influences		
Parent drug use	Parents are users (especially mothers)	Parents are abstainers
Religion	Not religious	Religious
Values	Nontraditional values	Traditional values
Conflict	More family conflict	Less family conflict
Sibling drug use	Siblings are users	Siblings are abstainers
2. Peer influences		
Peer drug use	Best friend is user	Best friend is abstainer
Peer power	Peers are more influential	Parents more influential
3. Individual factors		
Opportunity	Opportunity to take drugs	No opportunity to take drugs
History	Good experiences with drugs	Unpleasant drug experiences
Adjustment	May have adjustment problems	May have superior adjustment
Attitudes toward authority	More rebellious and questioning	More conforming
Tolerance of deviance	More tolerant	Less tolerant
Deviant behavior	More deviant behavior	More conforming behavior
School achievement	Less concerned about achievement	More achievement-oriented

Source: Gelfand, Jenson, and Drew (1982).

alcohol and marijuana, with peers and situational factors playing a relatively more important role in marijuana use. In addition, nonconformist attitudes, liberal political views, truancy, minor delinquent activities, poor academic records, and the desire to experiment with the drug are related to marijuana use. The use of illicit drugs seems to depend less upon situational factors and more on the response to psychological problems such as depression, anxiety, low self-esteem, or rejection. If marijuana has been used to resolve such personal or psychological problems rather than as a response to social situations, it is likely to lead to use of hard drugs. However, even with illicit drugs, use by a close friend facilitates drug abuse. Serious delinquent offenses, resistance to adult authority, drug dealing, social alienation, and the need to increase self-insight also are associated with the use of illicit drugs. The more of these risk factors experienced by adolescents the more likely the adolescent is to be involved in drug abuse (Newcomb, Maddahian, & Bentler, 1986). With all types of drugs, a close relationship with a responsible, stable family helps to buffer adolescents against drug abuse (Brook, Lukoff, & Whiteman, 1980; Kandel, 1980).

As is found in many other disorders, drug abuse in adolescence is related to a series of subsequent associated adverse events such as school dropout, instability in early marriage and childrearing, and high rates of divorce (Newcomb & Bentler, 1989).

Although much concern has been voiced about the issue of youthful substance abuse our social policies and intervention programs have not dealt

Children with unstable family situations, such as those of this runaway smoking crack, are vulnerable to a wide range of problem behaviors including substance abuse.

effectively with the problem. Drug-abuse rates remain high, treatment programs are not available for the majority of adolescents, and relapse rates across diverse treatment programs range from 35 to 70 percent (Newcomb & Bentler, 1989).

There is so great a co-occurrence in drug use, alcohol use, unprotected sexual intercourse, and delinquency that some investigators have argued that these behaviors involve a single syndrome of problem behavior (Jessor & Jessor, 1977). Furthermore, much controversy has surrounded the issue of whether conduct disorders differ from another narrow-band category of undercontrolled behavior disorders, usually called hyperactivity or attention deficit disorder.

ATTENTION DEFICIT/HYPERACTIVITY DISORDER

The behavior of children with *attention deficit/hyperactivity disorder* leads to difficulties in the home, classroom, and peer group (Barkley, 1990). A variety of studies have demonstrated that not only do hyperactive children run into conflict with the various adults in their environment, but they also perform more poorly in school, present classroom management problems for the teacher, have difficult peer relations, and often think of themselves as being "no good" (Ross & Ross, 1982). Perhaps even more important, for at least 60 percent of these children, some of these problems are known to persist into adolescence and early adult life (Weiss & Hechtman, 1986). Adults who have been hyperactive children often describe themselves as inattentive, restless, impulsive, depressed, and lacking in self-esteem. Attention deficit disorders occur more frequently in boys than girls and are more sustained in boys.

How does a hyperactive child differ from other children? The case of Billy presented at the beginning of the chapter provides a description of many of the problems hyperactive children encounter. Most hyperactive children, like Billy, go undiagnosed until they enter school or some similar, highly structured environment. However, this is not because their hyperactive behavior first appears around the ages of 6, 7, and 8. Like Billy, many children who are later diagnosed as hyperactive have a history of being active infants whose biological functions such as sleeping and eating were irregular and who progressed to become tireless and fearless preschoolers (Ross & Ross, 1982). Despite these early indications, hyperactivity is usually first identified in elementary school children because of the combination of the demands of the school environment and the particular cluster of problem behaviors that hyperactive children exhibit.

Clinical Features of Attention Deficit/Hyperactivity Disorder. Children with this disorder display overactivity, poor sustained attention, impulsivity, and problems with adherence to instructions and rules (Barkley, 1990). Probably the most marked symptom that parents and teachers notice about hyperactive children is their inappropriately high activity level. However, although hyperactive children do have higher levels of inappropriate activity than their normal peers, the difference between the two groups is not a simple one. Many observers have adopted the misguided notion that hyperactive and nonhyperactive children differ simply in terms of the quantity of their activity, whereas in reality the two groups differ more in the quality of their situationally appropriate activity level (Ross & Ross, 1982; Whalen, 1989). For example, research indicates that in free-play situations hyperactive children cannot be discriminated from their peers in terms of activity level (Barkley & Ullman, 1975). Activity level does discriminate the two groups in *structured* situations such as the classroom, however.

The above findings suggest one major reason that hyperactivity is usually first identified in school-age children. Although as infants and preschoolers hyperactive children are often more active than their peers, the increased structure of the school environment introduces both a more strict set of standards and more of the structured situations that are most difficult for them. The inappropriateness of the behavior of the hyperactive child becomes apparent in situations demanding controlled, task-oriented behavior. Furthermore, the behavior of the hyperactive child is likely to disturb peers and lead to further disruption of the classroom (Whalen, 1989; Whalen, Henker, Collins, Finck, & Dotemoto, 1979).

The inappropriate activity of the hyperactive child appears to diminish during adolescence; unfortunately, other clinically important problems persist through these years (Hechtman & Weiss, 1983). One of the most persistent problems that hyperactive children exhibit is *inattention*. Like hyperactivity, inattention is a particularly difficult problem for hyperactive children in school, where teachers may have to expend considerable effort to keep them interested in learning tasks (Whalen, 1989). The attentional problems of hyperactive children involve an inability to sustain attention and stay on task rather than an inability to screen out irrelevant distractions (Ross & Ross, 1982).

The third major problem experienced by some hyperactive children is *impulsivity*. Hyperactive children often seem to act before they think. Impulsivity, like inattention, appears to be a relatively stable aspect of hyperactivity; it not only can be seen in the frequent accidents of the preschooler and the poorly thought-out test answers of the school-age child, but also may continue into adult life, where more frequent changes in residence and a higher incidence of automobile accidents are found among formerly hyperactive children (Weiss, Hechtman, Perman, Hopkins, & Weiner, 1979).

It has recently been found that children with attention deficit hyperactivity disorder also have deficiencies in *rule-governed behavior*. Rules are constructed by the individual or by others such as parents or teachers to describe relationships among behavior, antecedents, and consequences. For example, "When your little brother takes one of your toys, don't hit him, or you will be sent to your room." In responding to such rules which describe contingencies—that is, what will happen if certain things occur—hyperactive children have special problems in *tracking*. Although these children may be able initially to inhibit undesirable behavior in response to a rule, they are unable to use rules to track or maintain their behavior over time (Barkley, 1990). Probably as a result of their difficulties with overactivity, inattention, impulsivity, and utilization of rules to govern their behavior, hyperactive children suffer academically. As measured by both classroom assessments and standardized achievement tests, hyperactive children typically are found to be functioning one to two years below grade level despite a normal IQ (Loney, Kramer, & Milich, 1981; Sassone, Lambert, & Sandoval, 1981). Retention in the same grade or placement in special classes is a fairly common consequence of the academic and behavioral problems of hyperactive children. Although academic problems persist throughout school for many hyperactive children, one optimistic finding is that they achieve occupational status and satisfaction that is equal to that of their peers (Weiss, et al., 1979). Perhaps this is a result of finding a job that rewards the hyperactive child's strengths and makes fewer demands in the areas of weakness.

Etiology and Treatment. What is the cause of this frustrating collection of problems and how can hyperactive children be helped? Among the potential answers to these questions, no single and unquestionable solution has been discovered. Research on this topic has been complicated because so many explanations for the etiology and treatment of hyperactivity have been offered, and some speculations test the limits of believability. Of the more credible explanations of hyperactivity, one suggests that the problem has a biological origin while the other implicates the role of the environment.

Biological Hypotheses. For years, the leading biological explanation of hyperactivity suggested that this particular cluster of problems was caused by some form of *minimal brain dysfunction*, although no brain damage or brain pathology could be detected or reliably measured among hyperactive children (Bax & MacKeith, 1963). Recent tentative evidence supports the position that in some children with attention deficit/hyperactivity disorder some brain dysfunction may occur. Different individuals respond in diverse ways to the same level of stimulation and require different levels of stimulation for optimal functioning. Some people are overreactive and may require less stimulation, others are underreactive and may seek out higher levels of stimulation. It has been suggested that attention deficit/hyperactive children are underreactive and their excessive activity and impulsive behavior are attempts to obtain more stimulation (Anastopoulos & Barkley, 1988; Whalen, 1989). This has been attributed to neurotransmitter abnormalities in the brain but this hypothesis is still speculative.

The strongest piece of evidence for some type of brain dysfunction was thought to be the paradoxical effect of *psychostimulant medication* on hyperactive children. Stimulant medications—such as amphetamines—are known to increase alertness in adults and are sometimes legally or illegally used to heighten arousal, increase energy, and combat fatigue. Paradoxically, "speed," as this class of medications is commonly referred to in street language, has consistently been found to slow hyperactive children down. In fact, psychostimulants are a common treatment for the disorder. This apparently paradoxical effect of psychostimulants on hyperactive children was taken as further evidence of the brain damage or dysfunction that was thought to characterize these children (Whalen & Henker, 1976).

A very important piece of data was missing, however. No one knew what the effects of psychostimulants were on normal children because it was deemed unethical to conduct an experiment to find out. It seems ironic that ethics prevented the testing of even a few "normal" children's responses to psychostimulants but did not prevent physicians from prescribing these drugs to hundreds of thousands of "abnormal" hyperactive children. A carefully planned study finally tested this obviously important question. Rapoport and her colleagues (Rapoport et al., 1978) obtained permission from a group of scientists working for the National Institutes of Mental Health to give experimental dosages of psychostimulants to their normal children. The results have proven to be extremely important. As measured by behavioral observations and a wide variety of laboratory tasks, psychostimulants were found to have the same effect on normal children as they do on hyperactives. The medication appears to increase attention and, as a result, reduce extraneous activity. This effect, in fact, appears to be the same result that is seen when adults are given *small* dosages of stimulant medications; thus the paradoxical effect appears not to be paradoxical after all.

As a result of studies such as this, the minimal brain dysfunction hypothesis has been abandoned by most researchers in the field (Rutter, 1982; Whalen, 1989). Other biological hypotheses appear more credible at this time. For example, although the potential benefits of the Feingold diet, a diet restricting the intake of food additives, appear to have been greatly exaggerated by its proponents, a small subgroup of children may become hyperactive in response to food additives (Conners, 1980). Other investigators have found subclinically elevated blood levels of lead in some hyperactive children and have suggested that this may sometimes be the cause of hyperactivity (David, Hoffman, Sverd, & Clark, 1977). Lead poisoning is known to cause serious intellectual and behavioral difficulties among children (Chaiklin, 1979), although it may be that rather than increased lead causing hyperactivity, hyperactive children may be more likely to ingest lead.

At present, perhaps the most popular biological hypothesis is that hyperactivity is a genetic disorder. Evidence suggests that activity level is more similar among normal monozygotic than dizygotic twin pairs, although this finding does not necessarily extend to hyperactivity, nor does it rule out environmental influences. The critical adoption studies needed to test the genetic hypotheses simply have not been done (Ross & Ross, 1982).

Psychological Hypotheses. As an alternative to biological explanations of hyperactivity, some researchers have suggested that hyperactivity is environmentally caused. Diverse social and familial stressors such as poverty, low education, marital discord and disruption, household disorganization, and inept parenting have been associated with attention deficit/hyperactivity disorder (Campbell, Breux, Ewing, & Szumowski, 1986; Goodman & Stevenson, 1989; Rutter, 1989). Much of the research has focused on parent-child relations and it has been found that the mothers of hyperactive children generally are more controlling and intrusive and less affectionate and reinforcing than the mothers of normal children, and this may be related to their children's behavior (Mash & Johnston, 1982; Goodman & Stevenson, 1989). The question arises, however, as to whether the mothers' behavior is a cause of, or a reaction to, the hyperactivity.

A number of different researchers have developed a clever method of testing this question (Barkley & Cunningham, 1979; Humphries, Kinsbourne, & Swanson, 1978). What these researchers have done is to compare the interactions of hyperactive child-mother dyads when the children are on psychostimulant medication with times when the children are merely taking placebos, sugar pills with no active ingredients. Since the psychostimulant directly affects the child's behavior, any differences in mother-child interaction between the two conditions suggest that mothers are reacting to the difficult behavior of the hyperactive child, not causing it. This, in fact, is exactly what the research suggests. When their children were on medication, mothers of hyperactives were found to interact with them much differently than when the children were off medication (Barkley & Cunningham, 1979; Humphries et al., 1978). During the medication condition, the hyperactive child-mother dyads were similar to normal child-mother pairs. Although this research once again underlines the importance of children's influences on adults, reciprocal influence in mother–hyperactive child interactions should not be ignored. While a mother's intrusive, nonreinforcing behavior may initially be a reaction to a hyperactive child, that reaction probably serves to exacerbate the child's problems and it seems worthwhile to direct at least some efforts toward altering mother-child interactions.

If there are problems with both the biological and environmental explanations of the cause of hyperactivity, what is the cause of this disorder? The best answer is that there is no one cause; rather, hyperactivity appears to be a heterogeneous disorder with multiple causes. Brain damage can cause hyperactivity in some instances, and genetics, lead poisoning, and dietary agents eventually may be shown to explain other cases. It also seems likely that some children's hyperactivity is caused by the environment in which they are reared. At present, it is not possible to determine the cause of hyperactivity for any one individual child, nor can it be predicted what treatment the child will respond to best. Two treatments—psychostimulant medication and behavior therapy—appear to hold the most promise, however.

Treatments for Hyperactivity. At this point, there is little doubt that psychostimulant medication improves the behavior of about 75 percent of all hyperactive children, at least in the short term (Cantwell, 1980). This improvement is quite rapid and noticeable to parents and teachers, who quickly become advocates of medication. Hyperactive children become less impulsive, oppositional, and disruptive and more attentive and manageable when on medication, and to say this is a relief to some tired and worried parents is an understatement (Dulcan, 1986; Hinshaw, Henker, Whalen, Erhardt, & Dunnington, 1989; Whalen, Henker, & Granger, 1990; Whalen & Henker, 1991). The impact of psychostimulants is so dramatic that it is estimated that between 1 and 2 percent of American schoolchildren are currently taking the drugs.

On the other hand, there are many observers who object to the use of psychostimulant medications with hyperactive children. Objections range from the philosophical stance that altering children's behavior with drugs is inappropriate (Maynard, 1970) to questions about the side effects of psychostimulants such as a suppression in the rate of physical growth, irritability, insomnia, weight loss, and abdominal pain (Dulcan, 1986).

Perhaps the most critical objections to treating hyperactive children with medication are concerned with just what changes psychostimulants are effective at bringing about. While short-term improvements in behavior and on cognitive and academic performance have been demonstrated (Richardson, Kupretz, Winsberg, Maitinsky, & Wendell, 1988), it is asked whether stimulants produce long-run benefits. In fact, available evidence suggests that the beneficial effects of psychostimulants for hyperactive children appear to be primarily limited to short-term improvements in behavior. Hyperactive children who are placed on medication are no better off in the long run than hyperactive children who never receive it (Jacobvitz, Sroufe, Stewart, & Leffert, 1990).

The major alternative treatment available for hyperactivity is *behavior therapy*, a psychological intervention that is based on social learning principles. In traditional behavior therapy programs, parents and teachers are taught to identify and monitor various specific, troublesome aspects of the hyperactive child's behavior (for example, not completing class assignments on time) and to systematically reward the child for making improvements in the targeted problem area. This might be done with the aid of a *daily report card* on which parents or teachers monitor and record the child's behavior. In related behavior therapy programs, teachers and parents also work directly with the child in an attempt to teach cognitive self-control strategies (Barkley, 1990; Kendall & Braswell, 1985).

Considerable evidence has been gathered that supports the short-term effectiveness of behavior therapy in changing both the behavior and the academic success of hyperactive children (O'Leary, 1980). Because the side effects are fewer, some professionals advocate this approach as an alternative to medication. Behavior therapy has its own problems, however. For one, it requires more effort on the part of parents and teachers than does medication, and this increased effort sometimes produces less dramatic change in the child's behavior than does medication (Gittelman et al., 1980). Further, there has been no demonstration that behavior therapy leads to long-term improvement in the hyperactive child's functioning. Clearly, the search for ways to further improve the treatments for hyperactivity needs to continue. In the meantime, medication, behavior therapy, or a combination of the two can provide at least short-term benefits.

Overcontrolled Disorders

Whereas undercontrolled childhood disorders like hyperactivity and conduct problems are identified by the negative impact they have on the environment, it is the adverse effect on the child that *overcontrolled disorders* share in common. Various negative emotions such as anxiety, fears, and sadness characterize this broad-band classification. Children with excessive fears or sadness seem overcontrolled in the manner in which they relate to others; they do not fit the ideal of the happy, spontaneous child. Although excessive fears may cause considerable discomfort for the child and the family, research suggests that there is room for optimism in this area of developmental psychopathology. Although treatment may speed the process, evidence indicates that 80 percent of children's phobias are alleviated within two years even without treatment (Hampe, Noble, Miller, & Barrett, 1973). Furthermore, early problems associated with anxiety and social withdrawal, unlike undercontrolled disorders, generally are not predictive of adjustment problems during adult life (Robins, 1979). In contrast, depression appears to be more persistent.

If it is difficult to define what should be considered an undercontrolled disorder, it is even more troublesome to identify overcontrolled problems. Since the definition of childhood psychopathology depends on an adult's social judgment, and because it is much more difficult for adults to evaluate children's inner feelings (like sadness) than it is to judge their overt behavior (like aggression), the narrow-band diagnostic categories for overcontrolled disorders are often quite vague and controversial.

Questions that could be raised about most of the narrow-band categories of overcontrolled disorders apply to a particular intriguing and controversial disorder of overcontrol: childhood depression. This topic is discussed below as an illustration of one type of overcontrolled psychological disorder of childhood.

DEPRESSION IN CHILDHOOD

Before addressing some of the research and controversy concerning childhood depression, it is important to define this term carefully. The word "depression" is popularly used as a synonym for feelings of sadness, loneliness, or "the blues." In its clinical use, on the other hand, the term has a much more specific meaning. In order to be judged clinically depressed, not only must an adult or child experience extreme sadness or *affective* disturbance, but there also must be changes in these individuals' cognitive functioning and in their behavior. Some of these behavioral symptoms include insomnia, changes in appetite and weight, agitation or slowing down in motor activity, apathy or loss of pleasure in usual activity (for example, a decrease in sexual activity in adults), or loss of energy. Possible changes in cognitive functioning include guilt and feelings of worthlessness, complaints about inability to concentrate, slowed thinking, recurrent thoughts of death, and speculations about suicide. It is plain that clinical depression involves more than what usually is meant when people say they are "feeling down" or depressed.

Considerable disagreement can be found in the discussions of childhood depression. It has even been argued that because of immature cognitive and personality development, it is not possible for children to be clinically depressed, or at least that it may be impossible for younger children to experience depressive disorders in the same manner as adults do.

Most clinicians and researchers agree, however, that some form of childhood depression exists; they just don't agree on what it is (Kazdin, 1989). One controversy about childhood depression involves whether or not it is possible to determine accurately when children are experiencing the affective, cognitive, and behavioral disturbances that constitute clinical depression (Lefkowitz & Burton, 1978; Kazdin, 1989; Cantwell, 1990). Many of the symptoms of depression such as appetite and sleep disturbances occur with such a high frequency among children as to be considered developmentally normal events (Lefkowitz & Burton, 1978), and other events such as crying do not carry the same significance for children as they do for adults (Cicchetti & Poggep-Hesse, 1981). Furthermore, there are questions about how aware children of different ages are of their inner lives. Moreover, if they are aware of unpleasant feelings and thoughts, can children label these states and accurately describe their feelings to an adult? Can a preschool child tell you that he or she is depressed? Some research indicates that 5-year-old children rarely admit to being sad, whereas 6- and 7-year-old children more commonly recognize the emotion in themselves, suggesting that the transition from preoperational thought to the stage of concrete operations is related to children's awareness of, and reports on, their inner feelings (Glasberg & Aboud, 1982). Even among 6- to 13-year-old children hospitalized for depression there is little agreement between parents' and children's reports on the degree of sadness the child is experiencing (Kazdin, French, & Unis, 1983).

The increase with age in the frequency of the diagnosis of depression among children probably reflects both the difficulty in making the diagnosis among younger children and the fact that depressive disorder is experienced at its fullest only when the child's cognitive capacities reach the stage of formal operations. At noted in Figure 17-2, depression is rarely diagnosed among inpatient or outpatient samples of children under the age of 10, but the diagnosis rises dramatically in frequency during adolescence and adult life. Indeed, in contrast to its rarity during childhood, depressive disorder is so frequent among adults as to be referred to as "the common cold of psychopathology" (Seligman, 1973).

One unfortunate consequence of the increased rate of depression during adolescence is a concomitant increase in the rate of suicide. Although suicide is very rare among children under the age of 10 (Cantor, 1983), it is estimated to be the third leading killer of adolescents, following only accidents and homicide as a cause of death. Furthermore, the suicide rate among older adolescents has tripled in the past three decades. A recent study reported that 20 percent of high school students were suicidal (Rubenstein, Huren, Horssman, Rubin, & Stockler, 1988), and that 75 percent of these students had received no intervention in the year following their suicide attempts. The most notable increases in successful suicides have been in males, particularly in white males. However, attempted suicides are much more common in females than in males. Females more often use passive methods of suicide such as overdoses of drugs or poisons, whereas males prefer to use active methods such as hanging, shooting, or explosives. Active methods are much more successful than passive methods.

Although childhood depression is of increasing concern to clinicians, its diagnosis is relatively unreliable.

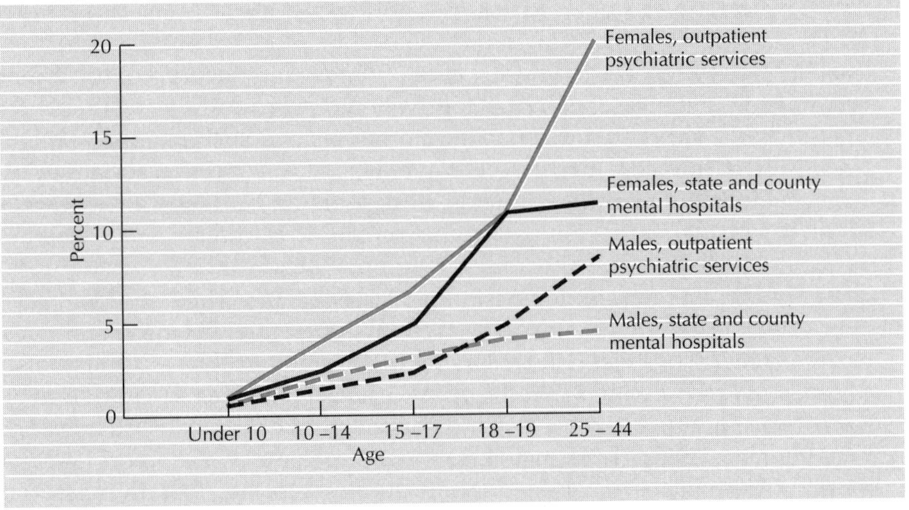

FIGURE 17-2

Percent of patients with psychoneurotic depressive reaction in psychiatric clinics and hospitals. From data in Mental Health Statistical Note No. 148 (1978) and Outpatient Psychiatric Services (1969). (*Source*: Weiner, I. B. (1982). *Psychopathology from infancy through adolescence*, p. 267. New York: Wiley.)

Basically, suicide is related to a general sense of overwhelming hopelessness, although it also may result from the accumulation of adverse life events such as family conflicts; loss of a family member due to illness, death, or divorce; breakups or problems in romantic relationships or friendships; school failure; being apprehended in a delinquent, forbidden, or embarrassing act or situation; or real or imagined mental or physical illness (Miller, Chiles, & Barnes, 1982; Cohen, Sandler, Bermann, & King, 1982). Adolescents who attempt suicide often feel they have no source of emotional support. They frequently are alienated from their families and may have had disruptions or losses in intimate relations and relations with peers that give them an increasing sense of isolation and helplessness.

Although not all teenagers who commit suicide alert others to their intentions, many do. Table 17-4 lists the reasons for attempting suicide that were given by eleven children of different ages. Any threats of suicide should be listened to and taken seriously, and if necessary, concrete action to prevent it must be taken regardless of the child's age.

TABLE 17-4

REASONS GIVEN FOR SUICIDE ATTEMPT

AGE (YEARS)	REASON GIVEN FOR SUICIDE ATTEMPT
5.2	"To be with my dead brother, so my mother will love me like she still loves him."
7.6	"So I won't get the cane from my father."
9.0	"I'm better off dead."
9.3	"To sleep for a long time . . . to get peace."
11.0	"The voice told me to kill myself so I won't kill my baby sister."
11.4	"Everybody blames me."
11.8	"I'm a burden on the family."
11.10	"The devil is in me."
11.11	"I'm just hopeless."
12.4	"I'm angry."
12.7	"I'm sad and I'm angry."

Source: Kosky (1983).

Social/Psychological Theories. One of the earliest theories of the causes of depression linked it to maternal deprivation or loss (Bowlby, 1960). Although research has supported this position, other factors, such as parental conflict, maternal depression, negative life events, lack of effective social supports, and, especially for girls, problems with peers and unpopularity have been linked with depression in children (Compas & Hamman, 1992; Downey & Coyner, 1990; Miller, Birnbaum, & Durbin, 1990).

The link between depression in parents and children has received considerable attention in the recent research literature. Children of depressed parents are not only at risk for having higher rates of depression but also for higher rates of a wide range of other disorders such as separation anxiety, academic failure, attention deficit disorders, and conduct disorders (Compas & Hamman, 1992; Weissman, Leckman, Merekangas, Gammon, & Prusoff, 1984). Although twin and adoption studies indicate that this association between depression in children and parents may be in part genetic, other studies show that the experiences of children with a depressed mother may differ from those with a nondepressed mother. Depressed mothers are more tense, disorganized, resentful, and ambivalent, and less responsive, communicative, and affectionate with their children (Radke-Yarrow, Cummings, Kuczynski, & Chapman, 1985). Furthermore they are more likely to perceive their children's behavior in a negative fashion. It is not surprising then that children of depressed mothers are more likely to be insecurely attached, fearful, lower in self-esteem, and to have problems in subsequent social relations (Downey & Coyner, 1990; Radke-Yarrow et al., 1985).

Cognitive Theories. An alternative theoretical explanation of depression is that it results from *learned helplessness* (Seligman, 1974). According to this view, depression results from the helplessness one feels at being unable to control the outcome of relevant events in one's life. Throughout this book we have emphasized that one of the developmental cornerstones of both cognitive and social competence is the development of a sense of self-efficacy, of an internal locus of control. However, the learned helplessness theory of depression proposes that not only must depressed people experience helplessness, but they also must attribute their failures in controlling the world to enduring personal problems or shortcomings. Essentially, then, learned helplessness is a cognitive theory asserting that depression results from the perception of being personally responsible for failing to succeed in achieving desired outcomes (Nolen-Holksema, Guigus, & Seligman, 1986).

Biological Theories. As with most psychological theories, biological theories of the cause of depression have focused more on adults than on children. Although a causal role has not been demonstrated, evidence has linked depression among adults with low levels of chemicals that facilitate the transmission of neural impulses; however, similar biochemical evidence has not been consistently obtained in depressed children (Burke & Puig-Antioch, 1990). Also, the use of antidepressant drugs with children has not been consistently associated with beneficial effects (Burke & Puig-Antioch, 1990). Finally, there is evidence that children of depressed parents are at an increased risk not just for developing depression but for developing a variety of behavior disorders (Beardslee, Bemporad, Keller, & Klerman, 1983). The relative contributions of family interaction and genetic influences remain an open question.

Children and adolescents with depressive disorders benefit from a wide range of interventions and respond more favorably to psychosocial and psychotherapeutic interventions than do children with conduct disorders.

In general, research on the etiology and treatment of childhood depression is in the very early stages. As is the case with most of the narrow-band overcontrolled disorders, sound research on etiology and treatment must await the development of better definitions of the disorders. In the area of childhood depression, such definitions must take into account children's differing behavioral, emotional, and cognitive capacities at various stages of development.

Pervasive Developmental Disorders

Although the problems of hyperactivity, delinquency, and depression are serious, some children exhibit even more marked forms of disturbance. The term *pervasive developmental disorders* is used to categorize these extremely disturbed children. Some researchers have referred to this category of psychopathology as *childhood psychoses,* indicating that the subjects are out of touch with reality. The disturbances found among these children are even more general and incapacitating than those in most psychoses, however, because the pervasive developmental disorders are characterized by gross deficits in many areas of cognitive, emotional, and social development.

Pervasive developmental disorders have often been confused with another serious emotional problem, schizophrenia. *Schizophrenia* is a common and seriously incapacitating disorder that, like the pervasive developmental disorders, is characterized by loss of contact with reality; thus, both disorders have been considered to be psychoses. The symptoms of the two problems are quite different, however; schizophrenia is characterized by hallucinations, delusions, and other thought disorders that are not found in the pervasive developmental disorders. Furthermore, the two problems have very different ages of onset. The pervasive developmental disorders begin in the first few years of life, whereas schizophrenia most commonly begins in later adolescence or early adult life. Thus, schizophrenia is not a narrow-band subcategory of the pervasive developmental disorders, and it is not a disorder that is found with any great frequency among children.

INFANTILE AUTISM

The mostly widely recognized of the pervasive developmental disorders is *infantile autism.* Children with this disorder were first identified by psychiatrist Leo Kanner (1943), who noted many of the most puzzling and disturbing characteristics of autism. These features include (1) *extreme autistic aloneness,* a lack of interest in other people that in some cases appears almost to be experienced as an aversion to contact with other human beings; (2) various *language abnormalities;* and (3) and intense *desire to preserve sameness* in the environment.

It is difficult to imagine just how disturbed an autistic child is, but once you have observed one of these unfortunate children the memory will last forever. If two autistic children are placed side by side in a room full of toys, chances are that they will ignore each other and most of the toys; these children seem to be living in a world much different from our own. In their aloneness, autistic children seem to prefer inanimate objects to human interaction. A failure to use eye contact and to modulate social interaction is a frequently observed feature of the disorder, and autistic children often appear to be unaware of people or even of themselves (see Box 17-3). However, studies using subtle measures of attending, such as heart rate, show that autistic children are aware of the presence of other people although this may not be reflected in their overt behavior. This disruption in social behavior also is found in a lack of attachment behavior and empathy in social relations, although attachment behaviors that seem normal appear in a small subgroup of autistic children (Sigman & Mundy, 1989).

Communication deficits constitute one of the most incapacitating problems autistic children face. These communication deficits are found both in nonverbal and verbal communication in autistic children. They have difficulty in understanding facial emotional expressions and in integrating or using instrumental gestures such as those meaning "be quiet" or "come here" or pointing gestures indicating "look" or "over there" (Hobson, 1989; Attwood, Frith, & Hermelin, 1985). In addition, about half of autistic children never develop meaningful, useful speech, and most others have limited and sometimes bizarre means of verbal expression. The development of useful speech by age 5 is the best predictor of adult outcome (Kanner, 1973). *Echolalia* is one frequent language problem found among autistic children who are not mute (Roberts, 1989). Echolalic children will repeat what is said to them, sometimes over and over again. It you were to ask an echolalic child, "What is your name?" the reply would be "What is your name?" Pronoun reversals are another common language problem found in autism. Autistic children often refer to themselves as "you" and to others as "I." Even when autistic children have acquired speech they often do not use it effectively for social communication. Autistic children rarely "chat" or respond to the verbal comments of other people (Baron-Cohen, 1988).

Many autistic children learn to master only a few of the tasks necessary to function in the world and need constant help with feeding, dressing, toileting, and cleaning. Autistic children spend much of their time engaging in *obsessive self-stimulatory behavior* such as repetitively spinning objects,

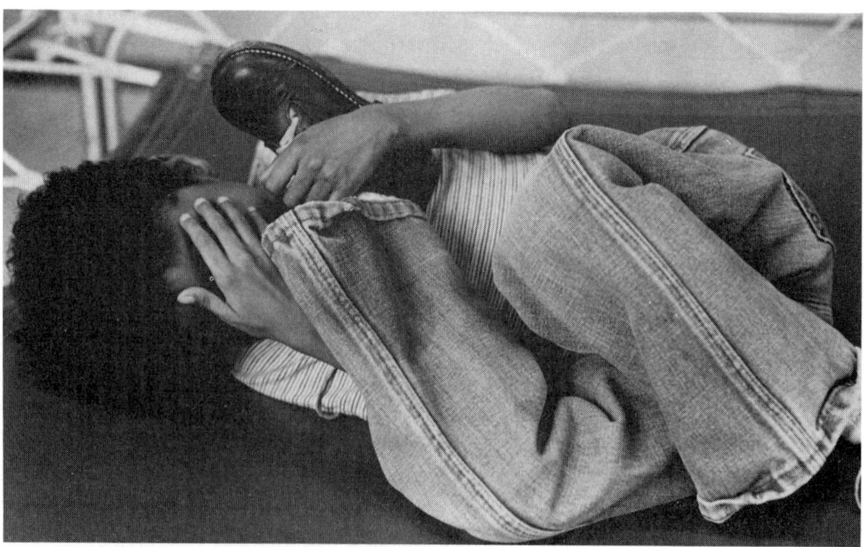

Extreme autistic aloneness in a young autistic child.

BOX 17-3 SELF-RECOGNITION OF AUTISTIC CHILDREN

The apparent lack of social awareness that autistic children frequently demonstrate may be so profound in some instances as to extend to a lack of awareness of themselves. That is, some autistic children not only may treat other people simply as additional objects in their environment but also may not be aware of themselves as independent social beings. Children without severely incapacitating disorders like autism or mental retardation develop the ability to recognize themselves around the age of 2. Do autistic children show deficits in self-recognition ability?

Donna Spiker and Margaret Ricks (1984) tested the self-recognition capacity of fifty-two autistic children who were 12 years old and younger. Because, for reasons that should be obvious, they did not want to rely on a task requiring verbal instruction, these investigators employed a procedure that has been used as a test of self-recognition in infants and toddlers. In this test, under the pretext of wiping the child's nose clean, the experimenter unobtrusively smears green makeup on the face of the child being tested. Children are then shown their image in a mirror. Children who touch their own (green) noses upon seeing the mirror image are thought to have the ability to recognize themselves; those who reach for the mirror image or who do not respond do not have self-recognition ability.

What did Spiker and Ricks find among the autistic children they tested? Fully 31 percent of the autistic children did not demonstrate recognition of their mirror image. Self-recognition ability was strongly related to the child's level of communicative speech: those children who demonstrated at least some communicative speech were much more likely to wipe their noses upon seeing the mirror image than were those children who had no communicative speech. However, even those autistic children who showed evidence of self-recognition demonstrated little emotional response during the task. Normal children of ages similar to those of the tested autistic children typically will respond with giggling when they see their green noses in the mirror, and will say something like "you tricked me." The autistic children had no such reactions. The social impairments of these children appear to be so great as to include disturbances in their concepts of themselves as social beings.

Source: Spiker, D., & Ricks, M. (1984). Visual self-recognition in autistic children: Developmental variations. *Child Development*, **55**, 214–225.

switching lights on and off, or flapping their hands in front of their eyes (Newsom, Hovanitz, & Rincover, 1988). While their senses function adequately when tested, autistic children behave as if they had sensory deficits. Thus, the major purpose of this bizarre-appearing behavior may be to provide sensory stimulation.

Whether autistic children are of normal, below-average, or superior intelligence has been the topic of much discussion. Kanner and others have suggested that autistic children have normal or even superior intelligence that is hidden beneath a blanket of psychopathology. Several pieces of circumstantial evidence support this speculation. The parents of autistic children are somewhat more likely to have higher than average IQs (Cantwell, Baker, & Trutter, 1978), and the normal physical appearance and motor development of the child does distinguish autism from many forms of mental retardation. Furthermore, some autistic children show what is called *idiot savant* capacities: They may have peculiar talents, particularly mathematical ones, such as being able to quickly and accurately predict the day of the week that some future date will fall on. (Is August 30, 1997, a Tuesday?) Some autistic children show remarkable memory in being able to repeat television commercials verbatim or to sing operatic arias or complete musical scores. Despite such indications that the psychological problems of some autistic children may shroud a superior intelligence, most autistic children would score as mentally retarded on psychological tests. About 70 percent of all autistic children score in the retarded range on measures of intelligence, and this below-average performance is quite stable over time (Rutter & Schopler, 1987).

In view of the problems autistic children have in social relations it is not surprising that recent research (Baron-Cohen, 1989; Perner, Frith, Leslie, & Leekman, 1989) indicates that some of the cognitive deficits of autistic children are found in what we described in Chapter 10 as metacognition and what others have called a "theory of mind." These children are unable to understand that mental states such as knowledge, beliefs and expectancies exist and are connected to people's behavior. This lack of a theory of mind or deficiencies in metacognition makes it difficult for autistic children to anticipate and predict the responses of others and interferes with appropriate social actions.

Etiology and Treatment. At present the cause of infantile autism is unknown. Some investigators, including Kanner himself, originally suggested that the cause might be of psychological origin and attributed the disorder to parents who were cold and aloof. Parents of autistic children have been described as "refrigerator parents" who just thawed out long enough to conceive an autistic child. Such assertions are unfounded and have tended to create unnecessary guilt and anxiety among the parents of autistic children. If these parents are somewhat distant from their children, it is much more likely to be a reaction to their child's social aversion than a cause of the disorder. Furthermore, the onset of the disorder comes so early in life, and other children have been found to be so resilient even in the face of catastrophic environmental events, that it hardly seems likely that a disorder as severe as autism could be caused by parents' "unconscious rejection" of their child.

Currently, it is almost universally accepted that autism has a biological cause that has yet to be specified. Genetics have been partially implicated by Folstein and Rutter (1977), who found that in four of eleven monozygotic twins both children had autism, while there was no case of both twins being autistic in dizygotic twins. In addition, a larger percent of families (2 percent) than would be expected by chance have two or more autistic children. Furthermore, parents and siblings of autistic children show more problems in cognition and language than are found in the general population (Genetic evidence, 1989; Folstein & Rutter, 1988). Biological dysfunction is also suggested by the fact that the fragile-X chromosome, brain damage, metabolic disturbance, and abnormally high levels of the neurotransmitter serotonin have been found in some autistic children (Folstein & Rutter, 1988; Gilberg, 1990). Still, the exact nature of the cause or causes of autism is unclear.

To date, autism has proven to be a discouraging disorder to treat. Although the use of medication, especially medication targeted at the reduction of the neurotransmitter serotonin, in the treatment of autistic children has increased, benefits of medication are not consistently obtained and such treatment is often accompanied by adverse side effects (Campbell & Spencer, 1988). Of the host of treatments that have been tried, operant behavior therapy appears to be most effective (Lovaas, 1987; Lovaas & Smith, 1988), but this is a time-consuming treatment producing change that may help the children in day-to-day functioning but usually still leaves them performing well out of the range of normal development (Rutter, 1983). By carefully monitoring the autistic child's behavior and by systematically rewarding appropriate behavior with such rewards as food, behavior therapy programs have been quite successful in teaching autistic children basic self-care skills. Such techniques have not been as successful in the teaching of generalizable language skills, however. While autistic children show improvement in their functional language as a result of behavior therapy programs, the process is often painfully slow. Furthermore, some of the autistic children who do learn words never seem to acquire the *meaning* of language (Cantwell et al., 1978). That is, they never generate new word combinations, and their new vocabulary and other therapeutic gains can quickly deteriorate if the children move from their highly structured teaching environment (Lovaas, Young, & Newsom, 1978). Teaching sign language rather than verbal language, intervening at earlier ages, and involving parents in training programs are alternatives that show some promise (Carr, 1979; Lovaas, 1987).

A recent study involving behavioral intervention offered evidence that an intensive program of one-to-one behavior modification directed at parents and their autistic children who were under the age of 4 at the start of the program could help some autistic children (Lovaas, 1987; Lovaas & Smith, 1988). The outcome of this intensive program involving forty hours a week of treatment for two or more years (Group I) was compared to the outcomes for a group of autistic children who received only ten hours a week of treatment (Group II) and a group who received no treatment (Group III). Although the children in the three groups had similar IQ scores with less than 10 percent scoring in the normal range before treatment, as can be seen in Table 17-5, after the intervention, the intensive treatment group had made considerable gain in intellectual functioning in comparison to the other two groups. In addition a follow-up showed that some of these gains were sustained into early adolescence (Lovaas, Smith, & McEachin, 1989).

While behavior therapy may not be the solution to all of the problems of the autistic child, it does offer these children the opportunity to develop many more skills than they would otherwise acquire, and the prognosis of autism without treatment is gloomy. Kanner himself noted that of ninety-six children diagnosed by him as autistic before 1953, only 10 percent had what was considered to be a good outcome—they could live independently (Kanner, 1973). The remainder required special care in institutions or other protected settings. These percentages are similar to those that have been found by other researchers (Lotter, 1978). Unfortunately, even what is called a "good" outcome, while a dramatic change, is far from the sort of life that most of us would consider to be ideal.

Despite the incapacitating symptoms and the pessimistic prognosis, there is one very positive aspect about infantile autism. It is rare. Only 2 to 4 children in every 10,000 are diagnosed as being autistic (Folstein & Rutter, 1988).

TABLE 17-5

EDUCATIONAL PLACEMENT AND AVERAGE IQ SCORE AT FOLLOW-UP IN THE LOVAAS INTENSIVE TREATMENT PROGRAM

	PERCENT OF CHILDREN COMPLETING REGULAR FIRST GRADE	PERCENT OF CHILDREN IN LANGUAGE-HANDICAPPED AND LEARNING-DISABLED CLASS	PERCENT OF CHILDREN IN FIRST GRADE FOR AUTISTIC-RETARDED
Group I (intensive)	47 IQ: 107	42 IQ: 70	11 IQ: 30
Group II (10 hours)	0	42 IQ: 74	58 IQ: 36
Group III (no treatment)	5 99	48 IQ: 67	48 IQ: 44

Adapted from Lovaas (1987).

THE TREATMENT OF DEVELOPMENTAL PSYCHOPATHOLOGIES

A parent seeking help for a child with a psychological problem may receive very different advice on what constitutes the appropriate treatment of the child. The treatment suggestions that mental health professionals make depend, in part, on their diagnosis of the problem; but since the diagnosis of developmental psychopathology is imprecise, treatment recommendations also are influenced by the clinicians' different theoretical views on the cause and treatment of the disorders. Although the variety of different treatments that have been tried as methods of intervening with disturbed children are far too numerous to attempt to describe here, the goals of five commonly used approaches will be briefly characterized; medication, play therapy, behavior therapy, family therapy, and community psychology.

Medication

Of the various *psychoactive medications* that have been used to treat abnormal behavior in children, by far, the most commonly used drugs are *psychostimulants*. As has already been discussed, psychostimulants have repeatedly been demonstrated to produce dramatic short-term improvements in the behavior of hyperactive children, although there is little evidence supporting their effectiveness in improving academic performance or producing long-term results (Campbell & Spencer, 1988).

In addition to noting limitations in its effectiveness, mental health professionals have voiced concern about the side effects of psychostimulant medication. Perhaps the cause of greatest concern is the observation that a suppression of growth can occur with long-term use of the drug. When use of the drug is discontinued, however, there appears to be a "growth rebound," that is, a period of rapid growth during which the child catches up with peers (Conners & Werry, 1979). A more subtle potential side effect of psychostimulants in the treatment of hyperactivity concerns the children's attributions for their improved behavior. Some hyperactive children seem to attribute their behavioral improvement to the drug rather than to themselves (Whalen, 1989; Whalen & Henker, 1976). "I didn't take my pill today" is not an uncommon answer to a teacher's inquiry about why the child had such a bad day in class.

Concerns about effectiveness and side effects notwithstanding, perhaps the two most controversial issues about the use of medication are philosophical and political. First, should drugs be used to alter children's behavior when there is no firm evidence to indicate that the disturbance is a result of a disease process? This issue subtly pervades the research on hyperactivity and, in many respects, underlies the debate as to whether hyperactivity and conduct disorders are different problems. If hyperactivity is viewed as a distinct disorder, the hidden implication often is that it is a "disease," and therefore, it is appropriate to treat the disease with drugs. If a hyperactive child is seen as just another "brat," on the other hand, it would seem that drug treatment is inappropriate. Second, there are a disproportionate number of minority and economically deprived children who are subjected to drug treatment. In view of what we know about the importance of "the eye of the beholder" in labeling behavior as deviant, this is a concern in the use of drug treatment. Ultimately, whether or not psychostimulants or other drugs should be used to alter children's behavior is a decision that parents must make for their own children. Mental health professionals can best help by informing them of the state of the art and of the available alternative treatments.

Play Therapy

Play therapy is a form of psychotherapy that is used with young children in response to their limited ability to express themselves verbally. In play therapy, children are encouraged to participate in free play with toys provided by the therapist. Often toys thought to be symbolically important are available—mommy and daddy dolls, for example. In psychoanalytic play therapy, the child's play is viewed in much the same way as free association is seen in psychoanalysis with adults: as an expression of the child's unconscious impulses and conflicts that gives the therapist a window into the child's unconscious mind. The therapist's goal in play therapy is to help the child gain insight into his or her unconscious psychodynamics through the process of interpretation of the play. More recently, some psychoanalytically oriented therapists have been broadening their treatment to include mother-child dyads (Stern, 1985), and a few rare analysts have even included home visits, education about development, and supportive services for at-risk parents and children (Laney, 1990; Musick, Clark, & Cohler, 1981; Fraiberg, Lieberman, Pekarsky, & Paul, 1981), in addition to play therapy.

Although there is very little evidence that psychoanalytic play therapy is an effective treatment in isolation, many clinicians agree that play, especially in combination with other interventions, can be an effective therapeutic tool. For most nonanalytically oriented clinicians, however, the goal of play therapy is not to help the child gain emotional insight, but to act as a means of building a trusting relationship with the child. Few can argue that play would not be helpful in achieving that important goal.

Behavior Therapy

Behavior therapy is not a single approach to intervening with children and families. Instead, the term refers to a collection of different treatment techniques that have been derived from the principles of social learning and

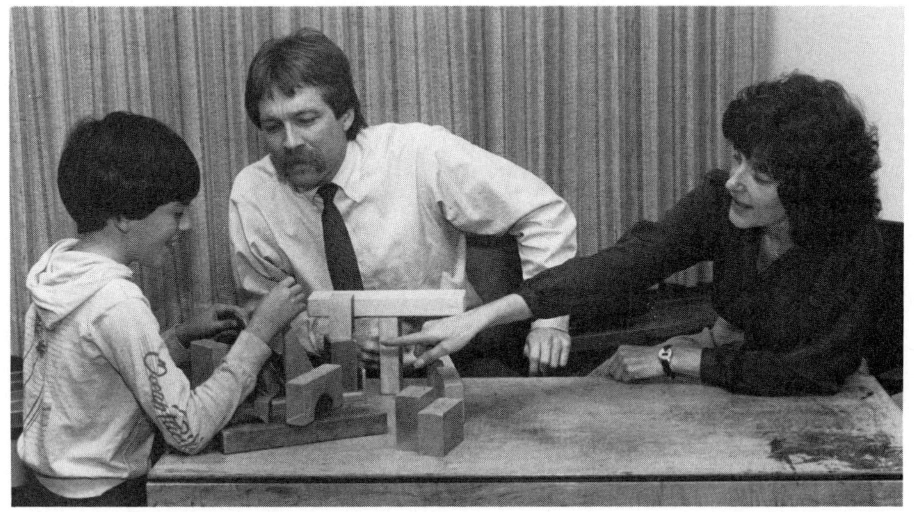

Sometimes structured family-interaction tasks, such as this building task, are used to gain an understanding of family relationships before beginning either behavior therapy or family therapy.

from the operant learning laboratories. One behavior therapy technique mentioned earlier is the daily report card, a system that allows schoolteachers to give parents daily feedback on their child's behavior in the classroom. Operant conditioning provides the crucial rationale for this technique, enabling the child's parents, in turn, to provide the child with positive reinforcement for achieving clearly specified behavioral goals.

The basic goal of behavior therapy is to teach the child new ways of behaving through changing the environment, teaching new skills, or changing cognitive and emotional processes. In teaching children and changing the environment, behavior therapists not only rely on operant conditioning but also use techniques based on classical conditioning, modeling, and cognitive processing. In general, behavior therapists can be applauded for carefully studying the effectiveness of their therapeutic interventions, and evidence suggests that behavior therapy procedures have proven to be useful in treating a variety of psychological disorders in children (Ross, 1978; Myers & Cohen, 1990).

Family Therapy

Family therapy is a treatment that is being used with increasing frequency as an intervention with children and their families. In family therapy, all relevant family members, not just the child, meet together with a therapist in an attempt to resolve their problems. Family therapists do not believe that psychological problems of childhood occur in isolation; rather, they see a child's behavior as an expression of a more general family disruption (Gurman & Kniskern, 1980). The child is viewed as a part of a *family system*, and presumably the child's behavior problem is an indication that something is wrong with the entire system, not just the child. Family therapists, therefore, view individual childhood psychopathologies as being ''symptoms'' that serve to cover up underlying family disturbances.

Functionally, the symptoms expressed by the child are thought to serve to maintain an equilibrium in the family. When the ''symptom'' is removed, it may precipitate a distressing crisis and a need to reorganize and restabilize the family system. For example, a passive father may gain vicarious gratification out of a child's aggressive assaults and verbal abuse on his dominant, sarcastic wife. If the child becomes less aggressive, the father may become more anxious and angry, and conflict between the husband and wife may escalate. In such cases, just when the child's behavior is improving, the parents may insist on the family's withdrawal from therapy.

While family therapy is a relatively new approach to treating childhood disorders, initial research suggests that it holds promise (Gurman & Kniskern, 1980; Hazelbrigg, Cooper, & Bordwin, 1987).

Community Psychology

In each of the four forms of treatment that have been discussed to this point, the focus has been on treating children who have already been identified as suffering from emotional difficulties. Furthermore, ranging from medication and play therapy to behavior therapy and family therapy, the interventions discussed represent a progressively broadening *ecological focus* from one that treats the child in isolation (medication) to one that treats the child in an important social context (family therapy). Community psychologists take an even broader ecological perspective and attempt the change of general

BOX 17-4 *PSYCHOLOGY IN ACTION* THE TREATMENT OF SERIOUS MULTIPROBLEM JUVENILE OFFENDERS

Adolescents, especially males, have higher crime rates in most categories than any other age group (Federal Bureau of Investigation, 1989) and are one of the most difficult groups to treat successfully. Recidivism rates among serious juvenile offenders, even those who receive treatment of some sort, tend to be over 70 percent. This is true in part because these delinquent adolescents have multiple problems and most treatment methods tend to be either too narrow, focusing only on one or two characteristics of the youth's ecology, or too broad, involving out-of-home placements.

Serious antisocial behavior is related to personal problems and difficulties in functioning in the family, peer group, school, and community (Henggeler, 1989). Henggeler, Melton, and Smith (in press) have used Bronfenbrenner's (1979) social ecological model of development, which was discussed in the first chapter of this book, to develop a multisystemic therapy (MST; Henggeler & Borduin, 1990) to treat serious juvenile offenders and their multiproblem families. MST attempts to change processes and systems—such as parental discipline, familial emotional reactions, peer association, and school performance—that research has identified as being related to antisocial behavior in adolescents. Thus, in addition to the focus on altering family relations found in traditional family therapy, MST attempts to therapeutically modify dysfunctional interactions in various settings. Principles of family therapy and behavior therapy are used to alter relationships and patterns of social responding, and the therapy is carried out in familiar settings such as the home or school. In addition, MST attempts to be sensitive to individual differences in juvenile offenders as well as to their sociocultural differences and the social systems in which they function.

In a recent study, Henggeler and his associates (Henggeler et al., in press) randomly assigned 96 juvenile offenders to either an MST treatment group or a typical treatment situation involving social agencies, curfew, enforced school attendance, and monitoring by a probation officer. Although these adolescents were on the average only 15 years of age, they were serious offenders, not just a group of rambunctious youths. They had averaged 3.4 previous arrests and 8.1 weeks of prior incarceration, and 59 percent had had at least one arrest for a violent crime. They were well down the road to a life of criminal activity. The average duration of treatment was 13.4 weeks, with the MST treatment involving 33 hours of direct contact with a therapist.

A multimethod battery of measures was used to assess pre- and posttreatment (59 weeks after referral) levels in criminal activity and incarceration; improvements in family relations, peer relations, and social competence; and decreases in psychopathology in both youths and their parents. At 59 weeks post-referral recidivism rates for the MST group was 42 percent and for the typical treatment group, 62 percent. Furthermore, 68 percent of the typical treatment group had been incarcerated versus 20 percent of the MST youth, who spent an average of 73 fewer days incarcerated. Increased family cohesiveness as well as less aggressive more positive relationships with peers, which were found among the MST group but not the typical treatment group, were important factors associated with the marked declines in criminal activity and incarceration in the MST group 59 months after treatment.

Henggeler, S. W., Melton, G. B., & Smith L. A. (in press). Multisystemic treatment of serious juvenile offenders: An effective alternative to incarceration. Journal of Consulting and Clinical Psychology.

Sources: Federal Bureau of Investigation, U.S. Department of Justice. (1989). *Uniform crime reports*. Washington, DC.

Henggeler, S. W. (1989). *Delinquency in adolescence*. Newbury Park, CA: Sage.

social conditions as a part of their interventions. Moreover, community psychologists focus much more on the prevention of the disorder than on the treatment of the disturbed.

Community psychologists generally recognize three levels of preventive intervention (Cowen, 1985). In *primary prevention* an attempt is made to alter social conditions that are thought to give rise to psychological difficulties. Improving school curriculums, teaching childrearing skills to new parents, and reducing the amount of lead in the environment all are primary prevention efforts. In *secondary prevention* there is an attempt to identify problems early and provide treatment to groups of children at risk for developing cognitive or social disorders. Project Head Start, a preschool program largely focused on economically deprived children, is one example of an effort at secondary prevention. Finally, *tertiary prevention* involves providing treatment to children

Project Head Start is one example of an attempt at secondary prevention.

and families who are already identified as suffering from a variety of problems. The various medical and psychological treatments that have been discussed in the chapter are examples of tertiary prevention.

Further efforts at preventing psychological disturbance are clearly needed, for the goal of prevention is a laudable one. It is unfortunate that psychologists are a long way from identifying the specific causes of most developmental psychopathologies, and it is inaccurate to assume that all such disorders can be prevented at this time. However, with continued research, the possibility of developing preventive interventions should become more of a reality. The recent work by Henggeler and his colleagues presented in Box 17-4 demonstrates how effective a research-based, ecological, multisystem intervention method can be in treating a most resistant group—serious juvenile offenders.

SUMMARY

Developmental Approaches to Psychopathology

- Developmental psychopathology involves the study of the origins, changes, and continuities in maladaptive behavior over the life span. The four basic principles of developmental psychopathology are: (1) The role of development must be considered in the origins of symptoms and in the course of disorders because the frequency and patterns of symptoms may vary with development; (2) psychopathology should be defined in terms of deviations from normal behavior and attainments for a person that age; (3) the earliest precursors of disordered behavior, such as noncompliant behavior and peer rejection, must be studied; and (4) there are multiple pathways to both normal and abnormal behavior.
- There is great variability in response to biological and environmental risk factors, including permanent developmental delays, sleeper effects that are exhibited later, resilience, and, even, enhanced adaptability due to the stress. The most positive effects occur when protective factors are available to promote good adjustment. The protective factors that have been identified are positive individual attributes (e.g., easy temperament), a

supportive family environment, and supportive extrafamilial individuals or systems.

What Is Abnormal?

- Most researchers and clinicians think that psychopathology is best thought of as problems in living. The perception of problems as pathological is based on social judgments that are themselves dependent on cultural and individual values.
- One way of defining abnormality is to use the *statistical model*, which views as abnormal any behaviors or feelings that differ from the average by a set amount. Although commonly used, this definition has the problem of arbitrary cutoffs. A second definition of abnormality is as a *deviation from the ideal*. This model has the problem of being based on what the decision maker thinks is ideal, a criterion that may or may not be shared by others.
- Children are usually referred to mental health professionals by their parents or other adults, and factors other than the child's behavior may influence the referring adult's judgment about the child. Three kinds of factors that may influence the adult's perceptions are child characteristics (e.g., gender, social skills), characteristics of the referring adult (e.g., standards, emotional problems), and contextual considerations (e.g., demands of the situation, family background).
- Whether or not a particular behavior is viewed as normal depends on the child's age and the likelihood that it will continue over time. Some problems, such as bed wetting, decline with age; others, such as nightmares, increase until adolescence and then decline. However, some childhood disorders, such as autism, are associated with later adult dysfunction. Continuity in some problem behaviors can be maintained by *cumulative continuity*, the selection of environments that support maladaptive behavior, or by *interactional continuity*, the evoking of negative responses from others that create and maintain dysfunctional interactions.

Classification of Child Psychopathology

- Two major ways of assessing and classifying developmental psychopathology are the diagnostic approach and the rating scale method. The *diagnostic approach* is based on descriptions of clusters behaviors and disturbing thoughts or feelings that are classified into various diagnostic categories. The most widely used diagnostic classification system is the DSM-III-R. Although this system has been revised over the past thirty years to reflect the trend away from viewing children as miniature adults, it still has problems of reliability and validity.
- The *empirical approach* involves having adults familiar with the child rate a large number of problem behaviors and then using statistical techniques to determine which disorders are related to one another. This approach typically agrees with the diagnostic approach on *broad-band diagnoses*, or the general categories of classification, even if there are disagreements on the more specific categories. These broad categories of psychopathology are also more reliable and valid than narrow band categories.
- *Undercontrolled behavior disorders* are the most frequently reported of all psychological problems of childhood because they are behaviors that cause problems for others because the child is not sufficiently controlled. The two most common diagnoses in this category are conduct disorders and

hyperactivity. *Conduct disorders* are characterized by a repetitive and persistent pattern of rule violations, including delinquency and illicit drug use. *Attention deficit/hyperactivity disorders,* which are often not diagnosed until children enter the structured environment of school, are characterized by higher than usual levels of situationally inappropriate activity.

- Although the inappropriate activity of hyperactive children diminishes with age, problems of overactivity, inattention, and impulsivity and an inability to use rules to guide behavior persist, resulting in poor academic performance. Although biological explanations for this disorder, such as minimal brain damage, have received little empirical support, some genetic component may be involved. Environmental explanations, such as dysfunctional parent-child interaction patterns, have received some research support. At present, it appears that hyperactivity may have multiple causes. It is often treated by psychostimulant medication, behavior therapy, or a combination of the two.
- *Overcontrolled disorders,* which are characterized by the negative impact they have on the child, include excessive anxiety, fears, and sadness. One form of an overcontrolled disorder is *childhood depression,* clinically defined as an affective disturbance accompanied by changes in cognitive functioning (e.g., guilt, thoughts of death) and behavior (e.g., insomnia, apathy, loss of appetite). Although most clinicians believe that depression exists in children, it is hard to diagnose because children may not be able or willing to talk about feelings of overwhelming sadness until they have reached a certain level of cognitive maturity. Thus, diagnoses of depression increase dramatically in adolescence, as does the rate of behaviors related to depression, such as suicide.
- A number of causes of depression have been hypothesized. Social-psychological theories suggest maternal deprivation and poor attachment to mothers as possible causes. Cognitive theories suggest that feelings of personal responsibility for being unable to control the environment, or *learned helplessness,* lead to depression. Finally, biological theories emphasize genetic and biochemical causes.
- The most extreme forms of childhood disturbances are found in *pervasive developmental disorders,* in which children are seen as being out of touch with reality and exhibiting gross deficits in cognitive, emotional, and social development. The most widely recognized of these disorders is *infantile autism,* which is characterized by a lack of interest in other people, various language abnormalities, and an intense desire to preserve sameness in the environment. Debate about the intelligence of autistic children exists; they sometimes exhibit specific talents in mathematics or the ability to repeat television commercials verbatim, but they score in the retarded range on IQ tests.
- Although the cause of infantile autism is unknown, it is thought to have a biological basis. Treatment has included medication and operant behavior therapy, with limited success. Although treatment allows the children to develop many skills that they would not otherwise acquire, their range of abilities remains quite limited.

The Treatment of Developmental Psychopathologies

- Five approaches to the treatment of developmental psychopathologies are commonly tried. The first is the use of *psychoactive medications* that result in short-term benefits but have some side effects. Controversy about this form of treatment centers on the use of a drug when there is no firm evidence to indicate the existence of an underlying biological disorder. The second approach is *play therapy,* used with children because of their limited ability to express themselves verbally. The therapist's goal is to help the child gain insight into his or her feelings and thinking by interpreting the child's play. *Behavior therapy,* the third approach, refers to a collection of different treatment techniques derived from the principles of social learning and operant conditioning. The goal is to teach the child new ways of behaving by changing the environmental contingencies. *Family therapy,* the fourth approach, views the child as part of a system and assumes that the child's behavior is an indication that something is wrong in the family system. Thus, the therapist meets with all members of the family and works on modifying family relationships and interactions. Finally, *community psychology* works to prevent disorders at the community level by providing interventions aimed at changing social conditions, identifying and providing services for at-risk groups, and treating families who have already been identified as having problems.

CHAPTER 18

EPILOGUE

Throughout this volume we have reviewed the results of many studies of children's development. A variety of theories have been offered to explain and interpret this complex and often only partially understood array of details about development. Neither the data nor the theories are final answers in our continuing attempt to unravel some of the puzzles of development. As in any field of science, our information about child development is constantly expanding and changing. Many findings and facts that we highlighted in earlier editions of this book were replaced in this edition; others were retained or elaborated. In spite of the temporary nature of many of the "facts," we have identified some broad themes that characterize our general views about the development and the process of research in child development. In closing this volume, we hope that a brief review of these themes, which are presented in Table 18-1, will be helpful.

1 *The child is competent*. In recent years a dramatic change has occurred in our view of the infant and child. Even infants and young children are no longer thought of as incompetent creatures with limited sensory, perceptual, and social capacities, awaiting the imprint of the adult world. Instead we recognize that infants and children possess a wide range of perceptual, motoric, cognitive, and social capacities from an early age.

2 *The child's behavior is organized*. The child's behavior is not just a disorganized bundle of responses, reflexes, and reactions. Instead, organization is evident in the child's behavior: even infant behaviors such as sucking, looking, and sleeping are highly structured response patterns.

3 *The domains of childhood are interdependent*. Social, emotional, physical, language, and cognitive development are often studied as separate domains, but these areas overlap and mutually influence each other.

4 *The child's behavior has multiple causes*. Current views stress that development is the outcome of the interaction among biological, environmental, and experiential factors.

5 *There is no single pathway to normal development*. Children may take alternative routes to normal development. No single pathway is necessarily the "best" one to follow, since socially and intellectually competent adults often have reached their goals by very different routes.

6 *The child influences the responses of other people*. The early unidirectional view of development under which adults influence children but children

THEMES OF DEVELOPMENT TABLE 18-1

1	The child is competent.
2	The child's behavior is organized.
3	The domains of childhood are interdependent.
4	The child's behavior has multiple causes.
5	There is no single pathway to normal development.
6	The child influences the responses of other people.
7	The child's behavior varies across situations and settings.
8	The child's behavior is influenced by social systems.
9	The child's behavior is culture-bound.
10	The child's behavior is time-bound.
11	Multiple research methods are necessary.
12	Multiple samples are necessary.
13	Multiple theories of child development are necessary.
14	Multiple disciplines are necessary.
15	Child development research influences, and is influenced by, social policy.
16	Development is a lifelong process.

do not alter adult behavior is no longer considered valid. Children play an active role in modifying and altering adult behavior even in infancy. A bidirectional view of child development is now widely accepted, with children playing an influential part in all aspects of their own development.

7 *The child's behavior varies across situations and settings*. The same child may behave in a very different manner in different situations or with different people—in the home, the laboratory, the school, or the peer play group. Thus, children should be studied in multiple settings, and caution should be exercised in making generalizations about children's behavior from one situation to another.

8 *The child's behavior is influenced by social systems*. The child is embedded in a variety of social systems and settings in which the members shape each other's behavior. These range from smaller immediate settings and systems, such as the family or peer group in which the child has considerable influence, to larger or more remote systems, such as the school, community, or greater society over which the child has less control. The nature of the interactions, stresses, and supports encountered in these systems will influence development.

9 *The child's behavior is culture-bound*. No single picture of development is accurate for all cultures, social classes, or racial and ethnic groups. Children develop different skills and competencies in different cultural milieus. Careful attention needs to be paid to *both* such cultural and ethnic variations within our own society as well as differences in other cultures around the globe. Both intracultural and cross-cultural perspectives are needed. No sweeping generalizations concerning children's development can be made without careful specification of a child's cultural background.

10 *The child's behavior is time-bound*. Knowledge about children is time-bound: as social conditions shift, children and families undergo changes that

alter their behavior. The experiences of children growing up in the Great Depression of the 1930s may be different from the experiences of children in the 1990s. Changing gender roles for mothers and fathers are altering household division of labor and women's employment patterns that, in turn, affect children's lives. Legal demands for ethnic integration are markedly altering the school experience for many children. One of the aims of child psychology is to constantly monitor these changes in order to show how these shifts affect children's behavior.

11 *Multiple research methods are necessary.* No single research method is sufficient to understand child development. A wide variety of methods, including naturalistic observations of children, experiments, self-reports, clinical studies, and standardized tests, contribute different types of information about child development. Information from different methods, sources, and situations presents a more accurate miultifaceted view of the complexity of human development.

12 *Multiple samples are necessary.* To fully understand child development, in all of its cultural and ethnic richness, multiple samples are needed that capture this diversity. Increasingly, developmental psychologists are using small samples to intensively study a process or issue in a particular region or ethnic group in combination with national samples that are representative of the groups found in our diverse society.

13 *Multiple theories of child development are necessary.* Just as there are multiple methods, there are multiple theories. Although there are grand theoretical schemes that attempt to provide a full and comprehensive account of development, such as those of Piaget, Freud, and Vygotsky, child psychologists are becoming more modest and restricted in the scope of their theories. As the complex and multidetermined nature of development becomes apparent, minitheories that aim to explain smaller pieces of the developmental puzzle are becoming more popular. Separate theories of sex typing, memory, aggression, and grammar development are more likely to be advanced by contemporary psychologists than elaborate theories aimed at explaining all of social or cognitive development.

14 *Multiple disciplines are necessary.* In spite of the fact that this is a volume on child psychology, many other disciplines contribute in important ways to our understanding of children. Anthropology provides a cross-cultural perspective, sociology offers a societal viewpoint, pediatrics shows the importance of the child's physical development, psychiatry examines the role of deviant and abnormal development, and history views childhood against the changing panorama of time. Multidisciplinary approaches are increasingly common in studies of children's development.

15 *Child development research influences, and is influenced by, social policy.* In contemporary child psychology, there is a close link between basic research and the application of research findings. Just as basic research concerning the importance of the early environment for the child's development stimulated government programs, such as Head Start and day-care programs, so, in turn, child psychologists have been more

actively involved in issues of concern to society and government, such as problems of poverty, divorce, and school integration. During the past decade there has been an increasing interdependence of child development as both a basic discipline and as an applied discipline.

16 *Development is a lifelong process.* Although this book focuses on development from conception through the adolescent years, development is a lifelong process that continues throughout adulthood. Individuals respond to, and are modified by, experiences throughout the course of development. Social, emotional, cognitive, language, and physical development are continuous processes across the life span. To understand children, it is important to recognize that parents continue their development across the life span, which, in turn, provides a changing context for children's development. Teenage parents provide a different context for children than do late-timed parents who begin parenthood in their late thirties. A life-course view of development helps us appreciate the interdependence of adult lives and children's development.

GLOSSARY

ABAB design A method in which a single person is studied experimentally. The participant serves as his or her own control and experimental condition. "A" represents the normal state and "B" the experimental state. For example, Jane, a toddler in toilet training, is being studied. First, the frequency with which she uses the toilet is recorded. As an incentive, Jane is given a jelly bean for using the toilet. The change in toilet use when Jane is given jelly beans is recorded (condition B). Condition A (no jelly beans) and condition B (jelly beans) are then repeated.

Abnormal A judgment made concerning an individual's behavior. This judgment utilizes one or more of the following criteria: (1) a statistical model, (2) a level of adaptive behavior, and (3) the amount of deviation from the theoretical ideal.

Accommodation (1) A process that involves the adjustment of an individual's schemata to meet environmental demands. (2) The ability to bring objects in the visual field into focus by changing the curvature of the lens.

Achondroplasia A congenital abnormal bone growth more commonly seen in the offspring of older fathers.

Adaptability The ability to modify attentional strategies to the demands of specific tasks or situations.

Adaptation The second functional principle, involving the process of assimilation and accommodation.

Adaptive behavior A means of determining the normalcy of behavior. This determination is made based on how functional the behavior is for that individual. Behaviors that decrease the individual's ability to get along in the world are considered abnormal.

Affective disturbances A disorder of mood.

Age of viability The point in fetal development when the fetus has a reasonable probability of survival if birth occurs; this point is at about 28 weeks.

Aggression Behavior that intentionally inflicts harm or injury on another person.

Alert inactivity A state in which the infant's eyes are open and have a bright and shining quality; the infant can pursue moving objects and make conjugate eye movements in the horizontal and vertical planes. The infant is relatively inactive. The face is relaxed, with no grimace.

Allele An alternate form of a specific gene at a particular locus on the chromosome.

Altruism Prosocial behavior such as helping, cooperating, and sharing.

Ambivalent attachment An attachment to the mother wherein the infant shows frequent distress, regardless of whether the mother is present or absent, and shows ambivalence about contact by intermittently seeking and rejecting contact with the mother.

Amenorrhea A condition of menstrual cessation that may strike girls who keep their weight low.

Amniocentesis A prenatal diagnostic procedure in which a needle is inserted into the amniotic sac, which surrounds the fetus, and fluid is removed. This fluid contains cells that have been sloughed off by the fetus. These cells can be examined for the presence of certain chromosomal and metabolic disorders.

Anal stage The second stage in Freud's psychodynamic theory during which the child is concerned with anal-related activities.

Androgen A male hormone.

Androgynous individuals Those who possess both masculine and feminine psychological characteristics.
Animistic thinking The tendency to attribute lifelike characteristics to inanimate objects; typical of children's thinking in the preconceptual period.
Anorexia nervosa A severe eating disorder most commonly found among teenage girls in which the individual diets to the point of starvation.
Anoxia The lack of sufficient oxygen to the brain, causing neurological damage or death.
Apgar A scoring scale used to assess the condition of the infant at birth.
Apneic periods Periods when breathing movements temporarily cease in the fetus; these periods are associated with moderate alcohol intake by the mother.
Assimilation A process by which an individual perceives and modifies an experience in accordance with the individual's existing schemata.
Associative learning (Level I) A term used by Arthur Jensen in referring to skills of short-term memory, rote learning, and attention. Level I intelligence is not highly correlated with school success and tends not to be measured by standard tests of intelligence.
Attachment The development of specific behaviors whereby an infant seeks to be near certain people.
Attention The act of focusing on a particular aspect of the environment.
Attention deficit/hyperactivity disorders A diagnostic category. The primary criteria employed in making this diagnosis are inattention, impulsivity, and hyperactivity.
Attribution Making inferences about the causes underlying a behavior in an attempt to understand the behavior.
Authoritarian control A style of discipline in which hostile, restrictive, power-assertive practices predominate.
Authoritative control A style of discipline in which parents permit children considerable freedom within reasonable limits, are responsive to the opinions and needs of their children, and communicate with their children. However, these parents do impose consistent limitations on children whenever they have greater knowledge or insight or when the children's behavior is inappropriate or unacceptable.
Automization The transformation of mental strategies and behaviors from conscious and controlled to unconscious and automatic.
Autonomic nervous system The body system closely related to emotional arousal and responsiveness.
Autonomous morality Piaget's second stage of moral development in which the child recognizes intention and the arbitrariness of social rules in his or her moral judgments.
Autonomy versus shame and doubt The second stage of Erickson's theory where the main conflict involves the child's emerging sense of autonomy versus the child's continuing dependency on adults and difficulty in meeting adult expectations.
Autosomes The 22 pairs of chromosomes possessed equally by males and females that determine the development of most body structures and attributes.
Autostimulation theory A theory that REM activity during sleep in infancy may stimulate the development of the central nervous system.
Avoidant attachment An attachment to the mother wherein the infant shows little upset about the mother's absence and avoids interaction with her upon reunion.
Basic capacity The amount of information that can be held in short-term memory.
Basic trust versus mistrust The first stage of Erikson's theory in which the main task for the infant is to determine the responsiveness of the environment and whether it can be trusted to satisfy the infant's needs.
Behavior therapy A variety of treatment strategies deriving from the principles of social learning and operant conditioning.
Behavioral perspective A perspective in psychology that views development as a continuous process governed by basic learning principles. The child is viewed as relatively passive, molded by environmental factors that modify behavior through either classical or operant conditioning.
Body cells All cells in the body except the germ cells.

Broad-band diagnoses A combination of several specific categories into one single or general category. (For example, oranges, apples, and pears are all classified as fruits. Fruit would be the broad-band classification.)
Bulimia An eating disorder that may occur in conjunction with anorexia nervosa in which the individual may indulge in "food binges," followed by purging through vomiting or the use of laxatives.
Canalization The limiting of phenotypes to one or a few developmental outcomes. The stronger the canalization, the fewer alternative paths there are from genotype to phenotype.
Case-study method A research strategy in which one individual is studied intensively.
Catharsis theory The theory which holds that aggression can be reduced by behaving aggressively against a safe target.
Centration The focusing on one dimension of an object when several must be considered to solve a problem correctly.
Cephalocaudal principle Developmental principle which states that development proceeds from the head downward.
Cerebral lateralization The specialization of function of the brain in one cerebral hemisphere.
Child development The scientific study of changes in the child's biological, social, cognitive, and emotional behavior during the period of childhood.
Childhood depression An affective disturbance accompanied by changes in cognitive functioning (guilt, thoughts of death) and behavior (insomnia, apathy, loss of appetite).
Chromosome A threadlike entity in the nuclei of cells. Genes are beaded along the length of the chromosomes.
Classical conditioning A procedure that enables a previously ineffective or neutral stimulus (the CS) to elicit a response (the CR), because of repeated pairings of the CS with another stimulus (the UCS), which could already elicit a response (the UCR).
Clinical depression A pervasive disorder of mood that is evidenced not only by extreme sadness but also by deficits in cognitive and physical functioning.
Coercive cycle A conflicted interaction between a parent and child in which the behavior of the parent becomes gradually more coercive in order to control the increasingly aversive behavior of the child. This destructive cycle is frequently found in divorced mothers and their sons.
Cognition The mental activity and behavior that allows us to understand the world; it includes concepts such as learning, perception, memory, and thinking.
Cognitive learning (Level II) A term used by Arthur Jensen to refer to intellectual skills that involve abstract thinking, symbolic processes, conceptual learning, and the use of language in problem solving. Level II intelligence is correlated with school performance and is measured by tests of intelligence.
Cognitive monitoring performance The ability to be able to monitor one's current level of success on a cognitive task and to evaluate the success of one's current strategy.
Cognitive style A relatively consistent way in which an individual processes, perceives, remembers, or uses information.
Cohort A term used to describe individuals who were born in the same year or in the same general time period and who therefore share the same historical experiences.
Community psychology A form of treatment that views psychological problems as a function of the general social condition; therefore, the major intervention strategy is to change counterproductive social conditions.
Competency The underlying capabilities of the individual that intelligence tests attempt to measure.
Complementary interactive stage The third stage of infant interaction. In this stage, children are engaging in complex social interchanges including imitation, reciprocal role relationships, and the expression of both positive and negative affect.
Componential analysis The analysis of both the steps through which the individual goes in solving a problem and the strategies the individual uses in deciding how to solve the problem.

Concordance rate A measure of the percent of cases in which a particular trait or disorder is present in both members of a twin pair if it is present in at least one member of the twin pair.

Concrete operational period Piaget's third stage of intellectual development, which is characterized by logical reasoning. Consideration in thought is limited to things actually present.

Conditioned response (CR) A response, closely resembling an unconditioned response, that is evoked by a conditioned stimulus after conditioning has occurred.

Conditioned stimulus (CS) A previously neutral stimulus that, by being consistently paired with an unconditioned stimulus, comes to elicit a response.

Conduct disorder A diagnosis defined by a repetitive, persistent pattern of rule violation. This acting out generally occurs in the company of a peer group. This disorder is considered to be socialized, whereas if this acting out is primarily done alone the disorder is said to be undersocialized.

Conservation A belief in the permanence of certain attributes of objects or situations in spite of superficial changes.

Continuity A term to denote aspects of development in cases when each new event or change simply builds upon earlier experiences in an orderly way.

Continuum of caretaking casualty The range of adverse factors in environmental and family situations.

Continuum of reproductive casualty The range of variations in reproductive complications that result in abnormalities in the child.

Conventional level The second level of moral judgment according to Kohlberg, in which morality is a matter of conformity.

Conversational rules Turn-taking, knowing when one is being addressed, and clues concerning the right words for the right situations.

Correlation coefficient (1) A numerical index of how closely two variables are associated with one another. The absolute correlation coefficient indicates the strength of association, whereas the sign of the correlation coefficient indicates the form of association. (2) An estimate of how two measures vary together.

Correlational research A research strategy that involves examining the relationship between two factors. If two factors are correlated, they are systematically related to each other, but it is not possible to determine if one caused the other.

Counterconditioning A method for reducing fear in which the fearful stimuli that typically evoke emotional reactions are presented in conjunction with pleasant activities.

Creole language The second-generation language spoken by the children of speakers of a pidgin language; this language is highly developed and rule-governed in contrast to the pidgin from which it originated.

Critical period A specific period in the child's development when he or she is sensitive to a particular environmental stimulus; the same stimulus coming either before or after the critical period does not produce the same effect in the individual.

Crossing-over A process that occurs during meiosis in which genetic material is exchanged between pairs of chromosomes.

Cross-sectional design A research design that involves comparing different groups of children at different age levels in the same situation.

Cross-section/short-term longitudinal design A research design in which longitudinal data are collected from an original set of subjects while new subjects are added from each age group.

Crying A state in which the individual has crying vocalizations associated with vigorous diffuse motor activity.

Cultural relativism A point of view that, when applied to child development, emphasizes the effects of the cultural setting on children's development.

Cultural universals The viewpoint that certain laws of development apply to all children regardless of culture.

Cumulative continuity Continuity of behavior, particularly maladaptive behavior, maintained by a selection of environments that support the behavior.

Cytomegalovirus (CMV) A type of herpes virus known to cause mental retardation, deafness, and blindness.

Cytoplasm The material that constitutes the cell other than the nucleus.

Deductive reasoning skills Techniques for solving problems, such as transitive inference and hierarchical classification.

Delinquent A legal designation for a juvenile who is found guilty of violating the law.

Deoxyribonucleic acid (DNA) A substance that contains the genetic code that directs the functioning of RNA. DNA is composed of phosphate, sugar, and the base pairs of cytosine and guanine, and thymine and adenine. The gene is composed of DNA.

Dependent variable That measure of behavior the experimenter anticipates will be affected by the change in environment that is introduced during the experimental procedure. For example, one group of children is fed nutritious breakfasts, whereas no food is provided for a second group. Afterwards, all the children's performances on a reading test are measured, with the presumption that eating breakfast will affect reading test performance. Reading test performance is the dependent variable in this experiment.

Depth perception The ability to perceive distance, usually in a downward direction.

DES (diethylstilbestrol) A synthetic hormone, prescribed to prevent miscarriages, associated with a number of reproductive abnormalities in adolescent and adult offspring of mothers who took the drug during pregnancy.

Desensitization A method for reducing fear in which a person is taught to relax in the presence of successively more fearful stimuli until there is no anxiety even with the most fearful events.

Developmental psychopathology The study of the origins, changes, and continuities in maladaptive behavior over the life span.

Deviation from the ideal A means of determining the normalcy of behavior. This determination is based on a comparison with a theoretical concept of the ideal healthy person. If behaviors do not conform to this theoretical concept, they are considered to be abnormal.

Deviation IQ An index of intelligence that indicates how far above or below the mean the individual's intelligence test score lies, relative to that of children the same age in the standardization group. The deviation IQ score was first used in tests designed by David Wechsler, but, more recently, it has been adopted by the Stanford-Binet Intelligence Scale as well. For all groups the average deviation IQ score is 100.

Diagnostic and statistical manual (DSM IV) The best known and most widely used diagnostic classification system in the United States. The DSM IV is published by the American Psychiatric Association.

Diagnostic approach An approach to developmental psychopathology based on description of behaviors and disturbing thoughts or feelings that are classified into various diagnostic categories.

Diagnostic categories A classification of similar patterns of behavior, disturbing thoughts, and feelings.

Diagnostic reliability A measure of how often two or more clinicians will arrive independently at the same diagnosis.

Differentiation theory A theory that proposes that perception becomes more differentiated as an individual learns to attend to, identify, and discriminate features in the complex sensory input available to him or her.

Direct observation A method of research that requires viewing of subjects in a variety of settings, ranging from naturalistic home settings to highly structured tasks in the laboratory.

Discontinuity A term to denote aspects of development which appear to occur as a series of steps or stages, in which each successive stage is qualitatively different from the preceding stage.

Distractability The inability to attend to only relevant aspects of an array of stimuli and to filter out or ignore the irrelevant.

Dizygotic twins or fraternal twins Two individuals, born to the same mother as the result of one pregnancy, who are no more genetically alike than siblings because they came from two separate zygotes.

Dominant allele An allele that will be expressed phenotypically when paired with another allele that is less powerful or recessive.

Down syndrome or trisomy 21 A disorder characterized by physical and mental retardation and a rather typical appearance, and attributed to either translocation or nondisjunction of chromosome 21. In the most common cases, individuals have 47 instead of 46 chromosomes, with three rather than two chromosomes at the twenty-first set.

Dream sleep or REM sleep A period of sleep characterized by rapid eye movements, as well as fluctuations in heart rate and blood pressure. In adults, dreaming occurs in this period.

Drowsiness A state in which the individual is relatively inactive; the eyes open and close intermittently; respirations are regular, though faster than in regular sleep; when the eyes are open, they have a dull or glazed quality.

Dyslexia A reading disorder striking 5 percent of all children which involves a fundamental difficulty in integrating visual and auditory information; it has been suggested that this disorder may be correlated with abnormal brain lateralization.

Echoing A technique for facilitating a child's verbal response that includes imitating part of the child's utterance but replacing unintelligible parts with one of the "wh" question-producing words in English.

Echolalia A child's constant repetition of a phrase that has been said to him or her. This is a common language problem found among autistic children.

Ecological perspective A perspective in child development that examines the impact of the child's daily social and physical environments on his or her development. The child's subjective experience or understanding of the environment and his or her active role in modifying it are important aspects of this perspective.

Encoding The transformation of specific aspects of the stimuli from the sensory registers into mental representations for placement into short-term memory.

Ego integrity versus despair The eighth and last stage of Erikson's theory in which the main conflict involves reviewing one's life and seeing it as meaningful or wasted.

Egocentricity An inability for a person to perceive situations from the perspectives of others; typical of children's thinking in the preconceptual period.

Elaboration A strategy for remembering that involves increasing the amount of information to be recalled by providing a common context into which several to-be-remembered items can fit.

Emotional display rules Strategies used by children to exaggerate, minimize, or mask their feelings.

Empathic stage The third stage of expectations about friends, which emerges at about grades 6 and 7 and in which self-disclosure, understanding, and shared interests occur; this is the stage of *chumship.*

Enrichment theory The theory that each time an individual perceives an object he or she learns a little more about the object.

Entity theory The belief held by some school children that they possess a fixed amount of intelligence which is displayed in their performances on cognitive tasks.

Estrogens Female hormones.

Ethological perspective The perspective in child psychology that development is a process of adaptation to the environment. In accordance with its evolutionary emphasis, this perspective places great importance on cross-cultural comparisons and on comparisons of children with other species.

Etiology The presumed cause of a disorder.

Executive control function This function directs the intake of information, as well as the selecting of strategies applied to the problem and the monitoring of the success of these strategies.

Executive processing space In the neo-Piagetian theory of cognitive development, the maximum number of independent schemes a child can activate at any one time.

Exosystem An environmental system that, according to Bronfenbrenner, comprises settings which affect the child but are *not* affected by the child, that is, settings in which the child plays no direct role.

Expansion A language technique whereby the adult responds to the child's incomplete utterance by imitating it while adding the omitted words.

Experimental research A research strategy by which the researcher assesses behavior in a controlled laboratory setting in response to the introduction of a systematic change or manipulation. This strategy allows the determination of cause-effect relationships.

Exposure to a fearless model A method for reducing fear in which a child watches a model act fearlessly, thereby reducing fear in the observing child.

Factor analysis A statistical procedure that groups together test items or tests that are highly related to each other and that are relatively independent from other groups of test items or tests.

Family scripts Repetitive patterns of interaction in which family members assume consistent roles.

Family system The notion that all behavior in a family is interrelated. In order for the behavior of any individual family member to change, the family patterns of interacting need to be changed.

Family therapy A treatment approach based on the notion that problems of individual family members can best be dealt with by working with the entire family.

Fast mapping A technique of early language development in which the child connects a new word with an underlying concept in order to build large vocabularies with greater speed.

Fetal alcohol syndrome A syndrome in offspring related to the mother's alcohol intake during pregnancy; its effects include facial and limb defects, abnormal behaviors, and mental retardation.

Field experiment Experimental strategy in which the investigator deliberately introduces a change into the naturalistic setting rather than into the laboratory.

Figurative language Language used in a nonliteral way, such as in similes and metaphors.

Formal operational period Piaget's fourth stage of intellectual development, characterized by flexible thought, complex reasoning, and mental hypothesis testing.

Fragile-X syndrome A sex chromosome abnormality in which individuals have an X chromosome that appears to be pinched or narrowed in some areas. These chromosomes are so fragile that the pinched areas may break and sections of the chromosomes separate off. The syndrome has been associated with mild to profound retardation in males and occasionally with mild mental retardation in women. It may be associated with autism.

Gender roles Behaviors typically exhibited by males and females within a culture.

Gender schema theory The theory which holds that a child's concept of gender is shaped by emerging abilities to create naive mental schemes about what is male and female.

Gender stereotypes Beliefs about gender held by members of a culture.

Gender typing The process by which children acquire the values, motives, and behaviors viewed as appropriate for males and females within a culture.

Gene A segment of DNA that forms the genetic code that will direct an individual's development.

General activity level A measure derived from general activity and from interruptions in the child's solitary play by others.

Generalization A process by which strategies learned while solving a previous problem are applied to new situations.

Generativity versus stagnation The seventh stage in Erikson's theory in which the conflict involves providing guidelines and assistance for future generations, which makes one's life meaningful, versus failing to do so, which results in stagnation.

Genital stage The last stage in Freud's psychodynamic theory in which heterosexual desires emerge.

Genotype The material, inherited from an individual's parents, that makes the individual genetically unique.

Germ cells The reproductive cells; the female ovum and the male sperm.
Gestures Nonverbal signals used in communication with or without words.
Grammar The structure of a language, including its syntax and morphology.
Habituation The decrease in responsiveness as a result of repeated presentation of a stimulus.
Helplessness In intelligence theory, the tendency for a child to give up easily or to deteriorate when working on difficult problems.
Hemispheric specialization A term referring to the differential functioning of the cerebral hemispheres, for example, the left hemisphere controls speech and language, and the right hemisphere controls visual-spatial information.
Herpes simplex A common venereal disease, which may be contracted by the infant during the birth process and which may lead to blindness, mental retardation, or death.
Heterozygous alleles Two differing alleles in an individual at a particular locus.
Homozygous alleles Two identical alleles in an individual at a particular locus.
Horizontal decalage Inability to solve some problems, although other similar problems involving the same operations can be solved.
Hormone A powerful and highly specialized chemical substance that interacts with cells capable of receiving the hormonal message and responding to it.
Hypothyroidism An endocrine problem involving a lack of thyroid gland secretion which can result in short stature.
Identification The Freudian process that serves as the basis for the acquisition of the behavior and values of a model.
Identity versus role confusion The fifth stage in Erickson's theory in which the main focus is the search for a stable definition of self.
Imitation or modeling The learning-theory term for the process involved in the acquisition of behaviors exhibited by a model.
Immanent justice The child's belief that punishment and other adversities are the direct, inevitable outcomes of transgressions.
Impulsivity The tendency to act suddenly without thinking.
Inattention The inability to be attentive.
Incremental theory The belief held by some school children that intelligence is composed of an ever-expanding set of skills and knowledge that is increased through effort.
Independent variable The characteristic that is changed by an experiment in order to assess its effect on a second measured behavior. For example, if one group of children is fed breakfast and no food is provided for a second group (the researchers hope to assess the impact of breakfast eating on reading performance), breakfast eating would be the independent variable.
Index of autonomic stability A composite measure of autonomic functioning, including blood pressure, respiration rate, galvanic skin response, salivation, and heart rate.
Industry versus inferiority The fourth stage of Erikson's theory where the main focus during middle childhood is on the mastery of intellectual, social, and physical skills so as not to feel inferior to one's peers.
Infantile autism A serious childhood disorder characterized by the following three features: (1) a lack of interest in other people or even an aversion to human contact, (2) language abnormalities, and (3) an intense interest in preserving sameness in the environment.
Inflections Variations in words that produce different grammatical relations.
Information processing theories A group of theories in psychology that view the human mind as a system that processes information according to a set of logical rules and limitations, similar to those of a computer. When applied to development, the theories focus on children's representations of information and how they operate on the information to achieve their goals in particular situations.
Initiative versus guilt The third stage (from 3 to 5 years) in Erickson's theory, in which the child deals with conflict-taking responsibility and with mastering the environment at the risk of possibly offending his or her parents.

Instrumental aggression A form of aggression involving quarrels and fights over possessions. This form of aggression is used most frequently by young children.
Intelligence quotient (IQ) An index of an individual's performance on a standardized test of intelligence relative to the performance of others his or her age. The original intelligence quotient was calculated as follows:

$$\text{Mental age} \times 100 = \text{chronological age}$$

In many cases, this formula has since been replaced by the use of the deviation IQ score.
Interactional continuity Continuity of behavior, particularly maladaptive behavior, maintained by the evocation of negative responses from others.
Interactionist One who stresses the interplay of biology and experience in producing behavior; in language development, one who believes that children are biologically prepared for language but require extensive experience with expressed language for adequate development.
Internalization The process by which the basis of moral behavior shifts from external factors to personal feelings and ethical beliefs.
Intersexuality or hermaphroditism The presence of some of the sexual characteristics or reproductive systems of both male and female in the same individual. It is believed that rare recessive or sex-linked genes may cause this condition in some cases.
Intimacy versus isolation The sixth stage (during young adulthood) in Erikson's theory in which the individual's main concern is the development of an intimate relationship with another adult.
Intuitive period A period of development, lasting from ages 4 to 7 years, marked by the appearance of certain mental "operations" to solve problems; however, the child is unable to explain the operations or strategies that he or she has used to solve the problems.
Invariants Attributes of objects or relationships among objects that do not change under different conditions.
Irony A figure of speech in which the intended meaning is the opposite of that expressed by the words used.
Irregular sleep A state in which the eyes are closed and the body engages in variable gentle limb movements, writhing, and stirring; grimaces and other facial expressions are frequent; respirations are irregular and faster than they are in regular sleep; there are also interspersed and recurrent rapid eye movements.
Irreversibility A characteristic of preoperational reasoning in which an individual fails to see that every logical operation is reversible—that is, can be returned to its original state.
Klinefelter's syndrome A sex chromosome abnormality in which an extra X chromosome is present in every cell. These XXY individuals are males, but they are sterile and have feminine breasts and hips.
Lability The frequency of spontaneous fluctuations, as in galvanic skin responses.
Latency period The stage in middle childhood, according to Freud's psychodynamic theory, in which sexual desires are submerged (or latent).
Learned helplessness (1) The pattern of attributing failure to lack of ability, task difficulty, or bad luck and of believing that successes do not reflect effort or ability. (2) A feeling of being totally ineffectual that results from the experience of being unable to control the outcome of previous salient life events.
Learning goals Goals adopted by children that focus on increasing cognitive skills in order to become smarter; these goals are associated with the incremental theory of intelligence.
Level of processing In information processing theory, the intensity with which information is processed into memory—along a continuum from shallow to deep—determining whether information can be recalled over shorter or longer periods of time.
Lifespan perspective The perspective within developmental psychology that development is a continuous process that begins at conception and continues through old age. The individual is susceptible to change in any of these periods, and, thus, all periods in the life cycle are of importance.

Locus The position of a gene on a chromosome.
Longitudinal design A research design that involves the examination of the same children at different age levels.
Long-term memory Knowledge of the world, strategies for problem solving, and memory for past events and experiences.
Macrosystem According to Bronfenbrenner, the environmental level that comprises the set of ideological institutional patterns of a particular culture.
Mainstreaming An educational practice whereby special children are integrated into the regular classroom.
Mastery orientation In intelligence theory, the tendency for a child to use failure feedback to guide or improve performance when working on hard problems.
Maternal deprivation An insufficient interaction with the primary caretaker. The lack of this interaction can have a profound negative effect on the physical and emotional development of an infant.
Mediational deficiency The inability to use verbal labels when they are available to assist memory.
Medical model The orientation that psychological disorders are a subset of physical disorders.
Meiosis The process by which reproductive, or germ, cells divide. It is a process of reduction division in which a cell divides in such a way that the two daughter cells include only one member of each pair of chromosomes.
Memory span The number of digits that can be remembered accurately from short-term memory.
Menarche The onset of menstruation which usually occurs two to three years after the beginning of the sexual maturation process.
Mental age An index of the child's absolute performance on a test of intelligence. If a child's performance is the same as that of the average 4-year-old, he or she is said to have a mental age of four years.
Mesosystem According to Bronfenbrenner, the environmental level that comprises the interrelationships among contexts of the microsystems in which the child actively participates, such as those between home and school.
Metacognition Knowledge about one's own cognitive processes, such as knowledge about oneself, the task, and the strategies to solve it.
Metacommunication skills The ability to understand one's own communication skills.
Metacomponents Strategies that the individual uses in deciding how to solve problems.
Metalinguistic awareness The ability to think and talk about language; emerges well after children are capable of complex communication.
Microsystem According to Bronfenbrenner, this represents the actual setting in which the child lives and interacts with other people.
Minimal brain dysfunction A presumed brain damage in hyperactive children. It cannot be reliably measured or detected, but is solely inferred on the basis of the child's behavior.
Mitosis A process of cell division in body cells in which each of the 46 chromosomes in the parent cell duplicates itself before division. Each of the two daughter cells includes 46 chromosomes.
Modifier gene A gene that influences the action of phenotypical expression of other genes.
Monozygotic twins or identical twins Two individuals, born to the same mother as the result of one pregnancy, who are genetically alike because they came from the same zygote.
Moral development The gradual process by which the child internalizes society's standards of right and wrong.
Moral realism Piaget's first stage of moral development in which the child views "right" behavior as absolute and the rules governing it as unalterable.
Moro reflex A reflex in which the arms are thrown out in extension and then toward

each other in a convulsive manner; hands are fanned out at first and then clenched tightly. This reflex is in response to a loud sound or jarring, or to a sudden head or body drop of a few inches.

Morphemes Modifiers and qualifiers that make the meaning of a word more precise, for example, cat*s*, cat*'s*, and look*ed*.

Motherese The simplified dialect used by mothers and others when addressing a young child.

Multischematic The ability of an individual to hold more than one schema for responding to the world, as in androgynous individuals.

Mutations Changes in genes that may produce new phenotypes.

Mutator gene A gene that controls the rate of mutation in other genes.

Myelination The development around the nerves of an insulating fatty sheath that facilitates the speed of transmission of neural impulses.

Narrow-band diagnosis A specific classification, a subset of a broad-band classification. A pear is a narrow-band classification of the broad-band classification of fruits.

Nativist One who stresses the innate bases of behavior; in language development, one who believes that children have an innate language acquisition device that enables them to learn language early and quickly.

Natural experiment An experimental strategy in which the investigator capitalizes on a change in the world that occurs naturally (for example, a court decision to bus children or a power failure), rather than deliberately causing the change to happen.

Neglecting A style of parenting in which parents are motivated to keep their children at a distance, focusing on their own needs rather than on the needs of the children.

Niche picking A process by which individuals seek out environments that are most compatible with their biological predispositions. The individual's genotype may direct this process.

Norms a statistical description of how a large group of people performs on a test; it can then serve as a guideline against which to measure an individual's performance or progress.

Object permanence A belief in the continued existence of objects even when these objects are no longer perceived.

Objective responsibility The child's concern with a specific behavior and its consequences rather than with its intent.

Open classroom A variation from the traditional classroom. The primary differences are reduced structure and more emphasis on individual and small-group work.

Operant conditioning A procedure for changing the probability that a certain response will be exhibited which involves repeatedly following the response with the same consequence.

Operation The internalized mental equivalent of a behavioral schema.

Oral stage The first stage in Freud's psychodynamic theory, during which the infant is preoccupied with activities associated with the mouth, such as sucking and eating.

Organismic perspective A perspective in child development that describes the child as actively seeking information and new experiences. Development results from increasingly complex reorganizations of mental structures as the child moves through an invariant sequence of stages to more advanced levels of cognitive functioning.

Organization The predisposition to integrate and coordinate physical or psychological structures into more complex systems.

Overcontrolled disorders Psychological problems that involve primarily fears, anxieties, and sadness.

Overextension A typical error in children's early word use in which a single word is used to mean different things.

Overjustification hypothesis A hypothesis suggesting that the persistent use of a contingent reward may overjustify an activity in a child's view, leading the child to discount its value.

Overregularization A typical error in children's early understanding of grammar in which the child ignores irregularities and exceptions and applies grammatical rules to all cases.

Ovum The female gamete or egg cell, a special cell that carries the genetic material of the mother.
Perception The intake of information from the environment.
Parental reports A method of gathering data in which the parents provide information about some aspect of their children's behavior or their own behavior, such as childrearing practices.
Parity The number of offspring a mother has previously borne.
Peers Social equals who are similar in characteristics such as age and functional level.
Performance anxiety Distress shown when one is asked to carry out a certain task in the presence of observers.
Performance goals Goals adopted by children that focus on avoiding errors and on gaining positive evaluations from others; these goals are associated with the entity theory of intelligence.
Period of the embryo The period of development during which differentiation of the most important organs and systems occurs. In humans, it extends from the beginning of the third week to the end of the eighth week after conception.
Period of the fetus The period of development marked by the growth of existing systems rather than by the establishment of new systems. In humans, it extends from the eighth week after conception until birth.
Period of the zygote The period of development of the fertilized ovum or zygote between fertilization and implantation. Also called the germinal period.
Permissiveness A parental practice in which few or no restrictions are placed on children.
Person-oriented or hostile aggression A form of aggression usually directed toward others, involving behaviors such as criticism and ridicule. This form of aggression is used more frequently by older children.
Pervasive developmental disorders The most extreme forms of childhood disturbances in which children are seen as being out of touch with reality and exhibiting gross deficits in cognitive, emotional, and social development—such as infantile autism.
Phallic stage (or Oedipal stage) The third stage in Freud's psychodynamic theory in which the child's interest shifts to the genitals.
Phenotype The way an individual's genotype is expressed in observable or measurable characteristics.
Phenylketonuria or PKU A disorder, caused by a recessive gene, that leads to the absence of an enzyme necessary to convert phenylalanine into tyrosine. This leads to an accumulation of phenylpyruvic acid, which has damaging effects on the developing nervous system of a child.
Phocomelia An anomaly associated with thalidomide. Limbs are missing, and the feet and hands are attached to the torso like flippers.
Phoneme The shortest speech unit in which a change produces a change in meaning.
Phonology The system of sounds for a language, that is, how the basic sound units (phonemes) are put together to form words and how the intonation patterns of phrases and sentences are determined.
Pidgin language The simplified hybrid language which is created when two different languages come in contact; this language lacks grammatical rules, and sentences are little more than strings of nouns and verbs.
Placebo An inactive treatment (for example, a sugar pill). Its effectiveness is based solely on expectations of change.
Placenta A fleshy disc attached to the uterus through which nutrients and waste products are exchanged between the maternal and infant systems.
Plane of action The level of behavior dominated by sensorimotor events.
Plane of thought The level of events dominated by mental operations.
Planfulness The ability to process certain selected types of useful information in accord with a plan or strategy.
Play A nonserious and self-contained activity engaged in for the sheer satisfaction it brings.

Play therapy A form of treatment utilized with young children because of their limited ability to verbally express themselves. The primary focus is to use the play materials as a means to symbolically express conflicts that the child may be confronting.
Pleiotropism The complex interactions among a set of genes acting together.
Postconventional level The third and highest level of moral judgment, according to Kohlberg. Morality is based on self-chosen, internalized ethical principles. This level is generally reached by mature individuals.
Pragmatics The rules governing the use of language in context by real speakers and real listeners.
Precocious puberty The onset of puberty abnormally early in childhood; this has adverse effects on adult stature, peer relations, and family relations.
Preconceptual period A period of development lasting from 2 to 4 years of age, in which systems of representation appear.
Preconventional level The first and lowest level of moral judgment according to Kohlberg. Morality is based on the desire to avoid punishment and to gain rewards. Young children generally function at this level.
Prematurity Birth occurring before the completion of the full-term gestation period and involving biological immaturity of the offspring.
Preoperational period Piaget's second stage of intellectual development, characterized by illogical thought based on intuitions, immediate perceptions, and direct experience.
Primary prevention This is an attempt to alter social conditions that give rise to psychological difficulties (for example, improving the school curriculum).
Problems in living The orientation that psychological disorders are based on social issues as opposed to medical causes.
Processes The underlying cause of developmental change within the individual.
Production deficiency The lack of production of verbal mediators that would assist in remembering.
Progesterone A female hormone.
Prompting A technique for facilitating a verbal response that includes rephrasing statements to make them easier to understand.
Prosocial behavior Positive behavior such as helping, sharing, cooperation, and altruism.
Prosocial skills Behaviors that facilitate interpersonal interaction and acceptance.
Proximal-distal principle Developmental principle which states that development occurs from the center outward.
Pseudodialogues The beginnings of conversational turn-taking between infant and caregiver when the infant is around 3 months of age.
Psychoactive medication A chemical compound that has psychological effects, such as the altering of mood or of thought processes.
Psychodynamic perspective The perspective in psychology that development is governed by unconscious drives and biological instincts; it is most often associated with Freud.
Psychosis A thought process which is out of touch with reality.
Psychostimulant medication An active chemical that heightens alertness and arousal in adults. However, it has the paradoxical effect of tranquilizing hyperactive children.
Puberty The attainment of sexual maturity; this attainment is a gradual process marked by a number of developmental changes.
Pygmalion effect See *Teacher expectation effect.*
Range of reaction Genetically-based variations of an individual's responsiveness to the environment.
Rating scale approach Approach to developmental psychopathology that involves having adults familiar with a child rate a large number of problem behaviors and using statistical techniques to determine which disorders are related to each other.
Realistic thinking A distortion in logical thinking. The child believes that his or her perspective prevails.
Recasting A language interaction in which the adult takes the child's incomplete

utterance, expands it, and modifies the grammatical form; for example, the child's utterance "Daddy go" becomes "Where is Daddy going?"

Recessive allele An allele that will not be expressed phenotypically when paired with a dominant allele. Recessive alleles are expressed only when they are paired with similar recessive alleles, that is, when they are homozygous.

Reciprocal imitation A behavior in which individuals imitate each other.

Reflective organism An individual whose thought process includes symbolic thought.

Reflex An involuntary response of the body to an external stimulus.

Reflexive organism An individual whose behavior is dominated by inherited perceptual and motor patterns.

Regular sleep A state in which the eyes are closed and the body is completely still; respirations are slow and regular; the face is relaxed, with no grimace; and the eyelids are still.

Rehearsal A strategy for remembering that involves repeating words subvocally or aloud.

Reliability The extent to which test results are stable or consistent over repeated administrations of the test.

Representation The form in which information is stored in the brain, such as in words, pictures, images, or actions.

Respiratory distress syndrome A disorder most commonly seen in premature infants who are incapable of producing sufficient quantities of surfactin, which results in respiratory difficulties.

Reward-cost stage The first stage of expectations about friends; it emerges at about 2 or 3 and is characterized by similar expectations, common activities,and propinquity (nearness).

Rh factor One aspect of blood type that can result in fetal erythroblastosis, when the child's blood is Rh-positive and the mother's is Rh-negative.

Ribonucleic acid or RNA The messenger carrying the DNA-originated directions from the nucleus of a cell to its cytoplasm. These directions lead to the synthesis of proteins which make up the body.

Rooting response A reflex in which the head is turned toward a nipple, finger, or other object touched lightly to an infant's cheek. The infant opens his or her mouth and tries to suck the object.

Rubella Also known as German measles. A common disease that generally is not serious in young children or adults. It can have effects such as blindness and mental retardation in children whose mothers contract the disease during the first three months of pregnancy.

Scaffolding A process of helping infants or children achieve more than they can on their own by skillfully structuring the social environment or the physical world to make it easier for them.

Schema A mental representation of an external event.

Schemata (Sing.: Schema) The cognitive structures underlying organized patterns of behavior.

Schizophrenia A seriously incapacitating thought disorder, characterized by the loss of contact with reality. Common symptoms are hallucinations and delusions.

Scripts Day-to-day routines which provide the person with a basic outline of what is expected and what should be done.

Secondary prevention An attempt to deal with psychological problems by providing early treatment for at-risk populations, for example, developing a preschool program for children who are economically disadvantaged, such as Head Start.

Secular trends Systematic changes within a culture that may influence a child's development, for example the increased percentage of women working outside of the home.

Secure attachment An attachment to the mother wherein the infant occasionally seeks to be close to her, intensifies the contact-maintaining behavior after being left alone in an unfamiliar situation, and is actively curious in dealing with new objects in unfamiliar situations when the mother is present.

Selective attention The ability to attend to only relevant aspects of an array of stimuli and to filter out or ignore the rest.

Self-control The ability to behave in accord with social or moral rules.

Self-disclosure The honest sharing of information of a very personal nature, often with the focus on problem solving. This is a central means that children ages 13 and 17 employ to develop friendship.

Self-identity The complex network of cognitions, emotions, motives, values, and behaviors that is unique to each person.

Self-report A data-collection strategy, such as an interview, questionnaire, or rating scale, in which parents, teachers, peers, or the child are asked to report on the child's behavior.

Self-stimulatory behavior The persistent engaging of repetitious behavior, such as hand-flapping or turning the lights on and off.

Semantic integration The extension of reinterpretation of information on the basis of reasoning or meaning.

Semantic organization The restructuring of information in order to make it more meaningful.

Semantics The study of the meaning of words and of sentences.

Semistructured lab research A research strategy by which the researcher duplicates many of the features of a natural setting in the laboratory. This approach allows control of the situation while preserving the "naturalism" of real situations.

Sensorimotor period Piaget's first stage of intellectual development, characterized by intelligent motor and perceptual acts and by experimentation with objects that results in increased knowledge of the surrounding world. The culmination of this period is the emergence of symbolic thought.

Sensory registers In the human information processing system, storage for information from the senses. This storage is fleeting; information in the visual sensory register lasts only briefly (e.g., a second).

Sex chromosomes Chromosomes that are responsible for sex-related characteristics in individuals. Females have two X chromosomes, and males have an X and a Y chromosome.

Sex-linked inheritance The inheritance of a characteristic through a recessive allele on the X chromosome. Since some genes on the X chromosome have no equivalent genes on the Y chromosome, sex-linked recessive characteristics appear more frequently in males.

Short-term longitudinal design A research design that involves tracking a group of individuals for a short time on key issues.

Short-term memory The process by which people remember over a brief period of time.

Sickle-cell anemia A severe, chronic, often fatal form of anemia caused by the recessive sickle-cell genes.

Sickle-cell trait or sicklemia Individuals who have the sickle-cell trait or sicklemia are heterozygous and carry only one of the recessive sickle-cell genes. There is a tendency for some of the red blood cells of these individuals to assume a crescent shape under conditions of low oxygen.

Single-subject design A research design in which the subject's baseline behavior is measured, and then change introduced, withdrawn, and reintroduced to discover what controls a particular behavior.

Size constancy The tendency of an object to retain its size in our perception regardless of changes in viewing distance, even though the size of the retinal image changes.

Sociability A personality attribute that can be described as the range from introversion to extroversion.

Social cognition The ability to understand the viewpoints, emotions, thoughts, and intentions of oneself and of others, and the ability to think about social relations and institutions.

Social learning theory A theory in psychology that, when applied to development, stresses the importance of observation and imitation in the child's acquisition of new behaviors.

Socialization The process by which an individual's standards, skills, motives, attitudes, and behaviors are shaped to conform to those regarded as appropriate for the society in which he or she lives.

Sociometric technique A peer nomination procedure whereby children rate other children in terms of the degree to which they like or dislike them. It is used to assess peer group status.

Special children Children who are either physically handicapped or who learn more slowly or more quickly than do average children.

Sperm cell The male gamete, a special cell that carries the genetic material of the father.

Stage of coordination of secondary schemata A period of development, lasting from 8 to 12 months of age, in which a child uses or combines previously acquired schemata as a means of attaining goals.

Stage of invention of new means through mental combination A period of development, lasting from 18 months onward, in which mental combinations replace the overt explorations and manipulations of the previous period.

Stage of moral realism The first or earliest stage of Piaget's cognitive-developmental theory of moral development. This early stage reflects a simplistic, conforming approach to morality.

Stage of primary circular reactions A period of development, lasting from 1 to 4 months of age, in which an infant repeats and modifies the basic sensorimotor functions of his or her own body.

Stage of reflex activity A period of development, lasting from birth until the end of the first month of life, in which infants refine their innate responses.

Stage of secondary circular reactions A period of development, lasting from 4 to 8 months, in which the infant's attention focuses on objects not just his or her body. Infants begin to intentionally manipulate and change their environment.

Stage of coordination of secondary schemata A period of development, lasting from 12 to 18 months of age, in which a child actively experiments with and adjusts schemata in order to learn more about objects.

Standardization In intelligence testing, constructing the scoring of test items such that test procedures will be the same when administered by different people.

State A point along the continuum of alertness or consciousness ranging from vigorous activity to regular sleep.

Statistical model A means of determining the normalcy of behavior. This determination is based totally on the frequency with which that behavior occurs. Behavior that occurs infrequently is considered abnormal.

Status offense Acts that are only illegal if the perpetrator is under the age of 18 (for example, possession of alcohol in some states or truancy).

Stimulus-augmenter An individual who subjectively experiences a stimulus as more stimulating than does the stimulus-reducer.

Stimulus-reducer An individual who subjectively experiences a stimulus as less stimulating than does the stimulus-augmenter.

Strange situation In attachment research, a means of assessing the quality of attachment relationships in infants through the infants' reactions to a series of situations involving the presence or absence of the mother and a stranger.

Strategy A conscious cognitive or behavioral activity used to enhance mental performance.

Sucking A highly organized response pattern, ready to operate at birth, which is both the principal means of feeding and also a distress-reducing activity.

Sudden infant death syndrome (SIDS) or crib death An as yet unexplained phenomenon in which infants under six months of age stop breathing and die.

Surfactin A liquid which allows the lungs to transmit oxygen from the air to the blood; this liquid is needed for adequate respiration in the newborn.

Sustained attention The ability to remain alert to a task over an extended period of time.

Symbolic function Systems of representation such as language.

Syntax The structure of the language; the underlying rules that specify the order and function of words in a sentence.
Teacher expectation effect A description of a finding (Rosenthal and Jacobson, 1968) that positive teacher expectations enhance children's performance, regardless of their actual ability. This has also been referred to as the Pygmalion effect.
Telegraphic speech Utterances made up of content words such as the messages in a telegram.
Temperament The characteristic style of responding, which is the biological substrate of personality.
Tempo of growth The tendency for the rate of physical development to be rapid or slow with the result that some children mature earlier and others later in relation to their peers.
Teratogen An agent that raises the incidence of deviations or produces malformations in the course of prenatal development.
Tertiary prevention A form of prevention involving the provision of treatment to children and families who are already identified as suffering from a variety of problems. Treatment methods are employed to alleviate adverse symptoms or to "cure" a disorder.
Test reliability An indication of whether the test performance of individuals is consistent and stable. If the test were to be taken on two separate occasions by the same person under identical circumstances, would that person's performance remain constant?
Test validity An indication of whether a test measures what it claims to measure.
Testosterones Male hormones.
Thalidomide A sedative and antinausea drug that, if taken by the mother early in pregnancy, may be associated with a number of anomalies, particularly phocomelia.
Transformation The process by which a change occurs.
Triarchic theory of intelligence Sternberg's theory that intelligence includes information processing skills, experience, and context.
Triple-X syndrome A sex chromosome abnormality in which the individuals have three, rather the normal two, X chromosomes. These individuals are female and appear normal but have deficits in verbal skills and in short-term memory.
Turner syndrome A sex chromosome abnormality in which only an X chromosome is present in each cell (XO pattern). These females are small and have a characteristic appearance. They do not develop secondary sex characteristics without estrogen therapy and generally have difficulty with spatial relationships and handwriting.
Ultrasound sonography A prenatal diagnostic procedure used to detect structural malformation. High-frequency sound waves are directed into the abdomen of the pregnant woman, and the echo from these sounds is transformed into a visual representation of the inner structures.
Unconditioned response (UCR) The particular response elicited by the unconditioned stimulus.
Unconditioned stimulus (UCS) A stimulus that can reliably elicit a particular response (the UCR) without any prior learning.
Undercontrolled disorders A broad-band class of problems involving difficulties in self-control and in conforming to social norms. Examples include conduct disorder and hyperactivity.
Underextension A typical error in children's early word use in which a word is used to mean only a particular instance rather than the more general category.
Universal features Properties that are thought to be common to all human languages; these properties may be innate.
Valid Indication of the correctness of the information that diagnosis provides regarding etiology and treatment.
Validity In testing, the extent to which a test measures what it is claimed to measure.
Visual acuity The ability to detect separation in parts of a visual target.

Visual cliff An apparatus for studying depth perception in infants; it consists of an elevated glass platform divided into a "deep" section and a "shallow" section.

Waking activity A state in which the individual frequently engages in diffuse motor activity involving the whole body; the eyes are open, but not alert, and respirations are grossly irregular.

World knowledge the knowledge one has about the world, as well as knowledge from past personal experiences.

Zone of proximal development According to Vygotsky, the gap between a child's current performance in a particular area and the child's potential performance when guided by someone more skilled.

Zygote The fertilized ovum formed by a sperm cell's penetrating and uniting with the ovum at conception.

REFERENCES

Aaronson, L. S., & MacNee, C. L. (1989). Tobacco, alcohol, and caffeine use during pregnancy. *Journal of Obstetrics, Gynecology and Neonatal Nursing,* **18,** 279–287.

Abraham, S., Collins, G., & Nordsieck, M. (1971). Relationship of childhood weight status to morbidity in adults. *Public Health Reports,* **86,** 273–284.

Abramovitch, R., Corter, C., Pepler, D. J., & Stanhope, L. (1986). Sibling and peer interaction: A final follow-up and a comparison. *Child Development,* **57,** 217–229.

Abramovitch, R., & Grusec, J. E. (1978). Peer imitation in a natural setting. *Child Development,* **49,** 60–65.

Abramovitch, R., Pepler, D., & Corter, C. (1982). Patterns of sibling interaction among preschool-age children. In M. E. Lamb & B. Sutton-Smith (Eds.), *Sibling relationships.* Hillsdale, NJ: Erlbaum.

Achenbach, T. M. (1990). Conceptualization of developmental psychopathology. In M. Lewis & S. Miller (Eds.), *Handbook of developmental psychopathology* (pp. 3–14). New York: Plenum.

Achenbach, T. M., & Edelbrock, C. S. (1978). The classification of child psychopathology: A review and analysis of empirical efforts. *Psychological Bulletin,* **85,** 1275–1301.

Adams, P. L., Mauer, D., & Davis, M. (1986). Newborns' discrimination of chromatic from achromatic stimuli. *Journal of Experimental Child Psychology,* **41,** 267–281.

Adamson, L. B., & Bakeman, R. (1985). Affect and attention: Infants observed with mothers and peers. *Child Development,* **56,** 582–583.

Adelson, E., & Fraiberg, S. (1974). Gross motor development in infants blind from birth. *Child Development,* **45,** 114–126.

Adler, A. (1990). Cocaine babies' reactions explored. *APA Monitor,* p. 8.

Agras, W. S. (1988). Does early eating behavior influence later adiposity. In N. A. Krasnegor, G. D. Grave, & N. Kretchmer (Eds.), *Childhood obesity: A biobehavioral perspective* (pp. 49–66). Caldwell, NJ: Telford Press.

Ahrens, R. (1954). Beitrag zur entwicklun des physionomie und mimikerkennens. *A. F. Exp. U. Angew, Psychol.,* **2,** 599–633.

Ainsworth, M. D. (1963). The development of infant-mother interaction among the Ganda. In D. M. Foss (Ed.), *Determinants of infant behavior* (Vol. 2, pp. 67–104). New York: Wiley.

Ainsworth, M. D. (1973). The development of infant-mother attachment. In B. Caldwell & H. Ricciuti (Eds.), *Review of child development research* (Vol. 3). Chicago: University of Chicago Press.

Ainsworth, M. D., Blehar, M., Waters, E., & Wall, S. (1978). *Patterns of attachment.* Hillsdale, NJ: Erlbaum.

Aitken, S. (1981). *Differentiation theory and the study of intersensory substitution using the sonic guide.* Unpublished doctoral thesis. University of Edinburgh.

Alexander, K. L., & Entwisle, D. R. (1988). Achievement in the first 2 years of school: Patterns and processes. *Monographs of the Society for Research in Child Development,* **53** (Serial No. 218).

Allen, L., & Majidi-Abi, S. (1989). Black American children. In J. T. Gibbs & L. N. Huang (Eds.), *Children of color.* San Francisco: Jossey-Bass.

Allen, V. L., & Feldman, R. S. (1976). *Children as teachers: Theory and research on tutoring.* New York: Academic.

Allison, A. C. (1954). Protection afforded by sickle-cell trait against subtertian malarial infections. *British Medical Journal,* **1,** 290–294.

American Psychiatric Association. (1987). *Diagnostic and statistical manual of mental disorders* (3rd Ed.). Washington, DC: Aumor.

Amiel-Tison, C. (1983). Neurological signs, aetiology, and implications. In P. Stratton (Eds.), *Psychobiology of the human newborn.* New York: Wiley.

Anastasi, A. (1988). *Psychological testing* (6th ed.). New York: Macmillan.

Anastopoulos, A. D., & Barkley, R. A. (1988). Biological factors in attention deficit-hyperactivity disorder. *Behavior Therapist,* **11,** 47–53.

Anderson, D. R., Choi, H. P., & Lorch, E. P. (1987). Attentional inertia reduces distractability during young children's TV viewing. *Child Development*, **58**, 798–806.

Anderson, D. R., & Levin, S. R. (1976). Young children's attention to "Sesame Street." *Child Development*, **47**, 806–811.

Anderson, D. R., Lorch, E. P., Field, D. E., Collins, P., & Nathan, J. (1986). Television viewing at home: Age trends in visual attention and time with TV. *Child Development*, **57**, 1024–1033.

Anderson, D. R., Lorch, E. P., Field, D. E., & Sanders, J. (1981). The effects of TV program comprehensibility on preschool children's visual attention to television. *Child Development*, **52**, 151–157.

Anderson, E. S. (1984). Acquisition of Japanese. In D. I. Slobin (Ed.), *The cross-linguistic study of language acquisition: Vol. 1. The data* (pp. 323–524). Hillsdale, NJ: Erlbaum.

Anooshian, L. J., & Siegel, A. W. (1985). From cognitive to procedural mapping. In C. J. Brainard & M. Pressley (Eds.), *Basic process in memory development*. New York: Springer-Verlag.

Apgar, V. A. (1953). A proposal for a new method of evaluation of the newborn infant. *Current Research in Anesthesia and Analgesia*, **32**, 260–267.

Aronfreed, J. (1976). Moral development from the standpoint of a general psychological theory. In T. Lickona (Ed.), *Moral development and behavior*. New York: Holt.

Aronson, E., Stephan, C., Sikes, J., Blaney, N., & Snapp, M. (1978). *The jigsaw classroom*. Beverly Hills, CA: Sage.

Asher, S. R. (1976). Children's ability to appraise their own and another person's communication preference. *Developmental Psychology*, **12**, 24–32.

Asher, S. R. (1980). Topic interest and children's reading comprehension. In R. Spiro, B. Bruce, & W. Brewer (Eds.), *Theoretical issues in reading comprehension* (pp. 525–534). Hillsdale, NJ: Erlbaum.

Asher, S. R. (1990). An overview of intervention research with unpopular children. In S. R. Asher & J. Coie (Ed.), *Assessment of children's social status*. New York: Cambridge University Press.

Asher, S. R., Hymel, S., & Renshaw, P. D. (1984). Loneliness in children. *Child Development*, **55**, 1456–1464.

Asher, S. R., & Markell, R. A. (1974). Sex differences in comprehension of high and low interest reading material. *Journal of Educational Psychology*, **66**, 680–687.

Asher, S. R., Oden, S. L., & Gottman, J. M. (1976). Children's friendships in school settings. *Quarterly Review of Early Childhood Education*, **1**, 1–17.

Asher, S. R., Oden, S. L., & Gottman, J. M. (1977). Children's friendships in school settings. In L. G. Katz (Ed.), *Current topics in early childhood education* (Vol. 1). Norwood, NJ: Ablex.

Asher, S. R., Parkhurst, J. T., Hymel, S., & Williams, G. A. (1990). Peer rejection and loneliness in childhood. In S. R. Asher & J. D. Coie (Eds.), *Peer rejection in childhood*. New York: Cambridge University Press.

Aslin, R. (1987). Visual and auditory development in infancy. In J. Osofsky (Ed.), *Handbook of infant development* (2nd ed.). New York: Wiley.

Aslin, R. N., Pisoni, D. B., & Jusczyk, P. W. (1983). Auditory development and speech perception in infancy. In P. Mussen (Ed.), *Handbook of child psychology* (Vol. 2). New York: Wiley.

Atkin, C. (1983). Effects of realistic TV violence vs. fictional violence on aggression. *Journalism Quarterly*, **60**, 615–621.

Atkin, C. K., Greenberg, B. S., & McDermott, S. (1978). *Television and racial socialization*. Paper presented at meeting of the Association for Education in Journalism, Seattle, WA.

Atkins, W. T. (1988). Cocaine: The drug of choice. In I. J. Chasnoff (Ed.), *Drugs, alcohol, pregnancy and parenting*. Boston: Kluwer Academic.

Atkinson, R. C., & Shiffrin, R. M. (1968). Human memory: A proposed system and its control processes. In K. W. Spence & J. Spence (Eds.), *Advances in the psychology of learning and motivation: research and theory* (Vol. 2). New York: Academic.

Attwood, A., Frith, W., & Hermelin, B. (1988). The understanding and use of interpersonal gestures by autistic and Down's syndrome children. *Journal of Autism and Developmental Disorders*, **18**, 241–257.

Au, K. H. (1979). Using the experience-test-relationship method with minority children. *Reading Teacher*, **32**, 677–679.

Auger, A., Bronfenbrenner, U., & Henderson, C. R. (1977). Socialization practices of parents, teachers and peers in Israel: Kibbutz, Moshav, and city. *Child Development*, **48**, 1219–1227.

Aylward, G. P., Pfeiffer, S. I., Wright, A., Verholst, S. J. (1989). Outcome studies of low birth weight infants published in the last decade: A meta-analysis. *Journal of Pediatrics*, **115**, 515–520.

Babson, S. G., Pernoll, M. C., Benda, G. I., & Simpson, K. (1980). *Diagnosis and management of the fetus and neonate at risk: A guide for team care* (4th ed.). St. Louis: Mosby.

Bai, D. L., & Bertenthal, B. I. (1989). The role of self-produced locomotion in the development of object localization skills. Unpublished manuscript, University of Virginia.

Bainum, C. K., Lounsbury, K. R., & Pollio, H. R. (1984). The development of laughing and smiling in nursery school children. *Child Development,* **55,** 1946–1957.

Bakeman, R., & Brown, J. V. (1980). Early intervention: Consequences for social and mental development at three years. *Child Development,* **51**, 437–447.

Bakeman, R., & Gottman, J. M. (1986). *Observing behavior.* New York: Cambridge University Press.

Baker, L. (1982). An evaluation of the role of metacognitive deficits in learning disabilities. *Topics in Learning and Learning Disabilities,* **2**, 27–35.

Baker, R. L., & Mednick, B. R. (1984). *Influences on human development: A longitudinal perspective.* Boston: Kluwer Nijhoff.

Baldwin, A. L., Cole, R. E., & Baldwin, C. P. (1982). Parent pathology, family interaction, and the competence of the child in school. *Monographs of the Society for Research in Child Development,* **47**(5, Serial No. 197).

Ball, S., & Bogatz, J. (1972). Summative research of Sesame Street: Implications for the study of preschool children. In A. D. Pick (Ed.), *Minnesota Symposia on Child Psychology* (Vol. 6). Minneapolis: University of Minnesota Press.

Baltes, P. B. (1987). Theoretical propositions of life span developmental psychology: On the dynamics between growth and decline. *Developmental Psychology,* **23**, 611–626.

Bandura, A. (1969). Social learning theory and identifactory processes. In D. A. Goslin (Ed.), *Handbook of socialization theory and research* (pp. 213–262). Chicago: Rand McNally.

Bandura, A. (1989). Cognitive social learning theory. In R. Vasta (Ed.), *Annals of Child Development* (Vol. 6). Greenwich, CT: JAI Press.

Bandura. A. (1989). Social cognitive theory. In R. Vasta (Ed.), *Six theories of child development.* Greenwich, CT: JAI Press.

Bandura, A., & MacDonald, F. J. (1963). Influence of social reinforcement and the behavior of models in shaping children's moral judgments. *Journal of Abnormal and Social Psychology,* **67,** 274–281.

Banks, M. S., Aslin, R. N., & Letson, R. D. (1975). Sensitive period for the development of human binocular vision. *Science,* **190**, 675–677.

Banks, M. S., & Salapatek, P. (1981). Infant pattern vision: A new approach based on the contrast sensitivity function. *Journal of Experimental Child Psychology,* **31**, 1–45.

Banks, M. S., & Salapatek, P. (1983). Infant visual perception. In P. H. Mussen (Ed.), *Handbook of child psychology* (Vol. 2). New York: Wiley.

Barcus, F. E. (1983). *Images of life on children's television.* New York: Praeger.

Barglow, P., Vaughn, B. E., & Molitor, N. (1987). Effects of maternal absence due to employment on the quality of infant-mother attachment in a low-risk sample. *Child Development,* **58,** 945–954.

Barker, R. G., & Gump, P. V. (1964). *Big school, small school.* Stanford, CA: Stanford University Press.

Barkley, R. A. (1990). Attention deficit disorders. In M. Lewis & S. Miller (Eds.), *Handbook of developmental psychopathology.* New York: Plenum.

Barkley, R. A., & Cunningham, C. E. (1979). The effects of methylphenidate on the mother-child interaction of hyperactive children. *Archives of General Psychiatry,* **36**, 201-208.

Barkley, R. A., & Ullman, D. G. (1975). A comparison of objective measures of activity and distractibility in hyperactive and nonhyperactive children. *Journal of Abnormal Child Psychology,* **3**, 231–244.

Barlow, F. (1952). *Mental prodigies.* New York: Greenwood.

Barnard, K. E., & Bee, H. L. (1983). The impact of temporally patterned stimulation on the development of preterm infants. *Child Development,* **54,** 1156–1167.

Barnard, K. E., Bee, H. L., & Hammond, M. A. (1984). Home environment and cognitive development in a healthy, low-risk sample: The Seattle study. In A. W. Gottfried (Ed.), *Home environment and early cognitive development* (pp. 117–149). Orlando, FL: Academic.

Barnes, D. M. (1989). "Fragile X" syndrome and its puzzling genetics. *Science,* **243,** 171–172.

Barnett, C. R., Leiderman, P. H., Grobstein, K., & Klaus, M. (1970). Neonatal separation: The maternal side of interactional deprivation. *Pediatrics,* **45,** 197–205.

Barnett, J. T. (1969). *Development of children's fears: The relationship between three systems of fear measurement.* Unpublished master's thesis, University of Wisconsin, Madison.

Baron, R. A. (1977). *Human aggression.* New York: Plenum.

Baron-Cohen, S. (1988). Social and pragmatic deficits in autism: Cognitive or effective? *Journal of Autism and Developmental Disorders,* **18**, 379–397.

Baron-Cohen, S. (1989). The autistic child's theory of mind: A case of specific developmental delay. *Journal of Child Psychology and Psychiatry,* **30**, 285–297.

Barr, H. M., Streissguth, A. P., Darby, B. L., & Sampson, P. D. (1990). Prenatal exposure to alcohol, caffeine, tobacco and aspirin: Effects on fine and gross motor performance in 4-year-old children. *Developmental Psychology,* **26**, 339–348.

Barrett, D. E. (1979). A naturalistic study of sex differences in children's aggression. *Merrill-Palmer Quarterly,* **25,** 193–203.

Barrett, D. E., Radke-Yarrow, M., & Klein, R. E. (1982). Chronic malnutrition and child behavior: Effects of early caloric supplementation on social and emotional functioning at school age. *Developmental Psychology,* **18,** 541–556.

Baruffi, G. (1982). *Review of the safety of maternity care in different birth locations.* In Committee on Assessing Alternative Birth Settings, Research Issues in the Assessment of Birth Settings. National Research Council, Commission on Life Sciences. Washington, DC: National Academy Press.

Baskett, L. M. (1985). Sibling status effects: Adult expectations. *Developmental Psychology,* **21,** 441–445.

Bates, E. (1976). *Language and context: The acquisition of pragmatics.* New York: Academic.

Bates, J. E. (1987). Temperament in infancy. In J. Osofsky (Ed.), *Handbook of infancy* (2nd ed.). New York: Wiley.

Bates, J. E., Maslin, C. A., & Frankel, K. A. (1985). Attachment security, mother-child interaction and temperament as predictors of behavior-problem ratings at age three years. In I. Bretherton & E. Waters (Eds.), Growing points of attachment theory and research. *Monographs of the Society for Research in Child Development,* **50**(1–2, Serial No. 209).

Baumrind, D. (in press). The average expectable environment is not good enough: A response to Scarr. *Child Development.*

Baumrind, D. (1967). Child care practices anteceding three patterns of preschool behavior. *Genetic Psychology Monographs,* **75,** 43–88.

Baumrind, D. (1971). Current patterns of parental authority. *Developmental Psychology Monographs,* **1,** 1–103.

Baumrind, D. (1991). Effective parenting during the early adolescent transition. In P. A. Cowan & E. M. Hetherington (Eds.), *Family transitions* (pp. 111–164). Hillsdale, NJ: Erlbaum.

Baumrind, D. (1991). To nurture nature. *Behavioral and Brain Sciences,* **14,** 386–387.

Bax, M. C. O., & MacKeith, R. C. (1963). Minimal brain damage: A concept discarded. In R. C. MacKeith and M. C. O. Bax (Eds.), Minimal cerebral dysfunction. *Little Club Clinics in Developmental Medicine* (No. 10.) London: Heinemann.

Bayley, N. (1965). Research in child development: A longitudinal perspective. *Merrill-Palmer Quarterly,* **11,** 184–190.

Bayley, N. (1969). Ch. 11. *Bayley scales of infant development.* New York, NY: Psychological Corporation.

Bayley, N. (1970). Development of mental abilities. In P. H. Mussen (Ed.), *Carmichael's manual of child psychology* (Vol. 1, pp. 1163–1210). New York: Wiley.

Beardslee, W. R., Bemporad, J., Keller, M. B., & Klerman, G. L. (1983). Children of parents with major affective disorder: A review. *American Journal of Psychiatry,* **140,** 825–832.

Beckwith, L. (1979). Prediction of emotional and social behavior. In J. D. Osofsky (Ed.), *Handbook of infant development.* New York: Wiley.

Bédard, J., & Chi, M. T. H. (1992). Expertise. *Current Directions in Psychological Science,* **1,** 135–139.

Bee, H., Barnard, K., Eyres, S., Gray, C., Hammond, M., Spietz, A., Snyder, C., & Clark, B. (1982). Prediction of IQ and language skill from perinatal status, child performance, family characteristics, and mother-infant interaction. *Child Development,* **53,** 1134–1156.

Beilin, H. (1992). Piaget's enduring contribution to developmental psychology. *Developmental Psychology,* **28,** 191–204.

Beitel, A., & Parke, R. D. (1990). *The role of maternal "gatekeeping" in father involvement.* Unpublished paper, University of Illinois, Urbana.

Bell, R. Q., & Harper, I. V. (Eds.). (1977). *Child effects on adults.* Hillsdale, NJ: Erlbaum.

Bell, R. Q., Weller, G. M., & Waldrop, M. F. (1971). Newborn and preschooler: Organization of behavior and relations between periods. *Monographs of the Society for Research in Child Development,* **36**(4, Serial no. 142), 1–145.

Belmont, J. M. (1989). Cognitive strategies and strategic learning: The socio-instructional approach. *American Psychologist,* **44,** 142–148.

Belsky, J., Long, M. E., & Rovine, M. (1985). Stability and change in marriage across the transition to parenthood: A second study. *Journal of Marriage and the Family,* **47,** 855–865.

Belsky, J., & Rovine, M. (1988). Nonmaternal care in the first year of life and infant-parent attachment security. *Child Development,* **57,** 1224–1231.

Belsky, J., Steinberg, L. D., & Walker, A. (1983). The ecology of day care. In M. E. Lamb (Ed.), *Nontraditional families.* Hillsdale, NJ: Erlbaum.

Bem, S. L. (1974). The measurement of psychological androgyny. *Journal of Clinical and Consulting Psychology,* **42,** 155–162.

Bem, S. L. (1981). Gender schema theory: A cognitive account of sex typing. *Psychological Review,* **88,** 354–364.

Bem, S. L. (1983). Gender schema theory and its implications for child development: Raising gender-aschematic children in a gender-schematic society. *Signs: Journal of Women in Culture and Society,* **8,** 598–616.

Bem, S. L. (1985). Androgyny and gender schema theory. In T. B Sonderegger (Ed.), *Nebraska Symposium on Motivation: Psychology and Gender* (Vol. 32). Lincoln: University of Nebraska Press.

Bem, S. L. (1989). Genital knowledge and gender constancy in preschool children. *Child Development,* **60,** 649–662.

Bem, S. L. (1991). *The lenses of gender: An essay on the social reproduction of male power.* Unpublished manuscript. Cornell University, Ithaca, NY.

Ben Tsvi-Mayer, S., Hertz-Lazarowitz, R., & Safir, M. P. (1989). Teacher's selections of boys and girls as prominent pupils. *Sex Roles,* **21,** 231–245.

Benbow, C. P. (1988). Sex differences in mathematical reasoning ability in intellectually talented preadolescents: Their nature, effects and possible causes. *Behavioral and Brain Sciences,* **11,** 169–232.

Benbow, C. P., & Stanley, J. C. (1980). Sex differences in mathematical ability: Fact or artifact. *Science,* **210,** 1262–1264.

Bender, B. C., Linden, M. G., & Robinson, A. (1987). Environment and developmental risk in children with sex chromosome abnormalities. *Journal of the Academy of Child and Adolescent Psychiatry,* **26,** 499–503.

Benedict, H. (1975). *The role of repetition in early language comprehension.* Paper presented at the biennial meeting of the Society for Research in Child Development, Denver.

Berg, W. K., & Berg, K. M. (1987). Psychophysiologic development in infancy: State, startle and attention. In J. Osofsky (Ed.), *Handbook of infancy* (2nd ed.). New York: Wiley.

Bergen, D. J., & Williams, J. E. (1991). Sex stereotypes in the United States revisited: 1972–1988. *Sex Roles,* **24,** 413–423.

Berman, P. W. (1987). Children caring for babies: Age and sex differences in response to infant signals and to the social context. In N. Eisenberg (Ed.), *Contemporary topics in developmental psychology.* New York: Wiley.

Bernard, H. W. (1962). *Human development in western culture.* Boston: Allyn and Bacon.

Berndt, T. J. (1986). Sharing between friends: Contexts and consequences. In E. C. Mueller & C. R. Cooper (Eds.), *Process and outcome in peer relationships.* New York: Academic.

Berndt, T. J., & Bulleit, T. N. (1985). Effects of sibling relationships on preschoolers' behavior at home and at school. *Developmental Psychology,* **21,** 761–767.

Berndt, T. J., & Ladd, G. W. (1989). (Eds.) *Peer relationships in child development.* New York: Wiley.

Berndt, T. J., & Perry, T. B. (1990). Distinctive features and effects of adolescent friendships. In R. Montemeyer, G. R. Adams, & T. P. Gullotta (Eds.), *From childhood to adolescence: A transition period?* London: Sage.

Bertenthal, B. I., Proffitt, D. R., & Cutting, J. E. (1984). Infant sensitivity to figural coherence in biomechanical motions. *Journal of Experimental Child Psychology,* **37,** 213–230.

Bertenthal, B. I., Proffitt, D. R., Kramer, S. J. (1987). The perception of biomechanical motions. Implementation of various processing constraints. *Journal of Experimental Psychology. Human Perception and Performance,* **13,** 577–585.

Berthoud-Papandropoulou, I. (1978). An experimental study of children's ideas about language. In A. Sinclair, R. J. Jarvella, & W. J. M. Levelt (Eds.), *The child's conception of language* (Vol. 2). Heidelberg: Springer.

Best, C. T. (1988). The emergence of cerebral asymmetries in early human development: A literature review and a neuroembryological model. In D. L. Molfese & S. J. Segalowitz (Eds.), *Brain lateralization in children* (pp. 5–35). New York: Guilford Press.

Best, D. L., & Ornstein, P. A. (1986). Children's generation and communication of mnemonic organizational strategies. *Developmental Psychology,* **22,** 845–853.

Best, D. L., Williams, J. E., Cloud, J. M., Davis, S. W., Robertson, L. S., Edwards, J. R., Giles, H., & Fowles, J. (1977). Development of sex-trait stereotypes among young children in the United States, England and Ireland. *Child Development,* **48,** 1375–1385.

Bhavnagri, N., & Parke, R. D. (1985, April). *Parents as facilitators of preschool peer-peer interaction.* Paper presented at the biennial meeting of the Society for Research in Child Development, Toronto.

Bhavnagri, N., & Parke, R. D. (1991). Parents as direct facilitators of children's peer relationships: Effects of age of child and sex of parent. *Journal of Social and Personal Relationships,* **8,** 423–440.

Bianchi, B. D., & Bakeman, R. (1983). Patterns of sex typing in an open school. In M. B. Liss (Ed.), *Social and cognitive skills: Sex roles and children's play.* New York: Academic.

Bigelow, B. J. (1977). Children's friendship expectations: A cognitive-developmental study. *Child Development,* **48,** 246–253.

Bigelow, B. J., & LaGaipa, J. J. (1975). Children's written descriptions of friendship: A multidimensional analysis. *Developmental Psychology,* **11,** 857–858.

Bigler, R. S., & Liben, L. S. (1990). The role of attitudes and interventions in gender-schematic processing. *Child Development,* **61,** 1440–1452.

Binet, A. (1909/1973). *Les idées modernes sur les enfants.* Paris: Flammarion.

Birch, H. G., & Gussow, J. D. (1970). *Disadvantaged children. Health, nutrition and school failure.* New York: Grune & Stratton.

Blake, J. (1989). Number of siblings and educational attainment. *Science,* **245,** 32–36.

Blasi, A. (1983). Moral cognition and moral action: A theoretical perspective. *Developmental Review,* **3,** 178–210.

Blass, E., Ganchrow, J. R., & Steiner, J. E. (1984). Classical conditioning in newborn humans 2–48 hours of age. *Infant Behavior and Development,* **7,** 223–234.

Block, J. (1971). *Lives through time.* Berkeley, CA: Bancroft Books.

Block, J., Bock, J. H., Keyes, S. (1988). Longitudinally foretelling drug usage in adolescents: Early childhood personality and environmental precursors. *Child Development,* **59,** 336–355.

Block, J. H. (1983). Differential premises arising from differential socialization of the sexes: Some conjectures. *Child Development,* **54,** 1335–1354.

Block, J. H., Block, J., & Gjerde, P. F. (1986). The personality of children prior to divorce: A prospective study. *Child Development,* **57,** 827–840.

Block, J. H., Block, J., & Harrington, D. M. (1974). *The relationship of parental teaching strategies to ego-resiliency in preschool children.* Paper presented at the meeting of the Western Psychological Association, San Francisco.

Block, J. H., Block, J., & Morrison, A. (1981). Parental agreement-disagreement on childrearing orientations and gender-related personality correlates in children. *Child Development,* **52,** 965–974.

Bloom, L. (1970). *Language development: Form and function in emerging grammars.* Cambridge, MA: M.I.T. Press.

Bloom, L. (1973). *One word at a time.* Hague: Mouton.

Bloom, L. (1976). *An interactive perspective on language development.* Keynote address, Child Language Research Forum, Stanford University.

Blough, H. A., & Guintoli, R. L. (1979). Successful treatment of human genital herpes infections with 2-deoxy-D-glucose. *Journal of the American Medical Association,* **241,** 2798–2801.

Bohannon, J. N., III, & Stanowicz, L. (1988). The issue of negative evidence: Adult responses to children's language errors. *Developmental Psychology,* **24,** 684–689.

Bohannon, J. N., III, & Warren-Leubecker, A. (1988). Recent developments in child-directed speech: We've come a long way, baby talk. *Language Sciences,* **10,** 89–110.

Boldizar, J. P. (1991). Assessing sex typing and androgyny in children: The children's sex role inventory. *Developmental Psychology,* **27,** 505–515.

Boothby, N. (1991). *Children of war: Survival as a collective act.* Paper presented at the meeting on vulnerability and resiliency in children and families: Focus on children with disabilities. Baltimore, MD.

Borke, H. (1971). Interpersonal perception of young children: Egocentrism or empathy. *Developmental Psychology,* **5,** 263–269.

Borke, H. (1975). Piaget's mountains revisited: Changes in the egocentric landscape. *Developmental Psychology,* **11,** 240–243.

Bornstein, M. H. (1978). Chromatic vision in infancy. In H. W. Reese & L. P. Lipsitt (Eds.), *Advances in child development and behavior* (Vol. 12). New York: Academic.

Bornstein, M. H. (1985). How infant and mother jointly contribute to developing cognitive competence in the child. *Proceedings of the National Academy of Sciences (U.S.A.),* 17–34.

Bornstein, M. H. (1989). Sensitive periods in development: Structural characteristics and causal interpretations. *Psychological Bulletin,* **105,** 179–197.

Bornstein, M. H., Kessen, W., & Weiskopf, S. (1976). The categories of hue in infancy. *Science,* **191,** 201–202.

Bornstein, M. H., & Sigman, M. D. (1986). Continuity in mental development from infancy. *Child Development,* **57,** 251–274.

Bornstein, M. H., & Tamis, C. (1986). *Origins of cognitive skills in infants.* Paper presented at the International Conference on Infant Studies, Los Angeles.

Bouchard, T. J., & McGue, M. (1981). Familial studies of intelligence: A review. *Science,* **212,** 1055–1059.

Bouchard T. J., & McGue, M. (1990). Genetic and rearing environmental influences on adult personality: An analysis of adopted twins reared apart. *Journal of Personality,* **58,** 263–292.

Bouchard, T. T., Lykken, D. T., Segal, N. L., & Wilcox, K. J. (1986). Development in twins reared apart: A test of the chronogenetic hypothesis. In A. Demirijian (Ed.), *Human growth: A multidisciplinary review* (pp. 299–310). London: Taylor & Francis.

Bower, T. G. R. (1979). Visual development in the blind child. In V. Smith & J. Keen (Eds.), *Visual handicap in children.* Clinics in Development Medicine, No. 73. London: Lippincott.

Bower, T. G. R. (1982). *Development in infancy* (2nd ed.). San Francisco: Freeman.

Bower, T. G. R. (1989). *The rational infant: Learning in infancy.* San Francisco: Freedman.

Bowlby, J. (1958). The nature of the child's tie to his mother. *International Journal of Psychoanalysis,* **39,** 35.

Bowlby, J. (1960). Grief and mourning in infancy and early childhood. *The Psychoanalytic Study of the Child,* **15.**

Bowlby, J. (1969). *Attachment and loss: Vol. 1. Attachment.* New York: Basic Books.

Bowlby, J. (1973). *Separation and loss.* New York: Basic Books.

Boyum, L. A., Dweck, C. S., & Hill, K. T. (1990, March). *Students' conceptions of their intelligence: Impact on academic course choice.* Poster presented at the biennial meeting of the Society for Research on Adolescence, Atlanta.

Brackbill, Y. (1958). Extinction of the smiling response in infants as a function of reinforcement schedule. *Child Development,* **29,** 115–124.

Brackbill, Y., McManus, K., & Woodward, L. (1985). *Medication in maternity: Infant exposure and maternal information.* Ann Arbor, MI: University of Michigan Press.

Bradley, R. H., Caldwell, B. M., & Elardo, R. (1977). Home environment, social status, and mental test performance. *Journal of Educational Psychology,* **69,** 697–701.

Bradley, R. H., Caldwell, B. M., Rock, S. L., Barnard, K. E., Gray, C., Hammon, M. A., Mitchell, S., Siegel, L., Ramey, C. T., Gottfried, A. W., & Johnson, D. L. (1989). Home environment and cognitive development in the first 3 years of life: A collaborative study involving six sites and three ethnic groups in North America. *Developmental Psychology,* **25,** 217–235.

Bradley, R. H., Caldwell, B. M., Rock, S. L., Casey, P. M., & Nelson, J. (1987). The early development of low birthweight babies. *International Journal of Behavioral Development,* **10,** 301–318.

Braine, M. D. S., & Rumain, B. (1983). Logical reasoning. In P. H. Mussen (Ed.), *Handbook of child psychology,* Vol. 3, New York: Wiley.

Brainerd, C. J., & Reyna, V. F. (1990). Inclusion illusions: Fuzzy trace theory and perceptual salience effects in cognitive development. *Developmental Review,* **10,** 365–403.

Brand, E., Clingempeel, W. G., & Bowen-Woodward, D. (1988). Family relationships and children's psychological adjustment in stepmother and stepfather families. In E. M. Hetherington & J. D. Arasten (Eds.), *Impact of divorce, single parenting and step parenting on children* (pp. 299–324). Hillsdale, NJ: Erlbaum.

Brandbard, M. R., & Endsley, R. C. (1984). The effects of sex-typed labeling on children's information seeking and retention. *Sex Roles,* **9,** 247–260.

Bray, J. H. (1988). Children's development during early remarriage. In E. M. Hetherington & J. D. Arasten (Eds.), *Impact of divorce, single parenting and step parenting on children* (pp. 279–298). Hillsdale, NJ: Erlbaum.

Brazelton, T. B. (1970). Effects of prenatal drugs on the behavior of the neonate. *American Journal of Psychiatry,* **126,** 1261–1266.

Brazelton, T. B. (1972). Implications of infant development among the Mayan Indians of Mexico. *Human Development,* **15,** 90–111.

Brazelton, T. B. (1984). *Neonatal behavioral assessment scale.* Philadelphia: Lippincott.

Brazelton, T. B., Nugent, J. K., & Lester, B. M. (1987). Neonatal behavioral assessment scale. In J. Osofsky (Ed.), *Handbook of infancy* (2nd ed.). New York: Wiley.

Brener, R. (1940). An experimental investigation of memory span. *Journal of Experimental Psychology,* **33,** 1–19.

Brenton, M. (1974). Mainstreaming the handicapped. *Today's Education,* **63,** 20–25.

Bretherton, I., Stolberg, U., & Kreye, M. (1981). Engaging strangers in proximal interaction: Infants' social initiative. *Developmental Psychology,* **17,** 746–755.

Briars, D., & Siegler, R. S. (1984). A featural analysis of preschoolers' counting knowledge. *Developmental Psychology,* **20,** 607–618.

Brody, G. H., Stoneman, Z., & Burke, M. (1987). Child temperaments, maternal differential behavior and sibling relationships. *Developmental Psychology,* **23,** 354–362.

Brody, L. E., & Benbow, C. P. (1987). Accelerative strategies: How effective are they for the gifted? *Gifted Child Quarterly,* **3,** 105–110.

Brody, N. (1985). The validity of tests of intelligence. In B. B. Wolman (Ed.), *Handbook of intelligence* (pp. 353–389). New York: Wiley.

Brodzinsky, D. M., Singer, L. M., & Braff, A. M. (1984). Children's understanding of adoption. *Child Development,* **55,** 868–878.

Bronfenbrenner, U. (1961). Some familial antecedents of responsibility and leadership. In L. Petrullo & B. M. Bass (Eds.), *Adolescents in leadership and interpersonal behavior*. New York: Holt.

Bronfenbrenner, U. (1970). *Two worlds of childhood: U.S. and U.S.S.R.* New York: Russell Sage.

Bronfenbrenner, U. (1975). Ecological systems theory. In R. Vasta (Ed.), *Annals of child development* (Vol. 6). Greenwich, CT: JAI Press.

Bronfenbrenner, U. (1975). Nature with nurture: A reinterpretation of the evidence. In A. Montague (Ed.), *Race and IQ* (pp. 114–144). New York: Oxford University Press.

Bronfenbrenner, U. (1979). *The ecology of human development*. Cambridge, MA: Harvard University Press.

Bronfenbrenner, U. (1986). Ecology of the family as a context for human development: Research perspectives. *Developmental Psychology*, **22**, 723–742.

Bronfenbrenner, U. (1989). Ecological systems theory. In R. Vasta (Ed.), *Six theories of child development*. Greenwich, CT: JAI Press.

Bronson, G. W. (1968). The development of fear in man and other animals. *Child Development*, **39**, 409–431.

Bronson, W. (1981). Toddlers' behaviors with age mates; Issues of interaction, cognition and affect. *Monographs on Infancy*, **1.**

Bronstein, P., & Cowan, C. P. (Eds.). (1988). *Fatherhood today: Men's changing roles in the family*. New York: Wiley.

Brook, J. S., Lukoff, J. F., & Whiteman, M. (1980). Initiation into adolescent marijuana use. *Journal of Genetic Psychology*, **137**, 133–142.

Brooks, J., & Lewis, M. (1976). Infants' responses to strangers: Midget, adult, and child. *Child Development*, **47**, 323–332.

Brooks-Gunn, J. (1988). Antecedents and consequences of variations in girls' maturational timing. *Journal of Adolescent Health Care*, **9**, 1–9.

Brooks-Gunn, J. (1990). Barriers and impediments to conducting research with young adolescents. *Journal of Youth and Adolescence*, **19**, 425–440.

Brooks-Gunn, J., Boyer, B., Hein, K. (1988). Preventing HIV infection and AIDS in children and adolescents. *American Psychologist*, **43**, 958–964.

Brooks-Gunn, J., & Petersen, A. C. (1992). The emergence of depression in adolescence. *Journal of Youth and Adolescence*, **21**,

Brooks-Gunn, J., & Ruble, D. N. (1984). The experience of menarche from a developmental perspective. In J. Brooks-Gunn & A. C. Petersen (Eds.), *Girls at puberty: Biological, psychological and social perspectives*. New York: Plenum.

Brooks-Gunn, J., & Warren, W. P. (1985). The effects of delayed menarche in different contexts: Dance and nondance students. *Journal of Youth and Adolescence*, **14**, 285–300.

Brophy, J. (1986). Teacher influences on student achievement. *American Psychologist*, **41**, 1069–1077.

Brophy, J. E. (1983). Research on the self-fulfilling prophecy and teacher expectations. *Journal of Educational Psychology*, **75**, 631–661.

Broverman, I. K., Vogel, S. R., Broverman, D. M., Clarkson, F. E., & Rosenkrantz, P. S. (1972). Sex-role stereotypes: A current appraisal. *Journal of Social Issues*, **28**, 59–78.

Brown, A. L., Bransford, T. D., Ferrara, R. A., & Campione, J. C. (1983). Learning, remembering and understanding. In J. H. Flavell & E. M. Markman (Eds.), *Handbook of child psychology: (Vol. 3). Cognitive development*. New York: Wiley.

Brown, A. L. & Campione, J. C. (1990). Communities of learning and thinking, or a context by any other name. In D. Kuhn (Ed.), *Developmental perspectives on teaching and learning thinking skills*. Basel, Switzerland: Karger.

Brown, A. L., Kane, M. J., & Echols, C. H. (1986). Young children's mental models determine analogical transfer across problems with a common goal structure. *Cognitive Development*, **1**, 103–121.

Brown, B. B., Lohn M. J., & McClenghan, E. L. (1986). Early adolescent's perceptions of peer pressure. *Journal of Early Adolescence*, **6**, 139–154.

Brown, J. V., & Bakeman, R. (1977, March). *Antecedents of emotional involvement in mothers of premature and fullterm infants*. Paper presented at the biennial meeting of the Society for Research in Child Development, New Orleans.

Brown, P., & Elliot, R. (1965). Control of aggression in a nursery school class. *Journal of Experimental Child Psychology*, **2**, 103–107.

Brown, R. (1973). *A first language*. Cambridge, MA: Harvard University Press.

Brown, R., & Bellugi, U. (1964). Three processes in the child's acquisition of syntax. In E. G. Lenneberg (Ed.), *New directions in the study of language*. Cambridge, MA: M.I.T. Press.

Brownell, C. A. (1990). Peer social skills in toddlers: Competencies and constraints illustrated by same age and mixed-age interaction. *Child Development*, **61**, 838–848.

Bruch, H. (1977). *The golden cage: The enigma of anorexia nervosa.* Cambridge, MA: Harvard University Press.

Bruner, J. (1983). *Children's talk.* New York: Norton.

Bruner, J. S. (1957). On perceptual readiness. *Psychological Review,* **64,** 123–152.

Bruner, J. S. (1966). On cognitive growth. In J. S. Bruner, R. R. Olver, & P. M. Greenfield (Eds.), *Studies in cognitive growth.* New York: Wiley.

Bryant, B., & Crockenberg, S. (1980). Correlates and discussion of prosocial behavior: A study of female siblings with their mothers. *Child Development,* **51,** 529–544.

Bryant, P. E., & Trabasso, J. (1971). Transitive inferences and memory in young children. *Nature,* **232,** 356–458, 457–459.

Bryden, M. P. (1982). *Laterality.* New York: Academic.

Bryden, M. P. (1988). Does laterality make any difference? Thoughts on the relation between asymmetry and reading. In D. L. Molfese & S. J. Segalowitz (Eds.), *Brain lateralization in children* (pp. 509–525). New York: Guilford Press.

Bryden, M. P., & MacRae, L. (1989). Dichotic laterality effects obtained with emotional words. *Neuropsychiatry, Neuropsychology & Behavioral Neurology,* **1,** 171–176.

Bryden, M. P., & Saxby, L. (1986). Developmental aspects of cerebral lateralization. In J. E. Obrzat & G. W. Hynd (Eds.), *Child neuropsychology: Vol. 1. Theory and research.* Orlando, FL: Academic.

Buchanan, C. M., Maccoby, E. E., & Dornbusch, S. M. Caught between parents: Adolescents' experiences in divorced homes. *Child Development,* in press.

Buchanan, C. M., Maccoby, E. E., & Dornbusch, S. M. (1992). Adolescents and their families after divorce: Three residential arrangements compared. *Journal of Research on Adolescence,* **2**(3), 261–291.

Buck, R. W. (1984). *The communication of emotion.* New York: Guilford.

Buckmaster, L., & Brownell, K. D. (1988). The social and psychological world of the obese child. In V. A. Krasnagor, G. D. Grave, & N. Kretchmer (Eds.), *Childhood obesity: A biobehavioral perspective* (pp. 9–28). Caldwell, NJ: Telford Press.

Bugental, D., Blue, J., & Cruzcosa, M. (1989). Perceived control over caregiving outcomes: Implications for child abuse. *Developmental Psychology,* **25,** 532–539.

Buhrmester, D., & Furman, W. (1987). The development of companionship and intimacy. *Child Development,* **58,** 1101–1113.

Bullinger, A., & Chatillon, J. (1983). Recent theory and research of the Genevan school. In P. H. Mussen (Eds.), *Handbook of child psychology* (Vol. 3). New York: Wiley.

Bullock, D. (1983). Seeking relations between cognitive and social-interactive transitions. In K. W. Fischer (Eds.), *Levels and transitions in children's development: New directions in child development.* San Francisco: Jossey-Bass.

Bullock, M. (1985). Animism in childhood thinking: A new look at an old question. *Developmental Psychology,* **21,** 217–225.

Burbury, W. M. (1941). The effects of evacuation and of air-raids on city children. *British Medical Journal,* **2** 361–369.

Burgess, R. L., & Conger, R. D. (1978). Family interaction in abusive, neglectful and normal families. *Child Development,* **49,** 1163–1173.

Burke, P., & Puig-Antioch, J. (1990). Psychobiology of childhood depression. In M. Lewis & S. Miller (Eds.), *Handbook of developmental psychopathology* (pp. 327–339). New York: Plenum.

Burks, B. S. (1928). The relative influence of nature and nurture upon mental development: A comparative study of foster parent–foster child resemblance and true parent–true child resemblance. *27th Yearbook of the National Society for the Study of Education* (Pt. 1, pp. 219–316). Chicago: University of Chicago Press.

Burnett, A., Beach, H. D., & Sullivan, A. M. (1963). Intelligence in a restricted environment. *Canadian Psychologist,* **4,** 126–136.

Burns, K. A., Deddish, R. B., Burns, K., & Hatcher, R. P. (1983). Use of oscillating waterbeds and rhythmic sounds for premature infant stimulation. *Developmental Psychology,* **19,** 746–751.

Burton, R. V. (1963). The generality of honesty reconsidered. *Psychological Review,* **70,** 481–499.

Burton, R. V. (1984). A paradox in theories and research in moral development. In W. M. Kurtines & J. L. Gewirtz (Eds.), *Morality, moral behavior, and moral development.* New York: Wiley.

Bussey, K., & Perry, D. G. (1977). The imitation of resistance to deviation: Conclusive evidence for an elusive effect. *Developmental Psychology,* **13,** 438–443.

Butterfield, E. C., & Siperstein, G. N. (1972). Influence of contingent auditory stimulation upon non-nutritional suckle. In J. F. Bosoma (Ed.), *Third Symposium on Oral Sensation and Perception: The Mouth of the Infant.* Springfield, IL: Charles C Thomas.

Butterfield, E. C., & Siperstein, G. N. (1974). Influence of contingent auditory stimulation upon non-nutritional suckle. In *Proceedings of the Third Symposium on Oral Sensation and Perception: The Mouth of the Infant*. Springfield, IL: Charles C Thomas.

Byrne, J. M., & Horowitz, F. D. (1981). Rocking as a soothing intervention: The influence of direction and type of movement. *Infant Behavior and Development*, **4**, 207–218.

Byrnes, J. P. (1988). Formal operations: A systematic reformulation. *Developmental Review*, **8**, 66–87.

Cadmus, H. (1974). *The behavioral and structural dynamics of social stratification as manifested in a racially integrated first grade classroom.* Doctoral dissertation, College of Education, University of Florida, Gainesville.

Cain, K. M. (1991, April). The relationship between conceptions of intelligence and motivational patterns: A developmental analysis. In C. S. Dweck & K. M. Cain (Chairs), Self-conceptions and motivational development. *Symposium presented at the biennial meeting of the Society for Research in Child Development*, Seattle.

Cairns, E. (1991). *Caught in the crossfire*. Syracuse, NY: Syracuse University Press.

Cairns, R. B., Cairns, B. D., Neckerman, H., Fergusen, L. L., & Gariepy, J. L. (1989). Growth and aggression: Childhood to early adolescence. *Developmental Psychology*, **25**, 320–330.

Caldera, Y. M., Huston, A. C., & O'Brien, M. (1989). Social interactions and play patterns of parents and toddlers with feminine, masculine and neutral toys. *Child Development*, **60**, 70–76.

Caldwell, B. M. (1973). Infant day care–The outcast gains respectability. In P. Robey (Ed.), *Child care—Who cares? Foreign and domestic infant and early child development policies*. New York: Basic Books.

Calvert, S. L., & Huston, A. C. (1987). Television and children's gender schemata. In L. S. Liben & M. L. Signorella (Eds.), *Children's gender schemata* (pp. 75–88). San Francisco: Jossey-Bass.

Camara, K. A., & Resnick, G. (1988). Interparental conflict and cooperation. Factors moderating children's post-divorce adjustment. In E. M. Hetherington & J. D. Arasten (Eds.), *Impact of divorce, single parenting and step parenting on children* (pp. 169–195). Hillsdale, NJ: Erlbaum.

Campbell, M., & Spencer, E. K. (1988). Psychopharmacology in child and adolescent psychiatry: A review of the past five years. *Journal of the American Academy of Child and Adolescent Psychiatry*, **27**, 269–279.

Campbell, S. B., Breux, A. M., Ewing, L. J., & Szumowski, E. K. (1986). Correlates and predictors of hyperactivity and aggression: A longitudinal study of parent-referred problem preschoolers. *Journal of Abnormal Child Psychology*, **14**, 217–234.

Campos, J., Barrett, K., Lamb, M., Goldsmith, H., & Stenberg, C. (1983). Socioemotional development. In M. M. Harth & J. J. Campos (Eds.), *Infancy and development psychobiology: Vol. 2. Handbook of child psychology*. New York: Wiley.

Campos, J., Hiatt, S., Ramsay, D., Henderson, C., & Svejda, M. (1978). The emergence of fear on the visual cliff. In M. Lewis & L. Rosenblum (Eds.), *The origins of affect*. New York: Plenum.

Campos, J. J., Barrett, K. C., Lamb, M. E., Goldsmith, H. A., & Stenberg, C. (1983). Socioemotional development. In P. H. Mussen (Gen. Ed.), *Handbook of child psychology* (4th ed.); M. M. Haith & J. J. Campos (Vol. Eds.), *Infancy and developmental psychobiology*. New York: Wiley.

Campos, J. J., & Bertenthal, B. I. (1989). Locomotion and psychological development in infancy. In F. Morrison, C. Lord, & D. Keating (Eds.), *Applied developmental psychology* (Vol. 3). New York: Academic.

Campos, J. J., Langer, A., & Krowitz, A. (1970). Cardiac responses on the visual cliff in prelocomotor human infants. *Science*, **170**, 196–197.

Campos, J. J., Svejda, M., Bertenthal, B., Benson, N., & Schmid, D. (1981, April). *Self-produced locomotion and wariness of heights: New evidence from training studies*. Paper presented at the meeting of the Society for Research in Child Development, Boston.

Campos, R. P. (1989). Soothing-pain elicited distress in infants with swaddling and pacifiers. *Child Development*, **60**, 781–792.

Camras, L. A., Malatesta, C., & Izard, C. (1991). The development of facial expressions in infancy. In R. Feldman & B. Rime (Eds.), *Fundamentals of nonverbal behavior*. New York: Cambridge University Press.

Canfield, R. L., & Haith, M. M. (1991). Young infants' visual expectations for symmetrical and asymmetrical sequences. *Developmental Psychology*, **27**, 198–208.

Cantor, N. L., Wood, D., & Gelfand, D. (1977). Effects of responsiveness and sex of children on adult males' behavior. *Child Development*, **48**, 1426–1430.

Cantor, P. (1983). Depression and suicide in children. In C. E. Walker & M. C. Roberts (Eds.), *Handbook of clinical child psychology*. New York: Wiley.

Cantwell, D. P. (1980). A clinician's guide to the use of stimulant medication for the psychiatric disorders of children. *Developmental and Behavioral Pediatrics*, **1**, 133–140.

Cantwell, D. P. (1990). Depression across the early life span. In M. Lewis & S. Miller (Eds.), *Handbook of developmental psychopathology* (pp. 293–309). New York: Plenum.

Cantwell, D. P., Baker, L., & Rutter, M. (1978). Family factors. In M. Rutter & E. Schopier (Eds.), *Autism: A reappraisal of concepts and treatment*. New York: Plenum.

Cantwell, D. P., Russell, A. T., Mattison, R., & Will, L. A. (1979). A comparison of DSM-II and DSM-III in the diagnosis of childhood psychiatric disorders. *Archives of General Psychiatry*, **36**, 1208–1228.

Capronk, C., & Duyme, M. (1989). Assessment of effects of socioeconomic status on IQ in a cross-fostering study. *Nature*, **340**, 552–554.

Cardoso-Martins, C., & Mervis, C. (1985). Maternal speech to pre-linguistic children with Down syndrome. *American Journal of Mental Deficiency*, **89**, 451–458.

Carey, S. (1978). The child as word learner. In M. Halle, J. Bresnan, & G. Miller (Eds.), *Linguistic theory and psychological reality* (pp. 264–293). Cambridge, MA: M.I.T. Press.

Carlson, A. J. (1902). Changes in Nissl's substance of the ganglion and the bipolar cells of the retinal of the brandt cormorant phalacrocorax pencillaturs during prolonged normal stimulation. *American Journal of Anatomy*, **2**, 341–347.

Carr, E. G. (1979). Teaching autistic children to use sign language: Some research issues. *Journal of Autism and Developmental Disorders*, **1**, 345–360.

Carraher, T. N., Schliemann, A. D., & Carraher, D. W. (1988). Mathematical concepts in everyday life. *New Directions for Child Development*, **41**, 71-87.

Carroll, J. B. (1976). Psychometric tests as cognitive tasks: A new "structure of intellect." In L. B. Resnick (Ed.), *The nature of intelligence*. Hillsdale, NJ: Erlbaum.

Carson, J., Burks, V., & Parke, R. D. (1992). Parent-child physical play: Determinants and consequences. In K. B. MacDonald (Ed.), *Parent-child play*. Albany: SUNY Press.

Carter, D. B., & Levy, G. D. (1988). Cognitive aspects of early sex-role development: The influence of gender schemas on preschoolers' memories and preferences for sex-typed toys and activities. *Child Development*, **59**, 782–792.

Case, R. (1984). The process of stage transition: A neo-Piagetian view. In R. Sternberg (Ed.), *Mechanisms of cognitive development*. New York: Freeman.

Case, R. (1985). *Intellectual development: Birth to adulthood*. New York: Academic.

Case, R., & Griffin, (1990). Child cognitive development: The role of central conceptual structures in the development of scientific and social thought. In C. A. Hauert (Ed.), *Developmental psychology: Cognitive, percetuo-motor and neuropsychological perspectives*. Amsterdam: North Holland.

Case, R., Sandieson, R., & Dennis, S. (1986). Two cognitive-developmental approaches to the design of remedial instruction. *Cognitive Development*, **4**, 293–333.

Caspi, A., Elder, G. H., & Bem, D. J. (1987). Moving against the world: Life course patterns of explosive children. *Developmental Psychology*, **23**, 308–313.

Cassidy, J. (1988). Child-mother attachment and the self in six-year-olds. *Child Development*, **59**, 121–135.

Cassidy, J., & Asher, S. R. (1992). Loneliness and sociometric status among young children. *Children Development*, **63**, 350–365.

Ceci, S. J. (1990). *On intelligence . . . more or less: A bio-ecological treatise on intellectual development*. Englewood Cliffs, NJ: Prentice-Hall.

Ceci, S. J. (1991). How much does schooling influence general intelligence and its cognitive components? A reassessment of the evidence. *Developmental Psychology*, **27**, 703–720.

Ceci, S. J., Ross, D. F., & Toglia, M. P. (1987). Suggestibility of children's memory: Psycholegal implications. *Journal of Experimental Psychology: General*, **116**, 38–49.

Cella, D. F., & Tross, S. (1986). Psychological adjustment to survival from Hodgkin's disease. *Journal of Consulting and Clinical Psychology*, **54**, 616–622.

Chaiklin, H. (1979). The treadmill of lead. *American Journal of Orthopsychiatry*, **49**, 571–573.

Chandler, M. J. (1973). Egocentrism and antisocial behavior: The assessment and training of social perspective taking skills. *Developmental Psychology*, **9**, 326–332.

Chandler, M. J., Greenspan, S., & Barenboim, C. (1973). Judgments of intentionality in response to videotaped and verbally presented moral dilemmas: The medium is the message. *Child Development*, **44**, 315–320.

Chang, H. W., & Trehub, S. E. (1977). Infants' perception of grouping in auditory patterns. *Child Development*, **48**, 1666–1670.

Charlesworth, R., & Hartup, W. W. (1967). Positive social reinforcement in the nursery school peer group. *Child Development*, **38**, 993–1002.

Charlesworth, W. (1988). Resources and resource acquisition during ontogeny. In K. MacDonald (Ed.), *Sociobiological perspectives on human development*. New York: Springer-Verlag.

Charlesworth, W., & Dzur, C. (1987). Gender comparison of preschoolers' behavior and resource utilization. *Child Development*, **58**, 191–200.

Chase, W. G., Simon, H. A. (1973). The mind's eye in chess. In W. G. Chase (Ed.), *Visual information processing*. New York: Academic.

Chasnoff, I. J., Griffith, D. R., MacGregor, S., Dirkes, B. M., & Burns, K. A. (1989). Temporal patterns of cocaine use in pregnancy. *Journal of the American Medical Association,* **261,** 1741–1744.

Chen, Z., & Daehler, M. W. (1989). Positive and negative transfer in analogical problem solving by 6 year old children. *Cognitive Development*, **4**, 327–344.

Cherlin A. J., Chase-Lansdale, P. L., Furstenberg, F. F. Jr., Kiernan, K. E., Robins, P. K., Morrison, D. R., & Teitler, J. O. (1991, April). *How much of the effects of divorce on children occurs before the separation? Longitudinal evidence from Great Britain and the United States.* Paper presented at meetings of the Society for Research in Child Development. Seattle, WA.

Cherry, R. S. (1981). Development of selective auditory attention skills in children. *Perceptual and Motor Skills*, **52**, 379–385.

Chess, S., & Thomas, A. (1972). Differences in outcome with early intervention in children with behavior disorders. In M. Roff, L. Robbers, & M. Pollack (Eds.), *Life history research in psychopathology* (Vol. 2). Minneapolis: University of Minnesota Press.

Chess, S., Thomas, A., & Birch, H. G. (1968). Behavioral problems revisited. In S. Chess & H. Birch (Eds.), *Annual progress in child psychiatry and development* (pp. 335–344). New York: Brunner/Mazel.

Chi, M. T. H. (1976). Short term memory limitations in children: Capacity or processing deficits? *Memory and Cognition*, **4**, 559–572.

Chi, M. T. H. (1978). Knowledge structures and memory development. In R. S. Siegler (Ed.), *Children's thinking: What develops?* Hillsdale, NJ: Erlbaum.

Chi, M. T. H., & Koeske, R. D. (1983). Network representation of a child's dinosaur knowledge. *Developmental Psychology*, **19**, 29–39.

Childs, C. P. & Greenfield, P. M. (1982). Informal modes of learning and teaching: The case of Zinacenteco weaving. In N. Warren (Ed.), *Advances in cross-cultural psychology* (Vol. 2). London: Academic.

Chittenden, G. E. (1942). An experimental study in measuring and modifying assertive behavior in young children. *Monographs of the Society for Research in Child Development,* **7** (Serial No. 31).

Chomsky, C. (1969). *The acquisition of syntax in children from 5 to 10.* Cambridge, MA: M.I.T., Press.

Chomsky, N. (1968). *Language and mind.* New York: Harcourt, Brace & World.

Christenson, S., Abery, B., & Weinberg, R. (1986). An alternative model for the delivery of psychology in the school community. In S. N. Elliott & J. C. Witt (Eds.), *The delivery of psychological services in schools: concepts, processes, and issues* (pp. 349–391). Hillsdale, NJ: Erlbaum.

Christoffel, K. K. (1990). Violent death and injury in U.S. children and adolescents. *American Journal of Disease Control,* **144**, 697–706.

Church, V. W. (1925). *Teachers are people, being the lyrics of Agatha Brown, sometime teacher in the Hilldale High School* (3rd ed.). Hollywood, CA: David Graham Fischer Corporation.

Cicchetti, D. (1990). A historical perspective on the discipline of developmental psychopathology. In J. Rolf, A. S. Masten, D. Cicchetti, Nuechterlein, & S. Weintraub (Eds.), *Risk and protective factors in human development.*

Cicchetti, D., & Lynch, M. (in press). Toward an ecological/transactional model of community violence and child maltreatment: Consequences for children's development. *Psychiatry.*

Cicchetti, D., & Olsen, K. (1990). The developmental psychopathology of child maltreatment. In M. Lewis & S. Miller (Eds.), *Handbook of developmental psychopathology* (pp. 261–279). New York: Plenum.

Cicchetti, D., & Pogge-Hesse, P. (1981). The relation between emotion and cognition in infant development. In M. E. Lamb & L. R. Sherrod (Eds.), *Infant social cognition: Empirical and theoretical considerations.* Hillsdale, NJ: Erlbaum.

Cicirelli, V. G. (1976). Siblings helping siblings. In V. L. Allen (Ed.), *Children as tutors.* New York: Academic.

Cicirelli, V. G. (1982). Sibling influence throughout the life-span. In M. E. Lamb & B. Sutton-Smith (Eds.), *Sibling relationships.* Hillsdale, NJ: Erlbaum.

Clancy, P. (1985). Acquisition of Japanese. In D. I. Slobin (Ed.), *The cross-linguistic study of language acquisition: Vol. 1. The data* (pp. 323–524). Hillsdale, NJ: Erlbaum.

Clark, E. V. (1983). Meanings and concepts. In P. H. Mussen (Eds.), *Handbook of child psychology* (Vol. 3). New York: Wiley.

Clark, H. H., & Clark, E. V. (1977). *Psychology and language: An introduction to psycholinguistics.* New York: Harcourt, Brace, Jovanovich.

Clark, J. E., Phillips, S. J., & Petersen, R. (1989). Developmental stability in jumping. *Developmental Psychology,* **25,** 929–935.

Clarke-Stewart, K. A. (1978). And daddy makes three: The father's impact on mother and young child. *Child Development,* **49,** 466–478.

Clarke-Stewart, K. A. (1987). Predicting child development from day care forms and features: The Chicago study. In D. A. Phillips (Ed.), Quality in child care: What does research tell us? *Research Monographs of the National Association for the Education of Young Children* (Vol. 1, pp. 21–42). Washington, DC: National Association for the Education of Young Children.

Clarke-Stewart, K. A. (1989). Infant day care: Maligned or malignant? *American Psychologist*, **44,** 266–273.

Clausen, J. A., & Williams, J. R. (1963). Sociological correlates of behavior. In *Yearbook: National Society of Education, Pt. 1* Chicago: University of Chicago Press.

Clegg, D. J. (1971). Teratology. *Annual Review of Pharmacology,* pp. 409–423.

Cline, V. B., Croft, R. G., & Courier, S. (1973). Desensitization of children of children to television violence. *Journal of Personality and Social Psychology,* **27,** 360–365.

Coates, T. J., & Thoresen, C. E. (1976). *Treating obesity in children and adolescents: A review.* Unpublished manuscript. Stanford University, Stanford, CA.

Cochi, S. L., Edmonds, L. E., Dyer, K., Grooves, W. L., Marks, J. S., Rovira, E. Z., Preblud, S. R., & Orenstein, W. A. (1989). Congenital rubella syndrome in the United States, 1970–1985: On the verge of elimination. *American Journal of Epidemiology,* **129,** 349–361.

Cohen-Sandler, R., Berman, A. L., & King, R. A. (1982). Life stress and symptomatology: Determinants of suicidal behavior in children. *Journal of the American Academy of Child Psychiatry,* **21**, 178–186.

Cohn, D. A. (1990). Child-mother attachment in six-year-olds and social competence at school. *Child Development,* **61,** 152–162.

Cohn, J. F., Campbell, S. B., Matias, R., Hopkins, J. (1990). Face-to-face interactions of postpartum depressed and non-depressed mother-infant pairs at 2 months. *Developmental Psychology* **26,** 15–23.

Coie, J. D., & Dodge, K. A. (1983). Continuities and changes in children's social status: A five-year longitudinal study. *Merrill-Palmer Quarterly,* **29,** 261–282.

Coie, J. D., & Dodge, K. A. (1988). Multiple sources of data on social behavior and social status in school: A cross-age comparison. *Child Development,* **57,** 815–829.

Coie, J. D., Dodge, K. A., & Kupersmidt, J. (1990). Peer group behavior and social status. In S. R. Asher & J. D. Coie (Eds.), *Peer rejection in childhood.* New York: Cambridge University Press.

Coie, J. D., & Kupersmidt, J. B. (1983). A behavioral analysis of emerging social status in boys' groups. *Child Development,* **54,** 1400–1416.

Colby, A., & Kohlberg, L. (1987). *The measurement of moral judgment* (Vols. 1–2). New York: Cambridge University Press.

Colby, A., Kohlberg, L., Gibbs, J., & Lieberman, M. (1983). A longitudinal study of moral judgment. *Monographs of the Society for Research in Child Development,* **48** (Serial No. 200).

Cole, M. (1985). The zone of proximal development: Where culture and cognition create each other. In J. V. Wertsch (Ed.), *Culture, communication and cognitive: Vygotskian perspectives.* Cambridge: Cambridge University Press.

Cole, M., & Scribner, S. (1977). Cross-cultural studies of memory and cognition. In R. V. Kail, Jr., & J. W. Hagen (Eds.), *Perspectives on the development of memory and cognition.* Hillsdale, NJ: Erlbaum.

Cole, P. M. (1985). Display roles and the socialization of affective displays. In G. Zivin (Ed.), *The development of expressive behavior: Biology-environment interaction* (pp. 269–290). New York: Academic.

Coleman, J. S., Campbell, E. Q., Hobson, C. J., McPartland, J., Mood, A. M., Weinfeld, F. D., & York, R. L. (1966). *Equality of educational opportunity.* Washington, DC: Government Printing Office.

Coleman, W. T., & Selby, J. J. (1983). *Educating Americans for the 21st century.* Washington, DC: National Science Foundation.

Collins, A., Brown, J. S., & Newman, S. E. (1990). The new apprenticeship: Teaching students the craft of reading, writing and mathematics. In L. B. Resnick (Ed.), *Cognition and instruction: Issues and agendas.* Hillsdale, NJ: Erlbaum.

Collins, W. A. (1973). Effect of temporal separation between motivation, aggression, and consequences: A developmental study. *Developmental Psychology,* **8,** 215–221.

Collins, W. A. (1983). Interpretation and inference in children's television viewing. In J. Bryant & D. C. Anderson (Eds.), *Children's understanding of television: Research on attention and comprehension.* New York: Academic.

Collins, W. A., Sobol, S. K., & Westby, S. (1981). Effects of adult commentary on children's comprehension and inferences about a televised aggressive portrayal. *Child Development,* **52,** 158–163.

Comer, J. (1988). The education of low-income black children. *Scientific American,* **259,** 42–48.

Compas, B. E., & Hammen, C. L. (1992, May). *Child and adolescent depression: Covariation and comorbidity in development.* Paper presented at the Grant Foundation Conference on Risk, Resiliency, and Development, Kiawah Island, SC.

Conger, J. J., & Petersen, A. C. (1984). *Adolescence & Youth* (3rd ed.). New York: Harper & Row.

Conger, K. J. (1992, March). *Sibling relationship quality as a mediator and moderator of the relationship between parental mood and behavior and adolescent self esteem.* Paper presented at the meetings of the Society for Research in Adolescence. Washington, DC.

Conners, C. K. (1980). *Food additives and hyperactive children.* New York: Plenum.

Conners, C. K., & Werry, J. S. (1979). Pharmacotherapy. In H. C. Quay & J. S. Werry (Eds.), *Psychopathological disorders of childhood* (2nd ed.). New York: Wiley.

Connolly, J. (1980). *The relationship between social pretend play and social competence in preschoolers: Correlational and experimental studies.* Unpublished doctoral dissertation. Concordia University, Montreal.

Cooper, C. R., & Cooper, R. G. (1992). Links between adolescents' relationships with their parents and peers: Models, evidence and mechanisms. In R. D. Parke & G. W. Ladd (Eds.), *Family-peer relationships: Modes of linkage.* Hillsdale, NJ: Erlbaum.

Corballis, M. C. (1983). *Human laterality.* New York: Academic.

Cornell, E. H., & Gottfried, A. W. (1976). Intervention with premature human infants. *Child Development,* **47**, 32–39.

Corner, G. W. (1961). *Congenital malformations: The problem and the task* (pp. 7–17). Papers and discussions presented at the First International Conference on Congenital Malformations. Philadelphia: Lippincott.

Corter, C. M., & Minde, K. K. (1987). Impact of infant prematurity on family systems. In M. Wolbraich (Ed.), *Advances in developmental and behavioral pediatrics* (Vol. 8). Greenwich, CT: JAI Press.

Cosgrove, J. M., & Patterson, C. J. (1977). Plans and the development of listener skills. *Developmental Psychology,* **13**, 557–564.

Cowan, C. P., & Cowan, P. A. (1992). *When parents become partners.* New York: Basic Books.

Cowan, C. P., Cowan, P. A., Heming, G., & Miller, N. B. (1991). Becoming a family: Marriage, parenting and child development. In P. A. Cowan & E. M. Hetherington (Eds.), *Family transitions.* Hillsdale, NJ: Erlbaum.

Cowan, E. L., & Work, W. C. (1988). Resilient children, psychological wellness, and primary prevention. *American Journal of Community Psychology,* **16**, 591–607.

Cowen, E. (1985). Primary prevention in mental health: Past, present, and future. In R. Felner, L. Jason, N. Mortsuger, & S. Farber (Eds.), *Preventive psychology.* New York: Pergamon.

Cox, B. D., Ornstein, P. A., Naus, M. J., Maxfield, D., & Zimmler, J. (1989). Children's concurrent use of rehearsal and organizational strategies. *Developmental Psychology,* **25**, 619–627.

Cox, M. J., Owen, M., Lewis, J. M., & Henderson, K. V. (1989). Marriage, adult adjustment, and early parenting. *Child Development,* **60**, 1015–1024.

Craik, F. I. M., & Lockhart, R. S. (1972). Levels of processing: A framework for memory research. *Journal of Verbal Learning and Verbal Behavior,* **12,** 599–607.

Crawley, S. B., & Spiker, D. (1983). Mother-child interactions involving two-year-olds with Down syndrome: A look at individual differences. *Child Development,* **54**, 1312–1323.

Crisafi, M., & Brown, A. L. (1986). Analogical transfer in very young children: Combining two separately learned solutions to reach a goal. *Child Development,* **57**, 953–968.

Crittenden, P. M. (1988). Distorted patterns of relationship in maltreating families: The role of internal representational models. *Journal of Reproductive and Infant Psychology,* **6**, 183–199.

Crnic, K. A., Greenberg, M. T., Ragozin, A. A., Robinson, N. M., & Basham, R. (1983). Effects of stress and social support on mothers and premature and full-term infants. *Child Development,* **54**, 209–217.

Crockenberg, S. B. (1979). The effects of cooperative learning environments and interdependent goals on conformity in school-age children. *Merrill-Palmer Quarterly,* **25,** 121–132.

Crockenberg, S. B. (1981). Infant irritability, mother responsiveness and social support influences on the security of infant-mother attachment. *Child Development,* **52,** 857–865.

Crockenberg, S., & Litman, D. (1990). Autonomy as competence in 2-year-olds: Maternal correlates of child defiance, compliance and self assertion. *Developmental Psychology,* **26**, 916–971.

Crockett, L. J., & Petersen, A. C. (1987). Pubertal status andpsychosocial development. Findings from the Early Adolescence Study in R. M. Lerner & T. T. Fochs (Eds.), *Biological-psychosocial interactions in early adolescence: A life-span perspective* (pp. 173–188). Hillsdale, NJ: Erlbaum.

Crouter, A. C., & MacDermid, S. M. (1991). *A longitudinal study of parental monitoring in dual and single-earner families.* Paper presented at the meetings of the Society for Research in Child Development. Seattle, WA.

Cummings, J. S., Pelligrini, D. S., Notarius, C. I., & Cummings, E. M. (1989). Children's responses to angry adult behavior as a function of marital distress and history of interparent hostility. *Child Development*, **60**, 1035–1043.

Cushna, B. (1966). *Agency and birth order differences in very early childhood*. Paper presented at the meeting of the American Psychological Association, New York.

Dale, P. S. (1976). *Language development: Structure and function* (2nd ed.). New York: Holt.

Damon, A., Damon, S. T., Reed, R. B., & Valadian, I. (1969). Age at menarche of mothers and daughters, with a note on accuracy of recall. *Human Biology*, **41**, 161–175.

Damon, W., & Phelps, E. (1989). Strategic uses of peer learning in children's education. In T. Berndt & G. Ladd (Eds.), *Peer relationships in child development*. New York: Wiley.

Daniels, D. (1987). Differential experiences of siblings in the same family as predictors of adolescent sibling personality differences. *Journal of Personality and Social Psychology*, **51**, 331–346.

Daniels, D., Dunn, J., Furstenberg, F. F., & Plomin, R. (1985). Environmental differences within the family and adjustment differences within pairs of adolescent siblings. *Child Development*, **56**, 764–774.

Dannemiller, J. L., & Stephens, B. R. (1988). A critical test of infant pattern perception models. *Child Development*, **59**, 210–216.

Dansereau, D. F. (1987). Transfer from cooperative to individual studying. *Journal of Reading*, **30**, 614–619.

Darvill, D., & Cheyne, J. A. (1981). *Sequential analysis of response to aggression: Age and sex effects.* Paper presented at the biennial meeting of the Society for Research in Child Development, Boston.

Darwin, C. (1872). *The expression of emotions in man and animals.* London: John Murray.

Dasen, P. E. & Heron. A. (1981). Cross-cultural tests of Piaget's theory. In H. C. Triandis & A. Heron (Eds.), *Handbook of cross-cultural psychology: Developmental Psychology* (Vol. 4). Boston: Allyn & Bacon.

David, O. J., Hoffman, S. P., Sverd, J., & Clark, J. (1977). Lead and hyperactivity: Lead levels among hyperactive children. *Journal of Abnormal Child Psychology*, **5**, 405–416.

Davidson, E. S., Yasuna, A., & Tower, A. (1979). The effects of television cartoons on sex role stereotyping in young girls. *Child Development*, **50**, 597–600.

Davis, S. W., Best, D. L., & Hawkins, R. C. (1981). *Sex stereotypes, weight, and body image in childhood and adolescence.* Paper presented at the biennial meeting of the Society for Research in Child Development, Boston.

Davison, A. N., & Dobbing, J. (1966). Myelination as a vulnerable period in brain development. *British Medical Bulletin*, **22**, 40–44.

Dawe, H. C. (1934). The influence of size of kindergarten group upon performance. *Child Development*, **5**, 295–303.

Day, M. C. (1975). Developmental trends in visual scanning. In H. W. Reese (Ed.), *Advances in child development and behavior* (Vol. 10). New York: Academic.

Dean A., Malik, M., & Richards, W. (1986). Effects of parental maltreatment on children's conceptions of interpersonal relationships. *Developmental Psychology*, **22**, 617–626.

DeCasper, A., & Fifer, W. (1980). Of human bonding: Newborns prefer their mothers' voices. *Science*, **12**, 305–317.

DeCasper, A. J., & Spence, M. (1986). Newborns prefer a familiar story over an unfamiliar one. *Infant Behavior and Development*, **9**, 133–150.

Delack, J. B. (1976). Aspects of infant speech development in the first year of life. *Canadian Journal of Linguistics*, **21**, 17–37.

DeLisi, R., & Staudt, J. (1980). Individual differences in college students' performance on formal operations tasks. *Journal of Applied Developmental Psychology*, **1**, 201–208.

DeLoache, J. S. (1989). The development of representation in young children. In H. W. Reese (Ed.), *Advances in child development and behavior.* Vol 22 (pp 1–39). New York: Academic Press.

DeLoache, J. S., & Brown, A. L. (1983). Very young children's memory for the location of objects in a large-scale environment. *Child Development*, **54**, 888–897.

DeMarie-Dreblow, D., & Miller, P. H. (1988). The development of children's strategies for selective attention: Evidence for a transitional period. *Child Development*, **59**, 1504–1513.

Dement, W. C. (1960). The effect of dream deprivation. *Science*, **131**, 1705–1707.

Demos, V. (1982). Facial expressions of infants and toddlers. In T. Field & A. Fogel (Eds.), *Emotion and early interaction* (pp. 127–160). Hillsdale, NJ: Erlbaum.

Dempster, F. N. (1985). Proactive interference in sentence recall: Topic similarity effects and individual differences. *Memory and Cognition*, **13**, 81–89.

Dennis, W. (1940). Does culture appreciably affect patterns of infant behavior? *Journal of Social Psychology*, **12**, 305–317.

DeRosier, M., & Kupersmidt, J. B. (1991). Costa Rican children's perceptions of their social networks. *Developmental Psychology,* **27,** 656–662.

deVilliers, J. G., & deVilliers, P. A. (1973). A cross-sectional study of the acquisition of grammatical morphemes in child speech. *Journal of Psycholinguistic Research,* **2,** 267–278.

deVilliers, P. A., & deVilliers, J. G. (1972). Early judgments of semantic and syntactic acceptability by children. *Journal of Psycholinguistic Research,* **1,** 299–310.

deVilliers, P. A., & deVilliers, J. G. (1979). *Early language.* Cambridge, MA: Harvard University Press.

deVilliers, P. A., & deVilliers, J. G. (1992). Language Development. In M. E. Lamb & M. H. Bornstein. (Eds.), *Developmental psychology: An advanced textbook* (3rd ed.). Hillsdale NJ: Erlbaum.

Dickinson, D. K. (1984). First impressions: Childrens knowledge of words gained from a single exposure. *Applied Psycholinguistics,* **5,** 359–373.

Diener, C. I., & Dweck, C. S. (1978). An analysis of learned helplessness: Continuous changes in performance, strategy and achievement cognitions following failure. *Journal of Personality and Social Psychology,* **36,** 451–462.

DiPietro, J. A. (1981). Rough and tumble play: A function of gender. *Developmental Psychology,* **17,** 50–58.

Dittrichova, J. (1969). The development of premature infants. In R. J. Robinson (Ed.), *Brain and early development.* London: Academic.

Dix, T. (1991). The affective organization of parenting: Adaptive and maladaptive processes. *Psychological Bulletin,* **110** (1), 3–25.

Dixon, S. D. (1991). *Infants exposed perinatally to cocaine or methamphetamine demonstrate behavioral and neurophysiologic changes.* Paper presented at the meeting of the Society for Research in Child Development, Seattle, WA.

Dobson, V., & Teller, D. Y. (1978). Visual acuity in human infants: A review and comparison of behavioral and electrophysiological studies. *Vision Research,* **18,** 1469–1483.

Dockrell, J., & Campbell, R. (1986). Lexical acquisition strategies in the pre-school child. In S. Kuczaj & M. Barrett (Eds.), *The Development of Word Meaning. New York: Springer.*

Dodge, K. A. (1985). A social information processing model of social competence in children. In M. Perlmutter (Ed.), *Minnesota Symposia on Child Psychology* (Vol. 18), 77–126. Hillsdale, NJ: Erlbaum.

Dodge, K. A., & Coie, J. D. (1987). Social information-processing factors in reactive and proactive aggression in children's peer groups. *Journal of Personality and Social Psychology,* **53,** 1146–1158.

Dodge, K. A., & Frame, C. L. (1982). Social cognitive biases and deficits in aggressive boys. *Child Development,* **53,** 620–635.

Dolgin, K. G., & Behrend, D. A. (1984). Children's knowledge about animates and inanimates. *Child Development,* **55,** 1646–1650.

Dollaghan, C. (1985). Child meets word: "First mapping" in preschool children. *Journal of Speech and Hearing Research,* **28,** 439–454.

Dominick, J. R., & Greenberg, B. S. (1972). Attitudes toward violence: The interaction of television exposure, family attitudes, and social class. In G. A. Comstock & E. A. Rubenstein (Eds.), *Television and social behavior: Television and adolescent aggressiveness* (Vol. 3, pp. 314–335). Washington, DC: Government Printing Office.

Dore, J. (1985). Holophrases revisited: Their logical development from dialogue. In M. D. Barrett (Ed.), *Children's single-word speech* (pp. 23–58). Chichester, England: Wiley.

Doris, J. (Ed.). (1991). *The suggestibility of children's recollections.* Washington, DC: American Psychological Association.

Dornbusch, S. M., Carlsmith, J. M., Bushwall, S. J., Leiderman, H., Hfastorf, A. H., Gross, R. T., & Rutter, P. (1983, April). *Single parents, extended households, and the control of adolescents.* Paper presented at the Pacific Sociological Meetings, San Jose, CA.

Douban, E., & Adelson, J. (1966). *The adolescent experience.* New York, Wiley.

Douglas, V. I. (1972). Stop, look and listen: The problem of sustained attention and impulse control in hyperactive and normal children. *Canadian Journal of Behavioural Science,* **4,** 259–282.

Downey, G., & Coyne, J. C. (1990). Children of depressed parents: An integrative review. *Psychological Bulletin,* **108,** 50–76.

Downs, R. M., & Liben, L. S. (1986). Children's understanding of maps. In P. Ellen & C. Thinus-Blanc (Eds.), *Cognitive processes and spatial orientation in animal and man. Vol. 1. Neurophysiology of spatial knowledge and developmental aspects.* Dordrecht, Holland: Martinius Nijhoff.

Drabman, R. S., & Thomas, M. H. (1976). Does watching violence on television cause apathy? *Pediatrics,* **52,** 329–331.

Drillien, C. M. (1964). *The growth and development of the prematurely born infant.* Baltimore: Williams & Wilkins.

Drillien, C. M., Ingram, T. T. S., & Wilkinson, F. M. (1966). *The cause and natural history of cleft lip and palate.* Edinburgh: Churchill Livingston.

Drillien, C. M., & Wilkinson, E. M. (1964). Emotional stress and mongoloid birth. *Developmental Medicine and Child Neurology,* **6,** 140–143.

Dubowitz, L., & Dubowitz, V. (1981). *The neurological assessment of the preterm and full-term newborn infant.* Philadelphia: Lippincott.

Duke, P. M., Carlsmith, J. M., Jennings, D., Martin, J. A., Dornbusch, S. M., Siegel-Gorelick, B., & Gross, R. T. (1982). Educational correlates of early and late sexual maturation in adolescence. *Journal of Pediatrics,* **100,** 633.

Dulcan, M. K. (1986). Comprehensive treatment of children and adolescents with attention deficit disorders: The state of the art. *Clinical Psychology Review,* **6,** 539–569.

Dumas, J. E., & Wahler, R. G. (1985). Indiscriminate mothering as a contextual factor in aggressive oppositional child behavior. *Journal of Abnormal Child Psychology,* **13,** 1–17.

Dunkeld, J. (1978). *The function of imitation in infancy.* Unpublished doctoral thesis. University of Edinburgh.

Dunn, J. (1983). Sibling relationships in early childhood. *Child Development,* **54,** 787–881.

Dunn, J. (1988). *The beginnings of social understanding.* Cambridge, MA: Harvard University Press.

Dunn, J. (1992). *Fights and fantasies: Siblings and their separate lives.* Invited address at the 4th annual convention of the American Psychological Society. San Diego, Calif.

Dunn, J., & Brown, J. (1991). Relationships, talk about feelings, and the development of affect regulation in early childhood. In J. Garber & K. Dodge (Eds.), *The development of emotional regulation and dysregulation.* New York: Cambridge University Press.

Dunn, J., Brown, J., & Beardsall, L. (1991). Family talk about feeling states and children's later understanding of others' emotions. *Developmental Psychology,* **27,** 448–455.

Dunn, J., & Kendrick, C. (1980). The arrival of a sibling: Changes in patterns of interaction between mother and firstborn child. *Journal of Child Psychology and Psychiatry,* **21,** 119–132.

Dunn, J., & Kendrick, C. (1982). Interaction between young siblings: Association with the interaction between mother and firstborn. *Developmental Psychology,* **17,** 336–343.

Dunn, J., & Kendrick, C. (1982). The speech of two- and three-year-olds to infant siblings: "Baby talk" and the context of communication. *Journal of Child Language,* **9,** 579–595.

Dunn, J. F. (1980). Individual differences in temperament. In M. Rutter (Ed.), *The scientific foundations of developmental psychiatry.* London: Heineman.

Dura, J. R., & Kiecolt-Glaser, J. K. (1991). Family transitions, stress and health. In P. A. Cowan & E. M. Hetherington (Eds.), *Family transitions.* Hillsdale, NJ: Erlbaum.

Duyme, M. (1988). School success and social class: An adoption study. *Developmental psychology,* **24,** 203–209.

Dweck, C. S., & Bempechat, J. (1983). Children's theories of intelligence: Consequences for learning. In S. G. Paris, G. M. Olson, & H. W. Stevenson (Eds.), *Learning and motivation in the classroom.* Hillsdale, NJ: Erlbaum.

Dweck, C. S., & Elliott, E. S. (1983). Achievement motivation. In P. H. Mussen (Ed.), *Handbook of child psychology* (Vol. 4). New York: Wiley.

Dweck, C. S., & Goetz, T. E. (1977). Attributions and learned helplessness. In J. H. Harvey, W. Ickes, & R. F. Kidd (Eds.), *New directions in attribution research* (Vol. 2). Hillsdale, NJ: Erlbaum.

Dweck, C. S., Goetz, T. E., & Strauss, N. L. (1980). Sex differences in learned helplessness: An experimental and naturalistic study of failure generalization and its mediators. *Journal of Personality and Social Psychology,* **38,** 441–452.

Dweck, C. S., & Leggett, E. L. (1988). A social-cognitive approach to motivation and personality. *Psychological Review,* **95,** 256–273.

Eaton, W., & VonBargen, D. (1981). Asynchronous development of gender understanding in preschool children. *Child Development,* **52,** 1020–1027.

Eccles, J. S. (1985). Sex differences in achievement patterns. In T. Sonderegger (Ed.), *Nebraska Symposium on Motivation.* Lincoln: University of Nebraska Press.

Eccles, J. S., & Hoffman, L. W. (1984). Sex roles, socialization and occupational behavior. In H. W. Stevenson & A. E. Siegel (Eds.), *Research in child development and social policy* (Vol. 1). Chicago: University of Chicago Press.

Eccles, J. S., Lord, S., & Midgley, C. (1991). What are we doing to early adolescents? The impact of educational contexts on early adolescents. *American Journal of Education,* (Vol. 99), pp. 521–542.

Eccles, J. S., & Midgley, C. (1989). Stage/environment fit: Developmentally appropriate classrooms for early adolescents. In R. E. Ames & C. Ames (Eds.), *Research on motivation in education* (Vol. 3). New York: Academic.

Eckerman C. O. (1989). *Imitation and the achievement of coordinated action.* Paper presented at the biennial meeting of the Society for Research in Child Development, Kansas City, KS.

Eckerman, C. O., & Didow, S. M. (1988). Lessons drawn from observing young peers together. *Acta Paeditrica Scandinavica,* **77** (Suppl. 344), 55–70.

Eckerman, C. O., Whatley, J. L., & Kutz, S. L. (1975). Growth of social play with peers during the second year of life. *Developmental Psychology,* **11,** 42–49.

Edelman, M. S., & Omark, D. R. (1973). Dominance hierarchies in young children. *Social Science Information,* **12,** 1.

Edwards, C. P. (1980). The comparative study of the development of moral judgment and reasoning. In R. L. Munroe, R. Munroe, & B. B. Whiting (Eds.), *Handbook of cross-cultural human development.* New York: Garland.

Edwards, C. P., & Lewis, M. (1979). Young children's concepts of social relations: Social functions and social objects. In M. Lewis & L. A. Rosenblum (Eds.), *The child and its family: Genesis of behavior* (Vol. 1). New York: Plenum.

Egeland, B., Breitenbucher, M., & Rosenberg, D. (1980). Prospective study of the significance of life stress in the etiology of child abuse. *Journal of Consulting and Clinical Psychology,* **48,** 195–205.

Egeland, B., Jacobvitz, D., & Stroufe, L. A. (1988). Breaking the cycle of abuse. *Child Development,* **59,** 1080–1088.

Egeland, B., & Sroufe, L. A. (1981a). Attachment and early maltreatment. *Child Development,* **52,** 44–52.

Egeland, B., & Sroufe, L. A. (1981b). Developmental sequelae of maltreatment in infancy. *New Directions for Child Development,* **11,** 77–92.

Ehrhardt, A. A. (1987). A transactional perspective on the development of gender differences. In J. M. Reinisch, L. A. Rosenblum, & S. A. Sanders (Eds.), *Masculinity/femininity: Basic perspectives.* New York: Oxford University Press.

Eichorn, D. H. (1979). Physical development: Current foci of research. In J. D. Osofsky (Ed.), *Handbook of infant development.* New York: Wiley.

Eilers, R. E. (1980). Infant speech perception: History and mystery. In G. H. Yeni-Kemshian, J. F. Kavanaugh, & C. A. Ferguson, *Child phonology,* Vol. 2, *Perception.* New York: Academic Press.

Eimas, P. D. (1982). Speech perception: A view of the initial state and perceptual mechanisms. In J. Mehler, M. Garrett, & E. Walker (Eds.), *Perspectives on mental representation.* Hillsdale, NJ: Erlbaum.

Eisenberg, N. (1992). *The caring child.* Cambridge, MA: Harvard University Press.

Eisenberg, N., & Fabes, R. (1991). Prosocial behavior and empathy: A multimethod, developmental perspective. In M. S. Clark (Ed.), *Review of personality and social psychology* (Vol. 12). Newbury Park, CA: Sage.

Eisenberg, N., Fabes, R., Miller, P. A., Shell, R., Shea, C., May-Plumee, T. (1990). Preschoolers' vicarious emotional responding and their situational and dispositional prosocial behavior. *Merrill-Palmer Quarterly,* **36,** 507–529.

Eisenberg, N., Lennon, R., & Roth, K. (1983). Prosocial development: A longitudinal study. *Developmental Psychology,* **19,** 846–855.

Eisenberg, N., & Miller, P. (1987). The relation of empathy to prosocial and related behaviors. *Psychological Bulletin,* **101,** 91–119.

Eisenberg, N., Murray, E., & Hite, T. (1982). Children's reasoning regarding sex-typed toy choices. *Child Development,* **49,** 500–504.

Eisenberg, N., & Mussen, P. H. (1989). *The roots of prosocial behavior in children.* New York: Cambridge University Press.

Eisenberg, N., Shell, R., Pasternack, J., Lennon, R., Beller, R., & Mathy, R. M. (1987). Prosocial development in middle childhood: A longitudinal study. *Developmental Psychology,* **23,** 712–718.

Ekman, P. (1972). Universal and cultural differences in facial expressions of emotion. In K. Cole (Ed.), *Nebraska Symposium on Motivation.* Lincoln: University of Nebraska Press.

Ekman, P. (1977). Biological and cultural contributions to body and facial movement. In J. Blacking (Ed.), *Anthropology of the body.* New York: Academic Press.

Ekman, P., Friesen, W. V., O'Sullivan, M., Chan, A., Diacoyanni-Tarlatzis, I., Heider, K., Krauss, R., LeCompte, W. A., Pitcairn, T., Ricci Bilti, P. E., Scherer, K., Tomita, M., & Tzavaras, A. (1987). Universals and cultural differences in the judgements of facial expressions of emotion. *Journal of Personality and Social Psychology,* **52,** 712–717.

Ekman, P., & Oster, H. (1979). Facial expressions of emotion. *Annual Review of Psychology,* **30,** 527–554.

Elbers, L., & Ton, J. (1985). Playpen monologues: The interplay of words & babbles in the first words period. *Journal of Child Language,* **12,** 551–565.

Elder, G. H. (1974). *Children of the Great Depression.* Chicago: University of Chicago Press.

Eldredge, L., & Salamy, A. (1988). Neurobehavioral and neurophysiological assessment of healthy and "at risk" full-term infants. *Child Development,* **59,** 186–192.

Elicker, J., Egeland, B., & Sroufe, L. A. (1992). Predicting peer competence and peer relationships from early parent-child relationships. In R. D. Parke & G. W. Ladd (Eds.), *Family-Peer relationships: Modes of linkage*. Hillsdale, NJ: Erlbaum.

Ellis, S., Rogoff, B., & Cromer, C. (1981). Age segregation in children's social interactions. *Developmental Psychology,* **17,** 399–407.

Emde, R. N., Gaensbauer, T. J., & Harmon, R. J. (1976). Emotional expression in infancy: A biobehavioral study. *Psychological Issues* (Vol. 10, No. 37). New York: International Universities Press.

Emde, R. N., Harmon, R. J., Metcalf, D., Koenig, K. L., & Wagonfeld, S. (1971). Stress and neonatal sleep. *Psychosomatic Medicine,* **33,** 491–497.

Emery, R. E. (1982). Interparental conflict and the children of discord and divorce. *Psychological Bulletin,* **92,** 310–330.

Emery, R. E., Binkoff, J. A., Houts, A. C., & Carr, E. G. (1983). Children as independent variables: Some clinical implications of child-effects. *Behavior Therapy,* **14,** 398–412.

Enright, R. D., & Satterfield, S. J. (1980). An ecological validation of social cognitive development. *Child Development,* **51,** 156–161.

Entwisle, D. R., & Alexander, K. L. (1987). Long-term effects of cesarean delivery on parents' beliefs and children's schooling. *Developmental Psychology,* **23,** 676–682.

Entwisle, D. R., & Doering, S. G. (1981). *The first birth.* Baltimore, MD: Johns Hopkins University Press.

Entwisle, D. R., & Frasure, N. E. (1974). A contradiction resolved: Children's processing of syntactic cues. *Developmental Psychology,* **10,** 852–857.

Epstein, J. L. (1980). *After the bus arrives: Resegregation in desegregated schools.* Paper presented at the meeting of the American Educational Research Association, Boston.

Epstein, L. H., & Wing, R. R. (1987). Behavioral treatment of childhood obesity. *Psychological Bulletin,* **101,** 333–342.

Epstein, L. H., Wing, R. R., Koeske, R., & Valoski, A. (1987). Long-term effects of family-based treatment of childhood obesity. *Journal of Consulting and Clinical Psychology,* **55,** 91–95.

Erickson, M. F., Sroufe, L. A., & Egeland, B. (1985). The relationship between quality of attachment and behavior problems in preschool in a high risk sample. In I. Bretherton & E. Waters (Eds.), Growing points of attachment theory and research. *Monographs of the Society for Research in Child Development,* **50,** (1–2, Serial No. 109).

Eriksson, M., Catz, C. S., & Yaffe, S. J. (1973). Drugs and pregnancy. In H. Osofsky (Ed.), *Clinical obstetrics and gynecology: High-risk pregnancy with emphases upon maternal and fetal well being* (Vol. 16, pp. 192–224). New York: Harper & Row.

Eron, L. D., & Huesmann, L. R. (1984). The control of aggressive behavior by changes in attitudes, values and the conditions of learning. In R. J. Blanchard & C. Blanchard (Eds.), *Advances in the study of aggression* (Vol. 2). New York: Academic.

Eron, L. D., & Huesmann, L. R. (1990). The stability of aggressive behavior—even into the third generation. In M. Lewis & S. Miller (Eds.), *Handbook of developmental psychopathology*. New York: Plenum.

Ervin-Tripp, S. (1979). Children's verb turn taking. In E. Ochs & B. Schieffelin (Eds.), *Developmental pragmatics*. New York: Academic.

Estrada, P., Arsenio, W. F., Hess, R. D., & Holloway, S. D. (1987). Affective quality of the mother-child relationship: Longitudinal consequences for children's school-related functioning. *Developmental Psychology,* **23,** 210–215.

Evans, E. D., & McCandless, B. R. (1978). *Children and youth: Psychosocial development*. New York: Holt.

Fagot, B. I. (1973). Sex-related stereotyping of toddlers' behaviors. *Developmental Psychology,* **9,** 429.

Fagot, B. I. (1977a). Consequences of moderate cross-gender behavior in preschool children. *Child Development,* **48,** 902–907.

Fagot, B. I. (1977b). *Sex-determined parental reinforcing contingencies in toddler children.* Paper presented at the biennial meeting of the Society for Research in Child Development, New Orleans.

Fagot, B. I. (1981). Male and female teachers: Do they treat boys and girls differently? *Sex Roles,* **7,** 263–272.

Fagot, B. I. (1985a). Beyond the reinforcement principle: Another step toward understanding sex role development. *Developmental Psychology,* **21,** 1097–1104.

Fagot, B. I. (1985b). Changes in thinking about early sex role development. *Developmental Review,* **5,** 83–98.

Fagot, B. I., & Hagan, R. (1991). Observations of parent reactions to sex-stereotyped behaviors: Age and sex effects. *Child Development,* **62,** 617–628.

Fagot, B. I., & Leinbach, M. D. (1987). Socialization of sex roles within the family. In D. B.

Carter (Ed.), *Current conceptions of sex roles and sex typing: Theory and research* (pp. 89–100). New York: Praeger.

Fagot, B. I., & Leinbach, M. D. (1989). The young child's gender schema: Environmental input, internal organization. *Child Development,* **60,** 663–672.

Fagot, B. I., & Leinbach, M. D. (1992). Gender-role development in young children: From discrimination to labeling. *Developmental Review.*

Fagot, B. I., Leinbach, M. D., & Hagan, R. (1986). Gender labeling and the adoption of sex typed behaviors. *Developmental Psychology,* **22,** 440–443.

Fairchild, H. H. (1988). Creating positive television images. In S. Oskamp (Ed.), *Applied social psychology annual* (Vol. 8). Newbury Park, CA: Sage.

Falbo, T., & Polit, D. F. (1986). Quantitative review of the only child literature: Research evidence and theory development, *Psychological Bulletin,* **100,** 176–186.

Falmagne, R. (1980). The development of logical competence: A psycholinguistic perspective. In R. M. Kluovie & H. Spade (Eds.), *Developmental models of thinking,* New York: Academic.

Faloon, J., Eddy, J., Wiener, L., & Pizzo, P. (1989). Human immunodeficiency virus infection in children. *Journal of Pediatrics,* **114,** 1–30.

Farnham-Diggory, S. (1990). *Schooling.* Cambridge, MA: Harvard University Press.

Farver, J. M. (1992). Cultural differences in scaffolding pretend play: A comparison of American and Mexican mother-child and sibling-child pairs. In K. B. MacDonald (Ed.), *Parents and children at play.* Albany, NY: SUNY Press.

Fein, G. (1978). *Child development.* Englewood Cliffs, NJ: Prentice-Hall.

Fein, G. (1981). Pretend play: An integrative review. *Child Development,* **52,** 1095–1118.

Fein, G. (1988). Mind, meaning and affect: Proposals for a theory of pretense. *Developmental Review,* **9,** 345–363.

Feingold, A. (1988). Cognitive gender differences are disappearing. *American Psychologist,* **43,** 95–103.

Feiring, C., & Lewis, M. (1987). The ecology of some middle class families at dinner. *International Journal of Behavioral Development,* **10,** 377–390.

Feld, S., Ruhland, D., & Gold, M. (1979). Developmental changes in achievement motivation. *Merrill Palmer Quarterly,* **25,** 43–60.

Feldman, N. S., Klosson, E. C., Parsons, J. E., Rholes, W. S., & Ruble, D. N. (1976). Order of information presentation and children's moral judgments. *Child Development,* **47,** 556–559.

Feldman, R. S., & Rimé, B. (Eds.). (1991) *Fundamentals of nonverbal behavior.* New York: Cambridge University Press.

Feldman, S. S., Nash, S. C., & Aschenbrenner, B. G. (1983). Antecedents of fathering. *Child Development,* **54,** 1628–1636.

Fendrich, M., Warner, V., & Weissman, M. (1990). Family risk factors, parental depression and psychopathology in offspring. *Developmental Psychology,* **26,** 40–50.

Ferguson, T. J., & Rule, B. G. (1980). Effects of inferential sex, outcome severity and basis of responsibility on children's evaluations of aggressive acts. *Developmental Psychology,* **16,** 141–146.

Ferguson, T. J., & Rule, B. G. (1982). Influences of inferential set, outcome intent and outcome severity on children's moral judgments. *Developmental Psychology,* **18,** 843–851.

Fernald, A. (1985). Four-month-olds prefer to listen to motherese. *Infant Behavior and Development,* **8,** 181–196.

Fernald, A. (1992). Meaningful melodies in mothers' speech to infants. In H. Papousek, U. Jurgens, & M. Papousek (Eds.), *Nonverbal communication: Comparative and developmental approaches.* Cambridge, England: Cambridge University Press.

Fernald, A., & Kuhl, P. K. (1987). Acoustical determinants of infant preference for motherese speech. *Infant Behavior and Development,* **10,** 279–293.

Fernald, A., & Mazzie, C. (1991). Prosody and focus in speech to infants and adults. *Developmental Psychology,* **27,** 209–221.

Ferrara, R. A., Brown, A. L., & Campione, J. C. (1986). Children's learning and transfer of inductive reasoning rules: Studies of proximal development. *Child Development,* **57,** 1087–1099.

Festinger, L. (1954). A theory of social comparison. *Human Relations,* **7,** 117–140.

Field, D. (1987). A review of preschool conservation training: An analysis of analyses. *Developmental Review,* **7,** 210–251.

Field, T., & Goldson, E. (1984). Pacifying effects of nonnutritive sucking on term and preterm neonates during heelstick procedures. *Pediatrics,* **74,** 1012–1015.

Field, T., Healy, B., Goldstein, S., & Guthertz, M. (1990). Behavior-state matching and synchrony in mother-infant interactions of non-depressed versus depressed dyads. *Developmental Psychology,* **26,** 7–14.

Field, T. M. (1978). Interaction behaviors of primary versus secondary caretaker fathers. *Developmental Psychology,* **14,** 183–184.

Field, T. M. (1984). Separation stress of young children transferring to new schools. *Developmental Psychology,* **20,** 786–792.

Field, T. M. (1986). Affective responses to separation. In T. B. Brazelton & M. W. Yogman (Eds.), *Affective development in infancy.* Norwood, NJ: Ablex.

Field, T. M. (1990). *Infancy.* Cambridge, MA: Harvard University Press.

Field, T. M., Cohen, D., Garcia, R., & Greenberg, R. (1984). Mother-stranger face discrimination by the newborn. *Infant Behavior and Development,* **7,** 19–25.

Field, T. M., Schanberg, S. M., Schafedi, F., Bauer, C. R., Vega-Lahr, N., Garcia, R., Nystrom, J., & Kuhn, C. M. (1986). Effects of tactile/kinesthetic stimulation on preterm neonates. *Pediatrics,* **77,** 654–658.

Field, T. M., & Walden, T. A. (1982a). Perception and production of facial expressions in infancy and early childhood. In H. W. Reese & L. P. Lipsitt (Eds.), *Advances in child development and behavior* (Vol. 16). New York: Academic Press.

Field, T. M., & Walden, T. A. (1982b). Production and discrimination of facial expressions by preschool children. *Child Development,* **53,** 1299–1311.

Fifer, W. P., & Moon, C. (1989). Auditory experience in the fetus. In W. P. Smotherman & S. R. Robinson (Eds.), *Behavior of the fetus* (pp. 175–187). Caldwell, NJ: Telford Press.

Finnie, V., & Russell, A. (1988). Preschool children's social status and their mothers' behavior and knowledge in the supervisory role. *Developmental Psychology,* **24,** 789–801.

Firsch, R. E. (1984). Fatness, puberty, and fertility. In J. Brooks-Gunn & A. C. Petersen (Eds.), *Girls at puberty: Biological, psychological, and social perspectives.* New York: Plenum.

Fischer, K. W., & Bullock, D. (1984). Cognitive development in middle childhood: Conclusions and new directions. In W. A. Collins & K. Heller (Eds.), *The elementary school years: Understanding development during middle childhood.* Washington, DC: National Academic Press.

Fischer, K. W., & Lazerson, A. (1984). A summary of prenatal development. In K. W. Fischer & A. Lazerson, *Human development* (p. 117). New York: Freeman.

Fischer, K. W., & Roberts, R. J. (1986). A developmental sequence of classification skills and errors in preschool children. Unpublished manuscript, Harvard University.

Fisher, C. B., & Brone, R. J. (1991). Eating disorders in adolescence. In R. M. Lerner, A. C. Petersen, & J. Brooks-Gunn (Eds.). *Encyclopedia of Adolescence* (Vol. 1). New York: Garland.

Fisher, S. F. (1973). *The female orgasm: Psychology, physiology, fantasy.* New York: Basic Books.

Flannagan, J. C. (1978). *Trends in male/female performance on cognitive ability measures.* Washington, DC: American Institutes for Research.

Flavell, J. H. (1963). *The developmental psychology of Jean Piaget.* Princeton, NJ: Van Nostrand.

Flavell, J. H. (1984). Discussion in R. Sternberg (Ed.), *Mechanisms of cognitive development.* New York: Freeman.

Flavell, J. H. (1985). *Cognitive Development.* Englewood Cliffs, NJ: Prentice-Hall.

Flavell, J. H., Beach, D. R., & Chinsky, J. M. (1966). Spontaneous verbal rehearsal in a memory task as a function of age. *Child Development,* **37,** 283–299.

Flavell, J. H., Friedricks, A. G., & Hoyt, J. D. (1970). Developmental changes in memorization processes. *Cognitive Psychology,* **1,** 324–340.

Flavell, J. H., Speer, J. R., Green, F. L., & August, D. L. (1981). The development of comprehension monitoring and knowledge about communication. *Monographs of the Society for Research in Child Development,* **46,** (5, Serial No. 192).

Folstein, S. E., & Rutter, M. L. (1977). Genetic influences and infantile autism. *Nature,* **265,** 726–728.

Folstein, S. E., & Rutter, M. L. (1988). Autism: Familial aggregation and genetic implications. *Journal of Autism and Developmental Disorders,* **18,** 3–30.

Ford, M. E., & Keating, D. P. (1981). Developmental and individual difference in long-term memory retrieval. *Child Development,* **52,** 234-241.

Fordham, S., & Ogbu, J. V. (1986). Black students' school success: Coping with the burden of acting white. *Urban Review.* **18,** 176–206.

Forehand, G., Ragosta, J., & Rock, D. (1976). *Condition and processes of effective school desegregation.* Final Report. Washington, DC: Office of Education.

Forssberg, H. (1985). Ontogeny of human locomotor control: I. Infant stepping, supported locomotion and the transition to independent locomotion. *Experimental Brain Research,* **57,** 480–493.

Forssman, H., & Hambert, C. (1966). Incidence of Klinefelter's syndrome among mental patients. *Lancet,* **1**(7284), 1327–1328.

Fox, H. E., Steinbrecher, M., Pessel, D., Inglis, J., Medvid, L., & Angel, E. (1978). Maternal ethanol ingestion and the occurrence of human fetal breathing movements. *American Journal of Obstetrics and Gynecology,* **132,** 354–358.

Fox, N. A., & Davidson, R. J. (1988). Patterns of brain electrical activity during facial signs of emotion in 10-month-old infants. *Developmental Psychology,* **24,** 230–236.

Fraiberg, S. (1977). *Insights from the blind.* New York: Basic Books.
Fraiberg, S., Lieberman, A., Pekarsky, J., & Pawl, J. (1981). Treatment and outcome in an infant psychiatry program. *Journal of Prevention Psychiatry,* **1,** 143–167.
Francis, P. L., Self, P. A., & Horowitz, F. D. (1987). The behavioral assessment of the neonate: An overview. In J. Osofsky (Ed.), *Handbook of infancy* (2nd ed.). New York: Wiley.
Freedman, D. G. (1974). *Human infancy: An evolutionary perspective.* Hillsdale, NJ: Erlbaum.
Freedman, D. G. (1976). Infancy, biology, and culture. In L. P. Lipsitt (Ed.), *Developmental psychobiology: The significance of infancy.* Hillsdale, NJ: Erlbaum.
French, D. C. (1988). Heterogeneity of peer-rejected boys: Aggressive and nonaggressive subtypes. *Child Development,* **53,** 976–985.
Freud, A., & Burlingham, D. (1943). *Children and war.* New York: Basic Books.
Friedrich, L. K., & Stein, A. H. (1973). Aggressive and prosocial television programs and the natural behavior of preschool children. *Monographs of the Society for Research in Child Development,* **38** (Serial No. 151).
Friederich, L. K., & Stein, A. H. (1975). Prosocial television and young children: The effects of verbal labeling and role playing on learning and behavior. *Child Development,* **46,** 27–36.
Frith, C., & Frith, U. (1978). Feature selection and classification: A developmental study. *Journal of Experimental Child Psychology,* **25,** 413–428.
Frodi, A. M., & Lamb, M. E. (1980). Child abusers' responses to infant smiles and cries. *Child Development,* **51,** 238–241.
Frodi, A. M., Lamb, M. E., Leavitt, L. A., & Donovan, W. K. (1978). Father's and mother's responses to infant smiles and cries. *Infant Behavior and Development,* **1,** 187–198.
Frost, R. (1959). The death of the hired man. In *The complete poems of Robert Frost* (pp. 49–55). New York: Holt.
Furman, W., & Gavin, L. A. (1989). Peers influence on adjustment and development. In T. J. Berndt & G. W. Ladd (Eds.), *Peer relationships in child development.* New York: Wiley.
Furman, W., & Masters, J. C. (1980). Affective consequences of social reinforcement, punishment, and neutral behavior. *Developmental Psychology,* **16,** 100–104.
Furman, W., Rahe, D., & Hartup, W. W. (1979). Social rehabilitation of low-interactive preschool children by peer intervention. *Child Development,* **50,** 915–922.
Furstenberg, F. F., Jr. (1976). *Unplanned parenthood: The social consequences of teenage childrearing.* New York: Free Press, Macmillan.
Furstenberg, F. F., Jr. (1988). Child care after divorce and remarriage. In E. M. Hetherington & J. D. Arasteh (Eds.), *Impact of divorce, single parenting and step parenting on children* (pp. 245–261). Hillsdale, NJ: Erlbaum.
Furstenberg, F. F., Jr., Brooks-Gunn, J., & Chase-Lansdale, L. (1989). Teenaged pregnancy and child bearing. *American Psychologist,* **44,** 313–320.
Gaines, L., & Esserman, J. (1981). A quantitative study of young children's comprehension of television programs and commercials. In J. F. Esserman (Ed.), *Television advertising and children: Issues, research and findings.* New York: Child Research Service.
Galler, J. R., Ramsey, F., & Solimano, G. (1985). A follow-up study of effects of early malnutrition on subsequent development to fine motor skills in adolescence. *Pediatric Research,* **19,** 524–527.
Garbarino, J. (1982). Sociocultural risk: Dangers to competence. In C. Kopp & J. Krakow (Eds.), *Child development in a social context* (pp. 630–685). Reading, MA: Addison-Wesley.
Garbarino, J. (1989). The psychologically battered child. San Francisco: Jossey-Bass.
Garbarino, J. (1990). *Children and youth in war zones: Coping with the consequences.* Testimony prepared for the U.S. Senate Committee on Human Resources.
Garbarino, J., & Grouter, A. (1978). Defining the community context for parent-child relations: The correlates of child maltreatment. *Child Development,* **49,** 604–616.
Garbarino, J., & Sherman, D. (1980). High-risk neighborhoods and high-risk families: The human ecology of child maltreatment. *Child Development,* **51,** 188–198.
Garcia Coll, C. T. (1990). Developmental outcome of minority infants: A process-oriented look into our beginnings. *Child Development,* **61,** 270–289.
Gardner, H. (1983). *Frames of mind: The theory of multiple intelligences.* New York: Basic Books.
Garmezy, N. (1983). Stressors of childhood. In N. Garmezy & M. Rutter (Eds.), *Stress, coping and development in children* (pp. 43–84). New York: McGraw-Hill.
Garner, D. M., Garfinkel, P. E., Schwartz, D., & Thompson, M. (1980). Cultural expectations of thinness in women. *Psychological Reports,* **47,** 524–527.
Garvey, C. (1990). *Children's talk.* Cambridge, MA: Harvard University Press.
Garvey, C. (1990). *Play.* Cambridge, MA: Harvard University Press.
Gash, D., Sladek, J. R., & Sladek, C. D. (1980). Functional development of grafted vasopressin neurons. *Science,* **210,** 1367–1369.

Gelfand, D. M., Jensen, W. R., & Drew, C. J. (1982). *Understanding child behavior disorders*. New York: Holt, Rinehart, and Winston.

Gelman, R. (1969). Conservation acquisition: A problem of learning to attend to relevant attributes. *Journal of Experimental Child Psychology*, **7**, 167–187.

Gelman, R. (1972). Logical capacity of very young children: Number invariance rules. *Child Development*, **43**, 75–90.

Gelman, R. (1978). Cognitive development. *Annual Review of Psychology*, **29**, 297–332.

Gelman, R. (1979). Preschool thought. *American Psychologist*, **34**, 900–905.

Gelman, R., & Baillargeon, R. (1983). A review of some Piagetian concepts. In J. H. Falvell & E. M. Markman (Eds.), *Handbook of child psychology: Cognitive development* (Vol. 3). New York: Wiley.

Gelman, R., & Gallistel, C. R. (1978). *The child's understanding of number*. Cambridge, MA: Harvard University Press.

Gelman, R., & Meck, E. (1983). Preschoolers' counting: Principles before skill. *Cognition*, **13**, 343–359.

Gelman, S. A., & Markman, E. M. (1987). Young children's inductions from natural kinds: The role of categories and appearances. *Child Development*, **58**, 1532–1541.

Gelman, S. A., & O'Reilly, A. W. (1988). Children's inductive inferences within superordinate categories: The role of language and category structure. *Child Development*, **59**, 876–886.

Genetic evidence for autism (1989, June 3). *Science News*, **135**, 349.

Gentner, D. (1982). Why nouns are learned before verbs: Linguistic relativity versus natural partitioning. In S. A. Kuczaj II (Ed.), *Language development: Vol. 2. Language, thought, and culture* (pp. 301–332). Hillsdale, NJ: Erlbaum.

Gentner, D., & Rattermann, M. J. (1992). Analogy and similarity: Determinants of accessibility and inferential soundness. Unpublished manuscript, Northwestern University.

Gentner, D., & Stuart, P. (1983, April). *Metaphor as structure mapping: What develops?* Paper presented at the biennial meeting of the Society for Research in Child Development, Detroit.

Gentner, D., & Toupin, C. (1986). Systematicity and surface similarity in the development of analogy. *Cognitive Science*, **10**, 277–300.

George, C., & Main, M. (1979). Social interaction of young abused children: Approach, avoidance and aggression. *Child Development*, **50**, 306–318.

Gerard, H. B., & Miller, N. (1975). *School desegregation: A long-term study*. New York: Plenum.

Gerbner, G., Gross, L., Morgan, M., & Signorielli, N. (1980). The "mainstreaming" of America: Violence profile No. 11. *Journal of Communication*, **30**, 10–29.

Gerbner, G., Gross, L., Signorielli, N., & Morgan, M. (1986). Television's mean world: Violence profile No. 14–15. University of Pennsylvania, Annenberg School of Communications, Philadelphia, PA.

Gesell, A. L. (1928). *Infancy and human growth*. New York: Macmillan.

Getchell, N., & Robertson, M. A. (1989). Whole body stiffness as a function of developmental level in children's hopping. *Developmental Psychology*, **25**, 920–928.

Gewirtz, J. L. (1967). The course of infant smiling in four child-rearing environments in Israel. In B. M. Foss (Ed.), *Determinants of infant behavior* (Vol. 3, pp. 105–248). Londong: Methuen.

Gewirtz, J. L. (1969). Mechanisms of social learning: Some roles of stimulation and behavior in early human development. In D. A. Goslin (Ed.), *Handbook of socialization theory and research*. Chicago: Rand McNally.

Gibbons, D. C. (1970). *Delinquent behavior*. Englewood Cliffs, NJ: Prentice-Hall.

Gibbs, J. T. (1989). Black American adolescents. In J. T. Gibbs & L. N. Huang (Eds.), *Children of color*. San Francisco: Jossey-Bass.

Gibson, D., & Harris, A. (1988). Aggregated early intervention effects for Down syndrome persons. *Journal of Mental Deficiency Research*, **32**, 1–7.

Gibson, E. J. (1969). *Principles of perceptual learning and development*. New York: Appleton-Century-Crofts.

Gibson, E. J. (1991). An odyssey in learning and perception. Cambridge, MA: MIT Press.

Gibson, E. J. (1992). How to think about perceptual learning: Twenty-five years later. In H. L. Pick, P. Van den Broek, & D. C. Knoll (Eds.), *Cognitive Psychology: Conceptual and Methodological Issues* (pp. 215–237). Washington, DC: American Psychological Association.

Gibson, E. J., & Walk, R. D. (1960). The "visual cliff." *Scientific American*, **202**, 64.

Gick, M. L., & Holyoak, K. J. (1980). Analogical problem solving. *Cognitive Psychology*, **12**, 306–355.

Gick, M. L., & Holyoak, K. J. (1983). Schema induction and analogical transfer. *Cognitive Psychology*, **15**, 1–38.

Gilberg, C. (1990). Autism and pervasive developmental disorders. *Journal of Child Psychology and Psychiatry*, **31**, 99–119.

Ginsburg, H. J., & Miller, S. M. (1982). Sex differences in children's risk-taking behavior. *Child Development,* **53,** 426–428.

Ginsburg, H. J., Pollman, V. A., & Wauson, M. S. (1977). An ethological analysis of nonverbal inhibitors of aggressive behavior in male elementary school children. *Developmental Psychology,* **13**, 417–418.

Girton, M. R. (1979). Infants' attention to intrastimulus motion. *Journal of Experimental Child Psychology,* **28**, 416–423.

Gittleman, R., Abikoff, H., Pollack, E., Klein, D. F., Katz, S., & Mattes, J. (1980). A controlled trial of behavior modification and methylphenidate in hyperactive children. In C. K. Whalen & B. Henker (Eds.), *Hyperactive children.* New York: Academic.

Gladwin, T. (1970). *East is a big bird:Navigation and logic on Pulawat Atoll.* Cambridge, MA: Harvard University Press.

Glasberg, R., & Aboud, F. (1982). Keeping one's distance from sadness: Children's self-reports of emotional experience. *Developmental Psychology,* **18**, 287–293.

Gleitman, H. (1991). *Psychology* (3rd ed.). New York: Norton.

Gleitman, L. R., Newport, E. L., & Gleitman, H. (1984). The current status of the motherese hypothesis. *Journal of Child Language,* **11**, 43–79.

Glucksberg, S., Krauss, R., & Higgins, E. T. (1975). The development of referential communication skills. In F. D. Horowitz (Eds.), *Review of child development research* (Vol. 4). Chicago: University of Chicago Press.

Goddard, H. H. (1912). How shall we educate mental defectives? *Traeniey School Bulletin,* **9,** 43.

Goetz, T. E., & Dweck, C. S. (1980). Learned helplessness in social situations. *Journal of Personality and Social Psychology,* **39,** 246–255.

Gold, D., & Andres, D. (1978). Developmental comparisons between 10-year-old children with employed and nonemployed mothers. *Child Development,* **49**, 75–84.

Goldberg, S. (1966). Infant care and growth in urban Zambia. *Human Development,* **15,** 77–89.

Goldberg, S. (1983). Parent-infant bonding: Another look. *Child Development,* **54,** 1355–1382.

Goldberg, W. A., & Easterbrooks, M. A. (1984). The role of marital quality in toddler development. *Developmental Psychology,* **20,** 504–514.

Golden, M., & Birns, B. (1971). Social class, intelligence, and cognitive style in infancy. *Child Development,* **42,** 2114–2116.

Golden, M., & Birns, B. (1983). Social class and infant intelligence. In M. Lewis (Ed.), *Origins of intelligence: Infancy and early childhood* (2nd ed.)(pp. 347–398). New York: Plenum.

Goldin-Meadow, S., & Morford, L. (1985). Gesture in early language: Studies of deaf and hearing children. *Merrill-Palmer Quarterly,* **31**, 145–176.

Goldsmith, H. H. (1983). Genetic influences on personality from infancy to adulthood. *Child Development,* **54,** 331–355.

Goldstein, N. (1990, January). *Explaining socioeconomic differences in children's cognitive test scores.* Unpublished manuscript, Malcolm Weiner Center for Social Policy, J. F. Kennedy School of Government, Harvard University.

Goodenough, E. W. (1957). Interest in persons as an aspect of sex differences in the early years. *Genetic Psychology Monographs,* **5**, 287–323.

Goodman, G. S., Bottoms, B. L., Schwartz-Kenney, B. M., & Rudy, L. (1991). Children's testimony for a stressful event: Improving children's reports. *Journal of Narrative and Life History,* **1**, 69–99.

Goodman, J. C. (1989). *The development of context effects of spoken word recognition.* Doctoral dissertation. The University of Chicago.

Goodman, R., & Stevenson, J. (1989). A twin study of hyperactivity: II. The etiologic role of genes, family relationships and perinatal adversity. *Journal of Child Psychology and Psychiatry,* **30**, 691–709.

Goodnow, J. (1988). Children's household work: Its nature and functions. *Psychological Bulletin,* **103,** 5–26.

Goodnow, J., & Collins, A. (1991). *Ideas according to parents.* Hillsdale, NJ: Erlbaum.

Gorn, G. J., & Goldberg, M. E. (1982). Behavioral evidence of the effects of televised food messages on children. *Journal of Consumer Research,* **9,** 200–205.

Gottesman, I. I. (1963). Genetic aspects of intelligent behavior. In N. Ellis (Ed.), *Handbook of mental deficiency: Psychological theory and research.* New York: McGraw-Hill.

Gottesman, I. I., & Shields, J. (1982). *Schizophrenia: The epigenetic puzzle.* Cambridge: Cambridge University Press.

Gottfried, A. E., Gottfried, A. W., & Bathurst, K. (1988). Maternal employment, family environment and children's development: Infancy through the school years. In A. E. Gottfried & A. W. Gottfried (Eds.), *Maternal employment and children's development: Longitudinal research* (pp. 11–53). New York: Plenum.

Gottfried, A. W., & Gottfried, A. E. (1984). Home environment and cognitive development in young children of middle-socioeconomic-status families. In A. W. Gottfried (Ed.), *Home environment and early cognitive development* (pp. 57–115). Orlando, FL: Academic.

Gottlieb, D. (1966). Teaching and students: The view of Negro and white teachers. *Sociology of Education,* **37,** 345–353.

Gottlieb, J., & Leyser, Y. (1981). Friendship between mentally retarded and non-retarded children. In S. R. Asher & J. M. Gottman, *The development of children's friendships.* New York: Cambridge University Press.

Gottman, J. (1989). Predicting the longitudinal course of marriages. *American Association of Marriage and Family Therapy Monograph* (pp. 39–44).

Gottman, J. M. (1983). How children become friends. *Monographs of the Society for Research in Child Development,* **48** (Serial No. 201).

Gottman, J. M. (1986). The world of coordinated play: Same and cross-sex friendship in young children. In J. M. Gottman & J. G. Parker (Eds.), *The conversations of friends.* New York: Cambridge University Press.

Gottman, J. M., & J. G. Parker (Eds.) (1986). *The conversations of friends.* New York: Cambridge University Press.

Gottman, J. M., & Mettetal, G. (1986). Speculations on social and affective development: Friendship and acquaintanceship through adolescence. In J. M. Gottman & J. G. Parker (Eds.), *The conversations of friends.* New York: Cambridge University Press.

Gould, R. (1972). *Child studies through fantasy.* New York: Quadrangle.

Graham, G. G. (1966). Growth during recovery from infantile malnutrition. *Journal of the American Medical Women's Association,* **21,** 737–742.

Graham, P., Rutter, M., & George, S. (1973). Temperamental characteristics as predictors of behavior disorders in children. *American Journal of Orthopsychiatry,* **43,** 328–399.

Graham, S. (1988). Children's developing understanding of the motivational role of affect: An attributable analysis. *Cognitive Development,* **3,** 71–88.

Graham, S., Doubleday, C., & Guarino, P. A. (1984). The development of relations between perceived controllability and the emotions of pity, anger and guilt. *Child Development,* **55,** 561–565.

Granrud, C. E. (1991). Visual size constancy in newborns. In C. E. Granrud (Ed.), *Visual perception and cognition in infants.* Hillsdale, NJ: Erlbaum.

Grant, C. A. (1990, September). Desegregation, racial attitudes and intergroup contact: A discussion of change. *Phi Delta Kappan,* pp. 25–32.

Grantham-McGregor, S., Schofield, W., & Powell, C. (1987). Development of severely malnourished children who received psychosocial stimulation: Six-year follow-up. *Pediatrics,* **79,** 247–254.

Gratch, G. (1982). Responses to hidden persons and things by 5-, 9-, and 16-month-old infants in a visual tracking situation. *Developmental Psychology,* **18,** 232–237.

Graves, S. N. (1975). *How to encourage positive racial attitudes.* Paper presented at the Society for Research in Child Development, Denver, CO.

Green, J. A., Gustafson, G. E., & West, M. J. (1980). Effects of infant development on mother-infant interactions. *Child Development,* **51,** 199–207.

Green, R. H., Asrat, D., Maurs, M., & Morgan, R. (1989). Children in Southern Africa. In United Nations Children's Fund (Ed.), *Children on the front line* (pp. 9–42). New York: United Nations.

Greenberg, B. S. (1986). Minorities and the mass media. In J. Bryant & D. Zimmerman (Eds.), *Perspectives on media effects* (pp. 165–188). Hillsdale, NJ: Erlbaum.

Greenberg, B. S., Fazel, S., & Weber, M. (1986). *Children's view on advertising.* Independent Broadcasting Authority Research Report, New York, N.Y.

Greenberg, J. W., & Davidson, H. H. (1972). Home background and school achievement in black urban ghetto children. *American Journal of Orthopsychiatry,* **42,** 803–810.

Greenberg, M., & Morris, N. (1974). Engrossment: The newborn's impact upon the father. *American Journal of Orthopsychiatry,* **44,** 520–531.

Greenberger, E., & Goldberg, W. A. (1989). Work, parenting and the socialization of children. *Developmental Psychology,* **25,** 22–35.

Greenfield, P. M. (1976). Cross-cultural research and Piagetian theory: Paradox and progress. In K. Riegel & J. Meacham (Eds.), *The developing individual in a changing world* (Vol. 1). The Hague: Mouton.

Greenfield, P. M. (1984). *Mind and media: The effects of television, video games and computers.* Cambridge, MA: Harvard University Press.

Greenfield, P. M., & Lave, J. (1982). Cognitive aspects of informal education. In D. A. Wagner & H. W. Stevenson (Eds.), *Cultural perspectives on child development.* San Francisco: Freeman.

Greenough, W. T., Black, J. E., & Wallace, C. S. (1987). Experience and brain development. *Child Development,* **58,** 539–559.

Greenough, W. T., & Green, E. J. (1981). Experience and the aging brain. In J. L. McGaugh, J. G. March, & S. B. Kiesler (Eds.), *Aging: Biology and behavior*. New York: Academic Press.

Gresham, F. M., & Reschly, D. (1988). Social skills and peer acceptance in the mildly handicapped. In T. R. Kratochwill (Ed.), *Advances in school psychology* (Vol. 6, pp. 203–247). Hillsdale, NJ: Erlbaum.

Grief, E. B., & Gleason, J. B. (1980). Hi, thanks, and goodbye: More routine information. *Language in Society*, **9**, 159–166.

Griest, D., Wells, K. C., & Forehand, R. (1980). Examination of predictors of maternal perceptions of maladjustment in clinic-referred children. *Journal of Abnormal Psychology*, **88**, 277–281.

Grobstein, C. (1979). External human fertilization. *Scientific American*, **240**(6), 57–68.

Grossman, K., Grossman, K. E., Spangler, G., Suess, G., & Unzer, J. (1985). Maternal sensitivity and newborn's orientation responses as related to the quality of attachment in northern Germany. In I. Bretherton & E. Waters (Eds.), Growing points in attachment theory and research. *Monographs of the Society for Research in Child Development* (Serial No. 209, pp. 233–256.)

Grotevant, H. (1986). Assessment of identity development: Current issues and future directions. *Journal of Adolescent Research*, **1**, 175–181.

Grotevant, H. D., Scarr, S., & Weinberg, R. A. (1977). Patterns of interest similarity in adoptive and biological families. *Journal of Personality and Social Psychology*, **35**, 667–676.

Grueneich, R. (1982). The development of children's integration rules for making moral judgments. *Child Development*, **53**, 887–894.

Grusec, J. (1973). Effects of co-observer evaluations on limitation: A developmental study. *Developmental Psychology*, **8**, 144–148.

Grusec, J. E., & Abramovitch, R. (1982). Imitation of peers and adults in a natural setting: A functional analysis. *Child Development*, **53**, 636–642.

Grusec, J. E., Covell, K., & Paucha, P. (1991). *Intergenerational transmission of discipline styles and associated belief systems*. Paper presented at the meetings of the Society for Research in Child Development. Seattle, WA.

Grusec, J. E., & Dix, T. (1986). The socialization of prosocial behavior: Theory and reality. In C. Zahn-Waxler, E. M., Cummings, & R. Ioannotti (Eds.), *Altruism and aggression*. New York: Cambridge University Press.

Grusec, J. E., Kuczynski, L., Rushton, P., & Simutis, Z. M. (1979). Learning resistance to temptation through observation. *Developmental Psychology*, **15**, 233–240.

Grych, J. H., & Fincham, F. D. (1990). Marital conflict and children's adjustment: A cognitive-contextual framework. *Psychological Bulletin*, **108**, 267–282.

Guerra, N. G., & Slaby, R. G. (1990). Cognitive mediators of aggression in adolescent offenders: 2. Intervention. *Developmental Psychology*, **26**, 269–277.

Guilford, J. P. (1966). Intelligence: 1965 model. *American Psychologist*, **21**, 20–26.

Gump, P. V. (1980). The school as a social situation. In. M. R. Rosenzweig & L. W. Porter (Eds.), *Annual review of psychology*. Palo Alto, CA: Annual Reviews.

Gump, P. V., & Ross, R. (1977). The fit of milieu and programme in school environments. In H. McGurk (Ed.), *Ecological factors in human development*. New York: North-Holland.

Gunnar, M. (1980). Control, warning signals and distress in infancy. *Developmental Psychology*, **16**, 281–289.

Gunnar, M., Leighton, K., & Peleaux, R. (1984). *The effects of temporal predictability on year-old infants' reactions to potentially frightening toys*. Unpublished manuscript, University of Minnesota, Minneapolis.

Gunter, B., & McAleer, J. L. (1990). *Children and television: The one-eye monster?* London: Routledge.

Gurling, H., Sherrington, R. P., Bynjolfsson, J., Read, T., Curtis, D., Monkoo, B. J. (1989). Recent and future molecular genetic research into schizophrenia. *Schizophrenia Bulletin*, **15**, 373–382.

Gurman, A. S., & Kniskern, D. P. (Eds.), (1980). *Handbook of family therapy*. New York: Brunner/Mazel.

Gusella, J. F., Wexler, N. S., Conneally, P. M., Naylor, S. L., Anderson, M. A., Tanzi, R. E. (1983). A polymorphic DNA marker genetically linked to Huntington's disease. *Nature*, **306**, 234–238.

Gustafson, G. E., & Green, J. A. (1988, April). *A role of crying in the development of prelinguistic communicative competence*. Paper presented at the International Conference on Infant Studies, Washington, DC.

Gustafson, G. E., & Harris, K. L. (1990). Women's responses to young infants' cries. *Developmental Psychology*, **26**, 144–152.

Gustafson, S. B., & Magnusson, D. (1991). *Female life careers: A pattern approach* (Vol. 3). Hillsdale, NJ: Erlbaum.

Guttentag, R. E. (1984). The mental effort requirement of cumulative rehearsal: A developmental study. *Journal of Experimental Child Psychology*, **37**, 92–106.

Guttentag, R. E. (1985). A developmental study of attention to auditory and visual signals. *Journal of Experimental Child Psychology*, **39**, 546–561.

Hagen, J. W., & Hale, G. A. (1973). The development of attention in children. In A. D. Pick (Ed.), *Minnesota Symposia on Child Psychology* (Vol. 7). Minneapolis: University of Minnesota Press.

Hagerman, R. J., & Sobesky, W. E. (1989). Psychopathology in fragile X syndrome. *American Journal of Orthopsychiatry*, **59**, 142–152.

Hahn, W. K. (1987). Cerebral lateralization of function: From infancy through childhood. *Psychological Bulletin*, **101**, 376–392.

Haight, W., & Miller, P. (1993). *The ecology and development of pretend play*. Albany: State University of New York Press.

Haith, M. M., Bergman, T., & Moore, M. J. (1977). *Eye contact and face scanning in early infancy*. Unpublished manuscript, University of Denver. Denver, Colorado.

Haith, M. M., Hazen, C., & Goodman, G. S. (1988). Expectation and anticipation of dynamic visual events by 3.5-month-old-babies. *Child Development*, **59**, 467–479.

Hale, G. A., & Taweel, S. S. (1974). Age differences in children's performance on measures of component selection and incidental learning. *Journal of Experimental Child Psychology*, **18**, 107–116.

Halford, G. S. (1990). Is children's reasoning logical or analogical? Further comments on Piagetian cognitive developmental psychology. *Human Development*, **33**, 356–361.

Hall, V. C., & Kaye, D. B. (1980). Early patterns of cognitive development. *Monographs of the Society for Research in Child Development*, **45**,(2, Serial No. 184).

Halliday, M. A. K. (1975). *Learning how to mean: Exploration in the development of language*. London: Arnold.

Hallinan, M. T., & Teixeira, R. A. (1987). Opportunities and constraints: Black-white differences in the formation of interracial friendships. *Child Development*, **58**, 1358–1371.

Halpern, D. (1992). *Sex differences in cognitive ability* (2nd ed.). Hillsdale, NJ: Erlbaum.

Halverson, H. M. (1931). An experimental study of prehension in infants by means of systematic cinema records. *Genetic Psychology Monographs*, **10**(2–3), 107–286.

Hamill, P., Drizd, T. A., Johnson, C. L., Reed, R. B., & Roche, A. F. (1976). HCHS growth charts. *Monthly Vital Statistics Report*, **25** (Suppl. HRA), 76–112.

Hamill, P., Johnston, F., & Lemeshow, S. (1973). Height and weight of youths, 12–17 years. *Vital and Health Statistics* (Serial 11, No. 124).

Hampe, E., Noble, H., Miller, L. C., & Barrett, C. L. (1973). Phobic children one and two years post-treatment. *Journal of Abnormal Psychology*, **82**, 446–453.

Harlow, H. F., & Zimmerman, R. R. (1959). Affectional responses in the infant monkey. *Science*, **130**, 421–432.

Harris, P. L. (1989). *Children and emotion*. New York: Basil Blackwell.

Harris, P. L., & Bassett, E. (1975). Transitive inferences by 4-year-old children? *Developmental Psychology*, **11**, 875–876.

Harris, P. L., Johnson, C. N., Hutton, D., Andrews, G., Cook, T. (1989). Young children's theory of mind and emotion. *Cognition and Emotion*, **3**.

Harris, P. L., Olthof, R., Meerum, Terwogt, M., & Hardman, C. E. (1987). Children's knowledge of the situations that provide emotions. *International Journal of Behavioral Development*, **10**, 319–344.

Harrison, A. O., Serafica, F., & McAdoo, H. (1984). Ethnic families of color. In R. D. Parke (Ed.), *Review of child development research: Vol. 7. The family*. Chicago: University of Chicago Press.

Harrison, A. O., Wilson, M. N., Pine, C. J., Chon, S. Q., & Buriel, R. (1990). Family ecologies of ethnic minority children. *Child Development*, **61**, 347–362.

Harter, S. (1983). Developmental perspectives on the self-system. In E. M. Hetherington (Ed.), *Handbook of child psychology: Socialization, personality & social development* (Vol. 4). New York: Wiley.

Harter, S. (1987). The determinants and mediational role of global self-worth in children. In N. Eisenberg (Ed.), *Contemporary topics in developmental psychology*. New York: Wiley.

Harter, S. (1990). Issues in the assessment of the self-concept of children and adolescents. In A. M. LaGrecca (Ed.), *Through the eyes of the child*. Boston: Allyn and Bacon.

Harter, S., & Whitesell, N. (1989). Developmental changes in children's emotion concepts. In C. Saarni & P. L. Harris (Eds.), *Children's understanding of emotions*. New York: Cambridge University Press.

Hartshorne, H., & May, M. S. (1928). *Moral studies in the nature of character: Vol. 1. Studies in deceit; Vol. 2. Studies in self-control; Vol. 3. Studies in the organization of character*. New York: Macmillan.

Hartup, W. W. (1974). Aggression in childhood: Developmental perspectives. *American Psychologist,* **29,** 336–341.
Hartup, W. W. (1976). Peer interaction and behavioral development of the individual child. In E. Shopler & R. L. Reichler (Eds.), *Psychopathology and child development.* New York: Plenum.
Hartup, W. W. (1983). Peer relations. In P. H. Mussen (Ed.), *Handbook of child psychology* (Vol. 4). New York: Wiley
Hartup, W. W. (1989). Social relationships and their developmental significance. *American Psychologist,* **44,** 120–126.
Hartup, W. W. (1992, August). Friendships and their developmental significance. Invited address, American Psychological Association Annual Meeting, Washington, D.C.
Hartup, W. W., Laursen, B., Steward, M. I., & Eastenson, A. (1988). Conflict and the friendship relations of young children. *Child Development,* **59,** 1590–1600.
Havinghurst, R. F., & Neugarten, B. L. (1955). *American Indian and white children.* Chicago: University of Chicago Press.
Hawkins, J., Sheingold, K., Gearhart, M., & Berger, C. (1982). Microcomputers in schools: Impact on the social life of elementary classrooms. *Journal of Applied Developmental Psychology,* **3,** 361–373.
Hawn, P. R., & Harris, L. J. (1983). Laterality in manipulatory and cognitive related activity. In G. Young, S. Segalowitz, C. Corter, & S. Trehub (Eds.), *Manual specialization and the developing brain.* New York: Academic.
Hay, D. F. (1979). Cooperative interactions and sharing between young children and their parents. *Developmental Psychology,* **15,** 647–653.
Hay, D. F., & Murray, P. (1982). Giving and requesting: Social facilitation of infants' offers to adults. *Infant Behavior and Development,* **5,** 301–310.
Hay, D. F., & Rheingold, H. L. (1983). *The early appearance of some valued social behaviors.* Unpublished manuscript. State University of New York at Stony Brook.
Hayden, L., Turulli, D., & Hymel, S. (1988, May). *Children talk about loneliness.* Paper presented at the biennial meeting of the University of Waterloo Conference on Child Development, Waterloo, Ontario, Canada.
Hayes, C. D., & Palmer, J. L. (Eds.). (1989). *Who cares for America's children? Child care policy for the 1990's.* Washington, DC: National Academy Press.
Hayes, D. S., Chemelski, B. E., & Birnbaum, D. W. (1981). Young children's incidental and intentional retention of televised events. *Developmental Psychology,* **17**, 230–232.
Hayes, K. J. (1962). Genes, drives and intellect. *Psychological Reports,* **10,** 299–342.
Hazebrigg, M. D., Cooper, H. M., & Borduen, C. M. (1987). Evaluating the effectiveness of family therapies: An integrative review and analysis. *Psychological Bulletin,* **101**, 428–442.
Hebb, D. O. (1946). On the nature of fear. *Psychological Review,* **53,** 250–275.
Hebb, D. O. (1949). *The organization of behavior.* New York: Wiley.
Hebert, C., & Dweck, C. S. (1985). *Mediators of persistence in preschoolers: Implications for development.* Unpublished manuscript, Harvard University.
Hechtman, L., & Weiss, G. (1983). Long-term outcome of hyperactive children. *American Journal of Orthopsychiatry,* **53**, 532–541.
Hecox, K., & Deegan, D. M. (1985). Methodological issues in the study of auditory development. In G. Gottlieb & N. A. Krasnegor (Eds.), *Measurement of audition and vision in the first year of postnatal life: A methodological overview.* Norwood, NJ: Ablex.
Henderson, V. L., & Dweck, C. S. (1990). Motivation and achievement. In S. Feldman & G. Elder (Eds.), *Adolescence: At the threshold* (pp. 308–329). Cambridge, MA: Harvard University Press.
Herbst, A. L. (1981). Diethylstilbestrol and other hormones during pregnancy. *Obstetrics and Gynecology,* **58,** 355–405.
Herrenstein, R. (1971). I. Q. *Atlantic,* **228,** 44–64.
Hertzog, M. E., & Shapiro, T. (1990). Autism and pervasive developmental disorders. In M. Lewis & S. Miller (Eds.), *Handbook of developmental psychopathology.* New York: Plenum.
Hess, R. D. (1970). Class and ethnic influences upon socialization. In P. Mussen (Ed.), *Carmichael's manual of child psychology* (Vol. 2). New York: Wiley.
Hess, R. D., & Holloway, S. D. (1984). Family and school as educational institutions. In R. D. Parke (Ed.), *Review of child development research* (Vol. 7). Chicago: University of Chicago Press.
Hess, R. D., & Shipman, V. (1967). Cognitive elements in maternal behavior. In J. Hill (Ed.), *Minnesota Symposia on Child Psychology* (pp. 57–81). Minneapolis: University of Minnesota Press.
Heston, L. (1966). Psychiatric disorders in foster-home reared children of schizophrenic mothers. *British Journal of Psychiatry,* **112,** 819–825.
Heston, L., & Denny, D. (1968). Interactions between early life experiences and biological factors in schizophrenia. *Journal of Psychiatric Research,* **6,** 363–376.

Heth, C. D., & Cornell, E. H. (1980). Three experiences affecting spatial discrimination learning by ambulatory children. *Journal of Experimental Child Psychology,* **30**, 246–264.

Hetherington, E. M. (1965). A developmental study of the effects of sex of the dominant parent on sex-role preference, identification, and imitation in children. *Journal of Personality and Social Psychology,* **2,** 188–194.

Hetherington, E. M. (1966). Effects of paternal absence on sex-typed behaviors in Negro and white preadolescent males. *Journal of Personality and Social Psychology,* **4,** 87–91.

Hetherington, E. M. (1967). The effects of familial variables on sex typing, on parent-child similarity and on imitation in children. In J. P. Hill (Ed.), *Minnesota Symposia on Child Psychology* (Vol. 1, pp. 82–107). Minneapolis: University of Minnesota Press.

Hetherington, E. M. (1972). Effects of father absence on personality development in adolescent daughters. *Developmental Psychology,* **7,** 313–326.

Hetherington, E. M. (1988). Parents, children and siblings six years after divorce. In R. Hinde & J. Stevenson-Hinde (Eds.), *Relationships within families* (pp. 311–331). Cambridge, MA: Cambridge University Press.

Hetherington, E. M. (1989). Coping with family transitions: Winners, losers and survivors. *Child Development,* **60,** 1–14.

Hetherington, E. M. (1991). The role of individual differences and family relationships in children's coping with divorce and remarriage. In P. A. Cowan & E. M. Hetherington (Eds.), *Family Transitions.* Hillsdale, NJ: Erlbaum.

Hetherington, E. M. (1991a). Families, lies and videotapes. *Journal of Adolescent Research,* **1**(4), 323–348.

Hetherington, E. M. (1991b). The role of individual differences and family relationships in children's coping with divorce and remarriage. In P. A. Cowan & E. M. Hetherington (Eds.), *Family transitions* (pp. 165–194). Hillsdale, NJ: Erlbaum.

Hetherington, E. M., & Clingempeel, W. G. (1992). Coping with marital transitions: A family systems perspective. *Monographs of the Society for Research in Child Development.* Chicago: University of Chicago Press. **57,** (2 and 3, Serial No. 227)

Hetherington, E. M., Cox, M., & Cox, R. (1979). Play and social interaction in children following divorce. *Journal of Social Issues,* **35,** 26–49.

Hetherington, E. M., Cox, M. J., & Cox, R. (1982). Effects of divorce on parents and children. In M. E. Lamb (Ed.), *Nontraditional families.* Hillsdale, NJ: Erlbaum.

Hetherington, E. M., & Morris, W. N. (1978). The family and primary groups. In W. H. Holtzman (Ed.), *Introductory psychology in depth: Developmental topics.* New York: Harper & Row.

Hetherington, E. M., Stanley-Hagan, M., & Anderson, E. R. (1989). Marital transitions: A child's perspective. *American Psychologist,* **44,** 303–312.

Heyman, G. D., Dweck, C. S., & Cain, K. M. (1992). Young children's vulnerability to self-blame and helplessness: Relationship to beliefs about goodness. *Child Development,* **63,** 401–415.

Higgins, A., Power, C., & Kohlberg, L. (1984). The relationship of moral atmosphere to judgments of responsibility. In W. M. Kurtines & J. L. Gewirtz (Eds.), *Morality, moral behavior and moral development.* New York: Wiley.

Hill, A. L. (1978). Savants: Mentally retarded individuals with specific skills. In N. R. Ellis (Ed.), *International review of research in mental retardation* (Vol. 9). New York: Academic.

Hill, T., K., & Eaton, W. O. (1977). The interaction of test anxiety and success-failure experiences in determining children's arithmetic performance. *Developmental Psychology,* **13,** 205–211.

Hilton, I. (1967). Differences in the behavior of mothers toward first- and later-born children. *Journal of Personality and Social Psychology,* **7,** 282–290.

Himelstein, S., Graham, S., & Weiner, B. (1991). An attributional analysis of maternal beliefs about the importance of childrearing practices. *Child Development,* **62,** 301–310.

Hinde, R. A. (1987). *Individuals, relationships and culture.* New York: Cambridge University Press.

Hinde, R. A. (1989). Ethological and relationships approaches. In R. Vasta (Ed.), *Six theories of child development.* Greenwich, CT: JAI Press.

Hindley, C. B., Filliozat, A. M., Klackenberg, G., Nicolet-Neister, D., & Sand, E. A. (1966). Differences in age of walking for five European longitudinal samples. *Human Biology,* **38,** 264–379.

Hines, M. (1982). Prenatal gonadal hormones and sex differences in human behavior. *Psychological Bulletin,* **92,** 56–80.

Hinshaw, S. P., Henker, B., Whalen, C. K., Erhardt, D., & Dunnington, R. E. (1989). Aggressive, prosocial and nonsocial behavior in hyperactive boys: Dose effects of methylphenidate in naturalistic settings. *Journal of Consulting and Clinical Psychology,* **57,** 636–643.

Hirayama, K. K. (1985). Asian childrens' adaptation to public schools. *Social Work in Education,* **7,** 213–230.

Hobbs, N. (1975). *The futures of children.* San Francisco: Jossey-Bass.

Hobson, R. P. (1989). Beyond cognition: A theory of Autism. In G. Dawson (Ed.), *Autism: Nature, diagnosis, and treatment*. New York: Guilford.

Hock, E. (1978). Working and nonworking mothers with infants: Perceptions of their careers, their infants' needs, and satisfaction with mothering. *Developmental Psychology*, **4**, 37–43.

Hoff-Ginsberg, E., & Shatz, M. (1982). Linguistic input and the child's acquisition of language. *Psychological Bulletin*, **92**, 3–26.

Hoffman, L. W. (1977). Changes in family roles, socialization and sex differences. *American Psychologist*, **32**, 644–657.

Hoffman, L. W. (1984). Work, family and the socialization of the child. In R. D. Parke (Ed.), *Review of child development research: Vol. 7, The family*. Chicago: University of Chicago Press.

Hoffman, L. W. (1989). Effects of maternal employment in the two-parent family. *American Psychologist*, **44**, 283–292.

Hoffman, M. L. (1984). Empathy, its limitations, and its role in a comprehensive moral theory. In W. M. Kurtines & J. L. Gewirtz (Eds.), *Morality, moral behavior and moral development*. New York: Wiley.

Hoffman, M. L. (1987). The contribution of empathy to justice and moral judgment. In N. Eisenberg & J. Strayer (Eds.), *Empathy and its development*. New York: Cambridge University Press.

Holden, G. W. (1988). Adults' thinking about a child-rearing problem: Effects of experience, parental status and gender. *Child Development*, **59**, 1623–1632.

Holden, G. W., & Edwards, L. A. (1989). Parental attitudes toward child rearing: Instruments, issues & implications. *Psychological Bulletin*, **106**, 29–58.

Hollenbeck, A. R., & Slaby, R. G. (1982). Influence of a television model's vocalization pattern on infants. *Journal of Applied Developmental Psychology*, **3**, 57–65.

Holtzman, W. H., Diaz-Guerrero, R., & Schwartz, J. D. (1975). *Personality development in two cultures: Cross-cultural and longitudinal study of school children in Mexico and the United States*. Austin: University of Texas Press.

Honzik, M. (1983). Measuring mental abilities in infancy: The value and limitations. In M. Lewis (Ed.), *Origins of intelligence: Infancy and early childhood* (2nd ed.) (pp. 67–105). New York: Plenum.

Honzik, M. P. (1976). Value and limitations of infant tests: An overview. In M. Lewis (Ed.), *Origins of intelligence*. New York: Plenum.

Hood, K. E., Draper, P., Crockett, L. J., Petersen, A. C. (1987). The ontogeny and phylogeny of sex differences in development: A biosocial synthesis. In D. B. Carter (Ed.), *Current conceptions of sex roles and sex-typing: Theory and research*. New York: Praeger.

Hook, E. B. (1973). Behavioral implications of the human XYY genotype. *Science*, **179**, 131–150.

Hook, E. B., & Lindsjo, A. (1978). Down syndrome in the live births by single year maternal age interval in a Swedish study: Comparison with results from a New York State study. *American Journal of Human Genetics*, **30**, 19.

Hopkins, B., & Westra, T. (1988). Maternal handling and motor development: An intracultural study. *Genetic Psychology Monographs*, **14**, 377–420.

Horowitz, F. D., Ashton, J., Culp, R., Gaddis, E., Leven, S., & Reichmann, B. (1977). The effects of obstetrical medication on the behavior of Israeli newborn infants and some comparisons with Uruguayan and American infants. *Child Development*, **48**, 1607–1623.

Horowitz, F. D., & Paden, L. Y. (1973). The effectiveness of environmental intervention programs. In B. Caldwell & H. Riccuiti (Eds.), *Review of child development research* (Vol. 3, pp. 331–402). Chicago: University of Chicago Press.

Householder, J., Hatcher, R., Burns, W., & Chasnoff, I. (1982). Infants born to narcotic-addicted mothers. *Psychological Bulletin*, **92**(2), 453–468.

Hovell, M. F., Schumaker, J. B., & Sherman, J. A. (1978). A comparison of parents' models and expansions in promoting children's acquisition of adjectives. *Journal of Experimental Child Psychology*, **25**, 41–57.

Howe, N., & Ross, H. S. (1990). Socialization perspective taking and the sibling relationship. *Developmental Psychology*, **26**, 160–165.

Howe, P. E., & Schiller, M. (1952). Growth responses of the school child to changes in diet and environment factors. *Journal of Applied Physiology*, **5**, 51–61.

Howell, R. R., & Stevenson, Jr., E. (1971). The offspring of the phenylketonuric women. *Social Biology Supplement*, **18**, 519–529.

Howes, C. (1987). Social competence with peers in young children: Developmental sequences. *Developmental Review*, **7**, 252–272.

Howes, C. (1988a, April). *Can age of entry and the quality of infant care predict behaviors in kindergarten?* Paper presented at the International Conference of Infant Studies, Washington, DC.

Howes, C. (1988b). Relations between early child care and schooling. *Developmental Psychology*, **24**, 53–57.

Howes, C., Phillips, D., & Whitebook, M. (1992). Thresholds of quality: Implications for the social development of children in center-based child care. *Child Development,* **63**, 449–460.

Howes, C., Rodning, C., Galluzo, D. C., Myers, L. (1988). Attachment and child care: Relationships with mother and caregiver. *Early Childhood Research Quarterly,* **3**, 403–406.

Hoy, E. A., Bill, J. M., & Sykes, D. H. (1988). Very low birthweight: A long-term developmental impairment? *International Journal of Behavioral Development,* **11**, 37–67.

Hubbard, R. (1980). Test-tube babies: Solution or problem. *Technology Review,* **85**(5), 10–12.

Hubel, D. H. (1988). *Eye, brain and vision.* New York: Scientific American Library.

Hudson, J. A. (1990). Construction processing in children's event memory. *Developmental Psychology,* **26**, 180–187.

Hudson, J., & Nelson, K. (1983). Effects of script structure on children's story recall. *Developmental Psychology,* **19**, 625–635.

Huesmann, L. R., Eron, L. D., Lefkowitz, M. M., & Walder, L. O. (1984). The stability of aggression over time and generations. *Developmental Psychology,* **20**, 1120–1134.

Huesmann, L. R., Guerra, N. G., Zelli, A., & Miller, L. (1992). Differing normative beliefs about aggression for boys and girls. In K. Bjorkquist & P. Niemele (Eds.), *Of mice and women: Aspects of female aggression.* Orlando, FL: Academic.

Huesmann, L. R., Lagerspetz, K., & Eron, L. D. (1984). Intervening variables in the TV violence-aggression relation: Evidence from two countries. *Developmental Psychology,* **20**, 746–775.

Humphries, T., Kinsbourne, M., & Swanson, J. (1978). Stimulant effects on cooperation and social interaction between hyperactive children and their mothers. *Journal of Child Psychology and Psychiatry,* **19**, 13–22.

Hunt, J. M. (1972). The role of experience in the development of competence. In J. M. Hunt (Ed.), *Human intelligence.* New Brunswick, NJ: Transaction Books.

Huston, A. C. (1983). Sex-typing. In P. H. Mussen (Ed.), *Handbook of child psychology* (Vol. 4). New York: Wiley.

Huston, A. C., Donnerstein, E., Fairchild, H., Feshbach, N. D., Katz, P. A., Murray, J. P., Rubinstein, E. A., Wilcox, B. L., & Zuckerman, D. (1992). *Big world, small screen.* Lincoln: University of Nebraska Press.

Huston, A. C., & Wright, J. C. (1989). Television forms and children. In G. Comstock (Ed.), *Public communication and behavior* (Vol. 2) (pp. 103–159). New York: Academic.

Huttenlocher, J., Haight, W., Bryk, A. Seltzer, M., & Lyons, T. (1991). Early vocabulary growth: Relation to language input and gender. *Developmental Psychology,* **27**, 236–248.

Huttenlocher, J., & Lui, F. (1979). The semantic organization of some simple nouns and verbs. *Journal of Verbal Learning and Verbal Behavior,* **18**, 141–162.

Huttenlocher, J., & Smiley, P. (1987). Early word meanings: The case of object names. *Cognitive Psychology,* **19**, 63–89.

Huttenlocher, J., Smiley, P., & Charnery, R. (1983). Emergence of action categories in the child: Evidence from verb meanings. *Psychological Review,* **90**(2), 72–93.

Huttenlocher, J., Smiley, P., & Ratner, H. (1989). What do word meanings reveal about conceptual development? In T. R. Seiler & W. Wannenmacher (Eds.), *Reader: Concept development and the development of word meaning.* Berlin, West Germany: Springer-Verlag.

Huttenlocher, P. R. (1979). Synaptic density in human frontal cortex: Developmental changes and effects of aging. *Brain Research,* **163**, 195–205.

Hwang, C. P. (1986). Behavior of Swedish primary and secondary caretaking fathers in relation to mothers' presence. *Developmental Psychology,* **22**, 749–751.

Hyde, J. S., Fennema, E., & Lamon, S. J. (1990). Gender differences in mathematics performance: A meta-analysis. *Psychological Bulletin,* **107**, 139–155.

Hyde, J. S., Krajnik, M., & Skuldt-Neiderberger, K. (1991). Androgyny across the life span: A replication and longitudinal follow-up. *Developmental Psychology,* **27**, 516–519.

Hyde, J. S., & Linn, M. C. (1988). Gender differences in verbal ability: A meta-analysis. *Psychological Bulletin,* **104**, 53–69.

Hymel, S. (1986). Interpretations of peer behavior: Affective bias in childhood and adolescence. *Child Development,* **57**, 431–445.

Hymel, S., Wagner, E., & Butler, L. (1990). Reputational bias: View from the peer group. In S. R. Asher & J. D. Coie (Eds.), *Peer rejection in childhood.* New York: Cambridge University Press.

Iannotti, R. J. (1978). Effect of role taking experiences on role taking, empathy, altruism and aggression. *Developmental Psychology,* **14**, 119–124.

Iannotti, R. J. (1985). Naturalistic and structured assessments of prosocial behavior in preschool children: The influence of empathy and perspective taking. *Developmental Psychology,* **21**, 46–55.

Imperto-McGinley, J., Peterson, R. E., Gautier, T., & Sturla, E. (1979). Androgens and the evolution of male-gender identify among male pseudohermaphrodites with 5-reductase deficiency. *New England Journal of Medicine,* **300**, 1233–1270.

Inagaki, K., Hatano, G. (1987). Young children's spontaneous personification as analogy. *Child Development*, **58**, 1013–1020.

Inhelder, B., & Piaget, J. (1958). *The growth of logical thinking from childhood to adolescence.* New York: Basic Books.

Inoff-Germain, G., Arnold, G. S., Nottleman, E. D., Susman, E. J., Culter, G. B., & Chrousos, G. P. (1988). Relations between hormone levels and observational measures of aggressive behavior of young adolescents in family interactions. *Developmental Psychology,* **24,** 129–139.

Isabella, R. A., & Belsky, J. (1991). Interactional synchrony and the origins of infant-mother attachment: A replication study. *Child Development,* **62,** 373–384.

Isabella, R. A., Belsky, J., & vonEye, A. (1989). Origins of infant-mother attachment: An examination of interactional synchrony during the infant's first year. *Developmental Psychology,* **25,** 12–21.

Israel, A. C. (1988). Parental and family influences in the etiology and treatment of childhood obesity. In N. A. Krasnegor, G. D. Grave, & N. Kretchmer (Eds.), *Childhood obesity: A behavioral perspective.* Caldwell, NJ: Telford Press.

Istvan, J. (1986). Stress, anxiety, and birth outcomes: A critical review of the evidence. *Psychological Bulletin,* **100,** 331–348.

Izard, C. E. (1991). *The psychology of emotions.* New York: Plenum.

Izard, C. E., Hembree, E. A., Dougherty, L. M., & Coss, C. L. (1983). Changes in two- to nineteen-month-old infants' facial expressions following acute pain. *Developmental Psychology,* **19,** 418–426.

Izard, C. E., Hembree, E., & Huebner, R. (1987). Infants' emotional expressions to acute pain: Developmental changes and stability of individual differences. *Developmental Psychology,* **23,** 105–113.

Izard, C. E., & Malatesta, C. Z. (1987). Perspectives on emotional development I. Differential emotions theory of early emotional development. In J. D. Osofsky (Ed.), *Handbook of infant development* (2nd ed., pp. 494–554). New York: Wiley.

Jacklin, C. N. (1989). Female and male: Issues of gender. *American Psychologist,* **44,** 127–133.

Jacklin, C. N., DiPietro, J. A., & Maccoby, E. E. (1984). Sex-typing behavior and sex-typing pressure in child-parent interaction. *Sex Roles,* **13,** 413–425.

Jacklin, C. N., Wilcox, K. T., & Maccoby, E. E. (1988). Neonatal sex steroid hormones and intellectual abilities of six year old boys and girls. *Developmental Psychobiology,* **21,** 567–574.

Jackson, C. M. (Ed.). (1933). *Human anatomy* (9th ed.). New York: McGraw-Hill.

Jacobvitz, D., Sroufe, L. A., Stewart, M., & Leffert, N. (1990). Treatment of attentional and hyperactivity problems in children with sympathomimetic drugs: A comprehensive review. *Journal of the American Academy of Child and Adolescent Psychiatry,* **29,** 677–688.

Jakobson, R. (1968). *Child language, aphasic, and phonological universals.* The Hague: Mouton.

Jencks, C. S., Smith, M., Acland, H., Bane, M. J., Cohen, D., Gintis, H. Heynes, B., & Michelson, S. (1972). *Inequality: A reassessment of the effects of family and schooling in America.* New York: Basic Books.

Jensen, A. R. (1969). How much can we boost IQ and scholastic achievement? *Harvard Educational Review,* **39,** 1–123.

Jensen, A. R. (1973). *Genetic, educability, and subpopulation differences.* London: Methuen.

Jensen, A. R. (1980). *Bias in mental testing.* New York: Free Press.

Jessor, R., & Jessor, S. L. (1977). *Problem behavior and psychosocial development.* New York: Academic.

Johnson, C. L., & Berndt, D. J. (1983). Preliminary investigation of bulimia and life adjustment. *American Journal of Psychiatry,* **140,** 774–777.

Johnson, C. L., Stuckey, M. K., Lewis, L. D., & Schwartz, D. M. (1982). Bulimia: A descriptive survey of 316 cases. *International Journal of Eating Disorders,* **2,** 3–16.

Johnson, J. S., & Newport, E. L. (1989). Critical period effects in second language learning: The influence of maturational state on the acquisition of English as a second language. *Cognitive Psychology,* **21,** 60–99.

Johnson, S. M., & Bolsted, O. D. (1973). Methodological issues in naturalistic observation: Some problems and solutions for field research. In L. A. Hamerlynck, L. C. Handy, & E. J. Mash (Eds.), *Behavior change: Methodology, concepts and practice.* Champaign, IL: Research Press.

Johnson, W., Emde, R. N., Pannabecker, B., Stenberg, C., & Davis, M. (1982). Maternal perception of infant emotion from birth through 18 months. *Infant Behavior and Development,* **5,** 313–322.

Johnston, J., & Ettema, J. S. (1982). *Positive images: Breaking stereotypes with children's television.* Beverly Hills, CA: Sage.

Jones, D. C. (1985). Persuasive appeals and responses to appeals among friends and acquaintances. *Child Development,* **56,** 757–763.

Jones, K. L., Smith, D. W., Ulleland, C. V., & Streissguth, S. P. (1973). Pattern of malformation in offspring of chronic alcoholic mothers. *Lancet,* **1,** 1267–1271.

Jones, L. V. (1984). White-black achievement differences: The narrowing gap. *American Psychologist,* **39,** 1207–1213.

Jones, M. C., & Bayley, N. (1950). Physical maturing among boys as related to behavior. *Journal of Educational Psychology,* **41,** 129–148.

Joos, S. K., Pollitt, E., Mueller, W. H., & Albright, D. L. (1983). The Bacon Chow study: Maternal nutritional supplementation and infant behavioral development. *Child Development,* **54,** 669–676.

Jost, H., & Sontag, L. (1944). The genetic factor in autonomic nervous system function. *Psychosomatic Medicine,* **6,** 308–310.

Juel-Nielsen, N. (1980). *Individual and environment: Monozygotic twins reared apart.* New York: International Universities Press.

Jusczyk, P. W., Rosner, B. S., Cutting, J. E., Foard, F., & Smith, L. B. (1977). Categorical perception of non-speech sounds by two-month-old infants. *Perception and Psychophysics,* **21,** 50–54.

Kagan, J. (1981). *The second year.* Cambridge, MA: Harvard University Press.

Kagan, J. (1983). Stress and coping in early development. In N. Garmezy & M. Rutter (Eds.), *Stress, coping and development in children.* New York: McGraw-Hill.

Kagan, J. (1984). *The nature of the child.* New York: Basic Books.

Kagan, J. (1989). Temperamental contributions to social behavior. *American Psychologist,* **44,** 668–674.

Kagan, J. J., Kearsley, R. B., & Zelazo, P. R. (1978). *Infancy: Its place in human development.* Cambridge, MA: Harvard University Press.

Kagan, J., & Moss, H. A. (1962). *Birth to maturity: A study in psychological development.* New York: Wiley.

Kagan, J. J., Reznick, S., & Gibbons, I. (1989). Inhibited and uninhibited life of children. *Child Development,* **60,** 838–845.

Kagan, J., Reznick, S., & Snidman, N. (1987). The physiology and psychology of behavior inhibition in children. *Child Development,* **58,** 1459–1473.

Kagan, J. S. (1969). Inadequate evidence and illogical conclusions. *Harvard Educational Review,* **39,** 274–277.

Kaler, S. R., & Kopp, C. B. (1990). Compliance and comprehension in very young toddlers. *Child Development,* **61,** 1997–2003.

Kallman, F. J., & Sander, G. (1949). Twin studies in senescence. *American Journal of Psychiatry,* **106,** 2–26.

Kandel, D. (1973). Adolescent marijuana use: Role of parents and peers. *Science,* **181,** 1067–1070.

Kandel, D. B. (1980). Drug and drinking behavior among youth. *Annual Review of Sociology,* **6,** 235–285.

Kanner, L. (1943). Autistic disturbances of affective contact. *Nervous Child,* **2,** 217–250.

Kanner, L. (1973). How far can autistic children go in matters of social adaptation? In L. Kanner (Ed.), *Childhood psychosis: Initial studies and new insights.* Washington, DC: Winston.

Karnofsky, D. A. (1965). Drugs as teratogens in animals and man. *Annual Review of Pharmacology,* **5,** 477–482.

Katchadourian, H. (1977). *The biology of adolescence.* San Francisco: Freeman.

Katzman, M. A., & Wokhik, S. A. (1984). Bulimia and binge eating in college women: A comparison of personality and behavioral characteristics. *Journal of Consulting and Clinical Psychology,* **52,** 423–428.

Kaufman, A. S., Kamphaus, R. W., & Kaufman, N. L. (1985). New directions in intelligence testing: The Kaufman Assessment Battery for Children (K-ABC). In B. B. Wolman (Ed.), *Handbook of intelligence.* New York: Wiley.

Kaufman, A. S., & Kaufman, N. L. (1983). *Kaufman assessment battery for children: Interpretive manual.* Circle Pines, MN: American Guidance Service.

Kaufman, J., & Zigler, E. (1978). Do abused children become abusive parents? *American Journal of Orthopsychiatry,* **57,** 186–192.

Kazdin, A. E. (1982). Applying behavioral principals in the schools. In C. R. Reynolds & T. B. Gutkin (Eds.), *The handbook of school psychology* (pp. 501–529). New York: Wiley.

Kazdin, A. E. (1989). Identifying depression in children: A comparison of alternative selection criteria. *Journal of Abnormal Child Psychology,* **17,** 437–453.

Kazdin, A. E., French, N. H., & Unis, A. S. (1983). Child, mother and father evaluations of depression in psychiatric inpatient children. *Journal of Abnormal Child Psycology.* **11,** 167–180.

Keating, D. P. (1990). Adolescent thinking. In J. Adelson (Ed.), *Handbook of adolescent psychology.* New York: Wiley.

Kee, D. W., & Howell, S. (1988, April). Mental effort and memory development. Paper presented at the meeting of the American Educational Research Association, New Orleans, La.

Keeney, T. J., Cannizzo, S. R., & Flavell, J. H. (1967). Spontaneous and induced rehearsal in a recall task. *Child Development,* **38**, 953–966.

Kellam, S. G., Ensminger, M. A., & Turner, J. T. (1977). Family structure and the mental health of children. *Archives of General Psychiatry,* **34**, 1012–1022.

Keller, M., & Wood, P. (1989). Development of friendship reasoning: A study of interindividual differences in intraindividual change. *Developmental Psychology,* **25,** 820–826.

Kendall, P. C., & Braswell, K. (1985). *Cognitive-behavioral therapy for impulsive children.* New York: Guilford.

Kennedy, W. A. (1969). A follow-up normative study of Negro intelligence and achievement. *Monographs of the Society for Research in Child Development,* **34,**(2, Serial No. 126).

Kennedy, W. A., VanDeRiet, V., & White, J. C. (1963). A normative sample of intelligence and achievement of Negro elementary school children in the southeastern United States. *Monographs of the Society for Research in Child Development,* **28,**(6, Serial No. 90), 13–112.

Kermonian, R., & Campos, J. J. (1988). Crawling experience: A determinant of spatial search performance. *Child Development,* **59**, 908–917.

Kessen, W., Leutzendoff, A. M., & Stoutsenberger, K. (1967). Age, food deprivation, non-nutritive sucking and movement in the human newborn. *Journal of Comparative and Physiological Psychology,* **63**, 82–86.

Kessen, W., Levine, J., & Wendrich, K. A. (1979). The imitation of pitch in infants. *Infant Behavior and Development,* **2**, 93–100.

Kestenbaum, J., Farber, E., & Sroufe, L. A. (1989). Individual differences in empathy among preschoolers: Relation to attachment history. In N. Eisenberg (Ed.), Empathy and related emotional responses. *New Directions for Child Development* (No. 44). San Francisco: Jossey-Bass.

Kimball, M. M. (1989). A new perspective on women's math achievement. *Psychological Bulletin,* **105,** 198–214.

Kitchen, W. H., Ford, G. W., Richards, A. L., Lissenden, J. V., Ryan, M. M. (1987). Children of birthweight $<$ 1000 g: Changing outcome between ages 2 and 5 years. *Journal of Pediatrics,* **110,** 283–288.

Klahr, D., & Wallace, J. G. (1976). Cognitive development: An information processing view. Hillsdale, NJ: Erlbaum.

Klaus, M. H., & Kennell, J. H. (1982). *Parent-infant bonding.* St. Louis: Mosby.

Kleiman, G., & Humphrey, M. (1982). Word processing in the classroom. *Compute,* **22,** 96–99.

Kleiman, G. M. (1984). *Brave new schools: How computers can change education.* Reston, VA: Reston Publishing.

Klesges, R., Malott, J., Boschee, P., & Weber, J. (1986). The effects of parental influences on children's food intake, physical activity and relative weight. *International Journal of Eating Disorders,* **5**, 335–345.

Kligman, D., Smyrl, R., & Emde, R. (1975). A "nonintrusive" longitudinal study of infant sleep. *Psychosomatic Medicine,* **37**, 448–453.

Knittle, J. L., Timmers, K., Ginsberg-Fellner, F., Brown, R. E., & Katz, D. P. (1979). The growth of adipose tissue in children and adolescents: Cross-sectional and longitudinal studies of adipose cell number and size. *Journal of Clinical Investigation,* **63,** 239–246.

Kobak, R. R., & Sceery, A. (1988). Attachment in late adolescence: Working models, affect regulation and representations of self and others. *Child Development,* **59,** 135–146.

Kochanska, G. (1991). *Affective factors in mothers' autonomy-granting to their five-year-olds: Comparisons of well and depressed mothers.* Paper presented at the meetings of the Society for Research in Child Development. Seattle, WA.

Kohlberg, L. (1963a). The development of children's orientations towards a moral order: 1. Sequence in the development of moral thought. *Vita Humana,* **6,** 11–33.

Kohlberg, L. (1963b). Moral development and identification. In H. W. Stevenson (Ed.), *Child psychology.* Sixty-second Yearbook of the National Society for the Study of Education. Chicago: University of Chicago Press.

Kohlberg, L. (1969). *Stages in the development of moral thought and action.* New York: Holt.

Kohlberg, L. (1985). *The psychology of moral development.* San Francisco: Harper & Row.

Kohlberg, L., & Candee, D. (1984). The relationship of moral judgment to moral action. In W. M. Kurtines & J. L. Gewirtz (Eds.), *Morality, moral behavior and moral development.* New York: Wiley.

Kohlberg, L. A. (1966). A cognitive-developmental analysis of children's sex-role concepts and attitudes. In E. E. Maccoby (Ed.), *The development of sex differences* (pp. 82–173). Stanford, CA: Stanford University Press.

Kohn, M. L. (1979). The effects of social class on parental values and practices. In D. Reiss & H. A. Hoffman (Eds.)., *The American family: Dying or developing* (pp. 45–68). New York: Plenum.

Kohn, M. L., & Schooler, C. (1978). The reciprocal effects of substantive complexity of work and intellectual flexibility: A longitudinal assessment. *American Journal of Sociology*, **84**, 24–52.

Kolb, B. (1989). Brain development, plasticity & behavior. *American Psychologist*, **44**, 1203–1212.

Kopp, C. B. (1982). The antecedents of self-regulation. *Developmental Psychology*, **18**, 199–214.

Kopp, C. B. (1983). Risk factors in development. In M. M. Haith & J. Campos (Eds.), *Infancy and developmental psychobiology: Vol. 2. Handbook of child psychology*. New York: Wiley.

Kopp, C. B. (1987). The growth of self-regulation: Caregivers and children. In N. Eisenberg (Ed.), *Contemporary topics in developmental psychology*. New York: Wiley.

Kopp, C. B. (1992). Emotional distress and control in young children. In N. Eisenberg & R. A. Fabes (Eds.), *Emotion and its regulation in early development*. San Francisco: Jossey-Bass.

Kopp, C. B., & Kaler, S. R. (1989). Risk in infancy: Origins and implications. *American Psychologist*, **44**, 224–230.

Kopp, C. B., & Krakow, J. B. (1983). The developmentalist and the study of biological risk: A view of the past with an eye toward the future. *Child Development*, **54**, 1086–1108.

Kopp, C. B., & Parmelee, A. H. (1979). Prenatal and perinatal influences on infant behavior. In J. D. Osofsky (Eds.), *Handbook of infant development*. New York: Wiley.

Korner, A. (1974). The effect of the infant's state, level of arousal, sex and ontogenic stage on the caregiver. In M. Lewis & L. Rosenblum (Eds.), *The effect of the infant on its caregiver*. New York: Wiley.

Korner, A. F. (1972). State as variable, as obstacle and as mediator of stimulation in infant research. *Merrill-Palmer Quarterly*, **18**, 77–94.

Korner, A. F. (1989). Infant stimulation: The pros and cons in historical perspective. *Bulletin of National Center for Clinical Infant Programs*, **10**, 11–17.

Korner, A. F., Kraemer, H. C., Hoffner, E., & Cosper, L. M. (1975). Effects of waterbed flotation on premature infants: A pilot study. *Pediatrics*, **56**(3), 361–367.

Korner, A. F., & Thoman, E. (1970). Visual alertness in neonates as evoked by maternal care. *Journal of Experimental Child Psychology*, **10**, 67–78.

Kosky, R. (1983). Childhood suicidal behavior. *Journal of Child Psychology and Psychiatry*, **24**, 457–468.

Krashen, S. (1975). The critical period for language acquisition and its possible bases. In D. Aaronson & R. W. Reiber (Eds.), *Annals of the New York Academy of Sciences: Vol. 263. Developmental psycholinguistics and communication disorders* (pp. 211–224). New York: New York Academy of Sciences.

Kreutzer, M. A., Leonard, C., & Flavell, J. H. (1975). An interview study of children's knowledge about memory. *Monographs of the Society for Research in Child Development*, **40**, 1–60.

Krogman, W. M. (1972). *Child growth*. Ann Arbor: University of Michigan Press.

Krosnick, J. A., & Judd, C. M. (1982). Transitions in social influence at adolescence: Who induces cigarette smoking? *Developmental Psychology*, **18**, 359–368.

Kubey, R., & Csikszentmihalyi, M. (1990). *Television and the quality of life*. Hillsdale, NJ: Erlbaum.

Kuchner, J. F. R. (1980). *Chinese-American and European-American: A cross-cultural study of infant and mother*. Unpublished doctoral dissertation. University of Chicago.

Kuczaj, S. A. (1982). *Language development: Syntax and semantics* (Vol. 1). Hillsdale, NJ: Erlbaum.

Kuczynski, L. (1983). Reasoning, prohibitions, and motivations for compliance. *Developmental Psychology*, **19**, 126–134.

Kuczynski, L., & Kochanska, G. (1990). Development of children's noncompliance strategies from toddlerhood to age 5. *Developmental Psychology*, **26**, 398–408.

Kuczynski, L., Kochanska, G., Radke-Yarrow, M., & Girnius-Brown, O. (1987). A developmental interpretation of young children's noncompliance. *Developmental Psychology*, **23**, 799–806.

Kuhn, D. (1984). Cognitive development. In M. H. Bernstein & M. E. Lamb (Eds.), *Developmental psychology*. Hillsdale, NJ: Erlbaum.

Kuhn, D. (1991). Reasoning, higher order in adolescence. In R. M. Lerner, A. C. Petersen, & J. Brooks-Gunn (Eds.), *Encyclopedia of adolescence* (Vol. 2). New York: Garland.

Kurtz, B. E., & Borkowski, J. G. (1987). Development of strategic skills in impulsive and reflective children: A longitudinal study of metacognition. *Journal of Experimental Child Psychology*, **43**, 129–148.

La Barbera, J. D., Izard, C. E., Vietze, P., & Parisi, S. A. (1976). Four- and six-month-old infants' visual responses to joy, anger, and neutral expressions. *Child Development*, **47**, 535–538.

Ladd, G. W. (1981). Effectiveness of a social learning method for enhancing children's social interaction and peer acceptance. *Child Development*, **52**, 171–178.

Ladd, G. W., & Emerson, E. S. (1984). Shared knowledge in children's friendships. *Developmental Psychology,* **20,** 932–940.

Ladd, G. W., & Golter, B. S. (1988). Parents' management of preschooler's peer relations: Is it related to children's social competence? *Developmental Psychology,* **24,** 109–117.

Ladd, G. W., Muth, S., & Hart, C. H. (1992). Parent's management of children's peer relations: Facilitating and supervising children's activities in the peer cultures. In R. D. Parke & G. W. Ladd (Eds.), *Family-peer relationships: Modes of linkage.* Hillsdale, NJ: Erlbaum.

Lader, M., & Wing, L. (1966). Physiological measures, sedative drugs and morbid anxiety. *Maudsley Monographs* (No. 14). London: Oxford University Press.

Lamb, M. E. (Ed.). (1987). *The father's role: Cross-cultural perspectives.* New York: Wiley.

Lamb, M. E. (1977). *The relationships between mothers, fathers, infants and siblings in the first two years of life.* Paper presented at the biennial conference of the International Society for the Study of Behavioral Development, Pavia, Italy.

Lamb, M. E. (1977). Father-infant and mother-infant interaction in the first year of life. *Child Development,* **48,** 167–181.

Lamb, M. E. (1979). Influence of the child on marital quality and family interaction during the prenatal, perinatal and infancy period. In R. M. Lerner & G. D. Spanier (Eds.), *Contributions of the child to marital quality and family interaction through the life span.* New York: Academic.

Lamb, M. E., & Campos, J. (1982). *Development in infancy.* New York: Random House.

Lamb, M. E., Easterbrooks, A., & Holden, G. W. (1980). Reinforcement and punishment among preschoolers: Characteristics, effects and correlates. *Child Development,* **51,** 1230–1236.

Lamb, M. E., Frodi, A. M., Hwang, P., & Frodi, M. (1982). Varying degrees of paternal involvement in infant care: Attitudinal and behavioral correlates. In M. E. Lamb (Ed.), *Nontraditional families.* Hillsdale, NJ: Erlbaum.

Lamb, M. E., & Roopnarine, J. L. (1979). Peer influences on sex role development in preschoolers. *Child Development,* **50,** 1219–1222.

Lamb, M. E., Suomi, S. J., & Stephenson, G. R. (1979). *Social interaction analysis: Methodological issues.* Madison, WI: University of Wisconsin Press.

Lambiotte, J.G., Dansereau, D. F., O'Donnell, A. M., Young, M. D., Skaggs, L. P., Hall, R. H., & Rocklin, T. R. (1987). Manipulating cooperative scripts for teaching and learning. *Journal of Educational Psychology,* **79,** 424–430.

Landesman-Dwyer, S., & Sackett, G. P. (1983, April). *Prenatal nicotine exposure and sleep-wake patterns in infancy.* Paper presented at the biennial meeting of the Society for Research in Child Development, Detroit.

Laneyz, M. D. (1990). Perspectives and interventions. In M. Lewis & S. Miller (Eds.), *Handbook of developmental psychopathology.* New York: Plenum.

Lang, P. J., & Melamed, B. B. (1969). Case report: Avoidance conditioning therapy of an infant with chronic ruminative vomiting. *Journal of Abnormal Psychology,* **74,** 1–8.

Langlois, J. H. (1985). From the eye of the beholder to behavior reality: The development of social behaviors and social relations as a function of physical attractiveness. In C. P. Herman (Ed.), *Physical appearance, stigma, and social behavior.* Hillsdale, NJ: Erlbaum.

Langlois, J. H., & Downs, C. A. (1979). Peer relations as a function of physical attractiveness: The eye of the beholder or behavioral reality? *Child Development,* **50,** 409–418.

Langlois, J. H., & Downs, C. A. (1980). Mothers, fathers and peers as socialization agents of sex-typed play behaviors in young children. *Child Development,* **51,** 1237–1247.

Langlois, J. H., & Stephan, C. (1981). Beauty and the beast: The role of physical attractiveness in the development of peer relations and social behavior. In S. S. Brehm, S. H. Kassin, & F. X. Gibbons (Eds.), *Developmental social psychology.* New York: Oxford University Press.

Laosa, L. (1982). School, occupation, culture and family: The impact of parental schooling on the parent-child relationship. *Journal of Educational Psychology,* **74,** 791–827.

Laosa, L. M. (1981). Maternal behavior: Sociocultural diversity in modes of family interaction. In R. W. Henderson (Ed.), *Parent-child interaction: Theory, research, and prospects.* New York: Academic.

Larrance, D. T., & Twentyman, C. T. (1983). Maternal attributions and child abuse. *Journal of Abnormal Psychology,* **92,** 449–457.

Larson, R., & Lampman-Petraitis, C. (1989). Daily emotional states as reported by children and adolescents. *Child Development,* **60,** 1250–1260.

Larson, R., & Richards, M. H. (1991). Daily companionship in late childhood and early adolescence: Changing developmental contexts. *Child Development,* **62,** 284–300.

Lasko, J. K. (1954). Parent behavior towards first and second children. *Genetic Psychology Monographs,* **49,** 96–137.

Lave, J. (1977). Cognitive consequences of traditional apprenticeship training in West Africa. *Anthropology & Education Quarterly,* **8,** 177–180.

Lazar, I., & Darlington, R. (1982). Lasting effects of early education: A report from the Consortium of Longitudinal Studies. *Monographs of the Society for Research in Child Development,* **47,**(2–3, Serial No. 195).

Leahy, A. M. (1935). Nature-nurture and intelligence. *Genetic Psychology Monographs,* **17,** 235–308.

Leary, M. A., Greer, D., & Huston, A. C. (1982, April). *The relation between T.V. viewing and gender roles.* Paper presented at the meeting of the Southwestern Society for Research in Human Development, Galveston, TX.

Lee, V. E., Brooks-Gunn, J., & Schnur, E. (1988). Does Head Start work? A 1-year follow-up comparison of disadvantaged children attending Head Start, no preschool, and other preschool programs. *Developmental Psychology,* **24,** 210–222.

Lee, V. E., Brooks-Gunn, J., Schnur, E., & Liaw, F. (1990). Are Head Start effects sustained? A longitudinal follow-up comparison of disadvantaged children attending Head Start, no preschool, and other preschool programs. *Child Development,* **61,** 495–507.

Lefkowitz, M. M., & Burton, N. (1978). Childhood depression: A critique of the concept. *Psychological Bulletin,* **85,** 716–726.

Lefrancois, G. R. (1973). *Of children.* Belmont, CA: Wadsworth.

Legg, C., Sherick, I., & Wadland, W. (1974). Reactions of preschool children to the birth of a sibling. *Child Psychiatry and Human Development,* **5,** 5–39.

Lei, T., & Cheng, S. (1989). A little but special light on the universality of moral judgment development. In L. Kohlberg, D. Candee, & A. Colby (Eds.), *Rethinking moral development.* Cambridge, MA: Harvard University Press.

Leiderman, P. H. (1978). The critical period hypothesis revisited: Mother to infant social bonding in the neonatal period. In F. D. Horowitz (Ed.), *Early developmental hazards.* Boulder, CO: Westview Press.

Leiderman, P. H. (1983). Social ecology and childbirth: The newborn nursery as environmental stressor. In N. Garmezy & M. Rutter (Eds.), *Stress, coping and development in children.* New York: McGraw-Hill.

Leifer, A. D., Leiderman, P. H., Barnett, C. R., & Williams, J. A. (1972). Effects of mother-infant separation on maternal attachment behavior. *Child Development,* **43,** 1203–1218.

Leinbach, M. D., & Fagot, B. I. (1992). *Gender-schematic processing in infancy: Categorical habituation to male and female faces.* Unpublished manuscript. University of Oregon, Eugene.

Leming, J. S. (1978). Cheating behavior, situational influence and moral development. *Journal of Educational Research,* **71,** 214–217.

Lenneberg, E. H. (1967). *Biological foundations of language.* New York: Wiley.

Lenneberg, E. H., Rebelsky, F. G., & Nichols, I. A. (1965). The vocalizations of infants born to deaf and hearing parents. *Human Development,* **8,** 23–37.

Leon, C. R., Kendall, P. C., & Garber, J. (1980). Depression in children: Parent, teacher, and child perspectives. *Journal of Abnormal Child Psychology,* **8,** 221–235.

Lepper, M., & Hoddell, M. (1988). Intrinsic motivation in the classroom. In C. Ames & R. Ames (Eds.), *Research on motivation in education* (Vol. 3, pp. 73–107). New York: Academic.

Lepper, M. R. (1982). Social control processes, attributions of motivation, and the internalization of social values. In E. T. Higgins, D. N. Ruble, & W. W. Hartup (Eds.), *Social cognition and social behavior: Departmental perspectives.* Cambridge, England: Cambridge University Press.

Lepper, M. R., & Gurtner, J. (1989). Children and computers: Approaching the twenty-first century. *American Psychologist,* **44,** 170–178.

Lerner, R. M. (1984). *On the nature of human plasticity.* New York: Cambridge University Press.

Lerner, R. M., & Lerner, J. V. (1983). Temperament-intelligence reciprocities in early childhood: A contextual model. In M. Lewis (Ed.), *Origins of intelligence: Infancy and early childhood* (2nd ed.) (pp. 399–421). New York: Plenum.

Lesser, G. S., Fifer, G., & Clark, D. H. (1965). Mental abilities of children from different social class and cultural groups. *Monographs of the Society for Research in Child Development,* **30**(4, Serial No. 102), 1–115.

Lester, B., Hoffman, J., & Brazelton, T. B. (1985). The rhythmic structure of mother-infant interaction in term and preterm infants. *Child Development,* **56,** 15–27.

Lester, B. M. (1988). Neurobehavioral assessment of the infant at risk. *Early identification of infants with developmental disabilities.* New York: Grune & Stratton.

Lester, B. M. (1991). *Neurobehavioral syndromes in cocaine exposed newborn infants.* Paper presented at the meeting of the Society for Research in Child Development, Seattle, WA.

Lester, B. M., Als, H., & Brazelton, T. B. (1982). Regional obstetric anesthesia and newborn behavior: A reanalysis toward synergistic effects. *Child Development,* **53,** 687–692.

Lester, B. M., Corwin, M., & Golub, H. (1988). Early detection of the infant at risk through cry analysis. In J. N. Newman (Ed.), *The physiological control of mammalian vocalization.*

Lester, B. M., & Dreher, M. (1989). Effects of marijuana use during pregnancy on the newborn cry. *Child Development,* **60,** 765–771.
Levant, R. F. (1988). Education for fatherhood. In P. Bronstein & C. P. Cowan (Eds.), *Fatherhood today: Men's changing role in the family* (pp. 253–275). New York: Wiley.
Levitt, M. J., Weber, R. A., & Clark, M. C. (1986). Social network relationships as sources of maternal support and well-being. *Developmental Psychology,* **22,** 310–316.
Levy, G. D. (1989). Developmental and individual differences in preschoolers' recognition memories: The influences of gender schematization and verbal labeling of information. *Sex Roles,* **21,** 305–324.
Lewis, D. (1975). The black family: Socialization and sex roles. *Phylon,* **36,** 221–237.
Lewis, M. (1983). On the nature of intelligence: Science or bias? In M. Lewis (Ed.), *Origins of intelligence: Infancy and early childhood* (2nd ed.) (pp. 1–24). New York: Plenum.
Lewis, M. (1989). Cultural differences in children's knowledge of emotional scripts. In C. Saarni & P. L. Harris (Eds.), *Children's understanding of emotion.* New York: Cambridge University Press.
Lewis, M. (1991). *Shame, the exposed self.* New York: Free Press.
Lewis, M., Alessandri, S. M., & Sullivan, M. W. (1992). Differences in shame and pride as a function of children's gender and task difficulty. *Child Development,* **63,** 630–638.
Lewis, M., & Brooks, J. (1974). Self, other and fear: Infants' reactions to people. In M. Lewis & L. Rosenblum (Eds.), *The origins of fear.* New York: Wiley.
Lewis, M., & Fiering, C. (1989). Infant, mother and mother-infant interaction behavior and subsequent attachment. *Child Development,* **60,** 831–837.
Lewis, M., & Freedle, R. (1973). The mother-infant dyad. In P. Pliner, L. Kranes, & T. Alloway (Eds.), *Communication and affect: Language and thought.* New York: Academic.
Lewis, M., & Michaelson, L. (1985). *Children's emotions and moods.* New York: Plenum.
Lewis, M. & Wilson, C. D. (1972). Infant development in lower-class American families. *Human Development,* **15,** 112-127.
Liben, L. S., & Bigler, R. S. (1987). Reformulating children's gender schemata. In L. S. Liben & M. L. Signorella (Eds.), *Children's gender schemata.* San Francisco: Jossey-Bass.
Liben, L. S., & Downs, R. M. (1989). Understanding maps as symbols: The development of map concepts in children. In H. W. Reese (Ed.), *Advances in child development and behavior,* Vol 22, pp. 145–201. New York: Academic Press.
Liberman, I. Y., Shankweiler, D., Liberman, A. M., Fowler, C., & Fischer, F. W. (1976). Phonetic segmentation and recoding in the beginning reader. In A. S. Reber & D. Scarborough (Eds.), *Reading: Theory and practice.* Hillsdale, NJ: Erlbaum.
Licht, B. G., & Dweck, C. S. (1983). Sex differences in achievement orientations: Consequences for academic choices and attainments. In M. Maryland (Ed.), *Sex differentiation and schooling.* London: Heinemann.
Liebert, R. M., & Baron, R. A. (1972). Some immediate effects of televised violence on children's behavior. *Developmental Psychology,* **6,** 469–475.
Liebert, R. M. & Sprafkin, J. (1988). *The early window: Effects of television on children and youth.* New York: Pergamon.
Liederman, P. H., Landsman, M., & Clark, C. (1990, March). *Making it or blowing it: Coping strategies and academic performance in a multiethnic high school population.* Paper presented at the biennial meeting of the Society for Research on Adolescence, Atlanta.
Lieppe, M. R., & Romanczyck, A. (1987). Children on the witness stand: A communication/persuasion analysis of jurors' reactions to child witnesses. In S. J. Ceci, M. P. Toglia, & D. F. Ross (Eds.), *Children's eyewitness memory.* New York: Springer-Verlag.
Lin, C. C., & Fu, V. R. (1990). A comparison of child-rearing practices among Chinese, immigrant Chinese, and Caucasian-American parents. *Child Development,* **61,** 429–433.
Lindberg, M. (1980). Is knowledge base development a necessary and sufficient condition for memory development? *Journal of Experimental Child Psychology,* **30,** 401–410.
Lindell, S. G. (1988). Education for childbirth: A time for change. *Journal of Obstetrics, Gynecology and Neonatal Nursing,* **17,** 108–112.
Linn, M. C., & Hyde, J. S. (1989). Gender, mathematics, and science. *Educational Researcher,* **18,** 17–27.
Linn, M. C., & Hyde, J. S. (1991). Trends in cognitive and psychosocial gender differences. In R. M. Lerner, A. C. Petersen, & J. Brooks-Gunn (Eds.), *The encyclopedia of adolescence.* New York: Garland.
Linn, S., Lieberman, E., Schoenbaum, S. C., Monson, R. R., Sutbblefield, P. G., & Ryand, K. J. (1988). Adverse outcomes of pregnancy in women exposed to diethylstilbestrol in utero. *Journal of Reproductive Medicine,* **33,** 3–7.
Linney, J. A., & Seidman, E. (1989). The future of schooling. *American psychologist,* **44,** 336–340.
Lipscomb, T. J., McAllister, H. A., & Bregman, N. J. (1985). A developmental inquiry into the effects of multiple models on children's generosity. *Merrill-Palmer Quarterly,* **31,** 335–344.

Lipsitt, L. P. (1986). Toward understanding the hedonic nature of infancy. In L. P. Lipsitt & J. H. Condor (Eds.), *Experimental child psychologist: Essays in honor of C. S. Spiker.* Hillsdale, NJ: Erlbaum.

Lipsitt, L. P., & Werner, J. S. (1981). The infancy of human learning processes. In E. Gollin (Ed.), *Developmental plasticity.* New York: Academic Press.

Little, R. (1975). *Maternal alcohol use and resultant birth weight.* Unpublished doctoral dissertation, Johns Hopkins University, Baltimore, MD.

Lobitz, G. K., & Johnson, S. M. (1975). Normal versus deviant children: A multi-method comparison. *Journal of Abnormal Child Psychology,* **3**, 353–374.

Lobitz, G. K., & Johnson, S. M. (1975). Parental manipulation of the behavior of normal and deviant children. *Child Development,* **46**, 719–726.

Loeb, R. B., Horst, L., & Horton, P. J. (1980). Family interaction patterns associated with self-esteem in preadolescent girls and boys. *Merrill-Palmer Quarterly,* **26**, 203–217.

Loehlin, J. C., Willerman, L., & Horn, J. M. (1988). Human behavior genetics. *Annual Review of Psychology,* **39**, 101–133.

Lollis, S. P., & Ross, H. S. (1992). Parents' regulation of children's peer interactions: Direct influences. In R. D. Parke & G. W. Ladd (Eds.), *Family-peer relationships: Modes of linkage.* Hillsdale, NJ: Erlbaum.

Loney, J., Kramer, J., & Milich, R. (1981). The hyperkinetic child grows up: Predictors of symptoms, delinquency, and achievement at follow-up. In K. D. Gadow & J. Loney (Eds.), *Psychosocial aspects of drug treatment for hyperactivity.* Boulder, CO: Westview.

Lorch, E. P., Bellack, D. R., & Augsbach, L. H. (1987). Young children's memory for televised stories: Effects of importance. *Child Development,* **58**, 453–463.

Lotter, V. (1978). Follow-up studies. In M. Rutter & E. Scholpler (Eds.), *Autism: A reappraisal of concepts and treatment.* New York: Plenum.

Loudal, L. T. (1989). Sex role messages in television commercials: An update. *Sex Roles,* **21,** 715–724.

Lovaas, O. I. (1967). A behavior therapy approach to the treatment of childhood schizophrenia. In J. P. Hill (Eds.), *Minnesota Symposia on Child Development* (Vol. 1, pp. 108–159). Minneapolis: University of Minnesota Press.

Lovaas, O. I. (1987). Behavioral treatment and normal educational and intellectual functioning in young autistic children. *Journal of Consulting and Clinical Psychology,* **55**, 3–9.

Lovaas, O. I., & Smith, P. (1988). Intensive behavioral treatment for young autistic children. In B. Lahey & A. Kazdin (Eds.), *Advances in clinical child psychology* (Vol. 2). New York: Plenum.

Lovaas, O. I., Smith, T., & McEachin, J. J. (1989). Clarifying comments on the young autism study: Reply to Schopler, Short, and Mesiboo. *Journal of Consulting and Clinical Psychology,* **57**, 165–167.

Lovaas, O. I., Young, D. B., & Newsom, C. D. (1978). Childhood psychosis: Behavioral treatment. In B. B. Wolman (Ed.), *Handbook of treatment of mental disorders in childhood and adolescence.* Englewood Cliffs, NJ: Prentice-Hall.

Loveland, K. A. (1987). Behavior of young children with Down syndrome before the mirror: Exploration. *Child Development,* **58,** 768–778.

Lowitzer, A. C. (1987). Maternal phenylketonuria: Cause for concern among women with PKU. *Research on Developmental Disabilities,* **8**, 1–14.

Lozoff, B. (1989). Nutrition and behavior. *American Psychologist,* **44,** 231–236.

Lummis, M., & Stevenson, H. W. (1990). Gender differences in beliefs and achievement: A cross-cultural study. *Developmental Psychology,* **26**, 254–263.

Luria, A. R. (1971). Towards the problem of the historical nature of psychological processes. *International Journal of Psychology,* **6**, 259–272.

Luthar, S. S. (1991). Vulnerability and resilience: A study of high-risk adolescents. *Child Development,* **62**, 600–616.

Luthar, S. S., & Zigler, E. (1991). Vulnerability and competence: A review of research on resilience in childhood. *American Journal of Orthopsychiatry,* **61**, 6–22.

Lykken, D. T., Iacono, W. G., Harocan, K., McGue, M., Bouchard, T. J. (1988). Habituation of the skin conductance response to strong stimuli: A twin study. *Psychophysiology,* **25**, 4–15.

Lytton, H. (1976). Do parents create, or respond to, differences in twins? *Developmental Psychology,* **13**(5), 456–459.

Lytton, H. (1980). *Parent-child interaction: The socialization process observed in twin and singleton families.* New York: Plenum.

Lytton, H., & Romney, D. M. (1991). Parents' differential socialization of boys and girls: A meta-analysis. *Psychological Bulletin,* **109**, 267–296.

Maccoby, E. E. (1967). Selective auditory attention in children. In L. P. Lipsett & C. C. Spiker (Eds.), *Advances in child development and behavior* (Vol. 3). New York: Academic.

Maccoby, E. E. (1969). The development of stimulus selection. In J. P. Hill (Ed.), *Minnesota Symposia on Child Psychology* (Vol. 3). Minneapolis: University of Minnesota Press.

Maccoby, E. E. (1988). Gender as a social category. *Developmental Psychology,* **24,** 755–765.

Maccoby, E. E., & Jacklin, C. (1980). Sex differences in aggression: A rejoinder and reprise. *Child Development,* **51,** 964–980.

Maccoby, E. E., & Jacklin, C. N. (1974). *The psychology of sex differences.* Stanford, CA: Stanford University Press.

Maccoby, E. E., & Martin, J. A. (1983). Socialization in the context of the family: Parent-child interaction. In E. M. Hetherington (Ed.), *Socialization, personality, and social development: Vol. 4. Handbook of child psychology.* New York: Wiley.

MacDonald, K., & Parke, R. D. (1984). Bridging the gap: The relationship between parent-child play and peer interactive competence. *Child Development,* **55,** 1265–1277.

Macfarlane, J. A. (1975). Olfaction in the development of social preferences in the human neonate. In M. A. Hofer (Ed.), *Parent-infant interaction.* Amsterdam: Elsevier.

MacFarlane, J. W., Allen, L., & Honzik, M. P. (1954). A developmental study of the behavior problems of normal children between 21 months and 14 years of age. Berkeley and Los Angeles: University of California Press.

Mackenzie, B. (1984). Explaining race differences in IQ: The logic, the methodology, and the evidence. *American Psychologist,* **39,** 1214–1233.

MacKinnon, C. C. (1989). An observational investigation of sibling interactions in married and divorced families. *Developmental Psychology,* **25,** 36–44.

MacMillan, D. L., Keogh, B. K., & Jones, R. L. (1986). Special education research on mildly handicapped learners. In M. C. Wittrock (Ed.), *Handbook of research on teaching* (3rd ed.). New York: MacMillan

MacTurk, R., Vietze, P., McCarthy, M., McQuiston, S., & Yarrow, L. (1985). The organization of exploratory behavior in Down syndrome and non-delayed infants. *Child Development,* **56,** 573–581.

Magenis, R. E., Overton, K. M., Chamberlin, J., Brady, T., & Lorrien, E. (1977). Parental origin of the extra chromosome in Down's syndrome. *Human Genetics,* **37,** 7–16.

Magnusson, D. (1988). Individual development from an interactional perspective: A longitudinal study. In D. Magnusson (Ed.), *Paths through life* (Vol. 1). Hillsdale, NJ: Erlbaum.

Main, M. (1973). *Exploration, play and level of cognitive functioning as related to child-mother attachment.* Unpublished doctoral dissertation, Johns Hopkins University, Baltimore, MD.

Main, M., & Cassidy, J. (1988). Categories of response to reunion with the parent at age 6: Predictable from infant attachment classification and stable over a 1-month period. *Developmental Psychology,* **24,** 415–426.

Main, M., & Solomon, J. (1989). Procedures for identifying infants as disorganized/disoriented during the Ainsworth strange situation. In M. Greenberg, D. Cichetti, & M. Cummings (Eds.), *Attachment in the preschool years.* Chicago: University of Chicago Press.

Main, M., & Weston, D. (1981). The quality of the toddler's relationship to mother and father: Related to conflict behavior and readiness to established new relationships. *Child Development,* **52,** 932–940.

Malatesta, C. Z. (1982). The expression and regulation of emotion: A lifespan perspective. In T. Field & A. Fogel (Eds.), *Emotion and early interaction* (pp. 1–24). Hillsdale, NJ: Erlbaum.

Malatesta, C. Z., Culver, C., Tesman, J., & Shepard, B. (1989). The development of emotional expression during the first two years of life: Normative trends and patterns of individual differences. *Monographs of the Society for Research in Child Development,* **54,** 1–2.

Malatesta, C. Z., Grigoryev, P., Lamb, C., Albin, M., & Culver, C. (1986). Emotion socialization and expressive development in preterm and full-term infants. *Child Development,* **57,** 316, 330.

Malatesta, C. Z., & Haviland, J. (1982). Learning display rules: The socialization of emotional expression in infancy. *Child Development,* **53,** 991–1003.

Malatesta, C. Z., & Haviland, J. (1985). Signals, symbols, and socialization. In M. Lewis & C. Saarni (Eds.), *The socialization of emotions.* New York: Plenum.

Malatesta, C. Z., & Izard, C. E. (1984). The facial expression of emotion: Young, middle-aged and older adult expressions. In C. Z. Malatesta & C. E. Izard (Eds.), *Emotion in adult development* (pp. 253–273). Beverly Hills: Sage.

Malcolm, L. A. (1970). Growth of the Asai child of the Madang district of New Guinea. *Journal of Biosocial Science,* **2,** 213–226.

Mallick, S. K., & McCandless, B. R. (1966). A study of catharsis on aggression. *Journal of Personality and Social Psychology,* **4,** 591–596.

Mandler, J. M. (1984). *Stories, scripts & scenes.* Hillsdale, NJ: Erlbaum.

Mandler, J. M., & Bauer, P. J. (1988). The cradle of categorization: Is the basic level basic? *Cognitive Development,* **3,** 247–264.

Manez, J. (1987). *Perception of impending collision in 3- to 6-week-old infants.* Unpublished doctoral dissertation. University of Minnesota.

Mangelsdorf, S., Gunnar, M., Kestenbaum, R., Lang, S., & Andreas, D. (1990). Infant proneness-to-distress, temperament, maternal personality and mother-infant attachment: Associations and goodness of fit. *Child Development,* **61,** 820–831.

Mann, J., Ten Have, T., Plunkett, J. W., & Meisels, S. J. (1991). Time sampling: A methodological critique. *Child Development,* **62,** 227–241.

A man's drinking may harm his offspring. (1975). *Science News,* **107** (8), 116.

Maratsos, M. (1983). Some current issues in the study of the acquisition of grammar. In P. H. Mussen, *Handbook of child psychology* (Vol. 3). New York: Wiley.

Maratsos, M. (1989). Innateness and plasticity in language acquisition. In M. Rice & R. L. Shiefelbusch (Eds.), *The teachability of language.* Baltimore, MD: Brooks/Cole.

Maratsos, M., & Chalkley, M. A. (1980). The internal language of children's syntax: The ontogenesis and representation of syntactic categories. In K. E. Nelson (Eds.), *Children's language* (Vol. 2). New York: Gardner Press.

Marcus, D. E., & Overton, W. F. (1978). The development of cognitive gender constancy and sex-role preferences. *Child Development,* **49,** 434–444.

Marini, Z., & Case, R. (1989). Parallels in the development of preschoolers' knowledge about their physical and social worlds. *Merrill-Palmer Quarterly,* **35,** 63–87.

Markman, E. M. (1973). Facilitation of part-whole comparisons by use of the collective noun "family." *Child Development,* **44,** 837–840.

Markman, E. M. (1977). Realizing that you don't understand: A preliminary investigation. *Child Development,* **48,** 986–992.

Markman, E. M. (1979). Realizing that you don't understand: Elementary school children's awareness of inconsistencies. *Child Development,* **50,** 643–655.

Markman, E. M. (1989). *Categorization and naming in children.* Cambridge, MA: MIT Press.

Markman, E. M., & Hutchinson, J. E. (1984). Children's sensitivity to constraints on word meaning: Taxonomic versus thematic relations. *Cognitive Psychology,* **16,** 1–27.

Markman, E. M. & Siebert, G. (1976). Classes and collections: Internal organization resulting in holistic properties. *Cognitive Psychology,* **8,** 561–577.

Martens, R. (1986). Youth sports in the USA. In M. Weiss & D. Gould (Eds.), *Competitive sport for children and youth.* Champaign, IL: Human Kinetics.

Martin, B., & Hoffman, J. A. (1990). Conduct disorders. In M. Lewis and S. Miller (Eds.), *Handbook of developmental psychopathology.* New York: Plenum.

Martin, C. L. (1992). New directions for assessing children's gender knowledge. *Developmental Review.*

Martin, C. L., & Halverson, C. F. (1981). A schematic-processing model of sex typing and stereotyping in children. *Child Development,* 1119–1134.

Martin, C. L., & Halverson, C. F. (1983). The effects of sex-typing schemas on young children's memory. *Child Development,* **54,** 563–574.

Martin, C. L., & Little, J. K. (1990). The relation of gender understanding to children's sex-typed preferences and gender stereotypes. *Child Development,* **61,** 1427–1439.

Martin, H. (1976). *The abused child.* Cambridge, MA: Ballinger.

Martin, J. A. (1981). A longitudinal study of the consequences of early mother-infant interaction: A microanalytic approach. *Monographs of the Society for Research in Child Development,* **46** (3, Serial No. 190).

Martin, J. B. (1987). Molecular genetics: Applications to the clinical neurosciences. *Science,* **238,** 765–772.

Martin, T. R., & Bracken, M. B. (1986). The association of low birthweight with passive smoke exposure in pregnancy. *American Journal of Epidemiology,* **124,** 633–642.

Martorell, R. (1984). Genetics, environment and growth: Issues in the assessment of nutritional status. In A. Velasquez & H. Bourges (Eds), *Genetic factors in nutrition.* Orlando, FL: Academic Press.

Mash, E. J., Johnson, J. L., & Kovitz, K. A. (1982). A comparison of the mother-child interactions of physically abused and nonabused children during play and task situations. *Journal of Clinical Child Psychology.*

Mash, E. J., & Johnston, C. (1982). A comparison of the mother-child interactions of younger and older hyperactive and normal children. *Child Development,* **53,** 1371–1381.

Massey, C. M., & Gelman, R. (1988). Preschooler's ability to decide whether a photographed unfamiliar object can move itself. *Developmental Psychology,* **24,** 307–317.

Masten, A. S., & Broswell, L. (1990). Developmental psychopathology: An integrative framework for understanding behavior problems in children and adolescents. In P. R. Martin (Ed.), *Handbook of behavior therapy and psychological science: An integrative approach.* New York: Pergamon.

Masten, A. S., & Garmezy, N. (1985). Risk, vulnerability, and protective factors in development. In B. B. Lahey & A. E. Kazdin (Eds.), *Advances in clinical child psychology* (Vol. 8). New York: Plenum.

Master, A. S. (1988). Toward a developmental psychopathology of adolescence. In M. D. Levine & E. R. McAnarney (Eds.), *Early adolescent transitions* (pp. 261–278). Lexington, MA: D.C. Heath.

Matas, L., Arend, R., & Sroufe, L. A. (1978). Continuity of adaptation in the second year: The relationship between quality of attachment and later competence. *Child Development,* **49,** 547–556.

Maurer, D., & Maurer, C. (1988). *The world of the newborn.* New York: Basic Books.

Maurer, D., & Salapatek, P. (1976). Developmental changes in the scanning of faces by young infants. *Child Development,* **47,** 523–527.

Maynard, R. (1970, June 29). Omaha pupils given "behavior" drugs. *Washington Post.*

McAdoo, H. (1978). Factors related to stability in upwardly mobile black families. *Journal of Marriage and the Family,* **40,** 761–776.

McCall, R. B. (1979). *Infants.* Cambridge, MA: Harvard University Press.

McCall, R. B. (1983). A conceptual approach to early mental development. In M. Lewis (Ed.), *Origins of intelligence: Infancy and early childhood* (2nd ed.) (pp. 107–133). New York: Plenum.

McCall, R. B., Applebaum, M. I., & Hogarty, P. S. (1973). Developmental changes in mental performance. *Monographs of the Society for Research in Child Development* **38,**(3, Serial No. 150), 1–84.

McCall, R. B., Hogarty, P. S., & Hurlburt, N. (1972). Transitions in infant sensorimotor development and the prediction of childhood IQ. *American Psychologist,* **27,** 728–748.

McCarthy, D. (1954). Language development in children. In L. Carmichael (Ed.), *Manual of child psychology.* New York: Wiley.

McCartney, K., Harris, M. J., Berniere, F. (1990). Growing up and growing apart: A developmental meta-analysis of twin studies. *Psychological Bulletin,* **107,** 226–237.

McCauley, E., Ito, J., & Kay, T. (1986). Psychosocial functioning in girls with Turner syndrome and short stature. *Journal of the American Academy of Child Psychiatry,* **25,** 105–112.

McCauley, E., Kay, T., Ito, J., & Treeler, R. (1987). The Turner syndrome: Cognitive defects, affective discrimination and behavior problems. *Child Development,* **58,** 464–473.

McCormick, C., & Mauer, D. M. (1988). Unimanual hand preferences in 6-month-olds: Consistency and relation to familial handedness. *Infant Behavior and Development,* **11,** 21–29.

McDavid, J. W., & Harari, H. (1966). Stereotyping of names and popularity in grade school children. *Child Development,* **37,** 453–457.

McGinty, M. J., & Zafran, E. I. (1988). Surrogacy: Constitutional and legal issues. Cleveland, OH: The Ohio Academy of Trial Lawyers.

McGraw, M. (1940). Neuromuscular development of the human infant as exemplified in the achievement of erect locomotion. *Journal of Pediatrics,* **17,** 747–771.

McGreal (1985, April). *The grandparent-grandchild relationship during the neonatal period.* Paper presented at the biennial meeting of the Society for Research in Child Development, Toronto, Canada.

McGue, M., & Bouchard, T. J. (1987). Genetic and environmental determinants of information processing and special mental abilities: A twin analysis. In R. J. Sternberg (Ed.), *Advances in the psychology of human intelligence* (Vol. 5). Hillsdale, NJ: Erlbaum.

McGue, M., & Gottesman, I. I. (1989). A single dominant gene still cannot account for the transmission of schizophrenia. *Archives of General Psychiatry,* **46,** 478–479.

McHale, S. M., Bartko, W. T., Crouter, A. C., & Perry-Jenkins, M. (1990). Children's housework and psychosocial functioning: The mediating effects of parents' sex-role behaviors and attitudes. *Child Development,* **61,** 1413–1426.

McKenzie, B. E., Tootell, H. E., & Day, R. H. (1980). Development of visual size constancy during the first year of human infancy. *Developmental Psychology,* **16,** 163–174.

McLoyd, V. C. (1990). The impact of economic hardship on black families and children: Psychological distress, parenting and socioemotional development. *Child Development,* **61,** 311–346.

McLuskey, K. A., Killarney, J., & Papini, D. R. (1983). Adolescent pregnancy and parenthood: Implications for development. In E. C. Callahan & K. A. McCluskey (Eds.), *Life span developmental psychology: Non-normative life events.* New York Academic.

McQueen, A. J. (1979). The adaptation of urban black families: Trends, problems and issues. In D. Reiss & H. A. Hoffman (Eds.), *The American family: Dying or developing.* New York: Plenum.

Mead, M. (1935). *Sex and temperament in three primitive societies.* New York: Morrow.

Mednick, S. A., Schulsinger, H., & Schulsinger, F. (1975). Schizophrenia in children of schizophrenic mothers. In A. Davies (Ed.), *Child personality and psychopathology* (Vol. 2, pp. 221–252). New York: Wiley.

Meicler, M., & Gratch, G. (1980). Do 5-month-olds show object conception in Piaget's sense? *Infant Behavior and Development,* **3,** 265–282.

Meltzoff, A. N. (1981). Imitation, intermodal coordination and representation in early infancy. In G. Butterworth (Ed.), *Infancy and epistemology.* Brighton: Harvester Press.

Meltzoff, A. N. (1988a). Infant imitation and memory: Nine-month-old infants in immediate and deferred tests. *Child Development,* **59,** 217–225.

Meltzoff, A. N. (1988b). Infant imitation after a 1-week delay: Long-term memory for novel acts and multiple stimuli. *Developmental Psychology,* **24,** 470–476.

Meltzoff, A. N. (1990). Towards a developmental cognitive science. *Annals of the New York Academy of Sciences,* **608,** 1–37.

Meltzoff, A. N., & Borton, R. W. (1979). Intermodal matching by human neonates. *Nature,* **282,** 403–404.

Meltzoff, A. N. & Moore, M. K. (1983). Newborn infants imitate adult facial gestures. *Child Development,* **54,** 702–709.

Mercer, J. R. (1971). Sociocultural factors in labeling mental retardates. *Peabody Journal of Education,* **48,** 188–203.

Mercer, J. R. (1972, September). IQ: The lethal label. *Psychology Today,* p. 44.

Meredith, H. V. (1975). Somatic changes during prenatal life. *Child Development,* **46,** 603–610.

Michals, K., Azen, C., Acosta, P., Koch, R., & Matalon, R. (1988). Blood phenylalanine levels and intelligence of ten year old children with PKU in the National Collaborative Study. *Journal of the American Dietetic Association,* **88,** 1226–1229.

Mickelson, R. (1990). The attitude-achievement paradox among black adolescents. *Sociology of Education,* **63,** 44–61.

Milham, J., Widmayer, S., Bauer, C. R., & Peterson, L. (1983, April). *Predicting cognitive deficits for preterm, low birthweight infants.* Paper presented at the biennial meeting of the Society for Research in Child Development, Detroit.

Miller, G. A. (1956). The magical number seven, plus or minus two: Some limits on our capacity for processing information. *Psychological Review,* **63,** 81–97.

Miller, K. F., & Paredes, D. R. (1990). Starting to add worse: Effects of learning to multiply on children's addition. *Cognition,* **37,** 213–242.

Miller, M. L., Chiles, J. A., & Barnes, V. E. (1982). Suicide attempts within a delinquent population. *Journal of Consulting and Clinical Psychology,* **50,** 490–498.

Miller, N. (1983). *The effect of school desegregation on black academic achievement: A meta analysis.* Paper commissioned by the National Institute of Education.

Miller, P. H. & Weiss, M. G. (1981). Children's attention allocation, understanding of attention, and performance on the incidental learning task. *Child Development,* **52,** 1183–1190.

Miller, S. (1973). Ends, means and galumphing: Some leitmotifs at play. *American Anthropologist,* **75,** 87–98.

Miller, S. M., Birnbaum, A., & Durbin, D. (1990). Etiologic perspectives on depression in childhood. In M. Lewis & S. Miller (Eds.), *Handbook of developmental psychopathology* (pp. 311–325). New York: Plenum.

Milstein, R. M. (1980). Responsiveness in newborn infants of overweight and normal weight parents. *Appetite,* **1,** 65–74.

Minuchin, P. P., & Shapiro, E. K. (1983). The school as a context for social development. In P. H. Mussen (Eds.), *Handbook of child psychology* (Vol. 4). New York: Wiley.

Mischel, W., & Mischel, H. N. (1983). Development of children's knowledge of self-control strategies. *Child Development,* **54,** 603–619.

Mischel, W., Shoda, Y., & Peake, P. K. (1988). The nature of adolescent competencies predicted by preschool delay of gratification. *Journal of Personality and Social Psychology,* **54,** 687–696.

Mistretta, C. M., & Bradley, R. M. (1985). Development of the sense of taste. In E. M. Blass (Ed.), *Handbook of behavioral neurobiology* (pp. 205–236). New York: Plenum.

Mitchell, R. G., & Farr, V. (1965). The meaning of maturity and the assessment of maturity at birth. In M. Dawkins & W. G. MacGregor (Eds.), *Gestational age, size, and maturity* (pp. 83–99). London: Spastics Society Medical Education and Information Unit.

Miyawaki, B. E., Strange, W., Verbrugge, R., Liberman, A. M., Jenkins, J. J., & Fujimura, O. (1975). An effect of linguistic experience: The discrimination of [r] and [l] by native speakers of Japanese and English. *Perception and Psychophysics,* **18,** 331–340.

Mize, J., & Ladd, G. W. (1990). Toward the development of successful social skills for preschool children. In S. R. Asher & J. D. Coie (Eds.), *Peer rejection in childhood.* New York: Cambridge University Press.

Moely, B. E., Olson, F. A., Halwes, T. G., & Flavell, J. H. (1969). Production deficiency in young children's clustered recall. *Developmental Psychology,* **1,** 26–34.

Moffitt, A. R. (1971). Consonant cue perception by twenty to twenty-four week old infants. *Child Development*, **42**, 717–732.

Mohn, G., & van Hof-van Duin (1986). Development of binocular and monocular visual fields of human infants during the first year of life. *Clinical Visual Science*, **1**, 51–64.

Mohr, P. J. (1979). Parental guidance of children's viewing of evening television programs. *Journal of Broadcasting*, **23**, 213–228.

Molfese, D. L. (1973). Cerebral asymmetry in infants, children, and adults: Auditory evoked responses to speech and musical stimuli. *Journal of the Acoustical Society of America*, **53**, 363.

Molfese, D. L., & Molfese, V. J. (1979). Hemisphere and stimulus differences as reflected in the cortical responses of newborn infants to speech stimuli. *Developmental Psychology*, **15**, 505–511.

Molfese, D. L., & Molfese, V. J. (1980). Cortical response of preterm infants to phonetic and nonphonetic speech stimuli. *Developmental Psychology*, **16**, 574–581.

Molfese, D. L., & Molfese, V. J. (1985). Electrophysiological indices of auditory discrimination in newborn infants: The bases for predicting later language development? *Infant Behavior and Development*, **8**, 197–211.

Molfese, D. L., & Segalowitz, S. J. (Eds.), (1988). *Brain lateralization in children*. New York: Guilford Press.

Money, J. (1985). Pediatric sexology and hermaphroditism. *Journal of Sex and Marital Therapy*, **11**, 139–156.

Money, J. (1987). Propaedeutics of diecious G-I/R: Theoretical foundations for understanding dimorphic gender-identity/role. In J. M. Reinisch, L. A. Rosenblum, & S. A. Sanders (Eds.), *Masculinity/femininity: Basic perspectives*. New York: Oxford University Press.

Money, J., & Annecillo, C. (1987). Crucial period effect in psychoendocrinology: Two syndromes abuse dwarfism and female (CVAH) hermaphroditism. In M. H. Bornstein (Ed.), *Sensitive periods in development: Interdisciplinary perspectives*. Hillsdale, NJ: Erlbaum.

Money, J., & Ehrhardt, A. A. (1972). *Man and woman, boy and girl*. Baltimore, MD: Johns Hopkins University Press.

Montessori, M. (1964). *Spontaneous activity in education*. Cambridge, MA: Robert Bentley.

Moore, D. R., & Arthur, J. L. (1989). Juvenile delinquency. In T. Oklendick & M. Hersen (Eds.), *Handbook of childhood psychopathology*. New York: Plenum.

Moore, K. L. (1989). *Before we are born*. Philadelphia: Saunders.

Morgan, G. A., & Ricciuti, H. (1969). Infants' responses to strangers during the first year. In B. M. Foss (Ed.), *Determinants of infant behavior* (Vol. 4, pp. 253–272). London: Methuen.

Moss, H. (1967). Sex, age and state as determinants of mother-infant interaction. *Merill-Palmer Quarterly*, **13**, 19–36.

Moss, M., Colombo, J., Mitchell, D. W. & Horowitz, F. D. (1988). Neonatal behavioral organization and visual discrimination at 3 months of age. *Child Development*, **59**, 1211–1220.

Moustakas, C. E., Sigel, I. E., & Schalock, N. D. (1956). An objective method for the measurement and analysis of child-adult interaction. *Child Development*, **27**, 109–134.

Mueller, E. (1989). Toddlers' peer relations: Shared meaning and semantics. In W. Damon (Ed.), *Child development today and tomorrow*. San Francisco: Jossey-Bass.

Mueller, E., & Lucas, T. A. (1975). A developmental analysis of peer interaction among toddlers. In M. Lewis & L. A. Rosenblum (Eds.), *Friendship and peer relations*. New York: Wiley.

Muir, D., & Clifton, R. (1985). Infants' orientation to location of sound sources. In G. Gottlieb & N. Krasnegor (Eds.), *Measurement of audition and vision in the first year of postnatal life. A methodological overview*. Norwood, NJ: Ablex.

Muir, D., & Field, T. M. (1979). Newborn infants orient to sounds. *Child Development*, **50**, 431–436.

Munroe, R. H., Shimmin, H. S., & Munroe, R. L. (1984). Gender understanding and sex role preference in four cultures. *Developmental Psychology*, **20**, 673–682.

Munsinger, H. (1975). The adopted child's IQ: A critical review. *Psychological Bulletin*, **82**, 623–659.

Murray, F. B. (1981). The new conservation paradigm. In I. Siegel, D. Brodzinsky, & R. Golinkoff (Eds.), *New directions in Piagetian research and theory*. Hillsdale, NJ: Erlbaum.

Musick, J., Clark, R., & Cohler, B. (1981). The mothers' project: A program for mentally ill mothers of young children. In B. Weissbound & J. Musick (Eds.), *Infants: Their social environments* (pp. 111–127). Washington, D.C.: NAEYC.

Myers, A. W. & Cohen, R. (1990). Cognitive-behavioral approaches to child psychopathology. In M. Lewis & S. Miller (Eds.), *Handbook of developmental psychopathology*. New York: Plenum.

Myers, N. A., Clifton, R. K., & Clarkson, M. G. (1987). When they were young: Almost-threes remember two years ago. *Infant Behavior and Development*, **10**, 123–132.

Myles-Worsley, M., Cromer, C. C., & Dodd, D. H. (1986). Children's preschool script reconstruction: Reliance on general knowledge as memory fades. *Developmental Psychology*, **22**, 22–30.

Nadelman, L., & Begun, A. (1982). The effect of the newborn on the older sibling: Mothers' questionnaires. In M. E. Lamb & B. Sutton-Smith (Eds.), *Sibling relationships.* Hillsdale, NJ: Erlbaum.

Naeye, R. L., Diener, M. M., & Dellinger, W. S. (1969). Urban poverty: Effects of prenatal nutrition. *Science,* **166,** 1206.

Nash, S. C., & Feldman, S. S. (1981). Sex role and sex-related attributions, constancy and change across the family life cycle. In M. E. Lamb & A. L. Brown (Eds.), *Advances in developmental psychology* (Vol. 1). Hillsdale, NJ: Erlbaum.

National Center for Health Statistics. (1976). *NCHS growth charts.* Washington, DC.

National Institutes of Health. (1979, April). *Antenatal diagnosis* (NIH Publication No. 79-1973). Washington, DC: U.S. Department of Health, Education and Welfare. Public Health Service.

Naus, M. J. (1982). Memory development in the young reader: The combined effects of knowledge base and memory processing. In W. Otto & S. White (Eds.), *Reading expository text.* New York: Academic.

Neal, M. V. (1968). Vestibular stimulation and developmental behavior of the small premature infant. *Nursing Research Report,* **3,** 2–5.

Neel, J. V. (1949). The inheritance of sickle cell anemia. *Science,* **110,** 64–66.

Neimark, E. D., Slotnick, N. S., & Ulrich, T. (1971). Development of memorization strategies. *Child Development,* **38,** 107–117.

Nelson, C. A. (1987). The recognition of facial expressions in the first two years of life. *Child Development,* **58,** 889–909.

Nelson, K. (1973). Structure and strategy in learning to talk. *Monographs of the Society for Research in Child Development,* **38** (1 & 2).

Nelson, K. (1977). Aspects of language acquisition and form use from age 2 to age 20. *Journal of the American Academy of Child Psychiatry,* **16.**

Nelson, K. (1989). Strategies for first language teaching. In M. L. Rice & R. L. Schiefelbusch (Eds.), *The teachability of language.* Baltimore, MD: Brooks/Cole.

Nelson, K., Carskadden, G., & Bonvillian, J. D. (1973). Syntax acquisition: Impact of experimental variation in adult verbal interaction with the child. *Child Development,* **44,** 497–504.

Nelson, K., & Gruendel, J. (1981). Generalized event representations: Basic building blocks of cognitive development. In A. Brown & M. Lamb (Eds.), *Advances in developmental psychology* (Vol. 1, pp. 131–158). Hillsdale, NJ: Erlbaum.

Netley, C. T. (1986). Summary overview of behavioral development in individuals with neonatally identified X and Y aneuploidy. *Birth Defects,* **22,** 293–306.

Nevin, M. M. (1988). Dormant dangers of DES. *The Canadian Nurse,* **84,** 17–19.

Newcomb, M. D., & Bentler, P. M. (1989). Substance use and abuse among children and teenagers. *American Psychologist,* **44,** 242–248.

Newcomb, M. D., Muddahian, E., & Bentler, P. M. (1986). Risk factors for drug use among adolescents: Concurrent and longitudinal analyses. *American Journal of Public Health,* **76,** 525–531.

Newcomer, S., & Udry, J. R. (1987). Parental marital status effects on adolescent sexual behavior. *Journal of Marriage and the Family,* **48,** 235–240.

Newell, K., Scully, D. M., McDonald, P. V., & Baillargeon, R. (1989). Task constraints and infant grip configurations. *Developmental Psychobiology,* **22,** 817–832.

Newman, D., Riel, M., & Martin, L. (1983). Cultural practices and Piagetian theory: The impact of a cross-cultural program. In D. Kuhn & J. Meacham (Eds.), *On the development of developmental psychology.* Basel, Switzerland: Karger.

Newport, E. L. (1982). Task specificity in language learning? Evidence from speech perception and American sign language. In E. Wanner & L. R. Gleitman (Eds.), *Language acquisition: The state of the art.* New York: Cambridge University Press.

Newport, E. L. (1990). Maturational constraints on language learning. *Cognitive Science,* **14,** 11–28.

Newport, E. L., Gleitman, H., & Gleitman, L. R. (1977). Mother, I'd rather do it myself: Some effects and non-effects of maternal speech style. In C. A. Ferguson & C. E. Snow (Eds.), *Talking to children: Language input and acquisition.* New York: Cambridge University Press.

Newsom, C., Hovanitz, C., & Rincover, A. (1988). Autism. In E. Mask & L. Ferdal (Eds.), *Behavioral assessment of childhood disorders. Selected core problems.* New York: Guilford.

Nicholls, J. G. (1984). Achievement motivation: Conceptions of ability, subjective experience, task choice, and performance. *Psychological Review,* **91,** 328–346.

Nicholls, J. G., & Miller, A. T. (1983). *Children's achievement motivation.* Greenwich, CT: Guilford Press.

Nickolls, K. B., Cassel, J., & Kaplan, B. H. (1972). Psychosocial assets, life crisis and the prognosis of pregnancy. *American Journal of Epidemiology,* **95,** 431–441.

Niemark, E. D. (1981). Confounding with cognitive style factors: An artifact explanation for the apparent nonuniversal incidence of formal operations. In I. Siegel, D. Brodzinsky, & R. Golinkoff (Eds.), *New directions in Piagetian research and theory*. Hillsdale, NJ: Erlbaum.

Niemiec, R., & Walberg, H. J. (1987). Comparative effects of computer assisted instruction: A synthesis of reviews. *Journal of Educational Computing Research,* **3,** 19–37.

Nisan, M., & Kohlberg, L. (1982). Universality and variation in moral judgment: A longitudinal and cross-sectional study in Turkey. *Child Development,* **53,** 865–876.

Nisbett, R., & Gurwitz, S. (1970). Weight, sex and the eating behavior of human newborns. *Journal of Comparative and Physiological Psychology,* **73,** 245–253.

Nolen-Holksema, S., Guigus, J. S., & Seligman, M. (1986). Learned helplessness in children: A longitudinal study of depression, achievement, and explanatory style. *Journal of Personality and Social Psychology,* **51,** 435–442.

Nord, C. W., Moore, K. A., Morrison, D. R., Brown, B., & Myers, D. (1991). Consequences of teenage parenting. *Journal of School Health.*

Norman, D. A. (1988). *The psychology of everyday things.* New York: Basic Books.

Nucci, L. P., & Turiel, E. (1978). Social interactions and the development of social concepts in preschool children. *Child Development,* **49,** 400–407.

Nugent, J. K., Lester, B. M., & Brazelton, T. B. (Eds.). (1989). *Biology, culture, and development.* Norwood, NJ: Ablex.

O'Brien, M., Huston, A. C., & Risley, T. (1983). Sex-typed play of toddlers in a day care center. *Journal of Applied Developmental Psychology,* **4,** 1–9.

Ochs, E. (1980). *Talking to children in western Samoa.* Unpublished manuscript. University of Southern California, Los Angeles.

Oehler, J. M., Eckerman, C. D., & Wilson, W. H. (1988). Social stimulation and the regulation of premature infant's state prior to term age. *Infant Behavior and Development,* **12,** 341–356.

Oething, E. R., & Beauvais, F. (1990). Adolescent drug use: Findings of national and local surveys. *Journal of Consulting and Clinical Psychology,* **58,** 385–394.

Ogbu, J. (1988). Black education: A cultural-ecological perspective. In H. P. McAdoo (Ed.), *Black families* (pp. 169–186). Beverly Hills, CA: Sage.

Ogbu, J. V. (1981). Origins of human competence: A cultural-ecological perspective. *Child Development,* **52,** 413–429.

Olds, D. L., Henderson, C. R., Tatelbaum, R., & Chamberlin, R. (1986). Improving the delivery of prenatal care and outcomes of pregnancy: A randomized trial of nurse home visitation. *Pediatrics,* **77,** 16–28.

O'Leary, K. D. (1980). Pills or skills for hyperactive children. *Journal of Applied Behavior Analysis,* **13,** 191–204.

O'Leary, K. D., & O'Leary, S. G. (Eds.). (1977). *Classroom management.* New York: Pergamon.

Oller, D. K., & Eilers, R. E. (1988). The rate of audition in infant babbling. *Child Development,* **59,** 441–449.

Oller, D. K., Wieman, L. A., Doyle, W. J., & Ross, C. (1976). Infant babbling and speech. *Journal of Child Language,* **3,** 1–11.

Olson, G. M., & Sherman, T. (1983). Attention, learning and memory in infants. In P. H. Mussen (Ed.), *Handbook of child psychology* (4th ed., Vol. 2). New York: Wiley.

Olweus, D. (1979). Stability and aggressive reaction patterns in males: A review. *Psychological Bulletin,* **86,** 852–875.

Olweus, D. (1982). Development of stable aggressive reaction patterns in males. In R. Blanchard & C. Blanchard (Eds.), *Advances in the study of aggression* (Vol. 1). New York: Academic.

Olweus, D., Mattson, A., Schalling, D., & Low, H. (1988). Circulating testosterone levels and aggression in adolescent males: A causal analysis. *Psychosomatic Medicine,* **50,** 261–272.

Omark, D. R., Strayer, F. F., & Freedman, D. G. (1980). *Dominance relations.* New York: Garland.

Opitz, J. M., & Sutherland, G. R. (1984). Conference report: International workshop on the fragile X and X-linked mental retardation. *American Journal of Medical Genetics,* **17,** 5–94.

Ornstein, P. A., Larus, D. M., & Clubb, P. A. (1992). Understanding children's testimony: Implications of research on the development of memory. In R. Vasta (Ed.), *Annals of Child Development* (Vol. 8). London: Jessica Kingsley Publishers.

Ornstein, P. A., Medlin, R. G., Stone, B. P., & Naus, M. J. (1985). Retrieving for rehearsal: An analysis of active rehearsal in children's memory. *DevelopmentaL Psychology,* **21,** 633–641.

Ornstein, P. A., & Naus, M. J. (1983). "Rehearsing" according to artificially generated rehearsal patterns: An analysis of active rehearsal. *Bulletin of the Psychonomic Society,* **21,** 419–422.

Ornstein, P. A., & Naus, M. J. (1985). Effects of the knowledge base on children's memory strategies. In H. W. Reese (Ed.), *Advances in child development and behavior,* (Vol. 19). New York: Academic.

O'Rourke, J. F. (1963). Field and laboratory: The decision making behavior of family groups in two experimental conditions. *Sociometry*, **26**, 422–435.

Ostrea, E. M., Chavez, C. J., & Strauss, M. E. (1979). A study of factors that influence the severity of neonatal narcotic withdrawal. *Journal of Addictive Diseases*, **5b**, 74–89.

O'Sullivan, J. T., & Pressley, M. (1984). Completeness of instruction and strategy transfer. *Journal of Experimental Child Psychology*, **38**, 275–288.

Overton, W. F., & Byrnes, J. P. (1991). Cognitive development. In R. M. Lerner, A. C. Petersen, & J. Brooks-Gunn (Eds.), *Encyclopedia of adolescence* (Vol. 1). New York: Garland.

Owen, M., & Cox, M. (1988). Maternal employment and the transition to parenthood. In A. E. Gottfried & A. W. Gottfried (Eds.), *Maternal employment and children's development: Longitudinal research.* New York: Plenum.

Palincsar, A. S., & Brown, A. L. (1984). Reciprocal teaching of comprehension fostering and comprehension monitoring activities. *Cognition and Instruction*, **1**, 117–175.

Palincsar, A. S., & Brown, A. L. (1987). Enhancing instructional time through attention to metacognition. *Journal of Learning Disabilities*, **20**, 66–75.

Palkovitz, R. (1985). Fathers' birth attendance, early contact, and extended contact with their newborns: A critical review. *Child Development*, **56**, 392–406.

Papalia, D., & Olds, S. (1975). *A child's world.* New York: McGraw-Hill.

Parke, R. D. (1977). Punishment in children: Effects, side effects and alternative strategies. In H. Hom & P. Robinson (Eds.), *Psychological processes in early education* (pp. 71–97). New York: Academic.

Parke, R. D. (1981). *Fathers.* Cambridge, MA: Harvard University Press.

Parke, R. D. (1990). In search of fathers: A narrative of en empirical journey. In I. Sigel & G. Brody (Eds.), *Methods of family research* (Vol. 1, pp. 153–188). Hillsdale, NJ: Erlbaum.

Parke, R. D., & Beitel, A. (1986). Hospital based intervention for fathers. In M. E. Lamb (Ed.), *The father's role: Applied perspectives.* New York: Wiley.

Parke, R. D., Cassidy, J., Burks, V. M., Carson, J. L., & Boyum, L. (1992). Family contributions to peer relationships among young children. In R. D. Parke & G. Ladd (Eds.), *Family-peer relations: Modes of linkage.* Hillsdale, NJ: Erlbaum.

Parke, R. D., MacDonald, K. B., Beitel, A., & Bhavnagri, N. (1988). The role of the family in the development of peer relationships. In R. D. Peters & R. J. McMahon (Eds.), *Social learning and systems approaches to marriage and the family.* New York: Breiner/Mazel.

Parke, R. D., & O'Leary, S. E. (1976). Father-mother-infant interaction in the newborn period: Some findings, some observations and some unresolved issues. In K. Riegel & J. Meacham (Eds.), *The developing individual in a changing world: Social and environmental issues* (Vol. 2). The Hague: Mouton.

Parke, D., O'Leary, S. E., & West, S. (1972). Mother-father-newborn interaction: Effect of maternal medication, labor and sex of infant. *Proceedings of the American Psychological Association*, **7**, 85–86.

Parke, R. D., & Slaby, R. G. (1983). The development of aggression. In E. M. Hetherington (Ed.), *Handbook of child psychology:* Vol. 4. *Socialization, personality and social development.* New York: Wiley.

Parke, R. D., & Tinsley, B. J. (1987). Family interaction in infancy. In J. Osofsky (Ed.), *Handbook of infant development* (2nd ed.). New York: Wiley.

Parker, J. G., & Asher, S. R. (1982). Peer acceptance and later personal adjustment: Are low accepted children at risk? *Psychological Bulletin*, **102**.

Parker, J. G., & Asher, S. R. (1992). The impact of friendship on loneliness of rejected children. *Child Development*, **63**.

Parker, J. G., & Gottman, J. M. (1989). Social and emotional development in a relational context: Friendship interaction from early childhood to adolescence. In T. J. Berndt & G. W. Ladd (Eds.), *Peer relationships in child development.* New York: Wiley.

Parkhurst, J. T., & Asher, S. R. (1992). Peer rejection in middle school: Subgroup differences in behavior, loneliness and interpersonal concerns. *Developmental Psychology*, **28**, 231–241.

Pasamanick, B., & Knoblock, H. (1966). Retrospective studies on the epidemiology of reproductive casualty: Old and new. *Merrill-Palmer Quarterly of Behavior and Development*, **12**, 7–26.

Pascual-Leone, J. (1980). Constructive problems for constructive theories. In R. H. Kluwe & H. Spada (Eds.), *Developmental models of thinking.* New York: Academic.

Pascual-Leone, J. A. (1989). Constructive problems for constructive theories: The current relevance of Piaget's work and a critique of information processing simulation psychology. In H. Spada & R. Kluwe (Eds.), *Developmental Models of Thinking.* New York: Academic Press.

Patterson, C. J., & Kister, M. C. (1981). Development of listener skills for referential communication. In W. P. Dickerson (Eds.), *Children's oral communication skills.* New York: Academic.

Patterson G. R. (Ed.). (1990). *Depression and aggression in family interaction.* Hillsdale, NJ: Erlbaum.

Patterson, G. R. (1982). *Coercive family process.* Eugene, OR: Castalia Press.

Patterson, G. R., & Bank, L. (1989). Some amplifying mechanisms for pathologic processes in families. In M. Gunnar & E. Thelen (Eds.), *Systems and development: The Minnesota Symposium on Child Psychology* (Vol. 22, pp. 167–209). Hillsdale, NJ: Erlbaum.

Patterson, G. R., Capaldi, D., & Bank, L. (in press). Two paths to delinquency: The early and late starter models. In K. B. Rubin & D. Pepler (Eds.), *The development and treatment of childhood aggression.* Hillside, NJ: Erlbaum.

Patterson, G. R., & Capaldi, D. M. (1991). Antisocial parents: Unskilled and vulnerable. In P. A. Cowan & E. M. Hetherington (Eds.), *Family transitions.* Hillsdale, NJ: Erlbaum.

Patterson, G. R., DeBarshyshe, B., & Ramsey, R. (1989). A developmental perspective on antisocial behavior. *American Psychologist.* **44**, 329–335.

Patterson, G. R., Reid, J. B., & Dishion, T. J. (1989). *Antisocial boys.* Eugene, OR: Castilia.

Patterson, G. R., & Stouthamer-Loeber, M. (1984). The correlation of family management practices and delinquency. *Child Development,* **55**, 1299–1307.

Payne, J. S., Kauffman, J. M., Brown, G. B., & DeMott, R. M. (1974). *Exceptional children in focus.* Columbus, OH: Merrill.

Pearl, R. (1985). Children's understanding of others' need for help: Effects of problem explicitness and type. *Child Development,* **56**, 735–745.

Pearson, J. L., Hunter, A. G., Ensminger, M. E., & Kellam, S. G. (1990). Black grandmothers in multigenerational households. *Child Development,* **61,** 434–442.

Pedersen, F. A., Zaslow, M. J., Cain, R. L., & Anderson, B. J. (1981). Cesarean childbirth: Psychological implications for mothers and fathers. *Infant Mental Health Journal,* **2,** 257–263.

Pederson, F. A., Zaslow, M., Cain, R., & Anderson, B. (1980). *Cesarean birth: The importance of a family perspective.* Paper presented at the International Conference on Infant Studies, New Haven, CT.

Pennington, B. F., Bender, B., Puck, M., Salenblatt, J., & Robinson, A. (1982). Learning disabilities in children with sex chromosome anomalies. *Child Development,* **53,** 1182–1192.

Pepler, D., Corter, C., & Abramovitch, R. (1982). Social relations among children. Comparisons of siblings and peer interaction. In K. Rubin & H. S. Ross (Eds.), *Peer relationships and social skills in childhood* (pp. 209–227). New York: Springer-Verlag.

Perner, J., Frith, U., Leslie, A. M., & Leekman, S. R. (1989). Exploration of the autistic child's theory of mind: Knowledge, belief and communication. *Child Development,* **60**, 689–700.

Perry, D. (1990). The socialization of aggression. In M. Lewis (Ed.), *Handbook of developmental psychopathology.* New York: Plenum.

Perry, D. G. (1990). The development of aggression. In M. Lewis (Ed.), *Handbook of Developmental Psychopathology.* New York: Plenum.

Perry, D. G., & Bussey, K. (1977). Self-reinforcement in high- and low-aggressive boys following acts of aggression. *Child Development,* **48,** 653–657.

Perry, D. G., Perry, L., & Boldizar, J. P. (1990). Learning of aggression. In M. Lewis & S. M. Miller (Eds.), *Handbook of developmental psychopathology* (pp. 135–146). New York: Plenum.

Perry, D. G., & Perry, L. C. (1974). Denial of suffering in the victim as a stimulus to violence in aggressive boys. *Child Development,* **45,** 55–62.

Perry, D. G., & Perry, L. C. (1983). Social learning, causal attribution, and moral internalization. In J. Bisanz, G. L. Bisanz, & R. V. Kail, Jr. (Eds.), *Learning in children: Progress in cognitive development research.* New York: Springer-Verlag.

Perry, D. G., & Perry, L. C. (1990). The development of aggression in childhood. In M. Lewis (Ed.), *Handbook of developmental psychopathology.* New York: Plenum.

Perry, D. G., Perry, L. C., & Weiss, R. J. (1989). Sex differences in the consequences children anticipate for aggression. *Developmental Psychology,* **25,** 312–320.

Peters, A. M. (1983). *The units of language.* New York: Cambridge University Press.

Peters, M. F. (1981). Parenting in black families with young children: A historical perspective. In H. McAdoo (Ed.), *Black families.* Newbury Park, CA: Sage.

Petersen, A. C., & Gitelson, I. B. (1984). *Toward understanding sex-related differences in cognitive performance.* New York: Academic.

Petersen, A. C., & Taylor, B. (1980). The biological approach to adolescence. In J. Adelson (Ed.), *Handbook of adolescent psychology.* New York: Wiley.

Pettit, G. S., Bakshi, A., Dodge, K. A., & Coie, J. D. (1990). The emergence of social dominance in young boys' play groups: Developmental differences and behavioral correlates. *Developmental Psychology,* **26,** 1017–1025.

Pettit, G. S., & Bates, J. E. (1989). Family interaction patterns and children's behavior problems from infancy to 4 years. *Developmental Psychology,* **25,** 413–420.

Phillips, D. (1991). With a little help: Children in poverty and child care. In A. Huston (Ed.), *Children and poverty.* New York: Cambridge University Press.

Phillips, J. (1969). *The origin of intellect: Piaget's theory.* San Francisco: Freeman.

Piaget, J. (1932). *The moral judgment of the child.* New York: Harcourt, Brace.

Piaget, J. (1951). *Play, dreams and imitation in childhood.* New York: Norton.

Piaget, J. (1952). *The origins of intelligence in children.* New York: International Universities Press.

Piaget, J. (1960). *The child's conception of the world.* London: Routledge.

Pianta, R., Egeland, B., & Erickson, M. F. (1989). The antecedents of maltreatment: Results of the mother-child interaction research project. In D. Cicchetti & V. Carlson (Eds.), *Child maltreatment: Theory and research on the causes and consequences of child abuse and neglect* (pp. 203–253). New York: Cambridge University Press.

Pick, A. D., & Frankel, G. W. (1974). A developmental study of strategies of visual selectivity. *Child Development,* **45**, 1162–1165.

Pick, A. D., & Palmer, C. F. (1989). Development of the perception of musical events. In J. Dowling & T. Tighe (Eds.), *The understanding of melody and rhythm.* Hillsdale, NJ: Erlbaum.

Pick, H. (1992). E. J. Gibson's contributions to developmental psychology. *Developmental Psychology, 28,*

Pietz, J., Benninger, C., Schmidt, H., Scheffner, D., & Bickel, H. (1988). Long term development of intelligence (I.Q. and EEG in 34 children with phenylketonuria treated early). *European Journal of Pediatrics,* **147,** 361–367.

Pillow, B. H. (1989). Early understanding of perception as a source of knowledge. *Journal of Experimental Child Psychology,* **47,** 116–129.

Pinker, S. (1987). Constant satisfaction networks as implementation of nativist theories of language acquisition. In B. McWhinney (Ed.), *Mechanisms of language learning.* Hillsdale, NJ: Erlbaum.

Pleck, J. H. (1979). Men's family work: Three perspectives and some new data. *Family Coordinator,* **28,** 481–488.

Pleck, J. H. (1984). Husbands' paid work and family roles: Current research issues. In H. Lapata & J. H. Pleck (Eds.), *Research in the inter-weave of social roles. Vol. 3. Families and jobs.* Greenwich, CT: JAI Press.

Plomin, R. (1986). *Development, genetics, and psychology.* Hillsdale, NJ: Erlbaum.

Plomin, R. (1989). Environment and genes: Determinants of behavior. *American Psychologist,* **44,** 105–111.

Plomin, R. (1990a). *Nature and nurture.* Pacific Grove, CA: Brooks/Cole.

Plomin, R. (1990b). The role of inheritance in behavior. *Science,* **248,** 183–188.

Plomin, R., & Bergeman, C. S. (1991). The nature of nurture: Genetic influence on "environmental" measures. *Behavioral and Brain Sciences,* **14,** 373–385.

Plomin, R., & Daniels, D. (1987). Why are children in the same family so different from one another? *The Behavioral and Brain Sciences,* **10,** 1–16.

Plomin, R., & DeFries, J. C. (1983). The Colorado adoption study. *Child Development,* **54,** 276–289.

Plomin, R., & DeFries, J. C. (1985). *Origins of individual differences in infancy.* New York: Academic.

Plomin, R., DeFries, J. C., & Loehlin, J. C. (1977). Genotype-environment interaction and correlation in the analysis of human behavior. *Psychological Bulletin,* **84,** 309–322.

Plomin, R., McClearn, G. E., Pedersen, N. L., Nesselroade, J. R., & Bergeman, C. S. (1988). Genetic influence on childhood family environment perceived retrospectively from the last half of the life span. *Developmental Psychology,* **24,** 738–745.

Plomin, R., & Rende, R. (1990). Human behavioral genetics. *Annual Review of Psychology,* **42,** 161–190.

Plomin, R., & Rowe, D. C. (1979). Genetic and environmental etiology of social behavior in infancy. *Developmental Psychology,* **15,** 62–72.

Pollitt, E., Gorman, K., & Metallinos-Katsaras, E. (1992). Long-term developmental consequences of intrauterine and postnatal growth retardation in rural Guatemala. In G. J. Suci & S. S. Robertson (Eds.), *Future directions in infant development research* (pp. 43–70). New York: Springer-Verlag.

Pomerleau, A., Bolduc, D., Malcuit, G., & Cossette, L. (1990). Pink or blue: Environmental gender stereotypes in the first two years of life. *Sex Roles,* **22,** 359–367.

Porac, C., & Coren, S. (1981). *Lateral preferences and human behavior.* New York: Springer-Verlag.

Porter, R. H., Cernock, J. M., & McLaughlin, F. J. (1983). Maternal recognition of neonates through olfactory cues. *Physiology and Behavior,* **30,** 151–154.

Powell, L. F. (1974). The effect of extra stimulation and maternal involvement on the development of low-birth-weight infants and on maternal behavior. *Child Development,* **45,** 106–113.

Power, T. G., & Parke, R. D. (1982). Play as a context for early learning: Lab and home analyses. In L. M. Laosa & I. E. Sigel (Eds.), *The family as a learning environment.* New York: Plenum.

Pratt, M. W., Kerig, P., Cowan, P. A., & Cowan, C. P. (1988). Mothers and fathers teaching 3 year olds: Authoritative parenting and adult scaffolding of young children's learning. *Developmental Psychology,* **24,** 832–839.

Pressley, M., Cariglia-Bull, T. Deane, S., & Schneider, W. (1987). Short-term memory, verbal competence, and age as predictors of imagery instructional effectiveness. *Journal of Experimental Child Psychology,* **43**, 194–211.

Pressley, M., Heisel, B. E., McCormick, C. G., & Nakamura, G. V. (1982). Memory strategy instruction. In C. J. Brainerd and M. Pressley (Eds.), *Progress in cognitive development research: Vol. 2. Verbal processes in children.* New York: Springer-Verlag.

Pulkkinen, L. (1982). Self-control and continuity from childhood to adolescence. In P. B. Baltes & O. G. Brim (Eds.), *Life-span development and behavior* (Vol. 4). New York: Academic.

Purcell, P., & Stewart, L. (1990). Dick and Jane in 1989. *Sex Roles,* **22,** 177–185.

Puttalaz, M. (1987). Maternal behavior and sociometric status. *Child Development,* **58,** 324–340.

Puttalaz, M., & Gottman, J. M. (1981). Social skills and peer acceptance. In S. R. Asher & J. M. Gottman (Eds.), *The development of children's friendships.* New York: Cambridge University Press.

Puttalaz, M., & Heflin, A. H. (1990). Parent-child interaction. In S. R. Asher & J. D. Coie (Eds.), *Peer rejection in childhood.* New York: Cambridge University Press.

Quigley, M. E., Shechon, K. L., Wilkes, M. M., & Yen, S. S. C. (1979). Effects of maternal smoking on circulating catecholamine levels and fetal heart rates. *American Journal of Obstetrics and Gynecology,* **133,** 685–690.

Quinn, B., & Goldberg, S. (1977, March). *Feeding and fussing: Parent-infant interaction as a function of neonatal medical status.* Paper presented at the biennial meeting of the Society for Research in Child Development, New Orleans.

Radin, N. (1976). The role of the father in cognitive academic and intellectual development. In M. E. Lamb (Ed.), *The role of the father in child development.* New York: Wiley-Interscience.

Radke-Yarrow, M., Cummings, E. M., Kuczynski, L., & Chapman, M. (1985). Patterns of attachment in two- and three-year-olds in normal families and families with parental depression. *Child Development,* **56**, 884–893.

Radke-Yarrow, M., & Zahn-Waxler, C. (1983). Roots, motives and patterns in children's prosocial behavior. In J. Reykowski, T. Karylowski, D. Bar-Tal, & E. Staub (Eds.), *Origins and maintenance of prosocial behaviors.* New York: Plenum.

Radke-Yarrow, M., Zahn-Waxler, C., & Chapman, M. (1983). Children's prosocial dispositions and behavior. In E. M. Hetherington (Ed.), *Handbook of child psychology: Vol. 4. Socialization, personality and social development.* New York: Wiley.

Ramey, C. T., Bryant, D. M., Campbell, F. A., Sparling, J. J., & Wasik, B. H. (1988). Early intervention for high-risk children: The Carolina early intervention program. In R. H. Price, E. Cowen, R. Lorien, and J. Ramos-McKay (Eds.), *Fourteen ounces of prevention: A casebook for practitioners.* Washington, DC: American Psychological Association.

Ramey, C. T., Bryant, D., Sparling, J. T., & Wasik, B. H. (1985). Educational interventions to enhance intellectual development. In S. Harel & N. Nastasiow (Eds.), *The at-risk infant: Psycho/socio/medical aspects.* Baltimore: Paul H. Brooks.

Ramey, C. T., Lee, M. W., & Burchinal, M. R. (1989). Developmental plasticity and predictability: Consequences of ecological change. In M. Bornstein & N. A. Krasnegor (Eds.) *Stability and continuity in mental development* (pp. 217–234). Hillsdale, NJ: Erlbaum.

Ramirez, O. (1989). Mexican-American children and adolescents. In J. T. Gibbs & L. N. Huang (Eds.), *Children of color.* San Francisco: Jossey-Bass.

Rapoport, J. L., Buchsbaum, M. S., Zahn, T. P., Weingartner, H., Ludlow, C., & Mikkelson, E. J. (1978). Dextroamphetamine: Cognitive and behavioral effects in normal prepubertal boys. *Science,* **199**, 560–563.

Raudenbusch, S. W. (1984). Magnitude of teacher expectancy effects on pupil IQ as a function of credibility of expectancy induction: A synthesis from 18 experiments. *Journal of Experimental Psychology,* **76,** 85–97.

Rauh, V. A., Achenbach, T. M., Nurcombe, B., Howell, C. T., & Teti, D. M. (1988). Minimizing adverse effects of low birthweight: Four-year results of an early intervention program. *Child Development,* **59,** 544–553.

Redd, W. H. (1988). Behavioral medicine in pediatric oncology. *Newsletter of the Society of Pediatric Psychology,* **12,** 7–13.

Reed, E. W., & Reed, S. C. (1965). *Mental retardation: A family study.* Philadelphia: Saunders.

Reese, H. W. (1962). Verbal mediation as a function of age level. *Psychological Bulletin,* **59,** 502–509.

Reid, J. B., Taplin, P. S., & Loeber, R. (1981). A social interactional approach to the treatment of abusive families. In R. B. Stuart (Ed.), *Violent behavior: Social learning approaches to prediction, management and treatment.* New York: Brunner/Mazel.

Reid, P. T., Tate, C. S., & Berman, P. W. (1989). Preschool children's self-presentations in situations with infants: Effects of sex and race. *Child Development,* **60,** 710–714.

Reilly, T. W., Entwisle, D. R., & Doering, S. G. (1987). Socialization into parenthood: A longitudinal study of the development of self evaluations. *Journal of Marriage and the Family,* **49,** 295–308.

Reiss, A. L., & Freund, L. (1990). Fragile X syndrome, DSM-III-R, and autism. *Journal of American Academy of Child and Adolescent Psychiatry,*

Reiss, D., Hetherington, E. M., & Plomin, R. (In press). The separate social worlds of teenage siblings. In E. M. Hetherington, D. Reiss, & R. Plomin (Eds.), *The separate world of siblings: Impact of non-shared environments on development.* Hillsdale, NJ: Erlbaum.

Reiss, D., & Klein, D. (1987). Paradigm and pathogenesis. In T. Jacob (Ed.), *Family interaction and psychopathology: Theories, methods, and findings* (pp. 203–205). New York: Plenum.

Reiss, D., Plomin, R., & Hetherington, E. M. (1991). Genetics and psychiatry: An unheralded window on the environment. *American Journal of Psychiatry,* **148,** 283–291.

Reissland, N. (1988). Neonatal imitation in the first hour of life. Observations in rural Nepal. *Developmental Psychology,* **24,** 464–469.

Renshaw, P. D., & Asher, S. R. (1983). Children's goals and strategies for social interaction. *Merrill-Palmer Quarterly,* **29,** 353–374.

Rescorla, L. A. (1980). Overextension in early language. *Journal of Child Language,* **7,** 321–335.

Resnick, M. B., Stralka, K., Carter, R. L., Ariet, M., Bucciarelli, R. L., Furlough, R. R., Evass, J. H., Curran, J. S., & Ausbon, W. W. (1990). Effects of birthweight and socio-demographic variables on mental development of neonatal intensive care unit survivors. *American Journal of Obstetrics and Gynecology,* **162,** 374–378.

Rest, J. R. (1979). *Development in judging moral issues.* Minneapolis: University of Minnesota Press.

Rest, J. R. (1983). Morality. In J. Flavell & E. Markman (Eds.), *Handbook of child psychology: Vol. 3. Cognitive development.* New York: Wiley.

Rest, J. R. (1986). Moral development: Advances in research and theory. New York: Praeger.

Rest, J. R., Davison, M. L., & Robbins, S. (1978). Age trends in judging moral issues: A review of cross-sectional longitudinal and sequential studies of the Defining Issues Test. *Child Development,* **49,** 263–279.

Revelle, G. L., Wellman, H. M., & Karabenick, J. D. (1985). Comprehension monitoring in preschool children. *Child Development,* **56,** 654–663.

Revill, S. I., & Dodge, J. A. (1978). Psychological determinants of infantile pyloric stenosis. *Archives of Disease in Childhood,* **53,** 66–68.

Rheingold, H., & Eckerman, C. (1970). The infant separates himself from his mother. *Science,* **168,** 78–83.

Rheingold, H. L. (1982). Little children's participation in the work of adults, a nascent prosocial behavior. *Child Development,* **53,** 114–125.

Rheingold, H. L., & Cook, K. V. (1975). The content of boys' and girls' rooms as an index of parent behavior. *Child Development,* **46,** 459–463.

Rheingold, H. L., & Eckerman, C. O. (1973). The fear of strangers hypothesis: A critical review. In H. Reese (Ed.), *Advances in child development and behavior* (Vol. 8, pp. 185–222). New York: Academic.

Rheingold, H. L., Hay, D. F., & West, M. J. (1976). Sharing in the second year of life. *Child Development,* **47,** 1148–1158.

Rice, M. L. (1990). Preschoolers QUIL: Quick incidental learning of words. In G. Gontiramsdem & C. Snow (Eds.), *Children's Language* (Vol. 7). Hillsdale, NJ: Erlbaum.

Rice, M. L. (1989). Children's language acquisition. *American Psychologist,* **44,** 149–156.

Rice, M. L. & Woodsmall, L. (1988). Lessons from viewing television: Children's word learning when viewing. *Child Development,* **59,** 420–429.

Rice, R. D. (1977). Neurophysiological development in premature infants following stimulation. *Developmental Psychology,* **13**(1), 69–76.

Richard, B. A., & Dodge, K. A. (1982). Social maladjustment and problem-solving in school-aged children. *Journal of Consulting and Clinical Psychology,* **50,** 226–233.

Richards, M. P., & Bernal, J. F. (1971). Social interactions in the first days of life. In H. R. Schaffer (Ed.), *The origins of human relations* (pp. 3–13). New York: Academic.

Richardson, E., Kupertz, S. S., Winsberg, B. G., Maitinsky, S. & Wendell, N. (1988). Effects of methylphenidate dosage in hyperactive reading-disabled children: II. Reading achievement. *Journal of the American Academy of Child and Adolescent Psychiatry,* **27,** 78–87.

Richardson, T. M., & Benbow, C. P. (1990). Long-term effects of acceleration on the social-emotional adjustment of mathematically precocious youths. *Journal of Educational Psychology,* **82,** 464–470.

Richman, N., Graham, P., & Stevenson, J. (1982). *Preschool to school: A behavioral study.* London: Academic.

Riesen, A. H. (1947). The development of visual perception in man and chimpanzee. *Science,* **106,** 107–108.

Rioux, J. W. (1968). The disadvantaged child in school. In J. Helmuth (Ed.), *The disadvantaged child.* New York: Brunner Mazel.

Ritter, P. L., Mont-Reynaud, R., & Dornbusch, S. M. (1990). Minority parents and their youth: Concern, encouragement and support for school achievement. Unpublished manuscript, Stanford University.

Robbins, L. C. (1963). The accuracy of parental recording of aspects of child development and of child rearing practices. *Journal of Abnormal and Social Psychology,* **66,** 261–270.

Roberts, G. C. (1987). The sporting life: Cultivating young minds. *1987 Medical and Health Annual* (pp. 156–169). Chicago, IL: Encyclopaedia Britannica.

Roberts, J. A. M. (1989). Echolalia and comprehension in autistic children. *Journal of Autism and Developmental Disorder,* **19,** 271–281.

Roberts, R. J. (1981). Errors and the assessment of cognitive development. *New Directions for Child Development,* **12,** 237–238.

Robertson, E. G. (1981). Adolescence, physiological maturity, and obstetric outcomes. In K. G. Scott, T. Field, & E. Robertson (Eds.), *Teenaged parents and their offspring.* New York: Grune & Stratton.

Robins, L. N. (1979). Follow-up studies. In H. C. Quay & J. S. Werry (Eds.), *Psychopathological disorders of childhood* (2nd ed.). New York: Wiley.

Robinson, J. L., Kagan, J., Reznick, J. S., & Corley, R. (1993). The heritability of inhibited and uninhibited behavior: A twin study. *Developmental Psychology,* **29.**

Roche, A. F. (Ed.). (1979). Secular trends: Human growth, maturation, and development. *Monographs of the Society for Research in Child Development,* **44** (Serial No. 179).

Rodin, J. (1981). Current status of the internal-external hypothesis for obesity: What went wrong? *American Psychologist,* **36,** 361–372.

Roffwarg, H. P., Muzio, J. N., & Dement, W. C. (1966). Ontogenetic development of the human sleep-dream cycle. *Science,* **152,** 604–619.

Rogoff, B. (1990). *Apprenticeship in thinking: Cognitive development in social context.* New York: Oxford University Press.

Rogoff, B., & Mistry, J. (1985). Memory development in cultural context. In M. Pressley & C. Brainerd (Eds.), *Cognitive learning and memory in children.* New York: Springer-Verlag.

Rogoff, B., & Waddell, K. J. (1982). Memory for information organized in a scene by children from two cultures. *Child Development,* **53,** 1224–1228.

Rolland-Cachera, M. F., Deheeger, M., Bellisle, F., Sempe, M., Guilloud-Bataille, M., & Patoid, E. (1984). Adiposity rebound in children: A simple indicator for predicting obesity. *American Journal of Clinical Nutrition,* **39,** 129–135.

Roopnarine, J. (1992). Father-child play in India. In K. MacDonald (Ed.), *Parent-child play.* Albany: State University of New York Press.

Roosa, M. W. (1984). Maternal age, social class and the obstetric performance of teenagers. *Journal of Youth and Adolescence,* **13,** 365–374.

Rosch, E., & Mervis, C. B. (1975). Family resemblances: Studies in the internal structure of categories. *Cognitive Psychology,* **7,** 573–605.

Rosch, E., Mervis, C. B., Gray, W. D., Johnson, D. M., & Boyes-Braem, P. (1976). Basic objects in natural categories. *Cognitive Psychology,* **8,** 382–439.

Rose, R., & Kaprio, J. (1987). Shared experiences and similarity of personality: Positive data from Finnish and American twins. *Behavioral and Brain Sciences,* **10,** 35–36.

Rosenblith, J. F. (1992a). *In the beginning: Development from conception to age two.* Newbury Park, CA: Sage.

Rosenblith, J. F. (1992b). A singular career: Nancy Bayley. *Developmental Psychology,* **28,** 747–758.

Rosenstein, D., & Oster, H. (1988). Differential facial response to four basic tastes in newborns. *Child Development,* **59,** 1555–1568.

Rosenthal, R. H., & Allen, T. W. (1978). An examination of attention, arousal, and learning dysfunctions of hyperkinetic children. *Psychological Bulletin,* **85,** 689–715.

Rosenthal, R., & Jacobsen, L. (1966). Teachers' expectancies: Determinants of pupils' IQ gains. *Psychological Reports,* **19,** 115–118.

Rosenthal, R., & Jacobsen, L. (1968). *Pygmalion in the classroom.* New York: Holt.

Rosenzweig, M. R. (1966). Environmental complexity, cerebral change, and behavior. *American Psychologist,* **21,** 321–332.

Rosenzweig, M. R., & Bennett, E. L. (1970). Effects of differential environments on brain weights and enzyme activities in gerbils, rats, and mice. *Developmental Psychobiology,* **2,** 87–95.

Rosett, H. L., Weiner, L., Zuckerman, B., McKinlay, S., & Edelin, K. C. (1980). Reduction of alcohol consumption during pregnancy with benefits to the newborn. *Alcoholism: Clinical and Experimental Research,* **4,** 178–184.

Ross, A. O. (1978). Behavior therapy with children. In S. L. Garfeld & A. E. Bergin (Eds.), *Handbook of psychotherapy and behavior change.* New York: Wiley.

Ross, D. M., & Ross, S. A. (1982). *Hyperactivity.* New York: Wiley.

Ross, H. S., & Goldman, B. D. (1977). Infants' sociability toward strangers. *Child Development,* **48,** 638–642.

Rothbart, M. K. (1971). Birth order and mother-child interaction in an achievement situation. *Journal of Personality and Social Psychology,* **17,** 113–120.

Rovee-Collier, C. K. (1986). Infants and elephants: Do they ever forget? Paper presented at a Science and Public Policy Seminar, Washington, DC.

Rovee-Collier, C. K. (1987). Learning and memory in infancy. In J. D. Osofsky (Ed.), *Handbook of infant development,* (2nd ed.) New York: Wiley.

Rovee-Collier, C. K., Cohen, R. Y., & Shlapack, W. (1975). Life span stability in olfactory sensitivity. *Developmental Psychology,* **11,** 311–318.

Rovee-Collier, C. K., & Lipsitt, L. P. (1982). Learning, adaptation and memory in the newborn. In P. Stratton (Ed.), *Psychobiology of the human newborn.* New York: Willey.

Rovet, J., & Netley, C. (1983). The triple X chromosome syndrome in childhood: Recent empirical findings. *Child Development,* **54,** 831–845.

Rubenstein, J. L., Huren, T., Horssman, D., Rubin, C., & Stockler, C. (1988, March). *Suicidal behavior in normal adolescents. Risk and protective factors.* Paper presented at the biennial meeting of the Society for Research in Adolescence, Alexandria, VA.

Rubin, J. Z., Provenzano, F. J., & Luria, A. (1974). The eye of the beholder: Parents' views on sex of newborns. *American Journal of Orthopsychiatry,* **43,** 720–731.

Rubin, K. H. (1982). Non-social play in preschoolers: Necessarily evil? *Child Development,* **53,** 651–657.

Rubin, K. H., Fein, G. G., & Vandenberg, B. (1983). Play. In P. H. Mussen (Ed.). *Handbook of child psychology* (Vol. 4). New York: Wiley.

Rubin, K. H., & LeMare, L. (1990). Social withdrawal in childhood: Assessment issues and social commitments. In S. R. Asher & J. D. Coie (Eds.), *Children's status in the peer group.* New York: Cambridge University Press.

Rubin, R. T., Reinisch, J. M., & Haskett, R. F. (1981). Postnatal gonadal steroid effects on human behavior. *Science,* **211,** 1318–1324.

Rubin, Z. (1980). *Children's friendships.* Cambridge, MA: Harvard University Press.

Rubin, Z., & Sloman, J. (1984). How parents influence their children's friendship. In M. Lewis (Ed.), *Beyond the dyad.* New York: Plenum.

Ruble, D. N. (1984). Sex role development. In M. H. Bornstein & M. E. Lamb (Eds.), *Developmental psychology: An advanced textbook.* Hillsdale, NJ: Erlbaum.

Ruble, D. N. (1987). The acquisition of self-knowledge: A self-socialization perspective. In N. Eisenberg (Ed.), *Contemporary topics in developmental psychology.* New York: Wiley.

Ruble, D. N. (1988). Sex role development. In M. H. Bornstein & M. E. Lamb (Eds.), *Developmental psychology: An advanced textbook* (2nd ed., (pp. 411–460). Hillsdale, NJ: Erlbaum.

Ruble, D. N., Boggiano, A. K., Feldman, N. S., & Loebl, J. H. (1980). Developmental analysis of the role of social comparison in self-evaluation. *Developmental Psychology,* **16,** 105–115.

Ruble, T. L. (1983). Sex stereotypes: Issues of change in the 1970's. *Sex Roles,* **9,** 397–402.

Rudy, G. S., & Goodman, G. S. (1991). The effects of participation on children's reports: Implications for children's testimony. *Developmental Psychology,* **27,** 527–538.

Ruff, H. A., & Lawson, K. R. (1990). Development of sustained focussed attention in young children during free play. *Developmental Psychology,* 26, 85–93.

Rugh, R., & Shettles, L. F. (1974). *From conception to birth: The drama of life's beginning.* New York: Harper & Row.

Rushton, J. P., Fulker, D. W., Neale, M. C., Nias, D. K. B., & Eysenck, H. J. (1986). Altruism and aggression: The heritability of individual differences. *Journal of Personality and Social Psychology,* **50,** 1192–1198.

Russell, A., & Finnie, V. (1990). Preschool children's social status and maternal instructions to assist group entry. *Developmental Psychology,* **26,** 603–611.

Russell, A., Russell, G., & Midwinter, D. (1991). Observer effects on mothers and fathers: Self-reported influence during a home observation. *Merrill-Palmer Quarterly.*

Rutter, M. (1977). Individual differences. In M. Rutter & L. Hersov (Eds.), *Child psychiatry: Modern approaches* (pp. 3–21). Oxford, England: Blackwell Scientific.

Rutter, M. (1979). Maternal deprivation, 1972–1978: New findings, new concepts, new approaches. *Child Development,* **50,** 283–305.

Rutter, M. (1982). Syndromes attributed to "minimal brain dysfunction" in childhood. *American Journal of Psychiatry,* **139**, 21–33.
Rutter, M. (1983). Cognitive deficits in the pathogenesis of autism. *Journal of Child Psychology and Psychiatry,* **24**, 513–531.
Rutter, M. (1983). School effects on pupil progress: Research findings and policy implications. *Child Development,* **54,** 1–29.
Rutter, M. (1987). Psychosocial resilience and protective mechanisms. *American Journal of Orthopsychiatry,* **51**, 316–331.
Rutter, M. (1989). Isle of Wight revisited: Twenty-five years of child psychiatric epidemiology. *Journal of the American Academy of Child and Adolescent Psychiatry,* **28**, 633–653.
Rutter, M., & Madge, N. (1976). *Cycles of disadvantage.* London: Heinemann.
Rutter, M., Quinton, D., & Yule, B. (1977). Family pathology and disorder in children. London: Wiley.
Rutter, M., & Schopler, E. (1987). Autism and pervasive developmental disorders: Concepts and diagnostic issues. *Journal of Autism and Developmental Disorders,* **17**, 159–186.
Rutter, M., & Tuma, A. H. (1988). Diagnosis and classification: Some outstanding issues. In M. Rutter, A. Juna, & I. Shann (Eds.), *Assessment and diagnosis in child psychopathology.* New York: Guilford.
Ryan, K. J. (1989). Ethical issues in reproductive endocrinology and infertility. *American Journal of Obstetrics and Gynecology,* **160,** 1415–1417.
Saario. T. M., Jacklin, C. N.., & Tittle, C. (1973). Sex role stereotyping in the public schools. *Harvard Educational Review,* **43**, 386–416.
Saarni, C. (1979). Children's understanding of display rules for expressive behavior. *Developmental Psychology,* **15,** 424–429.
Saarni, C. (1989). Children's understanding of strategic control of emotional expression in social transactions. In C. Saarni & P. Harris (Eds.), *Children's understanding of emotions.* New York: Cambridge University Press.
Saarni, C., & Crowley, M. (1990). The development of emotional regulation: Effects on emotional state and expression. In E. A. Blechman (Ed.), *Emotions and the family.* Hillsdale, NJ: Erlbaum.
Sachs, J. (1985). Prelinguistic development. In J. Berko-Gleason (Ed.), *The development of language.* Columbus, OH: Merrill.
St. John, N. H. (1975). *School desegregation.* New York: Wiley.
Salapatek, P. (1969, December). *The visual investigation of geometric pattern by the one- and two-month-old infant.* Paper presented at the meeting of the American Association for the Advancement of Science, Boston.
Salapatek, P., & Kessen, W. (1966). Visual scanning of triangles by the human newborn. *Journal of Experimental Child Psychology,* **3**, 155–167.
Salomon, G., & Perkins, D. N. (1987). Transfer of cognitive skills from programming when and how? *Journal of Education Computing Research,* **3,** 149–169.
Sameroff, A. J. (1972). Learning and adaptation in infancy. A comparison of models. In H. Reese (Ed.), *Advances in child development and behavior* (Vol. 7). New York: Academic.
Sameroff, A. J. (1977, February). *Caretaking or reproductive casualty determinants in developmental deviations.* Paper presented at the meeting of the American Association for the Advancement of Science, Denver.
Sameroff, A. J. (1983). Developmental systems: Contexts and evolution. In P. H. Mussen (Ed.), *Handbook of child psychology.* New York: Wiley.
Sameroff, A. J., & Cavanaugh, P. J. (1979). Learning in infancy: A developmental perspective. In J. Osofsky (Ed.), *Handbook of infant development.* New York: Wiley.
Sameroff, A. J., & Chandler, M. J. (1975). Reproductive risk and the continuum of caretaking casualty. In F. Horowitz (Ed.), *Review of child development research* (Vol. 4). Chicago: University of Chicago Press.
Sameroff, A. J., & Seifer, R. (1983). Familial risk and child competence. *Child Development,* **54,** 1254–1268.
Sameroff, A. J., Seifer, R., Barocas, R., Zax, M., & Greenspan, S. (1987). Intelligence quotient scores of 4-year-old children: Social-environmental risk factors. *Pediatrics,* **79,** 343–350.
Sameroff, A. J., Seifer, R., & Zax, M. (1982). Early development of children at risk for emotional disorder. *Monographs of the Society for Research in Child Development,* **47** (6, Serial No. 199).
Sameroff, A. J., & Zax, M. (1973). Perinatal characteristics of the offspring of schizophrenic women. *Journal of Nervous and Mental Disease,* **46,** 178–185.
Samuels, H. R. (1977). *The role of the sibling in the infant's social environment.* Paper presented at the biennial meeting of the Society for Research in Child Development, New Orleans.
Sanderson, J. A., & Siegal, M. (1991). *Loneliness in young children.* Unpublished manuscript. University of Queensland, Brisbane, Australia.
Santrock, J. W., & Sitterle, K. A., (1987). Parent-child relationships in step mother families. In

K. Posley & M. Ihinger-Tallman (Eds.), *Remarriage and step parenting: Current research and theory* (p. 135–154). New York: Guilford.

Santrock, J. W., & Warshak, R. A. (1979). Father custody and social development in boys and girls. *Journal of Social Issues,* **43,** 455–569.

Sassone, D., Lambert, N. M., & Sandoval, J. (1981). *The adolescent status of boys previously identified as hyperactive.* Unpublished manuscript. University of California.

Savin-Williams, R. (1987). *Adolescence: An ethological perspective.* New York: Springer-Verlag.

Savlin, R. E. (1987). Developmental and motivational perspectives on cooperative learning: A reconciliation. *Child Development,* **58,** 1161–1167.

Saxby, L., & Bryden, M. P. (1984). Left-ear superiority in children for processing auditory emotional material. *Developmental Psychology,* **20,** 72–80.

Saxby, L., & Bryden, M. P., (1985). Left visual field advantage in children for processing visual emotional stimuli. *Developmental Psychology,* **20,** 253–261.

Saxe, G. B. (1982). Developing forms of arithmetic thought among the Oksapmin of Papua New Guinea. *Developmental Psychology,* **18,** 583–594.

Saxe, G. B. (1988). The mathematics of child street vendors. *Child Development,* **59,** 1415–1425.

Saxe, G. B., Becker, J., Sadeghpour, M., & Sicilian, S. (1989). Developmental differences in children's understanding of number word conventions. *Journal for Research in Mathematics Education,* **20,** 468–488.

Saxe, G. B., Guberman, S. R., & Gearhart, M. (1987). Social processes in early number development. *Monographs of the Society for Research in Child Development,* **52,** 162.

Scarr, S. (in press). Developmental theories for the 1990s: Development and individual differences. *Child Development.*

Scarr, S., & Carter-Saltzman, L. (1980). Twin method: Defense of a critical assumption. *Behavior Genetics,* **9,** 527–542.

Scarr, S., & Kidd, K. K. (1983). Developmental behavior genetics. In M. M. Haith & J. J. Campos (Eds.), *Handbook of child psychology: Vol. 2. Infancy and developmental psychobiology* (4th ed.) (pp. 345–433). New York: Wiley.

Scarr, S., & McCartney, K. (1983). How people make their own environments: A theory of genotype environment effects. *Child Development,* **54,** 424–435.

Scarr, S., Phillips, D., & McCartney, K. (1990). Facts, fantasies and the future of child care in the United States. *Psychological Science,* **1,** 26–35.

Scarr, S., Webber, P. L., Weinberg, R. A., & Wittig, M. A. (1981). Personality resemblance among adolescents and their parents in biologically related and adoptive families. *Journal of Personality and Social Psychology,* **40,** 885–898.

Scarr, S., & Weinberg, R. A. (1976). IQ test performance of black children adopted by white families. *American Psychologist,* **31,** 726–739.

Scarr, S., & Weinberg, R. A. (1977). Intellectual similarities within families of both adopted and biological children. *Intelligence,* **1**(2), 170–191.

Scarr, S., & Weinberg, R. A. (1983). The Minnesota adoption studies: Genetic differences and malleability. *Child Development,* **54,** 260–267.

Scarr-Salapetek, S. (1971). Race, social class and IQ. *Science,* **174,** 1285–1292.

Scarr-Salapatek, S. (1971). Unknowns in the IQ equation. *Science,* **174,** 1223–1228.

Scarr-Salapatek, S., & Williams, M. (1972). The effects of early stimulation on low-birthweight infants. *Child Development,* **43,** 509–519.

Schaffer, H. R. (1966). The onset of fear of strangers and the incongruity hypothesis. *Journal of Child Psychology and Psychiatry,* **7,** 95–106.

Schaffer, H. R. (1971). *The growth of sociability.* London: Penguin.

Schaffer, H. R. (1977). *Mothering.* Cambridge, MA: Harvard University Press.

Schaffer, H. R., & Emerson, P. E. (1964). The development of social attachments in infancy. *Monographs of the Society for Research in Child Development,* **29**(3, Serial No. 94).

Schaivi, R. C., Thelgaard, A., Owen, D., & White, D. (1984). Sex chromosome anomalies, hormones and aggressitivity. *Archives of General Psychiatry,* **41,** 93–99.

Schank, R. C., & Abelson, R. P. (1977). Scripts, plans, goals and understanding. Hillsdale, NJ: Erlbaum.

Schieffelin, B. B., & Ochs, E. (1987). *Language socialization across cultures.* New York: Cambridge University Press.

Schiff, M. & Lewontin, R. (1986). *Education and class.* Oxford, England: Clarendon Press.

Schlossman, S., & Cairns, R. B. (1993). Problem girls: Observations on past and present. In G. Elder, Jr., J. Modell, & R. D. Parke (Eds.), *Children in time and place.* New York: Cambridge University Press.

Schnoll, S. H. (1986). Pharmacologic basis of perinatal addiction. In I. J. Chasnoff (Ed.), *Drug use in pregnancy: mother and child.* Lancaster, England: MTP Press.

Schofield, J. W. (1981). Complementary and conflicting identities: Images and interaction in an interracial school. In S. R. Asher & J. M. Gottman (Eds.), *The development of children's friendships.* New York: Cambridge University Press.

Scholnick, E. K., Fein, G. G., & Campbell, P. F. (1990). Changing predictors of map use in way finding. *Developmental Psychology,* **26,** 188–193.

Schultz, M. S. (1991). *Linkages among both parents. work roles, parenting style and children's adjustment to school.* Paper presented at the meeting of the Society for Research in Child Development. Seattle, WA.

Schwartz, R. G., & Leonard, L. B. (1984). Words, objects and actions in early lexical acquisition. *Journal of Speech and Hearing Research,* **27,** 119–127.

Schwartz-Bickenbach, D., Sculte-Hobein, B., Abt, S., Plum, C., & Nau, H. (1987). Smoking and passive smoking during infancy. *Toxicology Letters,* **35,** 73–81.

Scribner, S. (1985). Vygotsky's use of history. In J. V. Wertsch (Ed.), *Culture, communication and cognition: Vygotskian perspectives.* New York: Cambridge University Press.

Sears, R. R., Maccoby, E. E., & Levin, H. (1957). *Patterns of child rearing.* New York: Harper & Row.

Seashore, M. J., Leifer, A. D., Barnett, C. R., & Leiderman, P. H. (1973). The effects of denial of early mother-infant interaction on maternal self-confidence. *Journal of Personality and Social Psychology,* **26,** 369–378.

Seavey, C. A., Katz, P. A., & Zalk, S. R. (1975). Baby X: The effect of gender labels on adult responses to infants. *Sex Roles,* **1,** 103–109.

Sedlack, A. (1989). *National incidence of child abuse and neglect.* Paper presented at the meeting of the Society for Research in Child Development. Kansas City, KS.

Seitz, V. (1988). Methodology. In M. Lamb & M. Bornstein (Eds.), *Developmental psychology: An advanced textbook.* Hillsdale, NJ: Erlbaum.

Seitz, V. (1990). Intervention programs for impoverished children: A comparison of educational and family support models. *Annals of Child Development,* **7,** 73–103.

Seitz, V., Rosenbaum, L. K., & Apfel, N. H. (1985). Effects of family support intervention: A ten-year follow-up. *Child Development,* **56,** 376–391.

Seligman, M. (1970). On the generality of the laws of learning. *Psychological Review,* **77,** 406–418.

Seligman, M. E. P. (1973, June). Fall into helplessness. *Psychology Today,* pp. 43–48.

Seligman, M. E. P. (1974). Depression and learned helplessness. In R. J. Friedman & M. M. Katz (Eds.), *The psychology of depression: Contemporary theory and research.* Washington, DC: Winston-Wiley.

Selman, R. L. (1980). *The growth of interpersonal understanding.* New York: Academic.

Selman, R. L., & Byrne, D. F. (1974). A structural-developmental analysis of levels of role taking in middle childhood. *Child Development,* **45,** 803–806.

Selman, R. L., & Jacquette, D. (1978). Stability and oscillation in interpersonal awareness: A clinical-developmental analysis. In C. B. Keasey (Ed.), *The XXV Nebraska Symposium on Motivation.* Lincoln: Univ. of Nebraska Press.

Serbin, L., & O'Leary, K. D. (1975, December). How nursery schools teach girls to shut up. *Psychology Today.*

Shakin, M., Shakin, D., & Sternglanz, S. H. (1985). Infant clothing: Sex labeling for strangers. *Sex Roles,* **12,** 955–963.

Shantz, C. V. (1983). Social cognition. In J. H. Flavell & E. M. Markman (Eds.), *Handbook of child psychology: Cognitive development* (Vol. 3). New York: Wiley.

Shatz, M. (1983). Communication. In P. H. Mussen (Eds.), *Handbook of child psychology,* (Vol. 3). New York: Wiley.

Shedler, J., & Block, J. (1990). Adolescent drug use and psychological health. *American Psychologist,* **45,** 612–631.

Sherman, J. A. (1980). Mathematics, spatial visualization and related factors: Changes in girls and boys, grdes 8–11. *Journal of Educational Psychology,* **72,** 476–482.

Sherman, M. & Key, C. B. (1932). The intelligence of isolated mountain children. *Child Development,* **3,** 279–290.

Sherman, S. L., Jacobs, P. A., Morton, N. E., Froster-Iskenius, E., Howard-Peebles, P. (1985). Further segregation analyses of the fragile X syndrome with special reference to transmitting males. *Human Genetics,* **69,** 289–299.

Shirley, L. L., & Reynolds, R. E. (1988). Effect of interest on attention and learning. *Journal of Educational Psychology,* **80,** 159–166.

Shirley, M. M. (1933). *The first two years.* Minneapolis: University of Minnesota Press.

Shoda, Y., Mischel, W., & Peake, P. K. (1990). Predicting adolescent cognitive and self-regulatory competencies from preschool delay of gratification: Identifying diagnostic conditions. *Developmental Psychology,* **26,** 978–986.

Shweder, R. A., & Much, M. C. (1987). Determinants of meaning: Discourse and moral socialization. In W. M. Kurtines & J. L. Gewiretz (Eds.), *Moral development through social interaction*. New York: Wiley.

Siegel, A. W., & White, S. H. (1975). The development of spatial representatives of large scale environments. In H. W. Reese (Eds.), *Advances in child development and behavior* (Vol. 10). New York: Academic.

Siegel, L. S. (1981). Infant tests as predictors of cognitive and language development at two years. *Child Development*, **52,** 545–557.

Siegel, M. (1987). Are sons and daughters treated more differently by fathers than mothers? *Developmental Review*, **7**, 183–209.

Siegel, S. (1982). Reproductive, perinatal, and environmental factors as predictors of the cognitive and language development of preterm and full-term infants. *Child Development*, **53,** 963–973.

Siegler, R. S. (1983). Information processing approaches to development. In P. Mussen (Ed.), *Manual of child psychology*. New York: Wiley.

Siegler, R. S. (1987). The perils of averaging data over strategies: An example from children's addition. *Journal of Experimental Psychology: General*, **116,** 250–264.

Siegler, R. S. (1991). *Children's thinking* (2nd ed.). Englewood-Cliffs, NJ: Prentice-Hall.

Siegler, R. S. (1992). The other Alfred Binet. *Developmental Psychology*, **28**, 179–190.

Sigman, M., & Mundy, P. (1989). Social attachments in autistic children. *Journal of the American Academy of Child and Adolescent Psychiatry*, **28**, 74–81.

Signorella, M. L. (1987). Gender schemata: Individual differences and context effects. In L. S. Liben & M. L. Signorella (Eds.), *Children's gender schemata*. San Francisco: Jossey-Bass.

Signorielli, N. (1989). Television and conceptions about sex roles: Maintaining conventionality and the status quo. *Sex Roles*, **21,** 341–360.

Silverstein, B., Petersen, B., & Perdue, L. (1986). Some correlates of the thin standard of bodily attractiveness for women. *International Journal of Eating Disorders*, **5**, 895–906.

Simmons, R. G., & Blyth, D. A. (1987). *Moving into adolescence: The impact of pubertal change and school context*. Hawthorne, NY: Aldine.

Simmons, R. G., Blyth, D. A., & McKinney, K. L. (1984). The social and psychological effects of puberty on white females. In J. Brookes-Gunn & A. C. Peterson (Eds.), *Girls at puberty: Biological, psychological and social perspectives*. New York: Plenum.

Simmons, R. G., Blyth, D. A., Van Cleave, E. F., & Bush, D. M. (1979). Entry into early adolescence: The impact of school structure, puberty, and early dating on self-esteem. *American Sociological Review*, **44**, 948–967.

Simmons, R. G., Burgeson, R., Carlson-Ford, S., & Blyth, D. A. (1987). The impact of cumulative change in early adolescence, *Child Development*, **58**, 1220–1234.

Simmons, R. L., Conger, R. D., & Whitbeck, L. B. (1988). A multistage social learning model of the influences of family and peers upon adolescent substance use. *The Journal of Drug Issues*, **18,** 293–315.

Singer, D., (1976). Reading, writing and race relations. *Trans-action*, **4,**(7), 27–31.

Singer, D. G., & Benton, W. (1989). Caution: Television can be hazardous to a child's mental health. *Developmental and Behavioral Pediatrics*, **10**, 259–261.

Singer, J. L. (1977, August). *Television, imaginative play and cognitive development: Some problems and possibilities*. Paper presented at the meeting of the American Psychological Association, San Francisco.

Singer, J. L., & Singer, D. G. (1980). *Imaginative play in preschoolers: Some research and theoretical implications*. Paper presented at the meeting of the American Psychological Association, Montreal.

Singer, J. L., & Singer, D. G. (1981). *Television, imagination and aggression: A study of preschoolers*. Hillsdale, NJ: Erlbaum.

Singer, J. L., Singer, D. G., Desmond, R., Hirsch, B., & Nicol, A. (1988). Family mediation and children's cognition, aggression and comprehension of television: A longitudinal study. *Journal of Applied Developmental Psychology*, **9**, 329–347.

Siqueland, R. R. (1970). *Biological and experimental determinants of exploration in infancy*. Paper presented at the First National Biological Conference.

Sizer, T. (1984). *Horace's compromise: The dilemma of the American high school*. Boston: Houghton Mifflin.

Skeels, H. (1966). Adult status of children with contrasting early life experiences. *Monographs of the Society for Research in Child Development*, **31** (No. 9).

Skinner, B. F. (1957). *Verbal behavior*. New York: Appleton-Century-Crofts.

Skodak, M., & Skeels, H. (1949). A final follow-up study of one hundred adopted children. *Journal of Genetic Psychology*, **75**, 85–125.

Slaby, R. G., & Frey, K. S. (1975). Development of gender constancy and selective attention to same-sex models. *Child Development*, **46,** 849–856.

Slater, A. M., & Morison, V. (1985). Shape constancy and slant perception at birth. *Perception,* **14**, 337–344.
Slaughter, D. T. (1988). Ethnicity, poverty, and children's educability: A developmental perspective. *Science and Public Policy Seminars.* Washington, DC.
Slaughter-Defoe, D. T., Nakagawa, K., Takanishi, & Johnson, D. J. (1990). Toward cultural/ecological perspectives on schooling and achievement in African- and Asian-American children. *Child Development,* **61,** 363–383.
Slavin, R. E. & Madden, N. A. (1979). School practices that improve race relations. *American Educational Research Journal,* **16,** 169–180.
Slavin, R. E. (1983). *Cooperative learning.* New York: Longman.
Slobin, D. I. (1968). Imitation and grammatical development in children. In N. S. Endler, L. R. Boulter, & H. Osser (Eds.), *Contemporary issues in development in psychology.* New York: Holt.
Slobin, D. I. (1979). *Psycholinguistics.* Glenview, IL: Scott, Foresman.
Slobin, D. I. (1982). Universal and particular in the acquisition of language. In L. R. Gleitman & H. E. Wanner (Eds.), *Language acquisition: The state of the art.* New York: Cambridge University Press.
Slobin, D. I. (1985). *The cross-linguistic study of language acquisition* (Vols. 1 & 2). Hillsdale, NJ: Erlbaum.
Sluckin, A. M., & Smith, R. K. (1977). Two approaches to the concept of dominance in preschool children. *Child Development,* **48,** 917–923.
Smetana, J. G. (1984). Toddler's social interaction regarding moral and conventional transgressions. *Child Development,* **55,** 1767–1776.
Smetana, J. G. (1989). Toddlers' social interactions in the context of moral and conventional transgressions in the home. *Developmental Psychology,* **25,** 499–508.
Smetana, J. G., & Letourneau, K. J. (1984). Development of gender constancy and children's sex-typed free play behavior. *Developmental Psychology,* **20,** 691–696.
Smiley, P. A. (1989). *Individual differences in preschoolers' task persistence.* Poster presented at the biennial meeting of the Society for Research in Child Development, Kansas City, MO.
Smith, B. A., Fillion, T. J., & Blass, E. M. (1990). Orally mediated sources of calming in 1- to 3-day-old human infants. *Developmental Psychology,* **26**, 731–737.
Smith, C. L. (1979). Children's understanding of natural language hierarchies. *Journal of Experimental Child Psychology,* **27**, 437–458.
Smith, P. K., & Connolly, K. J. (1980). *The ecology of preschool behavior.* New York: Cambridge University Press.
Smith, P. K., & Sloboda, J. (1986). Individual consistency in infant-stranger encounters. *British Journal of Developmental Psychology,* **4**, 83–92.
Smith, R. T. (1965). A comparison of socioenvironmental factors in monozygotic and dizygotic twins: Testing an assumption. In S. Vandenberg (Ed.), *Methods and goals of human behavior genetics* (pp. 45–61). New York: Academic.
Smollar, J., & Youniss, J. (1982). Social development through friendship. In K. H. Rubin & H. S. Ross (Eds.), *Peer relationships and social skills in childhood.* New York: Springer-Verlag.
Snarey, J. (1987, June). A question of morality. *Psychology Today,* pp. 6–8.
Snarey, J. R., Reimer, J., & Kohlberg, L. (1985). Development of social-moral reasoning among kibbutz adolescents: A longitudinal cross-cultural study. *Developmental Psychology,* **21,** 3–17.
Snow, C. E., & Hoefnagel-Hohle, M. (1978). The critical period for language acquisition: Evidence from second language learning. *Child Development,* **49**, 1114–1128.
Solkoff, N., Yaffe, S., Weintraub, D., & Blase, B. (1969). Effects of handling on the subsequent developments of premature infants. *Developmental Psychology,* **1,** 765–768.
Sommer, R. (1969). *Personal space.* Englewood Cliffs, NJ: Prentice-Hall.
Sosa, R., Kennell, J., Klaus, M., Robertson, S., & Urrutia, J. (1980). The effect of a supportive companion on perinatal problems, length of labor and mother-infant interaction. *New England Journal of Medicine,* **303**(11), 597–600.
Sostek, A. M., & Anders, T. F. (1981). The biosocial importance and environmental sensitivity of infant sleep-wake behaviors. In K. Bloom (Ed.), *Prospective issues in infancy research.* Hillsdale, NJ: Erlbaum.
Spearman, C. (1927). *The abilities of man.* New York: Macmillan.
Speer, J. R., & Flavell, J. H. (1979). Young children's knowledge of the relative difficulty of recognition and recall memory tasks. *Developmental Psychology,* **15**, 214–217.
Spelke, E. S. (1979). Perceiving bimodally specified events in infancy. *Developmental Psychology,* **15**, 626–636.
Spelke, E. S. (1987). The development of intermodal perception. In P. Salapatek & L. Cohen (Eds.), *Handbook of infant perception: Vol. 2. From perception to cognition* (pp. 233–274). New York: Academic.
Spelke, E. S., & Cortelyou, A. (1981). Perceptual aspects of social knowing: Looking and

listening in infancy. In M. E. Lamb & L. R. Sherrod (Eds.), *Infant social cognition* (pp. 6–84). Hillsdale, NJ: Erlbaum.

Spellacy, W. N., Miller, S. J., & Winegar, A. (1986). Pregnancy after 40 years of age. *Obstetrics and Gynecology,* **68,** 452–454.

Spence, J. T. (1985). Gender identity and its implications for concepts of masculinity and femininity. In T. B. Sonderegger (Ed.), *Nebraska Symposium on Motivation: Psychology and Gender* (Vol. 32). Lincoln: University of Nebraska Press.

Sperling, G. (1960). The information available in brief visual presentations. *Psychological Monographs,* **73.**

Spiker, D., & Ricks, M. (1984). Visual self-recognition in autistic children: Developmental variations. *Child Development,* **55,** 214–225.

Spitz, R., & Wolf, K. (1946). The smiling response: A contribution to the ontogenesis of social relations. *Genetic Psychology Monographs,* **34,** 57–125.

Spitz, R. A. (1946). Anaclitic depression. *Psychoanalytic Study of the Child,* (1),.

Spock, B. (1957). *Baby and child care.* New York: Bantam.

Springer, S. P., & Deutsch, G. (1989). *Left brain, right brain* (3rd ed.). New York: Freeman.

Sroufe, L. A. (1979). Emotional development in infancy. In J. Osofsky (Ed.), *Handbook of infancy.* New York: Wiley.

Sroufe, L. A. (1983). Individual patterns of adaptation from infancy to preschool. In M. Perlmutter (Ed.), *Minnesota Symposium on Child Psychology* (Vol. 16). Hillsdale, NJ: Erlbaum.

Sroufe, L. A., Carlson, E., & Shulman, S. (1993). The development of individuals in relationships: From infancy through adolescence. In D. C. Funder, R. D. Parke, C. Tomlinson-Keasey, K. Widaman, (Eds.), *Studying lives through time: Approaches to personality and development.* Washington, DC: American Psychological Association.

Sroufe, L. A., Waters, E., & Matas, L. (1974). Contextual determinants of infant affectional response. In M. Lewis & L. Rosenblum (Eds.), *Origins of fear.* New York: Wiley.

Sroufe, L. A., & Wunsch, J. P. (1972). The development of laughter in the first year of life. *Child Development,* **43,** 1326–1344.

Stack, C. B. (1974). *All our kin.* New York: Harper & Row.

Stangor, C., & Ruble, D. (1989). Differential influences of gender schemata and gender constancy on children's information processing and behavior. *Social Cognition,* **7,** 353–372.

Stanley, J. C. (1976). Concern for intellectually talented youths: How it originated and fluctuated. *Journal of Clinical Child Psychology,* **5,** 38–42.

Stanley, J. C., & Benbow, C. P. (1983). SMPY's first decade: Ten years of posing problems and solving them. *Journal of Special Education,* **17,** 11–25.

Starr, A. S. (1923). The diagnostic value of the audio-vocal digit memory span. *Psychological Clinic,* **15,** 61–84.

Stassen, H. H., Lykken, D. T., & Bomben, G. (1988). The within-pair EEG similarity of twins reared apart. *European Archives of Psychiatry and Neurological Science,* **237,** 244–252.

Stattin, H., & Magnusson, D. (1990). *Pubertal maturation in female development* (Vol. 2). Hillsdale, NJ: Erlbaum.

Staub, E. (1975). To rear a prosocial child. In D. J. DePalma & J. M. Foley (Eds.), *Moral development, current theory and research.* Hillsdale, NJ: Erlbaum.

Stechler, G., & Halton, A. (1982). Prenatal influences on human development. In B. Buolman (Ed.), *Handbook of developmental psychology* (pp. 175–189). Englewood Cliffs, NJ: Prentice-Hall.

Stein, N. L., & Trabasso, T. (1989). Children's understanding of changing emotional states. In C. Saarni & P. Harris (Eds.), *Children's understanding of emotion.* New York: Cambridge University Press.

Stein, Z. A., & Susser, M. W. (1976). Prenatal nutrition and mental competence. In J. D. Lloyd-Still (Ed.), *Malnutrition and intellectual development* (pp. 39–80). Littleton, MA: Publishing Sciences Group.

Steinberg, L. (1985). *Adolescence.* New York: Knopf.

Steinberg, L. (1986). Latchkey children and susceptibility to peer pressure: An ecological analysis. *Developmental Psychology,* **22,** 433–439.

Steinberg, L. (1990). Interdependence in the family: Autonomy, conflict and harmony in the parent-adolescent relationship. In S. S. Feldman & G. L. Elliot (Eds.), *At the threshold: The developing adolescent* (pp. 255–276). Cambridge, MA: Harvard University Press.

Steinberg, L., Catalano, R., & Dooley, D. (1981). Economic antecedents of child abuse and neglect. *Child Development,* **52,** 975–985.

Steinberg, L., & Darling, N. (in press). The broader context of social influence in adolescence. In R. Silbereisen & E. Todt (Eds.), *Adolescence in context.* New York: Springer.

Steinberg, L., Dornbusch, S. M., & Brown, B. B. (1992). Ethnic differences in adolescent achievement: An ecological perspective. *American Psychologist,* **47,** 723–729.

Steinberg, L., Mounts, N. S., Lamborn, S. D., & Dornbusch, S. M. (1991). Authoritative parenting and adolescent adjustment across varied ecological niches. *Journal of Research on Adolescence,* **1,** 19–36.

Steinberg, L. (1985). *Adolescence.* New York: Knopf.

Steiner, J. E. (1979). Human facial expression in response to taste and smell stimulation. In H. W. Reese & L. P. Lipsitt (Eds.), *Advances in child development and behavior* (Vol. 13). New York: Academic.

Steinglass, P. (1987). A systems view of family interaction and psychopathology. In T. Jacob (Ed.), *Family interaction and psychopathology: Theories, methods, and findings* (pp. 25–65). New York: Plenum.

Stenberg, C., & Campos, J. (1989). The development of anger expressions during infancy. Unpublished manuscript. University of Denver, Denver, Colorado.

Stenberg, C., Campos, J., & Emde, R. N. (1983). The facial expression of anger in seven-month-old infants. *Child Development,* **54,** 178–184.

Stephan, W. G. (1978). School desegregation: An evaluation of predictions made in *Brown v. Board of Education. Psychological Bulletin,* **85,** 217–238.

Stephan, W. G. (1983). *Blacks and Brown: The effects of school desegregation on black students.* Paper commissioned by the National Institute of Education.

Stephan, W. G., & Rosenfield, D. (1982). Racial and ethnic stereotypes. In A. Miller (Ed.), *In the eye of the beholder.* New York: Praeger.

Stern, D. (1977). *The first relationship.* Cambridge, MA: Harvard University Press.

Stern, D. (1985). *The interpersonal world of the infant.* New York: Basic Books.

Stern, D. N. (1985). Affect attunement. In J. Call, E. Galenson, & R. Tyson (Eds.), *Frontiers in infant psychiatry,* (Vol. 2, pp. 3–14). New York: Basic Books.

Stern, M., & Karraker, K. H. (1989). Sex stereotyping of infants: A review of gender labeling studies. *Sex Roles,* **20,** 501–522.

Sternberg, R. J. (1985). *Beyond IQ: A triarchic theory of human intelligence.* Cambridge, England: Cambridge University Press.

Sternberg, R. J. (1988). *The triarchic mind.* New York: Viking.

Sternberg, R. J. (1989). *Mechanisms of cognitive development* (2nd ed.). N.Y.: Cambridge.

Sternberg, R. J., Conway, B. E., Ketron, J. L., & Bernstein, M. (1981). People's conceptions of intelligence. *Journal of Personality and Social Psychology,* **41,** 37–55.

Sternberg, R. J., & Powell, J. S. (1983). The development of intelligence. In J. H. Flavell & E. M. Markman (Eds.), *Cognitive development, Vol. III, Handbook of child psychology.* New York: Wiley.

Stevenson, H. W. (1983, April). Making the grade: School achievement in Japan, Taiwan, and the United States. *Report to Bush Center's Board of Trustees,* pp. 41–51.

Stevenson, H. W., Chen, C., & Uttal, D. H. (1990). Beliefs and achievement: A study of black, white, and hispanic children. *Child Development,* **61,** 508–523.

Stevenson, H. W., & Stigler, J. W. (1992). *The learning gap.* New York: Summit Books.

Stewart, G. D., Hassold, T. J., & Kunit, D. M. (1988). Trisomy 21: Molecular and cytogenic studies of nondisjunction. In H. Harris & K. Hirschhorn (Eds.), *Advances in human genetics* (Vol. 17). New York: Plenum Press.

Stewart, R. B., Mobley, L. A., Van Tuyl, S. S., & Salvador, W. A. (1987). The firstborns adjustment to the birth of a sibling: A longitudinal assessment. *Child Development,* **58,** 341–355.

Stillman, R. J. (1982). In utero exposure to diethylstilbestrol: Adverse effects on the reproductive tract and reproductive performance in male and female offspring. *American Journal of Obstetrics and Gynecology,* **142,** 905–921.

Stipek, D., & McCroskey, J. (1989). Investing in children: Government and workplace policies for parents. *American Psychologist,* **44,** 416–423.

Stipek, D. J., & MacIver, D. (1989). Developmental change in children's assessment of intellectual competence. *Child Development,* **60,** 521–538.

Stoch, M. B., Smyth, P. M., Moodie, A. D., & Bradshaw, D. (1982). Psychosocial outcome and findings after gross undernourishment during infancy: A 20-year developmental study. *Developmental Medicine & Child Neurology,* **24,** 419–436.

Stockard, J., Schmuck, P., Kempner, E., Williams, P., Edson, S., & Smith, M. A. (1980). *Sex equity in education.* New York: Academic.

Stocker, C., Dunn, J., & Plomin, R. (1989). Sibling relationships: Links with child temperament, maternal behavior, and family structure. *Child Development,* **60,** 715–727.

Stoel-Gammon, C., & Otomo, K. (1986). Babbling development of hearing-impaired and normally hearing subjects. *Journal of Speech & Hearing Disorders,* **51,** 33–41.

Stott, D. H. (1971). The child's hazards in utero. In J. G. Howells (Ed.), *Modern perspectives in international child psychiatry.* New York: Brunner/Mazel.

Stott, D. H., & Latchford, S. A. (1976). Prenatal antecedents of child health, development, and behavior: An epidemiological report of incidence and association. *Journal of the American Academy of Child Psychiatry,* **15,** 161–191.

Straughtan, R. (1986). Why act on Kohlberg's moral judgments? In S. Modgil & C. Modgil (Eds.), *Lawrence Kohlberg: Consensus and controversy.* Philadelphia: Falmer Press.

Strayer, F. F. (1980). Current problems in the study of human dominance. In D. Omark, F. F. Strayer, & D. Freedman (Eds.), *Dominance relations.* New York: Garland.

Strayer, F. F. (1984). Biological approaches to the study of the family. In R. D. Parke, R. Emde, H. Macadoo, & G. P. Sackett (Eds.), *Review of child development research: Vol. 7. The family.* Chicago: University of Chicago Press.

Strayer, F. F., & Strayer, J. (1976). An ethological analysis of social agonism and dominance relations among preschool children. *Child Development,* **47,** 980–989.

Strayer, J., & Roberts, W. (1988). Children's empathy and role-taking: Child and parental factors and relations to prosocial behavior. *Journal of Applied Developmental Psychology,*

Streissguth, A. P., Sampson, P. D., & Barr, H. M. (1989). Neurobehavioral dose-response effects of prenatal alcohol exposure in humans from infancy to adulthood. *Annals of the New York Academy of Sciences,* **562,** 145–158.

Stucky, M. F., McGhee, P. E., & Bell, N. G. (1982). Parent-child interaction: The influence of maternal employment. *Developmental Psychology,* **18,** 635–644.

Stunkard, A. J. (1958). The management of obesity. *New York Journal of Medicine,* **58,** 79–87.

Stunkard, A. J., & Burt, V. (1967). Obesity and the body image: II. Age at onset of disturbances in the body. *American Journal of Psychiatry,* **123,** 1442–1447.

Stunkard, A. J., Foch, T. T., & Hrubeck, Z. (1986). A twin study of human obesity. *Journal of the American Medical Association,* **256,** 51–54.

Stunkard, A. J., Sorenson, T. I., Hanis, C., Teasdale, T. W., Chakraborty, R., Schull, W. J., & Schulsinger, F. (1986). An adoption study of human obesity. *New England Journal of Medicine,* **314,** 193–198.

Sue, S., & Okazaki, S. (1990). Asian-American educational achievements: A phenomenon in search of an explanation. *American Psychologist,* **45,** 913–920.

Suess, G. L. (1987). *Consequences of early attachment experiences on competence in preschool.* Unpublished doctoral dissertation. Universitat Regensberg, West Germany.

Sugarman, S. (1987). *Piaget's construction of the child's reality.* Cambridge, England: Cambridge University Press.

Sullivan, H. S. (1953). *The interpersonal theory of psychiatry.* New York: Norton.

Sullivan, L. W. (1987). The risks of the sickle-cell trait: Caution and common sense. *New England Journal of Medicine,* **317,** 830–831.

Summers, M. (1987). *Imitation, dominance, agonism and prosocial behavior: A meta-analysis of sibling behavior.* Paper presented at the meeting of the Society for Research in Child Development. Baltimore, MD.

Suomi, S. J., & Harlow, H. F. (1972). Social rehabilitation of isolate-reared monkeys. *Developmental Psychology,* **6,** 487–496.

Super, C. M. (1981). Cross-cultural research on infancy. In H. C. Triandis & A. Heron (Eds.), *Handbook of cross-cultural psychology developmental psychology* (Vol. 4, pp. 17–53). Boston: Allyn and Bacon.

Super, C. M., Herrera, M. G., & Mora, J. O. (1990). Long-term effects of food supplementation and psychosocial intervention on the physical growth of Columbian infants at risk of malnutrition. *Child Development,* **61,** 29–49.

Sutton-Smith, B. (1976). Current research and theory on play, games and sports. In T. Craig (Ed.), *The humanistic and mental health aspects of sports exercise and recreation.* Chicago: American Medical Association.

Sutton-Smith, B., & Rosenberg, B. (1970). *The sibling.* New York: Holt, Rinehart & Winston.

Swensen, A. (1983). Toward an ecological approach to theory and research in child language acquisition. In W. Fowler (Ed.), *Potentials of childhood* (Vol. 2). Lexington, MA: Heath.

Tagatz, G. E. (1976). *Child development and individually guided education.* Reading, MA: Addison-Wesley.

Tanner, J. M. (1970). Physical growth. In P. H. Mussen (Ed.), *Carmichael's manuscript of child psychology* (Vol. 1, pp. 77–155). New York: Wiley.

Tanner, J. M. (1978). *Fetus into man: Physical growth from conception to maturity.* Cambridge, MA: Harvard University Press.

Tanner, J. M. (1987). Issues and advances in adolescent growth and development. *Journal of Adolescent Health Care,* **8,** 470–478.

Task Force on Pediatric AIDS. (1989). Pediatric AIDS and human immunodeficiency virus infection. *American Psychologist,* **44,** 258–264.

Tauber, K. (1990, September). Desegregation of public school districts: Persistence and change. *Phi Delta Kappan,* pp. 18–24.

Tavris, C. (1992). *The mismeasure of woman.* New York: Simon & Schuster.

Taylor, A. R., Asher, S. R., & Williams, G. A. (1987). The social adaptation of mainstreamed mildly retarded children. *Child Development,* **58,** 1321–1334.

Taylor, M. (1988). Conceptual perspective taking: Children's ability to distinguish what they know from what they see. *Child Development,* **59,** 703–718.

Taylor, N. K., & Kogan, K. L. (1973). Effects of birth of a sibling on mother-child interactions. *Child Psychiatry and Human Development,* **4,** 53–58.

Tellegan, A., Lykken, D. T., Bouchard, T. J., Wilcox, K., Segal, N., & Rowe, S. (1988). Personality similarity in twins reared apart and together. *Journal of Social and Personality Psychology,* **54,** 1031–1039.

Teller, D. Y., & Bornstein, M. H. (1984). Infant color vision. In P. Salapatek & L. B. Cohen (Eds.), *Handbook of infant perception.* New York: Academic.

Templin, M. (1958). Certain language skills in children: Their development and interrelationships. *University of Minnesota Institute of Child Welfare Monograph,* **26.**

Terman, L. M. (1954). The discovery and encouragement of exceptional talent. *American Psychologist,* **9,** 221–230.

Terry, R., & Coie, J. D. (1991). A comparison of methods for defining sociometric status among children. *Developmental Psychology,* **27,** 867–880.

Tharp, R. G. (1989). Psychocultural variables and constants: Effects on teaching and learning in schools. *American Psychologist,* **44,** 349–359.

Thelen, E. (1986). Treadmill-elicited stepping in seven-month-old infants. *Child Development,* **57,** 1498–1506.

Thelen, E. (1988). Self-organization in developmental processes: Can systems approaches work? In M. Gummar (Ed.), *Systems in Development: Minnesota Symposia in Child Psychology* (Vol. 22). Hillsdale, NJ: Erlbaum.

Thelen, E., & Fisher, D. M. (1982). Newborn stepping: An explanation for a "disappearing reflex." *Developmental Psychology,* **18,** 760–775.

Thelen, E., & Ulrich, B. D. (1991). Hidden skills: A dynamic systems analysis of treadmill stepping during the first year. *Monographs of the Society for Research in Child Development,* **58** (Serial No. 223) No. 1.

Thelen, E., Ulrich, B. D., & Niles, D. (1987). Bilateral coordination in human infants: Stepping on a split-belt treadmill. *Journal of Experimental Psychology,* **13,** 1405–1410.

Thevenin, D. M., Eilers, R. E., Oller, D. K., & LaVoie, L. (1985). Where's the drift in babbling drift? A cross-linguistic study. *Applied Psycholinguistics,* **6,** 3–15.

Thoman, E. (1987). Self-regulation of stimulation by prematures with a breathing blue bear. In J. Gallagher & C. Ramey (Eds.), *The malleability of children.* Baltimore/London: Paul H. Brookes.

Thomas, A., Chess, S., & Korn, S. J. (1982). The reality of difficult temperament. *Merrill-Palmer Quarterly,* **28,** 1–20.

Thomas, M. H., & Drabman, R. S. (1977, August). *Effects of television violence on expectations of others' aggression.* Paper presented at the annual meeting of the American Psychological Association, San Francisco.

Thompson, R. (1990). Vulnerability in research: A developmental perspective on research risk. *Child Development,* **61,** 1–16.

Thompson, R. A. (1987). Development of children's inferences of the emotions of others. *Developmental Psychology,* **23,** 124–131.

Thompson, R. A. (1989). Causal attributions and children's emotional understanding. In C. Saarni & P. L. Harris (Eds.), *Children's understanding of emotions.* New York: Cambridge University Press.

Thompson, R. A., Connell, J. P., & Bridges, L. J. (1988). Temperament, emotion and social interactive behavior in the strange situation: A component process analysis of attachment system functioning. *Child Development,* **59,** 1102–1110.

Thompson, R. A., Lamb, M. E., & Estes, D. (1982). Stability of infant-mother attachment and its relationship to changing life circumstances in an unselected middle-class sample. *Child Development,* **53,** 144–148.

Thompson, S. K. (1975). Gender labels and early sex-role development. *Child Development,* **46,** 339–347.

Thorne, B. (1986). Girls and boys together . . . but mostly apart: Gender arrangements in elementary schools. In W. W. Hartup & Z. Rubin (Eds.), *Relations and relationships.* Hillsdale, NJ: Erlbaum.

Thurstone, L. L. (1938). *Primary mental abilities.* Chicago: University of Chicago Press.

Tinsley, B. J. (1992). Multiple influences on the acquisition and socialization of children's health attitudes and behavior: An integrative review. *Child Development,* **63,** 1043–1069.

Tinsley, B. J., & Parke, R. D. (1988). The role of grandfathers in the context of the family. In P. Bronstein & C. P. Cowan (Eds.), *Fatherhood today: Men's changing roles in the family* (pp. 236–252). New York: Wiley.

Tobin-Richards, M., Boxer, A. O., & Petersen, A. C. (1983). The psychological impact of pubertal change: Sex differences in perceptions of self during early adolescence. In J. Brooks-Gunn & A. C. Petersen (Eds.), *Girls at puberty: Biological, psychological, and social perspectives.* New York: Plenum.

Tomlinson-Keasey, C. (1990). Developing our intellectual resources of the 21st century: Educating the gifted. *Journal of Educational Psychology,* **82,** 399–403.

Tomlinson-Keasey, C., & Keasey, C. B. (1974). The mediating role of cognitive development in moral judgment. *Child Development,* **45,** 291–298.

Toth, S. L., Manly, J. T., & Cicchetti, D. (in press). Child maltreatment and vulnerability to depression. *Development and Psychopathology.*

Trabasso, T., Issen, A. M., Dolecki, P., McLanahan, A., Riley, C., & Tucker, T. (1978). How do children solve class-inclusion problems? In R. S. Siegler (Eds.), *Children's thinking: What develops?* Hillsdale, NJ: Erlbaum.

Trabasso, T., Stein, N., & Johnson, L. R. (1981). Children's knowledge of events: A causal analysis of story structure. In G. Bower (Ed.), *Learning and motivation* (Vol. 15). New York: Academic.

Trevarthan, W. (1987). *Human birth: An evolutionary perspective.* New York: Aldine de Gruyter.

Trickett, P. K., Aber, J. L., Carlson, V., & Cicchetti, D. (1991). The relationship of socioeconomic status to the etiology and developmental sequelae of physical child abuse. *Developmental Psychology,* **27,** 148–158.

Trickett, P. K., & Kuczynski, L. (1986). Children's misbehavior and parental discipline in abusive and nonabusive families. *Developmental Psychology,* **22,** 115–123.

Trickett, P. K., & Susman, E. J. (1988). Parental perceptions of childrearing practices in physically abusive and non-abusive families. *Developmental Psychology,* **24,** 270–277.

Tronick, E., Wise, S., Als, H., Adamson, L., Scanlon, J., & Brazelton, T. B. (1975). *Regional obstetric anesthesia and newborn behavior: Effect over the first ten days of life.* Unpublished manuscript, Harvard Medical School, Cambridge, MA.

Truss, T. J. (Ed.). (1981, October). *Child health and human development: An evaluation and assessment of the state of the science* (NIH Publication No. 82-2304). Washington, DC: U.S. Department of Health and Human Services.

Tuchmann-Deuplessis, H. (1965). Design and interpretation of teratogenic tests. In J. N. Robson, J. M. Sullivan, & R. L. Smith (Eds.), *Symposium of Embryopathic Activity of Drugs* (pp. 56–87). Boston: Little, Brown.

Tuchmann-Deuplessis, H. (1975). Drug effects on the fetus. *Monographs on drugs* (Vol. 2). Sydney: ADIS Press.

Tulkin, S. R., & Kagan, J. (1972). Mother-child interaction in the first year of life. *Child Development,* **43,** 31–41.

Turiel, E. (1966). An experimental test of the sequentiality of development stages in the child's moral judgments. *Journal of Personality and Social Psychology,* **3,** 611–618.

Turiel, E. (1983). *The development of social knowledge: Morality and convention.* New York: Cambridge University Press.

Turiel, E., Killen, V., & Helwig, F. (1988). Morality: Its structure, functions and vagaries. In J. Kagan and S. Lamb (Eds.), *The emergence of morality in young children.* Chicago: University of Chicago Press.

Turkheimer, E. (1991). Individual and group differences in adoption studies of IQ. *Psychological Bulletin,* **110,** 392–405.

Turner, A. M., & Greenough, W. T. (1985). Differential rearing effects on rat visual cortex synapses: I. Synaptic and neuronal density and synapses per neuron. *Brain Research,* **329,** 195–203.

Turner, C. W., & Goldsmith, D. (1976). Effects of toy guns and airplanes on children's antisocial free play behavior. *Journal of Experimental Child Psychology,* **21,** 303–315.

Twain, M. (1976). The adventures of Tom Sawyer. In L. Teacher (Ed.), *The unabridged Mark Twain.* Philadelphia: Running Press.

Ungerer, J. A., Brody, L. R., & Zelazo, P. R. (1978). Long-term memory for speech in 2- to 4-week-old infants. *Infant Behavior and Development,* **7,** 177–186.

U.S. Bureau of Labor Statistics. (1988, March). *Marital and family characteristics of the labor force.* Washington, DC: U.S. Government Printing Office.

U.S. Department of Justice. (1989). *Crime in the United States, 1988.* Washington, DC: Government Printing Office.

Uzgiris, I. C. (1989). Infants in relation: Performers, pupils and partners. In W. Damon (Ed.), *Child development: Today and tomorrow.* San Francisco: Jossey-Bass.

Valian, V. (1986). Syntactic categories in the speech of young children. *Developmental Psychology,* **22,** 562–579.

Vandell, D. L., Henderson, V. K., & Wilson, K. S. (1989). A longitudinal study of children with varying quality day care experiences. *Child Development,* **59,** 1286–1292.

Vandell, D., & Wilson, K. (1987). Infants' interactions with mother, siblings and peer contacts and relations between interaction systems. *Child Development,* **58,** 176–186.
Vaughn, B., Gove, F., & Egeland, B. (1980). The relationship between out-of-home care and the quality of infant-mother attachment in an economically disadvantaged sample. *Child Development,* **51,** 1203–1214.
Vaughn, B. E., Kopp, C. B., & Krakow, J. B. (1984). The emergence and consolidation of self-control from eighteen to thirty months of age: Normative trends and individual differences. *Child Development,* **55,** 990–1004.
Vaughn, B. E., & Langlois, J. H. (1983). Physical attractiveness as a correlate of peer status and social competence in preschool children. *Developmental Psychology,* **19,** 561–567.
Vaughn, B. E., & Waters, E. (1981). Attention structure, sociometric status, behavioral correlates and relationships to social competence. *Developmental Psychology,* **17,** 275–288.
Vernon, M. D. (1955). The functions of schemata in perceiving. *Psychological Review,* **62,** 180–192.
Vincent, J. P., Harris, G. E., Cook, N. I., & Brady, C. P. (1979). *Couples become parents: A behavioral systems analysis of family development.* Paper presented at the biennial meeting of the Society for Research in Child Development, San Francisco.
Vorhees, C. V., & Mollnow, E. (1987). Behavioral teratogenesis: Long-term influences on behavior from early exposure to environmental agents. In J. D. Osofsky (Ed.), *Handbook of infant development* (pp. 913–971). New York: Wiley.
Vosniadou, S. (1987). Children and metaphors. *Child Development,* **58,** 870–885.
Vurpillot, E. (1968). The development of scanning strategies and their relation to visual differentiation. *Journal of Experimental Child Psychology,* **6,** 632–650.
Vygotsky, L. S. (1934). *Thought and language.* Cambridge, MA: M.I.T. Press.
Vygotsky, L. V. (1978). *Thought and language.* Cambridge, MA: M.I.T. Press.
Wachs, T. D. (1992). *The nature of nurture.* Newbury Park, CA: Sage.
Waddington, C. H. (1962). *New patterns in genetics and development.* New York: Columbia University Press.
Waddington, C. H. (1966). *Principles of development and differentiation.* New York: MacMillan.
Wagner, N. E., Schubert, H. J. P., Schubert, D. S. P. (1985). Family size effects: A revision. *Journal of Genetic Psychology,* **146,** 65–78.
Wahler, R. G. (1967). Infant social attachments: A reinforcement theory interpretation and investigation. *Child Development,* **38,** 1079–1088.
Wahler, R. G., & Dumas, J. E. (1987). Family factors in childhood psychology: Toward a coercion-neglect model. In T. Jacob (Ed.), *Family interaction and psychopathology: Theories, methods, and findings* (pp. 581–625). New York: Plenum.
Walker, A. (1980). *Perception of expressive behavior by infants.* Unpublished doctoral dissertation. Cornell University, Ithaca, NY.
Walker, L. J. (1980). Cognitive and perspective taking prerequisites for moral development. *Child Development,* **51,** 131–139.
Walker, L. J. (1988). The development of moral reasoning. *Annals of Child Development,* **5,** 33–78.
Walker, L. J. (1989). A longitudinal study of moral reasoning. *Child Development,* **60,** 157–166.
Wartner, U. G., & Grossman, K. (1988). Stability of attachment patterns and their disorganizations from infancy to age 6 in south Germany. Unpublished manuscript, Universitat Regensberg, West Germany.
Waterman, A. S. (Ed.). (1985). *Identity in adolescence: Progress and contents.* San Francisco: Jossey-Bass.
Waters, E. (1978). The reliability and stability of individual differences in infant-mother attachment. *Child Development,* **49,** 483–494.
Waters, E., Vaughn, G., & Egeland, B. (1980). Individual differences in infant-mother attachment relationships at age one: Antecedents in neonatal behavior in an urban economically disadvantaged sample. *Child Development,* **51,** 208–216.
Waters, H. F., & Malamud, P. (1975). "Drop that gun, Captain Video." *Newsweek,* **85,**(10), 81–82.
Watson, J. B. (1926). What the nursery has to say about instincts. In C. Murcheson (Ed.), *Psychologies of 1925* (pp. 1–35). Worcester, MA: Clark University Press.
Watson, J. B. (1928). *Psychological care of infant and child.* New York: Norton.
Watson, J. D., & Crick, F. H. C. (1953). Molecular structure of nucleic acid: A structure for deoxyribose nucleic acid. *Nature,* **171,** 737–738.
Watson, R. I. (1962). *Psychology of the child.* New York: Wiley.
Waxman, S., & Gelman, R. (1986). Preschoolers' use of superordinate relations in classification and language. *Cognitive Development,* **1,** 139–156.

Weber, J. M. (1988). The extent to which viewers watch violence containing programs. In B. Gunter (ed.), *Current Psychology,* **7,** 43–57.

Wechsler, D. (1952). *Wechsler Intelligence Scale for Children.* New York: Psychological Corporation.

Wechsler, D. (1958). *The measurement and appraisal of adult intelligence* (4th ed.). Baltimore: Williams & Wilkins.

Wehren, A., & DeLisi, R. (1983). The development of gender understanding: Judgments and explanations. *Child Development,* **54,** 1568–1578.

Weinberg, K., Gianino, A., Tronick, E. (1989). *Facial expressions of emotion and social and object oriented behavior are specifically related in 6-month-old infants.* Paper presented at the meeting of the Society for Research and Child Development, Kansas City, MO.

Weinberg, R. A. (1989). Intelligence and IQ: Landmark issues and great debates. *American Psychologist,* **44,** 98–104.

Weiner, I. B. (1982). *Psychopathology from infancy through adolescence.* New York: Wiley.

Weinraub, M., & Lewis, M. (1977). The determinants of children's responses to separation. *Monographs of the Society for Research in Child Development,* **42,** (Serial No. 172).

Weir, R. H. (1966). Some questions on the child's learning of phonology. In F. Smith & G. Miller (Eds.), *The genesis of language* (pp. 153–168). Cambridge, MA: M.I.T. Press.

Weisner, T. S., & Wilson-Mitchell, J. E. (1990). Nonconventional family lifestyles and multischematic sex typing in six year olds. *Child Development,* **61,** 1915–1933.

Weiss, G., & Hechtman, L. T. (1986). *Hyperactive children grown up.* New York: Guilford.

Weiss, G., Hechtman, L., Perman, T., Hopkins, J., & Weiner, A. (1979). Hyperactive children as young adults: A controlled prospective 10 year follow-up of the psychiatric status of 75 hyperactive children. *Archives of General Psychiatry,* **36,** 675–681.

Weissberg, R. P., Caplan, M. Z., & Sivo, P. J. (1989). A new conceptual framework for establishing school-based competence promotion programs. In L. A. Bond & B. E. Compas (Eds.), *Primary prevention and promotion in the schools.* Newbury Park, CA: Sage.

Weissman, M. B., Leckman, J. F., Merekangas, K. R., Gammon, D., & Prusoff, B. A. (1984). Depression and anxiety disorders in parents and children. *Archives of General Psychiatry,* **41,** 845–852.

Weisz, J. R., Seuwanlert, S., Chaiyasit, W., Weiss, B., Walter, B. R., & Anderson, W. W. (1988). Thai and American perspectives on over- and under-controlled child behavior problems: Exploring the threshold model among parents, teachers, and psychologists. *Journal of Consulting and Clinical Psychology,* **56,** 601–609.

Wellman, H. M. (1977). Preschoolers' understanding of memory relevant variables. *Child Development,* **48,** 1720–1723.

Wellman, H. M. (1978). Knowledge of the interaction of memory variables: A developmental study of metamemory. *Developmental Psychology,* **14,** 24–29.

Wellman, H. M. (1990). *The child's theory of mind.* Cambridge: M.I.T. Press.

Wellman, H. M., & Bartsch, K. (1988). Young children's reasoning and beliefs. *Cognition,* **30,** 239–277.

Wellman, H. M., Collins, J., & Glieberman, J. (1981). Understanding the combinations of memory variables: Developing conceptions of memory limitations. *Child Development,* **52,** 1313–1317.

Wellman, H. M., & Lempers, J. D. (1977). The naturalistic communicative abilities of two-year-olds. *Child Development,* **48,** 1052–1057.

Wender, P. H., Rosenthal, D., Kety, S. S., Schulsinger, S., & Welner, J. (1974). Cross-fostering: A research strategy for clarifying the role of genetic and experimental factors in the etiology of schizophrenia. *Archives of General Psychiatry,* **30,** 121–128.

Werker, J. F. (1989). Becoming a native listener. *American Scientist,* **77,** 54–59.

Werker, J. F., & McLeod, P. J. (1989). Infant preference for both male and female infant-directed talk: A developmental study of attentional and affective responsiveness. *Canadian Journal of Psychology,* **43,** 230–246.

Werner, E. E. (1988). Individual differences, universal needs: A 30-year study of resilient high risk infants zero to three. *Bulletin of National Center for Clinical Infant Programs,* **8,** 1–5.

Werner, E. E. (1989). Children of the garden island. *Scientific American,* **260,** 107–111.

Werner, E. E. (1991, March). *Vulnerability and resiliency: The children of Kauai.* Meeting on vulnerability and resiliency in children and families: Focus on children with disabilities. Baltimore, MD.

Werner, E. E., Bierman, J. M., & French, F. F. (1971). *The children of Kauai.* Honolulu: University of Hawaii.

Werner, E. E., & Smith, R. S. (1977). *Kauai's children come of age.* Honolulu: University of Hawaii.

Werner, E. E., & Smith, R. S. (1982). *Vulnerable but invincible: A longitudinal study of resilient children and youth.* New York: McGraw-Hill.

Werner, J. S., Minkin, N., Minkin, B. L., Fixen, D. L., Phillips, E. L., & Wolf, M. M. (1975). "Intervention package": An analysis to prepare juvenile delinquents for encounters with police officers. *Criminal Justice and Behavior*, **2**, 55–84.

Werner, J. S., & Siqueland, E. R. (1978). Visual recognition memory in the preterm infant. *Infant Behavior and Development*, **1**, 79–84.

Werry, J. S., Methuen, R. J., Fitzpatrick, J., & Dixon, H. (1983). The interater reliability of DSMIII in children. *Journal of Abnormal Child Psychology*, **11**, 341–354.

Wertsch, J. V. (1985). *Vygotsky and the social formation of mind.* Cambridge: Harvard University Press.

Wertsch, J. V., & Tulviste, P. (1992). L. S. Vygotsky and contemporary developmental psychology. *Developmental Psychology*, **28**, 543–553.

Westfield, G. E., Muczenski, I., Westfield, C., & Omark, D. R. (1989). Stability of boys' social success among peers over an eleven-year period. In J. A. Meacham (Ed.), *Interpersonal relations: Family peers and friends.* Basel: Karger.

Wetstone, H. (1977). *About word words and thing words: A study of metalinguistic awareness.* Paper presented at the second annual Boston University Conference on Language Development, Boston.

Whalen, C. K. (1989). Attention deficit and hyperactivity disorders. In T. Hollendick & M. Hersen (Eds.), *Handbook of child psychopathology.* New York: Plenum.

Whalen, C. K., & Henker, B. (1986). Psychostimulants and children: A review and analysis. *Psychological Bulletin*, **83**, 1113–1130.

Whalen, C. K., & Henker, B. (1991). Therapies for hyperactive children: Comparisons, combinations and compromises. *Journal of Consulting and Clinical Psychology*, **59**, 126–137.

Whalen, C. K., Henker, B., Collins, B. E., Finck, D., & Dotemoto, S. A. (1979). A social ecology of hyperactive boys: Medication effects in systematically structured classroom environments. *Journal of Applied Behavior Analysis*, **12**, 65–81.

Whalen, C. K., Henker, B., & Granger, D. A. (1990). Social judgment processes in hyperactive boys. *Journal of Abnormal Child Psychology*, **18**, 297–316.

White, C. B., Bushnell, N., & Regnemer, J. L. (1978). Moral development in Bahamian school children: A 3-year examination of Kohlberg's stages of moral development. *Developmental Psychology*, **14**, 58–65.

Whitehurst, G. J., Fischel, J. E., Caulfield, M. B., DeBaryshe, B. D., & Valdex-Menchaca, M. C. (1989). Assessment and treatment of early experience language delay. In P. R. Zelazo & R. Barr (Eds.), *Challenges to developmental paradigms: Implication for assessment and treatment* (p. 113–135). Hillsdale, NJ: Erlbaum.

Whitehurt, G. (1980). *Imitation, observational learning, and language acquisition.* Paper presented at the sixth biennial Conference on Human Development, Alexandria, Virginia.

Whiting, B., & Edwards, C. (1988). *Children of different worlds: The formation of social behavior.* Cambridge, MA: Harvard University Press.

Whiting, B. B., & Whiting, J. W. M. (1975). *Children of six cultures: A psychocultural analysis.* Cambridge, MA: Harvard University Press.

Wiesenfeld, A., Malatesta, C., & DeLoach, L. (1981). Differential parental response to familiar and unfamiliar infant distress signals. *Infant Behavior and Development*, **4**, 281–295.

Wilkie, C. F., & Ames, E. W. (1986). The relationship of infant crying to parental stress in the transition to parenthood. *Journal of Marriage and the Family*, **48**, 545–550.

Wilkinson, A. C. (1984). Children's partial knowledge of the cognitive skill of counting. *Cognitive Psychology*, **16**, 28–64.

Willerman, L., & Stafford, R. E. (1972). Maternal effects on intellectual functioning. *Behavior Genetics*, **2**, 321–325.

Williams, G. A., & Asher, S. R. (1987). *New approaches to identifying rejected children at school.* Paper presented at the annual meeting of the American Educational Research Association, Washington, DC.

Williams, J. E., & Best, D. L. (1990). *Measuring sex stereotypes: A multinational study* (rev. ed.). Newbury Park, CA: Sage.

Williams, R. L. (1970). Black pride, academic relevance and individual achievement. *Counseling Psychologist*, **2**, 18–22.

Williams, T. H., & Handford, A. G. (1986). Television and other leisure activities. In T. H. Williams (Ed.), *The impact of television: A natural experiment in three communities.* Orlando, FL: Academic.

Williams, T. M. (Ed.). (1985). *The impact of television: A natural experiment involving three towns.* New York: Academic.

Williams, T. M., Baron, D., Phillips, S., Travis, L., & Jackson, D. (1986, August). *The portrayal of sex roles on Canadian and U.S. television.* Paper presented to the International Association for Mass Communication Research, New Delhi, India.

Wilson, M. N. (1989). Child development in the context of the black extended family. *American Psychologist,* **44,** 380–385.

Wilson, R. S. (1983). The Louisville twin study: Developmental synchronies in behavior. *Child Development,* **54,** 298–316.

Wilson, R. S., & Harpring, E. B. (1972). Mental and motor development in infant twins. *Developmental Psychology,* **7,** 277–287.

Wimmer, H. (1980). Children's understanding of stories: Assimilation by a general schema for actions or coordination of temporal relations. In F. Wilkening, J. Becker, T. Trabasso (Eds.), *Information integration by children.* Hillsdale, NJ: Erlbaum.

Winick, M. (1970). Nutrition and nerve cell growth. *Federation Proceedings,* **29,** 1510–1515.

Winick, M. (1974). Childhood obesity. *Nutrition Today,* **9,** 6–12.

Winick, M., Knarig, K. M., & Harris, R. C. (1975). Malnutrition and environmental enrichment by early adoption. *Science,* **190,** 1173–1175.

Winn, M. (1990, April 29). New views of human intelligence. *The New York Times Magazine,* pp. 16–17, 28, 30.

Winner, E. (1988). The point of words: Children's understanding of metaphor and irony. Cambridge, MA: Harvard University Press.

Winner, E., McCarthy, M., Kleinman, S., & Gardner, H. (1979). First metaphors. In D. Wolf (Eds.), *Early symbolization: New directions for child development.* San Francisco CA: Jossey-Bass.

Witelson, S. F. (1977). Developmental dyslexia: Two right hemispheres and none left. *Science,* **195,** 309–311.

Witelson, S. F. (1978). Sex differences in the neurology of cognition: Psychological, social, educational and clinical implications. In S. Sullerto (Ed.), *La fait feminin.* Paris: Fayard.

Witelson, S. F. (1983). Bumps on the brain: Neuroanatomical asymmetries as a basis for functional symmetries. In S. Segalowitz (Ed.), *Language functions and brain organization* (pp. 117–144). New York: Academic.

Witelson, S. F., & Swallow, J. A. (1987). Individual differences in human brain function. *National Forum,* **67,** 17–24.

Witkin, H. A., Mednick, S. A., Schulsinger, F., Bakkestrom, E., Christiansen, K. O., Goodenough, D. R., Hirchborn, K., Lunsteen, C., Owen, D. R., Philip, J., Ruben, D. B., & Stocking, M. (1976). Criminality in XYY and XXY men. *Science,* **193,** 547–555.

Wolff, P. (1987). *The development of behavioral states and the expression of emotions in early infancy.* Chicago: University of Chicago Press.

Wolff, P. H. (1966). The causes, controls and organizations of behavior in the neonate. *Psychological Issues,* **5** (1, Whole No. 17).

Wolff, P. H. (1969). The natural history of crying and other vocalizations in early infancy. In B. Foss (Ed.), *Determinants of infant behavior* (Vol. 4). London: Methuen.

Wolff, P. H. (1987). *The development of behavioral states and the expression of emotions in early infancy: New proposals for investigation.* Chicago: University of Chicago Press.

Wood, D., Bruner, J., & Ross, G. (1976). The role of tutoring in problem solving. *Journal of Child Psychology and Psychiatry,* **17,** 89–100.

Woods, N. B. (1972). The unsupervised child of the working mother. *Developmental Psychology,* **6,** 14–25.

Woody-Ramsey, J., & Miller, P. H. (1988). The facilitation of selective attention in preschoolers. *Child Development,* **59,** 1497–1503.

Wright, J. C., St. Peters, M., & Huston, A. C. (1990). Family television use and its relation to children's cognitive skills & social behavior. In J. Bryant (Ed.), *Television and the American Family* (pp. 221–252). Hillsdale, NJ: Erlbaum.

Wright, P. J., Henggler, S. W., & Craig, L. (1986). Problems in paradise? A longitudinal examination of the transition to parenthood. *Journal of Applied Developmental Psychology,* **7,** 277–291.

Wyshak, G., & Frisch, R. E. (1982). Evidence for a secular trend in age of menarche. *New England Journal of Medicine,* **306,** 1033–1035.

Yarmey, A. D., & Jones, H. P). (1983). Accuracy of memory of male and female eyewitnesses to a criminal assault and rape. *Bulletin of the Psychonomic Society,* **21,** 89–92.

Yogman, M. W. (1981). Development of the father-infant relationship. In H. Fitzgerald, B. Lester, & M. W. Yogman (Eds.), *Theory and research in behavioral pediatrics* (Vol. 1). New York: Plenum.

Yonas, A., Arterberry, M. E., & Granrud, C. E. (1987). Space perception in infancy. *Annals of Child Development* (Vol. 4, pp. 1–34). Greenwich, CT: JAI Press.

Young, W. C., Goy, R. W., & Phoenix, C. H. (1967). Hormones and sexual behavior. *Science,* **143,** 212–218.

Youniss, J. (1980). *Parents and peers in social development.* Chicago: University of Chicago Press.

Yuill, N., & Perner, J. (1988). Intentionality and knowledge in children's judgments of actors' responsibility and recipients' emotional judgment. *Developmental Psychology,* **24,** 358–365.

Yussen, S. R., & Berman, L. (1981). Memory predictions for recall and recognition in first, third, and fifth grade children. *Developmental Psychology,* **17**, 224–229.

Zahn-Waxler, C., Cummings, M., McKnew, D., & Radke-Yarrow, M. (1984). Altruism, aggression and social interaction in young children with a manic-depressive parent. *Child Development,* **55,** 112–122.

Zahn-Waxler, C., & Kochanska, G. (1990). Socio-emotional development. In R. A. Thompson (Ed.), *Nebraska Symposium on Motivation,* 1988 (Vol. 36). Lincoln: University of Nebraska Press.

Zahn-Waxler, C., Kochanska, G., Krupnick, J., & McKnew, D. (1990). Patterns of guilt in children of depressed and well mothers. *Developmental Psychology,* **26,** 51–59.

Zahn-Waxler, C., & Radke-Yarrow, M. (1982). The development of altruism: Alternative research strategies. In N. Eisenberg-Berg (Ed.), *The development of prosocial behavior.* New York: Academic.

Zahn-Waxler, C., Radke-Yarrow, M., Wagner, E., & Chapman, M. (1992). Development of concern for others. *Developmental Psychology,* **28,** 126–136.

Zahn-Waxler, C., Robinson, J., & Emde, R. (1992). *The development of empathy in twins. Developmental Psychology,* **28.**

Zajonc, R. B., & Marcus, G. B. (1975). Birth order and intellectual development. *Psychological Review,* **82,** 74–88.

Zajonc, R. B., Marcus, H., & Marcus, G. B. (1979). The birth order puzzle. *Journal of Personality and Social Psychology,* **37,** 1325–1341.

Zarbatany, L., Hartmann, D. P., & Rankin, D. B. (1990). The psychological functions of preadolescent peer activities. *Child Development,* **61,** 1067–1080.

Zegoib, L. E., Arnold, S., & Forehand, R. (1975). An examination of observer effects in parent-child interactions. *Child Development,* **46**, 509–512.

Zelazo, N. A., Zelazo, P. R., Cohen, K. M., & Zelazo, P. D. (1988, April). *Specificity of practice effects on elementary neuromotor patterns.* Paper presented at the International Conference on Infant Studies, Washington, DC.

Zelazo, P. (1972). Smiling and vocalizing: A cognitive emphasis. *Merrill-Palmer Quarterly,* **18,** 349–365.

Zelazo, P. R. (1983). The development of walking: New findings and old assumptions. *Journal of Motor Behavior,* **15,** 99–137.

Zelazo, P. R., Kearsley, R. B., & Ungerer, J. A. (1984). *Learning to speak: A manual for parents.* Hillsdale, NJ: Erlbaum.

Zelazo, P. R., Zelazo, N. A., & Kolb, S. (1972). "Walking" in the newborn. *Science,* **176,** 314–315.

Zeskind, P. S., & Ramey, C. T. (1978). Fetal malnutrition: An experimental study of its consequences on infant development in two caregiving environments. *Child Development,* **49,** 1155–1162.

Zeskind, P. S., & Ramey, C. T. (1981). Preventing intellectual and interactional sequelae of fetal malnutrition: A longitudinal, transactional and synergistic approach to development. *Child Development,* **52,** 213–218.

Zigler, E., Abelson, W. D., Trickett, P. K., & Seitz, V. (1982). Is an intervention program necessary in order to improve economically disadvantaged children's IQ scores? *Child Development,* **53,** 340–348.

Zigler, E., & Seitz, V. (1982). Social policy and intelligence. In R. J. Sternberg (Ed.), *Handbook of human intelligence,* (pp. 586–641). Cambridge, England: Cambridge University Press.

Zill, N. (1986). *Happy, healthy and insecure.* New York: Cambridge University Press.

Zill, N. (1988). Behavior, achievement and health problems among children in step families. In E. M. Hetherington & J. D. Arasten (Eds.), *Impact of divorce, single parenting and step parenting on children* (p. 235–268). Hillsdale, NJ: Erlbaum.

Zill, N. (1991, Winter). U.S. children and their families: Current conditions and recent trends, 1989. *SRCD Newsletter,* pp. 1–3.

Zuckerman, B., Frank, D., Hingson, R., Amaro, H., Devenson, S. M., Kayne, H., Parker, S., Vinci, R., Aboagye, K., Fried, L., Cabral, H., Timperi, R., & Bauchner, H. (1989). Effects of maternal marijuana and cocaine use on fetal growth. *The New England Journal of Medicine,* **12,** 762–768.

Zukow, P. (1989). Siblings as effective socializing agents: Evidence from central Mexico. In P. Zukow (Ed.), *Sibling interaction across cultures.* New York: Springer-Verlag.

ACKNOWLEDGMENTS

Figure 1-2 Atkinson, R. C., and Schiffrin, R. M. (1968). Human memory: A proposed system and its control processes. In Spence, K. W., and Spence J. (Eds.), *Advances in the Psychology of Learning and Motivation Research and Theory*, Vol. 2. . Reprinted by permission of Academic Press.

Figure 1-3 Garbarino, J. (1982). From Kopp, G., and Krakow, J. *The Child*, © 1982, by Addison-Welsey Publishing Company, Inc. Reprinted with permission of the publisher.

Figures 3-1 and 3-2 Rugh, R., and Shettles, L. (1971). From *From Conception to Birth, the Drama of Life's Beginning* by Robert Rugh and Landrum Shettles. Copyright © 1971 by Robert Rugh and Landrum Shettles. Reprinted by permission of HarperCollins Publishers.

Figure 3-3 Watson, J. D., and Crick, F. H. C. (1953). Molecular structure of nucleic acid: A structure for deoxyribose nucleic acid. Reprinted by permission from *Nature*, Vol. 717, pp. 737–738; copyright © 1953 Macmillan Magazines Limited and Dr. James D. Watson.

Figure 3-5 Baumeister, A. A. (1967). The effects of dietary control on intelligence in phenylketonuria. *American Journal of Mental Deficiency*, Vol. 71, pp. 840–847. Reprinted by permission of the American Association on Mental Retardation.

Table 3-2 March of Dimes Birth Defects Foundation (1985). Reprinted with permission from the March of Dimes Birth Defects Foundation.

Table 3-3 Hook, E. G., and Lindsjo, A. (1978). Down syndrome in the live births by single year maternal age interval in a Swedish study: Comparison with results from a New York State study. *American Journal of Human Genetics*, **30**, p. 19. Reprinted by permission of The University of Chicago Press.

Figure 3-6 Bender, B. C., Linden, M. G., and Robinson A. (1987). Environment and developmental risk. *Journal of the Academy of Child and Adolescent Psychiatry*, **26**, pp. 499–503. © by the American Academy of Child Psychiatry.

Figure 3-7 Gottesman, I. (1983). Genetic aspects of intelligent behavior. In Ellis, N. (Ed.), *Handbook of Mental Deficiency: Psychological Theory and Research*, McGraw-Hill, Inc. Reprinted by permission of the author.

Table 3-4 Daniels, D., Dunn, J., Furstenberg, F. F., and Plomin, R. (1985). Environmental differences within the family and adjustment differences within pairs of adolescent siblings. *Child Development*, **56**, pp. 764–774. © The Society for Research in Child Development, Inc.

Table 3-5 Bouchard, T. J., and McGue, M. (1981). Familial studies of intelligence: A review. *Science*, **212**, pp. 1055–1059. Copyright © 1981 by the American Association for the Advancement of Science.

Figure 3-8 Wilson, R. S., and Harpring, E. B. (1972). Mental and motor development in infant twins. *Developmental Psychology*, **7**, pp. 277–287. Copyright 1972 by the American Psychological Association. Adapted by permission.

Table 3-6 Heston, L., and Denny, D. (1968). Interactions between early life experiences and biological factors in schizophrenia. *Journal of Psychiatric Research*, **6**, pp. 363–376. Copyright © 1968. Reprinted with permission of Pergamon Press Ltd.

Figure 4-1 Fischer, K. W., and Lazerson, A. (1984). A summary of prenatal development. Adapted from *Human Development* by K. W. Fischer and A. Lazerson. Copyright © 1984 by W. H. Freeman and Company. Reprinted by permission.

Figure 4-2 Moore, K. L. (1989). *Before We Are Born*. Reprinted by permission of W. B. Saunders Company.

Table 4-2 Apgar, V. A. (1953). A proposal for a new method of evaluation of the newborn infant. *Current Research in Anesthesia and Analgesia*, **32**, p. 267. Copyright © 1953. Published by John Wiley & Sons, Inc.

Figure 5-1 Jackson, C. M. (1933). In Jackson, C. M. (Ed.), *Human Anatomy*, 9th edition. Copyright © 1933. Reprinted by permission of McGraw-Hill, Inc.

Figure 5-2 Sostek, A. M., and Anders, T. F. (1981). The biosocial importance and environmental sensitivity of infant sleep-wake behaviors. In Bloom, K. (Ed.), *Prospective Issues in Infancy Research*, p. 108. Reprinted by permission of Lawrence Erlbaum Associates, Inc.

Figure 5-3 Roffwarg, H. P. (1966). Ontogenetic development of the human sleep-dream cycle, *Science*, **152**, p. 604. Copyright by the American Association for the Advancement of Science.

Figure 5-4 Korner, A. F., and Thoman, E. (1970). Visual alertness in neonates as evoked by maternal care. *Journal of Experimental Child Psychology*, **10**, pp. 67–78. Reprinted by permission of Academic Press.

Figure 5-5 Maurer, D., and Salapatek, P. (1976). Developmental changes in the scanning of faces by young infants. *Child Development*, **47**, pp. 523–527. © The Society for Research in Child Development, Inc.

Figure 5-7 Dannemiller, J. L., and Stephens, B. F. (1988). A critical test of infant pattern perception models. *Child Development*, **59**, pp. 210–216. © The Society for Research in Child Development, Inc.

Figure 5-8 Bertenthal, B. I., Proffitt, D. R., and Cutting, J. E. (1984). Infant sensitivity to figural coherence in biochemical motions. *Journal of Experimental Child Psychology*, **37**, pp. 213–230. Reprinted by permission of Academic Press.

Figure 5-10 Meltzoff, A. N., and Borton, R. W. (1979). Intermodal matching by human neonates. Reprinted by permission from *Nature*, Vol. 282, pp. 403–404; copyright © 1979 Macmillan Magazines Limited.

Figure 6-1 Rosenzweig, M. R. (1966). Environmental complexity, cerebral change, and behavior. *American Psychologist,* **21,** pp. 321–332. Copyright 1966 by the American Psychological Association. Reprinted by permission.

Figure 6-3 Shirley, M. M. (1933). *The First Two Years.* Copyright © 1933. Reprinted by permission of the University of Minnesota Press.

Figure 6-4 Zelazo, P. R., Zelazo, N. A., and Kolb, S. (1972). 'Walking' in the newborn. *Science,* **176,** April 22, 1972, pp. 314–315. Copyright 1972 by the American Association for the Advancement of Science.

Figure 6-5 Adelson E., and Fraiberg, S. (1974). Gross motor development in infants blind from birth. *Child Development,* **45,** pp. 114–126. © The Society for Research in Child Development, Inc.

Table 6-2 Martens, R. (1986). From "Youth Sport in the USA" by R. Martens. In *Sport for Children & Youths* (p. 28) by R. Weiss and D. Gould (Eds.), 1986. Champaign, IL: Human Kinetics. Copyright 1986 by Human Kinetics Publishers, Inc. Reprinted by permission.

Figure 6-7 Roche, A. F. (1979). Secular trends: Human growth, maturation, and development. *Monographs of the Society for Research in Child Development,* **44** (Serial No. 179). © The Society for Research in Child Development, Inc.

Box 6-2 Frank, A. (1952). *The Diary of a Young Girl.* Reprinted by permission of Doubleday, a division of Bantam, Doubleday, Dell Publishing Group, Inc.

Figure 6-8 Tobin-Richards, M., Boxer, A. O., and Petersen, A. C. (1984). The psychological impact of pubertal change: Sex differences in perceptions of self during early adolescence. In Brooks-Gunn, J., and Petersen, A. C. (Eds.), *Girls at Puberty: Biological, Psychological, and Social Perspectives.* Reprinted by permission of Plenum Publishing Corporation.

Figure 6-9 Simmons, R. G., Blyth, D. A., Van Cleave, E. F., and Bush, M. B. (1979). Entry into early adolescence: The impact of school structure, puberty, and early dating on self-esteem. *American Sociological Review,* **44,** pp. 948–967, Figure 2, p. 959. Copyright American Sociological Association. Reprinted by permission.

Figure 6-10 Epstein, L. H., Wing, R. R., Koeske, R., and Valoski, A. (1987). Long-term effects of family-based treatment of childhood obesity. *Journal of Consulting and Clinical Psychology,* **55,** pp. 91–95. Copyright 1987 by the American Psychological Association. Reprinted by permission.

Figure 7-1 Ahrens, R. (1954). Beitrag zur entwicklun des physionomie und mimikerkennens. *A. F. Exp. U. Agnew, Psyhcol,* **2,** pp. 599–633. Reprinted by permission of Verlag Fuer Psychologie.

Figure 7-2 Gewirtz, J. L. (1967). The course of infant smiling in four child-rearing environments in Israel. In Foss, B. M. (Ed.), *Determinants of Infant Behavior,* Vol. 3, pp. 105–248.

Figure 7-3 Sroule, L. A., and Wunsch, J. P. (1972). The development of laughter in the first year of life. *Child Development,* **43,** pp. 1326–1344. © The Society for Research in Child Development, Inc.

Figure 7-4 Schaffer, H. R., and Emerson, P. E. (1964). The development of social attachments in infancy. *Monographs of the Society for Research in Child Development,* **29** (3 Serial No. 94). © The Society for Research in Child Development, Inc.

Table 7-1 Ainsworth, M. D. (1973). The development of infant-mother attachment. In Caldwell, B., and Ricciuti, H. (Eds.), *Review of Child Development Research,* Vol. 3, Table 1. Copyright © 1973. Reprinted by permission of The University of Chicago Press.

Table 7-2 Main, M., and Cassidy, J. (1988). Categories of response to reunion with the parent at age 6: Predictable from infant attachment classification and stable over a 1-month period. *Developmental Psychology,* **24,** pp. 415–426. Copyright 1988 by the American Psychological Association. Adapted by permission.

Figure 7-5 Emde, R. N., Gaensbauer, T. J., and Harmon, R. J. (1976). Emotional expression in infancy: A biobehavioral study. *Psychological Issues,* Vol. 10, No. 37, International Universities Press.

Figure 7-6 Lewis, M., and Brooks, J. (1974). Self, other and fear: Infants' reactions to people. In Lewis, M., and Rosenblum, L. (Eds.), *The Origins of Fear.* Copyright © 1974. Published by John Wiley & Sons, Inc.

Figure 7-7 Barnett, J. T. (1969). *Development of Children's Fears: The Relationship between Three Systems of Fear Measurement.* Unpublished master's thesis, University of Wisconsin.

Figure 7-8 Kagan, J., Kearsley, R., and Zelazo, P. R. (1978). Reprinted by permission of the publisher from *Infancy: Its Place in Human Development* by Jerome Kagan, Richard B. Kearsley, and Philipo R. Zelazo. Cambridge, Mass.: Harvard University Press, copyright © 1978 by the President and Fellows of Harvard College.

Figure 8-1 Newport, E. L. (1990). Maturational constraints on language learning. *Cognitive Science,* **14,** pp. 11–28. Published by Ablex Publishing Corporation.

Table 8-1 Slobin, D. I. (1968). Table from *Contemporary Issues in Developmental Psychology,* by N. S. Endler, L. R. Boulter, and H. Osser, copyright © 1968 by Holt, Rinehart and Winston, Inc. Reprinted by permission of the publisher.

Box 8-4 McNeill, D. (1970). "Speech Samples" from *The Acquisition of Language: The Study of Developmental Psycholinguistics* by David McNeill. Copyright © 1970 by David McNeill. Reprinted by permission of HarperCollins Publishers. Brown, R., and Bellugi, U. (1984). Three processes in the acquisition of syntax. In Lenneberg, E. G. (Ed.), *New Directions in the Study of Language.* Copyright © 1984. Reprinted by permission of MIT Press.

Table 8-2 Slobin, D. I. (1979). From *Psycholinguistics* by Dan I. Slobin. Copyright © 1979, 1974 by Scott, Foresman and Company. Reprinted by permission of HarperCollins Publishers.

Figure 8-3 Reikehof, L. (1963). *Talk to the Deaf.* Published by Gospel Publishing House.

Figure 8-4 Entwisle, D. R., and Frasure, N. E. (1974). A contradiction resolved: Children's processing of syntactic cues. *Developmental Psychology,* **10,** pp. 852–857. Copyright 1974 by the American Psychological Association. Reprinted by permission.

Figure 9-1 *Peanuts* reprinted by permission of USF, Inc.

Figure 9-2 Phillips, J. (1969). Adapted from *The Origin of Intellect: Piaget's Theory,* by J. Phillips. Copyright © 1969 by W. H. Freeman and Company. Reprinted by permission.

Table 9-3 Selman, R. L., and Jacquette, D. (1978). Stability and oscillation in interpersonal awareness: A clinical-developmental analysis. In Keasy, C. B. (Ed.), *The XXV Nebraska Symposium on Motivation*. Copyright © 1978 by the University of Nebraska Press.

Table 9-4 Selman, R. L., and Byrne, D. F. (1974). A structural-developmental analysis of levels of role taking in middle childhood. *Child Development*, **45**, pp. 803–806. © The Society for Research in Child Development, Inc.

Figure 9-3 Lefrancois, G. R. (1992). *Of Children*, 7th edition. Published by Wadsworth Publishing Co.

Figure 9-4 Chi, M. T. H. (1978). Knowledge structures and memory development. In Siegler, R. S. (Ed.), *Children's Thinking: What Develops?* Reprinted by permission of Lawrence Erlbaum Associates, Inc.

Figure 9-6 Case, R. (1985). *Intellectual Development: Birth to Adulthood*. Reprinted by permission of Academic Press.

Figure 9-7 Radziszewska, B., and Rogoff, B. (1988). Influence of adult and peer collaborators on the development of children's planning skills. *Developmental Psychology*, **24**, pp. 840–848. Copywright © 1988 by the American Psychological Association. Reprinted by permission.

Figure 10-2 Vurpillot, E. (1968). The development of scanning strategies and their relation to visual differentiation. *Journal of Experimental Psychology*, **6**, pp. 632–650. Reprinted by permission of Academic Press.

Figure 10-3 *Peanuts* reprinted by permission of UFS, Inc.

Box 10-5 Carraher, T. N., Schliemann, A. D., and Carraher, D. W. (1988). Mathematical concepts in everyday life. *New Directions for Child Development*, **41**, pp. 71–87. Reprinted by permission of Jossey-Bass, Inc., Publishers.

Table 11-2 Gardner, H. (1984, 1985). *Frames of Mind* by Howard Gardner. Copyright © 1984, 1985 by Howard Gardner. Reprinted by permission of Basic Books, a division of HarperCollins Publishers.

Figure 11-1 Honzik, M. (1976). Value and limitations of infant tests: An overview. In Lewis, M. (Ed.), *Origins of Intelligence*. Reprinted by permission of Plenum Publishing Corporation.

Figure 11-2 Lesser, G. S., Fifer, G., and Clark, D. H. (1965). Mental abilities of children from different social class and cultural groups. *Monographs of the Society for Research in Child Development*, Vol. 30, No. 4, Serial No. 102, pp. 1–115. © The Society for Research in Child Development, Inc.

Figure 11-4 Scarr, S., and Weinberg, R. A. (1976). IQ test performance of black children adopted by white families. *American Psychologist*, **31**, pp. 726–739. Copyright 1976 by the American Psychological Association. Reprinted by permission.

Figure 11-5 Stevenson, H. H. (1983). Making the grade: School achievement in Japan, Taiwan, and the United States. Report to Center for Advanced Study in the Behavioral Sciences, Board of Trustees, pp. 41–51.

Table 11-3 Dweck, C. S., and Leggett, E. L. (1988). A social-cognitive approach to motivation and personality. *Psychological Review*, **95**, pp. 256-273. Copyright 1988 by the American Psychological Association. Reprinted by permission.

Table 12-2 and Figure 12-1 Baumrind, D. (1967). Child care practices anteceding three patterns of preschool behavior. *Genetic Psychology Monographs*, **75**, pp. 43–88, 1967. Reprinted with permission of the Helen Dwight Reid Educational Foundation. Published by Heldref Publications, 1319 Eighteenth St., N.W., Washington, D.C. 20036-1802. Copyright © 1967.

Figure 13-1 Eckerman, C. O., Whatley, J. L., and Kutz, S. L. (1975). Growth of social play with peers during the second year of life. *Developmental Psychology*, **11**, pp. 42–49. Copyright 1975 by the American Psychological Association. Reprinted by permission.

Figure 13-2 Ellis, S., Rogoff, B., and Cromer, C. (1981). Age segregation in children's social interactions. *Developmental Psychology*, **17**, pp. 399–407. Copyright 1981 by the American Psychological Association. Reprinted by permission.

Table 13-1 Hayden, L., Turulli, D., and Hymel, S. (1988). Children talk about loneliness. Paper presented at the biennial meeting of the University of Waterloo Conference on Child Development.

Table 13-2 Asher, S. R., Hymel, S., and Renshaw, P. D. (1984). Loneliness in children. *Child Development*, **55**, pp. 1456–1464. © The Society for Research in Child Development, Inc.

Figures 13-4 and 13-5 Dodge, K. A., Petit, G. S., McLaskey, C. L., and Brown, M. M. (1986). Social competence in children. *Monographs of the Society for Research in Child Development*, **51**, (2 Serial, No. 213), p. 40. © The Society for Research in Child Development, Inc.

Figure 13-6 Caspi, A., Elder, G., and Bem, D. (1988). Moving against the world: Life course patterns of shy children. *Developmental Psychology*, **24**, pp. 824–831. Copyright 1988 by the American Psychological Association. Reprinted by permission.

Table 13-3 Oden, S., and Asher, S. R. (1977). Coaching children in social skills for friendship making. *Child Development*, **48**, pp. 495–506. © The Society for Research in Child Development, Inc.

Table 13-4 Bigelow, B. J., and LaGaipa, J. J. (1975). Children's written descriptions of friendship: A multidimensional analysis. *Developmental Psychology*, **11**, pp. 857–858. Copyright 1975 by the American Psychological Association. Adapted by permission.

Table 13-5 Gottman, J. M. (1983). How children become friends. *Monographs of the Society for Research in Child Development*, **48** (Serial No. 201). © The Society for Research in Child Development, Inc.

Table 13-6 Gottman, J. M., and Mettetal, G. (1986). Speculations of social and affective development: Friendship and acquaintanceship through adolescence. In Gottman, J. M., and Parker, J. G. (Eds.), *The Conversations of Friends*. Reprinted by permission of Cambridge University Press.

Figure 13-8 Brown, B. B., Lohn, M. J., and McClenghan, E. L. (1986). Early adolescent's perceptions of peer pressure. *Journal of Early Adolescence*, **6**, pp. 139–154. Copyright © 1986. Reprinted by permission of Sage Publications, Inc.

Figure 13-9 Steinberg, L. (1986). Latchkey children and susceptibility to peer pressure: An ecological analysis. *Developmental Psychology*, **22**, pp. 433–439. Copyright 1986 by the American Psychological Association. Reprinted by permission.

Figure 14-1 Barker R. G., and Gump, P. V. (1964). *Big School, Small School*. Reprinted by permission of Stanford University Press.

Figure 14-2 Adams, R. S., and Biddle,

B. J. (1970). *Realities of Teaching: Explorations with Video Tape* by Raymond S. Adams and Bruce J. Biddle, copyright © 1970 by Holt, Rinehart and Winston, Inc., reprinted by permission of the publisher.

Cartoon, Chapter 14, p. 505 *Peanuts* reprinted by permission of UFS, Inc.

Cartoon, Chapter 14, p. 511 Drawing by Chon Day; © 1985 The New Yorker Magazine, Inc.

Figure 14-3 Asher, S. R., and Markell, R. A. (1974). Sex differences in comprehension of high- and low-interest reading material. *Journal of Educational Psychology*, **66**, pp. 680–687. Copyright 1974 by the American Psychological Association. Reprinted by permission.

Figure 14-6 Williams, T. H. (1986). *The Impact of Television: A Natural Experiment in Three Communities*, pp. 143–213, Figure 4.3, p. 161. Reprinted by permission of Academic Press.

Figure 15-1 Obrien, M., Huston, A., and Risley, T. (1983). Sex-typed play of toddlers in a day care center. *Journal of Applied Developmental Psychology*, **4**, pp. 1–9. Reprinted by permission of Ablex Publishing Corporation.

Figure 15-2 Zill, N. (1985). *Healthy and Insecure: A Portrait of Middle Childhood in the United States*. Reprinted by permission of Cambridge University Press.

Figure 15-3 Kagan, J., and Moss, H. A. (1962). *Birth to Maturity: A Study in Psychological Development*. Copyright © 1962. Reprinted by permission of John Wiley & Sons, Inc.

Cartoon Chapter 15, p. 547 © 1984, © 1984 Bil Keane, Inc. Distributed by Cowles Syndicate, Inc. Reprinted with special permission of King Features Syndicate, Inc.

Cartoon, Chapter 16, p. 571 *Miss Peach* © Mell Lazarus. By permission of Mell Lazarus and Creators Syndicate.

Figure 16-1 Kohlberg, L. (1963). The development of children's orientations towards a moral order. 1. Sequence in the development of moral thought. *Vita Humana*, **6**, pp. 11–23. Reprinted by permission of S. Karger AG, Basel, Switzerland.

Figure 16-2 Colby, A., Kohlberg, L., Gibbs, J., and Lieberman, M. (1983). A longitudinal study of moral judgment. *Monographs of the Society for Research in Child Development*, **48** (Serial No. 200). © The Society for Research in Child Development, Inc.

Table 16-1 Hay, D. F., and Rheingold, H. L. (1983). The early appearance of some valued social behaviors. Unpublished manuscript, State University of New York at Stony Brook.

Box 16-5 Zahn-Waxler, C., Radke-Yarrow, J., and King, R. A. (1979). Child-rearing and children's prosocial initiations toward victims of distress. *Child Development*, **50**, pp. 319–330. © The Society for Research in Child Development, Inc.

Table 16-2 Eisenberg, N., Lennon, R., and Roth, K. (1983). Prosocial development: A longitudinal study. *Developmental Psychology*, **19**, pp. 846–855. Copyright 1983 by the American Psychological Association. Reprinted by permission.

Figure 16-3 Huesmann, L. R., Eron, L. D., Lefkowitz, M. M., and Walder, L. O. (1984). The stability of aggression over time and generations. *Developmental Psychology*, **20**, pp. 1120-1134. Copyright 1984 by the American Psychological Association. Reprinted by permission.

Cartoon, Chapter 16, p. 599 *Calvin & Hobbes* by Bill Waterson. Reprinted by permission of Universal Press Syndicate.

Figure 16-5 Patterson G. R., DeBaryshe, D. B., and Ramsey, E. (1989). A developmental perspective on antisocial behavior. *American Psychologist*, **44**, pp. 329–335. Copyright 1989 by the American Psychological Association. Reprinted by permission.

Quotes, Chapter 16, p. 602 Landers, A. *Wisconsin State Journal*, February 24, 1969 and April 8, 1969. Permission granted by Ann Landers and Creators Syndicate.

Figure 17-1 Weisz, J. R., Serwanlert, S., Chaiyasit, W., Weiss, B., Waller, B. R., and Anderson, W. W. (1988). Thai and American perspectives on over- and under-controlled problems. *Journal of Consulting and Clinical Psychology*, **56**, pp. 601–609. Copyright 1988 by the American Psychological Association. Reprinted by permission.

Table 17-1 American Psychiatric Association. (1987). *Diagnostic and Statistical Manual of Mental Disorders*, Third Edition Revised. Reprinted by permission of the American Psychiatric Association, Washington, D.C.

Table 17-2 Oothing, E. R., and Beauvais, F. (1990). Adolescent drug use: Findings of national and local surveys. *Journal of Consulting and Clinical Psychology*, **58**, pp. 385–394. Copyright 1990 by the American Psychological Association. Reprinted by permission.

Table 17-3 Gelfand, D. M., Jensen, W. R., and Drew, C. J. (1982). *Understanding Child Behavior Disorders* by Donna M. Gelfand, William R. Jensen, and C. J. Drew. Copyright © 1982 by Holt, Rinehart and Winston, Inc. Reprinted by permission of the publisher.

Table 17-4 Kosky, R. (1983). Reprinted with permission form *Journal of Child Psychology and Psychiatry*, Vol. 24, R. Kosky, Childhood suicidal behavior. Copyright 1983. Reprinted by permission of Pergamon Press Ltd.

Table 17-5 Lovaas, O. I. (1987). Behavioral treatment and normal educational and intellectual functioning in young autistic children. *Journal of Consulting and Clinical Psychology*, **55**, pp. 3–9. Copyright 1987 by the American Psychological Association. Adapted by permission.

PHOTO CREDITS

Page 4: *above,* Diane Rawson/Photo Researchers. **4:** *below,* Ann Holmes/Photo Researchers. **10:** Children's Television Workshop. **15:** National Library of Medicine. **18:** Ira Kirschenbaum/Stock, Boston. **21:** The Bettmann Archive. **31:** *above,* Carolyn Hine/The Picture Cube. **31:** *below,* Ira Kirschenbaum/Stock, Boston. **37:** Mimi Forsyth/Monkmeyer. **46:** From Lang and Melamed, 1969; courtesy of Peter Lang. **49:** Bob Williams. **67:** M. M. Grumbach, University of California, San Francisco. **72:** From Smith & Wilson, 1973. **77:** Dr. Marion I. Barnhart, Wayne State University. **83:** *left,* Jerry Berndt/Stock, Boston. **83:** *right,* Peter Menzel/Stock, Boston. **113:** Elizabeth Crews. **116:** David Ward/UPI/Bettmann Newsphotos. **122:** *above & below,* Robert Goldstein/Photo Researchers. **127:** Courtesy of M. H. Klaus, M.D. **129:** Alan Carey/The Image Works. **143:** Arlene Collins/Monkmeyer. **146:** *a,* H. Prechtl and D. Beintoma, The neurological examination of the full-term newborn infant, *Little Clubs Clinic in Developmental Medicine,* 1964, number 12, 41. London: Spastics Society Medical Information Unit and William Heinemann Medical Books, Ltd. **146:** *b,* Eve Arnold/Magnum. **147:** *c,* Roy Pinney/Monkmeyer. **147:** *d,* Nolan Patterson/Black Star. **154:** Julie O'Neil/The Picture Cube. **159:** Fig. 5-9, Topham/The Image Works. **167:** Elizabeth Crews. **169:** Fig. 5-12, Breck P. Kent. **181:** Vivienne/Photo Researchers. **182:** Julie O'Neil/The Picture Cube. **184:** Rapho/Photo Researchers. **187:** Mac Donald/The Picture Cube. **188:** Spencer Grant/The Picture Cube. **193:** Barbara Alper/Stock, Boston. **210:** *top left & right,* Michael Weisbrot. **210:** *bottom left,* Frank Siteman/The Picture Cube. **210;** *bottom right,* George Bellerose/Stock, Boston. **213:** Elizabeth Crews. **229:** *left,* Hanna Schreiber/Rapho/Photo Researchers. **229:** *right,* Randy Matusow. **231:** Elizabeth Crews. **240:** Elizabeth Crews. **242:** Ulrike Welsch. **258:** Bob Daemmrich/The Image Works. **261:** Elizabeth Crews. **264:** Elizabeth Crews/The Image Works. **267:** Barbara Alper/Stock, Boston. **271:** Ulrike Welsch. **275:** Harvey Finkle. **284:** Judy S. Gelles/Stock, Boston. **299:** Elizabeth Crews. **301:** Elizabeth Crews. **303:** *top & bottom,* Nelson Zimbel/Monkmeyer. **308:** Anderson/Monkmeyer. **311:** Mimi Forsyth/Monkmeyer. **321:** Elizabeth Crews/Stock, Boston. **323:** Abigail Heyman. **343:** Ulrike Welsch. **355:** Jim Pickerell/Stock, Boston. **356:** Alice Kandell/Rapho/Photo Researchers. **361:** Lora E. Askinazi/The Picture Cube. **363:** Stephen Trimble. **367:** Elizabeth Crews/Stock, Boston. **379:** Peter Vandermark/Stock, Boston. **382:** *left,* Peter Buckley/Photo Researchers. **382:** *right,* Addison Geary/Stock, Boston. **384:** United Artists Pictures, Inc. **390:** James Holland/Stock, Boston. **392:** Ed Lattau/Photo Researchers. **411:** Virginia Blaisdell/Stock, Boston. **418:** Erika Stone. **419:** Marjorie Shostak/Anthro-Photo File. **422:** Jack Spratt/The Image Works. **426:** *left,* Joel Gordon. **426:** *right,* Hella Hammid/Photo Researchers. **427:** Cary Wolinsky/Stock, Boston. **428:** Erika Stone. **439:** Elizabeth Crews. **442:** Ulrike Welsch. **450:** Elizabeth Crews. **454:** Christian Poveda/Stock, Boston. **462:** Vivian Rodvogin/Black Star. **466:** Ulrike Welsch. **470:** Ulrike Welsch. **478:** Steve Takatsuno/The Picture Cube. **487:** Joel Gordon. **490:** Joseph Szabo/Photo Researchers. **498:** Jim Whitmer/Stock, Boston. **508:** Nita Winter/The Image Works. **510:** Elizabeth Crews/The Image Works. **517:** Elizabeth Crews. **525:** NBC Photo. **527:** Elizabeth Crews. **545:** Addison Geary/Stock, Boston. **551:** *left,* Elizabeth Crews. **551:** *right,* Elizabeth Crews/The Image Works. **552:** Peter Glass/Monkmeyer. **554:** Burk Uzzle/Magnum. **557:** Alan Carey/The Image Works. **562:** Gale Zucker/Stock, Boston. **572:** Elizabeth Crews. **577:** Patricia Hollander Gross/Stock, Boston. **588:** Michael Siluk/The Image Works. **597:** Elizabeth Crews. **605:** David Strickler/Monkmeyer. **610:** Maureen Fennelli:/Photo Researchers. **612:** Mimi Forsyth/Monkmeyer. **624:** Stock, Boston. **634:** Arthur Tress/Photo Researchers. **638:** David M. Grossman/Photo Researchers. **643:** Judy S. Gelles/Stock, Boston. **645:** Joel Gordon.

COLOR PHOTO CREDITS

Prenatal Development

Page 1: *top,* Francis Leroy, Biocosmos/Science Photo Library/Photo Researchers. **1:** *bottom,* C. Edelman/La Villette/Photo Researchers. **2:** *top left,* Petit Format/Nestle/Science Source/Photo

Researchers. **2:** *top right,* Petit Format/Nestle/Science Source/Photo Researchers. **2:** *bottom left,* C. Edelmann/La Villette/Photo Researchers. **2:** *bottom right,* Lennart Nilsson, *A Child Is Born,* Dell Publishing Company, Bonnierforlagen AB, Stockholm. **3:** *top,* S. J. Allen/International Stock Photo. **3:** *bottom left,* Lennart Nilsson, *A Child Is Born,* Dell Publishing Company, Bonnierforlagen, AB, Stockholm. **3:** *bottom right,* Bobbe Wolf/International Stock Photo. **4:** *top left,* Charles Gupton/ Stock, Boston. **4:** *top right,* Joseph Nettis/Stock, Boston. **4:** *bottom left,* S.I.U./Science Source/Photo Researchers. **4:** *bottom right,* Elizabeth Crews.

Motor Development

Page 1: *top left,* Sybil Shackman/Monkmeyer. **1:** *top right,* Laura Dwight/Peter Arnold. **1:** *bottom,* David Brownell/The Image Bank. **2:** *top left,* Laura Dwight/Peter Arnold. **2:** *bottom left,* Margaret Miller/Photo Researchers. **2:** *right,* Tim Davis/Photo Researchers.

Emotions

Page 1: *top,* Myrleen Ferguson/PhotoEdit. **1:** *bottom,* Tom McCarthy/PhotoEdit. **2:** *top left,* Erika Stone/Peter Arnold. **2:** *top right,* Ursula Markus/Photo Researchers. **2:** *center,* Bob Daemmrich/ Stock, Boston. **2:** *bottom,* John Yurka/The Picture Cube.

Cognitive Development

Page 1: *top & bottom,* Laura Dwight/Peter Arnold. **2:** *top left & right,* Laura Dwight/Peter Arnold. **2:** *bottom left,* Laura Dwight/Peter Arnold. **2:** *bottom right,* Bob Daemmrich/Stock, Boston.

Families around the World

Page 1: *top,* Mike Yamashita/Woodfin Camp & Associates. **1:** *center left,* Norbert Schiller/The Image Works. **1:** *bottom right,* Michal Heron/Woodfin Camp & Associates. **2:** *top,* Lawrence Migdale/Stock, Boston. **2:** *center,* Joel Gordon. **2:** *bottom,* Martha Cooper/Peter Arnold.

Extrafamilial Influences on Development

Page 1: *bottom,* Curtis Willocks/Brooklyn Image Group. **1:** *top,* Lawrence Migdale/Photo Researchers. **2:** *top,* Sybil Shackman/Monkmeyer. **2:** *center,* Peter Menzel/Stock, Boston. **2:** *bottom,* Lawrence Migdale. **3:** *top,* Kate Denny/PhotoEdit. **3:** *center,* Tony Freeman/PhotoEdit. **3:** *bottom,* Mary Kate Denny/PhotoEdit. **4:** *top,* Bob Daemmrich/The Image Works. **4:** *center left,* Dario Perla/International Stock Photo. **4:** *bottom left,* Billy E. Barnes/Stock, Boston. **4:** *bottom right,* Rhoda Sidney/Stock, Boston.

NAME INDEX

SUBJECT INDEX